| 8. | Gather relevant information from multiple print and digital sources, assess the credibility and accuracy of each source, and integrate the information while avoiding plagiarism. | Chapters 13, 15 |
| 9. | Draw evidence from literary or informational texts to support analysis, reflection, and research. | Chapters 12, 13 |

**Range of Writing**

| 10. | Write routinely over extended time frames (time for research, reflection, and revision) and shorter time frames (a single sitting or a day or two) for a range of tasks, purposes, and audiences. | Chapter 13 |

## College and Career Readiness Anchor Standards for Speaking and Listening

**Comprehension and Collaboration**

| 1. | Prepare for and participate effectively in a range of conversations and collaborations with diverse partners, building on others' ideas and expressing their own clearly and persuasively. | Chapters 11, 12, 13, 15 |
| 2. | Integrate and evaluate information presented in diverse media and formats, including visually, quantitatively, and orally. | Chapters 11, 12, 13 |
| 3. | Evaluate a speaker's point of view, reasoning, and use of evidence and rhetoric. | Chapters 11, 12 |

**Presentation of Knowledge and Ideas**

| 4. | Present information, findings, and supporting evidence such that listeners can follow the line of reasoning and the organization, development, and style are appropriate to task, purpose, and audience. | Chapters 11, 12, 13 |
| 5. | Make strategic use of digital media and visual displays of data to express information and enhance understanding of presentations. | Chapters 10, 11, 12, 15 |

D0215749

**FIFTH EDITION**

# Assessing and Correcting Reading and Writing Difficulties

## Thomas G. Gunning

*Professor Emeritus, Southern Connecticut State University*
*Adjunct Professor, Central Connecticut State University*

**PEARSON**

Boston   Columbus   Indianapolis   New York   San Francisco   Upper Saddle River
Amsterdam   Cape Town   Dubai   London   Madrid   Milan   Munich   Paris   Montréal   Toronto
Delhi   Mexico City   São Paulo   Sydney   Hong Kong   Seoul   Singapore   Taipei   Tokyo

*In memory of Joseph J. Gunning, 1944–2012,*
*loving husband, father, grandfather, father-in-law, and beloved brother.*

Vice President/Editor in Chief: Aurora Martínez Ramos
Editor: Kathryn Boice
Editorial Assistant: Michelle Hochberg
Executive Marketing Manager: Krista Clark
Production Editor: Paula Carroll

Editorial Production Service: Jouve North America
Manufacturing Buyer: Megan Cochran
Electronic Composition: Jouve India
Interior Design: Jouve North America
Cover Designer: Diane Lorenzo

Credits and acknowledgments borrowed from other sources and reproduced, with permission, in this textbook appear on the appropriate page within text.

Copyright © 2014, 2010, 2006, 2002, 1998 by Pearson Education, Inc. All rights reserved. Manufactured in the United States of America. This publication is protected by Copyright, and permission should be obtained from the publisher prior to any prohibited reproduction, storage in a retrieval system, or transmission in any form or by any means, electronic, mechanical, photocopying, recording, or likewise. To obtain permission(s) to use material from this work, please submit a written request to Pearson Education, Inc., Permissions Department, One Lake Street, Upper Saddle River, NJ, 07458, or you may fax your request to 201-236-3290.

Many of the designations by manufacturers and sellers to distinguish their products are claimed as trademarks. Where those designations appear in this book, and the publisher was aware of a trademark claim, the designations have been printed in initial caps or all caps.

CIP data on file. Data not ready at press time.

10  9  8  7  6  5  4  3  2  1

www.pearsonhighered.com

ISBN-10: 0-13-283810-9
ISBN-13: 978-0-13-283810-8

# About the Author

**THOMAS G. GUNNING** has taught courses in methods of teaching reading and writing for more than 20 years and was director of the Reading Clinic at Southern Connecticut State University. Before that, as a secondary English teacher, a reading specialist, and an elementary school reading consultant, he worked extensively with achieving and struggling readers and writers. Dr. Gunning, who recently served as a Reading First consultant, is currently working with teachers to help them implement Response to Intervention, as well as serving as an adjunct professor in the Reading/Language Arts Department at Central Connecticut State University.

Over the years, Dr. Gunning's research has explored reading interests, informal reading inventories, decoding strategies, readability, higher-level literacy skills, and response to intervention. As a result of this research, he has created a number of informal assessments and programs for developing decoding and comprehension skills.

As a well-known and highly regarded textbook author, Dr. Gunning has written and revised such titles as *Creating Literacy Instruction for All Students, Eighth Edition* (ISBN 0137009267); *Developing Higher-Level Literacy in All Students: Building Reading, Reasoning, and Responding* (ISBN 0205522203); *Closing the Literacy Gap; Building Literacy in the Content Areas* (ISBN 020545626X); *Best Books for Building Literacy for Elementary School Children* (ISBN 0205286259); and *Building Words: A Resource Manual for Teaching Word Analysis and Spelling Strategies* (ISBN 0205309224)—all published by Pearson Education. Dr. Gunning is also the author of a number of children's books, including *Dream Cars* (Dillon Press) and *Amazing Escapes* (Dodd, Mead) and an intervention program for students experiencing difficulty learning decoding skills. The program is entitled *Word Building, A Response to Intervention Program* (Phoenix Learning Resources).

# Contents

# 11 Building Comprehension 365

# 12 Reading to Learn and Remember in the Content Areas 425

# 13 Building Writing Strategies 491

# Preface

Although *Assessing and Correcting Reading and Writing Difficulties, Fifth Edition,* is grounded in theory and research, it is, above all else, a practical text. It describes in careful detail how to assess students and how to use assessment results to screen students, monitor progress, and provide effective instruction. Some 46 sample lessons, covering virtually every major skill or strategy, are presented. The lessons are described in an easy-to-follow, step-by-step fashion. The emphasis in the text is on teaching students strategies that they can use independently for developing skills in word recognition, vocabulary, comprehension, reading in the content areas, writing, spelling, and studying.

Recognizing that one reason low-achieving readers fall behind is that they typically read less than their higher-achieving peers, the text provides numerous suggestions for books and real-world and digital materials that can be used to provide additional reinforcement or that students might want to read for enjoyment. Because low-achieving readers read below grade level, books that are easy to read yet appealing to older students have been emphasized. Recognizing, too, that low-achieving readers and writers need a lot of practice, the text contains numerous suggestions for reinforcement activities.

To make the text as concrete as possible, numerous examples are presented of low-achieving readers being assessed and instructed. Most chapters also present an Exemplary Teaching box, which is a vignette of especially effective instruction, and a Mini–Case Study, which exemplifies the major principles explored in that chapter.

## Plan for the Text

The first portion (Chapters 1 and 2) of the text provides an overview of reading and writing difficulties and a summary of the factors that contribute to reading and writing problems. The second section (Chapters 3-6) presents ways of assessing the strengths and weaknesses of low-achieving readers and writers. Given the increased importance of progress monitoring in today's schools, it has been given extensive coverage in chapter 4 and is discussed in a number of other chapters as well. Because assessment and instruction are often intertwined, additional information on assessment is presented in the chapters on instruction. The emphasis is on obtaining information that will help teachers plan an effective program. The third section of the text (Chapters 7–10) features a chapter on improving emergent literacy skills (Chapter 7), with an emphasis on phonological awareness, along with chapters on phonics, high-frequency words, and fluency (Chapter 8), and syllabic analysis, morphemic analysis (meaningful word parts), contextual analysis, and dictionary skills and strategies (Chapter 9). The section ends with a chapter on developing vocabulary (Chapter 10).

The fourth portion of the text (Chapters 11 and 12) is devoted to understanding the written word and includes chapters on general comprehension and reading in content areas (together with study skills). The last section of the text (Chapters 13–15) explores writing strategies (Chapter 13) and intervention programs for students, with a section on helping students who have severe word-learning problems (Chapter 14). Chapter 14 describes programs for older problem readers and programs for students who are English language learners. The text concludes with a chapter on organizing a program for low-achieving readers and writers, including providing for materials, voluntary reading, and technology (Chapter 15). Suggestions are made throughout the text for implementing RTI and also for preparing students to be college- and career-ready.

With its broad coverage, detailed lessons, and numerous suggestions for reinforcement, it is my hope that this text will be both a practical guide and ready reference for teachers who work with low-achieving readers and writers.

## Changes in the Fifth Edition

Key changes in the fifth edition include the following:

### Chapter 1

- Explanation of Common Core State Standards and their impact on struggling readers and writers
- Introduction of the concept of executive functioning
- Update of RTI

### Chapter 2

- Discussion of positive identity as a reader
- Discussion of developing of executive functioning

### Chapter 3

- Explanation of interim assessments
- Discussion of CCSS assessments

### Chapter 4

- Explanation of multilevel screening
- Expansion of the discussion of mazes

### Chapter 5

- Explanation of DIBELS® Deep Word Reading and Decoding
- Explanation of Mystery Passages think-aloud
- Expanded coverage of assessing vocabulary knowledge

### Chapter 6

- Discussion of the Benchmark School Interactive Learner Profile

**Chapter 7**

- Discussion of Literacy Express, a high-quality pre-K program
- Discussion of dialogic reading

**Chapter 8**

- Discussion of differentiation of phonics instruction
- Discussion of the importance of integrating syllabic analysis with basic phonics
- Expansion of strategies for decoding words

**Chapter 9**

- Improved scope and sequence for syllabic analysis
- Expanded coverage of syllabic analysis strategies and dictionary usage

**Chapter 10**

- Discussion of the importance of vocabulary instruction for struggling readers
- Addition of the Adapted Academic Word List, which is especially designed for ELLs but may be used with struggling readers
- Description of programs to develop academic vocabulary

**Chapter 11**

- Expanded coverage of paraphrasing and summarizing
- Explanation of Mystery Passages as a technique for building higher-level comprehension
- Expanded coverage of providing evidence to support responses
- Discussion of the need to put strategies in perspective
- Expansion of techniques for building sentence-level comprehension

**Chapter 12**

- Expanded explanation of using text structure to improve comprehension
- Expanded explanation of using writing to improve comprehension
- Explanation of developing the ability to read complex text
- Updated listing of easy-to-read content texts
- Discussion of improved practice to enhance learning and retention
- Discussion of test-enhanced learning

**Chapter 13**

- Description of developmental stages of informational writing
- Discussion of techniques for improving informational writing
- Explanation of techniques for composing persuasive texts
- Explanation of Self-Regulated Strategy Development, a technique for improving the writing of struggling learners

**Chapter 14**

- Explanation of experimental teaching
- Update of intervention programs

### Chapter 15

- Expanded information on readability
- Updated information on using technology with struggling readers and writers

## Supplements for Instructors and Students for the Fifth Edition

The following resources are available for instructors to download on www.pearson highered.com/educators. Instructors enter the author or title of this book, select this particular edition of the book, and then click on the "Resources" tab to log in and download textbook supplements.

- Instructor's Resource Manual and Test Bank

  The Instructor's Resource Manual and Test Bank includes a wealth of interesting ideas and activities designed to help instructors teach the course. Each chapter includes a chapter-at-a-glance grid, the chapter purpose, underlying concepts, student objectives, vocabulary and key terms, activities and discussion questions, plus test questions for each chapter.
- PowerPoint Slides

  Ideal for lecture presentations or student handouts, the PowerPoint presentation provides dozens of ready-to-use graphic and text images.
- MyEducationLab Correlation Guide

  This guide connects chapter sections with appropriate assignable exercises on MyEducationLab.
- TestGen

  TestGen is a powerful test generator that instructors install on a computer and use in conjunction with the TestGen testbank file for the text. Assessments, including equations, graphs, and scientific notation, may be created for both print or testing online.

MyEducationLab is an online homework, tutorial, and assessment product designed to improve results by helping students quickly master concepts, and by providing educators with a robust set of tools for easily gauging and addressing the performance of individuals and classrooms.

MyEducationLab engages students with high-quality multimedia learning experiences that help them build critical teaching skills and prepare them for real-world practice. In practice exercises, students receive immediate feedback so they see mistakes right away, learn precisely which concepts are holding them back, and master concepts through targeted practice.

For educators, MyEducationLab provides highly-visual data and performance analysis to help them quickly identify gaps in student learning and make a clear connection between coursework, concept mastery, and national teaching standards. And because MyEducationLab comes from Pearson, it's developed by an experienced partner committed to providing content, resources, and expertise for the best digital learning experiences.

## CourseSmart, eBook, and other eBook Options Available

CourseSmart is an exciting choice for purchasing this book. As an alternative to purchasing the printed book, you may purchase an electronic version of the same content via CourseSmart for a PC or Mac and for Android devices, or an iPad, iPhone, and iPod Touch with CourseSmart Apps. With a CourseSmart eBook, you can read the text, search through it, make notes online, and bookmark important passages for later review. For more information or to purchase access to the CourseSmart eBook for this text, visit http://www.coursesmart.com.

Look for availability of alternative eBook platforms and accessibility for a variety of devices on www.mypearsonstore.com by inserting the ISBN of this text and searching for access codes that will allow you to choose your most convenient online usage.

## Acknowledgments

I am grateful to Aurora Martinez Ramos, Vice President/Editor in Chief at Pearson Education, who has graciously guided four revisions of the text, and to her capable assistant, Michelle Hochberg, who assisted in a timely but kindly fashion with the many tasks involved in preparing a manuscript for publication. I am also grateful to Paula Carroll, who guided the project through the production process; to Erin Grelak, literacy and ELL editor, who provided the overall direction needed to bring this project to completion.

Many thanks, too, to the following reviewers, who offered numerous suggestions that were both thoughtful and valuable: Anita Gail Choice, Stetson University; Wendy A. Ellis, Harding University; Chhanda Islam, Murray State University; Susan Kaye Jennings, Texas A&M University; and Mary C. Provost, College of Charleston.

My wife, Joan, provided a loving, supportive environment, which greatly aided the completion of this revision. I deeply appreciate her faith in this undertaking and in me.

T. G.

# 1 Introduction to Literacy Difficulties

The first chapter of this text serves as an overview and introduction to a complex topic: reading and writing difficulties. Before reading the chapter, think about the knowledge that you bring to the topic, so that you will be better prepared to interact with the information presented. Have you read books or articles on reading and writing difficulties? Do you remember from your school days what steps were taken to help those classmates who struggled with reading or writing? If you are teaching now, think about students of yours who may have difficulty with reading or writing. What problems are they manifesting? How are these students being helped?

After reflecting on your knowledge of the topic, complete the Anticipation Guide that follows. The Anticipation Guide is a device that will help you interact with the chapter's main concepts. Most of the statements in the Anticipation Guide are open ended and often do not have a right or wrong answer. These statements are designed to help you explore your beliefs and attitudes. They can also help indicate topics about which you might need additional information. The Anticipation Guide is a device that you can use with your students. Suggestions for teaching the Anticipation Guide are presented in Chapter 12.

## ANTICIPATION GUIDE

*Read each of the following statements. Put a check under "Agree" or "Disagree" to show how you feel about each one. If possible, discuss your responses with classmates.*

|  | AGREE | DISAGREE |
|---|---|---|
| 1. A problem reader is one who is reading below his or her grade level. | _____ | _____ |
| 2. In most instances, reading problems can be prevented. | _____ | _____ |
| 3. Most cases of reading difficulty should be handled by the classroom teacher. | _____ | _____ |
| 4. Low-achieving readers need to have tasks broken down into their component parts. | _____ | _____ |
| 5. There is no one best approach for working with low-achieving readers. | _____ | _____ |

## ▓▓ Reading Difficulty Defined

There are many ways of defining reading difficulty, but the most telling definition was uttered by Awilda, a fourth-grader in a large urban school. When asked how school was going, she replied, "I got trouble with my reading."

Counting the extra year spent in second grade, Awilda had received more than four years of formal instruction in reading. However, despite having average intelligence, she was reading only on an early first-grade level. Although she had a stable personality, a caring family, and dedicated, highly competent teachers, she was reading at a level far below what might reasonably be expected. Intervention attempts, including one-on-one instruction, had failed to help her. Further, Awilda's difficulty was interfering with her functioning both in school and the larger society. She lacked the skills necessary to read the literature, social studies, and science selections typically required of a fourth-grader. Outside school, she was unable to read the letters her grandmother sent from Houston, decipher the ads on cereal boxes, or engage in any of the literacy tasks that fourth-graders might encounter. Worst of all, Awilda's self-esteem was being eroded.

Awilda was manifesting a reading difficulty in three related but different ways. There was a discrepancy between her overall cognitive ability and reading achievement. Although she had average ability, she was reading well below grade level. And her lack of reading ability was interfering with the demands made by her life circumstances. Awilda was evidencing a functional difficulty. In addition, when provided with extra help, first by the classroom teacher and then by the reading specialist, who implemented an intervention approach that worked with most students, she failed to make progress. Currently there is an emphasis on preparing all students to be college- and career-ready by the time they graduate from high school. Given her current level of achievement, Awilda was not on track to become college- or career-ready.

---

**Discrepancy definition of reading disability:** a difference exists between the student's ability and achievement. A fifth-grader with the ability of a seventh-grader would be expected to read on a seventh-grade level.

A sizable discrepancy can be a sign of a severe difficulty. Badian (1997) found that students with large gaps between ability and achievement had a greater number of deficits.

**Response to intervention** is an approach to the identification of reading/learning disabilities in which struggling students are provided with reading instruction that increases in intensity from high-quality classroom instruction to specialized one-on-one intervention in order to assess the students' ability to learn. Instruction is typically combined with diagnosis.

---

### New Approach to Identifying Reading Disability

Until the reauthorization of the Individuals with Disabilities Education Improvement Act in 2004 (IDEIA 2004, PL-108-446), a **discrepancy** definition was used to identify students with learning disabilities. (About 80 percent of students judged to have learning disability [LD] receive their classification because of a reading disability.) According to a discrepancy definition, students were said to have a learning disability if there was a significant difference between their measured ability and their achievement. Because the difference needed to be a large one for classification purposes, identification of a learning disability wasn't made in many instances until students were in third or fourth grade. It took that long for students' performance to lag sufficiently so there was a significant difference. In addition, there were controversies surrounding the measuring of ability. One issue was that students with learning difficulties learn less and so perform more poorly on tests of academic ability. There was also the question of the cultural fairness of ability tests.

Now school districts no longer have to adhere to a discrepancy definition but may if they choose to. With IDEIA, they may be identified through **response to intervention** (RTI) complemented by other indicators or measures. The change in the way students are identified as having LDs is influencing the way that all reading difficulties are identified.

RTI is a commonsense approach in which struggling students are offered increasingly intensive additional instruction. A response to intervention means that the student has been provided with high-quality, research-based instruction but has failed to make adequate progress. This is typically a three-tier process. In Tier I, the student is provided with high-quality instruction in the regular general education program and may be provided with added help by the classroom teacher. If the student continues to lag behind, he or she is given supplementary instruction (Tier II)—usually in a small group. If the student still fails to make adequate progress, a more intensive intervention program is provided (Tier III). If progress is still inadequate, placement in special education is considered.

The advantage of the response to intervention approach is that the focus is on prevention and remediation, rather than on waiting for the student to fail. Under RTI, all students benefit. RTI emphasizes improving the classroom program and offering extra help to all students who are struggling. With high-quality classroom instruction, then supplementary instruction, and finally intensive instruction, most students will make progress (Vellutino et al., 1996; Vellutino, Scanlon, Small, & Fanuele, 2006). However, Berninger and O'Malley (2011) recommend conducting a diagnosis along with RTI, especially if students have severe problems: "The disadvantage of RTI is that it does not pinpoint, that is, diagnose why an individual failed to respond to instruction and identify how any teacher in general or special education might adapt instruction so that the individual begins to respond to instruction" (p. 168).

## Clarifying the Discrepancy Concept

Despite the shift to an RTI approach for identifying students with reading difficulties, each reader's intellectual capacity and/or language development should be taken into consideration. Theoretically, students should be able to read at a level equal to their intellectual capacity or level of oral language development. Gifted students should be expected to read above grade level because their capacity is above average (Rosenberger, 1992). On the other hand, a student with intellectual disabilities would not be expected to read at grade level when her or his capacity is well below average. In one study, students with IQs between 40 and 69 needed three years of intensive instruction before achieving an end-of-first-grade reading level (Allor, Mathes, Roberts, Cheatham, & Champlin, 2010).

Students with below-average intelligence are often denied corrective services because it is believed that diminished intellectual functioning is the cause of their reading problem. However, if a student with an intellectual disability is reading below the level indicated by his or her listening and/or cognitive ability test, that student is demonstrating a reading problem. In a sense, a struggling reader is one who is reading below intellectual capacity or oral language development.

Traditionally, discrepancies have been described in terms of students reading one or more years below their capacity—for instance, an average fifth-grader reading at a third-grade level. In many programs, discrepancies were expressed in **standard deviations**. A standard deviation is a measure of the degree to which a score is above or

A **standard deviation** is a measure of the degree to which a score is above or below average. Standard deviations are explained in more detail in Chapter 3.

below average. For placement in programs of students with serious reading disabilities, many states set the discrepancy at 1.5 standard deviations between performance on a test of academic ability and a test of reading achievement (Snow, Burns, & Griffin, 1998). This is a very large difference and explains why discrepancies that meet the criterion for placement take so long to show up. Using RTI is a better procedure than using large discrepancies for identification of a reading disability. However, being aware of the discrepancy between a student's cognitive and/or language ability and reading achievement can be diagnostically helpful, as long as the information is used judiciously. Judicious use of the discrepancy approach means being aware of some of the shortcomings of measuring cognitive and language ability. First of all, there is no agreement on a definition of intellectual ability or on how to measure it. Gardner (1999), for instance, speaks of many kinds of intelligences—linguistic, musical, logical–mathematical, spatial, bodily–kinesthetic, intrapersonal, and interpersonal—but concedes that there may be more. The fairness of intelligence (IQ) tests has also been called into question. IQ tests tend to discriminate against students from lower socioeconomic groups. Since IQ scores, at least in part, reflect the environment in which students grow up, students from disadvantaged environments tend to score lower on IQ tests (Siegel, 1998).

One solution to the IQ controversy has been to use listening tests as measures of students' potential (Badian, 1999; Kamhi, Catts, & Adlof, 2012; Spring & French, 1990). Listening comprehension is the level of material that students can understand when the material is read to them. If a student's listening comprehension is at a fifth-grade level and he or she is reading on a first-grade level, then there is a four-year discrepancy between listening capacity and achievement.

However, in both listening and intelligence tests, there is the issue of the confusion of cause and effect. Because poor readers are unable to fully utilize reading, which is a major source of intellectual and language development, they may do less well on verbal intelligence and listening tests (Stanovich, 1991). Through wide reading, verbal abilities such as word knowledge and using and comprehending language are fostered, so that the reading process actually makes students smarter (Stanovich, 1992). As Siegel (1998) notes, "It is a logical paradox to use IQ scores with learning disabled children because most of these children are deficient in one or more of the component skills that are part of these IQ tests and, therefore, their scores on IQ tests will be an underestimate of their competence" (p. 128).

Some students may have a discrepancy because of some internal characteristic that makes it difficult for them to learn. Others may have a discrepancy because of illness, absenteeism, a mismatched reading program, or high mobility. Recently, I worked with a fourth-grader reading at a first-grade level who had slightly above-average intelligence. She easily met the discrepancy definition. However, when instructed, she learned word-analysis skills easily and made rapid progress. Her family had moved often, so the student had missed large chunks of school. When her family finally settled down and she attended the same school for a sustained period of time and was given an appropriate program, she made rapid progress. Based on an RTI approach, she did not have a serious reading disability.

**Functional definition of reading disability:** achievement fails to meet a certain standard or interferes with the reader's functioning in or out of school.

## Functional Definition

Many programs also use a **functional** definition in identifying problem readers. They simply provide instruction for the lowest achievers in reading. All states now administer proficiency tests in grades 3 through 8 and in high school. In many areas, students who fail to reach the proficiency cutoff scores are provided with intervention, regardless of ability. Reading Recovery, a highly successful program designed to boost the reading performance of low-achieving first-graders, provides intensive one-on-one instruction for those students identified as being in the bottom 20 percent of reading achievement. Again, academic aptitude is not a factor. All students within the lowest 20 percent are provided with assistance. Although the functional approach may overlook some bright underachievers, it provides added help for the poorest readers, regardless of any labels that may have been attached to them.

Another way of looking at reading difficulty from a functional approach is to judge whether or not it interferes with the reader's life circumstances. Does it hinder her or him from engaging in reading and writing activities that others in similar circumstances encounter? Awilda was unable to e-mail her grandparents or complete her schoolwork. For high school students, it might take the form of reading so slowly that they cannot keep up with outside reading assignments. Barr, Blachowicz, and Wogman-Sadow (1995) define a reading problem as one in which "a student cannot adequately understand the materials used for regular classroom instruction" (p. 9). As Klenk and Kibby (2000) comment, the goal of remedial instruction is for every child to be able to read the "texts generally considered appropriate for children's age or grade" (p. 684).

From a functional point of view, current emphasis in literacy education is preparing all students to be college- and career-ready (U.S. Department of Education, 2010). This has led to widespread adoption of a challenging set of standards known as the Common Core State Standards (CCSS) so that every student will be college- and career-ready. The CCSS "define the knowledge and skills students should have to succeed in entry-level, credit-bearing, academic college courses and in workforce training programs" (National Governors Association and Council of Chief State School Officers, 2010a). There are 10 anchor standards for reading, writing, language, and content-area reading and writing. The anchor standards are broad statements of objectives, which are further broken down into more specific grade-specific objectives. The anchor standards are listed on the inside front cover.

> **▶ Using Technology**
>
> **Common Core State Standards Initiative**
>
> www.corestandards.org
>
> Lists and explains Common Core State Standards.

Thus, a current functional criterion is whether students are meeting CCSS or other agreed-upon standards. The ultimate criterion is whether students are on track to become college- and career-ready. Because the CCSS are more rigorous, chances are more students will be identified as needing help.

In this text, the emphasis will be on an RTI approach combined with ongoing assessment and diagnosis. However, the difference between students' ability and/or language development and achievement and their ability to meet literacy demands in and out of school will also be considered. Keeping in mind the limitations of intelligence and listening tests, it is recommended that one adopt a broad view of ability. Students can manifest ability in a variety of ways: by the thinking and language abilities they display in classroom discussions and collaborations with peers, by their ability to solve everyday problems, or by their knowledge of the world around them. One way of estimating students' learning abilities is by teaching them and seeing how much they learn. Many students who have been written off as incapable bloom when provided with the right kind of instruction (Hiebert & Taylor, 2000).

## ■■■ Incidence of Reading Problems

What proportion of the population has a reading difficulty? How many Awildas are there? The National Assessment of Educational Progress (NAEP), (National Center for Educational Statistics, 2011) found that the following percentages of students were unable to function on a basic level, which means that they could not comprehend text at a literal level, relate it to their lives, make simple inferences, or draw conclusions based on the text.

Grade 4: 33 percent

Grade 8: 24 percent

Grade 12: 26 percent

The basic level is a conservative estimate of grade-level reading (Allington, 2011; National Center for Education Statistics, 2011).

Based on NAEP and other data, it is estimated that up to 25 percent of the population has some difficulty with reading. Not all of these students have serious problems. Most have mild to moderate difficulty. They may be functioning a year or two below what might be expected. Only a small percentage has severe problems. (Awilda would be classified as having a severe reading problem.) Approximately 10 percent of the school population have a mild problem, 12 percent have moderate difficulties, and some 3 to 6 percent have a more serious difficulty (Badian, 1999; Fuchs, Fuchs, & Compton, 2012; McCormick, 1999; Torgesen, 2004b; Vellutino et al., 1996). These include students who are known as "nonresponders" because they fail to profit from carefully planned, expert instruction. Even so, only about 1 in 100 has a severe reading disability.

> ✳ For the latest information on NAEP performance, consult http://nces.ed.gov/nationsreportcard/

## ■■■ Persistence of Severe Problems

Unlike mild or moderate difficulties, severe reading problems, which are often referred to as "**reading disabilities**" (RDs) can be chronic and require intensive intervention. These are students "who have unusual difficulty learning to read and whose reading problems cannot be accounted for by other disabilities, broad intellectual limitations, impoverished home environment, or generally inadequate instruction" (Spear-Swerling, 2004, p. 517). RDs are intrinsic. They are not caused by inadequate instruction or lack of educational opportunity. A reading disability doesn't consist of a generalized learning problem. It typically involves a severe difficulty learning basic skills, such as the ability to decode printed words (Spear-Swerling, 2011). There are relatively few disabled readers, but they need intensive long-term instruction. In close to three decades of work with struggling readers, Morris (2008) has encountered just a few dozen children who don't respond to a traditional intervention program but need intensive long-term instruction that may last for several years.

> **Reading disability** refers to a significant difficulty learning to read that is not caused by other physical or mental disabilities or external factors such as poverty or poor instruction.

## ■■■ English Language Learners as Struggling Readers

Disproportionate numbers of English language learners (ELLs) are classified as struggling readers (Orosco & O'Connor, 2011). However, poor performance on an English reading test does not mean that a student who is an ELL is a struggling reader. Newly arrived students who are still learning the rudiments of the language would not be expected to be reading on grade level in English. It would be helpful to know how well the student is reading in his or her native language. If an ELL is having difficulty reading both English and the native language, then this is an indicator of a reading difficulty. On the other side of the coin, if an ELL is struggling to learn to read, you cannot dismiss this as being due to the fact that he or she speaks another language. You need to have some measure of the student's knowledge of English and opportunity to learn to read before that judgment can be made.

For most ELLs, progress in literacy is limited by their command of English. As they learn English, they will be better able to improve their English reading skills. However, because they are still learning the language, ELLs will need extra assistance learning to read. Most will improve in reading as they acquire English and are given appropriate instruction. Students who can read in their native tongue can transfer many of their skills to reading in English.

> **Using Technology**
> The National Clearinghouse for English Language Acquisition and Language Instruction Educational Programs can be accessed at http://www.ncela.gwu.edu/. This Web site provides information about programs for ELLs.

## The Nature of Intervention and Corrective Instruction

Intervention and corrective instruction come in many forms. Although specialized techniques are sometimes used, intervention and corrective instruction are often simply more individualized applications of methods employed in the regular classroom. Intervention and corrective techniques can be classified as being part-to-whole, whole-to-part, or interactive.

### Part-to-Whole Approach

> In a **bottom-up** (part-to-whole) approach, students are taught letters and sounds before being taught to read words. Emphasis is on processing the text rather than making use of the reader's background.

In a **bottom-up** or part-to-whole approach, students learn the nuts and bolts of reading and assemble them into a whole. Proceeding from the bottom of the process, they learn letter sounds and then blend them into whole words, which are then read in brief stories. Incorporating the belief that reading is easier if it is broken down into its parts and then reconstructed, many corrective programs have taken a part-to-whole or bottom-up approach.

### Whole-to-Part Approach

> A **top-down** (whole-to-part) approach emphasizes constructing meaning through the reader's use of background knowledge and language ability.

In a **top-down** or whole-to-part approach, students start at the top of the reading process and proceed downward to letters and sounds. Instruction is initiated by reading whole stories with teacher assistance. Through reading whole stories and by using their knowledge of language patterns, students learn individual printed words and letter–sound relationships. Holistic approaches are based on a top-down view of reading. Students learn to read and write by being immersed in meaningful literacy activities. Whereas in a bottom-up approach, meaning is constructed by decoding words and assembling sentences and paragraphs, in a top-down approach, meaning is predicted.

K. Goodman (1974) refers to reading as being a psycholinguistic guessing game in which readers use their background knowledge and language ability to predict the meaning of a sentence or passage. Instead of processing a word letter by letter, readers use as few cues as possible. For instance, according to this view, seeing the sentence "The sun is shining," readers need not decode *shining* letter by letter. Using their knowledge of what the sun does and the context of the sentence, readers predict that the word will be *shining*.

## An Interactive View

In this text, reading is viewed as an interaction between part-whole and whole-part or top-down and bottom-up processes. As Rumelhart (1985) hypothesized in his classic **interactive** model, reading is not linear. We don't proceed from letters to words to meaning in step-by-step fashion. Nor do we proceed from the whole to the part. Rather, we engage in parallel processing so that we simultaneously use knowledge of language as well as contextual and letter–sound cues for decoding and background knowledge and strategies as we construct understanding of what we read (Kamhi et al., 2012). Reading is simultaneously both top-down and bottom-up.

> An **interactive** approach stresses parallel use of text processing and background knowledge. Theorists with a bottom-up approach would posit that readers process all or most of the letters of *shining* and get little help from context. An interactive approach emphasizes that reading is a parallel, simultaneous process.

> One indication that students use parallel processing is that context aids their decoding. When students encounter words in context that they missed when presented in list form, they are able to read about 25 percent of the missed words correctly (Alexander, 1998).

The truth is that readers, especially ones who have serious problems, need to use all the reading processes. Because low-achieving readers often have difficulty decoding words, there is a temptation to focus on lower-level processes, such as sounding out words and literal comprehension. However, reading is very much a total language process. The most effective programs for struggling readers are those that include a strong decoding component along with plenty of opportunity to apply skills by reading (Santa & Høien, 1999). The efficient reader simultaneously uses background knowledge, facility with language, ongoing comprehension of a selection, and decoding skills. When reading the following sentence, Jason, a fourth-grade, low-achieving reader who has been receiving intensive instruction in decoding strategies, uses a variety of sources to help him decipher the word *cocoa*, which for him is an unfamiliar print form:

After shoveling the snow, Grandpa had a cup of hot cocoa.

Because Jason has had experience with hot cocoa, his ability to use the context of the sentence enhances his use of decoding skills so that he is able to process the word faster and more readily that he would have if the word *cocoa* had not been in his listening vocabulary. Top-down processes, including language ability and background knowledge, have made it easier for him to apply lower-level decoding processes. Had the context been weak or had the word *cocoa* simply been in a list, Jason would have had to rely more heavily on decoding.

Using a computer analogy, Adams (1990) theorizes that orthographic (letter), phonological (sound), meaning, and context processors all work simultaneously to decode words. However, the way that processors are brought into play is partly dependent on the nature of the task. As adept readers, our decoding skills become so well learned and rapid that they function automatically. There are occasions, however, when bottom-up processes are brought to the fore. Notice how consciously you use decoding skills as you read the following sentence:

Thēz wrdz ar speld fənetiklé.

Did you notice that you had to deliberately sound out each word? With your processes being slowed down, were you also able to notice how you used your knowledge of language and background of experience along with decoding skills to reconstruct the sentence?

Approaches to intervention can also be categorized as being cognitive-process or sociocultural or a combination of the two. A combination approach is probably more effective. As Stone (2004) noted, "Both perspectives have added to our understanding of language and literacy" (p. 4). A cognitive-process perspective focuses on the individual and emphasizes perceptual abilities, the limitations of memory, and the use of strategies to foster more efficient processing. Background knowledge is also stressed, and the learner is seen as an active participant who constructs meaning in terms of his or her background of experience. Socioculturalists see students as learning from more knowledgeable others. Reading and writing are seen as social processes in which participants learn from each other. What students learn is heavily determined by the social and cultural contexts in which it is learned.

When assessing a struggling reader from a cognitive-process perspective, the focus would be on the mental process and strategies that the student uses. From a sociocultural point of view, the emphasis would be placed on the student's culture and the environment in which he or she is being taught (McIntyree, 2011). Cognitive scientists emphasize the neurocognitive functioning of individuals. Socioculturalists emphasize the influence of the environment and cultural ties. Both, of course, are important. Problems are likely to arise when one approach is overemphasized to the detriment of the other. One of the most successful intervention approaches, reciprocal teaching, combines strategy instruction with collaboration.

## Impact of Literacy Difficulties

Reading and writing problems, especially when they are severe, affect all aspects of a student's life. Although Robert was easily the brightest student in first grade, he was facing possible retention. Robert had serious difficulty learning to associate spoken words with their printed symbols. Despite special assistance, he had learned only a half-dozen words by the end of the year. Unfortunately, he learned to fear reading in the process. By the time he was referred to a university reading clinic, he was refusing to attempt to read. Why try, when failure was virtually guaranteed? The wall he had built around himself to prevent further failure was so impenetrable that counseling was required.

Robert's reading problem also manifested itself physically. Complaining of stomach pains, Robert was given a thorough examination. Unable to find a medical cause for the pains, the doctor believed they were caused by stress at school. Even Robert's social relationships were harmed by his reading difficulty. Classmates teased him for his slowness in catching on to reading. Baffled by Robert's difficulty, his family was torn between sympathy for his plight and a suspicion that maybe the source of Robert's problem was lack of effort. Meanwhile, at school, Robert mentally withdrew from all tasks involving reading and writing. He noted that his favorite part of school was "the bus ride home."

Understanding a student's reading difficulty, especially when it is a severe one, means finding out how it affects and is affected by the significant aspects of his life: family, school, and friends. For older low-achieving readers, society at large and the world of work must also be figured into the equation. The understanding must be ecological. For instance, it is important to see how the low-achieving reader functions in her or his classroom. Questions that need to be answered include: How does the student interact in the classroom? How do other students respond to her or him? What changes might be made to improve the student's progress? If the student is in an intervention program, the key questions are: How might the intervention and regular classroom program be coordinated so as to achieve maximum benefit for the student? How can the classroom teacher and the reading or learning disabilities specialist support one another's efforts? What assistance might other staff members and the administration provide? How might the home be involved? A comprehensive plan of assistance must take into account how the school, the home, and other institutions might play a role in remediation. Whole-school efforts are generally most effective.

### Interacting Aspects of Reading

In addition to considering the student's literacy activities at home, in school, and in the wider world, a program of correction needs to take into account the five major interacting aspects of reading: reader, task, text, instructional approach, and situational context (Lipson & Wixson, 2009; Walker, 1992). At the center of reading is the reader. Reading is a highly personal activity. Each of us brings to reading a unique blend of background, ability, perspective, interests, and proficiency. We interpret a text in the light of who we are and what we know.

**Transactional theory:** The reader transforms text through personal perspective, yet is also changed by the text. Meaning is created by the transaction between reader and text.

Rosenblatt (1978, 1994) describes the interaction between reader and text as a **transaction**. The text is transformed by the reader, and the reader, in turn, is transformed by the text. The ease of reading, the degree of interest, the organization of the text, and the use of illustrations affect the quality of the transaction. The degree of involvement will be minimal if the text is boring, too difficult, or both.

The task is also a key factor. Will the reader be skimming the material, reading it casually, or studying it in preparation for a test? Will the material be read silently or orally? Interacting with the task is the instructional approach used. Some students may respond well to highly structured direct instruction. Others thrive with approaches that focus on student involvement and stress discovery learning. Teachers of low-achieving readers need to ask: What instructional approach works best with this student or group?

All the other factors—reader, text, task, and technique—are affected by the context. Discussions, for instance, are altered dramatically by context. Students who are stone silent in a large group may become very expressive in a small cooperative learning group.

## Principles of Intervention and Corrective Instruction

Problem readers are a diverse group. The majority have difficulty decoding; however, there are a number of excellent decoders who have difficulty understanding what they read. Degree of difficulty ranges from mild to severe. Possible causes run the gamut from inappropriate materials to poor nutrition. Depending on the nature, severity, and source of the problem, programs for low-achieving readers will vary. However, a number of basic principles should be incorporated in any program created to help students who are struggling with reading and writing.

## Prevention versus Correction

Prevention, of course, is vastly superior to remediation. Prevention safeguards self-esteem, eliminates ineffective strategies before they are hardened into habits, and saves limited corrective resources for those who most desperately need it. The best prevention is a high-quality literacy program. A national committee charged with making recommendations to help prevent reading difficulties concluded, "Excellent instruction is the best intervention for children who demonstrate problems learning to read" (Snow et al., 1998, p. 33). However, for older students, especially those who evidence persistent problems, the emphasis shifts from intervention to correction (Vaughn & Fletcher, 2012). Just as literacy problems may be persistent, so too should be intervention and correction. Students should be given whatever assistance they need to develop their literacy skills as fully as possible.

If needed, students should be provided with long-term support (Allington, 2011). Students who have difficulty with decoding in grade 1, may have difficulty with fluency in grade 2 and with vocabulary in grade 3. In addition, students may do well in their intervention programs but experience difficulty when the intervention ceases and they are totally reliant on classroom instruction. Transitional support should be provided until they are able to function on their own.

## Importance of Success

In reading as in life, nothing succeeds like success. With success, there is increased effort and more success. Marjorie Johnson (1966) describes the dawning of hope in a student with a severe reading problem who had spent several weeks laboriously, but successfully, learning a basic reading vocabulary:

> When Francis first learned that he could read a particular preprimer [beginning reading book] which happened to contain no words which he did not know at this point, he was amazed. It had been a long, hard struggle for him to acquire any immediate recognition vocabulary. His reaction showed both his recognition of his difficulty and his hope for the future—an awareness that he could and would progress. (p. 156)

## Building on the Known

A close corollary of teaching for success is building on what is known. All too often, corrective instruction focuses on what the student doesn't know or can't do. In this text, both assessment and instruction will be presented as positive forces. The emphasis will be on building on what the student already knows.

Building on the known also means taking into consideration the student's background. In today's highly diverse classrooms, students come from a variety of cultures. It is important to use examples with which the student will be familiar. It is important to use materials that incorporate the student's culture and to use discussion and responding styles that the student finds comfortable and familiar. If the student is learning English as a second language, it is important to be aware of his or her language proficiency and to build on that proficiency.

## Fostering Independence and Executive Functioning

The phrase "learned helplessness" is often used to describe low-achieving readers. Having a history of failure, they see themselves as unable to cope successfully with reading and writing tasks. In a study of poor readers, Butkowsky and Willows (1980) found that these students lacked confidence in their reading, had lower expectations of success, and gave up more easily. Poor readers are also more likely to attribute their success to luck (Wigfield & Asher, 1984) and failure to a lack of ability. Since luck and ability are beyond their control, they are inclined to give up too quickly or seek help, rather than rely on their own resources. Relying too heavily on others, their reading development is further stunted and they conclude that they are "helpless."

Often, well-meaning teachers fall into the trap of unwittingly reinforcing learned helplessness. Realizing that certain students have limited skills and are struggling, the teacher supplies answers or figures out hard words for them because she or he feels sorry for them. Over time, some students develop a negative reflex reaction to academic challenges. Upon encountering a difficult word, they immediately lift their heads from the page and look to the teacher for help. Upon answering a discussion question, they study the teacher's face for a sign indicating whether the answer was correct. They seldom venture opinions. Browbeaten by a cycle of failure and self-defeating behaviors, they feel like outcasts in the community of readers and writers. In addition to teaching these students strategies, the teacher must also build confidence, instill an openness to taking risks, and encourage taking responsibility for one's learning.

To foster independence, never do for students what they can do for themselves. A corollary is never to accept anything but the students' best. If students are accustomed to having substandard work accepted by overly sympathetic teachers, they internalize their lowered expectations. The greatest compliment teachers can pay students is to reject inferior efforts. By accepting only their students' best, teachers say, "I have faith in you." Expectations, of course, need to be realistic.

Part of fostering independence is building students' executive functioning, which is their ability to set goals and work toward reaching them. (Executive functioning is discussed in Chapter 2.)

## Personalized Instruction

In addition to providing direct instruction to low-achieving readers, it is important to adapt instruction to meet individual variations in interest and background and in preference for strategies. Some low-achieving learners do best with holistic instruction; others learn best when instruction is parceled out in manageable bits. No one intervention package fits all needs. The structured phonics system that works so well with some low-achieving readers is frustrating to students who prefer a more holistic approach.

## Continuous Assessment and Progress Monitoring

Teaching and assessment should merge. Initial instruction should be based on an assessment that highlights the students' strengths and weaknesses and establishes an appropriate level of instruction. As the instruction proceeds, the teacher is guided by the students' responses. If the materials are too hard or lacking in interest, the teacher obtains more appropriate materials. If students have difficulty applying a strategy, the teacher provides on-the-spot support and guidance. A key component in a highly successful RTI program is the use of frequent progress monitoring to plan instruction (Gunning, 2007). However, if students fail to make adequate progress despite increasingly intensive instruction, a diagnosis should be initiated.

## A Full Range of Literacy Experiences

Because low-achieving readers and writers often manifest difficulty with sub-skills such as decoding, oral reading, spelling, and handwriting, there is a natural temptation to remedy the deficiency by providing lots of extra practice in the poorly developed skill. As a result, struggling readers may end up working on fragmented skills. Instead of reading intriguing trade books or composing imaginative stories, they spend their time filling in blanks on worksheets or reading brief, unrelated selections and answering low-level multiple-choice questions. Worse, they are not prepared to read the kind of complex text that will prepare them for college or career. Fisher, Frey, and Lapp (2012) state, "We must commit to our students and help them read increasingly complex texts, and read those texts well" (p. 133).

Graves (1991) describes Billy, a third-grader with a learning disability who put so much effort into his spelling and handwriting that the final product was a badly smudged series of disconnected sentences. While Billy had serious handwriting and spelling problems, what he needed most was a program that encouraged him to express himself. Because he was focusing on the things that he did poorly, Billy failed to see himself as a writer. As far as he was concerned, he had nothing of value to say. An appropriate program for Billy would begin with Billy's concept of himself as a writer. Once he is convinced that he has something to say and begins to express himself on paper, Billy will see the need for conventional spelling and readable handwriting. At that point, Billy will be ready for helpful instruction related to his handwriting and spelling.

## Direct, Systematic Instruction

Although it is an essential ingredient, surrounding students with interesting, readable books and intriguing writing and reading tasks is not enough. The skills and strategies that achieving readers soak up through immersion all too frequently escape low-achieving readers unless they are provided with explicit explanations and demonstrations. Low-achieving readers and writers need a program of direct, intensive, systematic instruction presented in the context of lots of real reading and writing. In one instance, below-level readers were carefully taught strategies for making inferences; they were soon operating on the same level as the average readers (Hansen & Pearson, 1982).

Intervention programs should maximize success by developing needed background, vocabulary, concepts, and skills before students read a selection. As Curtis and Longo (1999) warn, "When you work with students who have a history of academic failure, you set them up to fail again unless you start with the first step: direct instruction" (p. 23). For instance, in some intervention programs, students are given books to read that contain unknown words or that contain phonic elements they have not been taught. Although the teacher prepares the students by conducting a book introduction, all of the difficult words or new phonic elements are not introduced directly. If the student has difficulty, the teacher provides prompts. However, students would undoubtedly be more successful if new words were more thoroughly introduced or if necessary phonic elements were taught beforehand. Direct instruction should be conducted within the context of real reading and writing and should focus on guidance in the purposeful use of strategies.

## An Integrated Approach

> A **unit** is a plan of study that includes objectives, teaching techniques, learning activities, materials, and assessment.

Poor readers and writers often have difficulty organizing and relating new knowledge to what they already know. Using a **unit** or theme approach is one way of helping low-achieving readers form the kind of cognitive connections that adept readers make on their own. By providing varied and sustained experience with key concepts or themes, students develop a depth of understanding. In addition, studying commonalities improves students' cognitive performance (Gelzheiser, Scanlon, & Hallgren-Flynn, 2010).

In a study in which low-achieving readers read and discussed a series of passages, those who read passages that developed a common theme showed a greater increase in overall comprehension. They also demonstrated significant improvements in their ability to construct generalizations and to infer the theme when reading about new topics (Palincsar & Klenk, 1992).

## Wide Reading

We literally learn to read by reading. In order to develop their capacities fully, poor readers need to make up for lost time. They need to read more, not less, than their higher-achieving peers. In a carefully controlled study of a program designed for struggling readers, Leslie and Allen (1999) found that the students who read the most in their free time made the most progress.

> Wide reading builds fluency, vocabulary, syntactical knowledge, and background knowledge. It also contributes to the development of thinking and memory skills (Stanovich & Cunningham, 1992).

Guthrie (2004) estimates growth based on the amount of time students spend reading, both in and out of school. Based on observations, questionnaires, and studies, Guthrie speculates that the average student in grade 4 reads about two hours a day. This includes 30 minutes in language arts, 30 minutes in the content areas, 30 minutes during self-selected reading, and 30 minutes at night doing homework or voluntary reading. With reading a total of two hours a day, the student achieves an average score on the typical standardized test. Students who read more achieve higher scores; those who read less have below-average scores. A fourth-grade student who has been reading just 30 minutes a day will be at the second-grade level. A student who reads three hours a day will be at the sixth-grade level. Each 30 minutes of additional reading is associated with about a year's growth in reading. However, assuming that students have been reading at an average rate since second grade, a fourth-grader would have to read an additional 270 hours (30 minutes times three years times the 180 days of an average school year) to gain an added year's growth. Of course, this is very approximate, but it can function as a rule of thumb.

## Providing Materials at the Appropriate Challenge Level

> Time on task increased from 20 percent to 50 percent when low-achieving readers were given a text that was one year below their grade level (Anderson, 1990). Allington (1995) comments, "The longer we allow children's development to lag behind that of their peers the more difficult it becomes to accelerate their learning" (p. 8).

If students are to engage in wide reading, reading should be relatively easy. In instructional settings, students apparently do best when they know 95 to 98 percent of the words in the selection (Berliner, 1981; Gambrell, Wilson, & Gantt, 1981; Nation, 2001). When trying out the revised version of the Developmental Reading Assessment, researchers found that students whose word reading accuracy was below 97 percent had difficulty comprehending (Pearson, 2009). In one study of struggling readers who were also second language learners, the key factor in how much progress students made was the number of texts each student read at 98 percent or higher accuracy (Ehri, Dreyer, Flugman, & Gross, 2007). Students who read at lower levels of accuracy did not make progress.

There is a belief that students will do better if given materials on their grade level, even if they are reading below grade level. However, research says otherwise. Fifth-graders who were given materials on their level did better than fifth-graders who were all given fifth-grade materials, even though the program was the same (Tracey & Young, 2005). When given texts on or close to the appropriate level, poor readers spend more time on task. Achievement also improves. When poor readers know most of the words, they are better able to use context clues and so do not have to overly rely on sounding out the words. They read with more fluency and understanding. Struggling readers who used texts on their instructional level did better in word recognition, fluency, and comprehension than students who used grade-level texts (O'Connor et al., 2002). When students are reading at their instructional level, there is a greater overlap of known words than when they are reading text at their frustration level. This means that they are more likely to see the same words over and over again. This fosters fluency.

One characteristic of all successful intervention programs is making sure that students are reading books that are on their level. Unfortunately, a number of intervention programs have set the criterion for instructional level at 90 to 95 percent word recognition. This means that students will have difficulty with as many as 1 word in 10. If students have difficulty with every 10th word, their reading is more likely to become halting and dysfluent. It will be more of a struggle than it need be. Students will make more rapid progress and will be more confident if they are given materials in which they can read at least 95 percent of the words.

All too often, students reading below grade level are given books that are too difficult for them. To help students with the many hard words they encounter in their basal readers or chapter books, the teacher proceeds slowly through the book. Perhaps the group spends an entire week on a single story. As a result, they end up spending a minimum amount of time reading. However, actual reading is what these students need most. Instead of inching their way through a book that is too hard, they should be given lots of books that have the appropriate level of challenge. Examples of easy reading materials are provided throughout the body of this text.

However, students also need to learn how to read complex text. In a desire to build struggling readers' confidence, teachers might give them a steady diet of simplistic materials. ACT (2006) researchers found that the ability to comprehend complex text provides the best preparation for college, and, by implication, career: "Performance on complex texts is the clearest differentiator in reading between students who are likely to be ready for college and those who are not. And this is true for both genders, all racial/ethnic groups, and all family income levels" (pp. 16–17). Literacy researchers Fisher, Frey, and Lapp (2012) explain,

> Perhaps one of the mistakes in the past efforts to improve reading achievement has been the removal of struggle. As a profession, we might have made reading tasks too easy. We do not suggest that we should plan students' failure but rather that students should be provided with opportunities to struggle and to learn about themselves as readers when they struggle, persevere, and eventually succeed. (p. 11)

This doesn't mean that struggling readers should be given materials that are frustratingly difficult. It does mean providing them with texts that have a depth of meaning and helping students delve into these texts. Thus, there needs to be a balance between texts that are relatively easy to read and those that are more challenging. However, struggling readers need thorough instruction in techniques for reading challenging, complex texts.

## A Sense of Community

Low-achieving readers also need a sense of community. By being accepted and valued in the classroom and in reading and writing groups, low-achieving readers are motivated to try harder. And, of course, they are then better able to learn from their peers. Describing the struggling readers and writers that they observed, Allen, Michalove, and Shockley (1993) noted, "Reggie learned how to choose classmates who could really help him read. Lee learned to write initially by copying what his friends wrote; eventually, he became a genuine collaborator, first in the oral composing of the story, and then in the physical writing" (p. 249).

## Using an RTI Approach

RTI is more than just a method for identifying students with learning disabilities. RTI is a whole-school improvement program that enlists all staff members, the community, and parents to ensure that all students' literacy potential is fully developed. The idea behind RTI is that all staff members will work together to provide each student with effective instruction. As Shanahan (2008) explains, "RTI tries to make sure that classroom teaching is 'up to snuff' and that when a student does falter, there will be a rich, and ultimately, sufficient response to his or her reading needs" (p. 106). Berninger and O'Malley (2011) recommend small-group differentiated classroom instruction that provides "appropriate and evidence-based instruction for all students, including those from low SES or low literacy homes and/or those who are learning English as a second language." (p. 168).

If improved classroom instruction isn't sufficient, then increasingly intensive instruction is implemented along with additional assessment and diagnosis. Special education placement is initiated if warranted. Under an RTI approach, the school does whatever it takes to bring all children to the fullest literacy possible. There is a shared responsibility. Classroom teachers, the reading specialist, special education personnel, the school psychologist, the speech teacher, ESL teachers, administration, and other staff members work together for the benefit of all students.

## ▦ Impact of the Elementary and Secondary Act and IDEIA

The Elementary and Secondary Act plays a highly influential role in literacy instruction and assessment and provides a wide range of services for struggling readers and writers. The Elementary and Secondary Act (currently known as No Child Left Behind or NCLB) is up for renewal. Although its basic purpose will remain the same, emphasis will be on improving the effectiveness of teachers, using measures of students' performance as part of teacher evaluation systems, using measures of growth rather than percentages of students passing a proficiency standard to assess the progress of schools, and providing assistance to underperforming schools and students. A key provision will be establishing standards that will prepare students to be college and career ready. Most states have adopted the Common Core State Standards, which emphasize developing students' ability to read complex text at and even beyond grade level. These more challenging standards mean that struggling readers and writers will need even more assistance than in the past.

## Individuals with Disabilities Education Improvement Act (IDEIA)

Another major source of funding for students with reading and writing difficulties is the IDEIA (Individuals with Disabilities Education Improvement Act of 2004). Some 6.5 million, or 13 percent, of the school-age population are served by IDEIA (Aud et al., 2012). Of those 6.5 million students, 38 percent have been classified as having a learning disability. Although a **learning disability** is defined as "a disorder in one or more of the basic psychological processes involved in understanding or in using language, spoken or written, which disorder may manifest itself in an imperfect ability to listen, think, speak, read, write, spell, or to do mathematical calculations" (PL 108–446), the disorder most frequently manifests itself as a reading difficulty. About 80 percent of students classified as learning disabled have a reading difficulty.

> **Learning disability:** "a disorder in one or more of the basic psychological processes involved in understanding or in using language, spoken or written, which may manifest itself in an imperfect ability to listen, think, speak, read, write, spell, or to do mathematical calculations" (PL 108–446).

> **Inclusion** is the policy of educating all students, including those with special needs, within the regular classroom. With partial inclusion, students may be included for some classes but not others.

Because of a past lack of coordination between intervention and classroom programs and a concern that pullout programs fragment instruction, current trends are toward collaboration and **inclusion**. Increasingly, Title I teachers are working within the classroom, as are special education teachers. Under RTI, struggling readers are being seen as the concern of all staff members, not just the responsibility of the reading or LD specialist.

## EXEMPLARY TEACHING

### Collaborating to Help Struggling Readers

Realizing that many students were coming to school with limited literacy experiences and were struggling with reading in the early grades, the principal of the Roosevelt School sought help in setting up a program that would provide the extra help these students needed. Believing that the program should be school-based, Karen Broadus, a literacy consultant, involved the teachers during the planning and the instructional stages as the group set up a one-on-one tutoring program. In fact, all three first-grade teachers and the two Title I teachers, along with community volunteers, became tutors. Arrangements were made for the first-grade teachers' aides to take over the class while they tutored. As a result, the professional staff got to know the program from the inside out. As they tutored the children, they got a close-up look at the kinds of techniques and materials that worked best with struggling readers. They adapted many of these for use with their classes. As one teacher explained:

> I'm really glad I was able to be part of this program. I can't say that enough because not only have I done it, but I understand it now and I understand a lot more about what I can do as a teacher. That's such a strength for all the children I'll ever work with. (Broadus & Bloodgood, 1999, p. 437)

With typical pullout programs, teachers are bypassed and may feel that they lack the necessary expertise to help struggling readers or that it is not their responsibility. However, the reality is that students spend only a small proportion of their time in intervention or remedial programs. Most of their instruction is provided in their regular classrooms. Without an effective classroom program, the best intervention programs will fall short.

## ▦  The Whys of Reading Problems

Although it is possible to remediate literacy difficulties without knowing their causes, it can help us plan a better program if we know why a student is struggling. For instance, there is a condition known as a word-finding difficulty, in which a student has a problem remembering common words. If, through a careful assessment, we become aware that a student has that difficulty, modifications can be made in the program that can help the student build word retrieval skills; there are also strategies that we can teach the student that will help him or her cope with this difficulty. The next chapter will take a look at the major factors involved in reading and writing difficulties to shed light on a vital area in hopes that we might better help the many students who suffer some form of reading or writing disorder.

## ▦  Summary

According to the response to intervention (RTI) concept, a problem reader is one who fails to benefit adequately from enhanced classroom instruction and intervention programs of increasing intensity. Approximately 25 percent of students have a reading problem. However, most of these have a mild or moderate problem. Only about 3 to 6 percent have a serious difficulty, and only about 1 in 100 has a severe reading disability. In general, disproportionate numbers of ELLs are classified as struggling readers.

Corrective instruction may be part-to-whole, whole-to-part, or interactive. Reading is a parallel rather than a sequential process, with four processes working simultaneously: orthographic, phonological, meaning, and context. Approaches to intervention can also be categorized as being cognitive-process or sociocultural or a combination of the two.

The Elementary and Secondary Act and Individuals with Disabilities Education Improvement Act (IDEIA) are changing the face of remedial and corrective reading. Under their provisions, struggling readers will be getting more assistance but will be held to higher standards.

Since reading affects all aspects of one's life, it is advisable to take an approach that considers the reader's functioning in school, in the family, with friends, and—for older low-achieving readers—in the workplace. Reading instruction also has five interacting aspects: reader, text, task, instructional approach, and context.

Although the nature and severity of reading difficulty may vary, a number of principles undergird the teaching of problem readers. These include emphasizing prevention, fostering success, offering a full range of literacy experiences, and providing direct instruction with integrated and personalized approaches. Also helpful is continuous assessment and progress monitoring and gearing instruction to ongoing assessment; building on the known, fostering independence and executive functioning; providing wide reading of material on an appropriate level of challenge; building a sense of community and using an RTI approach along with continuous assessment and, if needed, diagnosis.

In intervention programs, students are helped by a variety of professionals: classroom teachers, Title I personnel, reading/language arts specialists and consultants, learning disabilities specialists, and migrant and bilingual educators. Although taught by professionals from diverse fields, intervention programs tend to be similar. Current trends are toward collaboration between the specialist and the classroom teacher and the provision of corrective instruction within the classroom.

## Application Activities

1. Go back to the Anticipation Guide that you completed at the beginning of the chapter. Respond to the items once more. Have you changed your mind about any of the items? If so, what caused you to change your response? Even if your responses stayed the same, your reasons for agreeing or disagreeing may be different.
2. Interview the literacy specialist at a local school. Find out what kinds of help are given to students who are experiencing difficulty with reading.
3. Read "Beyond Strategy Instruction: Looking at Person, Situation, Task, and Text Variables" by Gaskins and Galloway (2010). What role did person, situation, task, and text variables play in Liam's difficulties?
4. Think about the way you process information. Which do you favor: a whole-to-part, part-to-whole, or interactive approach?

## My Education Lab

Go to the topic **Reading Assessment** in the MyEducationLab (www.myeducationlab .com) for **Assessing and Correcting Reading Difficulties,** where you can:

- Find learning outcomes for **Reading Assessment** along with the national standards that connect to these outcomes.

- Complete Assignments and Activities that can help you more deeply understand the chapter content.

- Apply and practice your understanding of the core teaching skills identified in the chapter with the Building Teaching Skills and Dispositions learning units.

- Examine challenging situations and cases presented in the Iris Center Resources.

- Check your comprehension of the content covered in the chapter with the Study Plan. Here you will be able to take a chapter pretest, receive feedback on your answers, and then access personalized Review, Practice, and Enrichment exercises to enhance your understanding of chapter content. After you complete the exercises, take a posttest to confirm your comprehension.

- Practice targeting instruction and making content accessible for all students with A+RISE activities.

# 2 Factors Involved in Reading and Writing Difficulties

**USING WHAT YOU KNOW**

This chapter explores factors involved in the attainment of proficiency in reading and writing. From your experience, what do you think might be essential factors in the attainment of reading and writing proficiency? What might be some factors that hinder progress? As you mull over these questions, think about possible intellectual, physical, environmental, psychological, and educational causes. Also, think in terms of the stages of reading and writing. What might make it difficult for a beginning reader to make adequate progress? What factors might be associated with a reading problem in the middle grades? In the upper grades?

**ANTICIPATION GUIDE**

*Read each of the following statements. Put a check under "Agree" or "Disagree" to show how you feel about each one. If possible, discuss your responses with classmates.*

|  | AGREE | DISAGREE |
|---|---|---|
| 1. The major cause of reading problems in young children is the schools' failure to teach phonics. | _____ | _____ |
| 2. Reversals can be a sign of a serious reading problem. | _____ | _____ |
| 3. Deficiencies in auditory processes are more likely to cause reading problems than are difficulties in visual processes. | _____ | _____ |
| 4. Fortunately, most low-achieving readers do not have emotional difficulties. | _____ | _____ |
| 5. The ultimate origin of severe reading difficulty is probably neurological. | _____ | _____ |
| 6. Low-achieving readers need to have tasks broken down into their component parts. | _____ | _____ |

## ▨▨ Interacting Factors in Reading and Writing Difficulty

Although Josh and Chip were eight years old, both were virtual nonreaders when their parents enrolled them in a special after-school program for struggling readers. Chip was able to read a few words such as *I* and *me* at sight and could write his full name and a few other words. Josh was only able to read the word *I* on the word-recognition test that was administered to him and was able to write his first but not his last name. Although the manifestations of their difficulties were similar, the boys had very different backgrounds. Josh was language delayed and neurologically impaired. He had extreme difficulty learning new words.

It was easy to see why Josh had failed to learn to read. Chip, however, was something of a puzzle. Although Chip experienced some difficulty learning new words, he had average intelligence, adequate language development, and no obvious physical, psychological, social, or emotional problems. During instructional sessions, however, Chip gave up easily. If he did not get a difficult word on the second or third try, he threw up his hands. Because there were so many words he did not know, he found reading very frustrating. Because he was also easily distracted, much of the instructor's time was spent getting and maintaining his attention. Although his parents expressed a sincere desire for him to succeed, they did not back up their words with supportive action. Chip was frequently absent or tardy and often failed to complete assignments, which his parents had been asked to supervise. Although he was showing some limited progress, Chip dropped out of the program.

Realizing that Josh would have difficulty attaining proficiency in reading and writing, his parents had vowed to support him in any way they could. They read to him regularly, conversed with him continuously, took him on frequent trips, and vigorously supported his academic efforts. Friendly and outgoing, Josh set about the task of learning to read with dogged determination. He was never late for his sessions and rarely absent. All assignments were completed. Noting Josh's interest in dogs and cats, the teacher built many of the activities around the topic of pets. Whenever possible, she gave Josh a choice of activities and materials. Working closely together, Josh's special program instructor and classroom teacher supported each other. Josh's progress surpassed the most optimistic predictions.

> ⚘ Chip might have been more successful if text, approach, and context had been adjusted until a mix was found that better met his needs.

The same factors that contributed to Josh's success—effort, drive, healthy self-esteem, parental support—were lacking in Chip's situation and so contributed to his lack of success. In addition, the suitability of the instructional programs differed. Josh's teacher built on his interests and gave him choices. Chip's teacher, however, had apparently given him material that was too difficult, which intensified his feelings of frustration and failure. Moreover, his teacher did not seem to have effective techniques for handling his distractibility.

As suggested by these two cases, reading difficulty is often the result of a host of interacting factors or contributing causes. These factors may be classified as cognitive, linguistic, psychological, social–emotional, physical, and educational. Although placed last, educational factors are often key. For instance, had Chip had a more satisfying, more appropriate program, he might have persevered. Perhaps, too, greater efforts could have been made to enlist parental support.

Although each of the major factors will be discussed in isolation, it should be emphasized that often no one factor causes reading problems. In general, the cause is an interaction of several factors.

## ▦ Cognitive Factors

A number of cognitive factors are possible causes of reading problems. These include overall cognitive ability or ability to learn, memory, associative learning, and the ability to pay attention.

### Overall Cognitive Ability

Generally speaking, the brighter the students, the better they read. Cognitive ability affects language development. Students with intellectual disabilities, for instance, are slower to develop language, show a depressed rate of vocabulary development, and have a lower final level of language development (Ratner, 1993). Language development, in turn, places limitations on reading development (Adlof, Perfetti, & Catts, 2011; Carroll, 1977). Reading requires bringing to a conscious level one's implicit knowledge of language (Menyuk, 1991). Delayed language development may hinder reading development.

Students with very limited language or cognitive ability—for instance, those who have profound cognitive or developmental disabilities—may never learn to read. Students with less severe disabilities, on the other hand, should meet with some success in learning to read but may not progress beyond a second- or third-grade level. Often these students do well with decoding but have difficulty with comprehension. As noted in Chapter 1, students' reading levels should match their level of cognitive or oral language development. An average fifth-grader who can understand fifth-grade selections that are read to her or him should be able to read on a fifth-grade level. A teen with a developmental disability who can understand language typical of third-graders should be able to read on a third-grade level. Of course, the relationship between cognitive ability or language development and reading achievement is not one to one. Other factors, such as the quality of the program, the amount of voluntary reading, and the motivation of the students, enter into the equation (Singer, 1977; Valencia, 2011a).

It should also be noted that the relationship between reading and language and cognitive growth is reciprocal. As Ratner (1993) notes, it seems likely that linguistic and cognitive ability develop in parallel fashion. Moreover, reading leads to fuller development in vocabulary and syntax and may also promote greater cognitive efficiency. Our ability to process information is based, in part, on how much we know. Through reading, we acquire a broader base of knowledge, which should foster cognitive growth (West, Stanovich, & Mitchell, 1993). As Resnick (1999) has pointed out, if given a well-planned challenging program, students can be taught to be smarter.

In addition to general cognitive capacity, a number of specific cognitive and linguistic abilities are involved in learning to read. These are discussed in the following sections.

### Memory

To investigate the role that memory plays in reading difficulty, it is important to understand the current concept of working memory. Memory is composed of three essential processes: encoding, storage, and retrieval. Simply put, outside data are translated into a code (encoded) that is placed into working memory and then long-term memory, from which they can later be retrieved through recall or recognition. The memory process begins when raw data enter the sensory register. The data are held there for only about a second. During that time, attentional processes select from the masses of data entering the sensory register those stimuli that we wish to process further. Stimuli not chosen fade away. Sensory data that have been chosen enter a short-term storage facility known as working memory.

**Working memory** "holds all the information that we are currently thinking about or are conscious of at any given time" (Gordon, 1989, p. 199). As such, it has a limited capacity that depends on the type of data being held there. Working memory is the system that temporarily stores information during the performance of such cognitive tasks as reading a sentence or working out a math problem in one's head (Hulme & MacKenzie, 1992). Working memory simultaneously stores and processes information and is composed of the following subsystems: the central executive; phonological memory, which temporarily stores verbal information; a visuospatial sketch pad, which temporarily stores visual images, and episodic buffer, which integrates verbal and visual information with input from long-term storage into a unitary episodic or story-like representation (Baddeley, 1992, 2000) (see Figure 2.1).

Most information is **encoded phonologically**. If we saw three geometric figures and wanted to remember them, we would most likely encode them by saying their names: "circle, square, triangle." People make use of both acoustic and articulatory encoding. "They may simultaneously hear a word and feel themselves saying it in their heads" (Carlson, Miller, Heth, Donahoe, & Martin, 2010, p. 222). New data entering working memory will replace old information. Therefore, we must rehearse the representations that we wish to retain or it, too, will fade away. Unless rehearsed, representations will fade away within about two seconds.

To see how working memory operates, try the following experiment (Carlson et al., 2010). Read the letters below and try to remember them. Look away from the book for a few seconds and then see if you can recite them.

PXMLR

How did you keep the letters in working memory? First of all, you probably verbally encoded the letters by retrieving their names from long-term memory. That is, you said the names of the letters. Then you probably rehearsed them. You said them to yourself or said them out loud over and over so you would not forget them.

> **Working memory:** temporarily holds all the information of which we are conscious, including what has just been perceived and what is being thought.

> **Phonological coding:** ability to use the sounds in a word to store that word in working and long-term memory and, later, to retrieve that word.

**■ FIGURE 2.1**
Model of Working Memory

Working memory, then, makes use of information stored in long-term memory as well as information that enters from the sensory store. In similar fashion, when you read words at the end of a sentence, you relate them to words at the beginning of the sentence (which are stored in working memory). However, you also relate the unfolding meaning of the gist of sentences and paragraphs read previously and now stored in long-term memory and relate it to experiences you have had, which is also information stored in long-term memory. As information is being placed into phonological memory, the executive system can retrieve information from other parts of the memory system and form associations so that data from working and long-term memory can be integrated.

How much information can be held in working memory? As a rule of thumb, as much verbal information as phonological memory will hold, which is approximately as much as you can say in two seconds (Baddeley, 1992). In a classic experiment, this averaged out to about seven bits of information for most people (Miller, 1956). However, the number varies depending on the type of units being placed in memory and the meaningfulness of the units.

Verbal encoding of the type noted by Baddeley is an essential process in reading. Inefficient verbal encoding may be at the heart of word recognition, comprehension, and vocabulary difficulties. As Brady (1991) notes, "The most striking characteristic of poor readers is the common occurrence of verbal memory problems" (p. 130). When compared with high-achieving readers, low-achieving readers have more difficulty remembering a series of letters, words, numbers, and similar verbal tasks. However, according to Brady (1991), low-achieving readers have no difficulty with tasks that require visual rather than verbal encoding. They do just as well as good readers when asked to remember a series of nonsense doodles or photos of unfamiliar people.

Torgesen and Hecht (1996) found a subgroup of children who have difficulty using a phonological code to store letter sounds or words. Because some children have difficulty encoding words and letter sounds into working and long-term memory, they have difficulty retrieving them and experience problems learning phonics and sight words.

The difficulty that low-achieving readers have remembering words or a series of verbal items such as digits apparently reflects a deficiency in verbal encoding (Brady, 1986). Poor readers can code incoming stimuli phonologically, but they apparently form less accurate and less stable representations. As a result, it is more difficult for them to hold onto information in working memory. Because of processing limitations, bits of data are lost. Both decoding and sentence comprehension suffer.

Based on their extensive study of memory, Gathercole and Baddeley (1990) concluded that phonological memory appears to make a critical contribution to reading development at the point at which relationships between letter groups and sounds are being acquired. Learning letter sounds and words requires acquisition of a stable phonological representation of the sounds, which is what phonological memory helps achieve. For instance, a student with weak phonological memory may only partially code the word *bug* when he learns it initially. Later, when he encounters the word in print, he may have difficulty retrieving its spoken form because it was stored without adequate phonological cues.

Inefficient use of working memory may also hinder comprehension. Good readers process information more efficiently and also store more information than do poor readers (Daneman & Carpenter, 1980). In addition, better readers pass information into working memory faster (Jackson, 1980). Because the words in the beginning of a sentence are stored in working memory while the rest of the sentence is being processed, an efficient working memory is crucial to comprehension. Otherwise, by the time the reader reaches the end of the sentence, she may have forgotten the content of the beginning of the sentence (McCormick, 1987). Deficient working memory makes it more difficult for students to make inferences.

They fail to retain information needed to make inferences (Karasinski & Weismer, 2010; Pike, Barnes, & Barron, 2010). Deficient working memory can also impact struggling readers' motivation:

> They may have to exert extra effort because of extreme difficulty in sustaining verbal processing in working memory over time. . . . Thus, the extra effort may be due to difficulty in sustaining working memory activity over time due to inefficiencies in phonological loop (RAN) or executive functions for flexible switching (RAS). This educationally handicapping condition (Berninger, 2008c) is not visible to others like many physical and communication disabilities are. That is why formal assessment is often necessary to diagnose . . . working memory problems. (Berninger & O'Malley, 2011, p. 170)

## Associative Learning

Randall is a 9-year-old third-grader. According to informal reading inventory results, Randall has a listening capacity of grade 3. However, Randall is operating on a beginning reading level. He is able to read just a few words at sight and knows initial but not final consonants. When presented with a word-learning test in which he was taught a series of seven words, with each word being presented a minimum of 10 times, Randall learned only one word (see the Word-Learning Test in Appendix A). Randall does no better in actual classroom teaching–learning situations. Even when new words are carefully presented in context, he fails to learn them.

When given this same word-learning test, Maria, a 10-year-old fourth-grader who was also reading on a beginning level, learned all seven of the words. However, when retested just 30 minutes later, Maria was able to read only two of the words. Both Randall and Maria have associative word-learning problems. They have extreme difficulty learning to associate printed words with their spoken equivalents. In kindergarten and first grade, both students, according to their teachers' reports, had difficulty learning to associate letters and their names and later, letters and sounds. Despite having had excellent teaching, they have made very little progress in reading.

The two students have a condition known as specific or primary reading disability. As described by Rosner, Abrams, Daniels, and Schiffman (1981):

> The dyslexic's major problem is symbolization or association. He experiences basic difficulty in the association of common experiences and the symbols (words) representing them. Since reading is a process of association, difficulty in this area means that the child will frequently encounter many problems in acquiring a sight vocabulary. . . . The major presenting symptom is the tremendous difficulty in decoding. (p. 442)

This description echoes the first account of a student identified as having a severe reading disability. The account was written more than a 100 years ago by Pringle Morgan, a physician, who was describing a 14-year-old who was struggling with beginning reading skills despite seven years of intensive tutoring. Morgan believed that the boy was showing the same signs as adults who had lost the ability to read because of brain damage. He believed that the boy's difficulty, which he termed "word blindness," was due to a congenital condition that involved defective development in the left angular gyrus:

> McGregor (2004) defined dyslexia as a "specific reading impairment in which the most prominent weakness is the inability to decode words" (p. 310).

> Percy F has always been a bright and intelligent boy, quick at games, and in no way inferior to others of his age. His great difficulty has been—and is now—his inability to learn to read. This inability is so remarkable, and so pronounced, that I have no doubt it is due to some congenital defect. . . . In spite of . . . laborious and persistent training, he can only with difficulty spell out words of one syllable. (Morgan, 1896, p. 1378)

**Associative word-learning difficulty:** serious difficulty learning to associate symbols and their spoken equivalents: letters and sounds; written words and their oral equivalents.

Although we do not know the cause of Percy's difficulty, he obviously had an **associative word-learning difficulty**. Associative word-learning problems are most likely rooted in phonological coding difficulties and inefficient memory and represent the most severe reading difficulty. As Vellutino, Fletcher, Snowling, and Scanlon (2004) note, "specific reading disability (dyslexia) in otherwise normal children has been and continues to be defined as a basic deficit in learning to decode print" (p. 6). There are several techniques for remediating this deficiency; these are discussed in detail in Chapter 14.

## Attention

**Attention:** act or state of directing one's consciousness to stimuli.

Another important condition for learning to read is **attention**. There can be no learning without attention (Simon, 1986). Attention fulfills three functions: screening out irrelevant stimuli, selecting relevant elements, and shifting from one stimulus to another (Robeck & Wallace, 1990).

Recently, I assessed and instructed a high school student who had a very low measured IQ and difficulty paying attention. Her progress was very limited, but it was not her low cognitive ability that was impeding progress; it was difficulty paying attention. When she was on task, she made quite encouraging gains. When she was off task, she made no progress. The most essential part of her program was planning ways to maximize her attention.

**Attention deficit hyperactivity disorder (ADHD):** "persistent pattern of inattention and/or hyperactivity-impulsivity that is more frequent and severer than is typically observed in individuals at a comparable level of development" (American Psychiatric Association, 2000, p. 78).

A condition that interferes with attention is the somewhat controversial **attention deficit hyperactivity disorder (ADHD)**. ADHD sometimes occurs with anxiety, depression, conduct difficulties, and learning disorders. In a national survey, 9.5 percent of parents of children 4 to 17 reported that their children had been diagnosed with ADHD (Centers for Disease Control and Prevention, 2010). The number of boys diagnosed outnumber the number of girls diagnosed by two to one. A large proportion of the girls referred have been diagnosed as having ADHD of the inattentive type. They are not hyperactive but have difficulty paying attention.

Students with attention deficit are said to have difficulty screening out stimuli. However, one firefighter diagnosed with ADHD explained how his condition allowed him to pay attention to everything that was happening in a fire scene simultaneously. This ability allowed him to size up a fire scene very rapidly. On one occasion his quick analysis and reaction resulted in the saving of four lives. In a sense this so-called disability may actually be a special ability.

According to the *DSM-IV-R* (American Psychiatric Association, 2000), the essential feature of ADHD is a "persistent pattern of inattention and/or hyperactivity-impulsivity that is more frequent and severer than is typically observed in individuals at a comparable level of development" (p. 78). Indications of inattention include difficulty sustaining attention to tasks in school and at play, not listening or following instructions, not completing tasks that require sustained effort, being easily distracted and forgetful, doing work in a careless fashion, shifting from one unfinished task to another, and losing items. Other indicators include lack of follow-through, difficulty organizing tasks, and frequently losing items. Signs of hyperactivity include not being able to sit still, excessive motion, inability to play quietly, talking excessively, and impulsivity. Impulsivity includes interrupting others, blurting out responses, and difficulty waiting in line or waiting for one's turn. Symptoms usually occur by the age of 7 and should be evident in a variety of situations: at home, at school, and at play. The symptoms should not be the result of anxiety, personality, or other mental disorder, and should not be occasioned by a temporary period of stress. One reason that ADHD is difficult to diagnose and controversial is that the symptoms are subjective and occur to some degree in many students.

**Using Technology**

CHADD (Children and Adults with Attention Deficit Hyperactivity Disorder) can be accessed at http://www.chadd.org/. This Web site provides a wealth of information on ADHD.

Although most children with ADHD will manifest signs of both inattention and hyperactivity-impulsivity, there are three subtypes of ADHD: a combined type that includes both inattention and hyperactivity-impulsivity, a predominantly inattentive type (ADD), and a predominantly hyperactive-impulsive type.

Students who have ADHD also seem to be at greater risk for a reading disorder. In a recent study, 51 percent of boys and 46 percent of girls who had ADHD were also judged to have serious reading problems (Yoshimasu et al., 2010). In contrast, only about 14.5 percent of boys and 7.7 percent of girls without ADHD were assessed as having serious reading problems. However, the two disorders, ADHD and reading disability, do not seem to be neurologically related. Students who have severe reading problems are characterized by increased brain activity, especially in areas in the left hemisphere, which are critical for reading, whereas those suffering from attention deficit disorder have a lowered pattern of brain activity (Wood, 1994). ADHD is additive: It adds to the disabled reader's woes. However, there may be a common genetic link between ADHD and reading disability (Yoshimasu et al., 2010).

Even if ADHD is overdiagnosed, as some critics contend, there are students who do have difficulty paying attention and who are overly active and impulsive. Some suggestions for working with these students include the following:

Some professionals wonder whether ADHD could be controlled by altering the instructional environment and teaching better self-management skills, using medication only as a last resort.

- If students have difficulty with tasks requiring sustained attention, have them read brief rather than lengthy selections, or break lengthy selections into segments.

- Use color or boxes or other means to highlight important details. This will call their attention to essential items.

- Plan assignments that involve the students in activities. This will help focus their attention. For instance, creating a web or semantic map or composing a timeline will sustain attention better than simply answering questions.

- Provide a variety of interesting practice activities to attract and hold students' interests.

Zentall (1993) sees ADHD as a bias rather than a deficit: ADHD students are biased toward strong stimuli, so a very strong stimulus may hold their attention more fully than it should and neutral or less attractive stimuli are ignored. The student may home in on an interesting fact and miss the main idea.

- Provide students with strategies that will help them compensate for their difficulties. For instance, impulsive students do poorly on multiple-choice items because they have difficulty delaying a response until they have read all the items (Zentall, 1993). Teach them a test-taking strategy that helps them read and consider all options before responding. Also teach strategies for planning and organizing work to impulsive students, who tend to jump in without thinking ahead.

- Provide structure and remove distractions or competing stimuli so that there is a better chance that students will focus in on relevant stimuli.

- Keep oral directions brief and to the point.

- Provide students with stretch breaks and opportunities to move around.

- Use positive reinforcement. Praise the students for rules followed and activities completed.

- Because ADHD students often respond better to visual stimuli, add visual elements to oral directions. A middle school teacher in Pennsylvania placed a model on the

## EXEMPLARY TEACHING

### Fostering Attention

Although ADHD can conjure up associations of a student who calls out answers, cannot sit still, bounces around the classroom, acts impulsively, and has difficulty getting along with the other children, Randy Lee Comfort (1994), an assessment and remediation specialist, has worked successfully with these students because she builds on their positive characteristics: their energy, creativity, spontaneity, and humor. Building on the students' creativity and energy, Comfort involves them in planning goals and the activities needed to achieve those goals. As she explains, "Too often we forget to talk to children about what they want and need; we forget to include them in their own growing up and learning process. Asking a child what kind of help is needed or listening to a student talk about when he or she wants to work on something independently might give teachers and parents clues as to the child's particular learning style" (Comfort, 1994, p. 67).

Being involved in the planning also gives the child a sense of being in control. ADHD children need structure and routine, but they also need choice and independence. As Comfort explains, they become anxious when they don't know the routine, and this increases their activity level. However, they also react to a structure that is too rigid, so they need to be able to make choices.

ADHD children also do better when the work is intrinsically interesting and involves higher thinking processes. If the work consists of completing low-level worksheets, they tend to rush through it. If the task requires thoughtful responses and is also interesting, then they become more deeply engaged and they are less likely to speed through the activity.

Working with Brad, a bright 7-year-old who could not seem to stay in his seat or concentrate on his work, Comfort and Brad set a goal of having Brad work for 10 continuous minutes. After that, Brad would be allowed to play for 5 minutes to get rid of tension that might build up as he worked for 10 minutes. In order to provide challenge and to make the task interesting, Comfort gave Brad a series of answers to word problems. Brad had to create the problems. Brad became so involved in the task, which used his creativity and analytic skills, that he skipped his 5-minute break. Given the right kind of situation, Brad's ADHD is minimized.

board to illustrate the steps in organizing assignments. Students were encouraged to compare their work with the model before turning it in. As a result, students' organizational skills improved (Burcham, Carlson, & Milich, 1993).

## Visual Processing Deficits

Although auditory and linguistic abilities are more important to reading than visual skills, visual processing does play a varied, sometimes surprising, role in reading. While linguistic coding and other deficits seem to be a major cause of reading disability, visual processing deficits may be complicating factors. In a series of studies, neuroscientists and vision specialists (Chase, 1996; Chase & Stein, 2003; Solan, Shelley-Tremblay, Hansen, & Larson, 2007) found that some poor readers were slower or less efficient at processing visual information.

Struggling readers sometimes complain that the words don't stand still on the page or that the letters move around. Stein (2001) found that there are some struggling readers who have slight deficits in detecting motion. Because motion detection is an important element in directing the movement of the eyes, a deficit in this process means that the eyes might have more difficulty keeping an image stable, and so the images might slide over each other and appear to move. Children with deficits in motion detection are slower at detecting the correct order of letters. This could make it difficult to decode printed words and establish a bond between the visual appearance of a series of letters and the sounds they represent. Irregular words would be more difficult to process (Au & Lovegrove, 2006). In contrast, Vellutino and colleagues (2003) emphasized phonological factors and concluded that visual processing deficits seem to be more correlate than cause and may be a biological marker for reading disability. However, based on their research and their review of the literature. Stainthorp et al. (2010) concluded that "though a phonological deficit has been firmly established as a cause of some children's dyslexia, there is now sufficient evidence to hypothesize that early visual perceptual processes may also be implicated in word reading difficulties" (p. 270).

## Reversals

As commonly used, reversals is a generic term that encompasses a number of confusions:

Orientation or rotation errors—*b* for *d* or *p* for *q*

Mirror images— Ǝ for E

Letter sequence or transposition errors—*was* for *saw*

As students first encounter print, it is natural for them to transpose, rotate, and reverse letters. Beginning at birth, perception develops and matures as the child grows older. Perception is selective. As visual perception develops, a student becomes more adept at searching out critical information in a display. Perception also becomes more differentiated. Thus, the child becomes better able to detect slight differences between *m/n, b/d,* and other easily confused letter pairs (Gibson & Levin, 1974).

At 4 years of age, children make a high proportion of mirror-image and rotation errors (Gibson, Gibson, Pick, & Osser, 1962). In a sense, however, these are not errors at all for a young child. Real objects do not change their identity when their position in space is altered. A chair is a chair whether it is upright, upside down, or lying on its side. However, depending on its orientation, a letter formed with a vertical line and a circle can be *b, d, p,* or *q.* Rotation errors, then, are natural. More than half of all kindergartners make these errors, with right–left rotation errors (*b/p*) posing special problems (Gibson & Levin, 1974).

The discrimination of graphic features is an ability that continues to develop through the age of 8. By age 8, most students make few mirror-image or rotation errors. However, low-progress readers may continue to make transposition and rotation errors beyond the age of 8 if they are still learning beginning reading skills. They may simply be going through the stages of letter and word discrimination that younger readers have already completed. In addition, according to Vellutino and Scanlon (1988), low-achieving readers make more reversal errors because their decoding skills are weak, and they are therefore less analytical in their processing of printed words. In their research, students taught through an approach that stressed phonological awareness and phonics made far fewer reversals than a control group.

Some classic confusions also seem to be memory rather than perceptual problems. Younger and low-achieving readers often confuse letter pairs such as *b* and *d* that have very similar appearance. However, this confusion, when it persists, is not because they cannot see the difference between a *b* and a *d*: They cannot remember whether the symbol they see is a *b* or a *d* (Badian, 2005). So what seems to a perceptual confusion may be a further indication of the difficulty that disabled readers have making associations between letters and their names. These students will be more likely to have difficulty with irregularly spelled words than regularly spelled words, since phonics can be more readily used to decode regularly spelled words. These children have difficulty storing and/or retrieving orthographic representations. "A child who has problems with recognition of the correct orientation of letters is likely to be a slow and inaccurate reader of both words and nonwords due to a problem in acquiring accurate and stable orthographic representations of words" (Badian, 2005, p. 48).

As far as sequencing errors are concerned, Gibson and Levin (1974) believe these may be caused by the manner in which novice readers process words. Inexperienced readers proceed letter by letter (*h-o-p*), whereas more mature readers use patterns of letters to read words (*h + op*). Because they process words letter by letter, rather than in chunks, poor readers are more likely to mix up the order of the letters.

## Delayed or Faulty Directionality

Although most children learn to process print naturally and with little difficulty, Marie Clay (1991) discovered students who continued to have problems processing print in proper order for a period of at least three years. Persistent errors in processing print may be caused by a faulty or slow developing sense of **directionality**. Clay speaks of the child developing "sensory postural awareness of one side as being different from the other" as being necessary to develop directionality (1991, p. 116). Our sense of left and right and up and down grow out of motor explorations (Kephart, 1966). As children reach to the left and to the right and up and down, they develop an internal sense of directionality. If the development of that sense is delayed or disturbed, students may have difficulty perceiving letters in a consistent left-to-right order and so transpose letters as was the case with Sam.

> **Directionality:** ability to detect left, right, up, and down consistently and automatically.

Although a bright student with supportive parents, Sam had difficulty learning the order of letters. Even in third grade he was transposing letters and often wrote his name in reverse order as *Mas*. An assessment using the Purdue Perceptual Motor Survey (Roach, 1966) revealed that Sam had poorly established directionality and was unable to shift from left to right. When walking on a balance beam or wall, Sam held his hands at his side. Holding his arms out as most people do to maintain balance would not have helped Sam since he was unable to move from left to right and right to left. When asked to move just his right arm or right leg, he moved both. He was unable to move one without the other. His parents reported that he was unable to ride a two-wheel bike because he couldn't maintain his balance. Time and performing exercises, such as dribbling a basketball with one hand and then shifting to the other hand, helped Sam develop directionality. With intervention, he eventually became a proficient reader but remained a poor speller.

Individual case studies sometimes reveal deficits that are averaged out in large-scale studies. Although language and phonological factors are the most frequent causes of reading disabilities, visual, perceptual, and motor proficiencies can also be a factor for some disabled readers.

In summary, rotating or transposing letters is a natural part of learning how to process print. In most instances, it is not a factor in reading disability. Although often equated in the popular press with letter transpositions and visual deficits, most cases of reading disability seem to spring from auditory language deficits. "Far from being a visual problem, dyslexia appears to be a limited facility in using language to code other types of information" (Vellutino, 1987, p. 34). However, if reversals persist beyond the age of 7 or 8, despite careful instruction, they may be a sign of an underlying disorder in directionality or memory (Badian, 2005; Harris & Sipay, 1990).

If students do manifest directional difficulties, observe and decide which of the following is the most probable description of the situation:

- The student is a novice reader and writer and is still learning to process print in a consistent manner. There is evidence that reversals or other signs of directional confusion are decreasing.

- Despite extended instruction and practice, there is continued evidence of directional errors. However, most of the errors have to do with substitution of *d* for *b* or *p* for *q* or other easily confused items. These suggests a memory or associative learning rather than a perceptual problem.

- Despite extended instruction and practice, there is continued evidence of directional errors. These errors involve confusing the order of letters in words, syllables in words, or words in sentences. Older low-achieving readers may make subtle transposition errors, such as mixing up the order of syllables in multisyllabic words, thus reading *enmentjoy* for *enjoyment* (Robeck & Wallace, 1990). If they persist, errors such as these may indicate an underlying processing problem.

Although in most instances poor readers simply outgrow orientation and sequencing errors, their progress is aided by good teaching practices, which stress consistent movement from left to right. These include the following:

- When reading from the board, chart paper, or a big book, emphasize that you read the words from left to right. Also note the return sweep. Demonstrate that after coming to the end of a line, you return to the beginning of the next line.

- When drawing objects on the board or decorating a wall, proceed from left to right.

- Insofar as possible, arrange and present displays from left to right.

- Using a chart with arrows or other devices, stress the need to form letters in a consistent fashion. For instance, when presenting the letter *t,* emphasize drawing the initial stroke from top to bottom and the second stroke from left to right. If students sometimes cross the *t* from left to right and at other times from right to left, they are opening themselves up to directional confusion.

- Directionality grows out of our physical sense of left and right. Plan a wide variety of games and activities, such as the Hokey Pokey, that foster development of that internal sense.

For those few children who continue to have difficulty with letter orientation and sequencing, try the following:

**Tracing.**   Tracing, especially if supervised, helps children with both orientation and directionality.

**Keyboarding.**   Encourage the use of word-processing programs. The slower, more deliberate selection of letters aids proper sequencing.

**Context.**   Always have students check their reading to make sure it makes sense. Children should be alerted to make adjustments when they read sentences like "I have on pets" for "I have no pets," or "I saw sad" for "I was sad."

**Sounding out.**   Encourage the use of sounding out along with context. Students are less likely to read "I saw sad" if they are using initial consonants or, preferably, all the letters in a word along with context to help them decode words. When such an error does occur, ask if the sentence makes sense and also ask them to tell what letter *saw* begins with so that they can see that, both semantically and phonologically, their response is wrong.

**Mechanical aids.**   Encourage the use of finger pointing and markers if they help. Although discouraged when used by more capable readers because it is believed to foster word-by-word reading, finger pointing can be a helpful aid for novice readers.

## Language Factors

Deficits in oral language are a major characteristic of low-achieving readers. According to Wiig (1994), approximately 70 to 80 percent of students classified as having LDs—most of whom have reading problems—have language disorders. They may have difficulty following a story, show little interest in verbal activities, and have difficulty with word retrieval (e.g., remembering the names of objects). Syntax may be similar to that of a younger child. Verbal concept development may also be deficient. Upon entering school, they may not be able to name colors, letters, or days of the week. These children may have limited vocabularies and difficulty with listening comprehension. Students who evidence language disabilities for which there are no obvious causes, such as hearing impairment or neurological damage, are referred to as having a language learning disability or specific **language impairment** (Kamhi & Catts, 2012).

> A **language impairment** is a condition in which children have difficulty learning or using language but there is no obvious cause.

> A **language delay** is a condition in which language development follows a normal but slower path of development.

Some students are **language delayed**. Their language development follows the same sequence as that of other children, but it is slower. For the most part, these children catch up to their peers. In contrast, the language of language-impaired children develops differently. They do not grow out of their impairment. Even when language-delayed children grow out of their difficulties, they may still have problems learning to read and write. Because of language delay, they may not have in place the necessary development for learning phonemic awareness when it is presented in kindergarten and first grade. Without adequate phonemic awareness, they are unable to learn phonics skills.

Children's expressive language milestones have been found to be particularly effective predictors of later reading achievement. Milestones include the age at which children say their first word, speak in sentences, and so forth. For more information on developmental milestones, see Chapter 6.

Students with language difficulties are almost sure to have problems with reading. However, in addition to instruction in reading, they will also need help developing needed language skills. Ideally, the language specialist and the reading teacher should map out a joint program. Here is how the reading specialist and the language specialist worked together to help Burt.

Burt, a third-grader, baffled his teachers. Burt had excellent decoding skills, but his comprehension was almost nonexistent. He had extreme difficulty answering questions about stories that he had read, and his score on the district's standardized test of comprehension was extremely low. While working with Burt, the reading specialist noted that he had difficulty understanding questions. When the specialist asked where the story had taken place, Burt gave the names of the main characters. When the specialist asked Burt when the story had taken place, he told where it was taking place. Burt also had difficulty answering questions in ordinary conversation. Referred to the language specialist, it was found that Burt had difficulty understanding and formulating questions. As the language specialist worked with Burt and the reading specialist implemented suggestions provided by the language specialist, Burt's reading comprehension improved.

Burt and other students with serious language problems need help from both language and reading specialists. Because their reading problems are rooted in language, the key to helping them is to build needed language skills.

## Articulation Difficulties

Speech articulation problems may also contribute to reading difficulties. Students may experience increased difficulty learning letter–sound relationships for sounds they are having difficulty forming, for instance. However, reading and speech should not be confused. Just because a child is unable to articulate a sound does not mean that the child cannot perceive that sound or cannot make sense of words in which the sound appears. When working with students who have articulatory or other language problems, it is best to consult with the school's speech and hearing specialist. Many children with articulation problems also have concurrent language disorders (Ratner, 1993).

Additional language difficulties that might contribute to a reading difficulty include poor phonological awareness, inadequate automatized rapid naming, and deficient word finding.

## Phonological Factors

A widely accepted theory of reading disability holds that a major cause is a deficiency in phonological processing. Phonological processing includes phonological awareness, phonics, working memory, and lexical retrieval. Phonological awareness includes detecting groups of sounds as in rhyming and individual sounds as in **phonemic awareness**. As novice readers process a printed word, they use phonological awareness to detect its separate sounds; retrieve orthographic and phonological information from the lexicon, which is a mental dictionary; and hold this in working memory as they connect sounds to the letters in the word they are reading (Troia, 2004). Phonological awareness, retrieval of information phonologically encoded, and phonological coding in working memory are key processes in decoding (Troia, 2004).

> **Phonemic awareness:** the ability to detect the separate phonemes (speech sounds) in a word: /b/ /a/ /t/.

A phonological-processing difficulty most often manifests itself in deficient phonemic awareness, which involves detecting sounds in words, and a phonological coding deficit, which is a slowness or difficulty in using the sounds of a word to help remember that word (discussed earlier). Students who are deficient in phonological awareness have difficulty dealing with language in an abstract way. For instance, although they can understand the word *hat* and use it in normal conversation, they are unaware that *hat* is composed of three sounds: /h/, /a/, /t/. These students might also have difficulty identifying initial consonants in words or even detecting rhyme. Not being able to perceive individual sounds in words, these students are unable to match up letters with sounds and are also unable to learn phonics. As might be expected, disabled readers have more difficulty learning phonological awareness (National Reading Panel, 2000) and so need more intensive instruction for longer periods of time.

Although it is often associated with young children, phonological awareness can be a problem for older disabled readers, too. Weaknesses in phonological awareness have been found in disabled readers of all ages (Bruck, 1992). This does not mean that older disabled readers will not be able to learn to decode words. It does mean that their program should include a very explicit phonological awareness element. In fact, without a strong foundation of phonological awareness, students may not acquire decoding skills, or they may learn phonics patterns but be unable to transfer that knowledge to new words (Lovett et al., 1994). (See Chapter 7 for a fuller discussion of phonological factors.)

## Rapid Automatized Naming

Even when students do have adequate phonological awareness, they may have difficulty naming or processing language rapidly and automatically. Famed neurologist Norman Geschwind (1972) conjectured that young children's ability to name colors would be an indicator of how well they would learn to read. Naming a series of colored blocks, explained Geschwind, would be a simulation of the cognitive processes activated in decoding, because the child would be required to attach a word to an abstract symbol, a block of color.

More than four decades of ensuing research have confirmed Geschwind's thesis (Swanson, 2011; Wolf, 1991). In a test known as **rapid automatized naming (RAN),** low-achieving readers, in numerous studies and at various ages, have been slower to name a series of colored squares, pictures of common objects, digits, and letters. In a RAN task, the student is asked to name a series of five different colors, objects, digits, or letters. These same five digits arranged in random order are repeated 10 times so that, for each subtest, the child is asked to name 50 items as quickly as possible. Figure 2.2 shows what a RAN digit-naming task would look like.

> **Rapid automatized naming (RAN):** ability to name letters, numbers, colors, or objects quickly with a minimum of cognitive effort. Slowness in naming numbers and letters is a sign of a slowness in underlying processes and could hinder decoding.

For most people, the order of naming speed from slowest to fastest is objects, colors, letters, and digits. The average adult can name digits or letters approximately twice as quickly as colors or objects. Naming letters and numbers is a more highly automated process than naming colors or pictures of objects. (Slowness in naming letters and numbers suggests a deficiency in automating the processing of the basic symbols of reading.) Naming pictures of objects and color squares requires semantic processing—you must attach meaning to the pictures and the squares—and so takes longer.

At the kindergarten and first-grade level, students who later become poor readers are slow at all four naming tasks. In grade 2 and beyond, they are generally slower at naming letters and digits than are achieving readers. However, only rate of naming letters and numbers correlates with achievement in reading. Poor readers are slower in reading letters, words in lists, and text. Biemiller (1977–1978) concludes that this may be due to slower visual processes. Poor readers may need to

**■ FIGURE 2.2**
Sample Automatized Naming Tasks

| | | | | | | | | | |
|---|---|---|---|---|---|---|---|---|---|
| 5 | 2 | 9 | 2 | 7 | 5 | 9 | 4 | 7 | 4 |
| 4 | 9 | 2 | 7 | 2 | 5 | 9 | 7 | 4 | 5 |
| 7 | 5 | 9 | 5 | 2 | 4 | 9 | 7 | 4 | 2 |
| 9 | 2 | 4 | 7 | 5 | 2 | 5 | 4 | 9 | 7 |
| 2 | 5 | 9 | 7 | 4 | 9 | 2 | 4 | 7 | 5 |

examine more features to identify letters. Slowness in recognizing letters may lead to slowness in word recognition or a disruption of the process.

A child who is slow to recognize letters is slow to retrieve the letter's sound and slow to build up awareness of the common letter patterns found in words. Without quick recognition of letters, they might process words letter by letter rather than in patterns (Bowers, Sunseth, & Golden, 1999). Struggling readers need more practice than achieving readers to learn to read words immediately and, even with added practice, still take longer to read high-frequency words (Ehri & Saltmarsh, 1995; Reitsma, 1989).

Some poor readers have slower lexical (word) access speed. This means that once they have processed the spelling of a word that they are reading, it takes them longer than the average reader to locate that word in their lexicon, which is a mental dictionary. RAN is an indicator of speed of lexical access. Theoretically, the slower the student is at rapid automatized naming, the slower she or he is at lexical access. Slowness in naming is persistent. Long after low-achieving readers are 100 percent accurate in naming letters and numbers, their speed at doing so remains less than that of achieving readers (Samuels, 1994).

## Word-Finding Problems

> **Word-finding deficiency:** persistent slowness or inability to generate a word to name a specific object, event, and idea, even though the word is in the speaker's vocabulary.

A process related to but on a higher level than speed of naming of familiar objects and symbols is word retrieval or word finding. **Word-finding deficiencies** affect comprehension and higher-level word-recognition skills, such as using context.

Burly, good-humored, and talkative, 10-year-old Mel was reading on a first-grade level, despite having average ability. In addition to his obvious reading disability, Mel's speech was marred by "you knows," hesitations, and roundabout expressions for common words. He referred to the carpet on the classroom floor as "the thing you walk on." It was not that the word *rug* or *carpet* wasn't in his vocabulary. Mel simply could not retrieve *rug* or *carpet* from his store of words. When the teacher said, "Do you mean *rug*?" Mel quickly responded, "Yes. The rug."

All of us have difficulty finding the right word on occasion—whether it be the name of a co-worker's spouse, a technical term, or a distinctive word that would be especially appropriate for a special situation. However, Mel's difficulty was ongoing and frequent. His word-finding difficulty interfered with reading and writing as well as speech. Although Mel's difficulty was so severe that it was noticeable to even the casual observer, many students suffer from less obvious forms of word finding.

Symptoms of word-finding difficulty include frequent pauses, circumlocutions or roundabout language, repetitions, misuse of nonspecific words such as *things* and *stuff*, frequent use of expressions such as "you know" or "I can't think of the word," and the frequent use of *ums* and *ahs* and similar meaningless sounds (Snyder & Godley, 1992). Frequent "I don't knows" when called upon to answer in class can also be a sign of word-finding difficulty. The "I don't know" may mean that the student cannot think of the words to express the answer.

Students with word-finding difficulties may have difficulty using picture and text clues. Stumped by the word *penguin*, Sandy was encouraged by her teacher to use the story's illustration, which showed a penguin, to help her decode the word. Unable to retrieve the name of the pictured animal, Sandy finally responded with the word *bird*. Deficient word-finding ability had hampered her use of a picture clue. Her use of other contextual clues will also be hampered by word-finding difficulties.

> Had Sandy used phonics along with picture clues, she would have had a better chance of retrieving the word.

Encountering a difficult word, she will be less able to predict what word might logically fit the sense of the sentence, because retrieving words from her mental storehouse is both slower and less accurate. However, this does not mean that students with word-finding difficulties should not use context. Ironically, although hampered in the use of context, they rely on context more heavily than students who have no difficulty retrieving words. Since context provides added clues, it aids in the retrieval of words.

Students with word-finding difficulties are better able to read words silently than orally (German & Newman, 2007). When given a silent retest, which consisted of identifying which of four words was the one spoken by the examiner, students with word-finding difficulties were able to identify most of the words that they had missed when reading them orally. Their correction performance was far better than that of students who did not have word-finding difficulties.

### Compensatory Programming

Traditionally, the speech therapist or communication disorders specialist works with students who have word-finding difficulty. However, there are a number of steps that you can take to help these students compensate for their difficulties:

> ✳ Having difficulty retrieving the necessary words, students with word-finding deficits will be less likely to join in class discussions of the selections they have read; if they do join in, they may not always be able to express the information they have garnered from their reading.

- In discussions, provide more clues and additional wait time. Keep in mind that these students may know more than they can say. (Remember how you felt taking a test and getting items wrong when you knew the date or name or word but could not remember it until after your test paper was turned in. Students with retrieval problems may experience these feelings on an almost ongoing basis.)

- Before reading, provide an overview of the selection or give a preview of the story. Place key words from the story on the board. Prominently displaying semantic maps and webs helps prepare students for the story. They also help cue retrieval during the reading of the selection and during the subsequent discussion.

- Stress the use of phonics in decoding unfamiliar words. Hampered in their use of context clues, these students should be taught to use phonics as a compensatory device. However, use of phonics should be integrated with context.

- Adjust evaluation procedures. Students with retrieval problems may have special difficulty with tests of expressive vocabulary that involve having the students retrieve words. They may also have difficulty with tests that require them to supply dates, names, and terms. Consider using a multiple-choice format with these students, because this lessens retrieval requirements.

- Since students might also have difficulty with oral-reading tasks, check their performance by providing a silent-reading task that is as equivalent as possible to the oral-reading task, or at least, double-check the oral performance.

## Orthographic Processing

Why might students be faster at saying that the spoken words *coat* and *boat* rhyme than they would be at saying that *boat* and *vote* rhyme, keeping in mind that the words were spoken and that they were not shown the printed versions of the words? This phenomenon, which has been found in several experiments (Zecker, 1991), highlights the importance of orthographic processing and also suggests that we process information in parallel fashion.

**Orthographic processing** is the visualization or visual awareness of letter patterns.

✱ Being able to process spoken rhyming words faster because they have similar spelling is known as the orthographic effect and provides evidence that the student is able to access, use, and integrate orthographic and phonological information automatically (Zecker, 1991). At age 7, normally achieving readers show the orthographic effect. However, reading-disabled students do not begin to show the effect until age 10, and the effect is smaller than that of normally achieving readers.

✱ Although weakness in orthographic processing may affect both reading and spelling, in some students it only affects spelling. These students may have sufficient orthographic memory for reading but not spelling (Orton, 1966).

✱ Speed in letter naming was found to be related to choosing the correct spelling, an orthographic task (Hultquist, 1997). Letter-naming speed is the speed with which students access orthographic representations.

**Orthographic processing** is the visualization or memory of letter patterns so that students can distinguish between or spell words such as *pear, pair,* and *pare.* Since the systems work in parallel, while the phonological processing system is detecting whether the two words end with the same sound, the orthographic system is being accessed. Words that are spelled the same often have the same sounds, so the orthographic system helps speed the detection process. There is a visual effect on what seems to be an auditory task. On the other hand, phonological similarities facilitate the recognition of visual similarities. Students were faster at recognizing that word pairs such as *pouch* and *couch* were spelled the same than they were at recognizing that word pairs such as *touch* and *couch* had the same spellings. Seeing the words activated both the orthographic and phonological codes.

When students learn to read, an orthographic identity is added to the phonological, semantic, and syntactic identities of words in their mental storehouse. Students with reading disabilities who have phonological deficits may have difficulty creating adequate orthographic images because the links between sound and letters or letter patterns are more difficult for them to grasp (Berninger, 1990). Although it is partially a visual skill, orthographic awareness is not the same as visual perception. As Berninger (1990) notes, "Children who mix up letter order in words may have inefficiencies in processing orthographic information, but that cannot be equated to an organically based deficit in visual perception" (p. 519).

Students may have strong phonological processing skills but weak orthographic processing ability. This can be seen in students who are good phonetic spellers but who have difficulty with words that are not phonetic. Orthographic processing takes on more importance after grade 3 (Badian, 2000). Experience with print builds orthographic awareness. Students who lack orthographic awareness overrely on phonics and are slower in their reading. In extreme cases, they may continue to sound out words that they have encountered many times—words that normal readers would recognize immediately. They are better at reading and spelling regular words (Stanovich, 1992). They tend to confuse words such as *what* and *want* that are orthographically similar and may continue to reverse and transpose letters longer than students who have a stronger orthographic ability (Badian, 2000).

Orthographic processing may be related to naming speed. Students who are slow at naming letters and numbers are less sensitive to orthographic information or letter patterns and may have difficulty with tasks such as recognizing the word spelled correctly when presented with *tite, tight,* and *tait.* Since both *tight* and *tite* have the same pronunciation, students have to rely on orthographic information to determine which spelling is correct. Difficulty in using orthographic information slows readers down because they have to rely more heavily on phonological information and do not get the extra boost that orthographic information provides. Notice how the following sentence is difficult to read because the orthographic information is misleading, and so you must rely strictly on a phonological coding:

Due ewe no hymn?

Orthographic ability is related to decoding ability. In the early stages of reading, students rely heavily on phonics to decode words. As decoding skills develop, orthographic processing becomes an important factor. Students who have difficulty with orthographic processing may have difficulty storing irregular words. Because they have difficulty with orthographic processing, they overrely on phonics, which means that their reading may be slow and laborious. They confuse letters and words that are similar in appearance, especially if the words are irregular. They frequently confuse word pairs such as *were* and *where*. Their spelling is phonetic. They spell what they hear and so have difficulty with irregular words such as *because* and *often*. They continue to misspell high-frequency words that they have encountered many times.

Unfortunately, many struggling readers are weak in both the phonological and orthographic areas (Roberts & Mather, 1997). In her study of disabled readers, Badian (1997) found that 90 percent of the students had a double deficit. They had difficulty with both phonological awareness and orthographic processing or rapid automatized naming. And 40 percent had a triple deficit: The most severely disabled readers evidenced weaknesses in phonological processing, orthographic processing, and naming speed.

## Social and Emotional Factors

> **Learned helplessness:** Children believe, based on repeated failures, that their efforts to learn will be ineffective and they must rely on others to help them.

Although she was gifted, Florence had difficulty learning to read in first grade. Seeing her friends learn with relative ease, she wondered why she could not make sense of the words on the page. The words that she had worked so hard to learn on Monday were forgotten by Tuesday. A naturally outgoing, confident child, she became withdrawn as her concept of herself as a competent learner plummeted. Within a few months, she gave up trying. She had acquired a condition known as **learned helplessness**.

According to Seligman (1975), learned helplessness is the response manifested by people who believe they are unable to exert any influence over a situation. Feeling that her efforts to learn to read were futile, Florence gave up trying. Instead of attempting to read the easy storybooks that her teacher gave her, she persuaded a friend or her mother to read them to her. When she came across a word she could not read, instead of trying to work it out, she immediately asked another student or the teacher for help. Believing that she could not learn to read became a self-fulfilling prophecy for Florence. Because she had judged her efforts to be futile, Florence no longer worked on reading, learned less, and fell further behind, thus confirming her feelings of defeat.

### Fight or Flight

Social and emotional maladjustment can be the cause of a reading problem, an effect, or a mixture of both. In Florence's case, learned helplessness was an effect of a reading difficulty, but in time it became a cause of her continued lack of progress. Being asked to read caused obvious stress in Florence.

Students who have serious reading difficulties often display a fight-or-flight reaction to escape the stress caused by having to engage in a behavior that they find virtually impossible. Students who adopt a fight reaction are soon noticed because they engage in confrontational or disruptive behavior, or they may simply refuse to read. They may criticize the reading material, complaining that it's a stupid book. They may say that reading is boring or deny having a reading problem. The student may refuse to begin an assignment, yell, or even have a tantrum (Gentile & McMillan, 1987). The

✳ Although the main reactions to danger or stress have been described as fight or flight, scientist have recently discovered a third alternative: tend and befriend. Seen mostly in females, tend and befriend is a reaction in which people turn to friends or family members in times of stress (Taylor et al., 2000).

purpose behind the behavior is to avoid reading at all costs. For the aggressive problem reader, being chastised, kept after school, or sent to the principal's office is preferable to reading.

The behaviors of students who exhibit a flight reaction are generally more subtle and more socially acceptable than those engaged in by the fight group. Instead of criticizing reading and displaying outward signs of anxiety, the students turn inward. They engage in self-criticism, blame themselves for their failure to read, become withdrawn and silent, and may escape into daydreams. When they do engage in reading activities, they adopt a learned helplessness approach and frequently seek help from peers and teachers.

## Developing a Sense of Self-Efficacy

Whether through fight or flight, students with negative associations with reading avoid it—or if they do read, they engage in the task with less intensity. Students are more likely to undertake an activity such as reading or writing if they have a sense of **self-efficacy**. Bandura (1977) describes self-efficacy as students' belief in their ability to complete a task successfully.

**Self-efficacy:** belief in oneself as a learner.

✳ Students' self-efficacy is enhanced when the learning task is perceived as being doable, the text is on the appropriate level, instruction is clear and well organized, and students feel comfortable.

Success breeds success. What students need above all else to build a sense of efficacy is a history of success. The tasks that students complete successfully must be at the proper level of challenge. Tasks that require too much effort or are judged to be very easy do not build a sense of self-efficacy. As Bandura (1977) comments, "To succeed at easy tasks provides no new information for altering one's sense of self-efficacy, whereas mastery of challenging tasks conveys salient evidence of enhanced competence" (p. 201). In reading, this means providing students with materials that they can handle. It also means carefully teaching strategies and making sure that students have ample opportunity to apply those strategies independently. Students who lack an adequate sense of self-efficacy need to see that they can use strategies successfully on their own. "Independent performance, if well executed, produces success experiences, which further reinforce expectations of self-competency" (Bandura, 1977, p. 202).

Strategy instruction is especially effective when students see the value of the strategy and understand when and where to apply it (Schunk & Rice, 1987). Praise and feedback also help. However, feedback should be specific. "I like the way you used context to figure out those hard words" is a more effective form of feedback than the general comment "You're doing great." Both effort and ability should be praised. "You're really working hard" should be complemented by "You really know what you're doing" or "You caught on fast." Struggling readers might need reattribution training. Struggling readers, especially older ones, may attribute success to luck and failure to a lack of ability and thus judge that they have no control over their learning. They needed to see a connection between effort and achievement. However, they may also judge that putting forth a lot of effort means that their ability is lacking. They need to see a connection between persistence and achievement. Therefore, attribution for effort should only be provided when the student has sufficient skill to complete the task (Berkeley, Mastropieri, & Scruggs, 2011). Students need to be able to say, "I tried hard, used the strategy, and did well" (p. 20) so that they can make this connection between effort and strategy use and success.

After an erroneous response, help the student see what she might do to achieve a successful experience: "You weren't able to sound that word out or find a part that you know, but try saying *blank* for the word and reading to the end of the sentence. Read the whole sentence again and then see if you can tell what word might be placed in the blank."

In summary, self-efficacy can be enhanced by group and individual goal setting, careful teaching with emphasis on building independence in use of strategies, positive expectations, using peers as models, and providing positive feedback. It also helps if you have high expectations and convey these to the class. Having materials and instruction on the proper level of challenge is also important.

## Lack of Positive Identity as a Reader

Some struggling readers will stop participating for fear that others will discover they are poor readers. As Hall (2008/2009) notes,

> I often hear kids say that they don't want anyone to identify them as poor readers. They frequently are ashamed of their perceived weaknesses and will do whatever it takes to cover them up. Sometimes they try to figure out what it takes to be identified as a good reader then try to emulate it. Others simply withdraw from class and from reading, believing that if they do not participate then no one can identify them as poor readers. (p. 354)

Ironically, struggling readers may resist instruction that would help them become better readers because they fear they will be identified as poor readers. However, Hall's research suggests that instruction is more effective if teachers relate it to students' identities. Asking such questions as "What kind of reader do you want to be?" and helping them set goals can help them construct a desired identity. To help students see themselves as readers, Reading Apprenticeship, a program for secondary school struggling readers, features activities in which students write and talk with others about reading experiences, habits, likes and dislikes, and reasons for reading. In doing so they set goals for literacy development (Schoenbach, Greenleaf, & Murphy, 2012).

## Executive Functioning

> **Executive functioning** includes a range of activities that are under an individual's cognitive control, such as setting goals, making plans to reach those goals, solving problems, and self-regulating.

Many struggling readers experience difficulty with executive functioning (Vaughn, Wanzek, Murray, & Roberts, 2012). **Executive functioning** is a broad term which includes a range of activities that are under an individual's cognitive control. These activities include setting goals, making plans to reach the goals, monitoring one's thought process—including whether goal-directed activities are being met, solving problems, and organizing. Attention, the ability to inhibit responses, and the ability to self-regulate are also a part of executive functioning. As Meltzer (2007) explains, "Academic success is thus dependent on students' ability to plan their time, organize and prioritize materials and information, distinguish main ideas from details, shift approaches flexibly, monitor their own progress, and reflect on their work" (p. xi). In addition to incorporating decoding and comprehension skills, successful reading requires a host of executive functioning and related skills.

The Benchmark School, a K–8 school for struggling readers, has shown hundreds of students how to overcome personal as well as academic obstacles so that they might take charge of their learning and persist in achieving their goals (Gaskins, Satlow, & Pressley, 2007). As part of the Benchmark curriculum, students are helped to set goals, make and implement plans for reaching those goals, check their progress, and modify their plans, if necessary. Development of executive control processes at Benchmark begins in grade 1 and continues through grade 8. Instruction is systematic and thorough. Teachers begin by modeling the target process. For instance, the teacher might do a think-aloud to show how she handles a situation where there is a conflict between starting on a long-term project and visiting a friend. Students are provided specific instructions for each process. Individual conferences are held to guide students with any questions or problems they may be experiencing. A detailed observation guide, the Benchmark School Interactive Learning Profile, is used to obtain information about executive functioning and other characteristics and attributes that play a role in successful reading (Gaskins & Galloway, 2010). After transitioning to high school, Benchmark graduates, despite having had serious learning difficulties, typically outperform their classmates because the Benchmark alumni have learned how to take control of their learning (Gaskins, 2005).

## Parental Pressure

Undue parental pressure to perform may also adversely affect the student with a reading disability. On the one hand, parental support is important as the child learns to read and write. The child sees that his parents value achievement and, in response, works hard, takes necessary risks, gives up play for work, and generally takes responsibility for learning. If undue pressure is added, however, the child may judge that "if I don't do well, Mom and Dad will be angry with me." If the pressure is increased even more, the child may see failure as catastrophic, thus creating in the child a genuine fear of failure (Bricklin, 1991). Under intense fear of failure, the child may engage in avoidance behavior or even give up trying, reasoning that if you don't try, you don't really fail.

## Helping Students Overcome Negative Behaviors

 **Using Technology**

For practical tips on handling behavior problems, visit Intervention Central at http://www.interventioncentral.org /behavioral-interventions.

Children with serious emotional and adjustment problems should be helped by the school social worker, psychologist, and other appropriate professionals. In addition to implementing the suggestions of mental health workers, try the following measures when working with students whose academic self-esteem is deficient:

- Provide a stable, caring learning environment. Be positive. Build on students' strengths, rather than focusing on their weaknesses. Supply clear instructions and establish orderly, consistent routines and high but realistic expectations. Be accepting of individual differences. Through example and instruction, teach mutual respect. Value each individual because of who he or she is, not because of what he or she does.

- Reprimand students in private rather than in public. Avoid sarcasm and condescending or demeaning remarks.

- Greet students when they enter the class; say good-bye when they leave (Curtis & Longo, 1999).

- Handle oral reading with care. Oral-reading practices that discourage low-achieving readers include asking them to read difficult passages or read parts in difficult plays orally; having them read books that are beneath their maturity level; frequently correcting them or allowing other students to correct them; and stopping them from reading but assigning a better reader to continue with their part or to help them (Gentile & McMillan, 1987). On the other hand, don't exclude low-achieving readers from oral-reading activities, but see to it that they are adequately prepared. Working with a disabled reader whose oral reading was dysfluent, Bradley and Thalgoot (1987) found that when the student read a selection silently before reading it orally, his rate of reading doubled and the number of misread words was significantly reduced. The student also seemed more relaxed and involved. In contrast, when reading orally at sight in the classroom, he mumbled the words, made frequent errors, and appeared both anxious and embarrassed.

■ Acknowledge difficulties. When students evidence obvious fight-or-flight reactions, judiciously acknowledge the difficulty and the emotion behind it: "You don't seem to like reading group," or "You seem to have a difficult time choosing a book to read," or "Tests seem to make you nervous." These acknowledgments need to be expressed "in an emotionally accepting way" (Bricklin, 1991, p. 212). The acknowledgment shows that you care and gives the child the opportunity to talk about the difficulty. Once the difficulty is acknowledged, steps can be taken to remedy it through encouragement, use of strategies, or, for more serious problems, sessions with a mental health professional.

■ Promote independence. Don't fall into the trap of providing unneeded assistance for students who have learned helplessness. As noted in Chapter 1, a general principle of remedial education is to never do for students anything that they can do for themselves. Don't sound out a word that a student can sound out for herself. And if she cannot sound out the whole word, encourage her to sound out as much as she can and then build on that. If she cannot recall an important fact from a selection she read, encourage her to go back and find it. Teach students strategies that they will be able to apply independently. Although they may need guidance in the beginning, gradually lead them to a stage of independence. Also, redirect questions that indicate a lack of independence, especially if asked by students who are overly dependent (Glazer, 1991). For instance, if a student asks "Should I read this again?" redirect the question so that the student must exercise her own judgment. Ask "Would you like to read it again?" or "Do you think you need to read it again?" If the student asks "Which book should I read?" redirect that to "Which book would you like to read?"

■ Give students choices whenever possible. Allow them to select books and stories to read and to choose activities. Involve them in setting up classroom rules and procedures. If they are involved, they will put more of themselves into their work. And you are also telling them that their thoughts and judgments are important. This will boost their self-esteem and give them a sense of control over their lives.

In many instances, students' mental health takes a turn for the better once they begin to make progress in reading. Because they feel good about themselves, they try harder and do better, which leads to even more success. It is the beginning of a very positive cycle. However, some students have such severe emotional problems that professional intervention is needed before they can make progress. For instance, a student who is deeply depressed may need mental health assistance before she or he is able to invest energy in improving reading skills or even take an interest in schooling. Although it is always a good idea to work collaboratively with other professionals, it is essential when teaching deeply disturbed students.

> ⚜ Ironically, undue fear of failure leads to behaviors that cause failure (Bricklin, 1991).

## ▓▓▓  Physical Causes

**I**n a holistic assessment, it is important to look at the student's mental and physical condition. Neurological and health factors, as well as vision and hearing, need to be considered.

### Neurological Factors

> ⚘ Mysterious as well as complex, the brain is organized in ways that may seem strange to us. For instance, the part of the brain responsible for sequencing letters also controls rhythmic activities (Luria, 1970). An awkward gait may be accompanied by letter reversals.

The most severe instances of reading difficulty—and, perhaps, some less severe cases—are caused or complicated by variation in neurological development, including subtle damage or changes in neurological organization that may not be readily apparent. Studies have shown underactivation in the left occipito-temporal, temporo-parietal, and inferior frontal cortical regions, but that after intervention, the areas showed increased activity (Keller & Just, 2009). These are areas involved in phonological processing, word reading, and orthographic processing (Davis et al., 2011). After 100 hours of instruction, 47 struggling readers ages 8–12 demonstrated an increase in white matter, which supplies connections to areas of the brain involved in reading and also increases in decoding skills. Control groups showed no changes in white matter.

Differences in lateralization were also noted. Lateralization means that one side of the brain, usually the left, is dominant for language activities. Participants whose brains were more lateralized were faster at processing words. Functional disruptions in the areas around the angular gyrus were also found. For participants with dyslexia there was a weakened connectivity in the left hemisphere between the angular gyrus and the temporal (responsible for hearing) and occipital (responsible for vision) lobes. This portion of the brain is thought to be the area in which associations between letters and sounds or printed words and their spoken equivalents are made (Shaywitz et al., 2000). However, research indicates that many parts of the brain are dynamically involved in reading. As Riccio and Hynd (1996) comment, "It is clear that there is no unitary neurological factor that results in dyslexia. Rather, the research to date suggests a combination of structural or functional differences" (p. 11).

### Hearing Impairments

> ⚘ The Individuals with Disabilities Education Improvement Act (IDEIA) defines hearing impairment as "an impairment in hearing, whether permanent or fluctuating, that adversely affects a child's educational performance." Deafness is defined as "a hearing impairment that is so severe that the child is impaired in processing linguistic information through hearing, with or without amplification."

In the past, most children with serious hearing problems were taught in residential schools or day schools that had special full-time programs. Today, more and more students are being taught within the regular classroom. This is due to a change in philosophy and advances in technology and techniques. With inclusion, it is important that the classroom teacher and reading specialist have a basic understanding of hearing difficulties.

#### Degree of Physical Loss

Hearing loss is measured in terms of pitch and intensity (National Dissemination Center for Children with Disabilities, 2010). Sound waves vibrate. The number of vibrations or cycles per second is the sound wave's pitch or **frequency**, which is measured in a unit known as hertz. The higher the frequency,

> **Frequency:** number of sound waves emitted per second.

**Hertz** (Hz): unit of measurement for sound waves. One hertz equals one cycle or sound wave per second.

**Decibel:** unit for measuring loudness of a sound.

the higher the **hertz**. Humans are sensitive to sounds in the 20–20,000 hertz range, but testing is generally done in the 125–8,000 range, which encompasses speech frequencies. There may be loss across all frequencies or a loss in specific frequencies.

In addition to measuring pitch, the intensity or loudness of sounds is also assessed. The higher the **decibel** level, the louder the sound. A whisper is 20 decibels, conversation about 55–60, heavy traffic 90, and thunder 120. Losses from 20 to 60 decibels are classified as mild or moderate, from 60 to 80 are severe, and 90 or above are profound.

## Extent of Impairment

While hearing loss can be measured in terms of frequencies and decibels, the extent of impairment depends on a number of factors. Generally speaking, the earlier the loss, the more profound its impact. Children who lose their hearing before acquiring speech are much more seriously impaired than those whose loss occurred after the acquisition of language. However, early intervention, which could include use of an assistive device such as a hearing aid or an amplification system used by the teacher, special teaching, use of preferential seating, and training of parents can significantly lessen negative effects. The use of sign language and other means of communication can also have a positive impact. For older students the use of caption videos and the assistance of a note taker or interpreter, can be helpful. Even so, children who are hearing impaired have a more difficult time learning vocabulary, grammar, word order, and idiomatic expressions.

## The Reading Teacher's Role

While cases of severe and profound hearing impairment are generally handled by speech and hearing specialists, you can help by noting children who seem to have undetected hearing difficulties and referring them for testing, by making appropriate program adjustments, and by collaborating with the speech therapist. Having deficits in vocabulary, syntax, and figurative language, students with hearing impairments generally lag significantly behind in reading comprehension. They may also be deficient in their knowledge of story structures and so experience difficulty comprehending narratives. Corrective students who are hearing impaired or who lost but regained hearing because of otitis media, which is an inflammation of the middle ear and is a fairly common and sometimes persistent and recurring condition in young children, may evidence language deficits and so need additional assistance.

Signs of a possible hearing problem include talking too loudly or too softly, poor articulation, asking to have directions repeated, difficulty listening, and frequent ear infections. An observational checklist of possible symptoms is presented in Figure 2.3. It is especially important for teachers of young children to be on the lookout for signs of otitis media.

## High-Frequency Loss

One type of impairment that sometimes evades detection is a **high-frequency hearing loss**. Students can hear sounds in the lower range, which include vowel sounds and, to a lesser extent, most consonants. However, students are unable to

**High-frequency hearing loss:** one in which students can hear low-frequency sounds but have difficulty hearing high-frequency sounds such as /f/, /s/, /th/.

hear certain consonants, such as /f/, /s/, and /th/, which are at the highest end of the range. Since these children can hear most speech sounds and understand some words, their impairment may escape detection, especially if only a few consonants are involved. However, because they miss some words, these students find school

**■ FIGURE 2.3**
Observation
Checklist: Signs of
Possible Hearing
Problem

| | |
|---|---|
| Faulty pronunciation or other speech difficulties | _____ |
| Poor spelling | _____ |
| Frequent requests to repeat directions and questions | _____ |
| Lack of attention | _____ |
| Inappropriate responses | _____ |
| Focusing on speaker's lips | _____ |
| Earaches | _____ |
| Frequent rubbing of the ear | _____ |
| Unnatural pitch of the voice | _____ |
| Cupping ear or turning ear toward speaker | _____ |
| Complaints of ringing or buzzing in ear, dizziness, or closed feeling in the ear | _____ |
| Sores in ear or discharge | _____ |
| Frequent sore throats, colds, or tonsillitis | _____ |

confusing and, of course, have special difficulty learning letter–sound relationships, especially consonant correspondences.

> ✳ A condition that might lead to a high-frequency loss is an enlarged vestibular aqueduct. The vestibular aqueduct is the canal that links the inner ear with the fluid that surrounds the brain. An enlarged vestibular aqueduct may allow the pressure changes in the fluid around the brain to pass through to the inner ear and adversely affect the hearing system.

Because her hearing impairment was subtle, Mandy's high-frequency loss was not detected until she entered school. As a result, her vocabulary was limited, as was her general background of knowledge and concepts. Once Mandy's impairment was discovered, she was fitted with a hearing aid and given special help by the speech therapist.

Mandy acquired a fairly substantial sight vocabulary, but she experienced difficulty learning decoding skills, and her comprehension was poor. Decoding skills showed an improvement when her reading teacher began using a modified version of a pattern approach. Through careful testing, the speech therapist had been able to determine which sounds Mandy could hear and which she still had difficulty with. The reading specialist taught those patterns that were composed of sounds that Mandy could hear. Working with the speech therapist, she also devised techniques in which she was able to show Mandy how high-frequency sounds, the ones she could not hear, were formed. In a sense, the therapist added a step to her phonics lesson. In order to compensate for Mandy's hearing impairment, she helped Mandy form difficult-to-hear sounds with her mouth. Mandy's teacher also helped Mandy with her writing. Because Mandy was overly concerned with spelling, she did virtually no writing. Mandy's writing consisted of a sentence or two of the plainest prose, devoid of all embellishment and elaboration. Encouraged by her teacher to spell as best she could, Mandy was finally convinced to try invented spelling. Little by little, her writing grew in content and quality of expression. Wide reading and lots of discussion helped expand Mandy's meager background.

## Use of Frequency Modulated Systems

Frequency modulated (FM) systems and other aids are frequently used to help students who have hearing impairments. An FM system amplifies the teacher's voice, but because the microphone is close to the teacher's mouth, it does not amplify background noises. For students with hearing loss, background noise, reverberation of sounds, and distance from the speaker can make hearing more difficult. An alternative to individual FM systems is a sound field system. Essentially, this involves placing speakers throughout the classroom so the teacher's voice is amplified throughout the room. Sound field systems are appropriate for students with mild hearing loss. Personal FM systems are appropriate for students who have a moderate loss.

It is also helpful if students with hearing loss are provided with preferential seating and steps are taken to reduce reverberations, such as putting tennis balls on the legs of chairs and desks. Although originally designed for students with hearing loss, FM systems are now being used with students who have auditory processing problems or attention difficulties.

## Vision Impairments

Vision impairment is one of the most prevalent disabling conditions among children. Approximately 6.8 percent of children younger than 18 years have a diagnosed eye and vision condition (Centers for Disease Control and Prevention, 2009c). According to Child Sight/Vision Correction, 2 million children have uncorrected refractive errors. The most common problem is nearsightedness. Although poor vision is rarely a cause of poor reading, blurred, fuzzy, or strained vision can certainly add to the problem.

Vision is initiated when light rays from an object enter the cornea and pass through the lens. The lens bends the rays so that they are focused on the retina. An optic nerve connects the retina with the visual cortex, which interprets the signal. In order for the light rays to be focused on the retina, the eye must be properly shaped. If the eyeball is too long, light rays fall in front of the retina, resulting in nearsightedness, or **myopia**. If the eyeball is too short, light rays fall behind the retina, resulting in farsightedness, or **hyperopia**. **Astigmatism**, a third major structural defect, results from an irregular curvature of the cornea and causes a blurred or misshapen image. All three of these conditions can be corrected with lenses.

> **Myopia:** condition in which the light rays fall in front of the retina so that distant objects are not seen clearly; also know as nearsightedness.

> **Hyperopia:** condition in which the light falls behind the retina so that close objects are not seen clearly; also know as farsightedness.

> **Astigmatism:** irregularity in the cornea that causes blurred vision.

### Accommodation and Convergence

Acuity of vision is not sufficient, however. Vision is both structural and functional. In order to have correct vision, our eyes need to be properly shaped. However, having properly shaped eyes is not enough. It is possible to have a vision system that is physically perfect but still have vision problems. Vision is functional, a learned act. Through experience, humans literally learn to see. Because of the physiology of the eyes, we should see two objects. However, we learn to fuse dual images into one.

A student's eyes must also function in such a way that she or he can see a single object at all working distances. **Accommodation** and **convergence** mechanisms must work in tandem. In accommodation, the shape of the lens is adjusted according to the distance of the target object. In convergence, a group of six pairs of muscles move the eyes so that they focus on the object. As an object gets closer, for instance, the lenses contract and the eyes turn inward.

> **Accommodation:** automatic focusing of the lens.

> **Convergence:** automatic adjustment of the pointing of the eyes in order to maintain clear vision.

**Strabismus:** muscular imbalance of the eyes so that the eyes point in different directions.

Two visual conditions that contribute to reading difficulties include **strabismus**, a condition in which the eyes are misaligned and point in different directions (Centers for Disease Control and Prevention, 2009b), and insufficient convergence, which means that the eyes are not fixating on the same spot at near point. Because these conditions strain the visual system, eyes may become tired, with resulting redness, itching, and burning. A headache may ensue. For some students, reading also may be disturbed. They may experience "letters and words that appear to overlap, letters and lines that appear to be crooked, parts of words that disappear, letters that become unclear, and problems with finding the next line of print" (Aasved, 1989, p. 192).

Struggling readers sometimes complain that the letters seem to be moving or that the words won't stand still. Reading requires, among other skills, binocular stability, which means that both eyes work together in such a fashion that they are able to fixate on small targets and maintain a single, clear fixation as the reader moves his eyes across and down a page. Binocular stability is developmental. Based on assessments of nearly 1,000 children, Stein (1996) found that only 54 percent of 6-year-olds had achieved binocular stability, but 70 percent of 7-year-olds and 85 percent of 9-year-olds had. However, a much higher proportion of binocular instability was found in disabled readers. When binocular instability was corrected through the use of special glasses, the disabled reader made nearly twice as much progress as did a group of controls. Fortunately, binocular instability can be partly alleviated by using large print.

## The Special Case of Amblyopia

Although 8-year-old Amy passed her vision screening test, frequent complaints of headaches and squinting alerted her teacher to a possible vision problem. An examination by a vision specialist revealed a serious problem. Amy had **amblyopia**, which can be caused by strabismus. Vision in her right eye was 20/20, but vision in her left eye was 20/100. Amy saw at 20 feet what people with average vision could see at 100 feet. Suppressing vision because of a lack of coordination with the right eye, the left eye had lost much of its power through disuse. Glasses and patching of the strong eye were prescribed. Patching the stronger eye forced the weaker eye to go back to work.

**Amblyopia:** suppression of vision in one eye. Because that eye is not used, it becomes weakened. Lost vision can be restored by stimulating the affected eye if the problem is detected early enough.

Amy was fortunate. According to Jobe (1976), amblyopia is best treated when the child is young. If untreated until the age of 8 or 9, there is danger of a complete loss of vision in the weaker eye. However, after months of patching, Amy's vision improved. Vision in her left eye improved to 20/50. Amblyopia, which is commonly known as "lazy eye," is the most common cause of vision impairment in children and is present in about 2–3 percent of the population (Centers for Disease Control and Prevention, 2009a)

## Color Vision

**Using Technology**

**Vision Health initiative (VHI)**

http://www.cdc.gov/visionhealth /basic_information/fast_facts.htm

Features easy-to-understand explanation of vision and vision impairments.

When the class was reading *Little Blue and Little Yellow* (Lionni, 1959), which explains how colors can be mixed to form new ones, Raphael seemed confused. Later, a visual exam revealed that Raphael is unable to distinguish the colors yellow and blue. The ability to see color ranges from individuals who can distinguish all hues to those who see only one color. In between are people who have difficulty detecting one or more of the primary colors: red, green, and blue. Most people who are color blind confuse red and green and are said to have red–green color blindness. However, some color-blind persons may also confuse blue and yellow. To them, blue is green, and yellow appears to be pink. A few color-blind persons are achromatic and see only white and shades of gray including black.

An inherited, X-linked trait, color blindness is far more prevalent among boys. About 7 boys in 100 have some degree of color blindness, but only about 1 girl in every 200 is color blind (Carlson, 1993).

It is important to be aware of children's ability to see color. Color blindness cannot be corrected and does not affect reading directly. However, it can be a source of confusion when teaching students how to read color names or when reading stories such as *Little Blue and Little Yellow,* in which color figures prominently, or when materials are color coded. Children who are color blind should be aware of their condition and should be taught strategies for adapting to it.

## Screening Vision

> While working with students, you might inquire if they have had a vision exam and whether glasses were prescribed. Often, students do not wear their glasses.

Although poor vision is usually not a cause of reading problems, it can make reading and related learning activities, such as copying from the board, more difficult. Therefore, it is important for the school to screen students for possible vision problems. Sometimes, signs of difficulty are obvious. The student holds the book too close or too far, or squints when copying from the board. Other signs are more subtle: tilting the head or covering one eye when reading, headaches or nausea after reading, or frequent tearing or redness in the eye. A list of symptoms is presented in Figure 2.4.

| | |
|---|---|
| Reddened eyes or lids | _____ |
| Frequent sties | _____ |
| Frequent tearing | _____ |
| Squinting | _____ |
| Headaches | _____ |
| Eyes turn in or out | _____ |
| Burning or itching sensation in eyes after reading or writing | _____ |
| Rubbing eyes while reading or writing | _____ |
| Excessive blinking while reading or writing | _____ |
| Double vision | _____ |
| Closing or covering one eye while reading or writing | _____ |
| Tilting head while reading or writing | _____ |
| Holding printed material too close | _____ |
| Frequently changing distance between eyes and printed material | _____ |
| Difficulty copying from board | _____ |
| Skipping or rereading lines | _____ |
| Omitting words | _____ |
| Using finger to keep his or her place | _____ |
| Difficulty writing on lines when writing or staying in lines when coloring | _____ |
| Writing with ragged left margin | _____ |
| Writing or doing math problems crookedly on page | _____ |

**■ FIGURE 2.4**
Vision Checklist
*Source:* Adapted from Beverstock (1991, pp. 10–11.)

## The Role of the Reading Specialist

Through your observations, note any students who may have visual problems and refer them for testing. Also encourage teachers to adopt practices that foster good vision. Lighting should be adequate, work on boards should be large enough so that it is easy to see, reading materials should be legible, students who need glasses should obtain and wear them.

## Vision Training

As noted earlier, there is more to vision than just acuity. Vision is a learned act. Although children may start kindergarten as early as age 4, vision does not mature until about the age of 7½. Young children tend to be farsighted. However, school demands a wide range of visual activities.

Years ago, noted child developmental researchers Ilg and Ames (1964) claimed that the following visual skills should be required for reading: ability to focus and point eyes together as a team, speed of perception, accuracy in looking from one object to another, ability to sustain focus at the reading distance, and eye–hand coordination. The authors recommended training for those found to be deficient in visual skills. They felt that for many children, visual therapy—that is, being taught how to move, focus, and fixate the two eyes so that they coordinate properly—is essential for efficient visual development.

Now, years later, visual training is controversial (American Academy of Pediatrics, Section on Ophthalmology, Council on Children with Disabilities; American Academy of Ophthalmology; American Association for Pediatric Ophthalmology and Strabismus; American Association of Certified Orthoptists, 2009; American Optometric Association, 2008 ), but its effectiveness has not been disproved. One conclusion that is clear is that visual training in isolation is ineffective. Visual training must be combined with instruction in reading and writing in order to have an impact. By and large, low-achieving readers and writers will improve in reading and writing when given careful instruction in these areas and lots of opportunities for practice and application. If students do evidence problems maintaining their place or sweeping their eyes across a line of print, steps can be taken to ease visual tasks. For one, the student can be shown how to use a marker. Clearly designed books with large print might be used. Periods of reading and writing might be interspersed with activities that involve far-point vision so as to give the child's near-point visual mechanism a rest. Copying from the board might be kept to a minimum, as the shifting from far to near point and back again makes maximum demands on the accommodation/convergence systems. Use of big books and chart stories, on the other hand, should be stressed, because these make use of the child's far-point vision.

> ✳ At one time, using a marker to help students keep their place as they read was discouraged, but one should be recommended for students who would benefit from its use. Older students might use a 6-inch ruler or similar device.

# Physical Health

> ✳ Kevin's case demonstrates the importance of an interactive approach. The first step in helping Kevin would be encouraging his family to make sure he is well rested.

Seven-year-old Kevin was having difficulty learning to read. Although he was in second grade, he still was operating at a beginning reading level. Observation indicated that Kevin was inattentive and seemed to lack energy. Kevin was also frequently absent due to colds and other minor illnesses. When questioned by his teacher, Kevin revealed that he stayed up late at night watching TV. Sleepy and irritable the next day, he had little energy to devote to the strenuous task of learning to read. His progress was further hampered by his frequent absences, which caused him to miss crucial instruction. Tragically, Kevin's reading difficulty was caused by inadequate care.

Unfortunately, more and more children are living in potentially stressful environments. The number of children raised in foster care has increased by more than half, from 200,000 to more than half a million. About one child in three is being raised in a single-parent home. Nearly one child in three lives in a home where no parent has full-time, year-round employment (Kids Count, 2011). There is also an increase in child abuse, homelessness, and violence in the lives of children. These factors are having a negative impact on the emotional and cognitive development of children and, of course, on their reading and writing development.

Also on the increase is asthma. Over 10 million U.S. children 17 years and younger (14 percent) have at one time been diagnosed with asthma; 7 million children still have asthma (10 percent) (Bloom, Cohen, & Freeman 2011). There is some evidence that low-achieving readers have a greater incidence of asthma and other allergic conditions (Hugdahl, 1993). Asthma and other chronic illnesses can impede progress in reading in one of five ways: increased absenteeism, side effects of medication, lessened ability to engage in learning activities because of the effects of the illness, interference from anxiety and other emotional facts caused by the illness, and teachers' or parents' perceptions that the student is too fragile to engage in learning activities (Celano & Geller, 1993). Research suggests that students who have asthma do not necessarily experience greater difficulty with reading. However, asthma may combine with other factors, such as low socioeconomic status and behavior problems, and then impede progress in reading (Celano & Geller, 1993).

Educational programs designed to help children better understand and manage asthma can help improve school performance. When planning programs for these children, it will be helpful to involve health care professionals and parents. Providing instruction in management of the illness and consulting with parents and health care professionals are effective procedures for working with any youngster who has a chronic health problem. The child's reading and writing difficulties should be considered in the total context of all of the child's needs.

## Educational Factors

On the basis of a longitudinal study, Vellutino and colleagues (1996) concluded that experiential and instructional deficits were at the heart of the reading difficulties of the middle-class students studied. All but 15 percent of students classified as being disabled readers made substantial progress in a carefully planned instructional program. In follow-up studies, Vellutino and colleagues (2006) found that most children at risk for having difficulty with reading overcame these risk factors when instructed in a well-planned literacy program in kindergarten and first grade. A small number needed additional help in first grade in order to overcome risk factors. As Vellutino, Fletcher, Snowling, and Scanlon (2004) concluded, "Early and long-term difficulties in the majority of impaired readers are caused primarily by experiential and instructional deficits rather than biologically based cognitive deficits" (p. 30). Factors that contribute to poor performance include failure to gear instruction to the needs of the student. Unfortunately, as a group, poor readers spend less time reading silently, do more oral reading, are asked a greater proportion of lower-level questions, are given fewer prompts, and have less time to answer (Allington, 1983; Barr & Dreeben, 1991).

Using inappropriate materials, especially materials that are too difficult, is also a major educational factor in reading difficulty. In her longitudinal study of poor readers, Juel (1994b) found that, on average, these students could only read about 50 percent of the words in their beginning readers. From first through fourth grade, they were able to read only between 70 and 80 percent of the words in their basal readers. In fourth grade, the average poor reader was able to read just 74 words in 100. In other words, for four years these youngsters were forced to read materials that were far too difficult for them. It is small wonder that they disliked reading. When interviewed in fourth grade, 26 of 29 expressed a distaste for reading. When asked whether they would rather read or clean their rooms, 40 percent opted for cleaning. Poor pacing, inadequate classroom management, and failure to develop independence are other factors that contribute to reading problems (Harris & Sipay, 1990).

> ✥ Goodman (1982) comments, "Coping with school texts, especially in upper elementary and secondary grades, is a problem that most troubled readers face even as they are improving in their ability and self-confidence" (p. 89).

Lack of effective instruction is also a major factor in reading difficulty. Although benefiting from immersion in print, many emergent readers require systematic instruction in phonological awareness and letter knowledge (Pinnell & McCarrier, 1994). Later, they need direct instruction in decoding, comprehension, vocabulary, and study skills. As Richek, Caldwell, Jennings, and Lerner (1996) comment, "Although the typical student often learns word recognition and comprehension strategies from extensive reading, low-achieving students may need direct, sequenced lessons" (p. 7). However, the program should be balanced. An overemphasis on phonics or oral reading can be detrimental (Allington, 1984). Students need ample opportunity to apply skills, so there should be an emphasis on reading a variety of materials. As Goodman (1982) notes, "Readers in trouble are more likely to be the victims of too much skill use than not enough" (p. 89). What they need, Goodman explains, are "opportunities to read and write, and most of all, the experience of success." They need to realize that "the easiest things for them to read are going to be the very ones they have the most interest in, the most background for, and that they get the most pleasure from" (p. 90).

Poor instructional planning can also be a factor in reading problems. As noted in Chapter 1, a small percentage of students who participate in Reading Recovery prove to be difficult to accelerate. Observations undertaken to note instructional factors that foster or hinder progress found that the major factor associated with a lack of success was failure to plan daily lessons. Other negative factors included not using consistent, specific language; not demonstrating enough; and not noting whether a student had gained control of a skill in a variety of contexts (Lyons, 1995).

## Scientifically Based Instruction

Concerned that schools adopted methods which had no validation and which often proved to be ineffective, federal legislation requires instruction that has been scientifically validated; that is, the technique or approach has been compared to another technique or approach and found to provide superior results. Key elements found to be a part of effective programs for the early grades are phonological awareness, phonics, fluency, vocabulary, and comprehension (National Reading Panel, 2000). The International Reading Association advocates evidence-based rather than scientifically based instruction. *Evidence-based validation* is a broader term and includes qualitative studies as well as those that had an experimental and control group.

## ▨ Social and Cultural Factors

✻ Students' behavior is a key factor in the amount of progress students make. In a study of early intervention programs, Torgesen (2000) found that students who benefited the least were those who had low scores on phonological awareness and were rated by their classroom teachers as having the broadest range and highest frequency of behavior problems.

In many ways, reading and writing are social activities. When we talk about a book we have read or ask a friend to explain a passage or, as members of a club, draft a letter to the editor, we are working with others to construct and create meaning. In schools, students read to each other, discuss books in small and large groups, work with a partner in reading, and share their writing in small and large groups. Students' learning is dependent, in part, on their role in the group, how the group perceives them, and how effectively they operate in the group.

Unfortunately, students who are poor readers are frequently rejected by their classmates (Richek et al., 1996). Feeling rejected, they become passive, stop participating, and fail to get help from their peers. Motivation and sense of self-efficacy also suffer. As noted in Chapter 1, building a sense of community in which everyone in the classroom is valued is essential for all students, especially those who are struggling.

Students also do better when materials reflect their cultural heritage and when the reading and writing activities in which they engage are ones that are important in their cultures. It is all too easy to underestimate the rich heritages that students from diverse cultures bring to the school (Taylor & Dorsey-Gaines, 1988). Teachers might use an approach known as "Cultural Modeling," in which commonalities between the literacy practices of home and school are identified and built upon. Raps, for instance, have been used to help students memorize key facts. Music lyrics, videos, and art have been used to expand students' writing (Orellana, Reynolds, & Martinez, 2011). Teachers have also built upon bilingual students' ability to translate for their caregivers. Orellana and Reynolds (2008) used this translation skill to develop students' "*para*-phrasing," which is a valuable writing and comprehension strategy. Orellana and Reynolds helped students apply the skills that they used to translate government forms and other complex text for their caregivers. The students used these same skills to comprehend difficult academic texts.

## ▨ Family Factors

Children of parents who had reading difficulties are three to six times more likely to experience reading difficulties themselves (Smith, Brower, Cardon, & Defries, 1998). Genetic studies suggest a complex interaction between several genes and environmental factors (Gilger & Wise, 2004).

The home literacy environment is, of course, a critical factor in children's literacy development. Key factors include the following:

- **Parental reading habits.** Children are more likely to value reading if they see their parents reading.

- **Reading to children by adults.** Reading to children is one of the most valuable things that parents can do. Reading to children develops language and literacy skills and builds a closer relationship between parent and child.

- **Availability of reading and writing materials.** Just having literacy materials available fosters their use.

- **Parental expectations.** By expressing high expectations and providing help, parents foster enhanced achievement.

- **Stimulating verbal interactions.** Discussions, explanations, dinner-time conversations, and reading to children and discussing what has been read all contribute to children's language and conceptual development. Research indicates that both middle-class and poor, uneducated parents engage in many of the same type of verbal interactions, but middle-class children are exposed to a greater quantity of interactions (Hart & Risley, 1995).

## Economic Factors

Some 21.9 percent (about 16 million) of the nation's school-age children live in poverty (U. S. Census Bureau, 2012). Poverty makes its mark early. At 18 months, all children have an equal vocabulary, regardless of the educational or economic status of their families (Hart & Risley, 1995). However, after that, vocabulary growth starts to diverge. Children raised in poverty may come to school knowing 3,000 or fewer words, whereas children from affluent families may have vocabularies of 8,000 or more words. By the time students enter kindergarten, 66 percent of students can recognize the letters of the alphabet. However, only 41 percent of children whose caregivers are receiving welfare can recognize the letters of the alphabet (West, Denton, & Germino-Hausken, 2000). According to National Assessment of Educational Progress (NAEP) data, children raised in poverty lag behind in reading. More than twice as many students eligible for free or reduced-price lunch programs read below the basic level (Grigg, Daane, Jin, & Campbell, 2003).

Although teachers want the best for their students, they may structure instruction for the poorest readers in such a way that their growth is unintentionally limited. Students who live in poor areas are also less likely to be taught comprehension strategies and may not be asked to do out-of-class reading, because the teachers judge they would not do it (García, Pearson, & Jiménez, 1994). When poor students receive similar reading instruction to that given to middle-class students, their achievement is similar.

Poverty can interact with other factors. Childsight, a division of Helen Keller International, estimates that approximately 25 percent of secondary school students who live in poverty cannot see what is written on the board. They need glasses but their families can't afford them. Targeting 11- to 14-year-olds, because that is the age group most likely to be hit with visual problems, Childsight has screened more than 200,000 students and distributed 30,000 pairs of eyeglasses (Helen Keller International, 2004).

## Summary

Reading problems are often the result of a host of interacting factors or contributing causes. Possible factors include cognitive, visual perceptual, linguistic, emotional, physical, educational, social, cultural, and economic factors. Having adequate intelligence is not a guarantee that one will not have a reading problem. Specific cognitive factors, such as memory, associative learning, and attention, apparently play roles in reading disorders. Although deficits in memory can affect reading in a variety of ways, inefficient verbal coding may be at the heart of word recognition, comprehension, and vocabulary deficiencies. Related to and possibly caused by inefficient verbal encoding is a deficit in associative learning. A deficiency in associative learning is characteristic of students who have the most serious reading difficulties.

Students who have difficulty paying attention have difficulty learning. As many as 51 percent of boys and 46 percent of girls who have reading problems have been diagnosed as having the somewhat controversial condition attention deficit hyperactivity disorder. Although auditory processing deficits seem to lie at the heart of many reading disorders, visual processing difficulties, including difficulty with orthographic processing, can contribute to the problem.

Deficits in oral language are a major characteristic of low-achieving readers. These deficits may take the form of articulation problems; auditory discrimination and phonological difficulties; deficiencies in vocabulary, syntax, and knowledge of story grammar; slowness in rapid automatized naming; and slowness in word retrieval.

Failure to learn to read can be both a cause and an effect of social and/or emotional problems. A multidisciplinary approach should be used when working with students who have social and/or emotional problems.

Reading difficulties can be rooted in physical factors or intensified by them. Both vision and hearing should be screened. Poor health does not necessarily affect reading development adversely. However, chronic conditions such as asthma, when combined with factors such as poverty, may hinder progress in reading.

Educational factors are at the heart of many instances of low achievement in reading. Inappropriate materials, poor pacing, lack of effective instruction, and overuse of skill and drill may lead to reading problems.

Failure to provide for the social nature of learning and the diversity that exists in today's classrooms can impede growth in reading. Poverty can also be a barrier to progress in reading and writing development.

## Application Activities

1. To get a concrete sense of a severe reading difficulty and what its effect might be, read the case study in "A Nonreader Becomes a Reader" by McCormick (1994). What are the possible causes of Peter's difficulty? How was his difficulty treated?
2. Read the Executive Summary of *Preventing Reading Difficulties in Young Children* by Snow, Burns, and Griffin (1998). What are the committee's major recommendations?
3. Choose one of the possible causes of reading difficulty and investigate it in more detail.

## My Education Lab

Go to the topic **Reading Assessment** in the MyEducationLab (www.myeducationlab .com) for **Assessing and Correcting Reading Difficulties,** where you can:

- Find learning outcomes for **Reading Assessment** along with the national standards that connect to these outcomes.
- Complete Assignments and Activities that can help you more deeply understand the chapter content.
- Apply and practice your understanding of the core teaching skills identified in the chapter with the Building Teaching Skills and Dispositions learning units.
- Examine challenging situations and cases presented in the Iris Center Resources.

- Check your comprehension of the content covered in the chapter with the Study Plan. Here you will be able to take a chapter pretest, receive feedback on your answers, and then access personalized Review, Practice, and Enrichment exercises to enhance your understanding of chapter content. After you complete the exercises, take a posttest to confirm your comprehension.

- Practice targeting instruction and making content accessible for all students with A+RISE activities.

# 3 Overview of Assessment

**H**ave you ever had the feeling, after taking a test, that the test was not a valid indicator of your knowledge, that you really knew more but the test did not allow you to show it, or that the test seemed unfair because it asked questions about topics not covered in the class? This chapter looks at some basic principles of assessment. It also looks at a number of different kinds of tests and the ways in which tests and other assessment devices can be chosen and used so as to provide the most accurate and useful information.

## ANTICIPATION GUIDE

*Read each of the following statements. Put a check under "Agree" or "Disagree" to show how you feel about each one. If possible, discuss your responses with classmates.*

|  | AGREE | DISAGREE |
|---|---|---|
| 1. In assessment, how a student gets an answer is more important than whether the answer is right or wrong. | _____ | _____ |
| 2. Most tests do not yield useful information because they distort the reading/writing process. | _____ | _____ |
| 3. In general, informal tests are better than formal ones. | _____ | _____ |
| 4. One of the best ways to assess a student is to teach him or her in a weak area and see how much and how well he or she learns. | _____ | _____ |
| 5. Time spent assessing low-achieving readers would be better spent instructing them. | _____ | _____ |

## ▚▚ Principles of Effective Assessment

Tracy, a fourth-grader, was a puzzle. She had above-average academic ability, and her word-recognition skills were superior. She could read multisyllabic words with ease. Her oral reading was smooth and expressive. However, her comprehension was surprisingly poor. On both informal and formal tests, she missed all but the easiest questions.

The test results revealed that Tracy had a comprehension problem, but they did not suggest any reasons for Tracy's problem, nor were there any suggestions in the results as to the best way to teach Tracy. The testing had been static. It provided the end product of Tracy's reading achievement, but it provided no information about the processes Tracy used. It did not indicate what Tracy needed in order to perform adequately. Nor did it suggest how much help Tracy might need. Also missing was information about other important aspects of Tracy's performance: How did she respond to classroom instruction? Were there some kinds of tasks that she enjoyed or found easier than others? How did she feel about herself as a learner? What was her relationship with her classmates? What was her family life like? Was her family supportive of her efforts in school?

> ✳ Although assessment and instruction are placed in separate sections in this text, assessment should be an integral part of instruction.

What Tracy required was an assessment that was interactive. An interactive assessment considers both top-down and bottom-up factors. It also postulates that the reader changes as the task changes. For instance, the student who daydreams her way through a science article may read a biography of her favorite sports star with intense interest. An interactive approach to assessment recognizes that five major factors have to be considered: the reader, the text, the techniques being used, the reading or writing task involved, and the situational context in which the reading or writing is performed (Walker, 1992). The student who is lost in a large-group situation may do quite well when taught in a small group. A student who responds negatively to a technique that is teacher directed might react more positively when taught by a method that relies more heavily on student input.

Because reading and writing are such complex activities, the assessment must also be multidimensional. Depending on the age and level of literacy development of the student and the nature of the difficulty, it should include the following areas: general cognitive ability; other cognitive processes, such as memory and associative learning; phonological and orthographic processing, the ability to use independent learning strategies in decoding, comprehension, and study skills; vocabulary knowledge; writing; spelling; and handwriting. Language development and physical factors, such as overall health, vision, and hearing, as well as home and school factors should be considered. Being holistic and interactive, the assessment needs to consider the interplay among the factors and how they affect each other. For instance, chronic ear infections might impair hearing, which might make learning phonics more difficult. This, in turn, will lower the student's self-image as a learner, which will reduce effort and achievement.

Assessment also needs to be realistic. The best assessment is that which is closest to the skill or strategy in its actual use in the classroom (Meltzer, 1993). The informal reading inventory, which is presented in Chapter 4, is one of the most effective assessment devices because it involves actual oral and silent reading and oral retellings or the oral answering of questions, which is similar to the way reading is conducted in the classroom. This assessment is even more realistic if the reading series, trade books, or content-area texts used in the students' program are a part of the assessment.

## ▨▨ Dynamic Assessment

Assessment must also be dynamic. It should not just measure what the student can do now; it should also predict the student's potential for change. For instance, two students may both do poorly on a test of word-reading ability. Although their scores may be identical, their potential for learning the words might be very different. But how does the teacher know this?

> ✳ Assessment must reflect changing academic demands as students move up through the grades and encounter higher-level comprehension and study tasks.

The solution is to teach the students a sampling of the unknown words and to note carefully what each student required in order to learn them. You might do this in a number of ways. First, select the words to be taught. You might choose, from those missed on the test, seven words of medium difficulty. Teach the words by using an approach that you feel should be effective for a particular student. Place the words on cards. Display a word and ask the student to read it. If the student is not able to read it, say the word and have the student repeat it. Point out distinctive features of the word or call attention to familiar phonic elements, and use it in a sentence. Each time you say the word, point to it. Then present the next word in the same way. After all the words have been presented, shuffle them, and present them again in the same way they were presented the first time. Keep a record of the number of words that the student is able to read correctly. See how many trials it takes the student to learn all seven words, but set a limit of approximately ten trials so that the student does not become frustrated. If the student learns all the words in a few trials, then you can infer that the student has good word-learning ability and should make rapid progress.

If the student has difficulty with the task, try other teaching approaches. You might use a word-building approach as explained in Chapter 8. In a dynamic assessment, you do not just find out what the student doesn't know; you also explore the student's level of knowledge, the amount of instruction needed to teach the element, and, in some instances, the way in which the student learns best. Dynamic assessment answers the all-important questions: How does the student learn? What must be done in order for the student to learn? As such, instruction is linked to assessment.

Dynamic assessment is based on Vygotsky's view of learning (Haywood, Brown, & Wingenfeld, 1990), which holds that children learn higher-level concepts through their interactions with peers and adults (Vygotsky, 1978). Vygotsky suggested that in addition to measuring a student's current functioning level, we should also assess how well the child might do if helped by an adult. The difference between what a child can do on his own and what the child can do with the assistance of an adult or more knowledgeable peer is known as the **zone of proximal development.** This is what is measured in dynamic assessment.

> **Zone of proximal development:** difference between what students can do on their own and what they can do under the guidance of an adult or more knowledgeable peer.

In a sense, dynamic assessment provides a more realistic estimate of students' potential because it yields information about their learning ability. As Feuerstein, Rand, and Hoffman (1979) have shown in their research, lack of knowledge may be mistaken for lack of ability to acquire that knowledge. Dynamic assessment has the potential for providing a more accurate, fairer estimate of learning ability in children who may not have had adequate opportunity to learn because of an impoverished home life or substandard schooling.

***Administering a Dynamic Assessment***   In general, administering a dynamic assessment involves the following steps:

*Step 1: Gather baseline data.* Administer the test the way it is normally given. This will provide baseline data.

*Step 2: Teach and record.* Provide assistance or instruction so that students can reach an acceptable level of performance on the task or a sample of the task. Record the amount and type of help required to reach an acceptable level.

*Step 3: Retest.* Give the original test once again and chart improvement from first to final testing. Degree of change suggests the extent to which students will benefit from instruction.

*Step 4: Evaluate intervention.* Note student responses to your assistance. What helped? What didn't? Are students able to apply or use in new context what they learned? Also note any difficulties students had during the learning trials. Then describe the conditions and procedures most likely to improve the skill or strategy tested (Haywood, 1993; Haywood et al., 1990).

Dynamic assessment is time-consuming, but for students with severe reading problems, dynamic assessment could mean finding techniques that work. "In such cases, the cost of dynamic assessment may be much less than the cost of not finding the answers to important educational questions" (Haywood et al., 1990, p. 417). Dynamic assessment also helps identify the number of students who have severe problems. Vellutino, Scanlon, and Tanzman (1998) found that when students initially identified as having serious reading problems were provided with well-planned instruction, most responded positively and made enough progress so that they were reclassified as achieving readers or as students with mild reading problems.

In one study, dynamic assessment was used to analyze the effectiveness of screening instruments that identify at-risk first-graders (Compton et al., 2012). The assessment measured proficiency on a decoding task and also the amount of scaffolding necessary for students to learn an unfamiliar decoding task. Use of this assessment effectively aided the identification of students at risk and reduced the number of false positives, students who would have been classified as needing intervention but who didn't really need it. *DIBELS Deep Word Reading and Decoding* (Sopris Learning) provides procedures for dynamic assessment, and notes responses obtained through teaching (Powell-Smith, 2012; Powell-Smith, Kaminski, & Good, 2011). Teachers can alter the directions or initiate instruction to elicit correct responses.

## Assisted Testing

In **assisted testing** you ask: "How much help and what kind of help do I have to provide in order for a student to perform successfully?" You start off by giving a little assistance and then increasing it until the student can respond correctly.

**Assisted testing** is an easy-to-apply form of dynamic assessment in which students are given cues or prompts to see how much help they need in order to respond correctly (Johnson, 1993). At first, provide an easy cue. Then gradually provide more substantial cues until the student is able to respond correctly or you run out of prompts. Based on the cues you have given, determine what the student already knows or can do and what she or he would need to know in order to be able to perform successfully.

For instance, on a test of word recognition, the student responded "I don't know" to many of the words. Going back over a sampling of the missed words, the teacher first asked the student if there was any part of a missed word that she knew. If that didn't work, the teacher covered up the first portion of the word and had the student read the second portion. Then uncovering the first portion, the teacher had the student read that, combine the two parts, and read the whole word. For instance, for the word *morning*, the student said she could not read any parts. But when the teacher covered up all but the *or*, the student had no difficulty reading it. When *m* was uncovered, the student was able to add *m* to *or* to form *mor* and then, reading the *ing,* add it to *n* and combine all the elements into the word *morning.* With similar help, the student was able to decode a number of the multisyllabic words that she had gotten wrong on the first pass through. The teacher concluded that the student knew the elements of which the words were composed but needed help locating known elements in multisyllabic words and then reconstructing the words.

On the basis of the initial testing, the teacher would have concluded that the student simply could not handle polysyllabic words. Using assisted testing, she could see that the student had some knowledge of multisyllabic words. The teacher also had discovered a way of helping the student learn what she needed to know in order to be more successful in decoding polysyllabic words. Figure 3.1 shows an analysis of the dynamic testing of the student, including recommendations for future instruction.

## Levels of Knowledge

> ✳ Finding a student's knowledge level provides a realistic starting point. Often we assume that problem learners have no knowledge in a particular area and we waste time reteaching what they already know.

When assessing students, also try to determine their level of knowledge. If they cannot respond on a higher level, move to a lower level. In the classic assessment, Durrell Analysis of Reading Difficulty (Durrell & Catterson, 1980), alphabet knowledge is tested on five levels. The highest level requires students to write the letters of the alphabet. If the students cannot do that, they are

---

**TITLE OF ASSESSMENT:** *Basic Reading Inventory, Graded Word Lists B*

**ORIGINAL RESULTS**

| Level | Number Correct |
|-------|----------------|
| *pp* | *20/20* |
| *p* | *19/20* |
| *1* | *17/20* |
| *2* | *17/20* |
| *3* | *10/20* |

*Did well with single-syllable words but had difficulty with multisyllabic words.*

**RETEST RESULTS**

| Level | Number Correct |
|-------|----------------|
| *pp* | *20/20* |
| *p* | *20/20* |
| *1* | *19/20* |
| *2* | *19/20* |
| *3* | *16/20* |

*Was able to read 11/17 multisyllabic words previously missed.*

**ASSISTANCE PROVIDED**

*Showed student how to look for familiar word parts in words she had difficulty with and use those familiar parts to reconstruct whole word. Needed four prompts.*

**RECOMMENDATIONS**

*Needs to be taught multisyllabic patterns, especially the less common ones. Needs more instruction in use of decoding strategies. Stress application of strategies.*

■ **FIGURE 3.1**
Dynamic
Assessment
Analysis

asked to identify a series of letters. Failing to do that, students recognize letters by choosing from four letters the one that the teacher says. Students who cannot do that are asked to match letters from memory. For example, shown the letter *m,* which is then removed from sight, the student picks the *m* from a series of four letters. The lowest level is a straight match. The students, while looking at the letter *m,* select its match from a series of four letters. The point of having these levels is to find out where the students are in terms of alphabet knowledge so that instruction can proceed from there.

> Assessment should emphasize the students' strengths so that these provide a foundation for instruction.

All too often, when students miss an item or a series of items, we assume they have no knowledge in that area. However, using a level-of-knowledge approach, we retest until we determine on what level the students are operating. For instance, if a student cannot read the word *where* on a test of word reading, the task could be made into one of recognition rather than recall by saying the word *where* and then having the student pick it out from among two or three other words.

Also vary the mode of response. If students are unable to write a summary, perhaps they can give one orally. If students have difficulty with certain questions, you might reword them. Perhaps they were too vague or too complex (Johnson, 1993).

## Trial Teaching

Also known as diagnostic teaching (Walker, 1992), trial teaching is based on the information yielded by an assessment. It works best if the assessment has been dynamic, because a dynamic assessment provides insight into the student's learning processes. Constructing hypotheses based on an analysis of assessment data, and in cooperation with the student, you construct a tentative approach that you feel will work best. You also carefully monitor the instruction to make necessary changes in the approach, materials, setting, pacing, or any other aspect of the situation.

> The Diagnostic Assessment of Reading (2nd ed.) is accompanied by online Trial Teaching Strategies, which are a series of brief lessons that can be matched to students' diagnostic profiles and used to try out and select teaching techniques.

Fittingly, the first step in trial teaching is to consult with the student. Discuss with the student the results of the assessment and explain that there are several ways of helping her or him and that you—teacher and student—will be trying out different ways of teaching and different materials to find out which works best (Roswell & Natchez, 1989). Depending on the skill or strategy being taught, the student is invited to choose materials and, in some instances, activities. Using your strongest hypothesis, try out one or more instructional procedures. If one doesn't work out, try another.

Diagnosis does not stop with dynamic or assisted testing or even trial teaching. It is an ongoing process. As Doris Johnson (1993) notes, "It goes on forever." In assessment, you create a hypothesis and evaluate it through testing, including dynamic testing, observation, trial teaching, and carefully monitoring the student's performance. In a sense, every lesson that you teach should be a trial or diagnostic one.

## Assessment Categories

Assessment measures fall into four main categories: screening, diagnostic, monitoring, and outcome. Screening devices are assessments used to identify students who need additional assessment because they appear to be at risk. For emergent

## Essential Steps in the Assessment Process

As adapted from Kibby (1995), the assessment process consists of six essential steps.

*Step 1:* Establish an estimate of the levels on which the students are operating.

*Step 2:* Gather and evaluate information about students' reading/writing strengths and weaknesses.

*Step 3:* Assess and evaluate students' teaching–learning situation. Through dynamic testing and trial teaching, determine under what circumstances students learn best. Also assess the students' home situations.

*Step 4:* Evaluate materials used in the students' program.

*Step 5:* Integrate information and design a long-term program.

*Step 6:* Continually assess and evaluate the program and make modifications as necessary. In general you will be asking the following questions:

- On what levels are students functioning?
- What are the students' potential for growth?
- What are the students' strengths and weaknesses in reading and writing?
- What are the students' most immediate or most essential needs in reading and writing?
- What would be the most effective materials for these students?
- Under what circumstances and in what setting would these students learn best?
- What are the most effective techniques or approaches for teaching these students?
- Are there any physical, psychological, social, or other factors that need to be considered?
- How might the home, larger community, and school work together to help students?

To answer these questions you will need assessment instruments, which are devices for gathering information about students' performance.

readers, tests of alphabet knowledge or phonological awareness might function as screening tests. Word-list tests composed of words that gradually increase in difficulty or oral or silent-reading selections might be used as screening tests for older students. Students are usually screened at the beginning of the school year or, if they are transfer students, when they enter the school. Students who score very low on screening measures should be provided with additional assessment and/or an intervention program. If students fail to make progress despite careful teaching and placement in intervention programs, an in-depth diagnosis may be required. Diagnosis is typically conducted by a team of professionals and might include assessment by the school psychologist, learning disabilities specialist, reading specialist, and other professionals.

Once they are in a program, students' progress is monitored monthly or even weekly to make sure they are making adequate progress. However, the progress of all students should be monitored three times a year to identify students who are falling behind and check the effectiveness of the classroom literacy program. By identifying students who are falling behind, the monitoring assessments perform a screening function.

Outcome measures are designed to indicate whether the goals of a program have been met. Outcome measures are generally given at the end of the semester or year. Assessment is sometimes described as being formative or summative. **Formative assessment** is ongoing assessment designed to provide teachers with data they can use to plan and revise instruction. Monitoring is an example of formative assessment. **Summative assessment** is given at the end of a program to evaluate its effectiveness. Outcome assessment is summative.

**Formative assessment:** ongoing assessment such as a quiz or teacher observation designed to be used to plan or inform instruction.

**Summative assessment** is the final measure of progress toward meeting a goal.

## ▓▓ Assessment Instruments

Given an interactive transactional theory of reading, which is based on the premise that students use both top-down and bottom-up processes to construct meaning, it follows that assessment should involve the kinds of reading and writing tasks that students are called on to perform in and out of school—reading whole books, studying texts, and writing stories or letters, which is authentic assessment. Although the term *assessment* might conjure up visions of tests, testing is just one way of getting information about students' reading and writing performance. You will also use observations, interviews, questionnaires, and samples of students' work. In addition, student records and portfolios can provide insight into students' reading and writing experiences and capabilities. Portfolios, which are collections of samples of students' writing and reading, are especially useful sources of information.

This chapter will provide an overview of the kinds of tests that are frequently used in literacy assessment and some basic measurement concepts. Chapter 4 will explore the informal reading inventory and related tests. Chapter 5 will focus on gaining insight into students' reading and writing processes using observations, interviews, questionnaires, work samples, and formal and informal tests. Appendix A contains word learning and decoding assessments.

> ❋ Every child can learn, given the right kind of instruction, materials, tasks, and situation. The purpose of assessment is to determine the optimal learning circumstances for a particular student.

## ▓▓ Tests

Although widely used, group tests have a number of shortcomings. Most do not require students to create meaning. Rather, most provide students with a series of multiple-choice items, so that they select rather than create responses. In addition, higher-level skills are neglected. Furthermore, group tests generally assess the product rather than the process of reading. Tests results may indicate the percentage of answers correct or compare students with others who have taken the test, but they do not generally provide insight into the strategies that students use to respond to test items.

Despite their shortcomings, results of group tests can provide useful information. They can function as screening devices. Low scores on group tests can indicate possible problems. Individuals with low scores might be given individual assessments. Low scores by groups of students in key areas such as comprehension or vocabulary development might suggest the need for changes in the instructional program or materials.

### Norm-Referenced versus Criterion-Referenced Tests

#### Norm-Referenced Tests

> **Norm-referenced test:** the performance of students is compared to that of a norming or sample group.

> **Standardized test:** tasks and administration are specified so that anyone taking the test does so under similar conditions. The term *standardized test* is also used to mean a norm-referenced test but a test can be standardized without being norm-referenced.

Group tests of reading and writing generally fall into one of two categories: **norm referenced** or criterion referenced. In norm-referenced tests, which are often referred to as **standardized tests,** students are compared with a norm group, which is a sample of others who are in the same grade or are the same age. The score indicates whether students' performance is average, above average, or below average compared to the norm group. Scores are commonly reported in one or more of the following ways:

- Raw score is the total number correct. It has no meaning until transformed into a percentile rank, grade equivalent, or other score.

> **Percentile rank:** the most-used score for norm- referenced tests of reading and writing. Percentile rank is a measure of comparative standing. If students progress at the same rate, their percentile ranks stay the same. To move up to a higher percentile, they must make a better-than-average gain.

- **Percentile rank** indicates where a student's score falls on a ranking of percentages from 1 to 99. A percentile rank of 10 indicates that the students did better than 10 percent of the norm group. A rank of 50 is average and indicates that the student did better than 50 percent of the norm group. Percentile rank is the most frequently used norm score. However, percentile ranks are not equal units. A percentile rank of 80 does not mean that the student did twice as well as a student with a percentile rank of 40. Therefore, percentile ranks should not be added, subtracted, divided, multiplied, or used for subtest comparison.

- Grade-equivalent scores characterize performance as being equivalent to that of other students in a particular grade. A grade-equivalent score of 6.2 indicates that the student answered the same number of items as the average sixth-grader in the second month of that grade. The grade-equivalent score does not indicate at what level the student can read. A score of 6.2 does not mean that a student is reading on a sixth-grade level.

  The International Reading Association opposes the use of grade-equivalent scores because they are open to misinterpretation. For instance, a grade equivalent of 6.2 earned by a third-grader does not mean that the third-grader can handle sixth-grade material. Chances are the third-grade test does not even contain selections on a sixth-grade level. On the other hand, a grade equivalent of 3.2 obtained by a sixth-grader does not mean that the sixth-grader is reading on a third-grade level. It does indicate that the student is reading significantly below grade level. Grade-equivalent scores are most meaningful when the test students have taken is at the right level and the score is not more than a year above or a year below average. Grade-equivalent scores are misleading and easily misunderstood and so should be used with care.

- Normal-curve equivalents (NCEs) place students on a scale of 1 through 99. The main difference between NCEs and percentile ranks is that NCEs represent equal units and so can be added and subtracted and used for comparing performance on subtests.

- The term *stanine* is a combination of the words *standard* and *nine* and describes a 9-point scale. The stanines 4, 5, and 6 are average points, with 1, 2, and 3 being below average and 7, 8, and 9 above average. Stanines are useful when making comparisons among subtests.

- Scaled scores are a continuous ranking of scores from the lowest levels of a series of norm-referenced tests through the highest levels—from kindergarten or first grade through high school. Scaled scores, which generally range from 000 to 999, are useful for tracking long-term growth. Two specialized forms of scaled scores are the DRP and Lexile units.

  DRP units are used to report performance on the Degrees of Reading Power tests. DRP units range from 15 for the easiest materials to 85 for the most difficult reading material. The advantage of DRP units is that the same type of measurement is used to indicate students' reading levels and also the difficulty level of reading material. A student with a DRP score of 50 is able to read materials that have a readability of 50 or below or slightly above.

  Lexile scores are also used for reporting test scores and the difficulty level of texts. The Lexile framework is a scale from 200 to 1700 with 200 being very easy reading material—about mid-first-grade level—and 1700 being very difficult reading material of the type found in scientific journals. A student with a

Lexile score of 600, which is about a sixth-grade level, is able to read materials below the 600 Lexile or slightly above it. Lexile units are also used to indicate both the students' level of reading proficiency and the difficulty level of reading material. Lexile scores are widely used on both tests and materials.

Many of the scores provided for norm-referenced tests are based on the concept of the *normal curve*. According to this concept, if a large number of people took a test and the scores were depicted graphically, most of the scores would fall in the middle. As scores fell more and more above or below average, there would be fewer cases, so that a bell-shaped curve would be formed as in Figure 3.2. A line drawn through the middle would depict the average or *mean score*.

In addition to having a mean, scores have a standard deviation. The *standard deviation* indicates the degree to which scores are above or below the mean. The more the scores vary, the higher is the standard deviation. Because of the shape of the curve, about 68 percent of the cases fall within 1 standard deviation above or below the mean, close to 96 percent fall within plus or minus 2 standard deviations, and nearly 100 percent fall within 3 standard deviations. Figure 3.2 shows standard deviations and how norm-referenced test scores relate to the normal curve and to each other.

Also shown are scores from two intelligence tests: the Wechsler scales and the Stanford-Binet. Both have a mean of 100, but the Wechsler scales have a standard deviation of 15 and the Stanford-Binet has a standard deviation of 16. This means that a score of 130 on the Wechsler is equivalent to a score of 132 on the Stanford-Binet, since both are exactly the same distance from the mean.

Standard deviations are sometimes used to classify students as being severely disabled readers. Typically, there must be a difference of 1.5 standard deviations between ability and reading achievement in order for a student to be classified as having a serious reading disability. A number of major ability and achievement tests have been constructed so that the tests have an average or mean score of 100 and a

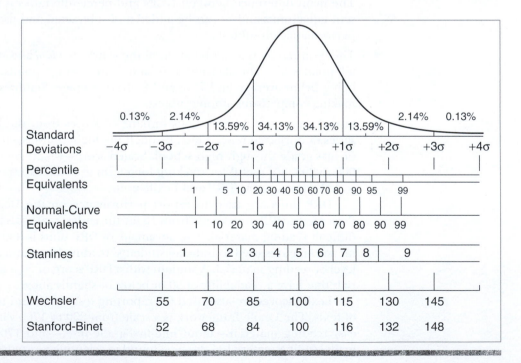

**FIGURE 3.2**
Comparison of Norm-Referenced Scores

standard deviation of 15. To meet the 1.5 standard deviation discrepancy, a student with an average IQ score of 100 would have to obtain a reading achievement score of 77.5 or lower and would place at about the 7th percentile on a test of reading. In other words, although the student did better than 50 percent of those who took the intelligence test, the student outperformed only 7 percent of the sample of students who took the reading achievement test. There is a wide discrepancy between ability and reading achievement.

***The Meaning of Norm Scores***   There seems to be an expectation that every student should be reading at grade level. However, norm-referenced tests are set up in such a way that 50 percent of those who take the test will score below the norm. The norm is where the average student scores. It is not a standard that all students should meet. The norm is the grade level of the test or the 50th percentile, the 5th stanine, or the 50th NCS. Here is how the publisher of a norm-referenced test explains the situation:

> If the norm group was tested in the sixth month of grade 4, the average score for the group would convert to the grade equivalent of 4.6. But note that even in that norm group, fully half of all pupils actually in the sixth month of fourth grade scored at or below that norm or "grade level." If the same test is then given to another group, it would not be surprising to find many pupils scoring "below the norm." Remember, half of the norm group itself scored at or below the norm; that's the meaning of the word. (Harcourt Educational Measurement, 2000)

If reading instruction improves and students start doing better on standardized tests, then the norms will be changed:

> Suppose that to score at the norm on a fourth-grade test, a pupil must answer 25 questions out of 40 correctly. Then, suppose we improve the teaching of reading so that all fourth-grade children in the nation score at least 25 and many score much higher than 25. Now all children are reading "at or above the norm," right? Wrong! As the scores have changed, so has their average—the norm. If you were to standardize the test again, you might find that the middle or average score for the national norm group is now 31 out of 40. So, the norm now is 31, not 25, and half the pupils are still reading at or below the norm and half are reading above the norm. In other words, if everybody is above average, it's not the average anymore! This is the reason that the norm is not an absolute goal for everyone to attain. It is simply a statement of fact about the average of a group. If they all read better, then the norm moves higher. You've done something worthwhile, indeed, but it didn't bring everyone "up to the norm"! (The norm for a test which was standardized in the 1950s is no longer the norm, since more than half the pupils now read better than that. This is one of the reasons new tests must be standardized by the publishers every few years.) (Harcourt Educational Measurement, 2000)

***Purpose of Norm-Referenced Tests***   Norm-referenced tests serve a sorting function. They indicate how students scored in comparison to the reference group. Were they average, above average, or below average? Teachers and school systems might want to know how their students did in comparison with other students.

However, if used to judge the effectiveness of a program—whether for an individual, a class, or a school district—norm-referenced tests have serious limitations. First and foremost, the tests might not measure what has been taught. Second, norm-referenced tests are designed to sort students, so most of the items are designed so that only 40 to 60 percent of the test takers will get them right. The tests are deliberately designed so that there are low, average, and high scores. Items that most students get right are likely to be removed from the test because they do not discriminate. As a result, norm-referenced tests tend to eliminate items on which most students do well. But the items on which most students do well are drawn from the areas that the teacher emphasized because they were the ones that encompassed the most important content or skills. In addition, norm-referenced tests often include items that students can answer because of knowledge they picked up outside school. In their attempt to include items that discriminate, test creators include items that require reasoning skills not typically taught as part of the content domain being assessed, so the items are assessing intellectual aptitude rather than content or skill achievement. As assessment expert W. James Popham (2000) comments, "Standardized achievement tests should be used to make the comparative interpretations that they were intended to provide. They should not be used to judge educational quality" (p. 401). However, norm-referenced tests can be used to indicate general strengths and weakness in a program. For instance, while serving as a consultant for an urban school, I analyzed test data and noted that vocabulary scores for each grade were below the national average and below performance on the comprehension and decoding subtests, thus indicating a schoolwide need for enhanced vocabulary instruction.

### Criterion-Referenced Tests

**Criterion-referenced test:** student performance is measured against a standard. A typical standard of performance on a criterion-referenced comprehension test is 75 percent.

Instead of comparing students with each other, a practice that fosters sorting and competition, **criterion-referenced tests** compare students' performance with a criterion or standard. The National Assessment of Educational Progress (NAEP) is criterion referenced, as are most state tests and tests now being constructed to assess Common Core State Standards. Students are expected to demonstrate a certain level of performance on key literacy skills. On measures of comprehension, a typical criterion is 75 percent. On measures such as knowledge of the letters of the alphabet or initial consonants, the criterion might be set at 100 percent.

One problem with criterion-referenced tests is that the standard is set arbitrarily. No one actually tries out the test with a representative group of students to see what a reasonable criterion or standard might be. For instance, the criterion for the proficiency level of the NAEP has, in the view of some experts, been set too high (Allington, 2011). The basic level seems to be a more reasonable standard for average performance. If they are constructed carefully, criterion tests provide information that can be used to plan instruction because they indicate how well students did on specific reading and writing tasks.

**Benchmark:** standard of performance against which students' achievement might be assessed. An end-of-first-grade benchmark might be the ability to read an excerpt from a *Frog and Toad* book with 95 percent word recognition and 75 percent comprehension.

One form of criterion-referenced assessment is the **benchmark,** a description of a key task that students are expected to perform. For instance, in one intervention program for struggling readers, the benchmark is that they be able to read the children's book *A Kiss for Little Bear* (Minarik, 1959; Hiebert, 1994). Benchmarks need not be tied to a specific book but might be stated in more general terms:

- Can read 95 percent of the first 200 high-frequency words.
- Can read fourth-grade material and retell the main events or details in the selection.
- Can read grade-level text at 100 words a minute with 70 percent comprehension.

Monitoring measures and interim tests are also used as benchmarks.

## Survey versus Diagnostic Tools

Reading tests can also be categorized as being survey or diagnostic tools. Survey tests typically provide an overview of general comprehension and word knowledge. Diagnostic tests assess a number of areas or assess key areas in greater depth. The Stanford Diagnostic Reading Test, one of the best known of the group diagnostic tests, assesses comprehension, reading or listening vocabulary, word analysis skills, and, at higher levels, the ability to scan. A list of survey and diagnostic tests is presented in Tables 3.1 and 3.2.

| | Name | Publisher | Grades | Skill Areas |
|---|---|---|---|---|
| **TABLE 3.1** Survey Reading Tests: Norm Referenced | *Group Tests* | | | |
| | Degrees of Reading Power | Questar | 1–college | Comprehension. |
| | Gates-MacGinitie Reading Test | Riverside | K–12 | Comprehension, vocabulary; early levels measure emergent literacy and decoding skills; trial teaching strategies provide teaching suggestions based on test performance. |
| | GRADE | Pearson | K–12+ | Listening, vocabulary, comprehension; early levels measure emergent literacy and decoding skills. |
| | Iowa Tests of Basic Skills (ITBS) | Riverside | K–12 | Comprehension, vocabulary, word analysis, listening, optional performance items, writing prompts. |
| | Iowa Tests of Educational Development | Riverside | 9–12 | Comprehension, vocabulary. |
| | Metropolitan Achievement Tests | CTB/ McGraw-Hill | K–12 | Comprehension, vocabulary. |
| | Nelson-Denny | Riverside | 9–16 | Comprehension, vocabulary, reading rate. |
| | Stanford Achievement Tests | CTB/ McGraw-Hill | K–12 | Comprehension, vocabulary. |
| | TABE (Tests of Adult Basic Education) | CTB/ McGraw-Hill | Adult (ranges from limited literacy to advanced literacy) | Comprehension, vocabulary. |
| | Terra Nova CAT, 3rd Edition (California Achievement Test 6) | CTB/ McGraw-Hill | K–12 | Comprehension, vocabulary. |
| | *Individual Tests* | | | |
| | Kaufman Test of Educational Achievement II (KTEA-II) | Pearson | 1–12 | Comprehension, decoding, spelling. |

*(continued)*

**TABLE 3.1**
(*Continued*)

| Name | Publisher | Grades | Skill Areas |
|------|-----------|--------|-------------|
| Peabody Individual Achievement Test Revised (PIAT-RR/NU) | Pearson | K–12 | Comprehension, letter and word recognition. |
| Wechsler Individual Achievement Test II | Pearson | K–12 | Word reading, comprehension (linked to WISC). |
| Woodcock–Johnson III NU Tests of Achievement | Riverside | K–13 | Decoding, word reading, reading vocabulary, comprehension, fluency, writing. |

**TABLE 3.2**
Diagnostic
Reading Tests

| Name | Publisher | Grades | Skill Areas |
|------|-----------|--------|-------------|
| *Group Tests* | | | |
| California Diagnostic Reading Test (CDRT) | CTB/ McGraw-Hill | 1–12 | Comprehension, vocabulary, decoding, reading speed, study skills. |
| Reading Power Essentials | Questar | 3–8 | Vocabulary, word reading, fluency |
| Stanford Diagnostic Reading Tests (SDRT) | Pearson | 1–13 | Comprehension, vocabulary, decoding, scanning; optional assessment for strategy use, interest and attitude questionnaire, and story retelling; has screening and online versions. |
| *Individual Tests* | | | |
| Diagnostic Assessment of Reading, 2nd Edition | Riverside | 1–6 | Comprehension, decoding, oral reading, reading levels, listening capacity. Accompanied by online Trial Teaching Strategies, which link instruction to assessment. |
| Durrell Analysis of Reading Difficulty | Pearson | 1–6 | Comprehension, oral reading, word reading, decoding, reading levels, letter knowledge, spelling, visual memory. |
| Woodcock Reading Mastery Tests—Revised Normative update | Pearson | K–13 | Comprehension, vocabulary, decoding, letter knowledge, visual–auditory (associative) learning. |
| Woodcock–Johnson III Diagnostic Reading Battery | Riverside | K–13 | Phonemic awareness, letter identification, word identification, word attack, reading vocabulary, comprehension, incomplete words, sound blending, oral vocabulary, listening comprehension, memory for sentences, and visual matching. |

## Formal versus Informal Tests

Tests can also be categorized as being formal or informal. Formal tests may be standardized. They are designed to be given according to a standard set of circumstances. These tests have sets of directions, which are to be followed exactly. They may also have time limits. All norm-referenced tests are standardized. The advantage of formal standardized tests is that typically they have been constructed with care and tried out on hundreds or thousands of students.

Informal tests generally do not have a set of standard directions, so there is a degree of flexibility in how they are given. In fact, the main advantage of informal tests is their flexibility. They may be designed to assess almost any skill or area, and may be tailored for any population. Informal tests are typically constructed by teachers. Their disadvantage is that they may not be constructed with sufficient care, and their reliability and validity may be unknown. One of the most widely used assessment devices in the field of literacy is the informal reading inventory, which is explored in the next chapter.

### Formative versus Summative Assessment

Assessment is summative or formative. As noted earlier, *summative* assessment summarizes students' progress at the end of a unit or a semester or at some other time and is administered after learning has taken place. Norm-referenced and high-stakes tests are generally summative. *Formative* assessment is ongoing and used to inform instruction. It takes place during learning. Combining characteristics of summative and formative tests is a type of test known as an "interim" test. **Interim assessments,** which are sometimes labeled as *through-course, benchmark,* or *short-cycle tests,* are often used to determine whether students are on track to reach key instructional goals or benchmarks or to predict how students will perform on the end-of-year state test or other high-stakes tests. They are given periodically: every quarter or month, for instance. Because they are given at intervals during the school year, they can be used to plan future instruction (Hamilton et al., 2009; Stiggins & Chapuis, 2005). As Valencia (2011b) comments, interim assessments can provide an early warning by indicating students who are at risk, but the assessments might not indicate what they need or how it should be taught.

> **Interim assessment:** administered periodically and used to assess students' progress and/or predict progress toward meeting an end-of-year goal.

*Assessing for Learning: Using Formative Assessments*    The purpose of assessing for learning is to obtain information about students and then provide the instruction they need. Assessing to learn begins with a clear explanation of the standards students are expected to meet. The classroom teacher or tutor might need to break down the state standards into a curriculum map or series of steps that, if followed, will lead to achieving the standard. The standard is expressed in terms that the students can understand. For a writing standard, for example, students are shown examples that meet the standard, so they have a clear idea of what is expected. They might also analyze samples that don't meet the standards, so they can see what needs to be done to be successful. As part of instruction, students are assessed to see where they are in relation to the standard and also what they need to do to achieve it. Progress is monitored and students are informed of their progress along the way. Results of the monitoring are used to inform instruction. Self-assessment is also developed.

Assessing to learn has a competency-building role. In the area of literacy, its purpose is to provide all students with the reading and writing skills they need to succeed (Stiggins, 2006). Assessments provide students with indicators of performance so they can track their progress. Because formative assessments are geared to what students are learning, students do well and their motivation is fostered. And if they have difficulty, they are provided with assistance.

Formative assessment when coupled with instruction can be powerful. Black and Wiliam (1998) found that its use increased average student performance by as much as 24 percentile points. Formative assessment was especially helpful for struggling learners: "While formative assessment can help all pupils, it yields particularly good results with low achievers by concentrating on specific problems with their work and giving them a clear understanding of what is wrong and how to put it right" (pp. 142–143). To be effective formative assessment must help the teacher understand what the student needs to be taught and also help the student understand what he or she needs to do to move ahead (Valencia, 2011b).

## ▦ Evaluating Assessment Devices

### Reliability

**Reliability:** the consistency of an assessment device. It is the degree to which the device would yield similar results if given to the same person or group again.

In order to be useful, assessment devices must be both reliable and valid. A reliable device is one that yields consistent results. For a test, **reliability** means that if students retook the test they would get approximately the same score. For an observation guide, it means that if two or three observers rated the same student at the same time, their ratings would be similar. In the rating of essays, it means that a single rater would give the same essays similar ratings if she or he rated them on different occasions or that the scores given by different raters to the same piece of writing would be similar.

### Validity

**Validity:** degree to which an assessment device measures what it intends to measure; also, the degree to which the results can be used to make an educational decision.

**Validity** means that a device measures what it says it measures, such as vocabulary, comprehension, rate of reading, attitude toward reading, and so forth. It also means that the device will provide information that will be useful in making an instructional decision—deciding, for instance, whether students' comprehension or word recognition is adequate or if a program or approach is working (Farr & Carey, 1986). Moreover, the way a skill or strategy is assessed should be dictated by the way it was taught and the materials used. If students were taught to write brief summaries of informational text using their science books, then a multiple-choice test that only requires them to select from four options the best summary of a brief, narrative piece would not be valid. Validity is also concerned with the interpretation of test results. When test results are used for purposes for which they are neither suited nor intended, then the interpretation is invalid, even if the test itself is valid.

For commercially produced tests, information on reliability and validity is generally contained in the test administration or technical manual. Reliability is expressed

**Correlation coefficient:** statistical measure that expresses in mathematical terms the degree to which two variables are related.

as a **correlation coefficient**. A correlation coefficient can range from 0, which means no relationship, to 1, which means a perfect relationship, and it can be positive or negative. For making decisions about a group, a correlation of 0.8 is adequate. However, when making individual decisions, a correlation of 0.9 is desired.

Validity may also be expressed as a coefficient of correlation. One way of indicating the validity of a new reading test, for instance, is to compare students' performance on the new test with their performance on an established test or some other criterion. The correlation should be high but not too high. A correlation of 0.9, for instance, would indicate that the tests are so closely related that they seem to be measuring the same thing, so what's the purpose of the new test? This type of validity is known as *statistical* or *concurrent validity*. Some tests also have *predictive validity*. That is, they predict how well a student will do on a related task at some later date. For instance, tests of alphabet knowledge and phonemic awareness given in kindergarten can be used to predict how students will do in reading in first grade. They typically yield correlations as high as 0.5 or 0.6, indicating a strong relationship between these factors and later success in reading.

Test makers also frequently include descriptions of construct and content validity. *Construct validity* is the degree to which a test measures a theoretical trait or construct such as critical reading, learning ability, or phonological awareness. The construct on which a test of phonological awareness is based is the theory that phonological processes are essential for the acquisition of reading skill. This theory is supported when students who have high scores in phonological awareness do well in beginning reading. *Content* or *curricular validity* is the degree to which the content of a test reflects reading or tasks as they are taught in the schools. Many of the national standardized tests are based on the content standards adopted by major professional organizations, such as the International Reading Association, state standards, and the content of basal readers and other materials used to teach literacy. The best way to judge content or curricular validity is to see how close a match there is between what you teach and what the test assesses. If possible, go beyond the general description of content validity in the technical manual and examine the test items themselves. Note whether the items are measuring behaviors or knowledge that is important. Also note what proportion of the content that you think is important is being assessed. Content validity is especially important in criterion-referenced tests.

> Some programs require the use of tests that have proven scientific technical validity and reliability. While tests might possess technical validity and reliability, they might be lacking in content validity. They might not measure skills that are essential in reading or might measure them in such a way that they do not provide helpful information to teachers.

## Standard Error of Measurement

**Standard error of measurement (SEM):** estimate of the difference between the obtained score and what the score would be if the test were perfect.

In judging the quality of a test, it is also important to know the **standard error of measurement** (SEM). The SEM is a statistical estimate of the amount that a test score might vary if the test were given again and again. Although tests yield a particular score, that score should be thought of as a range of likely scores. For instance, if a norm-referenced test has an SEM of 5 percentile points and you got a score of 50, that means that if you retook that test there is a two-thirds (1 standard deviation) chance that your score would fall between 45 and 55, which is plus or minus 1 SEM. Because standard error of measurement is an index of the consistency of test taker's scores, it is also a measure of reliability.

## Usefulness

Ultimately, assessment measures should provide information that can be used to foster students' learning. Results from assessments should not be used to convey a sense of failure and discourage effort. Instead, results should be used to promote students' growth and sense of self-efficacy. As Stiggins (2007) recommends:

> We must begin to evaluate our assessments in terms of both the quality of the evidence they yield and the effect they have on future learning. High-quality assessments encourage further learning; low-quality assessments hinder learning. Understanding the emotional dynamics of the assessment experience from the student's perspective is crucial to the effective use of assessments to improve schools. (p. 25)

Useful assessments answer the following questions: What decision is to be made? By whom? What information will be helpful? At the classroom level, teachers need to know: Where are my students? What is the next step on their way to reaching the standard? Students need to know: What do I need to learn next on my way to achieving the standard? At the program support level, which might be the grade-level team or the school learning team, a key question is: Who needs additional support? At the school and district levels, administrators and the public need to know: How many students are meeting the standards? Are a sufficient number of students meeting the standards?

At the classroom level, teachers need to go beyond identifying students who are or are not meeting standards and determine what needs to be learned so standards are met. This entails obtaining information about foundational skills that might be needed to meet a standard. Summative tests indicate which standards are being met but don't provide information about the steps needed to meet the standards. Observation, quizzes, discussions, and examination of students work are needed to reveal why a standard isn't being met. For instance, students might have difficulty understanding basic details or might have difficulty seeing how details are related or drawing a conclusion based on details or formulating a response (Gunning, 2010).

## Fairness

For additional information about tests, see the *Eighteenth Mental Measurements Yearbook* (Spies, Carlson, & Geisinger, 2010); *Tests in Print VII* (Murphy, Spies, & Plake, 2006), which lists nearly 4,000 tests; and *Test Reviews Online* at the Buros Institute (www.unl.edu/buros).

Tests, of course, should also be fair. As the Joint Task Force on Assessment (1994) notes, "Because traditional test makers have all too frequently designed assessment tools reflecting narrow cultural values, students and schools with different backgrounds and concern often have not been fairly assessed" (p. 41).

Test bias can take many forms. A test can be biased on the basis of geography, gender, socioeconomic status, ethnicity, or race. For instance, a reading selection on ice hockey would seem to favor middle-class males living in the Northeast. Today's tests are typically examined by teams of experts for bias. However, other forms of bias include opportunity to learn and familiarity with test situations. Students who have not been taught critical content will, of course, be at a disadvantage. So, too, will students from other countries who may not be familiar with U.S. testing situations. These youngsters should be provided with practice and instruction that will acquaint them with the form of the testing and the testing procedures (Popham, 2000).

## Functional-Level Assessment

When group tests are used, struggling readers are often assessed unfairly. It is a widespread practice to administer the same norm-referenced or criterion-referenced test to an entire class, even though there may be a wide range of reading ability in that class. For instance, a seventh-grade student reading on a second-grade level would find a typical seventh-grade test to be extremely frustrating. Moreover, the test would yield misleading results. Norm-referenced tests have a bottom. As soon as the student answers a question or two on a seventh-grade-level test, he might earn a grade-equivalent score of 3.5 or so. With a little bit of lucky guessing, the student might achieve a grade-equivalent score of fourth grade or higher. Thus, the teacher might assume that the student can read on a fourth- or fifth-grade level, so the student is given materials that are too difficult. In addition, the experience of taking a test that is far too difficult can be very demeaning and discouraging.

How can you tell if a test is too easy or too hard? A test is probably too hard if a student fails to obtain a score that is better than he would have gotten if he had merely guessed. If on a multiple-choice test there are four answer options, a student has one chance in four of getting an answer correct. If a student does not get more than 25 percent of the attempted items correct, his score is at a chance level. A test is too easy if a student gets all or most of the items correct.

The solution is to assess students on the level at which they are functioning (Gunning, 1982). This might mean giving a student an out-of-level test. For a seventh-grader reading on a second-grade level, this means giving the student a test that actually has second-grade material on it. If the material is too juvenile for the student, then you might use a test designed for older students or adults who are reading on a second-grade level. Grade-equivalent and scaled scores can be used with out-of-level testing. However, out-of-level norms should be used to report percentile and stanine scores, because these scores involve comparing students who are in the same grade.

Another possible solution is to select a test that assesses a wide range of reading levels. Administering the right-level test means that you need to know students' approximate reading levels. Approximate reading levels may be obtained from teacher judgment, informal reading inventories, running records, or observing which level of materials the students can handle. You may also use a locator test. A locator test is generally a brief test of reading vocabulary or reading comprehension that covers a broad range of levels. The GRADE Reader Level Indicator (Pearson) covers levels from grade 2 through secondary school and can be given to a group in about 10 minutes.

Another way of providing students with the appropriate level test is to use adaptive testing. Adaptive tests are usually taken on a computer. Based on the student's responses, the computer adapts to the student's level. If a student is getting all the questions correct, the computer presents higher-level questions. If the student is getting all or most of the items wrong, the computer switches to lower-level questions. Currently, there are two widely used adaptive tests: Measures of Academic Progress (MAP) and STAR Reading Enterprise. MAP tests consist of sentences or brief paragraphs and have a multiple-choice format. They can be given in grades 2 through 10, and they can be given four times a year to monitor progress. STAR Reading Enterprise uses multiple-choice items to assess how students are doing in relationship to individual state and Common Core standards. Plans for tests created by the Smarter Balanced Consortium to assess Common Core State Standards call for these assessments to be adaptive.

In some situations all students are required to take grade-level literacy tests. This creates a potential problem for struggling readers because they, by definition, read below grade level. The solution is to create tests that have enough "bottom" for virtually all students. Knowing that a large percentage of students will be reading below grade level, tests should be constructed so that there are some passages which are at the appropriate level for struggling readers. A fourth-grade test, for instance, might have a passage or two on the second-grade and third-grade levels. Taking a test with sufficient bottom allows below-grade-level readers to demonstrate what they know and can do. Struggling readers feel less humiliated; educators are provided with useful assessment information; and teachers of struggling readers feel better about having their students assessed.

## ▚▚▚ High-Stakes Tests

High-stakes tests, such as college entrance exams, have long been part of education. However, the number and uses of high-stakes tests have increased dramatically. High-stakes tests are now used in many school districts to determine whether young children pass or fail and, increasingly, are used as part of teacher evaluation systems.

Although assessment is an essential part of education, there are some problems with high-stakes tests. For one, tests provide only a limited sample of reading behavior and can yield misleading results. When important decisions are being made, it is important that several sources of information, such as actual samples of the students' work or teacher observations, be consulted. Second, when single tests are used to make important decisions, the tests take on inflated importance and may become the curriculum. This is especially true in high-poverty schools, where test scores tend to be low. When too much time is spent on test preparation, instructional time is lost. If the tests have a cutoff score, sometimes there is an overemphasis on those who just missed the cutoff and a consequent neglect of the lowest scorers. (Fortunately, there is a shift to assessments that measure students' growth.) Lastly, high-stakes tests reduce decision making at the local level. Teachers are forced to gear their curriculum to what is being tested. This thwarts the basic intent of assessment, which is to measure what has been taught so that adjustments can be made. Assessments geared to the Common Core State Standards will probably replace many of the instruments now being used to make high-stakes decisions.

## Common Core Assessments

The Common Core State Standards have been widely adopted. Assessments and curriculum aligned with the standards are now being created. Assessments are expected to be completed by the 2014–2015 school year. Information about the assessments and related instructional resources are available from PARCC (Partnership for Assessment of Readiness for College and Careers; http://www .parcconline.org/) and SBAC (Smarter Balanced Assessment Consortium; http:// www.smarterbalanced.org/). The assessments will emphasize higher-level literacy skills, will be delivered with the help of technology, will measure growth, and will provide both summative and formative data so that results can be used to evaluate and plan instruction. The ultimate goal is to provide information that will indicate whether students are on track to becoming college and career ready. Sample items are available at both sites.

## Measuring Growth

In the past, most states reported performance in terms of what percentage of students met the state's proficiency level. This is a threshold or status measure. Threshold testing might mask growth, especially when struggling students are being assessed. Results reveal what percentage of students have met a certain standard but not how much students' scores have changed. Struggling readers might have obtained two years' growth, but this might not be enough for them to reach the standard. Unless growth is measured, schools that have large numbers of struggling students might be misjudged.

Measuring growth requires comparing where students were at the point of initial assessment and where they are at the end of assessment. A growth model fits with the concept of meeting each student where he or she is and moving him or her upward. A growth model also fits in with the current trend to evaluate teachers not just on the quality of their presentations but also on the amount of growth that their students evidence. Growth measurement requires functional-level assessment. It is essential that an accurate measure of students' achievement be obtained. Otherwise, the amount of growth cannot be accurately ascertained. Struggling readers, by definition, are typically reading below grade level. Measuring students with materials that are on grade level, especially if students are reading significantly below grade level, lowers indicators of growth rates and may even invalidate the test results.

## Assessing English Language Learners

Because ELLs have diverse educational and language backgrounds, Jiménez (2004) recommends that a literacy profile be created for each student. The profile provides information about the language the student speaks at home and in school. Using information from the profile, records, or assessments, seek answers to the following:

- Language(s) spoken at home
- Educational background
- Reading and writing activities engaged in
- Favorite books in first language
- Proficiency in speaking first language
- Proficiency in speaking English
- Proficiency in reading and writing in first language
- Proficiency in reading and writing in English

The English as a second language (ESL) or bilingual specialist should be able to provide information about a student's literacy proficiency in her or his first language. Request that ELLs bring in books in their native languages and read them to you and then retell the selections in English. Also ask ELLs to bring in pieces of writing that they have done in their native languages and to read them to you and then retell them in English. Based on the proficiency with which they read, you can judge whether they are literate in their first language, even if you don't know the language. You might also obtain or construct a list of common words in each student's native language and ask him or her to read them. Figure 3.3 contains a list of 20 common Spanish words, phonetically respelled and with their English translations. You might use a list such as this to get a rough estimate of an ELL's reading proficiency. If the student can read all or most of these words, he can read at least at a basic level in Spanish (Gunning, 2010).

A distinguished panel of experts on English language learners (Gersten et al., 2007) recommends using the same standards for English learners as are used with native speakers of English:

> Schools with performance benchmarks in reading in the early grades can use the same standards for English learners and for native English speakers to make adjustments in instruction when progress is not sufficient. It is the opinion of the panel that schools should not consider below-grade-level performance in reading as "normal" or something that will resolve itself when oral language proficiency in English improves. (p. 3)

**■ FIGURE 3.3**
Spanish Word List

| Spanish Word | Pronunciation | Translation |
| --- | --- | --- |
| no | no | no |
| mi | me | me |
| uno | OO-no | one |
| esta | ES-tah | this |
| ella | AY-yah | she |
| señor | sen-YOR | mister |
| leer | lay-AIR | read |
| libro | LEE-bro | book |
| amigo | ah-ME-go | friend |
| pelota | peh-LOH-tah | ball |
| vaca | BAH-kah | cow |
| musica | MYEW-see-kah | music |
| sorpresa | sor-PRES-ah | surprise |
| leopardo | lay-oh-PAR-doh | leopard |
| abuela | ah-BWEH-la | grandmother |
| bicicleta | bee-see-KLAY-tah | bicycle |
| mañana | mon-YAH-nah | tomorrow |
| zapatos | sah-PAH-toes | shoes |
| primavera | pre-mah-BEAR-ah | spring |
| elefante | eh-leh-FAHN-teh | elephant |

Students should, of course, have sufficient command of English so that they understand the tasks required on a test and are able to respond correctly to some of the items. This might be a phonics or word-list test that begins with easy items that would be appropriate for the ELL's level of language development. It does not mean giving a fifth-grade ELL with limited language abilities a fifth-grade reading test that is far beyond her or his reading ability. The panel wants ELLs to take appropriate assessments so their needs can be revealed and they can be provided with assistance, if needed.

## ■■■ Reporting to Parents

Parents are understandably concerned about their children's performance. When discussing assessment results, focus on the child's strengths. Also avoid comparisons with other children, if possible. Discuss the student's performance in the light of what he might reasonably be expected to do. If the student has below-average scores, stress signs of progress: "Jan could read only one-syllable words when the school year began, but now she is able to read many words that have two or three syllables." If parents want to know how their child is doing in comparison with other children, use general categories rather than precise numbers. Instead of saying that Juan is reading at the 20th percentile, explain that he is reading below average. However, do explain that the child does have a reading problem.

When explaining assessment results, suggest ways in which the parents might build on strengths and try to shore up weaknesses. Show samples of the student's work. Highlight evidence of effort and improvement. End the conference on an encouraging, hopeful note.

## Summary

Assessment is an interactive process and should consider the reader, the text, the techniques being used, the reading or writing task involved, and the context in which the reading or writing is performed. Assessment should also be dynamic. Through instruction provided after initial testing or through trial or assisted teaching, assessment should attempt to discover what the student's true learning potential is and how the student learns best.

Assessment devices should be authentic. They should reflect the kinds of reading and writing tasks that students undertake in and out of school. Because they consist mainly of brief passages and multiple-choice items, traditional group tests have limited authenticity. Assessment measures fall into four main categories: screening, diagnostic, monitoring, and outcome. Assessment measures can also be classified as being formative or summative.

Tests can be norm referenced or criterion referenced. Norm-referenced tests compare a student's performance with that of a sample or norm group. Criterion-referenced tests compare students' performance with a criterion or standard, which may be a percentage of answers correct or a benchmark such as being able to read a book on a certain level. Tests can also be classified as being group or individual, survey or diagnostic, formal or informal. Some categories overlap. For instance, a test can be both criterion and norm referenced.

Tests are expected to meet standards of reliability and validity. A reliable test is one that yields the same approximate score if taken over and over again. A valid test is one that measures what it says it measures. In order to be valid, a test should also provide useful information for an educational decision. Kinds of validity include concurrent or statistical, predictive, curricular or content, and construct. Tests are not precise measures but have a standard error of measurement, which can be used to estimate the scores that students would achieve if they took the same test over and over.

High-stakes tests are those that are used as the basis for making important decisions. Although high-stakes tests can provide valid information about student performance, several sources of assessment should be used when making important decisions. In addition, tests should not be used to dictate curriculum. Assessment data should be shared with parents. Students' strengths and signs of progress should be emphasized. Measures of student growth generally provide better evaluative information than threshold measures.

## Application Activities

1. Start a collection of sample informal and formal tests and other assessment devices that you might use. Also, collect ideas for assessing students in reading and writing.

2. Examine a norm-referenced or criterion-referenced test. Note the skills being tested and the way they are being assessed. What does this suggest about the content validity of the test? What information does the test maker provide about reliability, validity, and fairness? What suggestions, if any, does the test publisher give for using test results?

3. Become acquainted with the literacy standards in your state and with tests or other systems used to assess students' performance on standards. Although the tests themselves are usually secure so that you cannot examine them, a list

of standards or skills assessed and sample items are usually provided. Note the consequences of not meeting the standards and whether assistance is provided for students identified as not meeting standards. Most state departments of education provide this information on their Web sites. If your state will be using the assessment from PARCC (Partnership for Assessment of Readiness for College and Careers; http://www.parcconline.org/) or SBAC (Smarter Balanced Assessment Consortium; http://www.smarterbalanced.org/), visit their sites to find out more about the assessments and the resources available.

## My Education Lab

Go to the topic **Reading Assessment** in the MyEducationLab (www.myeducationlab .com) for **Assessing and Correcting Reading Difficulties,** where you can:

- Find learning outcomes for **Reading Assessment** along with the national standards that connect to these outcomes.

- Complete Assignments and Activities that can help you more deeply understand the chapter content.

- Apply and practice your understanding of the core teaching skills identified in the chapter with the Building Teaching Skills and Dispositions learning units.

- Examine challenging situations and cases presented in the Iris Center Resources.

- Check your comprehension of the content covered in the chapter with the Study Plan. Here you will be able to take a chapter pretest, receive feedback on your answers, and then access personalized Review, Practice, and Enrichment exercises to enhance your understanding of chapter content. After you complete the exercises, take a posttest to confirm your comprehension.

- Practice targeting instruction and making content accessible for all students with A+RISE activities.

# 4

# Placing Students and Monitoring Progress

**H**ave you ever had to read a book that was simply too difficult for you? How did you feel? How would you feel if, day after day, you were asked to read books that were too hard for you? What do you think might be the overall effect on your attitude and your progress?

One of the most important decisions that you will make as a literacy teacher is matching students with materials that have an appropriate level of challenge. One of the best devices for placing students is the informal reading inventory or devices modeled on the inventory. A simple but powerful device, the inventory consists primarily of a series of selections that gradually grow more difficult.

**ANTICIPATION GUIDE**

*Read each of the following statements. Put a check under "Agree" or "Disagree" to show how you feel about each one. If possible, discuss your responses with classmates.*

|  | AGREE | DISAGREE |
|---|---|---|
| 1. Although they are subjective, informal tests are more useful than formal tests. | _____ | _____ |
| 2. When estimating a student's reading level, the most important factor is the ability to read words. | _____ | _____ |
| 3. When estimating a student's reading ability, silent-reading performance is more important than oral reading. | _____ | _____ |
| 4. For most students, group tests provide adequate data about reading performance. | _____ | _____ |
| 5. Monitoring students' performance should include assessment of higher-level skills. | _____ | _____ |

## ▪▪▪ The Informal Reading Inventory

> **Informal reading inventory (IRI):** a series of passages that gradually increase in difficulty, used to assess oral and silent reading and comprehension.

When properly administered and interpreted, the **informal reading inventory (IRI)** yields much of the information about a student that the reading teacher needs (Morris et al., 2012). Although it only takes about 30 minutes to administer, the informal reading inventory indicates the student's reading level and approximate level of language development. It provides insight into word-analysis and comprehension strategies, background knowledge, work habits, and interests. Once you are familiar with the IRI, it can be used as a framework with which to observe and interpret students' reading behavior.

One of the most valid and reliable measures of reading, the IRI is the basis for a number of commercially produced diagnostic assessments as well as the running record, which is an essential ingredient in Reading Recovery, and the technique of miscue analysis, an important element in reading assessment. Like many important developments in other fields, the IRI is simple and sensible. In its original form, administering an IRI was like having a customer try on shoes. The teacher had a series of graded readers and tried them on for size until finding the one that fit just right—neither too easy nor too difficult.

As originally conceived, inventories were constructed by teachers. Typically, IRIs were created using passages from basal readers. In keeping with the spirit of using children's books to teach reading, it is also possible to construct an inventory based on a series of children's books that increase in difficulty. (Instructions for creating an inventory can be found in Johnson, Kress, & Pikulski's [1987] *Informal Reading Inventories,* 2nd ed.) Teacher-constructed inventories are more valid because they reflect the types of materials you actually use in your class. Because of the time involved in creating a curriculum-based informal inventory, many teachers use commercially produced IRIs.

Although most inventories start at a preprimer level, which is early first grade, some inventories assess below the preprimer level. The Basic Reading Inventory (Johns & Elish-Piper, 2012) includes a selection on the picture and easy sight words level and also a number of early literacy assessments. The Stieglitz Informal Reading Inventory (Stieglitz, 2002) uses a procedure known as dictated story assessment to test students who are reading below a first-grade level. Students discuss a photograph and dictate a story about it, which they then read. Both the Basic Reading Inventory and the Bader Reading and Language Inventory (Bader & Pearce, 2013) contain a series of preliteracy assessments for students who are unable to read preprimer (beginning level) passages.

Unfortunately, most inventories are not properly aligned with the beginning levels of today's reading programs. Until recently, the major reading programs used a high-frequency approach to teaching beginning reading. This meant that the words of the easiest selections consisted mainly of frequently occurring words. However, today's major programs use a decodable text approach. Beginning reading materials are made up primarily of words that incorporate the phonics patterns that students have been taught plus some high-frequency words (Gunning, 2008a). Unfortunately, most commercial reading inventories still take a high-frequency approach and fail to incorporate phonics patterns. At the preprimer and primer levels, students are not being assessed on what they have been taught. If you are assessing students on the beginning reading levels, obtain passages that are representative of those levels. At the easiest levels, the 9th, 10th, and 11th editions of the Basic Reading Inventory and the 5th edition of the Qualitative Reading Inventory (Leslie & Caldwell, 2011) have passages containing decodable and high-frequency words. Most basal reading programs also have IRIs that are aligned with their instruction.

One problem with testing older low-achieving readers is that the easiest passages in most inventories are written for young children and are both demeaning and boring for older students. However, the Classroom Reading Inventory (Wheelock & Campbell, 2012) has three forms—one of which, Form C, contain passages, even at the easiest levels—that are appropriate for high school students and adults. The Bader Reading and Language Inventory (Bader & Pearce, 2013) also has a form designed for older students and one created for adults. A listing of commercial inventories is presented in Table 4.1.

> ✧ The Flynt–Cooter Reading Inventory uses brief sentences that gradually increase in difficulty rather than lists of words to establish a starting point. The Stieglitz Informal Reading Inventory provides both words in isolation and words in sentences.

**TABLE 4.1**
Commercial Inventories

| Name | Authors | Grades | Added Skill Areas |
|---|---|---|---|
| Analytic Reading Inventory | Woods & Moe | 1–9 | Contains science and social studies passages. |
| Bader Reading and Language Inventory | Bader & Pearce | 1–12 and adult | Also assesses phonics, language, spelling, and emergent literacy. |
| Basic Reading Inventory | Johns | 1–8 | Includes assessment of emergent literacy. |
| Burns/Roe Informal Reading Inventory | Roe & Burns | 1–12 | |
| Classroom Reading Inventory | Wheelock, Campbell, & Silvaroli | 1–8 | Forms C and D can be used with older readers. |
| Critical Reading Inventory: Assessing Students' Reading and Thinking | Applegate, Quinn & Applegate | 1–12 | Focuses on drawing conclusions and critical thinking. |
| Development Literacy Inventory | Temple, Crawford & Gillet | K–12 | Includes emergent literacy. |
| Ekwall/Shanker Reading Inventory | Shanker & Ekwall | 1–12 | Includes emergent literacy, word analysis, and interests. |
| Informal Reading-Thinking Inventory | Manzo, Mano, & McKenna | 1–11 | Includes assessment of prior knowledge and literacy thinking. |
| English-Espanol Reading Inventory for the Classroom | Flynt & Cooter | K–12 | Emergent literacy. Has an English-only version. |
| Comprehensive Reading Inventory | Cooter, Flynt, & Cooter | 1–12 | Features retellings, picture reading, and an observation guide to assess emergent literacy. Assesses phonemic awareness, phonics, vocabulary, and fluency. |
| Qualitative Reading Inventory V | Leslie & Caldwell | 1–12 | Features assessment of prior knowledge, retelling and think-alouds. |
| PALS | Invernizzi & Meir | K–3 | Emergent literacy, IRI, word reading, spelling. |
| Texas Primary Reading Inventory | Texas Education Agency | K–3 | Emergent literacy, phonics. Has a Spanish version. |

The typical IRI, whether teacher created or commercially produced, consists of two major components: graded word lists and graded passages. The graded word lists consist of separate lists of 10 to 20 words on a preprimer through an 8th- or 12th-grade level. The passages consist of a series of graded selections beginning at preprimer level and extending to 8th, 9th, or 12th grade. Generally, there are two passages at each level, one to be read orally and one to be read silently. Some inventories provide only an oral passage, and to save time, some teachers omit the administration of the silent-reading passages in inventories that assess both oral and silent reading. However, omitting silent-reading passages lessens both the validity and reliability of the IRI. Moreover, in some students, there is a marked difference between performance on oral and on silent-reading passages.

Besides the comparison of oral and silent-reading performance, other important information is lost when the administration of silent reading-passages is omitted. The teacher is unable to observe the strategies that a student uses when reading silently and is unable to gauge silent-reading speed. The teacher also misses the opportunity to note whether the students finger-point, subvocalize, or engage in other similar behaviors, which may indicate that the material is too difficult and/or that the readers are inefficient.

Administering the inventory is fairly straightforward. The inventory is administered individually and begins with the student being asked to read the words on the word lists, starting with the easiest list. Using the results of the word-list administration, the teacher locates a probable starting point for the reading of the graded passages. Beginning with passages where comprehension and word recognition are virtually flawless, the student continues to read until the material is obviously too difficult. As the student reads, the teacher carefully observes the student's comprehension, word recognition, use of strategies, oral language development, and how he or she handles the testing situation. The more careful the observation, the greater will be the insight obtained.

## The IRI as a Placement Device

**Independent level:** level of material that students can read with at least 99 percent word recognition and 90 percent comprehension.

**Instructional level:** level of material that students can read with at least 95 percent word recognition and 75 percent comprehension. The 95 percent word-recognition figure has recently been validated by ESL researchers (Nation, 2001). At the 90 percent level, a few students had limited comprehension. At 95 percent, most students were able to construct a reasonable understanding of the selection.

**Frustration level:** level of material at which students' word recognition is 90 percent or less or comprehension is 50 percent or less.

A primary purpose of the IRI is to obtain placement information. Teachers need to know what level of material is most likely to produce optimum results. This is especially crucial for low-achieving readers, who tend to be given materials that are too difficult for them, a condition that leads to frustration and makes it impossible for them to apply a balanced set of reading strategies (Clay, 1985).

The IRI yields four levels: independent, instructional, frustration, and listening capacity. As its name suggests, the **independent level** is the point at which students can read on their own, without any help from teachers, parents, or peers. They recognize at least 99 percent of the words, and comprehension is nearly perfect. At the **instructional level,** students can read at least 95 out of 100 words, and they recall at least 75 percent of what they read. If given instructional assistance, they can read with confidence and competence. At the **frustration level,** the material is simply too difficult for the students to read, even with assistance. Students miss 10 or more words out of 100 and/or remember only half of what they read. Students may exhibit lip movement during silent reading, may be easily distracted, or may engage in hair twisting, grimacing, or other stress-signaling behaviors (Johnson et al., 1987).

**TABLE 4.2**
Informal Reading
Inventory
Standards

| Level | Word Recognition in Context | | Comprehension |
|---|---|---|---|
| Independent | 99% | (and) | 95% |
| Instructional | 95% | (and) | 75% |
| Frustration | 90% | (or) | 50% |
| Listening capacity | | | 75% |

**Listening capacity:** level of material that students can understand with 75 percent comprehension when it is read to them.

✳ As a practical matter some kinds of reading, such as a set of directions require 100% word recognition; others, such as a novel being read for pleasure, don't require a high level of word recognition (Hasbrouck, 2012).

✳ There is some disagreement about the percentage of word recognition required for adequate comprehension. See Halladay (2012), Baumann (1989), and Powell (1971) for a discussion.

Once a student has reached the frustration level, the teacher reads the inventory selections to her in order to assess ability to understand written language when decoding is not a factor. The highest level at which the student can understand 75 percent of the material that is read to her is the **listening capacity.**

Although guidelines vary somewhat, the most accepted standards for the four levels are presented in Table 4.2. Powell (1971) and others have argued for lower standards and/or standards that vary according to grade levels. However, a study by Fuchs, Fuchs, and Deno (1982) found that levels obtained using the 95 percent word-recognition criterion agreed fairly substantially with levels obtained by teacher estimates and standardized tests. Using a lower word-recognition percentage resulted in placing a greater proportion of students above the level estimated by the classroom teacher.

As noted in Chapter 1, research indicates that students do best when they can cope with at least 95 to 98 percent of the words (Berliner, 1981; Biemiller, 1994; Gambrell et al., 1981; Nation, 2001). Indeed, Enz (1989) found that relaxing IRI standards resulted in a deterioration of both achievement and attitude. Students placed according to higher standards spent a greater proportion of time on task, had a higher success rate, and had a more positive attitude toward reading.

## Administering the Word-List Tests

The graded word lists provide a starting point for administration of the graded passages. They also yield valuable information about a student's ability to recognize words immediately and to use word-level processing strategies to decode words that are not immediately recognized. In a sense, the task is artificial because in actual reading words are generally encountered in running text, thus providing the opportunity to use context. Because the words in the word-list tests are presented in isolation, students have no recourse but to use word-analysis strategies; so this brief but important test provides excellent insight into a student's ability to use phonics, syllabic analysis, and other word-level decoding skills.

In order to get the most information from word-list tests, they should be given in both timed (flash) and untimed (analysis) administrations. In a timed administration, each word is flashed for a second, so that the student is assessed on her or his ability to pronounce words immediately, without recourse to decoding. The student should be seated to the side of you and should be reading from her or his copy. Use a second copy for marking, but keep that on your desk or a clipboard.

Using two three-by-five cards, flash each word for a second, as shown in Figure 4.1. A word is flashed by pulling down the card in the left hand while keeping the card

■▪ **FIGURE 4.1**
Administering
Word-List Test

home

in the right hand in place for one second. As the word is being exposed, it is important that the card in the right hand be held steadily and not dragged down, preventing the student from getting a clear, unobscured look at the word. To make sure that the word is exposed for a second but no longer, say "One thousand" to yourself and then snap the opening closed by pushing down the card in the right hand. Continue to flash the words in this fashion until the student misreads a word or is unable to read a word within one second. At that point, record the student's response in the flash column and open up the cards so the student can then analyze the word she or he missed. The student is then encouraged to use word-analysis skills to try to figure out the word. The student's response is recorded in the untimed column, and testing is resumed. Continue testing until the student misses half the words under the flash condition on two consecutive levels. Extending the testing to a level where the student is meeting difficult words provides you with the opportunity to observe the student's word-analysis skills in isolation and in full operation.

When the student makes an error, record her or his performance. If the student mispronounces or substitutes a word, write the mispronunciation or substitution. If the student says "I don't know," write *dk* in the blank. Write *o* if the student makes no response. A check indicates a correct response. (However, to keep the test moving, you need not record checks in the flash column until later. Because you don't need to write anything in the flash blank unless the student fails to respond or makes an error, you can assume that the blanks that have not been filled in are correct items.)

If a student reads correctly a word that she missed on flash, then place a check in the untimed column. If a student makes the same mistake, record it with a check with a tail. If the student gives a second mispronunciation or substitution, one that is different from the first, record that. It is important to record a student's errors, because they provide information about the kinds of elements he has mastered and those with which he is having difficulty. A list of symbols used to mark the word-list test is presented in Figure 4.2. A marked word-list test is presented in Figure 4.3.

Before giving the word-list test, explain its nature and purpose. Say "I am going to ask you to read some words for me. At first, I will only show you the word for a second, because I want to see how well you can read words without needing time to figure them out. If you are unable to read a word in one second, then I will give you

**■ FIGURE 4.2**
Marking Symbols

|        | Flash  | Untimed |       |                                                      |
|--------|--------|---------|-------|------------------------------------------------------|
| saw    | ✓      |         | ✓     | (Correct response.)                                  |
| then   | they   |         | they  | (Substitution. The substitution is written on the line.) |
| wet    | we     | ✓       | ✓     | (Made same error on untimed as on flash.)            |
| was    | dk     | dk      | dk    | (Said, "Don't know.")                                |
| boy    | 0      | 0       | 0     | (No response.)                                       |

|       |         | Flash  | Untimed |
|-------|---------|--------|---------|
| 1.    | me      | ✓      |         |
| 2.    | get     | ✓      |         |
| 3.    | home    | ✓      |         |
| 4.    | not     | no     | ✓       |
| 5.    | he      | ✓      |         |
| 6.    | tree    | tee    | ✓       |
| 7.    | girl    | ✓      |         |
| 8.    | take    | tack   | ✓       |
| 9.    | book    | ✓      |         |
| 10.   | milk    | more   | my      |
| 11.   | dog     | ✓      |         |
| 12.   | all     | ✓      |         |
| 13.   | apple   | ✓      |         |
| 14.   | like    | ✓      |         |
| 15.   | go      | ✓      |         |
| 16.   | farm    | ✓      |         |
| 17.   | went    | when   | ✓       |
| 18.   | friend  | dk     | dk      |
| 19.   | about   | above  | ✓       |
| 20.   | door    | do     | dot     |
| Percent correct: | | 60%    | 75%     |

**■ FIGURE 4.3**
Performance on
Test

time to figure it out. That will help me to see how you figure out words. As you go through the lists of words, they will become harder, but do the best you can."

## Interpreting the Results of the Word-List Tests

After the entire inventory has been administered, analyze the results, beginning with the words in isolation, the word-list tests. First, make a gross comparison between performance on the flash list and performance on the untimed list.

The flash score represents the student's ability to recognize words automatically, without resorting to decoding them. The untimed score indicates the student's ability to use phonics, syllabication, and morphemic analysis to decode words that are not recognized immediately. A high flash score indicates a high sight-word or immediate-recognition vocabulary. An improved analysis score is a gauge of decoding ability. The larger the difference between the two scores, the greater is the decoding ability. However, a very large difference may indicate that the student has few words that she or he can recognize at sight and so must sound out nearly all words. This can be a problem. If too much of a student's working memory is taken up by word analysis, too little will be left for comprehension (Samuels, 1994). What does the performance shown in Figure 4.3 suggest about the student's ability to recognize words immediately and her decoding skills?

After making a global analysis of a student's ability to recognize words at sight versus his ability to decode words, examine the kinds of words that were read correctly and those that were read incorrectly. Choose from the following questions those that apply to the student you have tested. The questions address gradually increasing levels of difficulty. The first questions are most appropriate for novice readers. The later questions are more suitable for advanced readers.

If word-list tests are analyzed carefully, they should yield as much or more information about decoding skills as a word-analysis or phonics test:

- What parts of the word can the student read? Beginning? Middle? End?
- Can the student read beginning consonants? Can the student read ending consonants?
- Can the student pronounce short-vowel patterns (*cat, pet*)?
- Can the student read double-letter long-vowel patterns (*goat, rain*)?
- Can the student read final-*e* long-vowel patterns (*wave, home*)?
- Can the student read *r*-vowel patterns (*car, chair, here, store, sir*)?
- Can the student read other-vowel patterns (*choice, how, crawl, brook, spoon*)?
- Can the student read multisyllabic words?
- Does the student's difficulty pronouncing words seem to be caused by a lack of familiarity with the words in oral language? Is this essentially a vocabulary problem?

To check to see whether a word the student has missed is in her listening vocabulary, say the word and ask the student to tell what the word means. For instance, if the student misread the word *solar*, say the word after the word-list test has been completed and ask the student to tell what the word means. If the student does not know what the word means, then the miscue is signaling a vocabulary need. If the student knows the meaning of *solar*, then a decoding need is being indicated (Jesse Turner, personal communication, October 10, 2000).

## Assisted Testing

As a further analysis, try assisted testing, which was explained in the previous chapter. Students might miss words on the word-list test because they were rushing, were nervous, or felt the pressure of being assessed. In an analysis of errors made by struggling readers, Cohn and D'Alessandro (1978) found that students were able to correct half the errors when each misread word was pointed out and they were asked "Please look at it carefully and try it again" (p. 342). If a student still got a word wrong, the examiner tried a series of prompts to direct the student's attention to the misread word. Another 28 percent of errors were corrected.

After administering the word-list tests, reassess the student on some of the missed items. First, give her another chance to say the word. If she is unable to respond, provide her with a prompt. A good prompt to use is "Are there any parts of that word that you can say?" This will tell you whether the student knows the element but needs the assistance of prompting. If the student is unable to respond to the prompt, cover up all but a part of the word that you think she might know and invite her to read that. Then uncover the rest of the word and see if she can read it. Make a note of the prompts you supplied and the student's response.

One student misread *ran/run, us/use,* and *got/goat.* Her results suggested difficulty with short vowels and long vowels. However, when asked to read the words again, she read all of them correctly. The student also had misread *struggle, sunup, several,* and *survive.* When given another chance to read them, she still had difficulty and was unable to respond to the prompt "Is there any part of this word that you can say?" However, when provided with a prompt that included covering up a portion of the word so that she could focus on a part of the word that was probably familiar, she was able to read all four words. (For instance, all of the word *struggle* was covered except for *rug.*) The results indicated that she was a better decoder than the original test results suggested. The improved performance also indicated that teaching her the pronounceable word part and other strategies would most likely be fruitful. As a side benefit, the student felt better about her performance because she could see that she had improved when given a second chance to read the words.

## Administering the IRI Passages

> Some informal reading inventories use longer passages to reflect the kinds of sustained reading that students actually do. The disadvantage is that these inventories take longer to administer.

Procedures for administering and interpreting inventories vary. The procedures presented in this text are drawn from those described in *Informal Reading Inventories* (Johnson et al., 1987), which is a widely used, highly respected source.

To determine the student's starting point for reading the oral and silent passages, locate his last perfect performance on the flash list. The starting point for the passages is the level below the last perfect performance. If the student's last perfect performance on flash was fourth grade, begin testing at the third-grade level. If you suspect a comprehension problem, you might start at an even lower level (Johnson et al., 1987). Looking at Sheila's scores (Figure 4.4), you can see that her starting point would be grade 2.

As conceived by Betts (1946), the IRI is modeled on the guided reading lesson (directed reading activity), except that the emphasis is on evaluation rather than instruction. A second major difference is that one passage at each level will be read orally without any preparation. Normally, passages are read silently before being read orally. The steps in administering the inventory, which, except for assessing

■ FIGURE 4.4
Sheila's Scores

| Word-List Scores | | |
| --- | --- | --- |
| Level | Flash | Untimed |
| PP | 100 | 100 |
| P | 100 | 100 |
| 1 | 100 | 100 |
| 2 | 100 | 100 |
| 3 | 100 | 100 |
| 4 | 75 | 90 |
| 5 | 50 | 60 |
| 6 | 40 | 50 |

> **Retelling:** process of recounting orally or in writing a story or an information piece. The purpose of a retelling is to assess comprehension.

listening comprehension, are similar to those in a traditional reading lesson, include preparing for reading a passage, assessing background knowledge, setting a purpose for reading, reading the passage, **retelling** the passage or answering questions about the passage, oral rereading of a selected segment of the silent passage (optional), and assessing listening comprehension.

The inventory begins with the reading of the oral passage at the level below the student's last perfect performance on the flash portion of the word-list tests. The oral passage is read at sight. The student does not read it silently first. Before a student reads the oral passage, explain the test and its purpose. Explain that he will be reading a series of stories (articles). State that you will be taking notes on the reading so that you can get some information on how he reads. Tell the student that after he has read the passage, you will ask him to answer some questions (or retell the story or article in his own words).

## Preparation for Reading a Passage

Ask a question or two about the title, topic, or illustration to explore briefly the student's knowledge of the topic. Before reading a selection about possums, you might direct the student's attention to the illustration of a possum and ask him what the picture shows. If there is no response, this might indicate a lack of background information about possums. To verify this, you might ask the student what he knows about possums. As the student responds, evaluate the depth and accuracy of his background knowledge.

Since reading is very much a matter of bringing meaning to a page or activating schema, it is important to have an estimate of the quality of the student's store of information. However, make sure that you don't give away major ideas or key vocabulary in the preliminary discussion. As part of a discussion, set a purpose for reading. This might be a general purpose, such as to find out more about the topic, or it may be more specific. Most commercial inventories contain a preliminary discussion and/or purpose-setting question. In the Basic Reading Inventory (Johns & Elish-Piper, 2012), for instance, the student is asked to read the title and tell the examiner what she thinks the passage will be about.

> As the student reads orally, note the quality of the reading and also time the reading to assess student's oral-reading fluency.

Once the purpose has been set, have the student read the selection aloud to answer the purpose question. As the student reads aloud, use a series of symbols to describe his reading behavior.

Note mispronounced words, omitted and inserted words, asking for help, correction of errors, hesitations, repetitions, misread punctuation, word-by-word reading, inaccurate intonation, head movement, finger-pointing, and other behaviors that might yield insight into the manner in which the reader processes print. Symbols for each of these behaviors are presented in Figure 4.5.

Mispronunciations that are occasioned by the student's dialect or because the student's native language is not English are not counted as errors. For instance, if students habitually omit endings in their speech, this is not counted as an error if they drop endings when they are reading. If a student who is not a native speaker of English pronounces *shoes* as *choose,* this is not counted as an error if this is the way the student pronounces the word in conversation and if the student understands that the word refers to footwear. In fact, translation of printed symbols into one's dialect is a positive sign (Goodman & Goodman, 1978). It indicates that the student is reading for meaning and not just making sounds.

---

**QUANTITATIVE ERRORS**

| | |
|---|---|
| the angry cat *(orange)* | Mispronunciation (Substitution) |
| the angry cat | Omission |
| the (angry) cat | Asked for word |
| the *big* angry cat | Insertion |
| the angry cat *angle* ✔ | Self-correction (not counted as an error) |

**QUALITATIVE ERRORS**

| | |
|---|---|
| the \|angry cat | Hesitation |
| <u>the</u> angry cat | Repetition |
| the angry cat *w × w* | Word-by-word reading |
| The angry cat hissed⊗ And away ran the dog. | Omitted punctuation |
| This is your cat. ↑ | Rising inflection |
| Is this your cat? ↓ | Falling inflection |
| *HM* | Head movement |
| *FP* | Finger pointing |

■■ **FIGURE 4.5**
IRI Oral Reading Symbols

As a practical matter, only uncorrected mispronunciations, omissions, insertions, and words supplied by the teacher count as errors. Repetitions and hesitations and other behaviors provide qualitative information about the student's reading. If a student reads so rapidly that it is difficult to record all his errors, then focus on noting those misreadings that count as errors. You may also record any other behavior that would shed light on the student's reading. In the sample marked-up inventory selection in Figure 4.6, the examiner included a comment in which the student stated that he likes animals. This information about the student's interests will come in handy when selecting materials.

As students are decoding difficult words, be sure to record all their attempts. This can yield valuable insight into their decoding processes. You might see, for instance, that a student is decoding a word sound by sound or using familiar word parts.

## Comprehension Check

After the student has read the passage, comprehension is checked. The traditional procedure for assessing comprehension of an IRI selection is to ask comprehension questions. The student's responses to questions should be recorded so you can take time later to examine any responses about which you are unsure. If the student has not supplied enough information for you to make a determination as to whether

The Biggest Nose (164 words)

Which animal has the biggest nose? Can you guess? The ‖ (elephant)

Commented, "I

does. The elephant's trunk is really its nose. The elephant smells with its

like

trunk, so its trunk is its nose. A full-grown elephant's trunk is about six feet

all

*waits*

kinds

long and weighs anywhere from 300 to 400 pounds. In a way the elephant's

of

trunk is like an arm and a hand, too. Although its trunk is very large, the

animals."

*odd* ✓

elephant can pick up an object as small as a peanut. The elephant also uses its

*drinks*

trunk to cool off. When it is hot, the elephant draws water up into its trunk.

*third* ✓

Then it lifts its trunk up and squirts water all over itself. When it is thirsty, it

*big*

squirts water into its mouth. Some ^ elephants even use their trunks to do

*far*

work. These elephants help men who are cutting down trees in the forests.

*heevy* ✓

After the trees have been cut into logs, the elephants pick up the heavy logs

and carry them away.

Source: From T. G. Gunning "Benchmark Passages Inventory." In *Building*

*Words: A Resource Manual for Teaching Word Analysis and Spelling*

*Strategies.* Boston: Allyn & Bacon.

**■ FIGURE 4.6**
Sample Informal
Reading Inventory
Performance
*Source:* From
Gunning, 2001.

the answer is right or wrong, you can ask the student to tell you more. However, do not supply any clues or hints. After scoring the comprehension responses, analyze them in terms of their quality. Were they complete? Was additional information volunteered? What level of language did the student demonstrate as she or he answered questions.

As an alternative to asking questions, you might check comprehension by requesting a retelling. In a retelling, a student is asked to recall a selection in her own words. Generally, the teacher uses a guide that indicates the main points that should be covered in a retelling. Figure 4.7 presents a sample retelling guide from the Qualitative Reading Inventory (Leslie & Caldwell, 2011).

The major advantage of the retelling procedure is that students reconstruct the piece according to their personal interpretations. The teacher is provided with the opportunity to observe how the student organizes her retellings and what kind of information she recalls or chooses to include. A retelling also shows what the reader inferred or added to the selection (Irwin & Mitchell, 1983).

Retellings, however, have to be interpreted with caution. Students generally do better on narrative retellings than they do with expository retellings. On the Quality Reading Inventory-5, average narrative retellings ranged from 17 to 41 percent,

**FIGURE 4.7**
Retelling Scoring Sheet Sample
*Source:* Leslie & Caldwell (2011). Reprinted by permission of the publisher.

SETTING/BACKGROUND

_____ John Chapman was born
_____ in 1774.
_____ He became a farmer
_____ and grew crops.
_____ John liked
_____ to grow
_____ and eat apples.
_____ People were moving west.
_____ Apples were a good food
_____ for settlers to have.

GOAL

_____ John decided
___5___ to go west.
_____ He wanted
___3___ to plant apple trees.

EVENTS

_____ John got many seeds
_____ from farmers
_____ who squeezed apples
_____ to make a drink
_____ called cider.
_____ He left
_____ for the frontier.
_____ He planted seeds
_____ as he went along.
_____ He gave them away.

_____ John walked miles.
___6___ He crossed rivers
___7___ and went through forests.
_____ He was hungry
_____ and wet.
_____ He had to hide
___8___ from Indians
_____ unfriendly Indians.
___9___ His clothes were torn.
_____ He used a sack
_____ for a shirt
_____ and he cut out holes
_____ for the arms.
___11___ He wore no shoes.

RESOLUTION

_____ John's fame spread.
___1___ He was nicknamed
___2___ Johnny Appleseed.
_____ Settlers accepted seeds
_____ gratefully.
_____ Thanks to Johnny Appleseed
___12___ trees grow
___13___ in many parts
_____ of America.

Other ideas recalled including inferences
*4   lived in Massachusetts*
*10   didn't give up*

whereas average retellings for expository text ranged from 13 to 31 percent. The low scores on retellings indicate that the average student's ability to retell a story is limited. Correlations between retellings and question answering was relatively low.

Because asking questions and requesting a retelling both have distinct advantages and provide different scores, you might assess comprehension by doing both. First, have the student provide a retelling. Then ask questions about any essential information not included in the retelling or follow-up probes.

### Administering Silent-Reading Passages

Immediately after discussing the oral passage, administer the silent-reading passage on that same level. After administering the third-grade oral passage, for instance, have the student read the third-grade silent passage. Do not administer all the oral passages at once and then the silent passages.

Just as was done when administering the oral passage, background should be explored in preparation for reading the passage and a purpose should be set. The student should be directed to read the passage silently. As the student reads silently, make notes on his behavior. Using the symbols presented in Figure 4.8, indicate lip movement, head movement, finger-pointing, and vocalization. Also note any words for which the student asks for assistance. (You may supply a word if the student asks for it, but if that word is part of the answer to a comprehension question, the student is not given credit for the answer even if she gets it correct. The rationale is that the student would not have arrived at the answer without the help you supplied.) At the conclusion of the silent reading, request a retelling or seek answers to traditional questions as you did for the oral passage.

Except as an optional procedure on the Qualitative Reading Inventory-5 (Leslie & Caldwell, 2011), students are not allowed to go back over the selection to locate information that would help them answer questions. This means that retention as well as comprehension is being assessed. Look-backs can be useful. Allowing students to look back would provide information about students' comprehension when memory is not a factor and also about their ability to locate appropriate information. However, the inventory should be scored according to students' ability to answer questions without using look-backs.

### Oral Rereading

Although it is not included in most commercial inventories, a valuable activity is to plan an oral rereading of a portion of the passage that was read silently. This rereading accomplishes three aims. It provides the following:

> (1) a gauge of the student's ability to skim for the relocation of specific information; (2) a measure of ability to read for a specific purpose and to stop when that purpose has been satisfied; and (3) an index of the ability to profit from previous silent reading of the material, and thus improve the fluency of oral performance over oral reading at sight at the same level of difficulty. (Johnson et al., 1987, p. 35)

| | |
|---|---|
| HM | Head movement |
| LM | Lip movement |
| FP | Finger pointing |
| SV | Subvocalization |
| PC | Use of picture clue |

■▪ **FIGURE 4.8**
Symbols for Silent Reading

✳ Because the student has already read the passage silently, the oral rereading should be more fluent than the reading of the oral passage at that level.

The oral rereading should be marked in the same manner as the oral selection was. A comment should also be placed on the teacher's copy to indicate how successfully the student reread the passage in question.

## Rate of Reading

✳ Although fluency includes quality of reading and comprehension along with rate of reading, a slow rate of reading at the independent and instructional levels suggests that students' reading is not fluent (Rasinski & Padak, 1996).

Another valuable piece of information that the inventory can yield is the rate of reading. The rate at which a student reads can provide insight into her fluency. Slow reading can be a sign that decoding is taking an excessive amount of time, that the student is reading word by word, or that she processes information slowly. Another possibility is that the student may be very anxious about remembering all the details in a selection and may believe that the best way to foster comprehension and retention is to read very slowly. Slow reading, especially among older students who have adequate decoding skills, is often a sign of an underlying problem.

Once students have mastered basic decoding skills, oral reading should match the student's rate of speaking (the average rate of speaking is 100 to 140 words per minute), and beyond grade 2, silent-reading speed should surpass rate of oral reading. To assess rate of reading, use a stopwatch but be unobtrusive. Students might feel pressured if they see that they are being timed.

Approximate average rates of reading for both oral and silent selections in grades 1 through 6 are presented in Table 4.3 (from Powell, cited in Lipson & Wixson, 1991). In seventh grade and beyond, students' rate of silent reading is approximately 200 to 250 words per minute (Harris & Sipay, 1990).

## Reaching the Frustration Level

Students continue reading oral and silent passages until they reach their frustration level. The frustration level is the point at which students have a score of 90 percent or less on the word recognition of the oral passages or when average comprehension of oral and silent passages is 50 percent or less. If students have acceptable word recognition but comprehension is 50 percent or less, test at the next highest level to make sure that the students have truly reached their frustration levels. Because of a lack of interest or inadequate background in a specific topic, students' comprehension may dip temporarily but rebound on a higher-level selection.

## Establishing Listening Capacity

Once students have reached the frustration level, you should have them stop reading. At that point, you begin reading the passages to them. The object is to

**TABLE 4.3**
Median Rates of Reading

| Instructional Reading Level | Oral Reading | Silent Reading |
|---|---|---|
| Grade 1 | 55 | 55 |
| Grade 2 | 85 | 85 |
| Grade 3 | 115 | 130 |
| Grade 4 | 135 | 155 |
| Grade 5 | 145 | 185 |
| Grade 6 | 150 | 205 |

> ✴ Because listening develops faster in the primary grades than reading does and some students have difficulty processing oral language, listening levels must be interpreted with care (Sticht & James, 1984).

locate the highest level at which students can understand printed materials, once the barriers posed by translating print have been removed. Two selections at each level are read to students in order to find the highest point at which students can understand 75 percent of the material. Again, be prepared for dips in performance. Do not stop as soon as the student reaches the 75 percent mark. Even if the performance slips below 75 percent, test at the next level. Listening comprehension may rebound.

Obtaining a listening-capacity level yields important information. The expectation is that students will be able to read up to their listening-capacity level. The listening-capacity task is an approximate measure of overall receptive language development. Students whose instructional level is below their listening-comprehension level are judged to be reading below their potential. Average students can typically grasp listening materials at their grade level. Below-average students generally have a listening level that is below grade level, and above-average students generally are able to comprehend material that is above their grade level.

Note the scores presented in Table 4.4. Although all three students whose scores are reported in the table are in the same grade and have different instructional levels; none is classified as a problem reader because all are reading up to their listening capacities. Jonathan, the first youngster, has a listening level of grade 2 but also is reading at a grade 2 level. Jonathan's language development seems to be below average. Maxine's instructional level of grade 4, which is at grade level, matches her listening level. Maxine's language development is apparently average. Benjamin, on the other hand, has an instructional and listening level of grade 8. His scores suggest superior language development.

As with the oral and silent passages, background should be explored and purposes set before the listening passages are read to students. For testing purposes, use the passages that the student has not yet read. However, if these are too hard, read easier passages from alternative forms. In the majority of cases a student's listening capacity will match or exceed the instructional level. However, some students have listening difficulties and will do even worse on a listening-comprehension test than they do on a reading test. They may have depressed listening scores because of emotional or attentional problems. A small percentage have difficulty processing information presented orally. For these students, it may be necessary to read passages to them that are below their instructional level. To get a measure of receptive language development in instances where the listening-capacity test does not seem to be working out, administer the Peabody Picture Vocabulary Test or a similar instrument.

Along with establishing the student's listening level, note his performance. Was he attentive during the reading of the selections? What kinds of questions was he able to answer with ease? What kinds of questions posed problems? How do listening and reading comprehension compare?

**TABLE 4.4**
Performance of Three Fourth Graders on an IRI

|  | Jonathan | Maxine | Benjamin |
|---|---|---|---|
| Independent | 1 | 3 | 4 |
| Instructional | 2 | 4 | 8 |
| Frustration | 3 | 5 | 6 |
| Listening capacity | 2 | 4 | 8 |

# Interpreting Inventory Results

Informal reading inventories do much more than just give reading levels. Because IRIs include a variety of lengthy selections and duplicate, in a controlled setting, the act of reading, they provide an excellent opportunity for insightful, in-depth observation. To interpret an inventory, begin with the most general information, the levels.

The listening-comprehension level provides information about the student's cognitive ability and language development. The higher the student's listening comprehension, the more fully developed are his language and cognitive abilities. Listening comprehension that is significantly above grade level indicates better-than-average potential.

Now take a look at the instructional level. Some students may have a range of instructional levels. Remember that a student is instructional if her word-recognition-in-context scores fall between 95 and 98 percent and comprehension is between 75 and 89 percent. Note Angela's levels in Figure 4.9. Her instructional levels are grades 2 and 3. Angela's basic instructional level, which is the highest level at which she meets the criteria, is grade 3. Her immediate instructional level is grade 2. That is the level at which the student begins to show needs. In deciding at which level to place Angela, a number of factors need to be considered. If Angela is older, it might be better to place her in the higher level, since that will make it easier to obtain materials that are age appropriate. If Angela seems insecure and gives up easily, it is advisable to give her lower-level materials, so she does not feel overwhelmed.

An examination of the levels yields other valuable information, too. They provide an estimate of the degree of discrepancy between ability and achievement in reading. For instance, the greater the difference between listening capacity and instructional level, the more serious is the problem. Note that Angela is reading three years below her listening capacity. Although both Orlando and Maria, whose levels are presented in Figure 4.10, have the same instructional level and are in the

---

Name __Angela__          Age _____

Date _____

Grade _____          School _____          Examiner _____

**Informal Reading Inventory Summary Sheet**

| | WORD-LIST SCORES | | | PASSAGE SCORES | | | | Reading Rate | |
| | | | Word Recog. | Comprehension | | | Listening | | |
| Level | Flash | Untimed | in Context | Oral | Silent | Avg. | Capacity | Oral | Silent |
|---|---|---|---|---|---|---|---|---|---|
| PP | 100 | — | | | | | | | |
| P | 100 | — | | | | | | | |
| 1 | 90 | 100 | 99 | 100 | 90 | 95 | | 120 | 130 |
| 2 | 85 | 90 | 98 | 80 | 90 | 85 | | 110 | 120 |
| 3 | 75 | 85 | 95 | 80 | 70 | 75 | | 100 | 120 |
| 4 | 60 | 70 | 89 | 60 | 50 | 55 | | 90 | 110 |
| 5 | 50 | 60 | | | | | 80 | | |
| 6 | 40 | 50 | | | | | 80 | | |
| 7 | | | | | | | 50 | | |
| 8 | | | | | | | | | |
| 9 | | | | | | | | | |

**LEVELS**

| | | **SUMMARY OF NEEDS** |
|---|---|---|
| Independent | 1 | Difficulty with main idea questions and multisyllabic words. |
| Instructional | 2–3 | |
| Frustration | 4 | |
| Listening Capacity | 6 | |

**■ FIGURE 4.9**
Sample IRI Levels

■▪ **FIGURE 4.10**
Comparison of IRI
Levels

| | ORLANDO | MARIA |
|---|---|---|
| Independent | 1 | 1 |
| Instructional | 2 | 2 |
| Frustration | 3 | 4 |
| Listening | 7 | 5 |

| LEVEL | WORD RECOGNITION IN CONTEXT | AVERAGE COMPREHENSION | WORD RECOGNITION IN CONTEXT | AVERAGE COMPREHENSION |
|---|---|---|---|---|
| PP | — | | — | |
| P | 100 | 100 | 100 | 90 |
| 1 | 99 | 90 | 100 | 90 |
| 2 | 95 | 80 | 96 | 80 |
| 3 | 86 | 60 | 93 | 70 |
| 4 | — | — | 91 | 60 |
| 5 | — | — | 90 | 60 |
| 6 | | | | |
| 7 | | | | |
| 8 | | | | |

same grade, Orlando apparently has the more serious problem. With a listening capacity of 7, Orlando is five years below capacity, whereas Maria, with a listening capacity of 5, is only three years below capacity.

Another comparison that should be noted is the magnitude of the difference between the instructional and the frustration levels. There is a buffer between the instructional and frustration levels that is at least 5 percent in word recognition and 25 percent in comprehension, because the criteria for the instructional level are at least 95 percent word recognition and 75 percent comprehension but 90 percent word recognition or 50 percent comprehension for the frustration level. The greater the distance between the instructional and frustration levels, the more likely it is that the student will make rapid progress because this indicates a gradual, rather than a steep, drop-off in skills.

Take a look at Orlando's and Maria's instructional and frustration levels. Orlando's word-recognition score takes a nose dive after he reaches the instructional level at grade 2. His 86 percent word-recognition score at grade 3 indicates that he will need lots of work in that area to bring word recognition up to an acceptable level. Maria's scores, on the other hand, taper off. With a little work, she should be able to bring up those 91 and 93 percentages to the 95 percent level.

After comparing levels, take a look at the student's scores in the two major areas assessed: word recognition and comprehension. Is there a discrepancy between the two? Is word recognition high but comprehension low, or vice versa? Or do both dip as the selections get harder, which is the typical pattern? Once you have a global sense of the student's reading performance, make an in-depth analysis of major areas, noting, of course, that reading is a holistic act so that ultimately information from all areas will need to be integrated.

## Word Recognition

Keeping in mind the information gathered from an analysis of the word-list tests, analyze the student's performance on word recognition in context. Is the student's percentage of word recognition in context higher at each level than her or his percentage of words recognized in isolation in the untimed condition? Was the student able to read some words in context that she or he had missed in isolation? Because of the availability of context clues, most students are better able to recognize words in context than in isolation.

On the other hand, there are a few students whose word-recognition skills are actually worse in context. These students have poor decoding skills. Deciphering words is a struggle for them. Given words in isolation, they are forced to apply their weak phonics skills. However, given words in running text, they overuse context, which is easier for them to apply than their weak phonics skills. If a picture is available, they may use that, too. Because they over rely on pictorial and verbal context and do not use the decoding skills they possess, they actually miss some words that they could read in isolation if they tried. They need to learn to use context along with phonics, not instead of phonics. They also need to have their phonics skills strengthened, with ample opportunity to apply them so they become automatic.

> If a student's performance on the word lists and oral passages portions of the IRI has been carefully analyzed, this should provide a wealth of information on word-analysis abilities, so it may not be necessary to give a separate phonics test.

Also observe the processes the student uses to decode words that posed problems. Did the student process the word sound by sound, saying /k/, /r/, /u/, /n/, /ch/ for *crunch*? Did the student use chunks of the word saying "un-run-crunch" or "run-crunch"? And what about the integration of strategies? Ideally, students should be making balanced use of the three language systems to decode words. These include the graphophonic, syntactic, and semantic. As you examine a student's errors, ask yourself the following questions:

- When the student encounters a difficult word, what does she or he do?
- Does the student try to sound the word out?
- Does the student use verbal context?
- Does the student use picture cues?
- Does the student ask for help or give up without trying to work out the difficult word?
- Are the student's miscues (misread words) meaningful?
- Does the student monitor her or his reading? Does the student self-correct when the text is not making sense or the word decoded does not fit? Self-corrections indicate that the student is reading for meaning and is monitoring her or his reading, and so are a positive sign. Self-correction of minor miscues, however, could indicate an overconcern with pronunciation. Good readers tend not to correct minor miscues that do not have an effect on the meaning of the passage (Y. Goodman, 1992).
- What strategies does the student use to correct an error?

At this point, take a look at the qualitative markings on the inventory. Slow or word-by-word reading, frequent hesitations, and repetitions are signs that the student is having difficulty with decoding. Take a little time, too, to examine the student's mastery of the "content" of phonics. What word-analysis elements was the student able to use? With what word-analysis elements did the student have difficulty? Using the list of word-recognition skills presented earlier in the chapter, examine the student's word-recognition-in-context performance. What phonic (consonants, consonant clusters, single vowels, vowel combinations, short vowels, long vowels, other vowels), syllabic, or morphemic elements (prefixes, suffixes, roots) was the student able to use? With which did she or he have difficulty?

Word recognition in isolation lends itself to dynamic testing. After students have completed the first run-through, go back and see if they can read some of the words they missed. For instance, pointing to a missed word, ask the student if there is any part of the word that she can read. If the student can read a part of the word, see if she can read the whole word. If the student says that she can't read any part of the word, cover up all but a part that seems relatively easy and see if the student can read that. (You might cover up all but the *par* in *particular*.) If the student can read that part, see if she can use that part to help her reconstruct the whole word. You may discover hidden strengths on which you can capitalize when you work with the student.

## Comprehension

Comprehension is affected by a number of factors, including language development, cognitive ability, background of experience, word recognition, and appropriate use of strategies. A good starting point for assessing comprehension processes is to look at the preparatory portion of each of the oral and silent selections. What background of information did the student bring to the selection?

If the student has answered traditional questions, analyze responses. What kinds of questions did the student answer best? What kinds of questions posed problems? Note in particular what the student's performance was on key questions and hypothesize what this implies about underlying cognitive processes. Literal questions, those whose answers are stated explicitly in the story, require selection and retention of details. Inferential questions and questions that require drawing a conclusion may require that a student integrate comprehension of details and background knowledge. Vocabulary questions hinge on word knowledge and, depending on the nature of the item, the ability to use context. Main-idea questions involve the ability to organize or categorize details and draw a conclusion as to what the main idea is. Instead of simply noting how many details, main idea, or inferential questions the student answered, take note of the basic comprehension processes that these responses suggest. Ask: "How is the student processing printed information? What are the student's strengths? What are the student's weaknesses?"

Most students have difficulty comprehending because the selection contains too many words that they don't know. However, there are students who are good decoders but poor comprehenders. To assess comprehension difficulties, probe responses so that you can gain some insight into the causes, which often have to do with the student's thinking processes. Some possible causes of poor comprehension are listed here, along with questions that might be asked to determine causes of difficulties (Dewitz & Dewitz, 2003):

■ Inadequate background knowledge. Ask questions about items that you believe the student might not know: "What can you tell me about planets? What is an asteroid? Have you ever seen a telescope?"

■ Difficulty with vocabulary. Go back to the passage, point to a key word that you believe may be unfamiliar to the student, and ask: "What does this word mean?"

■ Difficulty with syntax. Go back to the target sentence, and ask questions about it. Ask: "Who owns the dog that won the prize?"

■ Overuse of background knowledge. Ask: "What makes you think that the sun is closer to Earth in the summertime? How did you know that? Is that in the article?"

■ Failure to recall or comprehend directly stated information. Ask: "Can you find the answer to that in the article?"

- Failure to link ideas in a passage. Ask: "What happened because it rained? What else could have made Lee sad? Who else caused the team to lose?"

- Failure to make inferences. Ask: "Why do you think the family decided to head west? What do you think will happen because of the long, dry summer?" (Gunning, 2010)

### Supplementary Questions

To get a more complete look at the student's use of comprehension strategies, supplement the administration of the IRI with key questions about the use of strategies. After administering the comprehension portion of the IRI, ask such questions as: "What do you do before you read an article or story?" (Students should be surveying the text, predicting, setting purposes.) "What do you do as you read? What do you think about?" (Students should be selecting important details, organizing and evaluating information, relating new information to old, creating mental images.) "What do you do if there is a part that you don't understand?" (Students should be rereading, or perhaps using graphic cues.) "What do you do after you read?" (Students should integrate new and old information, evaluate information, and think about how the new information might be applied or used.) To get a fuller look at a student's use of strategies, you may wish to supplement the administration of the IRI with an administration of a think-aloud, which is discussed in Chapter 5.

### Shortcomings of IRIs

Commercial IRIs may overestimate the difficulty level of material that students can read. A possible consequence is that students may be given materials that are too difficult for them.

Despite the obvious utility, IRIs have their shortcomings. If they are not administered by a trained professional or if the professional does not heed the standards, they may yield inflated levels (Enz, 1989). If selections are unappealing, require backgrounds that students do not possess, or contain questions that are ambiguous or that can be answered without reading the selection, then they may yield erroneous results (Lipson & Wixon, 1997). In many inventories, the selections are very brief and so are easier to read than typical selections. Inventory selections for a particular grade may also be written at an easier level than the selections contained in basal readers and other materials designed for that grade. This is especially true of first- and second-grade selections (Gunning, 2000c).

## Selecting an IRI

Many of these shortcomings can be overcome by trying out several inventories and selecting the one that you feel gives the best results. Also, as you become familiar with an inventory, you will learn its strengths and weaknesses and can take steps to compensate. You may find that the sports selection on level 4 penalizes students who know little about sports but motivates reluctant readers who like sports to do their best and often reveals hidden strengths. In addition, levels yielded by an inventory should be thought of as estimates. Observe students' actual performance reading their texts and make adjustments as necessary.

In choosing an IRI, match it with your needs (Gunning, 2010). The Basic Reading Inventory (Johns & Elish-Piper, 2012, 2008) might be a good choice if you are assessing young children, since it has passages geared to materials now being used at the easiest levels. Because passages in the Basic Reading Inventory are 50 to 100 words long, it can be administered in a minimum of time. The QRI-5 might be a good choice for an in-depth analysis of comprehension at higher levels, because it includes lengthy content-area passages and think-alouds. If you are working with Spanish-speaking students you might want to use the Comprehensive Reading Inventory (Cooter, Flynt, & Cooter, 2007), which contains assessments in Spanish. See Nilsson (2008) for a detailed comparison of IRIs.

## Miscue Analysis

Miscue analysis, which is a way of examining and interpreting students' oral-reading errors, is based on the premise that not all oral-reading mistakes are equal or even negative. For instance, if a student substitutes the word *car* for *automobile* in the sentence "The automobile in the showroom window caught my eye," he is demonstrating that he is reading for meaning, because *car* is a synonym for

> **Miscues:** oral-reading responses that differ from the expected responses.

*automobile*. The word **miscues** rather than *errors* is used "to avoid the negative connotation of errors (all miscues are not bad) and to avoid the implication that good reading does not contain miscues" (K. Goodman, 1969, p. 12).

As noted earlier, according to K. Goodman, the reader draws on three basic sources of information: graphophonic or phonics, syntactic, and semantic, which includes the sum total of the reader's background of knowledge. By comparing miscues to the original text, we can gain insight into the reader's processes. For instance, we can surmise whether the reader is using a balanced strategy or is over-using graphophonic strategies or fails to use semantic cues. The promise of miscue analysis is that it provides insight into the reading process (K. Goodman, 1974).

### Adapted Miscue Analysis

Reading miscue analysis, originally designed for research purposes, can be time-consuming. Therefore, you may want to use the simplified miscue analysis procedures described below. To save more time, it is recommended that the procedures be used in conjunction with the oral-reading passages of an IRI. If miscues from an IRI are used, select only those miscues that occur at the independent and instructional levels and on any passages that occur between the instructional and frustration levels. Do not choose miscues from the frustration level. As material becomes too difficult, both good and poor readers tend to overuse graphophonics cues because they are not able to read enough words to use context.

On a sheet similar to the one in Figure 4.11, make a list of the student's miscues. List 25, if you can. If there are fewer than 25, list as many as are available. But remember that the fewer the miscues, the less dependable will be the conclusions that you can draw from the data. Next to each miscue, write the word that was misread—the actual text. Then compare the miscue with the text. Assess whether the miscue fits the sense of the selection. Ask: "Is the miscue meaningful? Does it fit the sense of the selection?" If so, put a check (✓) in the first column. If not, put a minus (–).

Next, determine whether the miscue is graphically similar. A miscue is graphically similar if at least half the graphic elements in the miscue are the same as those in the text. Note in the next three columns whether the beginning, middle, and end of the miscue are similar to the beginning, middle, and end of the text word. If the word has only two graphemes (*he, bee*), assess only the beginning and the end. A two-grapheme word is similar if one of the graphemes is the same. A three-grapheme (*goat, red*) word is similar if two of the three graphemes are the same.

**FIGURE 4.11**
Miscue Analysis

| Miscue | Text | Semantic Similarity | Graphic Similarity | DEGREE OF GRAPHIC SIMILARITY | | | Self-Corrections | Non-Words |
|---|---|---|---|---|---|---|---|---|
| | | | | Beg. | Mid. | End | | |
| 1. be | beyond | — | — | ✓ | — | — | ✓ | |
| 2. wild | wide | — | ✓ | ✓ | — | ✓ | | |
| 3. milk | Mike's | — | ✓ | ✓ | — | ✓ | | |
| 4. letter | leather | — | ✓ | ✓ | — | ✓ | | |
| 5. his | him | — | ✓ | ✓ | ✓ | — | | |
| 6. out | up | ✓ | — | — | — | — | | |
| 7. was | were | ✓ | — | ✓ | — | — | | |
| 8. title | titles | ✓ | ✓ | ✓ | ✓ | ✓ | | |
| 9. books | book | ✓ | ✓ | ✓ | ✓ | ✓ | | |
| 10. covers | covered | ✓ | ✓ | ✓ | ✓ | — | | |
| 11. full | fell | — | ✓ | ✓ | — | ✓ | | |
| 12. men | mean | — | ✓ | ✓ | — | ✓ | ✓ | |
| 13. talking | taking | — | ✓ | ✓ | — | ✓ | ✓ | |
| 14. out | ought | — | ✓ | ✓ | — | ✓ | | |
| 15. de-shed | demolished | — | ✓ | ✓ | — | ✓ | | ✓ |
| 16. schap | scrap | — | ✓ | ✓ | — | ✓ | | ✓ |
| 17. wreaked | wrecked | — | ✓ | ✓ | — | ✓ | | ✓ |
| 18. being | be | ✓ | ✓ | ✓ | — | — | | |
| 19. collection | collectors | — | ✓ | ✓ | ✓ | — | | |
| 20. budding | building | — | ✓ | ✓ | — | ✓ | | |
| 21. a | one | ✓ | — | — | — | — | | |
| 22. Claude | Claudia | ✓ | ✓ | ✓ | ✓ | — | | |
| 23. five | fife | — | ✓ | ✓ | ✓ | — | | |
| 24. tree | three | — | ✓ | — | ✓ | ✓ | ✓ | |
| 25. dis-tor | destroy | — | ✓ | ✓ | ✓ | — | | ✓ |
| Totals | | 32% | 84% | | | | 12% | 16% |

After assessing a miscue for graphic similarity, note whether it was self-corrected. Self-corrected miscues do not count as errors on an IRI but provide valuable information about a student's reading processes and so are included in the analysis. In the next column, note whether the miscue is a nonword. Production of nonwords is significant because it indicates a failure to read for meaning and suggests the overuse of decoding.

After filling in each column, tally the check marks and convert the total in each column to a percentage. Note which strategies the student is using. A high percentage of meaningful miscues and self-corrections indicates the use of context. A high percentage of graphically similar words indicates the use of graphophonics strategies. Compare percentages to determine whether strategies are being used in balanced fashion. Is there an overreliance on meaning or sounding out? Does one strategy area seem to be weak?

If phonics is a problem area, examine the columns to see which elements are being used. Most poor readers fail to use the middles of words because they have difficulty with vowel correspondences. Some rely too much on initial consonants. Reexamine the miscues to see if you note any particular needs in phonics or structural elements.

Most important of all, as you analyze the data, set up tentative hypotheses to describe the current state of the student's reading development and some steps that might be taken to foster the student's growth in literacy. As you administer additional assessment measures or work with the student, be prepared to amplify and revise your hypotheses.

Examine the sample miscue analysis in Figure 4.11. This is an analysis of the reading performance of Madeline, a fourth-grader who was receiving special help because of comprehension problems. The percentages tell the story. Madeline's miscues were graphically similar 84 percent of the time but fit the context only 32 percent of the time. In addition, she self-corrected only 12 percent of her miscues. It is clear from even a quick survey of the results that Madeline is neglecting context clues. Note that she produced four nonwords, a further sign that she does not always read for meaning.

A program for Madeline would emphasize reading for meaning and monitoring one's reading so the student is constantly asking: "Does this sound right? Does this make sense? What word would fit here?" Madeline also needs to integrate the use of context with her deciphering skills. With help from context, she should have been able to figure out words such as *leather* and *wrecked*. Although she overrelies on sounding out, Madeline needs some instruction in the use of word-analysis skills. She does well with single-syllable words but has difficulty with multisyllabic words. Vocabulary knowledge may also be a factor. She may have missed *demolished* because it is not in her listening vocabulary.

## Retrospective Miscue Analysis

In retrospective miscue analysis (RMA), the reader and teacher listen to a tape of the student's reading and discuss whether the miscue made sense, if it was corrected, and if it needed to be corrected. In their work with struggling readers in a detention facility, Moore and Aspegren (2001) found that students who used RMA improved their use of contextual clues and also improved their comprehension as indicated by richer and fuller retellings. The students also came to a better understanding of themselves as readers. Working with two seventh-grade struggling readers, Wilson (2005) used RMA to build the students' confidence and strategy use.

## ▨ Running Records

**Running record:** an oral-reading assessment with a dual purpose: determine (1) whether the material being read is at the appropriate level, and (2) which strategies the reader uses to decode hard words.

A useful adaptation of the informal reading inventory and miscue analysis, the **running record,** is a quick, easy assessment of a student's oral-reading behavior. Like miscue analysis, running records are designed to reveal the processes the student is using to read text:

> When the performance is less than perfect, there are opportunities to record the work done by the child to get it right, to puzzle it out. This reveals something of the process by which the child monitors and corrects his own performance. When he encounters something new we can observe how he approaches the novel thing, and what he learns from the encounter. (Clay, 1993, pp. 21–22)

✴ In a research study, schools that used running records to determine students' reading levels and their skill needs and used that information to plan and implement instruction outperformed schools that conducted action research (Ross, 2004).

Unlike miscue analysis, running records are quick and easy to administer, and no special material is needed. Generally, the student is given material felt to be at her instructional level and asked to read orally. As with other assessment procedures, the purpose of the running record is explained to the student. As the student reads, the teacher records the student's performance, using the symbols presented in Figure 4.12.

✴ Although running records are typically recorded on a blank sheet of paper, they may be recorded on a photocopy of the text that the student is reading.

A blank sheet of paper may be used to record a student's performance on a running record. Two lines of words and symbols are used to indicate each line of text. For most reading behaviors,

**FIGURE 4.12**
Running Record
Symbols

1. Words read correctly are marked with a ✓.
   *John ran home.*

   ✓  ✓  ✓

2. Substitutions are written above the line.
   All attempts to read the word are recorded.
   *Pam was hungry.*

   ✓  ✓  hunger/angry
           hungry

3. Self-corrections are marked "SC."
   *Pam was hungry.*

   ✓  ✓  angry | SC
           hungry

4. A dash is used to indicate no response.
   *I will see her tomorrow.*

   ✓  ✓  ✓  ✓  —
                    tomorrow

5. A dash is used to indicate an insertion
   of a word. The dash is placed
   beneath the inserted word.
   *A dog.*

   ✓  big  ✓
         —

6. A "T" is used to indicate that a child
   has been told a word.
   *I will see her tomorrow.*

   ✓  ✓  ✓  ✓  T
                    tomorrow

7. The letter "A" indicates that the child
   has asked for help.
   *A small mouse*

   ✓  ✓  A
            mouse

8. At times, the student becomes so tangled
   that it is suggested that she or he "Try
   That Again," which is coded with "TTA"
   and is counted as an error.
   *The horse ran into the barn.*

   (TTA)
   [ ✓  house  ✓  ✓  ✓  bus ]
        horse              barn

9. A repetition is indicated with an "R."
   Numerals show number of repetitions:
   R2, R3. If the repetition returns to an
   earlier portion of the sentence, the point
   to which the student returns is shown by
   an arrow.
   *The horse ran into the barn.*

   ✓  house | SC  ✓  ✓  ✓ bus | R
        horse                   barn

the student's performance is written on the top line. The bottom line is left blank; later, after the running record has been administered, it is filled in with the words from the text. A check mark is written on the top line to indicate each word read correctly. Substitutions are also written on the top line. If a student sounds out a word, that is indicated by using lowercase letters: *p-e-t*. Uppercase letters are used to indicate words that the student has spelled out (*L-I-O-N*). Insertions are indicated by writing the insertion above the line and a dash below it. Omissions are recorded by writing a dash above the line. An "SC" indicates a self-correction; "T," being told the word; and "A," an appeal for help. An "R" symbolizes a repetition with a line and arrow used to indicate going back over a series of words.

In general, you should take a neutral stance when assessing oral reading. Be supportive and encouraging but do not give assistance, as it will invalidate your results. Although as a teacher your natural inclination is to provide instruction, when you are assessing, you need to see what students can do on their own. Occasionally, however, students may make so many errors in a passage that they need to be redirected. This can be accomplished by asking them to "Try that again." If you resort to this intervention, which should be used sparingly, bracket the text in question and label it "TTA" for "try that again."

On some occasions, a student may be blocked by a key word that he is unable to decode but that is important to the sense and the flow of the passage. For instance, it might be the word *cheetah* in an informational piece about cheetahs. If he is unable to decode the word, the student will be blocked from using background knowledge to process the text. For this type of situation, you may tell the student the word, but code your assistance with a "T" to indicate "told word," and count it as an error.

As in the IRI, substitutions, omissions, insertions, appeals for help and being told a word are counted as errors. Self-corrections are not counted as mistakes. A repeated error, saying *there* for *this,* counts each time it occurs, but a proper noun, no matter how many times it is mispronounced, counts as only one error.

After scoring the running record, calculate the percentage of errors. Divide the number of errors by the number of words in the selection and subtract from 100 percent to get an accuracy rate. Using a more lenient standard than the IRI, guidelines for running records are presented in Table 4.5. The instructional level for word recognition, for instance, is 90 to 94 percent, rather than the 95 to 98 percent required by IRI standards. Note that only word recognition is included in the standards. As an option, you might also calculate the self-correction rate and assess comprehension. The self-correction rate is the percentage of errors that the student self-corrects. To determine the self-correction rate, divide the number of self-corrections by the number of errors. An acceptable rate would be approximately 25 percent, or one quarter. To check comprehension, have the student retell the story, or you might ask a series of questions as is done with the IRI.

## Analyzing Miscues in a Running Record

Just as with the informal reading inventory, it is important to code students' miscues and self-corrections when analyzing a running record. Note for each miscue and self-correction the cue or cues being used. To interpret the student's oral reading, Clay (1985) suggests that the teacher examine every error and ask: "Now what made him say that?" (p. 21). As you analyze miscues, ask yourself: "Is the student using meaning? Does the miscue make sense? Is the student using syntax? Does the miscue fit grammatically? Is the student using visual cues? Does the miscue fit the graphic construction of the word? Does it begin and/or end with the same sound? Does it have the same vowel sound?"

Code the miscues "M" to indicate use of meaning, "S" for syntax, and "V" for visual (phonics). Or students might be using two or even three strategies, so you

**TABLE 4.5**
Running Record
Standards

| Text | Word Recognition |
|------|------------------|
| Easy | 95–100% |
| Instructional | 90–94% |
| Hard | 80–89% |

Using running record procedures, you focus on what the students can do because you make a check mark for each word read correctly.

would code the miscue "MV, SV, SM," or "SVM." Also note whether the student engages in *cross-checking*—that is, using one type of cue to support another. For instance, a student reads "The dog were barking" for "The dogs were barking." Noting that *dog* does not fit with *were*, the student went back to the beginning of the sentence and saw that *dog* ends in an *s* and self-corrected by adding *s* to the noun. A syntactic cue alerted the student that she had misread, but a visual cue, the *s* at the end of *dogs*, was used to verify her correction, so the item should be coded "SV."

Look for a pattern. One or two miscues in the meaning category would be inconclusive. In order to obtain a sufficient number of miscues on which to base a valid conclusion, students should read a passage of about 100 words or more. The passage should be challenging but not overwhelming. As the text becomes too difficult, students' skills disintegrate, so the examiner will get a false impression of their reading. At the maximum, students should be making no more than 1 error for every 10 words read. For a thorough analysis of student's use of strategies, you might try a running record on easy, medium, and difficult selections but not one in which the student's error rate exceeds 10 percent. You might also compare a student's performance on a new story with one that has been read previously. Note the running record displayed in Figure 4.13. What strategies does the student seem to be using?

As you become familiar with the running record technique, you can make more detailed analyses of strategies used. This is especially true in the visual category.

For more information on running records, see M. M. Clay (1993, 2000). Still another source of information about running records is Johnston (2000).

Note, for instance, whether a student seems to sound out words letter by letter or is chunking sounds. Is the student breaking down a word such as *rat* into $r + a + t$, or is the student chunking sounds so that he analyzes it as $r + at$. Is he using the first letter and combining that with context, or is he attempting to use all parts of the word?

**FIGURE 4.13** Sample Running Record

The Elves and the Shoemaker

| | | | CUES USED | |
| --- | --- | --- | --- | --- |
| | | E  S | E | SC |
| The shoemaker was very poor. | ✓  T  ✓  ✓  ✓<br>shoemaker | 1 | M S V | M S V |
| He had just enough leather | ✓  ✓  ✓  every  letter<br>enough  leather | 2 | M S (V)<br>M (S)(V) | M S V<br>M S V |
| to make one more pair | ✓  ✓  ✓  ✓  \|poor<br>pair | 1 | M S (V) | M S V |
| of shoes. | ✓  ✓ | | M S V | M S V |
| He cut out the leather | ✓  ✓  ✓  ✓  letter<br>leather | 1 | M (S)(V) | M S V |
| for a new pair of shoes, | ✓  ✓  ✓ poor SC ✓  ✓<br>pair | 1 | M S (V) | (M)(S) V |
| and then he went to bed. | ✓  ✓  ✓  ✓  ✓  ✓ | | M S V | M S V |
| He was soon fast asleep. | ✓  ✓  ✓  first SC  ✓ R<br>fast | 1 | M (S)(V) | (M) S (V) |

Note how effectively and efficiently strategies are being used. Ask: "Are any strategies being overused or used inappropriately?" Are meaning strategies used when visual strategies are called for or vice versa? To what extent are strategies being used in a balanced, integrated fashion?"

As you assess, consider the student's stage of development. Overattention to one or another cue source is very common for brief periods of time in students' development. It is quite common for students just getting the hang of letter–sound relationships to devote an overabundance of effort to them, even to the extent that meaning is lost as attention is exhausted by the process of decoding words.

## Commercial Running Records

Based on the Reading Recovery model, Pearson's Developmental Reading Assessment (DRA) functions as an informal reading inventory/running record for students in grades 1 through 3. DRA2 (2nd edition; Pearson, 2009) is designed for grades 4–8.

The Fountas and Pinnell Benchmark Assessment System 1 (2nd edition; Fountas & Pinnell, 2010) which is designed for grades K–2, has an IRA–running record format that is similar to that of the DRA, with a feature called Comprehension Conversation that provides information about a reader's thinking. The Fountas and Pinnell Benchmark Assessment System 2, (2nd edition; Fountas & Pinnell, 2010) is designed for grades 3–8.

# Planning Instruction Based on IRI, Miscue Analysis, or Running Record Results

In addition to indicating instructional levels, IRIs, running records, and miscue analyses provide a wealth of data that can be used to plan a reading program for students, especially if the results have been carefully analyzed and you have carefully observed the student during the administration of one of these instruments and, if possible, during class time. After assessing a student, note strengths and weaknesses to help you determine what kind of instruction might be most effective. Consider strategies that might be used before, during, or after reading. Both decoding and comprehension strategies should be planned, along with ideas for book selection and fostering reading. Take your cues from the student's performance. For instance, if the student failed to preview before reading, stress previewing activities. If the student overused context, focus on decoding strategies.

Suggestions for developing the strategies and skills listed are developed in Chapters 7 through 14.

# Comparing IRI, Miscue Analysis, and Running Records

All three devices—the IRI, miscue analysis, and running record—play a role in assessment. The IRI is the most versatile of the three and the easiest to administer and interpret. The IRI is also the best of the three instruments for placing pupils and, when interpreted with care, can provide a wealth of information about a student's reading process.

The more specialized miscue analysis provides extensive information about the way a student processes printed language, information that can be used to plan a program of instruction. However, in an interview with Mellor and Simons (1991), K. Goodman warns that miscue analysis is of no value unless it is rooted in an understanding of its underpinnings.

The running record, a direct descendant of miscue analysis, is most valuable as an ongoing indicator of strategies that students are using and as a check on the suitability of materials they are reading. Easy to administer, the running record is a useful, practical instrument, but because of its focus on decoding, it works best with students who are operating on the earlier levels of reading.

The major benefit of the IRI, miscue analysis, and running record is that they provide a peek into students' reading processes. Using an IRI perspective whenever you examine students' reading performance, you are mentally estimating whether the material they are reading is on their independent, instructional, or frustration level. From a miscue analysis or running record perspective, you would be asking: What cues is the student using to process print? As Y. Goodman notes:

> Once you are aware of what is involved in miscue analysis, you are always listening with what I call a "miscue head"; you have the scheme of miscue analysis in your head. Sometimes, working with students whose strategies are not very efficient, you may need to do a very full, complete miscue analysis, but if kids are developing appropriately, it's not necessary to use a miscue inventory because you know that they're using the strategies in an appropriate way, and you just keep monitoring it yourself. (quoted in Mellor & Simons, 1991, p. 100)

## IRI-Based Tests

A number of reading assessment instruments are based on the concept or embody some of the major features of an IRI. These include oral-reading tests, group reading inventories, cloze and modified cloze tests, and word-opposites (Botel) and word-list tests.

### Oral-Reading Tests

As their title suggests, oral-reading tests do not include the assessment of silent reading. As such, they are quicker to administer, but they are less valid because they neglect silent reading and less reliable because they assess the student on just one passage for each level instead of two. One advantage of oral-reading tests such as the Gray Oral Reading Test (GORT) is that many of them are norm referenced and standardized so they may be used in situations that demand validated instruments, such as in pre- and posttesting for an experimental or government-funded program.

### Word-List Tests

To save time, teachers and diagnosticians sometimes administer word-list tests instead of IRIs. As discussed earlier, a word-list test consists of a series of words in isolation that gradually increase in difficulty. There is a close correlation between the ability to pronounce words in isolation and overall reading (Manzo & Manzo, 1993). However, because they require only the ability to pronounce words, these tests neglect comprehension and may report misleading levels for students who are superior decoders but poor comprehenders or vice versa. In a comparison of commercial and teacher-made IRIs with the reading subtest of the WRAT (Wide

Range Achievement Test), which requires only the pronouncing of isolated words, the WRAT yielded estimates that were one to two grade levels above the estimates yielded by IRIs (Bristow, Pikulski, & Pelosi, 1983). The two most popular word-list tests are as follows:

1. The Slosson Oral Reading Test (SORT) presents 20 words at each grade level from preprimer through grade 12. The student is required only to pronounce the words and does not have to know their meanings. Standardized and norm referenced, the Slosson yields grade equivalents, percentile ranks, and stanines.

2. Similar in format to the SORT, the Oral Reading Subtest of the WRAT also assesses reading through the pronunciation of isolated printed words. The WRAT is frequently administered by school psychologists.

## Group Inventories

Because of the time involved, it may be impractical to administer individual IRIs. However, you may choose to administer a group reading inventory. Information about constructing and administering group reading inventories can be found in *Informal Reading Inventories,* by Johnson, Kress, and Pikulski (1987). Some reading series contain group reading inventories. There are also two standardized tests that function as group inventories: the Degrees of Reading Power and the Scholastic Reading Inventory.

The major shortcoming of group inventories is that they assess only comprehension. They don't assess students' ability to read words. To obtain this information, you might use oral-words-reading tests such as the Slosson Oral Reading Test (norm referenced) or the Word Reading Survey (informal) (see Figure 4.14). Taking only about five minutes to administer, these tests give a quick estimate of the students' reading abilities. Because comprehension is not assessed, results have to be interpreted with care. Administer the Word Reading Survey just as you would an IRI word-list test. The student's estimated instructional reading level is the highest level at which she can read 7 or 8 words out of 10.

### Degrees of Reading Power (DRP)

**FIGURE 4.14**
Word Reading
Survey
*Source:* Gunning,
2003.

The Degrees of Reading Power is designed primarily to provide an instructional level. A modified cloze test, the DRP has no questions. Composed of a series of passages that gradually increase in difficulty, the DRP assesses overall reading ability by having students choose from among five options the one that best completes

| 1 | 2 | 3 | 4 | 5 | 6 | 7 | 8 | 9–12 |
|---|---|---|---|---|---|---|---|---|
| I | please | branch | reason | escaped | absence | continuously | calculator | administrative |
| the | never | middle | distant | business | instinct | application | agriculture | spontaneous |
| we | hour | stronger | lonesome | continue | responsible | incredible | prohibited | molecule |
| go | climb | picture | silent | obedient | evaporate | maximum | legislation | ritual |
| hat | field | hunger | wrecked | entrance | convenience | environmental | translucent | recipient |
| help | spend | several | decided | applause | commercial | accumulate | astronomical | conscientious |
| coat | side | empty | certainly | government | necessary | geographical | optimistic | infectious |
| are | believe | since | favorite | celebration | recognition | triangular | narrate | beneficiary |
| how | happen | impossible | realized | microscope | vertical | pollutant | persuasive | attribution |
| work | suddenly | straight | solution | navigate | starvation | currency | obnoxious | paralysis |

a portion of the passage from which words have been omitted. Each passage has nine deletions. As in a classical IRI, the passages gradually increase in difficulty and encompass a wide range of difficulty so that slow, average, and superior readers' ability may be assessed adequately.

Instead of yielding a grade-level score, the instrument provides a DRP score. The DRP score indicates what level of material a student should be able to read. A complementary readability formula is used to indicate the difficulty level of books in DRP units. The basic intent of the DRP is to match students with books that are on their levels.

### The Scholastic Reading Inventory

The Scholastic Reading Inventory, which also uses a modified cloze procedure, yields Lexile scores. Lexile units progress from 200 to 1700. Scholastic's inventories come in print and computer-adaptive versions. Very poor readers may need to be reassessed on a lower-level test than the one indicated for their grade level.

## Screening, Monitoring Progress, and Benchmarking

Screening, monitoring progress, and benchmarking are key elements in a response to intervention (RTI) approach but should be a part of any intervention program. To assess the quality of the classroom program and to identify students who need extra help, all students are screened three times a year. Students judged to be at risk are provided with extra help and closely monitored. Screening also serves benchmarking and progress-monitoring functions. Screening measures typically incorporate a key benchmark, such as being able to read an on-level passage with 95 percent accuracy at a designated rate of words per minute, depending on the grade level. The screening instrument administered three times a year can also be used to monitor progress. However, students who are at risk should have their progress monitored more frequently—in some instances, as often as once a week.

An economical but effective way to track students is to assess key skills. For emergent and very early readers, these skills might be alphabet knowledge and phonological awareness. Students are assessed on their ability to name the letters of the alphabet, provide initial sounds when shown illustrations, or segment spoken words into their separate sounds. For developing readers, it might be skills such as phonics and the ability to read words that become increasingly difficult. For more advanced readers, it might be comprehension of increasingly difficult passages. For secondary school students, a possible screen might be their performance on state or national literacy tests and progress they make in their individual content classes, as evidenced by performance on unit or other assessments (Vaughn et al., 2012). Tests now being created to accompany Common Core State Standards promise to include measures that can be used for screening and monitoring. Progress-monitoring measures can be informal. You might administer an IRI periodically or use running records or end-of-unit assessments. When monitoring students' progress, don't rely on just one or two sources of information. Work samples, checklists, and observations should be used to shed light on students' performance and track their progress. Charts of books read also enable you to monitor student progress. If students are lagging behind in their book reading, you can intervene.

Most screening consists of administering one or two assessments to all students. However, multilevel screening involves administering additional assessments to students judged to be at risk. The first stage of a two-stage screen would have the cutoff score set at a high enough level so that virtually all students at risk would be identified. The second-stage screen would be more thorough and would be designed to identify only those students who have a genuine need for intervention. Monitoring students' progress weekly for six weeks or so, obtaining information about students' attention and work habits, and dynamic assessment of phonics or other skills have been used as secondary screens (Compton et al., 2012). Multilevel screening enhances the accuracy of screening so that students who would do well without intervention are not mistakenly flagged as needing additional assistance. Multilevel screens can be used to identity students who might need a program that is more intensive than what is offered in Tier II and might ultimately need Tier III intervention (Fuchs et al., 2012).

## Curriculum-Based Measures

*Curriculum-based measures (CBMs)* are often used to monitor students' progress. Curriculum-based measures assess overall indicators of proficiency, rather than mastery of specific skills. Thus, being able to read lists of words and oral passages and to complete fill-in-the-blank maze passages are indicators of overall achievement in reading.

> **Using Technology**
>
> For additional information on CBM along with a web-based template for creating a progress monitoring graph, visit Intervention Central at http://www.interventioncentral.org/.

CBMs are quick probes that measure the same skill over and over again. They are designed in such a way that multiple but equivalent versions can be created so progress can be monitored frequently, in some cases as often as once a week (Hosp, Hosp, & Howell, 2007). CBMs are more effective when used to measure lower-level indicators. They don't do a very good job of measuring more complex processes, such as comprehension (Fletcher, Lyon, Fuchs, & Barnes, 2007). See Table 4.6 for a listing and sources of CBM measures.

### Emergent and Early Reading CBMs

Emergent and early literacy are assessed by measuring students' ability to name letters of the alphabet, give the sounds represented by letters of the alphabet, segment

**TABLE 4.6**
Sources of CBM Measures

| Source | Letter Name Fluency | First Sound Fluency | Phon Seg | Letter Sound Fluency | Nonsense Word Fluency | Word Reading Fluency | Oral Reading Fluency | Mazes | Modified Cloze | Voc. | Writing |
|---|---|---|---|---|---|---|---|---|---|---|---|
| AIMS Web | K–1 | | K–1 | K–1 | K–1 | | 1–8 | 1–8 | | | 1–8 |
| CBM Warehouse* | K–1 | | | | | 1–3 | | | | | |
| Dibels* | K | K | K | | K–2 | | 1–8 | 3–6 | | | |
| Edcheckup | | | | K–1 | | K–1 | 1–6 | 1–6 | | | 1–8 |
| Yearly Progress Pro | | | | | | | | 1–8 | | | |
| Monitoring Basic Skills Progress Pro-ED | | | | | | | | 1–7 | | | |
| Univ. Southern Maine | | | | | | | | 4–6 | | | |
| Vanderbilt Univ | K–1 | | | | 1 | | | | | | |

*Note:* Has assessments in Spanish.

*Source:* From *Creating Literacy Instruction for All Students* (7th ed.), by T. Gunning. 2010, Boston: Allyn & Bacon. Reprinted by permission of Allyn & Bacon.

spoken words, identify the first sound of a spoken word, read nonwords, and read high-frequency (sight) words.

*Letter Name Fluency*   The student names as many letters as she or he can within a minute's time. By timing the naming of the letters, the automaticity of the student's responses is being assessed. The student is asked to point to the letter name as she or he says it.

> **▶ Using Technology**
>
> DIBELS Next can be accessed at http://dibels.org/next.html/. This Web site provides extensive information about DIBELS along with downloads of the subtests.

*First Sound Fluency (DIBELS Next)*   The assessor says a word, and the student is asked to say the first sound for the word: "What sound does *man* begin with?"

*Letter Sound Fluency*   Letter sound fluency assesses the student's ability to provide the sounds typically represented by letters shown in isolation. For vowel letters, the student is only given credit for giving the short sound of the letter. Limiting the assessment to one minute indicates the student's automaticity or fluency and also speed of processing. In a tryout with 1,500 kindergarten students and 1,500 first-graders, Fuchs and Fuchs (n.d.) judged students to be at risk if they got a score of less than 12 at the end of kindergarten and less than 19 at the beginning of first grade. There were a number of false positives and false negatives in the assessment, so students' progress should be closely monitored. (A false positive means that a difficulty is predicted but the student does well. A false negative means that no difficulty is predicted, but the student does not do well.)

*Phoneme Segmentation Fluency (DIBELS)*   Given a spoken word, the student is asked to say all the sounds in the word. The tester pronounces the word *stop,* and the student is expected to say /s/, /t/, /o/, /p/.

*Word Identification Fluency*   The student is given a list of 50 to 100 high-frequency words and asked to read as many words as possible in a minute's time. Reading real words has proven to be a more valid predictor of reading achievement than reading nonsense words (Fuchs et al., 2004). Multiple copies of the Letter Sound Fluency and the Word Identification Fluency Test are available from Lynn Fuchs, Vanderbilt University, Peabody #328, 230 Appleton Pl., Nashville, TN 37203-5721.

## Fluency and Comprehension CBMs

**Oral-Reading Fluency** The most widely used CBM assesses oral-reading fluency, which measures how many words a student can accurately read in a minute. Oral-reading fluency is a general outcome measure and a rough indicator of a student's proficiency with lower-level reading skills. It has been compared to a thermometer in that it is an indicator of general reading health. However, in one study, 15 percent of students who had good oral-reading fluency had poor comprehension. These students also tended to have low vocabulary scores (Riedel, 2007). Measures of oral-reading fluency need to be complemented with measures of comprehension.

An oral-reading fluency test can be modified and administered in the same fashion as an IRI or running record. If given in both standard and modified fashions, the passages would yield reading rate scores, reading levels, and retelling scores. If a miscue analysis were administered, it would also yield qualitative data about the student's use of word-analysis skills and strategies. If adapted, oral-reading fluency tests such as the DIBELS would be more time-consuming to administer but would yield more valuable data (Gunning, 2010).

In addition to rate of reading fluency should also include accuracy, expression, and comprehension (Valencia et al., 2010). Reading with appropriate expression can be an indicator that the reader understands what he or she is reading well enough to voice the emotions indicated by the text. However, in some instances, monotonal readers have excellent comprehension and expressive readers have poor comprehension. Comprehension should still be checked with questions and/or a retelling. As noted earlier, measures of oral-reading fluency need to be complemented with measures of comprehension.

Screening and monitoring first-graders' oral-reading fluency with passages is problematic. Because they are still in the beginning stages of learning to read, first-graders aren't given passages to read until the winter of first grade. However, at that point, the skills of many students might still be too limited. For instance, the winter first-grade passage of the widely used DIBELS contains words with long vowels, *r* vowels, and other vowels. However, by the winter of the school year, many first-graders would not yet have been taught these more complex vowel patterns. The winter test passage would be more appropriate for spring administration. The passage would be overwhelming for struggling readers. A better assessment would be a word-list test, such as the Word Identification Fluency Test (Gunning, 2010). See Table 4.7 for rates of letter naming, phonological awareness, and word reading in grades K and 1.

*Maze Passages*   In grades 3 and beyond, maze passages are preferred to oral-reading passages because they provide a measure of basic comprehension, can be administered to groups, and take very little time from instruction. Maze passages are 150 to

**TABLE 4.7**
Rates of Letter Naming, Phonological Awareness, and Word Reading

| Grade | Fall | Winter | Spring |
|---|---|---|---|
| *K* | | | |
| Letter Name | (1) 2–8 (8+) | (0–19) 20–29 (30+) | (1–28) 29–39 (40+) |
| First Sound | (0–4) 5–9 (10+) | (1–9) 10–24 (25+) | NT |
| Phoneme Seg. | NT | (1–6) 7–17 (18+) | (1–9) 10–34 (35+) |
| Letter Sound Fl | 5 (0) | 17 | 27 (12) |
| Nonsense Wds | NT | (1–4) 5–12 (13) | (1–14) 15–24 (25+) |
| *Grade 1* | | | |
| Letter Name | (1–24) 25–36 (37) | | |
| Phoneme Seg. | (1–9) 10–34 (35+) | (1–9) 10–34 (35+) | (1–9) 10–34 (35+) |
| Letter Sound Fl | 28 (19) | 33 | 47 |
| Nonsense Wds | (1–12) 13–23 (24+) | (1–29) 30–49 (50+) | (1–29) 30–49 (50+) |
| Word Reading | 6–10 | 20–25 | 40–45 |

*Note:* Except for letter sound fluency, the figure in the middle indicates some risk. The figure in parentheses to the left of the middle figure indicates at risk. The figure in parentheses to the right of the middle figure indicates low risk. For letter sound fluency, the figure without parentheses indicates average score. The figure in parentheses indicates at risk. Figures for word reading are estimates of average performance.

*Source:* Adapted from Fuchs & Fuchs (n.d.), Good & Kaminski (2003), and AIMSweb (2006). From *Creating Literacy Instruction for All Students* (7th ed.), by T. Gunning. 2010, Boston: Allyn & Bacon. Reprinted by permission of Allyn & Bacon.

400 words in length. Every seventh word is deleted, but no words are deleted from the first or last sentence, and proper nouns are not deleted. Answer options include the word deleted from the selection and two other words. Distracter options do not make sense in the sentence and are usually a different part of speech but are approximately the same length as the answer. The distracters are usually chosen from words from other parts of the selection. Students read for three minutes.

Mazes can also function as a group reading inventory. Students who have low scores might be given a maze assessment on a lower level; those with higher scores might be assessed on higher levels in order to obtain approximate reading levels. Teachers should assess a student until an instructional level is obtained. The highest reading level at which the student reads with a score of 70 to 80 percent in an untimed administration is the estimated instructional level. These approximate levels might then be verified by observing the student's performance or by administering additional assessments, such as an IRI or oral-reading test.

One problem with maze passages is that are not very sensitive to growth. On average, students only gain about a half replacement per month. AIMSweb (http://aimsweb.com), a progress-monitoring system, has maze passages for grades 1–8. DIBELS Daze has passages for grades 3–6, which can be downloaded free of charge. You can also construct your own maze exercises. You can paste in a passage at the Maze Passage Generator Web site (http://www.rti2.org/rti2/mazes) to generate your own maze passage. Readability for the passage is also provided. Figure 4.15 shows a sample maze passage.

When used for benchmarking or screening, maze and other tests are typically given on grade level. The idea is to see if the student has reached the benchmark. When used for progress monitoring, tests are given on the students' reading level. The idea is to find out what level the student is operating on so that growth can be measured.

***IRIs and Running Records*** Running records and informal reading inventories (IRIs) have been criticized for use as progress-monitoring devices because they focus on specific skills, whereas curriculum-based measures are indicators of overall reading proficiency. Actually, both inventories and oral-reading fluency tests assess oral

■■ **FIGURE 4.15**
Sample Maze

*Source:* Gunning (2012). *Reading Success for All Students: Using Formative Assessment to Guide Instruction and Intervention,* p.222, San Francisco: Jossey-Bass.

---

**Sample Maze Passage**

*Kangaroos*

If you want to see one kind of kangaroo, you have to look up. One kind of kangaroo lives in (foods, trees, even). The tree kangaroo is small, but (it, that, from) has an extra long tail. It (and, also, in) has long curved claws. The long (tail, fruit, move) and sharp claws help it to (climb, eat, to) trees. The tree kangaroo is a good (person, jumper, up). It can leap 30 feet from (good, one, is) tree branch to another or (even, faster, and) from one tree to another. It (look, can, small) also jump as much as 60 (claws, as, feet) to the ground. But on the (kind, another, ground) the tree kangaroo hops slowly. It (only, quickly, long) hops about as fast as a (person, bird, main) walks. Trees are good places for (see, which, the) tree kangaroo. They can move much (faster, smaller, it) in trees. Besides, their main food (is, want, also) tree leaves. But they also eat (branch, fruit, sharp) and sometimes will even eat small (places, birds, to). In addition, being in a tree helps (keep, jump, but) tree kangaroos safe from enemies.

reading. Although some examiners skip this step, it is recommended that inventories be timed so that a rate of reading is obtained. In addition, through retelling and/or questioning, comprehension can be assessed. Comprehension is the ultimate aim of reading, so IRIs and running records are better indicators of performance when retelling and/or questioning is included. IRIs are time-consuming, but administration time can be reduced by assessing only oral reading and using brief passages. In addition, if students are tested several times a year, the examiner has a good idea of the level the student is on and thus can arrange for the student to read passages on that level (Gunning, 2013).

## Setting Benchmarks

Many progress-monitoring measures have benchmarks, or expected levels of performance. Benchmarks are typically set by noting the relationship between a student's performance on a benchmark and later performance on an outcome measure. For instance, according to the DIBELS Next, the benchmark for oral-reading rate at the beginning of fourth grade is 90 words per minute (wpm). Students who attained that benchmark are predicted to have an 80 to 90 percent chance of being successful. Reading rates at that level are associated with scores at the 40th percentile or above on the GRADE, a standardized and norm-referenced reading test (Good et al., 2011). The cut score for being at risk is 70 wpm. Scores below that level are associated with scores at the 20th percentile on the GRADE. Students at that level were judged to have only a 10 to 20 percent chance of being successful. Students reading below 90 wpm but above 70 wpm are predicted to be at some risk. They have a 40 to 60 percent chance of being successful. The benchmarks are less than perfect predictors, but they do provide helpful indicators. They need to be complemented with professional judgment and additional assessments. (Using composite scores from DIBELS Next provides a more accurate prediction than using just oral-reading fluency.)

Table 4.8 presents oral-reading rates of students at various percentiles. Note the variation of reading rate at each grade level. The table can be used to set benchmarks for students and cut points for determining at-risk performances. The cut point is the point that indicates a high probability the student will not reach the benchmark unless provided with intervention. The cut point might be set at the 25th percentile or lower. Table 4.9 shows replacement rates for maze passages. Table 4.10 shows average growth rates for students on a variety of CBMs. In grade 1, students gain about 1.5 words a week and are able to read 1 additional word on a 50-word phonics inventory. In oral fluency, they gain about 1 word per week in grades 2 and 3 but only 0.5 words a week in grades 7 and 8. Using the charts, you can estimate whether a student is making average progress.

## Constructing a Screening or Progress-Monitoring Assessment

You might decide to construct your own system, because of the overemphasis of existing assessments on speed of responding and lower-level skills and the lack of alignment between what you teach and what available progress-monitoring systems assess. First, decide what your key objectives are. Determine what your students should know and be able to do at the end of the year. This should include knowledge and skills set by school and district standards and any additional goals that you have for your students. Translate these standards into language your students can understand so they have a clear idea of what is expected of them. Also map out the

**TABLE 4.8**
Rates of Oral and
Silent Reading

| Grade | Fall | Winter | Spring | Silent |
|-------|------|--------|--------|--------|
| 1 | | 12 (23) 47 | 28 (53) 82 | |
| 2 | (25) 51 (79) | (42) 72 (100) | (61) 89 (117) | 121 |
| 3 | (44) 71 (99) | (62) 100 (120) | (78) 107 (137) | 135 |
| 4 | (68) 94 (119) | (87) 112 (139) | (98) 123 (152) | 149 |
| 5 | (85) 110 (139) | (99) 127 (156) | (109) 139 (168) | 163 |
| 6 | (98) 127 (153) | (111) 140 (167) | (122) 150 (177) | 177 |
| 7 | 128 (101) 156 | 136 (109) 165 | (123) 150 (177) | 191 |
| 8 | (106) 133 (161) | 146 (115) 173 | (124) 151 (177) | 205 |

*Note:* The figure in the middle shows reading rate at the 50th percentile. The figure in parentheses to the left of the middle figure shows reading rate at the 25th percentile. The figure in parentheses to the right of the middle figure shows reading rate at the 75th percentile.

*Source:* From *Creating Literacy Instruction for All Students* (7th ed.), by T. Gunning. 2010, Boston: Allyn & Bacon. Reprinted by permission of Allyn & Bacon. The figures for oral reading are drawn from Tindal, Hasbrouck, & Jones (2005) and Tindal & Hasbrouck, 2006. The figures for silent reading are drawn from Carver, 1990.

**TABLE 4.9**
Rates of
Completion for
Mazes

| Grade | Fall | Winter | Spring |
|-------|------|--------|--------|
| 1 | (0) 2 (6) | (2) 5 (10) | (3) 7 (13) |
| 2 | (2) 4 (8) | (6) 10 (15) | (9) 13 (18) |
| 3 | (8) 12 (17) | (10) 15 (19) | (10) 15 (21) |
| 4 | (9) 13 (17) | (13) 18 (25) | (14) 19 (25) |
| 5 | (12) 17 (22) | (15) 21 (27) | (18) 24 (30) |
| 6 | (10) 15 (22) | (13) 20 (28) | (14) 19 (27) |
| 7 | (13) 17 (22) | (13) 18 (24) | (15) 21 (28) |
| 8 | (14) 18 (23) | (14) 17 (22) | (17) 21 (28) |

*Note:* The figure in the middle shows completion rate at the 50th percentile. The figure in parentheses to the left of the middle figure shows the completion rate at the 25th percentile. The figure in parentheses to the right of the middle figure shows completion rate at the 75th percentile.

*Source:* From *Creating Literacy Instruction for All Students* (7th ed.), by T. Gunning. 2010, Boston: Allyn & Bacon. Reprinted by permission of Allyn & Bacon. The figures are adapted from AIMSweb, 2006.

**TABLE 4.10**
Estimated Growth
Rates per Week

| Skill | K | 1 | 2 | 3 | 4 | 5 | 6 | 7 | 8 |
|-------|---|---|---|---|---|---|---|---|---|
| Letter Name | 1 | | | | | | | | |
| Letter Sound | 1 | 1.2 | | | | | | | |
| Initial Sound | 1 | | | | | | | | |
| Segmenting | .5–1 | | | | | | | | |
| Word Reading | | 1.5 | | | | | | | |
| Phonics Inventory | | 1 | | | | | | | |
| Oral Reading Fluency | | | 1 | 1 | .75 | .75 | .75 | .5 | .5 |
| Mazes | | | | | .25 | .25 | .25 | .25 | .25 |

*Source:* Adapted from Good & Kaminski (2003), Gunning (2010), Hosp, Hosp, & Howell (2007), Fuchs & Fuchs (n.d.). From *Creating Literacy Instruction for All Students* (7th ed.), by T. Gunning. 2010, Boston: Allyn & Bacon. Reprinted by permission of Allyn & Bacon.

steps needed to meet the standards so students have a clear idea of what their learning journey will be.

Then create or adapt measures that assess those objectives. For instance, for phonics, you might use the Letter Sound Fluency Test, if students are at an early level of learning phonics, and the Phonics Inventory, explained in Chapter 5, if students are working with vowel patterns. For recognition of words in isolation, you might use the Word Identification Fluency Test or word lists from an IRI. For reading rate, you could use the DIBELS oral fluency passages. For comprehension, you might use the maze passages from AIMSweb or DIBELS Next, IRI passages, or DIBELS passages with retellings or questions added.

After determining the area or areas to be assessed, obtain baseline data on the student's performance (Wright, 2007). To set performance goals, determine as best you can what the norms for the grade are or what a reasonable expectation for desirable progress might be. For many literacy skills, it will be the ability to read grade-level material with 70 percent comprehension. For fluency, it will be the ability to read at the speed at which the typical student reads. Use Tables 4.7, 4.8, 4.9, and 4.10 to help you set performance goals.

The performance goal or target you set will also depend on the amount of time available for the intervention and the rate of progress you believe the student can make. For instance, suppose the student is a fourth grader reading at 40 words a minute who was assessed at the beginning of the year. You might estimate that this student can improve his reading rate by 2 words a week. Over a period of 30 weeks, you estimate the student can gain 60 words a minute in reading rate and so reach a target rate of 100 words a minute. Since the student is reading on a mid-third-grade level, you might also estimate that he will gain 1.5 years' growth. The progress-monitoring probes that you use will begin at the mid-third-grade level but continue through the fourth-grade level (Gunning, 2008).

Create a graph to show progress. Place reading rate on the vertical axis and time of year on the horizontal axis. Plot the student's beginning level and ending level. Draw a line to show his expected progress. Then weekly or monthly, plot the student's scores. If the student has a serious problem, monitor his progress more frequently. With frequent monitoring, you will be quicker to note when a student is lagging behind and so in need of additional instruction, more review, or better materials. The progress-monitoring chart in Figure 4.16 shows a first grader's scores on the Phonics Inventory. The student's beginning score was 2. A target score of 40 to 45 was set because it represents end-of-first-grade performance and seemed achievable, if the student were to be given extra tutoring. If the student fails to make adequate progress, strengthen the intervention. You might provide more intensive instruction or additional practice, or you might try an approach that seems more in keeping with the student's learning style (Gunning, 2010). For the student in Figure 4.16, it was necessary to intensify his intervention in order for him to reach his target.

## ▪▪▪ Mini–Case Study

Mike, the new boy in third grade, was something of a puzzle. Although he had been in the class for three weeks, he hadn't made any friends. The other children didn't pick on him, but they didn't seek him out for inclusion in their games.

Quiet and undemanding, Mike was easily overlooked in the hustle and bustle of the classroom. Although Mike did well with math calculations, he had difficulty

**FIGURE 4.16**
Monitoring Chart
*Source:* Gunning (2008c). Reprinted by permission of Galvin Publishing.

with any activity that required reading or writing. Because he was struggling with his third-grade basal reader, the school's reading specialist gave Mike an IRI.

The source of Mike's reading difficulties soon became obvious. According to the word-list tests, Mike's ability to recognize words at sight or immediately was adequate up through the preprimer grade level. Although he did better with word recognition in context, Mike's instructional level turned out to be first grade. Actually, Mike was able to read second-grade material with 80 percent comprehension, but his word recognition was only 85 percent. Having a rich background of information, Mike was able to make maximum use of context to reconstruct the story.

Mike also had excellent listening comprehension. When selections were read to him, Mike was able to answer at least 75 percent of the comprehension questions up through the seventh-grade level. This suggested that Mike had highly developed oral language and cognitive abilities.

Based on the IRI results and the classroom teacher's observations, Mike received additional assistance with word-recognition skills. The program included systematic instruction in phonics and in the use of context clues, with heavy emphasis on applying those skills by reading lots of books and other materials on the appropriate level. Writing also became a prominent part of the program.

In order to build on Mike's excellent cognitive and oral-language skills, he was encouraged to listen to recorded books and to view informational programs on DVDs. Mike was also placed in a cooperative learning group composed of students who were especially friendly and outgoing. After a slow start, Mike made rapid progress.

## Summary

The widely used informal reading inventory consists of graded word lists and oral and silent passages that extend from the preprimer through the 8th- or 12th-grade level. The IRI yields four levels: independent, instructional, frustration, and listening capacity. The independent level is the point at which the student's word recognition is 99 percent and comprehension is 90 percent. Figures for the instructional level are 95 percent word recognition and 75 percent comprehension. The frustration level is reached when word recognition slips to 90 percent or below, or comprehension is 50 percent or less. After a student has reached the frustration level, selections are read to her or him. The listening capacity, which provides an estimate of the level of material that a student could handle if she or he had the necessary processing skills, is the highest point at which the student can understand 75 percent of the material that is read to her or him.

When analyzed carefully, inventories are a rich source of information about a student's reading behavior. Miscue analysis, which can also be used with an IRI or a running record, builds on the concept of the IRI and yields information that opens a window on the strategies that the student is using and the reading process itself. In miscue analysis, an attempt is made to determine to what extent contextual and graphophonic cues are used.

Built on the concept of miscue analysis, the running record is an efficient way to assess students' oral reading. Used extensively in Reading Recovery, the main objectives of running records are to make sure students are reading on the appropriate level and to provide insights into the strategies they are using as they decode words.

A number of other tests are modeled on the format or purpose of the IRI. These include oral inventories, word-list tests, group inventories, and cloze tests.

Progress monitoring is a key element in every intervention. Progress monitoring may be formal or informal. One device used to monitor progress is curriculum-based measurement, which measures the same continuously developing skill, rather than a series of subskills, over and over again, often with brief probes.

## Application Activities

1. Compare two of the inventories mentioned in this chapter. Pay particular attention to the quality of the selections and questions. Which inventory seems to be better? Why?

2. Administer an informal reading inventory. Using the modified miscue analysis recommended in the chapter, analyze the inventory results. Based on this analysis, what strategies are used by the student you tested? What might be done to improve this student's reading?

3. Administer a running record to a student in a primary grade. Analyze the results and answer these questions: Was the text that you used on the appropriate level of difficulty? What strategies did the student seem to be using? What seemed to be the student's greatest strengths and weaknesses?

4. Administer a screening assessment, and note which students seem to be at risk. Monitor their progress.

## My Education Lab

Go to the topic **Reading Assessment** in the MyEducationLab (www.myeducationlab. com) for **Assessing and Correcting Reading Difficulties,** where you can:

- Find learning outcomes for **Reading Assessment** along with the national standards that connect to these outcomes.

- Complete Assignments and Activities that can help you more deeply understand the chapter content.

- Apply and practice your understanding of the core teaching skills identified in the chapter with the Building Teaching Skills and Dispositions learning units.

- Examine challenging situations and cases presented in the Iris Center Resources.

- Check your comprehension of the content covered in the chapter with the Study Plan. Here you will be able to take a chapter pretest, receive feedback on your answers, and then access personalized Review, Practice, and Enrichment exercises to enhance your understanding of chapter content. After you complete the exercises, take a posttest to confirm your comprehension.

- Practice targeting instruction and making content accessible for all students with A+RISE activities.

# 5

# Assessment of Reading and Writing Processes

This chapter complements the previous one on informal reading inventories, miscue analyses, and running records. It continues to look into ways in which reading and writing problems are assessed and analyzed and to provide techniques for assessing critical areas, such as decoding and comprehension, in more depth. It also discusses ways of assessing such related areas as spelling and writing. In addition, it goes beyond formal and informal tests to look at other ways of gathering information.

What do you know about assessing reading, writing, and spelling difficulties? In addition to knowing at what level the student is reading, what else would you wish to know if you were teaching a student with a reading difficulty? How would you go about gathering that data in order to get the most useful information in the shortest amount of time?

**USING WHAT YOU KNOW**

**ANTICIPATION GUIDE**

*Read each of the following statements. Put a check under "Agree" or "Disagree" to show how you feel about each one. If possible, discuss your responses with classmates.*

|  | AGREE | DISAGREE |
|---|---|---|
| 1. The most useful way to gather information about students' reading and writing processes is through observation. | _____ | _____ |
| 2. Decoding is the most important reading area to assess. | _____ | _____ |
| 3. When testing decoding skills, it is better to use nonsense words than real words. | _____ | _____ |
| 4. Having students retell a story is a better way to assess comprehension than asking them questions about the selection. | _____ | _____ |
| 5. If a student has good comprehension, you do not need to test decoding or vocabulary skills. | _____ | _____ |

## ▝▝▝ **Reading Processes: Decoding**

Having insight into students' decoding processes will help you decide on the most promising approaches to use when instructing them and determine what kinds of instruction they might need. In the previous chapter, you learned how to interpret the results of word-list tests and word recognition in context on informal reading inventories and also how to interpret running records. Through interviews, observation, and occasional informal questions, you can verify findings and gain additional information about students' decoding processes.

> ⁜ By asking students to tell you how they figured out a hard word, you are helping them become more aware of their thought processes.

As students read aloud, note the processes that they are apparently using. Note, first of all, whether they seem to have strategies that are effective. Do they use context? When they decode a word, do they sound it out letter by letter ($B + e + n$), or do they attempt to put large elements together ($B + en$)? Do they integrate context and sounding out? Do they try another pronunciation when the word they have reconstructed is not a real word or does not make sense?

For novice readers, note whether their errors or miscues are phonological. Reading *big* for *bag* or *run* for *ran* shows that students are beginning to use phonological skills. Reading *man* for *dad* would be a nonphonological representation. The point at which phonological errors outnumber nonphonological ones indicates that the student has attained functional phonological ability (Stuart & Colthheart, 1990).

After students have successfully decoded a difficult word, ask them how they figured out the word, or as they are unsuccessfully attempting to decode a word, ask what you might do to help them. For students who have serious decoding and word-learning problems, you might use the interview presented in Figure 5.1. It is not necessary to ask all the questions listed. Simply ask those that seem most pertinent.

If you want to find out what phonic elements a student knows, administer the Phonics Inventory in Appendix A. It consists of 50 words that include most of the major word patterns found in single-syllable words. If a student does poorly on the Phonics Inventory, administer the Beginning Consonant Correspondences test, which can be found on the author's Web site: http://wordbuilding.org. The Consonant Correspondences test consists of presenting the student with a letter

---

**■▝ FIGURE 5.1**
Word
Identification
Interview

| |
|---|
| **Name of Student** _____ |
| **Date** _____ |
| **Age** _____          **Grade** _____          **Reading Level** _____ |
|   1.  How do you feel about reading? |
|   2.  Is reading hard? |
|   3.  What do you think makes reading hard? |
|   4.  What is the hardest thing for you to do in reading? |
|   5.  Why do you think that it's hard for you to learn words? |
|   6.  What is the hardest thing about learning words? |
|   7.  What would make it easier? |
|   8.  What do you do when you come across a hard word? |
|   9.  What makes it hard to figure out words? |
| 10.  What kinds of words are the hardest to learn? |

and asking her to tell what sound that letter makes. If a student does well on the Phonics Inventory, administer the Graduated Syllable Survey in Appendix A to see how well she can decode multisyllabic words.

A number of tests use nonsense words to assess decoding. The rationale is that students will not have seen these items before and therefore will not be responding to them as words that they had memorized. However, as noted earlier, decoding involves using four processors: orthographic (letter), phonological (sound), meaning, and context. When students decode a word, there is a feedback step in which they note whether the item they have decoded is a real word. If the item being decoded is a nonword, then the semantic process cannot be brought into play.

Because of this missing feedback step, decoding nonsense words is apparently more difficult than decoding real words (Cunningham et al., 1999). Walmsley (1978–1979) also found that pseudo-words and rare words were more difficult to read than real words and words in common use. Moustafa (1995) noted a tendency for students to misread pseudo-words as real words. In all three studies, nonsense words were harder to read than real words. Using nonsense words provides some information about a student's ability to decode words. However, because the test task is more difficult than the task the student will actually face when reading, tests using nonsense words underestimate students' ability to decode words and may indicate a problem where there is none. Reading real words as opposed to nonsense words has proved a better predictor of future reading achievement (Fuchs, Fuchs, & Compton, 2004).

Sometimes spelling is used to assess students' knowledge of phonics. To assess knowledge of beginning consonant correspondences, students may be asked to spell such words as *ball, cat,* and *dog.* They are given credit if they are able to spell the first letter of each of the words, because that is what is being assessed. The problem with using spelling is that it is not the same process as that used in reading. In reading, the student must retrieve sounds for letters. In spelling, the student retrieves letters for sounds. Spelling is generally more demanding than reading. However, in some rare cases, a student can spell a word that he cannot read. Given the sounds of the words, he may be able to retrieve the letters that represent the sounds. Seeing the letters, however, he may not be able to retrieve the sounds.

## Published Phonics Tests

Many of the diagnostic tests listed in Chapter 3 assess decoding skills. There are also a wide variety of informal phonics tests. However, many of these either use nonsense words or spelling and so are of doubtful validity. Two published tests that use real words to assess phonics are the Beginning Phonics Skills Test (Shefelbine & Newman, 2000a) and the Phonics subtest of the Diagnostic Assessments of Reading (Riverside). Core Phonics (Honig, Diamond, & Gutlohn, 2008) assesses letter names, consonant sounds, and vowel sounds in isolation and key patterns, including syllables, in real and pseudo-words, thus providing an opportunity to compare students' performance on real and nonsense words. DIBELS Deep Word Reading and Decoding (Sopris Learning) has a Quick Screen that can be used to identify which of five in-depth assessments should be administered. Skills assessed range from beginning consonants to reading multisyllabic words. (For most skills, a subtest consisting of real words and a subtest consisting of nonsense words are provided). The testing is dynamic, which means that directions can be altered or teaching can be initiated in order to elicit correct responses. Reponses obtained through teaching are noted.

## ▨▨ Reading Processes: Comprehension

Dependent on but more complex than decoding, comprehension is more difficult to assess. Poor comprehension can be caused by a number of factors, including inadequate background, lack of necessary concepts or vocabulary, poor use of strategies, lack of basic decoding skills or fluency, lack of attention or concentration, poorly developed thinking skills, or inadequate language development. In addition to these internal factors, comprehension difficulties can be caused or made worse if the materials students are reading are too difficult or poorly written or if comprehension instruction is inadequate.

Comprehension can be assessed in a variety of ways. In addition to administering and analyzing an informal inventory, observing students in a discussion in class, noting students' performance on teacher-made comprehension tests or on end-of-book unit tests provides an overall sense of a student's ability to comprehend what has been read. Standardized norm-referenced tests, such as the Metropolitan, Iowa, Gates-MacGinitie, Terra Nova, GRADE, Stanford, and other similar tests, provide overall measures of comprehension. As noted in Chapter 3, guessing is a factor in most norm-referenced tests, because they generally have a multiple-choice format; in light of this, the tests are measures of recognition of information rather than recall or construction of meaning. A better test of comprehension is the informal reading inventory or a similar measure, because guessing does not play a role, and the students must construct their responses. Common Core assessments, which will contain both multiple-choice and constructed responses and will assess a wide range of comprehension skills, should provide more instructional information than the typical standardized or high-stakes test.

When assessing comprehension, make sure that students are reading material on their instructional level. If they are not able to read at least 95 percent of the words, comprehension will be hampered. Similarly, check reading rate. If students' reading rate is very slow—if they are reading grade 3 material or above and are reading at less than 80 words a minute—their reading rate is too slow. If they are reading second-grade material and their reading rate is less than 50 words a minute, their reading rate is too slow. In fact, their reading rate is so slow that it is probably interfering with comprehension (Monti & Cicchetti, 1996). To assess comprehension adequately, select a passage in which at least 95 percent of the words are known and the student can read the passage with a fair amount of fluency. Otherwise, a low comprehension score may be due to lack of fluency or inadequate word recognition.

Comprehension assessments have been criticized because they oversimplify the complexity of understanding texts. They focus on a few skills and don't provide teachers with very much information that they might use to help struggling readers (RAND Reading Study Group, 2004). Along with other recommendations, the RAND Reading Study Group called for comprehension assessments that contain

> capacity to identify individual children as poor comprehenders. An effective assessment system should be able to identify individual children as poor comprehenders, not only in terms of prerequisite skills such as fluency in word identification and decoding, but also in terms of cognitive deficits and gaps in relevant knowledge (background, domain specific, etc.) that might adversely affect reading and comprehension, even in children who have adequate word-level skills. It is also critically important that such a system be able to identify early any child who is apt to encounter difficulties in reading comprehension because of limited resources to carry out one or another operation involved in comprehension. (p. 746)

In addition to determining the status of struggling comprehenders, it is essential to find out what is causing their comprehension problems. Is it lack of background or vocabulary? Is it an attention problem? Are they failing to use strategies? Or are there some other factors at work? Retellings yield helpful insights.

## Retelling

A retelling of a piece of fiction takes a somewhat different format and is structured around the main elements of a story: setting, characters, plot, goal, story problem, and theme. After the student has read the selection, ask her to retell it. For a younger student you might say something like "Pretend I have never heard this story. Tell it to me." If necessary, use prompting questions, such as the following:

> Questions mold responses into a certain form. Retellings provide insight into the processes students use to construct meaning and organize information.

> After analyzing retellings, reflect on what this information tells you about students' reading–thinking–speaking processes and their ability to organize, integrate, and evaluate.

**Setting:** Where did the story take place? When did it take place?

**Characters:** Who are the main characters in the story? What can you tell me about them?

**Problem(s):** What problem(s) did the main character have to solve?

**Goal:** What is the main character's goal? What is she trying to do?

**Plot:** What are the main things that happened in the story?

**Outcome:** How was the story problem resolved?

When eliciting a retelling, tell students that they should pretend that they are telling the story to someone who has never heard it. Otherwise, they may assume that you know the story and omit important details because they believe you are familiar with the story events and characters (Benson & Cummins, 2000). In assessing a retelling, ask questions such as these:

- Are major events or ideas highlighted?
- Are appropriate inferences made about characters and events?
- Is the retelling accurate?
- Is information from the selection integrated with the student's background of information?
- Does the student evaluate information?
- Does the student use the author's organizational pattern?
- What does the retelling reveal about the student's oral language development and presentation style?

> You might try using five-finger retelling. As students retell, they make a fist and then release one finger for each story element in a piece of fiction or important idea in an information piece.

To make the assessment of a retelling more efficient and more accurate, list the main elements from an informational piece or story to check off as the student mentions them. You might use numbers to indicate the sequence of items included in the retelling. Put a "1" next to the plot element that the student mentioned first, a "2" next to the second element mentioned, and so forth. Code items with a *p* that were mentioned as a result of probing. (A sample retelling scoring sheet was presented in Figure 4.7.) Also note the overall completeness and quality of the retelling.

Because of difficulties with expressive language or other problems, some students may have difficulty retelling a story even though they fully comprehend it. Careful use of probes should help you discover to what extent students understood a piece. Using the levels-of-difficulty concept of assessment, start with a request for a retelling. If students are unable to retell the selection, use probes. Given follow-up questions after a retelling, third-graders reading below grade level were able to recall 40 percent more (Bridge & Tierney, 1981). Students also generally obtain higher scores on a retelling of a narrative than they do an expository article (Leslie & Caldwell, 2011). On the QRI 5 average narrative retellings ranged from 17 to 41 percent. Average retellings for expository text ranged from 13 to 31 percent. These low scores indicate that average students' retelling ability is limited. Students do better when answering questions (Leslie & Caldwell, 2011). If retellings are used to assess comprehension, they should be complemented by questions to get a more realistic appraisal of students' comprehension abilities (Gunning, 2013).

> ⚘ A written retelling assesses students' ability to construct meaning from what they have read and organize that in written form. Poor readers are typically penalized when written responses are required (Simmons, 1990).

If students have difficulty with probes, ask recognition-type questions in which they only have to recognize or select the right answer: "At the end of the story, did the dog return to its first owner, find a new home, or join a pack of wild dogs?" The idea is to find out at what level students understand the selection and in what format they are best able to respond. Students who have adequate comprehension but encounter difficulty in retelling should be taught how to retell a story. If it is not possible to obtain individual retellings, you might arrange for students to create written retellings.

## Retelling of Informational Piece

As noted when discussing informal reading inventories, an excellent way to assess comprehension is to arrange for a student to read a selection of the type typically read in class and then request a retelling. To use a retelling to probe comprehension of an expository piece, try the following procedures:

*Step 1: Provide material.* Provide a student with expository material on his level. The material should not be so hard that it is frustrating, but it should be challenging so that you can observe what strategies the student uses to read difficult materials.

*Step 2: Observe student reading.* Observe the student to see if he does anything before reading. Watch to see if he gets an overview of the selection, uses the title, headings, or illustrations, or simply dives right in. As the student reads, note whether he looks at illustrations, uses the glossary, or rereads.

*Step 3: Have student retell.* Have the student retell the selection. To elicit a retelling, start off with open-ended questions, so the student has complete freedom to formulate his responses. For an informational selection, ask such questions as: "Tell me in your own words as much information as you can from the selection that you just read." Or, "Tell me what you learned from the selection." If the student does not provide sufficient information, ask, "Can you tell me more about what you just read?" Note the quality and organization of the retelling. Is the student able to restate the main idea of the selection or provide a summary? Are most of the major points included in the retelling? Does the student seem to have an adequate understanding of the information? Does the student relate the information to his personal life or other information that he possesses?

*Step 4: Ask follow-up questions.* If the student was not able to retell the selection adequately, then ask follow-up or probing questions designed to assess how well the main idea and supporting details were comprehended. Ask: "What was this selection mostly about? What important details did the author include in the selection?" If the student has difficulty, provide assistance, but note what kinds of help are needed and how much help is required. Also try to gain insight into the student's reasoning processes so that you have a sense of what kind of help will be effective. If you are working with a group, you might have them write a summary of a brief expository piece.

## Think-Alouds

A key component in comprehension is the appropriate use of background knowledge when reading text. Poor comprehenders may read in bottom-up fashion, focusing on decoding rather than understanding the passage, or they may overly rely on background knowledge and insert their own information for what the text actually conveys.

> **Think-alouds:** readers or writers describe their thought processes as they read a selection or compose a piece.

One way to determine how students are processing text is to use a **think-aloud**. As its name suggests, a think-aloud involves having readers discuss what is going on in their minds as they read. This reveals the processes the reader uses. Think-alouds can be brief and informal. For instance, during a discussion of a selection, you might ask questions similar to the following:

- What was the selection mainly about?
- How did you get the main idea of the selection?
- What were you thinking about as you read the selection?
- What do you think will happen next in the selection? What makes you think so? (Gunning, 2000a)

To conduct a more formal think-aloud, use a selection that is 100 to 200 words in length. Mark off sections of the text where you want the students to stop and discuss their thought processes. This might be after each sentence or after brief segments of text. Ask questions designed to reveal students' thought processes. These might include the think-aloud prompts in Table 5.1.

If students have not previously engaged in thinking aloud, they may be reluctant to do so or may tell you what they think you want to know. To get students used to the idea, model the process. Tell them to take time every once in a while to think about what they are doing. This will get them used to noticing their thinking, and if done before you conduct a think-aloud, it should enhance the richness of the think-aloud. Think-alouds are also more productive if students feel secure and accepted (Johnston, 1992).

As students think aloud, record their responses word for word. Then analyze their responses. Note use of strategies listed below. (These strategies are discussed in Chapter 11.) Then come to conclusions about the effectiveness of the strategies that student are using and the extent to which they are monitoring for meaning:

- Made predictions
- Revised prediction or conclusion based on new information
- Considered information previously read
- Made inferences
- Drew conclusions
- Made judgments
- Visualized or created images
- Paraphrased
- Summarized
- Constructed questions
- Reasoned about reading

**TABLE 5.1**
Think-Aloud
Prompts

| Type of prompt | Think-aloud prompt(s) | Features to note |
|---|---|---|
| Before reading (Note whether student engages in any prereading activities, such as surveying the text.) | What do you think this selection might be about? What makes you think so? | Does student survey before reading? Does student predict? Are predictions based on survey? Does student activate background knowledge? What is extent of student's background knowledge? |
| During reading (Note whether student is apparently rereading portions or using text features such as illustrations.) | What was going on in your mind as you read the selection? What were you thinking about? What was the selection mainly about? Were there any parts that were hard to understand? What did you do when you came across parts that were hard to understand? Were there any hard words? What did you do when you came across hard words? What do you think will happen next in the section? What makes you think so? | Does student ask questions? Does student paraphrase or summarize? Does student make inferences? Does student make connections? Does student evaluate or judge the information? Does student make ongoing predictions? Does student use text features, such as headings and illustrations? Does student use imaging? Does student reread or use other fix-up strategies when a passage is puzzling? |
| After reading | What was this selection mainly about? | Does student include most of the main points in the summary? Student should be able to include 60 to 70 percent of the main ideas in the summary. If the summary is incomplete, encourage student to tell you more. |
| Connections | How does the information in this passage fit in with what you already know? Did anything in this passage make you think of something that you read about or heard about? Does anything in this passage remind you of something that has happened in your life? | Does student evaluate new information in terms of previously acquired information? Does student make connections between different parts of the text, with other texts he has read, and with the outside world? |

*Source:* Gunning, 2008b.

- Monitored for meaning
- Noted difficult words
- Noted confusing passages
- Reread difficult sections
- Used illustrations as an aid
- Used context or other decoding skills

If possible, think-alouds should be used with actual school texts. This increases the validity of the procedure and also increases the possibility that the results can be used to plan a program of intervention (Myers & Lytle, 1986). Myers and Lytle have constructed think-alouds specifically for use with low-achieving readers. They use passages that are 15 to 20 sentences in length and retype the passage so that each sentence is on a separate line. Sentences are uncovered one by one. After reading a sentence, students are asked to tell what they were thinking about or what event went through their minds as they were reading. Particular emphasis is placed on having the students tell what is going through their minds when they encounter difficult sentences, because it is at this point that insights into their way of processing difficult text are garnered.

Caroline, a fourth-grader, was referred to a university reading clinic because she was having difficulty comprehending what she read. Through administering a Think-Aloud Protocol Analysis, Myers and Lytle (1986) found that she used a number of strategies, including paraphrasing, inferring, and elaborating on the text by adding information and visualizing. However, Caroline failed to monitor for meaning, with the result that she sometimes failed to comprehend difficult passages and was not aware of her lack of comprehension.

Building on Caroline's strengths, the teacher affirmed her use of strategies and overall comprehension, and Caroline increased the use of her strategies and seemed more confident about her reading. She was also shown how to monitor her comprehension so she could take corrective action when she did not understand a passage. Strategies such as predicting and creating hypotheses about the reading were also demonstrated.

Based on work with struggling readers, Monti and Cichetti (1996) found that they tend to have the following profile:

- Focus on decoding and pronunciation rather than meaning
- Rarely activate background knowledge before reading a text
- Fail to monitor or take stock of their comprehension
- Rarely raise questions about meaning during reading (p. 16)

## Mystery Passages Think-Aloud

Mystery Passages are brief informational selections that have been inverted so that the identity of the creature or thing being described is not revealed until the last segment has been read (Wade, 1990). Students read the Mystery Passages in segments and after each segment predict what the passage is about. At the end of the think-aloud, students summarize by telling what they have learned. A Mystery Passage should be on the students' instructional level and should be about a familiar topic. Otherwise, students will not have the background knowledge needed to make predictions. For example, if a student has no knowledge of polar bears, a polar bear passage would not be appropriate.

### Administering a Mystery Passage as a Diagnostic Instrument

In preparation for reading a Mystery Passage like the one in Figure 5.2, the student is told that he will be reading an article about a mystery animal in parts and that after each part is read, he is to try to guess what the mystery animal is. After each segment is read, the student is asked: "What do you think the mystery animal is?" The student is then asked to explain the reasoning for his response: "What makes you think that?" After the student has completed reading all the separate segments, the student is asked to reread the passage and then retell the entire selection. The student's responses are analyzed in light of the following questions:

- How well was the reader able to hypothesize the identity of the animal?
- How well did the reader support her or his hypotheses with reasons, inferences, or predictions?
- At what point did the reader guess the identity of the animal?
- What information from the text did the reader use?
- Did the reader integrate information from the current passage with information from previously read passages? Were clues used in additive fashion?
- Were the reader's inferences and predictions logical?
- How did the reader use his background knowledge?
- How well was the reader able to identify key information in the passage?
- What strategies did the reader use?
- How did the reader handle unfamiliar words or puzzling portions of the text? (Gunning, 2010; Wade, 1990)

Note in particular how much background knowledge a student has and how well he makes use of it. Note also how well the student integrates information from succeeding segments and how logical his reasoning processes are.

Mystery Passages can be administered individually or in a group. In an individual administration the student's responses are recorded and then analyzed. In a group administration, ask the students to record their responses. After students have completed recording their responses to a segment discuss them. This gives students the opportunity to expand on their responses and gives you the opportunity to assess their thinking processes. Give students one clue segment at a time. Otherwise, they may read down the page and locate the identity of the mystery animal.

### Analyzing Students' Performance on Mystery Passages

Students to whom the think-aloud Mystery Passage was administered fell into five main categories.

1. **Good Comprehenders.** These students use information from the text and background knowledge to generate and support their hypotheses. They are flexible and change their hypotheses when they find new information in the text.

2. **Non-Risk-Takers.** These students stick closely to the text and are reluctant to offer a hypothesis. They fail to make adequate use of background knowledge. Nearly one in five students was a non-risk-taker. Most were younger readers or struggling readers.

3. **Nonintegrators.** These students fail to put together information from various segments of the text. They might pose a new hypothesis based on the current segment of text without regard to previously read segments.

**FIGURE 5.2**
Mystery Animal
Passage

■ It is a very large animal. When fully grown, it might weigh up to 1,500 pounds or even more.

My prediction: _____

Reason(s) for my prediction:

_____

_____

■ It is a powerful swimmer. It can swim for 10 hours or more.

My prediction: _____

Reason(s) for my prediction:

_____

_____

■ It is a fast swimmer. It can swim 6 miles in an hour's time.

My prediction: _____

Reason(s) for my prediction:

_____

_____

■ It doesn't mind the cold. It swims in icy water and sometimes floats on large sheets of ice.

My prediction: _____

Reason(s) for my prediction:

_____

_____

■ It has a built-in life jacket. It has two coats of hair. The inner coat is made of fine white hair and keeps it warm. The outer coat is made up of longer hairs. These hairs are hollow. The hollow hairs are like tiny life jackets or tubes.

My prediction: _____

Reason(s) for my prediction:

_____

_____

■ The two coats of hair help keep the polar bear floating on top of the water.

What were the main things that you learned about the mystery animal?

_____

_____

_____

_____

*Source:* From Gunning (2013). Administering a Mystery Passage as a Diagnostic Instrument, pp. 96–97. Reprinted by permission of Pearson.

4. **Schema Imposers.**　These students hold on to their first hypothesis. The information in succeeding passages is changed to fit the readers' schema. About 1 student in 10 is a schema imposer. Schema imposers might overly rely on background knowledge because of the difficulty they have processing the text.

5. **Storytellers.**　These students rely heavily on background knowledge to create a plausible scenario that might have little to do with the text. As with schema imposers, they may have difficulty processing the text and find it easier to create their own meaning rather than to construct meaning from the text. About 1 student in 12 is a storyteller (Wade, 1990; Gunning, 2010).

Students may fit more than one category. For instance, a third-grader that I assessed failed to integrate information from one passage to the next, held on to his original hypothesis, and was a storyteller. Although his decoding skills were flawless and he had no difficulty with any of the words in the selection, he obviously had problems processing the information and so made up his own version, which was only vaguely related to the details in the selection. Using information garnered from this think-aloud, I was able to plan a program that worked well. One of the techniques I used was presenting Mystery Passages as an instructional technique, which is explained in Chapter 11.

Different types of reading make different comprehension demands. Use discussions, quizzes, think-alouds, and other means to see how students cope with a variety of materials, how they read for a variety of purposes, and especially what kinds of support or assistance they require to be successful (Barr, Blachowicz, Bates, Katz, & Kaufman, 2007). When assessing students, provide them an opportunity to reread material for questions they had difficulty with and see if they can supply the correct information.

## Importance of Probing Responses

While working as a consultant in an urban school, I encountered a student who was crying while taking a comprehension test from the basal series the class was using (Gunning, 2008b). When I asked her what was wrong, she replied, "I don't know how to do this." The question that puzzled her was a constructed query that asked "Could this story have happened in real life the way it is told here?" (Valencia, 2001, p. 10).

I asked the student to read the question to determine whether she understood it. She read it smoothly. Thinking that maybe she didn't understand the story or that the story was written on too high a level for her, I asked her to read a few lines. She read them accurately. I then talked to her about the story, *Who Took the Farmer's Hat* (Nodset, 1963). It was about a farmer whose hat blew off. I asked the student if that could happen in real life. She replied that it could. We then discussed the part in which the farmer asks the squirrel if it has seen his hat. The student said that couldn't happen because animals can't talk. She said that the story was a fantasy. I suggested that she write down what she had just explained. However, her answer stated, "The story couldn't happen in real life. It is a fantasy."

The discussion with the student suggested that her comprehension of the selection was adequate, as was her reasoning about it. However, she apparently didn't understand the question or didn't realize that she knew the answer. Even after stating the answer, she had difficulty formulating a written response. She failed to tell why the story couldn't have happened in real life. In retrospect, I should have asked her to explain why it was a fantasy so that she might realize that she needed to prove it couldn't have happened in real life.

Interviews with other students revealed similar difficulties (Gunning, 2005). Although some students did have faulty comprehension, many could respond orally but had difficulty composing a written response. Ironically, in one study, college freshmen evidenced a similar problem. Calder and Carlson (2002) found that the oral responses of many middle-level students were superior to their written answers. The authors inferred, "For them, deep understandings seemed to evaporate when they tried to wrestle their thoughts to paper. This told us that we had work to do if we wanted to distinguish between assessing understanding and assessing students' ability to communicate their understanding" (p. 2). To get an accurate picture of students' comprehension, probing students' responses is essential (Gunning, 2008c). It is also essential to teach students how to compose responses so that they can better show what they know.

## Interviews and Questionnaires

Interviews and questionnaires are useful devices for getting information about reading processes. Some questions that might be asked include the ones listed in the comprehension interview presented below. Of course, all these questions would not be asked in one sitting. First, you would determine which area or areas of comprehension you want to explore and then choose or compose questions designed to tap into these areas. The five italicized questions are the most open ended. Encourage students to respond to these. If more information is desired, ask the probing questions listed under each italicized query.

### BEFORE READING

*What do you do before you read?*

Do you read the title and headings?

Do you look at the pictures?

Do you predict what the selection might be about?

Do you ask yourself what you know about the topic?

Do you plan how you are going to read the selection—fast, medium, or slow?

### DURING READING

*What do you do while you're reading?*

Do you think about what you're reading?

Do you stop every once in a while and ask yourself what you've read so far?

Do you picture in your mind the people, events, and places that you are reading about?

Do you make up questions in your mind as you read?

Do you imagine that you are talking to the author as you read?

*What do you do if the passage is confusing?*

Do you read it again?

Do you just keep on reading?

Do you try to get help from photos or drawings?

*What do you do if you come to a hard word?*

Do you use context to try to figure it out?

Do you try to sound it out?

Do you use a dictionary or a glossary?

### AFTER READING

*After reading the selection, what do you do?*

Do you think about what you've read?

Do you do something with the information that you've learned?

Do you compare what you've just learned from your reading with what you already know?

A less formal way to assess students' use of strategies is to include some of these questions in pre- and postreading discussions. An easy way to assess the difficulty students might be having with text—especially text that they're reading on their own—is to have students jot down the locations of words or passages that are posing problems or simply to place a sticky note under a difficult word or confusing passage (Gunning, 2000a).

## Observations

To enhance the validity and reliability of observations, determine which behaviors you wish to observe, for how long, and under what conditions. Construct an observation checklist so you can focus on target behaviors. Schedule several observations.

Direct observation is also a valuable source of information about comprehension and other processes. Although observations may be made at any time, some situations provide especially rich sources of information. In a reading conference or a group discussion of a selection, note the level of comprehension, the degree of interest and involvement, the grasp of strategies, and the immediate needs of students. During a period of voluntary reading, observe the kinds of books students select to read and the interest with which they read. In cooperative groups, note how students interact. During writing workshop, note how students approach their writing and how they use their time. It is especially helpful to observe students as they encounter a difficult word or confusing passage: What strategies do they use? How successful are they at applying these strategies?

Since memory is fleeting and deceptive, it is helpful to keep a record of observations. A checklist is useful for recording observations because it helps us to focus on key areas. You might also compose anecdotal records.

## Anecdotal Records

**Anecdotal record**: recording of an incident or behavior that provides information about a student. A convenient way to take anecdotal records is to summarize the behavior on a sticky note and, later, post it in a notebook set aside for keeping anecdotal records or to record observations on a handheld electronic device.

An **anecdotal record** is the recording of an event that sheds some light on the student's reading/writing behavior. An anecdotal record may be very brief but should contain a summary portrayal of the event, time, date, and names of persons involved and a description of the setting. In addition to providing information about comprehension and other reading processes, anecdotal records may be used to obtain data about interests, attitudes, strategy use, work habits, interaction with others, or other elements of the program. Records might be kept daily, weekly, or monthly. It is helpful to make records of the same type of behavior in a variety of situations. For instance, a student might achieve excellent comprehension under some circumstances but evidence poor comprehension under others.

When making anecdotal records, include a number of observations so that you do not form a conclusion based on limited data. Also take note of successful efforts as well as unsuccessful ones. There is a tendency to stress the failures and omit the successes, but this results in an inaccurate portrayal (Bush & Huebner, 1979).

In addition to being an accurate description of behavior, an anecdotal record should also describe the setting in sufficient detail "to give meaning to the event" (Thorndike & Hagen, 1977, p. 525). If the record includes an interpretation or evaluation of the event, that should be kept separate from the description of the event. The interpretation might be placed in parentheses. Presented in Figure 5.3 is a series of anecdotal records. What do they reveal about the student? How might this information be used in planning instruction for the student?

In order for anecdotal records to be used effectively, they should be reviewed periodically and summarized. Teachers should look for developmental trends or patterns. Strengths and weaknesses should be noted and used as a basis for gaining insight into a student's learning and planning instruction (Rhodes & Nathenson-Mejia, 1992).

## Background Knowledge

Because comprehension is a constructive process in which we build meaning based on what we know about a topic, background knowledge is a key component of comprehension. Background knowledge can be assessed informally through classroom discussions or discussions of IRI selections. The Qualitative Inventory (Leslie & Caldwell, 2011) uses two methods for assessing students' prior knowledge: concept questions and prediction. For each test passage, there are three to five questions created because they measure knowledge judged to be essential to an understanding of the selection. Students can also be asked to make predictions. Predictions are based on the title and concept questions. Predictions are assessed by counting the number of statements made by the students that are contained in the selection. A key observation is whether students are able to create idea statements that integrate

---

Student: _Marcia_                                                    Date: _10-11_

*During reading workshop, Marcia listened to "Three Billy Goats Gruff" on tape. I asked her if there were any books that she wanted to take home, but she said no and said that all the books in the room had too many hard words. I told her that I had some new books that she might like because they didn't have so many hard words. I showed her Have You Seen My Cat?, The Good Bad Cat, Cat on the Mat, and Let's Get a Pet. After looking over the books, she chose Have You Seen My Cat?, which I share-read with her.*

Student: _Marcia_                                                    Date: _10-12_

*Marcia rushed in this morning and claimed she could read Have You Seen My Cat? Relying heavily on pictures, she was able to retell the story. Marcia asked if she could take another book home and chose Cat on the Mat. I share-read it with her. I asked her to point to words as I read them, which she did.*

Student: _Marcia_                                                    Date: _10-14_

*When Marcia returned Cat on the Mat, she said she would like to read it to me. She was able to read it but continued to use pictures to help her. However, she was obviously using the print. She only used the pictures when she had difficulty with a word. She asked if she could take Let's Get a Pet home. She said that she was getting a pet and wanted to see if the book had any good ideas.*

**■ FIGURE 5.3**
Anecdotal Record

information from the title with information from the concept questions. Struggling readers have particular difficulty integrating ideas.

A number of teaching techniques include brainstorming to tap students' background knowledge. The quality and quantity of students' responses can also be used to assess their prior knowledge. A technique known as PReP was designed specifically to assess background knowledge. Brainstorming techniques are discussed in Chapter 12.

## Assessing Study Skills

Students are frequently required to go beyond comprehension. They are called on to remember and/or apply what they have read. This entails studying. Lack of adequate **study skills** is a major reason for referring older students for corrective help.

Study skills may be diagnosed through observation, interviews, questionnaires, and by subtests of standardized tests. One way to assess the effectiveness of study skills is to see how well students do on quizzes, tests, and assignments that require home preparation. If students are doing poorly, you might conduct an interview to determine the source(s) of the difficulty. Since effective studying involves habits, attitudes, and motivation as well as study strategies, your interview should cover all these areas. Because students may tend to tell you what they think you want to hear, ask questions in an open-ended fashion. Sample interview questions are presented in Figure 5.4.

> **Study skills:** strategies students use to help them learn and retain information, including outlining, note taking, and rereading to retain information.

> In preparation for assessing students' study skills, determine what skills and work habits students will need in order to complete assignments and prepare for tests.

---

I'm going to ask you some questions about the way you study. Your answers will help me understand how you study, so that I should then be able to give you suggestions for improving the way you study.

1. Which subject is your hardest to study for?
2. What makes that subject hard for you to study?
3. Which subject is easiest to study for?
4. What makes that subject easy for you to study?
5. What do you do when you are studying and there is something that you don't understand?
6. What do you do to try to help you remember the material you have studied?
7. How do you know when you have studied enough?
8. What do you think could be done to improve your studying?
9. What kinds of tests do your teachers give?
10. What's the best way to study for a test in which you have to fill in blanks?
11. What's the best way to study for a multiple-choice test?
12. What's the best way to study for an essay test?
13. Where do you study?
14. What supplies do you have in the place where you study?
15. When do you study?
16. Do you study at the same time each day?
17. How long do you study?
18. Do you listen to music or watch TV while you are studying?
19. Do you take breaks during your study periods? If so, when and for how long?
20. Do you ever study with other students? If so, do you find that helpful?
21. Which of your school books do you have to study the most? Pretend that you are studying for a quiz on a short section of this book. Show me how you would study for the quiz.

**FIGURE 5.4**
Study Strategies and Habits Interview

To save time, pick from the group of questions in Figure 5.4 the ones that are most pertinent. Also feel free to add questions and to reword questions to fit the needs of your students. If you are working with groups of students and do not have time for individual interviews, hold a group discussion on the topic. Often, students will be more open with their peers than they will be with their teachers. A checklist of study strategies is presented in Figure 5.5.

In order to see whether students possess study strategies, observe them as they use study strategies in the class. You might stage a study session in which they prepare for a test on a brief informational passage, study vocabulary words, memorize dates or facts, or study a list of spelling words. For more information on assessing and teaching study skills, see Chapter 12.

## Assessing Vocabulary Knowledge

Although vocabulary is a critical skill, teachers often lack information about the extent of children's vocabulary. By being able to obtain information about students' vocabulary, teachers establish data they can use to plan a vocabulary development program.

An easy-to-administer group measure of students' vocabulary knowledge, the Vocabulary Levels Test, is available at the School of Linguistics and Applied Language (University of Wellington; http://www.victoria.ac.nz/lals/resources/vocrefs/default.aspx). The Vocabulary Levels Test assesses students' knowledge of the 10,000 most frequently occurring words. Although designed for ELLs, the Vocabulary Levels Test can be used with native speakers of English.

Vocabulary knowledge can also be assessed informally. Assessing the vocabulary of younger children can be time-consuming because they lack the reading skill needed to take a group vocabulary assessment. However, a vocabulary assessment known as the Two-Questions Assessment can be used to assess the vocabulary of primary grade students (Kearns & Biemiller, 2010/2011). Word knowledge is assessed by asking the

| | | | |
|---|---|---|---|
| 1. Does the student use SQ3R (see Chapter 12 for explanation of SQ3R) or some other study approach? | usually | sometimes | never |
| 2. Does the student clarify difficult concepts or passages? | usually | sometimes | never |
| 3. Does the student take notes on her or his reading? | usually | sometimes | never |
| 4. Does the student outline important information? | usually | sometimes | never |
| 5. Does the student organize the information into a semantic map or another type of graphic organizer? | usually | sometimes | never |
| 6. Does the student rehearse the information by saying it over and over again, visualize the information, or use some other strategy for remembering it? | usually | sometimes | never |
| 7. Does the student integrate material from notes and text? | usually | sometimes | never |
| 8. Does the student self-test herself or himself on the material? | usually | sometimes | never |
| 9. Does the student take adequate notes in class? | usually | sometimes | never |
| 10. Do study efforts manifest themselves in the student's earning higher grades? | usually | sometimes | never |

**FIGURE 5.5**
Checklist of Study
Strategies

students two short yes–no questions about each test word. The correct response to one question is yes; the answer to the other questions is no as in the following sample item:

*signature*

Would a red stoplight be a signature?

Would you write your name if someone asked you for a signature?

Students are given a response sheet. To receive credit for knowing a word, the child must answer both questions correctly. Statistically, the probability for answering both questions correctly is 0.25, which is the same probability for answering a multiple-choice question that has four options. A good source of items for the Two-Questions Assessment would be Dale & O'Rourke's *Living Word Vocabulary* (1981), Kearns & Biemiller's (2010/2011) article, or Biemiller's (2009) *Words Worth Teaching,* as well as a district or school list or a listing of words that you judge are important for your students to know. Although designed for use with primary grade children, this assessment could be extended to higher levels and could be a useful instrument for assessing the oral vocabularies of struggling readers whose listening vocabularies typically exceed their reading vocabularies. When testing younger children a training session to familiarize them with the testing procedures should be included.

One of the easiest and most flexible vocabulary assessments is a self-reporting scale. In a self-reporting scale, students are given a list of words and asked to check one of four responses:

1.  I never saw it before.
2.  I have heard of it, but I don't know what it means.
3.  I recognize it in context—it has something to do with. . . .
4.  I know it. (Dale & O'Rourke, 1971, p. 3)

Standardized tests also provide information about students' word knowledge. The Peabody Picture Vocabulary Test and other similar tests yield a measure of students' receptive test vocabulary. Some diagnostic tests also assess oral vocabulary. The Diagnostic Assessments of Reading (2nd ed.) (Riverside); Assessing Reading, Multiple Measures (Honig et al., 2008); the first two levels of the Stanford Diagnostic Reading Test (Pearson); and all levels of the new Grade (Pearson) standardized tests assess listening vocabulary. Also look at the informal reading inventory results. How did the students do with items that involved difficult vocabulary? How did they do on the word-list tests? Were they able to pronounce the difficult words? Did they mispronounce some of the multisyllabic words in such a way that suggests that these words are not part of their listening vocabulary?

You can also get some sense of students' listening and speaking vocabularies by noting the kinds of words that they use in their conversations with you and the quality of their responses to questions. How does their use of words compare with the demands of the situation? Is it adequate? Is it more than adequate? Is it less than satisfactory? If the vocabulary portion of an individual intelligence test has been given, check to see how the student performed.

Note students' reading vocabulary as well as their listening and speaking vocabularies. If students have difficulty with decoding, there may be a number of words in their listening or speaking vocabularies that they do not recognize in print. Most norm-referenced tests contain a reading vocabulary subtest. Generally, vocabulary and comprehension scores are comparable. When vocabulary is high, comprehension is high.

When vocabulary is low, comprehension is low. A high-vocabulary, low-comprehension score suggests that the student has the potential to read better but is not using it. The cause could be an attention problem, weakness in strategy use, or difficulty seeing relationships among words or ideas. A low-vocabulary, high-comprehension score suggests that the student has a language difficulty or might still be learning English. Students who are still acquiring English may have a wealth of background to bring to a selection and so are able to answer a number of comprehension questions, but their English vocabulary is limited because they lack extended experience with the language.

## Assessing Writing

**M**ore than any other subject, writing lends itself to assessment. The product is there for all to see and can be analyzed in many different ways. Yet while an analysis of the final product will yield important information, it is also important to examine the process of writing. Combining product and process information provides a fuller understanding of your students as writers and so helps you to plan the best possible program for them. In your evaluation, include an assessment of the teaching techniques that you have used.

### Role of Students

Include students as an integral part of the evaluation process. Evaluation starts with the assessment of needs and the setting of goals. Discuss with students their goals for the writing program and discover what their needs are. These goals and needs do not have to be expressed all at one time and will change as the students' writing ability changes. An opportune time to discuss goals and needs is when examining

> **Portfolio:** collection of pieces of writing or other work samples, lists of books read, test results, and other data.

a student's writing **portfolio,** a collection of pieces of the student's writing or other work samples, lists of books read, test results, and other data. While going over the portfolio with the student, you might ask questions like these:

- What kinds of writing do you do in school?
- What kinds of writing do you do outside school?
- How do you feel about writing?
- What do you like about writing?
- What do you like best about writing?
- What is hard for you in writing?
- What kinds of writing would you like to learn to do better?

### Assessment Techniques

#### Observations

Observe students as they write. How do they go about choosing topics? About what kinds of topics do they like to write? What kind of preplanning do they do? How much effort do they put into composing? What are their work habits like? How do they go about revising and editing?

As you hold conferences with students, note strengths and needs. Also note strengths and needs during discussions and sharing. Keep a chart similar to the one

| STUDENT | DATE | SUBJECT | STATUS | STRENGTHS | NEEDS | PLANS |
|---------|------|---------|--------|-----------|-------|-------|
| Alberto | 1/9 | Letter to friend | 2nd draft | Lots of information | Show interest in other person | Ask person questions |
| Georgia | 1/9 | New sister | 1st draft | Warm tone | Weak beginning | Work on beginning |
| Latisha | 1/9 | Grandmother | 1st draft | Interesting personality | Examples of courage & kindness | |
| Raphael | | Editorial: rats | Researching | | | |
| Stephanie | | Dancing contest | Planning | | | |

**FIGURE 5.6**
Notes from a
Writing Conference

shown in Figure 5.6. Also keep anecdotal records on actions and events that offer special insight into the student as writer.

### Journals

Students' journals provide insight into their writing. Journal entries may include a description of the topics they have explored, some of the struggles they have had with their writing, and some of their achievements as writers. Of course, the journal itself might show how the students' writing has changed. Are the selections longer? Are they more specific and purposeful? Are they more alive?

## Using Rubrics to Evaluate Writing

**Using Technology**

Reading Apprenticeship Downloadable Resources http://www.wested.org/cs/ra/print/docs/ra/resource-downloads.htm

Offers a number of rubrics for assessing a variety of literacy activities.

A **rubric** is a set of guidelines used to assess the quality of a piece of work.

**Using Technology**

About 6+ 1 Trait® Writing

Explains this widely used system for assessing writing.

A *rubric* is a descriptive set of guidelines used to assess the comparative quality of a piece of work. Although frequently used to assess writing, rubrics can be used to assess media projects, oral and written reports, group work, and a wide variety of other activities.

Rubrics are more than just scoring guides. Rubrics have the power to improve instruction. They serve as "instructional illuminators." As Popham (2000) notes, "Appropriately designed rubrics can make an enormous contribution to instructional quality" (p. 292).

Well-constructed rubrics specify the essential tasks that the students must complete or the key elements that must be included in order to produce an excellent piece of work. This helps both the teacher and student focus on key skills. In order to be effective, rubrics should be concise. They should contain only four to seven evaluative criteria; otherwise, both student and teacher get lost in details. Second, each evaluative criterion must encompass a teachable skill. For instance, evaluative criteria for a persuasive piece might include effective introduction, use of examples and/or reasons to advance a position, effective organization, use of persuasive language, and correct use of conventions. All of these criteria are teachable.

The first step in developing a rubric is to identify the key characteristics or traits of the performance or piece of work to be assessed. For a rubric on a written piece, the key traits might include ideas (content), organization, voice, sentence fluency, and conventions. If possible, examine finished products to see what their major traits are. Write a definition of each trait. What exactly is covered by ideas, organization, voice, sentence fluency, and conventions? Develop a scale for the characteristics. It is usually easiest to start with the top performance. If you have examples of students' work, sort them into piles—best, worst, and middle. Look over the best pieces and decide what makes them the best. Look at the poorest and decide where they are deficient. Write descriptions of the best and poorest performances. Then fill in the middle levels. Divide the middle-level examples into two, three, or four piles from best to worst, depending on how many levels you wish to have. However, the more levels you create, the more difficult it becomes to discriminate between adjacent levels. You may find that four levels suffice.

Evaluate your rubric. Use the following checklist to assess your rubric:

- Does the rubric measure the key traits in the students' performance? Of the analytic scales, six-trait writing is the most popular and is used in virtually every state and a number of countries around the world. (See p. 146 for an adapted listing of key traits.)

- Are differences in the levels clearly specified?

- Does the rubric clearly specify what students are required to do? The criteria need to be constructed in such a way that they are geared to the skill being taught and to the specific task used to assess mastery of the skill. For instance, a task to measure students' ability to write a story might have students describe a day in the life of a talking pencil. If evaluative criteria assess the students' ability to make an inanimate object seem like a person, then the criteria are too task specific. A more universal and more valuable criterion might be "creating believable characters." This criterion applies to all fictional writing and leads to teaching a skill that can be applied in many situations rather than teaching to a specific task. On the other side of the coin, evaluative criteria can be too general, so that it is difficult to use them to discriminate between an average and above-average performance (Popham, 2000).

- Can the rubric be used as a learning guide by students?

- Can the rubric be used as an instructional guide by the teacher? (Chicago Public Schools, 2000)

Show the rubric to colleagues and discuss it with students and ask for feedback. Try out the rubric, revise it, and then use it. As you use the rubric with actual pieces of students' work, continue to revise it.

Rubrics are more effective if students participate in their construction. Through helping in the creation of the rubrics, students form a clearer idea of what is expected in the task being assessed. In one study with fourth graders, students used cooperatively created rubrics to assess their writing (Boyle, 1996) and also took part in peer-evaluation sessions in which the rubric was used. As a result of creating and using the rubric, students' writing of persuasive pieces showed significant improvement. A sample rubric is presented in Table 13.1.

## Using Portfolios to Assess Writing

Although portfolios are intended primarily as a way to assess writing, they can also be used to assess progress in reading and in content areas. Modeled on the artist's portfolio, a student's portfolio includes samples of the student's work. As such, it displays the breadth of her or his work and shows development over time. Given the current trend of using student progress as a key element in teachers' evaluations, portfolios are growing in popularity. Recognizing the inadequacy of using tests as the sole indicator of student progress, many school districts are using portfolios along with formal test results to evaluate teachers.

Portfolios serve the following purposes:

1. By assembling a portfolio and examining it periodically, students see how they have grown and developed as learners, what their strengths are, and in what areas they need to work. Portfolios help students to gain insight into themselves as learners and to be self-evaluative.

> ✳ To assess the processes a subject uses, include samples from various stages of a project. For writing, include prewriting sheets, first draft, revisions, and final copy.

2. Portfolios provide teachers with a means of assessing the growth of their students so they can plan activities to foster further growth. They also give teachers a deeper understanding of the way students develop as learners. Portfolios can also be used to demonstrate students' growth. They can show growth in areas that don't lend themselves to formal testing.

3. Portfolios can help parents better understand the development of their children's abilities. They can see areas in which their children have grown and areas in which they need additional work. Seeing how their children have developed is more meaningful to them than numerical or letter grades.

Physically, portfolios can be folders, oversized manila envelopes, small boxes, accordion folders, or can even be electronic. Contents can range from rough drafts through finished copies to video clips of an enactment of an original drama.

## Steps in Using Portfolios

In order to fulfill their promise, portfolios have to be carefully planned. There are five steps to using portfolios: establishing goals, deciding on indicator tasks, establishing standards, managing portfolios, and evaluating (Paris, 1993).

> ✳ Poor writers do better on portfolio assessment than on test compositions. Portfolios provide them with the time they need to do their best work (Simmons, 1990).

*Step 1:  Establishing Goals.* As with any evaluation, you must first establish goals. These will be overall goals for your program and individual goals or objectives for each student. If you have constructed an individualized education plan (IEP), required for students who are assigned special education services or if students in your class have such plans, that could be one source from which to draw objectives.

*Step 2:  Deciding on Indicator Tasks.* Once you have decided on your goals, you must select indicator tasks that you will be able to use to tell whether each goal has been reached. For instance, if one goal is to increase students' ability to write expository prose, then samples of expository writing could be used as a basis for assessing that goal.

*Step 3:  Establishing Standards.* You need to decide what counts as adequate performance. For example, what qualities must an expository essay meet before you can say that a student's performance is adequate? As noted earlier, a type of standard frequently used in the assessment of writing and other literacy tasks is the rubric. Rubrics can be composed for individual literacy tasks and also for the portfolio as a whole.

*Step 4:  Managing Portfolios.* Portfolios can get out of hand. They can become a warehouse for a student's work, including virtually every piece of writing he or she has done.

So that you and the student can focus on what is important, portfolios should include only key samples of work. These samples are chosen because they can be used as indicators of progress toward one or more of the goals that have been specified. Samples from the beginning, middle, and end of the instructional period should be included so that progress can be assessed. Encourage students to include samples of work done outside school in addition to work done in school. If students are composing poems, taking part in a play put on by a community group, reading books on their own, or engaging in other significant literacy activities outside school, this should be noted in their portfolios.

Both teacher and students should agree on a system for deciding which pieces of writing or other work samples are to be included in the portfolio. Students may want to include only their best pieces. However, you may want to select a variety of pieces so that the portfolios reflect multiple aspects of the students' literacy development. You might adopt a system in which students choose one-third of the pieces to be included, you choose one-third, and you agree mutually on one-third. Whichever system you choose, students should be involved in the process.

> ✳ To build students' sense of self-efficacy, demonstrate how much they have improved. Examine pieces written at different times of the year that show a progression.

A checklist or summary sheet placed on the inside cover or other suitable spot should provide an overview of the contents of the portfolio. Students should also provide statements in which they list their goals, the activities undertaken to reach their goals, and a reflection on their progress in meeting their goals. Students might also note continuing needs and future goals and plans for meeting those needs and reaching those goals. Some teachers use the three-column chart presented in Figure 5.7 to help students reflect on their progress (Hansen, 1987). This chart was designed for writing folders but can be used in portfolios as well.

*Step 5: Evaluating Portfolios.* Both teacher and students evaluate the contents of the portfolio. Portfolio conferences should be held at least four times a year (Farr & Farr, 1990) but may be held more frequently, especially if you are working one on one or with small groups of low-achieving readers and writers. Portfolios should also be assessed with a rubric, so that teachers and students can use the assessment of the portfolio to plan instructional activities (Popham, 2000).

## Assessing Writing Samples

If a portfolio is not available, the next best source of information is to obtain writing samples. Samples can be obtained in a number of ways. You might give students a drawing or photo and ask them to write a story about it. For young students, you might ask them to draw a picture of something they like to do and then have them write a story about the picture. This prompt could also be adapted for use with older students. Omitting the drawing portion, you might ask them to tell about things they like to do, including hobbies and sports and other interests.

Another prompt that can be used with students of varying ages is to have them write letters telling about themselves. Picture prompts might be used to elicit

| THINGS I CAN DO WELL | THINGS I'M WORKING ON | THINGS I PLAN TO LEARN |
|---|---|---|
| *Write a letter* *Capitalize, use periods and question marks* | *Writing pieces that explain or tell how to do something* *Spelling* *Better sentences* | *How to write interesting beginnings* *How to write better endings* |

**■ FIGURE 5.7**
Portfolio
Reflection

narrative tales. Prompts from topics such as those listed here might elicit a variety of narratives, informational, or persuasive pieces:

My Favorite Book

The Most Important Person in My Life

How to Make My Favorite Sandwich

The Importance of Taking Care of Our Home, the Earth

Why We Should or Should Not Build a Station in Space

Why Cats Make Better Pets than Dogs (or vice versa)

What I Would Do If I Had a Million Dollars

If I Had Three Wishes

If possible, obtain two or three samples of each student's writing. Also try to obtain pieces written for varied purposes. A student might be more proficient in narrative than in expository writing, for instance. When obtaining the samples, emphasize that students should do their best but should not worry about handwriting or spelling. Because you want to obtain an estimate of what the student can do independently, do not provide help with spelling or mechanics.

Analyze the writing samples along a variety of dimensions ranging from content (ideas) to handwriting. Start with the highest-level aspect—content—and work down to the lowest-level aspect—handwriting. Areas that might be assessed are as follows:

**Ideas:**   Does the piece have a main idea or theme? How well developed is the main idea or theme?

**Organization:**   How well organized is the piece? Do all the details support the main idea? Are the details in their proper order?

**Voice:**   How distinctive is the writing?

**Fluency:**   How well structured are the sentences? Are there a variety of sentence types? Are the sentences well developed?

**Word choice:**   What is the quality of the word choice? Are a variety of words used? Are words used correctly? Is there an attempt to use language in an imaginative way?

**Conventions:**   Has correct style been used? Is the capitalization, punctuation, spelling, and usage correct (Spandel, 2005)?

**Handwriting:**   How legible is the handwriting? Is the handwriting readable? Are all the letters formed correctly? Is spacing between words and letters accurate?

As students write their sample pieces, observe their performance. Note whether they spend time planning or revising. Note, too, how much effort they put into their writing.

## Commercial Tests of Writing

Commercial tests might also be used to assess writing achievement. One of the best-known writing tests is the Test of Written Language-4 (TOWL-4). The TOWL-4, which is designed for students ages 7 through 17, assesses the mechanics of writing, sentence combining, spelling, and the ability to write a story. The Wechsler

Individual Achievement Test (Pearson), the Diagnostic Achievement Battery 3 (Western Psychological Services), the PIAT-R/NU (Pearson), and the KETA II (Pearson) contain writing assessments. (For additional information on the assessment of writing, see Chapter 13.)

## Using Portfolio Assessment

An especially rich source of information is the portfolio. At the Simpson-Waverly School portfolios are used to make sure that every child is making adequate progress. Although 95 percent of its students live in poverty, Simpson-Waverly's (Hartford) scores on the demanding Connecticut Mastery Test are equal to those of suburban schools. Strong leadership, a dedicated staff, a push for excellence, and help from community institutions, such as lectures provided by Trinity College professors to students in grades 4 through 6, help account for the school's success. However, a key factor is the school's monthly portfolio review process. Once a month the school's review team meets with each teacher. The review team consists of the principal, reading specialist, curriculum specialists, and other staff members. Team members examine test scores, quizzes, writing samples, logs of books read, and any other artifacts that might shed light on students' progress. The team plans the program and makes suggestions for teachers, with special attention being paid to students who are not making progress. Although individual folders are analyzed, sometimes common needs are noted, so suggestions are made for techniques or materials that might be used with a group or the whole class. Cumulatively, the review process reveals schoolwide needs and so the review sessions are used to plan professional development (Gottlieb, 2004).

## Spelling

Although sometimes thought of as a visual memory process, spelling is that and more. Spelling is deeply rooted in linguistic knowledge. "These linguistic foundations include knowledge and awareness of phonology, orthography, semantics, and morphology, as well as clear and concise mental orthographic images" (Apel, Masterson, & Niessen, 2004, p. 645).

> Although poor spellers can be good readers, the reverse is almost never true. Poor readers are virtually always poor spellers.

Research conducted by Henderson (1990) and his colleagues indicates that spelling develops in stages. By knowing what stage a student is at, the teacher can build on that knowledge and teach spelling and decoding more effectively. However, in order to understand the developmental stages of spelling, it is important to understand the basic principles of spelling development.

Spelling is based on three principles: alphabetic, pattern, and meaning (Henderson & Templeton, 1986; Templeton & Morris, 1999). On its most primitive level, English spelling is *alphabetical*. Letters represent sounds. In the word *hat*, for instance, the letters *h-a-t* represent the sounds /h/, /a/, /t/. However, there are a large number of words in which there is not a one-to-one relationship between a word's letters and sounds. The *pattern* principle means that spelling is frequently determined by the patterning of letters within a word. For instance, the *e* marker at the end of a word indicates that a vowel is long rather than short, as in *hat/hate*.

According to *meaning*, the third principle, words that have similar meanings have similar spellings, even if their pronunciations differ. For instance, the boldface letters in the following word pairs have different pronunciations, even though the letter in each pair is the same: *compete/ competition, serene/ serenity*. Spellings have been kept the same to show the similarity in meanings.

As students' knowledge of spelling develops, they learn first the alphabetic principle, then the pattern principle, and finally, the meaning principle. As their understanding of the spelling system changes, it becomes more conceptual and more abstract.

## Stages of Spelling

Based on the alphabetic, pattern, and meaning principles, spelling development is divided into five broad stages: prephonemic, alphabetic (letter name), word pattern (orthographic, within-word pattern), syllabic (syllable juncture), and morphemic (derivational constancy).

### Prephonemic

The student in this stage does not use the alphabetic principle. The student may create letterlike forms, use a mixture of letters and numbers, or just use letters. However, the letters do not represent speech sounds.

### Alphabetic

> Students in the early alphabetic stage rely not only on how words sound but also on how the sounds feel as they are articulated. /v/ feels like /f/, so *love* is spelled *LF* (Bear, Invernizzi, Johnston, & Templeton, 2008).

The student's writing incorporates the alphabetic principle. In the earliest stages, a single letter may represent a whole word: *K* for *car*. Later, the student represents the first and last consonant sounds: *KR* for *car*. As the student progresses, she or he begins using vowels. Long vowels are spelled with letter names: *FET* for *feet*, *BOT* for *boat*.

Fortunately for the inventive speller, the names of the long vowels incorporate their sounds. Because short-vowel sounds are not incorporated by a distinctive set of letters, many inventive spellers use the letter name for the long vowel that is formed in approximately the same place in the mouth as the short vowel they are attempting to spell. Say "ay," the long-vowel sound for *A*, and "eh," the short-vowel sound for *E*, and you will notice that both are very close in their place of articulation. Since short *e* is articulated in approximately the same place as long *a*, *bed* is often spelled as *bad* in the alphabetic stage. This is known as the "close to" tactic. Other "close to" spellings include spelling short *i* with an *E* (*BET* for *bit*), short *o* with an *I* (*TIP* for *top*), and short *u* with an *O* (*COT* for *cut*) (Read, 1971).

> Spanish-speaking English learners apply their knowledge of Spanish pronunciations to their invented spellings (Nathenson-Mejia, 1989). For instance, /t/ and /th/ sounds in English are often pronounced /d/ by Spanish speakers, so a word like *the* would be spelled *de* or *di*. The word *little* might be spelled *ldl*.

For some consonant spellings, the spelling–sound connection is not apparent at first glance. For instance, *tr* is frequently spelled *ch*, as in *CHAN* for *train* and *dr* may be spelled *JR* as in *JROM* for *drum*. To see why these spellings are logical from the student's point of view, listen carefully as you say *chain* and *train*. Did you notice that the beginning sound of *train* is very similar to the beginning sound of *chain*? And if you say *chree*, it sounds like *tree* (Temple, Nathan, Temple, & Burris, 1993). In similar fashion, the *d* in *dr* has a /j/ sound, so *drop* may be spelled *JRUP* or simply *JUP*. During this stage, spellings with nasal sounds such as *m* and *n* are omitted when they occur before a consonant, so that *bump* is spelled *BUP*. At the end of this stage, students begin to spell regular short-vowel words (*hat, pet*) correctly.

## Word Pattern

> ⚘ The key understanding in the word pattern stage is that words are not spelled by sound alone. Orthographic patterns such as final *e* (*brave*) and digraphs (*plain*) must be incorporated.

Through encountering standard spelling in books and other printed matter in their environment, children begin to notice certain spelling conventions: The consonant cluster at the beginning of *train* is spelled with *tr*; *e* at the end of a word is a marker for a long vowel (*rake*), and so forth. Children begin to use visual features in addition to sound features to spell words and enter the orthographic word pattern stage. Their spelling is no longer based solely on sound. Although their spelling is not always correct (they may spell *rain* as *RANE*), it is becoming more standard and incorporates such features as final-*e* markers and double-vowel letters to spell long-vowel sounds. A sign that students have entered this stage is the use of silent letters (Templeton & Morris, 1999).

As students progress in this stage, they learn to spell most single-syllable words accurately. This is when students with poor orthographic processing ability begin to experience difficulty.

## Syllabic

> ⚘ The key characteristic of the syllabic (syllable juncture) stage is applying knowledge about spelling single-syllable words to spelling multisyllabic ones—for instance, knowing when to double the final consonant when adding inflectional endings (*hop* + *ping* = *hopping*).

With additional experience with print, students begin encountering multisyllabic words. They have a firm grasp of single-syllable patterns, but now they must be able to apply their knowledge to multisyllabic words. Students learn when to double the final consonant or drop the final *e* when an ending such as *ing* is added (*dropping* or *taking*). They also learn about the double-consonants in closed syllables, as in words like *battle,* which have syllables that end with a consonant (*bat-tle*), with the vowel usually being short. The word *battle* has a double-consonant just as the word *batting* does. Students also learn about open syllables, which are syllables that end with a vowel: *ba-by,* with the vowel usually being long.

## Morphemic

> ⚘ In the morphemic (derivational-constancy) stage, focus is on meaningful elements rather than sound elements. Students break up words into prefixes, suffixes, and roots rather than syllables.

In this stage, students apply the principle of meaning. Words that have similar meanings have similar spellings even though pronunciations may be different. From a phonemic point of view, a better way to spell *sign* would be *SINE*. However, the *g* is retained to maintain the semantic connection among *sign, signal,* and *signature* (Venezky, 1965). Other examples include *compose/composition,* where the long *o* in the second syllable of *compose* becomes the short *o* in the second syllable of *composition,* and *contribute/contribution,* where the short *i* in the second syllable of *contribute* becomes a schwa in the second syllable of *contribution* (Ganske, 1993). A chart of the major stages of spelling can be found in Figure 5.8.

As the description of the phases of spelling suggests, learning to spell is a constructive, conceptual process. Through the experience of reading and writing words, students create hypotheses about the way words are spelled and then test them. In the alphabetic phase, for instance, students conceive of spelling as being a process of writing one letter for each sound. In the orthographic pattern phase, they realize that the pattern of a word, not just its individual sounds, must be considered when the word is being spelled.

Because spelling is constructive, conceptual, and progresses through various phases, it is important that spelling instruction match students' level of word

**■ FIGURE 5.8**
Spelling Stages

| | | |
|---|---|---|
| **1. Prephonemic** | *zq* | Student uses random letters to spell words. Letters have no relation to sound. |
| **2. Alphabetic** | *td, tod* | Student understands that letters represent sounds. In early stage, an initial or an initial and a final consonant may be used to represent the whole word. Later, long-vowel sounds are spelled with their letter names, and short-vowel sounds are spelled with the long-vowel letter formed closest to the place where the short vowel is articulated. At end of stage, regular short-vowel words are spelled correctly. |
| **3. Word Pattern** | *tode, toad* | Student realizes that there is a visual component to spelling. Thus, a final *e* or another vowel letter would be added to *tod* (*toad*) to signify the long *o* sound. At the end of this stage, most single-syllable words would be spelled correctly. |
| **4. Syllabic** | *planning* | Student begins to form hypotheses about how to spell multisyllabic words. She becomes aware of dropping final *e* or doubling the final consonant when adding certain endings. |
| **5. Morphemic** | *sign, signal* | Student realizes that words with a common derivation and meaning have similar spellings even if the pronunciations vary. |

⚹ For a more thorough analysis of children's spelling, use the Developmental Spelling Analysis (Ganske, 2000) or the Spelling Performance Evaluation for Language and Literacy (SPELL 2; Masterson, Apel, & Wasowicz, 2006), a computer software assessment tool.

knowledge (Henderson & Templeton, 1986). Vowel markers or the doubling rule for consonant–vowel–consonant words (*hopped, planning*), for instance, is too difficult conceptually for students who are still grappling with alphabetic phonics. They might be able to memorize words like *hate* or *planned*, but they will not grasp the underlying principles that determine their spellings. Words should be presented that fit students' developmental levels so they can discover and make use of the underlying regularity of the language.

## Determining the Stage of Spelling

⚹ See Bear et al. (2008) for a variety of spelling inventories.

Spelling stages can be assessed by observing the kinds of spellings students create. You can also give a screening test to assess students' spelling development. One such test is presented in Table 5.2. The Informal Spelling Inventory presents 20 words that gradually grow more difficult. Start with the easiest item for each student, and continue testing until the words are obviously too difficult. Encourage students to spell the words as best they can. Before giving the test, explain its purpose. Tell students that you want to find out how they spell words. Explain that some of the words may be hard but that they should do their best to spell as much of each word as they can. Say each word, use it in a sentence, and then say the word once more.

To estimate students' stage of development, carefully analyze their spelling in terms of the major characteristics of each stage. For instance, students are in the early alphabetic stage if they are representing whole words by one or two consonant letters, as long as those letters are intended to represent sounds. They are in the late alphabetic stage if they are beginning to represent long vowels with single letters containing the vowels' names. They are in the word-pattern stage if they use two vowel letters or a final *e* to represent long-vowel sounds. Students might also show signs of being in two stages at the same time or moving back and forth between stages.

Verify the results of the Informal Spelling Inventory by analyzing spellings that appear in students' writing. Misspellings are better indicators of stages, because words spelled correctly might be ones that the student has memorized without

**TABLE 5.2**
Informal Spelling
Inventory

| Stages | Early Alphabetic (Early Letter Name) | Alphabetic (Letter Name) | Word Pattern | Syllabic (Syllable Juncture)/ Morphemic (Derivational Constancy) |
|---|---|---|---|---|
| 1. pet | p, pt, b, bt | pat | pet | |
| 2. sit | s, st | set | sit | |
| 3. stop | s, st, sp, stp | sip, stip | stop | |
| 4. jump | j, jp | jop, jomp, jom | jump | |
| 5. drum | jm, dm, jrm, drm | jrom, drom | drum | |
| 6. time | t, tm | tim, tym | tighm, tiem, time | |
| 7. wait | w, wt | wat | wayt, wate, wait | |
| 8. soap | s, sp | sop | soep, sope, soap | |
| 9. twice | ts, tws, tetwc | twis, twic | twighs, twise, twice | |
| 10. peach | p, pc, pch | pec, pech | peech, peche, peach | |
| 11. store | sr, str, | stor | store | |
| 12. shook | s, sk | sok, shok | shook | |
| 13. taught | tt, tgt | tot, togt | tought, taught, tawt. | |
| 14. shout | s, st, sht | shot, shut | showt, shout | |
| 15. heard | h, hd | hrd | hurd, herd, heard | |
| 16. plastic | | | pasik, pastic, plasik | plastik, plastic |
| 17. stopping | | | stopin, stopen, stoping | stoping, stopping |
| 18. rattle | | | radl, ratl, radol | ratel, radel, rattle |
| 19. baking | | | bakking, baiking, bakeing | baking |
| 20. treasure | | | trasr, trsaur, tresher, trejar | treshore, tresure, treasure |

*Source:* Adapted from: Gunning, T. (2011). *Teacher's Guide for Word Building Book D* (2nd ed.). Unionville, CT: Galvin; Honesdale, PA: Phoenix Learning Resources.

understanding the basic principles behind the spellings. For instance, a student might memorize the spelling of *like* without realizing that the final *e* marks the *i* as being long (Schlagal, 1992).

Based on the student's spelling stage, you can estimate his spelling level. The alphabetic stage is kindergarten and first grade. Word pattern encompasses grades 1 and 2. The syllabic stage is equivalent to grade 3+. Figure 5.9 shows the performance of a student on the Elementary Spelling Inventory (Bear & Barone, 1989). What stage is he in?

You can also give a placement test to assess students' spelling development. A Spelling Placement Assessment is presented in Table 5.3. The Spelling Placement Assessment has five levels. Level 1 consists of easy sight words and short-vowel patterns and is equivalent to grade 1 spelling. Level 2 consists of long-vowel patterns and is equivalent to grades 1 and 2 spelling. Level 3 features *r* vowels and other vowels and is equivalent to grades 2 and 3 spelling. Level 4 consists of multisyllabic words and is equivalent to grades 3 and 4 spelling. Level 5 is equivalent to grade 5 spelling.

To administer the Spelling Placement Assessment, explain to students that you will be dictating some words. Tell them that some words may be hard to spell, but

**■ FIGURE 5.9**
Student's
Performance

| | |
|---|---|
| 1 bed | bed |
| 2 Shep | ship |
| 3 Driv | drive |
| 4 Buph | bump |
| 5 Wan | when |
| 6 Thran | train |
| 7 Clist | closet |
| 8 Chas | chase |
| 9 Folt | float |
| 10 BiJes | beaches |

urge them to do their best. Tell them that even if they can't spell the whole word, they should spell as much as they can, even if it's just the first letter. Say each word in isolation, in a sentence, and then in isolation. Start with the first list, unless you know that the students are advanced spellers. Stop when students are missing most of the words in a list.

> ✳ A diagnostic spelling test can be found in Bader and Pearce (2013). Spelling placement tests can be found in Bear et. al (2008) and Wheelock & Campbell (2012).

The criterion for an instructional level for spelling is lower than it is for reading. Students are instructional at the level at which they are able to spell between 50 and 75 percent of the words correctly (Temple et al., 1993). After you have obtained students' level, analyze the results to determine which stage they are in and also major needs. Students who are unable to spell any of the words are at the emergent stage. Those who are able at least to represent initial consonants are at the beginning alphabetic stage. Those who are able to spell the short-vowel patterns are at the end of the alphabetic stage. Those who show some knowledge of long-vowel patterns, even if their spelling of long vowels is not always correct (they may spell *train* as *TRANE*), are in the word-pattern stage. Those who are able to spell most single-syllable words correctly are at the end of the word-pattern stage. Students who are able to spell multisyllabic words and who know when to drop final *e* (*hoping*) and when to double final consonants (*planning*) are in the multisyllabic stage. Spelling can lag behind reading. A student in the multisyllabic stage in reading may be in the word pattern stage in spelling.

As noted earlier, it is important to know what stage students are in so instruction can be geared to their conceptual understanding of the spelling system. For

**TABLE 5.3**
Spelling Placement Assessment

| Level 1 | Level 2 | Level 3 | Level 4 | Level 5 |
|---------|---------|---------|---------|---------|
| cat | name | star | happen | damage |
| the | what | guess | everyone | happiness |
| sad | like | care | metal | opposite |
| is | any | laugh | welcome | laughter |
| ten | read | school | between | adventure |
| one | want | build | holiday | passenger |
| not | show | farm | carried | caution |
| was | been | young | against | ninety |
| hop | train | turn | middle | voyage |
| you | from | touch | famous | president |
| get | sleep | should | question | magazine |
| were | put | learn | absent | government |
| sun | use | south | weather | probably |
| on | once | sure | yesterday | mention |
| sit | place | cloud | thousand | separate |
| do | are | month | success | continue |
| bug | night | join | student | description |
| give | your | knee | mountain | future |
| fish | smile | caught | neighbor | information |
| come | milk | warm | problem | electric |

instance, students in the early alphabetical stage do not have sufficient grasp of the spelling system to grapple with final-*e* words such as *hope* and *plane*. They still conceptualize spelling as being one letter for each sound. They might spell *eighty* as *A-T-E* (Gentry, 1997). They are not quite ready to spell by eye but will be ready to do so once they have encountered more final-*e,* long-vowel words in print.

Also note the kinds of words that students had difficulty with. Many words can be spelled auditorially. Words such as *hat, went,* and *stop* are spelled just the way they sound, so they can be spelled correctly if students sound them out. Some words, such as *mention* and *future,* require advanced knowledge of phonics before they can be spelled correctly. And some words, such as *money, do, where,* and *police,* are only partially spelled the way they sound and so require students to memorize them visually as well as auditorially. Still other words, such as *hopped* and *liked,* can be spelled correctly if students apply the correct rules for adding the past-tense marker. Knowledge of roots, suffixes, and prefixes helps students spell words like *finally* and *actually*. Realizing that *final* and *actual* are the base words, the student adds *ly* to create adverbs and so spells the words correctly as *finally* and *actually.*

In the first two levels of the Spelling Placement Assessment, the odd-numbered words are highly predictable and lend themselves to auditory spelling. However, the even-numbered words have less predictable spellings and so require the use of visual memory or orthographic processes.

To further assess the student's spelling, examine her written pieces and observe her during the writing process to see whether she is able to detect spelling errors. Note how she goes about correcting her errors. Does the student try several spellings? Does the student use a reference, such as a word wall or dictionary? Also assess the student's ability to learn to spell. Choose five words from the ones that the student has misspelled, and ask her to study them because she will be tested on them. Note how the student goes about studying the words. Retest the student on the words and note how effective her study techniques were. Also use the Student Spelling Interview in Figure 5.10.

Although the two processes of spelling and reading differ somewhat—spelling requires producing letter sounds, reading requires only the recognition of letter sounds—students' spellings can offer insights into their knowledge of the phonics system, especially in the early stages. If a student is only using initial consonants to spell words, for instance, that suggests that he has not grasped vowels yet. This could be a good time to introduce short-vowel patterns, but teaching long-vowel patterns is probably beyond the student's level of development. In general, spelling lags a bit behind reading. For example, students can usually read long vowels before they can spell them (Stahl, Stahl, & McKenna, 1998).

In addition to determining what stage students are in and what level they are operating on, it is important to know what strategies they are using. Are they using sound, visual, structural (roots, prefixes, suffixes), rules, and meaning strategies in balanced fashion, or are they neglecting a particular area? Chapter 13 provides additional suggestions for assessing students' use of strategies to spell words and also students' strategies for studying spelling words.

## Commercial Spelling Tests

In addition to the many informal tests of spelling, there are several commercially produced tests of spelling. The Test of Written Spelling-3 (Pearson), which can be administered to students ages 6 to 18, uses 50 predictable words and 50 unpredictable words to assess spelling. Norms are provided. A thorough assessment of spelling is presented in the Spelling Performance Evaluation for Language and Literacy (SPELL; Laureate), a software program that analyzes students' misspellings and makes instructional recommendations. The Reading and Language Inventory (Bader & Pearce, 2013) also contains a series of diagnostic spelling tests designed to show whether students can spell phonetically regular words, words with silent letters, words that follow key spelling rules, and high-frequency words. Ganske (2000) also has a very thorough spelling assessment in her book *Word Journeys: Assessment-Guided Phonics, Spelling, and Vocabulary Instruction*. Spelling Assessments can also be found in the *Words Their Way* series (Pearson).

---

**Name** _____        **Date** _____
**Grade** _____        **Age** _____

1. What kinds of words are easy for you to spell?
2. What words are hard for you to spell?
3. What makes a word hard to spell?
4. How do you go about spelling a hard word?
5. How do you go about studying spelling words? Show me how you might study a list of words for a test.
6. How do you check to see if the words are spelled correctly in a story that you have written?
7. What might you do to become a better speller?

---

 **FIGURE 5.10**
Student Spelling Interview

# ▓▓ Handwriting

**A**lthough poor handwriting is often associated with severe reading difficulty, it tends to be neglected in intervention programs. Perhaps because there are higher-level skills that need instruction, handwriting is given a low priority. However, even though it is a low-level skill, deficient handwriting can lead to lowered grades and lowered self-concept. Written work that is not neat or legible is frequently downgraded and is also a constant reminder to the student and her teachers of her other learning difficulties.

**Dysgraphia**: a neurological condition in which the person loses the ability to write. A dysgraphic student can read but has difficulty writing.

Because of the widespread use of keyboarding skills, cursive writing is being given less attention in many school systems and has even been phased out in some.

Although it is a low-level skill, handwriting is a complex task (Bain, 1991). Poor handwriting may reflect poorly developed motor skills, deficient visual or kinesthetic memory, or **dysgraphia,** which is a disorder that occurs between the visual memory system and the motor system (Bain, 1991; Johnson & Myklebust, 1967).

Because handwriting disorders may manifest in many ways, observation is an important element in their assessment. Different tasks make different demands, so students should be observed in a variety of situations: copying from material on their desk, copying from material on the board, composing a piece, and—if older—taking notes. Posture, grip, handedness, quality of writing, and speed of writing should be noted, and the product of a student's writing should be compared with a standard piece of writing (Bain, 1991; Rowell, 1992). When appropriate, both manuscript and cursive writing should be compared.

Observation of handwriting is important because this can lead to a better understanding of a handwriting deficiency. Slowness in copying from the board, for instance, may be caused by inattention, by forming letters one at a time rather than as part of a group, or by poor visual memory that requires the student to check the board for each new letter that is being copied (Bain, 1991). It can even be caused by a lack of automatized skill in letter formation, so that the student has to look several times at a single letter that is being copied to see how it is formed.

Scales for assessing quality of handwriting are available from publishers who distribute handwriting material, such as Zaner Bloser (traditional) and Scott-Foresman (D'Nealian). Cursive writing may be assessed on the Handwriting Scale of the Test of Written Language (TOWL; Pro-Ed), or the Test of Legible Handwriting (TOLH; Pro-Ed). The TOLH assesses the readability of handwriting, manuscript or cursive, in grades 2 through 12. The Test of Handwriting Skills Revised (Western Psychological Services) also assess cursive and manuscript writing. It is designed for students ages 5 to 18.

## ▓ Summary

**B**oth decoding and comprehension processes can be assessed in greater detail through the administration of formal and informal tests, observations, questionnaires, and think-alouds. The emphasis should be on gaining insights into the processes that students are using. For comprehension, retellings generally yield more information than asking questions. However, if students have difficulty with retellings because of language processing or other problems, then answering questions is a more appropriate means of assessment. Study skills, a leading area for referrals for corrective help for older students, should also be assessed. Questionnaires, interviews, observations, and an analysis of content area test results are among the methods that can be used to assess study skills.

Vocabulary knowledge can be assessed through observation and informal or formal tests. Writing can be assessed through examination of portfolios and obtaining and analyzing writing samples. A developmental spelling inventory can be administered and analyzed to estimate what stage students are in and to see how this data might be used to plan spelling and word-analysis instruction. The effectiveness of the methods students use to study spelling words can be assessed by providing them the opportunity to study five words that they misspelled and then giving a retest. Diagnostic and placement spelling tests are also available. Handwriting can be assessed informally or with the aid of commercial scales.

## Application Activities

1. Focusing on one aspect of behavior, observe a student and compose an anecdotal record. If possible, observe the student on three different occasions. Then compare the records. What conclusions can you draw?
2. Examine one or more of the tests presented in this chapter. Note what the test is measuring and its format. Note, too, its strengths and weaknesses.
3. Administer the Informal Spelling Inventory (see Table 5.2) or another developmental spelling test to a group of struggling students. Note the students' level of development, the spelling skills that they have apparently learned, and those that students might be in the process of learning. Based on an analysis of the assessment, plan an intervention program.
4. Pick a level and view the videos demonstrating PALS at http://pals.virginia.edu. What kinds of information are the assessment measures providing? How might you make use of this information?

## My Education Lab

Go to the topic **Reading Assessment** in the MyEducationLab (www.myeducationlab. com) for **Assessing and Correcting Reading Difficulties,** where you can:

- Find learning outcomes for **Reading Assessment** along with the national standards that connect to these outcomes.
- Complete Assignments and Activities that can help you more deeply understand the chapter content.
- Apply and practice your understanding of the core teaching skills identified in the chapter with the Building Teaching Skills and Dispositions learning units.
- Examine challenging situations and cases presented in the Iris Center Resources.
- Check your comprehension of the content covered in the chapter with the Study Plan. Here you will be able to take a chapter pretest, receive feedback on your answers, and then access personalized Review, Practice, and Enrichment exercises to enhance your understanding of chapter content. After you complete the exercises, take a posttest to confirm your comprehension.
- Practice targeting instruction and making content accessible for all students with A+RISE activities.

# 6 Assessment of Cognitive, School, and Home Factors

**USING WHAT
YOU KNOW**

This chapter looks at the ways of assessing students' cognitive and related capabilities: academic aptitude, memory, attention, and associative learning, which includes the crucial ability to learn printed words. Because of the interactive nature of assessment, personal, home, and school factors are also explored.

What has been your experience with intelligence and other tests of cognitive abilities? What might be some effective ways to gather information about personal, home, and school factors as they affect reading and writing development?

**ANTICIPATION
GUIDE**

*Read each of the
following statements.
Put a check
under "Agree" or
"Disagree" to show
how you feel about
each one. If possible,
discuss your responses
with classmates.*

|  | AGREE | DISAGREE |
|---|---|---|
| 1. The main problem with intelligence tests is that no one knows exactly what intelligence is; therefore, it cannot be measured accurately. | _____ | _____ |
| 2. Tests of listening capacity are more equitable measures of ability to learn to read than are tests of intelligence. | _____ | _____ |
| 3. Questionnaires and interviews lack validity because people are inclined to tell the questioners what they want to hear. | _____ | _____ |
| 4. Parents are reliable sources of information about their children. | _____ | _____ |
| 5. The best way to gain insight into students' reading problems is to talk to them. | _____ | _____ |

## ▦ Assessment of Capacity

One of the most basic questions asked in an assessment is: What is the student's aptitude for reading? Or, to ask the question in another way: Given optimum development—one in which any reading deficiencies might be remedied—on what level should the student be reading? There are three main ways to assess a student's capacity: administer a test of academic aptitude, ascertain the student's listening capacity, or provide the student with the opportunity to learn and see how she or he does.

> ✳ What we call intelligence is the result of interaction between heredity and environment. The richer the environment, the more fully our mental capabilities are developed (Carnegie Corporation, 1994).

Because of past misuse and misinterpretation, the testing of intelligence is highly controversial. Most intelligence tests are really measures of academic aptitude. They measure such behaviors as vocabulary development, background information, ability to see likenesses and differences, ability to complete verbal and figural analogies, ability to complete patterns, and other similar abilities that are good predictors of school performance (Salvia & Ysseldyke, 1998). However, intelligence tests fail to include items that assess practical problem-solving abilities, which may be a good predictor of how one does in life.

Resnick (1999) has challenged what she sees as an overemphasis on aptitude. As she explains:

> What we learn is a function of both our aptitudes for particular kinds of learning and the effort we put forth. However, there is a widespread belief that ability determines, in large measure, what we learn in school. Therefore, students who score low on aptitude tests or seem to be lacking in ability are not provided with challenging learning. Basic skills are emphasized. As a result, not having been presented with tasks and materials that demand higher level thinking these students score low on tests of reasoning ability. However, research over the past quarter-century has demonstrated that, when taught, students can and do learn higher level thinking skills. In experimental programs and in practical school reforms, we are seeing that students who, over an extended period of time are treated as if they are intelligent, actually become so. If they are taught demanding content, and are expected to explain and find connections as well as memorize and repeat, they learn more and learn more quickly. They think of themselves as learners. (p. 1)

According to Resnick, students can literally be taught to be smarter. Teaching students to be smarter starts with the belief that well-planned instruction combined with effort will improve students' ability to reason. The curriculum must be stated in clearly understood terms, focus on covering key concepts in depth, and provide opportunities for reasoning with those concepts.

### Lowered Expectations

The most significant criticism of intelligence tests is that they may lead to an underestimation of what students can do. As Carlson (1993) points out:

> Another problem with intelligence tests is that they may lead low-scoring students to underestimate themselves. Children who discover that they have scored poorly on an intelligence test are likely to suffer feelings of inferiority and may become disinclined to try to learn, believing that they cannot. (p. 448)

Low scores may also lead teachers to believe that students cannot achieve. Believing this to be so, they may not challenge them sufficiently or give them as rich a program as they should. Carlson (1993) comments, "Clearly, schools should use intelligence tests with great caution. If the results are not themselves used intelligently, such tests are actually harmful" (p. 418).

## ▓▓ Role of Intelligence Tests

Despite their obvious limitations, intelligence tests can play an important role in the assessment of reading problems, if results are interpreted with awareness of the above limitations. For one thing, intelligence tests provide an indication of the extent of a student's reading difficulty. They may also indicate potential. Problem readers, especially if they have retreated into themselves, may be judged to have lesser cognitive ability.

For instance, Frank, an 8-year-old reading on a first-grade level, spent much of his time daydreaming and seldom spoke in class. That, together with his unkempt appearance, created the impression of a student who had low-average ability. When he was tested, however, Frank achieved a score of 141, which put him in the top 1 percent of the population. Realizing that Frank was intellectually gifted and that his reading problem was even more severe than it had seemed—because Frank should have been reading far above grade level—Frank's teacher obtained additional services for him. A measure of IQ, especially verbal IQ, can be helpful in classifying students as having a severe reading difficulty (Swanson, 2011).

> ⚖ Frank meets the functional and discrepancy definitions. He was reading below grade level and was unable to handle his school texts. Achievement was also below ability.

In addition to identifying students who have serious learning problems and who need specialized instruction, intelligence tests can be used to identify children who aren't working up to their ability (Carlson, Donahue, Miller, Martin, & Heth, 2010). Intelligence tests can also yield information about students' cognitive processes.

> ⚖ Interpreted with caution, individual intelligence tests can provide insights into students' cognitive functioning and so can be used to plan a more effective intervention.

As a practical matter, most intelligence testing is conducted by a school psychologist. However, knowing the contents of the major intelligence tests and what scores on subtests signify will put you in a position to make use of that information. If it is analyzed carefully, information about a student's performance on specific elements of an intelligence test can shed light on the student's reading difficulty and can be used to plan a program of remediation.

### Wechsler Scales

> ⚖ Wechsler scales have a standard deviation of 15. Since 68 percent of the population have a score of 100 ± one standard deviation, this means that 68 percent have an IQ score of between 85 and 115. Some 14 percent have an IQ of between 115 and 130. Another 14 percent have scores that fall between 70 and 85. Only 2 percent have scores above 130 and 2 percent have scores below 70.

The most popular of the intelligence tests are the Wechsler scales, which define intelligence as the "overall capacity of an individual to understand and cope with the world around him" (Wechsler, 1974, p. 5). Although Wechsler conceived of intelligence as being global and multifaceted, he created scales that included a number of subtests. The WISC-IV (Wechsler Intelligence Scale for Children IV), which can only be administered by a qualified examiner, is designed for students between the ages of 6 and 16. The WISC-IV yields a full-scale score and four indices: Verbal Comprehension, Perceptual Reasoning, Working Memory, and Processing Speed. In addition to obtaining an estimate of a student's overall functioning intelligence level, the teacher can, by examining performance on subtests and indices, determine a student's relative strengths and weaknesses in several crucial areas.

A description of each subtest and its relevance follows.

### Verbal Comprehension

*Vocabulary*   The student is asked to name pictures (at the easiest level) and define words read aloud by the examiner. This subtest measures the student's store of concepts and is generally considered to be the best assessment of academic aptitude.

Older low-achieving readers may have somewhat depressed scores because they are cut off from one avenue of learning new words: reading. Their scores should not be too depressed, however, because there are many ways, besides reading, of learning new words. A low score suggests a need to develop vocabulary.

*Similarities*    The student tells how two items are alike. This subtest measures the ability to form concepts. Poor readers can do well on this subtest. A low score suggests the need to teach thinking skills such as noting similarities and differences and categorizing.

*Comprehension*    The student tells what she or he would do in a variety of social situations. The subtest measures common sense and social judgment. Since school-type learning is not being assessed, poor readers are not penalized.

*Information*    The student is asked questions about general knowledge. This subtest measures how well the student has interacted with the environment and recalls information. Because poor readers are cut off from one source of information, their scores may be somewhat depressed. A low score suggests a need to build a background of information.

*Word Reasoning (supplemental)*    The student is presented with one to three riddle-style clues and asked to determine what the tester is describing. Verbal comprehension, reasoning, and general knowledge are assessed.

## Perceptual Reasoning

*Block Design*    The student uses blocks to reproduce a design. The subtest measures nonverbal concept formation and the ability to detect and construct relationships. Poor readers are not penalized on this subtest, but students with neurological impairments may do poorly.

*Picture Concepts*    The student is shown two or three rows of pictures and asked to choose one picture from each row to form a group of images with a common characteristic. The student might choose a ball in one row and a doll in another because they are both toys. The ability to classify is assessed.

*Matrix Reasoning*    The student selects from among five options the missing portion of an incomplete matrix. This subtest assesses the ability to process visual information and reason based on that information. Since words are not involved, poor readers would not be penalized.

*Picture Completion*    The student is asked to identify the missing part in a picture. The subtest measures attention to detail and the ability to differentiate between essential and nonessential elements. Poor readers are not penalized on this subtest.

## Working Memory

*Digit Span*    The student says a series of numbers forward and backward. This subtest measures attention, concentration, and working memory. Because poor readers may have problems in one or all three of these areas, they tend to do poorly on this subtest.

*Letter–Number Sequencing*    The student is orally given sequences of numbers and letters and asked to repeat them in numerical and alphabetical order. Attention, concentration, and ability to keep in mind and manipulate symbols are assessed.

*Arithmetic*    This subtest requires students to solve arithmetic problems mentally. It measures the ability to pay attention and concentrate and to remember the elements that need to be manipulated. Poor readers frequently do badly in these areas, and so they tend to do badly on this test.

### Processing Speed

*Coding*    The student associates the code that goes with a symbol and writes it in a blank. The subtest measures the ability to make, remember, and record associations. Because some low-achieving readers have difficulty making associations, they may do poorly on this task.

*Symbol Search*    The student is shown rows of symbols and marks whether or not target symbols appear in each row; this measures visual attention, short-term memory, and processing speed.

*Cancellation (supplemental)*    The student marks lines through objects that do not belong in a page of randomly placed objects and in a page of arranged objects. Visual attention and processing speed are measured.

> ✳ Students with learning problems may evidence "scatter." Often, they have some surprisingly low scores on some subtests but surprisingly high scores on others and miss easy items but get difficult items correct.

As a group, poor readers tend to do poorly on the Arithmetic, Digit Span, Information, and Coding portions of the Wechsler scales. As Galvin (1981) notes, except for Information, the subtests have in common paying attention to and keeping in memory abstract symbols, an area in which poor readers often have difficulty. Of the four indices, disabled readers score the lowest on the Working Memory Index (Smith, 2003).

Subjects over age 15 are tested with the Wechsler Adult Intelligence Scale (WAIS), and children ages 3 to 7 years, 3 months are tested with the Wechsler Preschool and Primary Scale of Intelligence (WPPSI). These tests are similar to the WISC-IV, and are available in Spanish.

Results of the subtests can be used to plan instruction. Getting a low score on Vocabulary suggests the need for language development, whereas getting a low score on Information indicates the need for building background knowledge. Getting a low score on Similarities indicates the need to build reasoning skills, especially seeing similarities and differences. Low scores on Digits, Arithmetic, and Letter–Number Sequencing indicate the need for helping the student focus attention and process information. A low score on Coding indicates a possible problem with learning letter names, letter sounds, and printed forms of words.

## Stanford-Binet

The Stanford-Binet Intelligence Scales (5th ed.; Riverside), assesses the following areas: fluid reasoning, knowledge, quantitative reasoning, visual–spatial processing, and working memory. The Stanford-Binet can only be given by a qualified examiner.

> ✳ The Peabody Picture Vocabulary Test is frequently used as a measure of receptive vocabulary rather than of academic ability.

## Peabody Picture Vocabulary Test

Both teachers and reading specialists can administer the Peabody Picture Vocabulary Test (PPVT-4), which can be used with individuals ages 2 years, 6 months through 90 years and older. Sometimes used as a test of verbal ability, the Peabody measures only one aspect of verbal ability, receptive vocabulary, but "it can serve as a useful screening device" (Salvia, Ysseldyke, & Bolt, 2007, p. 331). The Peabody measures vocabulary by having the student point to the picture that best represents the meaning of the word that the examiner says.

Because the Peabody only requires the student to point to a picture, it works especially well with students who are shy or withdrawn or who have difficulty expressing themselves. However, guessing is a factor in this test. Moreover, the authors of the Peabody warn that it can only be used as a measure of verbal ability if the student is a native speaker of English (Dunn & Dunn, 1997). It may yield erroneous results if it is administered to those with hearing difficulties, to nonnative speakers of English, or to those who have in some other way not had a full opportunity to learn standard English vocabulary.

## Other Individual Tests of Cognitive Ability

Tests that are frequently used in the assessment of students with reading disabilities include the following:

### Woodcock–Johnson III NU Test of Cognitive Abilities (Riverside)

This test, for ages 3–70+, contains a wide range of cognitive and achievement subtests and features several working memory tests, language tests, and a reasoning subtest.

### Detroit Tests of Learning Aptitude, Fourth Edition (Pro-Ed)

Intended for students ages 6–17, this test includes 10 subtests: Word Opposites (vocabulary), Design Sequences (visual sequential memory), Sentence Imitation (auditory memory), Reversed Letters (auditory memory), Story Construction (using a picture to tell a story), Design Reproduction (visual memory and motor skill, visual–motor integration), Basic Information, Symbolic Relations (nonverbal reasoning), Word Sequences (auditory memory), and Story Sequences.

### Detroit Tests of Learning Aptitude—Primary, Third Edition (DTLA-P-3) (Pro-Ed)

Intended for younger students, ages 3–9. Subtests include Articulation, Conceptual Matching, Design Reproduction, Digit Sequences, Draw-a-Person, Letter Sequences, Motor Directions, Object Sequences (memory), Oral Directions, Picture Fragments, Picture Identification, Sentence Imitation (auditory memory), and Symbolic Relations.

### Kaufman Assessment Battery for Children II (Pearson)

For students ages 3–18, this test includes two scales, each of which has several subscales. The Sequential Processing Scale has these subscales: Hand Movements (recall and reproduce hand movements), Number Recall, and Word Order (remember names of objects in order). The Simultaneous Processing Scale has these subscales: Magic Window (identify a picture on the basis of seeing parts of it), Face Recognition (recognize faces previously shown), Gestalt Closure (complete a drawing and name it), Triangles (copy designs), Matrix Analogies (complete visual analogies), Spatial Memory, and Photo Series (arrange photos to tell a story). The Kaufman Battery also has a number of achievement tests.

## Group Intelligence Tests

Although group intelligence tests were once used widely, their use has decreased. Group tests of intelligence are even more problematic than individual tests of intelligence. Guessing is a factor, and the tests are timed. In addition, because the tests are administered in group fashion, there is no one-on-one administration designed to elicit each student's best performance. Beyond the primary level, group intelligence tests may involve reading. Unless students can read the test items with relative ease, they may be unfairly penalized: Scores will reflect both reading and intelligence.

The two most widely used group tests of academic aptitude are the Cognitive Abilities Test (Riverside) and the Otis–Lennon School Ability Test (8th ed.; Pearson). The Cognitive Abilities Test measures abilities in three areas: Verbal, Quantitative, and Nonverbal. The Otis–Lennon School Ability Test measures verbal and nonverbal reasoning. Despite their shortcomings, these tests do provide an indication of the reasoning abilities of students and can be used as screening devices. In addition, the tests can indicate whether students are reading up to their ability. The Cognitive Abilities Test has been co-normed with the Iowa tests. The Otis–Lennon has been co-normed with the Stanford and the Metropolitan. If students take both an aptitude test and an achievement test, it is possible to note whether reading and other scores are commensurate with measured academic ability.

## ▨  Tests of Listening

As noted in Chapter 3, tests of listening can also be used to estimate students' potential. Tests of listening from an informal reading inventory (IRI) can be used, or you might also use a test of listening vocabulary in which words and possible definitions are read to a student and she marks the correct definition. Tests of this type can be found on the GRADE, some levels of the Stanford Achievement Tests, the first two levels of the Stanford Diagnostic Reading Tests, and the WIAT-III, which includes a test of receptive vocabulary and comprehension of oral passages. The Diagnostic Assessment of Reading (2nd ed.) and other individual diagnostic reading tests feature listening vocabulary tests in which the student supplies definitions for target words that are read by the examiner. One advantage of a listening test is that it does not pigeonhole students into a particular cognitive category, as an intelligence test does. Another measure of ability is to provide students with opportunities to learn under optimum conditions and see how they do.

## ▨  Tests of Language

Through tests such as the Peabody and the informal reading inventory, you can assess students' vocabulary and listening abilities. Through analyzing students' responses, you can also informally assess the quality of their language. Students who seem to have speech or language problems should be referred for additional assessment.

One assessment device that is widely used by speech and language professionals is the Clinical Evaluation of Language Fundamentals–4 (CELF–4). The CELF–4

(Harcourt) is designed to assess students in grades K–12 in the areas of word meaning, sentence and word structure, and memory. Both expressive and receptive language are assessed. This is a lengthy but thorough test that would best be administered and interpreted by the speech–language specialist. The Woodcock–Johnson III NU Tests of Achievement (Riverside) also contain a number of tests of language. Test of Word Knowledge Test (TOWK; Pearson) evaluates receptive and expressive language. The Emerging Literacy and Language Assessment (ELLA; Super Duper) assesses students ages 4 years, 6 months to 9 years, 11 months in phonological awareness, sign reading, phonics, word reading, sentence comprehension, rapid naming, and story retelling.

## Assessment of Memory

Working memory may be assessed through both verbal and nonverbal tests. Auditory working memory can also be assessed by having students repeat a series of words, sentences, or nonsense syllables or recall orally a series of pictured objects.

A popular test for working memory is digit span, which involves having the student repeat a series of digits forward or in reverse. Digit Span is one subtest given on the Wechsler scales. The Arithmetic subtest may also be used to assess working memory. To see if there is a possible memory problem, you should compare the student's scaled score on Digit Span with scores on the other subtests to see if there is a significant difference. Each of the subtests on the Wechsler yields a score between 1 and 20, with 10 being an average score. Because the scores are all on the same scale, they can be compared. However, only a difference of 3 points or more is considered to be significant. (Working memory is assessed on the WISC-IV with the subtests Digit Span, Letter–Number Sequence, and Arithmetic.)

If Wechsler scores are not available, you can administer digit span items from the Slosson Intelligence Test. To use these items to assess auditory memory, simply regroup them and ask them, one series at a time, starting with the shortest span of numbers and working up to the highest number. Administer digits forward and then digits reversed. To analyze performance, note the highest age level at which the student is able to repeat all the digits. Memory for sentence items, which involves having the student repeat sentences, can also be regrouped, administered, and analyzed in the same way that digit span items are.

Other sources of auditory memory items include the following two subtests of the Detroit Tests of Learning Aptitude (Pearson):

1. **Sentence Imitation.** The student repeats sentences that gradually increase in length.
2. **Word Sequences.** The student repeats a series of unrelated words. A useful comparison is to see whether students do better with Word Sequences or Sentence Imitation. Are they able to use the sense and structure of the sentences in Sentence Imitation to remember more words? (Hammill & Bryant, 1991, p. 7)

The Detroit Tests of Learning Aptitude also have a test of visual memory, which is described as follows:

> **Design Sequences**. In Design Sequences, students choose from a set of six cubes, each of which contains five shapes, the ones that are the same as those presented by the examiner before being hidden from view. Because the figures are nonsense shapes, the student will have difficulty using a name to help him

remember the shapes, and so visual memory is tapped. A useful comparison is to contrast visual and verbal memory. Many low-achieving readers apparently have difficulty using a verbal code to help them store and/or retrieve items but do fine with visual memory. (Hammill & Bryant, 1991, p. 7)

Attention and concentration are also involved in memory tasks. Students may have difficulty with a memory task because they are tired, feeling anxious, distracted by a problem that is bothering them, or having difficulty paying attention or concentrating for some other reason.

## Associative Word Learning

Of all the diagnostic areas mentioned so far, associative word learning is probably the most crucial. Difficulty with associative word learning is the defining characteristic of a severe reading difficulty. All the students with the most serious reading problems that I have encountered have had a serious, dramatic, unmistakable problem in this area.

A problem in associative word learning can be diagnosed in many ways. One indication of a problem in this area is a noticeable difficulty learning letter names, letter sounds, and high-frequency words. Poor performance on the word-list tests of an IRI despite ample opportunity to learn is a possible sign of an associative word-learning problem.

> Difficulty learning the printed forms of words is the major hurdle faced by students who have the severest reading problems. To assess word-learning ability, note a student's performance when new words are presented. How many words does he learn? How many does he retain?

To assess a student's word-learning ability, use a procedure similar to that employed for dynamic testing. Gather seven words that are in the student's listening vocabulary but that she does not recognize in print. (These might be seven words that she missed on the word-list test.) After pretesting to make sure that the student cannot read the words, see how many presentations it takes before she learns all seven words. In the first presentation, help the student to analyze each word. Go over any elements, such as initial consonant, vowels, or vowel patterns, that the student might use to help her to learn and remember the word. For instance, when presenting a word such as *hat,* help the student sound out the word, /h/-/a/-/t/, if the student knows these elements. If the student knows vowel patterns, point out the *h* and the *-at* pattern. If the student knows only consonants, point out the *h* and the *t.* For the remainder of the presentations, simply tell the student what the word is if she gets it wrong. If the student gets the word right, simply say, "Yes, the word is _____." Stop after 10 presentations so that the student does not become too frustrated. Note the number of words known at the last presentation. Then retest 30 minutes later and then the next day to assess delayed recall. (A word-learning test is presented in Appendix A.)

The average student will learn all seven words within 10 trials and will be able to recognize most, if not all, the words 30 minutes later and the next day. Students with associative word-learning difficulties may learn only one or two words in 10 trials, but even if they do learn them all in the 10 trials, they will be able to recognize only one or two 30 minutes or a day later. These same students will also do poorly on other tests of associative learning that use visual symbols, such as the Coding subtest on the WISC-IV.

Additional tests of associative learning can be found in the Woodcock–Johnson Cognitive Abilities Battery (Riverside) and are listed below:

**Visual–Auditory Learning.**   The student learns to associate familiar spoken words with symbols in the context of a story.

**Memory for Names.**   The student learns to associate nonsense names with drawings of space creatures.

## Word Finding

Word-finding difficulties can be diagnosed by comparing performance on a test of receptive vocabulary, such as the Peabody or Receptive One-Word Picture Vocabulary Test (ROW-PVT), with that on a test such as the Boston Naming Test or the Expressive One-Word Picture Vocabulary Test (EOWPVT), both of which require the students to supply a word when shown an illustration, so that comparisons can be easily made between an individual's expressive and receptive language.

The Expressive Vocabulary Test (EVT–2) is sometimes used in conjunction with the PPVT–4. Because both tests were normed on the same sample, receptive and expressive vocabulary can be compared. Students with word-finding difficulty generally do better on receptive vocabulary tests because they do not have to retrieve words from memory. An instrument designed specially to diagnose word-retrieval difficulties is the Test of Word Finding-2 and Test of Adolescent and Adult Word Finding (Riverside).

Word finding can also be assessed through observation. A word-finding observation checklist is presented in Figure 6.1.

If you suspect that a student has a word-finding difficulty, involve the speech therapist. The speech therapist will be in a better position to evaluate the student's overall language ability and might work with the student if he turns out to have a word-finding difficulty. The speech therapist might also give you assistance as you plan a program for the student.

## Assessing the Instructional Situation

In an interactive assessment, the student's instructional situation should be observed and analyzed. At the Reading Clinic at Southern Connecticut State University, students who have severe reading problems may receive services for two or even three years. Having a different student teacher for each semester, they may

**FIGURE 6.1**
Observation Guide for Word-Finding Difficulties

| | | | | |
|---|---|---|---|---|
| 1. | Does the student use roundabout phrases (the thing that you cut with)? | rarely | sometimes | often |
| 2. | Does the student frequently answer "I don't know" when you believe that she or he does know the answer? | rarely | sometimes | often |
| 3. | Does the student frequently pause or use "ums" and "ahs" when speaking? | rarely | sometimes | often |
| 4. | Does the student frequently say "I forgot," "I can't remember," or "I can't think of the name of that"? | rarely | sometimes | often |
| 5. | Does the student frequently use vague or general words such as "that boy," "that place," "something" rather than the specific name of the person, place, or object? | rarely | sometimes | often |

have as many as six instructors over a period of three years. The amount of progress that students make varies from instructor to instructor, sometimes to a considerable degree. Although all the instructors are well trained and carefully supervised, each has a different personality and a unique style of interacting. Each has different preferences in materials and teaching approaches. When students have exceptional teachers, they generally make exceptional progress.

Although the teacher is the most important factor in determining the amount of progress, other essential elements include amount of instructional time, how the time is used, the degree to which the student is actively involved, the types of materials used, and the kinds of activities pursued. In general, time spent on actual reading—including voluntary reading—and writing has a greater payoff than time spent on worksheets. Students also benefit more when instruction is pegged to their interests and abilities. Overall, the instructional situation has an enormous impact on students' learning and is particularly crucial for low-achieving readers.

If you are assisting a student but are not her classroom teacher, explore her school situation as part of your assessment. Talk to the student's teachers. Get an overview of the major tasks that she is expected to complete and an assessment of her performance. Ask about the student's strengths and weaknesses in key subject areas. Ask, too, about the student's work habits and overall adjustment. Invite the student's teacher(s) to provide any insight they might have about her difficulty with reading and writing. Find out what kinds of approaches have been used with the student. Balanced programs seem to work best. The student may have been in a program that did not provide systematic instruction in crucial skills or in a program where there were insufficient opportunities for application. In particular, try to find out what kinds of activities and materials work particularly well and which don't.

Assessing the instructional setting is important. Knowledge of instructional presentation, feedback, class structure, and nature of materials used can provide insight into the kinds of interventions that might be planned (Shapiro, 1996). The assessment should consider classroom requirements. A student's ability to handle his texts and complete typical assignments should also be assessed. Analyzing the student's portfolio and completed class and homework assignments will shed light on his ability to function in the classroom and also the kinds of tasks he is required to complete and his proficiency in completing these tasks (Shapiro, 1996).

It is also helpful to get the student's perspective on the instructional setting. Does the student feel competent in the target area? Does the student understand typical directions? Does the student know what to do when he runs into difficulty? Are there areas or tasks, such as spelling, that pose particular problems?

Also observe the student on two or more occasions during reading and writing sessions. If the student attends subject matter classes, observe those. Use an observation guide such as the Functional Assessment of Academic Behavior (FABB; Ysseldyke & Christenson, 2002) or the Benchmark School Interactive Learner Profile (Gaskins & Galloway, 2010).

## Functional Assessment of Academic Behavior

The basic purpose of FABB is to observe both home and school factors that impact learning so that parents and educators can answer the question: "Under what type of conditions can the student operate most optimally?" (Ysseldyke & Christenson,

2002, p. viii). FABB assesses 23 alterable factors that impact leaning. Taking a problem-solving/consultation approach, FABB would be especially useful for Tier III students in an RTI program who are not responding to instruction. However, FABB could be used to observe and enhance the instructional environment of virtually any student. A classroom observation guide based on FABB is presented in Figure 6.2. The assessment and intervention planning incorporated in FABB includes eight steps:

1. Identify and clarify the problem or concern

2. See the student's instructional needs from the perspective of teacher and parents

3. Observe the student and collect data on her or his instructional environment

4. Plan an intervention

5. Identify ways the parents can help

6. Monitor progress and evaluate the effectiveness of the intervention

7. Revise the intervention as needed

8. Report the results

If a student is receiving special help, arrange for a conference with the specialist and observe her working with the specialist. In addition to conducting

---

**INSTRUCTIONAL MATCH**

_____ The student is on the appropriate level as determined by an IRI or other assessment and the student's performance.

_____ Responses indicate that the skill being taught or reviewed is one that the student needs but is not too advanced.

_____ The student has the necessary background and prerequisite skills.

_____ The student's rate of accuracy is 95 percent or above on word recognition and 70 percent on comprehension for instructional tasks but 98 percent on word recognition and 90 percent comprehension on independent tasks.

**CLASSROOM ENVIRONMENT**

_____ The classroom atmosphere is orderly and positive.

_____ Classroom rules and routines are established and enforced.

_____ The student completes assignments.

_____ The student is on task at least 80 percent of the time.

**INSTRUCTION**

_____ Objectives are clearly communicated. The student knows what is to be learned and why it is being taught.

_____ Instruction is clear, step-by-step, and thorough.

_____ Think-alouds, modeling, and demonstrations are used as appropriate.

_____ Varied guided and independent practice are provided.

_____ The student is proved with the necessary feedback.

_____ Application activities are provided.

_____ Systematic review is provided.

**ENGAGEMENT AND MOTIVATION**

_____ Learning tasks are interesting, varied, and challenging.

_____ The student's efforts are affirmed with specific praise.

_____ The purpose and value of learning tasks are explained.

_____ A sense of self-efficacy is fostered.

_____ The student is provided with choices.

_____ The student has the opportunity to work with others.

**FIGURE 6.2**
Classroom
Observation

observations and interviews, evaluate the student's ability to cope with her school books (Broaddus & Bloodgood, 1994). Ask the student how textbooks are used. Does the student read them in class, or is she expected to read them independently at home? If they are read at home, is the student provided with some sort of study guide? If they are read in class, are they read silently or are they read aloud?

Have the student indicate what chapter the class is on in each text and then read a portion of the next chapter. In IRI test style, assess whether or not the texts are on the student's instructional level. Also note the strategies the student uses to comprehend the text.

Assess the student's home assignments and how they are handled. Find out if the student makes a note of homework assignments so she knows what to do. If the student does, ask to see a record of the assignments. Note whether the record of the assignments is clear. If the student does not keep a record, ask her how she remembers what the homework assignments are. Also find out whether the student completes assignments on a regular basis (Meltzer, 1993).

## Benchmark School Interactive Learner Profile

The Benchmark School Interactive Learner Profile is an observation survey designed to "identify patterns in student's habits of mind and behaviors that may impede reading progress, but which are not usually measured on formal reading assessments" (Gaskins & Galloway, 2010, p. 200). Areas included on the profile are attention, reflectivity, active learning, persistence, adaptability organization, reasoning, memory, language, social awareness, self-awareness, motivation, volition, and physical and health factors. Also included is a list of supports that might be offered to students to develop needed skills, attitudes, and habits of mind. For instance, if students have difficulty in Person Variables such as reflectivity and active learning, the profile lists possible supports that include goal-setting conferences, reflectivity exercises, self-assessment, coaching self-regulation strategies, and creating plans for completing assignment. Overall, the profile is "intended to promote an understanding of person, task, text, and situation variables that interact to determine a student's academic success" (p. 223). With its practical suggestions for reading and developing areas in which there are needs, the profile provides a sound foundation for effective intervention.

## School Records

According to the Family Educational Rights and Privacy Act (20 U.S.C. § 1232g; 34 CFR Part 99), schools may not release information from school records without parental permission. When requesting information, it is advisable to obtain a written release from parents.

School records can be a valuable source of information, especially if the student has been tested extensively or if the school keeps a portfolio. If you are not working in the student's school, you need to get written parental permission to examine records. All information should be kept confidential. Pertinent information includes the following:

**Attendance.** Spotty attendance can interfere with learning.

**Retentions.** Students who spent a year in a transition class or who were retained in first grade or another grade may have a more serious problem than those who were not, because they have had an additional year of schooling.

**Grades.** Look at overall performance and areas of strength and weakness.

**Performance on achievement and aptitude tests.**   Look at all areas, not just reading and writing. Sometimes a student will show strengths in areas such as math or art, where reading and writing are not as important.

**Special help given.**   If the student has been given help and is still having difficulty, he may have a more serious problem.

**Transfers.**   Moving from school to school can cause gaps in students' learning.

## Case History

> When obtaining a case history, interview both parents together, if possible. Maintain a nonjudgmental, professional attitude.

In order to get a fuller understanding of a student's background, it is important to obtain a case history from the parents or other primary caregivers. A case history will provide a backdrop for interpreting test results and other data. The focus of the history is on obtaining data about the biological and environmental factors that affect the student's physical, emotional, social, and cognitive development (Abrams, 1988).

To obtain needed information, the following six areas should be explored:

1. Family constellation and student's role within the family.
2. History of the mother's pregnancy, and her child's birth and infancy.
3. Developmental milestones, such as the age at which the student sat up, crawled, and walked, with special emphasis on language development. Major developmental milestones are listed in Table 6.1. The sequence of these milestones is the same for all children. Children coo and babble and then say single words before they speak in sentences. However, there is enormous variation within each stage. For instance, although most children speak in two-word phrases or sentences by about the age of 2, some normal children may not do so until they are 3 or 4 (Lenneberg, cited in Stewig & Nordberg, 1995). A delay in reaching developmental milestones may not be significant in and of itself. However, a

| | |
|---|---|
| Lifts head | 2 months |
| Coos | 4 months |
| Babbles | 6–9 months |
| Sits without support | 6 months |
| Stands alone | 11 months |
| Walks | 12 months |
| Says one or more words | 12 months |
| Scribbles randomly | 18 months |
| Speaks in two-word sentences | 24 months |
| Speaks in three-word sentences | 36 months |
| Makes wordlike scribbles | 36 months |
| Writes letters but letters do not represent sounds | 48–60 months |
| May attempt invented spelling in which letters represent sounds | 48–72 months |

**TABLE 6.1**
Developmental
Milestones

pattern of late development takes on more significance, especially when accompanied by other indicators of slow development and learning problems.

4.  Medical and psychological history, with emphasis on factors that might influence reading and writing development.

5.  School history with emphasis on elements that might have an impact on reading and writing development (Abrams, 1988).

6.  Personal adjustment.

A case history should be obtained from both parents or the student's primary caregivers. The interview should be held in a relaxed, private setting. Take a few minutes to put the parents at ease and also explain the purpose of the interview: that you wish to obtain information which will give you a total picture of their child so that you can reach a fuller understanding of their child's reading and/or writing difficulty. Explain that it is important for you to gain an understanding of the problem from their perspective.

> ☀ If parents express feelings of guilt about their child's learning problems, explain that they should not blame themselves but should focus on working to improve their children's reading and writing.

In order to obtain a maximum amount of information, questions should be asked in open-ended fashion. Sample questions follow below. Some questions touch on sensitive areas. Be sensitive to parents' reaction. Adapt questions to fit your particular situation.

### FAMILY FACTORS

*Can you tell me about your family? Who lives in your home? What are the names and ages of the other children? Have any of your other children had problems in school? Did you or your spouse have any difficulty in school?*

### PREGNANCY

*How would you describe your pregnancy? Did you experience any illnesses during your pregnancy? Did you take any medications? How would you describe the birth? Did you have any difficulties or complications? Was the baby full term or did the baby come early? (Note: 37 weeks is considered full term.) How much did your child weigh? (Note: 5.5 pounds is considered full-term weight.)*

### EARLY YEARS AND OVERALL HEALTH

*What was _____ like as an infant? Was _____ easy or difficult to care for? What kinds of childhood illnesses did _____ have? Has _____ ever had her/his eyesight or hearing checked? Did she/he have any high fevers? Did _____ ever have any convulsions? Were there any head injuries? Did _____ ever lose consciousness? How would you describe _____ health now? Is _____ on any medication now? How much sleep does _____ get each night? Does she/he have any difficulty sleeping? How would you describe her/his appetite? Does she/he eat most foods? Does she/he eat breakfast? Has _____ ever been diagnosed as being hyperactive or having an attention deficit disorder?*

### DEVELOPMENTAL MILESTONES

*Did you keep any records telling when _____ talked or walked? At what age did _____ sit up? At what age did _____ crawl? Stand? Walk? Say first word? Say first sentence? How would you describe _____ speech as she/he was growing up?*

## EARLY LANGUAGE AND LITERACY DEVELOPMENT

*What language or languages are spoken in the home? What language does _____ use at home? Did _____ play with pencils and crayons? Did _____ try to write? Did _____ have favorite storybooks? Did anyone read to her/him? Did _____ ever pretend to read to you, to teddy bears or dolls, or to younger children? Did _____ watch TV? How often did she/he watch? What kinds of shows did she/he like best? Did _____ use electronic devices, such as an electronic tablet? What kinds of activities did _____ engage in with the electronic devices? As a young child did _____ ever ask questions about signs? Did _____ ever ask you how to write her/his name or other words? Did _____ try to write before going to school?*

## SCHOOL HISTORY

⚓ Parents can provide valuable insights
✴ into their child's attitude toward
school, response to different kinds of
instruction, and self-feelings as a learner.

*What can you tell me about _____ reading/writing difficulty? How do you see the problem? What do you think is the cause of the problem? When did you first notice that _____ had a difficulty? What has been done to help _____ solve the problem? What else, if anything, do you think should be done? Does _____ like school? What are _____ favorite subjects? Which subjects does she/he like least? Did _____ attend preschool? Kindergarten? In what ways have you or other members of the family tried to help _____? How is _____ school attendance? About how many days a year does _____ miss? Has _____ ever missed a long period of schooling because of illness or other reasons?*

## HOME FACTORS

⚓ Questioning parents about
✴ homework can yield valuable
information about the student's study
strategies and habits.

*Do you or anyone else in the family try to help _____ with homework? About how much homework does _____ have each evening? Where does _____ do homework? Do you take _____ to the library? If so, how often? Do you buy books, magazines, or software or apps for _____? Do you read to _____? Did you read to _____ when she/he was younger? Do you like to read? About how much reading do you do each day? Do you subscribe to any newspapers or magazines? What plans do you have for _____? What plans does _____ have for herself/himself? What does _____ plan to be when she/he grows up?*

## INTERESTS/PERSONAL ADJUSTMENT

*How does _____ get along with the other children at school? Does _____ belong to any clubs or teams? How does _____ spend her/his free time? Does _____ like to read? How much time does _____ spend reading each week? About how many books would you say _____ read last month? Does _____ have any hobbies or other interests? About how much time each day does _____ spend watching TV? Does _____ use a computer or other electronic devices? About how much time each day does _____ spend on these devices? How does _____ get along with the children in the neighborhood? How does _____ get along with the other members of the family? Is there anything else you would like to tell me about _____?*

The questions do not have to be asked in order. Rather, you should follow the natural flow of the interview. When asked a health question, parents may get into the area of school history because the child got sick in school. To get the most information, follow the parent's lead. Rearrange questions as the situation dictates. Also spend added time in those areas that seem to have the most bearing on the particular student you are examining. If chronic illness is a major factor, for instance, spend additional time discussing the student's medical background. Also, keep in mind that parents are not always objective. Some information may be omitted or distorted. And some information, such as the age of some of the developmental milestones, may not be remembered accurately. If parents have medical or developmental records, these should be consulted. All information should, of course, be kept confidential.

If you are unable to interview parents or school personnel, you might use a written questionnaire to obtain information. Although interviews are more effective in eliciting information, using a questionnaire is better than obtaining no information at all. Since school personnel are busy, questionnaires should be succinct. Because some parents of poor readers and writers may also have experienced difficulty with reading and writing, parent questionnaires should be easy to read and easy to answer. Sample questionnaires are presented in Figures 6.3 and 6.4.

## Students' Views

An essential element in assessment is to obtain the students' views of their reading and writing. How do they think they are doing? What kinds of skills would they like to learn? What kinds of help, if any, would they like to have?

> By asking students what they would like to learn to do in reading and what would help them to become better readers, you involve them in setting goals.

Some possible questions that might be asked are listed below. Choose the questions that seem most appropriate. Also feel free to add questions. Instead of using a formal interview approach, ask the questions in an informal, conversational style:

- What are your favorite school subjects? Why?
- Are there any subjects that are hard for you? What makes them hard? What might make them easier?
- What things are easy for you in reading? Writing?
- What things are hard for you in reading? Writing?
- What kinds of things would you like to learn to do in reading? Writing?
- What would help you to become a better reader? Writer?
- Do you read on your own at home?
- What kinds of things do you like to read?

> Students' responses can help you determine assessment/instructional priorities. If students say the words make reading hard, look into their decoding skills or the difficulty level of the reading material.

- What are your favorite books?
- Who are your favorite authors?
- Do you user a computer, tablet, or smart phone? If so, how do you use it? What are your favorite Web sites? What are your favorite programs or apps?

Questions can also be asked about content areas. Responses can be supplemented by observational data and other information that you obtain about the students and their perception of reading and writing.

**■ FIGURE 6.3**

Parent
Questionnaire

Name of child _____     Date of birth _____
Name of school _____    Grade in school _____
Mother's name _____     Occupation _____
Father's name _____     Occupation _____
Names and ages of brothers and sisters
_____
Main language spoken in home _____ Other languages spoken in home _____
How would you describe your child's overall health?
_____
_____
Does your child now have any major illnesses?
_____
_____
Has your child had any major illness or had any accidents that caused an injury?
_____
_____
Does your child wear glasses? _____ When was the last time your child's eyes were checked? _____
Has your child ever had any difficulty with hearing? _____
When was the last time your child's hearing was checked? _____
Has your child ever repeated a grade or been placed in a transitional class? _____
What difficulty does your child have in reading or writing? _____
When was this difficulty first noticed?
_____
_____
Has the school tried to help your child? If so, how?
_____
_____
Have you tried to help your child? If so, how?
_____
_____
Except for help that you have given, has your child been helped outside school? _____ If so, how?
_____
Has your child been tested for a learning problem? If so, what kind of testing was done?
_____
Is your child in any special programs for children with learning problems?
_____
Has your child missed a lot of time from school? _____ If so, please describe.
_____
What does your child like to do do when not in school?
_____
What special interests or hobbies does your child have?
_____
Is there anything else that you can tell us that would help us to understand your child's reading or writing difficulty?
_____
_____
_____

**Reading expectancy:** estimate of the level at which a student should be reading, based on tests of academic aptitude, listening capacity, or estimated ability to learn.

## ■■■ Reading Expectancy

An assessment should include some indication of the level at which the student should be reading. This is the student's **reading expectancy**. As a general principle, students should be able to read up to their cognitive or linguistic capacity. Tests of

**FIGURE 6.4**
School
Questionnaire

| Name of student _____ | Grade _____ | Date _____ |

Name of school _____ Teacher _____

School address _____ Phone _____

1. Student's reading level _____
2. Name and level of materials now being used _____
3. Results of standardized tests _____
4. Results of IEP or other special assessments _____
5. Grades for last marking period _____
6. Results of vision test _____ Hearing test _____
7. Description of speech or behavior problems, if any _____
8. Any extended or frequent absences _____
9. Grades repeated or placement in a transition class _____
10. Description of any extra help given or any intervention _____

Classroom teacher's or specialist's description of the child's problem in reading or writing and suggestions for helping the child.

_____
_____

Is the child now being considered for special placement or retention? If so, please describe.

_____

cognitive ability such as the WISC-IV and the Stanford-Binet can be used to estimate a student's reading capacity. The higher the scores on these tests, the higher is the student's reading expectancy.

As a rough rule of thumb, to get a measure of expectancy, subtract 5.6 from the student's mental age (5.6 is the average age at which students start kindergarten). If the test does not give a mental age, you can calculate that by multiplying the student's chronological age by the test's standard or IQ score. Thus, a 9-year-old with an IQ of 133 has a mental age of 12 (1.33 times 9) and a reading expectancy of 6.6 (11 years, 12 months minus 5 years, 6 months). The student can be expected to be able to read on a sixth-grade level.

Still another way to calculate reading expectancy is to use the following formula: (IQ/100 times years of reading instruction) + 1 = Reading Expectancy (Bond, Tinker, Wasson, & Wasson, 1994). Using this formula, the student's reading expectancy is grade 5 ([133/100 times 3] + 1 = 5), so this formula gives a more conservative estimate. In calculating years in school, begin with first grade, not kindergarten, even though there may have been some formal reading instruction in kindergarten. If a student repeated a grade or spent an extra year in a transition class, that should be included when calculating years in school.

When calculating reading expectancy, also consider opportunity to learn. A very bright first grader, for instance, who has a reading expectancy of 4.0 might not have had sufficient exposure to reading for this to be a realistic expectation.

When determining a reading expectancy, consider several sources of information. Use an IQ score if available and also the listening level yielded by an informal reading inventory.

Technical procedures are sometimes used to determine reading expectancy, reading achievement, and whether there is a significant gap between the two. Typically a substantial discrepancy is one in which there is a difference of 1.5 standard deviations between achievement and ability (Spear-Swerling & Sternberg, 1996). This means that if a student achieved an average score of 100 on the Wechsler scales, which have a standard deviation of 15 points, then his achievement on a standard measure of reading, also having a standard deviation of 15, would have to be 77.5 or lower.

As noted earlier, it is not necessary to administer a test of cognitive capacity to obtain a measure of a student's reading expectancy. There are also a number of measures of language development that may be used to gauge a student's reading expectancy. The simplest of these is a test of listening capacity. The informal reading inventory, which was covered in detail in Chapter 4, yields a listening level. This is obtained by reading stories to students and finding the highest level at which the students can understand 75 percent of the questions asked about a selection that has been read to them. If a third-grader reading on a first-grade level obtains a listening level of grade 5, that is the student's reading expectancy. Other sources of language capacity are listening vocabulary subtests found in some norm-referenced group tests and some individual diagnostic tests as noted in Chapter 5. The grade equivalent yielded by these subtests is an estimate of the student's reading expectancy.

## Summarizing the Data

Once you have assembled all the data from your assessment, it is important to organize the information so that trends can be noted and comparisons made. Use a form similar to the one in Figure 6.5 to help you group data about reading in one block, data about spelling and writing in another, data about emergent literacy in a third, and so on. Suggestions for placing data are presented in Figure 6.6.

After placing the data in blocks, examine each of the blocks in terms of the first one, which summarizes the student's estimated cognitive ability, listening capacity, and reading expectancy. Looking at the reading block, for instance, note how the student is doing in terms of reading expectancy or listening capacity. Is the student reading above or below reading expectancy or listening capacity? Looking at the writing and/or spelling block, note whether performance is above or below the student's estimated capacity or expectancy.

---

Name  Robert Lawlor                Date of Birth  4-19            Grade  3              Date  3-10

| COGNITIVE | IRI & OTHER RDG. TESTS | WORD RECOG. | EMERGENT | SPELLING/ WRITING | ORAL LANGUAGE | ASSOC. LRNG. | MEMORY | ACH. TESTS |
|---|---|---|---|---|---|---|---|---|
| WISC 110 | Ind.  pp | F  U | | Cr 1–50 | Seems | Word Lrng. | Digits 8 | Stanf. |
| High | Inst.  p | pp 75 85 | | Cr 2–20 | adequate | Imm.-7/7 | Arith. 9 | Rdg.  10 P.R. |
| Comp.-13 | Frus.  1 | p 65 75 | | Letter | | Delayed-6/7 | | Math 40 P.R. |
| Vocab.-12 | List.  5 | 1 50 55 | | name | | | | Lang.  11 P.R. |
| Low | | 2 40 40 | | stage | | | | |
| Block-7 | Stan. | Phonics | | writing | | | | |
| Coding-7 | Tot.-10 P.R. | Invent | | sample— | | | | |
| | Comp.-11 P.R. | diff | | very | | | | |
| LISTENING | Wd.St. 9 P.R. | with | | rudimentary | | | | |
| CAPACITY | Vocab. 9 P.R. | long | | | | | | |
| 5 | | vowels | | | | | | |
| READING EXPECT. | | | | | | | | |
| 5.4 | | | | | | | | |

CASE HISTORY HIGHLIGHTS

Repeated 1st grade
Lagged in overall motor & lang. dev.
Emotional outbursts
Likes sports

SCREENINGS

Vision—squints & holds book close

TRIAL TEACHING

Responded best to whole-part teaching of word analysis skills
Is making limited progress in Tier II intervention.

SUMMARY

High/avg. ability
Possible diff with memory & attention
Signif. behind in reading, writing, & spelling

RECOMMENDATIONS

Use easy-to-read sports books
Use whole-part approach to word analysis
One-on-one instr.

Note: P.R. stands for percentile rank.

**FIGURE 6.5**
Case Summary

FIGURE 6.6

**FIGURE 6.6**

Suggestions for Filling Out the Case Summary

| | |
|---|---|
| *Cognitive Ability* | Give results of IQ test. Note high and low scores on subtests or areas in which student did well and areas in which student did poorly. |
| *Listening Capacity* | Note listening capacity from IRI and/or results from other listening, oral vocabulary, or language development test. |
| *Reading Expectancy* | Use IQ or listening test or both to estimate reading expectancy. |
| *Reading Achievement* | List IRI levels. Give results of other reading tests, think-alouds, or observations of reading. |
| *Word Recognition* | Give results of word-lists tests. Provide information from the Phonics Inventory, Syllable Survey, the Word-Identification Interview, think-alouds, and observations. |
| *Writing/Spelling* | Give results of the Elementary Spelling Inventory, a test on graded lists of spelling words, and examination of writing samples and portfolio. |
| *Oral Language* | Provide test results of vocabulary assessment or other language measures and note observational data. Include word-finding data, if this area was assessed. |
| *Assoc. Learning* | Provide results of Word-Learning Test. Note results of symbol learning tests and observations. |
| *Memory/Attent.* | Note results of tests of memory and attention. |
| *Emergent* | If pertinent, note knowledge of concepts of print, letter knowledge, phonemic awareness, and beginning sounds. Note interest in reading and writing and awareness of the purposes of reading and writing. |
| *Case History* | Note both major positive and negative factors. Note school situation. |
| *Screenings* | Note hearing, vision, health, or other screenings. |
| *Trial Teaching, Response to Intervention* | Briefly describe trial teaching or response to intervention and note results. |
| *Summary* | Indicate reading expectancy; reading, writing and spelling levels; major strengths, weaknesses, and needs. |
| *Recommendations* | Suggest type of assistance (small group, one-on-one), major areas of needed instruction, and possible techniques or approaches and possible materials. Also recommend needed screenings. |

After examining each block in this way, make comparisons among the blocks. How do writing and spelling compare with reading or word analysis? Also look for strengths and needs. Examining the categories at the bottom of the page, note major findings from the case study. These might include long-term illnesses, grades repeated, or indications of interventions or extra help given at school. Including

## EXEMPLARY TEACHING

### Trial Teaching

Maria, a 15-year-old ninth-grader, was reading on a fourth-grade level despite having average ability as indicated by a WISC administered by the school psychologist. Her listening level indicated adequate language development. Based on the results of the listening comprehension score, Maria was reading five years below her capacity.

During interviews with teachers, Maria's parents, and Maria, it was revealed that Maria disliked school in general, and reading in particular. During her interview Maria stated that she hated reading because it was boring and she couldn't see any sense in reading all that dumb stuff. When the examiner looked over the texts from content-area subjects, she could see that they were all written at or above grade level, which was well above Maria's fourth-grade reading ability.

During the trial teaching session, the examiner explained to Maria that she could understand ninth-grade stories and articles that were read to her. This meant that she was a bright person and had a good vocabulary and knew lots of things. The examiner also explained to Maria that she was good at reading one-syllable words, but because she had difficulty reading words that had two or more syllables, she would have a hard time reading ninth-grade books.

Looking frustrated, Maria said she had been taught all the syllable rules but they didn't help much. The examiner explained that she had a special way of teaching multisyllabic words, one she had used to help other bright students who had trouble with long words. She showed Maria how she could use her knowledge of single-syllable words to read multisyllabic words. Writing the words *side, beside, divide, decide,* and *provide* on the chalkboard, she helped Maria use her knowledge of *side* to read *beside, divide, decide,* and *provide*. Maria had missed both *provide* and *decide* during her testing (McCabe, 2010).

Sensing that Maria had a negative attitude toward traditional classroom material, probably because she had been given texts that were too hard for her, the examiner displayed an array of easy-to-read novels, the local newspaper, and *Action* (Scholastic), a magazine written on a third- through fifth-grade level for students in grades 6 to 12. Maria found *Action* to be appealing, especially after reading the cover selection and seeing that it wasn't too long or too hard to read.

Based on Maria's reactions, a program was planned in which she was taught high-frequency syllable patterns and shown how to use her knowledge of single-syllable words to decode multisyllabic words. Patterns introduced were drawn from materials that she was reading, so that she would see the value of learning the skill and apply it in the context of real reading. She was also provided with high-interest materials on a fourth-grade level of difficulty. Because her content-area texts were too difficult for her, recordings were made so she could read along with them. A variable-speed player was obtained so she could set the reading speed at a comfortable pace. Because she was so far behind, she was given help in the classroom and also after school by the reading specialist. By year's end, Maria was able to handle sixth-grade material. Her attitude toward school also showed a marked improvement, as did her grades.

only the most essential information, such as reading level, reading expectancy or listening capacity, major strengths and needs, summarize the data. Hold off on making recommendations until you have conducted a trial teaching lesson (see p. 62).

## Making Recommendations

Make recommendations on the basis of the assessment data and trial teaching and/or interventions. Recommendations should include suggestions for level of help—one on one, small group, regular classroom—and for the approach that might be taken—language experience, reading workshop, and so forth. Recommendations might also be provided for major needs—comprehension

> ⚕ Suggest type of assistance (small group, one-on-one), major areas of needed instruction, and possible techniques or approaches and possible materials. Also recommend needed screenings. Upcoming chapters explore materials, methods, and settings for corrective instruction. You will be better able to plan an intervention program after reading the rest of the text.

of main ideas, application of study strategies, ability to read short-vowel patterns, or ability to decode multisyllabic words, for instance. Possible teaching techniques, especially if these have been tried and shown to be successful, should be listed. Recommendations should consider person, text, task, and situation variables (Gaskins & Galloway, 2010). Also included might be recommendations for setting and pursuing goals, making plans to complete long-term assignments, using self-talk to help student stay on task, preparing for tests, being an active learner in class, seeing oneself as a competent learner, organizing materials, working effectively in a group, and seeking help when needed. The recommendations should answer the key questions established in Chapter 3:

- On what level is the student functioning?
- What is the student's potential for growth?
- What are the student's strengths and weaknesses in reading and writing?
- What would be the most effective materials for this student?
- Under what circumstances and in what setting would this student learn best?
- What are the most effective techniques or approaches for teaching this student?
- Are there any physical, psychological, social, or other factors that need to be addressed in order for the student to do his best?
- How might the home, larger community, and school work together to help the student?

In a response to intervention (RTI) approach, students judged to be at risk on the basis of a screening assessment, teacher judgment, or both are provided with assistance. One of the benefits of RTI is that students are provided help as soon as a need is identified. The amount and intensity of help are increased if the student fails to respond. Therefore, students at risk might have been provided with help before being assessed in depth. The case study would then contain an account of the intervention(s) that the student had been provided and the student's responses to the intervention(s). Similarly, descriptions of dynamic assessment would be especially valuable, since these would also provide insight into the kinds of instruction that might be most beneficial.

## Professional Reports

> ⚕ When constructing reports, avoid judgmental language. Instead of "Frank was lazy during the testing sessions," say, "Frank needed encouragement to continue working." When sharing results, emphasize the student's strengths and the practical steps that the parents or teacher might take to help the child.

Reading specialists, along with psychiatrists, psychologists, communication disorders specialists, and other professionals are called upon to summarize the results of their assessments and make appropriate recommendations. Although they differ from profession to profession, these reports or case studies have a number of commonalties.

In terms of style, they are typically written in formal English and attempt to be both objective and conservative. Care is taken to base conclusions and recommendations on test data and observations. Since these reports may be used to place students, obtain additional services, or plan a program of remediation, they should be complete, clear, and precise.

Although the reports should embody a professional tone, they should be free of jargon and written in clear, simple language so they may be understood by parents and others outside the profession, as well as school principals, school counselors, and other professionals. Technical terms should be used with care and, if used, should be explained. For instance, instead of saying "Mario had difficulty with vowel digraphs," state that "Mario had difficulty with words like *rain* and *bean*, in which two letters are used to spell the vowel sound." Instead of talking about a student's independent level, translate this into a phrase that a nonspecialist would understand: "the level at which Mario can read on his own, without any help from the teacher."

The content of the assessment report will vary, depending on the complexity of the case and the extent of the assessment procedures. A diagnostic report may range from 2 or 3 pages to 20 or more. However, the reports written by reading specialists for schools are generally brief.

Although the assessment report may include information about the student's health, interests, social and psychological adjustment, school record, cognitive abilities, vision, and hearing, the emphasis should be on reading and writing and the kinds of programs that seem to work best with the student. Presented here is an outline for a full report. Reports vary somewhat in both format and content, so the outline should be adapted:

> The assessment outline is a sample and should be adapted to fit your situation. Include categories that may have been left out; delete areas that you do not assess.

> Some assessment reports also include a listing of tests administered along with test scores on the first page. This provides the person reading the report with an overview of the test results

I. Information (on cover sheet)
  A. Student's name
  B. Date of birth and chronological age at start of assessment
  C. Sex
  D. Grade in school
  E. Name of school
  F. Examiner and place of assessment
  G. Dates of assessment

II. Reason for Referral and Summary of Observations (on inside pages)
  A. Name, age, grade, school, reason for referral
  B. Test-taking behavior, best-liked and least-liked tasks
  C. Results of interview about reading/writing problems, interests, and vocational plans

III. School History
  A. Summary of progress in school
  B. Achievement in specific subjects
  C. Results of achievement and other tests
  D. Attendance, repeated grades
  E. Description of classroom program
  F. Notes on special placement, interventions, RTI efforts, or other special help given
  G. Classroom and special placement observations

> The focus of an assessment will vary, depending on the stage the student is in. For beginning readers, decoding might be the emphasis. For more advanced readers, focus might be on comprehension and study skills.

IV. Results of Assessment
  A. Physical
    1. Vision
    2. Hearing
    3. Other
  B. Cognitive
    1. Academic aptitude
    2. Memory

    **3.** Associative learning

    **4.** Auditory and visual discrimination

  **C.** Reading achievement

    **1.** Word recognition

    **2.** Informal reading inventory levels

    **3.** Fluency, reading rate

  **D.** Phonological awareness, letter knowledge, if applicable

  **E.** Concepts of print—if applicable

  **F.** Special phonics testing

  **G.** Writing

  **H.** Spelling

  **I.** Handwriting

  **J.** Results of dynamic testing, response to intervention, and/or trial teaching

**V.** Summary of Assessment

  **A.** Highlights of cognitive testing

  **B.** Highlights of reading achievement and other testing

  **C.** Conclusions

**VI.** Recommendations

  **A.** Setting and approach

  **B.** Major needs to be addressed, including recommendations for executive functioning

  **C.** Ways in which school can be supportive

  **D.** Ways in which parents can be supportive

**VII.** Description of Intervention (if applicable)

  **A.** Setting, approach

  **B.** Major needs that were addressed

  **C.** Skills/strategies taught

  **D.** Techniques used

  **E.** Materials employed

  **F.** Evaluation of progress

## Assessment: An Ongoing Process

Assessment should be ongoing and continuous. Whenever a student is engaged in a learning activity, assess the activity. How does the student cope with the activity? Which activities cause difficulty? Which are done with ease? What factors are hindering the student's progress? What factors are accelerating progress? What changes might be made to improve the student's chances for success?

For instance, one student was struggling with a word-pattern approach but began making progress when taught by a sound-by-sound approach. Apparently, his phonemic awareness was weak, and he needed added instruction in letter–sound relationships. Later, building on his improved phonemic awareness and solid knowledge of letter–sound relationships, he did quite well with a pattern approach. Another student made very little progress learning new words until a tracing technique was used.

Chances are that even the most comprehensive assessment would not yield this information. This is the kind of information that continuous assessment, trying out different approaches and materials, is most likely to reveal. The important thing is to ask two questions as you work with the corrective reader: How is this approach/material/setting working? If it isn't working out, what might work better?

## ░ A Multidisciplinary Approach

A reading problem, especially one that is severe, can have many causes and can affect many aspects of a student's life. It is important to involve other professionals, parents, and the individual student in the process of assessment and intervention. The school psychologist can shed light on cognitive and affective factors and perhaps provide help with the emotional aspects of the problem. The language therapist can test language abilities and provide help with articulation, word finding, and other difficulties. The learning disabilities specialist can test in math and cognitive processing areas. The nurse can provide insight into health issues and screen for auditory, visual, or health problems. The classroom teacher can provide insight into the student's work habits and relationships with others. Working collaboratively is an excellent way to enlist needed support.

## ░ Mini–Case Study

Josephine is an 8-year-old second grader, who, when tested, was able to read only a passage on the preprimer level. Referred for testing by the school psychologist, she was given the WISC-IV. What do the results of the test suggest about Josephine's cognitive functioning? How might the following information from the WISC-IV be used to plan a program of intervention for her?

WISC-IV Full Scale IQ, 97

**Verbal Comprehension**

Information, 8

Similarities, 12

Vocabulary, 13

Comprehension, 11

**Perceptual Reasoning**

Picture Concepts, 10

Block Design, 6

**Working Memory**

Digit Span, 6

Arithmetic, 9

**Processing Speed**

Coding, 9

Note that, overall, Josephine has average ability. However, there is weakness in the Information area, which suggests that building background would be an important part of her program. Her high score in Vocabulary and Similarities suggests good ability to form concepts. Her low score in Digit Span suggests a possible attention/concentration problem or difficulty with short-term/working memory for verbal, sequential material. Her low score on the Block Design suggests difficulty in the visual perceptual motor area. A program for Josephine would build on her strong language skills but include elements such as manipulatives and tracing that would help her pay attention and concentrate.

## Summary

A student's literacy capacity can be assessed through administering an intelligence or a listening test. Focusing as they do on academic aptitude and encompassing tasks that all students may not have had an equal opportunity to learn, intelligence tests need to be interpreted with care and should be supplemented by observation of what students can actually do. The most popular intelligence tests are the Wechsler scales, whose subtest scores can be analyzed to yield diagnostic information. Only qualified personnel can administer the Wechsler scales; however, reading professionals may administer the Slosson Intelligence Test and the Peabody Picture Vocabulary Test, a measure of receptive vocabulary.

Specific areas of cognitive functioning that should be examined in a thorough assessment include memory and associative word learning. If a student is showing symptoms of word-finding difficulty, this area should also be assessed.

As part of an interactive assessment, a student's school situation should be observed. If possible, observe the student in reading and writing and content area classes. Also interview the student's teachers and analyze school records. If it is not possible to interview teachers, ask the school to complete a concise questionnaire. A case history obtained by interviewing the student's parents provides a backdrop for interpreting other assessment data. To determine whether a student has a reading disorder and the degree of severity, if there is a disorder, it is essential to establish where the student should be in terms of reading achievement. In general, students are expected to read up to their capacity as indicated by an IQ test, a listening test, or an oral vocabulary test. If possible, complement test and observational data by conducting condensed trial teaching lessons in a key area.

Reading professionals may be expected to summarize assessment data in a professional report. Such a report follows the same general style and format of that in a psychological report.

## Application Activities

1. Talk to a school psychologist or a reading specialist about the kinds of measures that she or he administers. Discuss the value and limitations of the measures.
2. Complete an assessment and write a professional report based on your findings. If time and circumstances permit, write a full report. If not, write a minireport based on a reading assessment that focuses on informal reading inventory results.
3. Fill out the Benchmark School Interactive Learner Profile for a student with whom you are working.

## MyEducationLab

Go to the topic **Reading Assessment** in the MyEducationLab (www.myeducationlab. com) for **Assessing and Correcting Reading Difficulties,** where you can:

- Find learning outcomes for **Reading Assessment** along with the national standards that connect to these outcomes.
- Complete Assignments and Activities that can help you more deeply understand the chapter content.

- Apply and practice your understanding of the core teaching skills identified in the chapter with the Building Teaching Skills and Dispositions learning units.

- Examine challenging situations and cases presented in the Iris Center Resources.

- Check your comprehension of the content covered in the chapter with the Study Plan. Here you will be able to take a chapter pretest, receive feedback on your answers, and then access personalized Review, Practice, and Enrichment exercises to enhance your understanding of chapter content. After you complete the exercises, take a posttest to confirm your comprehension.

- Practice targeting instruction and making content accessible for all students with A+RISE activities.

# 7

# Emergent Literacy and Prevention Programs

E mergent literacy, which encompasses both reading and writing, acknowledges that all students come to school with some experience with reading and writing. The term *emergent literacy* refers to those early reading and writing behaviors that ultimately evolve into conventional literacy. What might be involved in making the transition from the informal literacy activities engaged in at home to a formal introduction to reading and writing? How might the literacy backgrounds of students differ? What difficulties might students encounter, especially those who are at risk because of poverty or other factors, as they enter into reading and writing programs? What might be done to alleviate these difficulties? What kinds of early intervention programs might be effective in helping students who otherwise might experience failure in their attempts to learn to read and write?

**USING WHAT YOU KNOW**

**ANTICIPATION GUIDE**

*Read each of the following statements. Put a check under "Agree" or "Disagree" to show how you feel about each one. If possible, discuss your responses with classmates.*

|  | AGREE | DISAGREE |
|---|---|---|
| 1. Children learn to read and write in much the same way as they learn to speak. | _____ | _____ |
| 2. Early interventions should not be started too soon, because some students may simply need more time to mature. | _____ | _____ |
| 3. For at-risk students, a structured emergent literacy program works best. | _____ | _____ |
| 4. Older students who are just learning to read and write may need to go through the same stages of learning to read and write as average kindergartners and first-graders do. | _____ | _____ |
| 5. A prevention program should be started in kindergarten or even preschool. | _____ | _____ |

## ▦ Emergent Literacy and Prevention Programs

Although **emergent literacy** recognizes that all students who come to school have some knowledge of and experience with reading and writing, that knowledge and experience can vary enormously. Some students will be able to write their names, recognize most of the letters of the alphabet, and perhaps read a few words. A few students, about 1 in 100, will be able to read on a level comparable to that of the average second- or third-grader. On the other end of the continuum, some will not be able to write their names or recognize any letters. A few will never have held a book or a pencil. In one study, 5-year-olds who came from impoverished backgrounds had approximately the same level of literacy development as 4-year-olds who came from enriched backgrounds. As Gillet and Temple (1994) comment:

> **Emergent literacy:** reading and writing concepts and behaviors of young children that develop into conventional reading and writing (Sulzby & Teale, 1991).

Four out of five children make a host of useful discoveries about print before and during kindergarten. From being read to, from reading back favorite storybooks, and from attempting to make messages with pencils, these children pick up a range of concepts about print that enable them to grow as readers and writers with the help of normal tutelage. One out of five children is not so fortunate, however. These children do not have their early print concepts in place when they begin first grade, and things do not go well for them. (p. 58)

## Prevention Programs

Children who end up in the one-out-of-five group would benefit from a program of prevention. One way of preventing reading problems is to develop children's language and preliteracy skills in the preschool. This does not mean that there should be formal instruction in reading. Reading aloud regularly, shared reading, setting up areas for dramatic play for reading and writing, creating a classroom library, developing oral-language skills, modeling reading and writing, and providing opportunities for children to write, draw, and explore language will naturally develop emergent literacy (Campbell, 1998). Low-income 4-year-olds showed encouraging gains when stories were read to them on a regular basis and the teacher engaged them in discussions in which they made predictions, reflected on the story, and talked about words (Dickinson & Smith, 1994). It is also helpful to develop phonological awareness skills, letter knowledge, and concepts of print. Since this instruction is designed for preschool students, the goal is exposure and awareness rather than mastery. Four excellent preschool programs are described in the following sections.

> ✳ Information about High Scope, one of the best-known of the preschool preventive programs, can be accessed at http://www.highscope.org. This Web site provides information about setting up a program using High Scope principles.

### High Scope

Designed for 3- to 5-year-olds, the High Scope preschool curriculum is built around teacher- and child-initiated learning activities in five content areas: approaches to learning; language, literacy, and communication; social and emotional development; physical development, health, and well-being; and arts and sciences.

### Opening the World of Learning (OWL)

Opening the World of Learning (OWL) emphasizes language development and background building. The program enriches the traditional read-aloud by providing suggestions for teacher talk and interactions that foster vocabulary building and related language development. Having language-building conversations

**EXEMPLARY TEACHING**

### Books for Preschool Children

In a project known as Books Aloud, 330 child care centers in poverty-stricken areas in and around Philadelphia were provided with libraries of five books per child (Neuman, 1999). The books became a focal point and impetus for a host of activities.

With attractive, high-quality books available, teachers began reading aloud to children and talking about books. They talked about how books are read and how to care for them. The children began examining books and "reading" them. Discussions of authors and stories ensued. Word games were introduced. Children began using story-type language, such as "Once upon a time." Library corners and writing centers were set up. The curriculum of the day care centers was expanded to include reading and writing and talking about books.

Children in the Books Aloud program, who were 3 or 4 years of age at the time, showed encouraging gains in a number of literacy measures. They also did better in kindergarten than children who attended control day care centers. Although some training was involved, the key change agent in the project was the presence of and access to books.

---

is emphasized throughout the program. The program's manual provides specific suggestions for holding conversations during mealtimes and transitions that are related to topics covered during the day. OWL has a comprehensive curriculum organized around thematic units: Family, Friends, Wind and Water, The World of Color, Shadows and Reflections, and Things That Grow.

### Literacy Express

Literacy Express is a preschool curriculum that revolves around 10 thematic units, covered in three to four weeks each. In addition to large-group activities, teachers use three small-group activities daily (dialogic reading, phonological awareness activities, and print knowledge activities) with groups of three to five children. Literacy Express obtained modest but positive effects for oral language (12 percentile points), print knowledge (15 percentile points), and phonological processing (12 percentile points) according to the What Works Clearinghouse (2010a). Although the gains were modest, they exceeded those of all other programs assessed by What Works Clearinghouse.

### Para Los Niños

 **Using Technology**

PALS PreK at the University of Virginia provides literacy assessment for preschool, available at https://pals.virginia.edu.

 **Using Technology**

Webbing into Literacy

http://curry.edschool.virginia.edu/go/wil/home.html

Is a downloadable program designed to provide Head Start teachers with materials and instruction that will foster language development, phonological awareness, alphabet knowledge, and concepts of print.

Designed for 4-year-old Spanish-speaking preschool children, the program included big books shared reading, writing and reading centers, and a take-home library and workshops for parents. The students outscored native speakers of English who had participated in other preschool programs despite the fact that the emergent literacy tests were administered in English (Yaden et al., 2001).

## Kindergarten Prevention Program

The foundation of a prevention program is to build an atmosphere that fosters emergent literacy as it builds self-regulation. Being developmental, emergent literacy is a natural outgrowth of learning oral language and is fostered in much the same way as oral language is fostered: through interaction with adults and peers. In the classroom this means providing a literacy-rich environment in addition to instruction.

**Literacy-rich classroom:** one in which children have many opportunities to read to themselves and each other and to write using invented and/or conventional spelling.

On the surface, a **literacy-rich classroom** is one in which the student is surrounded by the tools of literacy: books, signs, posters, labels, paper, envelopes, and writing instruments of every kind, including word processors and rubber stamps. On a deeper level, a literacy-rich environment is more than an impressive display of the artifacts of literacy; it is one in which "a thoughtful teacher capitalizes on opportunities to focus on . . . print and make children aware of its various functions in real contexts" (Learning Media, 1991, p. 55).

Because literacy is an outgrowth of oral language, language development should be the foundation of the program. Literacy activities should be accompanied by opportunities to discuss what, how, and why we read and write. Students should also share orally what they have read and written. Talking about an experience before writing about it, for instance, both develops oral language and fosters better writing.

## Benefits of Reading Aloud

✴ Reading aloud to students is a vital element in a literacy program for low-achieving readers. Because they are hampered in their ability to read, they are cut off from one source of developing language and background.

Reading aloud to a child builds a background of experience, vocabulary, syntax, and comprehension (Dickinson & Smith, 1994). It also builds an acquaintance with literary language and a sense of story so that students have a framework for understanding narratives. Discussing books that have been read aloud is also very valuable. Adults tend to use enriched language when discussing books with children, and children pick up this enriched language (Kaderavek & Sulzby, 1999).

Literally thousands of books are available for reading to students. The important thing is to read books that both you and the students enjoy. It is also a good idea to include informational books so that you build background as you build language. However, select books that will be understandable to the students. For fiction, you might start with simple narratives and work up to more complex selections. Let the students' responses be your guide. If they are interested in the text and can answer most of the questions that you ask, then you are probably on the right level. If they are restless and seem confused, try a simpler book. When reading informational texts, read about topics that students can comprehend and to which they can relate. Select books that introduce and explain new ideas or topics but without overwhelming students. As students' language and background develop, introduce more complex selections. Being introduced to more complex language patterns helps students to internalize these patterns (Kaderavak & Sulzby, 1999).

How a book is read has a bearing on how much students benefit. Students seem to benefit most when the book is given an introduction, read through without much interruption, and then discussed fairly thoroughly (Dickinson & Smith, 1994). An important component of the discussion is "child-involved analytical talk" (p. 117). Child-involved analytical talk includes analyzing characters or events, predicting events, making connections between events or characters in the story and events and people in the listeners' lives, talking about words and their meanings, summarizing portions of the story, evaluating the story, and clarifying comments students make about the story (Dickinson & Smith, 1994).

The greatest long-term need for most struggling readers is to develop vocabulary. Limited vocabulary is ultimately what constrains students' progress. Use Text Talk (as described on pages 356–357) to introduce two or three words to students. By systematically developing vocabulary from the very beginning, you will reduce

## Read-Aloud Lesson

### Before Reading

Read the title and display the cover, and encourage students to predict what the story might be about. Have them justify their predictions. Introduce any concepts that might hinder students' comprehension of the story. Have students listen to the story to compare their predictions with what actually happens.

### During Reading

Clarify any elements that might be confusing. Also check students' predictions, and when appropriate, encourage them to make new predictions. However, emphasize the story itself. Do not allow long discussions to interrupt the flow of the story. Also very briefly define or explain any words that children might not know and which are needed for an understanding of the selection.

### After Reading

Discuss students' predictions. Have them compare their predictions to what actually happened in the story. Discuss events in the story and characters. Have students justify and explain their responses so that they are analyzing the text and the language of the story. For instance, after reading *Anansi Goes Fishing* (Kimmel, 1992) and after discussing the main events of the story, ask why Anansi went to the justice tree. Also ask why the tree is called a "justice tree" and why the judge didn't believe Anansi. Discuss why Anansi didn't speak to Turtle for a long time. Talk over, too, the good that came out of the story and the meanings of some of the difficult words: *disgrace, justice, judge,* and *warthog*. Also have students relate characters and events to their own lives.

the gap that exists between the number of words known by struggling learners versus high-achieving students.

The above read-aloud lesson incorporates the principles just discussed, which lead to increased development of vocabulary, overall language, and comprehension.

**Dialogic reading:** a way of reading aloud in which the student or students being read to become active participants by responding to prompts to say something about the selection and to elaborate on their responses.

## Dialogic Reading

**Dialogic reading** is a form of reading aloud in which the questioning and prompts are used with a small group to develop deeper understanding (Doyle & Bramwell, 2006). Questions are asked on three levels: literal questions, open-ended questions, and connection questions in which the children relate events in the story to another story or an experience in their lives. Vocabulary is also developed through discussion of key ideas in a selection. For instance, a classroom discussion in one dialogic reading session became an extended discussion of why the character in the story was feeling frustrated (a new vocabulary word), about times in which the children had felt frustrated, and about some things they might do when they feel frustrated. Through this and similar discussions, dialogic reading is used to develop social and emotional skills as students read about and discuss challenging situations. Here is an example of dialogic reading used with a storybook about a fish.

Before reading the book, the teacher asks children to point to the title and make predictions about what might happen. This helps children anticipate what's to come and establish a personal incentive to see what happens—to see if their predictions come to pass.

During book reading, the teacher gives explanations, prompts comments, and poses questions to gauge how well students are following and understanding the story. The teacher might ask, "What could Fish do to make friends?" As students share their ideas, the teacher turns their attention back to the story to show how Fish tries to solve the problem. As she does, the teacher also builds print awareness by tracking with her finger to show that text is read from top to bottom and left to right.

After reading the book, the teacher discusses it with the children, often drawing connections between events in the story and their everyday lives. For example, she might ask, "How did Fish feel about losing his scales? Have you lost something you loved? How did you feel?" This final level of reflection helps children see reading as a gateway to understanding their own world, helping them establish a personal connection to literacy (What Works Clearinghouse, 2007).

Dialogical reading uses two key techniques: PEER sequence and CROWD prompts. The PEER sequence consists of the following steps:

**P**arent or teacher prompts the child to talk about something on the page being discussed.

**E**valuate the children's response so you can build on the response.

**E**xpand the child's response by prompting the child to say more or explain his or her response.

**R**epeat the prompt or gist of the response to check that the child has learned by explaining or expanding his or her response (Whitehurst, 2012).

For example, using PEER with *Bugs Are Insects* (Rockwell, 2001), the teacher draws students' attention to pages 6–7 and asks: "What do you see on this page?" (prompt). Child: "Bugs." "Yes, these are bugs." (evaluation). "Another name for bugs is insects." (expansion). "How many legs do these insects have? Let's count them." (prompt). Child: "Six." "Yes, insects have six legs." (repeat gist). PEER sequences need not occur on each page, but might occur five or six times or more in a book. PEER sequences are omitted during the first reading.

CROWD prompts consists of questions designed to develop a fuller discussion. The CROWD prompts are as follows:

**C**ompletion questions. The child supplies a word or phrase or repeated line to complete a sentence or line from the text: "Brown Bear, Brown Bear, _____?" (Child supplies repeated line, "What do you see?")

**R**ecall questions. Ask child to provide details from the selection (*The Mitten* by Jan Brett): What color were the mittens? These prompts often begin with *what, where, when.*

**O**pen-ended questions. These increase the amount of talk about a book. "Tell me what's happening on this page. What are the animals doing? Why do you think the animals are crawling into the mitten? What makes you think that the woods had lots of animals? Which of the animals in the story might be able to sleep in a mitten? Could this story happen in real life?" These prompts often begin with, *why* and *how.*

**"W**h" questions. These *what, where, when, why,* and *how* questions are also used to develop vocabulary. The questions might pose inquiries about the story's illustrations. "What is the name of the animal in this picture? Can you point to the owl's talons?" "In the story it says, 'When he (the big owl) decided to move in also, the mole, the rabbit, and the hedgehog grumbled.' How do you think the animals felt when the owl moved in? What were the animals doing when they grumbled? Do you thinking they were laughing, singing, or complaining?"

**D**istancing questions. These questions help the child bridge the material in the book to their real-life experiences. "Have you ever lost something, like a pair of mittens, or a hat or toy but then found it? How did you feel?"

Dialogic reading is an essential part of Literacy Express (a research-based preschool program for 3- to 5-year-olds). Guidance is provided in the program for conducting dialogic reading with 60 children's books.

## Fostering Emergent Literacy

Within the context of holistic reading and writing activities and being read to, students grow in literacy. Although many children may develop literacy naturally, with a minimum of instruction, low-achieving readers and at-risk students need direct instruction in addition to numerous opportunities to engage in reading and writing. Areas in which direct instruction are especially important are concepts about print, phonological awareness, letter knowledge, and knowledge of beginning consonant correspondences.

## Concepts about Print

Even though they may have been in school for a while and have had experience with reading and writing in their homes, low-achieving readers may not have acquired essential **concepts about print**. These include the following:

> **Concepts about print:** basic understanding about written language—printed words represent spoken words, are composed of letters that represent sounds, are read from left to right, and so on.

### Book-Orientation Concepts

- Locating the front and back of a book
- Recognizing the functions of the cover and title page
- Recognizing the functions of print and pictures

### Print-Direction Concepts

- Reading from left to right
- Reading from top to bottom

### Print Concepts

- Understanding that words can be written down and read
- Recognizing a letter, a word, and a sentence
- Understanding that printed words are composed of letters
- Understanding that words are composed of sounds
- Understanding that letters represent sounds
- Being able to point to separate words in print and match these with words that are being read by oneself or another
- Understanding the difference between uppercase and lowercase letters
- Understanding the functions of punctuation marks

Above all, students should understand that reading is a meaningful act. Reading is not primarily a task involving translating letters into sounds but is mainly a matter of constructing understanding.

Some of the print concepts are interdependent. For instance, students' concept of words and their ability to form letter–sound relationships are apparently related. One device students use to follow a line of print is the use of initial consonants. In fact, being able to segment and pronounce or spell initial consonants seems to be a prerequisite for following a line of print by pointing to each word with one's finger (Morris, 1992). Knowing initial consonants apparently helps students locate the beginnings of words. Being able to finger-point, in turn, seems to contribute to further development of letter–sound relationships. Once students are able to detect individual words, they are then able to note the functions of final and later medial letters.

## Informal Assessment of Concepts of Print

To assess a student's concepts about print informally, give him a copy of *Brown Bear, Brown Bear, What Do You See?* by Bill Martin (1983), or a similar book. Ask questions to probe the student's knowledge of print conventions: "Have you ever seen this book? What do you think this book might be about? How can you tell what a book is about? What do you do with a book?" Open to a page that has an illustration and text, say "I'm going to read this page to you. Where should I start reading?" (Lipson & Wixson, 1997). "Point to the first thing I should read. [Note whether the child points to print or an illustration and whether the child points to the first word.] Now I'm going to start reading. Point to each word as I read it." [Read two facing pages of text slowly. Note whether the child can point to each word as you read it. Note, too, whether the child goes from left to right, makes a return sweep, and goes from top to bottom and from the left page to the right page.] Pointing to a line of print, ask "How many words are in this line?" Pointing to a word, ask "How many letters are in this word? Can you read any of the words?" After assessing the child's knowledge of print, note his overall level of development, and fill in the Concepts about Reading section of the Observation Guide presented in Figure 7.1.

## Writing Sample

As part of your assessment of a child's emergent literacy, ask her to write her name. If the child seems hesitant, encourage her to write it as best she can. If she can write her name, then ask her to write any additional words that she knows. Also ask the child to write a story. Ask her to write a story telling about games that she likes to play or other things that she likes to do. Encourage her to write as best she can or to write the way she usually does. (Accept drawing, scribbling, letter-like symbols, and other forms of written expression.) Note the child's overall level of development. With this information, complete the Writing section of the Observation Guide.

In addition to observing the child's performance on the structured reading and writing observations, note whether she understands the functions of reading and writing. As you observe, ask: Does the child enjoy listening to stories? Is she able to retell a story? Does she enjoy browsing through books? Does she attempt to read or retell a story from a book? Does she attempt to write? Does she write for a variety of purposes: to tell a story, to send a message, to make a list? For additional suggestions for assessing young students, see Marie Clay's *An Observation Survey of Early Literacy Achievement* (2006) or PALS-PreK or PALS-K (http://pals.virginia.edu).

When assessing young children, it is essential that you consider their opportunity to learn. As Meisel (1998) cautions:

> Not only do children—especially young children—acquire skills at different rates and in different ways, children are also exquisitely sensitive to opportunity to learn. If a child has . . . not been exposed to opportunities to acquire these skills, then that information will not be available to the child. (pp. 16–17)

With young children, try dynamic assessment. If students are unable to name letters of the alphabet or identify rhyming words, for instance, teach them these skills and note how readily and under what circumstances they learn these skills. If they do not learn these skills, determine what seems to be hindering their learning.

**FIGURE 7.1**

Emergent Literacy
Observation Guide

Student's Name _____ Age _____

Date _____ Native Language _____

Put a check (✓) in the blank if satisfactory, a minus (−) if a need exists in that area, and a plus (+) if advanced. Comments may also be written on the blanks.

*Oral Language*

Can express self clearly _____

Asks questions when necessary _____

Uses a vocabulary appropriate for age _____

Uses sentence structure appropriate for age _____

Listens to and understands stories _____

Can retell a story _____

Can follow oral directions _____

Can converse effectively with peers _____

Can converse effectively with teacher _____

*Concepts about Reading*

Understands the main purpose of print _____

Recognizes environmental print _____

Can name the letters of the alphabet _____

Can point to each word as a line of print is read _____

Can detect individual sounds in words _____

Can detect rhyme _____

Can detect beginning sounds _____

Can read own name _____

Recognizes some words in print _____

*Interest in Reading*

Responds to being read to _____

Shows an interest in books _____

Pretends to read books _____

Attempts to read books _____

Asks questions about words, letters, or pictures
   in books _____

*Writing*

Understands the functions of writing _____

Writes or draws stories, letters, or lists _____

Uses invented spelling _____

Uses writing to communicate _____

Can write name _____

*Attitude and Work Habits*

Wants to learn to read and write _____

Can work independently _____

Is able to sustain attention _____

Can work with others _____

Is willing to experiment and risk making mistakes _____

Has confidence in own ability _____

## ▓▓ Developing Literacy Concepts

Literacy concepts are best developed through an immersion in reading and writing activities. As you read books to children, point out the cover, the front of the book, the title, and the author's name. Discuss illustrations as you read. As you write messages or lists of names or schedules on the board, reinforce appropriate literacy concepts. Display and discuss signs, labels, notes, letters, announcements, and students' writing. Also use techniques such as shared reading.

### Shared Reading

> **Shared reading:** technique in which the teacher reads aloud from a big book or other enlarged text and students follow along. It is used to introduce concepts of print and high-frequency words.

In a **shared reading**, you read an enlarged text as students follow along. In subsequent rereadings of the text, students join in the reading. In order to engage productively in shared reading, students should have some knowledge of initial consonant correspondences. Enlarged text may take the form of commercially produced big books, big books that you create yourself, poems or songs written on the board, or experience stories written on large sheets of paper or on the board. Because the text is enlarged, the class can follow along as you read a selection.

This procedure can be used to introduce or reinforce nearly any skill or understanding in early reading, from the concept of moving from left to right to the reading of words, phrases, and sentences. Just as with oral reading, it is essential that you select big books that are on students' conceptual level and that engage them. Start

### Shared Reading Lesson

*Step 1: Preparing to read the selection.* Prepare students for a shared reading by discussing the cover illustration and the title and, if you wish, some illustrations from the text. Based on a discussion of the cover (and text illustrations) and the title, have them predict what the selection might be about. (If the book is informational, have students predict what the author might tell them.) Set a purpose for reading. If the students have made a prediction, the purpose might be to compare their predictions to what actually happened in the text.

*Step 2: Reading the selection.* As you read the selection, run your hand under it, pointing to each word as you say it so students get the idea of going from left to right and that there is a one-to-one match between the spoken and the printed word. Stop and clarify difficult words and concepts. Discuss interesting parts and have students evaluate their predictions, revising them if they see fit.

*Step 3: Discussing the selection.* After students have followed along as you read the selection, discuss it with them. Begin by talking about their

predictions. Also try to relate the selection to experiences that students may have had. Try to elicit responses to the characters and situations portrayed, asking such questions as "Do you know anyone like the main character? Has anything like this ever happened to you?"

*Step 4: Rereading the selection.* During a second reading of the text, point out and discuss words, letters, punctuation marks, and other elements of print. During this second reading, encourage students to join in and read parts that they can handle. This may be a repeated word or phrase or a whole sentence. If the book is a popular one, schedule several rereadings. Each time, the students should take more responsibility for the reading.

*Step 5: Extending the lesson.* As a follow-up, students may want to listen to recorded versions of the big book, or read regular-size versions to a partner. Depending on the student's development, this may be a pretend reading, a retelling based on pictures, or a genuine reading.

off with big books that contain familiar rhymes or stories and that have just one line of print per page.

## Concept of Separate Words

One of the most essential print concepts for students to learn is that each printed word represents one separate spoken word. One way of developing a concept of separate words is through voice pointing. Beginning readers often memorize stories that have been read to them over and over again or use the illustrations in highly predictable books to "read" a text. Although these readers seem to be reading the words on the page, actually they are reciting a memorized story or constructing a story based on the picture. This is especially true of students who are experiencing difficulty learning to read.

✳ See Scaffolded Writing on p. 196 for added suggestions for developing concept of word.

To convey the concept of separate words and to teach children to begin to take note of the details of individual words, point to each word as the class share-reads a story and encourage the children to look at each word as you point to it. When you come to a repeated line of text, such as "Are you my mother?" slow down the pace, very deliberately point to each word, and make sure that the students say the word as you point to it. Have a volunteer read the repeated sentences, pointing to each word as he does so.

The concept of word is facilitated by awareness of beginning sounds. Using beginning sounds, students can mark the beginning of a word and use that as an anchor point. Once students have a concept of word and can follow along as a book is being read, they are better able to pick up additional letter–sound knowledge. Because they are able to follow along in shared reading, they begin to match sound with letter, and they learn whole words and additional letter–sound relationships. The process is aided if the teacher points to words in the big book and if the teacher reads big books that contain just one line of print so that students are better able to match spoken and printed words (Morris, Bloodgood, Lomax, & Perney, 2003).

As individual students are reading a predictable book with you, occasionally have them point to each word as they read it. Also request finger-pointing whenever you feel that a student is reciting a memorized sentence rather than really reading it. Besides helping to build a concept of separate words in a sentence, doing so helps students notice the details of printed words and to learn some printed words incidentally. After all, if students are not looking at words as they read on their own or through shared reading or are not looking at the right words, then they will not learn anything about the makeup of the words.

*Focused Shared Reading*   Although typical shared reading lessons benefit everyone, the benefit can be intensified for struggling readers if the students are grouped by their level of proficiency so that the shared readings can be geared to their needs (Koskinen et al., 1999). In focused shared reading, the teacher selects a book for struggling readers that would best fit in with the needs she has observed. For students who are still learning initial consonants, the teacher might pick a very simple book, one that contains a number of repetitions of the target consonant. The teacher provides an overview of the text and asks students to predict what the selection will tell if it is nonfiction or what will happen if it is fiction. The teacher then does a "text walk" or "picture walk," in which she gives the gist of the story and reviews difficult words or expressions that might occur or any other elements that might pose problems. The teacher then reads the book aloud, pointing to the words she is reading. The book is then share-read. The book is made available for students to reread during the day and/or take home and read.

## Students' Writing

To further foster the development of literacy concepts, encourage students to write. In the past, children were discouraged from writing, except for copying, until they had been taught how to form letters of the alphabet and were taught how to spell some words. As a result, their writing was limited to words that they could spell and whose letters they could form. The current conception is that writing is a developmental ability that has its roots in language, starts with scribbling, and evolves into drawing and ever more complex representations, including the use of random letters, invented spelling, and eventually conventional spelling (Calkins, 1994; Temple et al., 1993).

### Scaffolded Writing

Scaffolded writing helps children develop the concept of word. Until children know where a word begins and ends, they will have difficulty learning and applying phonics skills and high-frequency words.

In scaffolded writing the student initially dictates her message to the teacher. To help convey the concept of word, the teacher draws a line for each word the student says (Bodrova & Leong, 2007; Bodrova, Leong, Gregory, & Edgerton, 1999). The student then repeats the message and points to a line as she says the word that the line represents. Next, the student writes each word on the line or as much of each word as she can. As the student develops the concept of word, she draws the line herself and then writes the word on the line. Saying the word while drawing the line provides practice in delineating separate words. Because the line reminds the student of the word, she is able to repeat the word over and over, which helps her to focus on representing the sounds of the words. Once students have internalized the concept of word, they can compose sentences without first using lines. Here is an example of a teacher implementing scaffolded writing:

- The child draws a picture and makes up a story about the picture.
- The teacher says, "We are going to draw lines with the highlighter to help you remember what you want to write. We will plan your story one sentence at a time. Tell me what you want to write."
- The student provides the first sentence: "We got a new puppy."
- The teacher says, "You want to write. 'We got a new puppy.'"
- The teacher writes the lines, saying a word as each line is drawn.
- The teacher has the student say the word represented by each line: "Let's go back over our plan [pointing to the lines]. You said you wanted to write, 'We got a new puppy.'" The student points to the lines and says the words represented by the lines.
- The teacher hands the paper with the lines to the student and says, "Now that you can remember what you want to write, go ahead and write it out on the lines. Say each word as you write it on the line to yourself. If you can't remember the word, go back to the beginning of the message and say the sentence aloud again." (Bodrova & Leong, 1998, pp. 8–9)

## Shadow Writing

Struggling students are often reluctant to attempt to write. In addition to using scaffolded writing to boost their confidence, you might try shadow writing. In shadow writing, the student dictates a label or sentence for a drawing. You write the student's dictation in yellow highlighter. The student then traces the letters. Have the child say the word before tracing it, the letters as he traces them, and the word after he traces it. This reinforces letter formation, the concept of word, and, to a lesser extent, letter–sound relationships. As Chadwell (2002b) notes, "The child [does] the thinking and the writing" (p. 2).

As they progress, children create or invent a system of representing sounds that, in the early stages, might use a letter or two to represent a whole word, such

> **Invented spelling:** intuitive spellings that students create before being introduced to conventional spelling, or as they are learning to spell. Invented spelling is sometimes referred to as "developmental" or "transitional" spelling.

as *lion* (which might be spelled *LN*), but that becomes increasingly accurate. Through **invented spelling**, children explore the nature of the spelling system and advance in their ability to spell and to decode printed words. (See pp. 148–152 for additional information about the stages of spelling.)

Daily writing activities in which invented spelling is encouraged foster development in both reading and writing. Initially, the writing activities might start with drawing a picture and then writing a story about the picture. Other writing activities include describing trips and memorable events, writing pieces telling about themselves and others, composing lists, writing notes and letters, creating fictional pieces, and keeping a journal.

Unfortunately, many low-achieving readers have had negative experiences with writing and may be extremely reluctant to write. Having had their erroneous spelling corrected on many occasions, they may also be unwilling to try invented spelling. Part of fostering a willingness to write is the approach that one takes. Sulzby and Barnhart (1992) suggest incorporating three elements in your approach. First, accept whatever form of writing children choose to use, whether this be drawing or scribbling or using random letters. Second, make your request simple. Say "Write a story" or "Write a letter to your mother." Third, be reassuring. Say "It doesn't have to be like grown-up writing. Just do it your own way" (p. 126). You might even model some of the forms of writing that novice writers choose.

After a student has written her piece, have her read it back. If the writing is not decipherable, some teachers choose to write a translation beneath the child's writing so they have it for later reference. As the student reads her piece, note how she reads it. If the student is reading a story, does it sound like storybook reading? Does a friendly letter sound and look different from a story? As the student reads, does she attend to the symbols that she wrote? How close is the match between the symbols that the student wrote and the reading? Whether children use drawings, squiggles, or letters to write, the emphasis should be on using these representations to create meaning (Calkins, 2003a).

In general, students should be encouraged to write every day. One good way to start is to have them draw a picture and then write a story about it. The picture actually helps them to encapsulate their thoughts so they can better structure what they want to write.

Foster a variety of writing activities: stories, letters, lists, signs, advertisements, and announcements. Strike a balance between providing topics or story starters and having children choose what they want to write about. Also strike a balance between the writing children generate on their own and dictated pieces that are created through a language-experience approach.

## Language-Experience Approach

**Language-experience approach:** a single student or group dictates a story, which is scribed by the teacher and then used to teach reading and writing.

In a **language-experience approach**, students discuss an experience that they have had, such as a trip to a farm, getting a new classroom pet, the arrival of a baby brother, and so forth, and then dictate a story about the experience. Through careful questioning, the teacher may structure the story, but the language of the piece should be the student's own. The story can be one that is created by the group or one that a student dictates to the teacher or an aide. After the story has been written, the teacher reads it back as the student follows along. The student is invited to make any changes that he wishes. After changes have been made, the teacher reads the story, and the student joins in, just as in a shared reading lesson.

Because they incorporate their own experiences and their own language, many low-achieving readers and students learning to speak English find language-experience stories easier to read than texts composed by others. Another advantage of the language-experience approach is that it can be used with students of all ages and is an excellent method of instructing older novice readers. A sample language-experience story is presented in Figure 7.2.

Use conventional spelling when scribing a student piece. To avoid confusion between your mature writing and students' emerging form, you might explain that you use grown-up writing when you write down their stories and that someday they will use grown-up writing, too. But it's okay for them to write the way other students do.

## Shared Writing

**Shared writing:** differs from language experience because both the teacher and the student share in composing the piece. In interactive shared writing, students do some of the physical writing of the story.

Modeled on shared reading, **shared writing** is a collaborative process in which both teacher and students take part in composing, scribing, and reading a piece of writing (Pinnell & McCarrier, 1994). Just as in traditional language experience, the class writes about experiences they have had or books that have been read to them. Often a shared reading of a favorite book forms the basis for the class's writing. If the class's writing is to be based on a story, the story is read several times so that students have a firm grasp of the plot or content and are familiar with the language of the story.

A story-based piece of writing can take a number of forms. After hearing "Goldilocks and the Three Bears," one class created a labeled drawing of the interior of the three bears' home. Another class, after hearing a version of Tolstoy's *The Enormous Turnip*, summarized it by creating a mural in which each character had a completed speech bubble.

Whatever form the written piece takes, students play an active role in deciding the content. For instance, in creating the mural for *The Turnip* (Domanska, 1969),

■■ **FIGURE 7.2**
Language-
Experience Story

*Hermit Crabs*
*Hermit crabs are sneaky.*
*They do not have homes of their own.*
*They steal shells from snails.*
*Then they make their homes in the shells.*

each student drew one of the characters in the tale and, in a conversation bubble drawn by the teacher, decided what the character would say. One student decided that his character would say "One, two, three, pull" (Pinnell & McCarrier, 1994).

In addition to suggesting content, students also participate in the writing. In a form of shared writing known as shared interactive writing, the teacher encourages students to scribe initial consonants, parts of words, or even whole words. One strategy that these novice writers are encouraged to use is knowledge of the spellings of their names. For instance, Tiffany was able to supply the first letter of *turnip* because *turnip* begins like *Tiffany,* and Paul was able to supply the first letter of *pull.* The students' names are placed on the wall in alphabetical order so these can be used to help with the spelling of words. The teacher also uses prompts to call students' attention to the number of words in the sentence and to reinforce the concept of separate words and other print concepts. Some prompts that might be used include the following (Pinnell & Fountas, 1998):

- How many words are there in our sentence?
- Can you clap as I say each word?
- What is the first word that we want to write?
- Say the word slowly. What sounds do you hear?
- What sound do you hear at the beginning of the word?
- Whose name begins like that word?
- What letter stands for that sound?
- Can you write the letter that stands for that sound?

Here is sample dialogue to show how shared writing might be implemented. It is based on work by Martin (1995). After reading *All I Am* (Roe, 1990), students discuss things they can do. The class decides to compose a shared story telling what they can do:

**Robert:** I can sing.

**Teacher:** How shall we write that in our story?

**Tanya:** Robert can sing.

**Teacher:** (pointing to spot on board) Robert, will you write your name here?

**Teacher:** (pointing to and reading "Robert") What goes next?

**James:** *Can.*

**Teacher:** How does *can* begin? Who has a name that begins like *can*?

**Carmelita:** I do.

**Teacher:** How does your name begin?

**Carmelita:** With a *c.* My name begins with a *c.*

**Teacher:** Can you write a *c* here? (Judging that the class does not know the sound of the short *a,* she adds an *a* and reads /ca/.) What do we need to add to /ca/ to make *can*?

**Class:** *N.*

**Teacher:** Who can add an *n*?

**Nina:** I can.

**Teacher:** (after *n* has been added, reads while pointing to each word as she says it) Robert can. What can Robert do?

**Class:** Sing.

**Teacher:** How does *sing* begin? Whose name begins like *sing*? (Getting no response) How about *Sandra*? Does *sing* begin like *Sandra*?

**Teacher:** Sandra, can you make an *s* here?

**Teacher:** (Adds *ing* to *s* and reads) *Sing.* Robert can sing. Is this right? Is this what we wanted to write?

The scaffolding and explanations that the teacher offers are geared to the students' level of understanding. Skills and understandings that students are currently working on are the concepts of word and beginning sounds. Later, the teacher might focus on ending sounds and then medial sounds or high-frequency words. Stories are posted, and students are encouraged to read them from time to time. As a reference, all of the students' first names are listed in alphabetical order on a chart that is displayed prominently. Also listed are color words and other words that the class has studied. An alphabet strip is also available in case students forget how to form a letter. As students learn high-frequency words such as *the,* these are listed on the class's word wall.

## Individual Interactive Writing

In addition to its use with groups or whole classes, shared interactive writing can be implemented with individual students (Roser, 2011). Using it with individual students enables teachers to obtain a more complete picture of each child's literacy development and is especially helpful when working with struggling learners. The lessons are especially effective because they build on a student's abilities and focus on specific needs. Using a technique adapted from Ashton-Warner's (1963) organic approach, teachers invite students to dictate stories that are based on a particular word. Whereas Ashton-Warner asked students what word they would like to learn, in this approach the teacher asks, "What word is in your mind?" After saying what their word is, students are asked to tell about the word. A student who says *deer* is then asked to tell about the word and might say, "I saw a deer." Sharing the pen, the student might write "I" and, when prompted, write the *s* in *saw*. The teacher finishes the writing of *saw*, prompts the writing of *a* and initial *d* and then writes *eer* to complete the word *deer*.

Other prompts to initiate shared interactive writing include: "What do you want to write about today?" "What do you want to say?" For students who need extra support, the teacher might say, "Make a mark on the paper. Tell me about that mark." As the teacher, you might demonstrate how you decide what you want to write about and how you go about writing. This demonstration helps students get their thoughts down on paper. It is more effective than simply inviting them to write (Gunning, 2013).

 **Using Technology**

Use electronic devices such as VTech's Follow Me Writer or Leapfrog's Scribble and Write in which lighted figures and letters guide students as they form letters and numbers.

## Handwriting

Even though they may have been in school for several years, low-achieving readers may not have learned how to form correctly all of the letters of the alphabet. As they explore writing, students will naturally learn some aspects of letter formation. Displaying a large model alphabet and individual alphabet cards will help. However, these students should also receive direct instruction. (See Chapter 13 for suggestions for teaching handwriting to older students whose handwriting skills are deficient.)

## ▓▓ Phonological Processes and Reading

Reading demands that students be able to deal with the structure of language in an abstract way. For instance, students must be able to abstract the beginning sounds of words before they can learn that *b* represents the sound /b/, as in the beginning of *ball*. In conversation, students are not aware that words have separate sounds. They may not even have a concept of what a word is or may not be able to tell how many words are in a sentence. "What did you say?" may seem like a single speech event to them: "Whatyasay?" Without being able to detect the separate words in a sentence, students will not be able to match printed words with their spoken equivalents.

Clay (1991) found that a large percentage of 6-year-olds who were having difficulty learning to read could not detect the separate sounds in words. What makes detecting the sounds of a word like *sun* or *cat* so difficult? First of all, speech sounds are not articulated separately. "Spoken language is seamless. There are no breaks in speech signaling where one phoneme ends and the next begins" (National Reading Panel, 2000, Sec. 2, p. 11). For instance, the word *hat* is not articulated /h/-/a/-/t/, nor is it perceived as three sounds. The word *hat* is spoken as one continuous flow of sound. Its sounds are formed and perceived more or less simultaneously. Because of a speech phenomenon known as coarticulation, the lips form /h/ and at the same time the tongue articulates an /a/ and glides into a /t/. The /h/, /a/, and /t/ overlap and form a single pulse of sound (Liberman & Mattingly, 1989). This is an advantage for the listener. It speeds the perception of speech. However, coarticulation makes detecting individual sounds difficult.

> **Metalinguistic ability:** the ability to think of language as an object itself—to think of words as words and speech sounds as speech sounds.

In addition, phonological awareness requires dealing with language on an abstract or metalinguistic level. **Metalinguistic ability** requires that the child deal with the form as well as the content of language. Metalinguistic skills go beyond using language and involve playing with language, thinking and talking about language, and making judgments about the correctness of language. Children begin to show some evidence of metalinguistic awareness at the age of 3 (Snow et al., 1998). However, this ability develops slowly and continues into the school years. For a time, children have difficulty considering words apart from their meanings. For instance, when asked to tell which word is longer, *snake* or *caterpillar*, many children will respond that *snake* is longer because they are thinking of the creature named by the word, not the word itself. When they are asked to segment sentences into words, young children tend to supply meaningful phrases rather than individual words: *The little boy/has a red wagon.*

Metalinguistic awareness requires a certain degree of cognitive development. Speaking of tasks that require the manipulation of beginning sounds, Harris and Sipay (1990) note that "the ability to abstract a beginning sound from a spoken word and compare it with the beginning sound of another word is a cognitive ability that many five- and six-year-olds have not yet developed. In Piaget's terms, it requires 'decentration' " (p. 42).

> **Decentration:** cognitive operation in which a child has the ability to consider two or more aspects of an object or event at the same time.

**Decentration**, a hallmark of the stage of concrete operations, means that a child must be able to consider two aspects of a situation at that same time. In language, the child must realize that *cat* represents an animal and is a word composed of sounds. Watson (1984) posits a decentration lag for those who have difficulty noting sounds in words. Some students who perform normally on general language measures are slow to develop decentration ability, which in turn slows down development of phonemic awareness, which in turn blocks progress in reading. These students would need additional experience with phonemic awareness activities.

> ✳ Phonemic awareness goes beyond merely noting separate sounds in words. It requires mentally holding onto and manipulating sounds in words (Gentry & Gillet, 1993).

> **The onset:** is a word's initial consonant or consonant combination.

> **The rime** is the rhyming part of a word, the part that begins with a vowel (*-et, -oat*).

Phonological awareness develops from larger to smaller units. Students begin by detecting separate words in short sentences and then segment compound words into individual words and words into individual sounds or phonemes (*h* + *a* + *t*). Segmenting a word into individual sounds is a struggle for many kindergarten children (Liberman, Shankweiler, Fischer, & Carter, 1974; Yopp, 1995). Even among 6-year-olds, one child in six had difficulty segmenting a word into its individual phonemes (Sawyer, 1987). The other key phonological awareness task is blending, in which students are required to synthesize a series of speech sounds into words. Students blend individual words into compound words, then blend **onsets** and **rimes** (*m* + *an* = *man*), and then the individual sounds in a word.

Blending is easier than segmenting, and detecting sounds is easier than segmenting sounds. It is easier to detect that *ball* and *bat* begin with the same sound than it is to segment the sounds in *ball* and *bat*. A reasonable sequence for developing phonological awareness is to segment sentences into words, segment compound words, segment words into syllables, blend compounds, blend syllables, blend onsets and rimes, blend phonemes, detect beginning sounds, detect ending sounds, and segment words into phonemes.

> ✳ Perhaps because they are dealing with the beginning of words, ELLs may find detecting beginning sounds easier than detecting rhyme.

Most phonological awareness programs develop students' ability to detect rhyme. In years past, it was believed that rhyming was the easiest of the phonological awareness tasks. However, Gough, Larson, and Yopp (2001) found that some students were better able to identify words that begin with the same sound than to supply a rhyming word. In addition, research has indicated that tasks such as segmenting and identifying initial sounds are more effective for building phonological awareness than rhyming. Rhyming is an important concept in its own rite and should be developed. However, the focus should be on segmenting and blending.

## Phonological Awareness and English Language Learners

> ✳ See Yopp and Stapleton (2008) for a discussion of developing the phonemic awareness of Spanish-speaking students.

Students who are learning English as a second language do best if they learn phonemic awareness in their own language. These skills transfer. However, difficulties arise when English language learners (ELLs) are taught phonemic awareness in English. There will be a number of sounds in English that are not present in the students' native languages. They may be asked to detect sounds that are foreign to them.

When teaching phonemic awareness to ELLs, focus on sounds that are the same in both languages. For instance, there is no long *e* in Spanish but there is a long *o*, so start with the long-*o* sound. Table 7.1 compares sounds in English and Spanish.

## Assessing Phonological Awareness

Key skills to be assessed for initial reading are beginning sounds, blending, and segmentation. However, rhyming might also be assessed.

**TABLE 7.1**
Comparison of Speech Sounds in Spanish and English

*English Vowel Sounds Not Present in Spanish*

Short *a*: cat

Short *i*: wish

Short *u*: cup

Short double *o*: book

Schwa: sofa

*English Consonant Sounds Not Present in Spanish*

/j/: jump

/v/: vase

/z/: zipper

/sh/: shoe

/ŋ/: sing

*Possible Confusions*

/b/ pronounced /p/: *cab* becomes *cap*

/j/ pronounced /y/: *jet* becomes *yet*

/ŋ/ pronounced /n/: *sing* becomes *sin*

/ch/ pronounced /sh/: *choose* becomes *shoes*

/v/ pronounced /b/: *vote* becomes *boat*

/y/ pronounced /j/: *yet* becomes *jet*

/sk/, /sp/, /st/ pronounced as /esk/, /esp/, /est/

/i/ pronounced /ē/: *sit* becomes *seat*

/ē/ pronounced /i/: *seal* becomes *sill*

/u/ pronounced /o/: *cut* becomes *cot*

/oo/ pronounced /ōō/: *look* becomes *Luke*

*Source:* Adapted from C. A. O'Brien (1973). *Teaching the Language-Different Child to Read.* Columbus, OH, Merrill.

## Rhyming

Rhyming can be assessed informally by having students match picture cards of items whose names rhyme. For instance, give student three cards, two of which rhyme: *cake, snake,* and *dog.* Have students tell which two pictures have names that rhyme. Do several examples so that students understand the directions. Also be sure to name the pictures so that students do not misinterpret a picture of a snake for a worm, for instance. Supplying rhyming words—"Tell me a word that rhymes with *hat*"—is a more difficult task than identifying words that rhyme. Some students who can tell which words rhyme will not be able to supply rhyming words.

> ⚡ Asking students to supply a rhyming word or beginning sound is more difficult than asking whether two words rhyme or begin with the same sound. Students might be able to detect rhyme and beginning sounds but might not be able to supply a rhyming or alliterative word.

## Beginning Sounds

Beginning sounds can be assessed by having students match pictures whose names begin with the same sound. After being shown and naming a picture of the sun, students choose from two or three pictures the one that begins like *sun.* Or students can simply say the beginning sound of spoken or pictured words. Showing a picture of the sun, you would say, "What is the first sound in the word *sun?*" However, because it requires isolating or segmenting the sound, saying a beginning sound is more difficult than matching beginning sounds.

If students are unable to perceive most of the beginning sounds, it may be because they have little experience with beginning sounds or find the terminology unfamiliar. You might further probe low scores in this area by teaching beginning sounds to low-scoring youngsters and noting how they respond to instruction.

***Blending***    Blending consists of combining separate syllables (*foot + ball*), onset and rime (*f-oot*), or separate sounds (*f+oo+t*) to form a word. Blending is usually easier than segmenting. It is easier to blend /f/-/oo/-/t/ to form *foot* than it is to segment *foot* as /f/-/oo/-/t/. Blending is assessed by saying words in parts and having the student say what the word is. Students can be asked to blend syllables, onsets and rimes, or individual phonemes. To assess the ability to blend individual phonemes, begin with two-phoneme words (*boy, pie*) and work up to words having three phonemes (*cat, boat*). Some tests include words that have blends (clusters), which are groups of sounds (*st*op, be*lt*). This is probably overtesting. Students don't need to be able to blend or segment blends before beginning to learn phonics. They don't need these skills until they meet blends in their reading. A Blending Survey can be found at http://wordbuilding.org.

## Segmentation Ability

**Segmentation** is the ability to divide a word into its separate sounds.

**Segmentation** may be partial—noting the beginning sound in a word—or it may be complete—noting all the sounds in a word. Identifying a phoneme requires at least partial segmentation of a word. A student must first segment beginning sounds before being able to tell whether the words begin with the same sound. However, segmentation does not necessarily involve identifying the sound, which is critical in word analysis (Byrne & Fielding-Barnsley, 1995). Segmentation ability can be assessed on three levels: by having a student say a word in syllable parts, *cow–boy*; by having the student say a word in onset–rime parts, *b–ook*; and by having a student say the separate sounds in a word, *b–oo–k*. A Segmentation Survey can be found at http://word building.org. A copyright-free test of segmenting is available at Yopp (1995).

Students do not have to be able to segment words completely in order to start work on initial consonants, but they should be able to segment the first sound, and they should be able to detect beginning sounds. If students are unable to segment words sound by sound, they need continued work with phonemic awareness as they learn initial consonants. Work on phonemic awareness can be integrated with phonics instruction.

***Manipulating Sounds***    In some phonemic awareness assessments, students are asked to manipulate phonemes by deleting a phoneme or a syllable from a word. They are asked to tell what word would be left if they took off a sound ("What word would you have if you took the /m/ from *meat?*"). This is a complex task that requires the student to abstract a sound and then state the word that remains. The student must retain in working memory both the phoneme being abstracted and the remaining portion of the word. The processing required by this task is not a necessary prerequisite for instruction in beginning phonics. It makes considerable demands on working memory.

## Commercial Tests

A number of commercial tests assess phonological awareness.

- The Phonological Awareness Test 2 (Lingui Systems) assesses all aspects of phonological awareness and also basic phonics. The use of nonsense words limits the utility of phonological awareness and decoding tests, however.

- The Comprehensive Test of Phonological Processing (CTOPP; Pearson) assesses phonological awareness, phonological memory, and rapid naming. There are two versions: one for kindergarteners and first graders and a second for students in grades 2 through college.

- The Phonological Awareness Literacy Screening (PALS; University of Virginia) assesses phonological awareness on several levels. On the PALS-PreK, Rhyme Awareness is assessed having students select from three pictures the one that rhymes with the target picture. On the PreK Beginning Sound Awareness test, the teacher says a word and shows a picture of the word and asks the child to say the beginning sound. A unique feature of this assessment is that there are a number of practice items that can be repeated until the child understands what to do. During the test itself, students are told whether their responses are correct so that the test actually becomes a teaching activity. On the PALS-K, the Rhyme Awareness test is the same as on the PreK version. On the PALS-K Beginning Sound Awareness test, children choose from three pictures the one that begins with the same sound as the target picture. The PALS-K assessment can be given to small groups.

  Using PALS 1–3, students who show a need are assessed with the Blending and Sound to Letter tests. In the Blending test, students blend sounds spoken by the teacher, for example, blending /u/ and /p/ to form *up*. For the Sound to Letter test, the student tells what sound the target word begins with or says a word that has the same beginning sound as the target word. Demonstrations of the assessments are available at https://pals.virginia.edu/ by clicking on Tools and choosing Assessments from the drop-down menu.

- DIBELS Deep Phonemic Awareness (Sopris West) assesses blending word parts in compound words; blending syllables; blending two- and three-phoneme words; segmenting compound words; segmenting syllables; identifying initial sounds; identifying final sounds; and segmenting two-, three-, and four-phoneme words. The testing is dynamic, which means that directions can be altered or teaching can be initiated in order to elicit correct responses. Teaching suggestions are made at key points in the testing; however, teachers are free to try other approaches. Reponses obtained through teaching are noted. The purpose of dynamic testing is to see if a correct response can be elicited and, if so, what kind of support was effective. This information can then used for instructional planning.

- The Dynamic Measurement Group (DIBELS) offers the following two tests of phonemic awareness, which are free and can be downloaded from http://dibels.org/next.html:

  1. **First Sound Fluency:** The assessor says a word, and the student is asked to say the first sound for the word: "What sound does *man* begin with?"
  2. **Phoneme Segmentation Fluency.** Given a spoken word, students are asked to say all the sounds in the word. The tester pronounces the word *stop*, and the student is expected to say "/s/, /t/, /o/, /p/."

## Techniques for Building Phonological Skills

Developing phonological awareness should be seen as part of a program of over-all language development. Since phonological awareness apparently grows out of vocabulary knowledge, the more words children know, the easier it will be for them to develop phonological awareness. As their vocabularies develop, children acquire an increasing number of words that have similar sounds, so that they have to distinguish among words like *bat, bet, bit, but, beet,* and so on (Metsala, 1999).

As their vocabularies grow, children develop the ability to make finer discriminations and begin processing words on a phonemic rather than a holistic level. Because they have more experience with everyday words, students are better able to discriminate between familiar words with similar sounds than they are between unfamiliar or infrequently heard words that have similar sounds. Beginning elements are easier to segment or isolate than ending ones. Middle elements are the most difficult. Words with fewer sounds are easier to work with than words with more sounds (Troia, 2004).

One way to foster overall phonological awareness is through natural activities such as word play and listening to rhymes, riddles, puns, jokes, songs, and stories that call attention to words as words and sounds as sounds. When students play with language, instead of just listening to the meanings of words, they are drawn to words and sounds as abstract units of language.

### Rhyme

Detecting beginning sounds, segmenting, and blending are more important skills than rhyming. However, rhyming is one way of introducing phonological awareness, and it can be useful when introducing word patterns.

An enjoyable way to develop the concept of rhyme is to read nursery rhymes and other rhyming tales to students. At first, just read and discuss the rhymes, so that students build a kind of subconscious storehouse of rhyming knowledge. As students become familiar with rhyming pieces, stress the rhyming elements. As you develop the concept of rhyme, also build the language used to talk about rhyme: *same, sounds, rhyme, words,* and so forth.

To extend the concept of rhyme, build rhymes with students. Using the element *at,* here is how a rhyme might be built. Say "at." Have students say "at." Tell students that you are going to make words that have *at* in them. Say "c-at," emphasizing the *at* portion of the word. Ask students if they can hear the *at* in *c-at.* Holding up a picture of a cat, have them say "cat" and listen to the *at.* (By using pictures, you will reduce the burden on students' memories.) Next, hold up a picture of a hat. Have students tell what it is. Tell students that *h-at* has an *at* in it. Ask them if they can hear the *at* in *h-at.* Introduce *rat, bat,* and *sat* in the same way. Ask students if they can tell what sound is the same in *cat, hat, rat, bat,* and *sat.* Stress the *at* in each of these words. Explain that *cat, hat, rat, bat,* and *sat* rhyme because they all have *at* at the end.

Invite students to suggest other words that rhyme with *cat: mat, pat, fat, that.* Also have students tell whether word pairs such as the following rhyme: *cat–hat, hat–pan, mat–rat, can–man.* If the students give correct responses, affirm their answers and explain why they are correct: "Yes, *cat* and *hat* do rhyme. They both end with an *at* sound."

If students provide a wrong response, gently supply the correct response and an explanation, or rephrase the question so students have a better chance of getting it correct: "Do you hear the same sound at the end of *hat* that you hear at the end of *pan?* No, *hat* and *pan* do not rhyme. *Hat* ends with an *at* sound, and *pan* has an *an* sound. *An* and *at* are different sounds."

To make the task more concrete and to aid students' memories, show pictures of word pairs as you say them. From time to time, also re-explain what a rhyme is.

Here are some pairs of words that might be used in this activity:

| | |
|---|---|
| *bee–car* | *bee–tree* |
| *bag–rag* | *king–ring* |
| *cat–hat* | *ball–net* |
| *cake–man* | *fish–dish* |
| *car–star* | *boat–goat* |

Sorting is also an excellent way to reinforce the concept of rhyme. In sorting, students group objects or pictures whose names rhyme. If possible, begin with objects. They are more concrete than pictures and less likely to be misinterpreted.

Other activities for developing the concept of rhyme include the following:

- Call attention to rhyming sounds in nursery rhymes and rhyming tales.
- When reading a pair of rhyming lines, read all but the last word and have students suggest a word to complete the couplet:

*Twinkle, twinkle, little star,*

*How I wonder what you _____*

*Up above the world so high,*

*Like a diamond in the _____*

## Blending

Begin blending by having students combine words into compounds: *door + bell, door + knob, door + way, base + ball, foot + ball.* Explain to students that we sometimes put two words together to make a new word. Provide examples and have students combine words to make compounds. You might use illustrations as an aid. For the word *football*, show students illustrations of a *foot* and a *ball*; for *doorbell*, show a *door* and a *bell*; and so on.

Once students grasp the concept of a compound word, have them blend onsets and rimes. The onset is the consonant or consonant cluster preceding the rime: *s-, sl-, tr-.* The rime is the word's vowel or vowels and any consonants that follow: *-oap, -eep, -ee.*

Using a puppet, tell students that the puppet says its words in parts. Instead of saying *fish* the way we do, it says *f-ish.* Tell students that they have to help the puppet by putting together the parts of the word. Have students help put together the following words: *b-ee, h-at, b-ook, d-eer, s-un.*

Present the words in groups of five. As a way of involving all students, supply each student with a set of five pictures showing the five words. Be sure to discuss the names of the pictures. When you say the word to be blended, ask students to choose the picture that shows the word and hold it up. By observing the students, you can tell who is catching on and who is having difficulty. After students have held up their pictures for the word being blended, have them say the word. Confirm students' efforts but correct wrong responses. For a correct response, you might say "Hat. That is correct. When you put /h/ and /at/ together, you get *hat.*" For an incorrect attempt, you might say "That was a good try. But when I put /s/ and /un/ together, the word is *sun*. You say it: *s-un—sun*." After students have completed a set of words, go through them again. Challenge students to put the words together faster.

> **Continuants** are speech sounds that are articulated with a single stream of breath: /s/, /f/, /h/, /w/, /m/, /n/, /r/, /l/, /sh/, /th/, /th/, /y/, /v/, /z/, /zh/, and /ng/.

After students can blend onsets and rimes, have them blend all the phonemes in a word. Start with words that have just two sounds: *say, so, no, moo, knee, may, me, we, see, pay, way* (both sounds are **continuants**); *go, boy, bee, tea, pie, toe, cow, tie, two, toy* (first sound is a **stop**). Then have students blend words that have three sounds: *same, mess, rose, nose, hose, mouse, room, soon, moon, zoom* (all sounds are continuants); *hat, sat, rat, mat, soap, sit, mitt, sock, mop* (first sound is a continuant, last is a stop).

> **Stops** are consonant sounds that are articulated by partially obstructing the flow of breath: /b/, /d/, /k/, /g/, /p/, /t, /j/, and /ch/.

Blending might be difficult for students who have problems with articulation and short-term memory for sounds (Swanson & Alexander, 2001). Take steps to reduce the memory load. Stretch the sounds (*ffiish*), ask students to repeat the stretched form, and then ask them to identify the word. Doing so helps make the task easier, as does presenting words with just two sounds (O'Connor & Bell, 2004). Sounds that cannot be stretched can be iterated or repeated: *b-b-b-all*.

Blending and segmentation work together. Students segment words and then blend them. An effective program would teach both together (O'Connor, 2011). As students learn to segment they can also blend the elements they are segmenting.

## Segmentation

Segmentation begins with larger elements and progresses to smaller elements. Students are presented with exercises that segment compound words into their component words, words into syllables, and finally words into individual sounds or phonemes. To introduce segmenting words into compound words, explain that some words are made up of two words. Point out the separate syllables in compound words. You might have students clap out the syllables they hear in *baseball, football, playground, bluebird, outside, backpack, rowboat,* and *starfish*. After students are able to identify the words in compound words, introduce syllabication of two-syllable words that are not compounds. Remind students that words are made up of parts. Point out the separate syllables in two-syllable words: *pen-cil, ba-by*. You might have students clap out the syllables or word parts they hear in *puppet, window, table, basket, open, puppy*. Also have students clap out the syllables they hear in each other's names, for example, *David, Chin-Mae,* or *Maria*.

> **Using Technology**
> The following site provides an explanation and practice with segmenting syllables: http://www.smarttutor.com/home/lessons/PH_syllabification_L3_V1_T1a.swf.

To introduce the concept of individual sounds in words—which is phonemic awareness because a phoneme is an individual speech sound—play this game with students: Pointing to a picture of a goat, ask "Is this a /g/?" When the class says "no," agree and explain: "That's right. I didn't say all of the word's sounds. I said 'Is this a /g/?' " Then say, "Is this a /g/, /ō/?" (emphasize each sound). Explain that no, this is not a /gō/. It doesn't have enough sounds. Next, ask "Is this a goat?" Once again, carefully enunciate all three sounds, /g/, /ō/, /t/. When the class says "yes," explain that they are right. *Goat* has three sounds, and you said all three of them. Present *sun* and *cat* and other three-sound words in this same way.

If students have difficulty segmenting words into sounds, practice with words that have just two sounds: *go, no, me, he*. Also present two-sound words in which the vowel comes first: *ape, ate, at, eat, it*. Words that begin with a vowel are a little easier to segment than those that begin with a consonant (Uhry & Ehri, 1999). Avoid

■■ **FIGURE 7.3**
Easy-to-Segment
Words

| | | |
|---|---|---|
| at | moo | pie |
| ape | too | tie |
| age | zoo | toe |
| ate | bee | Joe |
| Ed | see | Sue |
| eat | we | new |
| it | he | who |
| us | she | my |

segmenting words that contain vowels followed by nasals (/n/, /m/, /ng/) such as *an, and, am, can, sang,* because a nasal tends to combine with the preceding vowel. A list of easy-to-segment words is given in Figure 7.3.

Detecting sounds in words is not only difficult because the sounds overlap but also because the sounds are fleeting; they quickly fade (Castiglioni-Spalten & Ehri, 2003). Calling attention to the way sounds are formed can also help students learn to detect sounds, especially when the means of articulation is readily detectable. For instance, have students say "mmm" and discuss how the lips are used to make this sound. Noting the separate movements can help students become more fully aware of the speech sounds they are making. This is a concrete way of experiencing phonemes. Realizing how phonemes are articulated helps lay a conceptual foundation for phonemic awareness (Lindamood & Lindamood, 1975, 1998). For instance, the three phonemes in *meat* can be seen in the three successive mouth movements needed to articulate meat. Lips are pressed together to form /m/, teeth are shown to form /ē/, and the tongue is used to articulate the final /t/ sound.

Using articulatory movements to explore sounds may help students who have difficulty perceiving them auditorially (Torgesen, 1994). It might also be that producing the articulatory gestures needed to make speech sounds requires more focus and more concentration (Castiglioni-Spalten & Ehri, 2003). Articulating the speech sounds also seems to be more motivational. In one study, students in an articulatory group required fewer corrections for inappropriate behavior than those in the comparison group. For students who are seriously struggling with developing phonemic awareness, including articulatory movements as part of instruction might mean the difference between learning and not learning. Skjelfjord (1976) reported on two students who made no progress learning to segment sounds until an articulatory component was added. At that point, their progress was rapid. Because an articulatory component creates strong bonds, requires more concentration, and seems to be motivational, it should probably be added to phonemic awareness training. See Table 7.2 for descriptions of how initial consonant sounds are articulated. Reword the directions for students as needed.

**Elkonin technique:** method that teaches phonemic awareness by having students put tokens in boxes to show how many sounds a word has.

*Elkonin Technique* Using markers can also help students segment sounds. To reinforce and to extend the concept of sounds in words, use the **Elkonin technique** (Elkonin, 1973). Through the use of sound boxes, Elkonin sought to "materialize" the analysis of a word into its component sounds (phonemes).

Children are given a picture of an object whose name contains two or three sounds. Underneath the picture appear boxes that match the number of sounds the picture's name contains. One block is drawn for each sound. For the word

**TABLE 7.2**
Articulation of
Consonants

| Sound | Articulation | Directions for Students |
|-------|--------------|-------------------------|
| **Stops** | | |
| /b/ | Lips popping, voiced. | Lips are pressed together and opened quickly to make a popping /b/ sound as in *ball*. Vocal cords vibrate. |
| /p | Lips popping, voiceless. | Lips are pressed together and opened quickly to make a voiceless popping /p/ sound as in *pen*. |
| /d/ | Tongue behind ridge, voiced. | Front and sides of the tongue touch the ridge behind the teeth. Tongue is lowered and makes a voiced burst of sound as in *dog*. |
| /t/ | Tongue behind ridge, voiceless. | Front and sides of the tongue touch the ridge behind the teeth. Tongue is lowered and makes a voiceless burst of sound as in *ten*. |
| /g/ | Tongue at back of mouth, voiced. | Tongue touches middle of roof of mouth. Tongue is lowered and makes a voiced burst of sound as in *goat*. |
| /k/ | Tongue at back of mouth, voiceless. | Tongue touches middle of roof of mouth. Tongue is lowered and makes a voiceless burst of sound as in *king*. |
| **Nasals** | | |
| m/ | Lips are pressed together. Sound partially absorbed by preceding vowel. | Lips are pressed together. Air is pushed through the nose as in *man*. |
| /n/ | Tongue behind teeth. Sound partially absorbed by preceding vowel. | The front and sides of the tongue touch the ridge. Air is pushed out through the nose as in *nail*. |
| /ng/ | Tongue at back of mouth. Sound partially absorbed by preceding vowel. | Tongue touches the roof of the mouth. Air is pushed out through the nose as in the last sound in *ring*. |
| **Fricatives** | | |
| /v/ | Teeth touching lower lip. Vocal cords vibrate. | Lower lip presses against upper teeth and pushes air out as in *vase*. Vocal cords vibrate. |
| /f/ | Teeth touching lower lip. Vocal cords do not vibrate. | Lower lip presses against upper teeth and pushes air out as in *fish*. Vocal cords do not vibrate. |
| /th/ | Tongue behind or just below teeth. Vocal cords vibrate. | Tip of tongue presses against or just below upper teeth and pushes out air to make /th/ as in *this*. Vocal cords vibrate. |
| /th/ | Tongue behind or just below teeth | Tip of tongue presses against or just below upper teeth and pushes out air to make /th/ as in *thumb*. Vocal cords do not vibrate. |
| /z/ | Tongue touching roof of mouth. | The tip of the tongue touches the middle of the roof of your mouth. The sides of your tongue touch your teeth. Air is pushed over your tongue and makes a zzz sound as in *zebra*. Vocal cords vibrate. |

| Sound | Articulation | Directions for Students |
|---|---|---|
| /s/ | Tongue behind teeth touching roof of mouth. Sides of tongue touch teeth. Students might not articulate this sound until they have their front teeth. | The tip of the tongue touches the middle of the roof of your mouth. The sides of your tongue touch your teeth. Air is pushed over your tongue and makes a snake sound as in *sun*. Vocal cords do not vibrate. |
| /zh/ | Tongue touching roof of mouth and teeth. | Tongue touches roof of mouth. Sides of tongue touch teeth and push out air to make a /zh/ sound as in the last sound in *garage*. Vocal cords vibrate. |
| /sh/ | Tongue touching roof of mouth. | Tongue touches roof of mouth. Sides of tongue touch teeth and push out air to make a "be quiet," /sh/ sound as in *shoe*. Vocal cords do not vibrate. |
| /h/ | Pushing air through throat. | Air is pushed up through the throat to make a /h/ sound as in *hat*. Vocal cords do not vibrate. |
| **Affricatives** | | |
| /j/ | Tongue touching ridge of mouth. | Tongue touches ridge of mouth. Tongue is lowered, and sound is pushed out as in *jar*. Vocal cords vibrate. |
| /ch/ | Tongue touching ridge of mouth. | Tongue touches ridge of mouth. Tongue is lowered, and sound is pushed out as in *chair*. Vocal cords do not vibrate. |
| **Glides** | | |
| /w/ | Lips are rounded. | Lips are rounded but shape changes to form the vowel that follows, as in *wagon*. Vocal cords vibrate. |
| /y/ | Tongue touching roof of mouth. | Tongue touches roof of mouth but moves to form vowel that follows, as in *yo-yo*. Vocal cords vibrate. |
| **Liquids** | | |
| /r/ | Tongue touching roof of mouth. | Tongue is pushed up to roof of mouth and pushes out sound as in *ring*. |
| /l/ | Tip of tongue touches ridge of mouth. | Tip of tongue touches ridge on roof of mouth and pushes out sound as in *lion*. |

*cat*, three blocks are drawn, one each for /k/, /a/, /t/. Three boxes are also drawn for the word *goat*. Although goat has four letters, it has only three sounds: /g/, /ō/, /t/. Students indicate the number of sounds in a word by placing a marker in the box for each sound they hear. Figure 7.4 shows Elkonin boxes.

> ✵ A book to introduce beginning sounds is *The Story of Z* (Modesitt, 1990), in which the letter *Z* leaves the alphabet. As you read this book aloud, highlight the missing sound and discuss beginning sounds in words.

### Beginning Sounds

A key segmentation skill is detecting beginning sounds. A delightful way to introduce beginning sounds is through reading Dr. Scuss's *There's a Wocket in My Pocket* (Geisel, 1974), which combines rhymes and perception of beginning sounds. After reading the text, discuss the rhymes and the words that Dr. Seuss made up.

■ **FIGURE 7.4**

Elkonin Boxes
*Source:* From
T. Gunning (1994a).
*Word Building:
Beginnings.* New York:
Phoenix Learning
Resources. Reprinted
by permission of
Galvin Publications.

# Sounds in Words

**Say the word that names the picture. Put a marker in the first box as you say the first sound of the word. Put a marker in the second box as you say the second sound of the word. Put a marker in the third box as you say the third sound of the word.**

Lead students to see that Dr. Seuss made up his silly words by changing the first sound of a real word: *pocket–wocket.* Supply real words and help students create silly words by changing the first sound. In the exercise below, students change the first sound in the last word in each sentence.

There's a _____ in my book.

There's a _____ in my lunch box.

There's a _____ in the room.

There's a _____ on my desk.

There's a _____ on the bus.

Also use names to convey the concept of beginning sounds. Ask students if you are Ms. "_____ eynolds." When they say no and say you are "Ms. Reynolds," ask them what was missing from "_____ eynolds." Lead them to see that the beginning sound was missing and that you are "Ms. RRReynolds," drawing out the initial /r/. Go around the room and ask: Is this "_____ am"? Is this "_____ eth"? Is this "_____uis"? Have students add the beginning sound to each name. Repeat the child's name, stretching the initial sound as you do so: "SSSam."

Follow the same procedure with objects or pictures of objects: Is this an "_____ ail" (*nail*)? Is this an "_____ en" (*pen*)? Is this an "_____ ook" (*book*)? Is this an "_____ orse" (*horse*)? If students have difficulty with this task, drop down to a lower level, one that requires only sound discrimination. For instance, holding up a real object or a picture, ask the following questions:

(Holding up a pen) Is this a *pen* or a *ten?*

(Holding up a pan) Is this a *pan* or a *fan?*

(Holding up a hat) Is this a *hat* or a *bat?*

(Holding up a ball) Is this a *ball* or a *wall?*

To further reinforce the concept of beginning sounds, choose a book that lends itself to this activity, such as *Morris and Boris* (Wiseman, 1959). Discuss how

※ Instruction in phonological awareness that is focused on one or two skills is more effective than instruction that includes a variety of phonological awareness skills. Segmenting is an especially essential skill (National Reading Panel, 2000).

※ Given intensive instruction, children who lack phonemic awareness can catch up to students whose phonological awareness is more advanced (O'Connor, 2000). However, the gap widens if students who are poor in phonological awareness do not receive instruction (McBride-Chang, Wagner, & Chang, 1997).

*Morris* and *moose* begin in the same way. Also read alliterative tales or alphabet books to students. If reading the *s* page of an alphabet book that contains a number of items that begin with /s/, discuss how all the items begin with the same sound. Emphasize the /s/ in each word so that students can clearly hear it. Say the sound in isolation and in the context of a whole word. Talk about the sound of /s/ as in *sun*. Discuss students' names that begin with /s/: *Sam, Sarah, Saada.*

Also read alliterative verses and sing alliterative songs. Discuss the names of common objects that begin with /s/, and create a bulletin board of objects whose names begin like *sun.*

During the normal course of the day's activities, take advantage of naturally occurring opportunities to reinforce awareness of beginning sounds. If it is a Monday in May, discuss how *Monday* and *May* begin with the same sound. If you are discussing animal sounds, note that cows make a moo sound.

Once students have begun to detect beginning sounds, introduce the letters that go with the sounds. Seeing the letters helps students mark the beginning sounds. Correspondences for sounds that are incorporated in the names of letters are easier to learn than those that aren't. Thus, it is easier to learn *b* = /b/ (*bee*) or *t* = /t/ (*tee*) than it is *h* = /h/ (*aich*). Long vowels and the following consonants incorporate their sounds in their names: *b, d, f, j, k, l, m, n, p, r, s, t, v, z* and the soft sounds of *c(city)* and *g* (*gym*) (Durrell, 1980; Ehri & Snowling, 2004; Piasta & Wagner, 2010). Students typically have a more difficult time learning correspondences for *h, w, y,* hard *g* (*girl*), and hard *c* (*can*). The letter name *y* is especially difficult because it begins with a /w/ sound.

## Sorting Beginning Sounds

In sorting, students group objects or pictures whose names begin with the same sound. If possible, begin with objects. As noted earlier, objects are more concrete than pictures and less likely to be misinterpreted. Using toys and dollhouse furniture, assemble sets of objects or pictures similar to the following: man, mouse, monkey, mirror, moon, mop and hat, horse, house, hammer, hose, heart. Display two boxes: one with a toy man in front of it and one with a hat in front of it. Tell students that they are to put the objects that begin with the same sound as *man* in the "man" box and those that begin like *hat* in the "hat" box. Sort one or two objects as examples. For instance, hold up a toy monkey and say its name, emphasizing the /m/. Then say "*Mmmonkey* begins like *mmman*. Both begin with an /m/ sound, so I'll put the monkey in the 'man' box."

Once students understand what they are to do, have them sort the objects. Have them name each object, tell which of the two boxes it should be placed in, and why. After all the objects have been sorted, have students name the objects in each box and note that they all begin with the same sound.

Also have students sort pictures. Pictures might be sorted in columns, with the model picture at the top of the column. Students can work individually, in pairs, or in small groups. After a sort has been completed, have students say the name of each picture in a category. If students are slow or hesitant, discuss any questions they might have and ask them to sort again. If students have completed a sort under your guidance, have them sort the items a second time independently for additional practice.

## Other Activities

Also have students do these activities:

- Have students identify which of two pictures begins with a target sound. Because the student only has to choose between two items, this is an easy task. Holding up a picture of a hat and a man, the teacher asks "Which picture, the hat or the man, begins with /m/ as in *moon*? Other possible practice items include these:

  | /s/ | *sun dog* |
  |-----|-----------|
  | /m/ | *man boy* |
  | /h/ | *hat pig* |
  | /k/ | *bird car* |
  | /r/ | *ring goat* |

- Have students create sound booklets. A sound booklet contains drawings or pictures of items that begin with the same sound. An /s/ booklet might contain drawings of the sun, a sock, a sandwich, a saw, and a six and a seven.

- Say a rime and have students make as many words as they can by adding initial consonants. For instance, say "-eep." Students might say *beep, deep, jeep,* and so forth. As an alternative, say a word and have students make new words by changing the first sound of the word, so that *cat* becomes *bat, hat, pat, sat,* and so forth.

- Give the rime of a word and a clue. Have students guess what the word might be. Say "ay." Monday is a _*ay*. Give me some money. _*ay* me. Feed this to a horse. _*ay*.

## Playing with Sounds

To further develop students' implicit knowledge of the sounds of language, sing songs and read books to them that play with language. For instance, read *Jamberry* (Degen, 1983), a humorous picture book in which the word *berry* is used to form dozens of words:

> One berry Two berry Pick me a blueberry.
>
> Hatberry Shoeberry In my canoe berry.

As you read the book, have the students clap out the rhythm of the piece—one clap for each syllable. After discussing the tale, ask students to form *berry* words, the sillier the better. Other children's books that play with language include the following:

Geisel, T. (1991). *Mr. Brown Can Moo! Can You?* New York: Random House.

Geisel, T. (1979). *Oh Say Can You Say?* New York: Random House.

Hutchins, P. (1976). *Don't Forget the Bacon.* New York: Morrow.

Hutchins, P. (1976). *Follow That Bus.* New York: Knopf.

Lunn, C. (1990). *A Buzz Is Part of a Bee.* Chicago: Children's Press.

*Riddles*   Read riddles and jokes to students, especially those that involve a play on words. Discuss riddles that call attention to sounds in words, like these:

> What kind of key can climb a tree?  (A mon-*key*.)
>
> What kind of pet can play in a band?  (A trum-*pet*.)
>
> What kind of vegetable can take you for a ride?  (A *cab*-bage.)

*Adding Sounds*   Say *and* and tell children that you will be making a new word. Say *sssand.* Discuss what sound you added to *and* to make *sand.* Create other words in this same way. Some possibilities include *eat–seat, ate–gate, air–hair, an–can, am–ham, at–rat, in–pin, it–sit, and–band.*

## A Reciprocal Relationship

Phonemic awareness apparently enjoys a reciprocal relationship with reading (Perfetti, 1992; Perfetti, Beck, Bell, & Hughes, 1988). Thus, adults who have never learned to read are lacking in phonological awareness (Alegria & Morais, 1991). Although some awareness of sounds in words is necessary for the acquisition of initial reading skills, experience with initial reading tasks further develops phonemic awareness.

You do not have to wait to introduce letter–sound relationships, sight vocabulary, and other beginning reading skills until children have mastered phonemic awareness. Based on their studies, Vandervelden and Siegel (1995) believe that initial phoneme recognition and some segmentation ability are all that is required for instruction in beginning phonics. Segmentation ability might be partial. Being able to isolate the first sound in a word should be sufficient for instruction in initial consonant correspondences.

## Phonological Awareness and Word Analysis

> "It is during writing that the relationship between individual letters and phonemes might be the most vivid. That is, a child with pencil in hand as she sounds the phonemes in her mouth and attempts to represent these." (Juel & Minden-Cupp, 1999, p. 30)

Phonemic awareness is most effective when students learn to segment and identify phonemes as part of learning to read and write rather than as an isolated skill (Vandervelden & Siegel, 1997; Bus & van Ijzendoorn, 1999). Because the letters in a word represent the word's sounds, working with letters is a way of marking sounds.

Students taught by an integrated approach outperform those who are taught either phonological awareness or phonics in isolation. Neither a literature immersion nor a skills-first program of phonological awareness is most effective. What works best is to combine both reading good literature and systematic instruction in phonemic awareness. "Letters may draw the child's attention to the sounds in spoken words, and a distinct visual symbol for each phoneme may anchor the phonemes perceptually" (Bus & van Ijzendoorn, 1999, p. 412).

Another effective technique is to gear the program to the students' level of understanding. One highly successful program used speech-to-print recognition. Students were required only to recognize the printed form of a word spoken by the teacher. This is a relatively easy task and can be used with students who are struggling with typical approaches. The teacher presented a correspondence and then asked students to point to the word that contained that correspondence. After two correspondences were presented, the students were shown two words, one of which started with the correspondence just taught. For instance, having taught the correspondences *s* = /s/ and *m* = /m/, the teacher presented the words *man* and *sun* and asked students to point to the word that says *man.* After a third correspondence has been taught, have them choose from all three. However, as additional correspondences are introduced, drop one so that students are not required to choose from more than three correspondences.

This activity works best with continuants, since they are articulated with a continuous stream of breath and so may be emphasized without being distorted.

(See page 208 for a listing of continuants.) Also choose correspondences whose letter names are known by students. At-risk students who took part in speech-to-print recognition activities of this type improved in phonemic awareness, letter–sound recognition, and the ability to learn new words (Vandervelden & Siegel, 1997). An adapted lesson is presented in the following box.

## Road to the Code

Road to the Code is a research-based, 11-week program designed to teach phonemic awareness and two short vowel and six consonant correspondences. Vowels are included so that a series of words can be created by combining consonants and vowels. The program consists of 44 lessons, each 15 to 20 minutes long, that feature three activities: Say-It-and-Move-It, Letter Name and Sound Instruction, and Phonological Awareness Practice.

Say-It-and-Move-It is similar to using Elkonin boxes. First the target word is spoken; then each sound is spoken in an elongated fashion as a disk is moved for each sound. As students say a sound in a word, they move a blank tile from a circle or square at the top of the page down the page past a solid line to a line that has a dot

---

### Speech-to-Print Lesson

*Step 1: Introducing the correspondence.* Present the correspondence *m* = /m/. Emphasize the way that the lips are pressed together to form the sound /m/. Explain that the letter *m* stands for the sound /m/ heard at the beginning of *mmman*.

*Step 2: Guided practice.* Assuming that *s* = /s/ and *f* = /f/ have been introduced, present groups of word cards similar to those below. To make the activity more concrete, you might have the students place a plastic letter on the word they have identified, placing an *m* on *man*.

| Which word says *man*? | sun | man | fish |
| Which word says *sun*? | sun | man | fish |
| Which word says *fish*? | man | fish | sun |
| Which word says *me*? | see | me | five |
| Which word says *five*? | me | five | see |
| Which word says *see*? | see | me | five |
| Which word says *mat*? | mat | sat | fat |
| Which word says *fat*? | mat | sat | fat |
| Which word says *sat*? | mat | fat | sat |

*Affirm students' responses:* "Yes, that word says *man*. You can tell it says *man* because it begins

with the letter *m*. The letter *m* makes the sound *mmm* that you hear at the beginning of *man*."

*Correct students' responses:* "No, that word does not say *fish*. That word says *man*. You can tell it says *man* because it begins with the letter *m*. The letter *m* makes the sound *mmm* that you hear at the beginning of *man*."

After students have learned initial consonants, they are introduced to final consonants and make matches based on both the initial and final consonants. Giving the students the word cards *cat, can, cap,* the teacher would say, "Which word spells *can*? Which word spells *cat*? Which word spells *cap*?" After vowels were introduced, choices are made on the basis of vowels. Given the word cards *bit, bet, but,* the students are asked, "Which spells *but*? Which spells *bet*? Which spells *bit*?"

*Step 3: Guided spelling.* The teacher articulates the word, and the student spells it. Initially, the student might select from three plastic letters the one that spells the beginning sound. Later, as the student learns to spell whole words, he might be asked to spell two- or three-letter words and might be given the letters in mixed-up order.

**FIGURE 7.5**
Say-It-and-Move-It

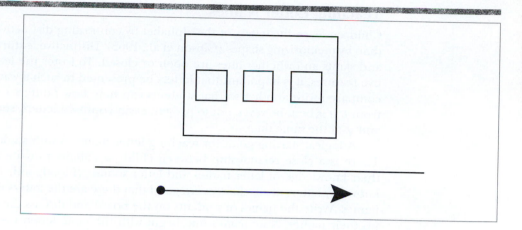

on the left end and an arrow tip on the right end (see Figure 7.5) (Blachman, Ball, Black, & Tangel, 1994, 2000). Hearing the word *mat,* the students would say /m/ while moving the first tile, /a/ while moving the second tile, and /t/ while moving the third tile. Students then tell how many sounds are in the word. After students learn the sounds for the letters *a, m, t, i, s, r, b,* and *f,* they use tiles that have letters to show the spelling of each sound.

## Letter Knowledge

> Some students can write their names but do not know the names or sound of the letters. They have simply memorized the shapes.

A key prerequisite to learning to read is knowing the letters of the alphabet (Piasta & Wagner, 2010). If students do not know the identity of the letter *s,* then they will not be able to associate it with the sound it represents. If they confuse *m* and *n,* they may assign the sound of /n/ to *m* and vice versa. The learning of letter–sound relationships will be greatly hindered. Knowing the name of a letter aids memory. Students who know the names of the letters are better able to learn letter–sound relationships (Ehri, 1983). According to Murray, Stahl, and Inez (1993), "Identifying letter names is a suboperation in the task of learning letters sounds" (p. 5).

Instruction in letter knowledge and phonological awareness helps students learn from other activities. For instance, students will not pay attention to or learn from environmental print in the classroom if they do not know any letters of the alphabet. And students have difficulty following along as the teacher reads a big book if they do not know beginning sounds. Knowing beginning sounds helps children determine where words begin (Morris, 1992).

### Assessing Letter Name Knowledge

To test students' knowledge of letter names, give the Letters Name Test presented on the author's Web site: http://wordbuilding.org. If students are unable to name the letters when they are shown them, drop down to a lower level of knowledge. Say the name of a letter, and have students pick it out from a series of four letters in a row.

## Teaching Letter Names

Children learn the letters of the alphabet by contrasting distinctive features rather than by memorizing shapes (Gibson et al., 1962). Distinctive features include curves and slants and whether lines are open or closed. To foster the learning of distinctive features, it is important that letters be presented in such a way that one can be compared with another so that students can note how *t* differs from *d* or *l* differs from *t*. It is best, however, not to present easily confused letters, such as *b* and *d* or *p* and *q*, at the same time.

A logical starting point for teaching letter names is with students' own names. There is a close relationship between children's ability to write their names and their knowledge of letter names and letter sounds (Bloodgood, 1999). If students know any letters at all, chances are good that these are the letters used to spell their names. Write the names of students on the board and discuss the letters that make up their names. Note names that begin with the same letter. List and discuss, for example, names that begin with *B* or *T*. If students cannot write both their first and last names, this is a good time to teach that skill.

At this point, you might also want to review correct letter formation, if necessary. Often low-achieving readers form some letters incorrectly or inconsistently. Forming letters consistently builds perceptual and organizational skills. Demonstrate the formation of the letters, and use simplified directions to talk students through what you show them. For lowercase *h*, you might say "Straight down, back up to the top of the first line, and curve around to the bottom of the line." However, do not overemphasize letter formation. Students who are overly conscious of forming their letters perfectly will have a difficult time moving beyond that task to writing. Because poor readers often have difficulty remembering visual–verbal material, it may be helpful if you supply them with copies of the alphabet that they can paste in their notebooks and refer to as needed. (See Chapter 13 for additional suggestions on handwriting instruction.)

One of the best ways to reinforce knowledge of letter names is to surround students with examples of letters and reasons to use them. Display a model alphabet and have available old typewriters, computers, stamp sets, letter stencils, magnetic and felt letters, and a wide assortment of writing instruments and paper. Encourage students to experiment with the alphabet and to play alphabet games. Also encourage wide writing with invented spelling. Most important of all, read and discuss alphabet books and encourage students to read them. Simply reading alphabet books to students seems to increase their letter knowledge and their sensitivity to sounds in words (Murray et al., 1993). Activities in which letters are presented in context and along with their sounds are apparently more effective than those in which letters are presented in isolation (Piasta & Wagner, 2010). Other activities that might be used to reinforce letter knowledge include the following:

- Using a magnetic letter board, mix several examples of the letter being taught with letters that have already been learned. Don't mix letters that are similar in form—*m* and *w*, for example. Have students assemble all the examples of the target letter—all the *s*'s, for example (Clay, 1993).

- Help students create an alphabet book. Set aside 26 pages in a composition book. As students learn a letter, write it on the appropriate page in upper- and lowercase forms. Write a model word that begins with the letter, so that students can see the letter in the context of a word and also begin to get a sense of the sound that the letter represents. Have students paste in or draw an illustration of the model word.

⁂ Just because students represent a whole word with a single letter, this does not necessarily mean that they are not aware of all the sounds in a word. At first the task of thinking what letter represents each sound may simply be too overwhelming to students (Hughes & Searle, 1997).

⁂ Watching and listening as children spell words is a good way to gain insights into the processes they are using. Writing slows down the student's processing, so it lends itself to observation (DeFord, 1997).

⁂ Children can make essential discoveries about letter–sound relationships through their attempts to write. Children "reinvent writing and thereby make it their own" (Ferreiro, 1986, p. 37).

- Use environmental print. This is an especially useful approach if you work with older students, who will see environmental print as being mature. Bring in cereal boxes, milk cartons, and other items that have labels. Have students read the labels and identify the letters that make up the labels.

- Develop letter knowledge as a natural part of your routines. As you list names or write messages on the board, spell out the words and names. Also surround students with the tools of writing, so that they are encouraged to experiment with writing and make discoveries about the alphabet as they do so. One especially useful device is to load talking software, such as Dr. Peet's Talk/Writer (Interest Driven Learning) or Write Out Loud (Don Johnston), into your computer so that when a key is pressed, it says the name of the key's letter. Later, as students move into letter sounds, the software's operation can be changed so that when a key is pressed, the sound of the letter, rather than its name, is spoken.

- Use well-designed apps such as Introduction to Letters (App Store), which features tracing of letters and saying the names and sounds of the letters and Kids ABC Letters (Android), which focuses on learning letter names.

- Present letters cumulatively. According to research by Reutzel (2008), it's better to present a new letter each day rather than devote a whole week to a letter, which is a common practice. A letter a week doesn't allow enough time for review. In a letter-a-day program, the letters can be reviewed every 26 days. In Reutzel's research, students who were taught a letter a day outperformed letter-a-week students by a wide margin.

## Invented Spelling

Encourage experimentation with writing and spelling. Through their attempts at spelling, students provide themselves with a valuable analysis of letter–sound correspondences. Invented spelling also opens a window onto the child's processing of letter–sound relationships. By examining samples of a student's invented spelling, it is possible to estimate where he is on the path to understanding the alphabetic system. Does the student understand that words are composed of letters? Does the student realize that letters can be used to represent sounds? Does the student know some basic letter–sound correspondences? If so, which ones? (See Chapter 5 for additional information about spelling development. See Figure 5.8 for a chart of stages of spelling development.)

## ▩ Mini–Case Study

Jan's performance was puzzling. Although she was a 7-year-old second grader, she was still struggling to learn initial consonants. She had learned a series of alliterative sentences for each consonant. If you asked her the sentence for /m/, she would reply "Mighty Mack made a muddy mess." And when she saw the letter *m*, she would say "mmm." All of this led Jan's teacher to believe that Jan had mastered initial consonants. However, Jan was unable to apply this knowledge. For instance, when Jan encountered the word *man* in a story, she responded with a very elongated "mmmm" and then said "dog."

Through rote memory, Jan had learned to associate /m/ with the letter *m* and could recite the alliterative sentence but could not manipulate individual sounds in words. Thus, when she saw the word *man*, she was unable to manipulate the sound /m/ and produce a word that began with /m/. When told "I am going to add /s/ to *ay*. What word will I make?" Jan was unable to respond.

In an informal survey, Jan was able to supply sounds for all of the consonant letters except *z* and *y*. However, this knowledge was built on a very weak foundation, one that did not include adequate phonemic awareness. Because Jan's previous program had consisted primarily of isolated drill work, it was decided to present phonemic awareness and related skills through the shared reading of easy, highly predictable children's books. After reading *Have You Seen My Cat?* (Carle, 1987) and *Brown Bear, Brown Bear, What Do You See?* (Martin, 1983), the sounds of key words in those books were discussed.

Rhymes, short poems, and word-play games were a regular part of the program. Jan was also encouraged to use invented spelling. Progress was slow and labored. However, the teacher noted that Jan responded with animation and enthusiasm to games. A colleague recommended a board game called Road Racer (Curriculum Associates). A fairly typical board game, Road Racer has a raceway composed of initial consonants and clusters. Students move their race cars by rolling dice. Printed on 10 dice are common rimes: *-at, -ame, -et.* The idea is to roll the dice and create words by combining the initial-consonant element with the rime. Forming words in this way involved manipulating sounds and was exactly the skill with which Jan had difficulty.

Jan's eyes lit up when the teacher introduced the game. Using a modified set of rules, the teacher read the rimes and asked Jan what sound needed to be added to make the target word. For instance, if the *et* rime turned up, the teacher read *et* and asked Jan to tell what sound would need to be added to *et* to make *pet.* Jan was far more successful with the game than she had been with any of the other devices or techniques that had been tried. She still needed hints and missed an item here and there. But, excited by the challenge of the game, she put forth maximum effort.

Animated by the fun of the game and flush with success, Jan attacked her lessons with increased vigor and renewed insight into the language's sound system and was able to apply this knowledge to her reading of beginning-level books. At long last, Jan was on the roadway to literacy.

## Summary

Although the concept of emergent literacy recognizes that all children come to school having some experience with reading and writing, the quantity and quality of this experience varies enormously. Because of limited literacy experiences or slow progress, at-risk learners should be taught literacy skills directly in the following areas: concepts of print, phonological awareness, and letter knowledge. These are taught within the context of holistic reading and writing activities and reading aloud to students.

Concepts of print that should be taught include understanding the purpose of print and being able to identify the basic parts of a book and the basic units of print, especially letters, words, and sounds. A crucial understanding for emergent readers is being able to point to separate words as they are read aloud.

A major cause of reading disorders is a deficiency in phonological awareness. In order to read, students must be able to detect and blend separate words, syllables, and sounds. They should also be able to note words that rhyme, and perceive beginning sounds. Playing with words; listening to rhymes, riddles, and alphabet books; and engaging in a variety of reading and writing endeavors are key activities for teaching necessary phonological skills. However, in addition to direct instruction and experiences, students apparently also need a degree of cognitive maturity in order to attain needed phonological awareness.

Letter knowledge can be presented through alphabet books, immersion in print, explicit instruction, writing, and a variety of other techniques. Students experiencing difficulty learning to read and write should be encouraged to write using invented spelling if they are unable to spell conventionally. Invented spelling, and writing in general, foster growth in phonemic awareness, concepts of print, writing, letter–sound relationships, and spelling.

There are a number of formal and informal measures for assessing emergent literacy. Three of the best known are the Observation Survey (Clay, 2006) and PALS-PreK and PALS-K (http://pals.virginia.edu).

## Application Activities

1. Make a list of five children's books that might be appropriate for a shared reading lesson.
2. Plan a shared reading or language-experience lesson. If possible, teach the lesson and evaluate its effectiveness.
3. Analyze five samples of young children's writing. What stages are the children in (see Chapter 5 for the Informal Spelling Inventory)? What does an analysis of their writing indicate about their knowledge of letter–sound relationships?
4. Plan a series of lessons on beginning sounds. Try out the lessons with a student who is struggling to learn to detect beginning sounds. Make adjustments in your lessons as necessary. Reflect on the effectiveness of the lessons.

## MyEducationLab

Go to the topic **Reading Assessment** in the MyEducationLab (www.myeducationlab.com) for **Assessing and Correcting Reading Difficulties,** where you can:

- Find learning outcomes for **Reading Assessment** along with the national standards that connect to these outcomes.

- Complete Assignments and Activities that can help you more deeply understand the chapter content.

- Apply and practice your understanding of the core teaching skills identified in the chapter with the Building Teaching Skills and Dispositions learning units.

- Examine challenging situations and cases presented in the Iris Center Resources.

- Check your comprehension of the content covered in the chapter with the Study Plan. Here you will be able to take a chapter pretest, receive feedback on your answers, and then access personalized Review, Practice, and Enrichment exercises to enhance your understanding of chapter content. After you complete the exercises, take a posttest to confirm your comprehension.

- Practice targeting instruction and making content accessible for all students with A+RISE activities.

# 8 Teaching Phonics, High-Frequency Words, and Fluency

**USING WHAT YOU KNOW**

**B**ecause our speech sounds can be represented by letters, we can write and read anything that can be spoken. Unfortunately, large numbers of students have difficulty learning phonics, the system of letter–sound relationships that enables them to translate printed symbols into meaningful language.

What has been your experience with phonics? What do you do when you encounter an unfamiliar name or a word you have never seen before? How do you decipher these words? Do you know any students who have difficulty decoding words? How might they be helped? What role do you think phonics should play in a program for low-achieving readers?

**ANTICIPATION GUIDE**

*Read each of the following statements. Put a check under "Agree" or "Disagree" to show how you feel about each one. If possible, discuss your responses with classmates.*

|  | AGREE | DISAGREE |
|---|---|---|
| 1. Inadequate instruction in phonics is a major cause of reading failure in the early grades. | _____ | _____ |
| 2. An effective way to learn phonics is through spelling. | _____ | _____ |
| 3. Vowel spellings are so irregular that instruction should focus on consonants, especially in the early stages of learning to read. | _____ | _____ |
| 4. The easiest way to decipher a printed word is to decode it sound by sound. | _____ | _____ |
| 5. Problem readers should learn phonics through reading rather than through formal instruction. | _____ | _____ |
| 6. Students who confuse words such as *where*, *what*, and *when* and read one for the other need to be taught to be more careful. | _____ | _____ |

## ▦ Phonics and the Poor Reader

Failure to master phonics and related word-analysis skills is easily the number-one cause of reading problems. In a longitudinal study that followed 54 students from first through fourth grade, Juel (1994b) found that of the 24 children who remained poor readers through all four grades, 22 were poor decoders and had, in fact, failed to reach the level of decoding achievement of average second graders.

In addition to generalized difficulty with processing words phonologically, poor readers have a variety of specific difficulties learning and using phonics. As a group, low-achieving readers are slower to learn phonics, rely on smaller units of sound, have difficulty applying phonics, tend to over rely on phonics, and fail to integrate context clues with their use of phonics (Adams, 1990).

Poor readers may also scan words less efficiently. Cohen (1974–1975) found that poor readers tend to use fewer letter cues. For instance, they may process only the word's first letter or the first and last letters. They may fail to process the medial vowel, even though the medial vowel is known. As Cohen notes, "One might say that the poor reader is confused with vowel sounds, but there are too many instances where it is more likely that the poor reader simply made a quick judgment based on first letter cue" (p. 647). Making judgments based on an incomplete scan could be developmental. According to the Piagetian concept of decentering, younger children make judgments based on a single perception. However, as children develop cognitively, they are able to use successive elements in a word. Responding on the basis of an incomplete scan of a word's letters could also be due to an impulsive style. Some poor readers may respond too quickly, without looking at all the letters (Gaskins, Ehri, Cress, O'Hara, & Donnelly, 1996–1997).

### Example of Decoding Difficulty

As discussed in Chapter 4, it is not necessary to give a phonics test to detect decoding difficulties. Problems will show up on informal reading inventories in both the graded word lists and oral-reading passages of the test.

Take a look at Figure 8.1, which shows Rachel's performance on the graded word list of an informal reading inventory. It is clear that the student has a very limited immediate recognition vocabulary. The flash column shows that Rachel recognized just six of the words immediately; the untimed column gives a picture of Rachel's ability to apply decoding skills. The student was able to decode initial and final clusters when given time to sound out the words: *wing, went, stick,* and *smell.* However, the student had difficulty with long-vowel words; note how she read *tack* for *take, hum* for *home, net* and *next* for *neat, man* and *men* for *mean,* and *sin* for *sign.* Rachel also had difficulty with *r* vowels patterns (*hurt, floor*) and other-vowel patterns (*move, shoe*). However, Rachel was able to read several high-frequency words: *on, off.*

> ✳ Looking at word recognition on both word-list tests and oral-reading passages provides a more valid assessment, because most students do better when reading words in context.

An examination of her performance on the oral-reading passages and classroom observations confirms this conclusion and also suggests that she overuses context and picture clues and underuses decoding strategies. Although she is in third grade, Rachel has failed to master rudimentary decoding skills and strategies. She needs a systematic program that follows the principles and techniques presented in this chapter. A possible starting point would be a review of clusters and instruction in long-vowel patterns.

**FIGURE 8.1**
Performance on
Word-List Test

| | | FLASH | UNTIMED |
|---|---|---|---|
| 1. | wet | ✓ | |
| 2. | with | ✓ | |
| 3. | take | tack | ✓ |
| 4. | off | ✓ | |
| 5. | home | hum | ✓ |
| 6. | hurt | her | hut |
| 7. | neat | net | next |
| 8. | tiger | tig | tigger |
| 9. | stick | sick | ✓ |
| 10. | move | mo | moo |
| 11. | wing | win | ✓ |
| 12. | mean | man | men |
| 13. | shoe | sh | shot |
| 14. | wish | ✓ | |
| 15. | went | wen | ✓ |
| 16. | on | ✓ | |
| 17. | sign | sin | ✓ |
| 18. | bit | ✓ | |
| 19. | smell | sell | ✓ |
| 20. | floor | fire | far |
| | | 30% | 50% |

## Incidence of Deficient Decoding among Older Students

Appendix A contains the Phonics Inventory, which assesses students' ability to read major word patterns. This test can be used to establish a starting point for phonics instruction.

Having poor decoding skills is a primary cause of poor reading, even among older students. In a study of fourth graders who failed a state proficiency test, Valencia and Buly (2004) found that 41 percent had significant difficulty with decoding. Some 9 percent were labeled as "reading disabled." They could decode single-syllable, short-vowel words but needed systematic instruction in more advanced skills.

## A Theory of Decoding

To correct decoding deficiencies, it is necessary to understand what processes students use to decode words and then construct a theory that accounts for these processes. Instruction should grow out of the theory.

Based on an extensive review of the research, Adams (1990) theorized that the reader uses interacting cues. She concluded that there are four processors at work: orthographic, meaning, context, and phonological, as shown in Figure 8.2. The orthographic processes letters, which are translated into speech sounds by the phonological processor. The meaning processor assigns an identity or meaning to the series of sounds translated by the phonological processor. This meaning is fed into the context processor, which constructs a continuing understanding of the text.

However, communication among processors is two way. Working in parallel fashion, the processors both send and receive information. Information from context, for instance, can speed up the other three processors and vice versa. And when

■ **FIGURE 8.2**
Modeling the
Reading System:
Four Processors
*Source:* Adams (1990).

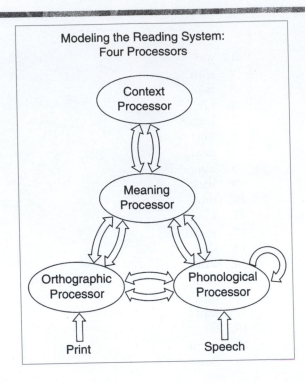

information from one processor is weak, the other processors work extra hard. For instance, when one encounters a word like *produce,* which can have different pronunciations, functions, and meanings, the context processor aids the meaning and phonological processors in assigning a meaning and pronunciation. Readers process most, if not all, of the letters in a word. However, at the same time and in parallel fashion, they also use context. In keeping with this view, this text will emphasize the use of both phonics and context.

As discussed in Chapter 2, although phonological processing is a key element in learning to read words, orthographic processing is also an essential but sometimes overlooked element. Orthographic processing is the visualization or memory of letter patterns so that students can distinguish between or spell words like *hear* and *here.* Students who lack orthographic awareness over-rely on phonics and are slower in their reading. They may continue to sound out words that they have encountered many times.

⁂ Orthographic processing skill fosters rapid, fluent reading (Barker, Torgesen, & Wagner, 1992). Because they are able to recognize words faster, students with good orthographic processing ability are more fluent readers.

## ▦ How Words are Read

Words are read in one of five ways: decoding, analogy, pronounceable word part, prediction, or memory/immediate recognition (Ehri & Snowling, 2004; Gunning, 2013). Students might decode words sound by sound (/h/ + /a/ + /t/) and then blend the sounds. Or they might decode words by sounding out the onset and then the rime (h + at). Or they might read new words by analogy (e.g., the new word *pen* is like the known word *ten*) or by pronounceable word part (noting the familiar word part *en* or *ben* in *bench* and then adding the other word parts to form *bench*). Words are also read by prediction. Students might use the first letter and context to predict what a word might be, or they might use an illustration as a clue. Memory/immediate recognition is used when the word has been encountered so many times that it is bonded in memory. Seeing the letters calls up the word. As Ehri and Snowling (2004) explain, "Knowledge of letter–sound relations provides a powerful mnemonic system that bonds the written forms of specific words to their pronunciations in memory" (pp. 436–437).

According to Ehri (1994), as a student processes words, connections are created between letters and sounds. Access speed increases as a result of processing the word in print many times. Even though words are analyzed element by element, this is done so rapidly that it is virtually instantaneous (Gough, Juel, & Griffith, 1992) and so we say that we recognize words at sight.

In time, all words, except for those we have never seen before, become sight words. Although words may be recognized just about instantaneously, they are learned through phonics. Through processing words phonologically, readers create bonds between a word's spelling and its pronunciation and meaning. This is true even for words such as *are* and *they,* which are only partly phonetic. As the National Reading Panel (2000) noted:

> The primary way to build a sight vocabulary is to apply decoding or analogizing strategies to read unfamiliar words. These ways of reading words help the words to become familiar. Processing letter–sound relations in the words through decoding or analogizing creates alphabetic connections that establish the words in memory as sight words. (Sec. 2, p. 99)

## Phases in Learning to Read Words

Readers' processes change as they become more skillful. From emergent literacy through mature reading, the developing reader seems to go through three phases: prealphabetic, alphabetic, and consolidated alphabetic (Ehri, 1994).

### Prealphabetic Phase

> **Prealphabetic** (logographic) **phase:** students learn words by memorizing their shapes or other distinctive features.

In the **prealphabetic** (logographic) **phase**, readers connect certain visual aspects of a word directly with its meaning. These visual features do not involve letter–sound relationships and may not involve letter identities. The word *McDonald's* is recognized because golden arches are in the background, not because the child realizes that McDonald's starts with an *m.* The word *look* might be remembered because the *o*'s in the middle of the word look like eyes. Since the connections are arbitrary and fail to grow out of an understanding that letters represent sounds, they are easily forgotten or confused or may result in the youngster producing a synonym for the target word. The student might read *see* for the word *look.* As Ehri (1992) explains, "Because the visual cues are connected to meanings rather than pronunciation, readers may produce synonyms rather than one specific word when they read spellings" (p. 125). Major characteristics of this phase include the following:

- Students can read a few high-frequency words.
- Students use word length, shape, and similar cues to remember words.
- Learning words at this stage requires many exposures (McCormick, 1995).
- Students' miscues are generally meaningful. Students might substitute *plane* for *jet* because the focus is on using meaning cues rather than letter–sound cues.

As students reach the end of the stage, they may balk at attempting to read words they don't recognize at sight. Beginning to realize that letters represent sounds but being unable to make full use of that information, students may stop responding (Biemiller, 1970).

- Not having made the connection between letters and sounds, students may spell words with random letters. *Ball* might be spelled *WOF.*
- Poor readers remain in this stage longer and may overrely on picture and meaning cues.

Cardoso-Martins, Rodrigues, and Ehri (2003) conducted a study of nonliterate adults, who knew the letters of the alphabet and a few beginning consonant correspondences. The researchers found that although the adults could read labels, signs, and other environmental print, they could not read these same words when they were not seen in the context of a label or sign but were simply printed in list form. Despite having seen the words many times, the adults did not recognize them out of context. The researchers concluded: "Processing of letter cues may be an unnecessary step when print is embedded in a sufficiently rich and distinctive context as is the case with most environmental print. It may be only when conspicuous nonalphabetic cues are absent that nonreaders who know letters are pushed to use their letter knowledge to perform a word reading task" (p. 353).

This conclusion has implications for young novice readers as well as older novice readers. If they can get by using picture cues, they won't bother processing the text. As Cardoso-Martins et al. (2003) cautioned, "The problem with using environmental print is that the environment is much easier to read than print. More effective instruction is that which teaches students how to process letters in the spellings of words in order to read them" (p. 354).

## Alphabetic Phase

> **Alphabetic** (letter name) **phase:** students use their knowledge of letter sounds to read and spell.

As novice readers begin to learn letter identities and letter–sound relationships, they enter the **alphabetic** (letter name) **phase** and begin to use this knowledge to make connections between the letters in words and their sounds. They note that the *b* in *boy* stands for /b/ and that *cat* ends with a *t,* which represents the sound /t/. Novices may not make all the necessary letter–sound connections in a word. They may only associate the first or the first and last letters with speech sounds. Even so, reading is more accurate and more reliable in this stage because the connections are between letters and the sounds they represent, not between a word's meaning and an arbitrary visual feature.

During the early portions of this stage, the student might use the initial consonant plus context to decode words. Confusion continues to arise, however, especially if the youngster is not using all the letters in the word. In time, most novices learn to use all of the letters in a word and use these to make more accurate and more reliable connections between letters and sounds. Switching from initial consonant plus context to the use of a more fully alphabetical strategy is characteristic of better readers. Poor readers tend to hang on to initial consonant plus context longer than good readers do (McGuinness, 1997). Major characteristics of this phase include the following:

- Students use letter–sound relationships to decode unfamiliar words.
- Students may analyze words sound by sound: *r–a–t.*

- Some students may begin to adopt a strategy of using known parts of a word to decode the whole word. If *fat* is not a word that they have seen in print before, they may read the *at* in *fat* and then add the *f*. Or they may use an analogy strategy: seeing the unfamiliar word *fat*, they relate it to the known word *cat*. Other students may not develop the ability to see patterns in words until they reach the next phase, consolidated alphabet (Invernizzi & Hayes, 2011).

- Students can read more words.

- Students can learn words more easily because they use the relationships between a word's letters and its sounds to help them remember the word.

- Students may overemphasize phonics and produce words that are graphically similar to the target words but that do not fit the sense of the selection: *bad* for *bank*. Because students are overly focused on sounding out, they may also produce nonsense words: *hep* for *help*. In time, students integrate the use of phonics and context so that they produce fewer nonwords or words that do not fit the sense of the selection (Biemiller, 1970).

- Students' spelling reflects their growing knowledge of letter–sound relationships. At first, they may use just initial consonants to spell words (*F* for *fire*). Later, they add final consonants (*FR* for *fire*) and, later still, vowel letters (*FIR* for *fire*).

## Consolidated Alphabetic Phase

> **Consolidated alphabetic** (orthographic, within-word) **phase:** students use their knowledge of patterns, rather than single letters, to read and spell.

In the **consolidated alphabetic** (orthographic, within-word) **phase**, students use more sophisticated print units to make associations between print and sound. For instance, the reader may use final *e* as a sign that the vowel sound in *cape* is $/\bar{a}/$ rather than $/a/$. Instead of reading *goat* as $/g/ + /\bar{o}/ + /t/$, the reader clusters the word into longer units and may read *goat* as $/g/ + /\bar{o}t/$.

Students' ability to learn new word patterns depends on their understanding of the spelling system. Students who are still learning short-vowel patterns may have difficulty with long-vowel patterns. At the short-vowel phase, students understand the writing system as having a one-to-one correspondence. Each letter represents a sound. Being able to grasp long-vowel patterns means that they have to acquire a more advanced understanding of the spelling system. They must see that sounds can be signaled by patterns of letters, such as the final-*e* marker or vowel digraph for long vowels (*ripe, raid*). This is cognitively more difficult than producing a sound for each letter that one sees. Students must both look at each letter and also note the *e* at the end or the two-vowel letters and translate these into sounds. For the final *e* as in *ripe*, they must process the letters from left to right, note the final *e*, and come back to the medial vowel letter. This entails carrying out two operations at the same time. Children who are not in the stage of concrete operations might have difficulty with this (Bear, personal communication, December 4, 2003). Major characteristics of this stage include the following:

- Because they recognize natural units in words, students use longer units to decode words. The word *ranch* might be decoded as *ran–ranch* or *an–ran–ranch*.

- Students use knowledge of such orthographic features as final *e* (*cape*) or two vowels appearing together (*goat*) to decode words.

- In their spelling, students begin to use orthographic information. They add final *e* and use double-vowel letters to spell vowel sounds.

## Syllabic and Morphemic Phase

Syllabic stage and morphemic analysis: students use their knowledge of syllables and morphemes (affixes and roots) to read and spell words.

In the **syllabic stage,** students apply what they have learned about single-syllable words to multisyllabic words. However, they must also learn to make a number of adjustments, such as noting the dropped final *e* in words like *making* and *writing*. Otherwise, they may mispronounce *whining* as *winning* (Invernizzi & Hayes, 2011). They must also learn to adjust the pronunciation of vowels in multisyllabic words that have unaccented syllables (*principal, human*). In **morphemic analysis**, they learn to use roots and affixes to segment words into pronounceable parts and also to derive the meanings of unfamiliar words.

## ▨ Types of Word-Recognition Difficulty

Students with decoding problems fall into a number of categories. Different kinds of decoding problems often have different causes and require different kinds of instruction. The following categories have been suggested by Spear-Swerling (2004).

### Deficient Decoders

These students lack basic decoding skills. They need systematic instruction with lots of opportunities to apply skills. They respond to effective instruction and opportunity to practice. Deficient decoders might have been slow to learn when decoding skills were presented in the early grades. Because often there is no systematic instruction in decoding beyond second grade, they end up with missing skills.

### Disabled Decoders

Despite ample instruction, disabled decoders learn new patterns extremely slowly or not at all. A fifth grader reading on a mid-first-grade level would be an example of a disabled decoder. He might need dozens of repetitions before learning a pattern and then forget it by the next day. Disabled decoders need long-term, intensive instruction that includes techniques, such as the Orton–Gillingham or Fernald (1943), for shoring up attention/concentration and memory.

### Inaccurate Decoders

Not having mastered basic decoding skills because of poor phonemic awareness or a lack of instruction or practice, inaccurate decoders misread patterns, especially those that are less common, such as the *oi* in *avoid*. They may compensate by overusing context clues and so they fail to fully analyze words. Because they fail to fully analyze words, their growth is hindered. They need systematic instruction and lots of practice. They also need to monitor for meaning.

### Nonautomatic Decoders

These students have solid basic word-recognition skills, but their skills are not automatic and so they read slowly and laboriously. They need lots and lots of practice with easy materials. Because they may see the purpose of reading as pronouncing words accurately, rather than constructing meaning, silent reading and reading for meaning should be emphasized.

## ▚ Principles of Teaching Phonics

⚘ This text recommends early, systematic instruction in phonics along with application in context. Context speeds the use of phonics, but does not replace it. For students who need it, there should be some instruction in phonics during every intervention session, accompanied by opportunities to apply what was learned by reading selections that incorporate the element taught.

The key to teaching phonics to poor readers is to gear instruction to the stage the students are in and to use an approach that is systematic and fits the needs of individual learners. Ample reinforcement in the form of extensive reading is also essential. In too many programs, students are given large doses of phonics but little opportunity to apply decoding strategies. Extensive reading is required for students to incorporate strategies to the point where they become automatic. Care needs to be taken that phonics is not overemphasized to the detriment of comprehension. Students may become so focused on sounding out words that they fail to read for meaning. Ironically, this cuts them off from context clues, a very valuable source of information about the identities of printed words.

Realizing that students are deficient in phonics, teachers may spend lengthy periods instructing students in word-analysis skills so that the students can catch up. While direct instruction in phonics is essential for poor readers, a little phonics instruction goes a long way. A brief period of direct phonics instruction should be complemented by fairly lengthy periods of reading or other form of application. As a rule of thumb, 10 or 15 minutes of phonics instruction a day is probably plenty.

It goes without saying that the skills taught should be those that are incorporated in the selection to be read. For instance, a good time to present the -*at* pattern would be when students are about to read a text such as a *Cat on the Mat* (Wildsmith, 1982). The skills taught should also be skills that the student needs to know.

To be effective, phonics instruction should be functional, useful, and contextual It also should be planned, systematic, and explicit (Fielding-Barnsley, 1997; Foorman, Fletcher, Francis, Schatschneider, & Mehta, 1998). It must also be differentiated.

## Differentiation of Phonics Instruction

Often, teachers doing intervention note that students are weak in phonics and decide to begin from the beginning. This is a poor practice. It fails to give students credit for what they know and undermines them by giving them material that is too easy. Assess students to find out where they are, and begin instruction there, making adjustments as necessary.

Similarly, whole-class instruction in phonics is a poor practice. In almost all classes, there is a range of phonics knowledge. Students have different levels of understanding of the alphabetic principle. Some are just beginning to grasp that letters represent sounds. Others have a concept that each sound in a word is represented by a letter—as with /h/, /a/, /t/ for *hat*—and are learning short-vowel patterns that, for the most part, show a one-to-one correspondence between letters and sounds. More advanced students realize that not all words can be processed sound by sound. They have come to the understanding that some words have a final-*e* marker that indicates that the preceding vowel is long, as in *hate,* or a vowel digraph that performs a similar function, as in *wait.* Instruction should be geared to students' developmental level. Students who are just beginning to grasp that each sound in a word is represented by a letter and have not mastered short-vowel patterns are not ready for instruction in final-*e* or digraph patterns. Research clearly indicates that students make the most progress when they are grouped according to their developmental level (Juel & Minden-Cupp, 2000). Some reading programs recommend whole-class instruction in phonics. However, the research clearly favors small-group, targeted instruction (National Reading Panel, 2000).

Differentiation also means gearing the nature of instruction to the needs of students. In one study, children low in alphabet knowledge did best when placed with the teacher who did the most phonics (Juel, 2010). The teacher shifted to more reading as students acquired decoding skills, and students were reading above grade level by year's end. On the other hand, students with low alphabet knowledge in a classroom in which reading of trade books and predictable books was emphasized did poorly. However, those high in alphabet knowledge did well. Being called on was a key factor in students' progress. Children who were called on the most (average of 10 times a session) made the most progress (Juel, 2010).

Buly and Valencia (2002) found a tendency to prescribe wholesale instruction in phonics to help the large numbers of fourth graders who were failing the state reading test. However, when they assessed students who failed the test, they found that the students had a variety of needs. While some did need phonics instruction, others needed work in fluency, comprehension, vocabulary, or a combination of areas (Gunning, 2013).

## The Content of Phonics: Consonants

Although there are only 26 letters in the alphabet, there are approximately 41 speech sounds in English. These include 25 consonant and 16 vowel sounds. Many of these sounds can be spelled in more than one way.

English vowels are notorious for the many ways in which they can be spelled. However, if you look at the list of consonant sounds and their spellings in Table 8.1, you can see that most have only one spelling. The consonant /b/, for instance, is regularly spelled *b* as in *baby*. Even the consonant /f/, which is one of the most variable consonant elements, is generally spelled *f*; it is only rarely spelled *ph* (*photo*) or *gh* (*laugh*). Because consonants are less variable than vowels in their spellings, they are usually presented first in most phonics programs. Coming in initial position as they do in many words, consonant letters also provide more essential and more usable cues than vowels. Also, in children's invented spelling, consonants are the first letters to appear (Read, 1971).

## Approaches to Teaching Consonants

> **Explicit** (synthetic) **phonics:** presents phonic elements in isolation and synthesized into whole words. Thus *t* = /t/, *e* = /e/, and *n* = /n/ are taught as separate elements and then blended to form the word *ten*.

The two major approaches to teaching phonics are the *explicit* and *implicit*, which are sometimes termed the *synthetic* and *analytic*. In **explicit phonics,** students are taught isolated sounds and then blend the sounds together to create a word. In deciphering the word *hat*, the student would say "huh-ah-tuh" and then blend the sounds into "hat." A major problem with an explicit approach is that it distorts sounds. Stop consonant sounds, such as /b/, /d/, and /p/, cannot be spoken in isolation without distorting them. (Try saying *b* without making a vowel sound.) In addition, blending sounds to form a word is a difficult task for many readers. Blending poses a short-term memory problem, especially if the word is a long one such as "s-t-r-a-p." By the time the student gets to the last sound, he may have forgotten the first one (National Reading Panel, 2000).

**TABLE 8.1**
Consonant
Spellings

| Sound | Spelling: Initial | Spelling: Final | Model Word |
|---|---|---|---|
| /b/ | boy | tub, tube | ball |
| /d/ | day | had | dog |
| /f/ | five, phone | life, graph | fish |
| /g/ | gate, ghost, guide | bag | goat |
| /h/ | hen, who | | hat |
| /hw/ | when | | whale |
| /j/ | jeep, giant | age, bridge | jar, giraffe |
| /k/ | cap, king, quit, character | bake, track, ache | cat, key |
| /l/ | little | well | lion |
| /m/ | me | am, time, hymn, tomb | man |
| /n/ | new, gnaw, pneumatic | | nail |
| /p/ | page | top | pen |
| /r/ | read | | ring |
| /s/ | side, cent | bus, pass, race | sun |
| /t/ | tail | bat, hopped | ten |
| /v/ | van | brave | vase |
| /w/ | wet, wheel | | wagon |
| /y/ | yes, onion | | yo-yo |
| /z/ | zoo | says, prize, quiz, zebra | zoo |
| /ch/ | church, cello | hatch, question | chair, future |
| /sh/ | she, sugar, Chicago | | shoe |
| /th/ | think | bath | thumb |
| /th/ | that | bathe | the |
| /zh/ | azure, version | garage | |
| /ŋ/ | | sing | ring |

*Note: Initial* and *final* refer to words *or* syllables.

> **Implicit (analytic) phonics:** presents letter–sound relationships within the context of a whole word. The correspondence $t = /t/$ is taught as "*t* represents the sound heard at the beginning of *t–en*."

The **implicit phonics** approach uses the context of whole words and is the method once espoused in most of the best-selling basal systems (Stein, Johnson, & Gutlophn, 1999). In an implicit approach, students are not taught that *h* makes a "huh" sound; they are told that *h* makes the sound heard at the beginning of *hat*. The major disadvantage of the implicit approach is that it is somewhat circuitous. For $m = /m/$, students are required to think about the sound they hear at the beginning of the word *moon* and abstract it from that word, which means that they must be able to segment the first sound in the word (Beck & Juel, 1995). Although it results in a distortion, it is easier to identify the sound of *m* as being "mmm."

> ⚓ Novice readers may process words sound by sound (/h/ + /e/ + /n/), but gradually learn to chunk sounds (/h/ + /en/).

Because explicit phonics breaks down phonics into its smallest elements, it is frequently used in intervention materials and today's basals. However, because of the distortion and the difficulty of blending, readers may not recognize the word they have sounded out. The best way to resolve this problem is to use elements of both explicit and implicit phonics. For instance, in teaching $m = /m/$, refer to *m* as the letter that stands for "mmm" as in *moon*. In this way, you are presenting the correspondence both in isolation and in context. Students encounter the correspondence in a real word but also hear it alone. Hearing the consonant pronounced in isolation is especially important for poor readers because some students have difficulty abstracting sounds from words—detecting the /m/ in *moon*, for instance. The following sample lesson combines the best features of an explicit and an implicit approach.

## Consonant Correspondence Lesson: *s* = /s/

### Objectives

- Students will understand that the letter *s* stands for the sound /s/.
- Students will use their understanding of /s/ to sound out and spell initial *s*.

**Step 1:  Phonemic awareness.** Hold up a series of objects or pictures of objects whose names begin with *s*: *saw, six, socks, seal, sandwich*. Have students say the name of each object. Repeat the names of all the objects, emphasizing the initial sound as you do so. Lead students to see that the words all begin with the same sound. Present the sound both in isolation and in the context of a word. (Although saying the sound in isolation distorts it, some youngsters have difficulty detecting a sound in the context of a word.) Say that *saw, six, socks, seal,* and *sandwich* begin with the sound /s/ as in *sun*. If any members of the class have first names that begin with *s*, ask them to raise their hands. Help the class determine whether the names actually do begin with /s/.

If students have difficulty detecting initial sounds, try asking silly questions that focus on *s*. Holding up a sock, ask, "Is this a lock? Is this a rock?" Lead students to see that *lock* and *rock* begin with the wrong sounds and must be changed to /s/ to make *sock*. Other silly questions might include the following: "Is this a wheel? (holding up a picture of a seal). Is this a bun?" (holding up a picture of the sun).

**Step 2:  Letter–sound integration.** Write the name of each of the objects from step 1 on the board: *saw, six, socks, seal, sandwich,* and *sun*. Read each name and have students tell with which letter each of the words begins. Lead students to see that the letter *s* stands for the sound /s/ heard at the beginning of *saw, six, socks, seal, sandwich,* and *sun*. (Create a model word for *s* = /s/. A model word is one that would most likely be a part of the students' listening vocabulary and is used to illustrate a correspondence such as *s* = /s/. Most model words are easy to depict so they can be accompanied by an illustration. A good model word for *s* = /s/ is *sun*. Place the model word along with an illustration on a consonant chart. If students forget the sound that a letter represents, the model word accompanied by its picture can be used as a reminder. Tell students that if they forget what sound *s* stands for, they can use the consonant chart to help them.)

**Step 3:  Guided practice.** Have students read sentences that contain easy *s* words: "I see the sun." "I see Sam." With the class read labels and signs that contain *s* words, as in the examples below.

> Salt
>
> For Sale
>
> Soda
>
> Seven-Up

**Step 4:  Application.** Have students read stories and real-world materials that contain easy *s* words. Easy picture books that feature *s* words include *Have You Seen My Cat?* (Carle, 1987) and *Brown Bear, Brown Bear, What Do You See?* (Martin, 1983). If students' skills are too limited for independent or guided reading, use shared reading of big books or create experience or interactive stories that contain the target consonant correspondence.

**Step 5:  Writing and spelling.** Review the formation of *s*, both upper- and lowercase. Dictate some easy *s* words (*see, sat*), and have students spell them as best they can. Encourage students to write sentences or stories that contain *s* words.

**Step 6:  Evaluation and reteaching.** Note whether students are able to read at least the initial consonant of *s* words and are using *s* in their writing. Review and reteach as necessary. Throughout the day, call attention to initial consonants that have been recently taught. As you prepare to write the word *Saturday,* for instance, ask students to tell what sound *Saturday* begins with and what letter makes that sound.

## ▨▨ Other Consonant Elements

After learning most of the initial consonant correspondences, students are introduced to consonant digraphs, final consonants, and consonant clusters.

### Consonant Digraphs

> **Digraph:** two letters that represent one sound, such as *sh* in *ship*. A trigraph consists of three letters that represent one sound, such as the *igh* spelling of long *i* in the word *sigh*.

Consonant **digraphs** (*di* = "two," *graphs* = "letters") are correspondences in which single consonant sounds are represented by two letters, as in *shore*. Note that two letters are used in *shore* to spell the initial consonant sound, but in *sure* a single consonant letter is used to spell the beginning consonant sound. Although the beginning sounds in both *shore* and *sure* have the same pronunciation, *shore* contains a digraph but *sure* does not. Common digraphs are listed in Table 8.2.

Digraphs are taught in the same way single consonant–letter correspondences are. However, you may want to point out to students that sometimes single sounds are spelled with two letters.

### Final Consonants

Final-consonant correspondences are generally introduced after most initial-consonant and consonant digraph correspondences have been taught. Final-consonant correspondences can be confusing. For instance, although initial *r, w,* and *y* represent consonant sounds, final *r, w,* and *y* are used to spell vowel sounds (*or, snow, wow, cry, holly*). Sounds represented by spellings may also change. *S* at the beginning of a word represents /s/, but it may represent /s/ or /z/ at the end of a word: *bus, has.*

### Consonant Clusters

> **Cluster:** two or more letters representing two or more sounds, such as the *sc* in *scale* and the *scr* in *scream*. Clusters are also referred to as *blends*.

As their name suggests, **clusters** (sometimes known as *blends*) are composed of two or more letters, but unlike digraphs, they represent two or more sounds, as in the *st* (/s/, /t/) in *stop* and the *spl* (/s/, /p/, /l/) in *splash*. Poor readers experience significant

**TABLE 8.2**
Consonant
Digraphs

| Digraphs | Examples |
|---|---|
| *ch* = /ch/ | **ch**ildren, **ch**urch |
| *ck* = /k/ | tra**ck**, sa**ck** |
| *gh* = /g/ | **gh**ost, **gh**etto |
| *gu* = /g/ | **gu**ess, **gu**est |
| *gh* = /f/ | lau**gh**, rou**gh** |
| *kn* = /n/ | **kn**ow, **kn**ot |
| *ng* = /ŋ/ | ri**ng**, bri**ng** |
| *ph* = /f/ | **ph**onics, **ph**easant |
| *sh* = /sh/ | **sh**op, **sh**ell |
| *th* = /th/ | **th**ink, **th**umb |
| *th* = /th/ | **th**is, **th**at |
| *wh* = /hw/ or /w/ | **wh**eel, **wh**eat |
| *wr* = /r/ | **wr**ong, **wr**ite |

difficulty with clusters. Knowing the individual consonant correspondences that make up a cluster does not guarantee students will be able to decipher it. Although they may be able to read *nail* and *sail,* they may stumble over *snail.*

When teaching consonant clusters to poor readers, build on what they already know. Most clusters are composed of *s, l,* or *r* combined with other common consonant letters. A list of clusters is presented in Table 8.3. When introducing a cluster, review the known correspondences that make up the cluster. Before introducing *sp,* for instance, review initial *s* and *p.*

The main obstacle students have learning clusters is separating the second sound in the cluster from the first. This is especially true of *l* and *r* clusters, because their sounds tend to merge with the preceding consonant. When teaching clusters, start with *s* clusters, which are more distinctive. Stress the separate sounds, and place

**TABLE 8.3**
Consonant
Clusters

| | Initial | | Final |
|---|---|---|---|
| **L** | | | |
| *bl* | **bl**anket, **bl**ue | *ld* | go**ld**, so**ld** |
| *cl* | **cl**am, **cl**oud | *lf* | wo**lf**, she**lf** |
| *fl* | **fl**ower, **fl**oor | *lk* | mi**lk**, wa**lk** |
| *gl* | **gl**ass, **gl**ad | *lt* | be**lt**, bo**lt** |
| *pl* | **pl**ate, **pl**ay | — | |
| *sl* | **sl**ide, **sl**ap | — | |
| **R** | | | |
| *br* | **br**ush, **br**ead | — | |
| *cr* | **cr**ab, **cr**ack | — | |
| *dr* | **dr**um, **dr**eam | — | |
| *fr* | **fr**og, **fr**ee | — | |
| *gr* | **gr**apes, **gr**ay | — | |
| *pr* | **pr**etzel, **pr**ize | — | |
| *tr* | **tr**ee, **tr**unk | — | |
| **S** | | | |
| *sc* | **sc**arecrow, **sc**out | — | |
| *sch* | **sch**ool, **sch**edule | — | |
| *scr* | **scr**eam, **scr**ub | — | |
| *shr* | **shr**ew, **shr**ink | — | |
| *sk* | **sk**unk, **sk**y | | de**sk**, ma**sk** |
| *sl* | **sl**ide, **sl**ed | — | |
| *sm* | **sm**ile, **sm**ell | — | |
| *sn* | **sn**ake, **sn**eeze | — | |
| *sp* | **sp**oon, **sp**in | | wa**sp**, gra**sp** |
| *spl* | **spl**ash, **spl**inter | — | |
| *spr* | **spr**ing, **spr**ead | — | |
| *st* | **st**ar, **st**and | | ve**st**, ma**st** |
| *str* | **str**ing, **str**eet | — | |
| *squ* | **squ**irrel, **squ**are | — | |
| *sw* | **sw**ing, **sw**eep | — | |
| **Others** | | | |
| *tw* | **tw**elve, **tw**ig | *ct* | a**ct**, effe**ct** |
| *qu* | **qu**een, **qu**ick | *m* | ju**m**p, la**m**p |

extra emphasis on the second sound. To develop phonemic awareness, slowly say a word containing the cluster, and have students count out the sounds, holding up a finger for each sound. For example, as you say "stop," hold up a finger as you say /s/, a second finger as you say /t/, a third as you say /o/, and a fourth as you say /p/.

Build on what students already know. In presenting the spelling of the cluster *st*, relate it to known words that begin with *s*. Place the word *sick* on the board, and have students read it. Stretch and count each out sound: /s/, /i/, /k/. Ask students to tell what needs to be added to *sick* to make the word *stick*. As you say "stick," emphasize the /t/. Present *sack–stack, sand–stand, sill–still*, and *sink–stink*. If students have had long-vowel words, you might also present *say–stay, sore–store*, and *seal–steal*. Lead students to see that all the words begin with *st*, the letters that spell the sounds heard at the beginning of *stick*.

Once students have caught on to the *st* cluster, present other *st* words: *stop, stamp, step*. For words like *spot* and *spark*, which don't form a word when the second consonant is removed, have students add an initial consonant. Write *pot* and *park* on the board, and have students read each word. Then ask what letter you would have to put in front of *pot* to make the word *spot*. After adding the *s*, read the word, stressing the /s/ and /p/. Point out that *spot* begins with an *s* and *p*. Ask volunteers to read the word. Form *spark* in this same way (Gunning, 2010).

To provide additional practice with *sp*, dictate a series of *s* and *sp* words to students. Have them write the beginning letter or letters. You might dictate words such as *soon, spoon, sank, spank, send*, and *spend*. As students write the beginnings of the words, tell them to say the sounds slowly so they can hear whether to write just an *s* or an *sp*. After students have attempted spelling the beginning of a word, write the whole word on the board and have students read it.

Students might also sort words containing *sp* or other clusters. The sort could take a number of forms. Initially, students might sort words according to whether they begin with a single consonant sound or a cluster of sounds. Students might then sort words according to which cluster they begin with.

Share-read with students selections that contain *sp* words, and have students complete a variety of practice exercises. Most important of all, have students read and write stories that contain *sp*. Easy picture books that contain *sp* words include *Spot Goes to the Circus* (Hill, 1986) and *More Spaghetti I Say* (Gelman, 1977).

## Confusing Consonants

Two consonant letters that offer special difficulty are *c* and *g*, because they can each represent two sounds (*c* = /k/ [*can*] or *c* = /s/ [*cent*]; *g* = /g/ [*girl*] or *g* = /j/ [*gym*]). When teaching these consonant letters, present the most frequently occurring correspondences in each pair first (*g* = /g/, *c* = /k/). Later, present the less frequently occurring correspondence (*g* = /j/, *c* = /s/). Teaching the following generalizations may also be helpful:

- The letter *c* stands for /k/ when followed by *a, o*, or *u*: *can, cot, cub*.
- The letter *c* stands for /s/ when followed by *e, i*, or *y*: *cent, city, cycle*.
- The letter *g* often stands for /g/ when followed by *a, o*, or *u*: *game, gone, gun*.
- The letter *g* often stands for /j/ when followed by *e, i*, or *y*: *general, giant, gym*. (There are a number of exceptions: *geese, get, girl, give*.)

When teaching the *c* and *g* generalizations, have students sort *c* = /k/ and *c* = /s/ words and later *g* = /g/ and *g* = /j/ words and discover the generalizations for themselves. An alternative to presenting the *c* and *g* generalizations is to teach students to be prepared to deal with the variability of the spellings of certain sounds. Students need to learn that letters in English can often stand for more than one sound.

After learning the two sounds for *c* and *g*, students should be taught to use the following "try-another-sound" strategy when they are unsure how to read a word that begins with *c* or *g*:

1.  Try the main pronunciation—the one the letter usually stands for.

2.  If the main pronunciation gives a word that is not a real one or does not make sense in the sentence, try the other pronunciation.

3.  If you still get a word that is not a real word or does not make sense in the sentence, try using context clues, skip it, or ask for help (Gunning, 2001).

Also stress the need to read for meaning. When a group of second graders who had been taught the *c* generalization encountered the sentence "We went to the city to catch a train," most read it as "We went to the kitty to catch a train" (Gunning, 1988b). Had they been taught to try alternative pronunciations and to use both phonics and context, they would have a better chance to read the sentence accurately.

To help build awareness of the major sounds that letters represent, create a consonant chart similar to the one in Figure 8.3. The chart depicts major consonant letters and the major sounds these letters represent. When students encounter a letter or letter combination for which they are unable to produce a sound, they can refer to the chart. The chart will be especially helpful for deciphering letters that represent multiple sounds. The chart clearly indicates, for example, that *c* represents two distinct sounds, as does *g*. After a correspondence has been introduced, add it to the chart. For students who have difficulty remembering initial-consonant correspondences, a consonant chart can be a very useful aid, one that fosters both learning and independence.

## Sequence of Teaching Consonants

Consonant correspondences can be taught in any order, but frequency of occurrence and ease of learning should be considered when determining which elements are taught first. Many low-achieving readers have difficulty with auditory discrimination and perception. Therefore, it is best to start with /s/, /m/, /f/, /r/, /n/, or /w/ or another continuant because they are articulated with a continuous stream of breath and so are easier to detect than stop consonants. A suggested scope and sequence for both consonants and vowels is presented in Figure 8.4. The sequence is based on the frequency with which the correspondences appear and their estimated level of difficulty (Gunning, 1975).

Although consonants are typically taught before vowels in most programs, it is recommended that consonants and vowels be taught together. After presenting four or five initial-consonant correspondences, introduce -*at* or another vowel pattern and form words. If the consonant correspondences *s* = /s/, *m* = /m/, *r* = /r/, and *f* = /f/ have been taught, you can then form the words *mat*, *rat*, *sat*, and *fat* and the sentence "The fat rat sat on the mat." After other consonant correspondences have been introduced, gradually introduce other high-frequency patterns. If the introduction of consonants and vowels is integrated in this fashion, it will be possible to form words from elements that have been taught and also to use knowledge of both consonants and vowels to decode words.

**▪▪ FIGURE 8.3**
Consonant Chart
*Source:* Gunning
(2008). Reprinted by
permission of Galvin
Publications.

## Consonant Chart

| | | | | |
|---|---|---|---|---|
| b | ball | | n | nail |
| c | cat | | p | pen |
| c | city | | qu | queen |
| d | dog | | r | ring |
| ch | chair | | s | sun |
| f | fish | | sh | shoe |
| g | goat | | t | ten |
| g | giraffe | | th | thumb |
| | | | th | the |
| h | hat | | v | vase |
| j | jar | | w | wagon |
| k | king | | x | fox |
| l | lion | | y | yo-yo |
| m | man | | z | zebra |

## ▪▪▪ Reinforcement Activities for Consonant Correspondences

### Reading

The best way to provide additional instruction and reinforcement with consonant correspondences is to use children's books. Alphabet books are especially appropriate for introducing and/or reinforcing consonant correspondences, as are books that are alliterative. Some books that are especially appropriate for providing practice with consonant correspondences are listed here:

Calmenson, S. ( 1993 ). *It begins with an A.* New York: Hyperion. Rhyming riddles challenge the reader to guess objects whose names begin with letters *A* to *Z.*

Cronin, D. ( 2005 ). *Click, clack, quackity-quack: An alphabetical adventure.* New York: Simon & Schuster. A summer adventure is told in alliterative phrases.

**FIGURE 8.4**
Sequence for
Teaching Vowels
and Consonants

## PREPARATORY LEVEL: LETTER NAMES, PHONEMIC AWARENESS

### LEVEL 1

High-frequency initial consonants

| | | |
|---|---|---|
| s = /s/ | r = /r/ | d = /d/ |
| m = /m/ | l = /l/ | c = /k/ |
| f = /f/ | b = /b/ | p = /p/ |
| h = /h/ | t = /t/ | n = /n/ |

Lower-frequency initial consonants and *y*

| | | |
|---|---|---|
| g = /g/ | r = /r/ | z = /z/ |
| w = /w/ | c = /s/ | x = /ks/ |
| j = /j/ | g = /j/ | |
| k = /k/ | y = /y/ | |

High-frequency initial-consonant digraphs

| | |
|---|---|
| ch = /ch/ | th = /th/ |
| sh = /sh/ | wh = /hw/ or /w/ |
| th = /th/ | |

Short vowels

a = /a/   (*hat*)
i = /i/   (*sit*)
o = /o/   (*not*)
e = /e/   (*pet*)
u = /u/   (*but*)

### LEVEL 2

Final consonants
High-frequency initial-consonant clusters

*L* clusters: *bl, cl, fl, gl, pl, sl*
*R* clusters: *br, cr, dr, fr, gr, pr, tr*
*S* clusters: *sc, scr, sk, sl, sm, sn, sp, st, str, sw*
Other clusters: *tw, qu, ct, mp*

Long vowels: final-*e* marker

| | |
|---|---|
| a-e = /ā/ | (*brave*) |
| i-e = /î/ | (*time*) |
| o-e = ō | (*hope*) |
| e-e = /ê/ | (*these*) |
| u-e = /û/ | (*fuse*) |

Long-vowel digraphs and trigraphs

| | |
|---|---|
| ai/ay = /ā/ | (*rain, hay*) |
| ee = /ē/ | (*tree*) |
| ea = /ē/ | (*seal*) |
| oa = /ō/ | (*goat*) |
| ow = /ō/ | (*crow*) |
| igh = /ī/ | (*night*) |

### LEVEL 3

*r*-Vowel correspondences

| | |
|---|---|
| ar = /ar/ | (*star*) |
| er = /er/ | (*her*) |
| ir = /er/ | (*sir*) |
| ur = /er/ | (*turn*) |
| or(e) = /or/ | (*for, store*) |
| air = /air/ | (*chair*) |
| ear = /eer/ | (*dear*) |
| eer = /eer/ | (*deer*) |

Other vowel correspondences

| | |
|---|---|
| au/aw = /aw/ | (*auto, claw*) |
| al = /aw/ | (*ball, walk*) |
| oo = /oo/ | (*look*) |
| oo = /ō̄o/ | (*food*) |
| oi/oy = /oy/ | (*boil, boy*) |
| ou/ow = /ow/ | (*out, cow*) |
| ue, ew = /ō̄o/ | (*true, grew*) |

### LEVEL 4

Advanced consonant correspondences

| | |
|---|---|
| ti = /sh/ | (*nation*) |
| ssi = /sh/ | (*mission*) |
| ch = /sh/ | (*chef*) |
| ch = /k/ | (*character*) |

Multisyllabic patterns (After teaching
short-vowel patterns, present two-syllable
words composed of those patterns.
Do the same with other patterns.)

Eastman, P. D. (1974). *The alphabet book.* New York: Random House. Each letter is accompanied by alliterative phrases.

Geisel, T. S. (1973). *Dr. Seuss's ABC.* New York: Random House. Each letter is accompanied by a humorous alliterative story.

Hofbauer, M. (1993). *All the letters.* Bridgeport, CT: Greene Bark Press. Each letter is illustrated with several objects beginning with that letter. Highly recommended.

Kellogg, S. (1987). *Aster Aardvark's alphabet adventures.* New York: Morrow. Each letter is accompanied by an alliterative story.

Laidlaw, K. (1996). *The amazing I spy ABC.* New York: Dial. Readers spy objects whose names begin with the target letter.

Wallace, N. E. ( 2005 ). *Alphabet house.* New York: Marshall Cavendish. Readers identify objects that begin with the letter sound featured on each page.

## Sorting

As noted earlier, an appealing but powerful way to help children discover basic principles of word construction is through sorting. Through sorting, children categorize words according to sound, spelling, meaning, or a combination of features. At the most basic level, pictures can be sorted according to beginning or rhyming sounds. On a more advanced level, words can be sorted according to the spelling patterns they incorporate or the meanings of the words' affixes. Through sorting, students examine each word's features and decide into which category it falls. Thus, they construct their own understanding of the underlying principles that they use to sort words. These principles are clarified and refined in discussions.

> Students' progress should be continuously monitored. Phonics knowledge builds. If students fail to master initial consonants, for instance, they will only be frustrated if they are pushed ahead to consonant clusters such as *st* and *gr*.

As soon as at least two correspondences have been introduced, students can sort them. When supplying correspondences for students to sort, choose ones that are distinctively different. Make letter cards for the sounds to be sorted, and assemble pictures that begin with the target sounds. Place each letter card at the head of a column, say the sound each represents, and then place under it an illustration of the sound's model word. For *s,* place an *Ss* card at the head of the column and say "*S* stands for /s/, the sound that you hear at the beginning of *sun.*" Place a picture of the sun under *Ss* and say "*Sun* is the model word for /s/." Follow this same procedure for the correspondence *m* = /m/ as in Figure 8.5.

Pointing to a stack of cards containing objects whose names begin with /s/ or /m/, tell students, "We're going to sort these picture cards. If the name of the picture begins with /s/ as in *sun,* we're going to put it in the *sun* column. If the name of the picture begins with /m/ as in *man,* we'll put it in the *man* column. Holding up a picture of a saw, ask "What is this? What sound does it begin with? What column should we put it in?" Affirm or correct students' responses. "Yes, saw begins with the sound /s/ that we hear in the beginning of *sssun,* so we put it in the *sun* column." Sort the remaining cards in this same way.

After all the cards have been sorted, have volunteers say the names of all the cards in each column and note that all the cards in the column begin with the same sound. Encourage students to suggest other words that might fit into the columns. Also have them re-sort the pictures on their own to foster speed of response. You might also add a third item to be sorted. If students seem to be using a picture card as a basis for sorting—they put *moon* under *man* because they both begin the same way—stop using the model cards and remove the picture cards as soon as they have been sorted so that they are matching the cards to the letter—*moon* is placed under the letter *m* because it begins with the sound /m/ (Morris, 1999).

Three correspondences should be the most that students are asked to sort. After students have mastered a group of three correspondences, drop the best-known correspondence and add a new one, or perhaps introduce three new correspondences.

After students have become adept at sorting cards, introduce a writing sort. In a writing sort, students write whole words or parts of them in columns headed by the target consonant sound. After sorting words beginning with /m/, /s/, or /f/, students fold their papers into three columns and head the columns: *m, s, f.* Dictate

**FIGURE 8.5**
Sorting

words starting with the target sounds. Students write the words in the appropriate column: *man* in the /m/ column, for instance. As you dictate the words, emphasize the initial sound.

Encourage students to say the words as they write them so that they are better able to detect each word's sounds. Also encourage students to write as much of each of the words as they can, but stress the writing of the initial sounds. Correct only the errors in placing the words in the wrong column or errors in writing the initial consonants. Students are to be held responsible only for what they have been taught, but they should be encouraged to explore letter–sound relationships and write as much of each word as they can. After students learn vowel patterns, they will be expected to spell whole words correctly in their writing sorts.

## Additional Reinforcement Activities

- Using magnetic or letter cutouts, students form *s* words.
- Students find and read *s* words in signs and food labels.
- Students create their own alphabet books.
- Students write as many *s* words as they can think of.
- Create an alphabet zoo. As a correspondence is introduced, add animals whose names begin with the target correspondence: *seal, salamander, salmon, sardine, sunfish.*

- Encourage students to use context and knowledge of s = /s/ to help them decode unfamiliar words that begin with s. However, once vowels have been introduced, encourage the use of all the word's letters and sounds.

## ▟▟ Using a Multisensory Approach to Learn Letter Names and Letter Sounds

Although Nathan, a second grader, had above-average intelligence and had been taught by highly competent classroom teachers as well as a learning specialist, he still did not know the names of the letters of the alphabet and in fact still could not name all the letters in his name. The teachers had tried all the usual methods for presenting the letters of the alphabet, as well as a number of imaginative and motivational activities, but nothing was working. Nathan apparently has an associative learning difficulty.

When students cannot seem to learn letter names and letter sounds in the normal way, try a multisensory approach. In a multisensory approach, students use their kinesthetic and tactile senses to reinforce auditory and visual senses. In addition to hearing and seeing the names of the letters of the alphabet, students say them and so get kinesthetic input and feedback and trace them, which provides tactile input

## Multisensory Lesson

**Step 1:  Introducing the letter.** The teacher says the name of the letter, *m,* and then has the class say the name of the letter. The teacher then calls on individuals to say the letter's name.

**Step 2:  Forming the letter.** The teacher demonstrates the formation of the letter. As the teacher demonstrates the formation of the letter, she describes the movements she is making: down, up and around and down, up and around and down again. Students trace the letter in the air, reciting the directions for forming the word as they do so. Saying the words and tracing helps the students remember the motor movements necessary to form the letter.

**Step 3:  Learning the letter name.** Once students have learned the movements necessary to form the letter, they begin to learn the letter name. Using a duplicated letter, students trace the letter with their fingers while saying its name. Students then copy the letter while saying its name, and, when they feel they can write the letter without looking at it, write it from memory.

**Step 4:  Learning the letter sound.** If students can tell when two words begin with the same sound and can segment the first sound in a word, they

can learn beginning-consonant correspondences. Share-read a story or a rhyme such as "The Three Little Kittens" that contains a number of /m/ words. Discuss how the words *mittens, meow,* and *mother* begin in the same way. To provide students with kinesthetic cues, demonstrate how the sound /m/ is formed. Have students note how the lips are pressed together to make the sound. Have students form the sound /m/. Going back over the nursery rhyme, note that *mittens, meow,* and *mother* all begin with the sound /m/ and are spelled with the letter *m.* Create a model word for /m/: *moon.* In practice activities, have students make the following associations.

- Visual–auditory–kinesthetic. Hold up the letter card. Students say its sound and the model word.

- Auditory–visual. Say the sound. Students, who have been given three or four alphabet cards, hold up the letter card that makes the sound.

- Auditory–visual–kinesthetic–tactile. Say the sound. Students write the letter that makes the sound. They say the sound as they form the letter.

and feedback. Pointing to the letter being taught, the teacher says the name of the letter and then traces it. The letter might be traced in the air, on the chalkboard, or on paper with a crayon or pencil.

Slingerland (1971) recommends tracing large letters. She recommends that they be at least a foot tall, so that students feel the flow of the movements needed to form the letter. Letters are traced using the index and middle fingers. As students trace the letter, they say its name. They should trace it enough times so that the motions involved in forming the letter become automatic. The box on page 243 shows how the letter *m* might be introduced. The lesson is based on the Slingerland approach (1971).

## The Content of Phonics: Vowels

There are fewer vowel than consonant sounds. There are approximately 16 vowel sounds in English. Table 8.4 shows 21 vowel sounds because these include vowels affected by *r*. Technically speaking, *r* vowels are not separate entities. However, they pose special problems for readers and so are treated as distinct elements.

Vowel correspondences are said to be irregular because a vowel sound may have a number of different spellings. However, although a vowel sound may have a dozen or more spellings, only three or four of those spellings are major. For example, long *i* has more than 10 spellings: *pine, night, tiger, bayou, aisle, height, geyser, lie, coyote, dye, aye, eye* (Mish, 1993) but is most often spelled *i-e, -igh, i,* or *-y* as in *line, night, spider,* or *try.* Only major spellings of vowels are presented in Table 8.4.

### Vowel Generalizations

> Poor readers often have difficulty applying generalizations; provide practice in applying words that incorporate generalizations.

> Short vowels are the most frequent (*cat, pet, hit, hot, cut*). Long vowels "say their own name" (*cake, sheep, like, boat, use*). R vowels are affected by r (*car, fair, for, hear, wire*). "Other" vowels fall into none of these categories (*paw, box, look, too, cow*).

Although English vowel sounds can be spelled in approximately 200 ways, the great majority of vowel spellings are covered by five generalizations (Gunning, 1975). These are discussed in the next section.

Except for the final *e*, second-graders who were observed attacking unfamiliar words made little use of phonics generalizations and rarely sounded out words letter by letter, even though half the students had been taught by an explicit phonics approach. Most sought out and used pronounceable word parts (Gunning, 1988a, 1999).

#### Short Vowels

A vowel is short when it is followed by a consonant (*bat, sit*). This generalization also applies to multisyllabic words. A vowel in a multisyllabic word is usually short when followed by two or more consonants: *batter, bitter.* More than one word out of every four follows this generalization.

#### Open Syllables

A vowel is long when it comes at the end of a word or syllable: *no, na-tion, e-qual.* This generalization occurs in only about one word out of every five.

**TABLE 8.4**
Vowel Spellings

| Vowel Sounds | Examples | Model Word |
|---|---|---|
| **Short Vowels** | | |
| /a/ | hat, batter, have | cat |
| /e/ | ten, better, bread | bed |
| /i/ | fit, little, remain | hit |
| /o/ | hot, bottle, father | mop |
| /u/ | cup, butter | bus |
| **Long Vowels** | | |
| /ā/ | made, nail, radio, hay, flavor | cake |
| /ē/ | he, see, seal, sunny, turkey, these, neither | tree |
| /ī/ | smile, night, pie, spider | bike |
| /ō/ | no, hope, grow, toad, gold, roll, local | goat |
| /ū/ | use, music | mule |
| **r Vowels** | | |
| /ar/ | car, charge, heart | star |
| /air/ | fair, bear, care, there | chair |
| /eer/ | ear, cheer, here | deer |
| /ir/ | sir, her, earth, turn | bird |
| /or/ | for, four, store, floor | door |
| **Other Vowels** | | |
| /aw/ | ball, walk, paw, song, caught, thought, off | saw |
| /oi/ | joy, join | boy |
| /o͞o/ | zoo, blue, grew, fruit, group, two, | moon |
| /oo/ | took, could, push | book |
| /ow/ | owl, south | cow |
| /ə/ | ago, telephone, similar, opinion, upon | banana |

### Final-*e* Markers

> ❋ One of the most frequent of the
> vowel sounds is *schwa*, which is
> the unaccented vowel sound heard
> in the second syllable of *sofa*.

A vowel is long when it is followed by a consonant and a final silent -*e* marker: *cane, time*. This generalization applies to about 1 word in every 20.

### Unstressed Syllables

A vowel is given a schwa pronunciation when it occurs in an unaccented syllable: *a-bout, di-vide*. This generalization occurs in nearly one word out of five. The problem with applying the rule is that the reader can only tell that a syllable is unstressed by pronouncing it.

### Digraphs

About one out of every six vowel sounds is spelled with two or more letters (Gunning, 1975). At one time, there was a generalization that stated "When two vowels go walking, the first one does the talking." As a blanket generalization, this one does not work very well. For one thing, many vowel combinations do not spell long-vowel sounds: *ou* (*out*) and *oy* (*joy*), for example. And some digraphs represent a variety of sounds. The digraph *ea*, for instance, represents at least six sounds: *bread, eat, earn, steak, dear,* and *bear.*

However, a number of vowel digraphs do occur with a high degree of frequency and consistency. These include the following:

| | | | |
|---|---|---|---|
| *ai/ay* = /ā/ | paid/pay | *oa* = /ō/ | boat |
| *au/aw* = /aw/ | cause/saw | *oi/oy* = /oi/ | boil/boy |
| *ea* = /ē/ | beak | *oo* = /o͞o/ | soon |
| *ea* = /e/ | bread | *oo* = /oo/ | book |
| *ew* = /o͞o/ | flew | *ou/ow* = /ow/ | out, town |
| *ee* = /ē/ | see | *ow* = /ō/ | snow |
| *ie* = /ē/ | field | | |

## Variability in Vowels

Since elements such as *ow* might represent a long-*o* sound (*tow*) or the /ow/ sound (*cow*), students need to apply the meaning test. If they try one pronunciation and that does not result in a meaningful word that fits the context, they should try the other pronunciation.

Although vowel correspondences are basically regular and fall, for the most part, into five spelling patterns, there are a number of exceptions. Therefore, students should be taught a flexibility strategy. They need to know that many individual vowel letters and vowel digraphs can represent more than one sound. They should also know what those vowel sounds are. Then, if they try one pronunciation and it doesn't work, they can try another.

One device that helps students deal with the variability of English spellings is a vowel-decoding chart, such as the one presented in Table 8.5. The decoding chart lists spellings and then gives the vowel sounds most frequently represented by those spellings. The vowel-decoding chart lists high-frequency vowel spellings such as *ea* that may represent more than one sound. Infrequently occurring items such as the vowel spellings of *said, says,* and *friend* are not listed.

**TABLE 8.5**
Decoding Chart for High-Frequency Variable Vowel Patterns

| Vowel Spelling | Corresponding Sound |
|---|---|
| bead | /ē/ |
| bread | /e/ |
| break | /ā/ |
| ear | /ēēr/ |
| bear | /air/ |
| find | /ī/ |
| wind (moving air) | /i/ |
| roll | /ō/ |
| doll | /o/ |
| wood | /oo/ |
| food | /o͞o/ |
| lost | /aw/ |
| most | /ō/ |
| cow | /ow/ |
| crow | /ō/ |

Here is how students might use the chart. Coming across the word *own*, the student reads "John had his /own/ (rhymes with town) money." Realizing that /own/ is not a word and the sentence does not make sense, the reader searches for *ow* on the chart. Noting that *ow* can also have long *o* in addition to an /ow/ pronunciation, the student constructs the word *own* (/ōn/). The student sees that own (/ōn/) is a real word and also makes sense in the sentence.

Like other strategies, this try-another-sound strategy should be modeled and reinforced with guided practice and application. As students learn alternative pronunciations for spellings, they should gradually learn to apply the strategy without the help of the chart.

> ⚡ Noting that some students were experiencing difficulty applying phonics strategies, Gaskins, Ehri, Cress, O'Hara, and Donnelly (1996–1997) revised the word-attack program so that students were taught to analyze words fully. To learn the word *will*, students noted the sounds in the word /w/, /i/, /l/ and matched these with the letters that represent the sounds *w, i, ll.*

## The Role of Phonological Processing in Teaching Vowel Correspondences

Phonological processing provides the foundation for learning to read words. When students have a firm phonological foundation, they can make connections between the sounds in words and the words' spellings. However, when phonological awareness is weak, adequate connections are not made. Students tend to learn words as specific entities and do not generalize. For instance, after learning the *eat* pattern in *meat*, *seat*, and *heat*, they fail to recognize the *eat* in *wheat* and so are unable to read the word. Instruction in the *eat* pattern must be accompanied by instruction in phonological awareness.

Once students can detect all the sounds in a word, they can connect them to their spellings (Harm, McCandliss, & Seidenberg, 2003). This is known as the *mapping hypothesis*. The mapping hypothesis holds that componential representation leads to generalization. Componential representation is the building of an awareness of the internal components of a word: the letters and the sounds represented by the letters.

As Gaskins (2011) explained, the sounds and spellings in the word must be fully realized. Intervention techniques must help students become aware of the separate sounds in the words and the letters that represent them. Word building, which is explained below, does this, as does the Benchmark Word Detectives program, a decoding program for severely disabled readers. Struggling readers might be able to read a word such as *meat* but be unable to read other *eat* words. That is because they have made a specific connection between the spelling of *meat* and the pronunciation and meaning of *meat*. However, the representation is holistic and not componential. The student is not processing the individual sounds in the word. Poor phonological representation has led to poor orthographic representation. Intervention must help the student break the word into its component parts and connect these sounds to the appropriate letters. Notice how this principle is applied in the word-building approach.

## Word-Building Approach to Teaching Vowel Correspondences and Patterns

Vowels may be taught implicitly or explicitly. In a way, vowels are easier to teach, because they can be pronounced in isolation without distortion. Vowels can be taught in isolation: *a* = /a/ or as part of a pattern –*at*, –*ad*, –*an*. Because it actively involves students in constructing words, an effective way to introduce vowels is through a word-building approach (Gunning, 2005). In a word-building approach, beginning consonants—onsets—are added to vowels or vowel patterns—rimes (*h* + *e* = *he*, *sh* + *ow* = *show*, *h* + *at* = *hat*). Common rimes and words containing those rimes are presented in Table 8.6.

**TABLE 8.6**
Major Word Patterns

## Short Vowels

| -ab | -ack | -ad | -ag | -am | -amp | -an | -and | -ang | -ank |
|---|---|---|---|---|---|---|---|---|---|
| cab | back | bad | bag | *ham | camp | an | and | bang | *bank |
| tab | jack | dad | rag | jam | damp | can | band | gang | sank |
| *crab | pack | had | tag | slam | *lamp | fan | *hand | hang | tank |
| | sack | mad | wag | swam | stamp | man | land | *rang | blank |
| | *tack | *sad | drag | | | *pan | sand | sang | thank |
| | black | glad | *flag | | | tan | stand | | |
| | crack | | | | | plan | | | |
| | stack | | | | | than | | | |

| -ap | -at | | -ed | -ell | -en | -end | -ent | -ess | -est |
|---|---|---|---|---|---|---|---|---|---|
| cap | at | | bred | *bell | den | end | bent | guess | best |
| lap | bat | | fed | fell | hen | bend | dent | less | nest |
| *map | *cat | | led | tell | men | lend | rent | mess | pest |
| tap | fat | | red | well | pen | mend | sent | bless | rest |
| clap | hat | | shed | yell | *ten | *send | *tent | *dress | test |
| slap | pat | | *sled | shell | then | tend | went | press | *vest |
| snap | rat | | | smell | when | spend | spent | | west |
| trap | sat | | | spell | | | | | chest |
| wrap | that | | | | | | | | guest |

| -et | -ead | | -ick | -id | -ig | -ill | -im | -in | -ing |
|---|---|---|---|---|---|---|---|---|---|
| bet | dead | | kick | did | big | bill | dim | in | king |
| get | head | | lick | hid | dig | fill | him | fin | *ring |
| jet | read | | pick | kid | *pig | *hill | skim | *pin | sing |
| let | *bread | | sick | *lid | wig | kill | slim | sin | wing |
| met | spread | | click | rid | twig | pill | *swim | tin | bring |
| *net | thread | | *stick | skid | | will | | win | sting |
| pet | | | thick | slid | | chill | | chin | thing |
| set | | | trick | | | skill | | grin | |
| wet | | | quick | | | spill | | skin | |
| | | | | | | | | spin | |
| | | | | | | | | thin | |
| | | | | | | | | twin | |

| -ink | -ip | -it | | -ob | -ock | -op | -ot | | -ust |
|---|---|---|---|---|---|---|---|---|---|
| link | dip | it | | job | dock | cop | dot | | bust |
| pink | lip | bit | | mob | *lock | hop | got | | dust |
| *sink | rip | fit | | rob | rock | *mop | hot | | just |
| wink | tip | *hit | | sob | sock | pop | lot | | *must |
| blink | zip | kit | | *knob | block | top | not | | rust |
| clink | chip | sit | | | clock | chop | *pot | | trust |
| drink | flip | knit | | | flock | drop | shot | | |
| stink | *ship | quit | | | knock | shop | spot | | |
| think | skip | split | | | | stop | | | |
| | trip | | | | | | | | |
| | whip | | | | | | | | |

| -ut | -ub | -uck | -ug | -um | -ump | -un | -unk | -us(s) |
|---|---|---|---|---|---|---|---|---|
| but | cub | *duck | bug | bum | bump | bun | bunk | *bus |
| cut | rub | luck | dug | hum | dump | fun | hunk | plus |
| hut | sub | cluck | hug | yum | hump | gun | junk | us |
| nut | *tub | stuck | mug | *drum | *jump | run | sunk | fuss |
| shut | club | struck | *rug | plum | lump | *sun | shrunk | muss |
|  | scrub | truck | tug |  | pump | spun | *skunk |  |
|  |  |  | chug |  | thump |  | stunk |  |
|  |  |  |  |  | stump |  |  |  |

## Long Vowels

| -ace | -ade | -age | -ake | -ale | -ame | -ape | -ate | -ave | -ail |
|---|---|---|---|---|---|---|---|---|---|
| *face | fade | age | bake | pale | came | ape | ate | *cave | fail |
| race | *made | *cage | *cake | sale | game | *cape | date | gave | jail |
| place | grade | page | lake | tale | *name | tape | *gate | save | mail |
| space | shade | rage | make | *scale | same | scrape | hate | wave | *nail |
|  | trade | stage | rake |  | tame | grape | late | brave | pail |
|  |  |  | take |  | blame | shape | mate |  | sail |
|  |  |  | wake |  | shame |  | plate |  | tail |
|  |  |  | flake |  |  |  | skate |  | snail |
|  |  |  | shake |  |  |  | state |  | trail |
|  |  |  | snake |  |  |  |  |  |  |

| -ain | -ay | | -eel | -ea | -each | -eak | -eal | -eam | -ean |
|---|---|---|---|---|---|---|---|---|---|
| main | bay | | feel | pea | each | *beak | deal | team | *bean |
| pain | day | | heel | sea | beach | leak | heal | *dream | lean |
| rain | *hay | | kneel | *tea | *peach | peak | meal | scream | mean |
| brain | lay | | steel | flea | reach | weak | real | stream | clean |
| chain | may | | *wheel |  | teach | creak | *seal |  |  |
| grain | pay | |  |  | bleach | sneak | squeal |  |  |
| *train | say | |  |  |  | speak | steal |  |  |
|  | way | |  |  |  | squeak |  |  |  |
|  | gray | |  |  |  |  |  |  |  |
|  | play | |  |  |  |  |  |  |  |

| -eat | -ee | -eed | -eep | -eet | | -ice | -ide | -ile | -ime |
|---|---|---|---|---|---|---|---|---|---|
| eat | *bee | deed | beep | *feet | | *mice | hide | mile | *dime |
| beat | see | feed | deep | meet | | nice | ride | pile | lime |
| neat | free | *seed | *jeep | sheet | | rice | side | *smile | time |
| *seat | knee | weed | keep | sleet | | lice | wide | while | chime |
| cheat | tree | bleed | peep | sweet | | twice | *bride |  |  |
| treat |  | freed | weep |  | |  | slide |  |  |
| wheat |  | speed | creep |  | |  |  |  |  |
|  |  |  | sleep |  | |  |  |  |  |
|  |  |  | steep |  | |  |  |  |  |
|  |  |  | sweep |  | |  |  |  |  |

| -ine | -ite | -ive | -ie | -ind | -y | | -o, -oe | -oke | -ole |
|---|---|---|---|---|---|---|---|---|---|
| fine | bite | dive | die | find | by | | go | joke | hole |
| line | *kite | *five | lie | kind | guy | | *no | poke | mole |
| mine | quite | hive | pie | *mind | my | | so | woke | *pole |
| *nine | white | live | *tie | blind | dry | | doe | broke | stole |
| pine |  | drive |  |  | fly | | hoe | *smoke | whole |
|  |  |  |  |  | *sky | | toe | spoke |  |
|  |  |  |  |  | try | |  |  |  |
|  |  |  |  |  | why | |  |  |  |

(continued)

**TABLE 8.6**
(*Continued*)

| -one | -ope | -ose | -ote | -oad | -oat | -ow | -old | | u-e |
|------|------|------|------|------|------|-----|------|---|-----|
| bone | hope | hose | *note | load | boat | bow | old | | use |
| cone | nope | *nose | vote | *road | coat | low | cold | | fuse |
| *phone | *rope | rose | quote | toad | *goat | tow | fold | | *mule |
| shone | slope | chose | wrote | | float | blow | hold | | Huge |
| | | close | | | | glow | *gold | | |
| | | those | | | | grow | sold | | |
| | | | | | | slow | told | | |
| | | | | | | *snow | | | |

## r Vowels and Other Vowels

| | | -air | -are | -ear, -ere | | -ar | -ark | -ard | -art |
|---|---|------|------|------------|---|-----|------|------|------|
| | | fair | care | *bear | | *car | bark | *card | art |
| | | *hair | hare | pear | | far | dark | guard | part |
| | | pair | share | there | | jar | mark | hard | *chart |
| | | chair | scare | where | | star | park | | smart |
| | | | spare | | | | *shark | | |
| | | | *square | | | | spark | | |

| -ear | -eer | | -or | -orn | -ort |
|------|------|---|-----|------|------|
| *ear | *deer | | *or | born | *fort |
| dear | cheer | | for | *corn | port |
| fear | steer | | nor | torn | sort |
| hear | | | more | worn | short |
| near | | | sore | | sport |
| year | | | tore | | |
| clear | | | wore | | |

| -all | -aw | -au | | -oss | -ost | -ought | | -oil | -oy |
|------|-----|-----|---|------|------|--------|---|------|-----|
| *ball | caw | fault | | boss | cost | ought | | *boil | *boy |
| call | jaw | *caught | | loss | *lost | *bought | | soil | joy |
| fall | paw | taught | | toss | fro | fought | | | toy |
| hall | *saw | | | *cross | | brought | | | |
| wall | claw | | | | | | | | |
| small | draw | | | | | | | | |
| | straw | | | | | | | | |

| -oud | -our | -out | -ound | -ow | -own | | -ood | -ould |
|------|------|------|-------|-----|------|---|------|-------|
| loud | our | out | bound | ow | down | | good | *could |
| *cloud | *hour | *shout | found | bow | gown | | hood | would |
| proud | sour | scout | hound | *cow | town | | *wood | should |
| | flour | spout | mound | how | brown | | stood | |
| | | | pound | now | clown | | | |
| | | | *round | plow | *crown | | | |
| | | | sound | | | | | |
| | | | wound | | | | | |
| | | | ground | | | | | |

| -ook |
|------|
| *book |
| cook |
| hook |
| look |
| took |
| shook |

* Possible model words.

✴ Looking at both individual letter–sound correspondences (*h-a-t*) and patterns (*h-at*) within the context of whole words helps students build a solid foundation of phonological knowledge and prepares them for using larger elements so that they become more efficient readers (Berninger et al., 1999).

Because some poor readers have difficulty with rimes (Bruck, 1992; Juel & Minden-Cupp, 2000), rimes are broken down into their individual sounds after being presented as wholes. After introducing the rime -*at* as a whole, the teacher should highlight its individual sounds: /a/ and /t/. In a study involving four first grades, only the two groups of struggling readers taught with an onset–rime approach were reading close to grade level by year's end (Juel & Minden-Cupp, 2000). And the students who did the best were those whose teacher broke the rimes into their individual sounds.

The word-building approach also fits the way students decipher printed words naturally. When they attack unknown words, both achieving and problem readers frequently seek out pronounceable word parts (Glass, 1976; Glass & Burton, 1973; Gunning, 1988a,1999; Hardy, Stennett, & Smythe, 1973; McGuinness, 1997). Encountering the word *trust,* for instance, students might read it as "*us-rus-trust.*" The word *chip* might be read as "*ip-chip.*"

## Preparation for Introducing Short-Vowel Words in a Word-Building Approach

Before presenting short *a,* short *e,* or another short vowel either as part of a word-building or pattern approach or as an individual vowel, introduce the vowel as it occurs at the beginning of words, since it is easier to perceive in that position. In preparation for introducing short *a,* say the words *apple, astronaut,* and *add.* Have students say them and note that they all begin with the same sound, which is /a/. Write the words on the board, read them, and lead the class to see that the words all begin with the letter *a* and that the letter *a* makes the sound /a/ as in *apple.* Tell students that the word *apple* will be the model word for the /a/ sound of *a.* On the board, write and say "*a, apple,* /a/." Explain to students that if they come across a word that has an *a* in it and they forget the sound of *a,* they can use the model word to help them. They can say "*a, apple*" and then think of the sound that *apple* begins with and say /a/ (Wilson, 1999).

Explain that there will also be a hand signal for "*a, apple,* /a/." Demonstrate by pretending to eat an apple, and explain that this signals *apple* and the sound at the beginning of *apple:* /a/. Elongate the sound of *a* at the beginning of *apple:* /a/. Have students practice saying "*a, apple,* /a/." Encourage them to use this mnemonic if they need it (E. Murray, personal communication, November 1, 2007).

Create a vowel chart, as shown in Figure 8.6, and place "*a, apple,* /a/" on it, along with a drawing of someone eating an apple. Use this same procedure for introducing the other short vowels. For short *e,* introduce the words *echo, Ed,* and *effort.* The hand signal is cupping your hands around your mouth and pretending to call out. For short *i,* introduce the words *itch, igloo,* and *iguana.* The hand signal is pretending to scratch your arm. For short *o,* introduce the words *octopus, October,* and *ostrich.* The hand signal is locking your thumbs and wiggling your eight fingers so they appear to be an octopus. For short *u,* introduce the words *up, us,* and *usher.* The hand signal is pointing up with your index finger (Gunning, 2008a). The box on page 252 shows how a word-building lesson might be structured.

✴ Keep a close relationship between the phonics you teach and the phonics students need; preview an upcoming selection, and choose a new phonics element they have not mastered.

## Adjusting Instruction

When presenting pattern words, limit the number introduced to five or six. Focus on the highest-frequency words and words that students will meet in upcoming selections.

■ **FIGURE 8.6**
Short-Vowel Chart

| | | |
|---|---|---|
| a | apple | /a/ |
| e | echo | /e/ |
| i | itch | /i/ |
| o | octopus | /o/ |
| u | up | /u/ |

## Word-Building Lesson: *-at* Pattern

**Step 1: Phonemic awareness and building the rime.** Read a selection such as *The Cat in the Hat* (Giesel, 1957), an easy version of The Gingerbread Man, or a rhyme in which there are a number of *-at* words. Call the students' attention to the pattern words from the selection: *cat, hat, sat*. Stressing the rhyming element as you say each word, ask students to tell what is the same about the words. Lead students to see that they all have an /at/ sound as in *cat*. Ask students to listen carefully so they can tell how many sounds the word *at* has. Articulate it slowly, stretching out the sound /a/ and emphasizing the /t/ as you do so: "aaat." Tell the students to say the word *at* and listen for the sounds as they do so. Discuss how many sounds the word *at* has. Then tell students that you are going to spell the word *at*. Ask students to tell

what letter would be used to spell the sound /a/ in *at*. Write *a*, commenting as you do so that it makes an /a/ sound. Have students tell what sound they hear at the end of *at*. Ask them what letter would be needed to spell /t/. Add *t*, saying /t/ as you do so. Explain that now you have the word *at*. Run your hand under each letter as you say its sound. Have several students read *at*.

**Step 2: Adding the onset.** Explain to students that you can use *at* to make other words. (Write a second *at* under the first one.) Ask students, "What do I need to add to *at* to make the word *cat*?" As you add *c* to *at*, carefully enunciate the *c* and the *at* and then the whole word. Have several students read the word. Then have students read *at* and *cat*. Then write *at* underneath *cat*. Ask students, "What do I need to add to *at* to make the word *hat?*" As you add *h* to *at,* carefully enunciate the *h* and the *at* and then the whole word. Have several students read the word. Then have students read *at, cat,* and *hat.* Introduce the words *sat* and *mat.* Then have students read all the words that have been formed. Lead students to see what is the same about the words—that they all end in *at.* Ask students if they know of any other words that rhyme with *cat.* If so, write these on the board and discuss them.

In a sense, word building takes a spelling approach. The teacher says a sound, and students supply the letter that would spell that sound. By slightly altering the directions, you can change to a reading approach when building words: Add the target letter, and then have students read the word. For instance, adding *c* to *at ,* ask, "If I add *c* to *at ,* what word do I make?" If students don't respond to a spelling approach, using a reading approach to building words provides another way of considering the elements in words.

**Step 3:    Adding the rime.** To make sure that students have a thorough grasp of both key parts of the word—the onset, which is the initial consonant or cluster—and the rime, which is the vowel and an ending consonant or cluster—present the onset or initial consonant and have students supply the rime or vowel–consonant element. Writing *c* on the board, have students tell what sound it usually stands for. Then ask them to tell what you would add to /k/ to make the word *cat.* After adding *-at* to *c,* say the word in parts, /k/–/a/–/t/, and then as a whole. Pointing to *c,* say /k/, pointing to *a,* say /a/, pointing to *t,* say /t/. Running your hand under the whole word, say "cat." Form *hat, sat,* and *mat* in this way. After all words have been formed, have students read them.

**Step 4:    Providing mixed practice.** Realizing that they are learning words that all end in the same way, students may focus on the initial letter and fail to take careful note of the rest of the word, the rime. After presenting a pattern, mix in words from previously presented patterns and have these read. For instance, after presenting the *-at* pattern, present a list of mixed *-at* and *-an* words: *cat, can, ran, rat, pat, pan, man, mat.* Besides being a good review, this trains students to use all the word's letters in their decoding processes. Otherwise, students might say the first word in a series of pattern words and then just use the initial consonant to say the rest. If students fail to use all the letters when reading on their own, they may misread *ran* for *rat* or *can* for *cat.* Reading mixed patterns also reviews previously presented patterns.

**Step 5:    Introducing the model word.** Choose one of the pattern words to be a model word. Select a word that has high frequency, is easy, and—if possible—can be depicted. For the *-at* pattern, you might choose *cat,* which is easily illustrated. Create a model words chart for your class. An illustrated chart of model words for short-vowel patterns is presented in Figure 8.7. After a pattern has been introduced, add its model word to the chart. If students forget the pattern, they can refer to the model words chart. Point out the model word *cat* and explain that it has a picture that shows the word. Tell students that if they forget how to say the model word, the picture will help them. As students encounter difficulty with *-at* words, help them to look for a part of the word they can say (*at*) and, if that does not work, use the model word *cat* as an analogy word to help them decipher the unknown word. Also encourage the use of context. Students should use context to assist in the use of pronounceable word-part or other sounding-out strategies and especially when sounding-out strategies do not work. Context should also be used to make sure that the word decoded is a real word and fits the sense of the selection.

**Step 6:    Guided practice.**

- Use functional reading materials to provide practice with the pattern. Holding up an advertisement for baseball bats, ask students to tell which word says "bat." Do the same with a hat label or advertisement.

- Compose a brief experience story using *at.* Say to students; "I can use *-at* words to write about some things that I have. I have a *cat.* I have a *hat.* I have a *bat.* (As you write each word, stress the word's sounds.)

- Have students sort *-an, -at,* and *-am* words (assuming that they have learned *-an* and *-am* patterns). They might complete a spelling sort as well as a card sort.

**Step 7:    Application.** To apply a correspondence that was just taught, choose a selection that

*(Continued)*

contains a number of words that fit the target pattern. Walk students through the selection. Discuss the title and illustrations, clarify unfamiliar concepts, point out and read to them difficult words (they should follow along with you in their books). Place particular emphasis on words that follow the pattern you just introduced. Note a sentence or caption that contains a pattern word and ask them to find the pattern word and point it out to you. Possible books include *Have You Seen My Cat?* (Carle, 1973) and *Cat on a Mat* (Wildsmith,1986).

*Step 8:   Spelling.* Learning to spell new pattern words is excellent reinforcement. Along with providing an opportunity for students to apply skills, it helps them to focus on vowel sounds and patterns within words. Choose pattern words for spelling that students will most likely use in their writing, for example, *cat, hat, sat, bat, mat.* Up to five words may be chosen for the spelling lesson. To introduce the spelling lesson, explain to students that they will be learning how to spell words that use the pattern just presented. To introduce the words, give a pretest. Dictate the words and have students attempt to spell them. Say each word, use the word in a sentence, and

then say each word: "*Cat.* My cat ran. *Cat. Hat.* The hat kept my head warm. *Hat. Sat.* She sat on the chair. *Sat. Bat.* I have a new baseball bat. *Bat. Mat.* I wiped my feet on the mat. *Mat.*" Have students say the word, enunciating it carefully before writing it. This will help them focus on the word's sounds. After the pretest, write the correct spellings on the board, and have students check their attempts, making any corrections necessary. They should focus their studying on words that were difficult for them.

*Step 9:   Writing.* Students compose an illustrated piece telling about a cat they know or have or a hat they would like to wear. Encourage the use of invented spelling. However, students are expected to spell pattern words correctly.

*Step 10:   Evaluation and review.* Note whether students are able to read words containing *-at* . Note, in particular, whether they are able to decode *-at* words that have not been taught. Note, too, whether students are spelling *-at* words in their writing. Provide additional instruction and practice as necessary.

*Step 11:   Extension.* Students learn other short-*a* patterns: *-an, -am, -ad,* and so on.

---

Nasal consonant sounds, such as /n/ and /m/, are partially absorbed by the preceding vowel. Therefore it is difficult to hear the separate sounds in *an* and *am.* When presenting the *an* and *am* patterns, present the rime as a unit. Do not attempt to say the separate sounds or have students say them.

For students having difficulty with word building, add letters to the rimes and ask them to tell what word you made. Adding *h* to *at*, have them read *hat.* Adding *s* to *at* have them read *sat.* Also use a speech-to-print approach. Hold up the words *hat* and *ham* and ask, "Which one says '*hat*'?" Ask students how they know the word says "hat" and not "ham."

⚕ For additional information on word
✳ building and other phonics
programs, go to Building Literacy at
http://wordbuilding.org/.

***Using a Sound-by-Sound Approach***   Having students build words by adding onsets to rimes is an efficient, effective approach to teaching phonics. However, at the earliest stages of learning to read, some students may have difficulty dealing with combinations of sounds. Younger students and students with poor phonological skills may need to work for a time with individual sounds (Walton, 1995). For this reason, word building presents rimes as units (*at, eep*) and as individual elements (*a-t, ee-p*). However, some students may still have difficulty with rimes. For these students, modify the approach by placing greater emphasis on the individual sounds in words. Later, as they begin to see patterns in words, place more emphasis on rimes.

**FIGURE 8.7**

Model Words

*Source:* Gunning (2008). Reprinted by permission of Galvin Publications.

**Model Words**

| | | | |
|---|---|---|---|
| -ad sad | | -ill hill | |
| -am ham | | -in pin | |
| -an pan | | -ing ring | |
| -at cat | | -it hit | |
| -ay hay | | -o no | |
| -e, -ee me, bee | | -oe toe | |
| -ed bed | | -op mop | |
| -ell bell | | -ot pot | |
| -en ten | 10 | -ug bug | |
| -et net | | -un sun | |
| -id lid | | -up cup | |
| -ig pig | | -us bus | |

## Integrating Syllabic Analysis with Basic Phonics

Multisyllabic words pose problems for struggling readers. Although students might know the words *car, pen,* and *her,* they have difficulty reading the word *carpenter.* Most multisyllabic words are composed of known word parts or patterns. After teaching several short-vowel patterns, present two-syllable words composed of those patterns. For instance, after students have studied the short-*a* and short-*i* patterns, present words such as *rabbit, napkin, distant,* and *instant.* Do the same with long-vowel and other patterns. When students encounter multisyllabic words, prompt them to use their knowledge of word parts to figure out the words. Also build words. After students have learned a word such as *swim,* have them make words that contain *swim* (*swims, swimming, swimmer*) so they get used to reading words that contain suffixes. Teaching multisyllabic words early provides a psychological boost for older readers who are learning basic phonics as is the case with Emilio.

Emilio, a fourth grader assessed as reading on a mid-first-grade level, looked distressed. Noting weaknesses in his knowledge of short-vowel patterns, the teacher was reviewing the *-am, -an,* and *-ad* patterns. As the review progressed, Emilio's stress increased, even though he was able to do the activities with ease. And then the teacher caught on: The work was too easy. Emilio felt as though he was doing baby work. The teacher commented, "These patterns are too easy. Let me give you some harder ones." The teacher then began working with two-syllable words composed of familiar patterns. With some guidance, Emilio was able to read words such as *rabbit,* *happen, magnet,* and *address.* Emilio's self-esteem was restored, and the teacher had provided a much-needed review of short-vowel patterns.

Working with teenage disabled readers, Curtis and Longo (1999) used an adult literacy series. However, they noticed that *oa* words presented in the program were already known by the students, so they provided more challenging words using the *oa* element: *boast, charcoal.* When placing students, especially struggling readers who are well aware that they lag behind their classmates, it is important to give students credit for what they know and provide them with interesting, challenging materials.

### Introducing Long-Vowel Patterns

*Final-e Words*   To introduce final-*e* words, dramatize the impact of final *e* on pronouncing a word. When presenting *a-e*, you might do the following: Holding up a can, tell students that you are going to change the can into a cane. (Hold up a cane.) Ask students to guess how you might do that. Explain that you are not actually going to change the can but that you are going to change the word *can.* Write *can* on the board. Adding *e,* explain that the word is now *cane.*

Write the following words on the board and then add an *e* so that they become long-vowel words: *cap, tap, mad, hat, plan, man.* Lead students to see that short *a* is spelled with an *a* in the middle or beginning of the word, as in *cap* and *at,* but long *a* has an *e* at the end of the word as a marker, as in *cape* and *ate.* Explain that long *a* is spelled *a___e,* with the blank being the space for a consonant letter (Gunning, 2008c).

Have students complete exercises similar to the following, in which they contrast consonant–vowel–consonant (CVC) and consonant–vowel–consonant-*e* (CVCE) words:

1.   The (*man, mane*) sees a lion.
2.   The lion has a (*man, mane*).
3.   The (*man, mane*) is the hair around the lion's face and on its neck.
4.   Lions like to rest in the (*shad, shade*) of tree.
5.   Lions (*can, cane*) hunt for food.

*Vowel Digraphs*   Present vowel digraphs as another way of spelling long vowels. Write the words *tale* and *tail* on the board. Explain that both are pronounced the same way. Point out that the *e* at the end of a word is often used to mark the vowel as being long. Explain that another way of marking a vowel as being long is to place two vowel letters side by side, as in *tail.* Discuss the different meanings of the two words.

Place the following homophone pairs on the board and discuss them with students: *male–mail, pale–pail, sale–sail.* Have students sort long -*a* words spelled with final *e* and long -*a* words spelled with a digraph.

## Make-and-Break Technique for Introducing or Reviewing Patterns

⚓ An interactive approach to decoding combines sounding out, meaning, and familiarity. For instance, *vat* is harder to decode than *cat* or *fat* because *vat* occurs less frequently and will not be in some students' listening vocabularies.

As an alternative to word building or along with it, you might use the make-and-break technique to introduce patterns. In this approach, students construct, break apart, and reconstruct common word patterns (Iverson & Tunmer, 1993). Choosing the word *and,* for instance, the teacher makes the word with magnetic letters, says the word, and has the student say it. The teacher then jumbles the letters and has the student reassemble the word and say it. This is repeated until the student is able to construct and say the word with ease. The teacher then puts an *s* in front of *and,* explaining that the word now spells *sand.* The student says the word. The letter *s* is removed, and the teacher explains that the word now says *and.* The student is asked to make the word *sand,* read it, and then make the word *and.* This process is repeated with *band* and *hand.*

## Whole–Part–Whole Approaches

Phonics lessons can proceed from the part to the whole or from the whole to the part. In a part–whole approach, the correspondence or pattern is presented and then is applied within the context of a whole story. However, some practitioners prefer starting with the whole, breaking the whole into parts, and reading a whole selection (Trachtenburg, 1990). Whole–part–whole approaches work especially well with students who have had negative experiences with intensive phonics programs.

Having failed with her school system's isolated phonics program, which consisted primarily of skills instruction and worksheets, Jana objected vehemently when her mother attempted to help her with the sheets. "I can't read those," she cried. Having been given too heavy a dose of phonics, Jana had learned very little about letter–sound relationships.

Jana should receive a holistic approach to reading through the use of easy predictable books or other techniques. Once she has a sense of what reading really is, she might be presented phonics through a holistic children's book technique. To acquaint Jana with the *oad* pattern, for instance, share-read with her books such as *Toad on the Road* (Schade, 1992) and *Railroad Toad* (Schade, 1994). During a rereading of the books, point out and discuss the *oad* words. Having provided a holistic, successful experience with the *oad* pattern, the teacher might then build the *oad* pattern through word building or the make-and-break technique or both. Because it is nonthreatening and allows the student to generate her own conclusions about patterns, sorting would also be an excellent extension activity for Jana.

## ▦ The Role of Dialect in Teaching Phonics

Although Justin had mastered all the vowel patterns, he was having a great deal of difficulty with the short-*o* patterns. Having just reviewed the *ot* pattern, the teacher was somewhat surprised when Justin, a third grader reading on a mid-first-grade level, spelled *hot* as *hat.* Thinking that it might be a handwriting issue and that the *a* was really a poorly formed *o*, the teacher asked Justin to name the letters. "H-a-t," responded Justin. Still perplexed, the teacher asked Justin to say the word. "Hot," answered Justin, pointing to his head. "Like the hot that you wear when it is cold."

Suddenly, the teacher understood. Justin had moved to the United States from Jamaica several months before. In his dialect, *hat* was pronounced /hot/; *man* as /mon/. No wonder he was struggling with short-*o* words. He had already learned to spell /hot/ as *hat.* Now the teacher was trying to tell him that it was spelled *h-o-t.* Backtracking, the teacher explained that *at* is pronounced /at/ in the United States but /ot/ in Jamaica. The teacher then explained that *hot* is a different word from *hat* and means "very warm." The teacher briefly discussed dialects and suggested that if Justin heard the word *hat,* he should listen to the way the word was used and that would help him decide if the word meant very warm or something that you wear on your head. The teacher also provided auditory discrimination exercises in which Justin noted whether the teacher was saying the same word twice or two different words: *cat–cot, hat–hat, pat–pot, not–not, sat–sat, hat–hot, nat–not, rat–rot, that–that*. The teacher used *at* and *ot* words in a variety of sentences and had Justin hold up the card that spelled the word she was saying: "I am wearing my new hat. It is a very hot day. The cook made soup in a large pot. Do not pat strange dogs."

When teaching phonics, it is important to be aware of your own dialect and the dialect that students speak if it is different from yours. Make adjustments in the way you introduce elements so that they fit the local dialect. For instance, in many areas, *egg* has a long-*a* pronunciation, *pen* has a short-*i* pronunciation, and *caught* has a short-*o* pronunciation so that it sounds like *cot*.

## Sequence for Teaching Vowels

Which vowel correspondences should be introduced first? Typically, short-vowel correspondences are taught first. These have more predictable spellings and occur with higher frequency. Most often, short-vowel sounds are spelled CVC (consonant–vowel–consonant), for example, with the vowel letter that typically represents that sound preceded and followed by a consonant (*cat, pen, tip, pot, tub*).

A suggested sequence for both vowel and consonant correspondences is presented in Figure 8.4. The sequence is based on frequency of occurrence of elements and ease of learning but should be adapted to fit the particular needs of the students. The ultimate determining factor for the sequence of introduction should be the phonics knowledge that your students already possess and their need to know.

## Application Through Reading

As students begin to learn phonics elements and decoding strategies, it is essential that they apply them by reading whole selections. For instance, students who have been introduced to long-*ee* correspondences might read *Sheep in a Jeep* (Shaw, 1986) and *Dark Night, Sleepy Night* (Ziefert, 1988). If students read materials that contain elements they have been taught, they will learn the elements better and also be better at applying them to new words (Juel & Roper-Schneider, 1985). Children's books that might be used to reinforce vowel patterns are listed in Figure 8.8. Except for *Sharks; Hungry, Hungry, Sharks;* and *Dinosaur Time*, these books would be most appropriate for students in grades one to three. High Noon Books (Academic Therapy Publications) has books designed for older readers that reinforce basic vowel patterns.

In addition to children's books that naturally reinforce key patterns, there are books known as *decodable texts* that have been written specifically for that purpose. Decodable texts have been created to provide practice with a specific phonic element: short-*a* or short-*e* words, for instance. Depending on the skill of the author, the books may seem natural or may seem contrived and artificial. Some of the story words may not even be in the students' listening vocabularies but are included because they incorporate the pattern being taught. Use of artificial language also makes it more difficult to make use of context clues.

However, some decodable texts are well done and can be used effectively. It is suggested that you judge each title for yourself. Here are some books to consider:

*A First Book* (Get Ready-Get Set-Read Series) (Barron's). Consists of 35 books in five sets that reinforce phonics patterns.

**FIGURE 8.8**
Books That
Reinforce Vowel
Patterns

**Level 1**
**Short-Vowel Patterns**
**Short *a***

Antee, N. (1985). *The good bad cat.* Grand Haven, MI: School Zone.
Cameron, A. (1994). *The cat sat on the mat.* Boston: Houghton Mifflin.
Carle, E. (1987). *Have you seen my cat?* New York: Scholastic.
Coxe, M. (1996). *Cat traps.* New York: Random House.
Maccarone, G. (1995). *"What is that?" said the cat.* New York: Scholastic.
Wildsmith, B. (1982). *Cat on the mat.* New York: Oxford.

**Short *i***

Coxe, M. (1997). *Big egg.* New York: Random.
Greydanus, R. (1988). *Let's get a pet.* New York: Troll.
Meister, C. (1999). *When Tiny was tiny.* New York: Puffin.
Ziefert, H. (2005). *Can you play?* New York: Sterling.

**Level 2**
**Short *o***

Flanagan, A. K. (2000). *Hot pot: The sound of short* o. Elgin, IL: Child's World.
McKissack, P. C. (1983). *Who is who?* Chicago: Children's Press.
Smee, N. (2006). *Clip-clop.* New York: Sterling.
Weston, M. (2002). *Jack and Jill and big dog Bill.* New York: Random House.
Worth, B. (2003). *Cooking with the cat.* New York: Random House.

**Short *e***

Ada, A. F. (2003). *Daniel's pet.* San Diego: Harcourt.
Flanagan, A. K. (2000). *Ben's pens: The sound of short* e. Elgin, IL: Child's World.
Gregorich, B. (1984). *Nine men chase a hen.* Grand Haven, MI: School Zone.
Snow, P. (1984). *A pet for Pat.* Chicago: Children's Press.

**Short *u***

Capucilli, A. S. (1996). *Biscuit.* New York: HarperCollins.
Gaydos, N. (2008). *The bus stop.* Norwalk, CT: Innovative Kids.
Gaydos, N. (2009). *Frog legs.* Norwalk, CT: Innovative Kids.
Gaydos, N. (2009). *The trip.* Norwalk, CT: Innovative Kids.
McKissack, P. , & McKissack , F. ( 1988 ). *Bugs.* Chicago: Children's Press.
Petrie, C. (1983). *Joshua James likes trucks.* Chicago: Children's Press.
Rylant, C. (2002). *Puppy Mudge takes a bath.* New York: Simon & Schuster.

**Levels 3 and 4**
**Review of Short Vowels**

Boegehold, B. D. ( 1990 ). *You are much too small.* New York: Bantam.
Kraus, R. ( 1971 ). *Leo, the late bloomer.* New York: Simon & Schuster.
Lewison, W. C. ( 1992 ). *Buzz said the bee.* New York: Scholastic.

**Level 5**
**Long-Vowel Patterns**

**Long *a***

Cohen, C. L. (1998). *How many fish?* New York: HarperCollins.
Flanagan, A. K. (2000). *Play day: The sound of long* a. Elgin, IL: Child's World.

(*Continued*)

Oppenheim, J. (1990). *Wake up, Baby!* New York: Bantam.

Raffi. (1987). *Shake my sillies out.* New York: Crown.

Robart, R. (1986). *The cake that Mack ate.* Toronto: Kids Can Press.

Stadler, J. (1984). *Hooray for Snail!* New York: HarperTrophy.

**Long *i***

Gelman, R. G. (1977). *More spaghetti I say.* New York: Scholastic.

Hoff, S. (1988). *Mrs. Brice's mice.* New York: HarperTrophy.

Kenah, K. (2004). *Animals day and night.* Columbus, OH: Children's Specialty.

Ziefert, H. (1984). *Sleepy dog.* New York: Random House.

Ziefert, H. (1987). *Jason's bus ride.* New York: Random House.

Ziefert, H. (2005). *No more TV, sleepy cat.* New York: Sterling.

**Level 6**
**Long *o***

Armstrong, J. (1996). *The snowball.* New York: Random House.

Buller, J., & Schade, S. A. (1998). *Pig at play.* New York: Troll.

Cobb, A. (1996). *Wheels.* New York: Random House.

Hamsa, B. (1985). *Animal babies.* Chicago: Children's Press.

Kueffner, S. (1999). *Lucky duck.* Pleasantville, NY: Reader's Digest Children's Books.

McDermott, G. (1999). *Fox and the stork.* San Diego, CA: Harcourt.

Oppenheim, J. (1992). *The show-and-tell frog.* New York: Bantam.

Rader, L. (2005). *Silly pig.* New York: Sterling.

Schade, S. (1992). *Toad on the road.* New York: Random House.

**Long *e***

Bonsall, C. (1974). *And I mean it, Stanley.* New York: Harper.

Milgrim, D. (2003). *See Pip point.* New York: Atheneum.

Shaw, N. (1986). *Sheep in a jeep.* Boston: Houghton Mifflin.

Ziefert, H. (1988). *Dark night, sleepy night.* New York: Puffin.

Ziefert, H. (1995). *The little red hen.* New York: Puffin.

**Review of Long Vowels**

Heling, K. , & Hembrook, D. (2003). *Mouse's hide-and-seek words.* New York: Random House.

Matthias, C. (1983). *I love cats.* Chicago: Children's Press.

Parish, P. (1974). Dinosaur time. New York: Harper.

Phillips, J. (1986). *My new boy.* New York: Random House.

Ziefert, H. (1985). *A dozen dogs.* New York: Random House.

**Level 7**
***r* Vowels**

Arnold, M. (1996). *Quick, quack, quick!* New York: Random House.

Clarke, G. (2001). *Sharks!* New York: Grosset & Dunlap.

Hooks, W. H. (1992). *Feed me!* New York: Bantam.

Penner, R. (1991). *Dinosaur babies.* New York: Random House.

Wynne, P. (1986). *Hungry, hungry sharks.* New York: Random House.

Ziefert, H. (1997). *The magic porridge pot.* New York: Puffin.

**Level 8**
**Long /oo/ Vowels**

Blocksma, M. (1992 . *Yoo hoo, moon!* New York: Bantam.

Marzollo, J. (2004). *I spy a scary monster.* New York: Scholastic.

Phillips, M. (2000). *And the cow said "moo."* New York: Greenwillow.
Silverman, M. (1991). *My tooth is loose.* New York: Viking.
Wiseman, B. (1959). *Morris the moose.* New York: Harper.
Ziefert, H. (1997). *The ugly duckling.* New York: Puffin.

*Short /oo/ Vowels*

Arengo, S. (2000). *The magic cooking pot.* New York: Oxford.
Brenner, B. (1989). *Lion and Lamb.* New York: Bantam.
Platt, K. (1965). *Big Max.* New York: Harper.

**Level 9**
**/ow/ Vowels**

Arengo, S. (2001). *The fisherman and his wife.* New York: Oxford.
Black, S. W. (1999). *Plenty of penguins.* New York: Scholastic.
Holub, J. (2001). *Scat, cats!* New York: Puffin.
Lobel, A. (1975). *Owl at home.* New York: Harper.
Oppenheim, J. (1989). *"Not now!" said the cow.* New York: Bantam.
Siracusa, C. (1991). *Bingo, the best dog in the world.* New York: HarperCollins.

**Level 10**
**/aw/ Vowels**

Crowley, N. ( 2006). *Ugh! A bug.* Minneapolis, MN: Millbrook Press.
Gaydos, N. (2008). *Where is my home?* Norwalk, CT: Innovative Kids.
Mann, P. Z. (1999). *Meet my monster.* Pleasantville, NY: Reader's Digest Children's Books.
Oppenheim, J. (1991). *The donkey's tale.* New York: Bantam.
Oppenheim, J. (1993). *"Uh-oh!" said the crow.* New York: Bantam.
Rylant, C. (1989). *Henry and Mudge get the cold shivers.* New York: Bradbury.
Wallace, K. (2001). *Diving dolphin.* New York: DK Publishing.

**/oy/ Vowels**

Marshall, J. (1990). *Fox be nimble.* New York: Puffin.
Witty, B. ( 1991 ). *Noises in the night.* Grand Haven, MI: School Zone.

**Review of r Vowels and Other Vowel Patterns**

Brenner, B. (1989). *Annie's pet.* New York: Bantam.
Hays, A. J. (2003). *The pup speaks up.* New York: Random House.
Hopkins, L. B. (1986). *Surprises.* New York: Harper.
Marshall, E. (1985). *Fox on wheels.* New York: Dutton.
Milton, J. (1985). *Dinosaur days.* New York: Random House.
Rylant, C. (1987). *Henry and Mudge: The first book.* New York.
Stambler, J. (1988). *Cat at bat.* New York: Dutton.

*Books to Remember* (Flyleaf Publishing). A series of beautifully illustrated 30-page books that provide a review of vowel patterns.

*Early Phonics Readers* (Continental Press). A series of 48 eight-page books that cover short vowels, long vowels, and consonant clusters. CD-ROM disks that read books aloud are available.

*High Noon Sound Out Chapter Books* (Academic Therapy Publications). Series of 32-page books designed for older readers.

*Let's Read Together Books* (Kane Press/Lerner). A series of five 32-page books that focus on short vowels.

*Ready Readers* (Modern Curriculum Press/Pearson). Includes 355 leveled books, organized into eight stages of decodable text. Books have a natural sound but some books need to be re-leveled.

*Real Kid Readers* (Millbrook Press/Lerner). A series of 32-page books illustrated with color photos.

*Wonder Books* (Child's World). A series of 35 books reinforcing consonants and vowel patterns. Very well done.

Decodable text can be a powerful aid. Until her teacher started giving her decodable text, Camatera, a second grader in the beginning stages of reading, was making virtually no progress (Mesmer, 1999). Even though she was being taught key patterns systematically, she wasn't learning to apply them. The text the teacher was using did not specifically reinforce the patterns that she introduced. In fact, the text contained so many patterns that Camatera was overwhelmed. When the teacher began using the Ready Readers series, which reinforced patterns but managed to retain a natural flow, Camatera began making progress. The match between materials and methods made all the difference.

## Leveling Books According to the Decoding Skills Needed to Read Them

The best possible practice for phonics is reading, but the materials students read should reinforce the skills they have been taught and be on the appropriate level of difficulty. All the major literacy programs present phonics in systematic fashion in the beginning levels. This means that students who are still learning basic phonics should be given books leveled according to the phonics skills needed to read them (Gunning, 2008a). In most basal reading programs, beginning reading (first grade) is divided into five texts, with each text covering two sublevels. Table 8.7 lists the key phonics elements in the sequence in which they are typically taught, along with the approximate levels in a first-grade reading program. This chart can be used to estimate the level of difficulty of beginning reading books in terms of the phonics skills needed to read them. To determine the level of a text, examine the book to see what key elements are needed to read it. For instance, if a book requires knowing all the short vowels but doesn't have words with clusters, it is assigned at the end of Level 1. To make the chart fit your program, you might need to make a few adjustments. (Note that the books listed in Figure 8.8 are organized by phonics element.)

The phonics readability chart (Table 8.7) is designed to be used with the Phonics Inventory in Appendix A. Each of the five levels is represented by ten words. For instance, if a student is able to read short-*a* and short-*i* words but has difficulty with short-*o*, short-*e*, and short-*u* words, then she should be given Level 1 books. If a student can read words containing long-vowel patterns but has difficulty with *r* vowel patterns, she should be ready for Level 4 books. Placement should be verified by observing the student as she attempts to read a book at the level at which she has been placed.

 **Using Technology**

**Word Family Sort**

http://www.readwritethink.org/files/resources/interactives/wordfamily/

Enables students to sort short-vowel words electronically.

## ▓ Additional Reinforcement for Vowel Patterns

### Sorting

Because it helps students make discoveries about printed words, sorting is one of the most valuable reinforcement activities.

Students can sort vowel patterns in much the same way that they sort consonant correspondences (see Figure 8.9).

## Modified Bingo

Modified bingo, which is a sorting activity in a game-like format, may be played with just three or four columns instead of five. The heading for each column is a pattern

**TABLE 8.7**
Phonics Readability Chart for Beginning Reading Programs

| Book Level | Sublevel | Key Elements |
|---|---|---|
| 1 | 1 | Consonants |
| | | Short *a, i* patterns |
| | 2 | Short *o, e, u* patterns |
| 2 | 3 | Short vowels with initial clusters |
| | 4 | Short vowels with final clusters |
| 3 | 5 | Long vowels (final -*e* marker): *a* and *i* |
| | 6 | Long vowels (final-*e marker*): *o, e, u* |
| | 7 | Long-vowel digraphs and open syllable: *ai/ay, e/ee/ea/ei, ie/igh/ind/ild/y (cry), o/oa/ow/oll/old* |
| 4 | 8 | *r* vowels |
| 5 | 9 | Other: vowel digraphs/diphthongs: *oo (book), ould (could), oo (too)/ew/ue/ui, ou (out)/ow* |
| | 10 | Other-vowel digraphs/diphthongs: *oi/oy, au/aw/all/alk/ong* |

*Source:* Gunning (2013) Figure 5.9, p. 236. Reprinted by permission of Pearson.

A book is placed at a level if at least 90 percent of the words at that level consist of phonic patterns introduced at that level or an earlier level, or the words are known high-frequency words or can be identified through the use of illustrations. Thus, a book is at Book Level 3, Sublevel 7, if 90 percent of the words contain long vowels or contain short vowels, or are known high-frequency words or can be identified through the use of pictures. Within each level, key elements are listed in sublevels in typical order of introduction. In Level 1, for example, short *o, e,* and *u* are introduced after short *a* and *i.* (**Exact scope and sequences vary somewhat from program to program, especially for placement of *r* vowels. Make adjustments as necessary.**)

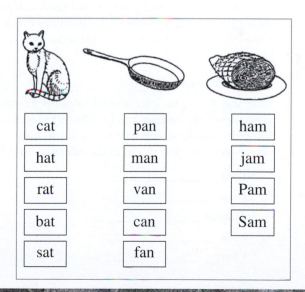

**FIGURE 8.9**
Word Sort by Pattern

**Word Bingo**

| hat | ham | can | map |
|-----|-----|-----|-----|
| cat | am | fan | |
| rat | | man | |
| | | ran | |
| | | van | |

word as in Figure 8.10. A row must be filled out with words in the same pattern or with wild cards. Cards for all players are placed in the center of the table, and players take turns choosing cards. After selecting a card, the player reads it and looks to see if it rhymes with one of his column-heading words. If so, the player can place it in one of the squares. After placing a card, the player reads the column-heading word and all the words that have been placed in the column. This provides added practice in reading pattern words (Morris, 1999).

Bingo cards can be created on a variety of levels. An early set might contain only short-*a* patterns. A later set might contain a short-*a*, short-*e*, short-*i*, or short-*o* patterns. A more advanced set might reinforce long-vowel, other vowel, or *r* vowel patterns.

## Modified Concentration

In the regular game of Concentration, pairs of cards are shuffled and placed face down. The first player turns over a card and then tries to guess where its match might be. If the player turns over a matching card, she removes it and places the pair in front of her. The player then continues to play until she fails to make a match. Then the second player attempts to make a match.

In modified Concentration, cards are composed of pairs of rhyming words. Students make a match by locating the rhyming partner of the word turned over, as shown in Figure 8.11. When a player turns over a card, she must read it. She then must find its rhyming partner and read it also. Concentration requires the player to keep the rime in mind as she searches for its match. It promotes focusing on the rime that the two words share (Morris, 1999).

## Little Books

One way to obtain easy-to-read books is to create your own. The books can simply contain words, or they can be illustrated with student or teacher drawings, photos, magazine illustrations, or clip art, if you have access to a desktop publishing system. Some patterns that might make effective little books include these:

I am _____.

I can _____.

The cat _____.

I like _____.

I play _____.

**■ FIGURE 8.11**
Modified
Concentration

| pet | wet |
|-----|-----|
|     |     |
|     |     |
|     |     |
|     |     |

I help _____.

I saw _____.

You might also create caption books devoted to a topic: numbers, colors, seasons, pets, dogs, cats, birds, farm animals, cars, trucks, toys, and so on.

## Using Writing to Reinforce Phonics

Through writing, students can make important discoveries about letter–sound relationships. Students who are at a rudimentary stage of spelling development should be allowed to use invented spelling. If a student has difficulty spelling a word, have him sound it out. Ask questions such as "What sound do you hear at the beginning of *bat*? What letter makes the /b/ sound? What sound do you hear next? Say the word slowly: 'baaaat.' What sound do you hear at the end of *bat*? What letter makes that sound?"

A good way to reinforce pattern words or another element that has been introduced is to have students write a brief story using some of the pattern words. Have students write the story and then, if necessary, help them with any words containing the target element that might have been misspelled. As always, give students credit for what they do correctly. Here is an example of how a teacher helped a student who wrote *got* for *goat*. She used the miscue as a minilesson in applied phonics: to help the student make the transition from the letter name to the word pattern stage.

> I see that you wrote *g-o* for the "go" sound in *goat* and that you wrote a *t* for the ending sound of *goat*. That's very good. But the *o* sound in *goat* is spelled *oa*, like this (teacher writes and carefully enunciates *goat*). The sound is /ō/, which is often spelled with an *oa*. If this is how I write *goat*, how might I write *boat*?

## Assembling Words

When working with large groups and/or as an alternative to using magnetic letters, have the group assemble letters to make words using procedures adapted from Cunningham (1991). Letter cards can be purchased or created by cutting up file folders. To keep the letters organized, place them in separate bags, one bag for each letter. Distribute a few letters at a time so that students are not overwhelmed with possible choices. Choose letters that reinforce familiar patterns and correspondences. To reinforce short *e*, for instance, you might distribute the following letters: *e, m, n, t, p*. Before having the words formed, tell students that they will be making words that have a short *e*, which is /e/ as in the word *ten*. Then say a short-*e* word, one that students are familiar with, and have students assemble the word with their letters. Say the word in a sentence to make sure that you and the students have the same word in mind. Also have students repeat the word. Assemble the letters to form a word for one or two examples. If students have difficulty, emphasize the separate sounds of the word: /t/, /e/, /n/. Using a larger version of the letter cards, have a volunteer form the word on the chalkboard ledge or a pocket chart.

After a word has been formed and its correct spelling demonstrated, make sure each student has formed the word correctly. Also write the word on the chalkboard. Words to be formed might include *men, ten, pen, met, net, pet*. Make sure that all the words you ask students to form are in their speaking vocabularies. After all words have been formed, discuss which ones rhyme, which ones begin with the same sound, and so forth.

## Word Wall

On the wall, place pattern words, high-frequency words, color words, names of the months, compound words, or any other words with which students are working. Because they are on the wall, the words are readily available for quick review. Troublesome words can be reviewed daily.

Putting words on the wall helps students to remember them. After a pattern has been introduced, place one or more of the pattern words on the wall. Arrange them alphabetically by pattern. The *ab* pattern would be placed first, followed by the *ack* and *ad* patterns, and so forth. Because the words are on the wall, they can be used as a kind of dictionary. If students want to know how to spell a pattern or high-frequency word, they can find it on the wall. Review wall words periodically, using the following or similar activities:

- Find as many animal names, color words, and number names as you can.
- Pantomime an action (sit, run) or use gestures to indicate an object or other item (pan, hat, cat, pen), and have students write the word and then hold it up so you can quickly check everyone's response. Have a volunteer read the word and point to it on the word wall. Before pantomiming the word, tell what pattern the word will be in: the *at* pattern. To make the task a bit more challenging and to get students to analyze the ending letters of patterns, tell students that the word will be in one of two patterns: the *at* or the *an* pattern.

## Secret Word

Select a word from a pattern, and jot it down on a sheet of paper but don't reveal its identity (P. Cunningham & Allington, 1994). Have students number their papers 1–5. Give a series of five clues to the identity of the word. After each clue, students write down their guesses. The object of the activity is to guess the word on the basis of the fewest clues. The clues might be as follows:

1. The secret word is in the *at* pattern.
2. It has three letters.
3. It is an animal.
4. It can fly.
5. Into the cave flew the _____.

After supplying the five clues, show the secret word (*bat*) and discuss students' responses. See who guessed the secret word first.

## Making Words

> ✳ Making Words is an excellent way to review a pattern or a series of related patterns. To enhance the value of Making Words, focus on a few patterns.

Making Words is a hands-on manipulative activity in which students put together letters to create words. It provides excellent reinforcement for word-building patterns. Beginning with two-letter words and extending to five-letter or even longer words, students assemble approximately a dozen words (Cunningham & Cunningham, 1992). The last word that the students assemble contains all the letters that they were given.

Here's how it works. Students are given the cutout or magnetic letters *a–d–n–s–t* and are asked to do the following:

- Use two letters to make *at*.
- Add a letter to make *sat*.
- Take away a letter to make *at*.
- Change a letter to make *an*.
- Add a letter to make *Dan*.
- Change a letter to make *tan*.
- Take away a letter to make *an*.
- Add a letter to make *and*.
- Add a letter to make *sand*.
- Now break up your word and see what word you can make with all the letters (*stand*).

## Building Words

One way of getting students to process all the letters in a word is to use a procedure in which they build words by changing a single letter: *cat, cap, can, pan, pat, pot, spot*. As a result of building words this way, disabled readers who overrelied on using just initial sounds made significant progress in processing medial and final sounds in words (McCandliss, Beck, Sandak, & Perfetti, 2003).

## Poems and Verses

> ✳ Poems can reinforce a variety of patterns. Some easy-to-read collections include *Surprises* and *More Surprises* (Hopkins, 1987) and *Soap Soup and Other Verses* (Kuskin, 1992).

Overusing their decoding skills or perhaps struggling so hard to decode words that meaning is neglected, poor readers often ignore substitutions that do not fit the sense of the sentence. Because of its rhythm and rhyme, poetry is harder to misread. The interrupted flow created by a miscue is more noticeable and more likely to be corrected. Some poor readers' mistakes seem due more to carelessness or an inexact style of reading than lack of skill. However, poetry demands an exact reading.

Having students read verses is a good way for them to experience accuracy in their reading (Broaddus & Bloodgood, 1994). Poetry can also be used to promote fluency, because poetry is meant to be read over and over again.

## ■■■ Technology

### Internet

The Web site Starfall (http://www.starfall.com) features activities, stories, and film clips designed to introduce single-syllable patterns. The program has a speech component so that words can be read. It highlights words in parts so that students can hear separate sounds in words and also match letters and sounds. In a number of activities Starfall builds words much as is done in word building.

Another Web site, Between the Lions (http://pbskids.org/lions), features a number of brief film clips of songs and stories that reinforce vowel patterns. The clips are fairly sophisticated so they could be used with older as well as younger students.

Words and Pictures (http://www.bbc.co.uk/schools/wordsandpictures/index .shtml) is produced by the BBC, so the exercises have a distinctive British flavor. Even so, they provide imaginative reinforcement.

### Software

Because of speech capability and interactive features, phonics software has the potential to provide excellent practice. The best software titles present phonics in a functional way that motivates students.

Simon Sounds It Out (Don Johnston), an award-winning software, pronounces and helps students build words by combining initial consonants (onsets) and word patterns (rimes). Featuring an electronic tutor, it provides especially effective practice for word building. Because it pronounces and shows parts of words, it also helps develop phonemic awareness.

Tenth Planet: Exploring Literacy (Sunburst) includes sorting activities, building words, and the writing of rhymes and songs. Programs include Letter Sounds, Vowels: Short and Long, Consonant Blends and Digraphs; Vowel Patterns; and Word Parts (working with multisyllabic words).

Lexia Reading has a variety of phonics lessons and activities in its phonics component. Activities range from working with initial consonants to working with multisyllabic words.

## ■■■ Word-Analysis Strategies

Struggling readers tend to have difficulty with the middles of words and so overrely on context and initial and final consonants (Ehri & Saltmarsh, 1995). Struggling readers also have difficulty in taking control of their learning. Even when they do know the elements in a word, they fail to use them. Struggling readers need to be taught strategies to guide them so that they analyze words fully and use what they know to analyze apparently unknown words. Tied in to the word-building instructional technique are the following key strategies: pronounceable word part, analogy, decoding, and context.

# Pronounceable Word-Part Strategy

> Some struggling readers may read words sound by sound. As they gain in skill, they should be encouraged to chunk sounds.

> **Pronounceable word parts:** chunks of words that lend themselves naturally to being pronounced, such as *an* or *ran* or *bran* in the word *branch*.

The word-building technique takes advantage of students' natural tendency to seek out pronounceable word parts by highlighting them. Rob, an 8-year-old struggling reader, is baffled by the word *slop* even though he knows the rime *op* and several words that begin with *sl*. The teacher asks Rob if there is any part of the word that he can say. Rob looks over the word, says "op," and then says "slop." The teacher's questioning helped direct Rob to a word part that he knew. Using the known element as a base, he was able to reconstruct the entire word. This step in the strategy is known as seeking out known or **pronounceable word parts**.

Later, Rob has difficulty with the word *tick*. He is unable to locate any pronounceable parts, so the teacher assists him by covering up the *t*. Rob reads "ick" and then "tick." Although the teacher provides help when needed, the objective is to have the student apply the strategy independently. The following box describes how the strategy might be taught.

## Teaching the Pronounceable Word-Part Strategy

**Step 1:   *Assessing strategy usage.*** Observe students as they encounter printed words whose meanings they know but that they cannot pronounce. Note the strategies they use and how successfully they are able to apply them. Discuss strategies for decoding words. Tell students that all readers, even you, run into difficult words. Ask students how they go about figuring out hard words. As you introduce strategies, build on what students know. Help them fit new strategies in with ones they are using.

**Step 2:   *Introducing the strategy.*** Explain to students that words that might appear difficult often contain parts that can be sounded out. Explaining that they will be learning a strategy called *pronounceable word parts,* model the strategy. Show how you might look for and use a known word part to help you sound out a word. After you have worked out the pronunciation of a word, show how you would check your reconstruction by seeing if your pronunciation was that of a real word and also seeing if the word fit the context of the sentence. Explain to students that, when seeking out pronounceable word parts, there is no one way to do it. In the word *bench,* for instance, *en* might be the familiar word part for some students. For others, the familiar word part might be *ben*. Do not ask students to look for the "little word" in the big word. For one thing, many big words do not contain little words. For another, using word units might make it more difficult to pronounce the entire word. Finding *hop,* the little word in *chop,* would actually make it harder to work out the pronunciation of *chop,* since the *ch* functions as a unit.

**Step 3:   *Guided practice for pronounceable word parts.*** Provide guided practice with the strategy. Have students seek out known word parts in the following or other words that contain elements familiar to your students. Pointing to each word, ask: "Is there any part of this word that you can say?"

lunch    spend    sting    stump

As students attempt to apply the strategy, provide assistance. If they are unable to find a pronounceable word part even though the target word has one, cover up all of the word except the pronounceable word part, and encourage them to say the part that is uncovered and use that part to reconstruct the whole word. For instance, if a student who knows the word *hen,* balks at *tent,* cover up all but the *en* and encourage the student to pronounce it. After *en* has been pronounced, uncover the initial *t* and have the student pronounce the *t* and then *ten*. Uncover the final *t,* have the student pronounce it, and then ask the student to read the whole word. Be sure to affirm students' efforts with specific comments: "I like the way you looked for a part of the word that you could say and then used that to help you figure out that hard word."

Do not encourage the use of the strategy with words like *of* or *you* or *wash,* or other words that are irregular and so do not lend themselves to this strategy. Encourage the use of context for these words. If it is obvious that a student cannot work out a word, tell the student the word, or ask, "Is that word _____ or _____ (you supply the target word and an option)?"

As part of your instruction, inform students that the pronounceable word-part strategy will not always work. For instance, pronouncing the *ow* in *knowledge* or the *ash* in *squash* won't help much. Students need to learn to check their constructions to make sure they are real words that fit the context. If not, they should try alternative pronunciations.

*Step 4: Application.* Before students read a selection, highlight some words that you feel they may have difficulty with. If they can't pronounce them, have students seek out pronounceable word parts

and see if they can construct the words' pronunciations. Emphasize the need to check to see that the word they construct is a real word and fits the story context. During reading, remind students to use the pronounceable word-part strategy if they encounter graphically unknown words. Supply help as needed. After reading, discuss words that students decoded successfully. Talk over the processes that they used to decipher the words so they become more fully aware of how the strategy works.

*Step 5: Assessment and Review.* Note students' ability to use the pronounceable word-part strategy and reteach as necessary. Review the pronounceable word-part strategy from time to time. Whenever a new word pattern is introduced, provide students with opportunities to note that pattern in words. For instance, after *-at* has been presented, have students note *-at* in words such as *chat, flat, patch,* and *rattle.* Encourage students to bring to class examples of encounters with newly taught patterns and instances where they were able to work out the pronunciation of words by using the pronounceable word-part strategy.

## Analogy Strategy

Although natural, effective, and relatively easy to teach, the pronounceable word-part strategy does not always work. When it doesn't work, students should try an analogy or compare–contrast strategy. Research suggests that the analogy or compare–contrast strategy is relatively easy to teach (Ehri & Robbins, 1992) and is highly effective (Cunningham, 1979; Gaskins, Gaskins, & Gaskins, 1991).

Here is how the analogy strategy works. While reading a sports story, Rob encounters the word *tame,* a word that is in his listening vocabulary but that he has never seen in print. Neither urging Rob to look for a familiar part nor covering up the *t* helps. Knowing that Rob can read the word *name*, the teacher uses an analogy strategy. She asks Rob if the word looks like any word that he knows. If Rob is unable to think of an analogy word, she may refer him to a list of analogy words known as the Model Words List (see words in Figure 8.7), or she might supply the analogy word. The teacher carefully prints the word *name* and immediately under it the word *tame.* She asks Rob to read the first word, which he does with ease. Noting that *tame* is similar to *name*, Rob reads it, too. If he had still been unable to read *tame,* the teacher would have used known *t* words (*to, toy*) to help him decode the initial consonant and then blend the two elements.

Beginning readers can use an analogy strategy to decode unfamiliar words if the analogy word is present (Goswami, 1988), but they must have some phonics skills if they are to draw an analogy word from memory (Ehri & Robbins, 1992). They can use the known word *cat* to read *mat* if the word *cat* is there before them but probably would not be able to retrieve it from memory. Use of analogy becomes more common as students' store of immediate recognition words increases (Ehri & Snowling, 2004). The next box describes how the analogy strategy might be taught.

## Teaching the Analogy Strategy

*Step 1: Introducing the analogy strategy.* Explain to students that sometimes they may not be able to find a word part that they can pronounce. Tell them that if this happens, they should try to think of a word they know that is similar. Model the strategy for them. For instance, show them how they could use the word *rain* to help decode *chain* or the word *him* to decode *trim*. Stress the need to see if the reconstructed word is a real one.

*Step 2: Guided practice.* Provide a number of words that may be new to students but that are analogous to known words. Have students use the known words to figure out the new ones. For instance, students might use the known words *pen* and *hit* to decipher *when, bent, spend, quit,* and *split.*

*Step 3: Practice and application.* Have students integrate the analogy and pronounceable word-parts strategies and apply them, as needed, to unfamiliar words in stories and articles. Post a list of model words similar to that presented in Figure 8.7 so that students can use these in case they can't think of an analogy word. To guide students in their use of the pronounceable word-part or analogy strategy, post a set of directions for using the strategies, model their use, and provide ample opportunity for practice and application. Whenever students encounter difficulty with a word, encourage them to apply the strategies. A sample set of instructions for using the strategies is presented in the section, "How to Figure Out Hard Words." You may want to reword the instructions to fit the level of your students.

*Step 4: Assessment and Review.* Note students' ability to use the analogy strategy and reteach as necessary. Review the analogy strategy from time to time. Encourage students to bring to class examples of encounters with newly taught patterns and instances where they were able to work out the pronunciation of words by using the pronounceable word-part or analogy strategy.

Both the pronounceable part and analogy strategies have been used extensively with struggling readers. Explicit instruction in the use of the pronounceable part and analogy strategies proved to be especially effective for severely disabled readers in grades 2 through 6 (Lovett & Steinbach, 1997). In just thirty-five lessons, the program produced significant and substantial gains in decoding. The analogy strategy has been used successfully with hundreds of disabled readers at the Benchmark School (Gaskins, 2005).

## Decoding Strategy

Students at the very beginning stages of learning to read may not be able to spot patterns in words or use a known word to read an unfamiliar one. These students can still use a pronounceable word part. For them, the pronounceable word part might be the first sound. They might then be encouraged to read the rest of the word sound by sound and to blend the sounds together. If students forget the vowel sound, prompt the use of the vowel model word routine in which they say the vowel letter, the mnemonic illustration from the Short-Vowel Chart in Figure 8.6, and the sound of the letter. For short *a*, students would say "a, apple, /a/."

## Context Strategy

Some words do not lend themselves to decoding or are composed of unfamiliar elements. Depending on the nature of the word and the context, students should be encouraged to use picture or verbal clues. Context should also be used as a cross-check. After students have decoded a word, they should make sure that it makes sense in the sentence.

## Advanced Strategies

As students encounter exceptions to the final-*e* generalization (*give, have*) and learn vowel digraphs (such as *ea* and *ow*) that have more than one pronunciation (*beak, bread; low, cow*), they will need to try more than one pronunciation. Model and provide practice with the variability or try-another-sound strategy. In using the try-another-sound strategy, students will, in most cases, try the long-vowel pronunciation, and if that doesn't work, they will try the short-vowel or another pronunciation. The strategy can also be used with the consonant letters *c* and *g*.

Steps for the try-another-sound strategy are as follow:

1. When decoding a word, if the word isn't a real word or doesn't make sense in the sentence, try another pronunciation.

2. Try the long-vowel pronunciation first. If that doesn't work, try the short-vowel or another pronunciation. For the consonant letters *c* and *g*, try the hard pronunciation first and then the soft pronunciation.

3. Check to see if the word is a real word and makes sense in the sentence.

Affirm students' use of a strategy. Doing so encourages students to use that strategy again: "I like the way you used a word part that you knew to read the whole word." At times, none of your prompts will work. In these cases, give students a prompt in which they choose between the correct word and an alternative: "Is that word *barked* or *howled*? How do you know?" Giving students a choice involves them in using phonics and/or semantics to respond and also prevents them from being embarrassed.

See Table 8.8 for a list of word-analysis strategies. Give students as much guidance as they need, but gradually lead them to the point where they can decode independently.

## Prompting Strategy Use

When a student encounters difficult words, use a "pause, prompt, praise" approach (Tunmer & Chapman, 1999). At first, say nothing. Simply pause, and give the student a chance to work out the word on his own. (If this is during a group activity, do not allow other students to respond.) If the student is not able to decode the word, supply a prompt. Unless the word is *were, of,* or another word that has an irregular spelling or contains phonics elements with which the student is not familiar, provide a phonics prompt. Although many programs urge the use of a context prompt, such as "What would make sense here?" phonics clues are more effective and promote the transfer of word-analysis skills to new words (Greaney, Tunmer, & Chapman, 1997; Tunmer & Chapman, 1999).

Because it is more direct and easier to implement, prompt the pronounceable word-part strategy first. Ask "Is there any part of that word that you can say?" If the student does not respond, provide additional assistance. For instance, if a student who has been taught the *ee* pattern has difficulty with a word such as *sweet* and is unable to note any known parts in the word, you might cover up all

> ✳ When prompting the use of the pronounceable word-part strategy, ask students if there is any part of the word they can say. Do not ask them to "look for the little word in the big word." Often there is none, but there is usually a pronounceable word part. Application of the pronounceable word-part strategy should be part of instruction in patterns. Once students have learned the *-en* pattern, they should be encouraged to use *-en* to help them read difficult words that contain this element.

but the middle *ee* and have her say what sound *ee* makes. Uncovering the *w,* have her pronounce *wee* and then, uncovering the *s,* lead her to pronounce *swee.* Uncovering the final *t,* encourage the student to pronounce the whole word.

If the student is unable to pronounce the *ee* in *sweet,* you might prompt the use of an analogy strategy. Ask the student if the word is like any word that she knows. If the student is unable to think of an analogy word, supply one. Using the model word *feet,* have her read *feet* and compare *sweet* with *feet.* (Cover the *sw* in *sweet* if necessary, so that she can read "eet" and then "sweet.")

Some students may be slow perceiving patterns in words, such as the *an* in *plan* or the *ip* in *trip.* For these students, the pronounceable word part might be the beginning consonant, or they may need to say each sound of the word individually: "p-l-a-n." If this is the case, encourage them to do so. In time, after being introduced to a number of word patterns, they should be able to perceive patterns in words.

If a student is unable to use a pronounceable word-part or analogy strategy or if the word does not lend itself to either of these strategies, prompt the use of context. Encourage the student to skip the word and read to the end of the sentence. Ask "What word would make sense here? What word would fit?" Even when a sounding-out strategy is used, context should be used as a cross-check. After a student has used the pronounceable word-part or analogy strategy, prompt the student to see if the word is a real word and fits the sense of the sentence.

How well do the pronounceable word-part and analogy strategies work? In a series of experiments, severely disabled readers taught to use pronounceable word-part and analogy strategies clearly outperformed students taught to use context (Greaney et al., 1997; Tunmer & Chapman, 1999). The authors recommended that "children should be encouraged to look for familiar spelling patterns first and to use context only as a back-up to confirm hypotheses as to what the word might be" (p. 82).

There are two problems with the overuse of context. First, it does not work as well as a decoding strategy. From context, students are only able to predict the pronunciation of about 1 out of every 10 content words. Functions words such as *of* and *the* are 40 percent predictable (Tunmer & Chapman, 1999). Second, unless students use their phonics strategies, they will fail to develop and so their word-analysis skills will be weakened. Ironically, use of phonics skills improves students' ability to use context. When presented with a series of irregular words presented in sentence context that they had missed when they were called upon to read them in list form, students who were better decoders outperformed the poor decoders (Tunmer & Chapman, 1999). Decoding ability facilitated the use of context.

To help students who rush through their oral reading and produce a host of "careless" errors, stress meaning. Have them focus on accurately reading short segments of text. For a while, they might read one sentence at a time. Initial reading should be silent so that they have time to work out difficult words. Encourage students to request help as needed. After their silent reading, have them read the sentences orally. Prompt the use of integrated clues. Students pay more attention to meaning and make fewer errors because they have spent more time carefully reading the segments. Where they request help, provide prompts that lead them to use effective strategies (Buettner, 2002). Gradually, they will incorporate these strategies and become meaning-based readers.

Sometimes, students fail to process all the letters in a word, even though they know all the correspondences in the word. They might glance at beginning and ending letters and guess at what the word might be. To help students process all the word's elements, have them write the word, saying each sound as they write the letter or letter group that represents that sound. For instance, after reading the word *problem* as *probably*, have the students write and read the word as "*p-r-o-b-l-e-m* problem" (Dorn, 2010).

## How to Figure Out Hard Words

Following is a series of steps that you might have students take when they confront a word that is unfamiliar in print:

1. See if there is any part of the word that I can say. If I can't say any part of the word, go to Step 4.

> ✳ The pronounceable word-part strategy is attempted first because it is less intrusive to the flow of reading and because it is faster and easier to apply than the analogy or contextual strategies.

2. Say the part of the word I know. Then say the rest of the word. If I can't say the rest of the word, go to Step 4.

3. Ask "Is the word I said a real word? Does it make sense in the story?" If not, try again or go to Step 4.

4. Is the word like any word I know? Is it like one of the model words? If not, go to Step 6.

5. Say the word. Is it a real word? Does it make sense in the story? If not, try again, or go to Step 6.

6. Say "blank" for the word. Read to the end of the sentence. Ask "What word would make sense here?"

Post a simplified list of steps that students might follow to decode challenging words and check the results of their efforts:

1. Make the word:
   - Can I say any part of this word? or
   - Is this word like any word I know? Is it like one of the model words? or
   - What word would make sense here?

2. Check the word:
   - Is the word I made a real word?
   - Does the word make sense in the sentence?

> To foster independence, review strategy use from time to time, provide lots of practice and application opportunities, and use prompts liberally.

Students should practice saying and eventually memorize the steps of the decoding strategies. In an experiment in which low-achieving readers rehearsed the steps of a strategy by saying the steps aloud and then to themselves, they did much better than a group who were simply taught the strategy. Affirming responses so that students could see they were using the strategy successfully also increased performance (Schunk & Rice, 1993).

## Balanced Use of Decoding Strategies

> ✳ An analysis of the performance of low-achieving readers suggests that those who use strategies make progress. Those who do not use strategies make very limited progress.

In addition to pronounceable word-part, analogy, decoding, and context strategies, a number of other strategies can be used to decipher words. These include using picture clues, using the initial letter of an unknown word, using phonics rules, using a picture glossary or picture dictionary, asking for help, and simply skipping the word altogether. Often, strategies are combined. For instance, decoding may be combined with a picture clue or context or both.

Strategy use may be inefficient or inappropriate. Using pictures clues is an early strategy that should give way to some form of using phonics clues and context. However, because some poor readers are deficient in higher-level decoding strategies, they continue to overuse picture and context clues. Because they overuse picture and context clues, they fail to develop other, more useful strategies.

Strategies should be taught directly, but careful instruction needs to be accompanied by extensive opportunities for application. After being taught a strategy, students need to be guided in its proper application. Their efforts also need to be affirmed with specific praise.

The degree to which students make progress is also a reflection of the teacher's guidance. Decoding instruction must go beyond teaching students a series of short-vowel patterns or consonant clusters. The instructor must teach students what to do when they encounter an unknown short-vowel or consonant-cluster word. That instruction cannot be limited to a few lessons or review sessions. It should include prompts that the teacher uses when the students encounter difficult words.

## Using Prompts to Foster the Use of Balanced Decoding Strategies

Julia, a 7-year-old second grader reading on a primer level, misread the sentence "The light is red now," from Eastman's (1961) *Go, Dog, Go*, as "The little is red new." Analyzing the misreading, the teacher realized that while Julia had made use of initial consonants (*little* and *light* and *new* and *now* begin with the same consonant sound), she ignored other sources of information. For instance, an illustration at the top of the page clearly shows a stoplight that has turned red, and in previous portions of the story, green and red lights have been mentioned. Apart from these picture and textual clues, Julia's knowledge of language should inform her that a noun will follow the article *the*. Her general knowledge of the world, as well as her knowledge of language, should also indicate that the sentence does not make sense as she reads it.

Julia had failed to make adequate use of all three cueing systems. Her miscues did not fit syntactically, semantically, or visually, except for the beginning sound. Through careful questioning or prompts, the teacher might lead Julia to the use of the semantic, syntactic, or phonic cueing strategies that would help her rectify her misreading. For instance, the following prompts might have been used:

- **Semantic:** "Does that sentence make sense? What would make sense here?"

- **Syntactic:** "Does that sound like real language? What would sound right here?"

- **Phonic:** "*Little* begins with an *l*, but how does it end? How does this word end?" (teacher points to *light*) "Can you think of another word that has *i-g-h-t*? What sound does it make?" (Earlier in the story, Julia had read *night* correctly. Using this as an analogy, she might be led to work out the word *light*.) Or you could try a pronounceable word-part strategy and ask "Is there any part of this word that you can say?"

> While picture clues might be fostered during the prealphabetic (logographic) and early alphabetic stages of reading, phonics and contextual clues should gradually replace them. Enlist a student's input by asking: "What would help you figure that word out?"

When choosing which prompt to use and therefore which cueing system to emphasize, you need to consider a number of factors.

> ⚓ Do not pose riddle-like prompts: "It rhymes with *shoots*. You wear these on your feet" (boots). Use a prompt that leads to strategy use: "Can you say any part of that word? What would make sense here?"

You need to ask "What prompt is most likely to lead to a correct response? Which prompt will provide the greatest payoff in terms of helping the student cope with difficult words in the future?" You also need to consider the student's development in reading. What strategies has she mastered? What strategies is she struggling to learn? If, for instance, a student learning about the final-*e* pattern read *cap* for *cape*, you might ask her "What is the vowel? What does the *e* on the end of the word tell you about the vowel?" (Wilson, 1999).

Although the pronounceable word-part approach is frequently a good strategy to start with because it is simple, direct, and easy to apply, a better choice for Julia might be to supply semantic prompts. First and foremost, students need to see that reading should make sense. A semantic prompt ("What word would make sense here?") would be a reminder of that fact. Since Julia neglected to relate *light* to the known word *night*, a phonic cue might be used as a cross-check. After the student supplies *light* on the basis of semantic cues, ask her if *light* begins with an *l* and ends with a *t*. Ask her if she can think of another word that ends in *i-g-h-t*. If she remembers *night*, have her say the word and compare *light* to this known word.

The nature of the text being read also has an effect on strategy choice. For instance, Tiffany, a third grader, had difficulty with the sentence "The bear fell from the tree." Since Tiffany was stuck on *from*, she hadn't read the phrase "the tree." Noting that *from* is irregular and believing that having more context would aid Tiffany, the teacher requested that Tiffany reread the beginning of the sentence, say "blank" for the unknown word, read to the end of the sentence, and then see if she could tell what the word might be. After rereading the entire sentence, Tiffany

> **Cross-check:** the use of one strategy to verify the results of another. For instance, a student uses context to verify that the word she sounded out makes sense.

had no difficulty identifying *from*. As a **cross-check**, the teacher asked Tiffany to tell what letters *from* begins with and what sounds these letters stand for. Noting some hesitancy and remembering that Tiffany had stumbled over other words that contained initial clusters such as *fr*, the instructor planned future lessons on clusters.

> ⚓ If you are not sure which is the best prompt to use with a student, enlist the student's input by asking, "What would help you figure that word out?"

Choice of strategies is also determined, in part, by the student's cognitive-processing abilities. Tiffany has difficulty remembering words and may miss the same word every time it appears in a story. In one story, Tiffany repeatedly missed the word *chance*. Hoping to provide some "hook" that would help Tiffany retrieve *chance*, the instructor asked Tiffany if there was any part of *chance* she could say. Tiffany recognized the *an*, added *ch* to it, said "chan," and then was able to read *chance*. In subsequent encounters with *chance*, Tiffany was able to use this strategy when she failed to recognize the word.

> ⚓ To gain insight into students' strategy use, occasionally ask them to tell how they figured out a hard word. You might ask, "How do you know that word was 'numb'?"

## Fostering Self-Correction

In reading, as in life, making errors provides the opportunity for growth. When a student misreads a word, don't immediately supply a correction. Let the student read to the end of the sentence or perhaps the paragraph. Often, reading additional text will indicate to the student that a miscue has been made and she will reread the text correctly. If not, supply a prompt that will lead her to self-correct: "Does that sound right? Does that make sense?"

If a student's misreading was partially correct, bring that to her attention. To confirm a student's use of context, you might say "The word *dog* fits the sense of the sentence. Dogs do howl. But the word begins with a *w*. What word that begins with a *w* might fit there?"

Provide prompts only after a reasonable interval and when it seems likely that the student will benefit from some help, and then give only as much help as is needed to nudge the student onto the right path. Use the least intrusive prompt possible.

Sometimes, despite your careful prompting, students will be unable to make use of any of the strategies. Provide the correct response as one of two options. For example, instead of simply telling them that the unknown word is *goat,* ask "Would *goat* or *got* fit here?" Then discuss why *goat* is appropriate. This "starter" prompt actively engages students and points out strategies that they might use in the future.

Self-correcting is a sign of a good reader. It means the student realizes that meaning is the ultimate aim of reading. It also means that the reader actively monitors his reading to make sure that it makes sense. When students self-correct without your help, reinforce this behavior by using an affirmation prompt in which you make comments such as "I like the way you corrected that mistake. That's what good readers do." From time to time, use an assessment prompt to ask students how they made a self-correction or figured out a hard word: "How did you know to change *green* to *grin*? How did you figure that word out?" These questions provide insight into the processes students are using. Because students are called on to explain what processes they are using, it leads them to a deeper understanding of the strategies and helps them generalize the strategies to other situations (Clay, 1993). Prompts for frequently used strategies are listed in Table 8.8.

Note particular difficulties that students have. Talk over the difficulties and work through them (Wilson, 1999): "I see you have difficulty with words that begin with *wh*. These words are tough. They have strange spellings. But if you read through the words, if you look at all the letters, especially the ending letters, that will help you. I'll give you some practice exercises that I think will help." Leading students to become aware of their areas of difficulty and providing strategies for overcoming those difficulties gives students a sense of self-efficacy. And, of course, it also makes them better readers (Gunning, 2008c).

## Effective Use of Strategies

Phonics programs for corrective readers are typically heavy on instruction and practice and light on application, with countless hours being spent on workbook pages. Actually, the corrective that students need most is the opportunity to apply skills to real reading.

Because decoding words is so difficult for some poor readers, they overuse context clues. This is especially true when they are asked to read material that is too hard for them. Other poor readers overuse phonics. Having poor decoding skills, they may have been drilled and skilled in phonics to such an extent that they view reading as primarily a matter of saying the right sounds.

Students need to learn to balance their use of strategies. The following sections provide tips about what to do when students are relying too heavily on one strategy.

### When Students Overuse Phonics Cues

To help students who overuse phonic cues, try the following:

■  Make sure the material they read is on the appropriate level. Students should know at least 95 percent of the words. If readers encounter too many unknown words or decode too slowly, they lose the sense of the selection and will resort to the overuse of phonics.

**TABLE 8.8**
Strategy Prompts for
Word Decoding

| Strategy | When Used | Prompt |
|---|---|---|
| Pronounceable word part | The word contains a pronounceable word part: *an* or *ran* in *ranch* | "Is there any part of this word that you can say?" (You might need to cover up all of the word except the pronounceable part.) |
| Analogy | The pronounceable word-part strategy doesn't work. The word is like one the student knows: *vain* is like *train*. | "Is this word like any word that you know?" "Is this word like any of the model words?" (You might need to write or show the known word so that the student can compare the two.) |
| Context | The word is irregular, or other strategies don't work. | "What word would make sense here?" |
| Sound by sound | Student doesn't see chunks or parts in words. Needs to decode the word sound by sound. | "What is the first sound? What is the next sound? The last sound? What word do you get when you put the sounds together?" |
| Try another sound | The vowel or consonant spelling has more than one pronunciation. | "What other sound can that letter (or letters) make?" (Student can refer to a model words chart.) The student also checks that the word is a real one and fits the context. |
| Sound correction/ model word routine | Student says the wrong sound for an element (says *pet* for *pit*) or can't recall the sound. The student is prompted to use model word routine and says the letter, model word from short-vowel chart, and sound of letter. For a long-vowel error (student says *cap* for *cape*), call attention to a final *e* or digraph. | "What is the vowel? What is the model word for *i*? What sound does *i* make? What would this word be if you put the *i* sound in it?" (Direct the student to refer to the model words chart, if you have one.) "What is the vowel? What does the final *e* tell you about the vowel? What would this word be if you put the long-*a* sound in it?" |
| Monitoring/ cross-check | Student produces a nonword or a word that doesn't fit. Student uses context to check the use of a phonological strategy or uses phonics to check the use of a contextual strategy. | Context: "Is that a real word? Does that fit the sense of the sentence?" Phonological: "With what letter does the word in the story begin? What sound does that letter make? What sound does your word begin with?" (Check other letters and sounds as needed.) |
| Writing | Student fails to process all the letters in a word, even though he knows all the correspondences in the word. | Write the word. As you write the letters, say the sounds that the letters stand for. |
| Choice | Student is unable to decode a word using any strategy. Provide a choice of two words. Have student select the correct one. | "Is the word *wolf* or *dog*? How do you know?" |
| Affirmation | Praise student for working out a word. Name the strategy used. This lets the student know what strategy she or he used and encourages the student to continue to use strategies. | "I like the way you used the pronounceable word part to help you read that word." |
| Diagnostic | To see what strategies a student is using, use a diagnostic prompt after the student has decoded a difficult word. | "How did you figure out that word?" |

*Source:* Gunning (2008c, p. 22 ). Some of the strategies are adapted from Clay (2003) and Wilson (1999).

- Stress reading for meaning. Spend extra time building background. As you build background, list key words on the board so students will be familiar with them and will be primed to read them when they are encountered in the selection. Have purposes set before students read.

- Stress silent reading. Oral reading can lead to a preoccupation with correct pronunciation of words rather than the construction of meaning.

- To provide practice with the use of context, construct a series of cloze or modified cloze exercises in which students complete stories in which words have been deleted. (See pp. 414–416.) Demonstrate cloze by modeling how you would go about filling in the blanks. Emphasize the need to use context clues and to read beyond the blank. After doing a few exercises cooperatively, have students complete some selections on their own. Be sure to discuss the completed exercises.

### When Students Overuse Context Clues

Students may overuse context cues for a variety of reasons. Their phonics skills may be weak, they may be holding on to strategies that worked with highly predictable books but are not appropriate for more mature materials, or they may not be demanding a high degree of accuracy from their reading. To build a more balanced use of phonics strategies, try the following:

- Make sure that materials are on an appropriate level of difficulty. Some students overuse context clues when they do not have the skills necessary to decode a large proportion of the unfamiliar words they encounter.

- Take several running records or informal reading inventory samples of a student's oral reading. Note whether decoding skills are adequate. If not, work to improve weak skills and teach missing ones, making sure that the student has plenty of opportunity to apply skills.

- Encourage wide reading of easy materials. Poor readers often need extra practice in order for their skills to become automatic.

- Before students read a selection, review key phonics patterns that appear in the piece, so the students will be better prepared to use needed phonics skills.

- Review the phonics strategies for attacking unknown words. When students are stumped by a word, ask, "What can you do to help you figure out that word? Are there any parts that you can say? Is the word like any word that you know?"

## Mini–Case Study

After intensive instruction, disabled readers ages 7 to 13 who took part in an intervention program doubled their reading vocabularies (Lovett, Warren-Chaplin, Ransby, & Borden, 1990). However, their skills were not transferring. Although students had been taught the words *line* and *mark*, for instance, they were unable to read the words *fine* and *dark*. The students weren't perceiving the *ine* and *ark* patterns. It was as though they had learned individual words, not the elements that made up the words.

To address this problem, the researchers changed their program in two ways. They revised instruction so that students became aware of onsets and rimes and also the letters and sounds that made up the rimes. They also directly taught the analogy, pronounceable word-part, and try-another-sound strategies and a strategy for decoding multisyllabic words. This program, which was dubbed Phast (Phonological and Strategy Training) Track, was highly successful with disabled readers.

## ▚▚ Scope and Sequence of Analogy Words and Patterns

Presentation of word patterns will vary according to the reading ability of your students and their oral language development. Younger students who are struggling with beginning reading skills should be presented with the easiest patterns: *cat, hat, fat, pet, wet*. Words introduced should be restricted to those generally known by primary-age pupils. Older students who are functioning at a beginner-reader level might also need to learn basic patterns such as *at*. The main difference in presentation should be in choice of words to be introduced. Having more extensive vocabularies, older readers might be able to handle more difficult words within each pattern: *chat, vat, slim,* and *whim,* for instance. A suggested sequence for introducing word-building patterns is presented in Figure 8.12.

The rate of introduction of patterns will vary. In the beginning, introduce only one pattern at a time and work on it until students seem to have a firm grasp of it. As students catch onto the concept of the patterns, you may be able to present two or three at a time. This is especially true if students have some phonics skills but need a systematic review. This does not mean that all low-achieving readers should be taught all the patterns. Give students credit for what they know. They are dismayed when retaught skills that they have already mastered. An informal reading inventory, observation, and/or the Phonics Inventory in Appendix A could be used to establish a starting point for instruction.

## ▚▚ Phonics Progress Monitoring

The Phonics Inventory, which is presented in Appendix A, can be used to monitor students' progress, assess their knowledge of single-syllable phonics, and place them in the appropriate level of instruction. The first 10 words in the

▚ **FIGURE 8.12**
Word-Building
Scope and
Sequence

---

**PREPARATORY**

Phonemic awareness
Letter knowledge
Initial-consonant correspondences

**LEVEL 1**

Short-vowel patterns

**LEVEL 2**

Short-vowel patterns with consonant clusters

**LEVEL 3**

Long-vowel patterns

**LEVEL 4**

*r* vowel patterns

**LEVEL 5**

Other vowel patterns: *oy (boy), ou (out), aw (paw), oo (book), oo (soon)* inventory assess short-vowel patterns; the next 10 words assess short-vowel patterns with clusters; the next 10 assess long-vowel patterns; the fourth group of 10 tests $r$ vowel patterns; and the last group assesses other vowel patterns. The criterion for proficiency is 80 percent. Students are instructed in the first level in which they correctly read fewer than 8 out of 10 of the words. For instance, students who get at least 8 out of 10 of the first 10 words correct but have difficulty with the next 10 should be instructed in short-vowel patterns that contain clusters.

The Progress Monitoring Chart (see Figure 4.16, page 119) shows the performance of a struggling first grader on the Phonics Inventory from October through May. The assessment is constructed so that phonics instruction is divided into 10 units, with each unit being represented by 5 words. The goal for first-graders is to be able to read 40 to 45 of the 50 words by year's end, which indicates that they will have mastered basic single-syllable phonics. Students are expected to be able to read an additional 4 or 5 words each month.

Because the student in Figure 4.16 was making slow progress in his regular program, he was placed in a Tier II program at the end of January, which provided more intensive instruction and more instructional time. Because the student had completed nearly five months of school, his expected performance was between 20 and 25 (4 to 5 words a month). However, his score was 13. The goal for this student was to be able to read 40 to 45 words by the end of the year. By the end of February, even with intervention, he was able to read only two additional test words. But then his progress accelerated. Notice the considerable jump he made from February to March and his accelerated progress through May. Progress monitoring is a valuable tool for tracking and accelerating progress.

## ▓ Mini–Case Study

Able to read only one or two words on the Phonics Inventory, the four first graders at an urban public school were provided extra help by their classroom teacher. Yet by October, it was clear that they were making very little progress. Next, they were given additional help by a trained tutor, who carefully coordinated her efforts with those of the classroom teacher. The help consisted primarily of using the supplementary program for struggling readers provided by the basal system the classroom teacher was using and reteaching the skills the students had failed to learn.

Observation and monthly monitoring indicated that the students were still making slow progress. It was clear that the supplementary program wasn't adequate. Instruction was intensified. Word building was initiated. Materials from Ready Readers (Modern Curriculum Press/Pearson) and books listed in Figure 8.8 (see pp. 259–261) were used to provide extra reading practice. Emphasis was placed on reading books that incorporated the skills taught. A lot of hands-on activities also were conducted, including sorting, making words, and composing sentences. Strategy instruction was emphasized. The program was adjusted so that students would follow the same sequence as that of the core classroom program. Most important of all, the tutor was knowledgeable, patient, and caring.

Students' progress accelerated. By year's end, all four had achieved a score of at least 40 on the Phonics Inventory. The progress monitoring chart in Figure 4.16 on page 119 shows the progress of one of the four students. All were reading very close to, on, or above grade level according to the TerraNova, a standardized norm-referenced reading test. In addition to receiving expert, caring tutoring and using a systematic program, the keys to the students' success were progress monitoring and reading a lot of books that reinforced the phonics patterns they had been taught (Gunning, 2007).

## A Means to an End

Phonics is a means to an end. The ultimate aim of decoding is to enable students to read independently. To accomplish that goal, decoding instruction must be functional and contextual. Skills taught should be related directly to selections that students are about to read. And students should have ample opportunity to put their skills to work by reading a wide variety of children's books, periodicals, and other real-world materials.

## High-Frequency Words

> **High-frequency words,** commonly known as "sight words," are the 200 or so most frequently occurring words in printed English, some of which have irregular spellings.

What are the most difficult words for reading-disabled students to learn to read? Ironically, the shortest, most frequently occurring words—**high-frequency words**—pose the most serious problem for many students. Compared to decoding *were, was,* or *where,* the words *rhinoceros* and *elephant* are a breeze. Compensating for their length by their distinctive spellings and specific meanings, *rhinoceros* and *elephant* are relatively easy to learn to read. After one or two presentations and a few encounters in a text, many students have these words mastered for life. After dozens, maybe hundreds of presentations, and countless encounters, some students still stumble over *was, were,* and *where.*

> ⚡ Students who are weak in orthographic processing may have special difficulty with irregularly spelled words because they have difficulty getting a visual fix on them.

Unfortunately, many of the most frequently occurring words in the language are abstract or lacking in concrete meaning, serving only as function words in a sentence (*the, of, with*); lack a distinctive appearance and so are easily confused with other words (*will, with, what*); and may have a spelling that gives little or no clue to their pronunciation (*one, of*).

### How High-Frequency Words Are Learned

> ⚡ Except for words like *of* and *one,* all words should be taught through a phonics approach so that connections are made between letters and sounds. As Torgesen (2004b) notes, a top myth in teaching reading is that if a student is a visual learner, the student should be taught through a visual approach. The truth is that decoding skills and high-frequency words must be learned phonologically. Using phonics to teach high-frequency words teaches students a reliable way of recognizing the words and provides a means by which the words can be stored in memory.

Because their spellings don't do a good job of indicating the sounds they represent, some high-frequency words, such as *of, you, was,* and *they,* don't lend themselves to a decoding approach. These words are taught in a logographic or paired-associate fashion. Students learn the words by associating the spoken words with visual features. In addition, there are other high-frequency words that do have predictable pronunciations but incorporate advanced phonic elements: *which, each, how.* Because these words occur with high frequency, it is difficult to read even the simplest of selections without encountering them. Therefore, they are often introduced in paired-associate or logographic fashion in the earliest stages of reading.

Novice readers can and do learn words through a sight or logographic approach. However, the number of words that they can learn in this way is limited to about 40 (Gough & Hillinger,

1980). At that point, the system begins to fall apart. The learner runs out of distinctive features by which to remember each word. In addition, since many high-frequency words are similar in appearance, they are easily confused because the "visual cues selected are not unique to individual words" (Ehri, 1994, p. 326). Such words are also hard to fix in memory because the cues used to establish the associations are arbitrary. The cues have no relationship to the sounds that the letters in the words represent.

Once students have reached the alphabetic stage, high-frequency words, insofar as possible, should be taught through a phonics approach. When taught through a decoding approach, they are easier to learn and remember. Many high-frequency words are completely regular: *and, in, that, it, at, this, but*. Their pronunciations can easily be predicted from their spellings. Except for a very few words, words like *of, one, on,* even the irregular words are mostly predictable. For most of them, the vowels are irregular: *was, from, some*. However, their initial and final letters can be used to determine beginning and ending sounds: *have, said, find, word*.

Not taking advantage of these regularities deprives students of a means of learning high-frequency words. For instance, disabled and novice readers typically confuse the *wh* words: *who, what, when, where, why, which*. However, *when* is completely regular. When presenting the word *when*, help students see the familiar word part *en* in *when* by relating it to *ten* or *pen* or other known *en* words. *Which* is also completely regular and can be related to words like *itch, pitch,* and *witch*. *Why* is completely regular. Relate it to *by, cry,* and other words that end in $y = /\bar{\imath}/$. *Who,* which incorporates the less frequent correspondence *wh* = /h/ and has an irregular spelling for its vowel sound, is more problematical. One way of teaching *who* is to present it with other high-frequency words that incorporate the $o = /\overline{oo}/$ correspondence: *do, to, two*. Although it is not completely regular, *what* can be distinguished from the other *wh* words because it ends in *t*.

Figure 8.13 shows the kinds of connections that readers might make between the spellings and sounds of regular and irregular words. The connections for *hat* are straightforward. There is a connection between the letter *h* and the sound /h/, the letter *a* and the sound /a/, and the letter *t* and the sound /t/. Similar connections are made for irregular words. Many of the connections in irregular words are between letters and the sound they typically represent. For letters that do not follow typical letter–sound rules, the reader might create special connections, such as the *o* in *from* having a short-*u* pronunciation and the sound /m/ in *lamb* being represented as *mb*. Or the reader might remember the *b* as being an extra or silent letter (Ehri & Snowling, 2004).

## Orthographic Processing and Learning High-Frequency Words

Orthographic ability is related to decoding ability. In the early stages of reading, students rely heavily on phonics to decode words. As decoding skills are developed and students encounter elements such as final-*e* words and vowel digraphs, orthographic or visual processing becomes an important factor.

**■■ FIGURE 8.13**

Connections in Memory between Letters and Sounds
*Source:* Ehri & Snowling (2004).

Students who have difficulty with orthographic processing may have difficulty storing advanced patterns and irregular words. Because they have difficulty with orthographic processing, they overrely on phonics, which means that their reading may be slow and laborious. They confuse letters and words that are similar in appearance, especially if the words are irregular. They frequently confuse word pairs such as *were* and *where*. Their spelling is phonetic. They spell what they hear and so have difficulty with irregular words such as *because* and *often*. They continue to misspell high-frequency words that they have encountered many times.

Although weakness in orthographic processing may affect both reading and spelling, in some students, it affects only spelling. These students may have sufficient orthographic memory for reading but not spelling (Orton, 1966). Students who have weak orthographic-processing ability need to have many encounters with words and might need a multisensory approach to learn irregular words.

## High Payoff of High-Frequency Words

> ✳ An efficient way of presenting high-frequency words is to teach patterns that incorporate these words. Present *he, be, me, we, see*; or *at, that*; or *way, may, day.*

The high-frequency list, which contains a number of irregular words and advanced patterns, is presented in Table 8.9 and consists of the 200 words that appear most frequently in books and other materials read by school children (Zeno, Ivens, Millard, & Duvvuri, 1995). These 200 words make up approximately 50 percent of the words in continuous text. The first word, *the*, occurs about 2 percent of the time. Because high-frequency words play such an important role in reading, they should be introduced periodically along with the patterns.

Presented in the next section is a sample lesson for direct instruction in high-frequency words. The approach taken to introduce high-frequency words will depend, in part, on students' stage of development and the nature of the words. Students in the alphabetic and word-pattern stages can be guided to use their knowledge of letter–sound relationships to learn high-frequency words as long as they are at least partly regular.

## ▦ Direct Teaching Approach for High-Frequency Words

> ✳ If the meanings of any of the words are unknown, discuss them. However, don't spend time developing meanings for words that are already in the students' listening vocabulary.

The direct teaching technique is adapted from an approach devised by Bryant, Kelly, Hathaway, and Rubin (1981). It emphasizes repetition and context and, in its adapted form, the use of phonics to help the student make solid, lasting connections between printed words and their spoken equivalents. A carefully structured, thorough technique, it has been effective with students who have had considerable difficulty learning high-frequency words.

## ▦ Indirect Teaching Techniques for High-Frequency Words

### Shared Reading

An excellent device for introducing and reinforcing high-frequency words, shared reading is a way of helping low-achieving readers read whole selections that they would not be able to read on their own. Instead of being limited to books on their

**TABLE 8.9**
High-Frequency
Words

| | | | | | | | | | |
|---|---|---|---|---|---|---|---|---|---|
| 1. | the | 41. | which | 81. | made | 121. | also | 161. | name |
| 2. | of | 42. | their | 82. | over | 122. | around | 162. | should |
| 3. | and | 43. | said | 83. | did | 123. | another | 163. | home |
| 4. | a | 44. | if | 84. | down | 124. | came | 164. | give |
| 5. | to | 45. | will | 85. | way | 125. | three | 165. | air |
| 6. | in | 46. | do | 86. | only | 126. | soon | 166. | line |
| 7. | is | 47. | each | 87. | may | 127. | come | 167. | mother |
| 8. | you | 48. | about | 88. | find | 128. | work | 168. | set |
| 9. | that | 49. | how | 89. | use | 129. | must | 169. | world |
| 10. | it | 50. | up | 90. | water | 130. | part | 170. | own |
| 11. | he | 51. | out | 91. | little | 131. | because | 171. | under |
| 12. | for | 52. | then | 92. | long | 132. | does | 172. | last |
| 13. | was | 53. | them | 93. | very | 133. | even | 173. | read |
| 14. | on | 54. | she | 94. | after | 134. | place | 174. | never |
| 15. | are | 55. | many | 95. | word | 135. | old | 175. | am |
| 16. | as | 56. | some | 96. | called | 136. | well | 176. | us |
| 17. | with | 57. | so | 97. | just | 137. | such | 177. | left |
| 18. | his | 58. | these | 98. | new | 138. | here | 178. | end |
| 19. | they | 59. | would | 99. | where | 139. | take | 179. | along |
| 20. | at | 60. | other | 100. | most | 140. | why | 180. | while |
| 21. | be | 61. | into | 101. | know | 141. | thing | 181. | sound |
| 22. | this | 62. | has | 102. | get | 142. | great | 182. | house |
| 23. | from | 63. | more | 103. | through | 143. | help | 183. | might |
| 24. | I | 64. | two | 104. | back | 144. | put | 184. | next |
| 25. | have | 65. | her | 105. | much | 145. | year | 185. | below |
| 26. | not | 66. | like | 106. | good | 146. | different | 186. | saw |
| 27. | or | 67. | him | 107. | before | 147. | number | 187. | something |
| 28. | by | 68. | time | 108. | go | 148. | away | 188. | thought |
| 29. | one | 69. | see | 109. | man | 149. | again | 189. | both |
| 30. | had | 70. | no | 110. | our | 150. | off | 190. | few |
| 31. | but | 71. | could | 111. | want | 151. | went | 191. | those |
| 32. | what | 72. | make | 112. | lot | 152. | tell | 192. | school |
| 33. | all | 73. | than | 113. | me | 153. | men | 193. | show |
| 34. | were | 74. | first | 114. | day | 154. | say | 194. | always |
| 35. | when | 75. | been | 115. | too | 155. | small | 195. | until |
| 36. | we | 76. | its | 116. | any | 156. | every | 196. | large |
| 37. | there | 77. | who | 117. | same | 157. | found | 197. | often |
| 38. | can | 78. | now | 118. | right | 158. | still | 198. | together |
| 39. | an | 79. | people | 119. | look | 159. | big | 199. | ask |
| 40. | your | 80. | my | 120. | think | 160. | between | 200. | write |

*Source:* Adapted from *The educator's word frequency guide,* by S. M. Zeno, S. H. Ivens, R. T. Millard, & R. Duvvuri, 1995, Brewster, NY: Touchstone Applied Science Associates.

## High-Frequency Word Lesson

*Step 1: Selecting words to be taught.* Choose between four and six words for instruction. Words chosen should be ones that students will meet in a basal-reader selection, children's book, or other reading material that they are about to read. The words should also appear more than once in the piece, are important to the piece, and will probably occur in other selections. Words such as *for* and *from* that are easily confused should not be presented at the same time. Print the words on three-by-five cards. To avoid wasting time with words that are already known, pretest students by holding up each card and asking them to read it. Discard words known by nearly everyone. Step 2 shows how the words *old, wore, green, hat,* and *man* might be introduced.

*Step 2: Presentation in isolation.* First, reconstruct each word sound by sound or pronounceable element by pronounceable element so that students establish and later learn to recognize familiar parts in words. Here's how the high-frequency word *old* might be presented. Write *old* on the board. Ask if anyone can read it. If no one can, build on any knowledge of letters or letter–sound relationships that students have. If students are in the alphabetic stage and know the letters *o-l-d* and the sounds they represent, ask students if there is any part of the word that they can say. If there are parts of the word that are familiar, have them read and use the familiar parts to reconstruct the word. If the word is totally unfamiliar, cover it up except for its vowel and reconstruct the word sound by sound. For the word *old,* cover up the *l* and *d,* and ask students to say the sound that *o* stands for. Give help if necessary. After students read *o,* uncover the *l* and have students read *ol,* giving help as necessary. After students have read *ol,* uncover the *d,* have students say what sound it stands for, and have them read *old.* Supply assistance as needed. Then ask each student to read the word. If a student misses the word, reconstruct it with him, having the student read "o-ol-old" as you uncover the word's letters. If students are in the prealphabetic stage, emphasize the appearance and spelling of the word, especially the first letter.

Present the word *wore* in the same way. If students are in the alphabetic stage, begin instruction with *or* and then build the word by adding final *e* (note that this *e* does not change anything) and then *w.* For *green,* start with *ee* and add *n* so that you have formed the ending portion of the word, then *r,* and finally, *g.* For *hat,* start with *at* and add *h.* For *man,* relate it to the known word *an.* Have students read *an.* Then add *m* and have the word *man* read. After this initial presentation of the

words, print them on cards, if you have not already done so, and present them once more. Continue presenting the words until students are able to read each one within one second on two consecutive presentations.

*Step 3: Presentation in context.* Present the words in phrases or short sentences. The phrases might include two or more of the high-frequency words and should be cumulative. Phrases for the words *old, wore, green, hat,* and *man,* for example, might be introduced as follows:

> old hat
>
> old green hat
>
> wore an old green hat
>
> The man wore an old green hat.

The phrases and sentences should be presented until students can read all of them fluently.

*Step 4: Application.* Introduce the selection from which the high-frequency words were drawn. Discuss the title and key illustrations. Assist students in finding and reading the target high-frequency words in the selection. Have them read the entire sentence in which the target high-frequency word appears. Then, after setting a purpose for reading based on a discussion of the title, key illustrations, and high-frequency words, have students read the selection silently. During or after the follow-up discussion of the story, have students once again read the story sentences in which the high-frequency words appeared.

*Step 5: Review.* The next day, go over the words in isolation and in phrase and sentence context. Also provide review sessions for high-frequency words learned in previous sessions. Focus on words that continue to cause difficulty. Provide a variety of opportunities for students to apply their growing knowledge of high-frequency words by completing the practice activities presented later in this chapter. Keep in mind that the best way to build a high-frequency vocabulary is to have students read lots of easy materials. A list of books containing high-frequency words is found in Figure 8.14 (see p. 290).

*Step 6: Assess.* Observe students' ability to read high-frequency words and periodically administer a test of high-frequency words. Reteach and review as needed.

reading level, which may be too simple or unappealing, low-achieving readers are given access to more mature, more interesting materials.

If you are working with groups, use a big book, or write the selection on the board or story paper, or show it on an overhead projector or document camera so that everyone can see the words. If working one-on-one, a regular-size book can be used. Introduce the text, share-read it with students, and discuss it with students in the way that was suggested in Chapter 7. During a second reading of the text, invite the students to read along with you. If the text has repeated phrases, stop as you come to them and have the students as a group or individual volunteers read them. Pay particular attention to the high-frequency words you wish students to learn. During the reading of the text, make sure that you point to each word as it is being read and that students look at the word as you point to it, so connections can be made between printed and spoken words.

In addition to share-reading and highlighting them in context, also have students read high-frequency words in isolation so that they can concentrate on each word's distinguishing features. As in the direct instruction lesson, lead students to see the pronounceable word parts or letter sounds in the high-frequency words, so that they will have additional memory pegs.

As an extension, invite students to read the text with a partner or on their own. If recorded versions of the text are available, also have students read along as they listen. If the text is a favorite, arrange for additional rereadings from time to time.

After students seem to have a grasp of the high-frequency words, place the words on cards and have students read them. Individual words might be recorded on three-by-five cards and put on rings, in envelopes, or filed in small boxes known as **word banks**. The words will then be available for sorting and other reinforcement activities. The sentences in which the high-frequency words appear might be placed on sentence strips so that students see the words in context as well as in isolation. Choose additional practice activities from those listed later in this chapter.

> **Word bank:** a collection of words that students have learned or are in the process of learning. They are used in a variety of reinforcement activities.

## Singing High-Frequency Words

> **Using Technology**
>
> The following sites have a variety of sing-along songs and rhymes.
>
> **NIEHS Kids**
>
> http://kids.niehs.nih.gov/games/songs/
>
> **Nicky's Nursery Rhymes**
>
> http://nurseryrhymes4u.com/

As a variation on shared reading, have students sing songs that contain high-frequency words. In addition to being motivational, songs are easier to process because of repeated refrains and the element of rhyme. Sing the song or play a recorded version of it, pointing to each word as it is sung. During the second singing, have students sing along. During a third singing, you might sing the main stanzas while students sing the refrain.

As a follow-up, have students sing the words as they follow along with a recorded version of the song. As they sing, they should be pointing to the words they are singing. The following sets of recordings and books are especially well done:

*Animal Songs.* Raffi. New York: Crown (2008).

*Down by the Bay.* Raffi. New York: Crown (1987).

*Nancy Cassidy's Kids Songs.* N. Cassidy. Palo Alto, CA: Klutz Press (2008).

*Shake My Sillies Out.* Raffi. New York: Crown (1987).

*Songs of Our World.* Raffi. New York: Crown (2008).

*Wheels on the Bus.* Raffi. New York: Crown (1987).

A number of children's videos and DVDs use a bouncing ball to draw attention to the words of a song so that the viewers can sing along. Have students sing along with the recordings. Once they feel they know the words to the song, they can turn down the volume and then attempt to sing along. If they have difficulty, they may turn up the volume and practice some more. Sing-along recordings that you might use include the following:

*Chicken Little Sing-Along Songs*. Walt Disney. Burbank, CA: Buena Vista Home Entertainment.

*Sing-Along Songs: Fun with Music*. Walt Disney. Burbank, CA: Buena Vista Home Entertainment.

*Sing-Along Songs: Under the Sea*. Walt Disney. Burbank, CA: Buena Vista Home Entertainment.

*Sing-Along Songs: Disneyland Fun*. Walt Disney. Burbank, CA: Buena Vista Home Entertainment.

*Toy Story Sing-Along Songs*. Walt Disney. Burbank, CA: Buena Vista Home Entertainment.

## Language-Experience Stories

As explained in the previous chapter, a language-experience story recounts in writing an event in the students' lives, such as a trip to a farm, getting pet hamsters for the classroom, or the arrival of a baby brother. The story might also be based on a piece the students have read or a classroom discussion. Dictated by the students and written by the teacher, the language-experience story becomes the students' reading material.

High-frequency words naturally appear in all language-experience stories. By choosing certain topics, you can ensure that special high-frequency words will find their way into the story. If, for instance, you want to reinforce the high-frequency words *like* and *do,* you might have the class dictate a piece on the topic "Things I Like to Do."

 The story might be composed on an electronic whiteboard.

Because it is based on the children's experiences and written in their language, the language-experience story is readily understood and usually easy to read, especially for students who are still learning to speak English. Individual stories are also an excellent device for reinforcing high-frequency words.

Individual language-experience stories are composed in much the same way as group stories. However, individual stories allow you to personalize the words being introduced. Individual stories can be illustrated and compiled into a booklet. The booklet may be taken home and later placed in the class library.

## Predictable Books

**Predictable books** and stories, can be used to develop high-frequency vocabulary in students reading at a beginning level. Predictable books, as their name suggests,

**Predictable books** are easy to read because they contain elements that enable the reader to read the print: repeated phrases, rhyme, and illustrations that depict much of the print.

are texts that have repeated elements or are told in such a way that after reading or hearing a portion of the text, it is easy to predict what the rest of the text will say. Some traditional examples include "The Gingerbread Man," "The Three Little Pigs," and "Goldilocks." (Figure 8.14 lists a number of predictable books.)

## Constructing an Experience Story

*Step 1: Introducing the experience story.* Students discuss the experience they have had. In the discussion, you draw out the children's ideas.

*Step 2: Writing the experience story.* Through questioning you help children frame their experience. You might say, for instance, "Let's write a story about our visit to the recycling center so that we can share it with others. What should we call our story?" Write the title that the children suggest: "Our Trip to the Recycling Center." As you write each word, say it so students match the written and spoken forms. After writing the title, read it, running your hand under each word as you do so. After writing and reading the title, have students suggest a good beginning sentence, a second sentence, and so on. As with the title, read each word as you write it and then read each completed sentence. After writing the whole story, read the story once more. Ask the students if the story says what they want it to. Ask students if they want to make any changes or add any details.

*Step 3: Rereading the story.* Read the story once more. Invite the students to read along with you. Stop before high-frequency words that you want to reinforce and invite the class or individual volunteers to read them.

*Step 4: Using sentence strips and word cards.* Some students may simply memorize the story or use context to such an extent that they are not attending to the printed words. This step is designed to have them focus on the printed forms of the words. After students are familiar with the target words and sentences in the story, create tagboard strips containing the sentences. Mix up the order of the sentences and have students rearrange the sentences in correct order. If available, use a pocket chart to hold the sentence strips. If you are working with a group of students, you may want to duplicate the story and cut it into strips so that each student has a series of sentences to manipulate. Once students have arranged the sentences in their personal copies of the story,

you can have a volunteer read the sentence that goes first and place the tagboard version at the top of the pocket chart and continue until all the sentences have been placed. The story is then read and checked to make sure sentences are in the right order. Students then compare their reconstructions with the one in the pocket chart. If you are working with older students and pocket charts seem too juvenile, have them rearrange ordinary strips of papers on their desks.

After students have reassembled the sentences in the story, cut the first sentence into individual words and have students reassemble it. Then proceed to the other sentences.

*Step 5: Reading the experience story to others.* Copy the story from the board, duplicate it, and distribute it to students. Have them read it to a partner. Once they can read the story with a degree of fluency, they may take it home and read it to their brothers and sisters, parents, and grandparents.

*Step 6: Adding words to the word bank.* Words that students have learned to read are added to their word banks. These words can be identified by having students underline words they can read or you can test them by putting the words on three-by-five cards and asking students to read them. Words that are partially known or that are not identified consistently and words that are not known but that you feel are important, could be set aside for additional instruction. You might have students keep two word banks (McCormick, 1995). Words that the student knows could be placed in a word bank entitled "Words I Can Read." Words that the student is still learning could be placed in the "Words I Am Learning" word bank.

*Step 7: Providing additional practice.* Review the words in the word bank on a daily basis if possible. Sorting and assembling words into sentences make excellent practice exercises. If your time is limited, you might have pairs of students test each other on their words and complete other practice activities.

## ■ FIGURE 8.14
Books Containing High-Frequency Words

---

LEVEL 1: PICTURE READING

Pictures illustrate all of the text. Generally one or two words label the picture: a drawing of an elephant is shown, and the word *elephant* appears under it.

Bruna, D. (1984). *Animal book.* Los Angeles: Price/Stern/Sloan.

Burningham, J. (1985). *Colors.* New York: Crown.

Burton, M. R. (1989). *Tail toes eye ears nose.* New York: Harper.

Cohen, C. L. (1986). *Three yellow dogs.* New York: Greenwillow.

Hoban, T. (1972). *Count and see.* New York: Macmillan.

LEVEL 2: CAPTION

Pictures illustrate most of the text. Often, the text is a frame, which is a repeated sentence or phrase that varies by one or two words. The subject or verb varies, but the rest of the sentence stays the same: *The dog sat on the mat. The tiger sat on the mat. The elephant sat on the mat.* The illustration may depict the part of the sentence that changes.

Arnosky, J. (2001). *Mouse colors.* Boston: Houghton Mifflin.

Brown, C. (1991). *My barn.* New York: Greenwillow.

Burningham, J. (1984). *Wobble pop.* New York: Viking.

Cameron, A. (1994). *The cat sat on the mat.* Boston: Houghton Mifflin.

Gomi, T. (1991). *Who hid it?* Brookfield, CT: Millbrook Press.

---

Inexpensive books that reinforce high frequency words can be found at Wilbooks http://www.wilbooks.com. A wide variety of downloadable books can be found at the Web sites: http://www.enchantedlearning.com and http://www.readinga-z.com. A listing of trade books containing high-frequency words can be found at http://www.wordbuilding.com.

Predictable books build confidence because students can use illustrations and the predictability of the books to help them read the text. However, the books might be so predictable that students aren't actually processing the words but are using pictorial and verbal context to read them. It is helpful, therefore, to have children read the text without the availability of picture clues. Here is how this might be done. Select a book that contains words that you want to teach, read the book to students, and then reread it, encouraging students to join in. You might read a big book version, if available, so that students can follow along.

After several rereadings, cover the pictures or write the text on the board and ask students to read the text. This gives them the experience of using phonics and context rather than relying on picture clues. You might also place words and phrases from the selection on cards or the chalkboard and have students read them.

## Exemplary Teaching: Balancing Decodable Text with Predictable Books

While working with a group of five first graders who were making very slow progress, the teacher introduced some predictable books to them and arranged for them to practice reading the books until they could read them fairly smoothly. Although it was important that students learn basic phonics patterns, it was also important that they see themselves as readers. Up to this point the teacher had been working primarily with decodable text but had noted that the children weren't having much fun reading. They were still having a difficult time with short-*a* and short-*i* patterns. The predictable texts, with their repeated language and heavy picture support, were easier to read.

Learning to read these books boosted the children's self-confidence. They were quite pleased that they could take books home and read to Mom, Dad, Grandma, Grandpa, and other family members.

Among the predictable books used with the five struggling readers, there was one that depicted a number of things that the main character could do: "I can read; I can sing; I can run." The book reinforced the *an* pattern, a pattern that the children were still slow in recognizing. Another predictable book had a number of *it* words, a pattern that was recently introduced. A judicious use of predictable books can foster both confidence and skill.

## Holistic Programs

Several series of books are designed to foster reading development through the presentation of high-frequency words in predictable books written at a variety of levels. These include Reading Corners (Dominie Press), Little Red Readers (Sundance), and Story Box (Wright Group).

## Creating Little Books

In addition to acquiring pattern books, you can create your own. The books might incorporate a particular theme: People in My Family, Foods I Like, Things I Can Do, Holidays, and so on. These books might also incorporate a particular pattern: I can _____, I see _____, I like_____, _____ got _____ on the bus (Johnston, Invernizzi, & Juel, 1998). You might create these on your own or recruit help from your students.

The books might be illustrated with pictures that you draw, pictures from a desktop publishing program, or student-drawn illustrations. Since instructional time is limited, be careful that students don't spend an excessive amount of time creating illustrations. You might also create open-ended books and have students complete them by placing words in the blanks. For instance, they might complete five "I can _____" or "I like _____" sentences.

## Read-Along Technique

Obtain an easy book, one in which the student has an obvious interest. If the book does not have an accompanying audio recording, create one. Have the student follow along as the recorded version is read. The student might read a book such as *Brown Bear, Brown Bear, What Do You See?* (Martin, 1983), which has only 32 different words, or *The Cake That Mack Ate* (Robart, 1986), which has just 30 different words. Start with shorter books and work up to longer ones. You might also use digital read-alongs. As the story is being read, the text is highlighted so that the viewer can read along. Read-alongs are available as traditional downloads that can be run on the computer or as apps that can be played on tablets or smart phones. Students can read along with the recorder until they are able to read the book on their own (Chomsky, 1978). This may require as many as 20 read-alongs. As students acquire a broader high-frequency vocabulary and begin to acquire decoding skills, fewer rereadings will be required.

### Using Digital Read-Alongs

Read-along texts include digital texts in which the words are read aloud. Usually the text being read is highlighted. Capstone and Lerner have the largest collections of read-along texts. Dozens of read-along apps can be found at Apple's App Store or at Appolicious or other sites that market apps. For some app read-alongs, the highlighting and reading of the text are not exactly synchronized. Check to make sure that the text being read aloud and the text being highlighted are in sync.

> Richek and colleagues (1996) describe a student who took 10 weeks to learn eight high-frequency words. The student may have had an associative word-learning problem of the type described in Chapter 6.

## Using a Multisensory Technique

If students experience serious difficulty learning high-frequency words, try using the Fernald or other multisensory technique. Multisensory techniques are explained in Chapter 14.

# Additional Practice Activities for High-Frequency Words

### Words on the Wall

> In a pantomime activity, pairs of students are given a series of five to eight words that can be pantomimed: *walk, run, fly, jump, throw.* One student pantomimes the words. The second holds up a card printed with the high-frequency word being pantomimed.

Add high-frequency words to the word wall described earlier in the chapter. You might want to separate them from the phonic pattern words, if these have been placed on the wall.

When adding words to the wall, be sure to discuss any parts that students can already say or any distinctive features that the word might have and any cues that students might use to help them remember the word or distinguish it from other words: "You can tell that *h-e-a-r* means to listen because it has an *ear* in it." Also discuss the word's meaning if it is unknown or vague.

Each day, if possible, review items on the word wall. You might have students find all the animal words, locate the opposites of *on, old,* and *dark,* or note words that incorporate a newly learned pattern. When words have been mastered, remove them.

### Sight-Word Commands

Create a series of cards that contain commands composed primarily of high-frequency, or sight, words. When the command is displayed, the class carries it out. Commands might be just for fun, or they may be functional. Some possible commands include the following:

| | |
|---|---|
| Count to three. | Sing a song. |
| Hold up a piece of paper. | Sit down. |
| Put up one hand. | Stand up. |
| Put up both hands. | Stand on one foot. |
| Line up in the front of the room. | Say your name. |

## Read the Label

Bailey's Book House (Riverdeep) presents high-frequency words in sentences and uses animated sequences to illustrate each word's meaning. It also helps students compose a story that uses high-frequency words.

Label appropriate items in your class. Label the light switch with an *on* and an *off,* for example. When writing directions, try to use high-frequency words: "Put blocks here. Put toys in the box." Introduce the sign, label, or set of directions. Read it for students, pointing out each word as you do so. Then have students, as a group, read the item along with you. Also encourage individual volunteers to read the item. From time to time, review the item.

Some possible functional, high-frequency word signs, labels, and directions include the following:

| | |
|---|---|
| In | Pull |
| Out | Walk. Don't run. |
| Up | Mrs. Doyle's Room |
| Down | Pet Corner |
| Push | Book Corner |

## Forming Phrases and Sentences

From a big book selection, language-experience story, or other source, copy a sentence that contains several high-frequency words onto oak tag. (If you are working with a large group, you might photocopy the sentences.) Cut the words apart and place them in an envelope. Have students arrange the words so they form a sentence. This builds sentence sense and comprehension while providing practice with high-frequency words.

## Sorting

Using their bank of high-frequency words, have students sort their words. They might group them semantically: all the color words, all the number words, all the action words. Or they might group them structurally or phonemically: all the words that begin with *s* or all the words that end with the *at* pattern.

## Fostering Fluency

Although the activities described so far help to introduce high-frequency words, they also build accuracy of recognition and fluency. Before students can recognize words rapidly or automatically, they must first achieve accuracy (Samuels, 1994). Low-achieving readers may take longer to achieve accuracy than higher-achieving readers. By one estimate, students may require 35 or more exposures to a word before learning it, with the slowest students needing almost three times as many exposures as the brightest students (Gates, 1931). Provide ample practice, so that the words are recognized accurately. Once students can recognize words accurately, emphasize speed so that words are recognized instantaneously, and fluent reading will be fostered.

Although one characteristic of fluent reading is processing words at an acceptable rate, fluency also entails reading in meaningful phrases and with appropriate expression. Table 8.10 presents the fluency scale used by the National Assessment of Educational Progress. Students at Levels 3 and 4 are generally considered to be

**TABLE 8.10**
NAEP Oral
Reading Fluency
Scale
*Source:* U.S.
Department of
Education, National
Center for Education
Statistics (1995).

**LEVEL 4**

Reads primarily in larger, meaningful phrase groups. Although some regressions, repetitions, and deviations from text may be present, these do not appear to detract from the overall structure of the story. Preservation of the author's syntax is consistent. Some or most of the story is read with expressive interpretation.

**LEVEL 3**

Reads primarily in three- or four-word phrase groups. Some smaller groupings may be present. However, the majority of phrasing seems appropriate and preserves the syntax of the author. Little or no expressive interpretation is present.

**LEVEL 2**

Reads primarily in two-word phrases with some three- or four-word groupings. Some word-by-word reading may be present. Word groupings may seem awkward and unrelated to larger context of sentence or passage.

**LEVEL 1**

Reads primarily word by word. Occasional two-word or three-word phrases may occur, but these are infrequent and/or they do not preserve meaningful syntax.

*Source:* U.S. Department of Education, National Center for Education Statistics (1995). *Listening to children read aloud, Oral fluency* 15. Wahington, DC: Author.

fluent, and those at Levels 1 and 2 nonfluent. However, fluency requires comprehension. Samuels (2006) notes, "The critical test of fluency is the ability to decode a text and understand it simultaneously" (pp. 39–41). Rapid expressive reading does not guarantee comprehension. As Alt and Samuels (2011) comment, "While the secondary characteristics (speed, accuracy, and prosody) are necessary for reading fluency, they are not sufficient" (p. 177). A test of fluency must include a measure of comprehension.

Model fluent reading when reading to students. Explain that as you read, you group words into meaningful phrases and read with expression. After reading aloud to students, ask them how they enjoyed hearing the selection. Discuss things that you might have done as a reader to dramatize the selection, to convey the author's meaning, and to keep the listeners' attention (Rasinski, 2004). Discuss and demonstrate these techniques and guide students as they adopt their use. The following suggestions and activities are designed to develop rapid word recognition and fluent reading.

## Repeated Reading

**Repeated reading:** reading a text over and over to build fluency.

A major technique for achieving fluency is through **repeated reading** (Samuels, 1979). One way of learning high-frequency words is to read the same story over and over again. Often poor readers stumble over their text, especially when they encounter words that are easily confused, such as *what, where,* and *when.* Repeated reading gives them the opportunity to achieve accuracy. At the same time, through providing practice, it fosters instantaneous recognition of high-frequency words. The box that follows gives an example for presenting a lesson in introducing repeated readings.

Through repeated readings, students improve in both accuracy and speed of reading. In one study, reading rate increased by about 50 percent after four

## Repeated Readings Lesson

**Step 1:** *Introducing repeated readings.* Explain the procedure to students. Tell them that they will be reading a short selection over and over again so that they will learn to read faster and better.

**Step 2:** *Selecting a passage.* Select or have the students choose short, interesting selections of approximately 100 words.

**Step 3:** *Obtaining an initial timing.* Obtain baseline data on the selections. Have the students read them orally. Time the readings and record the number of words read incorrectly. If students take more than two minutes to read the selection and make more than five errors in 100 words (not counting missed endings), the selections are too hard. If students make only one or two errors and read the selection at 85 words per minute or faster, the selection is too easy.

**Step 4:** *Rereading.* Go over the students' miscues with them. Help them read these words correctly. Then direct them to reread the selections until they feel they can read them faster and more smoothly.

Practice can take one of three forms: (1) reading the selection to oneself; (2) listening to a recorded version while reading the selection silently and then reading the selection without the aid of the recording; or (3) reading the selection to a partner.

**Step 5:** *Evaluating the reading.* The students read the selections to you or to a partner. The number of word-recognition errors and reading speed are noted. The students are informed of their progress. A chart, as in Figure 8.15, might be constructed to show the degree of improvement. The goal is to have students read at least 85 words per minute. Students should practice until they reach that criterion. Word-recognition errors should also decrease. However, do not insist on 100 percent word recognition. Insisting on perfection in word reading sends the wrong message to students. It makes them think that reading is a word-pronouncing rather than a meaning-making activity. It also impedes fluency. If they are afraid of making a mistake, students will slow their reading rate (Samuels, 1979).

readings (Rashotte & Torgesen, 1985). Gains in reading speed are most likely to transfer when there is a high overlap of words, so that students are meeting a number of words in a new story that had been presented in a previously read selection. The sheer amount of reading also influences fluency. Students made gains when they read a number of selections on the appropriate level. Perhaps the best feature of the technique is that students enjoyed it. When the experiment was discontinued, many students requested additional repeated-reading sessions.

Repeated reading also builds students' confidence. Because below-level readers struggle with reading, they might never have had a successful reading experience. Repeated reading accompanied by some coaching can help these students achieve proficient reading so that they might begin to think of themselves as readers.

### Variations on Repeated Reading

Selections can be reread on a less formal basis. The evaluation may also be informal. Instead of working with a teacher, students may work in pairs. However, model the procedure first. One student reads and attempts to reach criterion, while the other tracks her progress on the chart shown in Figure 8.15. Then they switch roles. Show students how to time the reading and count errors. To simplify the charting procedure, have students check 100-word samples only. The reader may actually read a lengthier selection, but only the first 100 words are used for charting progress.

Students may speed through a selection to beat the clock. Encourage students to read at a normal pace. Stress that the goal is to meet the criterion, not set a world record. Occasionally, use a song or a poem instead of a typical reading

**FIGURE 8.15**
Speed of Reading
Chart

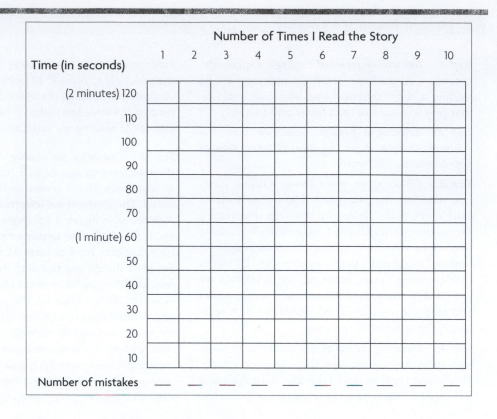

selection. Because of their rhythm, some narrative poems and songs lend themselves to speedy reading.

***Wide Reading***   Although repeated reading is a key technique for fostering fluency, wide reading also fosters fluency. Wide reading can be oral or silent. It can be supported or independent. In several studies, Kuhn (2011) compared the effectiveness of repeated reading versus wide reading. Both the group that read books three times each and those that engaged in a single choral or echo reading of a wider range of books improved in word recognition, reading speed, and oral expression. Both groups did better than a control group. However, the wide reading group also improved in comprehension. Kuhn hypothesized the wide reading group may have viewed the main purpose of reading as constructing meaning whereas the repeated reading group my have seen the main purpose as reading faster, more accurately, or with more expression. In addition, students who read more books were exposed to wider range of concepts and vocabulary. Wide reading is a better background builder than is repeated reading. Fluency activities should include procedures, such as preparatory and after-reading discussions, that foster comprehension.

## Silent Reading

Some low-achieving readers decode or attempt to decode every word they meet. They are able to read high-frequency words, but they are unable to read them as sight words. They seem to need to take time to sound them out. As a result, their reading is slow and laborious. These students may not have had enough time to practice newly learned skills or words, or phonics and oral reading may have been emphasized so much that they believe the purpose of reading is to pronounce written words correctly. Stress meaning by asking students to retell selections or answer questions about them, and reduce the amount of oral reading.

Fluency can also be fostered by having students read a wide variety of easy books. As they read books in which nearly all the words are known, their ability to recognize the words more quickly should increase. Students, especially if they are younger, may also be encouraged to read the same books a second, a third, or even a fourth time.

## Recorded Reading

Read Naturally (Read Naturally) and Reading Assistant (Scientific Learning) use recorded readings to foster fluency. Reading Assistant (Scientific Learning) listens to the student read a selection and provides help with words that she has difficulty with. The student can also listen to herself read aloud. This program also has a glossary of difficult vocabulary words and provides a comprehension component. If requested, the program will read aloud to the student. Selections are available for students in grades 1 to 11.

## Reading to Others

A natural way to foster repeated readings is to have students read aloud to younger students. Practicing their performance is a natural preparation for the read-aloud. Fifth-grade struggling readers improved their fluency and achieved significant gains on standardized reading tests as a result of reading to kindergarten students (Labbo & Teale, 1990). Before reading aloud to their younger partners, the fifth graders practiced their reading and planned ways to involve their kindergartners in a discussion of the books. Reader's theater also provides natural opportunities for reading text aloud (see pp. 299–300). In addition, it focuses students' attention on meaning and interpretation (Ivey, 2000).

## Buddy Reading

In buddy reading, two students who are on a similar level read together. They might read alternate pages or, if they are reading a script, take different parts. Or they might read silently and then discuss what they have read. Buddy reading can be used as a part of independent or self-selected reading. Buddy reading can even extend into reading done at home. Students might agree to read a certain number of pages each night and then discuss their reading the next day. This provides added incentive for completing reading assignments at home. Buddies won't want to let each other down (Rasinski, 2003).

## Choral Reading

Besides building fluency, choral reading is a way of building a sense of community. It brings both the poorest and the best readers together in a performance in which all can be successful.

Carol Tesch has her third graders chorally read a poem each day. The poem is placed on chart paper so all can see it. Each time the poem is reread, the struggling readers grow more proficient. As Tesh notes, "We'll read a poem once, twice, three times a day or even more. And each time we read their voices get stronger and more confident. Even the children who have the most difficult time in reading can read by the third time through" (Rasinski, 2003, p. 59).

Choral reading can take many forms. In its simplest form, the whole class simply reads a piece together. In refrain, one reader reads portions of the text and the other students supply the refrain. In antiphonal choral reading, students are divided into groups. One group (perhaps the boys or the left side of the class) reads the main part. The second group (the girls, the right side of the class) reads the refrain. Or the groups might read alternate stanzas.

As students read, it is essential that you point to the words so they connect printed and spoken words. The piece read should also be worthy of the time spent on it. It should develop background and vocabulary, for instance.

## Paired Reading

Paired reading, which is also known as *duolog reading* (Topping, 1998), is a highly effective technique that can be used with students of any age and is easily implemented by a professional or a volunteer with a minimum of training. The teacher, a parent, or a peer who is a more proficient reader teams up with a student. (Paired reading is different from partner or buddy reading, in which two students of similar reading ability read a book together.)

The low-achieving reader selects the book to be read. The book chosen should be one that would be a little too difficult for the student to read on his own. After a brief discussion of the title and cover illustration, the helper and student simultaneously read the book out loud. During this choral reading, the helper adjusts her reading rate so it matches that of the student. When the student feels that he can read a portion of the text on his own, he signals the helper by raising his left hand. When he wants the helper to resume reading with him, he raises his right hand. The helper automatically provides assistance when the student stumbles over a word or is unable to read the word within five seconds. The assistance provided should be immediate and nonjudgmental. The helper simply says the word and has the student say it. The reading then continues. Quick correction maintains the flow of the activity (Topping, 1987, 1989). Because the helper does not provide a prompt, the helper does not need extensive training. The helper also praises the student periodically.

*Echo Reading*   In echo reading the teacher (or more accomplished reader) reads a portion of text while the student follows. Students can follow along by tracking the words in their copies of the text or the teach might use a big book or enlarged text shown by a document camera. In that case the teacher would point to each word as it is being read. Text to be read at one time can be a title, a sentence, or several sentences. After the teacher reads the text, the student or students echo it by reading it. Text to be echo-read would typically be one that has too many words that would be too advanced for the student to read but not overwhelming. The text should not have more than about 10 percent hard words. Echo reading builds oral fluency and provides practice with word recognition and builds background and vocabulary by making it possible for students to read books with assistance that they couldn't read on their own. It could be used to enable below-level readers to read grade-level reading and content area texts as long as there aren't too many difficult words.

## Alternate Reading

✳ Oral reading can be overemphasized. Tierney and Readence (2005) caution, "Oral reading is a communication skill. It is a way of delivering information or providing entertainment to listeners. If used in this way, oral would seem best done for a specific purpose and a student's performance best evaluated in terms of its communicative value" (p. 244).

As an alternative to paired or echo reading, the teacher, parent, or tutor may take turns reading the selection with the student. At first, the teacher might do most of the reading. The student would read any words that he could. For some students, this might be a few high-frequency and short-vowel words or a repeated sentence. As the student becomes more proficient, he can read larger segments. For instance, the teacher reads the first page and the student reads the second page. Or the teacher might read the difficult parts and the pupil the easy parts.

The teacher also supplies whatever help the student needs. For instance, if the student stumbles over a word, the teacher tells him the word or helps him to figure out the word. The teacher might use the pronounceable word-part, analogy, or context strategy. The teacher also explains difficult or confusing passages and discusses key events in the story from time to time. Knapp (1998) found that parents and tutors as well as teachers were able to implement this technique with a high degree of success.

## Performance Reading

Repeated reading works best when there is a genuine purpose for reading. Rasinski (2003) refers to this as performance reading. Poems and nursery rhymes are designed to be read aloud. To get the proper expression, they should be read several times. Chants and cheers also lend themselves to repeated oral reading. Scripts are also designed to be read many times. In addition to prepared scripts, students might use scripts created for reader's theater.

## Reader's Theater

 **Using Technology**

**Reader's Theater Editions**

http://www.aaronshep.com/rt/RTE.html

Provides free scripts for students 8–15.

Since no stage or props are required and the script does not have to be memorized, reader's theater (RT) is easy to implement and highly effective in enhancing fluency, comprehension, and motivation. In reader's theater, participants dramatize poems, short stories, and even excerpts from historical biographies. Ready-made play scripts can be used, or participants can prepare their own. Reader's theater works especially well with low-achieving readers because it provides them with the opportunity to reread a text several times so that they become thoroughly familiar with it. It also gives them an in-depth look at a selection.

Reader's theater begins with a careful reading and discussion of the selection and is followed by the preparation of a script and its performance. The following box highlights the steps involved in reader's theater.

## Increasing the Amount of Reading

Fluency can also be fostered by increasing the amount of reading that students do. In one program in which students engaged in partner and echo reading of the basal text and silent reading in school and at home of self-selected books, the students gained nearly two years during the yearlong program (Stahl, Heubach, & Crammond, 1997). By the end of second grade, 90 percent were reading at grade

## Reader's Theater Performance

*Step 1:   Reading the selection.* The selection is read and discussed. Prereading preparation includes activating schema, building background and vocabulary, considering strategies to be used during the reading, and setting a purpose for reading.

*Step 2:   Preparing the script.* After the selection has been discussed in much the same way as it would be in a directed reading activity, students who will reenact the piece reread the piece, and discuss the characters, and perhaps create a character map (Hoffman, 1993). The teacher can let students decide who will take which parts, or he can assign parts himself. If the group includes both adept and low-achieving readers, the teacher might choose parts for the low-achieving readers that involve less reading and are easier to read. The script may be written by the teacher or by the group. Group writing is preferable, but guidance may be required. The group discusses how they want to write the script. Dialogue from the selection should remain intact. Narrative segments from the selection might be summarized, especially if they are lengthy, or they may be translated into dialogue. Additional narration may need to

be composed, for the sake of clarity. Students can highlight their own dialogue with markers. Narrations can be underlined. Narrator's lines can be added as needed to introduce scenes, provide transitions, or summarize events (Hoffman, 1993).

*Step 3:   Interpreting the script.* Once the script has been prepared, students discuss how they will portray each character: what facial expressions they will use, what gestures they will employ, and how they will use their voices to convey emotions (Tompkins & Hoskisson, 1991).

*Step 4:   Practicing.* Students practice reading their scripts. At the end of each reading, they discuss things that each did well and what might be done to improve the performance or the script.

*Step 5:   Performing.* The script is performed for the class. Pieces that work best for reader's theater are those that have a great deal of dialogue and a minimum of narration. Stories or even chapters from books and novels can be portrayed through reader's theater. For long works, it might be best to portray excerpts of key portions of the text.

level or beyond. The students who gained the most were reading at least on a pre-primer level. Apparently, students need some basic reading skill before they are ready for fluency instruction (Kuhn & Stahl, 2000).

Sometimes word-by-word reading persists despite teachers' best efforts. If this is the case, you might consider having students read selections in which phrases are marked so that they have practice reading in meaningful chunks. As always, stress comprehension. Don't overemphasize fluent reading, or students might focus on sounding good instead of constructing meaning.

Although fluency practice is often associated with oral reading, extensive silent reading should also produce gains in fluency. One danger of oral-fluency instruction is that students will focus on saying the words rather than constructing meaning. One sign of fluency is the students' ability to read silently at a reasonable pace with adequate comprehension.

Although it is possible to build the decoding abilities of older students, even those at the lowest level of reading achievement, the extent and results of the intervention depend on the severity of the difficulty. Students at the 30th percentile in decoding skills are readily brought up to grade level after a relatively brief period of remediation, about 60 hours (Torgesen, 2004c). Students at the 10th percentile need about 100 hours of instruction. Although their decoding skills are brought up to grade level, their reading rate remains a bit behind. The most severely disabled readers, those at the 2nd percentile, need a program of about 120 hours. Although their decoding skills are brought up to the near-average range, their reading rate remains slow.

Torgesen (2004c) speculates that because these students were poor readers, they read very little and so missed out on the opportunity to bring words into their immediate recognition vocabulary. Although their decoding skills have been brought up to an adequate level, they still have a limited store of immediate recognition words. There might also be neurobiological factors involved. Since these students missed out on opportunities to read, extensive silent reading of text on their level might help develop automaticity and fluency.

## Putting Fluency in Perspective

Because DIBELS and other widely used assessments measure rate of reading, in some instance reading speed has been overemphasized to the detriment of comprehension (Gunning, 2013). As Rasinski and Hamman (2010) explain,

> Reading instruction must be focused on the making of meaning. . . . The importance of speed should be minimized in the fluency debate. Reading requires a level of active awareness and thought about language which diminishes when reading speed is emphasized. Reading at an appropriate rate in meaningful phrases, with prosody and comprehension, should be the fluency goal for all readers." (p. 26)

## Closing the Gap by Providing Better Reinforcement

With the right kind of intervention, it is possible for struggling readers to catch up. In one study of first graders, struggling readers caught up to average readers in just 15 weeks (Menon & Hiebert, 2005). The control group used a typical basal. The intervention group was given a series of 150 little books that were designed to reinforce the phonics patterns they had been taught. However, the books were not written in the singsong fashion characteristic of some decodable texts. The little books were carefully resequenced so that in all instances, easier books were presented before more difficult books and the books gradually became more challenging.

In addition to reading books that were more carefully sequenced and did a better job of reinforcing patterns that had been taught, the intervention group read a greater variety of words (Menon & Hiebert, 2005). They read between 500 and 1,000 words a week. The basal group read an average of 250 words. The basal group, which devoted a full week to a selection, reread the same story several times, so they may have read as many words as the intervention group, but they did this by reading the same words over and over again. Reading several books seems to be more effective than reading the same book over and over again.

## ▚▚ Affirming Efforts

Students, especially those who are struggling with reading and writing, need to see signs of progress. You might use a picture of a thermometer, ladder, or football field or a simple graph to represent number of words learned. On the graph, the student colors in one block for every 10 words learned.

If, despite your best efforts, students cannot seem to learn high-frequency words or word patterns, they may have a serious word-learning problem. They may need to be taught with a multisensory approach such as VAKT, which is described in detail in Chapter 14. To test for a serious word-learning problem, administer the Word-Learning Test in Appendix A.

## Mini–Case Study

Despite being tutored by the Title I teacher over a period of two years and having an excellent classroom teacher, Alfredo was making very limited progress. Referred to a university reading clinic, Alfredo, who would soon be celebrating his ninth birthday, was tested and shown able to read only a dozen or so words. At school, Alfredo had been subjected to several intensive phonics programs, which obviously didn't work. The clinic instructor decided to try a more holistic approach. High-frequency words were taught in the context of easy children's books. After each session, Alfredo took home a set of five or six cards containing new words. At home, he studied the words.

Despite intensive studying and completing many activities with the words, Alfredo still experienced difficulty learning new words. Often, he would stumble over words such as *and* and *that,* which had been introduced and carefully reviewed. Words that were known one week were forgotten the next. Sometimes, by the end of a session, he had forgotten the words that had been taught at the beginning of the session. Encountering the words over and over again just didn't seem to help Alfredo. He seemed to need some type of mechanism that would help him remember the words.

Word building and the pronounceable word-part and analogy strategies were introduced to Alfredo. Progress was slow but steady. Encountering the word *that,* Alfredo balked and looked to the teacher for help. Realizing that the *at* pattern had been introduced to Alfredo, the teacher had Alfredo try the pronounceable word-part strategy. "Is there any part of that word you can say?" she asked. Recognizing *at,* Alfredo was then able to add *th* and say the whole word.

Sometimes, Alfredo needed additional guidance. He was unable to recognize any part of the word *silly,* even though he had just studied the *ill* pattern the day before. Covering up all of the word except *ill,* the teacher asked Alfredo if he could say that word part. After Alfredo read "ill," the teacher had him add *s* and read *sill* and then read the whole word. Two pages later, Alfredo failed to recognize *silly.* However, when his teacher asked him if there was any part of the word he could say, he was able to read *sill* and then the whole word.

As time passed and with lots of guidance and opportunities for application, Alfredo became more proficient at using the pronounceable word-part and other word-recognition strategies. He became more confident and began to rely on himself rather than simply giving up or asking the teacher for help. As he put more effort into his work, he learned more. Although he still had a lot of catching up to do, with the help of word building and several carefully taught and well-practiced word-recognition strategies, Alfredo had become a reader.

## Summary

The 41 speech sounds of American English can be spelled in more than 200 ways. However, most consonant sounds have only one or two spellings, and most vowel sounds have only three or four common spellings. Despite this regularity, many low-achieving readers have difficulty learning how to decipher words.

A program that is systematic, that is related to their specific needs, and that provides ample opportunity for reinforcement and application should help.

A number of approaches can be used to teach phonics: explicit, implicit, pattern, and word building. Because it combines the best features of the other three approaches and gives students a fresh start, the word-building approach is recommended. Although consonants are typically taught before vowels and short vowels are taught before long vowels, it is recommended that consonants and vowels be taught together.

Low-achieving readers need to be taught strategies for deciphering unknown words. These strategies include seeking out pronounceable word parts and using analogy. Context should be an integral part of any strategy that is used. Using appropriate prompts, the teacher should guide students in the use of varied but balanced strategies to decode words. Ultimately, students should apply these strategies independently.

Easy, high-frequency words, such as *was, of,* and *the,* which are known as sight words, are among the most difficult to learn to read. Because their spellings do not always adequately represent their sounds (*of, one*) or they are presented before students have learned the phonics elements necessary to decode them (*how, look*), they are taught through a logographic or paired-associate method. However, only about 40 words can be learned in this way, because the learner runs out of ways of creating distinguishing cues and the cues themselves are arbitrary. In actuality, most words are fully or partially regular. If feasible, high-frequency words should be learned through phonics, because this makes it possible for the student to use letter–sound cues to learn and remember them.

A direct approach to teaching high-frequency words incorporates phonics, repetition, and reading the words in the context of real stories. Indirect approaches to teaching high-frequency words include shared reading, language-experience stories, predictable books, and composing sentences.

Learning high-frequency words has a high payoff in reading. The 200 highest-frequency words comprise about 50 percent of the words in running text. In order to make reading fluent, it is important that these high-frequency words be recognized immediately. Procedures that promote fluent reading include wide reading, rereading familiar material, performance activities (such as reader's theater and choral reading), and reading along with recorded materials.

## Application Activities

1. Examine the phonics component of two sets of materials designed for low-achieving readers. How are the phonics elements taught? Is there adequate provision for reinforcement and application?
2. Observe a beginning reader. What skills has she apparently mastered? What skills does she need? What strategies does she use to decipher difficult words?
3. Create two phonics lessons: one using the word-building approach and one using the implicit, explicit, or pattern approach. If possible, teach the lessons. Which one seemed more effective? Why?
4. Add five books to the list of predictable books suggested as being appropriate for teaching high-frequency words. If you are working with young children, choose books that are appropriate for them. If you are working with older students, choose books appropriate for their maturity level.

**5.** View the video showing how oral-reading fluency is assessed at https://pals
.virginia.edu/tools-1-3.html. What are the major elements in oral fluency?
What specific oral-reading behaviors led to the classification of each of the
three students?

PEARSON
**myeducationlab**
Where the Classroom Comes to Life

## My Education Lab

Go to the topic **Reading Assessment** in the MyEducationLab (www.myeducationlab
.com) for **Assessing and Correcting Reading Difficulties,** where you can:

- Find learning outcomes for **Reading Assessment** along with the national
  standards that connect to these outcomes.

- Complete Assignments and Activities that can help you more deeply
  understand the chapter content.

- Apply and practice your understanding of the core teaching skills identified in
  the chapter with the Building Teaching Skills and Dispositions learning units.

- Examine challenging situations and cases presented in the Iris Center
  Resources.

- Check your comprehension of the content covered in the chapter with
  the Study Plan. Here you will be able to take a chapter pretest, receive
  feedback on your answers, and then access personalized Review, Practice,
  and Enrichment exercises to enhance your understanding of chapter
  content. After you complete the exercises, take a posttest to confirm your
  comprehension.

- Practice targeting instruction and making content accessible for all students
  with A+RISE activities.

# 9

# Syllabic, Morphemic, and Contextual Analysis and Dictionary Strategies

**USING WHAT YOU KNOW**

The previous two chapters have explored ways of learning single-syllable words. This chapter examines strategies for identifying polysyllabic words through syllabic, morphemic, and contextual analysis as well as dictionary usage. Both phonic and syllabic analysis strategies primarily involve some form of sounding out. In this chapter, word-identification techniques that rely on meaning-based strategies are also introduced. These include morphemic analysis—which is the analysis of meaningful units of words (prefixes, suffixes, and roots)—context clues, and dictionary strategies.

How useful do you find these strategies in your reading? Do you sometimes divide words into syllables to sound them out? Do you try to use prefixes, suffixes, and roots to help you figure out unknown words? Do you use context clues? The dictionary? How useful are these strategies to poor readers you have worked with?

**ANTICIPATION GUIDE**

*Read each of the following statements. Put a check under "Agree" or "Disagree" to show how you feel about each one. If possible, discuss your responses with classmates.*

| | AGREE | DISAGREE |
|---|---|---|
| 1. Most older low-achieving readers have been taught how to use word-analysis strategies but fail to apply them. | _____ | _____ |
| 2. Except for phonics, the most valuable word-analysis strategy is the use of context clues. | _____ | _____ |
| 3. In most instances, context does not provide adequate clues for the identification of a difficult word. | _____ | _____ |
| 4. Using roots and prefixes and suffixes to figure out the meanings of new words is of limited value. | _____ | _____ |
| 5. Because the dictionary is so difficult for struggling readers to use, using it is the least useful of the word-identification strategies. | _____ | _____ |

## ▓▓▓  Syllabic Analysis

> ✴ As students read, most automatically develop a sense of which letters occur together and patterns in words. As a result, they learn to recognize syllable boundaries (Adams, 1990). However, students who read very little or whose orthographic awareness is weak may have difficulty establishing syllabic boundaries.

As they progress through the grades, most students eventually learn phonics and may even become adept at deciphering single-syllable words. However, Shefelbine (1990) found that 15 to 20 percent of the students in the fourth- and eighth-grade classes that he tested had difficulty with multisyllabic words. Shefelbine and Newman (2000b) found that average and poor decoders were two to four times more likely than good decoders to omit syllables when reading multisyllabic words. However, when taught how to use affixes and vowel patterns to recognize and pronounce syllables, struggling readers made significant progress in a program that lasted just 30 days (Shefelbine, 1990).

Although students have mastered single-syllable phonics, they may have difficulty locating the known element in a polysyllabic word. For instance, *par* is a single-syllable word that appears as an element in *partial, parcel,* and *particle* but has a different identity in *parade* and *paradise.* As Shefelbine (1990) notes, "Identifying patterns of syllables requires more developed and complex knowledge of letter and spelling patterns than the knowledge needed for reading single syllable words" (p. 225).

Carmen is a fairly typical example of a student who has difficulty with multisyllabic words. Reading has never been easy for her. In first grade, while most of her classmates learned high-frequency words after just a few repetitions and seemed to catch on to phonics effortlessly, Carmen had to struggle to catch up. Now in fourth grade, Carmen has long since mastered phonics but has fallen behind once more. Despite working extra hours on her assignments, she can't seem to keep up with all the reading in science and social studies that she is required to do. Concerned, her classroom teacher administered an informal reading inventory (IRI). A copy of her performance on the IRI's word-lists test is presented in Figure 9.1 What do the test results show?

As you can see from the words she misread, Carmen has learned her phonics lessons well. She was able to read virtually all of the single-syllable words. However, she has difficulty applying her phonics knowledge to multisyllabic words. Note that Carmen was unable to read a number of multisyllabic words that should have been easy to decode. For instance, she could read *mess* and *cape* but stumbled over *escape,* which incorporates the sounds of both these words. She also misread *discover,* although she could read *miss, glove,* and *her.* And she misread *carpenter* and *passenger,* although she could easily read *car, pen, her,* and *pass.* She also had difficulty with words like *adventure* and *vacation,* which contain word parts such as *ture* and *tion,* which are found only in multisyllabic words. Carmen's syllabication skills, which are sometimes known as *syllabic analysis,* are weak.

Carmen is not alone. Difficulty in decoding multisyllabic words is a major problem for many older problem readers. Why is this so? Based on experience with single-syllable words, achieving students create syllable patterns and read long words syllable by syllable. This is done automatically as the long word is being read. Although you probably have never seen the following words, you probably have no difficulty using your knowledge of word patterns to put them into syllables: *corniculate, dimercaprol, elastomer.* Because struggling readers read less or because of a difficulty with orthographic processing, they are slower at developing recognition of patterns. Although they can read words like *car* and *soon,* they have difficulty reading the word *cartoon.* While they know the phonic elements that make up the word, they fail to see the patterns in the words and so cannot tell where one syllable ends and the next begins.

**FIGURE 9.1**
Carmen's IRI
Results

| | FLASH | UNTIMED | | FLASH | UNTIMED |
|---|---|---|---|---|---|
| 1. friend | ✔ | | 1. brief | ✔ | |
| 2. moment | moo | movie | 2. special | dk | dk |
| 3. squawk | ✔ | | 3. passenger | pass | passed |
| 4. mess | ✔ | | 4. settler | ✔ | |
| 5. entrance | en | enter | 5. wreck | ✔ | |
| 6. through | ✔ | | 6. discovery | dis | discuss |
| 7. calm | ✔ | | 7. cause | ✔ | |
| 8. glove | ✔ | | 8. invitation | dk | dk |
| 9. carpenter | car- | carpet | 9. distant | disease | ✔ |
| 10. vacation | dk | dk | 10. stroll | ✔ | |
| 11. beast | ✔ | | 11. escape | 0 | exit |
| 12. howl | ✔ | | 12. famous | ✔ | |
| 13. frighten | ✔ | | 13. adventure | 0 | advice |
| 14. nature | dk | dk | 14. breathe | bread | breath |
| 15. cape | ✔ | | 15. pilot | pile | ✔ |
| 16. country | county | ✔ | 16. judge | ✔ | |
| 17. fruit | ✔ | | 17. claim | ✔ | |
| 18. sly | ✔ | | 18. several | 0 | seven |
| 19. meal | ✔ | | 19. squirt | ✔ | |
| 20. absent | 0 | above | 20. voyage | dk | dk |
| **Totals** | 65 | 70 | Totals | 45 | 50 |

## Approaches to Teaching Syllabic Analysis

> **Syllabic analysis:** breaking a word into syllables, pronouncing each syllable, then blending the syllables to pronounce the whole word.

There are two major ways to teach **syllabic analysis**: through traditional rules and a pattern approach. These two approaches are not mutually exclusive and so may be used to support each other. Whichever approach is used to teach syllabication, its mission must be kept firmly in mind. In reading, the purpose of syllabication is to break a word into smaller, more manageable units so that each of these can be sounded out and then the units can be put back together to form a whole word. To accomplish this, it is not necessary for students to break the word at the syllable's exact boundaries. For instance, it does not make any difference whether readers divide the word *inspector* into *in-spec-tor* or *in-spect-or* or *ins-pec-tor*. As long as their analysis of the word enables them to pronounce it, that's all that counts.

### Rules Approach to Syllabication

Since so many low-achieving readers are poor decoders, they are generally discouraged by the sheer length of polysyllabic words. Seeing a long word, they immediately give up. Having a poor sense of orthographic awareness, they may have a poor sense of where one syllable ends and another begins.

## Concept of Syllables Lesson

*Step 1: Introducing the concept of syllables.* To introduce (or reintroduce) the concept of syllabication, say the names of some common animals, while emphasizing the separate syllables. Have students tell you how many parts the animal names have. You might also have the class clap for each syllable in a word. Say the following or similar names. If you have pictures of the animals, point to them as you say their names. Some animal names that you might use include the following:

| | |
|---|---|
| cat | monkey |
| yak | buzzard |
| ostrich | elephant |
| tapir | hippopotamus |

*Step 2: Presenting visual syllables.* Once students grasp the idea of syllables on an auditory level, write the names of the animals on the board. Point to each syllable while saying it. Have students say the syllables along with you. Start with two-syllable animal names and work up to longer syllables.

*Step 3: Presenting generalizations* When students have a firm grasp of the concept of visual syllables, introduce the traditional syllable generalizations, but use the names of animals, sports teams, brand names of products, or other interesting words to make the generalizations come alive. Listed below, in approximate order of difficulty, are the major syllabication generalizations and animal names that might be used to illustrate the generalizations. You might also use an animal name to characterize each generalization. Thus, *catbird* syllables refer to compounds; *tiger* syllables refer to single consonants occurring between vowels; *rabbit* syllables refer to double consonants occurring between vowels.

*Compound (catbird) words.* A compound word forms separate syllables.

| | |
|---|---|
| bobwhite | catbird |
| jellyfish | blackbird |
| waxwing | glassfish |

*Affix (anteater) words:* Prefixes and affixes usually form separate syllables.

| | |
|---|---|
| anteater | snowy owl |
| sidewinder | golden plover |

*Double-consonant (rabbit) words:* When two consonants are placed between two vowels, the word is usually divided between the two consonants.

| | |
|---|---|
| panda | gibbon |
| otter | penguin |
| possum | rabbit |

*Single-consonant (tiger) words:* When a single consonant is placed between two vowels, the consonant usually goes with the syllable to the right. (There are a number of exceptions: *robin, lizard*).

| | |
|---|---|
| tiger | spider |
| tapir | |
| zebra (*br* forms a single cluster) | |

*Final* le *(turtle) words:* Final *le* usually attaches to the preceding consonant to form a separate syllable.

| | |
|---|---|
| turtle | beetle |

*Step 4: Practice and application.* Practice and application should involve actually reading and/or writing words that follow the generalization that has been introduced. Having students divide words into syllables or count the number of syllables in a word is of little value, because both exercises can be performed without actually reading the words. In addition, you don't want to emphasize exact syllable division, since approximate division works just fine in most instances.

The best practice and application is to have students read selections that contain words that follow the pattern that has been introduced. Other profitable practice activities are described below.

- When introducing new multisyllabic vocabulary words, instead of saying the words, invite students to attempt to use their skills to pronounce them.

- Seek out books and magazines that respell words phonemically. Show students how to use the phonemic respellings. As part of the postreading discussion, have students pronounce the words or read the passages in which they appear. For instance, the Reading Rainbow book, *Dinosaur Time* (Parish, 1974)

*(Continued)*

respells the names of dinosaurs and provides excellent practice for students just learning how to apply syllabication skills.

- Have the class sing song lyrics. Song lyrics are typically divided into syllables.

- Using sorting to help students discover syllable patterns. Students might sort a mixed group or open and closed syllables, for instance. The patterns in Table 9.1 (see pages 311–313) are a potential source of words to be sorted.

- To help students differentiate between open and closed syllables, have them read contrasting word pairs (*super, supper*; *biter, bitter*; *later, latter*) or complete sentences by selecting one of two contrasting words: Although the fruit looked sweet, it was (*biter, bitter*). We had a (*super, supper*) time at the park.

- Give pairs of students syllables, one on each card. Have them match up their syllables to make words.

What they need is instruction that both builds their confidence and shows them how to handle multisyllabic words. Since they may already have been taught syllabication and failed to learn it adequately, they also need a fresh approach. Even if you are using a traditional rules approach, you can give it a new look by using animal names to illustrate generalizations as is done in the following box. If you are working with older students, you might try a sports motif. Animals' names are used to make the examples more memorable. However, you may choose to use ordinary words as examples.

## Pattern Approach to Syllabication

Presenting high-frequency syllabication patterns provides specific examples of generalizations and helps students detect and learn to use pronounceable word parts within multisyllabic words. For instance, instead of presenting the open-syllable (*tiger*) generalization, introduce a group of long-*i*, multisyllabic words that fit the pattern. If possible, include a one-syllable known word as a *contrasting element* so that students can more readily identify the familiar elements in each multisyllabic word, as in the following:

tie

tiger

spider

diner

miser

Reading *tie* should help students read *tiger*, which should help them read *spider*, and so on. This is actually an extension of word building to multisyllabic words. Steps for teaching syllabication are presented in A Lesson in Teaching Syllabication Patterns.

Table 9.1 presents a list of major multisyllabic patterns and the order in which their elements are introduced. Compound words are taught first but the items introduced should be composed of elements that have already been introduced, such as short-vowel words (*sunfish*) and high-frequency words (*someone*). Easy affixes, such as *ing*, can be introduced after the pattern has been taught. Other affixes can be introduced when they begin appearing in the texts that students read (see Table 9.3). Closed-syllable patterns can be taught as soon as students have learned the single-syllable patterns that make up the closed syllables. For instance, the multisyllabic words *admit* and *attic* can be analyzed after students have learned short-*a* and short-*i*

## A Lesson in Teaching Syllabication Patterns

*Step 1:   Teaching the patterns.* Explain the importance of being able to read multisyllabic words. Tell students that you will be teaching them the open *o* pattern, which will help them to read dozens of multisyllabic words. Write *go* on the board and have students read it. Write *ago* on the board. Write the separate syllables in contrasting colors or underline them. Say the syllables as you write them. Then have students read the word. Contrast *go* and *ago*. Present *over, broken, spoken,* and *frozen* in the same way. Point out that *go* is the model word for the *o*-pattern. Later, if students have difficulty with a word containing an *o*-syllable, encourage them to say each part of the word or as many parts as they can and then reconstruct the word. If necessary, they can use *go* or other model words to help them.

*Step 2:   Guided practice.* Have students use pronounceable word parts or the model words to read the following: *stolen, token, woven, opener.* Remind them that the words they construct must be real ones. If they analyze a word and it does not seem to be real, they should try again. Also have students complete reinforcement exercises. Sample exercises include the following:

1. Form words by combining two of the three parts in each line.

   | | | |
   |----|----|----|
   | wo | ven | ver |
   | ken | spo | ker |
   | ker | to | ken |
   | len | ler | sto |

2. Underline the word that best fits the sense of the sentence.

   a. The car locks are (*frozen, chosen*).

   b. The door is (*open, over*).

   c. Have you ever seen a four-leaf (*chosen, clover*)?

   d. You will need a (*stolen, token*) for the bus.

   e. This coat has been (*frozen, woven*) from fine wool.

3. Students read signs or labels that contain pattern words.

   *Cocoa*
   *Frozen Foods*
   *Open*
   *Buy Tokens Here*
   *Photo Shop*

4. Have students create a sentence or story using as many of the key words as they can.

*Step 3:   Application.* Provide practice in reading open-*o* multisyllabic words: *moment, rodent.* Also provide students with frequent opportunities to make use of this strategy by reading basal stories, trade books, periodicals, and real-world materials.

*Step 4:   Assessment and Review.* Note students' ability to read multisyllabic words. Provide additional instruction as needed. From time to time, review the patterns and model the process of using them. When students encounter difficult words, encourage them to seek out pronounceable word parts or use the model words to help them decode the words. Provide assistance as needed.

patterns. However, you might want to wait until most of the basic short-vowel patterns have been learned before presenting closed syllable patterns, but do not wait until all the major single-syllable patterns have been taught before introducing syllabic analysis.

In Table 9.1, sample multisyllabic words are presented that are restricted to elements previously introduced in single-syllable words. For instance, the first group of short-vowel patterns contains only words composed of short-*a* and short-*i* words but are gradually expanded to include short-*o*, short-*e*, and short-*u* words; then they move into long-vowel words, and then *r*-vowel words and other-vowel words. With this sequence, it is possible to introduce multisyllabic words before students have learned all the basic single-syllable patterns, which is the practice in most programs.

**TABLE 9.1**
Common Syllable
Patterns

**Compound-Word Patterns**

| some | day | out | sun |
|---|---|---|---|
| someone | daylight | out | sunup |
| sometime | daytime | outgrow | sundown |
| something | daybreak | outfield | sunfish |
| somehow | daydream | | sunlight |
| somewhere | | | sunbeam |

**Short-Vowel Patterns**

| rabbit | basket | expense | discuss |
|---|---|---|---|
| admit | magnet | accept | hundred |
| attic | happen | invent | puppet |
| plastic | splendid | comment | trumpet |
| traffic | absent | contest | |
| instant | eldest | suggest | |

**Open Long-Vowel Patterns**

| vacant | evil | minus | robot | human |
|---|---|---|---|---|
| raven | secret | tripod | focus | menu |
| | decent | ripen | nomad | emu |
| | react | silent | solo | humid |
| | recent | | open | |
| | | | hotel | |
| | | | motel | |
| | | | woken | |
| | | | vocal | |

**Final-*e* Vowel Patterns**

| locate | inhale | divide | invite | expose |
|---|---|---|---|---|
| escape | exhale | provide | despite | suppose |
| mistake | invade | advice | reptile | excuse |
| donate | exhale | entire | bicycle | |
| vibrate | | retire | recycle | |

**Vowel Digraphs Patterns**

| exclaim | succeed | approach |
|---|---|---|
| obtain | peanut | below |
| remain | repeat | shadow |
| display | | |

***y* as long-*I* Pattern**

try
reply
supply
deny
magnify

***r* Vowel Patterns**

| artist | batter | certain | explore | purpose |
|---|---|---|---|---|
| carpet | enter | perfect | fortunate | surface |
| harvest | corner | concern | important | murmur |
| margin | lumber | confirm | restore | disturb |
| market | member | | support | absurd |
| participate | | | | |

*(Continued)*

**TABLE 9.1**
(*Continued*)

## *le* Patterns

| | | | |
|---|---|---|---|
| saddle | pebble | juggle | beetle |
| paddle | dribble | paddle | people |
| rattle | pickle | rattle | circle |
| candle | tickle | candle | turtle |
| example | riddle | example | couple |
| | simple | | double |
| | puddle | | |

## Long *oo* Patterns / *ove* Spelling of Long *o* Patterns / *U* Spelling of Long *oo* Patterns

| Long *oo* Patterns | | *ove* Spelling of Long *o* Patterns | | *U* Spelling of Long *oo* Patterns | |
|---|---|---|---|---|---|
| igloo | roofer | prove | approve | Sue | studio |
| kangaroo | noodles | proven | remove | super | truly |
| scooter | typhoon | improve | movements | student | tuna |
| shampoo | | | | | |
| rooster | | | | | |

## Short *oo* Patterns

| | |
|---|---|
| cookie | woolen |
| rookie | looking |
| wooden | lookout |

## *al* Pattern Pattern / *au* Pattern Pattern / *aw* Pattern Pattern

| *al* Pattern Pattern | | *au* Pattern Pattern | | *aw* Pattern Pattern | |
|---|---|---|---|---|---|
| also | altogether | because | caution | draw | strawberry |
| always | although | saucer | faucet | drawing | awful |
| already | walrus | author | sausage | crawling | awesome |
| | | August | daughter | | |
| | | autumn | auditorium | | |
| | | audience | | | |

## *oi* Patterns Patterns / *oy* Patterns Patterns

| *oi* Patterns Patterns | | | *oy* Patterns Patterns | |
|---|---|---|---|---|
| oil | disappoint | noisy | joy | annoy |
| point | disappointment | avoid | enjoy | royal |
| poison | rejoice | moisture | destroy | loyal |
| appoint | | | employ | voyage |
| appointment | | | | |

## *ou* Patterns Pattern / *ow* Patterns Patterns

| *ou* Patterns Pattern | | *ow* Patterns Patterns | |
|---|---|---|---|
| round | compound | power | allow |
| surround | thousand | tower | allowance |
| mountain | | flower | |
| fountain | | | |

## Schwa *a* Patterns / Adjacent Vowel Patterns

| Schwa *a* Patterns | | Adjacent Vowel Patterns | | |
|---|---|---|---|---|
| ago | around | quiet | poet | area |
| away | along | trio | poem | create |
| alone | alive | piano | fluid | |
| about | apart | radio | ruin | |
| awake | across | period | studio | |
| among | | | | |

## *-ture* Pattern

| | | |
|---|---|---|
| capture | creature | gesture |
| fracture | future | mixture |
| pasture | sculpture | picture |
| nature | | |

*(Continued)*

| *-tion* Pattern | | | | *-sion* Pattern |
|---|---|---|---|---|
| fraction | description | decoration | illustration | conclusion |
| section | destruction | demonstration | information | explosion |
| fiction | direction | exaggeration | introduction | confusion |
| nation | election | exclamation | invitation | occasion |
| station | emotion | expectation | multiplication | persuasion |
| motion | abbreviation | explanation | population | |
| portion | conversation | investigation | | |

After presenting a pattern, call attention to the generalization that the pattern follows. For instance, after presenting open *i (mi-nus)* or open *a (va-cant)*, help students see that the vowel is long because it is in an open syllable. Older students frequently have difficulty with some single-syllable patterns. Using a pattern approach to multisyllabic words provides an opportunity to review single-syllable patterns. Since students are working on multisyllabic words, they don't feel that they are doing "baby" work as they might if they were just working with single-syllable words.

## Pronounceable Word-Part and Analogy Strategies Applied to Polysyllabic Words

Teaching syllable patterns is a useful activity in itself. It introduces words that students may have difficulty recognizing in print. However, the true value of teaching syllable patterns is that they can be used as a basis for providing students with strategies that will enable them to decode most multisyllabic words.

If students have already mastered single-syllable patterns, they can build on this knowledge to attack multisyllabic words. Basically, instruction consists of showing students how to use what they already know to attack unfamiliar words. The pronounceable word-part and analogy strategies, introduced in Chapter 8 as strategies for decoding single-syllable words, are also effective when used to decode polysyllabic words (Cunningham, 1978, 1979).

Using the knowledge they gained through studying syllabication generalizations and/or patterns and through experience coping with multisyllabic words, students should try to pronounce an unfamiliar multisyllabic word syllable by syllable. Students would pronounce the word *sudden* "sud, den, sudden." If they are unable to pronounce the syllable as a whole, students might pronounce the first syllable by seeking out the pronounceable word part, then go on to the second syllable, and so on. For the word *sudden*, students might decode it as "ud-sud, en-den, sudden." Often, the pronunciation of the first syllable will trigger pronunciation of the whole word, so students may pronounce it as "sud-sudden" or "ud-sud, sudden." (However, if they are unable to pronounce the first syllable, they might try their luck with a subsequent syllable. They may be able to pronounce enough syllables so that they can reconstruct the word, or pronouncing the medial or ending syllable may trigger the pronunciation of the entire word.)

If the pronounceable word-part strategy does not work, then students should try the analogy strategy. When used with multisyllabic words, this strategy works much the same way as it does with single-syllable words. However, instead of making only one comparison, it may be necessary to make two or three. Here is how it works. A student stumbling on the word *gander* uses the analogous words *fan* and *her* to sound it out. The word *locate* is sounded out by comparing its two syllables to *go* and *hate*.

The strategy does not work all the time. There are some syllables for which no analogies can be found. In addition, the pronunciation of a sound unit is often altered when it is found in a syllable, especially one that is unaccented. For instance, the *re* in *refer* is no longer analogous to *he*, because the long *e* has become a short *i* (*ri-fur*). Students need to be taught to make adjustments in pronunciation when applying this strategy.

In making comparisons, students can think up their own analogy words or can use the analogy (model) words presented in the word-patterns list (Table 8.6) in the previous chapter. The lesson that follows describes how students might be taught the pronounceable word-parts/analogy strategies to decipher multisyllabic words.

### Teaching the Strategies

As students encounter difficult multisyllabic words, help them to apply the pronounceable word-part and analogy strategies, along with context, so that ultimately they apply these strategies independently. Your aid might take the form of guiding questions such as "Are there any parts of the word that you can say? Can you say the first part? The next part? Can you put the word together? If you don't see any parts that you know, can you see if any of the word's parts are like any words that you know? Is the first part like any word that you know? Is the second part like any word you know?"

At times, your guidance might need to be highly directive. For instance, if a student has been taught the *o* pattern but has trouble with *frozen* and is unable to note any known parts in the word, you might cover up all but the *fro* and have the student say "fro." (If the student can't read *fro*, cover up all but the *o* and have the student read "o-fro.") Uncover *zen* and have the student say "zen." (If the student can't read *zen*, cover up the *z* and have the student read "en-zen.") Then put both parts together and see if it is a real word and fits the context of the selection. If students are unable to read *fro* or *zen*, you would use the analogy strategy and have them compare *fro* to the model word *no* and compare *zen* to the model word *ten*. Give students as much guidance as they need, but gradually lead them to the point where they can decode independently.

Post the following steps for decoding multisyllabic words:

1. Say each part of the word, or say as many parts as I can.

2. If I can't say a part, think of a word that is like the part I can't say, and then try to say that word part. (If I can't do Step 1 or 2, then go to Step 5.)

3. Put the parts together to make a word.

4. Ask "Is this a real word? Does it make sense in the story?" (If not, try again or go to Step 5.)

5. Say "blank" for the word. Read to the end of the sentence. Ask "What word would make sense here?"

6. If nothing else works, I can use the dictionary or glossary.

## Generalization Approach to Decoding Polysyllabic Words

Although the pronounceable word-part and analogy strategies are easy to apply, students sometimes have difficulty seeing patterns in words. In these instances, they should try to use generalizations to help them decode words. In his research, Shefelbine (1990) found that instruction in open (*mo-, ta-, fi-*) and closed (*-at, -em, -in*) syllables and affixes (*un-, pre-, -less, -ful*) was especially helpful. After teaching a number of closed-syllable patterns, help students construct a generalization about the pattern, such as "Syllables that end in a consonant are often short (*win-dow*)." After introducing a number of open-syllable patterns, help students construct a generalization about the pattern, such as "Syllables that end in a vowel are often long (*se-cret*)."

To use generalizations to decode polysyllabic words, students should identify the first syllable by locating the first vowel and note whether the syllable is open (followed by one consonant or digraph) or closed (followed by two or more consonants). Students should say the first syllable and then proceed in this same way, syllable by syllable. After they have pronounced all the syllables, they should blend them and try to say the word, making any adjustments that are required. Prompt students as needed. If students misread an open syllable as a closed one, for instance, reading *tiny* as *tin-ny*, ask them to tell where the vowel is so they can see that the vowel should be ending the syllable and should be long (Shefelbine & Newman, 2000b).

Often, vowel sounds are reduced when they appear in multisyllabic words, as in *educate,* where the *u* has a schwa pronunciation. Explain to students that they should change pronunciations if necessary so they can "read the real word" (Shefelbine & Newman, 2000b). Often, if the proper stress isn't given to a syllable in a multisyllabic word, it won't be a real word. Students should monitor to see if they have produced a real word, one that fits the context in which it appears. If not, they should try another pronunciation.

## Spot and Dot

> The key to developing strategy use is to provide many opportunities for students to apply them. For many students who have difficulty with multisyllabic words, it is partly a problem of confidence. They encounter lengthy words and give up. Students need to be encouraged to use their skills.

If students are unable to use the pronounceable word-part and analogy strategies, they might try the spot and dot strategy (Cheyney & Cohen, 1999). In the spot and dot strategy, students spot the vowels and then place a dot over each vowel or vowel digraph. Students then connect the dots and count the number of letters between the dots. To use this strategy, students need to be taught that if a vowel is followed by one consonant (*biter*), the consonant most often goes to the right and the vowel is long. If the vowel is followed by two consonants (*bitter*), the consonants are usually split. The syllable that ends with a consonant is closed and usually has a short vowel. There are exceptions, so students need to be flexible. They need to check to see that they have produced a real word and that the word makes sense in the sentence in which it is used. If not, they should try an alternate pronunciation. Pronouncing *robin* as *roh-bin* because there is a single consonant after the vowel, they would see that *roh-bin* is not a real word and so try an alternate pronunciation. If a word contains affixes, the prefix is circled, and then the suffix is circled. The spot and dot strategy is then applied, and the student reads the word syllable by syllable. Steps for spot and dot are listed below. The strategy doesn't work equally well with all syllables. It doesn't work with *tion* or *ture* or *r*-vowel or other vowel patterns (*aw, ow, oo, oo, oy*), and students may be confused by vowel digraphs (*succeed*) or vowels that appear to be digraphs but aren't (*idea*). However, it does help pinpoint separate syllables, which is a first step in reading multisyllabic words. Although a useful strategy, spot and dot needs to be used flexibly. Post the following steps for using spot and dot:

1. Spot and dot the vowels: *splendid* (Note place a dot over the *e* and over the *i*).

2. Connect the dots and count the number of consonants between the dots.

3. If there two vowels, separate between the consonants: *splen/did*.

4. If there is one consonant, separate after the vowel: *mo/to*.

5. If the word doesn't sound right, try separating after the consonant: *rob/in*.

## Reading by Syllables and Whole Words

An effective way to practice reading multisyllabic words is through an activity known as reading by syllables (Shefelbine & Newman, 2000a). Place a syllable on the board and have students read it. Then place another syllable on the board and have students read it and then read the word by putting the two syllables together. For example, students read *ab* and then *sent* and then *absent*.

Emphasize the need to adjust the pronunciation of a syllable to construct a real word. When occurring in unaccented syllables, vowels have a reduced pronunciation, so that the second syllable in *velvet* is pronounced *vit* instead of *vet*. Explain to students that they must adjust the pronunciations of words so that they sound like real words. If students are slow to read the words, present the words a second time and emphasize the speed of response.

Also have students use syllabic analysis skills to read whole words. In the reading by syllables activity, explained in the previous paragraphs, students are provided with practice in recognizing individual syllables and combining them to form words. Reading whole words by syllables is a more advanced activity. Students must note the word's syllables on their own and then reconstruct the word. (Students might use the pronounceable word-part, analogy, or spot and dot strategies first).

## Implementing a Systematic Program

On a regular basis, introduce a set of pattern words and show how these can be used to decipher multisyllabic words as in the sample lesson. It is recommended that the pattern words be introduced in sets of three. One or two sets might be introduced each week, depending on the needs of the class and the amount of instructional time available.

> One way of deciding which syllable patterns to introduce is to examine the materials students are about to read; note which multisyllabic words will probably be unknown, and then present the patterns they embody.

A listing of pattern words was presented in Table 9.1. The patterns are listed in the order in which they might be introduced. Although there are more than 200 syllable patterns, only about 100 of these occur with a high degree of frequency. The patterns listed were chosen on the basis of frequency of occurrence and ease of learning. However, add or delete patterns to fit the needs of your students.

When should multisyllabic words be introduced? It is not necessary to wait until students have mastered all the major single-syllable patterns before presenting multisyllabic words. As soon as students have learned most of the short-vowel patterns, you may introduce multisyllabic words that are composed of patterns they have learned: *napkin, hammer, cabbage, absent, invent, address*. After students have learned long-vowel patterns, they can be introduced to multisyllabic words composed of familiar short- and long-vowel patterns: *escape, even, secret, obtain, locate*.

Introducing multisyllabic words early has multiple payoffs. It provides an excellent opportunity for students to apply skills, familiarizes students with multisyllabic words at an early stage of reading, and boosts the self-confidence of older struggling readers by showing them that they can read "grown-up" words.

## Additional Syllabic Analysis Programs

### Benchmark Word Detectives Plus

There are a number of other programs for decoding multisyllabic words. In addition to Word Building, one of the most carefully constructed is the Benchmark Word Detectives Plus program. Designed specifically for low-achieving readers, Benchmark Word Detectives Plus is a multilevel program that was developed over a period of more than 30 years at the Benchmark School (Media, Pennsylvania), a school founded to assist students who have serious reading disorders. Designed for students in grades 1–12, the multilevel program can be used by students ranging from a beginning to a fifth-grade reading level.

> **▶ Using Technology**
>
> For additional information about the Benchmark programs, visit the http://www.benchmarkschool.org Web site.

At the beginning levels, students are introduced to a series of key words that represent high-frequency patterns. These key words are then used to help students decode unknown words. At the beginning level, the key word *it* can be used to help students read *bit* and *mitt*. In the intermediate component, students use key words developed in the primary program to figure out multisyllabic words. Students might use the key words *grab* and *it* to decode the word *rabbit*. In all, students learn 120 key words. Although the analogy strategy is stressed, the program features the use of four essential strategies for decoding words. (However, the pronounceable word-part strategy is not included. If you are using a program that fails to include the pronounceable word-part strategy, add it.) Sorting and other highly effective activities, spelling, and application through reading are also essential elements of the program. (For more information about the program, refer to http://www.benchmarkschool.org/pages/BenchmarkSchool.)

*Megawords.*   Designed for grades 4–12, Megawords (EPS) is a highly structured program that develops both decoding and spelling of multisyllabic words. The program consists of five levels and includes reading syllables, combining syllables to form words, spelling multisyllabic words, matching multiyllabic words and their definitions, and completing words by adding syllables. (For more information about the program, refer to http://eps.schoolspecialty.com.)

## REWARDS

REWARDS (Reading Excellence: Word Attack and Rate Development Strategies) (Sopris Learning). REWARDS Secondary (grades 6–12) and REWARDS Intermediate (grades 4–6) are short-term intervention programs for older students who have mastered basic reading of single-syllable phonics but experience difficulty reading multisyllabic words and/or who read slowly (60 to 120 words per minute). REWARDS Secondary has 20 50-minute lessons, and REWARDS Intermediate has 25 50-minute lessons. Initially, students listen to a word pronounced in parts and then blend the parts to form the word. Students also review vowel combinations, learn prefixes and suffixes, and learn a strategy for noting syllables. Vocabulary development and fostering comprehension are parts of the program as well. (For more information about the program, refer to http://www.soprislearning.com.)

## SIPPS

SIPPS (Systematic Instruction in Phoneme Awareness, Phonics, and Sight Words) (Developmental Studies Center). The Challenge program emphasizes multisyllabic words but, as an option, reviews single-syllable phonics. To provide opportunities for students to apply newly learned skills, SIPPS has decodable texts specifically written for the program. However, it also offers libraries of trade books to build fluency after students have completed most of the Challenge levels. Students are trained to read 90 syllable patterns and provided with useful strategies for decoding polysyllabic words. (For more information about the program, refer to http://www.devstu.org.)

### System 44

System 44 (Scholastic), which is designed for students in grades 3 to 12, uses computer technology and texts to build basic decoding skills and fluency. The program provides high-interest practice selections in social studies and science so students build background knowledge as they learn decoding skills. The program also uses adaptive technology to assess students and move them through the program as efficiently as possible. (For more information about the program, refer to http://teacher.scholastic.com/.)

### Word Work Program

Designed for struggling readers in grades 4 through 8, Word Work (Wright Group/McGraw-Hill), which is the word study component of the Fast Track intervention program, presents multisyllabic words by building on single-syllable patterns. For example, after short-vowel patterns are presented, two-syllable words containing short-vowel patterns are taught: *rabbit, mascot, attic, magnet*. In all, the program presents five patterns: closed (*rabbit*), open (*tiny*), silent *e* (*mistake*), *r*-controlled (*lobster*), two vowels (*teacher*), and *cle* (*cable*). Vowel digraph patterns are subdivided into those that represent long vowels (*remain*) and those that spell diphthongs or other vowel sounds (*downtown*). To help students determine how many syllables are in a word, the spot and dot strategy is recommended. Patterns are reinforced with decodable poems and stories. (For more information about the program, refer to https://www.mheonline.com/.)

## ▨ Morphemic Analysis

Unless you are in the medical field, the word *hemacytometer* is probably unfamiliar to you. However, there's a good chance that you can figure it out without referring to the dictionary. The form *meter* is already familiar to you. And if you compare *hemacytometer* to *hemophilia, hemoglobin,* or *hemorrhage,* you can see that *hem* refers to blood. The root *cyt* may seem unfamiliar, but if you think of *cytoplasm* or *cytology,* that may help you infer that *cyt* means "cell," so a *hemacytometer* is simply a device that measures blood cells.

> **Morphemic analysis:** identification of the meaningful parts of a word to derive the meaning of an unknown word. A morpheme is the smallest meaning-bearing unit in a word. The word *untimely* has three morphemes: *un-time-ly.*

Although the English language contains nearly a million words and is growing by leaps and bounds, a vast number of both its technical terms and general words have been constructed by joining roots or adding affixes to roots. **Morphemic analysis**, which is the study of meaningful word parts such as compound words, roots, prefixes, and suffixes, can help low-achieving readers recognize hundreds of words. It can also help them learn and remember words. It is easier to learn *chronology* if you can relate it to *chronic* and *chronometer*. And if you forget what *chronology* means, you can use your knowledge of the combining form *chron* and context to help you figure it out.

Although struggling readers do well when morphological tasks are presented orally, they do not make effective use of their knowledge of roots, prefixes, and suffixes in their reading (Champion, 1997). When tested on their knowledge of morphology, struggling readers knew only 15 percent of the prefixes, 17 percent of the roots, and 20 percent of the suffixes (Henry, 1990). With training, however, disabled readers may use their knowledge of morphology to compensate for weak phonological skills. Given training in morphology, adolescent disabled readers improved in both reading comprehension and spelling (Elbro & Arnbak, 1996). Using a morphological segmentation may help struggling readers by easing the burden on working memory, because they can concentrate on one meaningful segment at a time.

## Teaching Morphemic Elements

**M**orphemic elements should be taught inductively and build on what students know. For instance, students should use their knowledge of *pedal* to derive the meanings of *pedestrian, biped, pedicure,* and *pedometer.* By noting the use of *ped* in all five words, the students should also be able to derive a meaning for the morphemic form *ped.* Also present related forms at the same time—*podiatrist, tripod, gastropod*—so that students can see relationships among the words.

Provide a cumulative word wall of the morphemic elements that have been taught so that students can refer to it if they forget what an element means and can see relationships among elements, such as the suffixes used to form nouns and the prefixes that mean "not." If the elements have cognates, also place those on the wall—for instance, *idad* and *ity* in Spanish and English, respectively, as in *originalidad* and *originality* (Kieffer & Lesaux, 2007). In addition, provide charts of the various forms of a base word, such as Table 9.2.

Teach specific morphemic elements as part of a systematic program, but also teach them in the context of meaningful reading. Provide extensive modeling of how you use morphemic elements to derive the meanings of unfamiliar words, along with guided practice in the use of morphemic elements. From time to time, have students describe instances when they were able to use morphemic elements to derive the meaning of a difficult word. Properly taught, morphemic analysis improves both the vocabulary and the comprehension of students. Both English language learners (ELLs) and native English speakers benefit from this instruction (Carlo et al., 2004).

### Making Connections

Make connections whenever possible. For instance, in a chapter entitled "Below and Above Earth's Surface" in an easy-to-read geography series (Lefkowitz, 1990), the following technical terms are taught: *atmosphere, stratosphere, ionosphere,* and *hemisphere.* If students are led to see the common elements in the words, they will better

**TABLE 9.2**
Chart of Word Forms

| Noun | Verb | Adjective | Adverb |
|------|------|-----------|--------|
| origin, originality, origination | originate | original | originally |
| strength | strengthen | strong | strongly |
| courage | | courageous | courageously |
| preparation | prepare | prepared | preparedly |

understand them, remember them longer, and, if they forget their meanings, be able to use morphemic units to decode the words. Lead students to see that *sphere* means "ball," so that *atmosphere, stratosphere,* and *ionosphere* are layers of gas that form balls that surround the earth. Note, too, the meanings of the morphemic forms: *atmo* ("air"), *strato* ("layer"), and *iono* ("electrically charged"). When discussing *hemisphere,* lead students to see that *hemi* means "half," so a *hemisphere* is "half a ball."

The key to teaching morphemic units is to build students' awareness of these elements in words so that when they encounter a difficult word, they see if they can figure out its meaning by analyzing it morphemically. Just as you teach students to seek out pronounceable word parts when applying phonics or word building, you now teach them to seek word parts whose meanings they know. By teaching morphemics, you move students from the level of sound units to meaning units. Because of this new focus, students start noticing the meaningful components of words. Having been introduced to the root *mal,* they might note it in the word *malice* used in the Gettysburg address studied in history class, in the phrase *economic malaise* in their economics class, and in *malapropism* in their language arts class (Flanigan, Templeton, & Hayes, 2012). After his class engaged in a study of roots, one student exclaimed, "I see roots everywhere now!" (Flanigan et al., 2012, p. 138). To bolster this kind of awareness, Flanigan, Hayes, Templeton, Bear, Invernizzi, and Johnston (2011) recommend an activity entitled "It's All Greek (and Latin) to me!" in which students bring in and discuss words that contain roots that have been studied in class.

## Prefixes

> **A prefix** is a morpheme placed before a word or root that changes the word's meaning, as in *unafraid* or *preview.*

Although prefixes are easier to learn than suffixes, because there are fewer of them and their meanings are more concrete, they do not become an important factor in students' reading until they are reading second- or third-grade material. Common **prefixes** are listed in Table 9.3.

When teaching prefixes, teach them inductively and, if possible, have students derive the meaning of a prefix through analyzing known words: *unhappy, unafraid, unknown.* When teaching *pre-,* for instance, lead students to derive its meaning by discussing its effect in the following words: *preview, prepay, pretest.* In your instruction and practice activities, focus on having students develop a metacognitive awareness of prefixes as meaningful units. Students may not perceive *un-* as being a separate element in words such as *unhappy* and *unknown* and so would not seek out these elements when deriving the meanings of difficult words that contain the prefix *un-.*

As you introduce prefixes, inform students of prefix pitfalls (White, Sowell, & Yanagihara, 1989). The first is that many prefixes have more than one meaning. For instance, the prefix *in-* can mean "not," as in *incapable,* or "lack of," as in *inexperience.* Sometimes an apparent prefix is not a prefix at all. The word *indifference,* for instance, is derived from the Latin word *indifferentia.* Sometimes a prefixed word is not quite the sum of its apparent parts. The true meanings of *unbending* and *uncalled for* would be hard to infer if just the words themselves were examined. The presence of prefix pitfalls means that prefixes need to be taught with care and students need to integrate morphemic analysis and context clues.

One way to teach prefixes is to group them by families of meaning (Baumann et al., 2002). Possible groups include the following:

- Number: *mono-, bi-, di-, tri-*
- Negative: *un-, im-, in-, il-, ir-*

**TABLE 9.3**
Common Prefixes

| Prefixes | Meaning | Examples |
|---|---|---|
| **Easy Prefixes** | | |
| un- | (not) | **un**friendly |
| un- | (opposite) | **un**pack |
| under- | (under) | **under**ground |
| dis- | (not) | **dis**belief |
| dis- | (opposite) | **dis**agree |
| re- | (again) | **re**read |
| re- | (back) | **re**pay |
| im- | (not) | **im**polite |
| in- | (not) | **in**expensive |
| ir- | (not) | **ir**responsible |
| pre- | (before) | **pre**winter |
| sub- | (under) | **sub**marine |
| tri- | (three) | **tri**color |
| **Intermediate Prefixes** | | |
| anti- | (against) | **anti**war |
| bi- | (two) | **bi**cycle |
| co- | (with) | **co**captain |
| deci- | (one tenth) | **deci**meter |
| en- | (forms verb) | **en**circle |
| ex- | (out, out of) | **ex**haust |
| ex- | (former) | **ex-**owner |
| hemi- | (half) | **hemi**sphere |
| inter- | (between) | **inter**state |
| micro- | (small) | **micro**scope |
| mid- | (middle) | **mid**night |
| milli- | (one thousandth) | **milli**meter |
| mis- | (not) | **mis**understanding |
| mis- | (bad) | **mis**behavior |
| mono- | (one) | **mono**rail |
| multi- | (many) | **multi**purpose |
| non- | (not) | **non**fiction |
| poly- | (many) | **poly**syllabic |
| semi- | (half, part) | **semi**sweet |
| trans- | (across) | **trans**oceanic |
| pro- | (for) | **pro-**union |
| sub- | (under) | **sub**way |
| super- | (above) | **super**sonic |

- Below or part: *sub-, under-*
- Again and remove: *re-, de-*
- Before and after: *pre-, post-*
- Against: *anti-, counter-*
- Excess: *over-, super-, out-*
- Bad: *mis-, mal-*

## Introducing Prefixes Lesson

**Step 1:** *Introducing the concept of a prefix.* Read the portion of the Humpty Dumpty chapter in Lewis Carroll's (1871/1969) *Through the Looking Glass* that talks about unbirthdays. Discuss what an *unbirthday* might be and how it is different from a birthday. List other *un-* words on the chalkboard: *unafraid, unhappy, unclear.* Have students tell how *un* changes the words and tell what *un* means. Note than *un* is a prefix and that prefixes are placed at the beginning of words and change the word's meaning. Note, too, that a prefix forms a separate syllable.

**Step 2:** *Guided practice.* Have students read individual words that contain the prefix *un-* and tell what each word means. Also encourage students to complete cloze (fill-in-the-blank) exercises with *un-* words or read brief passages that contain

*un-*words. Students might also illustrate *un-* words (*unhappy, unlucky*) or create their own *un-* words.

**Step 3:** *Application.* Have students read materials that contain the prefix *un-.* As part of the application step, ask students to use their knowledge of *un-* to derive the meanings of new words. Encourage students to use a strategy similar to the one they used for decoding difficult words. However, instead of looking for word parts they can say, students should look for word parts they know.

**Step 4:** *Extension.* Discuss the fact that *un-* can also mean "opposite," as in *undo* and *unpack.*

**Step 5:** *Assessment and Review.* Note students' ability to use prefixes to decode difficult words. Review and reteach as necessary.

## Suffixes

A **suffix** is a morpheme added to the end of a word or root that changes or adds to the meaning of the word, as in *careful* or *fearless.*

There are two kinds of **suffixes**—inflectional and derivational. Inflectional suffixes have a grammatical function, indicating subject–verb agreement (rabbit *hops*), present participle *-ing* (*singing*), past tense *-ed* (*planned*), past participle *-en* (*written*), comparisons (*sooner, soonest*), plural *-s* (*cats*), and adverbial *-ly* (*suddenly*) functions.

Derivational suffixes either change a word's part of speech or function. Many suffixes form nouns: *-ance* (*resistance*), *-dom* (*freedom*), *-tion* (*action*). A number of others form adjectives *-(i)al* (*jovial*), *-ary* (*honorary*), *-ic* (*geographic*), *-ous* (*joyous*).

Do not spend a lot of time teaching inflectional suffixes. If students are reading for meaning and using their sense of the language, they will usually supply the necessary inflectional endings automatically. Besides, generally speaking, little or no meaning is lost if students omit inflectional suffixes as they read. Since low-achieving readers are lagging behind, you need to focus on instructional techniques that have the greatest payoff.

Derivational suffixes are another matter. They should be taught directly and reinforced periodically. When teaching students to apply knowledge of suffixes, it is also a good idea to review prefixes. Many words that have suffixes also have prefixes (White et al., 1989). Derivational suffixes begin appearing in students' reading material in grade 2. The suffixes *-en* and *-er* can be found on that level. In grade 3, the following suffixes appear with a fair amount of frequency: *-able, -ible, -ful, -ness, -y,* and *-tion* (Gunning, 2001). A good time to teach suffixes is when students are reading on a second- or third-grade level or when suffixes are appearing in their reading material with some regularity. Suffixes are listed in Table 9.4 in approximate order of difficulty. You may want to stress the following suffixes because they occur with the highest frequency: *-er, -(t)ion, -able, -al, -y,* and *-ness* (White et al., 1989). Suffixes should be taught inductively, with stress placed on application. Suffixes and other morphemic elements should be taught on a systematic basis and also when there is a need.

**TABLE 9.4**
Frequently
Occurring Suffixes

| Suffixes | Meaning | Examples |
|---|---|---|
| **Easy Suffixes** | | |
| -en | (made of; having) | gold**en** |
| -er | (one who) | farm**er** |
| -or | (one who) | inspect**or** |
| -able | (is, can be) | believ**able** |
| -ible | (is, can be) | vis**ible** |
| -ful | (full of; having) | thank**ful** |
| -ness | (having) | ill**ness** |
| -tion | (act of) | imagina**tion** |
| -y | (being; having) | chill**y** |
| **Intermediate Suffixes** | | |
| -age | (forms nouns) | mile**age** |
| -al | (being; having) | accident**al** |
| -an, -ian | (having to do with; of) | Americ**an**, Itali**an** |
| -ance | (state of) | import**ance** |
| -ary | (forms adjectives) | summ**ary** |
| -ence | (state of or quality of) | obedi**ence** |
| -ial | (of; having to do with) | adverb**ial** |
| -ian | (one who is in a field; one who) | musici**an**, guardi**an** |
| -ic | (of; having) | histor**ic** |
| -ify | (make) | terr**ify** |
| -ish | (having the quality of) | fool**ish** |
| -ist | (a person who) | motor**ist** |
| -ity | (state of) | activ**ity** |
| -ize | (make) | memor**ize** |
| -ive | (being) | secret**ive** |
| -less | (without) | hope**less** |
| -ment | (state of) | enjoy**ment** |
| -ous | (having) | danger**ous** |

Some suffixes have three or four or more definitions, and these definitions may be abstract. For instance, the suffix *-ic* is listed as having nine meanings in *Random House Webster's Unabridged Dictionary* (Random House, 2005). These definitions have been combined and simplified for Table 9.4. Because many suffixes have multiple, sometimes abstract definitions, it is important that students see many examples of the target suffix in use. Examples need to be used to convey the sense of the suffix. For instance, seeing the suffix-containing words *artistic, comic, historic,* and *poetic* in the context of sentences and whole selections will do a better job of helping students understand the suffix *-ic* than will providing abstract definitions.

When teaching suffixes, show students how the spelling of the base word or root might be affected. Adding suffixes can change spellings in one of three ways (White et al., 1989):

1. Consonant doubling: *sunny, runner*

2. Change of *y* to *i*: *penniless, reliable, happily, apologize*

3. Omitted final *e*: *hoping, activity, official, cubic*

Show students that they may have to mentally restore the letters that were removed or changed when the suffix was added. Otherwise, they may not recognize the *penny* in *penniless* or the *active* in *activity*.

---

**Root:** the morpheme that remains after all the affixes have been removed. *Sing* is the root for *singer, singing,* and *sings*. The root is also the historical source of a word.

---

Tenth Planet's Roots, Prefixes, and Suffixes (Sunburst) provides practice with morphemic elements. Activities include composing clues and writing "Mad Blab" stories.

---

**Using Technology**

PrefixSuffix.Com <http://www.prefixsuffix.com/> has an extensive listing of roots and a number of activities, and is also available as an app.

---

**Using Technology**

Funbrain Rooting Out Words at http://www.funbrain.com/roots/index.html has games for acquainting students with roots.

---

# Roots

The most complex of the morphemic elements is the root. A **root** is the part of a word that is left when all the affixes have been removed. It may be a word (the *help* in *unhelpfully*) or a portion of a word (the *ceive* in *receive*) (McArthur, 1992).

Common roots are listed in Table 9.5. The list contains both roots and elements known as *combining forms*. To avoid unnecessary distinctions, both combining forms and roots are referred to as "roots." Although there are hundreds of roots, only the most frequently occurring and most useful elements have been included. For a more complete listing, see *The Reading Teacher's Book of Lists* (Fry & Kress, 2006).

## Attacking Words That Have Multiple Parts

When decoding words that have multiple parts, generally, the first task is to put the word into syllables and then try to say it. If the word is unknown—one that is not in the reader's listening

| Roots | Meaning | Examples |
|---|---|---|
| **Easy Roots** | | |
| graph | (writing) | auto**graph** |
| tele | (distance) | **tele**scope |
| port | (carry) | **port**able |
| saur | (lizard) | dino**saur** |
| phon | (sound) | micro**phon**e |
| vid, vis | (see) | **vid**eo, **vis**ion |
| astro | (star) | **astro**naut |
| bio | (life) | **bio**graphy |
| **Intermediate Roots** | | |
| aud | (hearing) | **aud**ible |
| auto | (self) | **auto**biography |
| -ology | (study of) | ge**ology** |
| cred | (believe) | in**cred**ible |
| chrono | (time) | **chrono**meter |
| dict | (say) | pre**dict** |
| duct | (lead) | con**duct** |
| geo | (earth) | **geo**graphy |
| loc | (place) | **loc**ation |
| manu | (hand) | **manu**al |
| ped | (foot) | **ped**estrian |
| scrib, script | (writing) | in**scrib**e, manu**script** |
| therm | (heat) | **therm**os |

**TABLE 9.5**
Frequently Occurring Roots

## A Lesson in Teaching a Root

*Step 1:   Conveying the nature and importance of the element.* Before presenting the element, explain to students what roots are and show how they will help them to become better readers. Place some lengthy words containing roots on the board and model the process of pronouncing the word and deriving its meaning. For instance, putting *polychromatic* on the board, explain what a root is, and underline *chrom*. Then show how you would translate the root and the affixes into their meanings (*poly* = "many"; *chrom* (*at*) = "color"; *ic* = "having") and come up with the overall meaning of the word: "having many colors." Note that words are like puzzles, and often we can solve their meanings by thinking about and putting their parts together.

*Step 2:   Introducing the new element.* Build on whatever knowledge students might have of the new element. Present words with which they are likely to be familiar. By analyzing these words, help them derive the meaning of the element. For the root *bio*, discuss *biography* and *biology* and the common item *bio*. Help them to see that *bio* means "life" or "living." Help students determine the meanings of *biographer, biohazard, biotechnology,* and *biochemistry*. Note that it is sometimes necessary to check the meanings you derive through analysis with definitions given in a glossary or dictionary.

*Step 3:   Guided practice.* Have students read signs or articles containing *bio*. For instance, they might read a label that contains the word *biodegradable*. Or they may read a selection about *biofeedback*. After the selection has been read, have students explain what they think these *bio* words mean and how they derived these meanings.

*Step 4:   Application.* As students encounter new words containing morphemic elements that they know, help them to apply their knowledge by using the known part or analogy strategies. For instance, when students encounter the word *biorhythm,* ask them to see if there are any parts of the word whose meaning they know. If they recognize *rhythm* but not *bio*, use an analogy strategy. Compare the *bio* in *biorhythm* to the *bio* in *biology* and *biography* and help them derive the meaning of *bio* and the whole word. After they have derived a tentative meaning, they should test it out in context to see if it fits.

*Step 5:   Assessment and Review.* Note students' ability to use roots to derive the meanings of unknown words. Review and reteach as necessary.

vocabulary—then the task becomes one of using knowledge of affixes and the root to attempt to derive a meaning for the word. Context would also be used.

Steps for decoding a word with multiple parts are as follows:

1.   See whether the word has a prefix or suffix. If so, pronounce the prefix, then the suffix, and then the remaining part(s) of the word. If the word has no prefix or suffix, start with the beginning of the word and divide it into syllables. Say each syllable.

2.   Put the syllables together. Include the word's prefix or suffix, if any. If the word does not sound like a real word, try other pronunciations until you get a real word.

3.   See if the word makes sense in the sentence in which it appears. If it does not, try other pronunciations.

4.   If the word is one whose meaning you don't know, see if you know the meaning of the prefix, if there is one; then see if you know the meaning of the root and the meaning of the suffix, if there is one. Put all the meanings together. Also use context to get clues to the word's meaning.

5.   If nothing works, use a dictionary or ask the teacher for help.

## ▨▨ Contextual Analysis

> **Contextual analysis:** the use of verbal clues from a sentence or passage in order to derive the meaning of an unknown word.

Deriving the meaning of a word from the context is called **contextual analysis**. When students read materials on the appropriate level, they have a 15 percent chance of deriving the meanings of unfamiliar words from context (Swanborn & de Glopper, 1999). Less able readers, however, have about a 10 percent chance of using context successfully. These readers know fewer words, and their knowledge of the words that they apparently know is less extensive than that of more capable readers. Their backgrounds of experience are also less fully developed. Students can't use contextual analysis if the target word and key words in the context clues are unknown.

Struggling readers frequently fail to make full use of available context clues. They may focus on one or two details rather than consider the whole context. For instance, one middle school struggling reader focused on the dog's method of getting food when attempting to use context to derive the meaning of *ravenously,* and he concluded that *ravenously* means "licked":

> The satisfied Labrador had eaten ravenously that evening, cleaning up bowls of fresh milk and plates of food with a bottomless appetite. (Goerss, Beck, & McKeown, 1999, p. 163)

When carefully taught how to use context clues, students do improve. In one study, students nearly doubled their ability to derive the meanings of words from context (Jenkins, Matlock, & Slocum, 1989). However, in order to improve students' ability to use context clues, instruction needs to be significant. Students given only limited training did not improve. The best results are also achieved when strategy instruction is combined with instruction in types of clues (Fukkink & de Glopper, 1998).

### A Complex Process

Deriving the meaning of an unfamiliar word requires the following:

- Recognizing that a word is unknown (Nation, 2001).
- Deciding to use context to derive the meaning of the unknown word. Most use of context is virtually automatic (Rapaport, 2004). A decidedly deliberate use of context is not initiated until the reader notes that an unknown word is blocking the construction of meaning (Kibby & Wieland, 2004).
- Selecting clues to the word's meaning.
- Using the clues to compose a general meaning of the word. The reader combines text clues and background of experience to hypothesize a meaning. Background is a crucial factor because it enables the reader to make inferences about the unknown word (Rapaport, 2004). Therefore, to increase the effectiveness of students' use of context clues, it is important to model how to make inferences based on background knowledge.
- Testing the meaning of the word and changing or refining the meaning if necessary. The reader tries out the hypothesized meaning to see if it fits. If it doesn't fit, the reader repeats the process. (Good readers revise when they find the hypothesized definition is not working out. Poor readers start all over again.) In one study, readers required five or six encounters with a word before they could derive an accurate meaning (Kibby & Wieland, 2004).

## Steps for Using Context

Once students have decided to use contextual analysis, they should follow these steps for deriving meaning:

*Step 1: Seeking clues.* Students read the entire sentence, saying "blank" for the unknown word. They then look for clues that might help them guess the meaning of the unknown word. If the clues in the sentence are inadequate, students look at earlier and later sentences.

*Step 2: Combining clues.* Students put all the clues together.

*Step 3: Using background knowledge.* Students add background knowledge to the clues they have assembled and construct a tentative definition or meaning.

*Step 4: Trial substitution.* Students substitute the tentative word or phrase for the unknown word.

*Step 5: Checking the substitute.* Students check the context to see if the substitute word or phrase fits all the cues.

*Step 6: Revision.* If the substitute word or phrase does not fit, students revise the substitute and try another word or phrase.

> To spotlight the use of context clues, encourage students to bring in examples of instances where they were able to use context clues to get the meaning of an unfamiliar word.

When students are attempting to use context, use prompts to guide their efforts. Because struggling readers may not be using their understanding of the text as a context clue, it is important when providing them prompts to first ask them to tell what the target section is about. Often, the general sense of the passage will provide a clue as to the meaning of a word. However, students won't be able to use the overall sense of the passage if they don't comprehend it (Beck, McKeown, & Kucan, 2002). Ask students what's going on in the passage or what the passage says, and then discuss what the target word might mean.

To help students learn the process, the teacher models how to go about using context clues. The teacher also provides guided practice. During guided practice, the teacher might ask such questions as: "What are the clues telling us? What are the clues in the sentence that contains the word telling us? Are there any clues in the sentences before the hard-word sentence? Are there any clues in the sentences after the hard-word sentence? When you put all the clues together, what does the word seem to mean? What do I know that will help me figure out what this word means?"

Stress the need to think carefully. As McKeown and Beck (2004) concluded, "For many students the most difficult part of deriving word meaning from context is the process of reasoning about how to put information together from the context and what kind of conclusions are valid to draw" (p. 24). Using think-alouds, demonstrate for students the kind of reasoning that is required to derive the meaning of an unknown word. Also use prompts to help students apply their reasoning skills.

Here is how Angela, a middle school student, used some probes provided by the researcher and arrived at a tentative meaning for the word *qualms,* which was contained in a selection that she was reading:

> I had a few qualms at first about how Caroline and Julia would get along together. Julia was so different from all of our school friends that I felt sort of awkward with her myself. (Duncan, 1977, p. 55)

**Researcher:** Talk to me. What do you think?
**Angela:** That maybe there are questions or how they are going to get together.
**Researcher:** What do you mean by questions?
**Angela:** Like are they going to get together or are they not. Like she's thinking in her head how is she like going to get along with her friend.

**Researcher:** So what does that tell you about the word *qualms*?
**Angela:** That she might be thinking in her head.
**Researcher:** What else can you tell me? (long pause before Angela responds)
**Angela:** Ideas.
**Researcher:** Keep talking.
**Angela:** Maybe like an uneasy feeling. (Harmon, 1998, p. 586)

## Types of Context Clues

There are a number of different kinds of context clues, and some are easier to use than others. Context clues such as explicit definitions and synonyms are easier to use than those that require making inferences (Carnine, Kame'enui, & Coyle, 1984). And, of course, the number of clues makes a difference. Some difficult words are accompanied by multiple clues. Distance also has a bearing on the use of context clues. The closer the clue is to the target word, the easier it is to use.

When instructing students, especially younger ones, start with easier clues. Also, focus on words that have near, rather than distant, context clues. As part of your instruction in context clues, discuss the different types of clues, how to spot the clues, and the ways in which the clues might be used to derive the meanings of unfamiliar words. The next section lists some frequently occurring context clues (Sternberg, 1987). Discuss multiple examples of the clues and model and discuss how you the clues might be used. Also invite students to bring in examples of context clues for discussion.

> ☀ Periodically display a word that has such explicit context that it is possible to derive its meaning. Encourage students to use the context to construct a meaning for the word. Discuss the processes they use.

> ☀ From time to time, review and model the process of deriving the meaning of a word from context. As students encounter hard words in rich contexts and are not using clues, encourage them to do so.

### Definition

Quite often, authors supply definitions for difficult words, especially technical terms used in science and social studies. In some instances, the definition is detailed and conceptual, far better than what might be found in a dictionary. An extended definition for a *walker,* which is a key word in the story, is provided in the following passage: "What's a walker?" Donna asks. "It's a light metal frame that helps people walk," Mrs. Price says. "It has four legs, and handles for you to hold. When you take a step, you put the walker in front of you" (Cameron, 1990, p. 16). In many cases, however, the definition is concise and appears as an appositive directly after the difficult word or is defined in a separate sentence. Note the definitions provided for *planet* and *orbits* in the following sentences: "Earth is a planet. Planets are large bodies in our solar system that move around the sun. Each planet has its own path around the sun. This path is called its orbit" (Block, 2013 p. 5). Using this clue requires noticing whether a definition has been provided.

### Synonyms

Except for directly stated definitions, synonyms seem to be the easiest type of context clue. Synonyms are especially easy when they appear close to the difficult word (Carnine et al., 1984). In the following sentence, a student can use the synonym *snout* to derive an approximate meaning for *proboscis*: "The housefly has a long snout or proboscis" (Steele, 1991b, p. 15). Using this clue requires searching for a synonym, which might be in the target sentence or another sentence. Often a synonym or definition follows the difficult word and is set off by commas, dashes, or placed in parentheses.

### Comparison–Contrast

Comparison–contrast context clues are sometimes signaled by *not, but, however,* or *even so.* The words *even so* in the following excerpt indicate that the lepidoptera's ability to fly huge distances contrasts with the fact that it is fragile, and so suggests an approximate meaning for *fragile*: "Lepidoptera are fragile creatures. Even so, some of them can fly huge distances, or migrate to warmer climates" (Steele, 1991b, p. 18). Using this clue requires being aware that a comparison or contrast is being made and seeking out the comparison or contrast and using that information to gain insight into the meaning of the target word.

### Function Indicators

Sometimes, the reader can tell what a word means by noting what the difficult word does. By noting the function of the *incinerator* in the following passage, the reader can get a fairly clear sense of what it is: "The chassis oven, as well as the cab ovens, are heated with the help of the plant incinerator located out on the receiving dock. Freightliner burns all its scrap paper, lumber, and cardboard boxes in the incinerator" (Nentl, 1983, p. 35). Using this clue requires noting that the difficult word is doing something and seeing how that helps to derive the meaning of the difficult word. The reader would ask: "What is the incinerator doing?"

### Example

One or more examples of the target word are provided. This makes it possible for the reader to examine the example(s) and infer the meaning of the target word. The following passage, which includes *vegetarian,* gives a number of examples of foods that a vegetarian diet might include: "Some birds have a mostly vegetarian diet. They eat seeds, fruit, berries, nuts, grasses, shoots, waterweeds, and leaf buds" (Steele, 1991a, p. 13). Using this clue requires being aware that an example has been provided and noting what the example is showing about the target word.

### Experience

The target word may label or describe a common experience. Using his background of experience, the reader can often infer meanings. Through real or vicarious experience, the reader can infer the meaning of *celebration* by noting in the following excerpt the many ways in which people celebrate Juneteenth: "On Juneteenth, people celebrate African American culture and history. They hold parades and picnics. Many pray or attend church. People tell stories and share food. They also sing and play games" (Murray, 2012, p.4). Using this clue requires being aware that one's experience can help determine the meaning of a difficult word and using that experience to think about what the word might mean.

### Pictorial Clues

Encourage students to use illustration clues to get the meanings of unfamiliar words. In a geography text for low-achieving readers (Abbye & Donahue, 1993), *assembly line, prairie, plateau,* and other key words are explained with pictures. When preparing students to read a passage, point out the pictorial clues and stress the need to read captions to get the benefit of the clues. Often, pictorial clues are far superior to verbal ones. Using this clue requires searching visuals to see if they depict difficult words or provide other information about their meanings.

## ▚▚ Using the Dictionary

Dictionaries vary greatly in complexity. As a practical matter, students are unable to handle conventional dictionaries until they are able to read on a third-grade level (Halsey & Morris, 1977). Below that level, students need to use picture dictionaries, simplified glossaries, or digital dictionaries. However, learner dictionaries are written on a simplified level and might be used with both ELL and native speakers. *The Longman Dictionary of American English* (Pearson Education, 2008) defines words using only the most frequently occurring 2,000 words.

So that students will not become frustrated in their attempts to use the dictionary, obtain one that is as close to the students' reading level as possible. For an eighth-grader reading on a third-grade level, this would mean using a beginning dictionary or a learner dictionary. Along with ease of reading, also consider maturity. Select a beginning dictionary that is not obviously designed for primary students. Analyze the dictionary. Look for ease of use, definitions that are readable and understandable, and the generous use of illustrations. Or obtain an electronic dictionary that pronounces words being looked up and reads definitions.

Learner dictionaries for ELLs, such as *Collins Cobuild* and *Longman Dictionary of American English,* provide simplified definitions and more examples so that students can see how words are used. Special attention is paid to idioms and words that frequently occur together as common expressions: *missed opportunity, pose a question.* Both bilingual and learner dictionaries should be made available to English language learners. Consulting a bilingual dictionary is especially helpful when ELLs are trying to understand the meaning of a word. Learner dictionaries might also be made available to struggling readers.

## Teaching Dictionary Skills

Instruction should be functional. Nothing is quite as dull as completing dictionary worksheets. However, students will need some direct instruction in key dictionary skills. One of the best ways to teach dictionary skills is to model the use of the dictionary. When the spelling, meaning, or pronunciation of a word is questioned in class and you are unsure of the correct answer, freely admit it and model how you use the dictionary to answer questions that you have about words.

### Deriving Correct Meanings

The most difficult dictionary skill of all is to derive the correct meaning of the word being looked up. One problem is locating the correct definition. A second problem is understanding the definition. The language of definitions tends to be abstract. Even if the definition is written in understandable style, students may focus on a fragment of a definition and so misinterpret it (Scott & Nagy, 1997). In addition, when good readers go to the dictionary, they may already have a sense of the word's part of speech and may have constructed some possible meanings. Struggling readers go to the dictionary without any such expectations (Neubach & Cohen, 1988).

> Encourage the use of glossaries. Because glossaries have a limited number of words and fewer definitions, they are easier to use.

> Some dictionary definitions do not provide enough information for readers. For instance, if the word *laser* is essential to the meaning of a passage, a reader might need to consult an encyclopedia to acquire in-depth information.

Acquaint students with the various sources of information about a word's meaning. For instance, in the *Merriam-Webster Learner's Dictionary* (http://www.learnersdictionary.com/), the word *tripod* is shown in an illustration in addition to being defined. The word *triumphant* is defined, used in an illustrative phrase, and used in an illustrative sentence. The word *boycott* is defined and used in several example sentences. In some dictionaries the word *boycott* is accompanied by a brief account of its origin.

Also model the process of looking up a word. As you model the process, demonstrate to students how you use context to decide the word's part of speech and make some guesses about the word's meaning before looking it up. Show how you go about using context to select the right definition and carefully consider the whole definition, using both definitions and examples and also illustrations and word histories, if available. Because dictionary usage is a complex skill, it needs explicit, sustained instruction with many opportunities to apply the skill.

Students also need multiple encounters with words so that they get a feel for how these words are used. Additionally, the traditional assignment of looking up words in the dictionary and using them in sentences should probably be eliminated. In addition to being a tedious assignment, most students are not able to use a new word in a sentence (unless it is very concrete) until they have had multiple encounters with it.

When looking up words that have multiple definitions, struggling readers tend to select the first definition. Even when there is just one definition, these readers may focus only on a portion of the definition. For example, for *altercation*, which is defined as "a heated argument," struggling readers might focus on "heated" and ignore the "argument" portion (Nichols, 2007). Through modeling and think-alouds, demonstrate using context to get a sense of the word and then using the dictionary to confirm or adjust your guess.

### Determining the Correct Pronunciation

For reading purposes, it is not necessary to derive the correct pronunciation of a new word. Getting the meaning is all that is needed. One young reader thought *colonel* was pronounced /kol-uh-nul/. Since she understood that the word referred to a military officer, her comprehension did not suffer. However, not knowing the pronunciation of the word, she was unable to recognize it when she heard it and so was unable to add to her knowledge of the word when it was spoken by others. In addition, had she used it in her own speech, no one would have known what she was talking about. Learning how to derive the pronunciation of a new word is an important skill.

> Encourage students to take advantage of phonemically respelled words in periodicals, trade books, and texts. Students tend not to use aids such as this unless the teacher emphasizes them.

When teaching the pronunciation key, build on what students already know. Except for the symbol /ŋ/ used in *sing* and the /zh/ symbol for the sound heard near the end of *measure*, students will be familiar with all symbols for the consonant sounds, since they do not differ from the letters used to represent their sounds. Students will also be familiar with symbols for short vowels, since they are the same. Long-vowel symbols are easy to learn because they are symbolized by a macron (¯). The only symbols students will have to learn are those for schwa, *r* vowels, and the other vowels (those that are neither long nor short). Students also need to know that the pronunciation key may vary slightly from dictionary to dictionary.

> Electronic dictionaries can be found online and are appearing as features of word-processing programs, on e-readers, and as apps for tablets and smartphones. Most electronic dictionaries, provide pronunciations along with definitions and examples. Some electronic dictionaries can be searched by voice so that the student need not know how to spell the word.

After giving an overview of the pronunciation key, emphasize the familiar elements and model their use. Have students use the pronunciation key to construct pronunciations for short, straight-forward words. Choose words from trade books and content area books that they are reading. Select words whose spellings do not effectively represent pronunciations: *python, quartz, gnu, queue*. As they encounter words whose pronunciations are unknown, have students use the dictionary to reconstruct pronunciations. Online dictionaries and some dictionaries that are loaded onto digital devices provide oral pronunciations for words, but it is still useful for students to know how to use a pronunciation key, since an oral pronunciation might not be available. After reconstructing a pronunciation using a pronunciation key, students might check their reconstruction by comparing it with an oral pronunciation provided by an electronic dictionary.

As students encounter words like *route* and *tomato,* which have variable pronunciations (ro͞ot, rout), (tə mā tō, tə ma tō), lead them to see that people in different parts of the country speak different dialects so that their pronunciations of certain words differ. They may also use certain expressions and words in different ways. Discuss the fact that all dialects are equal and that many words may be pronounced in more than one way. Thus /ro͞ot/ and /rout/ are equally correct. The pronunciation chosen should be the one that matches the speaker's dialect.

### Glossaries

Glossaries can be found in reading programs beginning in first grade and in many informational books. An especially useful type of glossary is the eGlossary at http://www.eglossary.com, which is available for a number of reading and content area texts. With its speech component, an eGlossary says the target word, says its definition, and reads an example sentence. The eGlossary is especially beneficial for students who are unable to pronounce a word. Because it reads the word and its meaning and an example sentence, the eGlossary is also a helpful study aid. Hearing a word spoken fosters retention. In addition, the eGlossary also helps students review hard words independently before reading a selection.

## A Functional Tool

Knowing when to use a dictionary is just as important as knowing how to use it. When encountering a new word in their reading, students should use phonic, syllabic, and/or morphemic analysis strategies and context clues to derive the meaning and/or pronunciation of the word. If the word is not crucial to an understanding of the selection, the reader should skip it. The dictionary should be consulted only when the unknown word is essential to the meaning of the passage. Otherwise, looking up words disrupts comprehension.

However, looking up problem words after reading a selection is a good idea. It is also a good idea to look up words whose meanings have been derived from context. Again, this should be done after the selection has been read. Looking up a word gives readers feedback, allows them to revise their definitions, and provides more information about the word. For these reasons, the dictionary is an excellent vocabulary expander and builder.

## Balanced Use of Strategies

Given the complexity of the English language and the changing needs of readers as they encounter materials of increasing difficulty, there is a need for a variety of word-analysis strategies. Phonics and syllabic analysis are required for sounding out words. Morphemic analysis and dictionary usage are essential when the meanings of words are unknown. Context is useful for identifying words that the reader cannot sound out and for deriving the meanings of unknown words.

These strategies are often used in integrated fashion to support each other and as cross-checks. In a balanced program of word analysis, students need to know which strategy to use in which situation. They also need to be able to integrate strategy use.

## ▟▟▟  Using Think-Alouds

As they advance through the grades, struggling readers adopt strategies for dealing with unknown words. Unfortunately, these strategies may not be effective. In addition, because their strategies do not work very well, struggling readers may lack confidence in their ability to deal with unfamiliar words and may simply skip words that are difficult.

Such was the case with Angela, a below-level reader in the seventh grade (Harmon, 1998). Angela generally skipped words that she did not know. And when she did attempt to derive the meaning of an unknown word, she focused on attempting to pronounce the word, a strategy that does not work if the word is not in the reader's listening vocabulary. In addition, Angela used only the immediate context in which the word appeared; she failed to consider any of the text that appeared before or after the sentence in which the word was used. Angela never considered the use of the dictionary or another reference.

One way of guiding students in the use effective strategies is to conduct a think-aloud. In a think-aloud, students stop when they come to a difficult word and then give a thought-by-thought description of what they do to try to figure out the word. The teacher does not provide instructional guidance at this point but offers neutral prompts that encourage students to explain their thinking: "Can you tell me what you are thinking? Can you tell me more?" Once you know what strategies students are using, you can then use the think-aloud as an instructional tool. You might use such prompts as: "Is there any part of that word that you can say? Are there any parts of that word that you know? Is the word like any word you know? Can you find clues to the word's meaning in other sentences or other parts of the article? What else might you do to get help? Would a dictionary help?"

Strategies that can be used to derive the meanings of words are many and varied. The personal guidance provided in a think-aloud can help students integrate and apply strategies. Most important of all, the guidance provided can help build students' confidence in the use of word-analysis strategies and build their sense of competence. If individual think-alouds are impractical, group think-alouds may be used instead.

## ▟▟▟  Mini–Case Study

An eighth-grader, Andreas had a fifth-grade instructional level and difficulty keeping up with his school work. One of his difficulties was decoding multisyllabic words. Not only did Andreas have difficulty sounding out multisyllabic words, but he also failed to emphasize meaning. Many of the words he sounded out were not real words. For instance, he read *tretorius* for *treacherous*, *avication* for *aviation*, and *descrease* for *decrease*.

Andreas's teacher was puzzled. Did Andreas have difficulty putting the words into syllables? Was limited vocabulary part of the problem? For instance, if Andreas did not know the meanings of *aviation*, *treacherous*, and *decrease*, then decoding them would not have done any good, unless he could have derived their meanings from context.

To explore these unanswered questions and determine why Andreas had difficulty with the words, his teacher went back over the items that Andreas had missed. She determined that some of the words missed were in Andreas's listening vocabulary, but some were not. Also, she found that when Andreas was given a second chance and some support, he did a little better. As a result of these additional insights, a multifaceted approach was designed. Syllabication, morphemic analysis, and dictionary usage were taught. However, they were taught within the context of the content-area reading that Andreas was required to complete for school.

Multisyllabic words were drawn from selections that Andreas would be reading soon in his regular assignments. When possible, words were chosen that fit into one of the multisyllabic patterns that Andreas had difficulty with: the *-ence* pattern, as in *convenience* and *confidence,* for instance. In addition, Andreas was taught the pronounceable word-part and analogy strategies for identifying multisyllabic words. These strategies were integrated with context, and meaning was stressed so that the words Andreas constructed were real words and fit the sense of the sentence and passage.

Gradually, morphemic analysis and dictionary skills were added to the program so that Andreas had strategies for coping with the many new words that appeared in his content area texts. Emphasis was placed on learning roots and affixes that appeared in the content-area vocabulary that he was learning. Andreas also learned to make better use of context clues and to use the glossary when necessary. Over time, Andreas made gradual but encouraging progress.

## Summary

All too often, low-achieving readers have difficulty applying phonics knowledge to multisyllabic words and so need explicit instruction in this area. Approaches for teaching the decoding of multisyllabic words include traditional rules and patterns combined with word building. The strategies of seeking out pronounceable word parts and using analogy/comparison–contrast to decipher multisyllabic words should also be taught along with spot and dot or a similar routine for analyzing multisyllabic words.

Low-achieving readers should be taught a number of meaning-based strategies for identifying new words. These include morphemic analysis, context clues, and dictionary skills. Morphemic analysis involves the analysis of morphemes, or meaningful units of words, such as roots, prefixes, and suffixes.

Morphemic elements should be taught inductively and build on what students know. Morphemic elements should also be grouped in some way so that students can see relationships. Focus should be placed on teaching those elements that students have the greatest need to know and that are likely to transfer to new words they will meet. Being easier, prefixes should be taught before suffixes, but they should not be taught before students are reading on a second- or third-grade level. Roots, which are the most complex forms, should be taught last.

With instruction, low-achieving readers can double their ability to use context clues effectively. Using context is a two-stage process. In stage one, students use context and prior knowledge to construct a possible meaning. In stage two, students try out this possible meaning. Major context clues include definition, synonyms, comparison–contrast, function indicators, example, and experience.

The dictionary is an essential tool for low-achieving readers, helping them cope with difficult words and build their vocabularies. It is important that low-achieving readers use a dictionary that is on the appropriate level. Electronic dictionaries should also be introduced. Using the dictionary requires three major skills: locating the word, selecting the appropriate definition, and reconstructing pronunciation. The dictionary should be presented as a functional tool to be used as needed.

Think-alouds may be used to assess students' use of word-analysis strategies and to provide guidance in their application.

## Application Activities

1. Plan a lesson teaching an element in morphemic analysis, context clues, or dictionary usage. If possible, teach the lesson and evaluate its effectiveness.
2. Examine three children's dictionaries and one or more learner dictionaries. Pay particular attention to the way words are defined. Look up 5 to 10 words and compare the definitions provided in terms of accuracy, completeness, and understandability. Which of the dictionaries seems most useful for low-achieving readers? Why?
3. Examine an electronic dictionary. How does it compare with a regular dictionary? In what ways might low-achieving readers find it more useful than a regular dictionary? What difficulties might they have in using it?

## MyEducationLab

Go to the topic **Reading Assessment** in the MyEducationLab (www.myeducationlab .com) for **Assessing and Correcting Reading Difficulties,** where you can:

- Find learning outcomes for **Reading Assessment** along with the national standards that connect to these outcomes.

- Complete Assignments and Activities that can help you more deeply understand the chapter content.

- Apply and practice your understanding of the core teaching skills identified in the chapter with the Building Teaching Skills and Dispositions learning units.

- Examine challenging situations and cases presented in the Iris Center Resources.

- Check your comprehension of the content covered in the chapter with the Study Plan. Here you will be able to take a chapter pretest, receive feedback on your answers, and then access personalized Review, Practice, and Enrichment exercises to enhance your understanding of chapter content. After you complete the exercises, take a posttest to confirm your comprehension.

- Practice targeting instruction and making content accessible for all students with A+RISE activities.

# 10 Building Vocabulary

**USING WHAT
YOU KNOW**

The previous chapter discussed syllabic, morphemic, and contextual analysis, as well as dictionary usage, which are four key strategies for learning new words. This chapter presents principles and techniques for teaching new words and strategies for remembering them.

What are some words that you have learned recently? How did you learn these words? Have you ever taken a course in vocabulary development or embarked on a program of self-study to improve your vocabulary? What techniques did you use? How effective was the program? What might be the components of a vocabulary program for low-achieving readers?

**ANTICIPATION
GUIDE**

*Read each of the
following statements.
Put a check
under "Agree" or
"Disagree" to show
how you feel about
each one. If possible,
discuss your responses
with classmates.*

| | AGREE | DISAGREE |
|---|---|---|
| 1. Having a limited vocabulary is the major cause of poor comprehension. | _____ | _____ |
| 2. Nearly all low-achieving readers have a less well developed vocabulary than do achieving readers. | _____ | _____ |
| 3. Instruction in vocabulary is bound to have a positive impact on comprehension. | _____ | _____ |
| 4. New words are best taught when there is a need to know them. | _____ | _____ |
| 5. A certain amount of time should be set aside each day for vocabulary instruction. | _____ | _____ |

## ▚▚ Low-Achieving Readers and Vocabulary

When Valerie Anderson (Anderson & Henne, 1993) asked 60 low-achieving read-ers in the sixth grade what makes reading hard, the predominant response was "the words." When she asked them if they had any problems when they read, the answer was, once more, "the words." When asked to tell what good readers do, the sixth-graders noted that the good readers knew the words and read quickly. As Biemiller (2011) comments, "Vocabulary problems probably create as many serious reading comprehension limitations as do the more widely recognized reading dis-abilities" (p. 208).

In addition, students who are at risk because of poverty or other factors tend to come to school with limited vocabularies. Children from professional families know twice as many words as children raised in families on welfare (Hart & Risley, 1995; Risley, 2003). According to Biemiller's research, by the end of second grade, the lowest 25 percent of students have an average vocabulary of 4,000 words. Average students have a vocabulary of about 6,000 words and the highest 75 percent have a vocabulary of 8,000 words. Working with struggling readers, Curtis (2010) found that high school students had a receptive vocabulary equal to that of the average sixth-grader. As Perfetti (2010) notes, "Vocabulary is the reflection of unequal opportunity."

Limited vocabulary isn't much of a hindrance in the early grades. The words that students encounter are mostly known words. Working with at-risk second-graders, teachers were able to bring them up to an average level of performance on word recognition (Juel, 2010). However, oral vocabulary scores remained at a below-average level of 89, with 100 being average. Vocabulary does become an essential factor at about grade 3 when students are more heavily engaged in read-ing content materials and is a key factor in grade 4 and beyond (Chall, Jacobs, & Baldwin, 1990). For struggling readers, the gap widens. Having had less opportu-nity to acquire new words because they generally read less, struggling readers need a systematic program of vocabulary development. In fact, language development, with an emphasis on vocabulary, should be a part of virtually all intervention pro-grams. Note that in the Juel (2010) study the intervention program was highly suc-cessful in building word-recognition skills. However, chances are these students as they move into higher grades will experience comprehension problems because of limited vocabularies.

## ▚▚ Stages of Word Learning

Knowing a word's meaning is not an either-or proposition. Graves (1987) posited six tasks in word knowledge:

*Task 1:* *Learning to read known words.* Learning to read known words involves sounding out words that students understand but do not recognize in print. It also includes learning a sight vocabulary and using phonics and syllabication to sound out words.

*Task 2:* *Learning new meanings for known words.* Even a cursory examination of a dictionary reveals that most words have more than one meaning. A large part of expanding a student's vocabulary is adding new shades of meaning to words partly known.

*Task 3:* *Learning new words that represent known concepts.* Because the concept is already known, this really is little more than learning a new label.

***Task 4:*** *Learning new words that represent new concepts.* As Graves (1987) observed, "Learning new words that represent new concepts is the most difficult word-learning task students face" (p. 169). Moreover, in content texts, conceptually unknown words often appear in pairs or groups so that students have a number of difficult words to learn. They typically require extensive instruction, which includes learning relationships among words (Hiebert, 2010). It is the learning of large number of words that label unknown concepts which makes content or informational texts difficult. Literary texts may also contain large numbers of unfamiliar words, but often these words are labels for known concepts and so are easier to learn. The familiar concept *sad* might be labeled with the unfamiliar words: *gloomy, miserable, depressed, grief-stricken,* and *disconsolate.*

***Task 5:*** *Clarifying and enriching the meanings of known words.* Although this task is accomplished when students meet known words in diverse contexts, Graves felt that more systematic, more direct involvement is called for. Teachers have to help students forge connections among known words and provide a variety of enrichment exercises to ensure greater depth of understanding.

***Task 6:*** *Moving words from receptive to expressive vocabulary.* It is necessary to teach words in such a way that they appear in students' speaking and writing vocabularies. The ultimate test is whether students actually use newly learned words correctly.

Another way of looking at vocabulary knowledge is to assess the depth to which a word is known or how the student can use the word. Stahl and Fairbanks (1986) and Baumann and Kame'enui (1991) describe three degrees of word knowledge: associative–definitional, contextual–conceptual, and generative.

*Associative–definitional knowledge* means that the student can make an association between a word and a definition. A *monitor* is "a device used to check or control." A *nomad* is "a member of a tribe who moves from place to place to get food for cattle."

*Contextual–conceptual knowledge* means that the student understands the "core concept the word represents and how that concept is changed in different contexts" (Stahl, 1986, p. 663). The student would understand that although a monitor in the lobby of an apartment building and a monitor worn by a heart patient have something in common, they also have differences. Conceptual knowledge varies in depth. A student can have partial conceptual knowledge or deep conceptual knowledge.

*Generative knowledge* means that the student can use a word appropriately in speaking or writing. As Nagy and Scott (2000) note, knowing a word is more than just being able to state a definition: "Knowing a word means being able to do things with it. . . . Knowing a word is more like being able to use a tool than it is like being able to state a fact" (p. 273).

> ✳ With experience, students deepen their understandings of words stored in their lexicons. Initially, the word *cat* may refer to the family's pet. In time, it encompasses other cats, and eventually it becomes a category label for wild as well as domestic cats.

Before teaching new words, you must ask: "What does the student need to know about the word?" For novice readers, it may be simply a matter of learning the graphic form of a word. The word may be one that they recognize when they hear it, but they don't know its printed form. Although the word *pneumonia* may be in students' listening vocabulary, they may not recognize its printed form. When presenting a word of this type, teach only the part that is unknown. If the students know the meaning of the word, do not waste time defining it or using it in several contexts. Emphasize, instead, the *pneu* spelling of /nōō/, which is most likely to be the unknown part of the word.

**Concept:** generalization formed by considering particular examples or specific characteristics of objects, actions, or states that share certain characteristics.

When teaching vocabulary, it helps to think in terms of **concepts.** Through their life experiences, low-achieving readers may have acquired a number of concepts for which they have no labels. For instance, students have undoubtedly seen or read about hens but might be puzzled if they encounter the word *pullet.* It will not be necessary to talk about the characteristics of a hen. Teaching should center around helping students remember that the word *pullet* means "young hen." This is an instance where you are teaching a label for a familiar concept, so the teaching should be on the associative–definitional level.

Ironically, in many instances, students know the labels but not the concepts. This is especially true of abstract words such as *republic* and *democracy.* These are words that students may have seen or heard but whose meanings may not be clear to them. And then there are words that embody new concepts and have unfamiliar labels: *osmosis, photosynthesis, introvert.* Words such as *magenta* and *pullet* can be taught in a minute or two, but a word that embodies a new concept or a new concept as well as a new label will require considerably more time and effort. These words would be presented on the conceptual–contextual level.

Teaching vocabulary also involves clarifying and deepening students' understanding of known words and helping students use new words in their speaking and their writing. See Table 10.1 for a listing of states of word knowledge and recommended instruction for each stage.

## ▓ Word Knowledge and Comprehension

Although having a rich vocabulary is important in its own right, it is often taught as a means of improving comprehension. Instruction must go beyond simply supplying definitions for words, however. It must be thorough and deep. Students

**TABLE 10.1**
States of Word
Knowledge

| State | Instruction |
|---|---|
| 1. Knows word when hears it but does not recognize printed form. | Teach printed form. |
| 2. Knows word's oral and written form but does not use it. | Promote generative knowledge. Give examples of its use. Clarify word. Encourage its use in a safe environment. |
| 3. Knows the concept but not the label. | Teach the label and relate it to the concept. |
| 4. Has partial knowledge of the word. May have definitional but not contextual knowledge. | Develop fuller meaning of the word. Examine the word in several contexts. |
| 5. Recognizes the label but has no real conceptual knowledge of the concept: *republic.* Or the word may have a familiar everyday meaning but an unknown technical meaning: *energy, motion.* | Develop the concept. |
| 6. Both the concept and the label are unknown. | Develop the concept and the label. |

*Source:* Adapted from "Vocabulary Knowledge and Comprehension: A Comprehension-Process View of Complex Literacy Relationships," by M. R. Ruddell. In R. B. Ruddell, M. R. Ruddell, & H. Singer (Eds.), *Theoretical Models and Processes of Reading* (4th ed., pp. 414–417). Newark, DE: International Reading Association, 1994.

*Note:* In addition, there are some words for which a student has partial knowledge. Students may know that a *colonel* is someone who is in the armed services but may not realize that *colonel* designates a rank just below general. Or students may know a word but not use it because they are unsure of its meaning or pronunciation or both.

must have contextual knowledge; definitional knowledge is not adequate (Stahl & Fairbanks, 1986). They should be given examples of a word used in context, unless the word is one that can be pictured. Showing a picture of a butte, for instance, would be more effective than using it in a sentence, although doing both would be better still. According to Beck and McKeown (1991), two other features are also essential if comprehension is to be improved: "fluency of access to word meanings and richness of semantic network connections" (p. 806).

If students are reading passages similar to the following, in which the boldface terms are new words, comprehension will likely suffer unless students can access the meanings of those words rapidly and accurately and use them to help construct the meaning of the passage. If students have only been given definitions of the words, chances are that that in itself will not be sufficient to improve their comprehension of the selection. They will lack the kind of contextual knowledge needed to understand the words in their settings. And because they were only introduced to the words once, students may forget them or may require additional time to recall the words, either of which will hinder comprehension.

> Clovis people were very successful big game hunters who first appeared in the western plains soon after the **glaciers** began to retreat. Some scientists think the Clovis people were the first American settlers and that they arrived sometime 15,000 years ago. Others think they were **descendants** of **immigrants** who arrived much earlier. Scientists may disagree about who the Clovis people were, but everyone agrees that they were **thriving** over wide areas of North and South America by 11,500 years ago. Within just a few centuries they had spread from coast to coast. Thousands of their **artifacts** have been found linking river valley to river valley from Washington State to Nova Scotia and from Alaska to the southern tip of South America. Scientists identify Clovis people by the **distinctive fluted** (grooved) spear points they made. These points are called Clovis because they were first found near Clovis, New Mexico. Clovis points have since been found all over North America and places in Central and South America. (Sattler, 1993, p. 43)

If students have limited background and vocabulary, teaching a new word may actually involve presenting a series of related words. For instance, teaching the word *atom* might involve teaching the words *electron, neutron,* and *proton* (Baker, Simmons, & Kame'enui, 1998).

Teaching vocabulary to improve comprehension, then, will require the following:

1. Teaching to contextual–conceptual knowledge. Give a word's definition, and use it in context. Provide a student-friendly definition. Discuss its meaning and help students relate the new word to known words or familiar concepts.

2. Establishing relationships. Show students or help them discover how new vocabulary words are related to each other and to words they already know. For instance, talk about ways in which descendants of immigrants might thrive and what kinds of artifacts, besides spear points, they might leave behind. Also relate the new word *thriving* to the known phrase *doing well* and the new word *descendants* to the known phrase *children of*. This type of discussion both broadens and deepens knowledge of a word so that a student is better able to make connections between new words and known words. Help students make a personal connection with the new words. They might name conditions under which they thrive.

3. Providing multiple exposures. At least three exposures, and preferably more, should be provided. This promotes accessibility. Ideally, these exposures should

involve active manipulations of words—completing an analogy, giving an example, supplying an opposite, relating the word to one's own experience—so that the students must think about the words (Stahl & Fairbanks, 1986). It is also important to display words and make sure that students pronounce them. Seeing the spellings of words activates graphophonemic connections that help secure pronunciations and meanings in memory. Students who are shown the spellings of words and say the words learn more words than do students who simply hear new vocabulary words (Rosenthal & Ehri, 2008).

## ▨ Incidental versus Systematic Instruction

An **incidental** approach is one in which skills are taught when the need arises.

There are two main approaches to teaching vocabulary: incidental and systematic. In the **incidental** approach, vocabulary is taught as needed. Words likely to pose problems in a story or informational piece are taught before students read the selection. As an unknown word is encountered in class, it is discussed. The main advantages of the incidental approach are that students apply their knowledge immediately and can see a need for learning the new words.

A **systematic** approach is one in which skills are taught on a regular, planned basis.

In the **systematic** approach, words are taught as needed, but time is also set aside for the systematic study of vocabulary. This may be a few minutes of each day or one period a week. The main advantage of the systematic approach is that vocabulary study is given more emphasis. If it is tied in with word histories, crossword puzzles, and word games, systematic vocabulary study can create an interest in words. Realistically, a systematic program of vocabulary development might cover only 400 or so words in a year's time. However, at the same time that students are learning these new words, they should also be learning strategies and habits that will foster independent word learning. As Curtis and Longo (1999) note, "They see the importance of a wider vocabulary, and become motivated to increase their vocabularies on their own" (p. 37).

## EXEMPLARY TEACHING

### Fame (an Intensive Vocabulary Development Program)

Realizing that limited vocabularies were causing comprehension problems and poor comprehension was limiting vocabulary development in their struggling readers, Curtis and Longo (2001) devised an intensive vocabulary development program. Emphasis was placed on having students process the introduced words in many contexts so that both understanding and retention would be fostered. In the presentation of the word *persistent*, notice the varied contexts and note, too, how the teacher draws out from students contexts in which the word might be used.

A persistent person is someone who hangs in there despite difficulties. We often hear or read about people like this—people who overcame a bunch of obstacles to succeed. Like an athlete who was persistent even though he or she had injuries—they refused to give up. Can anyone think of someone they know or have heard about who was persistent, who refused to give up? Could persistence ever be a negative thing? Can anybody think of a situation when someone's refusal to give up or let go might be harmful? We had at least one word in an earlier unit that is related to *persistence*—can anyone think of one? The one I thought of was *endurance*. What connections do you see between *endurance* and *persistence*?

After the words were introduced, students completed unfinished sentences by providing examples of the words' meanings and then gave an example from their experience, for example, a time when they were persistent. Students then completed sentence and paragraph cloze activities as well as analogies and responded to yes-no questions that included a pair of the words studied (e.g., *persistent* and *extinguished*: Could something persistent ever be extinguished?). Opportunities to use the words in conversation and writing were also provided. Topics were chosen for conversations and for writing that lent themselves to the use of the new words. Students also read selections containing the new words. The new words were incorporated into questions about the reading selection.

After reading about Goodyear, for instance, students might respond to a question like "What incidents from the article indicate that Goodyear was persistent?"

Students' progress was monitored. For each unit students were given a pretest and a posttest. Words that most students had difficulty with on the pretest were given more reinforcement. In addition to a posttest given at the end of each unit, students were assessed on their recognition of the new words in their reading and the use of the words in their speaking and writing. Teachers held conferences with students to talk over their progress and determine steps that they might take to improve. Although FAME lasted only 12 weeks, students typically gained a year in both vocabulary and comprehension.

## Principles of Vocabulary Instruction

Whether you use a systematic or an incidental approach to teaching vocabulary, or a combination of the two, certain basic principles form the foundation of an effective program. The first principle is to establish goals.

### Establishing Goals

Establish vocabulary-learning goals with your students (Baumann & Kame'enui, 1991). Include them in the goal-setting process. Ask: "Why do you want or need to learn new words?" One goal might be to build self-confidence. Another goal might be to improve reading comprehension. Still another might be to improve written and spoken expression. Students, especially ones who are academically behind, delight in learning long words. Accustomed to doing "baby" work, learning new words gives students a sense of concrete accomplishment.

### Building on What Students Know

Carr (1985) directed students to establish personal clues for new words. Having been introduced to the words *jubilant* and *periodicals,* students noted favorite periodicals and events that made them jubilant.

When presenting new words, build on what students know. In presenting the word *periodical*, for instance, ask students if they or their families subscribe to magazines or newspapers. Ask them where they might go if they wanted to read old magazines. See if anyone knows in what room or section of the library magazines are kept. Note that the room is often called the "Periodicals Room" because magazines are known as *periodicals*. Explain that they are called *periodicals* because each magazine is issued after a certain period of time, such as a week or a month. Discuss what other publications might be found in the periodicals section. Have students give an example of a periodical that they read.

In developing the meaning of *jubilant,* ask students to tell what kinds of things make them very happy or jubilant. After introducing both words, have students tell how a periodical might make them jubilant.

## Building a Depth and Breadth of Meaning

Present a word in several contexts. Simply defining a word and supplying a single example of its use may lead to a false concept of the word's meaning. A *magnificent* sunrise may be translated as a *bright* sunrise. Hearing about a *magnificent* gift, a *magnificent* deed, and a *magnificent* speech should broaden the students' understanding of the word so that when they read about a *magnificent* statue, they understand that it is not a *bright* statue.

## Creating an Interest in Words

Use joke and riddle books to help students see that words can be fun. In addition to having a few laughs, students will become more aware of words, more receptive to learning new words, and more appreciative of words they already know. Explore the histories of words. Investigate the histories of words like *boycott, Braille, gardenia,* and *robot.* Discuss, too, how words change and note new words that have come into the language. Also have students note vivid use of vocabulary and encourage students to strive to use expressive words in their writing (Graves & Silverman, 2011).

## Relating Words to Students' Lives

Most important of all, relate the learning of new words to students' everyday lives. As Dale and O'Rourke (1971) noted, once we are introduced to a new word, it pops up in our reading, on the TV shows that we watch, and in conversations. Encourage students to note examples of the usage of words that they have studied recently. They can write on a card the word and the context in which it was used and share that with the class. Also have students share examples of ways in which they have used recently learned words in their writing or speaking.

In relating the word *gnarled* to students' lives, seventh-grade teacher Denise Stanton used the following examples:

> Have you ever seen an elderly person who has arthritis and their hands are all twisted? That's *gnarled.* Or have you ever seen a tree trunk that the trunk itself is twisted? That's *gnarled.* (Harmon, 1998, p. 523)

## Promoting Independent Word Learning

Show students how to increase and expand their vocabularies by using the tools of word learning: context, morphemic analysis, glossary, dictionary, and thesaurus. Research suggests that when students are taught how to use the tools of word learning, they acquire vocabulary at a faster rate (Baumann & Kame'enui, 1991).

## Selecting Words for Instruction

Beck, Kucan, and McKeown (2008) have divided words into three groups: Tier One, Tier Two, and Tier Three. Tier One words are "everyday, basic familiar words" (*look, see*) that are learned through speaking and listening. Tier Two includes "high-utility words that generally appear primarily in print rather than in conversation" (*gaze, glance, peer*). Tier Three words are "technical words drawn from specific content areas" (*nutrients, minerals*). Tier One words are learned through conversation and interaction with others. Tier Two words are learned mostly through reading and classroom discussions. Tier Three words are learned primarily through studying or exploring a specific content area.

Beck and her colleagues (2008) recommend providing instruction in Tier Two words. Most Tier Two words are synonyms for common words—*multitude* for *many, courageous* for *brave, hideous* for *ugly*—and so are easy to teach.

## Techniques for Teaching Words

In choosing a technique for teaching vocabulary, consider three factors:

1. What is the nature of the word? Is it abstract, concrete, common, rare? Is it a technical word? Does it have many meanings?

2. What background will students bring to this word? Will this be a word with which they are vaguely familiar? Do they have the conceptual background but lack the label? Do they lack the conceptual background but have the label? Do they lack both the label and the conceptual background?

3. How will the students use this word? Is it essential to the meaning of a story they are about to read? Is it a high-utility word that will appear again and again in this and other selections? Do you simply expect students to recognize it when they hear it? Will they be required to use it in their writing or speaking?

### Conceptual Teaching of Key Words

> When selecting words for instruction, choose words that are essential for an understanding of key concepts, words that are probably not known by students, and that are likely to occur in future selections. If the number of new words in a selection is unreasonably large, you may decide that the selection is simply too difficult. It may exceed the students' instructional level.

In some selections, especially lengthy content-area pieces, 20 or more words may be unfamiliar to students. This is too large a number of new words for students to learn. An upper limit of seven is more manageable, so you must make choices.

Because your overall objective in teaching words prior to the reading of a selection is to improve students' comprehension, decide first what you want students to comprehend and then choose the vocabulary words that they will most need to know in order to learn those ideas. For example, as a result of reading the first four pages of *Thurgood Marshall: Fight for Justice* (Bains, 1993), you might want students to learn the following concepts:

- Thurgood Marshall was learning about the Constitution.
- Marshall wondered why African Americans were not given equal rights that the Constitution said all Americans have.

Then go through the selection and choose those words that are needed for an understanding of the major concepts but that might pose problems for students. Emphasize high-utility words, words that are sure to occur in future reading. Listed below are words needed to understand the major concepts in *Thurgood Marshall: Fight for Justice:*

| | |
|---|---|
| Constitution | equal protection |
| Fourteenth Amendment | lecture |
| memorized | deny |

The concepts of denying someone that which is his due, lecturing someone who has misbehaved, and studying until one knows something by heart will be in students' background of experience, but they may not be familiar with the labels for these experiences: *deny, lecture,* and *memorize.* These are Tier Two words and can be presented briefly. Several of the words chosen—*Constitution, Fourteenth Amendment, equal protection*—are Tier Three words and will require building or expanding concepts.

Once the words have been chosen, you can then determine the best way to teach them. Conceptual learning needs techniques that lead students into deeper levels of processing. As Baumann and Kame'enui (1991) note, learning new concepts requires developing semantic relatedness and activating prior knowledge. This involves showing how new words are related to each other and how they relate to students' backgrounds and words they already know. When they integrate new words into their schema, readers are better prepared to use those new words to construct the meaning of a passage.

Actually, virtually all vocabulary instruction should involve some elements of semantic relatedness and prior knowledge. For example, although all students have been scolded for misdeeds, they may not have had the type of scolding that includes explaining why their actions were wrong and why they should not repeat them, a concept conveyed by the label *lecture*. Unless a connection is made through discussion or some other means between the label *lecture* and the experience of being scolded, students may not truly understand what *lecture* means. It is also important to develop the concept more fully by showing how a lecture is accompanied by an explanation of why the conduct is not appropriate and why the conduct should not be repeated.

Because most words can have many meanings, the meanings provided for the new words must match those that the words have in the selections. For instance, *lecture* can mean "a speech" or "a scolding," and *deny* can mean "to say something is not true," "to disavow," or "refuse to grant." If the students access the wrong meanings, they may misinterpret a portion of the passage.

Tier Two words that are needed for clarification of comprehension might be presented at point of use. If you are reading aloud, a difficult word can be clarified—that is, briefly explained—when it is encountered. For silent reading, words might be presented near the point of use. This works best if students are reading a work section by section. For instance, if students are reading about a boy who is *irate* because someone stole his lunch, you might explain, in parenthetical fashion, "In this section, you will read about a boy who is irate because someone took his lunch. *Irate* means 'very angry.' " Because you are providing the meaning as clarification, you would not go into a discussion about a time when you felt irate or a time when students were irate. If you want students to add the word *irate* to their store of vocabulary, you can go into this kind of discussion after the selection has been read. Beck and colleagues (2008) recommend providing brief vocabulary instruction before reading (unless you are developing conceptual knowledge of Tier Three words), parenthetical instruction during reading, and robust instruction after reading.

## Brainstorming Techniques

**Brainstorming:** group technique used to activate thinking by encouraging participants to volunteer whatever thoughts or associations come to mind when provided with a stimulus word.

One group of approaches that activates prior knowledge and helps students organize new concepts and their labels is **brainstorming**. In brainstorming, the teacher invites students to volunteer their mental associations with a word or topic. In addition to activating students' prior knowledge, brainstorming techniques provide the teacher with an opportunity to evaluate students' background of information. For instance, the teacher may not know whether students have any knowledge of the Constitution or, if they do, how extensive or accurate that information is. Brainstorming is a good way to find out. Once the teacher has some sense of the students' understanding of the Constitution, she or he "can then clear up misconceptions and make sure that new concepts and words are related to experiences that are meaningful to those particular students" (Lipson & Wixson, 1991, p. 560).

In one of its simplest forms, brainstorming can be presented through a list–group–label framework (Taba, 1967). The topic to be brainstormed is written on the board, and students are invited to tell what the topic makes them think about. Writing *Constitution* on the board, for example, you would invite students to tell what comes to mind when they think of this word. All responses are listed, even those that don't seem to have any connection to the topic. After responses have been listed, the class—working together—categorizes the words into groups of three or more. (A word may be placed in more than one group.) After all items have been classified, they are given category labels. As students group the words and label them, they explain why certain words should be placed together and why their category name is appropriate. Since grouping or categorizing is a difficult task for many poor readers, you might model the process of categorizing and labeling items for one of the categories. As students become more proficient, they can take more responsibility for grouping and labeling.

As students supply responses, you evaluate the accuracy and extent of their knowledge of the topic. As a member of the group, you may volunteer words during the brainstorming portion of the procedure. For instance, if students fail to mention *equal* and *equality,* you might add them to the list. Lest the number of items to be grouped grows unwieldy, limit the number of brainstormed items to 25 or so (Tierney & Readence, 2005).

If you notice that the students' knowledge of the Constitution is uneven, provide them with enough of an overview of the Constitution so that they understand its basic intent, especially that it guarantees certain rights to all Americans. Since your main goal is to instruct students in essential vocabulary so that they can better understand the biography of Thurgood Marshall, you need not provide an in-depth study of the Constitution. However, if you are the reading teacher, you might coordinate your lessons with those of the classroom teacher, who might undertake a study of the Constitution as part of a "Justice for All" unit.

## Using Imaging and Graphic Organizers to Learn Words

Linguistic modality is not the only way of representing a word. Words can and should be represented as images (Marzano, 2004). In one study, students learned words twice as well as when they created images of them as opposed to just learning definitions (Powell, 1980, as cited in Marzano, 2004). Where appropriate, have students create logographs or illustrations for their words (Beers, 2003). In a logograph, students use a symbol or drawing to illustrate the meaning of a word.

### Graphic Organizers

**Graphic organizer:** diagram used to show how words or ideas are related. Graphic organizers can be used to improve vocabulary knowledge and comprehension of a passage and as a preplanning device in writing.

**Graphic organizers** can also be helpful. Graphic organizers are semantic maps, charts, diagrams, and other visual devices that help students see and establish relationships among words and ideas. Graphic organizers seem to work especially well with students who may have difficulty seeing relationships when they are only expressed verbally. Using graphic organizers to process words at a deeper level led to students' increased retention of the words in one study (Boulware-Gooden, Carreker, Thornhill, & Joshi, 2007).

## Semantic Mapping

Semantic mapping is based on the list–group–label technique and combines brainstorming and graphically organizing information. After brainstorming, categorizing, and labeling, the class arranges items graphically to show their relationships. **Semantic maps** are also flexible. Items can be added to them during or after reading or even during subsequent lessons. Semantic maps are especially helpful to low-achieving readers who have difficulty organizing information and who may have negative associations with more verbal methods of arranging data, such as outlines.

> **Semantic map:** places the main idea in the center and uses a series of lines and circles to show how subordinate ideas are related to it.

The steps in semantic mapping include announcing the topic, brainstorming, grouping and labeling, creating a map, discussing and revising the map, and extending the map. The lesson that follows describes how a fourth-grade corrective group created a map for Earth in preparation for reading *Blastoff to Earth: A Look at Geography* (Leedy, 1992).

## Semantic Mapping Lesson

*Step 1: Announcing the topic and inviting brainstorming responses.* The teacher wrote the word *Earth* on the board and invited a student to read it. Then the teacher asked the class to tell what comes to mind when they think of the word *Earth*. Students responded with the following words: *land, water, ocean, mountains, United States, rivers,* and *South Pole*. No one mentioned the names of any specific oceans, so the teacher asked probing questions. Students volunteered *Atlantic* and *Pacific*. No one mentioned *continents* either, so the teacher added that word. The teacher asked the students if they knew what continents are. One student explained that they are "large pieces of land," so *large pieces of land* was added to the list. When asked to name the continents, students could only think of America. The teacher explained that America is actually divided into two continents: *North America* and *South America*. Both these terms were added to the list.

*Step 2: Grouping and labeling responses.* Students discussed ways of grouping the words and possible titles for word groups. A preliminary map was constructed.

*Step 3: Discussing and revising the map.* The class discussed the map. One student remembered that Africa is a continent, and so that was added to the map. During the discussion, concepts were clarified. The teacher noted that the continent in which the South Pole is located is Antarctica, and so the map was adjusted.

*Step 4: Using the map.* Students used the title and cover illustration to predict what *Blastoff to Earth* might be about. Students read *Blastoff to Earth* to evaluate their predictions and find out more about Earth. The semantic map was displayed so that students could use it as a reference as they read. After students read and discussed the selection, the map was reviewed, and students were invited to add additional elements. The names of the remaining oceans and continents were added, as were the names of additional land forms. During subsequent sessions, as students learned more about the Earth and its major features, they added to the map and made several other changes. Learning that Europe and Asia are considered to be one continent, they added Eurasia to the map. The map is presented in Figure 10.1.

In addition to being a prereading vocabulary development technique, semantic maps can also be used as a way to summarize the content of a selection or as a prewriting activity. However, for the technique to be of optimum value, students should participate in the creation of maps. If teachers create maps, they are the ones who sift the information and so students do not get an opportunity to organize and process the terms. According to research by Berkowitz (1986), students' performance does not show much improvement unless they have a hand in creating the maps.

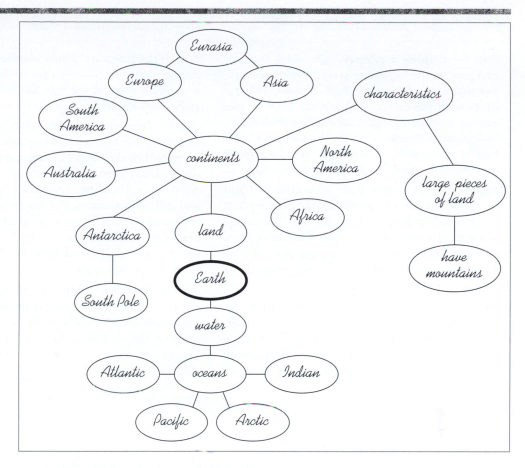

■ **FIGURE 10.1**
Semantic Map of
Earth

## Pictorial Maps

Maps need not be verbal. They can also be visual or a combination of verbal and visual items. The words in semantic maps can be illustrated with drawings, or drawings can be used instead of words. This works especially well when working with concrete items.

## Semantic Feature Analysis

**Semantic feature analysis:** uses a grid to compare objects, people, or ideas on a number of characteristics.

Like semantic mapping, **semantic feature analysis** (SFA), which involves comparing the characteristics of a series of related words, has been shown to be effective in improving both vocabulary and comprehension. SFA has been especially effective with poor readers and with students who have learning disabilities (Pittelman, Heimlich, Berglund, & French, 1991). Through having students assess the main features of words, SFA activates prior knowledge and helps students explore and organize relationships among words. Through eliciting the ways words in a category are the same or different, SFA helps students to establish relationships among words and to note shades of meaning. It fosters precision in word knowledge and usage.

Although it is a useful tool, SFA works best with words that have features that are either present (+) or absent (−). However, SFA can be adapted to include a graduated scale: A = always, S = sometimes, or N = never, for instance.

## Semantic Feature Analysis Lesson

*Step 1:   Choosing a category.*   Choose a topic or category. In the beginning stages, choose categories that are concrete and less complex. Tell students what the category is, and ask them to give examples. In preparation for reading *Pocket Facts, Wild Animals* (Steele, 1991c), the category *mammals* is presented. Students are asked to name mammals. Prompts are provided, if necessary.

*Step 2:   Creating a grid.* Place an outline of a grid on the board or on an overhead transparency. List "mammals" in a column on the left. Encourage students to suggest features or characteristics that at least one of the mammals possesses. Not all features have to be identified at this point. Some may be added later.

*Step 3:   Determining feature possession.* Put a plus (+) in the block if a particular mammal possesses the feature being considered or a (–) if it doesn't. The plus need not signal that the creature always possesses the feature; it can mean that it usually

does. If the group is not sure whether the mammal does or does not possess a particular feature, put a question mark in the box. Discuss items, especially those about which students are uncertain.

*Step 4:   Discussion of the grid.* Discuss the grid with the class. If it is missing some words or features important to the overall concept, add them. After the grid has been completed, discuss its overall significance. Have the class note major similarities and differences among the mammals. Encourage the group to sum up the ways in which mammals are the same and the ways in which they are different. Have students read *Wild Animals* to find out more about mammals.

*Step 5:   Extension.* After students have read *Wild Animals,* discuss it and extend the grid to include mammals described in the text but not listed on the grid. The class may also want to list additional features of mammals. The completed SFA grid is displayed in Figure 10.2.

### Venn Diagrams

**Venn diagram:** uses two or more overlapping circles to compare objects, people, or ideas. The overlapping spaces are used to show commonalities. The other spaces are used to show differences.

The **Venn diagram**, which is a device that uses overlapping circles, fosters the comparison and contrast of semantic features. In a Venn diagram, concepts are compared and contrasted. Features shared by the concepts are placed within overlapping circles. Characteristics peculiar to each concept are placed in the outer portions of the circles. A Venn diagram comparing and contrasting African and Asian elephants is presented in Figure 10.3. To make the comparisons more concrete, the diagram is illustrated with drawings of an African and an Asian elephant.

Although Venn diagrams may be used before reading, especially when students are reading a selection that compares and contrasts two items (electric-powered versus gas-powered cars, crocodiles and alligators, or toads and frogs), they probably work better as postreading organizers. Although Venn diagrams are widely used, frames matrices are often the better graphic organizer for making comparisons (Hyerle, 2001).

**Using Technology**

PBS Kids: Vocabulary Gameshttp:// pbskids.org/games/vocabulary.html

Features a variety of vocabulary games for younger students. Many of the games introduce new words.

**Using Technology**

NASA Vocabulary www.ueet.nasa .gov/StudentSite/vocabulary.html

Helps develop a space vocabulary.

## Other Vocabulary-Building Devices

Other vocabulary-building devices include possible sentences, predict-o-grams, simulations, word sorts, and the vocabulary self-collection strategy (VSS).

**FIGURE 10.2**
Semantic Feature
Analysis
*Source:* Gunning
(2010). Reprinted by
permission of Allyn &
Bacon.

| | eat plants | eat meat, fish, or bugs | babies born live | lay eggs | have pouches | can run or jump | can swim | can fly | hibernate | attack people | live on land | live in water |
|---|---|---|---|---|---|---|---|---|---|---|---|---|
| bats | ? | + | + | − | − | ? | − | + | + | − | + | − |
| bears | + | + | + | − | − | + | + | − | + | + | + | − |
| elephants | + | − | + | − | − | + | + | − | − | + | + | − |
| foxes | − | + | + | − | − | + | ? | − | − | − | + | − |
| giraffes | + | − | + | − | − | + | ? | − | − | − | + | − |
| kangaroos | + | − | + | − | + | + | ? | − | − | − | + | − |
| lions | − | + | + | − | − | + | ? | − | − | + | + | − |
| platypuses | − | + | − | + | − | + | + | − | − | − | + | − |
| seals | − | + | + | − | − | − | + | − | − | − | − | + |
| skunks | ? | + | + | − | − | + | ? | − | − | − | + | − |
| whales | + | + | + | − | − | − | + | − | − | − | − | + |

## Possible Sentences

Possible sentences, one of the simplest vocabulary-building techniques, may also be one of the most effective. It taps prior knowledge, arouses students' curiosity and interest, elicits predictions, fosters discussion, and helps students detect relationships among known and unknown words. As with many of the other vocabulary-building techniques, the first step in the possible sentences technique is to determine the major concepts that you want students to learn. Then list the key vocabulary needed to learn those concepts (Moore & Moore, 1986; Moore, Readence, & Rickelman, 1989). List six to eight potentially difficult words (Stahl & Kapinus, 1991). Then choose the same number of words that are necessary to understand the key concepts but that are easy.

Write the words on the board. Invite students to read them and tell what the difficult ones mean, but supply pronunciations and definitions if no one else can. Briefly discuss the words. Note that they are taken from a selection that students are about to read. Have them predict what the selection might be about. Then challenge students to create sentences in which at least two of the words from the list are used. The sentences should be ones that might appear in the text students are

**FIGURE 10.3**

Venn Diagram: Comparison of African and Asian Elephants

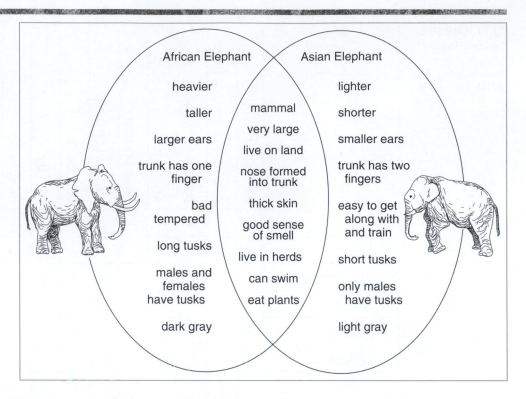

| African Elephant | | Asian Elephant |
|---|---|---|
| heavier | mammal | lighter |
| taller | very large | shorter |
| larger ears | live on land | smaller ears |
| trunk has one finger | nose formed into trunk | trunk has two fingers |
| bad tempered | thick skin | easy to get along with and train |
| long tusks | good sense of smell | short tusks |
| males and females have tusks | live in herds | only males have tusks |
| | can swim | |
| dark gray | eat plants | light gray |

about to read. Model the creation of one such sentence, explaining as you compose the statement why you think it might appear in the passage. Then have students create sentences. Note that words may be used in more than one sentence. Write students' sentences, including those that are not accurate, on the board. Stop after all the words have been used.

Next, have students read the selection to see how accurate their sentences are. After students have completed their reading, discuss the accuracy of their sentences. Encourage them to use the text as a reference to clarify confusions, resolve disputes, and back up assertions. Edit or delete sentences that are inaccurate. Students may also expand sentences to include new information garnered from the selection.

After discussing the sentences, encourage students to compose additional sentences using the words. This is especially important if students' sentences have not captured the key concepts in the selection. Since using new words in sentences is a difficult task, supply help as needed. Record the students' sentences on the board. Students may copy these sentences into their notebooks so that they have a record of key concepts contained in the selection.

A possible sentences exercise completed by a group of sixth-grade, low-achieving readers is presented in Figure 10.4. The exercise was written in preparation for reading the first chapter of *Ellis Island* (Reef, 1991), an easy-to-read book about the famous site.

### Predict-o-Grams

In an intriguing device called a predict-o-gram, the teacher has students group words that they believe will tell about characters, plot, setting, and other parts of a narrative (Blachowicz, 1986). Choosing words that are likely to be unfamiliar, as

**■ FIGURE 10.4**
Possible Sentences

| immigrants | ocean |
| voyage | ships |
| Ellis Island | America |
| processed | countries |
| descended | pass |
| inspection | harbor |

*Students' Sentences*

1. Immigrants from many countries came to America.
2. The immigrants made a long voyage by ship across the ocean.
3. After a ship docked, the immigrants were taken to Ellis Island.
4. Immigrants were processed at Ellis Island.
5. The immigrants had to pass an inspection at Ellis Island.
6. Many of us are descended from immigrants.

⚹ Predict-o-grams can also be used to reinforce the concept of story grammar, which is an analysis of the major parts of a story.

well as some known words, the teacher lists them on the board and discusses them with students. He then asks students to classify the words according to their prediction about how they will be used in the story. Will they be used to tell about setting, characters, problem, plot, or resolution? Students then predict the story.

Creating predict-o-grams helps students to think about new vocabulary words in terms of a story that is to be read. It also helps students relate the words to each other. After the story has been read, students should discuss their predictions in terms of the actual content and structure of the story. They should also revise their predict-o-grams, which provides them with additional experience with the new words. The predict-o-gram for "Hungry Spider," a trickster tale, is shown below.

| Setting | Characters | Story Problem | Plot | Resolution |
|---------|------------|---------------|------|------------|
| house | Spider | dinner | prepare | cried |
| river | Turtle | invite | refresh | floated |
|  |  | reluctantly | polite | surface |
|  |  |  | disappointed | morsel |
|  |  |  | famished |  |
|  |  |  | feast |  |
|  |  |  | pebbles |  |
|  |  |  | manners |  |

## Simulation

For certain abstract terms, where deep conceptual understanding is desired, you might try a simulation. For instance, to convey the concept of the Constitution, you might form cooperative learning groups and have students pretend that they were on a spaceship heading for Mars when the ship's guidance system broke down and they ended up on a distant planet. With no hope of ever returning to Earth, they have decided to set up a new country and to draw up a set of rules for the people in this new country. After students have completed drawing up their rules, discuss them. Lead students to see that this is what was done in 1789 in the United States. A meeting was held to set up a basic set of rules called the Constitution. Compare the rules set up by the group with the Constitution's major provisions.

## Word Sorts

As noted earlier, the word-sort technique is a categorization device that can be used to manipulate words. It can be especially useful for grouping technical terms (Tonjes, 1991). The words are placed on slips of paper or three-by-five cards, and the sorts can be open or closed. In a closed sort, students are given the category names. In an open sort, they must compose category names. An open sort forces students to see relationships and state what those relationships are.

Listed below is a completed sort taken from *Observing the Sky* (Stott, 1991):

| Planets | Constellations | Comets |
|---------|----------------|--------|
| Mercury | Scorpio | Halley |
| Venus | Taurus | Hale-Bopp |
| Earth | Ursa Major | Encke |
| Mars | Ursa Minor | |
| Jupiter | Draco | |
| Saturn | | |
| Uranus | | |
| Neptune | | |

## Vocabulary Self-Collection Strategy

When students personalize their learning, they become more active and more involved learners (Blachowicz & Fisher, 2000). One device designed to foster personal selection of new words is the vocabulary self-collection strategy (VSS) (Ruddell, 1992). In the VSS, each student chooses one word to learn. The word chosen should be one that the student believes is important enough for the whole class to learn. The teacher also selects a word. Each student records the sentence in which he or she found the word, if it is in a text, or describes the context in which he or she heard it, if it is from a lecture, conversation, TV show, movie, song, or other source. A student tells what she or he thinks the word means in the context in which it is found. He or she also explains why the class should learn the word.

Words are discussed and defined in context. Dictionaries and glossaries may be checked to make sure that the correct pronunciation and definition have been obtained. For the teacher, the discussion offers opportunities for modeling functional use of context clues and the dictionary. The teacher adds a word, and the class list is reviewed. Students choose words primarily because they seem important, useful, or interesting.

In addition to being an effective way to learn words, the VSS has the potential to turn passive students into active seekers of new words to learn. Realizing that they are responsible for selecting a word for the whole class to study, students suddenly become word conscious and begin noticing words as possible candidates for selection. As students, especially disabled readers, start attending to and thinking about words, they begin acquiring new vocabulary words at a sometimes surprising rate.

## Wide Reading

Once students are able to read challenging texts on their own, the best source of new words is through wide reading. If reading materials are on the appropriate level, average students have about a 15 percent chance of deriving the meanings of unfamiliar words from context (Swanborn & de Glopper, 1999). Out of 100 hard words, readers will be able to derive suitable meanings for 15 of those words. If students read a million words at 98 percent word recognition, they will encounter 20,000 unknown words. Learning 15 percent of them means that they will pick up

300 words through their reading. Of course, if they read more and learn to make better use of context clues, they will acquire more words.

Another reason wide reading is necessary for word learning is because readers might need to meet a word a number of times before deriving a meaning for it (Rapaport, 2004). Jenkins, Stein, and Wysocki (1984) estimate that it might require as many as six meetings before students accurately derive the meaning of a word from context and also have sufficient exposure to the word so that they remember it. One way of looking at word learning is the concept of layers of meaning. When first encountering an unfamiliar word, we might get a general impression of its meaning. With subsequent meetings of the word, we add to that general meaning and acquire a greater depth and breadth of knowledge of the word. In a sense, we learn a word bit by bit.

For free reading, students should be reading on or close to their independent levels (98 percent). Otherwise, they will be meeting too many unknown words and

## Vocabulary Self-Collection Strategy Lesson

A vocabulary self-collection strategy (VSS) lesson is initiated after the text has been read, because being familiar with the text helps students select words that are important. Here are the steps in the VSS procedure.

*Step 1: Selection of words.* Students select a word they would like to study. The selection process is usually done in small groups of two to five, with each group nominating one word. During the selection process, the students read the word as it is used in context, tell what they think the word means, and explain why they think the word is important to know. Some 8 to 10 words are nominated, and 5 or 6 are selected for the final list. If you are working with a small group of students, each student's word may be selected. The teacher may also nominate a word.

*Step 2: Discussion of words.* Words are listed on the board and their meanings as derived from context are discussed. If necessary, meanings are checked with a glossary or dictionary. Words selected are recorded in vocabulary notebooks or study sheets.

*Step 3: Extension.* Words are practiced and applied in a variety of activities.

## EXEMPLARY TEACHING

### Vocabulary Self-Collection Strategy

Using the vocabulary self-collection strategy as a part of an intervention program, middle-school reading teacher Brenda Shearer (1999) saw a dramatic improvement in her students' reading achievement and attitude toward learning new words and spelling. Students selected one word per week. The class's words were discussed on Monday. During the week there were additional discussions of the words and suggestions for learning their meanings and how to spell them. The students reflected on their word study in their journals. On Fridays they were tested on their ability to spell the words and were also required to use the words in meaningful sentences.

Students enjoyed choosing words. As one student explained, "I think that we should keep picking our own words because then we will want to study them more efficiently. If we get something handed or picked out by a teacher we don't want to study something we don't like" (Shearer, 1999). Another student explained how the activity had changed his attitude toward learning new words:

> Now I often catch myself and when I listen to music or listen to someone talk, I listen to the words they say and I find myself asking what the words mean. I try to make sure I understand what it means. I find that doing this helps me understand big words when I read them in a book or a textbook or even in a magazine. (Shearer, 1999)

so won't be able to use context clues. For vocabulary development, reading informational texts is especially important because these are the primary sources of an academic vocabulary (Nation, 2001).

The key to fostering reading among poor readers is to provide materials that are interesting to the students and that are on their level. These materials need not be books. They can be newspapers, magazines, Web sites, or how-to manuals. (See Chapter 15 for specific suggestions for motivating wide reading.) Books that are particularly effective for developing vocabulary are informational books and periodical articles, especially if they define words in context or provide illustrations that depict or clarify the meaning of terms. Listening to or reading along with recorded books is also a good way to build vocabulary.

## Developing Vocabulary through Reading Aloud

A rich source of vocabulary development comes from reading aloud. In one study, kindergarten-age children were able to pick up some new words through a single reading that involved no discussion of the new words (Senechal & Cornell, 1993). However, discussing the words resulted in even greater gains. Second graders learned 3 out of a possible 20 words through listening to stories. With discussion and teacher explanation, the students acquired eight of the words (Elley, 1989).

Since they generally do less reading, low-achieving readers, even older ones, should be read to on a regular basis. In addition to building background, this will also build vocabulary. Although a discussion or explanation of some hard words could be a natural nonintrusive aspect of reading aloud to students, care needs to be taken that you don't detract from the students' enjoyment of being read to.

To get the most out of reading aloud as a vocabulary builder, adopt a systematic approach such as that used in a technique known as Text Talk (Beck & McKeown, 2001). From each book or chapter two words were selected that were unfamiliar to students but that labeled known concepts. For younger students, these included words such as *reluctant, immense, miserable,* and *searched.* Unfamiliar words should usually be presented after the story has been read aloud. Although it is better to preteach words when students are reading on their own, it is preferable to discuss vocabulary words after a selection has been read aloud to students. If words are needed for an understanding of a selection, then they can be explained briefly as the selection is being read. This will enable students to use their knowledge of the new words to comprehend the selection.

Text Talk has six steps:

1. Present the word in story context after an initial reading.
2. Provide an easy-to-understand definition of the word. Be sure to display the written form of the word. This helps students store the word's pronunciation and meaning in memory (Rosenthal & Ehri, 2008).
3. Supply examples of the use of the word in other contexts, so that the word generalizes.
4. Help students relate the word to their lives.
5. Review the word.
6. Encourage students to use new words in their speaking and writing and also to note examples of hearing or seeing the words.

Here is how the word *reluctant* from *A Pocket for Corduroy* (Freeman, 1978) was presented:

*Step 1:* The teacher introduced the word *reluctant* to label Lisa's feeling. "In the story, Lisa was reluctant to leave the Laundromat without Corduroy."

*Step 2:* The teacher supplied an easy-to-understand definition of *reluctant* and also asked students to say the word so that they would use the spoken representation to help store the word in memory. "*Reluctant* means you are not sure you want to do something. Say the word with me."

*Step 3:* The teacher provided examples of the word. "Someone might be *reluctant* to eat a food that he or she never had before, or someone might be *reluctant* to ride a roller coaster because it looks scary."

*Step 4:* The teacher invited students to relate the word to their lives. To assist the children, the teacher provided a frame. "Tell about something you would be *reluctant* to do. Try to use *reluctant* when you tell about it. You could start by saying something like 'I would be *reluctant* to _____.' "

*Step 5:* The teacher reviewed the word. As appropriate, the teacher used the word in other contexts. "I am *reluctant* to go outside because it is so windy."

*Step 6:* One key to vocabulary development is to note other contexts in which new words are used. Students were urged to be on the lookout for examples of new words in the reading that they do or on TV shows that they watch or in conversations or discussions that they hear. In an activity known as Word Wizard, new words are posted on the wall. Underneath the words, the students' names are listed. Students are given a check when they report an instance of hearing the word spoken or using the word in their writing or speaking. Students with the most checks are given an award. In one study, Word Wizard proved to be a powerful reinforcer for helping students remember words. It was just as effective as a dozen or so practice exercises (Nagy, 2010).

## Teaching Vocabulary to English Language Learners

Having had excellent instruction in both English and Spanish, Miranda, an eighth grader, is reading on grade level in Spanish and is fluent in English. Although her decoding skills in English reading are on grade level, she has difficulty with comprehension. Because she has had less opportunity to develop English vocabulary, Miranda's English vocabulary development is limited. Especially lacking are the higher-level words she needs to comprehend her challenging content-area texts.

For Miranda and other ELLs, much of their word learning will involve learning the English equivalent of words already known in their first language. When Miranda learns the word *moon*, she need only associate it with the known Spanish word for moon, *luna*. Teaching cognates, words that have a common origin, also helps ELLs learn new words. The English word *insect* and the Spanish *insecto* both derive from the Latin *insectum* (see Table 10.2). Helping students recognize and use cognates will effectively build their English vocabulary.

For ELLs, word knowledge rather than pronunciation or grammar is the key concern. If you don't know the words, you have no chance of understanding what is being communicated or of communicating yourself. Miranda and other ELL students need a program of intensive vocabulary instruction, one that emphasizes acquisition of academic vocabulary.

Vocabulary poses a special problem for students who are still learning English. García (1991) found that more than 10 percent of the words used in a test passage were not known by Hispanic youngsters.

**Using Technology**

Spanish/English Cognates
http://www.moramodules.com/
MoraModules/SpEngCognates.htm
Provides practical suggestions for using cognates.

**TABLE 10.2**
Spanish Cognates

| | | |
|---|---|---|
| artista | famoso | música |
| autor | foto | necesita |
| bebé | favorito | nota |
| biografía | fruta | número |
| carácter | gigante | oficina |
| carro | gorila | página |
| causa | grado | papá |
| contento | hipopótamo | perfecta |
| describir | importante | rápido |
| diferente | insecto | teléfono |
| difícil | jirafa | tigre |
| elefante | mamá | tomate |
| enciclopedia | mágico | uniforme |
| eléctrica | mayo | vegetales |
| familia | minuto | zoológico |

*Source: Creating Literacy Instruction for All Students* (6th ed.), by T. Gunning. Boston: Allyn & Bacon. Reprinted by permission of Allyn & Bacon.

 **Using Technology**

Interesting Things for ESL Students
http://www.manythings.org

Provides a variety of vocabulary-building activities for ELLs that may be used by all students.

## Building Academic Language

English language learners acquire conversational language within a year or two, but it takes considerably longer—six years or more—to acquire the language of books and the classroom, which is known as academic language (Cummins, 1994). Academic language means learning Tier Two and Tier Three words, as well as the grammar and thinking skills necessary to formulate abstract thoughts and draw sound conclusions. The acquisition of background knowledge is also required so that students will have a range of topics and ideas to think about.

Academic vocabulary can be thought of as being made up of "bricks" and "mortar" (Dutro & Moran, 2003). The bricks are content-specific technical words, such as *carbohydrates, glucose, fats, calories*. The mortar consists of the words used to articulate the concepts represented by the technical words: *regulate, cause, supply*. The mortar words can be even more abstract than the brick words. Mortar words are also used to describe academic tasks: *analyze, contrast, evaluate*. Academic language also includes stock phrases, some of which use figurative language: *when all is said and done, what it all boils down to, read between the lines, see eye to eye* (Zwiers, 2008).

Although ELLs might be in the most need of learning academic language, their need is shared by at-risk students, students who speak a dialect other than mainstream English, and native speakers of English who have had limited exposure to academic language. These students require a deliberate and systematic introduction to the academic language needed to complete the kinds of discussion, reading, and writing tasks required of them. For instance, students should be taught the language that they will need to complete assignments: "Arrange the events in the order in which they occurred. Compare and contrast the two versions of the tale. Note three similarities." Students should also be taught what the words in directions for tests and assignments mean and how to respond to them. Sample questions should be answered as a group activity. You might supply starter sentences or frames to help students use academic language to respond: "_____ and _____ are similar in several ways. First of all, _____. Second of all, _____. Last of all, _____."

The Academic Word List (AWL) provides a practical starting point for developing the needed academic language skills. Because it has been drawn from college texts, the 510-word AWL presented in Table 10.3 has been adapted. Words not typically found in elementary or secondary texts have been eliminated, and words are listed according to three levels of tested difficulty: basic, intermediate, and advanced. Basic words are those known by 40 to 80 percent of students at the end of grade 2. Intermediate words are those known by at least 40 to 80 percent of students in grade 6.

Advanced words are those known by 67 percent or more of students in grades 8 to 12. Each level is split in two, with the first half being composed of the higher-frequency words and the second half being composed of the lower-frequency words in that level.

**TABLE 10.3**
Adapted Academic Word List

**Adapted Academic Word List: Basic A1 and A2**

**A1**

| | | | | | |
|---|---|---|---|---|---|
| accurate | enormous | positive | author | index | schedule |
| achieve | environment | previous | capable | initial | secure |
| adult | estimate | primary | channel | injure | structure |
| aid | expand | principal | clarify | insert | substitute |
| approach | expert | publish | conduct | inspect | sufficient |
| area | final | purchase | construct | instruct | sum |
| assume | function | remove | consume | investigate | summary |
| attach | goal | research | contribute | lecture | suspend |
| available | grade | respond | convert | likewise | target |
| aware | grant | reveal | convince | notion | text |
| challenge | image | route | cooperate | overlap | tradition |
| chapter | indicate | series | detect | overseas | transmit |
| chart | individual | shift | displace | participate | transport |
| chemical | involve | similar | display | plus | vehicle |
| code | issue | somewhat | dispose | precise | violate |
| communicate | label | task | draft | predict | visible |
| community | legal | team | drama | proceed | vision |
| compound | link | topic | edit | recover | |
| contact | locate | transfer | eliminate | register | |
| couple | major | uniform | emerge | reject | |
| create | medical | | error | relax | |
| culture | normal | **A2** | export | rely | |
| cycle | obvious | adjust | foundation | resolve | |
| design | occur | appreciate | furthermore | restrain | |
| device | paragraph | appropriate | globe | restrict | |
| encounter | period | assign | guarantee | retain | |
| energy | portion | assist | identical | reverse | |

*(Continued)*

**TABLE 10.3**
(*Continued*)

## Adapted Academic Word List: Intermediate B1 and B2

**B1**

| | | | B2 | | |
|---|---|---|---|---|---|
| abandon | expose | professional | **B2** | fee | preliminary |
| accompany | **feature** | project | access | flexible | prime |
| adapt | federal | range | accommodate | formula | priority |
| alter | file | react | assemble | fund | prohibit |
| alternative | focus | region | attain | generate | promote |
| apparent | fundamental | **release** | commence | ignorance | publication |
| approximate | generation | require | comment | imply | random |
| aspect | identify | resource | comprise | inevitable | reside |
| assure | illustrate | role | **confer** | insight | restore |
| attitude | impact | section | confirm | institute | revise |
| benefit | item | seek | consequent | intense | scheme |
| bond | journal | select | consult | **interval** | sole |
| brief | labor | sex | contrary | liberal | specify |
| capacity | layer | site | converse | license | sphere |
| category | maintain | source | core | manipulate | **strategy** |
| complex | mental | specific | correspond | manual | submit |
| conclude | method | stable | debate | margin | sustain |
| conflict | military | stress | derive | mechanism | tense |
| considerable | minimum | style | dimension | media | theme |
| consist | minor | survey | distribute | medium | trace |
| constant | nevertheless | survive | document | migrate | transit |
| credit | nuclear | symbol | domain | minimize | trend |
| data | obtain | tape | dominate | monitor | undertake |
| decade | odd | technique | duration | network | version |
| define | partner | technology | ensure | option | visual |
| definite | percent | temporary | equip | outcome | voluntary |
| demonstrate | phase | theory | equivalent | overall | welfare |
| depress | physical | unique | exceed | parallel | widespread |
| despite | policy | vary | exclude | perspective | |
| economy | potential | volume | exhibit | phenomenon | |
| element | principle | | exploit | philosophy | |
| establish | process | | extract | pose | |

## Adapted Academic Word List: Advanced C

**C1**

| | | | | |
|---|---|---|---|---|
| accumulate | evolve | ratio | commodity | integrate |
| acquire | explicit | regulate | compensate | integrity |
| adequate | external | revenue | compile | intermediate |
| affect | factor | revolution | complement | intervene |
| ambiguous | finance | rigid | comprehensive | levy |
| analyze | framework | sequence | compute | mode |
| annual | hence | significant | conceive | motive |
| authority | hypothesis | statistic | confine | mutual |
| bulk | impose | status | conform | nonetheless |
| cease | income | subsequent | contradict | offset |

| | | | | |
|---|---|---|---|---|
| circumstance | input | technical | controversy | passive |
| civil | instance | transform | crucial | quote |
| clause | intelligence | trigger | currency | rational |
| commission | internal | ultimate | denote | refine |
| component | interpret | whereas | diminish | regime |
| concentrate | invest | | discriminate | reinforce |
| concept | isolate | **C2** | distort | reluctance |
| consent | justify | abstract | diverse | scope |
| constitute | logic | academy | dynamic | straightforward |
| contemporary | mature | acknowledge | enhance | subordinate |
| context | modify | adjacent | erode | successor |
| contract | neutral | advocate | ethic | supplement |
| contrast | objective | amend | ethnic | terminate |
| decline | occupy | anticipate | format | thesis |
| deny | output | arbitrary | hierarchy | undergo |
| devote | panel | assess | highlight | underlie |
| distinct | perceive | attribute | implement | unify |
| domestic | precede | bias | incentive | utilize |
| emphasis | prior | cite | incline | valid |
| enable | proportion | classic | incorporate | via |
| enforce | prospect | coherent | induce | whereby |
| estate | psychology | colleague | initiate | |
| evaluate | pursue | commit | persist | |
| eventual | radical | coordinate | practitioner | |
| evident | thereby | corporate | predominant | |

*Source:* Adapted from Coxhead (2000).

***Word Generation and Alias*** Word generation is an interdisciplinary program designed to develop academic vocabulary. Words are drawn from the Academic Word List (AWL) and are embedded in content materials created for the program. The articles in which the words were embedded discuss high-interest but controversial topics, such as cyberbullying or paying students to do well in school. Each content-area teacher spends 15 minutes a week developing the words within his or her content area. On Monday, the English teacher introduces the words. On the next day, the math teacher presents the words in a word problem. On Wednesday, the science teacher presents the words in a science article. On Thursday, the social studies teacher has the students debate an article that contains the words. On Friday, the English teacher leads the students to develop a persuasive essay using the words. The persuasive essay is based on the controversial issue that was introduced on Monday. In addition to improving their academic vocabulary, students learn to discuss and write about controversial issues (Strategic Education Research Partnership, 2009).

Academic Language Instruction for All Students (ALIAS) is a vocabulary-building approach similar to Word Generation, except that it is designed to be implemented by language arts teachers. It was effective in building both academic vocabulary and, to a lesser extent, comprehension (Lesaux, Kieffer, Faller, & Kelley, 2010). Academic vocabulary was presented in 45-minute segments to sixth-graders four days a week in eight-day units.

Each unit was based on an interesting article from *Time for Kids,* a periodical published for students in grades 4 to 6. Words were introduced in the context of the selection. On day one, students read and discussed the article, and the eight or nine target words were introduced. On day two, use of context clues was discussed. Possible word meanings were brainstormed, and the class, under the teacher's direction, created an accurate definition. Class definitions were recorded. Students were encouraged to compose a personal definition by writing the class definition in their own words. On subsequent days, students, working in pairs, responded to questions about the text. The questions contained target words. In other activities, students drew representations of the words and completed similar reinforcement activities. Students then engaged in a morphological analysis of the target words and created a chart in which various forms of the target words were displayed: inflected forms, derived forms, and related words. For the word *suspicious,* the words *suspicion, suspiciously, suspiciousness,* and *suspect* were listed (Word Generation, 2010). Ultimately, words were used in speaking and writing. Discussions or mock interviews were held in which the target words were purposely used. Students then used the target words in written pieces. The writing activities were crafted so that they lent themselves to the use of the words. For instance, they responded to the prompt: "What *crucial* invention from the past one hundred years has most *affected* your daily life?" (Lesaux et al., 2010, p. 206). The italicized words are target words.

> **Using Technology**
>
> Word Generation
> http://wg.serpmedia.org/
> Provides a wealth of information about Word Generation.

## A Full Program of Vocabulary Development

Although this chapter has taken a strong stand in favor of direct, systematic instruction in vocabulary, it is important to take full advantage of informal incidental opportunities to learn new words. Don't restrict vocabulary study to a set amount of time each day or week. Bring in new words that appear in daily newspapers or TV shows, and encourage students to do the same. Often, words that are probably unfamiliar to students dominate the news: *inflation, recession, crimes against humanity, famine, scientific breakthrough.* If appropriate, bring these to students' attention and discuss them, or better yet, encourage students to contribute new words that they encounter. Pay special attention to the words that students are learning in science and social studies and other content areas. Reinforce these in many contexts.

Above all, create an interest in and enthusiasm for words. Play word games. Discuss puns and other verbal word play. Have a vocabulary bulletin board and a word of the day. Obtain a calendar that introduces new words. Discuss the etymologies of words, and track new words coming into the language. Take full advantage of digital dictionaries and glossaries. Use a variety of teaching techniques. Most importantly, provide students with the tools for learning new words and evoke the motivation to do so.

## Mini–Case Study

As you recall from the previous chapter, Andreas is an eighth grader who reads on a fifth-grade level. Although he has good solid average intelligence, good work habits, and a supportive family, he is struggling with reading, especially in the content areas. Although Andreas is able to decode single-syllable words, he stumbles over multisyllabic words. Instruction in multisyllabic patterns and the use of analogy and pronounceable word-part strategies improved his skill in that area.

However, because of a limited vocabulary, Andreas is struggling with his science and history texts, which at this level include many advanced, technical words. Andreas's score on the Peabody Picture Vocabulary Test and his struggle with words in his content-area texts indicate that his overall vocabulary development is lagging. For instance, in his reading, he did not know the meanings of words such as *haughty, sacrifices, circumference, decrease, aviation,* and *exaggeration,* words that the typical eighth grader knows.

In addition to teaching Andreas strategies for decoding difficult words and deriving meanings of new words using context or morphemic analysis, his teacher has devised a multifaceted program for developing new vocabulary. First of all, Andreas is encouraged to read widely from self-selected magazines, newspapers, Web sites, and books. Each week, he records on note cards 10 new words drawn from his reading. On one side of the card, he notes the word and the context in which it appeared and what he thinks the word means. On the other side of the card, he writes the dictionary or glossary definition, thus checking his use of context. He discusses his new words with a peer partner. The two also quiz each other on the new words. In addition, Andreas is encouraged to use his new words in his speaking and writing.

Efforts are being made to build Andreas's interest in words. When the word *narcissistic* cropped up, the teacher explained the history of the word. That led to a study of words based on the names of Greek and Roman deities. When Andreas had difficulty with *transportation,* other words containing *trans* and *port* were studied.

As he has an artistic bent, Andreas was encouraged to draw diagrams and label them. For instance, when studying the parts of the brain, he copied a diagram of the brain and labeled all of the major parts. Seeing relationships among words was also stressed. When studying words from a selection, Andreas has been encouraged to create a web, use semantic feature analysis, or use other graphic devices to help him understand how the new words were related.

Because Andreas's poor vocabulary was interfering with his comprehension of his science and history texts, an extra effort has been made to build a conceptual understanding of key terms before Andreas reads a selection. As a result, his understanding of content-area material has been showing an encouraging improvement.

## Summary

**B**ecause they do not read as much as achieving readers, problem readers usually don't have as large a store of vocabulary. This deficit grows worse as low-achieving readers progress through the grades. However, because it reflects background knowledge and speeds the reading process, vocabulary is the single most important factor in comprehension. To foster comprehension, vocabulary instruction must be intensive. It must go beyond definitional knowledge to a contextual or conceptual status, include multiple encounters, and develop relationships.

Vocabulary instruction can be incidental or systematic or both. In the incidental approach, vocabulary is taught as needed. In the systematic approach, time is set aside for vocabulary instruction on a regular basis, so there is more focus on direct vocabulary development. Approximately 400 words can be thoroughly taught in a systematic program in a year's time.

Principles of teaching vocabulary include establishing goals, building on what students know, building depth and breadth of meaning, creating an interest in words, relating words to students' lives, and promoting independent word learning.

Techniques for teaching words include conceptual teaching of key words and brainstorming techniques, such as the list–group–label and semantic mapping approaches. Graphic techniques include semantic mapping, pictorial maps and webs, semantic feature analysis, and the Venn diagram. Other vocabulary teaching techniques described in the chapter are possible sentences, predict-o-grams, word sorts, simulation, vocabulary self-selection strategy, and Text Talk. Wide reading and being read to were also discussed as ways of expanding vocabulary. Both English language learners and underachieving students need to have their academic language developed.

## Application Activities

1. Try creating a semantic map, Venn diagram, and semantic feature analysis for some words that you are learning. Evaluate the effectiveness of each device. What are the strengths of each? What are the weaknesses?
2. Compile a bibliography of vocabulary-building books, word games, or apps that you might use with current or future students.
3. Following the recommendations made in this chapter, plan a vocabulary development lesson. If possible, teach the lesson and evaluate its effectiveness.
4. Read about FAME, an exemplary vocabulary program, at http://www. readingonline.org/articles/art_index.asp?HREF=/articles/curtis/index.html. How might you use elements of this program with struggling readers that you are teaching or plan to teach?.

## MyEducationLab

Go to the topic **Reading Assessment** in the MyEducationLab (www.myeducationlab .com) for **Assessing and Correcting Reading Difficulties,** where you can:

- Find learning outcomes for **Reading Assessment** along with the national standards that connect to these outcomes.

- Complete Assignments and Activities that can help you more deeply understand the chapter content.

- Apply and practice your understanding of the core teaching skills identified in the chapter with the Building Teaching Skills and Dispositions learning units.

- Examine challenging situations and cases presented in the Iris Center Resources.

- Check your comprehension of the content covered in the chapter with the Study Plan. Here you will be able to take a chapter pretest, receive feedback on your answers, and then access personalized Review, Practice, and Enrichment exercises to enhance your understanding of chapter content. After you complete the exercises, take a posttest to confirm your comprehension.

- Practice targeting instruction and making content accessible for all students with A+RISE activities.

# 11 Building Comprehension

**USING WHAT YOU KNOW**

In a sense, this chapter is the core of the text. For the most part, the previous chapters covered techniques for teaching the kinds of beginning reading and word-level skills and strategies that make comprehension possible or enhance it. Three of the chapters that follow will explore ways of applying comprehension skills and strategies to the content areas, using comprehension skills to study, and using writing to improve comprehension.

This chapter presents comprehension as an active process in which the reader constructs meaning. When you are reading, what steps do you take to foster comprehension? What are some of the reasons students might have difficulty comprehending? What steps might be taken to help them?

**ANTICIPATION GUIDE**

*Read each of the following statements. Put a check under "Agree" or "Disagree" to show how you feel about each one. If possible, discuss your responses with classmates.*

|  | AGREE | DISAGREE |
|---|---|---|
| 1. A lack of background knowledge is the main cause of poor comprehension. | _____ | _____ |
| 2. How much readers comprehend depends mainly on the kinds of comprehension strategies that they use. | _____ | _____ |
| 3. Most low-achieving readers should have little difficulty learning highly effective comprehension strategies. | _____ | _____ |
| 4. The fastest way to improve comprehension is to use challenging materials. | _____ | _____ |
| 5. Generally speaking, comprehension deficiencies are easier to remediate than decoding difficulties. | _____ | _____ |

## ▦ Reading Complex Text

The Common Core State Standards (CCSS) call for a deep level of comprehension, a level that requires a significant amount of work on a reader's part, and often a struggle to construct meaning. In the past, perhaps feeling empathy for the difficulties that struggling readers endure, teachers tried to make the reading easy and so gave students simplified texts. While it is true that struggling readers need a firm foundation in decoding and fluency, these are not enough. Along with developing these essential skills, teachers need to develop struggling readers' ability to comprehend complex text. As Fisher, Frey, & Lapp (2012) note,

> Perhaps one of the mistakes in the past efforts to improve reading achievement has been the removal of struggle. As a profession, we might have made reading tasks too easy. We are not suggesting that we plan students' failure, but rather that students are provided with opportunities to struggle, and to learn about themselves as readers when they do struggle, persevere, and eventually succeed. (p. 11)

These next two chapters will emphasize techniques that lay a foundation for and also develop the ability to read complex text. However as the CCSS documents caution, "Students need opportunities to stretch their reading abilities but also to experience the satisfaction and pleasure of easy, fluent reading within them, both of which the Standards allow for" (National Governors Association Center for Best Practices and Council of Chief State School Officers, 2010b, p. 9).

## ▦ Theories of Comprehension

Comprehension was once seen as a passive process in which the reader's main mission was to grasp the author's message. Today comprehension is seen as an active process in which the reader plays a very active role, constructing meaning based on his or her cultural and experiential background, purpose for reading, and the overall setting. The most widely accepted description of this view of reading is schema theory. A related view of comprehension is expressed in the mental models theory of reading.

### Schema Theory

The ad sitting on the kitchen table caught my eye. In a boldface head, it was touting two books on farming. "Farm twice as effectively with half the effort!" A caption promised "Farming made easy with these two expert guides." The ad had been clipped by my wife, who intended to order the books. Since we don't even have a garden, much less a farm, I was puzzled by her interest in the books, until I read the rest of the ad.

What do you think the books will be about? What comes to your mind as you think about farming? My comprehension of the ad was based on my knowledge of farming. I pictured tall rows of corn, squealing pigs, bleating sheep, and a weathered barn. Even though I've never lived on a farm, I brought a fairly substantial background of knowledge to the ad. Had I grown up on a farm, I would have brought an even richer background to the ad. And that's what reading comprehension is. It isn't so much a matter of getting meaning from a selection; it's more a matter of bringing meaning to an ad, a story, or an article.

Comprehension is an active constructive process that activates our schema. A **schema** is a generic concept, composed of our past

> **Schema** (pl. schemata): abstract representation of knowledge organized and stored in memory. Schemata represent knowledge at various levels of abstraction. We can have a schema for baseball, growing tomatoes, liberty, and so on.

experiences and our knowledge organized and filed away (Rumelhart, 1980). Schemata (the plural of schema) are based on our background of experience. We have schemata for persons, places, objects, and events. We have schemata for apple orchards, zoos, air pollution, and vacations. The richer our experiences, both real and vicarious, and the better organized they are, the richer and more useful are our schemata.

In addition to our schemata based on life experiences, we also have schemata for the way stories are told and information is presented. Our schema for stories tells us that a fable teaches a lesson, so when we read a fable we search for the moral. Our schema for informational texts tells us that the main idea is often announced in the first sentence of a piece. Comprehension depends, to a large extent, on the adequacy of our schemata for world knowledge and our schemata for text. Schemata provide a framework for assimilating text information. If we are reading a mystery, our schema for mysteries tells us to look for clues. A schema helps us to make inferences. If there is a wolf in a fable, our schema for fictional wolves and fables alerts us to make the inference that the wolf will probably be intent on doing harm to someone.

Schemata also help us to determine what is important in a selection. Our schema for animals might alert us to focus on their life processes. Schemata also help the reader to monitor for meaning. If a story does not proceed as expected or the information does not fit in with what the reader knows, the reader may decide to reread to make sure that he has read the passage properly (Westby, 1999).

Comprehension is a flexible process. We may read something that conflicts with our ideas and concepts, so we must be prepared to modify our schema. And sometimes we have a schema but fail to activate it, or we activate the wrong schema, which is what I had done when I was reading the heading for the farming ad.

As I read further, I learned that the ad was about real estate farming, so I dropped my dirt farming schema and activated my schema about real estate farming. I realized that the word *farming* was being used in a figurative sense and referred to my wife's way of getting new clients. As a real estate agent, she has a "farm," an area assigned to her by the broker for whom she works. Each month she sends ads to the homeowners in her farm. Now the ad for the books made sense. However, had I not had indirect experience with real estate farming, I would not have had the proper schema to activate and so would have had some difficulty comprehending the ad.

---

The **surface code** is composed of the exact words and syntax of the written piece.

---

The **textbase** includes the ideas but not the exact words conveyed by the surface structure and low level inferences made by the reader.

---

A **situation model,** also known as a *mental model,* views comprehension as a "process of building and maintaining a model of situations and events described in text" (McNamara, Miller, & Bransford, 1991, p. 491). A situation model includes the reader's prior knowledge and inferences and judgments that the reader makes.

## Situation Models

Comprehension can also be thought of as the construction of a situation model or mental model. According to a situation model theory, comprehension consists of multiple levels of understanding and includes a surface code, propositional textbase, and the situation or mental model itself (Graesser, 2007; Kintsch, 1994). The **surface code** is composed of the exact words and syntax of the written piece. The **propositional textbase** contains the explicit propositions or ideas conveyed by the surface structure and some low-level basic inferences. The textbase retains the meaning of the text but not the form. Understanding a textbase involves making connections among words and phrases within sentences and making connections among sentences. The **situation model,** or mental model, consists of the representation of the situation constructed by the reader. A situation model is a representation of the ideas in the text enriched by the reader's knowledge (Hampton & Resnick, 2009).

A situation model for fiction is the imaginary world that the reader has created and features the main characters, including their emotional or mental states, the setting, and the story situation (Graesser & Bertus, 1998). The reader keys in on the apparent main character and creates a situation model of the circumstances in which the character finds himself or herself and also keeps track of the who, when, where, and why of a story (Zwaan, Radvansky, Hilliard, & Curiel, 1998).

The quality of the situation model is determined by the quality of the text-base representation and the richness of prior knowledge. When reading narrative text, readers are "explanation driven." They supply reasons for goals and actions. From their background knowledge, they generally have familiarity with situations depicted and so are to be able to establish connections (Coté, Goldman, & Saul, 1998).

In an expository text, the situation model reflects the key information in the text and the way it is organized. The situation model for a science article would include a representation or mental sketch of the physical parts of the system, the steps in the system's process, relationships among the parts of the system and the steps in its operation, and the ways in which people might use the system.

A situation model goes beyond what is explicitly stated and includes higher-level inferences the reader has made and the background knowledge the reader has. A textbase is an account of what the text says. A situation model is an account of what the text means. It relies more heavily on background knowledge and inferential processes (Duke, Pearson, Strachan, & Billman, 2011). A situation model is an example of knowledge transforming as opposed to knowledge memorizing, which is what the textbase represents.

Comprehension can be thought of as an interplay between construction of a textbase and use of prior knowledge. When prior knowledge is lacking, readers have a difficult time constructing a situation model. When constructing a textbase is difficult because there is a large proportion of unknown words, readers rely more heavily on prior knowledge and may even alter the text so that it fits in with their schema. When text is above the students' reading levels, they tend to create a fragmented textbase and fail to make connections among sentences. Processing becomes piecemeal, and retellings lack coherence (Coté et al., 1998).

Comprehension at a textbase level requires four main processing abilities: understanding key details at a literal level, integrating text across sentences and paragraphs, making basic inferences, and monitoring for meaning. Short-term, or working, memory is also an essential component (Cain, Oakhill, & Bryant, 2004). In a study of students classified as average readers, Beck and McKeown (2006) found a number of students who failed to construct even a basic textbase representation of what they had read. Note the following retelling, which is based on a reading of a passage about the Boston Tea Party:

> "It's about the Boston Tea Party, and it's about a whole bunch of, like, they were bringing loads over and its was rotten, and all that, so they went back and got more loads and dumped all the tea into the water." (p. 18)

The student recalled the name of the event but did not understand its significance. She failed to understand a key detail. She picked up a few scattered details but seemed to think the tea was dumped because it was rotten. She failed to integrate ideas across text and to infer the significance of details. She also seemed unaware that her representation of the text was confused and inaccurate. She was apparently not monitoring for meaning.

Similar confusion was seen in students' discussion of a story about horses on a farm that was struck by a hurricane. The story stated that the horses ran out of the barn. It then stated that Barney and Fred ran around wildly. No one in the small discussion group of fifth graders seemed to realize that Fred and Barney were horses. Although the students understood both sentences, they failed to connect the two sentences and infer that *Barney* and *Fred* were the names of horses.

One of the most basic but also most important skills that struggling comprehenders need to learn is how to make connections among sentences and among larger portions of text. Based on work with struggling readers who have difficulty making connections, Dewitz and Dewitz (2003) suggest that the teacher should model making connections and physically mark them. He should also note what kinds of connections are being made: between sentences, between paragraphs, to other texts, to background knowledge, and so on. Students should be encouraged to use sticky notes to indicate the connections that they are making as they read. As students become more proficient, sticky notes can be phased out and probes and prompts can be used to foster making connections. Probes can also be used to gain awareness of the processes the students are using so that adjustments can be made in instruction.

In the Dewitz and Dewitz (2003) study, the teacher also used texts that lent themselves to making connections. Before assigning a text, the teacher read the text twice. The first reading was to get an overview of the text. For the second reading, the teacher imagined himself to be a struggling reader. He noted the difficulties that the reader might encounter and the strategies and procedures that might be used to overcome those difficulties.

## Role of Surface Features

Compare the following two excerpts:

> Ford saw all this. But he didn't like it. The workers had to keep going back and forth to get parts. Again and again. Too many minutes and even hours were wasted. Ford was concerned. Such a great waste of _____ was disturbing. "There must be a better way," he thought. (DRP = 43)

> Henry Ford was the trailblazer of mass production in the automotive industry. When Ford began manufacturing, automobiles were usually assembled like houses, with the chassis fabricated at stationary locations where mechanics gathered around, attaching various parts. Assistants were constantly required to fetch materials, a practice that consumed numerous man-hours. Ford studied these production methods and was concerned. Such a great waste of _____ was disturbing. (DRP = 73)

Although both excerpts cover the same content, the second is written in a more complex style. In the second excerpt, vocabulary is more advanced, and sentences are longer and more complex. As might be expected, when presented with the full version of the more complex text, students' scores fell. Students were able to fill in 70 percent of the missing words in the less complex version but only 48 percent in the more complex one. As the sample passages suggest, surface features can impede comprehension (Touchstone Applied Science Associates, 2006, p. 2).

The performance on the sample passages highlights the importance of automaticity in decoding and of adequate language skills, including vocabulary. The difference in performance also underscores the importance of providing students with materials that are on their level.

## Causes of Comprehension Difficulty

Although schema deficiencies such as having inadequate background and poorly developed concepts, failing to activate relevant schema, and failing to use the four basic reading processes can cause comprehension problems, numerous other factors can also impede understanding.

Reader factors that might cause a comprehension problem include lack of basic decoding skills, limited vocabulary, overuse of background knowledge or a lack or flexibility in considering new ideas, failure to read for meaning, and a lack of strategies or failure to use **strategies** appropriately (MacGinitie & MacGinitie, 1989; Manzo & Manzo, 1993; Maria, 1990; Pressley, 2000). These factors, of course, interact with the task, the text, the techniques being used, and the situation. A reader may be successful with some kinds of tasks and in some environments but not with others. Although reader factors are emphasized in this chapter, other major reasons for comprehension difficulties involve inappropriate texts, teaching techniques, and instructional settings.

> **Strategies** are deliberate, planned procedures designed to help reach a goal. Previewing, predicting, summarizing, inferring, imaging, questioning, and monitoring for meaning are key comprehension strategies. When applied automatically strategies become skills.

## Approaches to Teaching Comprehension

There are two main approaches to teaching comprehension: strategy and content analysis. As McKeown, Beck, and Blake (2009) explain, "A major distinction between the two approaches is that strategy instruction encourages students to think about their mental processes and, on that basis, to execute specific strategies with which to interact with text. In contrast, content instruction attempts to engage students in the process of attending to text ideas and building a mental representation of the ideas, with no direction to consider specific mental processes" (p. 219). Of course, the approaches can be combined so that the reader attends to both strategies and content. In this chapter, strategy, content, and combined approaches are explored. This chapter also looks at approaches that are collaborative but that focus on content. That is, the approaches focus on analyzing ideas rather than the strategies used to comprehend those ideas.

## Comprehension Strategies

In breakthrough research, cognitive scientists discovered that when above-average learners were given a memorization task, they spontaneously used a series of strategies such as clustering like items and using mnemonic devices (Resnick & Hall, 2003). Given the same tasks, below-average learners did not use strategies. However, when taught strategies, they learned them quickly, and their performance improved significantly so that it was more in line with that of the above-average learners. However, when given the same tasks two weeks later, the below-average learners failed to use the strategies they had been taught.

From this and hundreds of similar experiments, cognitive psychologists have come to the conclusion that strategies are teachable and learnable. But it isn't enough to just teach them. It is essential to teach the strategies thoroughly enough so that they are learned deeply and so that they generalize to a variety of contexts. It is also essential that students learn when, where, and under what conditions to apply strategies.

## ▒▒ Implementing Strategies

The use of comprehension strategies strengthens the use of the main processes of basic comprehension: understanding, integrating, inferring, and monitoring. The use of strategies also bolsters working memory. Strategic readers are able to use four sources of knowledge in a flexible way: (1) knowledge of a variety of appropriate strategies; (2) knowledge of one's self as a learner; (3) knowledge of the demands of the reading task, which makes it possible for the reader to select, use, monitor, and evaluate strategies; and (4) background or world knowledge (Palincsar, Winn, David, Synder, & Stevens, 1993). In addition, readers must be motivated to use their knowledge of strategies (Paris & Okra, 1986) and have confidence that they will work (Dole, Brown, & Trathen, 1996). Garner (1994) concluded that a lack of interest in the text and a lack of confidence in strategies will diminish the students' willingness to use strategies.

Intensive step-by-step instruction is an essential element in strategy instruction. At the Benchmark School, a special school for disabled readers, students are taught one strategy at a time, with each strategy being taught, reviewed, and reinforced for nearly two months. A chart listing the steps of the strategy is displayed, and students discuss when, where, and how to use the strategy.

Strategy use is incorporated into reading lessons. Along with building background and introducing new vocabulary, Benchmark teachers introduce or review a strategy that students are expected to use in their reading. After reading a selection, students discuss it and describe ways in which they used the strategy in their reading. After a strategy has been thoroughly learned, a new strategy is introduced and related to the old one so that students learn how to integrate strategies. To foster transfer, strategies are applied to a variety of materials and especially to the content areas (Gaskins, 1998).

Intensive step-by-step instruction is also the foundation of the Strategic Instructional Model (SIM) developed by the University of Kansas Center for Research on Learning. SIM is a highly effective approach that uses learning strategies interventions to teach struggling readers. Students made impressive gains when instruction was thorough and intensive and they were given many opportunities for practice and application and received feedback on their performance. When instruction was minimal, gains were minimal.

> ▶ **Using Technology**
>
> Center for Research on Learning http://www.kucrl.org/sim/strategies.shtml
>
> Provides descriptions of a wide range of learning strategies.

### Steps in a Strategy Lesson

Strategy instruction has six steps: introducing the strategy, demonstrating and modeling the strategy, guided practice, independent practice and application, assessment and reteaching, and ongoing reinforcement and implementation. Each step can be described as follows:

*Step 1.    Introducing the strategy.* Explain what the strategy is, why it is being taught, how it will benefit students, and when and where it might be used.

*Step 2.    Demonstrating and modeling the strategy.* Show how to use the strategy. Model the process, and do a think-aloud as you demonstrate activation of the strategy. If possible, select a text that was difficult for you, so that the think-aloud seems real to the students. Have students note the difficulty you are having and the steps you are taking to resolve it. Provide examples of situations in which you or others have used the strategy effectively. Sum up by providing students with clear, specific directions for applying the strategy. If possible, incorporate a mnemonic. For instance, RAP is used as a mnemonic for a paraphrasing strategy: **R**ead a paragraph. **A**sk yourself: What are the main idea and details in this paragraph? **P**ut the main idea and details in my own words (Berry, Hall, & Gildroy, 2004). Post a list of the steps in the classroom.

*Step 3.    Guided practice.* The guidance provided might be extensive initially, but you should gradually turn over more responsibility to students. In the beginning, the teacher does most of the talking, but students help out. The teacher and students apply the strategy cooperatively to a brief paragraph. Students explain how they are applying a strategy so that the teacher can provide clarification or corrective feedback if necessary and other students gain insight into the process of applying a strategy (Berkeley et al., 2011). Later, students do most of the work, and the teacher provides assistance. Although a strategy might be taught to the whole class, Boyles (2004) recommends that guided practice be completed in small groups of from four to six in the earlier grades and up to eight in the upper grades. With this arrangement, students can be grouped according to reading ability, and instruction can be geared to their level of development. As part of guided practice, you might have students work in pairs, in which one student implements the strategy and the other checks the implementation; then have them switch roles. In the initial stages of guided practice, it is a good idea to use materials that are brief and relatively easy. That way, students can focus their full mental energies on applying the strategy. However, as students gain proficiency, they should apply the strategies to text that gradually increases in complexity. Strategy guide sheets might be used to provide directions for each step, examples of each step, and suggestions for additional things to try if the strategy wasn't working.

Strategy steps for student self-questioning might include (a) "turn headings and subheadings into questions," (b) "read the section," (c) "stop!" and (d) "try to answer your question." Repair strategies to be used in case the strategy didn't work included (a) "reread that section (in case you missed something important)," (b) "check your understanding of vocabulary," (c) "look for other text structures (maps, graphs, pictures) that can help you," and (d) "write down questions to ask your teacher" (Berkeley et al., 2011).

Strategy monitoring sheets might be used to check on students' use of a strategy. For the self-questioning strategy students record their questions and note whether they were able to answer them. Using the first heading in the book *Polar Bear, Shrinking Ice* (Person, 2011), which is "The Polar Bear Capital," students might pose the question "What is the polar bear capital?" (see Figure 11.1). If students are able to answer the question, they circle "yes" and go to the next section, "A Freezing Home," and repeat the process of using the heading to pose a question, then answering the question, and checking the monitoring sheet. If students are not able to answer either, they circle "no" and try a repair strategy. As students become proficient with a strategy, the strategy sheets and monitoring sheets are gradually phased out. As a part of the instruction, students discuss techniques they used to come up with good questions and also any difficulties they had applying the strategy (Berkeley et al., 2011).

In a study by Berkeley and colleagues (2011) using this same format, students were taught a summarizing strategy, and their performance was compared with a group who used a widely available commercial program. Both groups improved. The commercial group did as well as the strategy group on literal multiple-choice questions. However the strategy group, did significantly better on a test that assessed the ability to answer open-ended questions, thus indicating the value of carefully planned instruction.

**FIGURE 11.1**
Sample Self-Questioning Strategy Monitoring Sheet

Polar Bear, Shrinking Ice

Directions: Write down questions that you will answer while reading:

Heading: The Polar Bear Capital

Question #1: What is a polar bear capital?

_____

Can you answer your question? Yes    No

Heading: A Freezing Home

Question #2: What makes the polar bear capital a freezing home?

_____

Can you answer your question? Yes    No

Subheading: Staying Warm

Question #3: How do polar bears stay warm?

Can you answer your question? Yes    No

_____

Subheading: Staying Cool

Question #4: How do polar bears stay cool?

_____

Can you answer your question? Yes    No

Subheading: At Home on the Ice

Question #5: How do polar bears live on the ice?

_____

Can you answer your question? Yes    No

*Step 4. Independent practice and application.* Strategy learning is contextual. The application of a strategy tends to be limited to the context or subject in which it was learned. To promote transfer, have students apply the strategy to a variety of materials and content areas.

*Step 5. Assessment and reteaching.* Observe students to see if they can apply the strategy and can do so effectively. Also conduct a brief written assessment. Reteach and review as necessary.

*Step 6. Ongoing reinforcement and implementation.* After a month or so of practice and application, students should have a grasp of the strategy. They can then add it to their repertoire and move on to learning the next strategy. However, you should continue to review the strategy from time to time and also remind students to use it, perhaps by offering cues. Cues differ from scaffolds because they provide brief reminders but do not "tell us all that we are to do or say" (Beyer, 2001, p. 421). To cue students, simply mention the name of the strategy to be used or provide a brief description of it; you might also ask students to tell what strategy they might use in a particular situation, point out a chart containing the strategy, or refer to a mnemonic that reminds students of the main steps of a strategy. (For example, a mnemonic for one summarizing strategy is WITS: **W**rite the main idea. **I**nclude only the key details. **T**ake out unimportant details and unnecessary words. **S**mooth out the summary.) Mnemonics and other cues might be placed on charts or bookmarks.

To reinforce strategy use in your postreading discussion of a selection, talk over the strategies that were used. You might ask "What strategies did you use?" If there is no response, use more specific questions: "Did you ask questions as you read? Did pictures pop into your mind as you were reading?" Ask students to support their responses by reading portions of the text: "What part of the text caused that picture to pop into your mind? Can you read it for us? What part of the text led you to ask questions?" Also discuss how using a certain strategy helped students understand the text: "How did using that strategy help you to understand what you were reading?"

When teaching strategies, build on what students know. By the time students reach the intermediate grades or middle school, they might have been taught a number of strategies. Find out what strategies students have been taught, and build on that knowledge. Students might need a review to use these strategies effectively.

Also consider teaching strategies as part of a group, instead of individually. Doing so helps foster comprehension. Because skilled reading involves knowing not only how to apply strategies, but when and where to apply them and which ones work best together, it is helpful to implement a procedure that involves several complementary strategies so that students can see how these work together (National Reading Panel, 2000).

There are dozens of comprehension strategies. However, they can be classified according to the cognitive operations that they incorporate: preparing, selecting and organizing, elaborating, rehearsing (studying), and monitoring. There are also affective or motivational strategies (Weinstein & Mayer, 1986).

## Preparational Strategies

| This text has organized strategies according to the cognitive processes that they demand. There is some overlapping. For instance, all strategies should involve some degree of monitoring. |

Preparational strategies are those that a reader uses to prepare for reading. These include activating prior knowledge, previewing a selection, predicting what might happen in a story or what information a nonfiction piece will convey, and setting a goal for reading.

Before reading a selection about acid rain, the reader asks herself: "What do I know about acid rain?" If there is a prereading discussion, the teacher might activate prior knowledge. If poor readers fail to activate prior knowledge, they may not connect information in the text with what they already know. A good way to teach activating prior knowledge is through modeling. If you model the process, use a real-life example: a piece that you are reading. For instance, you might say "I'm taking a class at night. And for homework I have to read about the brain. At first, I thought, 'This article is going to be really hard. I don't know anything about the brain.' But then I said to myself, 'Yes, I do. Let's see. I know the brain has two sides: the right hemisphere and the left hemisphere. I also know the brain has parts called *lobes* and billions of nerve cells called *neurons*.' "

### Setting Purpose and Goal

The purpose for reading might grow out of activating prior knowledge. For instance, in the previous example, your activation of prior knowledge may cause you to realize that you know that the hemispheres of the brain are connected, but

The **purpose** for reading is the information that you seek, a question to be answered, or a prediction to be assessed. A **goal** is your objective for reading. Are you reading for pleasure, to follow a set of directions, or to prepare for a test?

Low-progress readers often lack a purpose or clear goal in reading. Discuss goals and purposes with students. Ask: "Why are you reading this? What do you hope to find out?"

you aren't quite sure how they are connected. Your **purpose** (question to be answered) in reading might then be to find out how the hemispheres of the brain are connected.

Readers also need to set a **goal** for reading. If you are reading just for your own information, your reading may be casual. If you are preparing for a test, then you would adopt a study style of reading. Your goal would be to both understand and retain what you had read. Model for students how you might set a purpose and a goal for your reading.

## Previewing

Previewing is a natural accompaniment of predicting. In previewing, the reader spends a minute or two reading the title, headings, the first paragraph or introduction, and the last paragraph or summary and then scanning any illustrations, charts, graphs, or tables that accompany the piece. As readers preview, they gain an overview of the piece they are about to read. They should also activate schema, make predictions, set a purpose for reading, and create a plan for reading the piece. Should it be skimmed? Should it be read slowly and carefully? Should it be read section by section? Should it be read as a whole? A good preview can function as a framework for organizing the main ideas in a selection or as "a kind of a blueprint for constructing a mental model" (Gunning, 1996, p. 198).

## Predicting

Making predictions depends on the students' background. Students have a more difficult time if they are reading about an unfamiliar topic, because they have little basis for predicting.

A highly popular strategy, **predicting** forces the activation of prior knowledge. Using a prediction strategy, a reader makes an educated guess about the course of events in a story or the kind of information that will be contained in a nonfiction piece. We make predictions on the basis of what we know. Predictions can also determine our purpose in reading. We may read the selection to compare our predictions with what actually happens.

It is important to use this strategy flexibly. Poor readers sometimes fail to modify their beliefs when they read information that contradicts these beliefs. These students need to be prepared to modify predictions based on information contained in the text.

# Selection/Organizational Strategies

Selection/organizational strategies involve integrating textual information in some way. Specific strategies include making connections between ideas, deriving the main ideas, selecting relevant details, organizing details, summarizing, and creating graphic organizers. Of these strategies, deriving the main ideas and summarizing are the most essential.

## Deriving Main Ideas

When the vocabulary in a selection is difficult, as it so often is for poor readers, readers' focus must be on decoding and processing smaller units of text, perhaps only two- or three-word segments (Kletzien, 1991). Caught up in looking at individual words and details, readers may fail to grasp main ideas. The main ideas provide the underlying pattern for organizing a passage's vital details. Being able to derive main ideas is a prerequisite for summarizing, note taking, outlining, and creating graphic organizers.

Definitions of what comprises a main idea vary as do the activities designed to promote grasping the main idea (Baumann, 1986). A **main idea** can be best thought of as a summary statement that subsumes all of the details in a piece of writing. The main idea of a paragraph would include what all the ideas in a paragraph are about. It is not necessarily the most important idea; rather, it is the gist of the piece, a one-sentence summary of its message. It fits in with the strategies of determining importance and summarizing.

> **Main idea:** what a piece of writing is all about—the gist or summary statement of the passage.

In essence, constructing the main idea is a classification exercise. The reader must note similarities among the details in a paragraph and then must choose the sentence that tells about all the others (if the main idea is stated) or construct a statement that includes all the details in a paragraph (if the main idea is not stated).

A good way to initiate main idea instruction is to have students classify items, ideas, and whole sentences. For instance, young children can be asked to sort objects in a classroom and give those sorted objects a name. Students might sort toys or tools. Later, they can categorize words, indicating which word tells about all the others: *lions, elephants, whales, animals, dogs*. To foster categorizing, have students play Twenty Questions. The student tells in which category the mystery item falls. Categories can vary depending on the age of the students. Possible categories include animals, sports, countries, food, people, sports, and hobbies. The person(s) trying to guess the identity of the item ask a series of questions, up to 20. For the category people, the person might ask "Is it a man? Is he living now? Is he famous?"

Once students have grasped the idea of categorizing, they can classify the sentences in a paragraph and tell which sentence tells about all the others. In the following paragraph, for example, students should be able to tell that the first sentence states the main idea:

> Soybeans can be eaten in many different ways. Soybean flour and oil are used to make pancakes, cookies, candy bars, soups, and many other foods. Soybean flour is used to make foods that look and taste like meat. Soybeans can also be used to make a sauce that adds flavor to foods.

After students have become adept at picking the sentence that "tells about all the others," omit the main idea sentence from the paragraph and have them generate a main idea statement. This is a far more difficult task, so provide guidance as needed. Also reinforce the concept of the main idea by helping students use titles, topic sentences, headings, and subheads as clues to main ideas in a text. In a study by K. K. Taylor (1986), many students, but especially poor readers, failed to use titles and topic sentences to derive main ideas in selections, even though both contained the main idea of the passage.

> Understanding main ideas is partly developmental. Over the years the ability to select a main idea improves. In addition, students' ideas of what is important in a selection change as they mature.

Eventually, students should derive main ideas from real paragraphs in real books. Start with brief paragraphs that have a clearly stated main idea in the first sentence. Then move into longer selections and include ones in which the main idea sentence appears in the middle or end of a paragraph. Although the main idea or topic sentence can appear anywhere in a paragraph or may even be implied, poor readers tend to select the first sentence as the topic sentence (Gold & Fleischer, 1986).

Drawing from children's books or textbooks, choose well-written paragraphs that contain topic sentences that appear in various places in the paragraph. Social studies texts are a good source. Nearly half of the paragraphs in social studies texts contain topic sentences. However, these appear as the first sentence of the paragraph only 27 percent of the time (Baumann & Serra, 1984). As students choose topic sentences, have them verify their selections by explaining how other sentences in the paragraph support the main idea.

Apply the concept of main idea to longer pieces of writing. In a well-written science or social studies text or informational children's book, point out main ideas. Discuss the fact that just as paragraphs have main ideas, so, too, do sections of text. Show how headings often indicate the main idea of a whole section.

***Implied Main Ideas*** Adapting the strategies used by expert readers (Afflerbach, 1990), teach students to imply main ideas by implementing the following steps:

1. Use textual cues (title, heading, major illustrations, introductory sentence) to construct a tentative main idea statement.

2. As you read the passage, judge whether the sentences support the tentative main idea. If not, revise the main idea statement.

3. After reading, judge whether all or most of the sentences support the main idea. (Often, in well-written prose, passages will contain a sentence or two that is kind of an aside, a detail that may be interesting and related to the overall topic but that does not support the main idea). If most of the sentences do not support the main idea, then see what all or most of the sentences have in common and construct a main idea statement that tells what they are about.

Begin with brief passages, and gradually introduce longer segments of text. If possible, have students apply the steps to texts that they use in their content-area subjects. Also use writing to reinforce the concept of main ideas. Help students develop topic sentences into well-constructed paragraphs. You might use paragraph frames similar to the ones in Figure 11.2 to assist students. Once students have achieved a basic understanding of topic sentences, encourage them to compose and develop their own.

## Summarizing

**Summarizing** is the most effective comprehension strategy of all (Pressley, Johnson, Symons, McGoldrich, & Kurita, 1989). Summarizing is a method for both improving and checking comprehension. Because it involves selecting, organizing, and restating the main details in a passage, summarizing enhances understanding and promotes retention. It also forces a self-evaluation of comprehension. If you have not comprehended a selection adequately, you will not be able to summarize it.

> **Summarizing** is difficult. In addition to selecting the most important information, the summarizer must condense information by combining and synthesizing ideas. One practical way to get students to summarize is to provide limited space for the summaries (Stahl, 2004).

Summarizing should not be confused with retelling. In a retelling, students may tell all that they know or all that they can remember. In a summary, only the important details are retold, and they are related in condensed form (Maria, 1990). Although it involves paraphrasing, summarizing should not be confused with paraphrasing. Paraphrasing consists of translating text into one's own words. It does not necessitate selecting only the most important information and condensing it. One of the reasons summaries are difficult to compose is that they involve two processes: selection of important details and reduction or condensation of these details (Hidi & Anderson, 1986).

***Teaching Summarizing.*** Although summarizing demands adequate comprehension, writing a summary involves more than just understanding a passage. It also

**FIGURE 11.2**
Paragraph Frames

FRAME 1

Some fish have names that tell what they look like.
The glassfish _____.
The pipefish _____.
The parrotfish_____.
These fish have names that really fit.

FRAME 2

Computers are one of our most useful tools. Computers are used

_____.
Computers also _____.
Computers can even _____.
Now we wonder how we ever got along without computers.

FRAME 3

My favorite day of the week is _____.
For one thing, _____.
For another, _____.
Best of all,_____.
It's too bad there aren't two _____ in every week.

entails using specialized writing skills (Taylor, 1986). Because written summaries involve complex writing skills, instruction might be initiated with oral summaries.

Although oral summaries are more exacting than retellings, retellings can provide solid preparation for summarizing. To make retellings more valuable, guide students so they emphasize essential details. Through careful questioning, help them highlight the most important information. Ask questions such as "What was the most important thing that Marisol did? What three things happened to James?"

The strategies used to grasp main ideas can also form a basis for summarizing. Surveying a text provides an overview of the main ideas in a selection. Predicting also tends to make the reader focus on major events and ideas.

Use naturally occurring occasions to model summarizing. For instance, after explaining that you are summarizing, sum up a demonstration, lecture, or discussion. Summarize the main events in a story or the major details in a science or social studies article. As students catch on to the idea, ask them to summarize a discussion, a current event, or a section from a story or article.

Some students believe that summaries should feature the most interesting or most difficult details in a selection or sentences from the selection that are richly detailed (Taylor, 1986; Winograd, 1984). Stress the fact that summaries should feature the most essential details. The most important ideas are those that are essential for an understanding of the text. If taken out, the text would not fully convey its meaning. They are details that have been stripped of elaborative sentences that might accompany them. To help students get a sense of the difference between essential and nonessential details, cooperatively examine a range of brief texts and select the most important details. You might also put the sentences of a paragraph to be summarized on a series of cards or slips of paper (Kissner, n.d.) and have the students sort the sentences according to those that are important and should be a part of the summary and those that are of minor importance and so could be left out. This is especially helpful for students who have working-memory problems. If students work in pairs or groups they can discuss how the sentences should be sorted. This helps them to think more deeply about their choices. Kissner (n.d.), who has worked extensively with summarizing, has pairs of students read an article and then put the scrambled sentences from the article in order. The pairs then sort the sentences according to those that are essential and those that are nonessential.

Paraphrasing is also a key skill in summarizing. Initially students may copy whole sentences or phrases or even whole blocks of text, instead of paraphrasing. This occurs especially when students are reading text about unfamiliar topics and don't understand the text well enough to paraphrase. However, this can be a practical starting point for struggling readers to come to a better understanding of what they have read. As they gain in skill, they can be led to copy less and paraphrase more. They can use a "reappropriation strategy" in which they use some of the text's words but also use some of their words (Collins & Madigan, 2010). However, they also need direct instruction in paraphrasing and lots of guided practice.

***Developing Written Summaries***   Written summaries can be private or public (Hidi & Anderson, 1986). Private summaries are written for the benefit of the student writing them, and so need not be polished. Public summaries are designed to be read by the teacher or others and so should be polished. Hence, public summaries are more difficult to write. To introduce summary writing, examine model summaries and discuss the qualities of an effective summary such as "Begins with a statement of the main idea, includes most important details, ideas are combined, unnecessary words are left out, summary is clear." Provide exercises in which students select from three or four summaries the one that is best. Discuss why the best summary is better than the other options. Model the process of composing a summary. List the steps for composing a summary and post these along with a model summary as in Figure 11.3.

Compose group summaries in which students help with the composition of the summaries and provide scaffolded practice, such as using frames and summary organizers to compose summaries as in the examples in Figure 11.4 and Figure 11.5. Initially, focus on the need to state the main idea and include essential information in a summary. Once students exhibit these skills, work on combining ideas and condensing.

---

1. Determine the main idea.
2. Write the main idea.
3. Write the most important details that support the main idea.
4. Shorten the summary. Combine ideas. Get rid of ideas that are not important. Get rid of unnecessary words.
5. Read over the summary. Make sure that it has the main idea and key details. Make sure that it is clear.

Model Summary

A bat uses its ears to find its way. It makes sounds and then listens for the sounds as they bounce off objects and return. It can tell where the object is by how long the sound waves take to return.

**FIGURE 11.3**
Steps for Writing a Summary

■▪ **FIGURE 11.4**
Service Dogs at
Work
*Source:* Gunning.
(2010), p. 127.

Many service dogs wear special vests. Some vests have patches on them. The patch tells what kind of work the dog is doing. The patch might say "Hearing Dog" or "Search Dog." The vest and the patch inform people that the dog is working. Most people don't know what to do when they see a service dog. If you notice a service dog at work, the best thing to do is to do nothing. Don't talk to the dog. Don't call it. Don't feed it. Don't pet it. The dog is working. It is helping its owner, so don't distract it. Taking the dog's attention away from its work just makes its job harder.

Many service dogs wear special vests to let people know _____

_____.

If you a see service dog at work, _____.

*Checking the Summary*   After the summary has been written, ask: "Did we begin the summary with a statement of the main idea or topic sentence? Did we include all the important information? Are there any ideas up there that we could leave out because they are aren't very important? Are the key ideas listed in order? Have we expressed our ideas clearly? Can we shorten our summary? Are there any unnecessary words that we might take out?" Also use a rubric, such as the one in Figure 11.6 that was adapted from Kissner (n.d.), for assessing students' summaries. Share the rubric with students so they understand what is expected of their summaries.

*Graphic Organizers as Summaries*   Graphic organizers can also be used to summarize text. Because they do not necessitate writing a paragraph, graphic organizers are easier to create than traditional summaries. Graphic organizers also do a better job of highlighting important information and showing relationships among ideas. Graphic organizers can be written in their own right or used in preparation for composing a written summary.

Graphic organizers that might be used to create summaries include semantic maps, which were introduced in Chapter 10. A sample semantic map summarizing a brief text on fruit is displayed in Figure 11.7. For additional examples of graphic organizers used with content-area texts, see Chapter 12.

Graphic organizers are only as effective as the manner in which they are made a part of the lesson. At a minimum, Merkley and Jefferies (2001) suggest following these steps when using graphic organizers:

▶ **Using Technology**

Visit http://www.graphic.org/goindex. html to find a wealth of information about graphic organizers. The site features a wide variety of downloadable text organizers.

- Verbalize relationships (links) expressed by the visual
- Provide opportunity for student input
- Connect new information to past learning
- Make reference to upcoming text
- Seize opportunities to reinforce decoding and structural analysis (p. 352)

■▪ **FIGURE 11.5**
Summary Graphic
Organizer

| What is the main idea? | |
|---|---|
| What are the key supporting details? | |

**◼ FIGURE 11.6**
Rubric for
Assessing a
Summary

| | Advanced | Basic | Developing |
|---|---|---|---|
| Main idea | States main idea clearly. | States main idea, but it may be awkwardly expressed. | Fails to state main idea. |
| Essential details | States all of the important details. | States most of the important details. | Missing some important details. Contains unimportant details. |
| Organization | Ideas or events are told in order. | Ideas may not be in best order. | Lacks organization. |
| Paraphrases | Summary is told in student's own words | Portions of summary are paraphrased. | Summary consist mainly of sentences directly copied from text. |
| Condenses ideas | Details are combined where possible. | Some details are combined. | Details are not combined. |
| Condenses language | Does not have unnecessary words. | Some words could be omitted. | A number of words could be omitted. |
| Clearly written | Summary is clear and easy to follow. | Summary is mostly clear. | Summary is not clear. Summary may be awkward and confusing. |

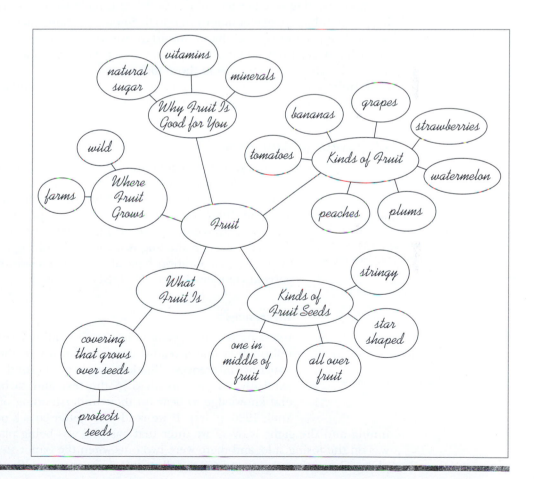

**◼ FIGURE 11.7**
Semantic Map
*Source:* Robinson
(1992).

■ **FIGURE 11.8**
*Somebody Wanted
But So* Summary

| Somebody | Wanted | But | So |
|----------|--------|-----|-----|
| [Bessie Cole-man | To learn to fly | She couldn't find anyone in the United States to teach her. | She saved her money and traveled to France to learn. |

### Summarizing with Somebody Wanted But So

*Somebody Wanted But So* is a structured way to help students summarize a narrative piece (Beers, 2003). As shown in Figure 11.8, the structure is simple. Students make four columns, one for each word. Under the *Somebody* column, students place the main character's name. Under the *Wanted* column, students list what the main character wanted to do. This is generally a statement of the main character's goal in the story. In the *But* column students add a statement of the conflict or the problem that the main character ran into. The resolution or the outcome of the main character's efforts to achieve a goal is placed in the *So* column.

In some instances, students might be able to sum up the whole story with one set of statements. In other instances, they might only note a part of the story and will need to add to it. Students can add a *then* and fill in another set of *Somebody Wanted But So* statements. If there is more than one main character, students can write more than one set of statements.

Summarizing is somewhat subjective. What is included in a summary depends, in part, on what the reader determines to be important. Summaries can be too brief or too lengthy. On the one hand important information is being left out; on the other hand, relatively unimportant information is being included. Summaries that are too lengthy are preferable to those that are too brief. It is easier to delete relatively unimportant information than it is to go back to the text and locate important details that should have been included but weren't.

## Elaboration Strategies

Using elaboration strategies, the reader transforms, judges, applies, or adds to information from the text in some way. Through elaboration, the reader may draw an inference, create a mental image, or evaluate the material that was read. Inferring is the main basic comprehension process in this set of strategies. However, higher-level processes are tapped, especially when evaluating is involved. Involving a deeper level of processing, elaboration typically improves comprehension by 50 percent (Linden & Wittrock, 1981).

⁂ Elaboration strategies are built on preparational and organizational strategies. Information cannot be transformed, evaluated, or applied unless it is first understood.

### Inferences

**Inferences:** the implied details, judgments, or conclusions that readers make based on their background knowledge and/or information in the text.

Inferring is a main elaboration at all reading levels. Much of the information that a reader derives from text is the result of constructing **inferences**. Readers must go beyond what is stated explicitly "to link up ideas in the text and to bring their general knowledge to bear on their understanding of it" (Oakhill & Yuill, 1996, p. 69). If we read "the batter struck out in the ninth inning and the game is over," we infer that baseball was being played, the batter was on the losing side, and there were two outs when the batter stepped up to the plate. The author does not have to tell us this. Inferences are the implied details, judgments, or conclusions that readers construct as they read. Inferences are based on readers' schemata and/or information contained in the text.

Because answering inferential questions requires combining information in the text with background or prior knowledge, having an impoverished background is one possible cause of having difficulty making inferences. Ironically, McCormick (1992) found that overreliance on background knowledge was a major cause of erroneous responses. In these instances, readers rejected or ignored text information and used personal background knowledge to respond to questions. McCormick explains, "It may be that low-achieving students have had less access to text information because of word recognition difficulties and over time have developed a pervasive strategy of simple guessing at possible responses based on knowledge already stored in their schemata" (p. 73). Other major errors included answers that were too specific or that were only marginally related to the question. In the first instance, students were distracted by irrelevant information. In the second instance, they failed to consider all the information in the selection, focusing instead on one specific detail, rather than considering several details.

> ✴ Possible reasons for having difficulty making inferences include not having the relevant knowledge to make inferences, having relevant knowledge but not being able to access it, or having relevant knowledge but not realizing that it should be integrated with information from the text.

As Wilson (1979) explains, poor readers tend to give intuitive answers, responses rooted in personal knowledge rather than in the text. In a similar vein, Phillips (1988) and Kimmel and MacGinitie (1984) found that low-performing readers used a kind of preservative strategy in which they held firmly to an erroneous response despite conflicting evidence. On the other hand, Oakhill and Yuill (1996) concluded that poor readers find it difficult to access relevant knowledge and integrate it with the information in the text. Poor readers may also emphasize literal comprehension and may not realize that they can and should make inferences.

Techniques designed to improve the inferencing ability of low-achieving readers need to compensate for their overreliance on prior knowledge, inadequate use of text, and lack of flexibility in reasoning about what one reads. Techniques also need to build students' confidence in their ability to draw inferences from text.

One approach that does an excellent job of incorporating these factors is Hansen and Pearson's (1982) prior knowledge prediction strategy. Although it is relatively simple to apply and teach, the strategy is powerful. After being taught the strategy, low-progress readers did just as well with inferences as did higher-achieving readers.

## Prior Knowledge Prediction Strategy Lesson

*Step 1: Creating questions.* As with a number of successful techniques, the first step in teaching the technique is to analyze the selection to be read for two or three central ideas. For each central idea, create two questions. The first question, which is designed to activate the appropriate schema, asks students about any experiences that they may have had that might be similar to the central idea. For instance, if the central idea is "A best friend moved away," then you would create a question similar to the following: "Have you ever lost a friend because your friend moved away or you moved away?" Then you would ask a prediction question that is related to the schema activation question and the central idea. "In the story we're about to read, Jeremy's best friend is moving away. What do you think Jeremy will do?"

*Step 2: Prereading discussion.* In the prereading discussion, the teacher asks the schema-activation question and then the prediction question. The discussion is critical. Low-achieving readers often have difficulty activating appropriate schema.

*(Continued)*

During the discussion, a student might think, "I've never had a friend move away" and so is unable to activate relevant schema. But then a student explains how he felt when his uncle and aunt moved away. He explains that they were young and had no children of their own, and had taken him many places. The discussion reminds the first youngster of how she felt when her cousin moved, so she is then able to activate the appropriate moving-away schema.

*Step 3:   Silent reading of selection.* Students read to assess their predictions.

*Step 4:   Postreading discussion.* The postreading discussion is also an important part of the technique. After discussing students' predictions, ask related inference questions. All too often, questions asked of low-achieving readers are restricted to the literal level. Or the higher-level questions that they are asked simply require an opinion. Inference questions should involve using both the text and prior knowledge: "How did Jeremy feel when his friend moved away?" Through discussions, students reveal their thought processes and help each other learn.

*Step 5:   Verifying inferences.* Since low-achieving readers overrely on prior experience, it is important that they be asked to justify inferences. If a student infers that the main character in the story, Jeremy, is sad because his friend moved away, then the student should be asked to supply evidence from the selection that indicates Jeremy is sad.

***Importance of Modeling***   Research by McCormick (1992) suggests that low-achieving readers may have limited experience drawing inferences. It is essential that the process be explained and modeled, with lots of opportunities for guided practice and application. You might also follow a gradual release of responsibility model (Pearson & Gallagher, 1983). Using brief passages, you draw an inference and have students find the supporting evidence. Once they have become proficient at locating evidence, switch roles. You supply the evidence and have them draw the inferences. Ultimately, students both draw the inferences and supply the evidence. Begin with short selections, and gradually work into longer ones.

❊ Based on observations of the most effective teachers, Fisher (2008) noted that they modeled their thinking processes and provided examples. If students were being asked to respond to a question, visualize, or engage in a discussion with a partner, the expert teachers gave students an example of the strategy or procedure before having them try it out.

Yuill and Oakhill (1991) improved the inferential comprehension of less skilled readers by modeling the process of using cues to make inferences and providing practice. For instance, after showing students how to make inferences using cues from single words, the students practiced making inferences about the sentence "Sleepy Tom was late for school again." With the teacher's help, they inferred that Tom was a boy because Tom is a boy's name and that Tom was a student. Otherwise, he would have been called "mister." From the word *sleepy,* students inferred that he was late because he overslept, and from the word *again* they inferred that this was not the first time he had been late. After working with single words in the context of sentences, the students made inferences from larger blocks of texts.

Students were then introduced to question generation. After being introduced to question words such as *who, what, where, when,* and *why,* they learned to create questions. Half of the students then created questions while the other half used their inference training to answer the student-generated queries. Students were also taught to use the question "What happened next?" to make predictions. This was used in connection with macro-cloze. In *macro-cloze,* a whole sentence is omitted, and students use experiential background and inferencing to predict what the missing sentence said. After students made their predictions, the omitted sentence is revealed. However, it is important to affirm all plausible responses.

Kerry wanted cereal for breakfast.

_____

_____

So she had to have toast instead.

Eduardo planned to shoot some baskets.

_____

_____

He did his homework instead.

Jeff thought the dog was friendly.

_____

_____

"Now I know why my mom told me never to pet a strange dog," Jeff told the doctor.

_____

_____

Tanya looked around for her homework.

_____

_____

"The teacher will never believe what happened to my homework," Tanya thought to herself.

After relatively brief periods of instruction and practice, the less skilled readers were operating at almost the same level as their more skilled counterparts.

> **Responsive elaboration:** the teacher analyzes a student's answer to determine what reasoning processes the student is using and then, building on that analysis, elaborates the student's response.

*Responsive Elaboration* Because faulty reasoning or use of inappropriate reasoning strategies is the cause of many erroneous inferences, a technique known as responsive elaboration may help students reason their way to credible inferences (Duffy & Roehler, 1987). As its name suggests, **responsive elaboration** is a teacher prompt or an elaboration made in response to a student's erroneous answer. The focus is on the process rather than the answer. Analyze the student's response and try to figure out how she arrived at that answer. Ask yourself: What strategies or thought processes did the student use? What can I do to correct the process? Here is an example of how a teacher used responsive elaboration to restructure an inference that was based on inadequate information:

**Student** (making erroneous inference): Jake was a coward.

**Teacher:** What leads you to believe that Jake was cowardly?

**Student:** The story says he was so filled with fear when he saw the snake that his knees were knocking. He felt like running away even though the snake was about to bite his baby sister.

**Teacher:** Did he run away?

**Student:** Yes.

**Teacher:** What did he do before he ran?

**Student:** He picked up a big rock and threw it on the snake.

**Teacher:** What else did he do?

**Student:** He grabbed his baby sister, and then he ran.

**Teacher:** Would that have taken courage? The snake might still have been alive.

**Student:** Yes. I suppose so.

**Teacher:** All of us have fears, but we show courage when we overcome our fears.

*QAR*    Although many low-achieving readers overrely on prior knowledge, some are textbound and respond to inferential questions with "I can't find the answer in the book" (Applegate, Quinn, & Applegate, 2006). This is especially true of younger low-achieving readers.

In addition to explaining the value and purpose of inferential questions, you might try using QAR (question–answer relationship). To show students that not all answers are in the book, QAR was created to help students locate the source of answers, whether they be literal or inferential (Raphael, 1984, 1986). QAR activities are designed to help students identify an answer as one of the following:

> To help students become more aware of the sources for answers to questions, have them create questions about a passage that are "right there," involve "putting it together," or are "on my own" or "writer and me."

1. **Right there:**    The answer is contained within a single sentence in the text.

2. **Putting it together:**    It is necessary to put together information from several sentences to obtain an answer.

3. **On my own:**    The answer is part of the student's prior knowledge.

4. **Writer and me:**    The reader must combine personal knowledge with information from the text to construct an inference.

To introduce QAR, write a paragraph similar to the following on the board. The selection and accompanying questions are designed to demonstrate the various sources of answers:

> With the sun in her eyes, the driver pulled over into the highway's slow lane and eased up on the gas. Glancing up at the large metal sign overhead, she was relieved to see that she had only two exits to go. She had started driving early in the morning, just before 6 a.m. Now it was nearly 6 p.m.

To show students where answers to questions can be found, ask questions of the following types:

- Where was the driver? (right there)
- How much farther did she have to go? (right there)
- How long had she been driving? (putting it together)
- In which direction was she heading? (writer and me)
- How do you feel after you've been in a car for a long time? (on my own)

As you discuss answers to the questions and the sources of the answers, emphasize the fact that answers are not always stated directly. During subsequent sessions, ask varied questions: some that can be answered with information in the text and some that require using background information and the text or just background knowledge. Along with discussing answers, also identify sources of answers.

### Making Inferences with *It Says–I Say–And So*

*It Says–I Say–And So* is a series of scaffolding statements that foster the drawing of inferences (Beers, 2003). As students are answering questions, they look to see what

**FIGURE 11.9**

It Says–I Say–And So

| QUESTION | IT SAYS | I SAY | AND SO |
|---|---|---|---|
| Read the question. | Find information from the text that will help you answer the question. | Think about what you know about that information. | Combine what the text says with what you know to come up with an answer. |
| How did the boy feel at the end of the story? | Johnathan wiped away a tear as the van pulled away. He would miss his best friend. But then he thought of the new home where he would have his very own room and a smile broke across his face. | You cry when you are sad. And you get sad when you lose your best friend. But getting your own room can make you happy. I remember how I felt when my brother moved out and I got his room. | And so that's why I think Johnathan had mixed feelings. He was sad and happy at the same time. |

the text says (*It*), and then what they have to say about that (*I Say*), and what happens when you put what the text says and what I say together (*And So*).

Students make four columns, as shown in Figure 11.9. Under the Question column, students write the question to be answered. Under It Says, they write information from the text that will help answer the question. Under I Say students think about what they know about the text information and write that. Under the And So column, they combine text and personal information and make an inference or draw a conclusion. Using responses to the items, students go through the process of making an inference step by step. When responses are placed on the board and discussed, students have the opportunity to see how their peers make inferences.

Start off with fairly simple questions, ones that have just one piece of information, under It Says. Gradually move to questions that have a number of items under It Says so that students need to record and consider several details.

### Difficulty Drawing Conclusions

Working with students who were having difficulty drawing conclusions, McMackin and Witherell (2005) observed that the students failed to consider information provided in the text. Students were urged to think about the passage they had just read, to note what they knew for sure because it was contained in the passage, and then to stop and think about this information so that they could draw a conclusion: "I must combine what I know for sure from the text with what I think about it and then determine what else I can figure out from the information provided." Students were asked, "What were you able to figure out from the passage you read?" They were also asked to cite support for their conclusions. McMackin and Witherell also used graphic organizers to scaffold students' efforts. They differentiated instruction by providing different levels of organizers.

### Mystery Passages

Introduced in Chapter 5 as a think-aloud for assessing comprehension, Mystery Passages also serve as a highly effective technique for developing students' ability to predict, make inferences, draw conclusions, and integrate information from several sentences or passages (see Figure 11.10 for a sample lesson). Mystery passages are riddle-like segments of text whose main idea or topic is not revealed until the last

■■ **FIGURE 11.10**
Instructional Mys-
tery Passage
*Source:* Gunning
(2010), p. 15.

Use the clues to solve the mystery. After each clue, write down what you think the mystery animal is.

The Most Dangerous Animal

■ What is the most dangerous animal in all of Africa?
My prediction: _____
Reason(s) for my prediction: _____

■ The most dangerous animal in all of Africa is a huge beast. It can weigh more than 8,000 pounds. Even though it is huge and has short legs, it can run very fast. It can run faster than any human and most animals.
My prediction: _____
Reason(s) for my prediction: _____

■ Its mouth is gigantic and it has huge teeth. It has chomped alligators and small boats in half.
My prediction: _____
Reason(s) for my prediction: _____

■ Many animal scientists believe that the hippo is the most dangerous creature in Africa. Hippos have killed more people than any other wild animal.
What are the main things you learned about the mystery animal?
_____

segment. To create a Mystery Passage, write or adapt articles so that the identity of the object or creature being described is not revealed until the end (Gunning, 2010).

Here is how the Mystery Passages activity works. Students read a brief segment of text, write down what they predict the mystery entity is, and then briefly explain in writing what makes them think that. Their prediction is discussed along with their reasons. The teacher might use prompts such as "What makes you say that? Tell me more about your thinking. What does the passage say about that?" to elicit a brief discussion. Then they go on to the next segment, which provides an additional clue. Students can retain or change their predictions. During the discussion of their predictions, the teacher again uses prompts. The prompts vary according to the processes students are using. If students fail to integrate information from previous segments, the teacher might prompt, "How does that fit in with what you read in previous segments?" If students are not using background knowledge, the teacher might prompt, "How does that fit in with what you know about African animals?" If the student is overusing background knowledge and neglecting the text, the teacher might prompt, "What did the passage have to say that?" or "Was that in the passage that you just read?" Students continue make predictions as they read additional passages. After completing all the segments, students reread the entire passage and tell what they learned about the mystery animal, person, or object.

When using the Mystery Passage activity, distribute the clues one by one so that students don't read ahead. Students are encouraged to use their background knowledge and thinking skills. Prompts might be used that lead them to make more carefully considered predictions or to integrate details from the passage.

The Guess Who series (Benchmark Marshall Cavendish), which is designed for beginning readers, has a format similar to a Mystery Passage selection. In the book *Who Swims?* (Rau, 2009), for instance, students use information about a penguin's behaviors, physical characteristics, and habitat to guess its identity. Some Mystery Passages exercises are available on the author's Web site (http://www.wordbuilding.org).

**EXEMPLARY TEACHING**

## Motivating Strategy Use with Mystery Passages

Here is an excerpt from a session in which a fifth-grade teacher is helping a struggling reader by using Mystery Passages (Smith, 2006). Clues, which consisted of single sentences, were written on separate slips of paper.

Sentence 1. Suddenly I could hear it making noise pounding on the roof of the house.

> **Teacher:** What do you know from your experience that does that?
>
> **Student:** A storm.
>
> **Teacher:** Good

Sentence 2. I could see something bouncing onto the sidewalk and gathering into little white piles.

> **Student:** Still thundering and raining. . . .
>
> **Teacher:** Well, what are those white piles?
>
> **Student:** Huh? [rereads] Hah. Snow!
>
> **Teacher:** Really? What does it say besides "white piles"? Is there another clue?
>
> **Student:** Gathering . . . bouncing? Let's see what the next sentence says.

> **Teacher:** Good thinking! Keep your mind thinking while you read more.

This next one might really throw you.

Sentence 3. It was summertime, but cold bits were falling from the sky.

> **Student:** Oooh, so it was raining?
>
> **Teacher:** What makes you think so? Does that fit with what you read right before?
>
> **Student:** Uh huh.
>
> **Teacher:** But you said "snow" right before.
>
> **Student:** Oh, man, snow.
>
> **Teacher:** Okay, let's review what we've read so far. So you have a storm. What else do you have?
>
> **Student:** Ice. [laughs delightedly and reads next sentence]

Sentence 4. I've heard that sometimes it could get the size of golf balls or break car windshields.

> **Student:** Oh, I know it . . . but I can't get the word out for it!
>
> **Teacher:** What's it like?
>
> **Student:** Hail!
>
> **Teacher:** You think? All right, let's see. (Smith, 2006, p. 769)

### The Magic of Indexing

I once worked with a third grader whose comprehension was virtually nonexistent, despite his command of basic decoding skills, obvious intelligence, and effective language skill. The student experienced difficulty answer literal questions about single sentences. Although he responded with enthusiasm to Mystery Passages, he failed to integrate clues and also created his own version of the segments by citing details not present in the passage. However, when I tried a technique known as indexing, his comprehension was 100 percent.

According to Bruner (1964), we make sense of our environment through three modalities: enactive representation (action), iconic representation (imagery), and symbolic (language, representation). Glenberg, Gutierrez, Levin, Japuntich, and Kaschak (2004) have proposed the indexical or enactive hypothesis of language comprehension, which asserts that the first step in comprehending language is indexing or relating the words to their objects or referents. Manipulating objects assists the indexing process and improves a student's ability to visualize a representation of the text. According to the indexical hypothesis, words and syntax are indexed to actions. Thus, students can be led to understand a passage by performing the actions specified by the text. If a passage said, "The enraged rhino charged at the jeep and smashed its grill," the reader would use toys to show the rhino changing at the jeep. In experiments, students who manipulated objects after reading sentences were able to answer more than twice as many questions as students who simply read the sentences twice. Even students who simply viewed the manipulations had improved comprehension. The technique worked when students were guided individually, in small groups, in whole classes, and when working in pairs (Glenberg, 2011; Marley, Szabo, & Glenberg, 2011). It was effective with both listening and reading comprehension and with achieving and at-risk populations (Marley, Levin, & Glenberg, 2007).

In the following paragraph about giraffes, figures of animals and trees were used to simulate the actions or ideas expressed in the sentences preceded by an asterisk. This and similar paragraphs were used to instruct and provide reinforcement for the third-grader who had a severe comprehension difficulty.

### Giraffes

Giraffes are tall animals. *A giraffe is taller than an elephant. *A giraffe is so tall that it can eat the leaves on the tops of trees. Giraffes have many enemies. *Lions, hyenas, and Nile crocodiles hunt giraffes. Because they stand tall and have excellent eyesight, giraffes can see far away. *A giraffe can see a lion or hyena that is a mile away. (Gunning, 2010)

The activity was easy to set up. A plastic elephant, giraffe, lion, and hyena and plastic trees were assembled. After reading that a giraffe is taller than an elephant, the student placed the giraffe next to the elephant. After reading that a giraffe is so tall that it can eat the leaves from the tops of trees, the student showed the giraffe eating the leaves. After reading that "Lions, hyenas, and Nile crocodiles hunt giraffes," the student assembled the animals and showed them approaching the giraffe. After reading "A giraffe can see a lion or hyena that is a mile away," the student showed the giraffe spotting a lion that was far away. Actively involved and motivated by the task, the third-grader's comprehension was perfect. Over time, more complex tasks were arranged and the student was led to use imaging.

Obtaining appropriate manipulatives can be time-consuming and expensive. However, toys can be obtained from parents whose children have outgrown them. Illustrations downloaded from free clip art sites can also be used. Older students might use maps, globes, diagrams, replicas of sports fields, or other manipulatives.

Indexing seems to be especially effective with students who fail to read for meaning and may not understand how one goes about reading for meaning or even that the purpose of reading is to construct meaning. As Glenberg (2011) explains, indexing "demonstrates for the child how written texts can be meaningful and how to uncover that meaning." Indexing may provide some students with a foundational understanding that enables them to begin to comprehend text.

***Books That Lend Themselves to Indexing***    Books with activities and experiments lend themselves to indexing. All or most of the sentences of science experiment can be enacted. However, informational or fictional books that include statements that can be enacted also lend themselves to indexing. For some brief texts, the whole book can be indexed. For instance, most of the sentences in *Polar Bears* (Freeman, 1999) can be indexed. The statement "Polar bears are some of the largest bears in the world" might be enacted by making available a number of different kinds of bears and having the student select the polar bear, which is the largest of the bears present. For the sentence, "Polar bears live in the Arctic," readers can place a polar bear on a map depicting the Arctic. In other instances, only a portion of the book might be indexed. In a book on castles, the description of the castle and an attack on the castle might be indexed. Books that lend themselves to indexing include the following:

Adler, D. A. (2011). *Time zones.* New York: Holiday House. Portions of the text can be illustrated with a globe and a desk lamp or flashlight.

Branley, F. M. (1985) *Sunshine makes the season* (rev.). New York: HarperCollins. Directions for indexing are embedded within the text.

Brett, J. (1989). *The mitten.* New York: Putnam's Sons. Props for indexing are available at the author's Web site (http://www.janbrett.com/put_the_animals_in_the_mitten.htm).

Kolpoin, M. (2012). *Polar bears.* Manakota, MN: Capstone Press. Simple text can be indexed with a few props.

Landau, E. (2008). *Earth.* New York: Scholastic. Using replicas of the solar system as props, many of the key concepts in this or similar books can be indexed.

Sweeney, J. (1996). *Me on the map.* New York: Dragonfly Books. Selected segments can be indexed with the help of a world, U.S., and state maps.

Teitelbaum, M. (2008). *Baby elephant's fun in the sun.* San Anselmo, CA: Treasure Bay. Simple text can be indexed with a few props.

### Providing Evidence: A Key Standard

Drawing conclusions, making inferences, deriving a main idea, noting character traits, detecting a theme, and a number of other key skills and strategies require that students provide support or evidence. Indeed, Smarter Balanced Consortium (2012) concluded that citing evidence is a part of the first nine CCSS anchor standards. As a result, Smarter Balanced recommended, "Given the emphasis the standards place on supporting analysis with evidence, reading items will as often as possible provide the opportunity to cite specific evidence from the text or texts" (p. 41). This could include multiple-choice items where students might be required to underline supporting evidence.

However, this ability is more than just locating and retrieving information from a selection. As Smarter Balanced explains,

Depending on the particular item or task, students may support responses with details drawn directly from the text (text-referential responses) or may do so by providing a rich, text-based synthesis that clearly reflects deep understanding of the text. Given a question such as "Based on what you read, why did Jean's mood improve?" a student might respond by noting that Jean's mood improved because the <u>daffodils began to bloom</u> and <u>leaves began to form on the trees</u>" (underlined words taken directly from the text); however, an entirely different but text-relevant way to respond would be "Jean's spirits lifted because the world around her changed and became more colorful as it turned to spring." (p. 29)

The process of citing evidence should be modeled. Students should be encouraged to cite evidence during many of their text-based questions, whether oral and written. They should also explain how the evidence supports their response. Initially, students might cite evidence that entails citing one or two details directly stated. They should then be guided to cite evidence that requires making inferences and paraphrasing and synthesizing.

**Imaging:** process of creating visual, auditory, or other representations as one reads, listens, views, or thinks. While the verbal coding system might analyze and organize information in the form of words, the imaging system generates mental images (Sadowski, Goetz, & Fritz, 1993).

## Imaging

Indexing can build a foundation for imaging. In **imaging**, students create visual, auditory, or other sensory-based mental representations of characters, objects, events, or other elements in a selection. In one experiment, students who used indexing were able to solve more than twice as many math story problems as students who simply read the problems twice (Glenberg, 2011). Students who used imaging did nearly as well as the students who used indexing. After students have become proficient at indexing, they move on to imaging by visualizing how they move objects instead of actually moving them. First they index the objects; then they imagine indexing them. Eventually, they visualize moving the objects without first having indexed them. Imaging the objects is a more specific activity than following the prompt that is typically given to "make pictures in your head." Imaging is developmental. Younger students have a more difficult time imaging (Levin & Pressley, 1978). However, they do better with specific prompts that help them encode a story in images and also retrieve the story's images.

Imaging is a powerful strategy for poor comprehenders (Oakhill & Yuill, 1996). Imaging helps them to integrate information in text in a way that they would not normally use. It is particularly helpful for inferential questions, especially when students have to infer descriptive information that is not stated explicitly. Imaging may help less able readers integrate text and use working memory more effectively insofar as it provides them with a strategy for integrating information in text. Imaging may also help poor comprehenders overcome some of the limitations they have in processing information by providing them with a more economical way of representing information from text. However, imaging may not be helpful for lengthy passages, because it may be too difficult to sustain (Yuill & Oakhill, 1991).

When they used visualizing, low-achieving readers were better able to understand what they read and to integrate new and old information (Pressley, 1977). Images can call forth ideas and words, and words and ideas can evoke images. For instance, we can create images for *justice* and *democracy* and other abstract concepts (Sadowski et al., 1993).

Both imaging and indexing are examples of dual coding. According to a dual coding theory of cognitive processing, information can be coded verbally or nonverbally. The word *robot*, for instance, can be encoded verbally. It can also be encoded visually as a mental picture of a robot. And if indexed by operating a toy robot it can be encoded motorically. Because it can be encoded as a word or mental picture or, if indexed, as a movement, it can be retrieved from memory either verbally, visually, or motorically so it is twice or more than twice as memorable. In one research study, participants who encoded words visually remembered twice as many words as those who only encoded the words verbally (Schnorr & Atkinson, 1969). Students who pretended to perform actions associated with words they were studying also learned more words (Marley, Levin, & Glenberg 2007).

When providing imaging prompts, be as specific as possible. Instead of providing generic prompt, such as "Make a movie in your head," be more specific: "Imagine what the main character is doing as he tries to escape from his captors" (Levin & Pressley, 1978). Use high-imagery passages. Start with single sentences and then move on to short paragraphs and, later, longer pieces. Have students read the sentence or paragraph first, and then create their image by imaging what the main character is doing as he tries to escape from his captors.

Questions that ask students to create visual images should become a natural part of postreading discussions. Auditory and kinesthetic or tactile imaging should also be fostered. You might ask students to tell how the thunder in the story sounded, or what the icy water they read about felt like. In discussing images that students have formed, remind them that each of us makes our own individual mental picture. Ask

## Imaging Lesson

**Step 1: Introducing imaging.** To introduce imaging, explain what it is and why it is a valuable comprehension strategy. Then model the process. Show how you would create images of a concrete passage.

**Step 2: Focusing.** Encourage students to relax and clear their minds of distracting thoughts. Have students close their eyes and listen to a brief, concrete passage, forming pictures in their minds as they do. Direct students to draw pictures of their images. This fixes the images so that when the class discusses them, individual students don't forget what their original images looked like (Maria, 1990). In the beginning, you might use single sentences or very brief paragraphs. Once students have begun to grasp the idea of imaging, try using longer pieces.

**Step 3: Discussing.** Discuss students' images, but before doing so, talk over the fact that because each of us is a different person and has different experiences, each of us will create individual images. To show students how different people create different images, compare the illustrations in different versions of classic stories, or compare illustrations of similar events or scenes from several content-area texts. When discussing students' images, use probing questions to get more detail and also to focus on important ideas. As with other activities, students can get bogged down in unimportant details.

**Step 4: Guided practice.** After students have caught on to the idea of creating images, ask them to create pictures of text in their minds as they read. Start off with brief concrete text and then move into longer pieces, including content-area texts. After students have read the passage and sketched their images, ask questions that focus on the main content. Also pose questions that help them to create fuller images. If the passage lends itself to it, ask questions that go beyond the visual. In addition to asking, "What did you see?" ask: "What did you hear? What did you feel? What did you touch? What did you smell?" If students have difficulty creating an image or have left out elements, encourage them to reread the passage and create an image of the piece, adding elements to their mental representation. One interesting activity is to visualize the main character of a story or a setting and then compare one's mental picture with that created by the illustrator.

**Step 5: Review and application.** After introducing imaging, continue to review and reinforce it. Suggest its use where it might be especially appropriate: imaging scenes, characters, or events in fiction; imaging events or scenes in history, places in geography, and processes in science. Encourage students to use drawings, even if they consist mainly of stick figures. Also encourage the creation of charts, diagrams, geographic and semantic maps, and other graphic displays to organize information that they have read. Periodically, make imaging a part of prereading activities, assignments, and discussions, so that it becomes second nature to students.

**Step 6: Assessment.** Observe students as they create images. Note how well they can do the following:

- Create images from narrative text
- Create images from informational text
- Create images that convey the gist or main idea of a selection
- Create images that include essential details
- Create images that include inferred details

### Reviewing the Strategy

Learning a strategy may take a month or more. In subsequent lessons, review and extend the strategy. To review the strategy, ask the following kinds of questions.

- What strategy are we learning to use? (Imaging)
- How does this strategy help us? (Helps us to picture what we have read. Helps us to remember what we read.)
- When do we use this strategy? (With fiction or informational text that can be pictured.)
- How do we use this strategy? (Review the steps of using the strategy.) Also ask students to tell about instances when they used the strategy on their own (Scott, 1998).

(This same format may be used for reviewing all of the strategies presented in this and other chapters.)

a variety of students to tell what pictures they formed. Through prompting, encourage students to elaborate on their images: "What did the spaceship look like? Was it round or triangular? What color was it? Did it have any special features? What kind of engine did it have? What did the engine sound like?"

*Verbal Visualizing*   Instead of or along with drawing pictures to develop imaging, verbal prompts can be used. To stimulate visualizing, students study pictures, put them aside, and then describe what they saw. The teacher uses a series of questions to flesh out the students' descriptions and also to develop language that can be used to describe images (Bell, 2007). Students then proceed to describe known words. They might be asked to describe a car or a character in a story. Again, the teacher uses questions to help students elaborate: "What make is the car? What color is it? How large is the car? What does the grille look like?"

In the next stage, students image single sentences: "Because its body is soft and flexible, an octopus can squeeze its rounded body and eight dangling arms into a crack in an undersea wall when it is chased by a hungry predator." Prompting questions might include: "What are you picturing? What does the octopus look like? What does its body look like? How many arms does it have? Where is it? What does the wall look like? What is it doing? Is it moving slowly or quickly? What other creature do you picture? What does that creature look like?"

Students then image whole paragraphs. Emphasis is on building a cumulative image and on making connections among the sentences. After students have provided an image of each sentence in the paragraph, they provide a verbal summary of the entire paragraph. For more information on this approach, see the text *Visualizing and Verbalizing* (Bell, 2007).

As with any other strategy, students should learn when, where, and why to use imaging as well as how to use it. As part of your instruction, explain why imaging is a useful strategy. Also point out that it works better with some kinds of writing than with others. Consider individual differences in the use of imagery. Some students thrive on imaging. Others have difficulty creating or describing images. They may need more instruction and practice. If their difficulty is significant they may prefer using other strategies. Younger students in particular may have difficulty using imaging.

## Metacognitive Awareness

Although Anna, a fifth grader, spent 30 minutes poring over an article on the formation of rocks, she had little to show for her effort. When asked questions about the article, she was unable to respond. As she was reading, Anna wasn't really getting much meaning from the text. She didn't understand what she was reading, and she didn't realize that she didn't understand. She wasn't monitoring her reading. She lacked **metacognitive awareness**.

**Metacognitive awareness:** being conscious of one's thought processes.

All of us have difficulty with comprehension from time to time, but usually we are aware of the difficulty. We realize that our attention was diverted and don't have the slightest idea of what we just read. Or we realize that we have gotten lost in a tangle of legalese when reading a contract. Or we don't understand the steps for installing a new piece of software. Realizing that we are not comprehending, we take corrective action: reread, get help with difficult terms, or examine a clarifying illustration. However, since low-achieving readers often don't realize that they are not understanding, they fail to take steps to repair faulty comprehension.

To build metacognitive awareness, Reading Apprenticeship, a program for struggling readers, plans activities in which students have conversations about what a text means and how they know what it means. This helps them to become of aware of the processes they are using (Schoenbach et al., 2012).

Metacognitive awareness is the ability to think about our cognitive processes. It is knowledge about "ourselves, the tasks we face, and the strategies we employ" (Garner, 1994, p. 717). According to Paris (1991), "As children gain experience with a task such as reading, they begin to understand their own abilities, the characteristics of a text that make reading easy or difficult, and the strategies that can be employed to aid comprehension" (p. 34).

In addition to being less likely to detect a comprehension problem, low-achieving readers are also less likely to choose a corrective strategy even when they do detect a problem. While achieving readers report rereading a confusing passage, poor readers are more likely to say that they would "skip it" (Garner & Reis, 1981).

The four crucial areas in metacognition are (1) knowing oneself as a learner; (2) regulating; (3) monitoring; and (4) repairing (Baker & Brown, 1984; Garner, 1994).

## Knowing Oneself as a Learner

Generally, a student knows what his background of knowledge is and knows himself as a reader. He may realize that he is a fast, global reader with a poor background in science. Self-knowledge, however, can be faulty. A student may believe that he knows all there is to know about snakes and so fail to read with an open mind an article that contradicts his deeply held but erroneous concepts. Or the student may believe that he is dumb and that he will not learn new material no matter how hard he tries (Paris, 1991). Beaten before he starts because of a poor self-concept, the student may not exert a wholehearted effort and may not apply the strategies that he has mastered. Helping low-achieving readers know themselves as learners often involves both correcting false notions and building confidence.

## Regulating

Regulating means that the student exercises cognitive control over her learning. The student knows strategies and knows how, when, and where to use them. The student also knows what to read to fulfill a specific purpose. For instance, in studying for a science quiz, the student with a fast, global style will shift to a slower-paced analytic approach when she realizes that the quiz will be factual. She may choose to use a specialized study technique or simply take notes or engage in some form of self-questioning. She may focus on the textbook sections that describe areas that the teacher emphasized in class.

## Monitoring

**Monitoring:** mental checking of one's cognitive processes. In reading, monitoring is an awareness of whether a passage is making sense or not.

**Monitoring** means that the student evaluates his understanding. After each section, he may attempt to summarize what he has read or engage in self-testing by asking himself questions about what he has read. If a section doesn't make sense, he may reread it, look up difficult words in the glossary, refer to illustrations, or ask a friend, parent, or teacher for help. Imaging or summarizing can be another form of monitoring for meaning. If a student has difficulty creating images or summaries, it may be due to faulty comprehension.

✳ Poor readers' difficulty with
✳ monitoring may be caused by
material that is too difficult. If they spend
too much time grappling with unknown
words, they may become accustomed to
reading "nonsense" and do not develop
the habit of monitoring for meaning.

Poor monitoring may also be related to poor comprehension strategies and the material's level of difficulty. In several experiments, inconsistencies and nonsense words were inserted in selections read by good and poor readers in the fourth grade. When low-achieving readers' understanding and recall of a passage was inadequate because the text was apparently too difficult, they noted fewer inconsistencies or nonsense words in the text (Paris & Myers, 1981). However, when the text was simplified, poor readers noted as many errors as good readers. When the reading material is too difficult, poor readers are unable to make full use of the strategies they possess. If too many of the text's words are unknown, the poor reader may not comprehend well enough to see that there are inconsistencies.

Learning to monitor one's comprehension is partly developmental. In general, older students are better at monitoring than younger ones. The nature of monitoring also changes as students develop. Young students and low-achieving readers tend to focus on lower-level elements. They are concerned about processing words and sentences, whereas older readers and more competent students are more aware of their understanding of paragraphs and larger sections of text.

## Repairing

Being aware of a problem in comprehension is a necessary first step in solving that problem. The second step is repairing the problem. Repair strategies consist of pausing, slowing reading rate, reading aloud, skipping portions of a text (jumping over), looking back, rereading, and taking other steps to make sense of a puzzling passage (see Table 11.1, which is adapted from Walczyk & Griffith-Ross, 2007).

Struggling readers apparently make better use of repair strategies when the text is interesting. When the text is dull, these readers repair less and so comprehend less. High motivation and conscientious compensation can make up for weak skills, however (Walczyk & Griffith-Ross, 2007).

A second group of repair strategies involves using illustrations, maps, charts, graphs, and other graphic materials to provide clarification. A third group of repair strategies involves using references, such as a glossary, dictionary, or encyclopedia, to clarify a confusing concept or to obtain needed background information.

All too often, struggling readers are programmed for failure and need to know what steps they can take when comprehension falters. Repair strategies should be modeled, and many opportunities should be provided to apply them both under teacher guidance and independently.

Realizing that older struggling readers might operate under the misconception that reading is effortless and automatic for teachers and other proficient readers, Chris Tovani (2000) demonstrated to her students how she had to struggle to understand a difficult article. On other occasions, she used editorials, poems, directions, and excerpts from a novel to show how she used repair strategies on challenging texts. Hearing that their teacher had difficulty with the word *trisyllabic* and the expression *contextually defined conditions,* the students began to see that reading was an active process that even adept readers have to work at. And so the stage was set for them to learn effective repair strategies.

## Instruction in Metacognition

Struggling readers might not realize the mental effort that goes into constructing meaning. They might look at achieving readers and believe that they breeze their way through the text and that comprehension is something that takes place automatically for them. Struggling readers need to know that constructing meaning takes effort,

**TABLE 11.1**
Repair Strategies

| Strategy | Description | When Used |
|---|---|---|
| Slowing reading rate | Reads at a pace that allows deeper concentration. | Text is difficult, complex, and/or confusing. |
| Pausing | Stops momentarily. | Pauses to figure out a word or expression or to figure out what might be done to solve a confusion. |
| Reading aloud | Deliberately whisper reads or reads aloud to self. | Reads aloud to obtain greater focus or overcome distraction. |
| Jumping over | Skips a confusing word or text. | Skips a word a word or phrase thought to be unimportant or in hopes that added reading will clarify a confusion. |
| Looking back | Checks back to locate a forgotten or misunderstood piece of information. | Obtains information lost from working memory or gets information overlooked on the first pass through text. |
| Rereading | Reprocesses a portion of text. | Rereads a sentence or passage to obtain meaning not gotten first time or to clarify a confusion. |
| Paraphrasing | Puts text in own words. | Translates a difficult passage into easier-to-understand language. |
| Using text aids | Uses illustrations, maps, charts, graphs, etc. | Consults an illustration or other graphic to clarify a confusion or get more information. |
| Using references | Uses glossary, dictionary, encyclopedia, or other reference. | Checks an unknown word or concept. Obtains information to clarify a confusion. |
| Reading an easier version | Uses an easier-to-read or less complex version. | Uses when target text is too complex or confusing. |

*Source:* Gunning, T. (2010). *Creating Literacy Instruction for All Students* (7th ed.). Boston: Allyn & Bacon. Reprinted by permission of Allyn & Bacon.

but that effort pays off. They might not realize either that proficient readers reread text when it is complex or confusing. They might not even realize that you should reread the text if it doesn't make sense. As Beers (2003) commented, "Rereading is probably the number one strategy independent readers use when something stumps them in text. It's probably the last strategy dependent readers use" (p. 113).

## Use of Graphic Guides

As an aid to strategy use, Paris, Cross, and Lipson (1984) used posters and slogans, such as "Be a reading detective," to remind students to use strategies as they read. A list of metacognitive strategies emphasized in the program include the following (Alverman et al., 1989, p. R8):

### Think Ahead

- What is this selection about?
- What do I already know about it?

## A Lesson in Teaching Metacognitive Strategies

*Step 1: Describing the strategy.* The strategy is explained in detail. The teacher provides a description and examples of the strategy so that the students know what the strategy is and how it works.

*Step 2: Explaining why the strategy is important.* Explain and model why the strategy is valuable. Low-achieving readers may not realize that even the best readers have difficulty with comprehension at times and need to be aware of whether or not their reading makes sense. Also note that checking one's reading periodically enables the reader to clear up puzzling parts and helps the reader to remember the material longer.

*Step 3: Demonstrating the strategy.* Using modeling or another technique, show how you would use the strategy. Placing a brief selection on the board or an overhead, show how you pause at the end of a paragraph and ask "Does this make sense?" Choose a tricky paragraph, one that you misread the first time, and show students how you stopped when the piece stopped making sense. You might also discuss the steps you would take to repair the comprehension gap.

*Step 4: Explaining when and where to use the strategy.* When teaching a strategy, be sure to note when and where it is to be used. For instance, when teaching correction strategies, note when it is appropriate to reread the sentence or the paragraph. Also point out when it might be a good idea to read ahead because the next sentence or paragraph explains the word or idea with which you were having difficulty.

*Step 5: Explaining how and why to evaluate a strategy.* Explain how to evaluate a strategy and why evaluation is important. For instance, explain that you need to see if rereading a sentence works, because if it doesn't you will need to use another strategy.

*Steps 6 and 7: Guided practice and application.* As part of instruction in metacognitive strategies, students need opportunities to try out strategies with guidance and feedback from their teachers so they can clarify misunderstandings, make necessary adjustments, and get the feel of the strategy. Be sure to affirm students' successful efforts with specific praise: "I like the way you reread that sentence when you saw that it didn't make sense" or "I like the way you used the diagram to help you understand the paragraph." They also need ample opportunity to apply the strategy to a variety of texts in a variety of situations so that the strategies become automatic, and they can see which ones work best in which situations.

*Step 8: Assessment and review.* Note students' use of strategies. From time to time, ask them to tell what they are doing to help them understand what they are reading and what they do when they don't understand what they are reading. Review strategies as needed.

- What do I want to find out?
- What is my goal?
- How should I go about reading in order to meet my goal?

### Think While Reading

- What have I read about so far?
- Do I understand it? If not, what should I do?
- What is the author saying and what do I think about it?

### Think Back

- Have I learned what I wanted?
- How can I use what I read?

## Informal Instruction

In addition to formal instruction, take advantage of informal, on-the-spot opportunities to promote metacognitive awareness. Before students read a selection, ask them how they will read it—quickly or slowly? Also ask what they will do to check their understanding. If a selection has confusing or densely written sections, discuss ways in which those sections might be read. In the after-reading discussion, have students tell how they handled difficult or confusing portions of a selection. Ask questions that lead students to discuss their use of metacognitive strategies: "Were there any confusing passages in this article? How did you handle the confusing parts? What do you do when the selection stops making sense?"

From time to time, model metacognitive strategies that you use, and have students explain the metacognitive strategies that they use. To reinforce monitoring for meaning, have students use sticky notes to indicate passages that were difficult. Discuss those passages with students. Talk over strategies that they might use to understand the passages better.

## ■ Importance of Using Appropriate Materials

Regardless of what technique is used to teach comprehension strategies, it is absolutely essential that the text be on the appropriate level of difficulty. In a study of good and poor readers in high school, Kletzien (1991) found that strategy use declined as the text grew harder. Both good and poor readers used the same strategies at the independent reading level. At the instructional level, the better readers demonstrated somewhat greater flexibility in the use of strategies. However, at the frustration level, poor readers "evidenced a precipitous decline in strategy usage (both in variety of strategies and in number of times strategies were used)" (Kletzien, 1991, p. 79).

> ✣ Frequently faced with materials on their frustration level, struggling readers often focus on low-level literacy processes. Seeing reading as getting the words right, they devote their energies to pronouncing each word correctly and neglect comprehension.

At the frustration level, strategy use deteriorated to a focus on small segments of text: individual words or phrases. Complaining that there were too many hard words, some of the subjects simply gave up. Explaining the drastic change in strategy use as texts grew too difficult, Kletzien (1991) commented:

> Because vocabulary and sentence structure were much more complex at this level, subjects had to work much harder at the lower-level tasks of word recognition and understanding of individual sentences, leaving less cognitive capacity available to understand the meaning of the passage as a whole and to integrate the content with what they already knew. Even subjects who reported using prior knowledge appeared to have done so out of desperation. One subject, obviously overwhelmed by the difficulty of the material, reported, "I have no idea what this is talking about; I am just trying to remember anything I know about Africa." (p. 82)

## ■ Beyond Strategies

There is more to using strategies than knowing how, when, and where to use them. There is also an essential affective component. Just as you build on what students know in word recognition, you should also consider what they know when building comprehension strategies. Besides being an effective instructional strategy, this fosters students' self-esteem.

In typical discussions, there is an emphasis on the correctness of the answer. However, students can reach the right answer for the wrong reason or the wrong answer for the right reason. Besides, the object of instruction is not to obtain answers, right or wrong; the goal is to improve students' use of strategies.

When students respond correctly and the strategy or thinking process they used to obtain the response is obvious, affirm their use of the strategy: "I like the way you used pieces of information from the story to conclude that the main character is kind." If the thinking or strategy isn't obvious, have the student explain it: "Why do you think the main character is kind?" If the student gives no response, rephrase the question or provide a probe that gives support. If the response is not fully correct, build on what the student provided. If the student responded that the main character is selfish, ask the student why she thinks so. (It could be a perfectly legitimate interpretation.) If the student has not considered all the evidence, encourage her to do so. You might say "Let's go back to the story and take a look at the main character's actions."

If a student is unable to respond at all, even with rephrased queries, help her use a strategy that will lead to a response. You might say "Let's look at what it says about the main character on page 22." In this way, you are showing the student how to use a strategy (looking back at the text), and you are involving her in obtaining the answer. This is far better than simply supplying the answer, which leaves her no better off than she was, and in fact, may confirm or contribute to a sense of academic powerlessness.

Once the focus is shifted from task completion or getting right answers to the process of learning how to comprehend, your natural tendency will be to choose activities that foster strategy building and independence. The question that you need to keep in mind is not: Is the answer correct? It should be: How I can build on what the student knows?

In a study involving primary- and middle-grade students who were low-achieving readers, Thames and Reeves (1994) found that when cognitive instruction that built on what students know was combined with self-selection of reading materials, poor readers maintained their academic self-esteem. The academic self-esteem of the members of a control group, who were taught in traditional ways, plummeted. However, Hall (2012) in a study of middle-school students' use of strategies found that students who identified themselves as high-performing readers made more effective use of strategies than students who identified as being average or low-performing readers. Students who identified themselves as being high performing chose strategies based on what they believed would be most helpful, whereas students who identified as being average or low performing used one or two favorite strategies, regardless of whether or not the strategies proved to be effective. Differences in strategy use were not due to differences in reading ability. A number of students who identified as being high-performing readers actually were average or below-average readers. A number of students who identified as being average or below were actually above-average readers. Changing students' identities as readers has the potential to foster more effective strategy use. As Hall concluded," … students' identities can … play a role in how they think and talk about texts" (p. 263).

## Approaches to Teaching Strategies

Two major approaches to teaching strategies include direct explanation and transactional strategy instruction (National Reading Panel, 2000). In *direct explanation (DE),* emphasis is placed on explaining the reasoning process in reading and the steps for applying strategies. Strategies are taught as problem-solving procedures that help readers construct meaning. *Transactional strategy instruction (TSI)* also attempts to provide insight into the reasoning processes of comprehension but does so through explanation, modeling, and discussion. In TSI, teachers and students work together to create meaning from a text. Emphasis is on the interchange of ideas and interpretations among teachers and students.

Although DE and TSI have construction of meaning as the ultimate goal and use many of the same procedures, TSI places more emphasis on discussion and group interpretation. In a version of TSI known as *collaborative strategy instruction*, disabled readers in grades 6 through 11, three-quarters of whom were reading on a third-grade level or below, gained significantly more than did a group taught using conventional approaches (Anderson & Roit, 1993).

## ▦ Collaborative Strategy Instruction: An Exemplary Program

From a teaching standpoint, the students looked virtually hopeless. The failures of a group of low-achieving sixth through tenth graders had left them apathetic and discouraged. All were operating at least two years below grade level (Anderson & Roit, 1993).

Taking part in an experimental program that combined strategy instruction with collaborative learning, the students made substantial progress. The key idea of the experimental program was that students have natural problem-solving abilities that they use in their everyday lives but fail to apply to reading and writing tasks. In the program, reading was presented as a problem to be solved by the group. Each group consisted of five students and a teacher. Strategies were not prescribed but were decided on by the group. As a member of the group, the teacher was an active participant who discussed and modeled strategies but did not dictate them.

Recognizing that these students, having been in school for a number of years, have strategies for dealing with text but might not use them, the teachers built on these strategies. Based on observations of 80 students involved in the project, the researchers compiled a list of 10 strategies that students used in their everyday lives, some of which included recognizing a problem, knowing what matters, making sense, getting back on track, explaining, wrapping up experiences, and so forth. (These are actually students' labels for widely used text-reading strategies, such as predicting, summarizing, and monitoring.) Teachers helped students adapt and refine their everyday strategies so that they could be applied to understanding text.

Having endured criticism from themselves and others, older low-achieving readers are reluctant to talk about or even admit their problems with reading. Using a quality termed *cognitive empathy,* teachers looked for signs that a student was struggling: a quizzical look, a sigh, a discouraged expression. Teachers capitalized on these teachable moments to show empathy and to encourage students to reveal their thinking. In the following exchange, in which a group of students are having difficulty with the term *human aging,* the teacher's role as a facilitator is demonstrated:

**T:** I see a confused look here. Which part is confusing you?

**S1:** The part that says, "human again."

**T:** I guess it isn't really "again." Does anyone have a strategy to figure that one out? You usually have very good ones.

⚡ This is an excellent example of responsive elaboration. In response to the students' statements, the teacher leads them to use the overall sense of the passage to obtain the correct identification of *aging*.

⚡ Collaborative strategy instruction helped the students become aware of the strategies they already possessed and build on that knowledge. Students were active participants in their learning. They selected materials to read and identified the vocabulary words they felt might be difficult. They also discussed problems they had understanding the text.

**S2:** "Agging."

**T:** Do you know what "agging" means?

**S2:** To bother?

**T:** I think that if I relate this word to the title, "Growing Old," that would help me to get an idea.

**S1:** Aging.

**T:** Aging. What helped you get that?

**S1:** After you said growing old, I looked at the title and I just remembered that someone growing old is aging. (Anderson & Roit, 1993, p. 6)

Imitating the teacher's behavior, the students soon began to show cognitive empathy toward each other. Students began giving suggestions to each other and discussing strategies that they used.

Throughout the project, the emphasis was placed on the processes used to understand text rather than on getting the right answers. "The learning goal—becoming a more active reader in order to understand text better—was clear and consistent" (Anderson & Roit, 1993, p. 28). Discussions were conversational. Instead of simply asking content-specific, factual questions, teachers asked and encouraged students to ask the kinds of questions that might pop up in a natural discussion of text: What is this passage about? What is important here? These are questions that students might well ask themselves during their reading. Although lessons might vary from day to day and from teacher to teacher, the box below contains the steps in a typical lesson.

## Putting Strategies in Perspective

You need to guard against making strategy instruction too intrusive or too burdensome. Students need time to read just for pleasure or for their own purposes (Keene &

### Collaborative Strategy Instruction Lesson

*Step 1: Choose a text.* Students choose a text. Each group had a library of informational pieces that students might read.

*Step 2: Survey the text.* Students survey the text to get an overview and look for possible problems that might hinder comprehension. At this point, students pick out vocabulary that is unfamiliar. The difficult vocabulary from the text is then discussed.

*Step 3: Predict.* Students decide what they think the text might be about and what they would like to learn from it.

*Step 4: Read in segments.* Students read the text in segments. Problems with the text are discussed.

Text is discussed in terms of purposes set initially. Students also discuss any problems they experienced comprehending the text. They talk over strategies used, which ones worked and which didn't and how they might apply what they learned about reading to other texts. During discussions, teachers might also model how they use strategies to solve reading problems. For instance, a teacher might show the group how she read to the end of a sentence to get sufficient context so that she could guess the meaning of an unfamiliar word.

Cognitive strategies do require a certain amount of mental input, especially when students are learning to use them. As students become more proficient, however, the strategies become more automatic and take little or no extra effort (Graesser, 2007).

Zimmermann, 2007). Keene recalls her daughter stating that she hated strategies. The girl's overzealous teacher was having students mark five things that they thought were important on every page (Keene & Zimmermann, 2007). It's important to keep in mind that strategies are a means to an end and not an end in themselves. As Scanlon, Anderson, and Sweeney (2010) warn, "When too much emphasis is placed on strategies and too little on the materials being read, children may come to believe that it is the application of strategies that is valued and important rather than comprehension of the text" (p. 286). As Duke and her colleagues (2011) explain, "Primary focus should actually be reading for compelling purposes, with teachers guiding and helping students select strategies to meet their comprehension goals while working through the tough parts of the texts they encounter."

## Importance of Prior Knowledge

Prior knowledge has been shown to make a greater contribution to text comprehension than decoding or reported use of strategies (Samuelstuen & Bråten, 2005). Building background knowledge is especially effective if facts are tied together into generalizations or concepts so that they represent a depth of understanding. The main component of effective reading comprehension is well-organized, accessible knowledge that is cumulatively acquired and organized so that it is available for future use (Romance & Vitale, 2006).

## The Role of Reasoning

Deriving a main idea, drawing a conclusion, comparing and contrasting, making inferences, making judgments, and performing similar higher-level comprehension require the ability to reason. Reasoning can be developed. You can create the conditions that make your students smarter:

> People can become more intelligent by living and working every day in a particular kind of environment: one that coaches them in using problem-solving skills and praises them for using the skills; one that holds them accountable for using them well because it assumes they are smart and capable. This kind of learning environment can create the beliefs and dispositions that constitute intelligence. (Resnick & Hall, 2001)

## Accountable Talk

One of the most powerful techniques for fostering higher-level thinking skills and improved reading and writing is through talk. But not all talk is equal. For talk to be an efficient means for learning, it should be accountable (Resnick & Hall, 2001). Through accountable talk, students learn to think carefully about their responses and base assertions on passages from a text or other source of information. Accountable talk respects and builds on what others say. Accountable talk takes place throughout the day in teacher–student conferences, in small-group discussions, in whole-class discussions, and in student presentations. Teachers develop accountable talk by explaining, demonstrating, modeling, and coaching. They elicit accountable talk through a number of questions and probes:

- They seek clarification and explanation when called for.
- They ask for proof or justification for positions or statements.
- They recognize and help clarify erroneous concepts.
- They interpret and summarize students' statements (Resnick & Hall, 2003).

Here are some prompts that help students carry on thoughtful, accountable discussions. These prompts might be used by teachers or students:

**Drawing conclusions:**   What conclusion might we draw from these facts?

**Making within-the-text connections:**   What is the connection between losing the game in the first part of the story and the way Shauna treats the new kid?

**Making text-to-text connections:**   What story that we have read does this one remind you of?

**Making text-to-world connections:**   Do you know anyone like the main character?

**Clarifying:**   Can you explain what you mean by that? I'm not sure I understand.

**Explaining:**   Can you tell us step-by-step how Homer's invention worked?

**Predicting:**   What do you think will happen next? Why?

**Hypothesizing:**   If we added salt, what do you think would happen to the freezing temperature?

**Comparing:**   How are the twins similar in their actions?

**Contrasting:**   How are the twins different?

Here are some prompts that might be used to facilitate a discussion:

**Restating:**   Here is what you seem to be saying . . .

**Summarizing:**   So far, this is what the author has told us . . .

**Affirming:**   I like the way you gave three examples to prove your point.

**Including:**   We haven't heard from _____ yet.

**Agreeing:**   I agree with Justin, because . . .

**Building on what others have said:**   I'd like to add to what Justin said.

**Disagreeing:**   I can see how Justin came to the conclusion that the main character was unselfish. But when I think of why he did favors for others, I believe that he was just trying to get on their good side. And here is why I think that, . . .

## Questions

A key element in accountable talk is the kinds of questions that are asked. Questions are a powerful tool. You can improve students' reading performance simply by using the right kinds of questions (Hansen & Pearson, 1980). Questions also serve a multitude of purposes. They can be used to evaluate, to highlight important information, to lead a student to a conclusion or to a higher level of thinking, to get a discussion going or to keep it going, to review content, or to start a strategy lesson (Hyman, 1978). Questions also serve affective purposes. We can use questions to make a student feel part of a group, to share feelings, or to display her knowledge on a particular topic.

Teachers can also use questions to trap a student who has not been paying attention. However, this is done at a price. If questions are used to embarrass or control, then they become threatening, and the accepting atmosphere is corroded. Hyman (1978) recommends that the teacher handle the issue of paying attention by simply "calling for the students' attention in a straightforward way" (p. 4).

Judging from research and experience, low-achieving readers have been ill served by questions. In general, they are asked lower-level questions, given fewer prompts, and given less time to respond than are achieving readers. And the teacher is more likely to call on another student "to help out" the poor reader (Allington, 1984).

## Creating Questions

### For Narrative Selections

Since questions are such an important element in instruction, especially for poor readers, questioning techniques need to be planned with care. Analyzing narrative selections, Beck, Omanson, and McKeown (1982) identified the key elements in a story and constructed a map that linked these units. The key elements map (sometimes known simply as a *story map*) became a blueprint for constructing questions. The revised questions were especially helpful to the less skilled readers. The researchers found that less skilled readers had difficulty structuring the content of the story into a cohesive whole; however, responding to questions that focused on the story's main happenings significantly assisted less able readers in their attempts to create a mental map of the selection.

Creating a key elements map can be done informally by following these steps:

- List the theme, moral, starting point, or basic premise of the story.
- List the major events in the development of the plot. Include implied as well as stated events.
- List concepts or ideas that you feel students will need to know to understand the theme and other major elements in the story.

Prereading questions should prepare students for the theme and major plot occurrences. There should also be questions that guide students through the selection. Postreading questions should help students understand the basic facts of the story: Who were the main characters? What happened? Once students understand the basics of a selection, they can build on those basics and answer higher-level questions about theme, quality of story, use of literary techniques, and so forth. For an example of a simplified key elements map and questions based on the map, see Figures 11.11 and 11.12.

### For Informational Pieces

The discussion questions for an informational piece should be based on the major concepts covered in the selection. The teacher should list two to four ideas that he feels are important. Prereading questions should be designed to activate relevant schema and build background necessary to understand the article. Questions should also be posed that will help students focus on the main concepts in the selection. Postreading questions should help students clarify and organize concepts and relate new information to old. Once students have a grasp of basic

**FIGURE 11.11**
Story Elements
Map
*Source:* From Wang,
M. L. (1989). *The Ant
and the Dove.* Chicago,
IL: Children's Press.

| | |
|---|---|
| *Theme (Moral):* | You don't have to be big or strong to help someone. |
| *Plot:* | 1. A dove saves an ant from drowning.<br>2. A hunter is about to catch the dove.<br>3. The ant bites the man.<br>4. The dove flies free. |
| *Needed Concepts or Ideas:* | A dove is a bird.<br>A fable is a story that teaches a lesson. A fable usually has animals as main characters but the animals act like people. |

*Source:* From Wang, M. L. (1989). *The Ant and the Dove.* Chicago, IL: Children's Press.

information, they can respond to questions that involve evaluating information and applying it.

## Levels of Questioning

Having had an unbalanced diet of low-level questioning, low-achieving readers need questions that involve all cognitive levels. However, this does not mean that literal questions should be neglected. Poor readers do show improvement when given low-level questions (Medley, 1977). They need to know what happened in the story or what the main facts in the article are. At that point, they are ready to be lifted to higher levels.

---

**BEFORE READING**

Have you ever been in danger or trouble?
Have you ever been chased by a dog or been lost?
Have you ever been sick? Have you ever fallen down and hurt yourself?
Who helped you? Have you ever helped anyone?
Read *The Ant and the Dove.* Find out how the ant and the dove helped each other.

**AFTER READING**

How did the dove help the ant?
How did the ant thank the dove?
What did the ant promise to do?
What question did the dove ask?
Why did the dove ask "What could an ant do?"
How did the ant help the dove?
What lesson does the story teach?
Is this lesson true? Have you ever known of a small person helping a big person or a child helping a grown-up?
Do you know what kind of story this is? What kind of story teaches a lesson and has animals that act like people?

---

**FIGURE 11.12**
Questions Based
on a Story
Elements Map
*Source:* From Wang,
M. L. (1989). *The Ant
and the Dove.* Chicago,
IL: Children's Press.

A revision of Bloom's taxonomy can be found in *A Taxonomy for Learning, Teaching, and Assessing* by Anderson and Krathwohl (2001).

Questions can be classified in a number of ways. One way of arranging questions is according to the cognitive processes involved. Adapting Weinstein and Mayer's (1986) system, which was used to classify strategies, the following taxonomy evolves. The first level, comprehending, is drawn from Bloom's taxonomy (1957):

**Comprehending.** Students understand prose on a literal level. They can recite five facts stated in a selection, name the main characters, and indicate dates and places. This level also includes having students put information in their own words. This is similar to portions of Bloom's Comprehension level.

**Organizing.** Students select important details from the selection and construct relationships among them. This involves identifying or constructing main ideas, classifying, noting sequence, and summarizing. This is similar to portions of Bloom's Comprehension level.

**Elaborating.** Elaborating entails making connections between information from the text and prior knowledge and includes a wide range of activities: making inferences, creating images and analogies, and evaluating or judging. Evaluating and judging are similar to Bloom's Analysis level.

**Monitoring.** Monitoring involves being aware of cognitive processes. It involves knowing whether a selection makes sense and knowing what steps might be taken to repair comprehension.

Listed below are examples of each type of question. They are based on *Baseball's Best: Five True Stories* (Gutelle, 1990), an easy-to-read book that should appeal to older readers:

**Comprehending:** Which of the five players hit the most home runs? Which has the longest hitting streak? Which one was both a good pitcher and a good batter?

**Organizing:** In what ways were the five players alike? In what ways were they different?

**Elaborating:** Which player was most generous? Why? Which player changed baseball the most? Why? Which player was the best? Why do you think so? Picture Jackie Robinson stealing his first base in the major leagues. What do you see? What do you hear?

**Monitoring:** Did you find any confusing parts? Did you run into any words that you couldn't read or whose meanings you didn't know? If so, what did you do? Can you summarize each player's main accomplishments? If you forget how many home runs Hank Aaron hit or the number of games in which Joe DiMaggio hit safely, what might you do?

## Atmosphere

*How* questions are asked is almost as important as *what* questions are asked. Having had negative experiences with questions, low-achieving readers need an accepting, supportive atmosphere. Instead of being oral quizzes, discussions should be genuine opportunities to build the concepts, background, and thinking skills so necessary for comprehension.

### Wait Time

One small but particularly positive change that literally takes seconds to implement is to increase wait time. Typically, students are given a second or less to respond to

✳ Speaking about wait time, Hyman (1978) comments, "If the teacher does not begin to talk after each student finishes, the teacher nonverbally encourages the students to talk" (pp. 102–103).

a teacher's questions. If there is no response, the teacher repeats the question or, most often in the case of poor readers, calls on another student. After the student responds, the teacher waits less than a second before reacting to the answer (Hyman, 1978). However, studies by Hyman (1978), Lake (1973), and Rowe (1969) have shown that when a teacher increases the wait time from one second or less to three to five seconds, the following occurs: fewer no responses and "I don't knows"; greater number of correct answers; longer, more thoughtful responses; greater number of alternative responses; more evidence of reasons for answers; fewer responses that convey a "Is this what you wanted?" tone; greater confidence, as indicated by a tone of assurance in the voice; and greater number of responses from lower-achieving students.

Students weren't the only ones who benefited from longer wait times. Teachers demonstrated increased adaptability, asked fewer but more varied questions, and raised their expectations for slower students (Hyman, 1978).

## Probes and Prompts

✳ Questions can be used to help students focus on a topic, expand their responses, substantiate their answers, and lift students to higher levels of thought (Taba, 1965).

While establishing an encouraging atmosphere and using wait time are essential elements in a discussion, prompts and probes are also important. At times, low-achieving readers know the information requested by higher-level questions, but they have difficulty formulating their responses. This may be especially true of students who are still learning English. Prompts can help them shape their answers (Hyman, 1978).

For instance, to help students form concepts by grouping similar data, you might ask such questions as these: "Which of these items go together? What do all of these have in common? What would you call all of these items?" If students' answers are too brief, use an elaboration probe: "Would you please tell me more? Would you please explain?" If students are offering unsubstantiated opinions, use a specific probe: "You said you didn't like the story. What was there about the story that you didn't like? You said the main character was sly. What did she do that was sly?"

If a response is unclear, you might use a restating–crystallizing probe. In this probe, you restate what you believe the student said and then ask if your restatement is correct: "You seem to be saying that Roger was the cause of the family's problems. Is that right?" The purpose of a restating–crystallizing probe is to help the speaker clarify his thoughts. It can also be used to keep the speaker on track if he has gotten off the topic. You are also telling the speaker that you are paying close attention to him and that his opinions are worth hearing (Hyman, 1978).

English language learners might need more explicit assistance with responding to questions. They might be provided with models of responses in the form of sentence starters (Olson & Land, 2007):

- From this article, I learned that _____.
- This reminds me of _____.
- I have a question about _____.
- The character that I identify with is _____.
- I agree with Maria because _____.

## Think–Pair–Share

Think–Pair–Share is a highly effective routine for fostering discussing and thinking (Lyman, 1981). In the Think step, the teacher poses a question or topic and the students reflect on it. At the teacher's discretion, students can be directed to write a brief response. This gives them time to reflect. In the Pair step, students share their reflections with partners. This helps students develop, organize, and articulate their thoughts and provides each partner with a different perspective. To further develop students' thinking, have two sets of partners share their ideas. In the Share step, a spokesperson for each pair or group shares with the whole class her conclusion and that of her partner and/or group. The technique can be streamlined by simply having pairs of students share with each other. This is sometimes referred to as Turn and Talk.

Model the sharing technique. If possible, use the so-called fishbowl technique, in which you and another teacher or you and a student use the technique. Also provide specific questions to be answered: "Tell whether or not you think electric cars are a good idea, and give reasons for your opinion." Class discussions are usually deeper and more thoughtful after students have engaged in Think–Pair–Share.

## Lesson Plans that Foster Comprehension

Questions and discussions and direct instruction in strategies designed to improve comprehension are often conducted within the framework of a lesson plan. The best known and most widely used lesson plan formats are the directed reading activity and the directed reading–thinking activity.

## Directed Reading Activity (Guided Reading)

> **Directed reading activity (DRA):** traditional five-step plan for conducting a reading lesson that has as its core the reading of a selection. Today the DRA is often used as part of guided reading.

The **directed reading activity (DRA)** incorporates the following five steps: preparation, silent reading, discussion, rereading, and follow-up or extension. Updated to incorporate recent research and practice, today's DRA focuses on activating prior knowledge, applying strategy instruction, and gearing activities to the major concepts and structure of the selection to be read. The steps in the DRA, which have been modified for use with low-achieving readers, are described in the box that follows.

### A Directed Reading Activity Lesson

*Step 1: Preparing.* In this step, do whatever is necessary to prepare students for a successful, engrossing reading of the selection, which could be a newspaper article, a story in a basal reader, a chapter from a children's book, or an article from a magazine. As part of the preparation, introduce the selection, activate prior knowledge, build background, and develop needed vocabulary and concepts and whatever thinking skills or reading strategies might be needed to handle the selection.

The introductory phase might use discussion, demonstrations, video clips or other audiovisual aids, and/or simulations to build background. In general, background-building activities should remind students of what they already know about a topic, tie new information to students'

(Continued)

background knowledge, and focus on the important ideas in the selection to be read (Adoption Guidelines Project, 1990). At times, students have the necessary background or schema but need help activating it. Students don't automatically activate their schema.

Also engender interest in the selection and set a purpose for reading. The purpose can be set in cooperation with the students. It can be a question or series of questions to answer or a prediction to evaluate. It can also be a strategy guide of thoughtful questions (see page 445) or a graphic organizer to be completed. Build interest and engagement by helping students make connections between what they are about to read and their own lives (Neubert & Wilkins, 2004). If they are reading about recycling, for instance, they might talk about efforts they or their families or community are making to recycle. If possible, involve students in selecting the piece to be read. Also involve them in choosing the difficult vocabulary to be introduced and discussing how the story should be read and what strategies might work best with it. Because poor readers are often alienated by past failures, they need to feel involved. (The preparational stage should only take about 10 to 15 minutes. Don't spend so much time preparing students that they don't have time to read. The outcome of the preparing stage of the DRA is to set a purpose for reading. The purpose can be set by the teacher, by the students, or both.)

*Step 2:   Silent reading.* In general, the initial reading of a selection should be silent. The purpose of the DRA is to foster comprehension. When students read orally, they focus on pronouncing the words correctly. When students read silently, they focus on constructing meaning. Reading silently also provides students the opportunity to apply word-identification skills. Free from the pressure of reading aloud, students can use pronounceable word-part, analogy, context, or other word-identification strategies to figure out difficult words.

During this portion of the lesson, observe students, note their needs, and provide help to them. Students can read the whole selection all at once or read it in sections. After each section,

hold a brief discussion. Breaking up a suspenseful narrative piece into sections may lessen students' enjoyment of the selection. However, it might be wise to read a fact-packed informational text in segments. Students may need and welcome the additional guidance provided by discussing segments of the text.

During silent reading, students might take notes, complete a graphic organizer or strategy guide, use sticky notes to flag puzzling passages, or write brief responses (Neubert & Wilkins, 2004). The teacher might also break into the silent reading to remind students to use visualizing or another strategy that has been the focus of a recent lesson (Neubert & Wilkins, 2004).

*Step 3:   Discussion.* The discussion generally begins with students responding to the purpose question. If students read to find out how skyscrapers are built, for instance, the opening question might be "How are skyscrapers built?" To help students get started, the question might be "sliced" (Pearson & Johnson, 1978), or broken into easier segments: "What is the first step in building a skyscraper? The second?" During the discussion, confusions are clarified and concepts are expanded. Ideas from the selection are organized, and students relate new information in the story to information already in their background. Low-achieving readers may not see the relationships among ideas and may have difficulty constructing the main idea from a series of details. Asking students carefully crafted questions can help them organize and integrate information.

You might also do some on-the-spot teaching. For instance, one student was unsure of the word *piles*. He wondered how piles of steel could be used to hold up a skyscraper. The class discussed the word as it was used in context: "Long, thick piles of steel are sunk into the land, down to a bed of hard rock. Those piles hold up the base of the building" (Blaine, 1986, p. 164). They concluded that *piles* had a different meaning from its ordinary use as "a heap." Checking in the dictionary, they learned that a *pile* is a heavy beam driven into the ground or a riverbed.

During the discussion, be alert to students' needs. For instance, you might notice that they have difficulty with some of the compound words that appear in the selection, such as *landfill* and *framework*. Perhaps they also have problems keeping the sequence of events in mind. Mentally plan to review these areas during the rereading or follow-up portion of the lesson. The discussion can also provide an opportunity to use new vocabulary words. If the word *excessive* has been introduced, the teacher might ask "according to the author of this article, what kinds of packaging are excessive?" Discussions might also occur between or among students. Students might meet with a partner or in a small group to discuss a text. Later, the group might meet with the teacher.

*Step 4: Rereading.* Students reread the selection for a new purpose: to obtain information they missed during the initial reading, to clarify misconceptions, to focus on a particular aspect of the selection, to gain a deeper appreciation or understanding, or for a similar purpose. The rereading often offers an opportunity for a purposeful oral reading: to dramatize a portion of the selection,

to read a humorous or descriptive passage, or to clarify a disputed point, for instance. Although listed as a separate step, rereading often flows into the discussion stage, when you ask a student to read the sentences in which *piles* appears or the passage that explains how the crane is taken down from the top of a skyscraper, for instance. The rereading can also be an entirely separate step. For example, you may want to review strategies for comprehending sequence and have students apply these strategies as they reread the selection.

*Step 5: Follow-up.* The follow-up, which is an optional part of the lesson, can take many forms but should extend the main concepts or strategies stressed in the lesson or build on the lesson's content. For the skyscraper lesson, students might observe one being built and write about it, read a book on their level about skyscrapers, or read and discuss the poem "Giants of the City" by Marge Blaine (1986). Whatever the activity, it should provide opportunities for further development of reading and writing skills.

---

The DRA differs from the text walk. Depending as it does on illustrations, a text walk is best used with heavily illustrated books. As students grow in skill, shift to the DRA or a similar format.

To create a directed reading activity, first analyze the selection to be read. Note the main ideas, concepts, or principles that you wish students to learn. (If the selection is fiction, compose a key elements map.) These become the focal point for your lesson. Then list the vocabulary necessary to understand the key ideas. For instance, the major ideas in "Amazing Rescue Underground" (Shea, 1992), which is written on a second-grade level but will appeal to older students, include the following:

- Jessica, a toddler, was trapped in an abandoned water well.
- A team of rescue workers saved Jessica.

After listing the major ideas, go back over the story and jot down the vocabulary words or concepts in the story that need to be known in order to comprehend the major ideas in the selection. "Amazing Rescue Underground" has more than 20 words that might be potentially difficult. However, that is far too many for students to learn at one time. The list can be narrowed down to the following six:

| | | |
|---|---|---|
| abandoned well | backhoe | paramedics |
| rescue | microphone | cable |

After listing the difficult words, examine the article and determine its structure and what strategies will be needed to understand it. The piece has a dual structure. Primarily, it is sequential. It narrates and describes a series of steps taken to rescue the child. But it also has a cause-and-effect structure. A helpful strategy for students would be to ask "What did the rescue workers do and why?" Drawings in the article also contribute to an understanding of the story. For instance, it mentions that a rathole rig was used to dig. Drawings depict a rathole rig better than any words could.

At this point, you are now ready to structure a preparatory discussion that will activate schema, build background and vocabulary, set a purpose, guide students in the use of reading and thinking strategies, and, last but not least, motivate the students to want to read the selection. Note how this is done in the sample DRA presented in the following box, keeping in mind that this selection could have been handled in a number of different ways.

## Directed Reading Activity for "Amazing Rescue Underground"

**Step 1: Preparing.** Writing the title, "Amazing Rescue Underground," on the board, ask the class what they think the story might be about. To make sure that the class knows what *rescue* means and will recognize it in print, point to it as you say it and amplify and clarify students' responses, if necessary. Direct the class to turn to the story on p. 28 and to examine the illustration. Ask, "Based on the illustration, what do you think the story will be about?" As the illustration is being discussed, point out the cover for the abandoned well in the foreground. Write "abandoned well" on the board. As students discuss the possible content of the story, point to the vocabulary, previously written on the board, and ask why each might be needed in a rescue at an abandoned well: *microphone,* a *backhoe, paramedics,* and a *cable.*

Assessing the students' knowledge of each term, devote as much time to each as is needed. Having built the needed vocabulary and background and activated students' prior knowledge, set a purpose for reading. Pointing out that Jessica, the child in the purple overalls, falls in the well, ask students to read to find out what steps were taken to rescue her and why. Suggest that, as students read, they use the pictures in the selection to help them understand what has happened and also to picture in their minds important scenes that are not shown.

**Step 2: Silent reading.** As the students read silently, note whether they are having any difficulty. For instance, if you see that several students are trying to sound out *petroleum* and one seems stumped by *inquiries* and *ambulance,* make a note to review pronounceable word-parts and analogy strategies as applied to multisyllabic words. Also review context clues.

**Step 3: Discussing.** Begin the discussion with the purpose question: "What steps were taken to rescue Jessica and why?" The class talks over the steps that were taken and why each was taken. Having been engrossed in the story, they have a good sense of the sequence of events. However, there may be some confusion. For instance, some students might believe that the paramedics helped with the digging. If so, ask students to locate and read passages that clarify that point. (This is a valid purpose for orally rereading passages.) Other issues are also discussed as they come up: why the second hole had to be dug, why it had to be dug by hand, how the mother helped, how Jessica must have felt, what it was like to drill the tunnel, how long it took to drill the tunnel, what petroleum jelly is and why it was used.

**Step 4: Rereading.** During the discussion, you might note that the students had difficulty explaining why the rescue took two days. Have the class skim through the selection to find passages that tell why the rescue took so long. Help them calculate the time that it took to dig the tunnel. Also review strategies for figuring out some troublesome words: *petroleum, ambulance, inquiries.*

*(Continued)*

*Step 5: Follow-up.* Building on the words *microphone* and *paramedic,* extend students' understanding of the forms *micro* and *para*. If the class still has some questions about the rescue and they want to know what happened to Jessica since the rescue, bring in a magazine article that gives her last name. Then, with the help of the media specialist, the class might locate updates on Jessica McClure. The class might also view a made-for-TV movie of the rescue and compare the TV version with the selection they have read.

## Directed Reading–Thinking Activity

> **Directed reading–thinking activity (DR–TA):** form of the DRA in which students make predictions and read to verify their predictions. The DR–TA requires that students bring some background knowledge to a selection. Without adequate background, students will have difficulty making predictions.

Based on the DRA, the **directed reading–thinking activity (DR–TA)** places greater emphasis on student involvement. In the DR–TA, students predict what the selection might be about and then read to evaluate their predictions. Because they are more active participants in a DR–TA, students also shoulder greater responsibility for their learning. They must be able and willing to generate questions, know how to ignore irrelevant material in their quest to have their questions answered, suspend judgment, and read flexibly. They must also be able to modify their predictions if they encounter information that conflicts with their ideas (Stauffer, 1969). The DR–TA can be an especially effective technique for use with low-achieving readers because it involves them more directly and more personally in the reading process. Like the DRA, the DR–TA also has five steps.

## A DR–TA Lesson

*Step 1: Preparing.* The preparation stage of the DR–TA is less extensive than that of the DRA. Under your guidance, students discuss the title and predict what they believe the story might be about. They then examine and discuss illustrations and say whether they would change their predictions. Headings and the first paragraph might also be used if the title and illustration(s) are not helpful. In order to involve all students, make sure that each one makes a prediction, or at least agrees with a prediction that someone else has made. List the predictions on the board and have students say with which one they agree. After making or choosing their predictions, students read to evaluate them. For instance, in preparation for reading the first chapter of *The Chalk Box Kid* (Bulla, 1987), you might discuss the title and have students predict what the story seems to be about. Discuss the cover illustration and encourage students to use additional information to adjust or elaborate on their predictions. Because the title and illustration provide a very limited basis for making predictions, read the initial portion of the text, down to the sentence on the second page of the story that says, "So far it was his very worst birthday." Discuss that segment of the text and have students make a final prediction as to what might happen in the first chapter. Write their predictions on the board. Make sure that everyone is involved either in making a new prediction or supporting a prediction that has already been made.

Although not typically included in a DR–TA, provision might also be made for prereading assistance with difficult vocabulary words and concepts. Write key vocabulary words on the board and discuss each one. You might suggest to students that they use the words as an added basis for making their predictions.

*(Continued)*

*Step 2:    Silent reading.* Students read until they are able to respond to their predictions. This might occur after a page of reading or at the end of the selection. As students read, they should be prepared to revise their predictions if necessary.

*Step 3:    Discussing.* The discussion stage of the DR–TA is very similar to that of the DRA, except that the discussion is initiated with a consideration of students' predictions. Students evaluate their predictions. If they stayed with their original predictions, they supply reasons or details to support their positions. If they revised them, they tell how and why they did so. The discussion can also be expanded to encompass major elements in the selection just as was done in the DRA discussion.

*Step 4:    Rereading.* Same as in the DRA.

*Step 5:    Follow-up.* Same as in the DRA.

The DR–TA, with its emphasis on making, verifying, and revising predictions, is an excellent technique. Because it requires students to justify and verify predictions, it fosters higher level thinking (Stahl, 2004). However, it does not work well if students need extensive guidance or have such a limited background for a selection that they have very little basis for making predictions. It does, however, provide a bridge from heavily teacher-directed procedures, such as the DRA, to strategies that the student applies independently, and it is an excellent device for turning passive readers into active ones.

## ▓▓▓  **Other Techniques for Building Comprehension**

### Cloze Procedure

**Cloze:** way of assessing comprehension by having a student fill in missing words that have been deleted from a selection. The cloze procedure can also be used as a comprehension test or as a way to estimate the difficulty level of a text.

Short for *closure,* **cloze** is a procedure that has students read selections in which words have been deleted. Generally, every 5th, 7th, or 10th word has been removed, but other patterns of deletion are possible. As they read, students attempt to restore the omitted words.

Try the following cloze exercise. As you fill in the blanks, ask yourself: "What does this task require me to do? What strategies does it require me to use? What kinds of readers would benefit from this type of activity?"

**A Famous Author**

The only daughter of rich parents, Beatrix Potter spent most of her days by herself. There were no other _____ and boys around to _____ with. But she did _____ to draw. She spent _____ happy hours drawing pictures _____ plants and animals.

Later, _____she was grown up, _____ sent letters to a _____ little boy. The little _____ was sick. In her _____, she told stories. One story _____ about a rabbit who _____ into trouble when he _____ into a farmer's garden. _____ little boy liked the _____. So did other boys _____ girls.

Beatrix Potter decided _____ make a book out _____ the story about the _____. Some people cautioned her _____ to. They believed she _____ only sell a few _____ and would lose a _____ of money. But Beatrix Potter_____ ahead with plans for _____ the book. As it _____ out, boys and girls _____ over the world liked _____ book. Can you guess _____ the title of Beatrix Potter's _____ is? If you said *The Tale of Peter Rabbit,* _____ are right.

Beatrix Potter_____ 22 other books and _____ a famous children's author. _____ books were mostly about _____, kittens, and other animals. _____ the book that boys _____ girls liked best was_____ first book. Although *The Tale of Peter Rabbit* _____ been around for close _____ 100 years, it is _____ being read today. In fact, it is one of the best-liked children's books of all time.

Here are the words that were omitted: *girls, play, like, many, of, when, she, friend's, boy, letters, was, got, sneaked, The, story, and, to, of, rabbit, not, would, books, lot, went, publishing, turned, all, her, what, book, you, wrote, became, Her, ducks, But, and, her, has, to, still.* Check your responses. How did you do?

✲ Cloze fosters reading for meaning and use of context. It is especially effective for students who fail to read for meaning, but should only be used with students reading at least on a third-grade level. Cloze is an excellent device for fostering sentence-level comprehension but is not a particularly effective way to develop passage-level comprehension.

Because words are omitted, cloze forces readers to use their background knowledge and knowledge of language to restore the missing words. Cloze also demands a close attention to meaning. The reader can't fill in a blank if he doesn't have a good grasp of what he has read. If the reader hasn't comprehended what he has read, he will have no basis for filling in the blanks. Cloze works especially well with students who overuse phonics clues, fail to use context, or fail to read for meaning.

Discussion is an essential element in the application of cloze (Jongsma, 1980). Students should justify their choices, especially if exact replacements aren't required. Explaining their responses clarifies students' thinking, and it is also helpful for them to hear why others made the choices they did. Discussion also makes for a livelier lesson.

Although you might choose to accept reasonable substitutes in lieu of exact replacements, have students compare their finished products to the originals. Comparison of their choices with the words used by the author should be interesting and should help students see the importance of word choice. If you do make this kind of comparison, inform students that they are doing fine if their responses match those of the author half of the time. The standard for a cloze score at the instructional level is 44 to 57 percent. Table 11.2 presents the criteria for cloze levels based on exact replacements. When the standards in Table 11.2 are applied and only exact replacements are counted as being correct, cloze can be used as a placement test.

Before students start a cloze exercise, give them some tips for completing it. They should read the whole piece first to get an overview. During their second reading of the selection, they should read to the end of each sentence or beyond before attempting to fill in the blank. Students naturally stop at the blank, but often the words beyond the blank provide essential information. Clues may even be found in the next sentence or two. After students have filled in the blanks, they should go back and see if there are any changes they wish to make.

Tell students to ignore spelling. If students worry about spelling, they will lose their focus and also restrict their responses to words they can spell.

| Level | Percentage of Correct Replacements |
|---|---|
| Independent | > 57 |
| Instructional | 44–57 |
| Frustration | < 44 |

**TABLE 11.2**
Criteria for Cloze

### Constructing Cloze Exercises

Choose material that is interesting and on the appropriate level of difficulty. Don't use material that presents a number of new concepts, because this makes it extra hard to fill in the blanks. In classical cloze, which was originally used to assess the difficulty level of printed materials, selections were 250 words in length and every fifth word was omitted, so there would be a total of 50 deletions. Having fewer deletions makes the task easier. Controlling deletions also simplifies the task. Content words, such as nouns and verbs, are more difficult to restore than structure words, conjunctions, prepositions, and articles. Deletions made at the middle or end of a sentence are also easier to restore than are deletions made at the beginning of a sentence (Rye, 1982). Deletions are also easier to restore if the clues to the deletion precede it rather than come after it.

The types of deletions you make depend on the strategies you wish to reinforce. Restoring deleted content words, especially nouns and verbs, requires comprehension of details. Restoring structure words involves using language cues and noting relationships. Whether using classical or adapted cloze, do not delete any proper nouns or any words from the first or last sentence.

Although many students enjoy the challenge of cloze, it needs to be introduced with care. Students, especially those who lack confidence, may be upset by the task if they don't understand its nature. When introducing cloze, explain the nature of the activity and tell students what it is called and why. Students respond positively when they are treated as competent individuals capable of learning mature concepts. Also model the process of filling in the blanks in a sample cloze exercise. Emphasize the need to use language as well as content clues and to go beyond the blanks when necessary. Provide guided practice.

Because cloze is a fairly difficult activity, it is not recommended, in its classical form, for students reading below a third-grade level. However, students operating on a lower level can engage in modified cloze or masking.

---

**Using Technology**

Intervention Central: Maze Passage Generatorhttp://www
.interventioncentral.org/tools/
maze-passage-generator

If you want to use maze passages, Maze Passage Generator is a helpful aid. Paste a passage in and a maze passage is generated.

---

### Modified Cloze

In modified cloze, also known as *mazes,* students fill in the blanks by choosing one of three or more options so that cloze becomes a multiple-choice activity. Modified cloze, although not as valuable as classical cloze, is a reasonable alternative for students who have difficulty with classical cloze because of word-retrieval problems or students who are overly concerned with spelling. Mazes are frequently used for monitoring basic comprehension.

### Masking

Masking is a form of cloze that is frequently used in shared reading situations. After an initial reading of the selection, the teacher covers predictable words with masking tape. Then as she comes to the word, she asks students to predict what the covered word might be. After students make and discuss their predictions, the covered word is unmasked. This exercise is especially valuable for students who neglect context clues.

## Think-Alouds

As noted in Chapter 5, think-alouds can be used to obtain additional information about the processes that a student uses in reading comprehension or word analysis. Think-alouds can also be used as an instructional technique. For instance, one way for you to demonstrate the thinking processes that go on as you make a prediction, summarize a story, use context to figure out a hard word, or engage in any number of reading or writing processes is to let students know your thought processes through thinking aloud. You simply tell what is going on in your head as you make a prediction: "Based on this heading, I predict that this section will tell about some helpful kinds of beetles."

When introducing think-alouds to students, first explain what they are, how they might help comprehension, and how, when, and where they might be used. Then model a think-aloud, and provide for guided and independent practice. As you model a think-aloud, stress comprehension strategies that you have previously taught, such as predicting and summarizing, and metacognitive strategies, such as checking and repairing.

Still another use of think-alouds is to have students apply them as they read a selection. They can think aloud with a partner, with the two of them reading alternate paragraphs and telling each other what they were thinking about as they read. The listening partner can ask probing questions such as "What were you thinking about? Were there any confusing parts? Were there any hard words?" The listening partner might fill out a brief think-aloud form, which can be a vehicle for discussion between the two.

Think-alouds help students become more aware of the ways in which they process text and use monitoring and other comprehension strategies. Think-alouds also provide insight into the students' thought processes and the manner in which they are applying strategies. Therefore, think-alouds provide a unique opportunity for on-the-spot guidance. For instance, if a student admits to being confused by a passage and does not seem to know what to do about it, you can lead her to some possible repair strategies, asking such questions as "What don't you understand? What is blocking your understanding? What do you need to know? What might you do to make this clear? Would rereading the sentence help? Would starting over help?"

## Developmental Retelling

Retelling is used both to assess and foster readers' comprehension of stories. To retell a selection, the student must comprehend the story, be aware of the structure of stories, be able to analyze the story, possess the language required to retell the story, and be able to organize the events of the selection in sequence (Benson & Cummins, 2000). Some students might have a vivid mental representation of the story but lack the language or processing skills needed to retell it.

Developmental retelling is a way of improving the student's comprehension of selections, as well as his language and cognitive skills, by building prerequisite skills and fostering retelling skills that match the student's level of development (Benson & Cummins, 2000). Developmental retelling levels include pretelling, guided retelling, and written retelling.

### Pretelling

In pretelling, students explain an everyday task, such as assembling a toy, playing a game, dribbling a basketball, or using a new computer program. Students must be able to think backward to reconstruct the steps of the task and then think forward to put the steps in order.

As with other strategies, you should model the process. In demonstrating the steps in making a booklet, for instance, show each step while explaining what you are doing. Then in reconstructing the steps, hold up the booklet and show and explain what you did first, second, and so forth. Stress the use of the words that denote sequence: *first, second, third, next,* and *last.* Summarize the demonstration by listing the steps in order on the board. After more demonstrations, have students share in the pretellings and then pretell with partners and on their own.

## Guided Retelling

When students have become adept at pretelling, introduce guided retelling. Students retell a story aided at first by illustrations and then by artifacts. Read the selection aloud, and show how you use the illustrations to aid in your retelling. Select pieces that have illustrations that clearly depict the key parts of the story. After demonstrating and reviewing the technique with students, invite them to join in as you retell with illustrations. Then have students engage in illustration-supported retellings with a partner, a small group, and a larger group. Encourage students to use only the illustrations when retelling.

After students are able to retell with illustrations, introduce the use of props, such as puppets, items from the story, or pictures of objects or people from the story. Unlike the illustrations, which depict all the key elements in a selection, props might consist of four or five pictures or artifacts that represent the highlights of the selection. Felt boards or pocket charts might be used to hold the props.

*Written Retelling*   After successfully using props, have students create graphic organizers, such as story maps and time lines, to support their retellings.

Graphic organizers also provide good preparation for written retelling. Students use a story map or other graphic organizer as a plan for composing a written retelling. At each stage, model the process of retelling, and provide lots of practice. Then gradually turn the process over to students (Gunning, 2010).

## ▚ Sentence-Level Comprehension

Students with severe comprehension problems may have difficulty understanding the simplest paragraphs. For these students, it may be necessary to start with the comprehension of single sentences. Begin by discussing and asking questions about simple sentences. Ask the student to read a sentence similar to the following and tell what it says:

The boy ran.

**Ask:** Who ran? What did the boy do?

Expand the sentence and have the student answer questions about the expansion. The boy ran home.

**Ask:** Where did the boy run?

The boy ran home because it was getting dark.

**Ask:** Why did the boy run home?

Gradually work up to sentences that contain embedded clauses and other complex structures. *Embedded clauses* are clauses that have been placed within a sentence through subordination and are one of the most complex structures, especially if the embedded clause interrupts the flow of the sentence:

The boy who yelled to us ran home.

**Ask:** Which boy ran home?

Reassembling cut-up sentences, performing sentence-level cloze, paraphrasing, completing sentences by adding clauses (Sarah was late for class because …), indexing and composing sentences are good reinforcement activities. As the student learns to comprehend single sentences, proceed to brief paragraphs and then to longer pieces. ReQuest, which is explained in Chapter 12, is also an excellent technique for use with students who have severe comprehension problems.

Ultimately, comprehension requires building an accurate textbase, which means that students need to understand individual sentences and the relationships among sentences (Dewitz, 2012). Complex syntax can trip up students, especially those who struggle. The structures in Table 11.3 pose particular problems.

One way to improve comprehension is to increase students' familiarity with many kinds of sentences. Read to your class regularly. Include both fiction and non-fiction and include a variety of authors so that students internalize a variety of literary patterns. Discuss the meanings of sentences that seem especially difficult. Also invite students to bring in confusing sentences and have the class discuss and interpret them (Schoenbach et al., 2012).

Written directions often require special attention. Discuss their meanings; they are often written in a single sentence that prescribes several actions. Talk about the actions that such a sentence might be describing. Model how you might take the sentence apart to understand it better.

Ask "who," "what," "where," "when," and "why" questions about sentences that are complicated. This encourages students to get used to questions and also focuses attention on complex elements. The questions also can direct students' attention to the main parts of a text and will model the kinds of questions students might ask themselves as they encounter puzzling sentences. For the sentence below, you might ask the questions that follow.

Alex, Fred's little brother, was not unhappy with the new toy, a robot that could be programmed to speak 10 words.

"Who was Alex? How did he feel?" If a student says, "unhappy," ask questions that will help direct him to the correct response: "What does unhappy mean? How do you feel when you are not unhappy?"

| Structure | Example |
|---|---|
| Passive voice | The heavy wooden plow was pulled by a team of oxen. |
| Negation | Clearing the land was not an easy task. |
| Relative or embedded clauses | The settler who did not lend a hand to those who needed help was scorned. |
| Appositives | His uncle, a short but muscular jack-of-all-trades, supervised the raising of the barn. |
| Clauses or verbals as subjects | Growing sufficient food despite drought or plant disease was necessary for survival |
| Sentences in which events are not recorded in the order they happened | Before hitching up the horses, Ben fed them. |

**TABLE 11.3**
Structure Problems

Show students how it might be necessary to paraphrase sentences that are especially complex or confusing, such as the following:

> The boy who broke the bat that had belonged to Jack's father who had briefly played for the Yankees volunteered to buy Jack a new one.

Reconstructing sentences can boost comprehension. Weaver (1979) found that third graders who used word cards to compose sentences demonstrated a significant improvement in comprehension. Research indicates that the most vital parts of a sentence are the verb or action, the agent, objects, and recipients. Thus students were taught to locate the action word first and then construct a sentence by asking *who, what, where, when, how,* and *why.* After constructing the sentence, students were to ask themselves, "Does the order of the words in the sentence make sense? If not, have I tried ordering the words in other ways? Have all the words been used? If not, have all the questions been asked?" Questions were explained as were action words. The procedure was carefully modeled, and guided practice was also provided.

An element that sometimes causes confusion in sentence comprehension is anaphora. **Anaphora** is the use of a word to substitute for a preceding word or group of words. The most common example is that of a pronoun and its antecedent; for example, "The dog ate its food," where *its* substitutes for *dog.* Common examples of anaphora include the following (Baumann & Stevenson, 1986):

Selective Taxonomy of Anaphoric Relationships

| | | |
|---|---|---|
| 1. Noun substitutes | | |
|   **a.** Pronouns | | *Will and George* were here, but *they* left about an hour ago. |
|   **b.** Synonyms or more general words | | *The polar bear* started toward us, but a loud noise distracted the *beast.* |
| 2. Verb substitutes | | I can't *sing* but Melanie *can.* |
| 3. Causal substitutes | | He believes *our team will win,* but I don't think *so.* |

Anaphora: use of a word to substitute for a preceding word or group of words.

The ability to handle anaphora increases with age and reading ability (Irwin, 1986). Instruction can be helpful, especially when students are facing potentially confusing sentences, such as "The teacher told John that he would be staying after school."

The reader would be rightfully confused because it isn't clear who will be staying after school, the teacher or John. In this instance, readers should be told to use other information in the selection and/or their knowledge of social situations and the way the world works to decipher the sentence (McNeil, 1987). For older students you might bring in ambiguous headlines or brief excerpts from periodicals and other sources. Demonstrate in a think-aloud how you might resolve ambiguities.

Explain the function of anaphora and provide practice in identifying anaphoric elements and the words they refer to. While discussing reading selections, you might question students about the overall meaning of sentences containing anaphoric elements and about their antecedents: "Who is laughing? Who are *they?* Who is in the group? What other word did the author use for *kid?* What is the author referring to when he uses the word *vehicles?* What does *latter* refer to?" Texts in which the pronoun and antecedent are more than a sentence apart can be especially challenging for struggling readers (Dewitz, 2012). For complex or tangled relationships, have students draw arrows to show pronoun–antecedent relationships.

Also model how you handle a sentence in which it isn't clear what the antecedent is. Include sentences in which careful analysis will help, as well as others where the sense of the passages, common sense, or reader's knowledge might be used.

Writing should also help students become familiar with anaphoric elements. Emphasize that pronouns should clearly refer to their antecedents. Show students how sentences of this type are written. Help students correct unclear faulty references that appear in their writing. The use of manipulatives might also be used to straighten out tangled syntax.

## ▦ Mini–Case Study

Although Jennifer was a 9-year-old third grader and had no difficulty with decoding at grade level, her comprehension was poor (Sawyer, 1985). When asked to retell selections at the second- and third-grade levels, Jennifer's responses were brief, very general, and involved simply stating the topic: "It's about bears and honey." She was unable to supply details about a selection, and when asked specific questions, she based her responses on her background knowledge and not on the text. For the most part, her responses were only marginally related to the questions.

Further testing indicated that Jennifer was able to understand simple sentences but had difficulty with complex sentences, especially those that had embedded clauses, as in "It was the first time Bill went to camp." Jennifer also had difficulty integrating information across paragraphs. In addition, Jennifer experienced problems following directions, apparently because she failed to focus on key words. Jennifer was able to organize information, but she had difficulty explaining how or why she organized it. Although she was able to categorize items correctly, she was unable to supply a category name or title.

A program of intervention focused on comprehension and, in particular, the thinking skills that are an essential element in comprehension. Instruction was initiated with materials on a late-first-grade to beginning-second-grade level. Activities designed to foster application of prediction strategies on the sentence level included cloze exercises (President _____ freed the slaves.) and complete-the-sentence exercises (Columbus sailed west because _____.). To foster comprehension across sentences, Jennifer was also asked to complete unfinished paragraphs (The day was dark and gloomy. Hurricane warnings were in effect and the winds were howling around the house. Suddenly, sheets of rain began to blow toward the beaches. May's father rushed in through the door and said, _____.").

To activate Jennifer's schemata and to help set a purpose for reading, semantic maps or structured overviews were suggested for use with her before she read a selection. Because Jennifer spoke mainly in short, simple sentences, activities to develop oral language were also recommended (Sawyer, 1985).

## ▦ Summary

According to schema theory, comprehension is an active, constructive process that activates a reader's schemata. Comprehension can go awry if the reader lacks the necessary schema, fails to activate it, or activates the wrong schema. The situation (mental model) model complements the schema theory of comprehension. According to the situation model point of view, readers create mental representations as they read. Comprehension consists of multiple levels of understanding and includes a surface code, propositional textbase, and the situation or mental model. The surface code is composed of the exact words and syntax of the written piece. The textbase includes the ideas but not the exact words conveyed by the surface structure and also includes low level inferences made by the reader. A situation model includes the reader's prior knowledge and inferences and judgments that the reader makes. Comprehension requires four main processing abilities: understanding key details at a literal level, integrating text across sentences and paragraphs, making inferences, and monitoring for meaning. Short-term memory is also an essential component.

Causes of poor reading comprehension are multiple and involve an interaction of reader, task, text, teaching technique, and situation. Major causes within the reader include limited vocabulary, language deficiency, deficient decoding skills, inadequate background or poorly developed schema, lack of intellectual curiosity or interest or flexibility in considering new ideas, inadequate use of thinking skills, lack of strategies, and failure to apply strategies. Overreliance on background and failure to read for meaning also cause comprehension difficulties. Although reader factors were emphasized in this chapter, teaching techniques, using appropriate texts, and the quality of the overall learning situation have a critical impact on comprehension.

One key to comprehension is the effective use of strategies. Strategies can be classified according to the cognitive processes they incorporate: preparing, selecting and organizing, elaborating, rehearsal (studying), and monitoring (metacognition). Strategies should be regarded as a means to an end and not as ends in themselves.

Higher-level comprehension demands higher-level thinking skills. Accountable talk and well-chosen questions can develop both thinking and comprehension and improve attitudes. Questions should be balanced and include items from all levels: comprehending (literal level), selecting/organizing, elaborating, and monitoring (metacognition). Creating an accepting atmosphere is important to questioning. Using wait time and prompts enhances the effectiveness of questions.

The directed reading activity (DRA), which includes guided reading, is an instructional framework that incorporates the activation of schema, building of background and vocabulary, and the use of strategies and questions to build comprehension. The directed reading–thinking activity (DR–TA) is modeled on the DRA but gives the student a more active role.

Cloze, which is short for *closure,* is a procedure that has students read selections in which words have been deleted. As they read, students restore the deletions. In simplified versions, students use multiple-choice items to fill in the cloze blanks (mazes) or respond to one item at a time under the teacher's guidance (masking).

Some severely disabled comprehenders may need help with sentence-level comprehension and understanding questions. They might be aided by using indexing.

Another technique for teaching comprehension is think-alouds, which include Mystery Passages. Think-alouds can be used by the teacher to model comprehension processes. Think-alouds, when used by students, help them to become more aware of their thinking and reading processes. Developmental retelling scaffolds the skills required by retelling. For students with serious comprehension problems, it may be necessary to work on understanding sentences and questions.

## Application Activities

1. Plan a lesson presenting one of the strategies described in the chapter. If possible, teach the lesson and evaluate it.

2. If you are now teaching, try using wait time and probes for a week. What changes do you notice in your students? In yourself? Ask a colleague to act as a coach and observe your performance and give you suggestions for improvement. If you are not teaching, try the technique in a small discussion group.

3. Plan a DRA (guided reading) or DR–TA, and teach your lesson if possible. If you teach the lesson, write an evaluation of it.

4. Construct a cloze or maze activity, and try it out with a class. How did the class react?

5. Do a think-aloud with a partner on a challenging informational piece or a difficult piece of fiction. What strategies did your partner use? What strategies did you use?

## My Education Lab

Go to the topic Reading Assessment in the MyEducationLab (www.myeducationlab .com) for Assessing and Correcting Reading Difficulties, where you can:

- Find learning outcomes for Reading Assessment along with the national standards that connect to these outcomes.

- Complete Assignments and Activities that can help you more deeply understand the chapter content.

- Apply and practice your understanding of the core teaching skills identified in the chapter with the Building Teaching Skills and Dispositions learning units.

- Examine challenging situations and cases presented in the Iris Center Resources.

- Check your comprehension of the content covered in the chapter with the Study Plan. Here you will be able to take a chapter pretest, receive feedback on your answers, and then access personalized Review, Practice, and Enrichment exercises to enhance your understanding of chapter content. After you complete the exercises, take a posttest to confirm your comprehension.

- Practice targeting instruction and making content accessible for all students with A+RISE activities.

# Reading to Learn and Remember in the Content Areas

**A**lthough most of the skills and strategies needed to comprehend content-area texts were introduced in the previous chapter, research shows that students often fail to transfer general skills and strategies to specific areas. A number of techniques and approaches for teaching the application of literacy skills to content areas will be discussed.

**USING WHAT YOU KNOW**

What has been your experience reading in content areas? Which subject-matter texts in your undergraduate or graduate courses did you find particularly difficult? What made them difficult? What strategies did you employ to improve your comprehension? What special difficulties might low-achieving readers experience as they attempt to read content-area material? What steps might you take to help low-achieving readers read content-area texts?

**ANTICIPATION GUIDE**

*Read each of the following statements. Put a check under "Agree" or "Disagree" to show how you feel about each one. If possible, discuss your responses with classmates.*

|  | AGREE | DISAGREE |
|---|---|---|
| 1. The content-area teacher is not responsible for teaching reading or study strategies to poor readers. | _____ | _____ |
| 2. The main reason that low-achieving readers have difficulty with content-area texts is because they lack general reading skills and strategies. | _____ | _____ |
| 3. A major barrier to comprehension of content-area texts is a lack of background knowledge in that area. | _____ | _____ |
| 4. Low-achieving readers should get most of their content-area information from lectures, discussions, experiments, and audiovisual aids, rather than from books. | _____ | _____ |
| 5. The biggest obstacle to effective studying is a lack of discipline. | _____ | _____ |
| 6. Study skills are neglected at all levels of schooling. | _____ | _____ |

## ⬛⬜⬛ The Challenge of Content-Area Texts

A n extensive assessment of seventh graders that included disabled and nondisabled students revealed that both groups had difficulty highlighting main ideas
and supporting details, taking notes, creating graphic organizers, or writing coherent reports (Englert et al., 2009). In general, the students had difficulty selecting,
organizing, and reporting on essential information. They were ill prepared to use
content texts. This was especially true of students with LDs or other learning difficulties. As Englert and colleagues noted, "Students with disabilities did not know
how to organize, classify, and label their expository ideas" (p. 157). For the most
part, they simply copied passages or portions of passages. They did not engage
with the ideas in the texts in any meaningful way. The study authors recommended
instruction in the "specific learning strategies that will help them to comprehend,
compose, study, and learn. . . . Based on this research, it is apparent that such
instruction must include a focus on the organizational and rehearsal strategies that
support students as they attempt to read to learn and write to learn" (p. 158).

Fortunately, research on comprehension instruction for struggling learners is
encouraging. Teaching strategies and study techniques, careful questioning, enhancing the text with visuals or embedded questions, and providing basic reading instruction, such as phonics or vocabulary instruction if needed, should improve students'
ability to engage with content texts. Peer tutoring, use of computer-assisted instruction, and use of graphic organizers also have the potential to build improved comprehension. What most of these treatments have in common is "an effort to teach
students to attend more carefully or to think more systematically about text as it [is]
being read" (Scruggs, Mastropieri, Berkeley, & Graetz, 2009, p. 433).

## ⬛⬜⬛ Content Enhancement

**Using Technology**

Center for Research on Learning:
Content Enhancement

http://www.kucrl.org/sim/content.shtml

Provides information on Content
Enhancement.

O ne way to help students learn content is through Content
Enhancement. Content Enhancement is an approach to
teaching curriculum content that is designed to assist struggling
readers, but it also helps achieving readers (Fisher, Schumaker, &
Deshler, 2002). Content Enhancement, which is also known as strategic teaching, is instruction "in which the teacher compensates
for students' lack of strategies and models and guides students in
learning how to learn" (Bulgren & Scanlon, 1997/1998, p. 293).
Content Enhancement organizes and presents the curriculum in such a way that
key concepts are easier to learn and more readily learned.

Here are the steps for implementing Content Enhancement, as adapted from
Torgesen (2004a):

*Step 1:*   Compose two or three key questions that the unit should answer.

*Step 2:*   Create a concept map of the key content for the unit.

*Step 3:*   Based on an examination of the key questions and the content map and
text, note the difficulties that your students, especially the struggling readers, might
experience.

*Step 4:*   Use the potential difficulties and the nature of the material to be learned
to select Content Enhancement Routines that will help learners understand key
concepts by relating them to prior knowledge and noting defining characteristics.
Content Enhancement includes lesson organizer routines in which students are

shown how the key ideas in a lesson are related to each other, to past and future lessons, and to the unit of study. A framing routine helps students see how details and main ideas are related. And a survey routine highlights the most important content.

*Step 5:* Based on the potential difficulties and the nature of the text, decide on key learning strategies that students will need to use. Strategies are similar to those presented in this text.

*Step 6:* Incorporate the Content Enhancements and student strategies in your instruction.

*Step 7:* Monitor students' progress, and make adjustments as necessary (Gunning, 2012, p. 421).

## Framework for Teaching Content-Area Reading

Teaching content-area reading consists mainly of applying and adapting techniques and approaches described in Chapter 11 and includes adaptations of the Content Enhancements discussed above. A convenient way to look at a content-area reading lesson is to view it within the framework of a directed reading activity (guided reading). A content-area reading lesson is basically an adaptation of the directed reading activity or directed reading–thinking activity. Implemented within the context of Content Enhancement, it includes establishing key ideas, preparation for reading, guided reading, rereading, extension, application, and monitoring of student progress.

### Establishing Key Ideas

As noted when discussing the directed reading activity and a number of other teaching techniques, the starting point of effective instruction is to decide which key ideas or concepts you want your students to learn and then to structure questions and activities around them. Barron (1969) recommends that you analyze the selection to be read and select two to four key concepts. (Key concepts for lessons are easier to determine if you have established key questions for the unit and a concept map.) Creating key questions will give focus to your lesson and help you to determine how to prepare students for the reading of a selection and how to guide their efforts.

### Preparing for Reading

Preparation for reading in the content areas can take many forms but generally includes activating schema and building background, expanding vocabulary, building reasoning skills and reading strategies, establishing a purpose for reading, and motivating students. Special emphasis is placed on removing barriers to learning.

> To help students relate their background of experience to content-area concepts, express the concepts in such a way that students can bring their prior knowledge to bear (Herber & Herber, 1993). A key concept such as that of representative government might be expressed as "Sometimes we let others speak for us."

#### Activating Schema and Building Background

No matter how arcane the topic, students will usually have some background knowledge to bring to it. What is important is helping students use what knowledge they have to build a bridge to the new material they are about to read. One characteristic of low-achieving readers is that even when they have relevant background knowledge, they may not realize it. An essential element in the preparation process is to help students discover what they do know about a topic.

Part of helping them discover what they know is to create questions that tap into their prior knowledge. For instance, when developing the concept of representative government in preparation for reading about the Revolutionary War, you might relate this to how a class votes for a representative for the school's student council. Building on this concrete experience, lead students into a discussion about how the colonies were governed by Great Britain and had no representatives to speak for them.

### Expanding Vocabulary

Once you have established the key ideas that you wish to emphasize, choose the vocabulary words that you feel students may have difficulty with but that are essential for an understanding of the key ideas. A selection may include 20 to 25 or more words that you feel might be difficult for your students. Learning all those words would be overwhelming. By concentrating on those words that are most essential for an understanding of the key ideas, you limit the number of words that need to be introduced. When introducing new words, keep the number to 6 or 7.

### Building Reasoning Skills and Strategies

When you are analyzing the selection, note the reasoning skills or strategies required to read it. If the selection is fiction, it may demand making inferences. A social studies selection may require drawing a conclusion or making an evaluation. A description of a science process may entail imaging.

Also note the structure of the piece. Readers may be able to use the structure to help them organize the information. For an article on air pollution, they may be able to use the structure to organize the information into a series of causes and effects. For a piece on regions of the United States, they may be able to organize the information in a comparison–contrast format.

### Establishing Purpose and Motivating Students

A purpose for reading should also be set. This purpose might involve questions the students have about a topic. The students should also be motivated to read. Getting them involved in setting purposes, arousing their curiosity about intriguing topics, and helping them to relate topics to their lives generate interest in reading.

## Guiding the Reading

The first reading should be silent and might be guided by questions, as in the directed reading lesson, or by a prediction, as in the directed reading–thinking activity. Or you might use a study or strategy guide, a gloss, an anticipation guide, or self-constructed questions. These procedures are explained later in the chapter.

## Discussing the Reading

The discussion of material read might be similar to that conducted in a directed reading activity, or it might be part of a lecture on the topics covered in the text. Discussions might also take place in cooperative groups as students reflect on what they have read.

Students who are learning English may do better in a small discussion group. They are more likely to participate and will probably find that language is less of a barrier in a small group. These students may also benefit from the opportunity to use their home language to discuss new concepts. As Barba (1995) notes, "New knowledge can be integrated with existing knowledge only when existing knowledge (which may have been constructed in the student's native language) is restructured and students elaborate on what they already know" (p. 15).

## Rereading

In the content areas, rereading is used to expand on, clarify, and organize information rather than to focus on reinforcing reading skills and strategies. By continuously monitoring students' progress, you can address problem areas.

## Extending and Applying

Extension and application activities might take the form of additional reading about the topic, conducting a survey, performing an experiment, or writing an essay or report. Extending and applying often involve putting the new information to use in some way.

# Text Structure

Fostering comprehension in the content areas also entails building an awareness of text structure. To get the most out of their reading, students need to be able to recognize and make use of narrative and expository text structures. Knowledge of text structure can also help them improve their writing skills.

## Narrative Text Structure

What comes to mind as you read or hear the following passage?

> One fine afternoon Anansi the Spider was walking by the river when he saw his friend Turtle coming toward him carrying a large fish. Anansi loved to eat fish, though he was much too lazy to catch them himself. (Kimmel, 1992)

Because you are familiar with stories, chances are you expect to hear a tale in which Anansi and Turtle are the main characters. You expect the tale to have a problem that, after a series of events, will be resolved in some way. In other words, you have a schema for stories, a cognitive framework that tells you stories have characters, a setting, a problem, major events, and a resolution of the problem. If your sense of a story—your **story schema**—is well developed, you may also know that a story may also have a theme or moral or may be used to explain the origin of some natural phenomenon.

> **Story schema:** the reader's concept of a story, including setting, problem, goal, characters, major episodes or plot, and resolution.

Unfortunately, low-achieving readers may have a poorly developed sense of story. When retelling stories, they tend to omit important information about the setting, characters, and the ending, and they may have difficulty with the sequence (Garnett, 1986). Poor readers have a difficult time producing coherent summaries of stories they have read, and the stories that they compose tend to be made up of a series of unconnected or loosely connected events (Oakhill & Yuill, 1996). Poor readers' difficulties with stories include comprehending or retelling stories that have been read to them as well as stories that they have read. Their difficulties are also evident when they write stories. Their stories are less well structured than those of good readers when they are given a title as a prompt (Cain, 1996). However, they do better when they are given a series of illustrations that depict key events in the story, whereas good readers do not. This indicates that poor comprehenders do not have an adequate grasp of story structure. Cain (1996) concluded that poor story structure was a cause of poor comprehension.

Narrative content can be action oriented or consciousness oriented or a mixture of the two (Bruner, 1986). In action-oriented narratives, the tale is generally told from the perspective of a third-person narrator. The material usually consists of a series of episodes arranged in the order in which they took place. Little text is devoted to the psychological states of the main characters. Action-oriented stories are relatively easy to comprehend and require only an understanding of the actions being described (Westby, 1999).

More complex are stories that embody the consciousness of the characters. These are often told from the perspectives of several characters and require an understanding of human motivation. This involves understanding the actions of others in terms of their goals and plans (Bruce, 1980). Even relatively simple stories may require complex understandings. In order to understand a trickster tale, a student must realize what deception is, recognize that false information can be given, understand that the intention is more important than the actual content of the message, and be able to detect deceit using cues that indicate the speaker is not telling the truth (DePaulo & Jordan, 1982). See the following Exemplary Teaching box.

Fostering the comprehension of narratives requires being aware of the students' level of knowledge of narratives. One way of assessing students' comprehension of narrative schema is to ask them to retell a familiar story or to create a story based on a wordless picture book (Westby, 1999). Ask questions that probe the depth of students' understanding of a story: "How did Jan feel in the story? Why do you think she felt that way? What might she do to make up for her embarrassing mistake?" Students with poorly developed story schema will retell stories as a series of isolated

## EXEMPLARY TEACHING

### Developing Narrative Schema

We often associate disabled readers with decoding problems. However, there are also a large number of students whose decoding is adequate, who can pronounce all the words, but who do not understand what they have read. Sometimes their comprehension problems are quite severe. They can't seem to answer the simplest questions about a selection that seems relatively easy. One such student was Glenda, a second-grader in an urban school. Glenda read "The Hen and the Apple Tree," a fable in which Wolf, disguised as an apple tree, tries to trick Hen into coming outside. However, Hen notices that the apple tree was not there the day before, and it had four furry feet, pointed ears, and a mouthful of sharp teeth. She refuses to come out and Wolf leaves in a rage. Glenda had difficulty constructing a story map of the fable. In fact, despite all the clues provided, Glenda did not realize that the tree was not a real tree but was Wolf disguised as a tree.

Discussion revealed several areas of need. Glenda apparently did not have a schema for fables. Her teacher, Thomas Christopher, began reading and discussing fables to the group. Glenda, a good decoder, also seemed to believe that the mark of a good reader was how you sounded. She did not realize that meaning is reading's bottom line. Christopher deemphasized oral reading and began stressing meaning. Glenda was also inexperienced at making inferences. Christopher began teaching the students strategies for making inferences. Realizing that he had not given Glenda much before-reading guidance, Christopher also began providing more preparation for reading. During the preparation periods, he emphasized building and activating schema. He also broke the reading into shorter segments. As the year progressed, Christopher introduced other key comprehension strategies, such as monitoring for meaning, summarizing, and questioning.

incidents or will have information about isolated incidents but will have difficulty creating a coherent story. They will have a difficult time making inferences about the characters' goals and motivation. They may be able to tell what the character did but not why or what the effect of the actions might be (Dewitz, 2012). They will also have difficulty inferring emotions and characteristics and predicting outcomes (Westby, 1999). They may have difficulty with stories told in the first person and difficulty making causal connections (Dewitz, 2012).

## Developing a Sense of Story

The best way to develop a sense of story is to read to students and discuss stories with them. After hearing and discussing many stories, students naturally acquire a series of expectations about what takes place in a story. If your students lack a strong sense of story, start out by reading brief action stories told in relatively simple language. As students' comprehension of stories becomes more advanced, read stories that emphasize the development of characters and that provide insight into motivation and emotions.

As you discuss stories, you might also highlight the most important elements in a story, asking questions such as these:

Where did the story take place?

Who were the most important characters in the story?

What did Anansi plan to do?

How did Turtle trick Anansi?

How do you think Anansi felt after he discovered that he had been tricked?

Why didn't Warthog believe Anansi?

What did Anansi learn?

What lesson do you think the story teaches?

Questions should be geared to the key elements of the story. These help students form a solid sense of story. One way to make sure questions are keyed to the major elements in a story is to create a key elements map (Beck et al., 1982). The creation of a key elements map is described in Chapter 11.

**Story map:** graphic display showing the major elements in a story. Often the focus is on the plot.

Student versions of key elements maps, which are also known as **story maps,** can be used to enhance low-achieving readers' comprehension (Cunningham & Foster, 1978; Fitzgerald & Spiegel, 1983). A sample student story map is presented in Figure 12.1.

Just about the most difficult element in a story is its theme. Identifying a story's theme requires moving to a higher level of understanding and generalizing about the events of the tale. A technique known as the "Theme Scheme" consists of a series of 14 lessons that use organizing questions to help students discover a story's theme or moral (Williams & Pao, 2011). The first organizing questions summarize the plot: "Who is the main character? What is the main character's problem? What did the main character do about the problem? And then what happened?" (p. 262). The next four lead into the theme. "Was what happened good or bad? Why was it good or bad? The main character learned that he should _____. We should _____." (p. 262). The final questions help students generalize the theme or moral to real life: "When is it important to _____? In what situation is it easy to _____?" (p. 262). At first the teacher models the responses to questions but then guides students as they analyze stories.

■ FIGURE 12.1
Story Map

| Setting: | By the river |
| --- | --- |
| Characters: | Anansi |
| | Turtle |
| | Warthog |
| Problem: | Anansi wanted a fish. |
| Main Happenings in Story: | Anansi asked Turtle to teach him to fish. |
| | Anansi made a net. |
| | Anansi put the net in the river. |
| | Anansi caught a fish and cooked it. |
| | Turtle ate the fish. |
| | Anansi asked Warthog for justice. |
| | Warthog did not believe Anansi. |
| Outcome: | Spiders learned how to weave nets. |

Questions, as well as the type of story being read, should be geared to the students' level of story knowledge. As Westby (1999) notes, "Children with limited narrative abilities frequently do not enjoy listening to or reading complex stories" (p. 193). If students have difficulty retelling a story or responding to questions about a story that you have read to them, try selecting less complex stories and working up to more complex stories.

Writing also helps develop a sense of story. Students might begin by imitating a simple, predictable pattern, such as the one in *Millions of Cats* (Gág, 1928). In time, they can try more complex patterns. As students develop a sense of story, they can also take a deeper look at theme, more complex plots, and more realistic characterization. Composing group stories provides reluctant writers with support and also models the process for them.

Wordless picture books or a series of illustrations can also be used as a prompt for a story. The advantage of using a series of illustrations is that this helps structure the story for the student.

In addition to story knowledge, students must also know the language of stories to be able to read and write stories. As you read stories to students and discuss and write stories with them, highlight the language of storytelling.

### Other Techniques for Developing a Sense of Story

**Story grammar:** shows how the major parts of a story are interrelated. A story grammar might include setting, problem, goal, characters, major episodes, and resolution.

Techniques that involve the use of **story grammar** to predict and build comprehension are the probable passages, predict-o-gram, and story impressions techniques. Probable passages are similar to possible sentences and predict-o-gram, which were discussed in Chapter 10.

In probable passages, students use their inferential skills to predict which vocabulary words tell about which story grammar category: setting, characters, problem, resolution, or ending. Once they have placed vocabulary words in story grammar categories, students predict what the story might be about. This can be done orally, or students might create a written probable passage that summarizes the story. In addition to fostering a sense of story grammar, comprehension, and vocabulary knowledge, probable passages also promote summarizing skills.

Story impressions also use vocabulary from the story to activate students' story schema. Story impressions are designed specifically for corrective readers and have been shown to be an effective technique for fostering improved comprehension (McGinley & Denner, 1987). In story impressions, students use a series of words and phrases from a selection to reconstruct the story. Words and phrases that offer useful clues are chosen. Although students are encouraged to structure a story that is as close as possible to the actual story, faithfulness to the original tale is not the essential factor in assessing students' achievement. The ability to use the clues to construct a logical tale is the main factor in improved comprehension. To present story impressions, try the steps outlined in the following box.

A list of story impression clues based on Isaac Asimov's "The Fun They Had" and a low-achieving reader's construction of a story based on the clues is presented in Figure 12.2.

Story impressions has been used successfully with students in grades 2 through 12. McGinley and Denner (1987) found that when used as a previewing device, story impressions "had a significant facilitative effect on subsequent story comprehension" (p. 251). This was true even when the stories the students composed were not closely related to the originals. As the authors concluded, "The process of developing the story guess itself, whether it was parallel to the original or not, and then actively testing it was apparently the major factor in facilitating comprehension" (p. 251). Being involved in composing a story and comparing it to the original, students also gained greater insight into the creative process and began to see themselves as authors.

## A Lesson in Developing Story Impressions

*Step 1:  Developing a set of story impressions.* First, read the whole story. Then reread it and select words that highlight characters, setting, and key elements of the plot. Whenever possible, use the exact words from the story. Use single words, or phrases limited to three words. Choose 10 to 15 clues and arrange them in order. Use arrows to show that one element leads to another.

*Step 2:  Explaining story impressions.*  Explain the purpose of story impressions and how it works. Have a student read the title of the story and tell students that clues from the story are listed on the board. Explain that they will be using the clues to create a story and then they will read the actual story to compare what they have written to what the author has created.

*Step 3:  Reading the clues.* Read the clues with students. Discuss any words that may be unfamiliar. Encourage students to think about the kind of story that might be created based on the words listed.

*Step 4:  Creating a story impression.*  After discussing the clues, you and the class create a story impression based on the clues. Students may add words and phrases not presented. Focus on creating a story that is interesting and logical. After the story has been composed and written on the board, discuss it, and encourage students to evaluate it and make revisions if needed.

*Step 5:  Reading of author's story.*  Direct students to read the author's story and compare their version with the author's story.

*Step 6:  Discussing the story.*  Discuss the author's story. Compare the author's and students' versions. As students become proficient in this technique, they might create and discuss story impressions in small cooperative learning groups. Story impressions can also be used as part of the writing program (McGinley & Denner, 1987). They provide excellent practice in constructing narrative pieces.

■▪ **FIGURE 12.2**

Story Impressions
*Source:* McGinley &
Denner (1987,
December).

| STORY IMPRESSIONS GIVEN TO A CLASS | A REMEDIAL EIGHTH-GRADER'S STORY GUESS WRITTEN FROM THE STORY IMPRESSIONS |
|---|---|
| left side<br>↓<br>May 17, 2157<br>↓<br>Margie<br>↓<br>Tommy<br>↓<br>mechanical teacher<br>↓<br>homework slot<br>↓<br>telebooks<br>↓<br>hated school<br>↓<br>centuries ago<br>↓<br>paper books<br>↓<br>children<br>↓<br>help one another<br>↓<br>fun<br>↓<br>laughing and shouting<br>↓<br>in the schoolyard<br>↓<br>move period | Margie and Tommy were students in the year 2157. They had a mechanical teacher. The mechanical teacher had a homework slot where students could have their homework checked. The mechanical teacher also had telebooks. These were books that used videos to show stories and explain ideas. The words ran at the bottom of the screen and were spoken by the mechanical teacher. This made reading very easy. But Margie and Tommy hated school.<br><br>Centuries ago children read paper books. They had to figure out all the words and there were no videos showing them what was in the book. The children had to help each other. Still, the children had fun. They could be heard laughing and shouting in the schoolyard. |

## Expository Text Structures

What makes the following paragraph easy or hard to read?

> Skin has four important jobs. One, it keeps harmful bacteria out of your body. Two, it keeps the water in your body from drying up. The outer layer of skin is water-proof. And oil glands in the skin produce oils that keep the skin moist. Three, skin regulates the temperature of your body. Layers of fat in the skin help to keep you warm. Sweat glands in the skin let the body give off moisture through the skin. This helps you cool off. Four, skin is the sense organ of touch. (Bledsoe, 1990, p. 185)

⚕ We organize information from our
reading according to the structure of
the ideas in a selection. The main idea is
at the top of the structure. Supporting
details are organized around the main
idea.

The paragraph, which was taken from *Fearon's Biology*, a text for below-level readers, is well structured. It has a main idea, announced in the first sentence, followed by a listing of four details. By using the structure of that paragraph, the student can better understand its content. In fact, the structure provides a map of the information presented in the paragraph. Using that map should improve the encoding of the information. Students will know that they will be looking for four items as they read the paragraph. The structure also helps the readers organize the information: one main idea and four details. Knowing the structure, the student will be better able to take notes, create a semantic map, or outline the paragraph.

Using the text structure strategy, good readers seek the author's main idea and then relate the details to that main idea. The students then create a mental representation of the text that reflects the text structure (e.g., problem–solution, cause–effect). When recalling the text, they retrieve the major idea first and then the details. Poor comprehenders, on the other hand, do not organize information and simply encode a passage as a list of unrelated items. As Meyer, Brandt, and Bluth (1980) comment: "The reader has no focus and simply tries to remember something from the text" (p. 80). The result is a "list-like collection of descriptions about the passage topic with no attempt to interrelate them" (p. 80).

## Types of Expository Text Structure

Expository texts are organized in a variety of ways. Major types of organization are discussed in the following sections.

*Time Sequence*   This structure is a listing, but time order is indicated. Signal words include *after, afterwards, at last, before, finally, later, long ago, then, recently, today, tomorrow,* and *yesterday* and the names of specific days, times, and dates. Time sequence is frequently found in fiction and in history texts, such as this:

> Ferdinand Magellan, a Portuguese captain, was commissioned to sail in search of the Far East in 1519. He sailed across the Atlantic Ocean and reached the coast of South America. He then journeyed south, to the southern tip of South America. There he found a waterway that became known as the Strait of Magellan. The stormy waters led from the Atlantic to the Pacific Oceans. Magellan had found the water route around the new world. (King & Napp, 1998, p. 39)

*Enumeration/Description*   This structure also may present details in a simple list, provide a series of descriptive details, or give a series of examples. No cause–effect, time, or other relationships are used. The structure may be cued by words such as *and, another, for example, one,* and *two* and other number words. Enumeration/description is frequently found in fiction and social studies but may also be found in science. Here's an example:

> The early colonists were mostly wealthy men and women. They were used to living in warm homes where food was plentiful. They had no idea how to farm or hunt for food. They learned much from the American Indians on how to survive in the wild land. (Fajardo, 2012, p. 4)

> Knowledge of text structure can be used to organize in one's mind information that one has read and can also be used to structure information that one is writing.

*Explanation/Process*   This structure explains how something works or is done, such as how a laser disk player works, how plants make food, how a president is elected, how rocks are formed, or how we hear. Explanation/process passages dominate scientific writing, as shown in this passage:

In conduction, heat is moved along by molecules bumping into one another. Suppose you put a spoon in a cup of hot coffee. The top of the spoon doesn't touch the coffee at all. Yet it will soon be hot. This is because of conduction. The coffee heats the bottom of the spoon. The hot molecules on the bottom of the spoon bump into other spoon molecules. This warms them up. In turn, these molecules warm up the next ones up the spoon. The heat moves right on up to the tip of the spoon. (Bledsoe, 1994, p. 199)

***Comparison–Contrast***    This structure focuses on similarities and/or differences, using cue words such as *although, but, however, instead, similar, different, on the one hand, on the other hand,* and *in contrast*. Comparison–contrast structures are frequently found in social studies texts but are also found in science writing. Consider this example:

> Rabbits are much like rodents. There are two big differences. Rabbits have four cutting teeth while rodents have only two. Also rabbits have very strong back legs. These make rabbits very good hoppers and leapers. (Bledsoe, 1988, p. 165)

> ⚹ Newspaper articles often follow a journalism structure (Simonsen, 1996). The main idea of the article is highlighted in the first paragraph, and the details follow in the remaining paragraphs.

***Problem–Solution***    In this type of structure, a problem is presented and then its solution specified, using cue words such as *problem, solution, in response to, as a result*. Here's an example about eliminating solid waste:

> Kids in the U.S. throw away more than four billion little drink boxes a year. Drink boxes can sit for 300 to 400 years in a landfill. As an answer to this problem some cities and school systems have drink-box recycling programs. If there isn't a drink-box recycling program in your area, ask your student council to start one. Better yet, try filling a Thermos or sports bottle with juice instead of buying drink boxes—and urge your friends to do the same. (Lowery & Lorbiecki, 1993, p. 17).

***Cause–Effect***    In this structure, a cause is described and then its effects are presented. In a variation, the effect or effects are presented and then the causes are given. Cue words used include *cause, effect, due to, because of, as a consequence of, accordingly, therefore, hence, thus*. This text illustrates the traditional cause–effect structure:

> Fishing, hunting, and trapping are one cause of animal extinction. Another cause is the clearing away of plant life. Animals that lived in these places die because their homes have been destroyed. (Bledsoe, 1988, p. 247)

However, in some texts, the cause-effect structure is more subtle as in the following passage:

> Krill are small, shrimp-like animals. They feed on algae, small organisms that often grow on the underside of sea ice. As temperatures rise in Antarctica, areas of sea ice have grown smaller. With less ice, there are fewer algae for the krill. Krill is a food source for whales, seals, penguins, seabirds, squid and fish. Without enough krill, these animals cannot live. (Arnold, 2012, p. 190)

***Combinations of Structures***    Although a piece of writing may have a predominant structure, most combine two or more organizational patterns. The following piece is composed primarily of a comparison–contrast pattern that compares plant and animal cells, but the pattern flows naturally into an enumeration/description pattern as cell walls are described and the function of chloroplasts is explained:

> Plant and animals cells have a few important differences. First, plant cells have cell walls. The cell wall is outside the membrane. It is harder and stronger than the membrane.

> Plant cells usually have bigger vacuoles than animal cells. This is because plant cells must store a lot of water. Often, however, animals' cells have more vacuoles than plant cells.

> The most important difference is that plant cells have something called chloroplasts. Chloroplasts store a green coloring. This green coloring traps sunlight. Plants use the trapped sunlight to make their food. (Bledsoe, 1994, p. 43)

## Teaching Text Patterns

To teach text structures, start with the easiest pattern. For younger children, the time sequence pattern seems easiest (Englert & Hiebert, 1985). For older students, the comparison–contrast pattern seems to be the best choice for initial instruction (Meyer & Rice, 1984). The problem–solution pattern is apparently the most difficult structure. Students tend to miss the solution portion of the structure (Meyer & Ray, 2011). Especially difficult are articles containing a combination of problem–solution and cause–effect structures, in which there is a statement of a problem and its cause(s) and then a solution to the problem.

To teach a time sequence pattern, begin with everyday activities. Compose a list of the day's activities, or recount a recent trip in an experience story. Include and emphasize time signal words: *next, after, soon*. Next, read a brief, well-structured selection with the class. Using a think-aloud procedure, show how you would use text features of the selection, such as the title and headings and opening sentence and also cue words, if available, to determine the structure of the passage and, in turn, use the structure to organize the text's ideas (Meyer & Ray, 2011). Explain that as you read the text, you will note whether the text's key ideas fit into the structure you have chosen. If not, you will select a more appropriate structure.

Discussing the time sequence passage about Magellan, you might say, "The first sentence tells me that Magellan started out in 1519. This paragraph looks like it will have a time sequence order. Yes, here it says he sailed across the Atlantic and then went south. This is definitely a time sequence passage. As I read this passage, I'll try to keep the events in order." You might also say, "You can tell a time sequence passage by the way the events happen one right after another and also because there are words that signal time order. Dates such as 1519 signal time order. Can you find other words that signal time order?" The class would discuss the role that *then, finally,* and *at last* play in cueing time order. For added practice using structure words, provide students with selections in which the structure words are highlighted (Meyer & Ray, 2011). Ask questions of text structure. For time sequence ask: "How are the events or steps organized? How is time sequence signaled?" (Kissner, n.d.). See Table 12.1 for sample questions for the major text structures.

Under your guidance, have students read brief, well-structured time sequence passages. Help them examine the text feature and signal words to determine the text structure and use this structure to organize their ideas. When discussing the selection, ask questions that incorporate time structure. For instance, for the Magellan passage, you might ask students to trace in order the main parts of

**TABLE 12.1**
Text Structure Questions

| Text Structure | Possible Questions |
| --- | --- |
| Sequence: Process | What is the process? What materials are needed? What are the steps in the procedure? |
| Sequence: Events | What are the events? How are they sequenced? What are the dates? |
| Comparison–Contrast | What two things are being compared? How are they alike? How are they different? |
| Problem–Solution | What is the problem? What are the solutions? |
| Cause–Effect | What is the critical event? What caused the event? What are the effects? |

*Source:* Englert et al. (2009).

**FIGURE 12.3**
Sequence Chart

Magellan's journey around the world. Asking how many ships or men took part in the journey are valid questions but don't take advantage of the structure of the passage, which is what you are emphasizing.

Have students compose graphic organizers that show the structure of the piece. For time sequence passages, you might use a timeline or a series of boxes, as in Figure 12.3, that show time order. For explanation/process, show the steps in the explanation or process in a series of boxes. For comparison–contrast, you might use a Venn diagram (see Figure 10.3, page 352). For enumeration/description, you might use a semantic map or web (see Figure 10.1, page 349).

To reinforce the use of signal words, have students highlight the clue words in a passage (Williams & Pao, 2011). On a more advanced level, cut up a passage that incorporates cue words and have students reassemble it as in the following exercise. Select a passage similar to the one shown, in which putting the passage back together again would be difficult without cue words.

Have you ever wondered how dolphins are trained?

Next, the dolphin is taught to look at the trainer.

At last, the dolphin is taught to do easy tricks like taking a bow.

First of all, a dolphin has to be trained to eat dead fish, because in the wild, dolphins only eat live fish

Have students compose time order passages. You may want to have them use well-structured passages as models or supply frames, as in Figure 12.4. Starting with simplified sequence patterns, Cudd and Roberts (1989) report using frames as early as the second half of first grade.

If you do use frames, gradually phase them out so students are creating their own pieces. Also encourage the use of signal words, but as students grow in writing skills, lead them to see that the overuse of signal words can produce prose that is wooden. After students have a fairly good grasp of one pattern, introduce another. (For more information on using text structures in writing, see Chapter 13.)

Once students have grasped basic patterns introduce texts that have more than one pattern. Show students how you identify the top level or main structure and

**FIGURE 12.4**
Frame for an Explanation/ Process

| | |
|---|---|
| _____ is easy. First, you _____. | |
| The next step is to _____. | |
| Then you _____. | |
| Finally, you _____. | |
| Just four simple steps, and you're finished. | |

then fit the other patterns into the top level structure. Show how graphic organizers might be used to show the organization of a combined structure.

Encourage students to use their knowledge of patterns in their studying as well as in their reading and writing. For instance, when taking notes, students should take advantage of the text pattern so that major historical events are listed in order and effects are listed under causes or vice versa.

## Using a Structural Organizer

**Structural organizer:** helps students take advantage of the organization of a selection in order to enhance comprehension and retention.

A **structural organizer** is a strategy guide in which the organization of the text is briefly explained and a partially completed outline or other organizer is supplied. The reader is told how and why to finish the outline. Figure 12.5 shows a structural organizer.

---

### CHAPTER 15: HOW WE USE THE LAND

In this chapter, which talks about using land, William Lefkowitz, the author, uses two types of writing patterns: main idea and details and cause and effect. Read the section to answer the cause-and-effect and main idea questions:

Why is there a limited amount of usable land? (p. 175, par. 1)

*Causes for Limited Amount of Usable Land*

1. _____
2. _____
3. _____
4. _____
5. _____

What are the seven major uses of land in the United States? (pp. 176–177)

*Seven Major Uses of Land*

1. _____
2. _____
3. _____
4. _____
5. _____
6. _____
7. _____

What are the three causes of shrinking farmland in the United States? (pp. 180–181)

*Three Causes of Shrinking Farmland*

1. _____
2. _____
3. _____

*Source:* Exercise based on W. Lefkowitz, *Fearon's United States Geography.* Belmont, CA: Fearon Education, 1990.

**FIGURE 12.5**
Sample Structural
Organizer

A structural organizer can be a powerful technique for guiding students in the use of text organization as a reading strategy. In one study, ninth graders who used a structural organizer recalled 77 percent more than did those who read as they usually did (Slater, Graves, & Piche, 1985).

## Using Headings and Subheads

Show students how headings and subheads reflect the organization of text. Before reading, headings and subheads provide an overview of topics covered and a guide to learning. After reading, they can be used as a summary of what was read and an aid to locating information (Dickson, 2004).

Model for students how you survey a selection to get an overview of the information being presented. Using a think-aloud, demonstrate how you make use of the titles, headings, and subheads. Demonstrate how you use these aids to activate background knowledge and predict the content of the selection. After you get an overview of the selection, use each of the subheads as a guide to the particular section that you are reading.

Provide activities in which students survey a section and discuss what they believe the section will be about. Have them read specific sections, using subheads as a guide. Discuss how the subheads helped them comprehend the section. Ask, "How did the author organize information?" Discussing why the author chose a particular form to write in helps students use the author's form to organize their reading. It also introduces them to forms or devices that they might use in their writing.

## Using Text Features

Examining text features before reading the text can build needed background. A chart, for example, might display an overview of the events being described. Text features, such as maps, charts, diagrams, illustrations, graphs, and marginal notes can provide valuable information during reading. Students who struggle understanding words might be aided by the visual features embedded in a text. A diagram might show what the words in the text explain. One student recounted how visuals enabled her to understand a difficult biology text. She looked upon diagrams as being movies that were showing biological processes. She also took the diagrams apart and added her own labels (Schoenbach et al., 2012).

Model the use of text features to get students into the habit of using them. During a discussion of a text, ask questions based only on text features: "What does the chart tell us about the change in the farmers' income? What information was presented in the map?" (McDonald & Thornley, 2005). Have students work in pairs to discuss visuals, asking such questions as: "What is the diagram showing? What is the purpose of the diagram? What symbols are being used? How does the diagram add to our understanding?" (Schoenbach et al., 2012).

A program known as *Strategies for Literacy Independence across the Curriculum (SLIC)* (McDonald & Thornley, 2005) emphasizes the use of text structure and text features. It is based on the theory that students' comprehension improves if they understand the ways in which different text forms present information and make use of those understandings. Instruction and feedback are based on students' performance. Students are closely observed, and their work is carefully analyzed in order to provide them the help they need. If students have difficulty using comparison–contrast structures, for instance, they are provided with instruction in that area.

## ▓▓ Instructional Techniques for Fostering Learning From Text

There are numerous techniques for fostering comprehension in general reading and in the content areas. It is important to use a variety of techniques, as this sparks interest. Some techniques are especially effective in building background, whereas others can be effective in activating schema, generating interest, or organizing information. Some are teacher directed; others are more student centered. The well-prepared reading teacher has knowledge of a variety of techniques but, more important, knows which techniques work best in which situations.

As you read about each technique, think of its advantages and disadvantages and consider in which situations it might work best. Techniques have been grouped according to when they would most likely be used: before, during, or after reading.

### Before-Reading Techniques

The purpose of before-reading teaching techniques is to help students get an overview of the selection to be read, activate prior knowledge, build background knowledge and vocabulary, set goals, and establish strategies for reading and reasoning. Before-reading techniques feature the anticipation guide and Frayer model. In the previous chapter, the directed reading activity and directed reading–thinking activity were presented as devices to prepare students to read. The initial portions of these techniques may also be used to prepare students for reading a content-area selection.

### Anticipation Guide

At this point, you should be fairly familiar with the anticipation guide. One has appeared at the beginning of each chapter in this book. An **anticipation guide** consists of a list of three to six controversial or debatable statements. Students respond to the statements by indicating whether they agree or disagree with them.

**Anticipation guides** have the potential to spark a lively discussion and interest in the topic. This activates prior knowledge and fosters motivation for active reading.

An anticipation guide forces students to think about a subject before they read about it. While activating their prior knowledge, it may also bring to the fore erroneous concepts that they have about a topic. Low-achieving readers tend to hold on to beliefs even when they are contradicted in print (Lipson, 1984; Maria & MacGinitie, 1987). Anticipation guides, by bringing forth erroneous beliefs, make these easier to deal with. The steps for creating and using an anticipation guide are outlined in the next box (Head & Readence, 1986).

### Steps for Introducing an Anticipation Guide

*Step 1: Identifying major concepts.* Note two or three major ideas that you wish students to learn.

*Step 2: Determining students' background.* Considering students' general store of knowledge and beliefs and content of the selection to be read, what

misunderstandings might they have about the topic? Jot these down.

*Step 3: Creating the guide.* Write three to six statements that encompass key concepts. Compose statements that tap areas in which students have

*(Continued)*

misconceptions or doubts. Do not compose statements about areas in which students have no knowledge, because they won't be able to say whether they agree or disagree. The best kinds of statements are those for which the students have enough information so they can respond, but not so much that they won't be acquiring new information as they read. Be careful not to write statements that are really true–false items and that do not require students to assess their knowledge, beliefs, and opinions (Head & Readence, 1986).

*Step 4:   Introducing the guide.* Explain the guide. It may be placed on the board or on sheets of paper. Read the directions and the statements orally and ask students to respond to each statement by checking "Agree" or "Disagree." Students may work independently or in small groups. Small groups may be more effective in getting students to consider their ideas on the topic, including misconceptions.

*Step 5:   Discussing responses.* Discuss each statement. You might have students raise their hands to indicate if they agree or disagree. Have students explain their reasons. Try to elicit at least one agree and one disagree statement for each item so students are better able to evaluate both sides of an issue. The discussion should help students open their minds as they consider their beliefs in relationship to the beliefs of others. The discussion should also motivate students to want to read, so they can evaluate their beliefs.

*Step 6:   Reading the text.* Restate the gist of students' responses. Then have them read the selection to evaluate their answers.

*Step 7:   Discussing the text.* Students can discuss the text and their responses to the original statements once more, this time in the light of having read the selection. They can talk over how reading the text had an impact on their original responses.

*Extended Anticipation Guide*   The extended guide adds a second part, in which readers indicate whether they have found support in the text for their responses (Duffelmeyer, Baum, & Merkley, 1987). If they did not find support, they rewrite in their own words information from the text that conflicts with their beliefs. Because the extended anticipation guide requires students to paraphrase information that conflicts with a misconception, it should be more effective in motivating them to revise erroneous information.

### Frayer Model of Conceptual Development

Because they are small, crawl on the ground, and have a somewhat similar appearance, spiders, insects, mites, and ticks are often lumped together. Even students who know that spiders are not insects are surprised to learn that neither are ticks or mites.

The **Frayer model** works best with high-level, complex concepts that have a hierarchical organization. Through seeing superordinate, coordinate, and subordinate categories, students can better grasp how key concepts are interrelated.

A procedure that has been used successfully to teach concepts to low-achieving readers in both social studies and science is the **Frayer model** of conceptual development (Peters, 1979). A carefully thought-out, systematic procedure, the Frayer model develops concepts through discovering relevant attributes, considering irrelevant attributes, and noting examples and nonexamples. The concept is also placed within a hierarchy so that students see superordinate, coordinate, and subordinate categories. This allows students to see how the concept fits in within an overall conceptual scheme. Seeing all these relationships, students learn concepts better because they have more semantic cues. The following box shows how the concept of insects might be taught.

## During-Reading Techniques

As students read content-area texts, they hone in on critical information, information that answers the purpose question that was established for their reading. Students

## Frayer Model Lesson

**Step 1: Brainstorming the concept.** To involve students and find out what they know about a topic, write the topic word on the board and ask students to say what comes to mind when they hear, for example, the word *insect*. List students' responses on the board.

**Step 2: Discussing examples of the concept.** From the information listed on the board, note examples of insects. If there are few examples, list additional ones.

**Step 3: Discussing relevant characteristics.** Talk over what insects have in common—six legs and three body parts.

**Step 4: Arranging concepts in a hierarchy.** Show where insects fall in the hierarchy. Show superordinate categories. Insects are arthropods. Arthropods are invertebrates. Invertebrates are animals. Then show coordinate categories. Insects belong in the same group of arthropods as do crustaceans, arachnids, chilopods,

and diplopods. Discuss subordinate categories: *Coleoptera* (beetles), *Lepidoptera* (butterflies and moths), *Hymenoptera* (ants, bees, wasps), and *Diptera* (flies).

**Step 5: Discussing common characteristics.** Help students decide what the relevant characteristics of an insect are, that is, three pairs of legs and three body parts.

**Step 6: Discussing irrelevant characteristics.** Discuss irrelevant characteristics of insects: color, size, whether they have eyes, the climate in which they are found.

**Step 7: Discussing nonexamples.** Discuss why a spider, a scorpion, a tick, a mite, or a centipede is not an insect.

**Step 8: Testing the concept.** Provide the students with examples and nonexamples of creatures and have them tell whether they are insects and explain their responses. An example of Frayer's model is shown in Figure 12.6.

distinguish between relevant and irrelevant information and between important and unimportant details. They organize information using main ideas that they have recognized as they read or constructed. They make inferences about causes; visualize settings, characters, and processes; generate questions; summarize; predict; integrate

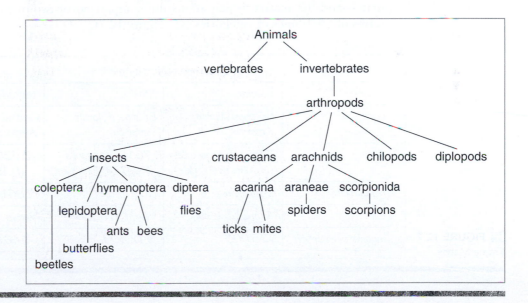

**◼ FIGURE 12.6**
Frayer Model

new information with old; and modify schema if necessary. They also make use of heads and subheads, charts, photos, drawings, other graphical features, and the overall organization and layout of the chapter or section being read. In addition, they monitor for meaning and use correction strategies, such as rereading, as necessary.

In general, adept readers use many of the strategies highlighted in the previous chapter. In addition, they employ a strategy introduced earlier in this chapter: using chapter organization and text structure to enhance comprehension. The techniques that promote the use of during-reading strategies include frame questions, frame matrixes, strategy guides, glosses, and WIRC thinksheets.

## Frame Questions

In a sense, each content area attempts to answer a series of questions. Much of science is devoted to asking questions about mechanisms, processes, systems, and theories. For instance, the following questions are regularly asked about major systems of the body: "What are the parts of the system? Where is the system located? How does the system work? What is the system's function? What are some signs that the system is not functioning properly?" In geography, frequently asked questions include: "Where is it? What are its major physical characteristics? How was it formed? How is it changing?" History is concerned with questions of time and causes and effects.

> ✳ One key to learning the content of a subject matter is to know what questions to ask. The questions help determine what information is most important and how that information is organized.

> **Frames:** categories of information that reflect the structure of content-area text (Armbruster & Anderson, 1981). A history frame, reflecting the content area's concern with causes and effects, may detail the causes of the Revolutionary War.

**Frames** are visual representations of the answers to implied or explicit content-area questions (Armbruster & Anderson, 1981). Frames reflect the structure of the content area. For instance, a history frame, reflecting the content area's concern with causes and effects, may detail the major causes of the Revolutionary War. One way to take advantage of the frame organization is to construct a frame matrix.

## Frame Matrix

As its name suggests, the frame matrix has two major aspects: a frame, which highlights essential categories of information—such as location, area, population, climate—and the matrix, which allows the comparison of two or more elements in terms of the frames or categories (see Figure 12.7).

| Countries of North America | | | |
|---|---|---|---|
| | Canada | Mexico | United States |
| Location | Northern North America | Southern North America | Central North America |
| Area | 3,851,809 sq miles (9,976,186 sq km) | 761,600 sq miles (1,972,547 sq km) | 3,536,341 sq miles (9,159,123 sq km) |
| Population | 34 million | 107 million | 306 million |
| Climate | Temperate-Cold | Warm | Varies |
| Income per person | $38,000 | $12,800 | $46,000 |

■ **FIGURE 12.7**
Frame Matrix

Frame matrices work best when comparisons are being made or when the focus is on key categories of information.

To construct a frame matrix, seek out the important categories of information for a topic. Then note how each category might be subdivided. If you are familiar with a topic, you might set up a tentative frame and then verify it by checking the text that students are about to read (Armbruster, 1991). You might also check the topic in an encyclopedia. Encyclopedias often organize their articles around major topics or questions.

Possible frame questions for a chapter or a book on weather disasters might include: "What is it? What are its main characteristics? What causes it? What damage does it do? How is it forecast? What are the signs of it? How can you protect yourself against it? What are some of the most notorious ones?"

In a study of states, possible frame questions might include: "What is its name? Where is it? How big is it? How many people does it have? What is the average income of its people? What are its main industries? What are its natural resources? What is its capital?"

A frame matrix helps students see relationships. Students can see at a glance what entities are being compared and what the major categories of information are. Making comparisons is facilitated because categories being compared are lined up side by side. The matrix also makes it obvious when information is missing (Heiman & Slomianko, 1986).

## Strategy Guides

**Strategy guide:** written set of questions or other activities designed to assist students in their reading of a segment of content-area text.

**Strategy guides,** which evolved from study guides, are flexible devices that help students comprehend and organize information during as well as after reading, listening, and/or viewing. The main purpose of strategy guides is to help students become independent, strategic learners (Wood, Lapp, Flood, & Taylor, 2008). Strategy guides come in many shapes and sizes, may take a variety of forms, and serve a number of purposes.

To create a strategy guide, follow these steps:

1.  Analyze the selection to be read, listened to, and/or viewed. Note the major concepts that you want students to learn. Mark the segments that discuss those concepts so students can focus on them.

2.  Keeping in mind the skills and abilities of your students, mark the difficult vocabulary, unfamiliar language, confusing explanations, or complex organization that might pose problems. In your guide, provide assistance with the difficulties noted.

3.  Identify the organizational pattern(s) of the segment, such as enumeration/ description, sequential, explanation/process, and so on.

4.  Identify the strategies needed to understand the selection.

5.  Create a guide that highlights key content, helps students overcome any obstacles to understanding the selection, and guides them in the use of effective strategies.

*Content Guides*    One of the simplest guides is the content guide. Low-achieving readers often find a fact-packed, content-area text to be overwhelming. Through questions, statements, matching items, sentence-completion exercises, and the completion of graphic organizers, a content guide leads students to the significant content in the chapter. As an additional aid, the pages on which the essential information is located are generally noted.

*Pattern Guides*   Pattern guides make use of the structure of text. Noting the pattern of a piece of writing (time sequence, cause–effect, problem–solution) enhances comprehension because it gives the reader a plan to follow. In most pieces of extended writing, however, the author uses several patterns. In the section covered by the pattern guide in Figure 12.8, the author used both a problem–solution and a cause–effect pattern.

## Glossing

Glossing is a guide for helping low-achieving readers cope with the complexities of content-area texts. The normal interaction or transaction in reading is between reader and author. Glossing places the teacher in the interaction as an expert adviser (Stewart & Cross, 1991).

> **Gloss:** guide in which segments of the text are clarified through notes, usually placed in the margin.

A **gloss** is a series of notes or suggestions designed to improve a student's reading of a passage. The notes and suggestions are written on a sheet of paper lined up with the text or written directly on a photocopy of the text or embedded in a digital text. The gloss

---

READ CHAPTER 32: LIVING IN COMMUNITIES, PP. 229–234

**Problems:**

What was Borneo's main problem?

_____

_____

_____

What was the second problem?

_____

_____

_____

**Solutions:**

How was the first problem solved?

_____

_____

_____

How was the problem solved?

_____

_____

_____

*Cause and Effects*

What were the unwanted effects of using chemicals? Fill in the boxes to show what happened when chemicals were used.

**Cause**                                                        **Effects**

| Chemical was spread. | → | Made roaches sick. | → | Lizards ate | → | Cats ate | → | | → | |

*Source:* From L. J. Bledsoe, *Biology, The Kingdom of Life.* Castro Valley, CA: Quercus, 1988.

**◼ FIGURE 12.8**
Pattern Guide
*Source:* Bledsoe (1988).

may contain definitions of difficult terms, an explanation of a difficult concept, a paraphrase of a confusing sentence, a suggestion to tap prior knowledge, or a suggestion that may in some other way enhance students' comprehension or metacognition. The notations in the gloss might consist of a statement, a question, a brief paragraph, or even a fill-in-the-blank or complete-the-statement activity.

Various kinds of questions might be included: those that help students tap prior knowledge or integrate new information with old, those that help students set a purpose for reading, those that help students use an essential comprehension or word-recognition strategy, or those that help readers check their understanding of the text (Richgels & Hansen, 1984).

Designed to integrate content and process, glosses typically include activities that focus on both. A gloss may also be designed to focus on a particular area, such as difficult vocabulary, or a particular strategy, such as using the organization of the passage. A gloss can also be used to make a text more readable. All too often, there is a gap between the reading ability of low-achieving readers and the difficulty level of the text.

Steps you can take in preparing glosses that make texts more accessible include the following:

- Give the reader an easy-to-read overview of the text.
- Highlight the most important information.
- Paraphrase in more understandable language essential segments that may be too difficult for students to read on their own.
- Give the meanings of essential vocabulary.
- Gloss photos, drawings, charts, and other graphic pieces of information. Even if the text is virtually indecipherable for students, they can learn from the diagrams and other illustrations and from the gloss that you provide.
- Provide an easy-to-read summary of the most important information.

## Creating a Gloss

**Step 1:  Examine the text.**  Decide which two or three concepts you would like students to learn. Note the difficult vocabulary that will be needed to understand the key concepts. Note also the organization of the passage and the main strategies that might be used to understand the passage, such as inferring, summarizing, evaluating, and imaging.

**Step 2:  Write the gloss.**  Keeping in mind the students' prior knowledge and command of strategies, decide which elements you would like to emphasize, and write a gloss accordingly. Focus on a few elements. Limit your gloss to one or two items per page. Students find it difficult and tiresome to cope with too many items (Stewart &

Cross, 1993). This also makes the task less burdensome for you.

**Step 3:  Consider and refine.**  Line up a sheet of paper with the text and print your gloss next to the target text. If this is a duplicated sheet, write your gloss directly in the margin and photocopy the page. As you write your gloss, imagine that you are with your students as they are studying. Think of the questions they might have about the material, the words they might stumble over, and the elements they might find confusing. Imagine, too, what you might say to help them read purposefully and strategically, monitoring for meaning as they progress through the passages. Let the answers to those questions guide your construction of a gloss.

## Writing to Comprehend

Writing about a text enhances comprehension because it provides students with a tool for "visibly and permanently recording, connecting, analyzing, personalizing, and manipulating key ideas in text" (Graham & Hebert, 2010, p. 13). However, struggling readers and writers don't seem to benefit if they are not taught how to write about texts. Writing about a text, summarizing, or taking notes is more effective than reading the text a second time or even studying it. Writing responses to questions or creating questions and responding to them is more effective than answering questions orally. Increasing the amount of writing also improves reading comprehension (Graham & Hebert, 2010).

*Using WIRC (Writing Intensive Reading Comprehension) Thinksheets*     Using a research-based approach that was refined and validated during a three-year tryout in inner-city schools, Collins and Madigan (2010) employed writing to foster comprehension while students read, rather than after they have finished. Typically, students write after they read. As an after-reading activity, writing becomes a way of responding to and extending reading. However, writing can also be a during-reading tool for fostering comprehension.

Collins and Madigan (2010) devised an approach in which students use thinksheets to promote a transaction between reading and writing, in which the writing supports the reading and the reading supports the writing. The thinksheets guide students through brief segments of text by providing specific questions to be answered. This is known as "targeted reading." Students read to answer specific questions. Students read and write in segments that last about 5 to 10 minutes. The brief reading and writing periods allow students to focus their attention without being overwhelmed.

With the typical reading guide, students read the text and then respond to the items on the guide. They do not refer to the text as they fill in the guide. Thinksheets are designed to be used while students are reading. The thinksheets are laid out in such a way that the text and questions are aligned, as shown in Figure 12.9. This leads to so-called two-handed reading, as students read with one hand and take notes or answer questions with the other. (After students have become adept at using thinksheets, you can simply list the page number where the target text can be found.) Struggling readers who have difficulty responding to questions that they attempt to answer after reading a whole piece have improved comprehension when they use thinksheets and respond to brief segments of text (Collins & Madigan 2010). Struggling readers literally "write their way through reading problems" (Collins & Madigan, 2010, p. 114).

Note that thinksheets ask students to provide written answers to the questions and also provide evidence from the text. Evidence can be noted by underlining it as is required in the sample thinksheet in Figure 12.9 or by having students copy the text that provides support. Citing support is a critical element in the effective use of thinksheets. Through experimenting with thinksheets, researchers found that having students provide evidence from the text forces them to refer back to the text, which is a key but often neglected step in responding to questions.

Although breaking tasks down into more manageable segments helped struggling readers, they then had difficulty integrating the segments. A graphic organizer was added to the thinksheets (see bottom of Figure 12.9) to help students integrate their responses. In the final step, students put all the information together and composed an extended response (see Figure 12.10). In summary, thinksheets have a three-part structure: targeting and exploring information, organizing information, and guiding extended writing to foster improved comprehension (Collins & Madigan, 2010).

Just as invented spelling is an accepted strategy for novice writers, copying is an accepted strategy as students learn to paraphrase text. Initially students may copy whole sentences or phrases or even whole blocks of text, instead of paraphrasing. This occurs especially when students are reading about unfamiliar topics and don't understand the text well enough to paraphrase. However, this can be a practical starting point for struggling readers to come to a better understanding of what they have read, as they organize their responses and compose an extended response. As they gain in skill, they can be led to copy less and paraphrase more (Collins & Madigan, 2010). They can use a "reappropriation strategy" in which they use some of the text's words but also use some of their own words (Collins & Madigan, 2010).

An essential component of the WIRC program is teacher involvement and the use of discussion to foster comprehension. Teachers model and discuss the use of thinksheets and conduct brief minilessons with students in preparation for having them use their thinksheets. Each 5- to 10-minute segment of reading/writing is

**FIGURE 12.9**

Thinksheet: Making Inferences/ Drawing Conclusions

How did Fizo save his owner?

_____

_____

What proof do you have that Fizo was brave?

_____

_____

What proof do you have that Fizo was very sick?

_____

_____

**Fizo**

Sitting on the balcony of his home in Sydney, Australia, Fizo, a Silky Terrier, watched as his 9-year-old owner and three friends played below. Then Fizo spotted a large poisonous brown snake. The snake was getting ready to strike. Fizo leaped onto the snake's back and grabbed it with his jaws. The snake bit Fizo several times. But Fizo held on until the snake died. Fizo then passed out. Fizo was rushed to the vet. He was given antivenom. An antivenom is a medicine that fights poison. Fizo didn't wake up for three days. And it took him six months to recover fully. Fizo was given a medal for his bravery.

What makes you think that Lulu knew her owner needed help?

_____

_____

What makes you think that Lulu was brave?

_____

_____

How did Lulu save her owner?

_____

_____

**Lulu**

Lulu's owner had fallen and passed out. Lulu, a pet pig, saw that no one was coming to help. The trailer in which the owner lived had a pet door. A pet door is a special door cut out of the bottom of a regular door so that a pet can go in and out of the home. Lulu shot through the pet door and out into the street. Then she lay on her back in the middle of the street and kicked her legs in the air. When a car stopped and the driver got out, Lulu ran back to the trailer. The driver followed her and discovered Lulu's owner. The driver called for an ambulance. Help was soon there. Later, doctors said that Lulu had saved her owner's life. Her owner would probably have died if help hadn't gotten there as quickly as it did.

**FIGURE 12.9**
*Continued*

Why did Fido run to his owner's bedroom door?

_____

_____

How did Fido save the Gumbley family?

_____

_____

What makes you think that Fido was brave?

_____

_____

**Fido**

    Once, a rat saved a family of three. A pet rat by the name of Fido was awakened at two o'clock in the morning by the smell of smoke. The rug in his owner's living room had caught fire. Luckily, Fido's cage door had been left open. Fido jumped to the floor and ran to the door of his owner's bedroom. Inside, Lisa Gumbley and her two daughters, 9-year-old Megan and 3-year-old Shannon, were sleeping. The door was closed. Fido began scratching on the door. When no one came, he scratched harder. Finally, Megan heard the scratching. She figured that Fido had escaped from his cage. Megan picked up Fido and was taking him downstairs to put him back in his cage when she spotted flames. Still carrying Fido, she ran back upstairs and shouted to her mother and little sister. All three quickly ran out of the house. Their lives had been saved by an 8-month-old pet rat.

**COMPARISON OF THE THREE PETS**

Write your answers in the blocks. Use information from your notes or the article.

| Animal | Kind of Animal | Who They Saved | How They Saved Their Owners | Danger Pets Were In |
|--------|----------------|----------------|------------------------------|---------------------|
| Fizo | | | | |
| Lulu | | | | |
| Fido | | | | |

*Source:* From Gunning T., (2008). *Read, Reason, Respond: Boosting Literacy*. Unionville, CT: Galvin Publications. Reprinted by permission.

followed by a brief discussion. Generally, there are three of these segments in a class period. Over time, the periods of work are extended. Teachers observe students at work and hold conferences with them. Students also confer with partners and in small groups. As students progress, the amount of assistance provided by the think-sheets is reduced. Students gradually become more independent.

## After-Reading Techniques

After reading content-area material, students should engage in some activity that will help them integrate the information they have just read with what they already know. Students should also evaluate new information and apply it in some way, if possible. The directed reading (guided reading) and directed reading–thinking lessons, which were presented in the previous chapter, include provision for after-reading activities. Other techniques that incorporate after-reading techniques are reflection, graphic organizers, and extending and applying.

> Allow students who are still acquiring English to discuss new concepts in a small discussion group in their own language. This will allow them to use their old knowledge to help them understand new knowledge.

**FIGURE 12.10**
Frame:
Constructing a
Response

| After reading about these three animals, what conclusion can you draw about them? Write your conclusion. Use information from your notes, the graphic organizer, or the article to support your conclusion. | |
|---|---|
| Write a beginning sentence that announces your conclusion. | |
| Give three examples to support your topic sentence. | |
| Write a closing sentence. | |

| Which animal do you think was the bravest? Use information from your notes and the chart to support your judgment. | |
|---|---|
| Write a sentence that states which animal you believe was the bravest. | |
| Tell why you think the animal you chose was the bravest. Use information from the story to support your opinion. | |
| Write a closing sentence. | |

*Source:* From Gunning T., (2008). *Read, Reason, Respond: Boosting Literacy.* Unionville, CT: Galvin Publications. Reprinted by permission.

## Reflection

Simply comprehending a content-area text is not enough. Readers must integrate it with their own knowledge and retain it. One of the best ways to accomplish this dual goal is to reflect upon one's reading. Although reflective reaction can take place within a whole-class discussion, it works better in a small-group setting. Students have more opportunity and are more willing to talk when there are just a few of them.

Students need a topic or series of questions on which to focus. If students have completed a strategy, anticipation, or other guide, then that can become the basis of their discussion. Cooperative learning of the type involved in reflection encourages them to clarify and expand their thinking as they explain their responses. As mentioned previously, small discussion groups are especially helpful for English language learners (ELLs).

## Graphic Organizers

A graphic organizer is an effective device for organizing and displaying key concepts, main points, or basic steps. The content of the material and the way it is organized dictate the kind of graphic display that is used. Hyerle (2001) matched each of eight kinds of thinking with a graphic organizer that fosters that specific kind of cognitive processing (see Table 12.2). The table shows only a basic form of each kind of map. Each of the maps can be expanded or modified to reflect higher degrees of complexity. The key graphic organizers are an adaptation of Hyerle's Thinking Maps®. They are arranged according to approximate complexity of thinking involved. The first organizer, a descriptive map, simply requires noting details that support a main idea. The second organizer, a classification map or semantic map, requires that items be categorized. Other maps require arranging by sequence or process, arranging in hierarchical fashion, comparing and contrasting, and inferring causes and effects.

Hyerle recommends that schools adopt a common set of organizers and introduce them in a systematic fashion so that students not only learn to construct the maps but also reach a point where they decide which map is most appropriate. Most important of all, students should also be taught the thinking skills that undergird each map.

Graphic organizers have several crucial uses. They can be used to prepare for writing, as a way of organizing essential information, and as a device for learning vocabulary words. Because they are visual and are less dependent on language, graphic organizers are especially effective when used with, and by, struggling readers and writers and English language learners.

## Extending and Applying

Students can extend and apply content-area reading in a variety of ways. They can read trade books or periodicals that elaborate on and extend information presented in the text. They can conduct experiments, surveys, and observations. They can seek information from nonprint sources like interviews and audiovisual materials. They can keep a journal of observations, write letters to the editor, create posters or ads, write plays, or compose reports.

Students can also apply what they have learned to their own lives. As an application of information learned in health units, for instance, they can change their diets and get more sleep and exercise. After an ecology unit, they can take steps to increase recycling and decrease waste.

> KWL provides students the opportunity to learn from each other and also gives the teacher insights into the students' level of knowledge about a topic.

# KWL Plus: A Before-, During-, and After-Reading Technique

The widely used KWL Plus (Know, Want to know, and Learn, plus what we still want to know) technique incorporates before-, during-, and after-reading strategies.

## Group Brainstorming

KWL begins with brainstorming a topic. In preparation for reading an article about the Pacific Ocean, you might write the word *ocean* on the board and have students tell what they know about oceans. You would then write words and phrases

**TABLE 12.2**
Key Graphic Organizers

| Organizer | Thinking Skill | Example |
|---|---|---|
| Descriptive map (web) | Locate and assemble main idea and details | |
| Classification map (semantic map) | Categorize and classify | |
| Sequence map | Arrange in chronological order | |
| Process map (chain or flow map) | Arrange in step-by-step fashion | |
| Cyclical map | Arrange in circular fashion to show a process | |
| Tree diagram | Categorize and classify in hierarchical fashion | |
| Frame matrix (or Venn diagram) | Compare and contrast | |
| Cause–effect map | Locate or infer causes and/or effects | |

*Source:* Gunning, T. (2008). *Creating Literacy Instruction for All Students* (7th ed.). Boston: Allyn & Bacon. Reprinted by permission of Allyn & Bacon.

volunteered by students. Writing on the board what some students know and what some students want to learn provides a model for struggling readers so that they will be better prepared to write what they know and want to learn on their individual sheets (Ogle & Blachowicz, 2002). Conflicting information may be offered. If so, this can be posed as a question to be answered. For instance, if students disagree about the number of oceans, one of the items under "What we want to find out" would be "How many oceans are there?"

According to Ogle and Blachowicz (2002):

> The group discussion is the catalyst for raising questions that students might not have formulated on their own. It is these questions and the diversity of ideas and knowledge that capture the students' interest and propel their desire to read and learn. Once students have framed their inquiry around their knowledge and questions, they are stimulated to read the text materials in an active way and to keep notes of their learning and new questions. (p. 262)

Students might also work in pairs so that they can help each other. Based on the class discussion, the teacher can adapt the lesson. She might find out that students have so little background information that reading a particular selection would be too difficult or that they would need extensive preparation before reading it (Ogle & Blachowicz, 2002).

### Individual Brainstorming

After the group brainstorms, students list what they know about the topic on their personal KWL Plus sheets. The KWL Plus form contains four columns—What We Know, What We Want to Find Out, What We Learned, What We Still Want to Know—and a space for noting categories of information that are expected to be addressed in the text that will be read. A sample KWL Plus sheet is shown in Figure 12.11.

The group brainstorming helps students activate their background knowledge and so aids them in assessing what they know about the topic. Because you have listed the group's ideas on the board, spelling should not be a barrier for students who have difficulty in this area.

### Categorizing

After completing their lists, students are asked to categorize what they know. They can use a single letter or abbreviation to indicate categories: $l$ for location of ocean, $s$ for

> If you wish to simplify KWL, both categorizing and anticipating may be omitted. Although they are recommended by Ogle (1989), most teachers do not use them.

size of oceans, $c$ for creatures who live in the ocean, and so forth. If students are not familiar with categorizing, discuss which of the ideas that have been listed on the board should be grouped together and what their group names might be. You might also model the process of categorizing and constructing category names.

### Anticipating

As an optional step, after completing the classification activity, students anticipate the categories of information that might be presented in the article they are about to read. Ask students to tell what topics the author will probably cover in the article: "If you were the author, what would you tell about the oceans? What main topics would you write about?" Anticipating categories should help students organize information as they read. On their sheets, students record the categories that they believe the author will probably address.

**FIGURE 12.11**
KWL Plus Sample

Name _____ Date _____
Topic _____

| What We Know | What We Want to Find Out | What We Learned | What We Still Want to Learn |
|---|---|---|---|
| H   Dolphins live in the sea. | Are dolphins fish? | Dolphins are mammals. Have to breathe air. Give milk to babies. Are warm blooded. | |
| C   Dolphins can swim fast. | Do dolphins have enemies? | Orca whales and sharks. | |
| C   Dolphins are smart. | How do dolphins protect themselves? | Swim away from danger. Bulls make circle and bump enemies. | Are dolphins found in all oceans? |
| F   Dolphins eat fish. | How do dolphins find food? | Use clicking sounds that bounce off sea animals and come back to them. | Are there different kinds of dolphins? |
| C   Dolphins can be taught to do tricks. | How are dolphins trained to do tricks? | No answer | How are dolphins trained to do tricks? |

Categories of Anticipated Information:

Where Dolphins Live
What They Eat
How They Look
What Their Main Characteristics Are
How They Care for Their Young
What Their Living Habits Are
How They Get Food

*Source:* From R. A. Morris, *Dolphins.* New York: Harper, 1975.

## Questioning

The final activity in the prereading stage involves posing questions. Students tell what they want to find out. As in the brainstorming portion of the lesson, this is both a group and an individual endeavor. Throughout the lesson, note areas with partial, conflicting, and missing information; through discussion, help students consider these areas and later pose questions about them. After asking the class to tell what they want to find out, list their questions on the board. If the questions do not cover the essentials, probe in order to lead students to create additional questions.

Ogle cautions that the text should not be read until "some real questions to guide the reading have emerged from the group" (1989, p. 214). On their KWL sheets, students list the questions that are most important to them. If they wish, students can simply copy the group's questions. However, with experience, students tend to personalize their lists of questions.

### Reading

> As students note the answers to their questions, they might also list information that they weren't looking for but that is valuable and interesting.

Students read the selection to get the answers to their questions. New information is written in abbreviated form under the "What We Learned" column. If questions are not answered or if new questions arise, these can be noted in a fourth column, "What We Still Want to Know."

### After Reading

After students have completed their reading, the article is discussed. Students talk over what they learned. Information is elaborated and clarified. Comparing what students said they knew and what they learned provides an opportunity to correct misconceptions, if they still exist. Information students learned is written on the board. This models note taking and gives students a chance to revise their notes. Students also discuss questions that they still have about the topic.

## Sample KWL Plus Lesson

### Before Reading

*Step 1: Brainstorming.* In preparation for reading *Dolphins* (Morris, 1975), a mature-appearing paperback written on a second-grade level, encourage students to brainstorm the topic of dolphins. Writing the word *dolphins* on the board, ask, "What do you know about dolphins?" List students' responses on the board. If one student says that dolphins are fish and another says they are not, ask each student to explain her or his reasoning. The class might decide to make the classification of dolphins one of the things they want to find out. After the group brainstorms, students write down in the first column what they know about dolphins.

*Step 2: Categorizing.* Information is categorized, and students discuss the kinds of topics the book might present. They might decide that the book will tell where dolphins live, what they eat, how they look, what their main characteristics are, how they care for their young, what their living habits are, how they get food.

*Step 3: Discussing what you want to find out.* Students then discuss what they want to find out. They might want to find out whether dolphins are fish, how they get food, whether they have enemies, how they protect themselves, how they learn

to do tricks, and how smart they are. The class's questions are listed on the board or a large sheet of paper. Students list their individual questions on their sheets.

### During Reading

*Step 4: Discussing what you found out and what you still want to learn.* The class reads and notes what they found out and what they still want to learn. They see that the author gives information about the birth and care of a young dolphin, which was not an area in which they were seeking information. The class might construct a semantic map highlighting information they acquired.

### After Reading

*Step 5: Discussing, rereading, and seeking additional information.* Students discuss what they learned. If there is still a bit of confusion about whether the dolphin is a fish or a mammal, reread the section of the text dealing with that subject. To further clarify the matter, you might discuss with the class the characteristics of mammals. Students might note questions that were not answered: "How smart are dolphins? How are they trained?" The class may also have wanted to know whether dolphins are found in all oceans and how many different kinds of dolphins there are. The class discusses where that information might be found.

If the information is important, students might also create a semantic map that depicts major details graphically, or they might prepare an information map, which uses frame questions. If the students wish, they might also pursue any unanswered questions or new ones that may have cropped up. As part of their discussion, they can talk over possible sources of information for their unanswered questions.

## Outstanding Collaborative Approaches

Working collaboratively with the teacher and other students has proved to be a powerful technique for improving the comprehension of low-achieving readers. Three of the most carefully documented and highly effective of the collaborative techniques are ReQuest, reciprocal teaching, and Questioning the Author. ReQuest, which is easier to implement, can be used along with or as a stepping-stone to reciprocal teaching.

### ReQuest

✳ In collaborative discussions, there is more focus on processes, as the teacher explains his or her thinking and provides evidence or justification (Palincsar, 2003). The teacher also pays more attention to the processes that students use to compose their responses.

✳ ReQuest was designed so that teacher and student would discuss one sentence at a time; however, some users have analyzed whole paragraphs as a unit, rather than single sentences.

✳ "The greatest strength of ReQuest seems to be in that it gets students to overcome some of the subtle liabilities that tend to inhibit questioning—such as having to admit ignorance, and not knowing how to frame questions, and simply not realizing what it is that they don't know" (Manzo & Manzo, 1993, p. 317).

Although William had excellent word-recognition skills, his comprehension was just about nil. Even when the task was reduced to reading short, easy paragraphs, William's comprehension barely improved. At that point, William's teacher decided to try ReQuest (Manzo, 1969; Manzo & Manzo, 1993). ReQuest is a rock-bottom technique that approaches comprehension at the sentence level but that activates even the most passive student.

ReQuest requires both teachers and students to construct questions and answers about single sentences. The teacher is the master craftsperson and the student, an apprentice. In the procedure, the teacher models both asking and answering questions. Although initially designed to be a corrective one-on-one technique, ReQuest may be adapted for group use.

However ReQuest is used, Manzo and Manzo (1993) caution that teachers should model higher-level questioning. Students tend to construct the same kinds of questions that have been asked in their classes. Unfortunately, many of these are on a low level. Manzo and Manzo suggest that the teacher do two things to improve the level of questioning: "(1) Try to ask the types of questions that you would hope someone might ask you; and (2) try to ask questions that reflect the highest objectives of your teaching as well as more literal or reconstructive ones" (p. 317).

Presented below is an excerpt from a ReQuest lesson.

Living things play a part in soil creation from the beginning. Lichens and mosses can colonize bare rock surfaces. They produce acids that eat into the rock surface, releasing the minerals that plants need to grow. The mosses and lichens also help to trap wind-blown particles in cracks and depressions in the rock surface. Over long periods, soil begins to form. (Snedden, 1999, p. 36)

**Student:** What plays a part in soil creation?

**Teacher:** Living things.

**Student:** When do the living things start playing a part in the creation of soil?

**Teacher:** From the very beginning.

**Teacher:** Do you have any more questions for me? Okay. It's my turn. My question is what does the sentence mean when it says "living things"?

**Student:** The sentence doesn't say. From the picture I would guess that living things means plants. But maybe it means earth creatures, too.

**Teacher:** Good thinking. That's my only question.

**Student:** What is the correct pronunciation for *l-i-c-h-e-n-s*?

**Teacher:** The *ch* has a *k* sound, so the word is pronounced "Ligh-kenz."

**Student:** What are lichens?

**Teacher:** Lichens are plants.

**Teacher:** Where do lichens grow?

**Student:** It says that lichens colonize bare rocks, so I suppose that means that they grow on bare rocks.

**Teacher:** Good answer. Lichens are made up of lots of tiny plants known as algae and fungi. Because there are many of them growing together, they are said to colonize or set up colonies.

**Student:** What do lichens produce?

**Teacher:** Acids.

**Student:** What do the acids do?

**Teacher:** The acids eat into the rocks, and this begins to break them down.

**Student:** What is released?

**Teacher:** Minerals.

The discussion continues until concepts and vocabulary are clarified and a purpose for reading the rest of the article is set. (Gunning, 2012, p. 162)

## Introducing ReQuest

*Step 1:   Prepare to read.* You and the student read the title and first sentence of the selection. You might also look at any illustrations or other graphic elements that may be part of the introduction.

*Step 2:   Explain.* Explain to the student that she may ask as many questions about the first sentence, title, and illustrations as she can. The student is told to ask the kinds of questions that a teacher might ask.

*Step 3:   Set a purpose for reading.* The student asks questions, and you answer them. Then you ask questions about the first sentence, title, and illustrations. The objective of your questions is to model questioning behavior, to orient the student to the material, and to provide background for setting a purpose for reading.

*Step 4:   Continue questioning.* Questioning proceeds as in step 3. First, the student asks questions about the next sentence. Then you do. As the two of you move through the selection sentence by sentence, you ask questions that involve putting together information from several sentences. ReQuest continues until a purpose for reading is established but lasts no longer than 10 minutes. Usually this entails going through a paragraph or two. The concluding question is "What do you think the rest of the selection will be about?"

*Step 5:   Student continues reading.* The student reads the rest of the selection silently for the purpose or prediction that has been established. The student is encouraged to read flexibly and to adjust her purpose for reading, if necessary.

*Step 6:   Discuss the selection.* The ReQuest procedure can be used with any subject, in any grade, but seems to work best with informational text. However, Maria (1990) reports using ReQuest successfully with narrative material. ReQuest has also been used with students in such a way that the paragraph rather than the sentence is used as the basis for analysis.

### Using ReQuest

Although Josh's word recognition was adequate, his comprehension was extremely poor, especially when he was required to read informational texts. As a result of his woefully inadequate comprehension, Josh, a sixth grader, was failing science. Informal reading inventory results confirmed Josh's poor comprehension. Although word recognition was adequate up through the sixth-grade level, Josh's comprehension was poor at every level from the third grade up.

Using a think-aloud, the reading specialist determined that Josh's goal in reading was to complete the assignment. He was not seeking meaning from his reading. A very passive reader, he had few strategies and simply plunged into his text without previewing, activating schema, or setting a specific purpose. Once he started reading, Josh did not monitor to see if the text made sense. Nor did he stop at key points in the chapter or at the end to summarize what he had read. When queried, Josh was unable to answer a single question about the section on rocks that he had read as part of a think-aloud. The reading specialist also noted that the text was a bit too difficult for Josh. Because Josh's comprehension was so poor, the reading specialist tried ReQuest with him. Intrigued by the idea of creating questions for the teacher, Josh's comprehension improved while he was working directly with the teacher but deteriorated when he read on his own. Focusing on short segments, the teacher adapted the procedure so that it included the whole text. As Josh's comprehension improved, the teacher began gradually increasing the length of the selections and decreasing the amount of direct guidance. The teacher also began introducing previewing, predicting, self-questioning, and other strategies.

Because the science text was too difficult for Josh, easy-to-read trade books that explored the same concepts as the science texts were used. The teacher also provided lots of opportunities for Josh to engage in hands-on activities and use audio-visual aids to build background. As Josh became a more active and a more strategic reader, his grasp of content-area material improved.

## Reciprocal Teaching

**Reciprocal teaching:** fosters the development of key strategies—predicting, questioning, summarizing, and monitoring—within a teacher-guided cooperative learning framework.

In a sense, **reciprocal teaching** (RT) is both an expansion and extension of the ReQuest procedure. Designed for use with small groups, reciprocal teaching also involves students as active participants and, like ReQuest, uses a teacher–apprentice model.

Incorporating four powerful comprehension strategies—questioning, summarizing, predicting, and clarifying—reciprocal teaching has had a great deal of success with corrective readers of various levels, including at-risk students in college (Brown & Palincsar, 1986, Hart & Speece, 1998; Rosenshine & Meister, 1994). Because it is a complex technique, it is recommended that it be used for an extended period of time.

Although reciprocal teaching is an outstanding example of cooperative learning, the teacher is very much an active participant. A key element in reciprocal teaching is the scaffolding that the teacher provides to support the learners, much as a master craftsperson supports apprentices. The student apprentices take on greater responsibility as they acquire increased expertise.

The focus of the lesson is a brief text. At first, the teacher conducts the lesson. Later, a student is appointed to be a teacher. The student teacher makes a prediction based on the title and illustration or the beginning of the selection being read. (If the class has read a segment of the selection, then the prediction is based on what has been read.) A segment is then read silently by the group.

After the segment has been read, the student teacher generates and poses one or more questions. Questioning is a highly effective strategy because it requires students to determine essential information, create a question, and self-check their comprehension by seeing if they can answer the question. Just as with summarizing, students can ask questions at many levels. Initial questions may simply require recall of facts or details. More advanced questions require inferring, drawing conclusions, or evaluating.

After the questions have been discussed, the student teacher summarizes the selection. Summarizing is an essential skill because it requires students to determine essential information, paraphrase it, and integrate or synthesize it (Palincsar, 2003). Summarizing can take place on many levels, from single paragraph, to section, to whole selection. When starting out with reciprocal teaching, students typically summarize at the paragraph level. With instruction and practice, they begin to summarize longer sections of text.

At the end of the discussion, the student teacher makes a prediction about the upcoming segment. Predicting is a difficult skill because it requires hypothesizing about what will occur in the future (Graesser & Bertus, 1998). To predict well, students must use background knowledge as a basis for reasoning about what is likely to occur. Predicting also involves the use of text structure, as students use headings and subheads to aid in forecasting (Palincsar, 2003). Predicting, of course, also provides students with a purpose for reading: to assess their prediction.

At any time during the discussion, students can ask for clarification if there is a word they don't know or if any other aspect of the story is puzzling. Poor comprehenders typically fail to realize that they don't understand what they are reading. Clarifying is a way to show them how to monitor for meaning and to take steps to repair faulty comprehension. Clarifying is especially effective for students who glance over the words and make the sounds that correspond to the symbols but don't get the words' message. As part of clarifying, students need to note when the words fail to make sense and to determine ways in which they might repair comprehension by rereading, using illustrations, using the glossary, and so on (Palincsar, 2003). Members of the groups are also given a chance to ask questions that might have occurred to them as they read. If students are struggling readers, the teacher might read the text aloud.

In introducing reciprocal teaching, the purpose of the technique is explained, and students are taught how, when, where, and why to use each of the four strategies: predicting, questioning, summarizing, and clarifying. One of the strengths of the procedure is that strategies are modeled and monitored in the context of actual reading. In the beginning, the teacher's efforts will be very direct, as she explains and models strategies. Later, as students become increasingly more expert in the use of strategies, the teacher can function as a coach, make corrections and adjustments, provide useful suggestions, and urge students onward.

Direct instruction, plenty of practice, and gradual release of responsibility underlie the success of reciprocal teaching (Brown & Palincsar, 1986). Note in the sample dialogue in Figure 12.12 how the teacher worked with a small group of low-achieving readers. Student A is the leader for this segment. The teacher is T.

---

**Using Technology**

Reading Apprenticeship Downloadable Resources

http://www.wested.org/cs/ra/print/docs/ra/resource-downloads.htm

Provides a description of roles that students might take during a reciprocal reading session.

---

At first, the teacher may have to create summaries, predictions, and questions for students to imitate. Gradually, students should begin to generate their own questions, predictions, and summaries.

■ **FIGURE 12.12**
Sample Reciprocal
Teaching Dialogue

**CAN SNAKES STING WITH THEIR TONGUES?**

No—snakes' tongues are completely harmless. They're used for feeling things and for sharpening the snakes' sense of smell. Although snakes can smell in the usual way, the tongue flickering in the air picks up tiny particles of matter. These particles are deposited in two tiny cavities at the base of the nostrils to increase the snakes' ability to smell.

1. A: Do snakes' tongues sting?
2. K: Sometimes.
3. A: Correct.
   This paragraph is about do snakes sting with their tongue, and different ways that the tongue is for and the senses of smell.
4. T: Are there any questions?
5. C: Snakes' tongues don't sting.
6. T: Beautiful! I thought, boy, I must have been doing some fast reading there because I missed that point. A, could you ask your question again?
7. A: Do snakes' tongues really sting?
8. T: Now, A, since you have asked the question, can you find in that paragraph where the question is answered?
9. A: No, snakes' tongues are completely harmless.
10. T: So we'll try it again. Can you generate another question that you think a teacher might ask?
11. A: What are the tongues used for?
12. T: Good!
13. L: The sense of smell.
14. T: Is that correct? A, do you disagree? Yes.
15. A: That answer was right, but there are other things that the tongue can do.
16. L: But she only said tell one, she didn't say tell all of them.
17. T: O.K.
18. B: It is used to pick up tiny particles.
19. T: O.K. I think that this is an important point. You have the basic concept which is correct, O.K., but what the question really is saying is, is it used for smell? O.K.?
20. B: They are used for feeling things for sharpening snakes' sense of smell.
21. T: O.K. They are used for sharpening the snakes' sense of smell. Are they used for smelling? That's the point we aren't clear on.
22. L: In my answer I said it is for the sense of smell.
23. T: This is fine; this is what the technique is all about. What it means is not that you are right or wrong or good or bad. What it says is that we have just read something and have had a disagreement about what it says. We need to work it out.
24. A: My prediction is that they will now talk about the different things about snakes. Where they live, and what they eat and stuff like that.

*Source:* From A. Brown & A. Palincsar, *Reciprocal Teaching of Comprehension Strategies: A Natural History of One Program for Enhancing Learning* (Tech. Rep. 334), Table 5. Champaign, IL: University of Illinois, 1985.

# Questioning the Author

*⁎ Like reciprocal teaching, Questioning the Author is also a collaborative technique. Instead of using strategies to construct meaning, students respond to a series of queries. Queries are questions designed to prompt students to use the text and their background knowledge to construct meaning.*

One technique that is especially effective in helping struggling readers comprehend content area texts is Questioning the Author (QtA) (McKeown, Beck, & Sandora, 1996). In most approaches, students, including the poorest readers, are essentially left on their own to make sense out of texts that are stuffed with facts and loaded with technical terms. In QtA, the students and teacher construct meaning cooperatively in an ongoing fashion. Instead of having struggling readers become overwhelmed by being asked to read and understand a large segment of text, perhaps even a whole chapter, the class reads a small segment, collaboratively constructs meaning, and then moves on to the next segment. "We teach students that readers should 'take on' a text little by little, idea by idea, and try to understand, while they are reading, what ideas are there and how they might relate those ideas to one another" (Beck & McKeown, 2006, p. 31).

The segment read and discussed first provides a solid foundation for the comprehension of the next segment. Because the discussion is distributed throughout the reading of the selection, instead of only at the end, students have many opportunities to discuss and clarify complex ideas and to integrate information. The purpose of discussion is to "ensure that students are indeed comprehending what they read" (Beck & McKeown, 2006, p. 29). The teacher's role is to make sure everyone gets it. Consequently, active construction of meaning is emphasized. Instead of evaluating responses, as often happens in an after-reading discussion, the teacher encourages students "to consider an author's ideas and to respond to one another's interpretations of those ideas" (p. 36). Although QtA was originally designed for use with informational texts, it has also been used to help struggling readers understand complex literacy pieces (Sandora, Beck, & McKeown, 1999).

Unlike the approach in reciprocal teaching (RT), the focus in QtA is on content, rather than strategies. "A potential drawback of strategy-based instruction, however, is that both teachers' and students' attention may be drawn too easily to the surface features of the strategies themselves rather than to the meaning of what is being read" (Beck & McKeown, 2006, p. 24). A second difference between RT and QtA is that students construct and discuss text during reading, rather than after reading.

*⁎ Ultimately, students should incorporate these QtA queries into their reading. QtA lends itself to deeper discussion and more critical analysis.*

The core of QtA lessons is a series of queries. Queries are designed as collaborative inquiries that provide general guidance as students construct meaning. These queries are different from the usual kinds of questions asked at the end of the reading, which are often designed to assess students' grasp of the material. Initiating queries are used to get the meaning-making discussion started and include "What is the author trying to say here? What is the author's message? What is the author trying to tells us?" Follow-up queries are designed to help the students extend and deepen their understanding. If a passage did not seem clear, the teacher might ask "What did the author mean here? Did the author explain this clearly?" Questions can also be asked that help connect ideas that had been read previously: "How does this connect to what the author told us before? How do these two ideas fit together?" Other kinds of questions lead students to seek reasons: "Does the author tell us why? Why do you think the author included this information?" Questions might also help students see how what they are learning relates to their background knowledge: "How does this fit in with what you know?" A key purpose of QtA is to have students refer back to the text to find evidence or support, which is a skill stressed in Common Core State Standards (Fisher et al., 2012). QtA also encourages students to go beyond surface responses and dig deeper (M. Beck, 2010).

To keep discussions on track and constructive, the teacher uses six QtA moves: marking, turning back, revoicing, modeling, annotating, and recapping.

1. *Marking.* The teacher highlights a student's comment or idea that is important to the meaning being built. The teacher might remark, "You are saying that some good things came out of the Great Depression. It led to Social Security, unemployment insurance, and regulation of banks." Or the teacher might simply say, "Good point!"

2. *Turning back.* The teacher turns students' attention back to the text so that they can obtain needed information, correct a misreading, or clarify a point. "Yes, I agree the stock market collapse was a main cause of the Great Depression. But what were some other causes? What does the author tell us about some things that were happening years before the stock market collapsed?"

3. *Revoicing.* The teacher helps students express clearly what they are trying to say. "So what you're telling us is that the people who grew up during the Depression worked extra hard and saved money because they were afraid there might be another Depression."

4. *Modeling.* The teacher demonstrates how she might go about creating meaning from text. She might show how she rereads a confusing passage, makes an inference, or summarizes a section. The teacher might say "As I was reading this passage, I realized that it didn't make sense, so I read it again" or "Here's how I used the diagram to figure out how supply and demand works."

5. *Annotating.* The teacher supplies information that is missing from a discussion but that is important for understanding key ideas. It could be information that the text failed to mention. "The author tells us that businesses were making a lot of money because they didn't pay their workers much. What the author didn't say was that low wages were one cause of the Depression. Because of low wages, workers didn't have the money to buy the goods that the factories were making. Factories began losing money and had to close down."

6. *Recapping.* The teacher highlights essential points and summarizes. "Now we understand that there were a number of causes of the Great Depression and that some of those causes had been building for years." Implementing the six moves in a discussion might be a bit overwhelming initially. You might focus on the first two, and after you feel comfortable, add the second two, and then the last two.

The steps in a Questioning the Author lesson are listed in the following box.

In the following excerpt from a QtA lesson, note the depth of students' thinking and how they construct meaning. The class has just read a text segment about the presidency of James Buchanan, which stated that many people believed that he liked the South better than the North because he said that owning slaves should be a personal choice. The teacher began the discussion by posing a general query. After a student responded, the teacher asked a follow-up question:

**Teacher:** This paragraph that Tracy just read is really full of important information. What has the author told us in this important paragraph?

**Laura:** They think that Buchanan liked the South better because he said that it is a person's choice if they want to have slaves or not, so they thought that he liked the South better than the North.

## Questioning the Author Lesson

*Step 1:* Analyze the text and decide what you want students to know or understand as a result of reading the text. List two or three major understandings.

*Step 2:* Note any potential difficulties in the text that might hinder students' comprehension. These could include unfamiliar vocabulary, confusing concept, or needed background information.

*Step 3:* Divide the text into readable segments. A segment might be a single sentence or paragraph or several paragraphs. A segment will generally encompass one major idea.

*Step 4:* Based on the understandings you wish students to attain and the possible difficulties

posed by the text, plan your queries. Queries should be planned for each segment.

*Step 5:* Introduce the selection. Introduce unfamiliar vocabulary and other blocks to comprehension in a particular segment before that segment is read.

*Step 6:* Students read the first segment silently.

*Step 7:* Students and teacher discuss the first segment and construct meaning.

*Step 8:* Students go on to the next segment.

*Step 9:* At the conclusion, the class, with the teacher's guidance, summarizes what has been read.

**Teacher:** Okay. And what kind of problem did this cause Buchanan when they thought that he liked the South? What kind of problem did that cause?

**Janet:** Well, maybe less people would vote for him because like in Pennsylvania we were against slavery and might have voted for him because he was from Pennsylvania. But now since we knew that he was for the South, we might not vote for him again.

**Jamie:** I have something to add on to Janet's cause I completely agree with her. We might have thought that since he was from Pennsylvania and Pennsylvania was an antislavery state, that he was against slavery. But it turns out he wasn't.

**Teacher:** Just like someone whom you think is your best friend, and then all of a sudden you find out, oh, they're not. (McKeown et al., 1996, pp. 113–114)

At this point, students read and then discuss another text segment.

## ▞▚ Developing the Ability to Read Complex Text

As noted in Chapter 1, there is a commitment to preparing all students to be college- and career-ready. The best indicator of being college- and career-ready is the ability to read complex text. However, the emphasis in many intervention programs has been on shoring up deficient decoding skills and building basic comprehension skills, but today's work and school environments demand a higher level of comprehension. While it is essential that struggling readers acquire basic decoding and basic comprehension skills, intervention programs must also include higher-level skills that enable struggling readers to cope with complex text.

Complex texts are ones that present complex ideas and that invite thoughtful consideration. They are not necessarily ones that have longer sentences and more advanced vocabulary. One way of developing the ability to read complex text is to teach the kinds of skills and ask the kinds of questions that lead students deeper into a text. In addition to "what" and "where" questions, ask more "why" and "how" and comparison questions. Also spend additional time teaching techniques needed to read complex texts. Occasionally tackle texts that may be somewhat above the students' reading levels but not impossibly so. Just be sure to provide the preparation and support needed to cope with the text. One of the best educational decisions I made was to have my struggling ninth graders read Shakespeare's *Julius Caesar*. They needed more help than my achieving classes, but they were enthusiastic and worked extra hard. It was obvious that being given a challenging text created by the world's greatest writer did wonders for their self-esteem.

All readers, but especially those who struggle, need to experience giving a text a "close reading." Some actions that students can take to engage in a close reading of complex text include the following:

- Engage in individual conferences with students to see if they are reading complex texts and also are applying the close reading skills that have been presented. Pose higher-level questions during conferences and discussions.

- Use dialogue journals to scaffold and guide students reading as they tackle complex text.

- Engage in rereading of complex text. Select short, worthy passages for a close reading. A close reading will require rereading. It's easier to reread a brief passage than it is a lengthy one (Fisher et al., 2012). Teach students how to reread. Used to struggling through an initial reading, below-level readers will need guidance to engage in additional rereadings, but they may be relieved to know that if you don't get it on the first reading, you can go back and read it again.

- Read with a note-taking device. When reading complex text, it is helpful to underline key passages or make notes on the text (Fisher et al., 2012). If the text can't be written on, students might mark key passages with sticky notes. If they are reading e-books they might create electronic notes. You might teach them a system for marking text in which they use question marks to indicate pages they don't understand, circle key words, underline key ideas, and use an asterisk to mark the most important ideas.

- Note confusing parts. Noticing confusing parts builds metacognitive awareness. It also provides the teacher with information about items that are causing problems for students. This information can be used for planning and intervention.

## Additional Techniques for Scaffolding the Reading of Complex Text

Use extended explanations, prompts, probes, partially written responses, partially completed graphic organizers, and other scaffolds. The following techniques are especially helpful in scaffolding the reading of and responding to complex informational text:

- **Extended explanations.** Give an example that guides students through the construction of the response.

  Give one example that shows what kind of a person Dan West was. For instance, tell what Dan West did when he went to Spain. Now finish your answer by writing a sentence that tells what the example shows.

  Why is it a good idea to ask each family that is given a heifer to give a calf away? Use information from the article and your own ideas to help you answer the question. Give two reasons. For the first reason, think how getting a heifer calf helps other families. For the second reason, think how you might feel if you were able to help someone in need. (Gunning, 2010)

- **Prompts and probes.**   Use prompts and probes to help students expand and clarify responses and, if needed, to redirect their thinking or to locate information that will help them supply essential information.

    Can you tell me more about that? What does the article say about the kinds of poisonous snakes found in the United States?

- **Partially written responses or frames.**   Partially supplying a response helps get students started and provides the language they need to provide a constructed response.

    Write a summary of the first two paragraphs.

    Many service dogs wear special vests to let people know _____.
    If you see a service dogs at work, _____. (Gunning, 2010)

- **Partially completed graphic organizers.**   Graphic organizers help students to focus on key information, such as the main steps in a process or the key supporting details. Providing a partially completed graphic organizer gives them examples of key information.

    In the chart, write the missing steps in order. Refer back to the article to help you.

The Beginnings of a Desert

- **Providing an introduction.**   Add an introduction that supplies key background information or a helpful introduction. Include a purpose question (Hess, McDivitt, & Fincher, 2008).

- **Segment text.**   Divide the text into logical sections. Questions or activities follow each section. Because they are shorter, the segments are easier to comprehend.

- **Passage marking.**   Mark or highlight key elements.

- **Gloss vocabulary.**   Provide easy-to-understand definitions of key vocabulary in parentheses next to the target words or in the margin (Hess, McDivitt, & Fincher, 2008).

- **Hints and clues.**   Provide hints for difficult questions as noted below (Hess et al., 2008).

Based on the root and suffix and the way it is used in the article, what does the word *elevations* mean? Hint: Think of the word *elevator*.

   **a.** cold places

   **b.** high places

   **c.** faroff places

   **d.** places that are difficult to reach

Many of these elements can be used to make tests more accessible. These elements could be used with practice tests as a way of helping students practice effective test-taking skills. They could be faded gradually so that students would be able to apply them independently by the time they take target tests.

## ▚▚ Content Knowledge

Throughout this book, the emphasis has been on the processes of reading and writing, especially the teaching techniques and strategies used in learning text. However, process and content must be integrated. Content shapes the techniques and strategies that we and our students use. It is difficult to make inferences in areas in which we have limited knowledge. Noting main ideas is easier when we are acquainted with a subject and have a sense of what the subject's major and minor issues are. The process is somewhat circular. The more students know, the more they are prepared to learn. The more they know, the better they can apply strategies. The better they apply strategies, the more they learn. Use of strategies increases knowledge, which fosters more effective use of strategies.

## ▚▚ Textbooks in the Content Areas

The amount students learn also depends on the quality and appropriateness of their textbooks. All too often, texts in the content areas are too difficult for low-achieving readers. Many content-area texts are written a year or more above grade level (Chall & Conard, 1991; Kinder, Bursuck, & Epstein, 1992).

If the regular text is simply far too difficult for students, consider obtaining a text that is written on a simpler level. (Easier textbooks might be read in preparation for reading the core textbook.) A list of some easy-to-read language arts, social studies, science, and math texts is presented in Table 12.3. You might also use easy-to-read trade books that cover the topics you wish to explore. Because easy-to-read texts may be less detailed than the regular texts, you might want to supplement the information in the text with discussions, use of audiovisual aids, and other activities. For students with severe reading problems, consider using recorded versions of the text. Many publishers have recorded or e-book versions of their texts. Discovery Education has secondary content texts that it calls "techbooks" that include embedded film clips, assessments, explanatory activities, and a text-to-speech feature that reads and highlights the text in one of three speeds. There are also apps, such as Book Place that have a text-to-speech feature. Windows to the Universe (http://www.windows2universe.org/) presents articles on space and science. Articles are written on three levels: elementary, middle school, and high school reading levels.

Students who are unable to read their texts because of a documented reading disability may qualify for books recorded for the blind. Talking Books, a service sponsored by the National Library Service for the Blind and Physically Handicapped (Library of Congress, Washington, DC 20542), provides recorded versions of periodicals and popular books, including children's titles, for individuals who are blind, who have physical disabilities, or who have organic reading disabilities. Recording for the Blind and Dyslexic (20 Roszel Road, Princeton, NJ 08540), a private organization, provides recorded versions of school textbooks for students with reading problems.

### Adapting Texts

Another possibility is to adapt a textbook, a procedure that may result in significant gains for low-achieving readers (Lovitt, Rudsit, Jenkins, Pious, & Benedetti, 1986). Adapting an entire text would be a monumental undertaking. Choose only those chapters that contain the most essential concepts, and focus on the most important information in the chapter. Adapting a text to make it easier is more than just

**TABLE 12.3**
Easy-to-Read
Content-Area Texts

| Text | Publisher | Grade Level | Reading Level | Lexile Level |
|------|-----------|-------------|---------------|--------------|
| AGS Language Arts and Literature | Pearson | 6–8 | 4–5 | 720–760 |
| AGS World Literature | Pearson | 8–12 | 3–4 | 710 |
| AGS American Literature | Pearson | 8–12 | 3–4 | 820 |
| AGS British Literature | Pearson | 8–12 | 3–4 | 820 |
| AGS Exploring Literature | Pearson | 8–12 | 3–4 | 880 |
| Pacemaker® World Literature | Pearson | 6–12 | 3–4 | 620 |
| Pacemaker® American Literature | Pearson | 6–12 | 3–4 | 710 |
| Pacemaker® Basic English Composition | Pearson | 6–12 | 3–4 | 560 |
| Pacemaker® Basic English Grammar | Pearson | 6–12 | 3–4 | 590 |
| Pacemaker® Basic English | Pearson | 6–12 | 3–4 | 650 |
| **Social Studies** | | | | |
| AGS World Geography and Cultures | Pearson | 6–12 | 4–5 | 770 |
| AGS World History | Pearson | 6–12 | 4–5 | 760 |
| AGS Economics | Pearson | 6–12 | 3–4 | |
| AGS History of Our Nation: 1865 to the Present | Pearson | 6–12 | 3–4 | 870 |
| AGS History of Our Nation: Beginnings to 1920 | Pearson | 6–12 | 3–4 | 870 |
| AGS United States Government | Pearson | 6–12 | 3–4 | 930 |
| AGS United States History | Pearson | 6–12 | 3–4 | 880 |
| AGS Career Planning | Pearson | 6–12 | 3–4 | 880 |
| AGS Economics | Pearson | 6–12 | 3–4 | 860 |
| Pacemaker® World History | Pearson | 6–12 | 3–4 | 760 |
| Pacemaker® Careers | Pearson | 6–12 | 4–5 | 890 |
| **Science** | | | | |
| AGS Globe Earth Science | Pearson | 6–12 | 4 | |
| AGS Globe Physical Science | Pearson | 6–12 | 4 | |
| AGS Chemistry | Pearson | 6–12 | 3–4 | 880 |
| AGS Environmental Science | Pearson | 6–12 | 3–4 | 870 |
| AGS Biology: Cycles of Life | Pearson | 6–12 | 3–4 | 870 |
| AGS Chemistry | Pearson | 6–12 | 3–4 | 880 |
| AGS Life Skills Health | Pearson | 6–12 | 3–4 | 840 |
| Pacemaker® Health | Pearson | 6–12 | 3–4 | 800 |
| Wonders of Science | Houghton Mifflin Harcourt | 7–12 | 2 | |
| **Math** | | | | |
| AGS Mathematics: Concepts | Pearson | 6–12 | 3–4 | 720 |
| AGS Geometry-Revised | Pearson | 7–12 | 4–5 | 820 |
| AGS Algebra | Pearson | 6–12 | 3–4 | 760 |
| AGS Algebra 2 | Pearson | 6–12 | 3–4 | 790 |
| AGS Pre-Algebra | Pearson | 6–12 | 3–4 | 750 |
| Essential Math Skills | Phoenix | 9–12 | 5–6 | |

## Directed Listening–Thinking Activity

**Step 1: Making predictions.** Under your guidance, students survey and discuss the title, headings, and illustrations of the chapter or section to be read. You read the titles and headings to students. Based on the survey and discussion, students predict what the content of the selection might be. Predictions are written on the board.

**Step 2: Listening to the selection.** As you read, the students listen. Stop periodically to involve students in modifying predictions, summarizing text, asking questions about the text, evaluating what is being read, relating new information to old information, noting hard words and key terms, and using diagrams, charts, graphs, and other illustrative materials. During your oral reading, you can model the use of effective strategies and gradually lead students to use those same strategies as they listen, so they learn how to summarize, question, and monitor for meaning.

**Step 3: Discussion.** Students discuss the selection in light of their predictions. Discuss how the content differed from students' predictions. Provide needed elaborations and explanations and clarify confusing concepts. Note how the information relates to the students' background of knowledge and how they might apply information in the text. After the selection has been discussed, you might guide students as they dictate a summary of the material presented. Write their dictated summary on the board and review it with them. It can be copied by students into their notebooks, or you can duplicate it so that students have material to read and study on their own. A dictated summary is found in Figure 12.13.

substituting easy words for hard words or short sentences for long ones. One reason informational texts are so difficult is that they try to cover too much and end up being a dense recitation of facts. One way of making a text easier is to expand on key concepts and omit or eliminate nonessential details.

Here are some suggestions for adapting text:

- *Signal main ideas.* Use headings and topic sentences to announce key concepts. Also provide a brief preview, perhaps in the form of a graphic organizer, and a concise summary.

- *Develop key concepts fully.* Do not introduce extraneous details, even though they may be interesting.

- *Use signal words to foster cohesiveness.* Use lots of *buts, ands, on the other hands,* and other words/phrases that help show relationships among ideas.

- *Use straightforward language patterns.* Avoid passive voice and long, involved sentences.

---

**HOW PLANTS MAKE FOOD**

Green plants make their own food. They use sunlight to do this. The light causes a gas called carbon dioxide to combine with water. When water and carbon dioxide combine, they form sugar. The plants use this sugar to grow and stay well. Using light to make food is called photosynthesis (foh·tuh·SIN·thuh·sis).

By making food, plants help us to breathe. When water and carbon dioxide combine, oxygen is made. We need oxygen to breathe. Without plants, we would have no air to breathe. Plants keep us alive.

**FIGURE 12.13**
Student-Dictated Summary

- *Use fewer pronouns than you normally would.* That way, students will not become confused wondering what the pronoun's antecedent is.
- *Use concrete language and give lots of examples.*

**Using Technology**

**CAST UDL Book Builder**

http://bookbuilder.cast.org/

Use this tool to create e-books that have a variety of learning aids along with a text-to-speech feature.

## Directed Listening–Thinking Activity

Another option for handling a text that is too difficult is to use the format of a directed listening–thinking activity (DL–TA) to read it to students (Gillet & Temple, 1994). Similar in structure to the directed reading–thinking activity, except that students listen instead of read (Stauffer, 1969), the directed listening–thinking activity is presented in the box above.

## Hands-On Inquiry Approach

In the typical science text, the student reads about a concept and then performs an experiment. In an inquiry approach, the experiment comes first and is used to introduce concepts and important information. Students observe the experiment and then discuss the science concepts and related information illustrated by the experiment. Vocabulary for these science concepts is introduced at this time. Vocabulary and concepts are easier to learn because they are based on students' hands-on experiences.

The teacher might lead the students to compose a written summary of the unit's major concepts. This summary, which might include illustrations, could be used instead of the text or as an introduction to the text. Once they are familiar with the major concepts covered and related technical vocabulary, students will be in a better position to handle the text.

## The Interactive Strategies Approach

To prepare below-level readers to comprehend the challenging texts that are used to cover key concepts and that are typically used in content-area classes, an intervention program known as the Interactive Strategies Approach first identifies the

 **EXEMPLARY TEACHING**

### Hands-On Learning

Particularly because they have failed with books and paper-and-pencil tasks, low-achieving readers often appreciate hands-on experiences. Taking advantage of the opportunities offered by her seaside home, one literacy specialist enlivened a unit on sea creatures by bringing in specimens from Long Island Sound. A youngster who normally couldn't think of a word to write had no difficulty recording his observations of the live crab that his teacher brought in. As he examined the crab, he had lots of questions, the main one being, "Will the crab pinch me with its claws?" Questions led to the reading of a nonfiction book on sea creatures. Since that book didn't

answer all of the youngster's questions, other texts were consulted.

When the teacher brought in a lobster, the youngster wanted to know how a lobster was different from a crab. At the teacher's suggestion, the youngster recorded his observations. With the help of his teacher, a chart was constructed comparing the two creatures. Again, books on sea creatures were consulted to supply information not provided by observation. As the weeks passed, the chart grew, as did the student's knowledge of sea creatures and his ability to read for information, take notes, create charts, and summarize information. Poems and fiction books related to the theme were also read, and sea songs were read and sung.

key concepts that students will be studying in their social studies classes. They then analyze the challenging target text that covers these concepts and identify the skills and understandings needed to understand them (Gelzheiser, 2010). The teachers choose a graduated series of easier texts that provided preparation for reading the challenging text.

✵ Reading Apprenticeship uses "vertical reading" in which students read easier textbooks on a topic and then use the background and vocabulary that was developed to enable them to read more difficult texts (Schoenbach et al., 2012).

For instance, for an American history unit, a teacher might select key biographical figures, such as Benjamin Franklin and Abigail Adams, and then locate five biographies of gradually increasing difficulty for both of these historical figures. In stepping-stone fashion, students read the easier texts first. These easier texts prepare them for the more difficult text. By the time they finish reading as many as five preparatory books, they have increased their background knowledge and vocabulary and are experts on the subjects they have read about. For struggling readers, this can be quite a boost to their identity of themselves as students. Having never been experts in school, they begin to see that they are capable students.

A key objective of the program is to have students set a high standard of comprehension (Gelzheiser, Scanlon, & Hallgren-Flynn, 2010). Used to reading texts beyond their level in which they skipped over unknown words, struggling readers might not notice when comprehension has gone astray. To help them focus on meaning, teachers provide brief, easy-to-read texts that are readily comprehended by students and thus build an expectation that what they read should make sense. Students are gradually led to read more complex texts. Extensive reading is emphasized. Students read 40 short books and 4 or 5 chapter books in 50 to 60 sessions.

Discussions are collaborative and content focused. Both teachers and students are encouraged to initiate discussion topics, ask questions, and provide evidence to support an interpretation of a text. Realizing that they are working with students who might find questions threatening because they have a history of being asked questions that they couldn't answer, the teachers ask open-ended questions in conversational fashion: "I bet Hannah is upset about her father and brother arguing." "I wonder what Hannah is feeling now." (Gelzheiser et al., 2010, p. 222). Students are also taught a routine in which, after reading a section, they comment on what they read. If students' comments are incomplete or demonstrate misunderstanding, they are asked to share the basis for their comments. They are also shown how to go back to the text to verify or find additional information. Students are also instructed to use their knowledge of text genre to foster understanding.

Although discussions are collaborative, teachers frequently share their thinking about the text. Rather than correcting students' responses, teachers guide students to improve or elaborate on responses by prompting strategy use or having them return to the text. Discussion is concluded by affirming students' ideas and interpretation of the text and efforts. Based on the premise that the foundation of comprehension is the development of schema, emphasis throughout is placed on building content knowledge.

Sessions begin with a minilesson tailored to the student's needs. It might be a phonics lesson or word-recognition strategy lesson aligned with the selection to be read or it might be devoted to key vocabulary words from the selection.

Students then read a selection in which they apply the skills taught or reviewed in the minilesson and then discuss the selection. At the end of the session, students write a brief reflection based on the text they read. The purpose of this reflection is to have students think about the text as a whole.

To obtain books on the same topic but on a range of levels, use Titlewave or Renaissance Learning. Titlewave lists books by topic and level. For books on polar bears, for instance, Titlewave listed more than 100 books with readability ranging from 1.4 to 6.5. You can also check Renaissance Learning's site (http://www.arbookfind. com), which provides readability estimates for texts along with a brief description of the text and number of words in the text. Readability figures are estimates. Examine the books and note especially the number of hard words, sentence length, concepts, illustrations, and other factors that have an impact on the difficulty level of the text.

## Teaching Literature

In teaching literature to low-achieving readers, a key question is which works will be introduced. Often, as students move up through the grades, there is an expectation that certain literary works will be introduced. Because of their reading problems, low-achieving readers may have difficulty reading some literary selections. The issue is one of providing students with quality literature that they can understand and appreciate.

There are several ways of accomplishing this goal. Choose selections that students can read. A number of the classics are surprisingly easy to read. Table 12.4 provides estimated readabilities for a number of well-known works. The readability scores factor in only sentence complexity and difficulty of vocabulary. Background of experience, conceptual development, and emotional maturity are essential elements in understanding a piece of literature and need to be considered along with readability estimates.

**TABLE 12.4**
Sampling of Easy-to-Read, High-Quality Books

| Book | Reading Level |
| --- | --- |
| Fritz, J. (1958). *The Cabin Faced West*. New York: Coward-McCann. | 4–5 |
| George, J. (1959). *My Side of the Mountain*. New York: Scholastic. | 4 |
| Goodall, J. (1988). *My Life with the Chimpanzees*. New York: Simon & Schuster. | 5–6 |
| Hamilton, V. (1985). *The People Could Fly: American Black Folktales*. New York: Knopf. | 3–4 |
| Hamilton, V. (1967). *Zeeley*. New York: Macmillan. | 4–5 |
| Hemingway, E. (1952). *The Old Man and the Sea*. New York: Scribner. | 4–5 |
| Kumgold, J. (1953). *And Now Miguel*. New York: Harper. | 4 |
| Lowry, L. (1989). *Number the Stars*. Boston: Houghton Mifflin. | 5–6 |
| Mowat, F. (1961). *Owls in the Family*. Boston: Little, Brown. | 5–6 |
| O'Dell, S. (1986). *Streams to the River, River to the Sea*. Boston: Houghton Mifflin. | 3 |
| Paterson, K. (1977). *Bridge to Terabithia*. New York: Avon. | 4 |
| Paulsen, C. (1987). *Hatchet*. New York: Simon & Schuster. | 4 |
| Saroyan, W. (1943). *The Human Comedy*. New York: Harcourt Brace Jovanovich. | 4–5 |
| Steinbeck, J. (1939). *The Grapes of Wrath*. New York: Bantam. | 5–6 |
| Uchida, Y. (1978). *The Journey Home*. New York: Atheneum. | 5 |
| Voight, C. (1982). *Dicey's Song*. New York: Fawcett. | 5 |
| Yepp, L. (1977). *Child of the Owl*. New York: Harper. | 5 |

Other measures that can be taken to make literary works accessible to low-achieving readers include the following:

- Provide extra support. If the selection is challenging but not overwhelming, build background and vocabulary, provide glosses or other study guides, and read difficult portions to the students.

- Use audiovisual aids. If students simply cannot handle the reading, read the piece to them or obtain a recorded version of the work. Many of the classics are available as recordings or have digital versions that have text-to-speech capability. Students might read along as they listen to a recorded reading of the text. Even though students will not have to decode the words, they will still need assistance with comprehension and appreciation, so working with vocabulary, concepts, background, and esthetic elements will be essential.

- Use abridged or adapted versions. Abridged versions are simply shortened versions. The author's language has not been simplified. Literacy Volunteers of New York has abridged and added explanatory notes to a wide variety of contemporary literature and popular pieces, including Jane Goodall's *In the Shadow of Man* (1992), Alice Walker's *The Temple of My Familiar* (1992), and excerpts from classic American plays. Although they are designed for adult new readers, some of these pieces, if selected with care, can be used with secondary school students.

Adaptations of literary works are more controversial than abridgements, because adaptations involve changing and possibly distorting the author's words. If the issue is one of having students read an altered version of the original versus not reading it at all because it is too difficult, you may decide to use an adaptation. Selected sources of adapted and abridged classics are presented in Table 12.5.

## Personal Response

Reading literature, of course, involves much more than just understanding the words and ideas. For instance, a class that reads a genuinely humorous story, such as O. Henry's "The Ransom of Red Chief," and does not laugh did not understand the story, even though they may be able to give you a detailed account of the plot.

| | Adapted Text(s) | Publisher | Description |
|---|---|---|---|
| | Globe's Adapted Classics | Wieser Educational | Classics from American and English literature. Reading levels: 3–4 to 7–8 |
| | Lake Illustrated Classics | Lake | British and American classics are presented in illustrated strips. Reading level: 4 |
| | Longman Classics | Longman | Classics in British and American literature. Reading levels: 3–6 |
| | Pacemaker Classics | Wieser Educational | Classics from English and American literature. Audiotapes are available. Reading levels: 3–4 |
| | Phoenix Everyreaders | Phoenix | Presents classics from American and British literature. Reading level: 4 |
| **TABLE 12.5** Adapted and Abridged Classics | Saddleback Classics | Wieser Educational | Classic novels. Reading level: 4 |

⚛ The reader's stance is on a
continuum from efferent to esthetic.
Reading directions to assemble a bicycle
would be efferent. Reading a poem
about death could be highly esthetic if it
evoked strong emotion.

When literature is read, the emphasis should be on an esthetic reading, on evoking a personal response from the reader. Eliciting a genuine reader response involves setting up situations in which students feel encouraged to respond freely. First of all, selections should be chosen that lend themselves to reader response. Second, activities and questions should be geared to a personal response. Questions that encourage readers to relate some aspect of the selection to their own lives are especially helpful. In discussions of the piece, emphasis should be on personal response and interpretation. Small-group discussions work especially well, because students are more likely to share honestly and openly in such a setting. Struggling readers are more likely to do their best when they can relate what they are reading to their own lives.

## Self-Selection

One element that fosters response is reader selection. If possible, readers should have a choice in at least some of the pieces they read. This need not be a fully open choice. You might have students choose which of three novels they would rather read, for instance. Students become more involved when they are part of the selection process.

## Close Reading

The first standard in the Common Core English Language Arts Standards calls for a close reading of text: "Read closely to determine what the text says explicitly and to make logical inferences from it; cite specific textual evidence when writing or speaking to support conclusions drawn from the text" (National Governors Association Center for Best Practices and Council of Chief State School Officers, 2010a, p. 10). There is a distinct emphasis on analysis and interpretation. Other standards call upon readers to analyze the development of themes, actions of characters, and author's craft. In contrast to reader response's emphasis on making personal connections to text, a close reading is based on a careful examination of the text. This doesn't mean that personal connections can't or shouldn't be made, but they should be based on a careful consideration of the text. In a balanced approach, reader response can be based on a close reading of the text (Fisher et al., 2012).

Close reading typically requires a rereading of the text and going beyond the surface level. Because they are read with intensity, short texts are recommended for a close reading so that students are not overwhelmed. Excerpts might be used for a close reading. Texts might be chosen in which the language is fairly straightforward, but the meaning is complex. That way struggling readers can focus on the deeper meaning without being thwarted by unfamiliar vocabulary. In a close reading of fiction, readers analyze how the theme is developed, characters are brought to life, the plot is constructed, point of view is expressed, and the contribution of the author's craft. In a close reading of informational text, readers analyze the author's main points, development of those points, point of view, and the author's craft. A first reading of text reveals the surface meaning and may also be used to evoke a reader response. A second reading takes a closer look at the content of the text. A third reading might focus on the author's craft. Because in the past they may have been restricted to a surface look at text, struggling readers need extensive modeling along with carefully planned instruction and practice. Making text-to-text connections can be especially effective as students compare a current text with one read previously, especially if the comparison includes key points in the selections being compared. One highly effective example of close reading is Shared Inquiry.

## Shared Inquiry Discussion

Of nine discussion approaches examined, Junior Great Books and its Shared Inquiry Discussion approach resulted in the greatest gains (Wilkinson, 2009). Shared Inquiry is the foundation of Junior Great Books (Great Books Foundation, 1999). In Shared Inquiry Discussion, students respond to interpretive questions posed by the leader. The expectation is that each student will develop his or her personal interpretation based on a careful analysis of the text. Three kinds of questions are posed: factual, interpretative, and evaluative. A factual question has only one correct answer, which can be found directly stated in the text or can be easily inferred. An interpretive question has more than one answer. Although not explicitly stated in the text, the answer can be supported with evidence from the text. In Langston Hughes's "Let America Be America Again," the question "What will be necessary, according to the speaker, to redeem the land?" has no definite answer but is subject to a variety of interpretations that might be supported by the text (Great Books Foundation, 1999). An evaluative question asks the reader to make a judgment based on his or her experiences and values. It also requires an understanding of the text. After reading "Let America Be America Again," students are asked, "How can the products of injustice be redeemed?" After the discussion, students revise their responses in light of what they learned during the discussion. As a closing activity, students reflect on the discussion and its impact on them. They discuss such questions as "Did you change your answer? Did you hear an idea you especially liked?" They also talk about what went well during the discussion.

On the secondary level, Great Books provides materials for literature, science, and history. Discussions vary somewhat according to content area. In discussions of scientific texts, for instance, content questions are included to help readers grasp the scientific information in the selection. Application questions require going beyond the information expressed in the text (Great Books Foundation, 1999). In literature units, questions geared to a close reading of the text are featured.

Great Books recommends the following moves to make discussions more effective:

- **Ask questions when something is unclear.**   Simply asking someone to explain what he or she means by a particular word, or to repeat a comment can give everyone time to think about the idea in depth.

- **Ask for evidence.**   Asking "What in the text gave you that idea?" helps everyone better understand the reasoning behind an answer, and it allows the group to consider which ideas have the best support.

- **Ask for agreement and disagreement.**   "Does your idea agree with hers, or is it different?" Questions of this type help the group understand how ideas are related or distinct.

- **Reflect on discussion afterward.**   Sharing comments about how the discussion went and providing ideas for improvement can make each discussion better than the last (Great Books Foundation, 1999, p. 5).

The lively but deep Junior Great Books discussions feature an open-ended, intriguing interpretive question that elicits thoughtful responses that are supported by evidence from the selection as in this discussion by fourth graders:

**Leader:** What does Toto want? Why does Toto decide that winning races is more important than getting along with other the animals? Why does Toto grow to dislike the other animals? Did Toto get the respect he was looking for?

**Ian:** They hated him more. I have proof on p. 117.

**LaToya:** I disagree with Ian, but I agree with Eric and Misha. (LaToya cites evidence by reading from p. 118.)

**Charles:** "I have evidence that they didn't like him at all. (Charles cites evidence from the text.)

**Teacher:** So is he looking for revenge or respect? Why can't he have both?" (Wheelock, 1999, p. 47)

Although it focuses on challenging literature and higher-level reading skills, Junior Great Books has been used successfully with below-level readers. Often provided with scripted programs that focus on lower-level skills, below-level readers fail to develop the higher-level skills needed to become college- and career-ready. Implemented in three inner-city schools in grades ranging from K to 8, the program proved that students living in poverty and who were reading below grade level readily acquired higher-level skills when provided with carefully planned instruction and guidance (Wheelock, 1999). As one teacher commented,

> I was surprised that it would work this well in this socioeconomic area. I thought it would be much more difficult. I have been surprised by students' answers. I've had children with severe learning disabilities give interesting, intuitive, thoughtful answers. (p. 50)

Junior Great Books (grades Pre-K to 5) and Great Books (grades 6–12+) have been used successfully with below-level readers in New York and Washington, DC (Great Books Foundation, 2012) and in Bridgeport, Connecticut (Waters, 2010). What enables Junior Great Books to be effective with below-level readers is its expert scaffolding. Students are carefully guided through their reading. The text is read twice. The teacher has the option of reading the text aloud if students have difficulty reading it on their own. Although becoming a Great Books leader requires two days of training, the basic principles may be applied without formal training. The steps on page 477 incorporate many of the principles of Great Books.

## Sheltered English

**B**ecause of the integration of the language arts, reading, writing, listening, and speaking reinforce each other. Increasingly, reading and writing are used to build oral-language skills among English language learners (ELLs). Instead of using isolated drills on syntax and vocabulary and contrived conversations, ELLs now develop English speaking skills by reading quality literature or content-area materials and discussing them and writing about themt. Known as **sheltered English**, bilingual immersion, or cognitive academic language learning, the approach blends content and language development (Gersten & Jiménez, 1994).

> **Sheltered English:** the practice of teaching subject-matter content in English to English language learners who have learned conversational English but not academic language.

A major advantage of integrating second language acquisition and content exploration is that it fosters the development of both everyday and academic language as well as higher-level thinking skills. In sheltered instruction, teachers make a special effort to make content instruction understandable to all students, including those who are still acquiring academic English. This is something that conscientious teachers have always done. However, sheltered instruction has a second component. While presenting content, the teacher also takes steps to foster language development. Colburn and Echevarria (1999) comment that sheltered classes are "distinguished by careful attention to students' needs related to learning another language" (p. 36). In a sense, content and language objectives are combined.

## Steps for Conducting a Close Reading of a Complex Literary Text

*Step 1:*   Start with a high-quality-text that has the potential for deep discussion and that students will want to discuss. Before presenting the selection, the teacher reads the story and analyzes it for its central idea or theme and also any barriers to understanding that students might encounter. Questions are composed that will enable students to consider the selection's central idea or theme.

*Step 2:*   In a preparatory discussion, the teacher has students survey the text's title, illustrations, and headings and make predictions about what the story might be about. The teacher creates a previous-experience question that elicits from students any similar experiences that they may have had. This is a "have-you-ever" question (Pearson, 1985). In a story about moving, the teacher might ask, "Have you ever had a friend or uncle or aunt move away? How did you feel? What did you do?"

*Step 3:*   For the previous-experience question, an accompanying prediction question is created. This is a "what-do-you-think-will-happen" question. During the first reading, students also note anything that they have a question about. It could be a difficult vocabulary word, a figure of speech, a complex paragraph, or a confusing passage.

*Step 4:*   The teacher reads the selection aloud. Students read along to check their predictions and note their questions. As the teacher reads, she stops periodically and thinks aloud as she poses a question (Great Books Foundation, 2006). The teacher provides examples of the kinds of questions that might be raised. The teacher also briefly explains any vocabulary words, expressions, or concepts that might be unfamiliar to students. This helps prepare students to engage in an independent reading of the selection.

*Step 5:*   Students discuss their predictions. They also pose their own questions. Literal and vocabulary questions are answered. For literal questions, the teacher shows students how they might go back to the text to locate information that would answer the question. For vocabulary questions have students use morphemic analysis or a dictionary to respond. If there are unanswered questions, leave those on the board and see if they can be answered during a second reading. Discussing and answering their questions, especially about items that confuse them, will prepare them to read the selection independently.

*Step 6:*   The teacher creates an open-ended discussion question. This is an interpretive question to which there is no definite answer. However, it lends itself to a reasoned discussion in which students can use the text to provide support for their responses.

*Step 7:*   Students read the story a second time in order to answer the discussion question. They also take notes on a key essential idea. They might, for instance, note Jeremy's feeling about his friend's moving by noting: *S* for sad, *A* for angry, *D* for disappointed, *G* for glad.

*Step 8:*   After reading the story, students discuss the discussion question and related follow-up or supporting questions using a Shared Inquiry format, in which the teacher poses but does not answer questions and prompts students to provide support by reading pertinent passages.

Some steps that teachers take include the following:

- Make the input as comprehensible as possible. Use simple sentence structures and understandable vocabulary. Speak slowly but distinctly, and use gestures freely. Pantomime actions and demonstrate processes. Avoid idioms and jargon.

- Make directions as clear as possible. Show students what to do in addition to telling them. If possible, model the process for them.

- Whenever possible, use the visual to reinforce the verbal. When introducing a new word, show a picture of it, if possible, and write it on the board. When mentioning a place, write its name on the board and show it on a map.

- Use audiovisual aids whenever possible. Use timelines, graphs, videos, and film clips.

- Use realia such as nutrition labels, menus, job applications, and bank deposit slips.

- Use brainstorming, quickwrite, and similar techniques to tap prior knowledge.

- Use demonstrations and skits to make the language as meaningful as possible.

- Emphasize hands-on activities, drawings, webs, and maps, so that students can use techniques that are less language dependent to deepen and express their knowledge.

- Modify use of text. If necessary, read portions of the text with students, or do a "text walk," as explained in Chapters 7 and 14. Obtain texts that use a simpler language and more visuals.

- Encourage students to discuss content in their native language.

- Provide opportunities for students to talk over ideas. This could be in whole-class discussions, in pairs, or in small groups.

- Check students' understanding of the material frequently by asking questions about the material covered. Ask students to retell what they have learned or explain the significance of what they have learned.

- When assessing, allow students to demonstrate their knowledge in multiple ways. Where possible, include ways that do not rely heavily on language. These might include conducting an experiment, drawing a diagram, or completing a project.

## Reading to Learn and Remember

Studying involves the interaction of the ability, background knowledge, and motivation of the student; the nature of the course, its content, materials, task requirements, and teacher expectations; and the students' perception of the course and its requirements (Nist & Simpson, 2000). As Kletzien and Bednar (1988) note, students need to take control of their studying. This, in turn, involves four variables: knowing oneself as a learner, setting goals, assessing tasks, and applying thinking processes and strategies.

### Knowing Oneself as a Learner

Successful studying requires metacognition in addition to a command of useful study strategies. Students must know how and when to use strategies.

Low-achieving readers often have poor opinions of themselves as learners. Having failed in the past, they may see themselves as not being able to study adequately. They may even have given up trying to experience success in their schoolwork. Too often, students attribute a lack of success to a lack of ability. If failure is attributed to lack of ability, students have little recourse but to give up trying. They may lack a sense of self-efficacy.

Students need to see a connection between success and hard work and a link between high achievement and working smart. The assessment task also has to be moderated so that it allows for a successful performance. If tests are so hard that low-progress readers have little chance of passing them, they will soon give up trying.

## Setting Goals

When giving an assignment, purposes should also be made clear: to learn about the two major types of trees, deciduous and evergreen, for instance.

All too often, the student's only goal is to complete the assignment. The focus should be on learning, rather than on task completion. Students need a goal for reading: to read for enjoyment, to learn how to perform a task, or to learn and remember material for a test. The goal will help determine the nature of the task.

## Assessing Tasks

Analyze the study demands that are made of students by you and other teachers in your school. Also consider tasks, such as taking phone messages, that students engage in outside of school.

The task includes the type of material to be read, its difficulty, and its length. The goal also has a bearing on the task. Reading a novel for pleasure is a much different task from reading it for a test. Reading directions so that one can plant a tree requires a different kind of reading than reading about trees in order to pass an objective test.

## Applying Thinking Processes and Strategies

Once students have a clear idea of their learning goal (what they hope to be able to do), their purpose for reading (questions to be answered), and the task, they are in a better position to determine what thinking processes are involved in learning the material and then selecting strategies that incorporate those processes. Thinking processes and strategies include those that help students prepare for the reading (surveying, predicting), those that foster comprehension during reading (summarizing, inferring, imaging, judging), and those that aid retention (taking and studying notes, creating and studying graphic organizers, using mnemonic devices). Students need to ask themselves: "What do I need to do to learn this material?"

While reading a chapter on the effects of World War II and realizing that there will be an essay test on the chapter, a student might decide that selecting and organizing is required because he will have to provide essential information in an organized fashion. The student might then choose a strategy that involves creating a semantic map. If the student believes that he will be called upon to make critical judgments, then he might select an elaboration strategy, one that requires making judgments as he reads and reflecting after reading.

There are a number of popular strategies for studying textbooks. These include but are not limited to underlining, outlining, taking notes and completing strategy guides or graphic organizers, and the venerable SQ3R.

## ▓ Aids to Studying

Successful studying requires more than simply comprehending, because it bears the extra burden of retrieval. If you cannot remember information, it does not matter whether you understood it when you first read it. However, as a practical matter, understanding is a key component of information retrieval. Material that is well understood is easier to understand. As Memory and Moore (1992) note, there are three time-honored aids to studying: principles, organization, and association.

## Principles

**Principles:** generalizations or rules that underlie events, concepts, or processes.

The best way to promote both comprehension and retrieval of information is by teaching **principles**. If students understand the principles behind certain actions, events, or processes, they will be better able to understand new information and to retrieve it later on. For instance, readers who understand the principle of supply and demand will be better able to understand why prices fell during the Great Depression. They will also be better able to understand how the loss of jobs caused a drop in demand and the drop in demand, in turn, caused even more jobs to be lost.

In human biology, students are faced with learning that arteries are thick and elastic and carry oxygen-rich blood away from the heart but veins are thin and less elastic and carry blood laden with carbon dioxide back to the heart. The difference between veins and arteries seems arbitrary and so is difficult to remember (Bransford, 1994). However, if a principle is invoked or an explanation supplied, then the information becomes more meaningful and easier to remember. If readers are told that arteries are thicker and more elastic because blood is pumped through the arteries in forceful spurts, and therefore arteries must be elastic so they can expand and contract as they push the blood forward, readers will be better able to remember which is thicker and more elastic, a vein or an artery. The readers will be able to use a principle to help them remember whether a vein or an artery is more elastic and thicker, rather than rely on sheer memory or some mnemonic device.

The moral is clear: Make learning as meaningful as possible. If a selection provides a principle, the teacher should make sure that it is emphasized. If the underlying principle has not been stated, then help students discover it. Bransford (1994) discusses a content-area selection that describes various types of shelters that Native Americans constructed, but does not explain why some were permanent while others were easily disassembled and some had slanted roofs while others did not. Again, the information would be arbitrary until the teacher helped the students discover the principles behind the construction of the dwellings: living habits, climate, and availability of materials.

If neither the teacher nor the text makes the material meaningful, then students need to seek underlying principles. One of the study strategies that students need to be taught is how to make information meaningful.

One way of helping students retain principles is to have them apply those principles (Memory & Moore, 1992). For instance, after explaining why dwellings are built in different ways, you might ask students to survey the construction of homes in their area and discuss why they were built that way. You might ask such questions as "Why do homes in cold areas have sharply pitched roofs? Why are homes in warm places painted in light colors?" In order to build knowledge of principles, you need to ask a lot of "why" questions—after, of course, basic facts have been established.

## Organization

Organization: the manner in which ideas, events, processes, or other items are related.

The second-best comprehension and memory aid is organization. When students see the **organization** of a passage—main idea/details, cause–effect, or comparison–contrast—they are better able to see major ideas and cluster or chunk information. By grouping the following animals into categories—dogs, horses, cows, and cats—you will find that you can learn them faster and recall them more easily than if you just tried to memorize them as listed:

| | | | |
|---|---|---|---|
| Collie | Manx | Siamese | Morgan |
| Holstein | Bulldog | Jersey | Pomeranian |
| Calico | Clydesdale | Beagle | Guernsey |
| Ayrshire | Tabby | Brown-Swiss | Bloodhound |
| Palomino | Arabian | Appaloosa | Persian |

Questions and graphic organizers that mirror the organization of the selection help students cluster information. Previewing helps students detect the organization of a selection. The headings, for instance, may provide an outline of the chapter (Memory & Moore, 1992). Certain study techniques, such as outlining and using graphic organizers, also help students detect the organization of a piece.

## Organizational Study Strategies

A number of study strategies can help students organize information. In these strategies, some form of noting and recording major ideas is advocated.

> **SQ3R:** five-step study technique: survey, question, read, recite, review.

The oldest and the most widely advocated system for learning from text is **SQ3R**, which stands for survey, question, read, recite, review. Devised by Francis Robinson (1970) in the 1940s and updated over the years, SQ3R is based on sound psychological principles of learning. The five steps to be implemented are outlined in the following box.

When taught and applied properly, SQ3R has been shown to be an effective study technique. However, it does take low-achieving readers longer to learn to use the technique (Caverly & Orlando, 1991), and it should be taught early, before students have a chance to pick up ineffective study habits (Early & Sawyer, 1984).

When teaching SQ3R, build on what students already know about reading and studying. Chances are, they are already being taught to survey and generate questions and read to answer those questions. Also begin with easy, well-structured

## Steps in SQ3R

**Step 1: Survey.** Survey the chapter to obtain an overview of what you are about to read and to see what you already know about the topic. Read the title, introductory paragraph or overview, headings and subheads, and summary. Predict what the section is about. Activate prior knowledge. Ask yourself: "What do I know about this topic?"

**Step 2: Question.** Turn each heading into a question. The heading "Fruits Protect Seeds" is transformed into the question, "How do fruits protect seeds?" If you are taking notes, you might jot the question down.

**Step 3: Read.** Read the section to answer the question that you posed. Reading to answer a question keeps your focus active and purposeful.

**Step 4: Recite.** When you come to the end of a section, recite. See if you can answer the question that you posed: "How do fruits protect seeds?" This step is metacognitive. It forces you to check

your comprehension. If you cannot answer the question, go back over the section and find the necessary information. Recitation may be oral or written. A written recitation can later be used as notes for study. Use two-column notes, putting the question on the left and the answer on the right. If you record your responses, make sure they are very brief so the procedure doesn't become time-consuming and tiresome. Also, refrain from taking notes until you have read the entire section.

**Step 5: Review.** After the entire assignment has been completed, review what you have read. This will help you see the overall significance of what you have read, organize information, and integrate new information with prior knowledge. In addition to deepening your understanding of the material, it will help you remember it. Some authors suggest inserting a sixth step, an R for *reflection*. After reading, you might think over what you have read (Pauk, 1984).

content materials. Although you can teach SQ3R in a few sessions, learning to apply the technique may take months.

You might have conferences with students periodically to discuss their application of SQ3R. At that time, you might go over their SQ3R notes. Since studying is idiosyncratic, allow individual adaptations of SQ3R.

# Association

> **Association:** link between ideas, processes, events, or other items.

Although principles and organization are powerful study aids and should be used if at all possible, simple **associations** can also be helpful, especially if the material to be learned is arbitrary. Memory devices have been successful throughout the ages to help learners better remember facts, terms, and similar types of information.

## Associational Strategies

> **Mnemonics:** strategies such as rhymes and acronyms that rely on creating artificial rather than meaningful associations. For more information on mnemonic strategies, see Mastropieri and Scruggs (1989).

How many days are there in May or September? Most of us, when asked that question, resort to the rhyme "Thirty days hath September, April, June, and November." We can't use understanding because there is no particular principle for determining that, except for February, some months have 30 days and some 31. Rather than resort to brute memory, we use a **mnemonic**. Levin (1993) states that a mnemonic strategy "involves a transformation of otherwise difficult-to-remember material into something more memorable" (p. 236).

Most of the association devices explored in this section incorporate mnemonic devices. Mnemonic devices have a long history. Many of the traditional nursery and other rhymes are mnemonic devices designed to help schoolchildren in bygone years memorize important facts.

# Acronyms

In an acronym, each letter stands for a word. A word is made up of the first letter of each of the words to be memorized. The best-known example is probably *HOMES,* for the names of the Great Lakes: Huron, Ontario, Michigan, Erie, and Superior. In recalling the names of the Great Lakes, students use *HOMES* as a mnemonic aid: the letter *h* reminds them that the name of one of the Great Lakes begins with an *h,* the letter *o* reminds them that the name of another of the Great Lakes begins with an *o,* and so on. Another well-known acronym is *ROY G. BIV,* which helps retrieve the colors of the spectrum: *red, orange, yellow, green, blue, indigo,* and *violet.*

# Rhymes

Rhymes are another mnemonic device that have been used for hundreds of years to aid students' memories. When the associations between the pieces of information to be learned are arbitrary and no meaningful connections can be constructed, rhymes are used to assist memory. Two of the best-known rhymes include the one indicating how many days each month has and the one used to help with the spelling of words containing adjacent *i* and *e*:

Use *i* before *e* except after *c.*

Or when sounded as *a*

As in *neighbor* and *weigh.*

## Acrostics

**Acrostic:** sentence or rhyme or series of words in which the first letter in each word stands for a word or spells out a word.

An **acrostic** is a sentence or rhyme in which the first letter of each word stands for the first letter in a series of words to be memorized. For instance, the sentence "My Very Educational Mother Just Served Us Noodles" could be used to help recall the names of the planets: *Mercury, Venus, Earth, Mars, Jupiter, Saturn, Uranus,* and *Neptune.*

## Importance of Practice

The Adventures in Memory Series by Brian Cleary, published by Lerner, provides mnemonics to help students memorize key facts in science, geography, and history.

Practice is important to struggling readers for a number of reasons. Practice enables students to reach a certain level of competence (Willingham, 2009). Practice also builds automatic skills. Periodic practice also aids retention. If reviews are spaced, the skills or information is retained longer. Because it deepens understanding, practice also fosters transfer to new situations. If students apply a comprehension strategy to passages in the same genre or content area so that the strategy has been thoroughly practiced, they are more likely to be able to apply the strategy to a passage that is in a different genre or content area, but they should also be given opportunities to apply strategies to a variety of genres in a variety of content areas (Willingham, 2009).

Effective practice requires intentionality and feedback. Intentionality means that the students want to improve and are taking steps to do so. Feedback from a knowledgeable source is also required. The knowledgeable source can inform students when they need to make adjustments or move on to a higher level (Willingham, 2009).

## Interleaving for More Effective Practice

One method of helping students learn to apply a process or strategy is to provide them with model examples. This activity is typically set up so that a model example and explanation is provided followed by examples for students to work on independently. A more effective setup is to alternate or interleave studying of model examples with exercises that have to be completed independently (Pashler et al., 2007). Students who alternate back and forth between analyzing completed examples and doing exercises on their own do better than students who work a series of exercises after having read a single model exercise. By interleaving exercises to be completed with models or explanations, students get a chance to try out the strategy, work a few examples, and see which elements they might not understand. When they get to the next model example, they can seek explanations for elements not understood. For instance, students selecting a main idea statement might realize that they have been choosing statements that are too narrow, but they might then be aided by the interleaved model and explanation. For homework, rather than having to select the main idea for nine paragraphs, it would be more effective if students were given three sets in which each set consist of a worked example and two practice paragraphs. Having the sample example provides students with help for judging the next set of items, so they are motivated to consider the sample carefully because it will help them make better judgments on items they have to classify on their own. This is especially helpful to struggling readers.

## The Importance of Carefully Planned Review

Presenting a concept twice or more promotes deeper understanding and retention. In one experiment, middle school students taught mitosis in one lesson were compared with students taught mitosis over several sessions. Three weeks later, when quizzed, students taught under spaced conditions demonstrated that they had learned 50 percent more.

Re-presentation requires retrieving information from long-term memory. Doing so requires active engagement and so fosters retention. In addition, each presentation may have a different context. For instance, students taught mitosis in a spaced approach learned about mitosis in terms of animal reproduction and plant reproduction. These spaced presentations allow "'variable encoding'—chances to encode the information in different ways, get different perspectives on it, understand it a little bit differently, relate it to prior knowledge. All of these things are instrumental in learning and good retention"(McDaniels, 2008).

However, if the review or re-presentation is too close in time, it is not very effective. It is also not effective if the re-presentation is delayed for a very long period of time. Pashler and colleagues (2007) recommend that the interval between presentations should not be less than 5 percent nor more than 20 percent of the time that the information has to be retained. If the information has to be retained for 60 days, then it would probably be better to wait two or three days (5% of 60 days) or two weeks or so (20% of 60 days). The delayed reexposures can take the form of homework, quizzes, review sessions, applications, or similar exercises (Gunning, 2013).

## Test-Enhanced Learning

Quizzes can be a device for facilitating understanding and retention of material. Self-testing is one of the reasons why SQ3R is effective. Quizzes might contain items, such as filling in the blanks, or constructed responses that require retrieval of information. Tests that require students to produce answers, even if the answers to be produced are brief, are more effective than multiple-choice tests because production of responses requires active retrieval rather than recognition.

Taking a test is more effective than spending extra time studying. The act of recalling information to answer a question helps to establish it in memory. The quiz could be in a game-like format and doesn't have to count toward a grade. Corrective feedback should be provided. Otherwise, incorrect information will be retained. Students can also be taught to test themselves. This is known as test-enhanced learning. In their advice to students, researchers Roediger, McDaniel, and McDermott (2011) recommend:

> As you read text material, make up questions (or use the ones supplied at the end of the chapter) and then later test yourself. If you can retrieve the information from memory, great; having retrieved it once, you will remember it even better. If you can't retrieve the answer, study the material again and retest yourself until you're sure you know it. But even if you were able to retrieve the answer once, don't stop. Test yourself repeatedly and keep retrieving answers. Repeated retrieval is the key to long-term retention. (p. 66)

## Study Habits

Poor or ineffective study habits are a major cause of failure. A large proportion of students have inefficient study habits. When asked how they would study a section of expository text in order to recall as much as they could, most students typically respond that they would simply reread the material or just concentrate. Some will admit to having no strategy for remembering the material.

A first step in helping students who have become discouraged or have given up is to show them that they can learn. In a number of studies cited in earlier chapters, low-achieving readers achieved higher grades when they were taught effective strategies.

To determine how best to break the cycle of failure, survey the students. Find out how they study for tests. Find out which subjects or which kinds of tests are most troublesome, and plan a program of intervention. Enlist the aid of the subject-matter teacher.

## Metacognitive Aspects of Studying

⚹ Students may not be aware of how much studying is required in order to learn a list of new words or several concepts thoroughly. They may need to learn a criterion for adequate performance.

Students also need to know what to study: all of the chapters covered? selected portions of the chapters, handouts, notes? They also need to know whether the test is cumulative: Will it cover all the information from the beginning of the term or just the information for the last unit or since the last major test. In addition to knowing what to study, students need to know how, when, where, and how long to study. When students get high grades on a test, you might discuss with them how they went about studying for that particular test. A key element in studying is becoming aware of when the material being studied is known. Students tend to overestimate how well they know the material and so fail to allocate an adequate amount of study time (Pashler et al., 2007). To get a more accurate estimate of how well they know the material, students should use a technique known as "cue-only delayed judgment" to self-test themselves after there has been a delay of an hour or more from the time they finished studying. They should not have access to the answers when self-testing, and they should ask themselves, "How likely is it that I will answer this correctly on a test?" A technique that can be used after completing a reading assignment is to attempt to summarize the segment read and note four or so key words.

Cue-only delayed judgment can also be used with the whole class. Students are given a series of 10 or so questions and are asked to judge on a scale of 1 to 100 how likely they are to be able to answer the questions. They then write their answers and check to see whether they were able to answer the question correctly. If they did not get an answer, they can look in the book or ask the teacher. Better informed about what they know and do not know, they are in a better position to study more effectively (Pashler et al., 2007).

## Overcoming Obstacles to Studying

Teachers should also help students discover impediments to study: (1) lack of self-discipline, (2) lack of time, (3) boredom, (4) lack of perseverance, and (5) distractibility. Work out with students ways of overcoming these obstacles.

### Lack of Discipline

Set a routine. Study at the same time and the same place. The place should be free of distractions, although if the student works better with background music, that should not be considered a distraction. Break large tasks into smaller, more manageable ones. Instead of tackling a whole chapter, break it up into three-page or five-page sections. Start with the easiest and most enjoyable task to build a sense of accomplishment. Use rewards such as a 10-minute break for every 50 minutes of studying. Or you might encourage students to keep a chart showing number of minutes spent studying each night. At the end of each week, give the students checks or stars for completing their charts.

The best motivator is success. If students do well after studying, they will have an incentive for studying harder. Counseling may be in order for students who cannot seem to make themselves study.

### Lack of Time

Have students chart how they spend their time during a typical day. By analyzing the time spent, determine when might be the best time to study. Also select a place to study. If students live in a crowded apartment, they might decide to study in school or at the local library or to study early in the morning while everyone else is still in bed.

### Boredom

Show students how to set goals and become active learners. Tell them to use self-testing to challenge themselves and to tackle boring tasks in short but concentrated segments.

### Lack of Perseverance

Begin with short periods of study, perhaps just 10 minutes. Gradually build up to longer periods. Also use self-rewards. Try beginning with the easiest or most interesting task.

### Distractibility

To aid in avoiding distractions, use self-talk: "I will read three pages. I will concentrate on my reading. I will ask myself questions about what I have read. If I can answer the questions, I will reward myself and take a break." Stress with students that brief periods of focused study are better than long periods interrupted by internal and external distractions.

### Creating Study Plans

Help students devise individual study plans. Each student's plan might include when and where the student plans to study. Plans should be long term and short term. If students have long-term projects, they might indicate how they plan to complete those projects.

In the beginning, students might evaluate their study sessions by using a form such as the study log shown in Figure 12.14, reflections they have written in a learning log, or through discussions. The evaluation should include what study tasks the students undertook, what study strategies they used, and approximately how much time they spent on each task. They should also report any problems they had and assess the effectiveness of their study efforts. This will help students gain a greater awareness of what it means to be an effective learner. Students will also be able to see which strategies work best and how much time tasks take.

## Preparing for Tests

The best time to start preparing for a test is the first day of class. Grasping material from the start is essential, as is organizing it and reviewing it from time to time. Using two-column or three-column notes, creating information maps, and using other organizers are good ways to prepare for a test. Note taking should be geared, in part, to the type of test the student will be taking. If the test will be an objective one, for instance, then more attention should be paid to essential details.

**FIGURE 12.14**
Study Log

| Name _____ |
| STUDY TASK | DATE, TIME, AND PLACE OF STUDYING | TIME SPENT STUDYING | STUDY METHOD USED (OUTLINE, SQ3R, ETC.) | QUESTIONS, DIFFICULTIES, COMMENTS | RESULTS (TEST GRADES, QUIZZES, CLASS DISCUSSION) |
|---|---|---|---|---|---|
| Read chapter about kinds of rocks | 1–6 7–8:10 | 1 hr, 10 min | Frame | Many hard words | Quiz—90 |
| Read chapter on WWI | 1–6 8:30–9 | 30 min | SQ3R & Review notes | Many names & dates | |
| Study for test on WWI | 1–7 7–7:50 | 50 min | | | Test—C Knew causes of war but not names & dates |

Students should also learn the value of periodic review. Spaced review is generally better than massed review, especially when facts or processes are being studied. *Spaced review* means that students space out their studying over a period of days or weeks. In *massed review*, students study for lengthy periods of time. Cramming is a form of massed review.

Students should study the material in the same way that they will be expected to demonstrate their knowledge of it. If they will be asked to identify the parts of a frog in a lab practicum, then they should practice doing just that. Or if they will be asked to write essay questions, they should create skeletal answers to possible essay questions.

In their study of standardized test taking among elementary school students, Calkins, Montgomery, and Santman (1998) found that many of the students did not know how to take a test. Among the flaws in the students' test taking were the following:

- Not reading or following directions
- Using a casual reading style that was more suitable for reading a novel
- Not making educated guesses
- Not realizing that it was possible and even desirable to look back over a passage to find the answer to a question
- Not checking answers
- Using personal knowledge rather than text knowledge

As an experienced test taker, model how you go about taking a test. Explain your thinking processes as you read and follow directions. Show how you go about eliminating distracters when you are not sure of an answer. Model the process of checking answers and pacing yourself. Invite successful test takers to discuss their strategies. Provide extra coaching for students whose responding style lowers their scores: those who work too rapidly and fail to check answers as well as those who work too slowly and are overly concerned with making a mistake. If the test has a high ceiling and has advanced items, provide students with strategies for reading difficult passages and answering tough questions.

Also explain the correction factor. On some tests, students lose extra points for wrong responses and so are better off leaving an answer blank if they have no idea which of the options is correct. However, if they can eliminate more than one of the options, the odds of getting the right answer will be even or in their favor. If there is no penalty for guessing, students should make their best guess.

A strategy such as QAR adapted to test taking should be effective in helping students decide whether the answer is right there, so that if they don't recall it, they can go back over the passage and find it, or whether it's an author-and-me question, so they have to make an inference based on information contained in the passage.

Probe low-scoring students to find out how they handle difficult passages. Do they give up? Do they make random guesses? Or do they try to make as much sense out of the passages as they can and, when all else fails, match up unknown words in the answer options with the same words in the selection? Students need to know that they can sometimes answer questions correctly even when they don't know every word in the passage.

Test preparation must be ethical. Obviously, giving students examples from the actual test is wrong. However, it is also unethical to raise students' scores without also increasing their underlying knowledge and skill. As assessment expert Popham (2000) states, "No test preparation practice should increase students' test scores without simultaneously increasing student mastery of the assessment domain tested" (p. 82). The aim of test preparation should be to instruct students so that they have the test-taking skills they need so that their performance will reflect their true state of knowledge and/or skill. In fact, teachers are remiss if they do not help students attain the level of test-taking competence that will allow them to demonstrate what they truly know.

See pages 521–522 in Chapter 13 for suggestions for teaching students to create written responses to test questions.

## Motivating Students to Put Forth Needed Effort

Summarizing, questioning, imaging, and other reading strategies take more effort than simply glancing over the page. As Irene Gaskins (2003) comments, "Implementing strategies almost always entails more effort than students are accustomed to putting forth when they read" (p. 149). Therefore, it is essential that students see the payoff for the extra effort.

Explain to students that their grades are almost sure to improve if they use appropriate strategies. Tell them that research studies show that students' marks on quizzes increase by 30 or 40 points after learning strategies (Fisher et al., 2002). A more direct approach is to teach half of the class a strategy and then give a quiz to the whole class and compare how students do.

## Mini–Case Study

Carmen's teacher, noting her low grades, discussed her performance with her and arranged for her to obtain specialized help from the reading teacher. Through an informal interview and by using a think-aloud as Carmen demonstrated how she studied for quizzes, the reading teacher determined that Carmen was not studying efficiently or effectively. She had virtually no study skills and no specific goals, except to obtain passing grades.

The first thing the specialist did was to help Carmen set specific learning goals for each reading assignment. She also helped Carmen set up a study schedule and determine the best time and place to study.

Noting that Carmen seemed to lack confidence and did not give herself credit for what she did know, the specialist used KWL Plus with her. Discussing what Carmen knew and deciding what she wanted to learn helped her personalize her learning. As Carmen's comprehension and sense of personal involvement grew, the specialist introduced SQ3R. Emphasis was placed on preparing for the types of questions that the teacher typically asked in classroom recitations and written tests.

Carmen was also instructed in the use of text structure to help her comprehend and organize key ideas in science and social studies, the two areas in which she was having the most difficulty. As Carmen progressed, the reading teacher helped her construct frame maps based on her SQ3R notes. The reading teacher also showed Carmen how to use frames to prepare for quizzes and tests.

Carmen's grades gradually improved. As she began to see rewards for studying, she put more effort into her work, and by year's end, she was passing all subjects.

## Summary

Teachers of below-level readers can seek easier texts, use trade books written on the appropriate level of difficulty, provide additional assistance with the text, use glosses, use recorded versions of the text, make greater use of sources of information that do not require reading, and use hands-on activities. Texts can also be adapted, but this is time-consuming.

Content Enhancement organizes and presents the curriculum in such a way that key concepts are easier to learn and more readily learned and so fosters understanding. Teaching students how to use text structures also fosters comprehension. Other instructional techniques that can be employed to foster comprehension in the content areas can be categorized as those that are used before, during, or after reading. Before-reading techniques feature the anticipation guide and the Frayer model. During-reading techniques feature frame questions and strategy guides, including glosses. After-reading techniques include reflecting, graphic organizers, applying, and extending. KWL Plus is an approach that encompasses before-, during-, and after-reading techniques. Collaborative techniques that incorporate several highly successful comprehension strategies are ReQuest, reciprocal teaching, and Questioning the Author.

To prepare struggling readers and writers to be college- and career-ready it is essential that they be taught how to read and write complex text. Techniques that develop this ability include guided close reading and rereading, conferences, dialogue journals, taking notes, marking confusing passages, and teachers' use of prompts, probes, and scaffolding of responses.

Dealing as it does with material that is predominantly narrative, literature books are somewhat easier to comprehend than are social studies or science texts. For low-achieving readers, teachers may choose texts that are of high quality but are less demanding to read.

To study effectively, students must know themselves as learners. There are three approaches to studying: principles (understanding), organization, and association. The most widely used study strategy is SQ3R: survey, question, read, recite, review, to which a sixth step, reflect, is sometimes added. SQ3R is an organizational strategy. Other organizational study strategies include various forms of note taking. Associational memory devices include mnemonic approaches such as rhymes, acronyms, and acrostics. Spaced practice that is interleaved, carefully planned, spaced reviews, and test-enhanced review improve learning and retention.

Poor or ineffective study habits are a major cause of academic failure. Assessing students' study strategies and habits, building students' knowledge of self as a learner, instructing, coaching, and counseling are techniques that can help to improve students' study habits.

## Application Activities

1.  Examine texts written for low-achieving readers. Analyze the texts. What makes them easy to read? What are the major disadvantages and advantages of using easy-to-read texts?
2.  Construct a strategy guide or a gloss. If possible, introduce it and arrange for a group of students to use it.
3.  Try out SQ3R with some material that you wish to learn. Use it for at least five sessions. Assess its effectiveness. What are its advantages? What are its disadvantages?
4.  Teach one of the study strategies covered in this chapter to a disabled reader or a group of low-achieving readers. Assess the effectiveness of the lesson.
5.  Read and try out the suggestions made in *Organizing Instruction and Study to Improve Student Learning* at http://ies.ed.gov/ncee/wwc/PracticeGuide .aspx?sid=1

## My Education Lab

Go to the topic **Reading Assessment** in the MyEducationLab (www.myeducationlab .com) for **Assessing and Correcting Reading Difficulties**, where you can:

■   Find learning outcomes for **Reading Assessment** along with the national standards that connect to these outcomes.

■   Complete Assignments and Activities that can help you more deeply understand the chapter content.

■   Apply and practice your understanding of the core teaching skills identified in the chapter with the Building Teaching Skills and Dispositions learning units.

■   Examine challenging situations and cases presented in the Iris Center Resources.

■   Check your comprehension of the content covered in the chapter with the Study Plan. Here you will be able to take a chapter pretest, receive feedback on your answers, and then access personalized Review, Practice, and Enrichment exercises to enhance your understanding of chapter content. After you complete the exercises, take a posttest to confirm your comprehension.

■   Practice targeting instruction and making content accessible for all students with A+RISE activities.

# 13   Building Writing Strategies

**USING WHAT YOU KNOW**

**B**eset by difficulties in organizing their ideas and frequently handicapped by poor spelling and illegible handwriting, low-achieving readers find writing even more difficult than reading. The process approach, with its emphasis on the message as opposed to the mechanics, is a powerful tool for teaching disabled writers and will be emphasized in this chapter. However, focus will also be placed on presenting strategies that have proved to be effective with low-achieving readers and writers.

How do you feel about writing? What kinds of writing do you find relatively easy? What kinds do you find difficult? What strategies or routines do you use to help you write? How would you go about helping low-achieving writers?

**ANTICIPATION GUIDE**

*Read each of the following statements. Put a check under "Agree" or "Disagree" to show how you feel about each one. If possible, discuss your responses with classmates.*

|  |  | AGREE | DISAGREE |
|---|---|---|---|
| 1. | Good writers are born, not made. | _____ | _____ |
| 2. | If you can say it, you can write it. | _____ | _____ |
| 3. | The more planning you do beforehand, the better the writing. | _____ | _____ |
| 4. | The hardest part of writing is revising. | _____ | _____ |
| 5. | The major problem that struggling readers and writers have with writing is spelling. | _____ | _____ |

# Extent of Writing Problems

How many students have writing problems? In the 2003 (report of most recent testing at grade 4) and 2011 National Assessment of Educational Progress writing assessments, at grades 4, 8, and 12, the percentages of students performing below the basic level of writing achievement were 14, 20, and 21 percent, respectively (see Table 13.1) (National Center for Education Statistics, 2012; Persky, Daane, & Jin, 2003). These students have such limited writing skills that they lack even partial mastery for the writing demanded by their grade level. Students do better on narrative writing than informative, and better on informative than persuasive tasks.

# The Changing Nature of the Writing Process

As students mature as writers, the nature of their writing changes. Inexperienced writers use a knowledge-telling process, in which writing is similar to telling a story orally or providing an oral explanation. It requires "no greater amount of planning or goal setting than ordinary conversation" (Bereiter & Scardamalia, 1982, p. 9). Beginning writers use a "what next" strategy, in which they write from one sentence to the next without having an overall plan for the whole piece (Dahl & Farnham, 1998). The sentence currently being written provides a springboard for the next sentence.

> ✳ Writing is both more complex and more abstract than talking. When people talk to each other, they are aided by cues to start, to stop, to continue, to clarify, or to elaborate. When composing, writers are on their own (Bereiter & Scardamalia, 1982).

Over time, writers acquire the ability to transform knowledge, in which they develop and revise their thoughts as they write so that writing becomes a way of exploring and learning. As more experienced writers compose, their writing affects their thinking, and their thinking affects their writing. Instead of merely summarizing thoughts, writers reconsider old ideas and draw new conclusions, which are reflected in their writing.

Struggling writers, often because of poorly developed skills, get stuck in the knowledge-telling stage of writing. Asked to respond to a narrative poem or short story, struggling writers frequently resort to providing a plot summary. If the story is a challenging one, they might use all their mental energies to understand the story, so they are unable to evaluate it at the same time. Or they might not have a schema for the kind of writing that requires a critical analysis. The knowledge-telling strategy is adopted because the task is so challenging for the writers that they are unable to go beyond simply recording content. The problem with knowledge telling is that the writers do not provide their own interpretations, and a written voice or distinctive style is lacking.

| Grade | Below Basic | Basic | Proficient | Advanced |
|-------|-------------|-------|------------|----------|
| 4 | 14 | 26 | 58 | 2 |
| 8 | 20 | 54 | 24 | 3 |
| 12 | 21 | 52 | 24 | 3 |

**TABLE 13.1**
Writing Levels for a National Sample of Students

*Source:* National Center for Education Statistics (2012). *The nation's report card: Writing 2011* (NCES 2012–470). Institute of Education Sciences, U.S. Department of Education, Washington, D.C. Persky, H. R., Daane, M. C., & Jin, Y. (2003). *The nation's report card: Writing 2002* (NCES No. 2003-529). Washington, DC: U.S. Department of Education, Institute of Education Services, National Center for Education Statistics

One form of knowledge telling is a copying strategy. Using a copying strategy, students simply retell what they have read or heard. They may paraphrase or use their own words. Copying could be more of a reading than a writing issue. It may mean that the reader is still constructing the meaning of the passage and so is dependent on the author's words to say what the passage means. If the author's ideas are difficult to understand, writers may solve the problem by retelling these ideas in the author's words (Collins, 1998).

As with developing reading skills, the emphasis in writing instruction is on building on what students know. And that means digging deeply. When working with problem writers, it is easy to be stopped cold by surface features and go no further. You need to look beyond awkward wording, dysgraphic handwriting, bizarre spellings, and random use of capital letters and look into the message the students are attempting to convey and the processes they are using. The process approach to writing emphasizes composing and revising and puts mechanics in perspective so that they don't become the be-all and the end-all of writing instruction.

> **Writing process:** model of teaching writing that views writing as being composed of planning, composing, revising, editing, and publishing.

The five steps in the **writing process** are prewriting, composing, revising, editing, and publishing. Although these steps are discussed separately in the following sections, they operate in a circular or recursive fashion. Before I write, I plan and prepare, but actually I am composing in my head as I plan, and as I write I might revise and even edit and also plan what comes next. I might do much of my planning after I have started writing. I may not even know what I'm going to write until I have actually written it. Fiction writers report being motivated to write so they can see how the story comes out. With this type of writing, characters often take on a life of their own.

## Prewriting

> **Prewriting:** part of the writing process that includes all the things a writer does before composing, including selecting a topic and planning.

**Prewriting** consists of all those things that a writer does to prepare for writing. It may take 10 minutes, or it may be an idea that someone has been mulling over for 10 years.

The core of prewriting is topic selection. If students are going to invest time and energy and put themselves into their writing, they must have a sense of personal involvement in their writing. The best topics are those that students select for themselves because they have a personal interest in them and know a great deal about them or want to explore them. However, this does not mean that students should get bogged down in biographical narratives.

Graves (2004) emphasizes the need to move beyond the personal narrative. He cautions that students might "latch on to stale TV plots, violent actions scenarios, or insipid sentiments involving Care Bears—the kinds of stories they encounter on television and in computer games" (p. 29). To revitalize students' writing, Graves recommends that teachers "read the world," which means that they help students explore the important things that are happening in their lives and all around them. As Graves comments, "Children need to choose most of their own topics. But we need to show them all the places writing comes from, that it is often triggered by simple everyday events" (p. 91).

Struggling writers need to acquire a command of the major types of writing. They need to be able to write explanatory and persuasive pieces. However, they should be encouraged to write a persuasive piece about an issue that touches their lives or explain a process that is of interest to them.

## Modeling Topic Selection

Since underachieving writers may have limited experience in selecting topics, model the process for them. For instance, if the students are writing about famous Americans as part of a biography unit, list some of the people you might want to write about. List four or five names on the board and think-aloud your reasons for your choices, as in the following example:

Martin Luther King Jr.

Sally Ride

Roberto Clemente

Thomas Edison

Give an honest appraisal of which one you would like to write about. You might give the pros and cons of each topic, saying "I know Martin Luther King worked hard for justice and equal rights, and Sally Ride was the first woman astronaut. Roberto Clemente was an outstanding baseball player and tried to help poor people, but I'm most interested in Thomas Edison. He went on to become one of the most famous inventors of all time, but I heard that he had trouble with school. I'd like to find out more about his growing-up days and write about that."

Sources of topics are endless. Students can write about their everyday lives: what they have seen, heard, or read about in class or outside school. The topic might be a class trip, an interesting project, being the new boy or girl in class, the school principal, a guest speaker, a piece of information in a science or social studies book, or an article in *Sports Illustrated for Kids.*

Research is another possibility. Students can explore topics about which they have limited knowledge but which interest them. They can explore and write about how to take care of a new puppy, how to grow tomatoes, or how to make a lay-up. They can find out more about sharks, deserts, or the stars. They can write to their favorite basketball player or pop singer. They can interview their grandparents to find out about life in the 1970s, or talk to a dietitian about eating the right kinds of foods. You might also encourage students to talk to family members and friends about possible topics and to keep a notebook or file of possible subjects. A writer's notebook should be a place to generate ideas, explore topics, or jot down observations (Calkins & Harwayne, 1991).

> ✳ Notebooks provide their owners with the opportunity to collect ideas and information over a period of time before setting out to write. Choosing a topic becomes a matter of selecting ideas that have had time to ripen.

If students are really stuck for a topic, you might suggest some surefire generic topics. For instance, play the song "My Favorite Things" or read the book *Honey, I Love and Other Poems* (Greenfield, 1978), and talk over your favorite things or the things that you love. Then have students make a list of their favorite things and develop it into an autobiographical piece.

Reading is also a rich source of topic ideas. A brief article about bird watching or seeing-eye dogs may motivate students to explore this topic and report on their findings. In their notebooks, students might also record favorite passages, realistic characters, unusual settings, imaginative phrases, and humorous or wise expressions that might become the basis for future writing.

## Planning

After a topic has been selected, students gather and organize information. This is a crucial step for underachieving writers. Their compositions are typically very brief, suggesting that they lack adequate content knowledge or are unable to make use of the knowledge they do have (Graham & Harris, 1993). They may not realize how much information they have on a topic or may have difficulty organizing it and putting it in written form.

To help students make use of information that they already possess, drawing and brainstorming are effective techniques. Drawing helps younger students encapsulate their ideas. When they write in response to a drawing they have created, the drawing provides them a stable prompt for suggesting what details they might develop. Because it taps another dimension, drawing also helps older students retrieve details that they may not have thought of. After J. L. Olson (1987) encouraged her students to draw illustrations of their subjects before writing about them, the detail in their written pieces increased markedly. An essential element in the procedure was discussion. Olson discussed students' drawings with them before they began writing. This helped them translate into words the details recorded in their drawings.

Students may have a number of ideas that they wish to express, but they might not know how to organize them. Completing a semantic map or a preplanning sheet will help them organize their thoughts. However, they should be encouraged to add new ideas or details as they write. Since writing is, in part, a discovery process, writers often think up new ideas as they write.

## Brainstorming

An effective technique for helping students access details is to have them brainstorm a topic. The stimulus for brainstorming can be the topic or a single word. Model the process, emphasizing that in brainstorming, you come up with as many ideas as you can think of. Then encourage students to brainstorm. Urge them to listen to ideas expressed by others, because that may help them think of other ideas.

## Rehearsal

**Writing rehearsal:** practice of mentally composing a piece before actually writing it down. Drawing can be a rehearsal for writing. Moore and Caldwell (1991) devised a program in which students drew storyboards showing characters, setting, story events, and main ideas before composing their pieces.

A valuable planning technique is to provide students with time to mull over their topics. Before they begin composing, professional writers may have **rehearsed** the piece they are about to write for days or weeks or even years. When they sit down at their desks, they are ready to write. They have already shaped the piece in their minds. Encourage students to rehearse topics. Try giving them previews of writing assignments a day or so ahead of time, so that they have time to think over possible topics and how they might develop them.

## Audience

An important part of planning is considering the audience. Novice writers have a difficult time adjusting their writing for an outside reader. They believe that if they can understand it, so can anyone who happens to read it. To help build audience awareness, discuss the concept of audience before students start writing. Ask such questions as "For whom are you writing? Who will read your piece? What will you need to tell your readers so they will understand your piece?"

In the past, much of the writing that students did in school was for the teacher. Students wrote to complete an assignment or to be evaluated. This limited the range of students' writing. In today's schools, students write real pieces for a variety of audiences.

### Approaches to Prewriting

The amount of time and effort devoted to prewriting will depend, in part, on your approach to writing or the nature of the particular writing task (Collins, 1998). Some teachers take a write-it-now, fix-it-later approach, in which the focus of instruction is on revising first drafts to incorporate key features. The other approach is to supply a maximum of prewriting instruction so that students include key features in their first drafts. Neither approach is more effective than the other. However, getting it right the first time can be a confidence builder and allows more opportunity for refinement or fine-tuning.

## Composing

Low-achieving writers may be hindered by poor spelling ability, labored handwriting, possible difficulty in retrieving the right words to express their thoughts, and a negative association with writing, so they may scrawl only a sentence or two before calling it quits. The first order of business when working with low-progress writers is to emphasize content over mechanics. Stress with these students that the important thing in a first draft is to get one's thoughts down and not to worry about spelling, punctuation, capitalization, handwriting, or the appearance of the paper until later.

Tell students to spell as best they can. You might show them examples of first drafts in which the author may have used one or two letters to represent whole words or used invented spelling. (See Chapters 5 and 7 for more information on invented spelling.) Explain that there will be plenty of time to check spelling, punctuation, and capitalization, but that will come later.

> **Composing:** act of writing. The focus should be on getting one's thoughts down, rather than creating a finished, error-free piece on the first attempt.

Model the **composing** process for students, and show them some rough drafts that you have written in which wholesale changes were later made. If students need more convincing, invite reporters from the local newspaper or other professional writers to talk to the class about how they write their first drafts. If labored handwriting is a serious problem, you might try having students dictate their pieces or write using a computer if they have adequate keyboarding skills.

As students compose, they may reach a point where they can't seem to continue. Encourage them to seek additional information, or they may have a conference with a peer, with you, or with a writing group. These **writing conferences** serve some of the same functions in eliciting more writing that speaker–listener interactions in conversations do. They help elicit output. It is also a good idea to circulate around the room as students write, providing support for students or brief miniconferences to help them access additional information. If students are still stuck, they might consider putting the piece aside and coming back to it later or trying another topic.

> **Writing conferences:** meetings between student and teacher or student and peer editor for the purpose of discussing the student's writing.

### Writing Conferences

Conference questions are of three general types: opening, following, and process (Graves, 1983). *Opening questions* are icebreakers designed to start the flow of the conference. These are open-ended, nonthreatening inquiries: "How is it going? What are you writing about? Where are you now in your piece?"

*Following questions* are designed to maintain the flow. Often, they are simply restatements or summaries, in question form, of what the student has told you: "You're having difficulty getting started?" or "Your team lost the championship game

✳ Graves (1983) comments: "Listening is hard work. It isn't easy to put aside personal preferences, anxieties about helping more children, or the glaring, mechanical errors that stare from the page. I mumble to myself, 'Shut up, listen, and learn!'" (p. 100).

and you feel you're to blame?" or "You like your new school but miss your old friends?"

*Process questions* focus on the writing process itself. Process questions might be of a general nature: "What do you think you'll do next? What do you want to do with this piece? Where will you start? What part do you like best? Is there a part you aren't happy with?" Or the questions can be more specific: "What happened after this? Can you explain this? As a reader, I'd like to know more about this. What can you do to make your beginning stronger? Can you think of a different way to say this?" (Turbill, 1982). Process questions help students become aware of the strategies they are using so they can exert greater control over them. After students have solved a writing problem or finished a piece, you might ask questions that will lead them to reflect and comment on the processes they have used: "Your new ending is more interesting. How did you go about writing it?" (Graves, 1983).

Process questioning should also help you discover the writer's strengths and weaknesses, the strategies the writer is using, and ways in which you might build upon the writer's knowledge and strategies. In his work with struggling writers, Collins (1998) asked students to tell what made writing hard and to ask for help whenever they had questions about their writing or when they were encountering difficulty. This helped him to discover underlying writing problems and allowed him to suggest useful strategies.

In the writing conference, praise at least one aspect of the student's writing. However, also emphasize one element that could be improved. It can be an area that the class is focusing on for this particular writing task. Make a teaching point (Calkins, 2003a). For instance, perhaps the student didn't fully explain a process. You might ask her to reread the piece to see if others will be able to understand how she taught her dog to sit when she commanded it to do so. If the student fails to note missing steps, you might then ask her to read the piece and see if all the steps for teaching the dog to sit have been included. If the student fails to notice that a key step is missing, point out the difficulty and help her revise her piece. After the missing step has been added, summarize what has been done so that the student can apply this technique to future writing: "Rachel, you did a good job revising your piece. Good writers check their explanations to make sure that all the steps are there. They put themselves in the place of the reader and ask 'Would I be able to follow this explanation?'"

## Revising

**Revising:** procedure in the writing process in which the writer reviews what has been written and makes changes in content and expression.

Real **revising** means taking a fresh look at what you have written and asking yourself such basic questions as "What am I trying to say here? Have I said what I want to say? Have I said all that I want to say? Is my writing clear? Is it as fresh and vivid as I can make it? Does it sound right? Does it feel right? Do all the parts fit?"

To help students gain a sense of what it means to revise, model the process. Show them how you add or delete details, rewrite sentences, move elements around, and change words. However, focus on those aspects of revising that your students can handle. In the past, students were reluctant to revise because it meant recopying the entire piece. Demonstrate the shortcuts that students can take. Show them how they can use copyediting marks: arrows to move elements, carets to add. They can cross out items or even manually cut and paste elements. If possible, demonstrate how word-processing software might be used in the revision process. One of the advantages of using this software is that the mechanics of revising are made so much simpler.

As students look over their rough drafts, encourage them to see whether they have any questions about what they wrote. Have them put themselves in the readers' place and ask, "Will the readers understand what I'm trying to say? Have I told the readers enough? Will the readers want to know more?" Often, the major problem with struggling writers' pieces is that they haven't told enough. They have supplied a few bare-bone facts without elaborating. Or they have written "hodge-podges of anything-I-can-think-of-that-relates-to-this-topic pieces" (Calkins & Oxenhorn, 2003, p. v), instead of focusing on a key moment or incident (see Exemplary Teaching: Focusing in on Key Events).

When modeling the revising process, focus on one or two key items that the class as a whole seems to need. For instance, if students are not including enough details in their pieces, demonstrate adding information. Also alert students to the fact that revisions can sometimes be less effective and less clearly written than the originals. Encourage students to reread the piece after they have revised it to make sure the revised version sounds better than the original.

Revising should be cumulative. After students have mastered one revising strategy, introduce a second. For instance, after students have learned to add details to flesh out a piece of writing, you might find that they need to work on creating interesting beginnings. As students revise, they can focus on writing interesting beginnings but should also be responsible for making sure that they included sufficient detail. You might have students compose a revision checklist and add elements as these are taught. (Also consult the Revision Think Sheet in Figure 13.6, later in the chapter.)

## EXEMPLARY TEACHING

### Focusing in on Key Events

For struggling writers, a common flaw is failure to focus on a key event or even what Calkins and Oxenhorn (2003) term a small moment. Instead they attempt to recount all the events of a day or experience. Here is how teacher Lois Burdett used a writing conference to help a student hone in on an important event. "Here you told me your hamster died, but then you went right into your shopping trip at Kmart. How did you feel when your hamster died? Who buried it? Where did you bury it?" (Spandel, 2005, p. 233).

Responding to her teacher's queries, the writer described in vivid terms a description of the pet's last moments and how she touched its body to see if she could detect any signs of life. She followed with a description of her tears as she realized her pet was gone. She describes her rush into the basement to break the sad news to her dad. The piece ends with a description of the burial and the marker that contained the hamster's name and e-mail address.

A few well-thought-out questions by the teacher transformed a dull recounting of a day's events into a poignant piece.

When revising, struggling readers and writers tend to focus on surface features such as capitalization and spelling. Guide them in looking for and reworking substantive elements, such as using examples to develop a topic and using colorful adjectives. During the process, emphasize things that students have done well so that they have something to build on.

In writing narratives, struggling readers often fail to develop their characters. They fail to show why they acted the way they did or how they were feeling (Newcomer & Barenbaum, 1991). In preparing students to write narratives, read aloud to them or have them read selections in which the characters' motivations and emotions are developed. Discuss how the characters' motivations and emotions are revealed. Using these as models, have the class compose a group narrative in which motivation and emotion are revealed, and then have students write

(Continued)

their own pieces. As you conference with students, ask them why the characters were acting in a certain way and what they were thinking and feeling.

In writing expository texts, struggling readers and writers often fail to develop their topics. They may give just one example or one reason or one detail.

Just as with narratives, discuss model paragraphs and later longer pieces that are well developed. Note in particular how the authors developed their ideas and have students follow suit in a group story and then individual pieces. During prewriting, composing, and revising, emphasize the development of the topic.

## Editing

Up until this point, the focus has been on the content of the piece. Emphasis was rightfully placed on composing rather than on the mechanics of writing. In this final

> **Editing:** process of making corrections in a written piece. Often there is a focus on mechanical errors rather than on making changes in content.

step, students edit their pieces for mechanical errors. Normally, in the **editing** process, all errors are corrected. Since disabled writers tend to make an excessive number of errors, you may choose to focus on just one or two areas of concern. However, if pieces are to be published, then you may want to have all errors corrected.

As with the other conventions in writing, capitalization, punctuation, and usage should be taught directly and related to the writing that students are doing. To decide which elements to teach, examine students' first drafts to see what is needed. Focus on one element—capitalization of proper names or question marks, for instance.

### Editing Strategies

Once you have analyzed students' errors, discuss with them the kinds of mistakes they make. Keeping in mind any error patterns that you note, teach them strategies for minimizing errors and detecting those that do crop up. If students mix up the order of the letters in words, have them slowly and carefully read the piece exactly as it is written, so that *turly* is read as *turly* and the student can note that the word is misspelled. If students omit endings, have them be especially aware of the endings of words. If students omit syllables, have them pronounce each syllable in any multi-syllabic words they have written. Also, students might circle any words that they feel might be misspelled.

Better yet, as part of the revising/editing process, have students read their drafts out loud to themselves. When reading silently, we tend to read what we think should be there. When we read orally, we are more likely to note awkward expressions, missing words, and other problems or errors. Reading aloud is also an effective technique for peer editing. One student reads the other's draft out loud so he can detect needed changes. As Collins (2004) comments, "Listening to your own writing and listening to others read your writing is the best single editing technique" (p. 3).

### Skills Lessons

While group skills lessons should be taught on a regular basis, also provide instruction as needed on an informal basis. Whether taught as part of whole-group direct instruction or a repair-it-on-the-spot basis, skill instruction works best if it is taught when needed.

As students edit, it is helpful if they have a checklist to guide them. Checklists can be generic, or they can be individualized and geared to the needs of specific students. A sample editing checklist is presented in Figure 13.1.

**FIGURE 13.1**

Editing Checklist

> 1. Is the piece clear?
> 2. Are all the sentences complete?
> 3. Does each sentence end with a period, question mark, or exclamation point?
> 4. Is the first word of each sentence capitalized?
> 5. Are the names of people *(George, Uncle Fred)* and places *(New York, the United States, Main Street)* capitalized?
> 6. Are all the words spelled correctly?

For older students, you might provide them with a mnemonic strategy for editing, such as SCOPE:

**S**   Spelling: Is the spelling correct?

**C**   Capitalization: Are the first words of sentences, proper names, and proper nouns capitalized?

**O**   Order of words: Are the words in the right order?

**P**   Punctuation: Does each sentence end with a period, question mark, or exclamation mark? Are commas and apostrophes placed where needed?

**E**   Express complete thought: Is each sentence complete? Does each sentence have a subject and a predicate? (Bos & Vaughn, 1994)

## Publishing

Writing real pieces for real people is an essential element in the writing process. Writing for a real audience changes the nature of students' writing. For instance, several studies of poor writers in the intermediate and secondary grades found that these students expressed themselves effectively when writing on their own to peers or family members. Ironically, many of these same students had been judged to be poor writers on the basis of performance on school-related writing tasks (Dyson & Freedman, 1991).

> **Publishing:** part of the writing process in which students share their writing in some way. The piece could be printed in a booklet or newspaper, or it could be read or dramatized.

Developing as a writer requires getting a response to one's writing. One of the advantages of **publishing**, or making public one's writing, is that it invites feedback. Without feedback, the writer has no way of gauging whether her or his work was understood and enjoyed by the audience. Response from others also helps students learn to see their writing as others see it, which builds a sense of audience. Through audience reaction, writers can see which parts of their pieces are most effective and which parts may need clarifying or elaborating.

## Composing Explanatory/Informational and Persuasive Texts

> Narrative writing is less complex than expository or persuasive writing. As Bruner (1986) explains, there are two types of thinking: narrative and logical-scientific. Narrative thinking is more basic. Students have much more experience with narrative than they do with logical-scientific thinking, which is more complex and abstract.

Common Core State Standards place more stress on reading and writing informational text. In general, writing informational text is more difficult than writing narrative text. The first step in teaching students to compose informational text is to find out where students are. In their extensive studies, Donovan and Smolkin (2011) and Smolkin (2011) analyzed the expository writing of students in grades K to 5 and noted a series of stages or phases. The earliest writing consists of composing labels: "This is a robin" or simply "Robin." In subsequent stages students add information about the labels, elaborate on details they have included, organize their writing into paragraphs and sections, and increasingly use effective cohesive devices (see Figure 13.2). Although, informational writing development generally follows the stages listed in Figure 13.2, students can and do move back and forth between stages and that the stages overlap. In addition, students may be in one stage for informational writing and another for narrative.

When making instructional suggestions, plan activities and use prompts that are based on the student's current level of writing and that have the potential to

■▪ **FIGURE 13.2**
Developmental Stages of Informational Writing
*Source:* Adapted from Donovan & Smolkin (2011); Georgia Department of Education (2000); Hampton & Resnick (2009); and Salahu-Din et al. (2008).

**Emerging**

- Limited topic development. Topic might simply be stated and might be a label that identifies a person, place, or thing but provides no information beyond a label.
- Labels pictures with single words, phrases, or sentences.
- May draw, scribble, use random letters, or partial invented spelling.
- Little sense of audience.

**Expressing**

- Expresses details related to topic. Details go beyond label to provide information.
- Details are written in list-like fashion, but details are not explained or elaborated on.
- Uses simple words and sentence patterns.
- Limited sense of audience.

**Elaborating**

- Begins to expand on details by explaining how or why.
- Information lacks overall organization. There are no headings or subheadings. Little or no use of connecting words or transitions.
- Uses simple words and sentence patterns.
- Limited sense of audience.

**Organizing**

- Begins to organize details. May address a number of subtopics.
- Uses repetition of key ideas and connectives, such as *and* and *also,* to show relationships among ideas. May use headings and subheadings. Provides a concluding sentence.
- Begins to use varied sentence patterns. Combines some ideas into compound and complex sentences, but may string clauses together with a series of *ands*.
- Demonstrates ability to see similarities and differences.
- Shows emerging sense of audience.

**Expanding**

- Uses a variety of details and examples to develop a topic.
- Uses title; headings; connectives such as *therefore, for example,* and *however*; and sequencing to organize information.
- Has a well-developed beginning, middle, and end, but writing may be formulaic. Composes a conclusion that flows from the information provided.
- Uses technical vocabulary, more formal language, and a greater proportion of complex sentences.

*(Continued)*

FIGURE 13.2
(*Continued*)

- Demonstrates clear and logical thinking.
- Demonstrates a basic sense of audience.

Extending

- Uses well-chosen details and examples to develop a topic fully and clearly.
- Uses various devices to compose a smooth flowing, interesting, logically developed piece.
- Uses a varied sentence structure and carefully chosen vocabulary to develop ideas in an interesting fashion.
- Uses various techniques to keep audience engaged and informed. May use analogies, illustrations, examples, anecdotes, or figurative language.
- Demonstrates analytical and evaluative thinking and creativity.
- Demonstrates a keen sense of audience.

move the student forward, as in the following groups of information, elaboration, and organization prompts.

*Information prompts* ask for more details. The student might have simply written a label or not have supplied enough information. For instance, if a student has produced the label "This is a cheetah," the teacher can use the prompt: "Yes, that is a cheetah. Can you tell me something about the cheetah?" or "Make up a sentence that begins with the words *the cheetah* and tell me something about the cheetah," so that the student produces a fact statement: "The cheetah can run fast." To prompt more information, ask the student what else he can tell you about cheetahs. If the student has difficulty providing information, have him take a closer look at the illustration or book being used or seek out a suitable reference.

*Elaboration prompts* ask the student to explain facts or flesh out details. To elaborate the fact statement: "Cheetahs run fast," the teacher might ask: "How fast can cheetahs run?" How and why prompts are especially effective: "How are cheetahs able to run fast? Why do cheetahs run fast?"

*Organization prompts* are designed to help the writer show relationships by grouping details and/or by making greater use of cohesive devices, such as repeating key words (*cheetahs,* for instance), using pronouns–antecedents (*cheetahs–they*), or using words that signal relationships (*because, and, also*). If the student has a long list of unconnected facts, the teacher might have him cut the individual facts into strips and then group them: "Which ones describe the cheetah? Which ones tell how fast it runs? Which ones tell how it is built for speed? Which ones tells how it protects its young?" In future activities the student might also be encouraged to compose a topic sentence and, in a later activity, use signal words. Creating a graphic organizer also helps students organize their information (Donovan & Smolkin, 2011).

Mentor texts can be used as models of organization. Mentor books exist on a variety of levels of organization, from labels and lists of facts to carefully organized paragraphs. For instance, the text *Stegosaurus up Close* (Dodson, 2011) has a very clear organizational pattern that uses both headings and topic sentences to group major categories of information. The key to effective instruction is to determine the processes students are currently controlling and what kinds of scaffolding will enable them to use more advanced processing. Table 13.2 presents some common writing situations or difficulties that students encounter and the prompts teachers might use to scaffold students' efforts.

Writing boxes containing manipulatives can be used as physical rehearsals for composing (Karlowicz, personal communication, March 31, 2012). Supply a writing box that contains a toy cheetah and other animals with whom the cheetah's

| TABLE 13.2 | Writing Situations | Prompts |
|---|---|---|
| Prompts for Improving Writing | Has written a label sentence.<br>This is a cheetah. | Yes, that is a cheetah. Can you tell me something about the cheetah? Make up a sentence that begins with the words *the cheetah* and tell me something about the cheetah. |
| | Has not supplied enough information.<br>Cheetahs are cats. | What else they can tell you about cheetahs? What special ability do cheetahs have? (Supply a writing box that contains a cheetah.) Here is a cheetah. Show me what the cheetah can do. Show me how fast the cheetah runs in comparison with other animals. |
| | Has supplied a list of unconnected or unordered details but details are not explained.<br>Cheetahs are in the cat family.<br>Cheetahs are built to run fast.<br>Cheetahs can be found in Africa and the Middle East. | You said that cheetahs are built to run fast. How are they built for speed? What makes them fast? |
| | Lack of coherence or unity.<br>Cheetahs are the fastest animals on land. Cheetahs hunt for their food. Cheetahs can pull their claws in when they run. Cheetahs cannot roar. Cheetahs growl and hiss when they sense danger. Cheetahs have long powerful legs. Cheetahs yowl when danger gets close. Cheetahs hunt mostly medium-size mammals. Cheetahs have large hearts and lungs. Cheetahs chirp when searching for other cheetahs. | What is your main purpose here? Do all your ideas fit? Are your ideas in the best order? Let's cut your paragraph apart and group the sentences that go together. Which sentences explain why the cheetah is fast? Which sentences tell how the cheetah gets food? Which sentences tell about the sounds that cheetahs can make? Let's look at how (mentor author) organizes information. How might we use her organization? How might we use the signal words like *first, next,* and *last* to organize our explanation |
| | Topic is too broad. | What is your purpose in writing this? What's the most important or most interesting idea here? How might you develop that? |
| | Piece lacks details or examples. | I like your piece about _____.<br>But I don't know very much about _____. Can you tell more about it? |
| | Needs an interesting beginning sentence. | How might you start this? What might you say to pull your reader into this story (or article)? |
| | Inadequate conclusion or lack of ending. | How might you sum up what you've said? What thought or idea do you want your reader to take away from this? |

*Sources:* Adapted from Donovan & Smolkin (2011); and Muschla (1993).

running speed can be compared or that might be preyed upon by the cheetah: "Here is a cheetah. Show me what the cheetah can do. Show me how fast the cheetah runs in comparison with other animals."

## Composing Explanatory Text

When asked to provide explanations, students tend to write descriptions but fail to include causes (Donovan & Smolkin, 2012). For example, when asked to explain how a fire extinguisher worked, students provided a series of steps for operating the extinguisher but failed to explain why the extinguisher was able to put out the fire, even though in their science class the students had discussed how carbon dioxide smothered fire (Klein & Rose, 2010). Students described key steps but failed to explain why the steps occurred. When discussing processes, especially those in science, teachers should provide clear explanations of causes. In writing, teachers should model the process of creating clear explanations and emphasize the how and the why. Of course, a clear explanation begins with a clear understanding of the process. Students should be directed to do the following:

- Obtain the necessary information.
- Describe each step.
- Tell why each step works.

Students also need to be taught the language required to express relationships found in explanations. One way of familiarizing students with the rhetoric of explanations is to provide them with step-by-step hands-on experiences and then have students explain them. For instance, they might observe a dancing raisins experiment in which raisins are dropped into cups of diet soda and then explain what happened and why. The key is to stop at each step and get a clear description of what happened and then a reasoned explanation (Klein & Rose, 2010).

## Composing Argumentation and Persuasive Texts

Composing arguments is a key writing task. Students are asked to take positions on issues and support them, respond to literacy pieces and justify their responses, write persuasive essays and letters to the editors, and respond to prompts that call for taking a position and justifying it.

Composing an effective argument involves clearly stating a claim and supporting it, while at the same time refuting counterclaims. The evidence should be relevant, credible, and compelling. The piece should be well organized, with a clear introduction and a strong conclusion. Students do best in writing about claims that they agree with: being able to choose their own books, for instance. Students should also be taught to focus on their audience so they can anticipate what kinds of arguments would be convincing and what kinds of opposition might be presented. Students are typically better at supporting their claims than they are at answering possible objections.

Students have difficulty learning content and a rhetorical structure at the same time. Begin with topics or issues that are familiar so that they grasp the rhetorical structure before applying it to complex content (Klein & Rose, 2010). Activities that might be used to build the skills needed to compose an argument include

- Holding debates in which students are taught how to formulate arguments. Debating an issue helps students bring to the fore their arguments and support.
- Encouraging students to support their positions in class and small-group discussions and modeling how to do so.
- Having students read and analyze opinion pieces in newspapers and magazines and note how the authors state and support their claims and refute the claims of others. Older students might also read current editorials or historical documents that discuss issues of the day. Students might underscore with a single line the support provided for the author's claim and underscore with two lines details refuting reasons the other side has made or might make for its claim.

- Having students read and discuss two sample arguments and decide which one is better and why. List on the board the rhetorical features that are especially effective. Students should try out the rhetorical devices that they found to be effective.

- Having students read several pieces and rank them, and explain their ranking (Gunning, 2013).

- With the class, compose a checklist that contains the key elements of an effective persuasive piece.

Designed for secondary school students, iCivics (http://www.icivics.org/teachers/) has an outstanding program for developing students' ability to compose a persuasive piece (argument). The Persuasive Writing program is presented in a series of eight thorough, carefully crafted lessons beginning with "Lesson 1: So You Think You Can Argue."

## Using Rubrics

As explained in Chapter 5, rubrics can be used to guide students' writing as well as assess it. An effective rubric can be used to guide student writing and can also be used by teachers to plan instruction. The rubric in Table 13.3 lists the key elements for writing an explanatory piece. Looking at the rubric, students can see that they are expected to write a clear beginning that states the topic and develop ideas with general and specific details and examples. (If used with younger students or students reading on a low level, the rubric should be simplified.) Using the rubric to assess the finished piece, the teacher might find that beginnings are not clear or not enough details are supplied and so work with students on those elements. The sample rubric contains seven elements. You might wish to focus instruction on just two or three items.

## Guided Writing

Just as students benefit from structured guidance in reading, they also do better when given guidance as they write. Although some skills can be taught to the whole class, students' specific needs can be targeted more effectively if they are members of small groups. Instead of being grouped by reading level, students are grouped by reading and writing level. Just as with oral-language acquisition, students' understanding of the writing process and ability to write develops over time and with experience. Students' concepts of writing and abilities become deeper, more complex, and broader. Although the development of writing is not a linear process, it may be helpful to think of students' writing as occurring in overlapping stages. Writing level is determined by analyzing sample written pieces or portfolios. Instruction is geared to the students' level of development. Guidelines for determining students' stages of informational writing are listed in Figure 13.2. Students are grouped by their level of development and are given instruction geared to their stage.

## Strategic Writing Instruction

Strategic writing instruction also provides needed guidance. Strategic writing instruction, which can be integrated with guided writing, has four steps:

1. Identify a strategy worth teaching
2. Introduce the strategy by modeling it

**TABLE 13.3**
Rubric for
Assessing Writing
to Explain

| | Skillful | Sufficient | Developing | Needs Support |
|---|---|---|---|---|
| Introduction | States topic clearly and invokes reader's interest. | States topic. | States topic but statement is not clear or is not fully stated. | Does not state topic or topic is stated incorrectly. |
| Development of ideas | Clear explanation of whole subject and full discussion of main parts. | Explanation of most parts of the subject. | Some explanation of the subject. | Little or no explanation of the subject. |
| Details and examples | Clear general and specific details and examples to support understanding. | Details and examples support explanation, but some are not developed enough. | Some supporting details and examples, but they are not developed enough. | Not enough details or examples to support understanding. Details are not developed or may be incorrect. |
| Organization | Ideas are grouped. Transitions show relationships among ideas. | Ideas are grouped. Relationships among ideas are mostly clear. Few or no transitions. | Some ideas are grouped. Relationships among ideas are sometimes unclear. Few or no transitions. | Ideas are not grouped. Relationships among ideas are mostly unclear. |
| Word choice | Uses precise language and subject-specific vocabulary to inform the reader about the topic or to explain the topic. | Language is usually precise, with some use of subject-specific language. | Language is general and not precise. Limited use of subject-specific language. | Language is not clear and may be used incorrectly. |
| Conclusion | Provides a strong concluding statement or section related to the information or explanation presented. | Provides a concluding statement or section related to the information or explanation presented. | Concluding statement is weak or vague. | Lacks a concluding statement or the concluding statement is not related to the subject. |
| Conventions | Grammar, use of words, punctuation, and capitalization are usually correct with a few errors, but meaning is clear. | Grammar, use of words, punctuation, and capitalization are mostly correct with some errors, but meaning is clear. | Grammar, use of words, punctuation, and capitalization are mostly correct but with some errors that may make the piece harder to understand. | Grammar, use of words, punctuation, and capitalization are sometimes correct but with many errors that may make the piece harder to understand. |

*Source:* Adapted from National Assessment Governing Board (2010); and National Governors Association Center for Best Practices and Council of Chief State School Officers (2010c).

3. Help students try out the strategy with workshop-style teacher guidance

4. Help students work toward independent mastery of the strategy through repeated practice and reinforcement (Collins, 1998, p. 65)

To identify a strategy worth teaching, examine students' writing and discuss it with them. Note their struggles. Select a strategy that would seem to be of most assistance to them. Some strategies that have been of help to struggling writers include creating webs, drawing, talking over a story or expository piece before writing it, listing supporting details or examples, brainstorming, and using models. The strategy can be introduced through teacher modeling to a whole class, a small group, or an individual.

After the strategy has been introduced, it is essential that students have an opportunity to try it out in a workshop-style situation. At this point, the teacher and students work together to implement the strategy. As they work, they make necessary adaptations, and the students personalize the strategy so that the strategy is co-constructed by teacher and students. One student, for instance, personalized topic sentence and supporting details by noting that paragraphs have a lead sentence and following sentences (Collins, 1998). Using his personalized strategy helped him to write a coherent, well-developed paragraph. Repeated practice and application to other situations lead to independent mastery of the strategy.

## Writing Workshop

The writing workshop is a way of providing students with the opportunity to try out newly introduced strategies under the teacher's guidance (Collins, 1998). Through individual or small-group conferences, the teacher can help students adapt and implement strategies that were taught in whole-class or guided writing sessions. A flexible structure, the workshop generally includes whole-class instruction, guided writing, time to write while individual and small-group conferences are held, and sharing time.

---

### EXEMPLARY TEACHING

#### Writing Strategy Instruction

When Margarita, a ninth grader, was assigned to summarize and evaluate a newspaper article, she used a strategy adopted by many struggling writers. She simply retold the article and copied many of the article's details (Collins & Collins, 1996). When questioned about the strategies that she used, she replied that she knew she needed facts and so simply went back to the article and got them. Deciding that Margarita needed strategy instruction that would help her go beyond the author's words and do some interpretive and evaluative writing, Kathleen Collins suggested a read–think–summarize–interpret strategy in which the writer would read the article carefully, maybe several times, summarize what was said, and then interpret what was said.

To help students go beyond summarizing to interpreting, Kathleen Collins decided to use DEN (Double-Entry Notebook). To use DEN, students create two columns. In the first column they summarize or record what they have read. In the second column they react to or reflect on what they have read.

Kathleen modeled using double-entry notes to the class. She then had students apply the strategy under her guidance. Using double-entry notes, Margarita wrote a longer essay that included more details and that was the product of Margarita's construction and interpretation. Margarita found DEN to be helpful because "It helped me write down what I'm thinking about while I'm reading."

If possible, the writing workshop should be held every day. Daily writing keeps student writers connected to the pieces that they are developing. If several days pass without engagement with their pieces, the writers often lose the flow of the writing.

Whole-class instruction might cover the structure of a persuasive piece or the format of a business letter, if that is what the class is working on. Writing time follows and may last for 30 minutes or longer. During writing time, students work on their writing, have peer or teacher conferences, or meet in small groups to discuss their writing. Guided writing lessons tailored to the needs of small groups of students are held at this time.

At the end of the writing time, the class meets as a whole, and individual students share their pieces. Listeners are encouraged to offer affirming comments and positive suggestions or to ask questions about any portion of the piece that was not clear. By asking questions, responding students are suggesting to the writer parts of the piece that might be expanded or clarified.

The writing workshop needs to be well organized. Necessary supplies should be available. Student works in progress should be kept in folders. Charts of students' progress and needs should be maintained. For suggestions for assessing writing, see pages 141–147.

## ▨ Writing Programs for Low-Achieving Readers and Writers

Although research on the writing of low-achieving readers sometimes paints a picture of students who have little knowledge of the writing process (Englert et al., 1988), intervention research by a number of experts portrays a very hopeful scene. In one study, neutral examiners assessed pieces written by achieving and low-achieving readers and could not tell which were which. Incredibly, the pieces written by the low-achieving readers had the same high quality as those written by the achieving readers. What wrought this magic? A carefully conceived program known as Cognitive Strategy Instruction in Writing (CSIW), which makes generous use of scaffolding (Dixon, Carnine, & Kame'enui, 1993).

### Cognitive Strategy Instruction in Writing

Cognitive Strategy Instruction in Writing (CSIW) focuses on using text structures to improve writing and features "conspicuous strategies." Through modeling and think-alouds, the teacher demonstrates and makes visible the writing process and the strategies used in his own writing (Dixon et al., 1993; Raphael & Englert, 1990). Using modeling, coaching, discussion, and other techniques, the teacher focuses on the following features of process writing: topic selection, purpose (the kinds of questions the text might be expected to answer), identification of audience, brainstorming, use of text structure, grouping ideas, using key or signal words, revising, editing, and publishing. The instructional program is broken down into four phases: analyzing the text, modeling the writing process, guiding students, and providing opportunities for independent writing (Raphael & Englert, 1990).

A key feature in Cognitive Strategy Instruction in Writing is the use of writing think sheets, which are different from the thinksheets used for reading. Teaching CSIW on page 512 explains how writing think sheets are used.

Depending on how much help students need, separate think sheets might be used for each major phase of the writing project. The think sheet in Figure 13.3

**■ FIGURE 13.3**
Plan Think Sheet

**Author's Name** _____ **Date** _____

**Topic** _____

**Who: Who am I writing for?** _____

**What: What do I want to tell my readers?**

_____

_____

_____

_____

**How: How can I organize my ideas?**

_____ Explanation       _____ Problem/Solution

_____ Comparison/Contrast       _____ Other

_____ Main Idea/Details

*Source:* Adapted from C. S. Englert, T. E. Raphael, & L. M. Anderson, *Cognitive Strategy Instruction in Writing Project.* East Lansing, MI: Institute for Research on Teaching, 1989.

provides an example of prompts that a student might use to plan a piece. After completing a Plan Think Sheet, the student might then work on an Organize Think Sheet (Figure 13.4), which answers such questions as "What is being explained? What materials and the like are needed? What are the steps?"

Once both the Plan and Organize Think Sheets have been completed and discussed, students write their rough drafts. When students write their rough drafts, they write them on colored paper. This is a reminder that they are writing an initial draft, one that must be revised before being copied onto white paper.

**Author's Name** _____ **Date** _____

**What is being explained?** _____

_____

**What materials are needed?** _____

_____

**What are the steps?**
First, _____

Next, _____

Third, _____

Then, _____

Finally, _____

*Source:* Adapted from C. S. Englert, T. E. Raphael, & L. M. Anderson, *Cognitive Strategy Instruction in Writing Project.* East Lansing, MI: Institute for Research on Teaching, 1989.

**■ FIGURE 13.4**
Organize Think Sheet

**FIGURE 13.5**
Self-Editing Think Sheet

Author's Name _____          Date _____

1. After rereading my paper, what do I like best?
_____
_____

2. Did I tell what was being explained?
_____
_____

3. Did I tell what materials were needed?
_____
_____

4. Did I write down all the steps?
_____
_____

5. Is each step clearly explained?
_____
_____

6. Did I use signal words?
_____
_____

7. What parts do I want to change?
_____
_____

8. What questions do I have for my editor?
_____
_____

*Source:* Adapted from C. S. Englert, T. E. Raphael, & L. M. Anderson, *Cognitive Strategy Instruction in Writing Project.* East Lansing, MI: Institute for Research on Teaching, 1989.

The last two major think sheets are the Self-Editing and Revision Think Sheets. Self-Editing Think Sheets are filled out by students before they submit their pieces for peer editing. The Self-Editing Think Sheets have three concerns (see Figure 13.5). After asking writers to tell what they like best, the Self-Editing Think Sheet requests that writers reexamine their pieces and note any parts that they might want to change. Writers are then asked to list any questions that they have for their editors. After having conferences with peer editors, students use the Revision Think Sheet to complete a plan for revising the piece.

The Revision Think Sheets ask students to note their plans for revision because the researchers found that, unless they make specific plans, students tend to simply recopy their papers, making only a few surface revisions, despite having gone through self-editing and peer-editing procedures (Raphael, Englert, & Kirschner, 1989). When carefully monitored and guided, peer editing also provided students with a sharpened sense of audience, which in turn may lead to more substantive revisions. When a peer editor states that he would like to know more about a topic and that a part of a piece is not clear, then the writer is more likely to add information and clarify. A Revision Think Sheet is shown in Figure 13.6.

### ■ FIGURE 13.6
Revision Think Sheet

---

**SUGGESTIONS FROM MY EDITOR**

What suggestions has your editor given you?

1. _____
2. _____
3. _____
4. _____
5. _____
6. _____

Decide on the suggestions you want to use. Put an X next to each of the suggestions you would like to use in revising your paper.

**MY IDEAS FOR REVISING MY PAPER**

Now decide on any other changes that you might like to make. Ask yourself:

Is there any way I can make my paper more interesting?

_____

Is there any way I can make the paper clearer or easier to understand?

_____

**RETURNING TO YOUR DRAFT**

On your draft, make all the changes you think will make your paper better. Use ideas from the list above, from your Self-Editing Think Sheet, and any other ideas you have for your paper. When you are ready, you can write your final copy.

*Source:* Adapted from C. S. Englert, T. E. Raphael, & L. M. Anderson, *Cognitive Strategy Instruction in Writing Project.* East Lansing, MI: Institute for Research on Teaching, 1989.

---

### Guiding Students

Students write several pieces under your guidance. Students are asked to use the text structure being studied but are free to write on any topic that makes use of that structure. The first paper may be composed by a group. The second paper can be written by individual students, but the students receive extensive teacher and peer support. A third paper is also written by individual students, but the students take increased responsibility for their work. However, peer or teacher support is provided as needed (Dixon et al., 1993). Gradually, students learn to write pieces that incorporate two or more text structures.

In using CSIW, keep in mind that the heart of the program is the modeling and careful guidance that the teacher provides and the guided sharing in which the students engage. The think sheets are simply helpful scaffolds that prompt students to use strategies they might not have been able to apply without some guidance or that they may have overlooked. In time, students should be helped to incorporate the strategies prompted by the think sheets so that they are able to use the strategies on their own, without the reminders.

> ✳ Strategy instruction is tied to students' goals. Once students have formulated a goal for their writing, they are taught a strategy that helps them to reach that goal.

### Self-Regulated Strategy Development (SRSD)

Strategy instruction is also the centerpiece of Self-Regulated Strategy Development (SRSD), a writing program devised by Harris and

## Teaching CSIW

*Step 1: Analyzing the text.* Since low-achieving readers show little awareness of text structure, either in their reading or their writing, examining text structures is emphasized. Samples from basals, trade books, periodicals, or content area texts can he used to illustrate a particular structure. It is also a good idea to use examples written by students, perhaps from previous years.

As you analyze the text, which can be written on the board or chart or on an overhead, or electronic white board point out and discuss the following:

- the topic of the text
- its purpose
- the kinds of questions the reader might expect the text to answer
- the audience
- the text structure itself
- signal words that might be used in the text structure

You might also note some areas in which the piece might be improved.

Perhaps there is a part that is not clear, or a step may have been omitted from a process. Or signal words might he added to improve the comprehensibility of the piece.

*Step 2: Modeling the writing process.* After analyzing and discussing the text, demonstrate the composing of an informational piece by writing one yourself. If a new game is to be introduced to the class, you might write a how-to piece explaining how the game is to be played. As you go through the process, think aloud, so the class can see how you plan and compose a piece. Make explicit your sense of audience, your purpose for writing, and strategies you might use to help your planning, such as listing the steps in a process and indicating needed materials. Also talk about the text structure that you plan to use, why you are using that structure, and what might be some signal words that could be used to "glue" the structure together. Later, after a discussion with students, model the revising and editing processes.

*Step 3: Guiding students: Introducing Think Sheets.* As you model the process, introduce the concept of Think Sheets. These are prompts that help students plan, organize, revise, and edit their pieces. Each type of writing or text structure should have its own Think Sheet. Although sample Think Sheets are presented here, it should be emphasized that Think Sheets can take a variety of forms and should be tailored to meet the needs of your students. Think Sheets might provide prompts for the following (Dixon, Carnine, & Kame'enui, 1993):

- Who is my audience?
- What is my goal?
- What do I know about this topic?
- What can I tell the readers at the beginning to get them interested?
- What do I need to tell my audience so they will understand what I am trying to say?
- How can I group my ideas? (steps in a process, similarities or differences in a comparison–contrast piece, reasons in a persuasive piece, solution to a problem, causes of a problem, etc.).
- What signal words might I use *(first, then, because, and, but, however, moreover,* etc.).
- What might be a good ending sentence? (sum up, leave with a thought or question).

*Step 4: Providing opportunities for independent writing.* As students become more proficient, Think Sheets are phased out.

Graham (1992). However, SRSD is broader than CSIW. Whereas CSIW focuses on text structure, the Harris–Graham program includes a wide range of strategies and emphasizes goal setting.

SRSD was designed for students with LD but has been shown to work with all students (Graham et al., 2012). Writing is a complex, demanding activity. It requires will as well as skill. Discipline and persistence are foundational attributes of effective writers (Santangelo, Harris, & Graham, 2008). To address the discipline aspect of writing, SRSD features strategies for self-regulation along with strategies for effective writing. Self-regulation components include goal-setting, self-assessment, self-instruction, and the writing environment. As Santangelo et al. (2008) warn, students with learning difficulties are often beset by "self-doubts, learned helplessness, low self-efficacy, maladaptive attributions, unrealistic pretask expectancies, and low motivation and engagement in academic areas" (p. 81).

SRSD features six basic stages of instruction, which have been slightly adapted:

1. Developing background knowledge and skills
2. Discussing the strategy
3. Modeling the strategy
4. Memorizing the strategy
5. Supporting the strategy
6. Applying the strategy independently

Four strategies for self-regulation are developed along with the writing strategies:

1. **Goal setting**
2. **Self-instructions**—Students talk themselves through a process or to overcome an obstacle. For instance, in applying the SWEAT procedure explained in A Lesson in Teaching Writing Strategies, the student might say, "I have stated my topic and I have added one example, but I need another example. I will think of some times in which I have seen pets help older people." Students also make statements that encourage them to keep on trying. " I can do this. I just have to put some SWEAT into it" (Graham, Harris, & Olinghouse, 2007).
3. **Self-monitoring**—Students ask themselves the following questions: "Did I meet the goals I developed for my writing? If not, what changes should I make to meet my goals? Did I correctly use strategies that were appropriate for this task? If not, what should I change?" Students record their answers on a chart or teacher-provided questionnaire in order to track their progress toward writing goals and strategy use.
4. **Self-reinforcement**—Students congratulate themselves, and inform their teacher, when they meet their goals. (Graham et al., 2012, p. 16).

Mnemonics are used to help students remember and implement the steps of a strategy. For instance, POW is used for planning: **P**ick ideas (i.e., decide what to write about); **O**rganize their notes (i.e., brainstorm and organize possible writing ideas into a writing plan); **W**rite and say more (i.e., continue to modify the plan while writing) (Graham et al., 2012, p. 16).

Struggling writers require 8 to 12 lessons of 20 to 40 minutes to learn a strategy, but learning subsequent strategies takes less time. It helps if strategies are applied in other content areas. It is recommended that SRSD be integrated with the process approach to writing. The approach needs to be adapted go meet the varying needs of struggling writers (Harris, n.d.).

## CRISS Writing Strategies

Using writing as a means of learning is emphasized in CRISS® (Creating Independence through Student-owned Strategies), an exemplary program designed

## A Lesson in Teaching Writing Strategies

*Step 1: Introducing strategies and setting goals.* Help students set individual or group goals. Once goals have been decided, explain what strategy instruction is. Explain that almost any operation that improves writing can be taught as a strategy. Discuss with students the strategies you use when you write. In collaboration with the students, you decide which strategy might be introduced to help them reach their goals. For instance, if the students have difficulty generating content and if their goal is to write more elaborated pieces, brainstorming might be chosen as a strategy to be presented.

*Step 2: Preskill development.* Students are taught any skills needed to understand and apply the strategy about to be taught. For instance, if students are going to be taught how to use paragraph patterns to organize their writing, they would first need to be taught how paragraphs are organized.

*Step 3: Discussing the strategy.* Explain the strategy, its steps, its value, and when and where it might be used. A very basic strategy that you might teach students is how to develop a paragraph using examples. You might have students examine pieces of writing in which examples are used to develop a topic. Discuss the paragraphs and the value of using examples to writing convincing pieces. Discuss when and where examples might be used. Have students tell how they might use the strategy in their writing.

*Step 4: Modeling the strategy.* Model the strategy using any prompts, charts, mnemonics, or other aids that students might find helpful. For instance, you might write a piece telling why you think your cat is smart. Model the process of writing the piece. Note the steps that you use in writing your piece:

**S**tate the topic.

**W**rite examples to prove the topic sentence.

**E**xplain each example.

**A**dd an interesting ending.

**T**ake a look at the piece to see if you have used convincing examples.

*Step 5: Providing scaffolding.* Use think sheets, mnemonics, visual displays, or other devices to prompt students so that they follow all the steps. As incorporated into Stage 4, the mnemonic prompt for using examples is SWEAT. "With a little SWEAT, you can write an interesting piece." Using the mnemonic, students memorize the steps in the strategy.

*Step 6: Collaborative practice.* Students try out the strategy. During conferences, emphasize the strategy that has just been taught. Provide feedback and guidance. Feedback should be specific, "I like the way you used SWEAT to help you put three exciting examples in your piece."

*Step 7: Application.* Students apply the strategy on their own. However, review sessions are held to refine strategy use and to foster transfer.

---

**▶ Using Technology**

**Project CRISS**

http://www.projectcriss.com/
Provides additional information about CRISS®.

*Framed paragraphs should be presented in such a way that, over time, they require more and more input from students until, ultimately, students don't need to use them anymore.*

to help students learn content-area materials. Highly successful with low-achieving readers and writers, the writing component of CRISS stresses direct instruction and plenty of support for the learners. One form of support is the use of a series of highly structured writing formats, including framed paragraphs, opinion/proof paragraphs, and RAFT, a procedure that focuses on four major aspects of writing (Santa, Havens, & Maycumber, 1996). CRISS writing strategies can be taught within the framework of A Lesson in Teaching Writing Strategies.

## Framed Paragraphs

The most highly structured form of writing is the framed paragraph. A framed paragraph provides the main idea of the piece, indicates how many details the piece will contain, supplies transition words,

**◼ FIGURE 13.7**
Frame Paragraph

> STARTING A COIN COLLECTION
>
> If you want to start a coin collection, follow these steps.
>
> First, _____.
> Next, _____.
> Then, _____.
> Finally, _____.
>
> Once you've followed these steps, you'll have a hobby that you can enjoy for many years to come.

and may even provide a conclusion. While providing a maximum of support, framed paragraphs show students ways of organizing their ideas.

A sample frame paragraph is shown in Figure 13.7. Also refer to the Exemplary Teaching Lesson to see how one teacher made use of her version of framed paragraphs.

## Opinion/Proof

If students seem to need extra support for their writing, you might have them try an opinion/proof piece. The opinion/proof is a basic type of writing in which students back up an opinion with evidence or reasons. Opinion/proof pieces can be used in connection with informational texts or as the basis for developing a piece on any topic.

> ⁂ The opinion/proof format can be used with other kinds of writing: cause–effect, problem–solution, main idea–details.

To structure an opinion/proof piece, students divide a sheet of paper in two. Their opinion is placed in the left-hand column. Their proof is placed to the right. Once the opinion has been stated and the proof written down, the students can then develop their pieces. As students write their pieces, they should be encouraged to elaborate so that the piece they write is not just a restatement of the outline. They also need to compose a conclusion. A sample opinion/proof piece is shown in Figure 13.8.

| OPINION | PROOF |
|---|---|
| Basketball is the best sport. | Basketball has a lot of action.<br>Basketball can be played just about anywhere.<br>Basketball can be played inside or outside.<br>You don't need a lot of equipment to play basketball.<br>You don't need a lot of people to play basketball.<br>Anyone can play basketball. |

**◼ FIGURE 13.8**
Opinion/Proof
Paragraph

**EXEMPLARY TEACHING**

### Building on Interests

Discouraged by years of perceived failure, Jason, a seventh grader, decreed that he would no longer write. No more essays or book reports. Not even journal entries. He couldn't write, and that was that.

Capitalizing on Jason's interest in baseball, his corrective specialist, Carigan-Belleville (1989), asked him how his team had done on the previous Saturday. After discussing the game with him, she asked if he would give her three reasons why his team deserved to win. After Jason did so, she suggested that he put that in writing, using the following format:

Question: Who won Saturday's baseball game?
Five-sentence paragraph:

1. Topic sentence (answer to the question)
2. Reason #1
3. Reason #2
4. Reason #3
5. Conclusion (restate topic sentence in different words) (pp. 57–58)

Although the format might have hindered the free expression or creativity of some young writers, it was just what Jason needed. Using clear cues and a highly structured format, Jason was able to write a paragraph successfully.

Later, Jason started using story starters such as "If I had more money . . ." Jason also began writing in his journal. In addition, Carigan-Belleville arranged for Jason to dictate his stories into a tape recorder, using the recorded versions as a kind of rehearsal for the written pieces. Jason's willingness and ability to write improved significantly. As a side benefit, Jason also became more interested in reading.

---

### RAFT

> **RAFT:** structured approach to writing that helps students focus on four key elements: role of the writer, audience, format, and topic.

When writing essays for content-area subjects, students often turn in pieces that lack clarity and depth, two flaws that are occasioned by an assignment that is too general and too vague (Santa et al., 1996).

**RAFT** is an approach that sharpens the writing by helping the student focus on four elements: role of the writer, audience, format, and topic. RAFT pieces can be written from the student's viewpoint, but quite often they are not.

Here is an explanation of each element:

**R** *Role of the writer.* The writer can be a historical figure, a scientist, the president, a rock star, lawyer, police chief, or even an animal or inanimate object.

**A** *Audience.* Typically, students write for the teacher, so their pieces tend to be bland. The audience could be a judge, a legislator, future generations, the people of the world, a historical figure, a sports star, parents, or whomever else the writer wants to address.

**F** *Format.* The piece can be a letter to the editor, an essay, a news story, a TV script, a diary entry, a speech, a memo, or whatever format seems appropriate.

**T** *Topic.* The statement of the topic is accompanied by a strong verb so that it is an expression of the writer's purpose: demand a refund for a faulty product, persuade a radio station to let the town's teens have an hour show each week, convince an investor to back your new invention.

To introduce RAFT, explain its purpose and components and model writing a RAFT piece. Once students understand RAFT, brainstorm possible topics. The topics might fall under a general theme. For instance, if you are studying immigration, have students suggest possible RAFT pieces: a shipowner composing an ad to persuade Italian peasants to sail to America, an Irish teen describing in a letter to his parents his first few days in Boston, an editorial writer hailing the newcomers.

Science teacher Melissa Harrell of Luray, Virginia, had her students take on the role of a cell and write thank you notes to each organelle (Project CRISS, 2012).

In time, students should create their own RAFT topics. They should also go through all the stages in the writing process, including revising, editing, and publishing, as well as preplanning and composing. Refer to the Mini–Case Study at the end of the chapter to see how RAFT was used to help an extremely reluctant writer.

## Collins Program

Although not created specifically for struggling writers, key elements in the Collins program would be of help to students who have difficulty writing. The core of the Collins (2004) program is the concept of focus correction areas and planning and composing writing assignments that are clear and cover all the essentials.

As Chadwell (2002b) notes, an "everything counts" approach to improving, correcting, and assessing writing can be overwhelming for students. He recommends focusing on one to three areas. These focus correction areas, or FCAs, can be anything from capitalizing the first word in a sentence to writing an interesting lead. However, Collins (2004) recommends that the selected FCAs include at least one devoted to improving content. Others might deal with organization, style, or mechanics.

FCAs are emphasized in prewriting discussions and instruction, in conferences, in revision, and in assessment. Papers are written, revised, and assessed with the FCAs in mind. Focus correction areas can be provided for individuals, groups, or the whole class. Writing assignments are accompanied by focus correction areas. In fact, students note the FCAs at the tops of their papers. Focus correction areas are not applied to informal writing, such as quickwrites and journals. However, when students write a paper that is to be formally published, FCAs might be applied in the early drafts, but the final copy is subject to complete editing. Although students write on a regular basis, only four or five of their papers are published each year.

> **Using Technology**
> Visit http://collinsed.com/PDFs/collins_autobiography.pdf for an excellent example of a clear assignment from the Collins program.

Providing clear assignments is also a hallmark of the Collins program. Collins (2004) recommends noting the key elements of an assignment and then involving students in fleshing it out. Key elements include the four components of RAFT plus the focus correction areas, a description of procedures (which consists of a description of the steps that will be taken to complete the assignment), and a summary of the assignment. The summary provides a rationale for the assignment and a description of the final product. The summary statement clarifies the project for both teacher and students. Note the sample summary presented below:

**Describing a Special Place**

Project Summary. Each of us has a "getaway," a special place where we like to go to relax, think, read, or just be alone. For some of us, our special place is our bedroom, a clubhouse, or our backyard that we can visit most anytime. For others, a special place might be a relative's house or a vacation spot that can be visited only on special occasions. In this project you will write about your special place so that the reader knows what it is like there and why you like it. (Chadwell, 2002a, p. 22)

For this assignment, the key focus correction areas were explaining what the special place was and why it was chosen and using descriptive details.

## Collaborative Strategy Approach

> At the beginning of the Collaborative Strategy Instruction study, students were reluctant to write. At the end of the four-month period, the students were writing four to six double-spaced, typed pages (Anderson & Henne, 1993).

Less structured and more student centered than the four previously presented systems, the collaborative strategy approach combines instruction in writing strategies and text models. Students' writing is related to their reading. After completing a selection, students note the kinds of information covered in the text and the text's structure. Students then decide how they might use the kinds of structure and information presented in the text in their own writing. For instance, if the author used a problem–solution organization in a selection the students have read, the students would talk over problems they have and possible solutions. Using the selection they have read as a model, they would then compose a problem–solution piece (Anderson & Henne, 1993).

## Why the Programs Work

Although the programs just described vary in the way they are organized and implemented, they have several essential procedures in common. All incorporate direct instruction and emphasize strategies and writing process. All also provide additional support in the form of frame paragraphs, planning sheets, mnemonic reminders, or collaborative instruction and discussion. Most of the programs also provide model pieces of writing.

All of the programs also met with encouraging success. This success presents a clear message: When low-achieving readers and writers are provided with a carefully planned, thoroughly implemented, supportive program of writing instruction, they improve, sometimes dramatically. Students respond positively to techniques or strategies that make it easier for them to apply their skills.

## EXEMPLARY TEACHING

### The Hochman Program

The Hochman Program uses expository writing as a means of boosting students' overall achievement in reading, writing, and content areas. Many students entered New Dorp High School (Staten Island, New York) only able to write a few disjointed sentences (Tyre, 2012). Teachers noticed that a key difference between achieving students' writing and that of the struggling readers and writers was the ability to use conjunctions and complex sentences to show relationships between ideas. Because it taught basic writing skills such as writing clear but varied sentences, building paragraphs, and using connecting words, the Hochman approach was adopted as a school-wide program in which all teachers taught writing and created assignments in which students had to use connectors such as *although, unless, because* and write increasingly complex sentences and paragraphs.

Basic writing instruction translated into improved comprehension. As students learned how ideas were connected, they were better able to understand what they read. As one student explained, "Before, I could read, sure. But it was like a sea of words. The more writing instruction I got, the more I understood which words were important." The student's writing also improved. As the student commented, "There are phrases—*specifically, for instance, for example*—that help you add detail to a paragraph."

The Hochman program (Hochman, 2009) begins by developing students' sentence writing skill by having them develop sentences more fully, combine simple sentences into complex ones, and use a variety of connecting words to show varied relationships. Instruction in composing paragraphs and compositions emphasizes developing topic sentences, organizing information, using transitions, and writing for a variety of purposes. What makes the Hochman approach especially effective for struggling writers is the step-by-step manner in which basic skills are developed.

## ◼◼◼ Motivating Reluctant Writers

Understandably, low-achieving readers and writers frequently are extremely reluctant to write. If they do write, often it is just a sentence or two composed entirely of words that they can spell. Three kinds of writing that are especially effective for helping students overcome their reluctance to engage in composing are writing aloud, written conversation, and journal writing.

### Writing Aloud

In writing aloud, the teacher and the students create an experience story together. Although the teacher scribes the story, the students make suggestions about both content and form. The teacher invites the students to help her write a story. Based on the teacher's prompts, they make suggestions about details that might be added. They also help with the mechanics.

For instance, the teacher might ask students to help her spell a word or ask what kind of punctuation mark is needed at the end of a sentence. Using her knowledge of what the students know and what they need to know, she might decide that this is a good opportunity to reinforce the *-ed* ending. Writing *wait,* she might ask them what needs to be added to *wait* to make *waited.* Emphasizing that the first copy is a draft, the group rereads it and revises and edits it during subsequent sessions (Dorn, French, & Jones, 1998).

Although group-composed selections are often used with young children to reinforce beginning reading skills, they are an excellent technique for modeling the composition of both narrative and expository pieces at all levels. They give students, especially those who are struggling, guided practice in writing.

### Written Conversation

> **Written conversation:** writing-improvement technique in which a teacher and student talk to each other on paper. Instead of speaking words to each other, they write them.

An effective technique for promoting fluency is arranging for the student to talk to someone on paper. A **written conversation** is generally between the teacher and the student. You and the student sit side by side. You might initiate the conversation by posing a written question that helps the student describe an event or idea: "How is your basketball team doing this year?" After the student reads your question, she responds in writing. You reply with another written question, and the student answers it with a written response.

Sitting at a round table, you might carry on a written conversation with a small group of students. While one student responds to your written query, you can write a note to a second student. As students grow in proficiency, they can converse in writing with each other. The activity could also be extended into writing letters or leaving e-mail messages (Rhodes & Dudley-Marling, 1988).

Written conversations work well with problem writers because you gear your writing to each student's level of reading and writing proficiency and also consider each student's interests. In addition, through modeling good writing, you provide scaffolding so students can move up to higher levels of writing performance. Written conversations are also nonthreatening. Although a written conversation can be as brief as a single sentence, output generally increases as a result of using this device. Written conversations also have a positive effect on reading (Rhodes & Dudley-Marling, 1988).

## Journal Writing

| Journal: daily record of events, thoughts, ideas, or feelings. |
| --- |

**Journal** writing allows students to respond to their world in a personal way. In their journals, they can react to something they have learned in school, discuss an exciting TV show or a Little League game in which they played a key role, or describe the acquisition of a new pet. Through journal writing or the use of writer's notebooks, students can explore topics and techniques. It helps them discover that the events in their lives are worth writing about. Journal writing promotes fluency and exploration. Because journal writing is personal, it should not be subject to revision or correction. Focus should be on the message, not the mechanics.

## Quickwrites

A quickwrite is an informal, multipurpose, brief, one-draft paper written to respond to reading a short piece of literature, to express an opinion, to react to a topic introduced in a content area, to summarize a lesson, to respond to an idea or question, or to respond to a prompt. Quickwrites enable students to get their ideas down on paper and to write frequently. Because the task is brief—usually 10 minutes or less—and limited, quickwrites can be especially effective with struggling writers.

Students who have difficulty responding with words can use stick figures to represent their responses. They might also use stick figures to describe an event or tell a story. After telling a story in stick figure format, students can then add words. If the writers wish, they can expand their quickwrites into more extended pieces. Rief (2003), a middle school teacher, has her students collect their quickwrites in a section of their response journals. From time to time, students reexamine their quickwrites and may decide to expand some of them.

Since quickwrites are informal and designed to foster fluency, the mechanics of writing are not assessed (Chadwell, 2002b). Modeling the creation of quickwrites and discussing them increases their quality.

## ▓▓ Writing Instruction for English Language Learners

**B**ecause the vocabulary, knowledge of grammatical structures, and organizational patterns of English language learners (ELLs) are generally less well developed, they will need more intensive instruction in writing. To foster writing, it will be necessary to build vocabulary and syntax. Before students write a sequence piece, for instance, introduce words that signal sequence: *first, next, at last*. When writing a how-to piece, introduce words and phrases used to explain: *first you; then you; after that; be careful to* (Calkins, 2003). ELLs might be able to express themselves better in writing than speaking.

An excellent way to familiarize ELLs with syntactical patterns is to engage in written conversation with students or to use dialogue journals. A written conversation can be very informal. You might write a note that asks students a question, such as "What is your favorite book? What are your favorite TV shows?" Students can use key words in the question to formulate a reply. In your response, include a question or cue that leads to additional writing.

You might also model a response. Note the following interchange:

**T:** What do you find hardest about living in a new country?

**S:** I find the hardest thing is trying to talk to people.

**T:** When I lived in Mexico for a summer, I also found that talking to people was the hardest thing for me to do. I was afraid that people would laugh at the way I said the words. What makes talking to others the hardest thing for you?

The language-experience approach can be used effectively with ELLs. Topics should be selected in such a way as to control syntax. Language-experience stories may be written so that they focus on declarative sentences, questions, or another syntactical element. A story in which students write about things they like or can do would focus on statement sentences. A story on favorite animals could be structured in such a way that it includes both a question and a statement: "What is my favorite animal? My favorite animal is _____." Other stories might reinforce more complex patterns: "I like Saturdays because _____." The language-experience approach is flexible. Students can write on any topic and in virtually any format; assignments can be geared to the student's level of English language development.

ELLs need to develop a "writer's ear" for what sounds right in written language. They need to learn to read as writers, analyzing texts to see how writers express themselves in English. Before writing a descriptive paragraph, ELLs should read a variety of descriptive paragraphs to note the techniques and language used. English language learners need to learn the more formal language of writing. Reading aloud and discussing model selections will also help develop ELLs' writer's ear.

## Preparing for Assessment Prompts

One writing skill that struggling writers need to learn is how to respond to an assessment prompt. In writing workshop, students have the luxury of time to preplan, compose, and revise. Often, they select their own topics. All that is changed when they must respond to an assessment prompt. Because time is limited, they might be tempted to rush through the assigned piece. However, they should take a moment or two to read and reread the prompt carefully to be sure they understand what the prompt is asking for. They should also take a moment or two to jot down a brief but tentative outline or map (Spandel, 2005).

To prepare students for writing to a prompt, group struggling writers according to writing needs. In preparation for writing to a prompt, struggling writers should become familiar with the rubric that will be used to assess the prompt. They also should have some experience writing to similar prompts.

Show students how you would go about writing to a prompt. Do a think-aloud, so that they get insight into the thought processes involved. Model how you would preplan, compose your piece, and revise and edit.

As a cooperative venture, have the group of struggling writers respond to a prompt. After students have responded, discuss their work in light of the rubric. Praise what is effective and provide suggestions for improvement. Provide guided writing instruction in terms of writing needs.

In a program to prepare students for constructed responses on high-stakes tests, Boyles (2002) recommends two aids: an answer organizer and an answer frame. In the answer organizer, you lay out step-by-step what students are to do: "Write the topic sentence first, add three supporting details and write a concluding sentence." Answer frames provide even more assistance than answer organizers do. In an answer frame, you fill in a portion of the answer and have students finish it. (See frame paragraphs on pages 378 and 515.)

Do not spend an excessive amount of time on writing to prompts. Once students are familiar with writing to a prompt, added practice will have a diminishing effect. Students will be better off engaged in the regular writing program. As Fletcher and Portalupi (2001) note, a writing workshop properly implemented should prepare students for whatever writing assessment they encounter:

> Your students need time to write their hearts out; to explore many different subjects; to write deeply about a single one. They need to write for the fun of it, and at times they need coaches by their sides stretching them to write with more precision and craft.
>
> It boils down to this: Your students will perform fine on these tests as long as you provide them with regular opportunities for writing in the workshop. (p. 110)

## The Need for a Balanced Program

Writing is a complex task that has three interacting major components: generating appropriate content in sufficient quantity, organizing the content, and using appropriate grammatical and mechanical elements (Collins, 1998). Underachieving writers have problems in all three areas.

An effective way to help underachieving writers develop needed proficiency is to teach writing through a balanced process and strategy approach. Students who report using elements of the process approach, especially planning and composing more than one draft, outperform those who don't (Greenwald, Persky, Campbell, & Mazzeo, 1999).

For struggling writers, however, co-construction of key strategies also needs to be an essential component of the program. If workshops fail to provide effective strategy instruction, students may spend most of their time writing about what they know and using familiar forms of writing, usually personal narrative. Writing about familiar topics in familiar forms hinders struggling writers' progress (Collins, 1998). Struggling writers need more opportunities to learn different forms and explore new topics, not fewer.

## Spelling

Spelling can pose two problems for writers. If a student is spending an excessive amount of time trying to figure out how to spell words, then she has less cognitive energy left for actually composing the piece. Deficiency in the lower-level process of physically producing text can impede the higher-level processes of composing a message or an imaginative tale. Poor spelling may also inhibit the writer in another way. A writer who is ashamed of her poor spelling may not look beyond the spelling to the story she is trying to tell and so may restrict her writing to words that she can spell.

> One characteristic of struggling readers is their reluctance to take risks with their writing. The stories they write are restricted by the words they know how to write rather than by the story they want to tell or the feelings and ideas they would like to express (Dorn et al., 1998).

What is needed is a three-pronged approach. In addition to providing systematic instruction in spelling and extra support, focus on the content of the writing so that the student doesn't let spelling restrict her writing or, worse yet, begin to equate poor spelling with poor writing.

Spelling is harder to learn than decoding skills. Given the same amount of instruction, struggling readers learn more than twice as much phonics as they do spelling. Spelling is especially difficult to learn if students have difficulty with phonological or orthographic processes or both. If students have difficulty with phonological processes, sounds may not be adequately represented in the mind's ear. Thus, students may omit a sound or confuse a sound while spelling a word. They have particular difficulty with sounds that are hard to detect, such as the second sound in a cluster: the *t* in *stop* and the *r* in *brave*. They also have difficulty with sounds such as /l/, /r/, /m/, and /n/ when they are in the middle or at the end of a word. The inflectional endings *s* and *ed* also pose problems and are frequently omitted (Moats, 1995). If the student has difficulty with orthographic processes, letters representing sounds may not be adequately represented in the mind's eye, especially when these letters comprise irregular, infrequent, or complex spellings. The student will then have difficulty retrieving the correct spelling of an irregular or advanced pattern word from memory (Berninger et al., 1999).

These students lack what Gentry (1997) terms the "spelling gene." They have serious difficulty visualizing words, which is the main characteristic of average and good spellers. Although a small number of students experience difficulty learning to spell because of poor orthographic-processing ability, this doesn't mean that they can't improve their spelling. As Apel, Masterson, and Niessen (2004) warn, "Frequently, students and adults are heard to say, 'I'm just not a good speller,' as if to imply that they have no control over their spelling abilities and that their spelling proficiency can never change" (p. 644). This becomes a self-fulfilling prophecy. One element in a program for struggling spellers should be to build their sense of self-efficacy.

If students have a weaknesses in their phonological system, their spelling may not contain all the sounds in a word. Thus, *treasure* might be spelled *tessar*. However, if their phonological system is functioning well but there are weaknesses in the orthographic system, the word's sounds may be represented phonetically, but they may not be spelled accurately. *Treasure* might be spelled *trezur*.

Correct spelling requires being able to use phonological processes; orthographic processes; spelling rules, such as when to double the final consonant of a word; and a knowledge of roots, prefixes, and suffixes. Students may also use an analogy process, so that they use their knowledge of a known word such as *chance* to spell a word such as *trance*, which they may have never written before.

When analyzing spelling errors, ask the following questions:

- Is the student able to use knowledge of sound–spelling relationships to spell words?

- Is the student applying spelling rules?

- Is the student able to use orthographic knowledge or visual sense to spell words that cannot be spelled strictly phonetically?

- Is the student able to use an analogy strategy to spell words?

- Is the student able to use morphemic analysis to spell words?

- Is the student able to use meaning clues, so that when spelling a word such as magician he uses his knowledge of the word magic?

- Are some apparent misspellings due to faulty handwriting?

- Is the student making careless errors? (Bos & Vaughn, 1994)

## Teaching Spelling

A program for teaching spelling should be individualized, since students' abilities in spelling vary greatly. The program should be based on the student's current level of functioning in spelling and an analysis of the kinds of errors made. In a study in which one group of struggling third graders was given a second-grade spelling program, they outperformed the third graders on a spelling test made up of second-grade words and did as well on the test made up of third-grade words, even though they had not been taught these words. The researchers concluded that the experimental group learned more about the spelling system because instruction was pitched to their level of understanding as opposed to the third-grade comparison group, who were being taught "over their heads" and so did not learn as much (Morris, Blanton, Blanton, Nowacek, & Perney, 1995).

To find a student's current level of spelling ability, administer the Spelling Inventory from the Classroom Reading Inventory (Wheelock & Campbell 2012), the Gentry Spelling Grade Level Placement Test (Gentry, 2004), or the Spelling Placement Inventory in Chapter 5. The student's instructional level is the highest level at which between 50 and 75 percent of the words are spelled correctly. However, the student's level of spelling tells only part of the story. Also analyze the types of errors students make to get a sense of the kinds of processes the students are using to spell words.

Note, too, the stage of spelling at which the student is operating. As discussed in Chapter 5, research conducted by Henderson (1990) and his colleagues (Templeton & Bear, 1992) indicates that students' spelling develops in stages. By knowing what stage a student is in, the teacher can build on that knowledge and teach spelling more effectively. The Informal Spelling Inventory, which can be found in Chapter 5, can be used to estimate students' spelling stage.

It is also a good idea to note what kinds of strategies students use to help them spell words correctly. Do they attempt to visualize the words? Do they try to go through them sound by sound? Do they use rules or knowledge of word structure? Does writing them out seem to help? See, too, if students attempt to correct misspelled words in their written pieces. If they do, what strategies do they use? This information can be obtained through observation and through interviews with the students.

Words chosen for spelling instruction should be those that students need in their writing. If students are about to write about football, the spelling words might include *football, sports, kickoff, score, quarterback, halftime,* and similar words. High-frequency words should also be presented. In order to help students see patterns in words, it will also be helpful to present high-frequency patterns. (A listing of patterns can be found in Table 8.6 on pages 248–250.)

When introducing new words to poor spellers, use active teaching procedures, such as the test–study–test method. In this method, students take a pretest, study the words they missed, and then take a retest. It is also important to teach students a strategy for studying words. A popular strategy that emphasizes seeing the word in the mind's eye is the Fitzgerald method (Fitzgerald, 1951):

1. Look at the word carefully.
2. Say the word to yourself.
3. Close your eyes and picture the word.
4. Cover up the word and write it.
5. Check the spelling.
6. If the word is misspelled, repeat steps 1–5.

### Building Conceptual Understanding

A valuable activity for fostering a conceptual understanding of spelling is word sorting, especially if the sorting is geared to the students' level of spelling development. If students are in the alphabet stage and are having difficulty deciding whether words that begin with a /k/ sound are spelled with a *c* or a *k*, then they might engage in sorting activities in which they categorize words according to whether they begin with a /k/ sound, regardless of spelling, and then sort /k/ words according to their spelling. Instead of memorizing rules about the use of *c* and *k* to spell /k/, students form their own generalizations.

In the word-pattern stage, students can, through sorting, form generalizations about the use of final *e* and digraphs to spell long-vowel sounds. In the syllabic stage, students might, through sorting, form a generalization about when to double the final consonant when adding -*ing* or -*ed*. In the morphemic analysis stage, students might discover when to use the prefixes *im-*, *in-*, *ir-*, and *un-*. As they group words and construct understandings that they would not have developed if they had just looked at words individually, students develop a deeper understanding of the spelling system and in the process become better decoders as well as better spellers.

Help students see the meaning connections in spelling. One fourth grader failed to see the relationship between *nature* and *naturally*, even when it was pointed out to her, and another fourth grader thought that the presence of *round* in *surround* was merely a coincidence (Hughes & Searle, 1997). A word such as *granddad* is easier to spell if the student goes beyond the sound pattern, which could lead to spelling the word *grandad*, and thinks about the meaning in which *grand* is added to *dad* to form the word *granddad*. Word sorts can help students describe some of the principles that underlie such perplexing decisions as when to use the -*ible* versus when to use -*able* spelling or when to use the *ir-*, *im-*, *in-*, or *il-* prefix. At this stage, students should focus on or even spell the base word first and then add prefixes or suffixes. For instance, students will not compose misspellings such as *realy* or *unecessary* if they focus on *real* and *necessary* as the base words and then add the suffix -*ly* or the prefix *un-* (Snowball & Bolton, 1999).

Spelling can also be tied to the phonics patterns they are learning. Select the most useful words from the phonics patterns that they are studying. In general, students should only be taught to spell words that they can read. Patterns are especially useful elements because once students can spell one pattern word, they can build on that knowledge to spell other words in that pattern. For instance, once students can spell *ten*, they should be able to learn to spell *men*, *pen*, and other words fairly easily. To show students how to use their knowledge of one word to spell other words, ask "If you can spell *ten*, then what others can you spell?" (Snowball & Bolton, 1999). Lead them to see that *men* and other *en* words are spelled just like *ten* except for the first letter. Using this same principle of building on what students know, show them how if they can spell a base word, they can spell its inflected forms. If they can spell *help*, they can spell *helps*, *helping*, and *helped*.

Poor spellers may have a poor visual sense of how words should be spelled, so use mnemonic devices, overpronunciation, and overlearning to help them learn to spell words, especially those that are not very predictable. The mnemonic for *friend* might be "Friend has an *i* and an *end* at the end." In overpronunciation, students articulate sounds that are normally not spoken but are represented in the spelling of the word, saying *dif-FER-ence, av-ER-age, in-TER-est*. Overlearning entails studying a tricky word even after its correct spelling has been learned.

## Electronic Aids

Students should be shown how to use the spell checkers incorporated into most of today's word-processing programs. Handheld electronic spelling aids such as Spelling Ace (Franklin) might also be introduced. When users type in misspelled words, these devices use data about typical patterns of phonetic misspellings to help the learner locate the correct spelling of the misspelled word. They also feature spelling games and have the capacity to store words for later review.

## The Role of Writing

Frequent opportunities to write play an essential role in the development of spelling skills and strategies. Writing provides a reason for learning to spell, along with opportunities for students to apply their skills.

## ▒▒ Handwriting

Writing makes heavy demands on memory, discrimination, perception, and fine motor skills—areas in which low-achieving readers are often weak. Thus, reading problems are frequently accompanied by deficiencies in handwriting. Because instructional time is limited and handwriting seems a less vital skill than reading, handwriting instruction may be condensed or neglected. However, if it is taught as a functional part of the overall language arts program, handwriting can reinforce a number of skills necessary for reading.

⚓ Previously, students were taught letter formation and then taught to write. Today, students are urged to write as best they can. As they experience what writing is and have a need to form letters, then letter formation is introduced.

For instance, Benjamin has a poor sense of directionality, frequently reverses letters, and on occasion forgets what a letter looks like. Good handwriting instruction will help Benjamin proceed in consistent fashion from left to right and top to bottom. A focus on proper letter formation will also help him to commit to memory the shapes of letters. This should help reduce mirror images of letters and help him to remember letter forms.

If it is tied in with phonics instruction and composing activities, handwriting can be used to reinforce and extend writing and reading instruction. Last but not least, legible handwriting can build self-esteem. Although students' reading difficulty may go undetected, their handwriting is on display for teachers, parents, and peers to see. Legible handwriting can be a source of pride. And as a practical matter, students are often judged, rightly or wrongly, on the quality of their handwriting. All other things being equal, neatly written papers receive higher grades than barely legible ones. (See Chapter 5 for suggestions for assessing writing.)

⚓ *Preventing Academic Failure* (Bertin & Perleman, 1999) is an excellent source of handwriting and spelling activities for struggling spellers.

It is not unusual to find older students who are still not sure how to form all the letters of the alphabet. A program for students who have not mastered handwriting skills should be systematic and functional. As with other types of learning, instruction should build on what students know. In addition to being able to form letters, students should use proper spacing between words, have consistent slant, align the letters, create lines that are smooth, and create letters that are consistent in size. Students should also learn to evaluate their handwriting.

**Using Technology**

Literacy Center

http://www.literacycenter.net/
Demonstrates formation of shapes and letters.

Instruction should have a kinesthetic base so that students get a feel for how letters should be produced. When presenting letters, have students write them in the air and trace them on their desks before they use a pencil to form them. As students write letters, they should recite the movements necessary to make the letter. In forming a lowercase manuscript *t*, the student might say "Stroke down, stroke across." Periods of short instruction work best. About

10 or 15 minutes of instruction per day is adequate. However, handwriting skills can be applied during spelling, writing workshop, or whenever students are writing.

In addition to being able to write legibly, students also should be able to write quickly enough that they can copy material from the board, take notes, and complete writing assignments within a reasonable amount of time. Writing that is labored will hamper students' progress.

> ⁎ In one study, explicit instruction in handwriting and spelling for students having difficulty in those areas resulted not only in better handwriting and more accurate spelling but also improved writing performance (Graham, 1999).

If students fail to respond to instruction or if their difficulties seem to be rooted in physical problems, consult with an occupational therapist. Occupational therapists assist children who have difficulty performing functional tasks, including handwriting. Signs that a student may need specialized help include inconsistent use of the left or right hand for writing or drawing, avoidance of writing tasks, difficulty copying from the board, illegible handwriting, difficulty maintaining proper posture or grip, and failure to profit from instruction (Vreeland, 1998). If the student does have difficulty copying, have his vision checked. The student may have difficulty with far vision or may experience strain when switching from far-point (looking at the board) to near-point (writing on his paper) tasks.

## Mini–Case Study

One student in George Rusnak's class had had such bad experiences with writing that when asked to write, he responded, "Fail me if you want. I won't write!" Wisely, Rusnak decided to take two important steps: find out why the student's attitude toward writing was so negative, and provide a structure that would help the student feel that he could be successful.

Rusnak started off the writing unit by asking "What are your experiences with writing?" As students related their experiences with writing, most of which were negative, Rusnak talked over some of the bad experiences he had had when he was a student and how he coped with them.

Rusnak then introduced RAFT to support the students' attempts to write. To get students started, Rusnak provided them with an intriguing writing activity:

Role—worm in an apple

Audience—farmer

Format—persuasive letter

Topic—explaining to farmer why he shouldn't take the worm's apple

This lighthearted assignment was followed by one in which students took the role of a historical character and was related to the students' study of history. The piece had to be factual but affective. The student's personal involvement had to be evident. Supported and motivated through three drafts, the youngster who would rather fail than write transformed a 72-word empty letter into a 423-word, superbly written piece. A writer was born (Rusnak, 1994).

## Summary

On a nationwide assessment, from 14 to 21 percent of students were unable to write on a basic level. Effective instruction for struggling writers combines balanced instruction in writing strategies with the process approach to writing. The five steps in the writing process are prewriting, composing, revising, editing, and publishing. Prewriting includes topic selection and planning. An important component of the planning process is considering one's audience. Composing is the creation of the written piece. When composing, students should focus on the message, rather than the mechanics. Rehearsing what one plans to write can aid the composing process. Revising is an essential but often neglected part of the writing process. True revising involves taking a fresh look at what one has written and making substantive changes, if necessary. Editing involves checking and correcting mechanical errors. Publishing is an important element in writing because it provides students with a genuine purpose for writing and helps them gain a sense of audience. Although they are presented separately, the steps in the writing process overlap, and several may occur simultaneously.

Instruction in writing is carried out through modeling, formal and informal lessons, guided writing, strategy instruction, and conferences. A major purpose of writing conferences is to help students discover that they have something to say. A second major purpose is to discover difficulties that students may be having and help them overcome those difficulties.

Exemplary writing programs for low-achieving readers and writers include CSIW (Cognitive Strategy Instruction Writing), collaborative strategy instruction, self-regulated strategy development (SRSD), CRISS® writing, and the Collins program. Although the details of implementation vary, the programs all provide direct instruction in the use of strategies and support in the form of planning sheets, mnemonics, frames for writing, and/or discussion.

Journals, logs, and writer's notebooks provide opportunities for disabled writers to apply their skills in a personal way. Freewriting, quickwriting, and conversational writing also promote fluency in written expression. Current emphasis is on writing expository text. This includes composing explanatory/informational and persuasive texts.

Instruction for ELLs should include development of the language required by the writing activity. A language–experience approach is particularly appropriate for these students. A writing program should include an appropriate amount of instruction and practice in writing to assessment prompts, but this should not be overdone.

Although the focus in writing is on the message, mechanics are also important. Spelling instruction should be individualized, since students' achievement in spelling varies considerably. In addition, disabled writers need both formal and informal instruction in the mechanics of writing, with emphasis on those elements for which a need is demonstrated. Low-achieving readers and writers may also need special help with handwriting.

## Application Activities

1. Observe a guided writing class or writing workshop in action. Note the organization of the class and the major activities in which the students are engaged. What do you like best about the class? How might it be improved?

2. Design a planning sheet similar to those created in CSIW, or plan a strategy lesson similar to SRSD. If possible, present the planning sheet or strategy and evaluate its effectiveness.

3. Use RAFT, opinion/proof, or another structured writing device to write a piece. Evaluate the effectiveness of the device. How might these structured devices help low-achieving writers? How might they be inhibited by them?

4. Design a rubric for scoring a piece of writing that your students have written or will write. Try out the rubric. Revise it in the light of any shortcomings that you note. Also select from your students' writing anchor pieces that illustrate each of the rubric's categories.

5. Read the practice guide "Teaching Elementary School Students to Be Effective Writers," which you can access at http://ies.ed.gov/ncee/wwc/pdf/practice_ guides/writing_pg_062612.pdf. How might the guide's suggestions be adapted for use with struggling writers?

## My Education Lab

Go to the topic **Reading Assessment** in the MyEducationLab (www.myeducationlab .com) for **Assessing and Correcting Reading Difficulties**, where you can:

- Find learning outcomes for **Reading Assessment** along with the national standards that connect to these outcomes.

- Complete Assignments and Activities that can help you more deeply understand the chapter content.

- Apply and practice your understanding of the core teaching skills identified in the chapter with the Building Teaching Skills and Dispositions learning units.

- Examine challenging situations and cases presented in the Iris Center Resources.

- Check your comprehension of the content covered in the chapter with the Study Plan. Here you will be able to take a chapter pretest, receive feedback on your answers, and then access personalized Review, Practice, and Enrichment exercises to enhance your understanding of chapter content. After you complete the exercises, take a posttest to confirm your comprehension.

- Practice targeting instruction and making content accessible for all students with A+RISE activities.

# 14 Tier II and III Programs for Students of All Ages

**M**ost low-achieving readers will learn to read if taught by the methods described in previous chapters or one of the intervention programs described in this chapter. However, about 1 in 100 low-achieving readers has such a severe difficulty learning to read words that she may need to be taught through special word-learning techniques.

Teens and adults who have reading and writing problems often bring with them a long history of failure and may have a "can't do" attitude. It is important that they see themselves as competent learners and adopt a "can do" outlook. Students who are learning English and are struggling with reading and writing face the dual task of learning a new language and overcoming reading and writing difficulties. What is your experience with intervention programs? What is your experience with students who have such severe reading problems that they have not benefited from early intervention programs? Have you worked with older problem readers or students whose struggle to learn to read and write is compounded by their struggle to master a new language?

**USING WHAT YOU KNOW**

**ANTICIPATION GUIDE**

*Read each of the following statements. Put a check under "Agree" or "Disagree" to show how you feel about each one. If possible, discuss your responses with classmates.*

|  | | AGREE | DISAGREE |
|---|---|---|---|
| 1. | If taught properly, all students can learn to read. | _____ | _____ |
| 2. | Word-learning techniques that use tracing are successful because they establish additional connections in memory. | _____ | _____ |
| 3. | Intervention programs that provide extensive guidance for the teacher are more effective than those that require considerable planning. | _____ | _____ |
| 4. | The older a low-achieving reader is, the harder he is to teach. | _____ | _____ |
| 5. | If possible, English language learners should be taught to read in their native language. | _____ | _____ |

## ▚▚ Approaches to Intervention

Response to intervention (RTI) has two major approaches: problem solving and standard protocol. In a problem-solving approach, the intervention program is tailored to the apparent needs of the student being instructed. The program might be constructed by the school's intervention team. The standard protocol is an intervention program that has been validated and is delivered in a consistent, standardized fashion. The Reading Mastery and Wilson programs are examples of the standard protocol approach. Because these types of programs are standardized, they can be easier to deliver; instructors don't have to be as highly trained. Commercial programs, especially those that are scripted and/or contain detailed instruction for the teacher and that have been validated by research, fall into the standard protocol category. Of course, it is possible to use both problem-solving and protocol approaches.

However, programs, especially those designed for readers with the most severe disabilities, need a degree of flexibility and data-based input from expert instructors. Approximately, 5 percent of students fail to profit from Tier II instruction. For these students RTI experts Fuchs, Fuchs, and Compton (2012) recommend experimental teaching. Experimental teaching is data based. Using data obtained through observation and frequent monitoring, the teacher adjusts instruction. The teacher might use a standard protocol but intensifies or alters instruction as necessary. Tier III requires instruction by an expert because it involves using a broad base of knowledge and experience in order to fashion a program that will work with students for whom both primary (Tier I classroom or core) and secondary (Tier II intervention) programs have failed. Students do best when taught one-on-one by experts who might use a standardized approach but adjust instructions so that the student makes optimal progress (Vaughn & Fletcher., 2012). Students in intensive programs do make promising gains, but if students are older and are considerably behind, it may take them a significant amount of time to catch up.

## ▚▚ Early Intervention Programs

Children who experience difficulty reading do learn. Unfortunately, what they most often acquire from the learning experience are ineffective strategies and a concept of themselves as nonlearners. Speaking of delaying instruction until a child has experienced failure, Marie Clay (1985) notes, "The difficulties of the young child might be more easily overcome if he had practiced error behavior less often, had less to unlearn and relearn, and still had reasonable confidence in his own ability" (p. 10).

### Reading Recovery

The most widely implemented of the intervention programs is Reading Recovery. The plan of the program is to accelerate children's progress by providing intensive one-on-one instruction 30 minutes a day, five days a week, for a period of 12 to 20 weeks. The intent is to develop struggling students' skills and abilities so that they can function as well as the average students in their class. In the United States, the recovery rate is approximately 75 percent, not including students who dropped out or, because of absenteeism or did not complete at least 60 lessons (Reading Recovery Council of North America, 2012). There is also a Spanish version of Reading Recovery, Descubriendo La Lectura.

One study of the effectiveness of Reading Recovery concluded that students who failed to make adequate progress had lower pretest scores on tests of phonemic awareness, word analysis, and oral cloze (a test that requires students to use their knowledge of language to fill in the blanks of a story that has had words deleted from it) (Center, Wheldall, Freeman, Outhred, & McNaught, 1995). In view of this and an earlier study in which Reading Recovery students did better when systematic phonics were added to the program (Iverson & Tunmer, 1993), the authors concluded that the addition of systematic instruction in phonological awareness and phonics might strengthen the program.

Reading Recovery does not have a systematic approach to teaching phonological awareness and phonics. These skills are taught through spelling, the Make and Break technique, discussions with students when they have difficulty reading certain words, and an activity known as *fluent write*. However, over the years, these components have been given increased attention.

## A Reading Recovery Lesson

A typical 30-minute Reading Recovery lesson includes the following six components:

***Fluent Write***     Reading Recovery teachers dictate one or two words for the student to practice writing. If the student seems unable to write a word but knows an analog, the teacher might prompt him to use the analog to write the unknown word. For instance, when one student balked at writing the word *rake,* the teacher reminded him that he knew the word *make* and asked him to write it. After writing the word *make,* the student was then able to use his knowledge of *make* to write *rake.*

***Reading of Familiar Books***     The student rereads orally two or more familiar books for the purpose of building fluency and confidence. Doing so gives the student the chance to apply previously taught strategies, such as using context and letter–sound relationships. Because she has read the books previously, the student should find it easier to apply the strategies.

***Rereading of Previous Day's Book and Taking a Running Record***     As the child reads the book out loud and generally without any help from the teacher, a running record is taken. An analysis of the running record provides an assessment of the child's progress and yields information about the kinds of strategies he is using. At the end of this segment, the teacher praises the student for the quality of the reading, notes an instance or two when he applied strategies effectively, and points out one or more instances in which a strategy that was not used could have been applied or a strategy that was used could have been applied more effectively.

***Working with Letters and/or Words***     While reviewing the student's rereading or whenever appropriate, the teacher and student can build words together using magnetic letters and a metal board. The magnetic letters might be used to help the child see the similarities in pattern words (*cat, hat, sat*), note -*s* or -*ed* endings, or focus on the sequence of letters in a high-frequency word. Magnetic letters are also used to present the Make and Break technique, in which students construct, break apart, and reconstruct common word patterns (Clay, 1993).

***Writing a Story***     One of the basic assumptions of Reading Recovery (Clay, 1991) is the concept that reading and writing are closely related and that writing can be used as a means for understanding reading. Depending on the student's level of competence, she is asked to dictate or write a one- or two-sentence story or message, with the teacher's help, if necessary. The piece might be related to a previously read book, some event in the student's life, or another topic of interest.

A notebook or loose-leaf binder containing unlined paper opened up so facing pages are displayed and turned sideways is used. The student tells the story to the teacher, who jots it down on a separate piece of paper so it is not forgotten or distorted. The teacher repeats the story exactly as the student dictated it, and the student writes as much of the story as she can on the bottom page. The top of the double page functions as an instructional or practice area. Here, the student attempts to write words she is unsure of.

The teacher may provide assistance by drawing Elkonin boxes and coaching the student as she fills in the letters of the target word. If the student knows just one or two letters in the word—the initial and final consonants—for instance, she might write those in the appropriate boxes. The teacher then helps the student fill in the rest of the boxes. The teacher might also write words here, if the student has little or no chance of writing them successfully. A sample story is presented in Figure 14.1.

*Assembling a Cut-Up Story*    After the one- or two-sentence story has been written by the child on the bottom of the double page and it has been read and reread, the teacher rewrites it on a strip of tagboard. Each sentence is then cut up, and the student reassembles it and reads it. Reassembling the sentences fosters comprehension and knowledge of syntactic structures. The cut-up sentences are placed in an envelope so the student can practice reading the story at home.

*Reading a New Book*    The culmination of a Reading Recovery lesson is the reading of a new book. This step is done last so that the child can apply and integrate the strategies introduced earlier. If a variety of books is available, the child should take part in the selection process. The books provided by the teacher should present some challenge but not too much. Students should know at least 90 percent of the words in the text. (This book advocates a 95 percent standard.)

> In a storybook introduction or text walk, the teacher provides a scaffold so that students can get more out of the story and are better able to use strategies. For additional examples of a text walk, see Clay's (1991), "Introducing a New Storybook to Young Readers."

Having previewed the book in terms of the child's capabilities, the teacher "walks" through the book with him, pointing out the title and author and using illustrations to provide an overview of the text. The child is invited to relate the text to other books he has read or to relevant experiences he has had. The teacher may recite from the text unfamiliar terms, expressions, or syntactic structures. The teacher may point these out in the text and ask the student to repeat them (Clay, 1991). The basic purpose of this orientation is to prepare the child for a successful reading of the text.

**FIGURE 14.1**
Sample Story

## Introducing a Book

*Step 1: Analyzing the text.* Analyze the text. Note concepts, background information, words, or language structures that might be barriers for the prospective reader. In the book *The Hungry Giant* (Cowley, 1980, 1990), for instance, the word *bommy-knocker* would be unfamiliar. To understand the story, the reader would need to have a concept of a giant and background information about bees, beehives, and honey.

*Step 2: Introducing the title and topic.* Introduce the title and the topic of the text to the student. Help the student relate the topic to her own background of experience. Do not dwell on the title, as this will detract from the main purpose, which is a successful reading of the text. When introducing *The Hungry Giant,* read the title to the student and ask her to point to the giant on the cover. You might note that the giant is angry because he is hungry.

*Step 3: Highlighting the story.* Walk the student through the story page by page so that she has an overview of the tale. Knowing the gist of the story and who the main characters are, the student will be better able to use contextual and other clues to achieve a successful reading. As you walk the student through the story, preview words, concepts, and language structures that you think she might have difficulty understanding. Paraphrase key portions of the text that contain difficult items. Then help the student point out these items. For instance, after paraphrasing the first page, in which the unfamiliar word *bommy-knocker* is used, ask the student to point to the bommy-knocker in the illustration and tell how a bommy-knocker might be used. Then ask the student to point to the word *bommy-knocker* on the page. Also have the student point to *bread, roared,* and *giant,* which are words that would be in her listening-speaking vocabulary, but which she might have difficulty reading. As you walk through the text, paraphrasing the story, have the student point out other words that might be hard for her to read: *people, butter, honey, everywhere,* and *beehive.* To build necessary background, briefly discuss with the student what a beehive is and the fact that bees make honey and store it in a beehive. Do not display the last page. Instead, ask the student to tell what she thinks will happen when the giant smashes the beehive with his bommy-knocker. Although the student will know most of the story before she reads the book, she will still have the enjoyment of finding out how the story ends.

*Step 4: Reading the story.* As the student reads the story, note whether the selection seems to be on the appropriate level and also analyze the student's performance to see what strategies she is using and which strategies she might need to improve. Encourage the student to read the story on her own, but provide guidance and support as needed. If the student has difficulty with the word *with* in the sentence, "Get me some honey, or I'll hit you with my bommy-knocker," prompt the use of context. Have the student read "blank" for the unknown word *with* and then reread the sentence and use context to see what word would make sense there (these strategies are described in detail in Chapters 8 and 9).

*Step 5: Discussing the story.* Discuss the story. Start with the student's purpose for reading, which was to find out what happened when the giant hit the beehive with his bommy-knocker. Discuss, too, what the people did when ordered to bring the giant food and why they brought him a beehive.

*Step 6: Skill/strategy instruction.* Praise the student for her use of strategies: "I like the way you used the meaning of the story to help you read *with*." Call attention to strategies that might need introducing or refining. "You read this word (pointing to *zoomed*) as *ran*. The word *ran* makes sense in the story. But what letter does *ran* begin with? What letter does this word begin with? What word that begins with *z* might make sense here?"

*Step 7: Rereading.* Encourage the student to dramatize the story. You might take the part of the people while the student takes the role of the giant.

The new book may be reread, if there is time. It is always read the next day, during which time the teacher prepares a running record of the child's reading. Because introducing a book is a highly effective technique and can be used in any program, an adapted version of this procedure is presented in the box on page 535.

## Other Intervention Programs

Most early intervention programs use a framework similar to that incorporated in Reading Recovery. However, some programs take a more systematic approach to word-analysis instruction, and some use decodable texts rather than predictable texts.

### Early Steps

The Early Steps program added systematic phonics to the Reading Recovery framework (Morris, 2008). Early Steps may reach some students who need a more intensive, more explicit approach to phonics than that offered by Reading Recovery (Santa & Høien, 1999). Early Steps has the following components:

1.  **Rereading books (14 minutes).**   The student rereads a familiar book. A beginning reader will echo read a pattern book, a mid-first-grade reader will partner read or read every other page, and an end-of-first-grade reader will read with limited support from the tutor.

2.  **Word study (8 minutes).**   Depending on the student's knowledge of phonics, he will sort beginning consonants, short-vowel patterns, long-vowel patterns, or whatever element he is working on. Sorting is the way that phonics is presented in this program. (This textbook recommends direct instruction in phonics but using sorting to reinforce phonics.) During word study, the student might also play any one of a number of word games.

3.  **Sentence writing (8 minutes).**   The student composes a sentence about a topic of interest. Although the teacher provides some support, the student writes much of the sentence on his own. The purpose of having the student write the sentence is to encourage him to make discoveries about the spelling system, so some of his words will not be spelled conventionally. This is a departure from the procedure used in Reading Recovery, in which all words are written correctly. After the student has written the sentence, the teacher writes it correctly on a strip of tagboard, cuts it up, mixes up the words, and has the student reassemble the sentence. This activity is dropped once the student is able to read long-vowel patterns.

4.  **Introducing a new book (10 minutes).**   The teacher previews the new book. After discussing the title and predicting what the book might be about, the teacher "walks" through the book, discusses its illustrations, and has the student point to words that have been discussed but may still pose problems. Then the child reads.

5.  **Reading to the child (7 minutes, if time allows).**   The tutor reads a high-quality selection to the student and then discusses it with the child.

### Road to Reading

This program complements Road to the Code. Its focus is on decoding skills that range from initial-consonant correspondence to two-syllable and three-syllable words. Road to Reading also builds fluency. It can be used as a preventive or intervention program in grade 1 or a corrective/remedial program in grades 2 to 4.

**Using Technology**

Literacy Trust

http://literacytrust.org/

Provides additional information about Reading Rescue.

The program provides lessons and materials for games and word and sentence reading, and it lists suggestions for decodable books and children's trade books that might be used to provide reinforcement. The Road to Reading program has been validated by research (Blachman & Tangel, 2008).

## Reading Rescue

Although modeled on Reading Recovery, Reading Rescue features an intensive decoding program and the use of Ready Readers, decodable but readable texts, to reinforce phonics skills that have been taught. To be accepted into the program, students must be able to identify 17 letters. When results of instruction were analyzed, the major predictor of success was students' ability to read a text on which they were coached the previous day with at least 98 percent accuracy (Ehri et al., 2007). This finding has two implications: (1) students were given text on the appropriate level of challenge; and (2) systematic, effective instruction enabled students to read virtually all the words in the texts they were assigned. Progress in Reading Rescue was nearly twice that found in the typical intervention program for beginning readers. Reading Rescue incorporates many of the instructional principles recommended throughout this text but especially providing materials that students can read with a high rate of success, monitoring progress, and providing systematic instruction based on students' needs. Instruction can be provided by the classroom teacher or another trained professional.

## Key Factors

Key factors in early intervention programs include the number of rimes introduced, the amount of reading students do at home, and the level of parental involvement in the students' at-home reading (Leslie & Allen, 1999), as well as progress monitoring, systematic instruction in phonics, placing students at the appropriate level, and fostering a high rate of success (Ehri et al., 2007). Although many students benefit from a 20-week or full-year program, some may need a second year of instruction to catch up.

In addition to these research-based programs, there are a number of packaged or commercial intervention and corrective programs. These are listed in Table 14.1.

## Model Program for Early Intervention

Based on a review of the research, a careful look at successful group intervention programs, and practical experience, a program for group intervention should include the following elements:

- Conduct a beginning assessment to find out where students are. This should include alphabet knowledge, ability to segment words into sounds and/or identify beginning sounds, knowledge of letter–sound relationships, and knowledge of high-frequency words. The teacher's own judgment should also be a factor.

- Provide instruction on one-to-one basis or in small groups of three to five.

- As needed, cover phonological awareness (segmentation, identification of beginning sounds), decoding (initial consonants and patterns), high-frequency words, essential conventions of print, and comprehension. Each session should

**TABLE 14.1**
Commercial
Intervention
Programs

| Title | Publisher | Interest Level | Grade Level | Main Characteristics |
|---|---|---|---|---|
| Bookshop | Mondo | K–3 | K–3 | Workshop approach. PA, decoding, comprehension, writing, language. |
| Corrective Reading | SRA | 4–12 | 1–5+ | Scripted direct instruction. Decoding, comprehension. |
| Edge | Hampton-Brown | 9–12 | 1–9 | Decoding, vocabulary, comprehension, writing. |
| Edmark | Great Source | P–12 | K–1 | Whole-word approach, simplified text. Designed for students with cognitive deficits. Focuses on 150 high-frequency words in Level 1 and 200 in Level 2. Has a software version. |
| Fast Track | McGraw-Hill | 4–8 | 1–5+ | Decoding, comprehension. |
| High Noon | High Noon | 3–12 | 1–4+ | Decoding, comprehension. |
| High Point | Hampton-Brown | 4–12 | 1–6 | Decoding, comprehension, writing, oral language. Emphasis on ELLs. |
| inZone Books | Hampton-Brown | 9–12 | 1–9 | Voluntary or guided reading. |
| Language! | Sopris West | 1–12 | 1–9 | Decoding, comprehension, spelling, writing, oral language. |
| Leveled Literacy Intervention | Heinemann | K–3 | K–3 | Separate phonics/word study, oral language, and writing. Emphasis on reading predictable texts. |
| Lightspan Early Reading | Lightspan | K–3 | K–3 | Computer-based program. PA, decoding, comprehension, vocabulary, background knowledge. |
| Read Naturally | Read Naturally | 1–8 | 1–8 | Fluency. Also has materials for reinforcing phonics. |
| Reading 180 | Scholastic | 1–12 | 1–9 | Computer-based program. Decoding, comprehension, vocabulary, writing, oral language. |
| Reading Edge | Success for All Foundation | 6–8 | 1–8 | Decoding, fluency, vocabulary, comprehension, writing. |
| Reading Mastery | SRA | K–6 | K–6 | Scripted direct instruction. Decoding and comprehension. |
| Reading Milestones | PRO-ED | 1–5+ | K–4 | Language-controlled sight approach recommended for students with hearing impairments or language delays. |
| Reading Rescue | Literacy Trust | 1–2 | 1–2 | PA, decoding, fluency, vocabulary, comprehension. Uses Ready Readers. |
| Ready Readers | Modern Curriculum Press | K–3 | K–3 | PA, decoding. Stresses sorting. Texts are decodable but readable. |
| REWARDS | Sopris West | 4–6<br>6–12 | 2–4+<br>2–4+ | Syllabic analysis, fluency, vocabulary, comprehension. |

| Title | Publisher | Interest Level | Grade Level | Main Characteristics |
|---|---|---|---|---|
| Road to Reading | Brookes | 1–2+ | 1–2+ | Decoding single-syllable and multisyllabic words, fluency. |
| Sidewalks | Scott Foresman | 1–5 | 1–5 | PA, decoding, fluency, vocabulary, comprehension. |
| SIPPS | Developmental Studies Center | K–3 4–12 | K–3 1–4+ | PA, single-syllable phonics, syllabic analysis. Single-syllable phonics, syllabic analysis. |
| Soar to Success | Houghton Mifflin | K–8 | K–8 | Phonemic awareness (at K–2), phonics, fluency, and comprehension. Uses high-interest trade books. |
| S.P.I.R.E. | EPS | P–8 | P–5+ | OG. Decoding, spelling, fluency, comprehension. |
| Success for All | Success for All Foundation | K–8 | K–8 | Whole-school program. PA, decoding, comprehension, writing. |
| System 44 | Scholastic | 3–12 | 1–2 | Word analysis, fluency, vocabulary, comprehension. |
| Voyager Reading Intervention | Voyager | K–8 | K–8 | PA, decoding, comprehension, writing. |
| Word Building | Phoenix | K–4 | K–3 | PA, decoding, modified cloze comprehension. |
| Word Detectives | Benchmark School | 1–5+ | 1–5 | PA, decoding. |
| Wright Group Early Reading Intervention | Wright Group | K–3 | K–3 | PA, decoding, spelling, fluency, comprehension. |

Separate phonics programs are those in which the phonics skill taught in a particular lesson is not then reinforced by the selection read during that lesson.

PA = Phonological awareness.

OG = Orton–Gillingham.

include a 5- to 10-minute lesson on a consonant, pattern, or other element that appears in the text to be read. An approach known as word building, which was explained in Chapter 8, is highly recommended. Because students do not always apply skills, have them examine in the selection to be read sentences containing words that incorporate the element that has been taught. This should be done in preparation for reading the selection.

- Read and reread books that reinforce the pattern or other element that has been taught. These books should be on the appropriate level of difficulty, so that students should be able to read them with 95 percent accuracy. To achieve this high level of performance, books should be carefully selected (see Figure 8.8 on pages 259–261) and thoroughly introduced using the Reading Recovery procedure for introducing a book, described earlier. This introduction ("text walk") includes introducing difficult words and concepts before students read the book. This should be done in addition to conducting the word-analysis lesson.

- As the opportunity arises, guide students in the use of word-analysis and comprehension strategies. Word-analysis strategies should include using the pronounceable word-parts, analogy, and context strategies and, in some cases, letter-by-letter sounding out. (See Chapters 8 and 9 for a full discussion of these strategies.) Students should also be monitoring for meaning.

- Provide students with as many opportunities as possible to read one-on-one with the teacher, an aide, a volunteer, or even an older student. Helpers should receive training so they are able to guide the student in the use of strategies.

- Have students read independently as much as possible. This could include rereading familiar books or reading easy books for the first time. Students should take books home to read or reread on a daily basis.

- Include a writing component. Students might write, with your guidance, a single sentence about a book that they have read, as in Reading Recovery. The sentence may be cut up and taken home to be put together and read to parents.

- Involve parents. Parents need to understand the program so that they can support their children's efforts by listening to them as they read their books and segmented sentences.

- Provide ongoing monitoring. The use of running records is an excellent means of observing the student's use of strategies and to check the difficulty level of the material. This is a time-consuming procedure, so you might conduct a running record once a week and assess brief segments of text. You might also administer the Phonics Inventory (see Appendix A), the Word Fluency Indicator (see http://wordbuilding.org for a copy) or another progress-monitoring device. Other means of assessment include observing students and filling out an observation checklist (an observation checklist for word-analysis strategy use can be found in Chapter 4), quizzing students on patterns and high-frequency words that have been previously taught, and evaluating writing samples.

- Keep the program structured. Students feel more secure when they have a routine to follow. However, don't be so structured that you lose sight of students' individual needs (Barnes, 1996–1997).

- Closely coordinate the intervention program with the core program.

- Build vocabulary and background knowledge and develop comprehension.

- Track students' progress after they have graduated from the program and provide follow-up help as needed.

## Instructional Routines for an Intervention Program

A typical routine for a 30- to 40-minute group session might include the following activities:

- Rereading of a familiar book (5 minutes)

- Word study (5 to 10 minutes), in which a new pattern, initial consonant, or other element is presented

- Introduction and reading of a new book (10 minutes)

- Writing a sentence (5 minutes)

- Previewing a book to be taken home to read (5–10 minutes)

The 10 to 30 percent of students who don't make adequate progress in a yearlong intervention program may do so in a second year of intervention. A one-on-one program known as Book Buddies II was provided for children who had been tutored during first grade but were still below grade level. After an additional year of intervention, which included twice-a-week, one-on-one tutoring sessions of 45 minutes, all of the students were at or above grade level. The sessions included systematic instruction and practice in word recognition, comprehension, and writing. Students also took home books to read after each session (Fowler, Lindemann, Thacker-Gwaltney, & Invernizzi, 2002).

## The Need for Specialized Techniques

Approximately, 5 percent of students fail to benefit adequately from intervention programs that are effective with most students (Fuchs et al., 2012). A number of these struggling students, approximately 1 in 100 (McCormick, 1994), seem to have such extreme difficulty learning printed words or letter–sound relationships that they may need to be taught through specialized programs. One such student is Martha.

Although she had high-average intelligence, 8-year-old Martha was making very little progress in reading. Because she was experiencing difficulty learning to read new words, she was referred to a nearby university reading clinic. Despite intensive one-to-one instruction, she made very limited gains. Martha seemed to forget the high-frequency words she was taught soon after they were introduced. After a year of supplementary instruction, Martha was only reading on a primer level. She was able to read only 9 of 20 first-grade high-frequency words on an informal reading inventory word-list test.

## VAKT Tracing Technique

The struggle to learn to read was taking its toll on Martha. A vivacious youngster on the playground, she was quiet and subdued during her reading lessons. She seemed discouraged and was putting forth less and less effort. Feeling somewhat desperate, her teacher decided to try a technique that she had recently learned in her corrective reading methods class: the VAKT (Visual–Auditory–Kinesthetic–Tactile) tracing technique (Johnson, 1966).

> ✳ Both the Fernald and VAKT techniques use visual, auditory, kinesthetic (sense of movement), and tactile senses to help the student concentrate on the words they are learning. Use of various modalities may help students produce representations in memory that are more detailed and more lasting. Use of multiple modalities may also create more connections so that words are stored and retrieved more easily (Moats & Farrell, 1999).

> ✳ An essential element in Martha's success was the enthusiasm of her teacher, who made learning interesting and fulfilling and affirmed Martha's successes.

VAKT is an adaptation of the Fernald tracing technique (Fernald, 1943), which is estimated to be the most widely used approach for teaching severely disabled readers (Tierney & Readence, 2000a). Designed for the most severely disabled readers, Fernald/VAKT is a Tier III intervention. VAKT is a language-experience approach. As students attempt to write letters to relatives, summarize selections that have been read to them, describe experiences they have had, label diagrams, or make written observations about scientific experiments, they learn the words they don't know by seeing, saying, hearing, and tracing them (VAKT) or, in later stages, by seeing, hearing, and saying them (VAK). Although most words are learned in a writing context, some words from reading selections may also be learned through VAKT or VAK.

Long touted by experts in the field of reading difficulties (Clark & Uhury, 1995; Clay, 1993; Fernald, 1943; Johnson, 1966; Johnson & Kress, 1966; Manzo & Manzo, 1993; Roswell & Chall, 1994), the tracing technique worked as promised with Martha.

Revived by her initial success and the support of her sensitive teacher, Martha was soon learning new words with enthusiasm. Within just four weeks, she learned to read more than 50 words, which was nearly as many words as she had learned in two full years of schooling.

A technique of last resort, VAKT is recommended only for students who have serious word-learning problems. While most students have no difficulty learning to read by seeing and hearing, a small percentage of the population has such a serious difficulty learning to associate printed symbols with the words they represent that they need special methods that use kinesthetic (sense of movement) and tactile (sense of touch) as well as visual and auditory stimulation. In a guidebook on Reading Recovery for teachers, Clay (1993) advises using a tracing approach with students who are not learning words by visually analyzing them or by reconstructing them with magnetic letters. "If visual analysis and word reconstruction do not produce good results, introduce tracing and add the feel of the movements to the child's sources of information" (p. 56). Because VAKT is a method quite different from those typically used, it can give students a fresh start.

## Signs of Need

The major sign that VAKT is needed is failure to learn or remember printed symbols despite adequate ability and opportunity. A candidate for VAKT stands out because he is extremely slow to learn printed words and, even after apparently learning them, soon forgets them.

Jonathan, when tested at age 12, knew fewer than half the words on a primer list. Awilda had to trace the word *where* 25 times before learning it and then was unable to recognize it when she encountered it in a story minutes later. There may also be signs of stress associated with reading. Obviously distressed when her teacher handed her a book, one gifted student who had a serious word-learning problem blurted out, "Excuse me! We're not going to read, are we?"

## Prerequisites for VAKT

Although designed for students who have the severest reading problems, VAKT does have a number of prerequisites (Johnson & Kress, 1966). The child must be able to hear, see, say, and trace the words. A child with a profound hearing loss cannot use the technique. In addition, the learner needs enough phonological awareness so that she can detect separate syllables in a word. Since the technique also involves tracing and writing letters, the child should also know how to form most of the letters of the alphabet.

## Introductory Stage of VAKT

> The purpose of the introductory stage of VAKT is to acquaint the student with procedures for using the technique and to demonstrate that this technique will enable him to learn.

VAKT works, in part, because both the teacher and learner believe in it (Johnson & Kress, 1966). The purpose of the introductory stage is to show the student how the technique works and, more importantly, to convince the student that she can learn to read words by using it.

In introducing the technique, you will need the following materials:

- Dictionary
- Large black crayon

- Strips of 4-inch × 12-inch paper
- Stapler
- Recording sheet

## Establishing Rapport

As you establish rapport, find out whether the student is left-handed or right-handed. The teacher and student should be seated side by side, and the student should be able to observe the teacher as she traces new words. A right-handed teacher working with a right-handed learner sits to the student's right. You should also determine whether the student uses cursive or manuscript handwriting. Although Fernald (1943) and Johnson and Kress (1966) recommend cursive, because there is smoother flow and better sense of the wholeness of words written in cursive, manuscript is preferred by some because it matches the print that students will read.

Once you have established rapport with the learner, explain the technique. Tell the student that she will be using a new way to learn to read and spell words, one that a lot of bright students just like herself have used. Invite the student to suggest a word that she would like to learn. Tell the student that it can be a long word or a difficult word, any word that she would like to learn. One student requested that he be taught how to spell his last name. Up until that time, he had been using an initial to signify his surname. The student was 10 years old.

## Using the Dictionary

Except for proper names, all new words are looked up in a dictionary. This ensures that accurate syllabic division is obtained and familiarizes the student with the dictionary. Involve the student in the task by asking her what letter the word begins with and where it might be found in the dictionary. The student may also be asked to turn to the section in the dictionary where the word might be found. If she is looking up the word *tiny*, the student locates the *t*'s and not the word *tiny* itself, since this would involve knowing how to spell the word and would also be too time-consuming.

Before looking up the word, ask the student how many parts (syllables) it has. Then look up the word and tell the student the number of syllables that the word contains. Alerting the student to watch carefully, you say the word and write it in blackboard-size script on a strip of 4-inch × 12-inch paper placed horizontally. Say each syllable as you initiate the writing of the syllable. If you are using cursive, cross *t*'s and dot *i*'s from left to right, and then say the whole word once more. Also underline the separate syllables (as in Figure 14.2) if the word is multisyllabic. With your index and ring fingers, trace the word. Continue demonstrating the tracing technique until the student feels that she can do it.

**■ FIGURE 14.2**
Model Word
Prepared by
Teacher

| MANUSCRIPT | CURSIVE |
| --- | --- |
| dinosaur | dinosaur |

## Student Tracing

> ⚡ Martha had to trace the word *dinosaur,* one of her introductory words, 13 times before she was able to write it correctly from memory. However, as time went on, she required fewer tracings to learn words.

The student traces the word until he feels he can write it from memory. Tracing should be conscientious and accurate. Unless the student is totally involved in the process, it will not work.

Do not allow any inaccurate tracings. Inaccurate tracing includes faulty tracing of the individual letters. For reference, have a cursive or manuscript chart available. If the student begins to trace a manuscript *b* by going around and up, stop him and show him how to trace it. The tracing should be accompanied by an explanation: "When I trace *b,* I start at the top, come straight down, and then go up and around."

In addition to seeing that tracings are accurate, make sure that the student does the following:

- Says the whole word.
- Says a syllable as she begins to trace the syllable.
- Dots *i*'s and crosses *t*'s after tracing the whole word. If the student is using manuscript writing, the *i*'s are dotted and the *t*'s crossed as they are formed.
- Says the whole word again.

If the student skips a step or fails to follow the procedure exactly, stop him immediately. A major aim of VAKT is to establish correct habits, so you want to avoid reinforcing erroneous responses. The student may ask for a demonstration if his tracing procedures are not accurate, or he may undertake additional tracings. You may suggest additional tracings or demonstrations if you feel these are needed.

## Writing from Memory

Once the student feels that she knows the word, she writes it twice from memory. With the teacher's copy turned over, the student writes the word in normal-size script across the top of a second strip of 4-inch × 12-inch paper positioned vertically. The student compares her copy with the model copy. If it is correct, the student covers her writing with the teacher copy turned over and writes the target word once more. If the word is again written correctly, the student copy is dated and stapled to the teacher's copy. It is then filed in a box that has alphabetic dividers. If the student has difficulty, she may be asked to trace the word again.

## Keeping Records

Records should be kept of words learned and the numbers of demonstrations and tracings. (The symbols used to record the student's performance are presented in Figure 14.3.) These records provide an ongoing means for monitoring progress and can also be used as a basis for deciding when to move into another stage. The record displayed in Figure 14.4 shows that the word was presented in the introductory stage and indicates that the teacher demonstrated the tracing five times. The student traced the word correctly seven times in succession, then wrote the word from memory incorrectly twice in a row, and finally wrote the word correctly twice in a row.

Students remain in the introductory stage until they have mastered the tracing procedures. Some students may enter Stage 1 after tracing just one or two words. Others may need additional experience and should not be rushed.

**FIGURE 14.3**
VAKT Symbols

| | |
|---|---|
| *d* | demonstration tracing |
| │ | accurate tracing |
| ┢ | partial tracing—student was stopped because of faulty procedures |
| ✓ | correct writing of word from memory |
| ✓ˋ | incorrect writing of word from memory |

## Stage 1 of VAKT

In terms of tracing procedures, Stage 1 is identical to the introductory stage. The major difference is the source of the words to be learned. Words learned in the introductory stage are chosen by students. Words to be learned in Stage 1 are those the students need to know for their writing.

> As used in VAKT, the language-experience approach has an added step. After being scribed by the teacher and read by the teacher and student, the teacher dictates to the student, who then scribes the story. Because it is based on student-dictated stories, VAKT can be used with disabled readers of all ages, including adults.

VAKT is the word-learning component of a language-experience approach. The student may be composing a letter, a set of instructions, a shopping list, an account of a trip he has taken, or a summary of an experiment. After the experience has been discussed and organized, the student dictates what he plans to write. The teacher records the student's dictation. After the story has been recorded, the teacher then dictates it back to the student. Any words that the student is unable to write are presented, traced, and written from memory just as in the steps of the introductory stage.

Here is how Martha, the student taught at a university literacy center, was helped as she composed an experience story. Martha told about going swimming in a pool, which the teacher wrote down and then read back to her:

> When I go swimming, I walk in the water first. Then I swim under the water. I
>
> hold my breath and get the diving sticks from my mom. Sometimes I get the
>
> sticks at nine feet. I like to do this because it is fun.

Now that the story was composed, Martha began the physical writing of it. Following the teacher's oral reading of the first sentence, Martha was able to write the first three words "When I go," but she asked for help with *swimming:*

**Teacher:** How many syllables do you hear in *swimming*?

**Martha:** (after some hesitation) Two?

**Teacher:** We'll check and see. Do you know where in the dictionary it might be?

**Martha:** In the middle.

**Teacher:** Open to it.

**FIGURE 14.4**
VAKT Record

| | |
|---|---|
| *dinosaur* (I) | *d d d d d* │ │ │ │ │ │ ✓ ✓ ✓ ✓ |

After opening to *s*, Martha handed the dictionary to the teacher, who located the word and reported, "Here it is. You were right. Swimming has two syllables. Watch me while I write it for you." The teacher said the word as a whole, in syllables, and again as a whole: *swimming, swim • ming, swimming.* As the teacher said the word in syllables, she traced each syllable.

After some demonstrations and several practice tracings, Martha was able to write the word correctly twice. Although Martha was able to write a few words, such as *I, go, when, the, my, get, at, to,* and *do,* she needed to trace most of the words in the story.

At the end of each session, words that had been learned by tracing were underlined. After the session, the selection was typed so Martha would have the opportunity to see it in print. Newly learned words—those that had been underlined—were typed in list form. On the following day, Martha read the words that had been put in list form and the portion of the experience story that had been typed. The words that Martha forgot were practiced once more. When Martha missed a previously learned word, she retrieved it from the file—which provided incidental practice with initial consonants and alphabetical order—traced it, and again rewrote it twice from memory. The additional spelling attempts were dated and stapled to the original attempts.

When the student reads the previous day's words typed in list form, her performance is noted just as on the word-list test of an informal reading inventory. Performance is recorded on a second copy. If the student cannot read the words in isolation, she is given the opportunity to read them in the context of the experience story. A sample experience story with words underlined is shown in Figure 14.5.

**■ FIGURE 14.5**
Sample VAKT
Story

In addition to tracing and using new words in stories, numerous opportunities should be provided for students to read newly learned words in other contexts. These contexts might include rhymes, poems, songs, recipes, and similar pieces. Target words should be mixed with known words so that students are almost sure to be successful (Johnson & Kress, 1966).

## Moving from One Stage to Another

As students gain skills and learn words with greater ease, they move to more advanced stages. Signs that students are ready to move to a more advanced stage include making fewer repetitions and relying less on the word-learning technique that is characteristic of that level. Signs that a student in Stage 1 is ready to move into Stage 2 include needing fewer tracings before learning a word and learning an increasing number of words with no tracing at all. Students demonstrate the ability to learn words by looking, saying, and hearing, rather than by looking, saying, hearing, and tracing. If students in Stage 1 say they can learn a word without tracing it, give them the opportunity to do so. Have them try using Stage 2 procedures.

As they near the completion of Stage 1, students may use VAKT with some words and VAK with others. The transition from Stage 1 to Stage 2 is made when students can learn all their new words without the use of tracing.

## Stage 2 of VAKT

Stages 1 and 2 are the same, except that in Stage 2, the student is not required to trace. Since there is no tracing in Stage 2, 4-inch × 6-inch cards may be used instead of sheets of 4-inch × 12-inch paper. Instead of tracing the word, the student studies it from the card.

## Stage 3 of VAKT

In Stage 3, the student uses the dictionary rather than teacher-written copy as a model. If the word is not in the file box, the student, with the teacher's help, if necessary, locates the word in the dictionary and checks syllabication. The student studies the word from the dictionary, saying it as a whole, in syllables, and then as

---

### Steps in Stage 2 of VAKT

**Step 1:  Identify the word to be learned.** The student asks for the word or makes an error as she or he attempts to write it.

**Step 2:  Analyze the word.** You ask how many parts or syllables the word has. The student checks the word file to see if the word is there. If not, you and the student find it in the dictionary. Note how many syllables the word has and inform the student.

**Step 3:  Review the word.** If the word is in the file box, review the word. If the word is not in the file box, say the word, say each syllable as you write each syllable, and, after having written each syllable, say the word as a whole. Syllables are underlined.

**Step 4:  Say the word.** The student studies the word by saying it as a whole, saying each syllable, and saying it as a whole once more.

**Step 5:  Spell the word.** The student attempts to spell the word correctly twice on a second card, which is held vertically.

**Step 6:  Use the word.** The student writes the word in the story.

a whole. When the student feels that she has mastered the word, she writes it twice on a 4-inch × 6-inch card held vertically. After writing the word the first time, she compares it with the word in the dictionary. If the word has been written correctly, she covers the first writing, and writes the word from memory once more. If new, the word is then written on the front of the card held horizontally and is filed. The word is then written in the story. Stage 3 is discontinued when the student no longer seems to need it.

## Need for a Total Approach

> ✱ Along with VAKT, Martha used word building, read a variety of children's books, and composed stories using invented spelling.

VAKT is just one part of a total program for students who have severe reading problems. While the focus of the explanation of VAKT has been on mechanical procedures, the approach includes providing opportunities for investigating topics of interest, composing language-experience stories, reading children's books, participating in discussion groups, and doing all the things that might be done in an exemplary classroom.

VAKT should also be combined with a systematic word-analysis program such as word building. Initial patterns to be taught might be those that the student needs in his writing. For instance, noting the word *might* and *night* in a story, the teacher might initiate a study of the *ight* pattern. Johnson (1966) cautions that VAKT and VAK are not substitutes for the development of word-analysis skills. However, the high-frequency words learned in VAKT may become the basis for teaching phonics and other word-recognition skills.

As with any technique, the heart of VAKT is in the quality of the teaching. VAKT works best when the teacher carefully observes the student's learning strategies and builds on what he knows. If the student is using initial consonants, for instance, build on that strength. When that student is hesitant about writing a word, ask him to tell how he thinks it might begin. Also have the student use his knowledge of initial consonants to help locate words being looked up in the dictionary.

The overall program should be both systematic and incidental. Using word building or another phonics program, gradually introduce needed word-analysis elements. However, also take advantage of opportunities that arise naturally. For instance, if the student dictates a story about a time when he and some friends had to start rowing to shore when the motor on their boat conked out but they got a tow from a passing Coast Guard boat, then do a spontaneous study of the *ow* and *oa* spellings of long *o*.

## Adapted VAKT

Classical VAKT emphasizes the wholeness of words. When tracing single-syllable words, the student says it as a whole and does not break it into its constituent sounds. Multisyllabic words, however, are broken down into separate syllables. Research suggests that struggling readers, especially in the beginning stages, benefit by noting the separate sounds in words and also seeing words as a whole. The following adaptation of VAKT has been tried out with struggling readers and found to be effective.

First, the teacher shows how many sounds are in a single-syllable word and which letters represent those sounds. The teacher says the word, checks its spelling in a dictionary, writes the word while saying each sound, and then says the whole word. The teacher says the whole word, underlines each letter or letter group that represents a sound, says each sound while underlining it, and then says the whole word. The teacher demonstrates tracing by saying the whole word, saying each sound while tracing the letter(s) that makes that sound, and saying the whole word. The student says the whole word, says each sound while tracing the letter that makes that sound, and says the whole word. Learning the word *stop*, the student would say, "stop, /s/, /t/, /o/, /p/, stop." For words in which some sounds are spelled with two letters, the teacher puts one line under both letters to show that they represent just one sound: s̲h̲-o-p. An irregular word such as *laugh* would be written l̲-a̲u̲-g̲h̲. Multisyllabic words are traced in syllables, just as in classical VAKT.

## Why Is VAKT Effective?

> ⚹ Multisensory processing results in multiple memory traces, with the kinesthetic and tactile modalities reinforcing visual and auditory pathways (Hulme, 1981). VAKT also strengthens phonological awareness.

In addition to establishing a kinesthetic and tactile link and focusing attention, VAKT provides structure and support, builds on what a student knows, instills confidence, and sets high expectations for the student. VAKT also forces the student to note all the letters in a word (Gates, 1927). The technique removes the association of failure by providing students with a method they have never seen before. It is also firmly grounded in language development and the student's interests. Speaking of multisensory techniques, Moats and Farrell (1999) commented, "Most likely it is not simply the multimodal nature of such practice that explains its power but the mediating effect of various sensory and motor experiences on attention and recall" (p. 15).

## Orton–Gillingham Approach

> **Orton–Gillingham approach:** specialized word-learning technique that uses intensive synthetic phonics reinforced by tracing.

A no-nonsense, highly structured, skill-and-drill synthetic phonics technique, the **Orton–Gillingham approach** presents the isolated sounds of letters and then builds these individual sounds into words "like bricks into a wall" (Gillingham & Stillman, 1983, p. 40). It is also a Tier III intervention.

In a typical drill, the teacher shows the letter, and the student supplies its sound. The teacher says a sound, and the student names the letter. The teacher says a sound and the student writes the letter that represents that sound. After the sounds of the letters *a, b, f, h, i, j, k, m, p, t* have been taught, they are blended together to make words: *bat, hat, jab, it.* To avoid distorting consonant sounds, the student is encouraged to pronounce the first two sounds together, /ba/, and then add the final sound, /t/.

After learning to read a few words, spelling is initiated. The teacher says the word. The student repeats it, names its letters, *m-a-n,* writes each letter as he says it, *m-a-n,* and then reads the word: *man.*

Later on, this spelling technique will be used to teach nonphonetic words. As in the VAKT technique, students use their kinesthetic and tactile senses. They say and write the words. However, there is a crucial difference. In the VAKT technique, the student says each word or syllable as a whole as he traces it. In the Orton–Gillingham approach, the student says the letter name as he writes the letter, so that the association is between the name of the letter and its form. This is done, according to Gillingham and Stillman (1983), because words like *laugh* do not lend themselves to being pronounced letter sound by letter sound. One of the problems inherent in a letter-by-letter or sound-by-sound approach is that it fails to take advantage of the regularities that can be found in an approach that uses patterns.

Although in widespread use, the Orton–Gillingham approach needs to be modified in the following ways in order to embody current research and practice:

- Start where the student is. Pretest the student with an informal reading inventory or similar instrument, and begin instruction at the point where the student has difficulty.

- Encourage wide reading. Students do learn to read by reading. However, make sure that students are given books on the appropriate level.

- Orton–Gillingham advocates skill and drill on isolated phonics exercises. Phonics instruction should be functional and contextual. Skills taught should be those that are needed and are best taught when students are about to apply them in reading or writing.

- The Orton–Gillingham technique requires learning a series of phonics generalizations. Eliminate or simplify the teaching of rules, except for the ones suggested in Chapter 8. Students make very limited use of rules when attacking unfamiliar words (Gunning, 1988, 1999).

In addition, as Tierney and Readence (2005) have pointed out, "Students who learn by highly structured methods such as Orton–Gillingham have a tendency to emphasize pronunciation over meaning. The synthetic letter-by-letter approach, with its emphasis upon word-perfect reading, places an undue emphasis on the mechanics rather than reading for meaning" (p. 185).

Based on close to three decades of work with struggling readers, Morris (2008) notes that he has encountered a few dozen children who don't respond to a traditional intervention program that includes word study, guided reading, fluency, and writing. One such student was Greg. Despite participating in 40 lessons using sorting to reinforce short- and long-vowel patterns, Greg, a fifth grader, wasn't transferring these skills to contextual reading. Realizing that it was time to try another approach, Morris used Orton–Gillingham procedures (Gillingham & Stillman, 1983). He drilled Greg on letter–sound relationships and blending letters into words. Greg began making progress and was soon applying his skills to contextual reading. Yet after a year's instruction, he was only reading on a third-grade level. Because he was ready to enter the sixth grade, he was still three years behind. Morris speculates that had Greg been placed in a systematic program earlier, he could have caught up.

Morris (2008) is quick to point out that no single program is an absolute panacea. The Orton–Gillingham approach didn't work as well with Jason. At the end of first grade, Jason still didn't know all the letters of the alphabet and recognized fewer than 10 words. Morris realized Jason had a retrieval problem. He was slow in retrieving words from memory. (See page 166 for a discussion of word finding.) For instance, after several years of instruction, when Jason was presented first-grade words, he was able to read just 2 of them when flashed; when given time, however, he was able to read 17 out of 20 words. His performance in reading second-grade words was similar. Tests of the rapid naming of letters and digits supported a diagnosis of slowness in retrieving the names of symbols. Morris added a lot of opportunities for Jason to read and reread connected text. With the added practice, Jason's reading rate slowly increased.

Morris (2008) also warns against using techniques designed for severely disabled readers with readers who have less severe problems. Because specialized techniques are time-consuming and costly, they should be reserved for those who need them.

## ▦ **Other Orton-Based Approaches**

Although the Gillingham–Stillman approach is perhaps the best known of the Orton-based approaches, there are a number of other approaches that grew out of Orton's work. (Orton–Gillingham approaches are noted in Table 14.1.) All have in common systematic instruction in synthetic phonics and the use of visual, auditory, and kinesthetic modalities. However, one major difference is the connections that are emphasized. In the Gillingham–Stillman approach, students say the name of each letter as they trace it. In some Orton-based approaches, students say the sound of each letter as they trace.

▶ **Using Technology**

**Wilson Reading System**

http://www.wilsonlanguage.com/
w_wrs.htm

Provides information about this
Orton–Gillingham approach.

Which works better? Sheffield (1991) has tried both and claims that both work well. She believes that making the connection between the sound and the letter yields faster progress in reading, but the student who makes the connection between the letter and its name does better in spelling.

One of the best known of the Orton–Gillingham approaches is the Wilson Reading System. The Wilson Reading System grew out of Barbara Wilson's experience teaching adult struggling readers at Massachusetts General Hospital. Designed originally for older students, the Wilson System is now used in grades 2 and up. However, younger students use Level A workbooks, while older students use Level B.

The program is highly structured and designed specifically as a remedial program for students in grades 2–12 who have decoding problems. Although the program includes some work on comprehension and development of background and vocabulary, its main focus is on building decoding skills.

A typical lesson starts with a card drill in which students review previously presented sounds by saying the sound shown on the card. A new pattern or card is then introduced. Students practice the new element by reading words and sentences containing the new element. They are then given a quick drill in which the teacher pronounces a sound and the student names the letter that represents that sound. This is followed by reviewing or teaching students how to spell the element introduced and the dictation of words, sounds, and sentences. Students then read a passage designed specifically to reinforce the patterns taught so far. The lesson ends with the teacher's reading of a literature selection to build the students' background and vocabulary and acquaint them with good literature.

Active participation and manipulatives are key elements in the program. The program also introduces multisyllabic words early on. After students learn several single-syllable patterns, they learn multisyllabic words that incorporate those patterns: *limit, happen.*

Like other programs that use highly controlled vocabulary, the reading materials tend to be contrived: "Tim sat in the shop. A mom and a tot came in. The mom got gum for the tot."

Other widely used Orton–Gillingham-based approaches include Recipe for Reading (Bloom & Traub, 2004), Slingerland (King & Slingerland, 2008), Alphabetic Phonics (Educators Publishing Service), Project Read (PO Box 20631, Bloomington, MN 55420, phone 800-450-0343), and Go Phonics (http://www.gophonics.com). Slingerland (http://www.slingerland.org) is a classroom-based version of Orton–Gillingham, and Go Phonics is a commercial version of the Slingerland approach.

Although the Orton–Gillingahm has been widely used, the research is not strong enough to validate it as an effective approach. More research needs to be done (Ritchey & Goeke, 2006; What Works Clearinghouse, 2010). The same can be said for the Fernald approach (Myers, 1980).

## ▧ **Adapted Word Building**

⚹ If students have difficulty with word building, assess their phonemic awareness. Inadequate phonemic awareness can make learning phonics more difficult.

⚹ VAKT should be added to word building only if the student is having difficulty learning words through a word-building approach. If word building with adapted VAKT is not successful, try classical VAKT.

An adapted form of word building has been used with encouraging success with severely disabled readers and is highly recommended. As described in Chapter 8, word building focuses on the learning of patterns. Although patterns are presented as both individual sounds, /a/+ /t/, and as patterns, /h/ + /at/, the emphasis is on the pattern as a unit.

For most students, this is an efficient, effective way to learn phonics. However, if students are having difficulty learning patterns, adapt the technique so that they learn individual letter sounds. When presenting the *at* pattern, for instance, point out the separate sounds in *at*: /a/ + /t/. If students have difficulty using pronounceable word parts—if they cannot pronounce the *ap* in *map,* for instance—then see if they are able to process the word sound by sound. In other words, if the student is struggling, make whatever adjustments are necessary. Although decoding a word sound by sound distorts speech sounds and is burdensome, it may be a necessary procedure for some students.

In most cases, the use of a sound-by-sound approach will be temporary. As students become proficient in recognizing individual sounds in words or patterns, they will grow in their ability to perceive larger elements in words. Eventually, you should be able to present new elements through patterns, and students will be able to decode unfamiliar words by using pronounceable word parts.

If you adapt word building, Benchmark, or another word-learning system and students are still struggling, use VAKT along with the phonics system. A major drawback of using VAKT is that it is so time-consuming. If time is an issue, shorten VAKT by adapting the writing portion. Instead of having the student dictate a paragraph, help her construct an oral sentence, as is done in Reading Recovery (see pages 533–534). So that the tracing portion of the approach will reinforce the pattern being taught in word building, encourage the student to dictate a sentence using one or more of the pattern words. After studying the *et* pattern, a student might dictate a sentence similar to the following: "I took my pet to the vet."

After the student has dictated the sentence, dictate it back to him and have him write it just as in the VAKT approach. Words with which the student has difficulty should be traced. At the conclusion of the session, copy the sentence onto a strip of tagboard, as in Reading Recovery. It can then be cut up and taken home to be read for practice. The segmented sentence should be reassembled and read the next day.

Classical VAKT is designed to help students learn a basic store of words that they can read immediately. Phonics skills also need to be taught. The adapted version of VAKT recommended for use with word building is designed to reinforce patterns being taught. The reason sentences are written, rather than whole stories, as in VAKT, is to simplify the approach and make it easier to use and less time-consuming. However, if possible, VAKT should be used as described earlier in the chapter.

The following box shows how a sample lesson using adapted word building might be taught.

## ▧ **A Total Program**

The special word-learning techniques discussed in this chapter are just one part of a total program for low-achieving readers. Writing and wide reading and content-area learning should also be a part of the low-achieving reader's program.

## Sample Adapted Word-Building Lesson

**Step 1:** *Presentation of pattern*. Present pattern according to detailed lessons in Chapter 8.

**Step 2:** *Creation of pattern sentence*. Have student create a sentence using one or more pattern words and dictate that sentence to you.

**Step 3:** *Writing of sentence by student*. Dictate the sentence to the student and have the student write it. Have the student trace any words that are difficult.

**Step 4:** *Tracing of words (Stage 1)*. The student says the whole word, traces and says each syllable, and then says the whole word. The student continues tracing the word until he feels he can write it from memory.

**Step 5:** *Writing the word from memory*. Turning the tracing copy over, the student says the whole word, says each syllable as he writes each syllable, on a strip of 4-inch × 12-inch paper placed vertically,

and then says the whole word. The student checks the spelling of the word, covers the word that he has just written, and writes the word a second time and once again checks it for accuracy. The correctly written words are dated, stapled to the tracing copy, and filed alphabetically.

**Step 6:** *Writing the word in the sentence*. The student writes the new word in the sentence and reads it. As in VAKT, keep a record of demonstrations and tracings and words learned each time. The sentence can be written on tagboard and cut up for practice reading at home.

**Step 7:** *Application of word patterns*. Word patterns taught should be applied. A list of easy trade books that can be used for the application phase are presented in Figure 8.8 on pages 259–261. Crossword puzzles, riddles, jokes, signs, and ads can also be used to reinforce the pattern.

An integrated program that builds on students' strengths is best. Because students are probably well aware of their difficulties with reading and writing, attempts should be made to recognize and foster abilities that they have in athletics, the arts, or other areas. Although specialized word-learning techniques require one-on-one instruction, low-achieving readers can be part of a group or the whole class for other learning activities.

## Programs for Older Problem Readers

In general, the principles and procedures for teaching older problem readers are the same as those for teaching younger struggling readers. However, it is doubly important that instruction be tied to the learner's goals. Find out from students why they wish to improve in reading and writing. For older students in school, it might be the desire to pass or to graduate. Or they may want to learn how to read the manual that prepares them for the state driver's license test. Students might bring to class the actual materials that they want to read: a newspaper article, a letter from a friend, a form for school or work, or a text from a content-area class. And you might help them with any literacy tasks that they wish to master: filling out a job application or writing a thank-you note.

Because older problem readers have probably been given an overdose of skill-and-drill material, start with an approach that is holistic and use materials that reflect real life: signs, labels, menus, newspapers, magazines, novels, or stories on the appropriate level. However, if they have not mastered basic decoding skills, they will still need a systematic approach with lots of reinforcement, but skill instruction will need to present exercises and materials that

If older students are on a beginning reading level, you might build a high-frequency reading vocabulary or initial decoding skills by using easy functional-level materials, such as signs or food labels (Roswell & Chall, 1994).

are interesting and mature. Do not use children's picture books, easy readers from a basal series, or other materials that will be demeaning to students. There are lots of materials on the second-grade level and up. However, there are few materials written below the second-grade level that would be suitable for older learners.

If you are working with older beginning readers, you might want to try a language-experience approach. Since language-experience stories are based on the reader's experiences, they match her maturity level and should also be of interest to her. Topics chosen should reflect the needs and interests of the learner. They can be autobiographical or be related to a hobby, the learner's work, or an interest the learner wishes to explore. You might also use programs specifically designed for older struggling readers (see Table 14.1).

A program for older struggling readers should include the following elements:

- **Systematic instruction in learning strategies.** This might be provided by the English or language arts teacher or a reading or other specialist. The English or language arts teacher can provide instruction in summarizing, note taking, outlining, SQ3R, and other skills and strategies, but these should not be taught in isolation. They should be taught in context and in such a way that students learn how to apply them in the other content areas.

- **Embedded instruction in learning strategies in all content areas.** Coordinating with the language arts teacher, the reading coach, and other specialists, content-area teachers foster the skills and strategies their students need to learn content and are encouraged to read and write like historians, scientists, mathematicians, and other subject-area experts. In programs in which content teachers taught students to use text structures and strategies to foster comprehension of content text, the students' ability to understand and use text structures and strategies improved as did their grasp of content (Meyer & Ray, 2011).

- **Strategic tutoring.** Students who are reading significantly below grade level—those who are still struggling with decoding skills and fluency, for instance—need systematic intervention. Students who have mastered basic decoding skills but are still struggling should also receive special help. Tutoring is said to be strategic because, in addition to learning content, students learn how to learn (Biancarosa & Snow, 2006). As part of strategic tutoring, students complete content-area assignments while acquiring key reading, studying, and writing strategies.

## California's Expository Reading and Writing Course

Used in underperforming high schools, the Expository Reading and Writing Course (ERWC) contains reading and writing activities whose purpose is to provide students in grades 9 through 12 the expository reading and writing skills they need to be successful in college. Although the course predates Common Core Standards, the activities reflect the intent of CCSS and mirror many of the CCSS standards. In addition to providing suggested reading and writing activities, the course features a template that guides teachers through the planning of lessons designed to bolster expository reading and writing skills (California State University Expository Reading and Writing Task Force, 2008). Results of ERWC have been encouraging. Instruction at ERWC schools showed significant improvement. ERWC students had also higher scores on high-stakes tests. More importantly, more ERWC students attended college, and more of them were still in college after one year. Fewer ERWC students required remedial courses in college (Fong, Huebner, Fong, & Calisi, 2012).

**EXEMPLARY TEACHING**

### Working with Struggling Readers on the Secondary Level

Working with struggling readers on the secondary level, reading specialist Cynthia Fischer emphasizes affective as well as cognitive factors (Fischer, 1999–2000). After assessing below-level readers and noting the literacy process they use, she confers with them. They must show at least a minimum of motivation and commit to a five-day-a-week program. Because she complements her instruction with volunteer tutors, much of the instruction is one-on-one. Since students vary widely at the secondary level, instruction is tailored to their needs. In addition, the individual attention boosts their self-esteem.

The program includes instruction in key strategies at the students' reading level. Content-area texts are used so that students can see an immediate payoff for their efforts. Since wide reading is a key element in any reading improvement program, students spend substantial amounts of time reading self-selected materials. Although Fischer has a library of materials for students, she keeps some money aside so she is able to acquire additional books or periodicals when there is nothing suitable

for a particular student. For homework, students are required to read portions of a book of their choosing and keep a running account in their notebook of plot and character development or main ideas.

In addition to content-area and self-selected reading, students read to kindergarten children once a week. During the week they practice with the book they plan to read aloud. Again, this provides valuable reading practice and also builds the struggling readers' self-concept.

Since the tutors help out only two days a week, Fischer works with groups of three or four students three days a week. During this time she introduces strategies that all need, conducts book shares, or provides writing opportunities. Students' writing is published in a newsletter. The newsletter also features such items as accounts of students reading to kindergarten children and suggestions for outside reading. The newsletter motivates students to write and also affirms their efforts.

Students gain an average of 2.2 years during the school year. And they also stay in school. Only about 1 percent of the students who take part in the program drop out.

---

Key elements in ERWC include composing essential questions, curriculum mapping, focusing on the products that students would produce as a result of instruction, use of common formative assessments, breaking down key tasks into teachable segments, and collaboration. In some situations teachers adopted the yearlong course. In other situations, teachers used ideas or units from ERWC. ERWC is now being revised so as to be more closely aligned with CCSS (WestEd, 2012).

## Working with English Language Learners

Currently, there are almost 5 million elementary and secondary school students (10 percent) who are English language learners (ELLs). These are students "who are being served in appropriate programs of language assistance" (Aud et al., 2012). Some of these students come to school speaking no English at all. Others have varying degrees of English proficiency. The largest segment of these students speak Spanish as their home language. As a group, Latino students read significantly below average and have a higher dropout rate, although the dropout rate has declined lately (Aud et al., 2012).

The techniques recommended throughout this text should be effective when working with English language learners. However, special provision must be made for language and cultural variations. A program for English learners should emphasize the building of English language skills, especially academic language (see pages 358–362). If at all possible, initial reading instruction should be in the student's native language. Students who are literate in their native language can transfer these skills to reading English once they learn English. A firm foundation in their native language enables students to learn a second language more readily. Learning to read builds on students' vocabulary, ability to manipulate language, and awareness of environmental print. In addition, students use their knowledge of language to help them decode difficult words and to self-correct. Students with limited command of English lack these resources for learning to read in English. As the Committee on Preventing Reading Difficulties in Young Children concluded:

> It is clear that initial reading instruction in the first language does no harm, and it seems likely from research findings and from theories about literacy development that initial reading instruction in the second language can have negative consequences for immediate and long-term achievement. The conclusion leads us to urge initial literacy instruction in a child's native language whenever possible and to suggest that literacy instruction should not be introduced in any language before some reasonable level of oral proficiency in that language has been obtained. (Snow et al., 1998, p. 238)

As students acquire English, they first learn everyday conversational skills. Conversational English is contextualized and supported by such nonverbal aids as gestures, pointing to objects as you talk about them, and pantomiming. On average, it takes about two years for ELLs to become relatively proficient in everyday English. However, being decontextualized and more abstract, the language of school, in which procedures and concepts are explained, may take five or more years to acquire (Cummins, 1994).

When teaching English learners, make sure that they understand the language of instruction. Depending on the level and topic being covered, carefully explain such terms as *sounds, letters, beginning, ending, consonant, vowel, title, author, illustrations, setting, characters, main idea, conclusion, summarize, planning, revising,* and *editing,* and use them consistently. Interchanging the terms *artist* and *illustrator,* for instance, could be confusing. Avoid figurative language and idioms: *beat around the bush, has a big heart, turn over a new leaf* (Gersten & Jiménez, 1994). Use demonstrations, illustrations, and real objects whenever possible. When introducing the correspondence $b = $ /b/, for instance, show a button, ball, and bag or pictures of these objects as you talk about words that begin with /b/.

When working with ELLs, stress content rather than form. When acquiring a language, content is learned first and then form. Olivares (1993) suggests:

> When asking students to answer questions or give explanations orally, teachers should attend to what students are saying rather than to how they are saying it. Interrupting the message to correct a language error will discourage students from participating and remove the focus from how well they are mastering the content. (p. 44)

Also provide prompts that encourage students to clarify or expand responses. Make comments such as "That's interesting. I'd like to hear more about that. Can you explain that? Can you tell us more? So what happened next?"

## Special Comprehension Strategies for English Language Learners

For ELLs, reading and comprehending in English is more difficult. Fortunately, successful ELLs do use a repertoire of strategies to aid them.

One of the major obstacles is vocabulary. If students have recently learned to speak English, chances are that they will encounter a greater number of unknown words than will their same-age English-speaking counterparts. One strategy that students can use is to seek out cognates. A Spanish-speaking student who does not recognize the word *carnivorous* searches her vocabulary and notes that it is similar to the Spanish word *carnivoro* (Jiménez, García, & Pearson 1995). Another strength that ELLs may possess is that they are more metacognitively aware. Learning a second language has provided them with greater insights into language on an abstract level. They also use their native language as a source of help by activating prior knowledge in both languages and by translating when encountering a difficult passage, especially when they are in the early stages of learning English. Transferring prior knowledge, translating passages into their native language, and reflecting on text in their native or stronger language has the potential for improving comprehension (Jiménez, 1997).

Even though English language learners may have a rich background of knowledge, the background may not match the background required for the reading of a particular selection. For instance, they may come from a culture where parents, teachers, and other authority figures are treated more formally, and so they may have difficulty comprehending a selection such as *Help I'm Trapped in My Teacher's Body* (Strasser, 1993), in which student–teacher relationships are more casual.

## Selecting Materials

Just as when selecting texts for native speakers of English, choose books and other materials that are on the English language learners' reading and interest levels. However, also seek books that have illustrations that support the text and that use straightforward, predictable language.

Carefully chosen materials can foster language development. For instance, books with repetitive patterns such as *Brown Bear, Brown Bear, What Do You See?* (Martin, 1983) can provide practice with two basic sentence patterns: the question and the statement. English language learners can model a discussion or a piece of writing on the patterns found in *Brown Bear.*

> **▶ Using Technology**
> The Official Gary Soto Web site
> http://www.garysoto.com/
> Lists a number of books written in English but which contain Spanish expressions.

However, be sure to seek out materials that are culturally relevant. Books that contain expressions in the students' native language are especially desirable. ELLs find the use of their native language reassuring, even if only occasional use (Jiménez, 1997). A number of books are written primarily in English but include some Spanish expressions.

Some English language learners have essential concepts that they are unable to express in English because they lack the English words that label these concepts. For instance, on the beginning reading level, counting books and books that name colors may help ELLs learn the names of numbers or colors in English. There are also concept books that provide the names of farm animals (*Big Red Barn*, Brown, 1989), farm implements (*Tractor*, Brown, 1995), vegetables (*Growing Vegetable Soup*, Ehlert, 1987), tools (*Tools*, Morris, 1992a), and many other items.

Reading real-world materials, such as signs, menus, advertisements, announcements, phone books, and job applications, should be an integral part of the program. The youngest students need to know how to decipher common signs such as *in, out, open, up, down, closed, men, women, exit, emergency exit, office, nurse.* Older students need to know how to read and fill out job applications.

> **✳ If students can read in another language, they should be urged to continue reading materials in that language. This builds background.**

## Adapting Instruction

Krashen (1996) advocates comprehensible input for developing English. This includes learning language in classes, in informal conversations, through voluntary reading, and through sheltered English. Krashen (1996) also recommends voluntary reading of easy books to build vocabulary and the ability to handle complex grammatical constructions. Cho and Krashen (1994) cite the case of Karen, an adult ELL who, as a result of reading an easy series of books, gained five years in reading ability, going from a second- to a seventh-grade level.

Learning to read in a second language, of course, makes greater demands on a student. In addition to learning decoding and comprehension skills and strategies, the student must also deal with unfamiliar words and sentence structures (Chamot & O'Malley, 1994).

Before presenting a selection, you may want to analyze the text for sources of possible difficulty and confusion. Some possible problem areas include the following:

- **Syntax.** Does the selection contain sentence structures such as passives or contractions with which the student might have difficulty?

- **Semantics.** Does the selection use terms, figures of speech, or idiomatic expressions that might pose problems for English language learners?

- **Culture.** Are there cultural items, such as might appear in a story about foods or sports, that might be unfamiliar to ELLs?

To foster both reading and oral-language skills, allow lots of time to discuss stories. Also establish an accepting atmosphere and use prompts. Students may have ideas that they wish to contribute but may have difficulty formulating them. Also paraphrase responses and encourage students to expand on them (Gersten & Jiménez, 1994). For instance, if a student answers "Because he was afraid" to the question "Why did the little boy hide?" you might rephrase that as "Yes, the little boy hid because he was afraid." To expand the response, you might ask such questions as "Where did the little boy hide? What was he afraid of? What are some things that make you afraid?"

Sometimes teachers misinterpret students' lack of fluency in English as reflecting a low level of knowledge or ability. It is important that literacy programs for ELLs foster higher-order cognitive processes, lead to higher levels of student involvement, and enable students to engage in extended discourse (Gersten & Jiménez, 1994).

Although many formal tests are available for assessing students' language proficiency, observing students as they converse with friends and respond to discussions in class will provide some sense of their grasp of language. However, it is important that you observe them in several situations. Students might talk more freely in informal situations but might be more inclined to use academic language when responding in class. The listening capacity test of an informal reading inventory can be used as a rough gauge of students' ability to understand language. The highest level at which students can answer 75 percent of the questions is the approximate level at which they can understand English and the level at which they should be able to read with understanding if they have adequate decoding skills (Crawford, 1982).

## ▦ Mini–Case Study

When 14-year-old John was accepted for instruction at the Fernald School (a special school for students with severe reading problems) of the University of California at Los Angeles, he was described as being "defeated, troubled, and angry" (Berres & Eyer, 1970). A behavior problem since kindergarten, John howled like a wolf and rolled on the floor when asked to sit in the back of the room because of his distracting behavior.

Despite having average intelligence, John was reading on a first-grade level. Not surprisingly, he avoided academic tasks, and when the teacher offered him a book, he "broke out into a cold sweat" (p. 34).

The first order of business was to deal with John's perception of himself. John had to learn to see himself as a capable student and act like a learner. Because John was hyperactive, he was given tasks of brief duration, was allowed to choose activities, and was encouraged to run around the school track or spar with a punching bag whenever his excess energy seemed too much to handle.

Instruction capitalized on John's main interest: He wanted to be a plumber and often helped his father, who was a plumber. Plumbing supply catalogs, invoices, and sales slips were used to foster John's literacy skills.

Because of John's severe word-learning difficulty, the Fernald (VAKT) tracing technique was used with him. This was tied into his interest in plumbing. The first word that John learned was *tools*. He planned to use the word to fill out an order blank.

Because of the novelty of the Fernald technique and because it was helping John learn words that he wanted to write, he responded favorably to the approach. John remained in Stage 1 for seven months. During that period, he built up enough reading vocabulary that he was able to begin reading easy books. John enjoyed high-interest, low-readability books because they didn't seem "babyish."

In John's second year, he expressed a desire to read Edgar Allan Poe's tales of horror. Given extra help by the teacher, John did surprisingly well with a collection of Poe's stories. As John experienced success, his inappropriate behavior faded away. After three years at the Fernald School, John was reading at an eighth-grade level. He had gained the literacy skills and confidence he needed to attend high school.

## Summary

Following the lead of Reading Recovery, a variety of early intervention programs have been created and met with encouraging success. About 1 student in 100 has a serious word-learning problem and may need to be taught through specialized word-learning techniques. Two of the best known and most widely used word learning techniques are VAKT (Fernald) and Orton–Gillingham.

VAKT, which is based on the Fernald tracing technique, advocates using visual, auditory, kinesthetic, and tactile senses to learn words. Using these four senses may forge connections that will help the student remember new words. VAKT also fosters fuller attention and concentration and builds confidence. Classical VAKT can be adapted to strengthen phonological processing and to make it easier to implement.

The Orton–Gillingham approach is a highly structured, intensive phonics method that makes use of a form of tracing in which students name the letters as they write words. A number of programs are based on the Orton–Gillingham approach. Some involve having students say the individual sounds of words as they trace the words.

Specialized word-learning techniques should be presented within the context of a total program. Wide reading of appropriate-level texts and writing are highly recommended. Word building, adapted if necessary, can also be used with students who have serious word-learning problems.

With their history of failure, older poor readers and writers may feel too discouraged to try. Help them see that they are competent learners. Build on their strengths and construct a program that addresses their needs but uses appropriate materials and ties in with their personal goals.

Problem readers and writers who are English language learners face the double burden of acquiring a second language and overcoming their literacy difficulties. If possible, they should be taught to read and write in their native language. Acquisition of reading and writing in English is far easier if the students can read and write in their own language. Oral language and reading and writing skills are best acquired in the context of learning content. The language-experience approach and cooperative learning are especially appropriate for students who are still acquiring English.

## Application Activities

1. Read Fernald's (1943) classic text *Remedial Techniques in Basic School Subjects,* or the annotated version published by Pro-Ed (Idol, 1988). What kinds of suggestions did Fernald make that are still valid today?
2. If possible, observe the use of Fernald (VAKT), the Orton–Gillingham approach, or a program based on the Orton–Gillingham approach. How did the student respond to the program? What are the strengths of the program? What might be its weaknesses?
3. With a partner, try the tracing component of VAKT. Follow the steps exactly, and make sure you have the proper materials: a dictionary, stapler, large black crayon, and slips of 4-inch × 12-inch paper.
4. Try out word building in its adapted form, if necessary, with a student who has a serious word-learning problem. How does the student respond to the technique? What are the strengths and weaknesses of the program?
5. Refer to the National Center for Intensive Intervention (http://www .centeroninstruction.org) for the latest information on interventions for disabled readers.

## My Education Lab

Go to the topic **Reading Assessment** in the MyEducationLab (www.myeducationlab .com) for **Assessing and Correcting Reading Difficulties,** where you can:

- Find learning outcomes for **Reading Assessment** along with the national standards that connect to these outcomes.

- Complete Assignments and Activities that can help you more deeply understand the chapter content.

- Apply and practice your understanding of the core teaching skills identified in the chapter with the Building Teaching Skills and Dispositions learning units.

- Examine challenging situations and cases presented in the Iris Center Resources.

- Check your comprehension of the content covered in the chapter with the Study Plan. Here you will be able to take a chapter pretest, receive feedback on your answers, and then access personalized Review, Practice, and Enrichment exercises to enhance your understanding of chapter content. After you complete the exercises, take a posttest to confirm your comprehension.

- Practice targeting instruction and making content accessible for all students with A+RISE activities.

# 15 Organization of Intervention and Corrective Programs

**USING WHAT YOU KNOW**

**I**ntervention and corrective instruction are changing. They are moving away from an isolated skills emphasis in a resource room and becoming more balanced and collaborative. With the implementation of response to intervention (RTI), there is greater coordination between intervention specialists and classroom teachers, and increasingly, intervention and corrective instruction are taking place in the classroom.

With what corrective reading and writing programs are you familiar? What are the components of the program? How effective is the program? What do you think should be the components of an exemplary corrective program?

**ANTICIPATION GUIDE**

*Read each of the following statements. Put a check under "Agree" or "Disagree" to show how you feel about each one. If possible, discuss your responses with classmates.*

|  | AGREE | DISAGREE |
|---|---|---|
| 1. Intervention has been proven effective. | _____ | _____ |
| 2. Except for the most severe cases, classroom teachers should have major responsibility for the instruction of their pupils. | _____ | _____ |
| 3. Small-group intervention/corrective instruction is more practical than one-on-one teaching. | _____ | _____ |
| 4. Students in the earliest grades should be given the highest priority for intervention/corrective instruction. | _____ | _____ |
| 5. The intervention program should build on the classroom program. | _____ | _____ |

## ▦ The Changing Face of Intervention

✿ Allington (1994) stresses the need for enhancement of classroom instruction. "The primary role of special program funds and personnel would be to enhance the quality of classroom literacy instruction available to children finding learning to read and write difficult" (p. 25).

There is a growing realization that meeting the current goal of preparing every student to be college- and career-ready and implementing RTI will take an all-out effort by the school, parents, and the community at large. Preparing every student to be college- and career-ready means that struggling readers will need special attention and that there needs to be more focus on higher-level skills. RTI is an especially promising approach for providing struggling readers with the help they need. RTI is both a do-whatever-it-takes and we-are-all-in-this-together approach to helping all students reach their fullest potential. If properly implemented, the two initiatives are complementary.

### Setting Up a Literacy Committee

The first step in bringing everyone together is to set up a literacy committee. The committee's first order of business is to adopt a research-based core program, if one does not already exist, and to make it as effective as possible so fewer students will need extra help. The committee also undertakes the following:

- Constructing a mission statement and goals for the core and intervention/corrective program
- Setting criteria for selecting students who need additional help
- Constructing a curriculum for low-achieving readers
- Selecting approaches and techniques to be used
- Selecting materials
- Constructing a parent involvement component
- Setting procedures for reviewing progress and revising the program
- Establishing criteria for discontinuing students
- Coordinating the efforts of all professionals
- Planning appropriate professional development

The program needs to be both comprehensive and coordinated, and it should reflect an overall commitment to fostering literacy for all students. As appropriate, the strategies taught in language arts or reading classes should be applied in content-area classes, and a common terminology should be adopted. Providing multiple opportunities for students to apply skills is the most effective way to develop their literacy skills to the fullest.

### Grade-Level/Team Meetings

One way to foster ongoing assessment and improvement is to hold grade-level meetings once a week or once every two weeks. At these meetings, the focus should be on student achievement. For teachers, grade-level meetings provide an excellent opportunity to discuss underachieving students and to elicit suggestions from peers for assisting them. Inviting the literacy and learning disabilities teacher and other specialists to attend not only provides expert advice but also fosters collaboration. So-called vertical meetings, in which teachers from different grade levels confer, are also useful, since they help teachers understand the skills that students arrive with and the skills they will need to advance to the next grade. At the upper grade levels, it is especially important for teachers from different content areas to meet and coordinate their efforts.

*Study Groups*  Areas of need and promising practices can be explored by study groups of teachers. Study groups might meet once a month or more often. In these groups, participants choose a topic to investigate, such as improving comprehension or developing vocabulary, and then seek information through reading professional books and journals, attending conferences, or inviting experts to provide presentations. Effective study groups develop an action plan, so they can implement the techniques or procedures they have been studying.

*Review Conferences*   In a review conference, classroom teachers meet with the principal and specialists to review students' progress. The group examines formal test data, progress-monitoring results, and informal assessment data; it might also look at students' portfolios. Suggestions are made for how to help students who aren't making adequate progress and also for how to improve the classroom program.

## Collaboration

> **Collaboration** entails having classroom teachers and resource personnel work together. Collaboration may be between teachers and specialists, and also between specialists from different disciplines. Increasingly, specialists are functioning as coaches to help classroom teachers improve their programs so that literacy problems will be prevented or ameliorated in the classroom.

Collaboration is the key to providing the best possible program for low-achieving readers and writers. In a **collaboration**, the reading specialist works with the student's classroom teacher(s), other specialists and administrators, the parents, and the student to plan, implement, and monitor a program. The classroom teacher should be involved in every phase of the program, from assessment through instruction. During assessment, it is essential to obtain information about the student from the classroom teacher. He can shed light on the student's work habits, ability to get along with others, and strengths and weaknesses in a variety of academic areas, not just reading and writing. Specialists and the classroom teacher working together should decide on the best program for the student.

It is also essential that specialists collaborate. The reading specialist might have some helpful suggestions for a student identified as having a learning disability due to difficulty with reading. The learning disabilities specialist might have helpful suggestions for ways the reading specialist might work with students who need more structure to be successful.

## A Coordinated Program

If students are placed in an intervention program, that program should be coordinated with the classroom program. The intervention teacher may use intensive phonics, VAKT (Fernald; see Chapter 14), or some other specialized technique. Through discussions and careful planning, the specialist and classroom teacher can create programs that are mutually supportive.

For instance, the classroom teacher may schedule extra reading of books that contain short vowels, because short vowels is the topic being taught in the intervention program. Conversely, if the classroom teacher is presenting short vowels, the intervention teacher may provide complementary instruction, perhaps through word building. Both should agree, too, on which strategies the student will use to attack new words and in what order these strategies should be applied: pronounceable word part, analogy, and context, for instance. The teachers may decide to have

**EXEMPLARY TEACHING**

### Collaboration and Coordination

Programs for struggling readers are most effective when they are coordinated with the classroom program. Although pleased with the progress of the majority of her students, first-grade teacher Dodie McGill always felt a bit frustrated at the end of each school year. There were always a handful of students who still had not made what she felt was adequate progress. When she noticed the gains made by students in Reading Recovery, which had just been implemented in her school, Partee Elementary School in Gwinnett County, Georgia, she and the other first-grade teachers began to discuss with the Reading Recovery teachers how instruction might be improved for all students.

Adopting the name Reading Express, the group created a collaborative structure that would benefit all students. For one hour each day, the Reading Recovery teacher met with a whole first-grade class. During that time the Reading Recovery teacher taught and modeled key strategies. That way both teachers and students learned the strategies. The teacher also demonstrated a book introduction, guided reading, and how to take and use running records. Classroom teachers were able to adapt successful Reading Recovery techniques and use them in their classrooms.

As a result of the collaboration, first-grade teachers achieved a better understanding of their students' literacy development and were able to improve the quality and effectiveness of their program. Because first-grade teachers were now using, in adapted form, many of the techniques used in Reading Recovery, there was a greater continuity between the Reading Recovery and the classroom program. As a result, students were better able to extend the gains they made in Reading Recovery. And students who were not chosen for Reading Recovery but were still a bit behind had the benefit of more effective instruction and better materials. As a result, the first-graders' reading achievement rose dramatically (Kinnucan-Welsch, Magill, & Dean, 1999).

---

the student seek pronounceable word parts and reconstruct the word by building on them or to use an analogy strategy.

To foster coordination, the classroom and intervention teachers might share a notebook that the student carries back and forth and in which they briefly jot down what each worked on during the instructional session. Regularly scheduled meetings to discuss the student's progress should also be held.

### Leadership

An effective literacy program requires leadership. Support from the administration is essential. The principal not only provides encouragement and needed resources but also coordinates the efforts of the staff. The program also needs expert day-to-day guidance. In helping staff work with low-achieving readers and writers, the literacy and other learning specialists can provide assistance through modeling techniques and approaches, coaching, taking part in grade-level and other meetings, and helping staff interpret assessment data and plan instruction based on it.

## ▦ Components of an Intervention Program

Although the intervention program should be an integral part of the regular academic program, it should also have certain key elements. These elements are explored in the following sections.

## Goals and Objectives

**Goal:** general statement of what students are expected to learn.

**Objective:** specific statement of what students are expected to learn. Instructional objectives should be stated in terms that students can understand. One source of goals and objectives is the Common Core State Standards Web site at http://www.corestandards.org.

A clear statement of **goals** is the first step in creating an effective program. A statement of philosophy is also helpful. From the statement of general goals should flow specific objectives. Successful programs have overall goals and specific **objectives**, and concrete ways of determining whether both have been met.

As a practical matter, the goals of an intervention program are often tied, at least in part, to the state's or local school district's standards, which may be tied to Common Core State Standards This is especially true if the attainment of these standards is assessed by high-stakes tests.

## Selecting Students

Because of the fallibility of tests and other assessment instruments, it is wise to use more than one selection device.

A major practical concern of intervention programs is selecting pupils who need special help and scheduling instruction. In the past, students falling below a certain cutoff point—the 20 percentile of a standardized reading test, for example—were chosen for Title I programs. Reading Recovery and a number of other early intervention programs simply select the lowest-achieving students. This might be the lowest-achieving 20 percent or the neediest three students in a class. Screening tests are now being used in many systems as part of the selection process.

In a sense, the best criterion might be failure to reach a certain benchmark or cutoff score that is associated with future success in reading. For instance, one study found that beginning first graders who could not supply at least 19 letter sounds in one minute's time did poorly in reading in first grade (Fuchs & Fuchs, n.d.). In the author's experience, beginning first graders who were unable to read at least five words on the Phonics Inventory experienced difficulty. For older students, benchmarks might be based on oral-reading fluency, performance on benchmark books, or scores on maze or modified cloze tests. To prevent false positives, use of cutoff scores should be accompanied by other indicators. For instance, students might be chosen for intervention on the basis of failure to meet the cutoff score and subsequent failure to respond to extra help given by the classroom teacher.

In some instances, laws and regulations govern the selection process. For identification of a learning disability, federal legislation permits but does not require an ability–achievement discrepancy but allows for use of a response to intervention approach or another research-based alternative procedure. State departments of education determine the criteria to be used. If RTI is used, it is accompanied by another identification procedure.

### Screening Devices

Universal screening is recommended. Since everyone will be screened, the screening test should be valid and reliable but also easy and quick to administer. For secondary students, screening might take the form of performance on content-area or other suitable tests. It is also recommended that the progress of all students be monitored three times a year, so that students who were doing well at the beginning of the year but have run into difficulty later can be identified. The thrice-a-year monitoring also acts as a check on the classroom and school program. As a general rule, 80 percent of students are expected to do well in the classroom program. If a larger percentage is identified as needing intervention, this could be a sign that the classroom program needs bolstering.

✳ Take care when interpreting measures used with students who have not had an equal opportunity to learn. As McGill-Franzen (1994) notes, the role of prior knowledge or experience on assessment devices is "often grossly underrated" (p. 19).

Numerous assessment devices can be used to select students for a program. The selection devices chosen will depend on the goals of the program, the philosophy of reading, and the corrective or intervention procedures. A program that emphasizes letter–sound relationships will probably include a measure of phonics, for instance. One that emphasizes comprehension might use mazes and/or other assessments of comprehension.

Group tests, whether norm referenced or criterion referenced, might be used as a screening or monitoring device to identify students who may need intervention or a corrective program. Such a test should not be used as the sole selection device, however. Group tests, because of the guessing factor, can provide erroneous information for individuals. Portfolios, observations, and individual tests, together with recommendations by professionals, should also be used in the selection process.

## Curriculum

✳ The intervention strand of the program should be coordinated with the school's language arts curriculum. The program, however, should be based on evidence that it is effective and that it follows evidence-based principles.

The curriculum for an intervention program should reflect the school's philosophy of reading; goals or standards, such as Common Core State Standards; the nature of the program; and the students' needs. The curriculum should also be balanced and mesh with what is being done in the classroom.

Although the specific needs of a student or group should be addressed, the program should not be too narrow. For instance, if a child has difficulty with word identification, there should be an emphasis on word-level skills and strategies. However, these need to be applied within the context of real reading, lest you create a competent decoder who fails to read for meaning or dislikes reading. Too broad a program, on the other hand, might result in one that is unfocused and so is ineffective. The curriculum should also incorporate areas that have a long-term payoff, such as vocabulary, comprehension, and background knowledge, so that students will be college- and career-ready.

The curriculum should also be research based and delivered in the way it was designed to be delivered. There should be a fidelity of instruction. This doesn't mean that the teacher doesn't have input. Rather, it means that key elements are fully implemented.

## Instructional Approaches

The core of an intervention or corrective program is the instructional approach. The program planner has many decisions to make: Will the program use direct instruction? Will it use holistic approaches? Or will it use some type of combination of the two? Will there be an emphasis on application of skills and strategies? Will voluntary reading be fostered? Will specialized word-learning techniques, such as VAKT, be used with students who have severe reading problems? Will process writing be part of the program? Will a highly structured writing approach, such as CSIW, be used?

The instructional activities should fit in with the philosophy and overall goals of the program. Above all, the instructional components should consider the strengths and needs of the students.

## Instructional Schedule

Scheduling students for fewer than two sessions a week is probably not worthwhile. There would be a lack of continuity and too much forgetting because of the lapse of time between sessions. Five sessions a week is ideal but may be impractical if a large number of students need help.

Instruction supplied for the intervention should be provided in addition to that supplied in the classroom. Students also need extensive opportunities to apply and further develop their skills. In addition to engaging in reading and writing in language arts classes, students need to apply their developing skills in their content-area classes (Biancarosa & Snow, 2006). This, of course, requires a coordinated effort in the upper grades, where students have several teachers. Content-area teachers need to make texts accessible to all students and to teach the literacy skills needed to read and write in their areas.

> ✳ The number of sessions will vary depending on the severity of the difficulty. For primary grade students, Torgesen (2004c) recommends an additional 30 to 60 minutes a day of instruction for students who have fallen behind.

For a program to make a difference, a significant amount of time is needed. Based on an analysis of a number of studies, Guthrie, Seifert, and Kline (1978) concluded that a minimum of 50 hours of instruction is required for sustained gains. In the Boulder Project (Hiebert, 1994) and Early Intervention in Reading (Taylor, Strait, & Medo, 1994), two corrective programs for at-risk first graders, many students needed a full year before showing adequate progress, and about one in four needed a second year of extra help.

## Typical Intervention Session

> ✳ Strategies taught through corrective instruction should be those the student can apply in his or her regular classroom.

Time is limited in an intervention class, so it is important for sessions to be well planned and energetic. The typical session lasts from 30 to 50 minutes and might include three to seven students. The greater the needs of the students, the smaller the group should be. A daily session might include review of past material, introduction or extension of a skill or strategy, reading of a new selection, discussion and extension of the selection, and writing, if time allows. There might also be time for reading of a selection by the teacher or an activity chosen by the student.

## Discontinuing Students

> ✳ After students have been discontinued, meet with them periodically to make sure that they are having success and are able to apply strategies they learned.

According to Harris and Sipay (1990), one practice that can negate the effects of an intervention program is setting arbitrary time limits, with the result that students are discontinued from the program too soon. In a study of struggling second graders, Vaughn, Denton, and Fletcher (2010) found that 25 percent made adequate progress in 10 weeks, 25 percent made adequate progress in 20 weeks, and 25 percent made adequate progress in 30 weeks. However, 25 percent failed to make adequate progress after two years of instruction and obviously needed a more specialized, more intensive program. Harris and Sipay (1990) suggest using two criteria to determine if students are ready to be discontinued: (1) Is the student able to meet the reading demands of the regular classroom; and (2) does the student read voluntarily? If the reading demands of the classroom are too great, the student may be overwhelmed unless she is given extra help. If the student does not read on her own, improvement may cease. After students have been discontinued, they should be given follow-up support. Vaughn and colleagues (2010) found that some students who met criteria for success in an RTI program failed to thrive when placed back in the regular classroom.

## Organizational Patterns

How should low-achieving readers be organized for instruction? One-on-one teaching? Small group? Whole class with supplementary instruction? The organizational pattern to be followed depends on the nature of the student's difficulty, the resources available, and the policies and philosophy of the local school district.

### One-on-One and Small-Group Instruction

As can be seen from the dramatic results achieved by Reading Recovery, one-on-one tutoring by expert teachers provides effective instruction. While one-on-one instruction works best for the neediest students, it is not always possible to supply because of resource limitations.

> ✳ The question of how many is too many in an intervention group depends on the severity of the students' difficulties. The greater the needs, the smaller the group should be.

The next best organization pattern is the small group. In a review of the research, Fletcher and colleagues (2007) found that in some instances, groups with a ratio of three students to one teacher did as well as students taught individually. In a review of studies of successful corrective programs, Guthrie, Seifert, and Kline (1978) found that the effective ratio of students to teacher was no higher than four to one. Apparently, as ratios grow higher, the teacher's efforts are stretched too thin. Based on the research, then, three to four seems to be the optimum number for small-group instruction.

## Small-Group versus Whole-Class Instruction

In-the-classroom instruction should be differentiated so that the needs of all students are met. Struggling readers should be given extra help by the classroom teacher. Struggling readers do better when taught in small groups and when they are grouped according to common needs (Foorman & Torgesesen, 2001; Juel & Minden-Cupp, 2000; National Reading Panel, 2000). In small groups, students' needs can be met more easily, they have more opportunities to respond, and the teacher is better able to assess their progress and adjust instruction accordingly.

### Guided Reading

One way of providing small-group instruction is through guided reading. Guided reading is a framework within which the teacher supplies whatever assistance or guidance students need to read successfully (Fountas & Pinnell, 1996). Guided reading is used with individuals or groups who are on approximately the same level of reading development. Selections are provided that match the students' level of development.

> ▶ **Using Technology**
>
> **Success for All Foundation**
>
> http://www.successforall.org/
>
> Provides extensive information about Success for All.

The amount of guidance provided varies depending on the students' abilities and the complexity of the selection to be read. For beginning readers, the guidance might consist of going through the text page by page and discussing the selection and highlighting unfamiliar expressions, unknown concepts, and difficult words. Although designed for all students, guided reading is a way of ensuring that struggling readers are given materials and instruction that are on their level.

### Regrouping

The more groups a teacher has, the less time she or he has to spend with each group. One way of reducing the number of groups is to use a regrouping plan. In this plan, which is used in Success for All, a whole-school reform program that emphasizes scripted lessons, students are redistributed for reading instruction according to their reading levels. One teacher may take the lowest-level readers, another the second-lowest, and so on.

Special education teachers, the reading specialist, and other resource personnel might also work with groups within classrooms. This reduces the overall group size. The reading specialist, special education teachers, and others who have special expertise in reading might be assigned struggling readers with the most serious problems.

## Catching Up

Summer can be an excellent time for struggling readers to catch up. All too often, however, struggling readers, because reading is difficult, don't read over the long summer months and fail to maintain the gains they made during the school year. Summer school programs that are well planned, have small classes and good teachers, provide conscientious evaluation, and encourage parental involvement are especially effective (Cooper, Nye, Kelly, & Greathouse, 1996). Saturday, before-school, and after-school programs are also good times for providing additional instruction. Voluntary reading over the summer months can result in substantial gains. In a program in which teachers provided students with lessons that showed them how to sustain comprehension when reading on their own and in which parents listened to their children discus books that they had read, students gained an average of 2.5 months, with at-risk students gaining 4 to 5 months (White & Kim, 2008).

## Retention

Retention is not an effective tool for closing the achievement gap and, in fact, may contribute to it. Although students who have been retained may do somewhat better, those gains fade after two or three years. Underachieving students who have been promoted do just as well as comparable underachieving students who have been held back. Moreover, students who have been retained are more likely to have social and emotional problems and to drop out of school. In fact, retention is the best predictor of future dropout.

## Need for an Extended Program

Although prevention is preferable to remediation, there is a need for specialized reading and writing instruction throughout all the grades. Moreover, as students pass through the grades and the demands of reading change, different types of reading and writing difficulties may surface. The student who had a word-identification problem that was successfully remediated in grade 1 may evidence a comprehension difficulty in grade 3 or 4, when the comprehension of informational text of a more technical nature is required. In addition, students whose reading and writing abilities were adequate in the elementary grades may encounter difficulties in secondary school. The corrective reading/writing program must be multifaceted so it can meet a variety of demands.

## Pacing

> **Pacing:** rate at which instruction is provided, and the rate at which students are guided through materials. Ironically, students most in need of an accelerated pace are often the ones who are provided with a slower-moving program in which expectations are set low (McGill-Franzen, 1994).

Pacing is crucial in an intervention program. **Pacing** is the rate at which students are introduced to new learning and move through materials. The ideal is to accelerate students' progress so that they can catch up with their classmates and so profit from instruction in the regular program. Having caught up, they should not need corrective services, except perhaps for some follow-up or short-term intervention from time to time. Energized teaching, careful sequencing of tasks, not wasting time on activities that have little or no payoff, and promoting independence so that students can extend their learning all promote accelerated progress. Involving parents and emphasizing out-of-school reading both help, too (Goldenberg, 1994).

Accelerated pacing does not mean pushing children beyond their limits or exerting undue pressure. Students' progress should be monitored to make sure that the pace is appropriate.

## Monitoring

> Struggling readers should be monitored with an IRI, running record, or similar device at least once a month. Some programs recommend weekly monitoring.

A key element in successful programs is the monitoring of progress, and the essential ingredient in monitoring programs is making changes when they are needed. Specialists often have a favorite program, one that fits their philosophy of teaching and that has worked well over the years. From time to time, however, they may encounter a student for whom the program doesn't work yet be tempted to persist because the program has worked so well for so many other students.

Morris (2008) recounts admitting that a program he had used consistently with a high degree of success simply wasn't working with a particular student. Wisely, he sought another program—one that did work. Continuous monitoring is needed to point out when a program or approach isn't working and needs to be changed.

## Involving Parents

Parents need to know the nature of their child's difficulty. It will be helpful if they are told that many bright children have reading difficulties. There should be an ongoing dialogue between the parents and the school to inform parents of the student's progress, enlist the parents' help, and answer questions. If, because of illness, death, divorce, neglect, or some other difficulty, it is not possible to involve parents, then a substitute caregiver or a willing relative should be involved (Comer, 1988).

Working with a disabled reader can be slow and intense and sometimes frustrating. These students may need a great deal of repetition and often show no sign today of knowing today what they seemed to know yesterday. Progress can be painstakingly slow. Lacking training and objectivity, parents may not be well equipped to teach their children. However, they can help in other essential ways. First, they can provide love and support and see to it that the child comes to school well rested, fed, and with all the necessary equipment. They can monitor homework, provide praise for progress, and supply encouragement and keep in contact with the school and carry out routines that the teacher believes would be appropriate for parents to carry out.

Knowing that their youngster, who had a serious word-learning problem, would have difficulty in school, the parents of one reading-disabled youngster played up his strengths. They enrolled him in arts and crafts and sports activities—areas in which he showed ability—so that he could experience success. An easy-to-implement but highly effective technique that parents might use to help their children is paired reading, which is explained in Chapter 8.

## Family Literacy

One special way of working with parents who have problems with reading and writing is by helping them with their own literacy difficulties so they can better help their children. Parents who are not proficient readers and writers may not realize the essential role they play in the literacy development of their children and so may fail to support their children's literacy-learning efforts.

> **Family literacy:** all the types of reading and writing in which a family engages, as well as attempts to foster increased ability in reading and writing within the family.

A **family literacy** program can take many forms. Parents and children may attend sessions held after school or during the summer. They may be given separate programs, or the program might be coordinated in such a way that the parents spend some of the time working directly with their children. In other versions, just the parents attend sessions, but they are taught reading and writing skills, which they pass on to their children. Able to read on a basic level, the parents are then able to read storybooks to their children or help out with homework. In a third version, parents are taught ways to foster their children's reading and writing skills by reading to them, talking with them, or supervising homework. As they learn ways to help their children, their own literacy skills improve.

Parents may need extensive guidance in the use of techniques to help foster their children's literacy development. For instance, while working with parents from diverse cultures, Paratore (1995) found that it was not enough to provide parents with storybooks and demonstrations on how to read to children. The parents needed many opportunities to observe read-aloud sessions as well as opportunities to practice reading aloud and to discuss their read-aloud sessions.

## The Role of Test Preparation

Study after study has shown that when struggling readers are given a well-planned intervention program, their test scores rise. It isn't necessary to institute a program of test practice. In fact, implementing extensive programs of test preparation may actually limit students' progress. Test-prep programs often focus on lower-level skills. However, there are steps that can be taken to make sure that test results reflect the genuine gains that your students have made.

The most effective step is to integrate key content and skills that are tested into your curriculum. In her study of high-performing versus low-performing schools, Langer (2004) found that schools in which teachers incorporated test skills into the curriculum outperformed schools that focused on test preparation. Higher-performing schools used tests to examine their language arts programs. They analyzed the tests so as to note which skills and strategies were being assessed and then revised their programs to include the assessed skills.

It is important that struggling readers be taught in systematic fashion to answer questions that demand higher-level thinking and/or constructed response. Some time, but not an excessive amount, was spent instructing students in test-taking skills and in familiarizing them with the test format (Langer, 2004).

## Professional Development

The most essential element in any program of remediation and assessment is the quality of instruction. Successful programs provide ongoing professional development, including follow-up, active supervision, and feedback. They also have a clearly stated approach and philosophy and a full description of instructional procedures.

When the change in an intervention program is significant, then the inservice should be substantial. Many of the exemplary procedures and programs discussed in this text took months or even years to implement fully. Even relatively minor changes should be given adequate time and attention. An introduction of a new procedure should be accompanied by follow-up sessions, a plan for its gradual implementation, feedback, and coaching (Radencich, Beers, & Schumm, 1993).

## Tutors

While there is no substitute for one-on-one instruction by a highly trained professional, volunteer tutoring can achieve excellent results and may be the best alternative when funds are lacking.

The following factors were felt to be the foundation for effective tutoring (Juel, 1991, 1994a):

- **Caring, supportive attitude.**    Tutors showed that they cared. Many also were able to empathize with their students because they remembered struggling with reading and writing when they were in the primary grades.

- **Teaching the system.**    The tutors showed students how words are deciphered and how comprehension is achieved. They helped them gain insight into the process, or the "tricks of the trade."

- **Breaking down word recognition and spelling into small steps.**    Tutors dealt with individual sounds and letters so the students could see how words were composed.

- **Reinforcement.**   Tutors provide ample verbal and nonverbal praise and affirmation.

Tutoring programs work best when the tutors are trained and provided with ongoing support and professional supervision. The tutors need to know that they are on the right track and that their efforts are paying off. They also need to receive praise and affirmation.

### Peer Tutoring

**Using Technology**

Peer-Assisted Learning Strategies

http://kc.vanderbilt.edu/pals/

Provides information about PALS.

Peer tutoring typically has a double payoff: Both the tutor and tutee learn. Peer tutoring can be set up on an informal basis so that achieving students can help students who are struggling or who lack information on a topic or those having difficulty applying a certain skill. Or you can make use of structured peer-tutoring programs, such as Class Wide Peer Tutoring (CWPT), which has been validated in several scientific studies (Greenwood, Abbott, & Tapia, 2001), and Peer-Assisted Learning Strategies (PALS), which is a version of classwide peer tutoring (PALS, 2004).

## Materials

All too often, low-achieving readers end up with materials that are too difficult for them. The first step in teaching reading to underachieving readers is to match students and books.

The first step in making the match involves finding out what level of material the student is able to read. This can be done by administering an individual or group reading inventory, as was explained in Chapter 4. It is also helpful to obtain information about the reader's background of knowledge in terms of the book about to be read (Chall & Dale, 1995). An easy book on ice hockey could be difficult if the student knows nothing about the sport.

The second step in making the match is finding material on the appropriate level of difficulty and the appropriate level of maturity. This is not an easy task. By and large, most books are written for children of average or above-average reading ability (Gunning, 1998b). Finding appropriate books for older low-achieving readers can be especially challenging. However, if you know what to look for and where to look, the task is manageable.

### Readability: The Other Half of the Match

A three-part approach to estimating the readability of a text is recommended: quantitative measures of text difficulty, qualitative measures of text difficulty, and professional judgment in matching texts to reader and task (National Governors Association Center for Best Practices & Council of Chief State School Officers, 2010b). Quantitative measures consist of the use of formulas. Qualitative measures include leveling systems and checklists. Professional judgment involves considering reader factors in terms of the material to be read and the task to be performed.

Publishers of school materials generally provide reading levels for their texts. Using a formula or subjective leveling scale, they estimate that the material is at a third-, fifth-, or eighth-grade level, which means that the average third, fifth, or eighth grader should be able to read it.

> **Readability:** ease with which a book or other piece of written material can be understood.

Some publishers of children's books also supply **readability** levels. If no readability level is indicated for a book that you wish to use, you might use one of the following sources.

**AR Bookfind.** Readability estimates for more than 100,000 books can be found at AR BookFind (http://www.arbookfind.com). If an ATOS score is not provided for a text that you wish to use, you can obtain an ATOS readability by submitting a text file of the text to ATOS Analyzer.

**Metametrics.** Readabilities for more than 100,000 books and 80 million articles can be found at the Metametrics Lexile Framework site (http://lexile.com). Metametrics, the creators of the Lexile system, also has a Lexile Analyzer that anyone can use free of charge to obtain estimated Lexile levels (www.lexile.com/analyzer).

**Questar.**    Readabilities for more than 36,000 books can be found in an easy-to-use piece of software known as BookLink (Questar; http://www.questarai.com). Questar's Web site supplies readabilities for a wide array of content-area texts.

**Titlewave.**    Titlewave (http://titlewave.com) also provides a number of different readability estimates for many thousands of books.

**Google.**    Readabilities of Web sites are available from Google. Click *More search tools* on the left side of the search results page and then click *Reading Level.* Or using the *Advanced Search,* click on *Reading Level.* Reading Levels are designated as being basic (junior high or lower), intermediate (high school), and advanced. Search results can be narrowed by reading level.

**Coh-Metrix.**    Coh-Metrix's Text Easability Assessor (http://141.225.42.101/cohmetrixgates/Home.aspx?) provides more than simply a readability level. In addition to giving a Flesch-Kincaid readability for passages up to 1,000 words that have been pasted in, it provides information on the cohesion of the text.

- **Narrativity.**    Measures storytelling ability. Texts dealing with unfamiliar topics would have a low narrativity score.
- **Syntactic simplicity.**    Measures sentence length and familiarity of sentence structures.
- **Word Concreteness.**    Measures concreteness of words. Words that are concrete are easier to visualize and understand.
- **Referential cohesion.**    Measures number of words and ideas that overlap across sentences and the entire text and so form connections among parts of text. Gaps in cohesion require that the reader make more inferences and place greater demands on background knowledge.
- **Deep cohesion.**    Measures number of causal, intentional, and temporal connectives. These help the reader to form an understanding of the causal events, processes, and actions in the text. Use of connectives fosters comprehension.

Easability Assessor provides teachers with helpful information for planning instruction. Noting a lack of cohesiveness in text, for instance, teachers could use prompts and other scaffolds to help students see the relationships among key ideas and teach them to use inferencing to relate ideas when connections are implied but not directly stated.

### New Dale–Chall Readability Formula

One of the most carefully validated of the readability formulas is the New Dale–Chall Readability Formula (Chall & Dale, 1995). The New Dale–Chall can be used to estimate the difficulty level of material from grade 1 through grade 16, but it is most valid for materials in the range from grade 3 to grade 12. The New Dale–Chall's estimate of difficulty is based on average sentence length and the number of words not found on the Revised Dale List. The Revised Dale List is a compilation of 3,000 words known by most fourth graders.

### Fry Readability Graph

The Fry graph bases its estimate on two factors: sentence length and number of syllables in a word. Number of syllables in a word is a measure of vocabulary difficulty. In general, the more syllables a word has, the harder it tends to be. The Fry Readability Graph (Fry, 1977b) is presented in Figure 15.1.

### Flesch–Kincaid Readability Estimate

A revision of the Flesch formula that yields grade levels, the Flesch–Kincaid's readability estimate is based on the number of syllables in a word and average sentence length (Kincaid, Fishburne, Rogers, & Chissom, 1975). It also correlates rather closely with the Fry graph (Fusaro, 1988) and is bundled into Microsoft Word.

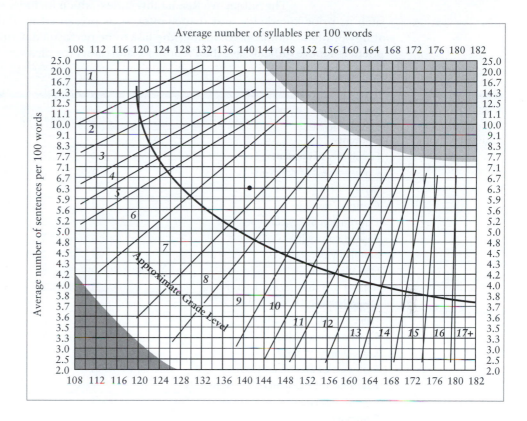

**Directions:** Randomly select three 100-word passages from a book or an article. Plot the average number of syllables and average number of sentences per 100 words on the graph to determine the grade level of the material. Choose more passages per book if great variability is observed and you conclude that the book has uneven readability. Few books will fall in gray area, but when they do, grade-level scores are invalid.

Count proper nouns, numerals, and initializations as words. Count a syllable for each symbol. For example, "1945" is 1 word and 4 syllables and "IRA" is 1 word and 3 syllables.

**Example:**

|  | Syllables | Sentences |
|---|---|---|
| 1st Hundred Words | 124 | 6.6 |
| 2nd Hundred Words | 141 | 5.5 |
| 3rd Hundred Words | 158 | 6.8 |
| Average | 141 | 6.3 |

Readability 7th Grade (see dot plotted on graph)

**FIGURE 15.1**
Fry Readability Graph
*Source:* From Edward Fry, Rutgers University Reading Center, New Brunswick, NJ. 08904. For further information and validity studies, see the *Journal of Reading*, December 1977.

# Subjective Factors

Making a match between the reader and the book requires teacher judgment. The teacher evaluates a text in terms of students' background of knowledge, interests, and purpose for reading.

Most readability formulas measure only difficulty of vocabulary and length of sentences. There are, of course, other factors that should be considered when choosing books for students. For informational texts, these factors include use of graphics, page layout, clarity of writing style, abstractness, and density of concepts. These are factors that do not lend themselves to measurement by a formula.

The Subjective Readability Index, which includes subjective factors such as prior knowledge and reader interest, is presented in Table 15.1. A readability estimate should also consider the task to be performed. Critically analyzing a poem is a more difficult task than reading a short story for pleasure (see Table 15.2).

**TABLE 15.1**
Subjective
Readability Index

| Text Factors | Low | | | | High |
|---|---|---|---|---|---|
| **Content** | | | | | |
| Familiarity of concepts | 1 | 2 | 3 | 4 | 5 |
| Concreteness of concepts | 1 | 2 | 3 | 4 | 5 |
| **Style** | | | | | |
| Clarity of writing | 1 | 2 | 3 | 4 | 5 |
| Elaboration of key concepts | 1 | 2 | 3 | 4 | 5 |
| Ease of vocabulary | 1 | 2 | 3 | 4 | 5 |
| Simplicity of sentences | 1 | 2 | 3 | 4 | 5 |
| Use of anecdotes | 1 | 2 | 3 | 4 | 5 |
| Relates text to students' background | 1 | 2 | 3 | 4 | 5 |
| **Organization** | | | | | |
| Use of heads, subheads | 1 | 2 | 3 | 4 | 5 |
| Focus on major ideas | 1 | 2 | 3 | 4 | 5 |
| Logical flow of ideas | 1 | 2 | 3 | 4 | 5 |
| Exclusion of irrelevant material | 1 | 2 | 3 | 4 | 5 |
| **Features That Enhance Comprehension** | | | | | |
| Chapter overview | 1 | 2 | 3 | 4 | 5 |
| Summary | 1 | 2 | 3 | 4 | 5 |
| Questions | 1 | 2 | 3 | 4 | 5 |
| Graphics | 1 | 2 | 3 | 4 | 5 |
| Phonemic respellings | 1 | 2 | 3 | 4 | 5 |
| Definitions provided in text | 1 | 2 | 3 | 4 | 5 |
| Glossary | 1 | 2 | 3 | 4 | 5 |
| **Total** | | | | | |
| (The higher the total, the easier the text) | ___ | ___ | ___ | ___ | ___ |
| **Reader Factors** | | | | | |
| Background of knowledge | 1 | 2 | 3 | 4 | 5 |
| Vocabulary | 1 | 2 | 3 | 4 | 5 |
| Overall reading ability | 1 | 2 | 3 | 4 | 5 |
| Interest | 1 | 2 | 3 | 4 | 5 |
| Motivation | 1 | 2 | 3 | 4 | 5 |
| Study/work habits | 1 | 2 | 3 | 4 | 5 |
| **Total** | | | | | |
| (The higher the number, the better the reader) | ___ | ___ | ___ | ___ | ___ |

| **TABLE 15.2** Task Difficulty | | Narrative | Expository | Poetry |
|---|---|---|---|---|
| Purpose for Reading | | | | |
| _____ Following directions | | | | |
| _____ Learning a new procedure | | | | |
| _____ Reading for pleasure | | | | |
| _____ Evaluating/analyzing a text | | | | |
| _____ Learning a new concept | | | | |
| Complexity of Questions | | | | |
| _____ Locate and recall | | | | |
| _____ Integrate and interpret | | | | |

_Source:_ Gunning T. (2013), Table 3.16, p. 119.

Assessing both subjective and objective factors should provide you with the optimum information for judging the suitability of a text and enable you to make appropriate matches.

## Holistic Estimate of Readability

⚡ The Qualitative Assessment of Texts (Chall, Bissex, Conard, & Harris-Sharples, 1996) helps you take a look at key elements in a text and plan activities that help students better understand the text.

An alternative to using formulas is to judge the material holistically by comparing it with a series of model passages or a series of benchmark books written on a range of difficulty levels. The rater decides which passage the material is most like. If it is most like the third-grade passage, then it is estimated to be on a third-grade level of difficulty. The most carefully developed of these instruments is the Qualitative Assessment of Texts (Chall et al., 1996).

## Leveling Books

Although traditional formulas provide reasonably accurate estimates of the difficulty levels of most reading materials, they don't work at the beginning levels. Formulas don't consider such factors as the usefulness of illustrations and number of lines per page, which are major determinants of the difficulty level of beginning materials. Formulas do indicate with reasonable accuracy that materials are on a first-grade level. However, first-grade reading encompasses a wide range of material, including counting and color books, which have just one or two easy words per page, as well as books such as the _Frog and Toad_ and _Henry and Mudge_ series, which contain brief chapters and may contain a thousand words or more.

Fountas and Pinnell (2009) have compiled a list of leveled books for students in grades K through 8 and also have a fee-based Web site that lists leveled books. Lists of leveled books can also be found in Gunning (2000a, 2005). Lists of leveled books can also be found on the author's Web site (http://wordbuilding.org). As discussed in Chapter 8, beginning materials should be leveled according to the phonics skill needed to read them. A list of books leveled in that way are presented in Figure 8.8 on pages 259–261.

Readability sources indicate estimated levels in different ways. AR BookFind uses grade equivalents, as do most formulas. However, Lexile readabilities are expressed in Lexile units, and Questar scores are expressed in DRP (Degrees of

**TABLE 15.3**
Comparison of
Readability Levels

| Grade | DRP Score | Lexile | Guided Reading | DRA | Reading Recovery Equivalent |
|---|---|---|---|---|---|
| Caption | | | A–B | A–2 | 1–2 |
| Preprimer 1 | | | C | 3 | 3–4 |
| PP2 | | | D | 4 | 5–6 |
| PP3 | | | E | 6, 8 | 7–8 |
| Primer | | 200–300 | F | 10 | 9–10 |
| 1 | | 300–400 | G–I | 12, 16 | 11–17 |
| 2a | 24–28 | 400–500 | J–K | 18, 20 | 18–20 |
| 2b | 29–33 | 400–500 | L–M | 24, 28 | |
| 3 | 34–42 | 500–700 | N–P | 30, 34, 38 | |
| 4 | 43–49 | 700–800 | Q–S | 40 | |
| 5 | 50–55 | 800–900 | T–V | 50 | |
| 6 | 56–59 | 900–1000 | W–X | 60 | |
| 7 | 60–63 | 1000–1100 | Y | 70 | |
| 8 | 64–66 | 1000–1100 | Z | 80 | |

Reading Power) units. Reading Recovery and Fountas and Pinnell's (2009) version of guided reading use a series of letters to indicate difficulty levels. Table 15.3 provides a comparison of key ways of indicating difficulty levels.

## ▪▪▪ Voluntary Reading

⁜ Even slight increases in time spent reading lead to gains (Anderson, 1996). Students show significant gains when they engage in as little as 10 minutes of free reading a day (Fielding, Wilson, & Anderson, 1986).

⁜ Include in your collection books of jokes, riddles, puns, and songs. Also feature heavily illustrated books and e-books. Reluctant readers can start on these fast reads and move up to more substantive works.

Although this text features dozens of techniques designed to help low-achieving readers and writers move up the literacy ladder, the key to success to any reading improvement program lies in fostering voluntary reading. Unfortunately, low-achieving readers, who start out having difficulty with reading, read less. Because they read less, they fall further behind. In first grade, good readers have been observed reading three times as much as poor readers (Allington, 1983).

Stanovich (1986) calls this the "Matthew effect," and it is essentially the same as the idea of the poor getting poorer and the rich getting richer. "The very children who are reading well and who have good vocabularies will read more, learn more word meanings, and hence read even better" (p. 381). By the middle grades, the difference in the time spent reading between the best and the poorest readers might be tenfold.

No matter how fine a library your school has, it is important that you also have books close at hand. Students are far more likely to borrow books if they are readily available. The classroom library should be as extensive and diverse as you can make it. Because they are inexpensive and have a mature look, paperbacks are recommended, especially for older students. However, also include hardcover books. Include, too, young people's magazines and newspapers. *Sports Illustrated for Kids,* which is written on a fifth-grade level, is highly popular with young people who like sports. Even if the text is a little difficult, they can get help from the photos in this generously illustrated periodical. Be sure to feature *Scholastic Action* (reading level: 3–5, interest level: 6–12) and *News for You* (reading levels for two versions: 2–3 & 4–6, interest level: adult) (New Reader's Press).

# ▨ Technology for the Reading/Writing Program

> In addition to tablets designed for the general populations, tablets such as LeapPad (LeapFrog), Nabi (Nabi), and Archos (Arnova) have been created for younger students.

Technology plays a dual role for low-achieving readers and writers. Through computers, DVDs, electronic tablets and apps, traditional topics can be presented in new and more interesting ways. In addition, with some programs, students are able to obtain help with background information and vocabulary, receive additional instruction, have segments read aloud, or branch into an easier portion.

## Assistive Technology

> **Assistive technology:** use of devices to assist people who have a physical disability or learning problem to perform tasks that would otherwise be difficult or impossible for them.

One of the most promising developments in **assistive technology** is the appearance of voice-activated computers. Using a voice-recognition device, the computer responds to speech, so the student does not have to type in text. Four of the best-known programs are Dragon Naturally Speaking (for PCs) and Dragon Dictate (for Mac), Via Voice (Nuance Communications), and Windows Speech Recognition (free program). (Students would need training in the use of each program.) Commands can also be spoken rather than typed. Each program can be used by students whose ability to spell is very limited and by students who are physically unable to type.

For students who have serious reading problems, reading systems such as the Kurzweil 3000 system, Read and Write Gold (Text Help), and Wynn Wizard (Freedom Scientific) are available. These typically consist of a scanner, optical character recognition (OCR) software, a word-processing program, and a speech synthesizer. The text that the student wishes to read is scanned into the word-processing program. Once scanned in and analyzed by the OCR software, it is read aloud by the computer's voice synthesizer. Anything that can be scanned in can be read. The reader will have to supply the occasional word that the scanner's software is unable to pronounce or that it mispronounces. OCR software continues to increase in both accuracy and ease of use.

Talking word-processing programs, such as Dr. Peet's Talk/Writer (Interest-Driven Learning), Special Writer Coach (Tom Snyder), and Write Out Loud (Don Johnston), are especially helpful for students who have difficulty reading or writing. By hearing their piece read back to them, they will be more likely to note awkward expressions, missing *-ing* and *-ed* endings, and omitted words. Even the best writers read over glaring errors but will probably recognize them if they hear them read aloud. Co-Writer (Don Johnston) helps students construct sentences and make spelling and word choices by predicting what word might come next. It lists the words and will also read them. The student then chooses the word that seems most suitable, or he can reject all the choices.

Programs that read texts to students provide struggling readers access to text that they might not be able to read on their own and also provide practice for building fluency. For instance, Start to Finish Books (Don Johnston) is a series of high-interest books designed for students ages 9 to 17. Books are written on a second- to third-grade level. Students can have the whole book read aloud or can have individual words pronounced.

Additional information about assistive technology and software is available from national, regional, and local sources. One of the best overall sources is Alliance for Technology Access (http://ataccess.org), which provides links to a large number of sites.

## Using e-books

▶ **Using Technology**

University of Oregon

http://ces.uoregon.edu/intersect/default.html

Web site has suggestions for creating and using digital materials; it also has links to many sources of digital books for secondary students.

Because they are in a digital format, e-books have a number of advantages. For one thing, in most instances, they can be read by a screen reader, which is built into most computers, or a talking word-processing program. On a Mac, for instance, Text-to-Speech can be found in System Preferences under Speech. Although the voice may be robotic, this makes e-books accessible to struggling readers. To make them even more accessible, e-books can be linked to a dictionary so that students can readily get help with difficult words. A third advantage is that it may be possible to alter the text. You might be able to add explanatory notes or illustrations or even rewrite difficult portions.

E-books are readily available on the Internet from a number of sources. The International Children's Digital Library (http://en.childrenslibrary.org) features a collection of multicultural e-books in dozens of languages for children ages 3 to 13. Other extensive sources of digital books include Project Gutenberg (http://www.promo.net/pg) and the University of Virginia (http://etext.virginia.edu/subjects/Young-Readers.html), which has a Young Readers collection of public domain texts. Bookshare™ (https://www.bookshare.org) is an online library of digital books for people with print disabilities. Bookshare offers free memberships to U.S. schools. The Awesome Talking Library (http://www.awesomelibrary.org/Awesome_Talking_Library.html) has links to a large number of e-books. E-books are also available from commercial publishers. These may have text-to-speech and highlighting capability so that the words are highlighted as they are spoken. MyON (http://www.thefutureinreading.com/) by Capstone has hundreds of e-books that feature an embedded dictionary, professional recorded audio and highlighting, and optional end-of-book quizzes. Rosen Publishing, Lerner Books, and Raz-Kids.com also offer interactive spoken e-books. Titlewave (http://titlewave.com/) has an extensive listing of e-books and notes whether they have text-to-speech or other features. The highlighting in some texts that are read aloud are not synchronized so that the words being spoken may move at a faster pace than the highlighting or vice versa. In addition, some e-readers lack text-to-speech capability or don't have them for all texts.

## Using the Internet

Because many Internet sites include illustrations and video clips, they can assist poor readers. Even greater assistance is provided by talking web browsers. As noted earlier, many computers and computer programs have a built-in text-to-speech feature. Awesome Talkster (http://www.awesomelibrary.org/Awesome_Talking_Library.html) combines a browser, directory, search engine, and text-to-voice technology. Students can have whole pages read to them, or they can select the text they wish to have spoken. Awesome Library is accessible to all computers. Awesome Talkster is only accessible to PCs. Programs such as Cool Speech (http://www.bytecool.com/voices.htm) offer text-to-speech in several languages.

In addition, there are a number of online programs designed for struggling readers and writers. These range from virtual schools to courses designed for struggling students. See Archambault et al. (2010) for a description of online resources for struggling readers and writers.

### Technology and ELLs

Technology can be especially helpful to English language learners. Using text-to-speech software, ELLs can hear words pronounced and listen to stories. If words are unfamiliar, students can obtain their meanings and pronunciations in an electronic dictionary.

Some text-to-speech programs are multilingual. Students can find the equivalent of an English word in their native tongue. Or the student can use translation software such as Google Translate (http://translate.google.com/) or Yahoo's Babel Fish (http://www.babelfish. com) to have passages translated from English into their native language or from their native language into English.

## Teacher Tools

Technology provides a number of tools for the teacher. For instance, using iBooks Author teachers can create multimedia texts for iPads, iPhones, or iPods. The Read.Write.Think site (http://www.readwritethink.org/materials/crossword) and EDHelper (http://www.edhelper.com), which is a paid site, have a variety of tools for creating puzzles and other teaching resources.

Inspiration (Inspiration Software, Don Johnston), which includes clip art, can be used to make graphic organizers. Teacher Tube (http://teachertube.com) is an online community for sharing instructional videos. Free-Reading (http://www.freereading.org) has a variety of resources: decodable stories, phonics exercises, and materials for phonological awareness, syllabic and morphemic analysis, fluency, vocabulary, and comprehension. Also available is a phonological awareness–phonics intervention program for students reading at an early or beginning level. WatchKnowLearn (http://www.watchknowlearn.org/) is a free online collection of educational videos for students ages 3 to 18 and includes more than 30,000 videos that have been reviewed and recommended by educators and are conveniently organized by category.

## Evaluation

Each student needs to be evaluated in terms of the goals established for him or her. Students may spend years in an intervention program and make little progress. Anytime a student makes limited progress, the situation needs to be examined and changed.

Programs should also undergo periodic evaluation. They need to be evaluated in terms of their overall goals and objectives. If one goal is to increase in-class corrective instruction, then that should be assessed. If another goal is to set up an early intervention program to help the lowest-achieving 20 percent of first graders, then the program should be assessed to see if it is actually reaching and helping those children.

Data gathered for evaluation should be broad based and include a variety of assessment devices. Gathering data is only a part of evaluation. The data should then be used to make a judgment about the effectiveness of the reading program. The question you want to answer is "To what extent were the goals of the program met?" Once a judgment has been made, the next step in the evaluation program is to make necessary changes. If the intervention or corrective program is not reaching enough students or fails to remediate a high proportion of them, then the program needs to be analyzed and revamped.

The components of an effective literacy program are listed in Figure 15.2. Above all else, a successful program for low-achieving readers and writers requires caring, well-trained professionals, the belief that low-achieving readers can learn, and a willingness to build on the unique gifts that each student possesses.

**FIGURE 15.2**
Components of an
Effective Literacy
Program

**GOALS**

Are clearly stated
Based on a statement of philosophy
Translated into specific objectives

**SELECTION OF STUDENTS**

Based on discrepancy between achievement and potential (optional)
Based on failure to achieve a set standard
Based on a variety of selection devices
Based on response to intervention (RTI)

**ORGANIZATION**

Uses one-on-one instruction
Uses small-group instruction
Makes provision for students who need extended instruction
Attempts to implement an inclusion model

**PACING**

Accelerates students' progress
Proceeds at a rate that is challenging but not overwhelming
Promotes out-of-school reading

**SCREENING/MONITORING**

Screens all students
Monitors progress on an ongoing basis
Uses several devices for monitoring
Adjusts program as necessary

**GROUPING**

Uses various grouping patterns
Does not use patterns that stigmatize low-achieving readers
Uses cooperative grouping

**INVOLVING PARENTS**

Explains program to parents
Keeps parents informed of child's progress
Involves parents in supporting the child's efforts

**LEADERSHIP/STRUCTURE**

A designated person or group is responsible for planning,
    supervising and monitoring the program.
The program is part of a coordinated effort that involves all staff.

**PREOFESSIONAL DEVELOPMENT**

Provision is made for ongoing professional development.

Professional development is based on achievement data and tied to students' performance.

Professional development includes grade-level meetings, study groups and coaching.

**VOLUNTEERS**

Parents and other volunteers from the community tutor students or act as aides. Volunteers are instructed, supervised and affirmed.

**EVALUATION**

The program is evaluated in terms of its goals.

Evaluation is broad based and uses many sources of assessment information. Uses several devices for monitoring.

Evaluation is used to improve the program.

## Summary

Since the goal of CCSS is that all students will be prepared to be college-and career-ready, there is a growing effort to help struggling readers at all levels. Key elements in the effort have been to intervene early, to provide added instructional time, and to place greater emphasis on developing the abilities needed to read complex text.

Components of a reading/writing intervention program include goals, student selection, curriculum, instructional approaches, instructional schedule, organizational patterns, pacing, materials, monitoring, grouping, involving parents, leadership, professional development, and evaluation.

Although one-on-one intervention is highly effective, small-group intervention, if carefully planned, can also achieve significant results. Modifications and additional assistance are provided as needed when struggling readers are instructed within the context of the whole class. While short-term intervention succeeds with most students, a small percentage need extensive, long-term assistance. Programs that are properly paced are more successful.

Ongoing monitoring to ensure that appropriate adjustments can be made is an important ingredient of effective programs. Although there are many ways of grouping students, heterogeneous and cooperative grouping foster increased achievement in low-achieving readers and writers. Whole-class instruction, if used, should be supplemented with small-group instruction or reading or writing workshop or some other form of individualization.

Parents should be informed of any difficulties their children are experiencing in acquiring literacy skills. They should also be involved in supporting their children's efforts.

Leadership and professional development are also important components of an effective program. An often untapped source of additional assistance is the volunteer tutor. Tutors should be trained, supervised, and affirmed.

Subjective assessment should be used along with objective formulas to obtain the most valid assessment of the difficulty level of texts. If low-achieving readers do not read voluntarily, they have little chance of making satisfactory progress.

Technology can assist low-achieving readers by providing them with materials that are interesting, instructive, and interactive. Technological tools and adaptive technology can help students compensate for learning difficulties.

Programs should be evaluated in terms of their goals. Evaluations should consider a variety of assessment information and should lead to program improvement.

## Application Activities

1. Observe a successful intervention program in your locality. What are the outstanding features of the program? What provision is made for Tier III students, that is those students who did not do well in the Tier II intervention program?
2. Read "Intervention Programs for 'At Risk' Students" (Tierney & Readence, 2005), which contains information about a number of early intervention programs. What are some similarities among the programs? What are some differences? What do the programs suggest about early intervention?
3. Use the Fry Readability Graph, the Lexile Analyzer, and the ATOS Analyzer to estimate the readability level of a content-area text or a trade book that your class is reading or might read. How does your assessment compare with that supplied by the publisher?
4. Use Coh-Metrix's Text Easability Assessor to analyze a text. How might you use the information yielded to plan lessons that will help struggling readers better comprehend the text?
5. Using one of the resources listed in the chapter, locate five high-interest, low-readability books. What makes them easy? With whom might you use them?

## My Education Lab

Go to the topic **Reading Assessment** in the MyEducationLab (www.myeducationlab .com) for **Assessing and Correcting Reading Difficulties,** where you can:

- Find learning outcomes for **Reading Assessment** along with the national standards that connect to these outcomes.

- Complete Assignments and Activities that can help you more deeply understand the chapter content.

- Apply and practice your understanding of the core teaching skills identified in the chapter with the Building Teaching Skills and Dispositions learning units.

- Examine challenging situations and cases presented in the Iris Center Resources.

- Check your comprehension of the content covered in the chapter with the Study Plan. Here you will be able to take a chapter pretest, receive feedback on your answers, and then access personalized Review, Practice, and Enrichment exercises to enhance your understanding of chapter content. After you complete the exercises, take a posttest to confirm your comprehension.

- Practice targeting instruction and making content accessible for all students with A+RISE activities.

# APPENDIX A

# Informal Assessment Measures

---

**Word-Learning Test**

Name of Student _____     Date _____
Grade _____

WORD-LEARNING TEST

**Directions:** Ask the student to read the following words until she or he misses at least seven of them, or use seven words that the student missed on a word-list or similar test. Write these words on cards and teach them to the student. Follow the instructions following the test.

both _____
few _____
much _____
eight _____
think _____
great _____
year _____
found _____
large _____
sure _____
learn _____
group _____
word _____
come _____
front _____
hold _____
gone _____
talk _____
dark _____
warm _____

## TEACHING PRESENTATION

Present the seven words chosen to be test words. Hold the word so that the student can see it readily. After you say it, have the student say it. Shuffle the word cards and present them in the same way a second time.

## TESTING TRIALS

Present each word and ask the student to read it. If the student gives a correct response, say "Yes, that's correct. The word is _____." If the student gives an incorrect response, say "No, that is not correct. The word is _____." Put the correct responses in a separate pile. Note the correct responses on the Learning Trials Sheet. Do not record incorrect responses. Shuffle all the cards after each trial. Continue presenting testing trials until the student gets all the words correct on two consecutive trials or until the student has had 10 learning trials. If the student has not gotten all seven words within 10 trials, note the number correct. To check long-term retrieval, give a single test trial one hour later and then twenty-four hours later.

## Learning Trials Sheet

Name of Student _____    Date _____

Examiner _____

**LEARNING TRIALS**

| WORD | 1 | 2 | 3 | 4 | 5 | 6 | 7 | 8 | 9 | 10 |
|---|---|---|---|---|---|---|---|---|---|---|
| 1. | | | | | | | | | | |
| 2. | | | | | | | | | | |
| 3. | | | | | | | | | | |
| 4. | | | | | | | | | | |
| 5. | | | | | | | | | | |
| 6. | | | | | | | | | | |
| 7. | | | | | | | | | | |

**RESULTS**

Number of trials _____

| | Words Known | Symbols for Correct Response |
|---|---|---|
| Immediate (first test) | _____ | ✓ |
| At end of 60 minutes (first retest) | _____ | C |
| Next day (second retest) | _____ | + |

Comments _____
_____
_____
_____

## Phonics Inventory

Name _____     Date _____     Score _____/50

1. hat _____
2. man _____
3. sit _____
4. big _____
5. can _____
6. top _____
7. hen _____
8. bug _____
9. hot _____
10. wet _____
11. stand _____
12. clap _____
13. trick _____
14. drip _____
15. spill _____
16. block _____
17. step _____
18. trunk _____
19. must _____
20. black _____
21. make _____
22. ride _____
23. place _____
24. hope _____
25. sheep _____

26. use _____
27. sail _____
28. play _____
29. coat _____
30. night _____
31. nurse _____
32. steer _____
33. share _____
34. smart _____
35. fair _____
36. shirt _____
37. clear _____
38. floor _____
39. smart _____
40. torn _____
41. brook _____
42. true _____
43. broom _____
44. ground _____
45. yawn _____
46. growl _____
47. joy _____
48. fault _____
49. noise _____
50. could _____

**Directions**: Explain to the student that he or she will be asked to read a series of words. Say that some of the words might be difficult but that the student is expected to try her or his hardest. Put the words on cards or have them read from the list. Mark each response with a check (✓) for correct or with a check with a tail for incorrect, and write incorrect responses in the blanks as time allows. If the student doesn't respond within 5 seconds, supply the word. Stop when the student gets five words in a row wrong. The student's level is the highest one at which she or he gets 8 out of 10 words correct. Students should be instructed at a level if they get more than 2 out of 10 wrong. Each level has ten items: 1–10, short-vowel patterns; 11–20, short vowels with clusters; 21–30, long vowels; 31–40, *r*-vowels; 41–50, other vowels.

*Source*: From T. Gunning (2008). *Teacher's Guide for Word Building* (2nd ed.). Honesdale, PA: Phoenix Learning Resources. Reprinted by permission of Galvin Publications.

## Graduated Syllable Survey

Name _____          Total number correct _____

Date _____

| | | |
|---|---|---|
| 1. admit _____ | 18. charter _____ | 35. subdivided _____ |
| 2. minus _____ | 19. approach _____ | 36. vulture _____ |
| 3. dentist _____ | 20. lumber _____ | 37. invention _____ |
| 4. vacant _____ | 21. voyage _____ | 38. discussion _____ |
| 5. discuss _____ | 22. awkward _____ | 39. special _____ |
| 6. human _____ | 23. loosen _____ | 40. treasure _____ |
| 7. problem _____ | 24. avoid _____ | 41. famous _____ |
| 8. frozen _____ | 25. powder _____ | 42. enclosure _____ |
| 9. plastic _____ | 26. wooden _____ | 43. conclusion _____ |
| 10. music _____ | 27. pronounce _____ | 44. partial _____ |
| 11. remain _____ | 28. destroy _____ | 45. courageously _____ |
| 12. barber _____ | 29. continue _____ | 46. observation _____ |
| 13. indeed _____ | 30. applause _____ | 47. disadvantage _____ |
| 14. former _____ | 31. complicated _____ | 48. astonishment _____ |
| 15. increase _____ | 32. disadvantage _____ | 49. communicate _____ |
| 16. further _____ | 33. responsibility _____ | 50. circumstances _____ |
| 17. frighten _____ | 34. advisable _____ | |

*Directions*: Give one copy of the Graduated Syllable Survey to the student and keep one copy for marking. Mark each response with a check (✓) for correct or with a check with a tail for incorrect. (When you use a check with a tail rather than a minus sign, x, or zero, the student can't tell whether her answers are being marked correct or incorrect, so a source of stress is reduced.) If possible, write down each incorrect response for later analysis. Start with the first item and continue testing until the student gets five in a row wrong. A score of 5 or below indicates that the student probably needs instruction in basic decoding skills. Administer the Phonics Inventory. A score of 6 to 44 indicates a need for instruction in syllabic analysis. A score of 45 or higher indicates mastery of basic syllabic analysis. The test words assess key syllabic patterns. Words 1–10: odd numbers, short vowels; even numbers, long vowels and short vowels. 11–20: odd numbers, long-vowel digraphs and short vowels; even numbers, *r* vowels and short vowels. Words 21–30: other vowels: /aw/, / oy/, / ow/, short and long *oo*; 31–35: prefixes and suffixes. Words *36–45*: *ture, tion, ion, cial, ous*. Words 46–50: words that have four or more syllables. Note areas where students had difficulty and plan instruction accordingly.

*Source:* Adapted from: Gunning, T. (2011). *Teacher's Guide for Word Building Book D* (2nd ed.). Unionville, CT: Galvin Publishing; Honesdale, PA: Phoenix Learning Resources.

# APPENDIX B

# Sample Assessment Report

**Reading Report**

| | |
|---|---|
| *Student:* | *James Lawlor (not his real name)* |
| *Evaluator:* | *Thomas G. Gunning, Ed.D.* |
| *Dates of Evaluation:* | *5-1-12, 5-2-12* |
| *Student's Birthdate:* | *4-20-02* |
| *School:* | *P. T. Barnum Elementary School, 501 North St., South Haven, CT* |
| *Grade:* | *3* |
| *Parents:* | *Mildred and Frank Lawlor* |
| *Address:* | *127 Whale St., South Haven, CT* |
| *Phone:* | *123-4567* |

## REASON FOR REFERRAL

James Lawlor is a ten-year-old, third-grade student at the P. T. Barnum School in South Haven, Connecticut. James was referred for testing by Mr. Alvarez, his teacher. Mr. Alvarez is concerned because James is struggling with both reading and writing and is operating well below grade level.

## OBSERVATIONS

During the two-day test period, James was very cooperative and worked very hard on the many tasks that were presented to him. He never said or showed that he was either tired or bored with the tests. In fact, on some of the tests that had to be ended because of a time limit, James expressed a desire to continue. On other tasks that were concluded because he had missed a number of items, James said that he wanted to try again or study the items so that he could do better.

James also frequently inquired about his performance on a number of the tests. He asked such questions as "How am I doing? How many did I get right? Did I fail that test?" Although the frequent inquiring about performance suggests a certain amount of anxiety, James did not exhibit any overt signs of feeling anxious, except on those tests that demanded reading. On the silent-reading selections of the Basic Reading Inventory, for instance, James's performance was accompanied by a great deal of lip movement, audible vocalization, and finger pointing. These signs of anxiety were present even when the material being read was well within James's capacity.

Of all the tests that were given, James seemed to enjoy most the one that required him to put blocks together to form a series of increasingly complex designs. This test was a part of the Weschler Intelligence Scale for Children–IV. James' best performance was on that part of the Weschler Intelligence Scale for Children–IV that required him to explain what he would do in certain social situations and that asked him to explain why certain social rules and conditions were necessary. His poorest performance was on a test that entailed connecting a series of numbers with their corresponding symbols.

James's favorite subject in school is math. He likes reading least of all, but he feels that he does "okay" in reading. He said that he feels that some words are long, the books have too many hard words, and they are boring. He feels that reading would be easier if he knew the words. James doesn't have a favorite book or author and doesn't read at home. James's favorite activities are playing sports and building models. He plays on Little League baseball and Midget football teams.

James wants to be a builder when he grows up. He said it would be fun to build houses. He understands that this occupation demands training and the ability to follow instructions. James's mother said that his brothers and he have helped their father with a number of projects and that James is a good worker.

## CASE HISTORY

A case history was obtained from Mrs. Mildred Lawlor, James's mother, who was openly cooperative and responsive to all questioning. The Lawlor family includes fifteen-year-old John, thirteen-year-old Lawrence, ten-year-old James, Mrs. Mildred Lawlor, and Mr. Frank Lawlor. The family appears to be closely knit and cooperative. As an example, while the father has been recuperating from injuries resulting from work, the three boys have been cooking meals and taking care of minor repairs under the father's direction. Mrs. Lawlor is employed full-time as a practical nurse. Mrs. Lawlor noted throughout the course of the interview that John's maturational development seemed to lag behind that of her other children almost from the very beginning. She cited that James sat by himself at the age of 11½ months, walked at 2 years, and talked at 2½ years. At the present time, however, she believes that James exhibits physical skills that surpass those of his brothers when they were at this age. He enjoys participation in baseball, basketball, and football.

## SCHOOL HISTORY

James's formal education began at the age of 5½, when he attended kindergarten in the South Haven Public Schools. Because James was still not reading at the end of first grade, he repeated the grade. During his second year in first grade, James was given help twice a week by the school's Title 1 teacher. Assistance was increased to four days a week in second grade. Despite increased assistance, progress has been minimal. James's current teacher reports that James is cooperative and works hard, but lately has been beginning to show signs of avoidance when asked to read and write. Mr. Alvarez reports that James becomes restless during reading time, often asks to leave the room, and can't seem to focus on the selection the group is reading.

## CLASSROOM OBSERVATIONS

James is in a class in which reading of basals is combined with the reading of trade books. Because James and several other students would have difficulty reading the third-grade basal on their own, they follow along as the teacher reads the selection to them. Meanwhile, the other class members read the basal on their own. For a twenty-minute period each day, the classroom teacher also provides special instruction and materials for James and the other students in his group. They are given material that is below grade level and additional instruction in decoding strategies.

Because this group has a limited store of words that they can recognize immediately, the teacher is currently supplying instruction in this area. The words that the teacher presents are drawn from a children's book that the students are about to read. The books used with this group are easier than the basal reader. However, even in this group James is struggling. He is much slower than the others in his group to learn the new words and forgets them more easily. Although James was able to read each of the new words correctly when they were presented on the board, he stumbled over them when he encountered them in the selection. The teacher told James that "he knew the words" and reminded James that they had just studied them, but that didn't help James. When James missed a word, the teacher suggested that he use context; but there were so many words in the selection that James didn't know, he was unable to use context.

After the lesson, the observer and teacher discussed James's difficulty remembering printed words and decided to use a word-building approach because James didn't seem to do well with a sight approach. It was also decided to teach James pronounceable word-part and analogy strategies in addition to context strategies and to give James easier materials. It was also decided to use the Phonics Inventory along with running records to monitor James's progress.

A follow-up observation revealed that the recommendations seemed to be working. Even in the easier book, James had to struggle with some of the words, but, because he knew most of the words, he was better able to use context. He also seemed more confident and more willing to take risks. According to the teacher, James also found the pronounceable word-part and analogy strategies to be helpful. As the teacher explained, James no longer had to rely solely on memory, which often failed him. During the session, James was able to decode the word *chimney* by reading the pronounceable word-part *im*, adding *ch* to make *chim*, and then using context to figure that the word must be *chimney*.

## ASSESSMENT RESULTS

### Physical

The Keystone Telebinocular was administered by the school nurse in order to assess James's visual functioning. James is functioning within the normal limits. The Maco Audiometer was used as a screening device to measure James's hearing capacity. The results seem to indicate that his capacity to hear is within the normal range.

James was given a physical at the walk-in clinic at South Haven General Hospital. James had been complaining of stomach pains. Unable to find a physical cause, the examining physician suggested that James might be experiencing stress but has scheduled a follow-up exam. Other than complaints of stomach distress, James is apparently in good health.

### Academic Aptitude

The Weschler Intelligence Scale for Children IV (WISC-IV) was administered by the school psychologist in preparation for a conference on James's reading difficulty. The WISC-IV is an individually administered intelligence test that consists of a series of subtests in four areas: Verbal Comprehension, Perceptual Reasoning, Processing Speed, and Working Memory. The Verbal Comprehension section of the test is designed to measure the child's ability to deal with verbal tasks in a variety of situations and to form concepts. The Perceptual Reasoning section is designed to measure the child's ability to deal with nonverbal tasks in a variety of situations and to form nonverbal concepts. The Processing Speed section measures the ability to work quickly and accurately. Working Memory assesses the ability to pay attention, concentrate, and to hold information in short-term memory while manipulating or working with the information. James's overall score on the WISC-IV fell within the average range. His scores on the Verbal Comprehension and Perceptual Reasoning sections were higher than his scores on the Processing Speed and Working Memory sections. James did particularly well on Verbal Comprehension subtests that required him to define words, use social judgment, and use his general fund of knowledge and on the Perceptual Reasoning subtest that required manipulating blocks to reproduce designs that grew in complexity. On the Processing Speed subtest, James had difficulty on the subtest that measured his ability to make new associations and to work rapidly and accurately by requiring him to connect a series of numbers with their corresponding symbols. On the Working Memory subtest, James had difficulty reciting a series of numbers forwards and backwards.

## Memory

The Word Sequences and Design Sequences subtests of the Detroit Test of Learning Aptitude (Third Edition) were administered in order to assess James's ability to pay attention, concentrate, and use auditory or visual memory to remember a series of words or designs. Although James did somewhat better on the tasks requiring him to remember a series of designs, his performance on both tasks was well below his expected level of achievement. Performance was similar to his below-average ability to recite numbers forwards and backwards on the WISC-IV.

## Rapid Automatized Naming

A portion of the Rapid Automatized Naming Tests (R.A.N.) was administered in order to assess how fast and how accurately James could name a series of letters and numbers. On the letters and numbers subtests, James's performance was similar to that of the average five-year-old. The results suggest a slowness and lack of automaticity in recognizing and naming letters and numbers.

## Reading

The Word-Lists portion of the Basic Reading Inventory (10th ed.) was administered, with the following results:

| Grade Level | Flash Score | Untimed Score |
|---|---|---|
| *Preprimer* | *75* | *85* |
| *Primer* | *60* | *75* |
| *First* | *30* | *40* |
| *Second* | | |
| *Third* | | |
| *Fourth* | | |
| *Fifth* | | |

The results of the Graded Words List of the Basic Reading Inventory indicate that James's ability to recognize words immediately, without taking time to figure them out, is adequate only at the preprimer (beginning first-grade) level. When given time to figure out words that he wasn't able to recognize immediately,

James was only able to read five additional words correctly. James was able to figure out three-letter words that began with a single consonant and ended with a single consonant (*top, pet, hen, met*) but had difficulty with words that began with two or more consonants (*truck*) or had complex vowel spellings (*brave, hurry*).

The passages section of the Basic Reading Inventory was also administered. The Basic Reading Inventory is an individual reading test. It is designed to indicate the level of reading material a student can profitably handle with instruction in a classroom or small-group setting. It also indicates the level of material that a student can read without any assistance, and the level of material that would be very difficult for him to handle, even with assistance. The Basic Reading Inventory also gives information about the student's oral reading, his ability to analyze and sound out words in context, and his ability to understand what he had read. The passages portion of the Basic Reading Inventory yielded the following results:

| Reading Level | Grade |
| --- | --- |
| *Independent* | *Preprimer* |
| *Instructional* | *Primer* |
| *Frustration* | *First* |
| *Hearing Capacity* | *Fifth* |

According to the results of this test, James can read preprimer (beginning first-grade) material without any assistance. His comprehension and ability to read the words are nearly perfect at this level. However, because he had difficulty reading several of the words in the selection at the primer (middle-first-grade) level, James would need the teacher's assistance with material at this level. James missed so many words at the end-of-first-grade level that this material would be too difficult for him even with the teacher's help.

Even at the easiest level, James's oral reading was slow and laborious. During silent reading, James moved his lips, and he vocalized several of the words. As the selections grew more difficult, his vocalizations became more frequent and more audible. James seemed to recognize few words automatically and needed time to attempt to sound out most of the words. However, he was attempting to read for meaning. Often, when he misread a high-frequency word such as *when* or *are*, he would self-correct his miscue (word misread) when he saw that it didn't fit the sense of the sentence. When James's miscues were analyzed, most fit the context. However, often the miscue was graphically quite different from the expected response. James was using context but failed to integrate context with phonics cues. Because of weak deciphering skills, he was overrelying on context.

James's comprehension of the selections that he read was perfect. However, because of deficient decoding skills, he was restricted to first-grade material. When selections were read to him, James was able to comprehend material on a fifth-grade level. This suggests that if James had adequate decoding skills, he would be able to read fifth-grade-level material.

## Writing

Writing was assessed by examining James's portfolio and asking him to write a letter telling about himself. James has written on a variety of topics, but the content of his written pieces lacks elaboration. For instance, in his letter he told that he works with his father on Saturdays, but he didn't tell what kinds of things he did. James also has difficulty with format and mechanics. He didn't use standard letter form and did not capitalize names or use end punctuation consistently. He also was reluctant to write any word that he couldn't spell.

## Phonics

The Phonics Inventory was administered in order to assess James's ability to use phonics to decipher words. James had no difficulty reading three-letter, short-vowel patterns (*wet, sit, hop, fun*) but had problems with long-vowel patterns (*game, road, wheel*). He also had difficulty with words that contained consonant clusters at the beginning or end of the word (*drop, jump*).

## Word Learning

Because James had significant difficulty reading printed words, a number of additional tests and procedures were used to obtain further information in this area.

### Assisted Testing of Word Lists

After the Word-Lists subtest was completed, portions of the subtest were readministered under assisted-testing conditions. James was given another opportunity to read some of the easier words that he had missed. If he missed a word again, he was given assistance. The idea was to see how much help and what kind of help he would need in order to be able to read the words. For instance, James was able to read the *il* and *en* in *children* when the teacher asked him if there were any parts of the word he could read. After pronouncing *il* and *en* in *children,* he was able, with a little coaching, to construct the word *children.* Given this same kind of assistance, James was also able to read *silver* and *smell.*

### Word-Learning Test

The Word-Learning Test was given to assess James's ability to learn to read new words. In this test, the student is presented seven words that were previously missed. Each word is printed on a card and shown to the student, who is asked to say the word. If he is unable to read the word or misreads it, the examiner tells the student the word. After all seven words have been presented, they are shuffled and presented again. After 10 trials, James knew just four of the words. The next day James knew just one of the words. His performance was similar to that of other students who have serious word-learning problems.

### Visual-Auditory Learning Subtest

The Visual-Auditory Learning subtest of the Woodcock-Johnson Cognitive Abilities Battery was administered. This subtest assesses the student's ability to link spoken words with printed symbols. This task is similar to what is required when a student learns sight words. James's performance was equal to that of the average four-year-old.

### Spelling

According to the Elementary Spelling Inventory, James is operating in the early word pattern stage. James is able to spell regular short-vowel words such as *hat, pet, hit, lot,* and *cut* correctly and is ready to learn long-vowel patterns, such as *late, made, hope, boat,* and *bean.*

## ADDITIONAL TESTING

### Trial Teaching

Because James did poorly on the Word-Learning Test, which presented words in sight-word style, James was taught seven words using a word-building approach, in which the student builds words by adding a consonant to the vowel portion of the word ($g + ate$) and also matches up the word's sounds with the letters that spell them. For a period of fifteen minutes, magnetic letters and other devices were used to help James learn the words. Several sentences using the words were constructed, so that James could see the words in context. At the end of fifteen minutes, James was able to read all seven of the words. The next day, after a brief review, James was able to read all seven again.

### Progress Monitoring

A word-building approach has been incorporated into Jame's small group instruction and also in his intervention program. According to the results of progress monitoring with the Phonics Inventory and running records, James is making slow progress. Although he is responding to the word-building approach, he is still significantly behind.

## SUMMARY

James appears to have at least average academic ability. His ability to define words and use social judgment and general knowledge suggest that his true academic ability might be above average. In addition, he is able to understand fifth-grade-level material when it is read to him. This suggests that his ability to comprehend language is equal to that of the average fifth-grader. This is the level of reading that James might be expected to achieve if he were not held back by poorly developed decoding skills. However, James did have difficulty with tasks that involve paying attention and concentrating and remembering a series of numbers, words, or pictures. James also was slow in naming letters and numbers. James's poorest perfor-mances were on those tests that required him to associate printed words or wordlike symbols with spoken words or to associate numbers with symbols. Apparently because of poor memory and underlying processing abilities, James has significant difficulty learning to read words. Learning new words is a struggle for him, and he soon forgets them. However, James does do better when a phonics rather than a sight approach is used.

Insofar as his reading ability is concerned, James is able to read preprimer (beginning-first-grade) material on his own. However, he needs assistance with any reading selections that are on a primer (middle-first-grade) level. Reading material on an ending-first-grade level and beyond is, at this time, so taxing for James that he would not be able to handle it. However, when material is read to James, he is able to understand selections on the fifth-grade level. James is reading well below his capacity. James's spelling and writing are also well below grade level and significantly below James's capacity.

James's low level of achievement in reading is apparently caused by his lack of a store of words that he recognizes instantly or at sight, his limited knowledge of phonics or word patterns, and his lack of strategies that he might use to figure out hard words.

## RECOMMENDATIONS

Because James is reading significantly below level and is making limited progress, it is recommended that he be considered for a more intensive intervention. It is recommended that the classroom teacher and intervention team meet and plan a coordinated high intensity program. The possibility of Tier III intervention should be considered. Enrollment in the school's summer camp reading program is also recommended.

Because James seems to learn best through a sounding-out approach, a systematic program of phonics should be taught. James should also be taught a series of strategies for deciphering hard words. These strategies should include looking for parts of the word he can say and then using known parts to build the word, thinking of a known word that is like the hard word, and using context.

James also needs to be given reading material that is on his level. Books that have too many unknown words are discouraging and don't provide James with the opportunity to apply his reading skills. In fact, James needs as much opportunity as possible to read books and other materials that are easy for him. In addition to showing him that reading need not be a struggle, reading easy books will provide practice in recognizing words so that the speed and ease with which he reads improves. Because James expressed an interest in animals and sports, he might enjoy books such as the following, which are on a primer (middle-first-grade) level:

> *Kick Pass and Run.* Leonard Kessler; *Oliver.* Syd Hoff; *A Dog Named Sam.* Janice Poland.; *Old Turtle's Riddle and Joke Book.* Leonard Kessler; *The Day the Teacher Went Bananas.* James Howe; *Dinosaur Time.* Peggy Parish.

Games might also be used to reinforce James's ability to decode vowel patterns. One possible choice is Road Racer (Curriculum Associates). Puzzles, riddles, songs, verses, and poems that incorporate patterns should also be motivating.

Writing might also be used to reinforce James's word-analysis skills. Because James's spelling ability is limited, he should be encouraged to use invented spelling so that he can give full expression to his ideas. He would also profit from the language-experience approach, in which he discusses an experience, dictates a story, and then reads the dictated story. This technique can also be used to explore topics in which James is interested. The teacher or an aide can read aloud to James books and articles that are too difficult for James to read on his own. The information is discussed and then summarized in an experience story. Also take judicious advantage of recorded books, ebooks that have speech capability, talking software, a text-to-speech reader, and other technology that might assist James with reading and writing tasks that otherwise would be too difficult for him.

Because of his low level of reading ability, James is restricted in the range of books that he can read. In order to continue building James's excellent background of knowledge, James should be read to in the classroom and at home. Another way of building on James's excellent background of information is to involve him in activities that don't require reading and writing. In class discussions, for instance, make it a point to call on James. Also encourage James to engage in art, sports, and other activities that don't require reading and writing, so that he experiences a sense of achievement.

James's parents can help by focusing on the things that James does well. They should encourage him to engage in activities that he enjoys, such as playing sports and helping his father. The parents might also continue to read to James and provide books that are on his reading level and in which he is interested. The parents should continue to build his background of information by taking him to the zoo, museums, and other places and discussing topics of interest with him.

# References

**PROFESSIONAL REFERENCES**

Aasved, H. (1989). Eye examinations. In H. Gjessing & B. Karlsen (Eds.), *A longitudinal study of dyslexia* (pp. 192–209). New York: Springer-Verlag.

Abrams, J. C. (1988). A dynamic-developmental approach to reading and related learning disabilities. In S. M. Glazer, L. W. Searfoss, & L. M. Gentile (Eds.), *Reexamining reading diagnosis: New trends and procedures* (pp. 29–47). Newark, DE: International Reading Association.

ACT. (2006). *Reading between the lines: What the ACT reveals about college readiness in reading.* Iowa City, IA: Author. Available online at http://www.act.org/research/policymakers/pdf/reading_report.pdf

ACT. (2011). *The condition of college and career readiness.* Iowa City, IA: Author. Available online at http://www.act.org/research/policymakers/cccr11/index.html

Adams, M. J. (1990). *Beginning to read: Thinking and learning about print.* Cambridge, MA: MIT Press.

Adoption Guidelines Project. (1990). Comprehension I: The directed reading lesson. In Adoption Guidelines Project, *A guide to selecting basal reading programs.* Champaign: University of Illinois, Center for the Study of Reading.

Adlof, S. M., Perfetti, C. A., & Catts, H. W. (2011). Developmental changes in reading comprehension: Implications for assessment and instruction. In S. J. Samuels & A. E. Farstrup (Eds.). *What research has to say about reading instruction* (4th ed., pp. 186–214). Newark, DE: International Reading Association.

Afflerbach, P. (1990). The influence of prior knowledge on expert readers' main idea construction strategies. *Reading Research Quarterly, 25,* 31–46.

Alegria, J., & Morais, J. (1991). Segmental analysis and reading acquisition. In L. Rieben & C. A. Perfetti (Eds.), *Learning to read: Basic research and its implications* (pp. 135–148). Hillsdale, NJ: Erlbaum.

Alexander, J. C. (1998). Reading skill and context facilitation: A classic study revisited. *Journal of Educational Research, 91,* 314–318.

Allen, J., Michalove, B., & Shockley, B. (1993). *Engaging children, community and chaos in the lives of young literacy learners.* Portsmouth, NH: Heinemann.

Allington, R. L. (1983). The reading instruction provided readers of differing reading ability. *Elementary School Journal, 83,* 548–559.

Allington, R. L. (1984). Oral reading. In P. D. Pearson, R. Barr, M. L. Kamil, & P. Mosenthal (Eds.), *Handbook of reading research* (pp. 829–863). New York: Longman.

Allington, R. L. (1994). The schools we have: The schools we need. *Reading Teacher, 48,* 14–29.

Allington, R. L. (1995). Literacy lessons in the elementary schools: Yesterday, today, and tomorrow In R. L Allington & S. A. Walmsley (Eds.), *No quick fix, Rethinking literacy programs in America's elementary schools* (pp. 1–15). New York: Teachers College Press.

Allington, R. L. (2011). Research on reading/learning disability interventions. In S. J. Samuels & A. E. Farstrup (Eds.), *What research has to say about reading instruction* (4th ed.). Newark, DE: International Reading Association.

Allor, J. H., Mathes, P. G., Roberts, J. K., Cheatham, J. P., & Champlin, T. M. (2010). Comprehensive reading instruction for students with intellectual disabilities: Findings from the first three years of a longitudinal study. *Psychology in the Schools, 47*(5), 445–446.

Alt, S. J., & Samuels, S. J. (2011), Reading fluency: What is it and how should it be measured? In A. McGill-Franzen & R. L. Allington (Eds.). *Handbook of reading disability research* (pp. 173–181). New York: Routledge.

Alvermann, D. E., Bridge, C. A., Schmidt, B. A., Searfoss, L. W., Winograd, P., Paris, S. G., Priestly, M., & Santeusanio, R. D. (1989). *Heath reading.* Lexington, MA: Heath.

American Academy of Pediatrics, Section on Ophthalmology, Council on Children with Disabilities; American Academy of Ophthalmology; American Association for Pediatric Ophthalmology and Strabismus; American Association of Certified Orthoptists. (2009). Joint statement—Learning disabilities, dyslexia, and vision. *Pediatrics, 123,* 837–844.

American Optometric Association. (2008). *Care of the patient with learning related vision problems.* Available online at http://www.aoa.org/documents/CPG-20.pdf

American Psychiatric Association. (2000). *Diagnostic and statistical manual of mental disorders* (4th ed., text rev.). Washington, DC: Author.

Anderson, A. W. (2011). Functional correlates of children's responsiveness to intervention. *Developmental Neuropsychology, 36,* 288–301.

Anderson, L. W., & Krathwohl, D. R. (Eds.). (2001). *A taxonomy for learning, teaching, and assessing: A revision of Bloom's taxonomy of educational objectives.* New York: Longman.

Anderson, R. C. (1990, May). *Microanalysis of classroom reading instruction.* Paper presented at the Annual Conference on Reading Research, Atlanta, GA.

Anderson, R. C. (1996). Research foundations to support wide reading. In V. Greaney (Ed.), *Promoting reading in developing countries* (pp. 55–77). Newark, DE: International Reading Association.

Anderson, V., & Henne, R. (1993). *Collaborative, integrated reading and writing strategy instruction.* Paper presented at the annual meeting of the National Reading Conference, Charleston, SC.

Anderson, V., & Roit, M. (1993). Planning and implementing collaborative strategy instruction for delayed readers in grades 6–10. *Elementary School Journal, 94,* 121–137.

Apel, K., Masterson, J. J., & Niessen, N. L. (2004). Spelling assessment frameworks. In C. A. Stone, E. R. Silliman, B. J. Ehren, & K. Apel (Eds.), *Handbook of language and literacy development and disorders* (pp. 644–660). New York: Guilford Press.

Applegate, M., Quinn, K., & Applegate, A. J. (2006). Profiles in comprehension. *Reading Teacher, 60,* 48–57.

Archambault, L., Diamond, D., Brown, R., Cavanaugh, C., Coffey, M., Foures-Aalbu, D., Richardson, J., & Zygouris-Coe, V. (2010). *Research committee issues brief: An exploration of at-risk learners and online education.* International Association for K-12 Online Learning. Available online at http://www.inacol.org/research/docs/iNACOL_AtRiskStudentOnlineResearch.pdf

Archer, L. E. (2010, December). Lexile reading growth as a function of starting level in at-risk middle school students. *Journal of Adolescent & Adult Literacy, 55,* 281–290.

Armbruster, B. B. (1991). Framing: A technique for improving learning from science texts. In C. M. Santa & D. C. Alvermann (Eds.), *Science learning: Processes and applications* (pp. 104–113). Newark, DE: International Reading Association.

Armbruster, B. B., & Anderson, T. H. (1981). *Content area textbooks* (Technical Report No. 23). Champaign: University of Illinois, Center for the Study of Reading.

Ashton-Warner, S. (1963). *Teacher.* New York: Simon & Schuster.

Au, A., & Lovegrove, W. (2006). Rapid visual processing by college students in reading irregular words and phonologically regular pseudowords presented singly and in contiguity. *Annals of Dyslexia, 56,* 335–360.

Aud, S., Hussar, W., Kena, G., Bianco, K., Frohlich, L., Kemp, J., & Tahan, K. (2011). *The condition of education 2011* (NCES 2011-033). U.S. Department of Education, National Center for Education Statistics. Washington, DC: U.S. Government Printing Office.

Baddeley, A. (1992). Working memory. *Science, 255,* 556–559.

Baddeley, A. (2000). The episodic buffer: A new component of working memory? *Trends in Cognitive Science, 4,* 417–423.

Bader, L. A., & Pearce, D. L. (2013). *Bader reading and language inventory* (7th ed.). Boston: Pearson.

Badian, N. A. (1997). Dyslexia and the double deficit hypothesis. *Annals of Dyslexia, 47,* 69–87.

Badian, N. A. (1999). Reading disability defined as a discrepancy between listening and reading comprehension: Longitudinal study of stability, gender differences, and prevalence, *Journal of Learning Disabilities, 32,* 138–148.

Badian, N. A. (2000). *It's not just phonological awareness! The importance of orthographic processing in reading.* Paper presented at the 27th Annual Conference on Dyslexia and Related Reading Disorders, New York.

Badian, N. A. (2005). Does a visual-orthographic deficit contribute to reading disability? *Annals of Dyslexia, 55,* 28–52.

Bain, A. M. (1991). Handwriting disorders. In A. M. Bain, L. L. Bailet, & L. C. Moats (Eds.), *Written language disorders: Theory into practice* (pp. 43–64). Austin, TX: Pro-Ed.

Baker, L., & Brown, A. L. (1984). Megacognitive skills and reading. In P. D. Pearson, R. Barr, M. L. Kamil, & P. Mosenthal (Eds.), *Handbook of reading research* (pp. 353–394). New York: Longman.

Baker, S. K., Simmons, D. C., & Kame'enui, E. J. (1998). Vocabulary acquisition: Research bases. In D. C. Simmons & E. J. Kame'enui (Eds.), *What research tells us about children with diverse learning needs* (pp. 183–218). Mahwah, NJ: Erlbaum.

Bandura, A. (1977). Self-efficacy: Toward a unifying theory of behavioral change. *Psychological Review, 84,* 191–215.

Barba, R. H. (1995). *Science in the multicultural classroom: A guide to teaching and learning.* Boston: Allyn & Bacon.

Barker, T. A., Torgesen, J. K., & Wagner, R. K. (1992). The role of orthographic processing skills on five different reading tasks. *Reading Research Quarterly, 27,* 335–346.

Barnes, B. L. (1996–1997). But teacher you went right on: A perspective on Reading Recovery. *Reading Teacher, 50,* 284–292.

Barr, R., Blachowicz, C., & Wogman-Sadow, M. (1995). *Reading diagnosis for teachers: An instructional approach* (3rd ed.). New York: Addison-Wesley.

Barr, R., Blachowicz, C. L. Z., Bates, A., Katz, C., & Kaufman, B. (2007). *Reading diagnosis for teachers: An instructional approach* (5th ed.). Boston: Allyn & Bacon.

Barr, R., & Dreeben, R. (1991). Grouping students for reading instruction. In R. Barr, M. L. Kamil, P. Mosenthal, & P. D. Pearson (Eds.), *Handbook of reading research, Vol. II* (pp. 885–910). New York: Longman.

Barron, R. R. Research for the classroom teacher: Recent developments on the structured overview as an advanced organizer. In H. L. Herber & J. D. Rilesy (Eds.), *Research in reading in the content areas: The first report* (pp. 28–47). Syracuse, NY: Syracuse University, Reading and Language Arts Center.

Baumann, J. F. (1986). The direct instruction of main idea comprehension ability. In J. F. Baumann (Ed.), *Teaching main idea comprehension* (pp. 133–178). Newark, DE: International Reading Association.

Baumann, J. F. (1989). *Reading assessment: An instructional decision-making perspective.* Columbus, OH: Merrill.

Baumann, J. F., Edwards, E. C., Font, G., Tereshinski, C., Kame'enui, E. J., & Olejnik, S. F. (2002). Teaching morphemic and contextual analysis to fifth-grade students. *Reading Research Quarterly, 37,* 150–173.

Baumann, J. F., & Kame'enui, E. J. (1991). Research on vocabulary instruction: Ode to Voltaire. In J. Flood, J. M. Jensen, D. Lapp, & J. R. Squire (Eds.), *Handbook of research on teaching the English language arts* (pp. 604–632). New York: Macmillan.

Baumann, J. F., & Serra, J. K. (1984). The frequency and placement of main ideas in children's social studies textbooks: A modified replication of Braddock's research on topic sentences. *Journal of Reading Behavior, 16,* 27–40.

Baumann, J. F., & Stevenson, J. A. (1986). Identifying types of anaphoric relationships. In J. W. Irwin (Ed.), *Understanding and teaching cohesion comprehension* (pp. 9–20). Newark, DE: International Reading Association.

Bear, D. R., & Barone, D. (1989). The elementary spelling inventory (with error guide). *Reading Psychology, 10,* 275–292.

Bear, D. R., Invernizzi, M., Johnston, F., & Templeton, S. (1996). *Words their way: Word study for phonics, vocabulary, and spelling instruction.* Upper Saddle River, NJ: Merrill.

Bear, D. R., Invernizzi, M., Templeton, S., & Johnston, F. (2008). *Words their way: Word study for phonics, vocabulary, and spelling instruction* (4th ed.). Upper Saddle River, NJ: Pearson.

Beck, I. L., & Juel, C. (1995). The role of decoding in learning to read. *American Educator, 9*(2), 8, 21–25, 39–42.

Beck, I. L., & McKeown, M. G. (1991). Conditions of vocabulary acquisition. In R. Barr, M. L. Kamil, P. Mosenthal, & P. D. Pearson (Eds.), *Handbook of reading research, Vol. II* (pp. 789–814). New York: Longman.

Beck, I. L., & McKeown, M. G. (2001). Text talk: Capturing the benefits of read-aloud experiences for young children. *Reading Teacher, 55,* 10–20.

Beck, I. L. & McKeown, M. G. (2006). *Improving comprehension with questioning the author: A fresh and expanded view of a powerful approach.* New York: Scholastic.

Beck, I. L., McKeown, M. G., & Kucan, L. (2002). *Bringing words to life: Robust vocabulary instruction.* New York: Guilford Press.

Beck, I. L., Kucan, L., & McKeown, M. G. (2008). *Creating robust vocabulary: Frequently asked questions and extended examples.* New York: Guilford Press.

Beck, I. L., McKeown, M. G., & Omanson, R. C. (1987). The effects and uses of diverse vocabulary instructional techniques. In M. G. McKeown & M. E. Curtis (Eds.), *The nature of vocabulary acquisition* (pp. 147–163). Hillsdale, NJ: Erlbaum.

Beck, I. L., Omanson, R. C., & McKeown, M. G. (1982). An instructional redesign of reading lessons: Effects on comprehension. *Reading Research Quarterly, 17,* 462–481.

Beck, M. (2010). Another side of Isabel. In M. G. McKeown, & L. Kucan (Eds.), *Bringing reading research to life.* New York: Guilford Press.

Beers, K. (2003). *When kids can't read: What teachers can do—A guide for teachers 6–12.* Portsmouth, NH: Heinemann.

Bell, N. (2007). *Visualizing and verbalizing for language thinking and comprehension.* Avila Beach, CA: Gander.

Benson, V., & Cummins, C. (2000). *The power of retelling: Developmental steps for building comprehension.* Bothell, WA: Wright Group/McGraw-Hill.

Bereiter, C., & Scardamalia, M. (1982). From conversation to composition: The role of instruction in a developmental process. In R. Glass (Ed.), *Advances in instructional psychology, Vol. 2* (pp. 1–64). Hillsdale, NJ: Erlbaum.

Berkeley, S., Mastropieri, M. A., & Scruggs, T. E. (2011). Reading comprehension strategy instruction and attribution retraining for secondary students with learning and other mild disabilities. *Journal of Learning Disabilities, 44,* 18–32.

Berkowitz, S. J. (1986). Effects of instruction in text organization on sixth-grade students' memory for expository text. *Reading Research Quarterly, 21,* 161–178.

Berliner, D. C. (1981). Academic learning time and reading achievement. In J. T. Guthrie (Ed.), *Comprehension and teaching: Research reviews* (pp. 203–226). Newark, DE: International Reading Association.

Berninger, V. (1990). Multiple orthographic and phonological codes: Keys to instructional interventions for developing word identification. *School Psychology Review, 19,* 518–533.

Berninger, V. W., Abbott, R. D., Zook, D., Ogier, S., Lemos-Brilton, Z., & Brooksher, R. (1999). Early intervention for reading disabilities: Teaching the alphabet principle in a connectionist framework. *Journal of Learning Disabilities, 32,* 491–503.

Berninger, V. W., & O'Malley, M. M. (2011). Evidence-based diagnosis and treatment for specific learning disabilities involving impairments in written and/or oral language. *Journal of Learning Disabilities, 44,* 167–183.

Berres, R., & Eyer, J. T. (1970). Cases from full-time remedial students: John. In A. J. Harris (Ed.), *Casebook on reading disability* (pp. 25–47). New York: David McKay.

Berry, G., Hall, D., & Gildroy, P. G. (2004). Teaching learning strategies. In B. K Lenz, D. D. Deshler, & B. R. Kissam (Eds.), *Teaching content to all: Evidence-based inclusive practices in middle and secondary schools* (pp. 258–278). Boston: Allyn & Bacon.

Bertin, R., & Perleman, E. (1999). *Preventing academic failure: A multisensory curriculum for teaching reading spelling, and handwriting in the elementary school classroom.* White Plains, NY: Monroe Associates.

Betts, E. A. (1946). *Foundations of reading instruction.* New York: American Book.

Beyer, B. (2001). What research says about teaching thinking skills. In A. L. Costa (Ed.), *Developing minds: A resource book for teaching thinking* (3rd ed., pp. 275–282). Alexandria, VA: Association for Supervision and Curriculum Development.

Biancarosa, C., & Snow, C. E. (2006). *Reading next—A vision for action and research in middle and high school literacy: A report to Carnegie Corporation of New York* (2nd ed.). Washington, DC: Alliance for Excellent Education.

Biemiller, A. (1970). The development of the use of graphic and contextual information as children learn to read. *Reading Research Quarterly, 6,* 75–96.

Biemiller, A. (1977–1978). Relationships between oral reading rates for letters, words, and simple text in the development of reading achievement. *Reading Research Quarterly, 13,* 223–253.

Biemiller, A. (1994). Some observations on acquiring and using reading skill in elementary schools. In C. K. Kinzer & D. J. Leu (Eds.), *Multidimensional aspects of literacy research, theory, and practice. Forty-third yearbook of the National Reading Conference* (pp. 209–216). Chicago, IL: National Reading Conference.

Biemiller, A. (2001). Teaching vocabulary: Early, direct, and sequential. *American Educator, 25,* 25–28.

Biemiller, A. (2009). *Words worth teaching.* Columbus, OH: SRA/McGraw-Hill.

Biemiller, A. (2011). Vocabulary development and implications for reading problems. In A. McGill-Franzen & R. L. Allington (Eds.), *Handbook of reading disability research* (pp. 208–218). New York: Routledge.

Bisson, S. A., Phillips, S. A., Creamer, S. M., & Baker, T. K. (1999). Shared reading, books, and audiotapes: Supporting diverse students in school and at home. *Reading Teacher, 52,* 430–444.

Bjorklund, B., Handler, N., Mitten, J., & Stockwell, G. (1998). *Literature circles: A tool for developing students as critical readers, writers, and thinkers.* Paper presented at the 47th Annual Conference of the Connecticut Reading Association, Waterbury, CT.

Blachman, B. A. (2000). Phonological awareness. In M. L. Kamil, P. B. Mosenthal, P. D. Pearson, & R. Barr (Eds.), *Handbook of reading research, Vol. III* (pp. 483–502). Mahwah, NJ: Erlbaum.

Blachman, B. A., Ball, E. W., Black, R. S., & Tangel, D. M. (1994). Kindergarten teachers develop phoneme awareness in low-income, inner-city classrooms: Does it make a difference? *Reading and Writing: An Interdisciplinary Journal, 6,* 1–18.

Blachman, B. A., Ball, E. W., Black, R. S., & Tangel, D. M. (2000). *Road to the code.* Baltimore, MD: Brookes.

Blachman, B. A., & Tangel, D. M. (2008). *Road to reading.* Baltimore, MD: Brookes.

Blachowicz, C. L. Z. (1986). Making connections: Alternatives to the vocabulary notebook. *Journal of Reading 29,* 643–649.

Blachowicz, C. L. Z., & Fisher, P. (2000). Vocabulary instruction. In M. L. Kamil, P. B. Mosenthal, P. D. Pearson, & R. Barr (Eds.), *Handbook of reading research, Vol. III* (pp. 503–523). Mahwah, NJ: Erlbaum.

Black, P., & Wiliam D. (1998). Inside the black box: Raising standards through classroom assessment. *Phi Delta Kappan, 80* (2), 139–148. Available online at http://www.pdkintl .org/kappan/kbla9810.htm

Blaine, M. (1986). Giants of the city. In J. Stanchfield & T. Gunning (Eds.), *Wings* (New Directions in Reading) (pp. 162–169). Boston: Houghton Mifflin.

Bloodgood, J. W. (1999). What's in a name? Children's name writing and literacy acquisition. *Reading Research Quarterly, 34,* 342–367.

Bloom, B. (Ed.). (1957). *Taxonomy of educational objectives.* New York: McKay.

Bloom B., Cohen R. A., & Freeman G. (2011). Summary health statistics for U.S. children: National Health Interview Survey, 2010. National Center for Health Statistics. *Vital Health Statistics 10*(250).

Bloom, F., & Traub, N. (2004). *Recipe for reading* (4th ed.). Cambridge, MA: Educators Publishing.

Bond, G. L., Tinker, M. A., Wasson, B. B., & Wasson, J. B. (1994). *Reading difficulties: Their diagnosis and correction* (7th ed.). Boston: Allyn & Bacon.

Bodrova, E. & Leong, D. J. (1998). Scaffolding emergent writing in the zone of proximal development. *Language, Literacy, and Learning, 3*(2), 1–18.

Bodrova, E., & Leong, D. J. (2007). *Tools of the mind: The Vygotskian approach to early childhood education* (2nd ed.). Upper Saddle River, NJ: Merrill.

Bodrova, E., Leong, D. J., Gregory, K., & Edgerton, S. (1999). *Scaffolded writing—A successful strategy for promoting children's writing in kindergarten: A research report and discussion.* Paper presented at NAEYC Annual Conference, New Orleans, LA.

Bos, C. S., & Anders, P. L. (1990). Effects of interactive vocabulary instruction on the vocabulary learning and reading comprehension of junior-high learning disabled students. *Learning Disability Quarterly, 13,* 31–42.

Bos, C. S., & Vaughn, S. (1994). *Strategies for teaching students with learning and behavior problems* (3rd ed.). Boston: Allyn & Bacon.

Boulware-Gooden, R., Carreker, S., Thornhill, A., & Joshi, R. (2007). Instruction of metacognitive strategies enhances reading comprehension and vocabulary achievement of third-grade students. *Reading Teacher, 61,* 70–77.

Bowers, P. G., Sunseth, K., & Golden, J. (1999). The route between rapid naming and reading progress. *Scientific Studies of Reading, 3,* 31–53.

Boyle, C. (1996). *Efficacy of peer evaluation and effects of peer evaluation on persuasive writing.* Unpublished master's thesis, San Diego State University, San Diego, CA.

Boyles, N. (2002). *Teaching written response to text: Constructing quality answers to open-ended comprehension questions.* Gainesville, FL: Maupin House.

Boyles, N. (2004). *Constructing meaning.* Gainesville, FL: Maupin House.

Bradley, J. M., & Thalgoot, M. R. (1987). Reducing reading anxiety. *Academic Therapy, 22,* 349–358.

Brady, S. (1986). Short-term memory, phonological processing, and reading ability. *Annals of Dyslexia, 36,* 138–153.

Brady, S. A. (1991). The role of working memory in reading disability. In S. A. Brady & D. P. Shankweiler (Eds.), *Phonological processes in literacy: A tribute to Isabelle Y. Liberman* (pp. 129–151). Hillsdale, NJ: Erlbaum.

Bransford, J. D. (1994). Schema activation and schema acquisition: Comments on Richard C. Anderson's remarks. In R. B. Ruddell, M. R. Ruddell, & H. Singer (Eds.), *Theoretical models and processes of reading* (4th ed., pp. 483–495). Newark, DE: International Reading Association.

Bricklin, P. M. (1991). The concept of "self as learner": Its critical role in the diagnosis and treatment of children with reading disabilities. *Reading, Writing, and Learning Disabilities, 7,* 201–217.

Bridge, C. A., & Tierney, R. J. (1981). The inferential operations of children across text with narrative and expository tendencies, *Journal of Reading Behavior, 13,* 201–214.

Bristow, P. S., Pikulski, J. J., & Pelosi, P. L. (1983). A comparison of five estimates of reading instructional level. *Reading Teacher, 37,* 273–279.

Broaddus, K., & Bloodgood, J. (1994). *Working with severe reading problems: Remediation.* Paper presented at the annual meeting of the International Reading Association, Toronto.

Broaddus, K., & Bloodgood, J. (1999). "We're supposed to already know how to teach reading": Teacher change to support struggling readers. *Reading Research Quarterly, 34,* 426–451.

Brown, A. L., & Day, J. D. (1983). Macrorules for summarizing text: The development of expertise, *Journal of Verbal Learning and Verbal Behavior, 22*(1), 1–14.

Brown, A. L., & Palincsar, A. (1986). *Reciprocal teaching of comprehension strategies: A natural history of one program for enhancing learning* (Technical Report No. 334). Champaign: University of Illinois, Center for the Study of Reading.

Bruce, B. (1980). Plans and social actions. In R. Spiro, B. Bruce, & W. Brewer (Eds.), *Theoretical issues in reading comprehension* (pp. 367–384). Hillsdale, NJ: Erlbaum.

Bruck, M. (1992). Persistence of dyslexics' phonological awareness deficits. *Developmental Psychology, 28,* 874–886.

Bruner, J. S. (1964). The course of cognitive growth. *American Psychologist, 19,* 1–15.

Bruner, J. S. (1986). *Actual minds, possible worlds.* Cambridge, MA: Harvard University Press.

Bryant, N. D., Kelly, M. S., Hathaway, K., & Rubin, E. (1981). *A summary of directions for the "LD-Efficient" teaching manual.* New York: Research Institute for the Study of Learning Disabilities, Teachers College, Columbia University.

Buettner, E. G. (2002). Sentence by sentence self-monitoring. *The Reading Teacher, 56,* 34–44.

Bulgren, J. A., & Scanlon, D. (1997/1998). Teachers' instructional routines and learning strategies that promote understanding of content-area concepts. *Journal of Adolescent and Adult Literacy, 41,* 292–302.

Buly, S. R., & Valencia, S. Below the bar: Profiles of students who fail state reading assessments. *Educational Evaluation and Policy Analysis, 24,* 219–239.

Burcham, B., Carlson, L., & Milich, R. (1993). Promising school-based practices for students with attention deficit disorder. *Exceptional Children, 60,* 174–180.

Bus, A. G., & van Ijzendoorn, M. H. (1999). Phonological awareness and early reading: A meta-analysis of experiential training studies. *Journal of Educational Psychology, 91,* 403–414.

Bush, C., & Huebner, M. (1979). *Strategies for reading in the elementary school* (2nd ed.). New York: Macmillan.

Butkowsky, I. S., & Willows, D. M. (1980). Cognitive-motivational characteristics of children varying in reading ability: Evidence for learned helplessness in poor readers. *Journal of Educational Psychology, 72,* 408–422.

Byrne, B., & Fielding-Barnsley, R. (1995). Evaluation of a program to teach phonemic awareness to young children: A 2-year and 3-year follow-up and a new preschool trial. *Journal of Educational Psychology, 87,* 488–503.

Byrne, B., Fielding-Barnsley, R., & Ashley, L. (2000). Effects of preschool phonemic identity training after six years: Outcome level distinguished from rate of response. *Journal of Educational Psychology, 92,* 659–667.

Cain, K. (1996). Story knowledge and comprehension skill. In C. Cornoldi & J. Oakhill (Eds.), *Reading comprehension difficulties: Process and intervention* (pp. 167–192). Mahwah, NJ: Erlbaum.

Cain, K., Oakhill, J., & Bryant, P. (2004). Children's reading comprehension ability: Concurrent prediction by working memory, verbal ability, and component skills. *Journal of Educational Psychology, 96,* 31–42.

Calder, L., & Carlson, S. (2002). *Using "think alouds" to evaluate deep understanding.* Policy Center on the First Year of College. Available online at http://www.brevard.edu/fyc/listserv/remarks/calderandcarlson.htm

California State University Expository Reading and Writing Task Force. (2008). *The Expository reading and writing course: Semester one.* Author. Available online at http://writing.csusuccess.org/uploads/qg/-C/qg-CVWRUJJbipnJw1m77Ew/Content-Lit-Preservice-Final-052609.pdf

Calkins, L. M. (1994). *The art of teaching writing* (2nd ed.). Portsmouth, NH: Heinemann.

Calkins, L. M. (2003a). *Nuts and bolts of teaching writing.* Portsmouth, NH: Heinemann.

Calkins, L. M. (2003b). *Units of study for primary writing: A yearlong curriculum* (K–2). Portsmouth, NH: Heinemann.

Calkins, L. M., & Harwayne, S. (1991). *Living between the lines.* Portsmouth, NH: Heinemann.

Calkins, L. M., Montgomery, K., & Santman, D. (1998). *A teacher's guide to standardized reading tests.* Portsmouth, NH: Heinemann.

Calkins, L. M., & Oxenhorn, A. (2003). *Small moments: Personal narrative writing.* Portsmouth, NH: Heinemann.

Campbell, R. (1998). Looking at literacy learning in preschool settings. In R. Campbell (Ed.), *Facilitating preschool literacy* (pp. 70–83). Newark, DE: International Reading Association.

Cardoso-Martins, C., Rodrigues, L., & Ehri, L. (2003). Place of environmental print in reading development: Evidence from nonliterate adults. *Scientific Study of Reading 7,* 335–355.

Carlo, M. S., August, D., McLaughlin, B., Snow, C. E., Dressier, C., Lippman, D., Lively, T., & White, C. (2004). Closing the gap: Addressing the vocabulary needs of English language learners in bilingual and mainstream classrooms. *Reading Research Quarterly, 39,* 188–215.

Carlson, N. R. (1993). *Psychology: The science of behavior* (4th ed.). Boston: Allyn & Bacon.

Carlson, N. R., Miller, H. L. , Heth, D. S., Donahoe J. W., & Martin, G. N. (2010). *Psychology: The science of behavior* (7th ed.). Boston: Allyn & Bacon.

Carnegie Corporation. (1994). *Starting points: Meeting the needs of our youngest children.* New York: Carnegie Corporation.

Carnine, D., Kame'enui, E. J., & Coyle, G. (1984). Utilization of contextual information in determining the meaning of unfamiliar words. *Reading Research Quarterly, 19,* 188–204.

Carr, E. M. (1985). The vocabulary overview guide: A metacognitive strategy to improve vocabulary, comprehension and retention. *Journal of Reading, 28,* 684–689.

Carroll, J. B. (1977). Developmental parameters in reading comprehension. In J. T. Guthrie (Ed.), *Cognition, curriculum and comprehension* (pp. 1–15). Newark, DE: International Reading Association.

Castiglioni-Spalten, M., & Ehri, L. C. (2003). Phonemic awareness instruction: Contribution of articulatory segmentation to novice beginners' reading and writing. *Scientific Studies of Reading, 7*, 25–52.

Catts, H. W., & Kamhi, A. G., & Adlof, S. M. (2012). Causes of reading disabilities. In A. G. Kamhi & H. W. Catts (Eds.), *Language and Reading Disabilities* (3rd ed., pp. 77–111). Boston: Allyn & Bacon.

Caverly, D. C., & Orlando, V. P. (1991). Textbook study strategies. In D. C. Caverly & V. P. Orlando (Eds.), *Teaching reading and study strategies at the college level* (pp. 86–165). Newark, DE: International Reading Association.

Celano, M. P., & Geller, R. J. (1993). Learning, school performance, and children with asthma: How much at risk? *Journal of Learning Disabilities, 26*, 23–37.

Center, Y., Wheldall, K., Freeman, L., Outhred, L., & McNaught, M. (1995). An experimental evaluation of Reading Recovery. *Reading Research Quarterly, 30*, 240–263.

Centers for Disease Control and Prevention. (2009a). *Vision health initiative, common eye disorders, amblyopia.* Available online at http://www.cdc.gov/visionhealth/basic _information/eye_disorders.htm

Centers for Disease Control and Prevention. (2009b). *Vision health initiative, common eye disorders, strabismus.* Available online at http://www.cdc.gov/visionhealth/basic _information/eye_disorders.htm

Centers for Disease Control and Prevention. (2009c). *Vision health initiative, fast facts.* Atlanta, GA: Author. http://www .cdc.gov/visionhealth/basic_information/fast_facts. htm

Centers for Disease Control and Prevention. (2010). *Increasing prevalence of parent-reported attention-deficit/hyperactivity disorder among children—United States, 2003 and 2007.* Available online at http://www.cdc.gov/mmwr/preview/ mmwrhtml/mm5944a3.htm

Chadwell, G. B. (2002a). *Developing an effective writing program for the elementary grades.* West Newbury, MA: Collins Education Associates.

Chadwell, G. B. (2002b). *Writing projects for the elementary grades.* West Newbury, MA: Collins Education Associates.

Chall, J. S., Bissex, G. L., Conard, S. S., & Harris-Sharples, S. H. (1996). *Holistic assessment of texts: Scales for estimating the difficulty of literature, social studies, and science materials.* Cambridge, MA: Brookline.

Chall, J. S., & Conard, S. S. (1991). *Should textbooks challenge students? The case for easier or harder books.* New York: Teachers College Press.

Chall, J. S., & Dale, E. (1995). *Readability revisited: The New Dale-Chall Readability Formula.* Cambridge, MA: Brookline.

Chall, J. S., Jacobs, V. A., & Baldwin, L. E. (1990). *The reading crisis: Why poor children fall behind.* Cambridge, MA: Harvard University Press.

Chamot, A. U., & O'Malley, J. M. (1994). Instructional approaches and teaching procedures. In K. Spangerberg-Urbschart & R. Pritchard (Eds.), *Kids come in all languages: Reading instruction for ESL students* (pp. 82–107). Newark, DE: International Reading Association.

Champion, A. (1997). Knowledge of suffixed words: A comparison of reading disabled and nondisabled readers. *Annals of Dyslexia, 47*, 29–55.

Chase, C., & Stein, J. (2003). Visual magnocellular deficits in dyslexia. *Brain, 126*, E-2.

Chase, C. H. (1996). A visual deficit model of developmental dyslexia. In C. H. Chase, G. D. Rosen, & G. F. Sherman (Eds.), *Developmental dyslexia: Neural, cognitive, and genetic mechanisms* (pp. 127–158). Baltimore, MD: York Press.

Cheyney, S., & Cohen, E. J. (1999). *Focus on phonics : Assessment and instruction.* New York: McGraw-Hill.

Chicago Public Schools. (2000). *How to create a rubric from scratch.* Available online at http://intranet.cps.kl2.il.us/ Assessments/Ideas_and_Rubrics/Create_Rubric/create rubric.html

Child Welfare Information Gateway. (2011). *Foster care statistics 2010.* Available online at http://www.childwelfare.gov/ pubs/factsheets/foster.cfm

Cho, K., & Krashen, S. D. (1994). Acquisition of vocabulary from the Sweet Valley Kids series: Adult ESL acquisition. *Journal of Reading, 37*, 662–667.

Chomsky, C. (1978). When you still can't read in third grade: After decoding, what? In S. J. Samuels (Ed.), *What research has to say about reading instruction* (pp. 13–30). Newark, DE: International Reading Association.

Clark, D. B., & Uhury, J. K. (1995). *Dyslexia: Theory and practice of remedial instruction* (2nd ed.). Parkton, MD: York Press.

Clay, M. M. (1985). *The early detection of reading difficulties* (3rd ed.). Auckland, NZ: Heinemann.

Clay, M. M. (1991). Introducing a new story book to young readers. *Reading Teacher, 45*, 264–272.

Clay, M. M. (1993). *Reading Recovery: A guidebook for teachers in training.* Portsmouth, NH: Heinemann.

Clay, M. M. (2000). *Running records for classroom teachers.* Portsmouth, NH: Heinemann.

Clay, M. M. (2006). *An observation survey of early literacy achievement* (2nd ed.). Portsmouth, NH: Heinemann.

Coe, M., Hanita, M., Nishioka, V., & Smiley, R. (2011). *An investigation of the impact of the 6+1 Trait Writing model on grade 5 student writing achievement* (NCEE 2012–4010). Washington, DC: National Center for Education Evaluation and Regional Assistance, Institute of Education Sciences, U.S. Department of Education.

Cohen, A. S. (1974–1975). Oral reading errors of first grade children taught by a code emphasis approach. *Reading Research Quarterly, 10*, 616–650.

Cohn, M., & D'Alessandro, C. (1978). When is a decoding error not a decoding error? *Reading Teacher, 32*, 341–344.

Colburn, A., & Echevarria, J. (1999). Meaningful lessons. *Science Teacher, 66(2)*, 36–39.

Collins, J. J. (2004). *Selecting and teaching focus correction areas.* West Newbury, MA: Collins Education Associates.

Collins, J. L. (1998). *Strategies for struggling writers.* New York: Guilford Press.

Collins, J. L., & Madigan, T. L. (2010). Using writing to develop struggling learners' higher level reading comprehension. In J. L. Collins & T. G. Gunning (Eds.), *Building struggling students' higher level literacy: Practical ideas, powerful solutions* (pp. 103–124). Newark, DE: International Reading Association.

Collins, K. M., & Collins, J. L. (1996). Strategic instruction for struggling writers. *English Journal, 85*, 54–61.

Comer, J. P. (1988). *Maggie's American dream: The life and times of a black family.* New York: New American Library.

Comfort, R. L. (1994). Understanding and appreciating the ADHD child in the classroom. In C. Weaver (Ed.), *Success *at last: Helping students with AD(H)D achieve their potential* (pp. 63–74). Portsmouth, NH: Heinemann.

Compton, D. L., Gilbert, J. K., Jenkins, J. R., Fuchs, D., Fuchs, L., Cho, E., Barquero, L., & Bouton, B. (2012). Accelerating chronically unresponsive children to tier 3 instruction: What level of data is necessary to ensure selection accuracy? *Journal of Learning Disabilities, 45,* 204–216.

Connor, C. M., Piasta, S. B., Glasney, S., Schatschneider, C., Crowe, E., Underwood, P., Fishman, B., & Morrison, F. J. (2009). Individualizing student instruction precisely: Effects of child instruction interactions on first graders' literacy development. *Child Development, 80*(1), 77–100.

Cooper, H., Nye, B. C., Kelly, L. J., & Greathouse, S. (1996). The effects of summer vacation on achievement test scores: A narrative and meta-analytic review. *Review of Educational Research, 66,* 227–268.

Cooter, R. B., Flynt, E. S., & Cooter, K. S. (2007). *Comprehensive reading inventory.* Upper Saddle River, NJ: Merrill.

Coté, N., Goldman, S. R., & Saul, E. U. (1998). Students making sense of informational text: Relations between processing and representation. *Discourse Processes, 25,* 1–53.

Council of the Great City Schools. (2009). *Urban indicator: High school reform survey, school year 2006–2007.* Available online at http://www.cgcs.org/publications/achievement.aspx

Coxhead, A. (2000). A new academic word list. *TESOL Quarterly 34,* 213–238.

Crawford, A. N. (1982). From Spanish reading to English reading: The transition process. In M. P. Douglass (Ed.), *Claremont Reading Conference Yearbook* (pp. 159–165). Claremont, CA: Claremont Reading Conference.

Cudd, E. T., & Roberts, L. (1989). Using writing to enhance content area learning in the primary grades. *Reading Teacher, 42,* 392–404.

Cummins, J. (1994). The acquisition of English as a second language. In K. Spangenberg-Urbschat & R. Pritchard (Eds.), *Kids come in all languages: Reading instruction for all ESL students* (pp. 36–62). Newark, DE: International Reading Association.

Cunningham, J. W., Erickson, K., Spadorcia, S. A., Koppenhaver, D. A., Cunningham, P. M., Yoder, D. E., & McKenna, M. C. (1999). Assessing decoding from an onset-rime perspective. *Journal of Literacy Research, 31,* 391–414.

Cunningham, J. W., & Foster, E. O. (1978). The ivory tower connection: A case study. *Reading Teacher, 31,* 365–369.

Cunningham, P. M. (1978). Decoding polysyllabic words: An alternative *strategy. Journal of Reading, 21,* 608–614.

Cunningham, P. M. (1979). A comparison/contrast theory of mediated word identification. *Reading Teacher, 32,* 774–778.

Cunningham, P. M. (1991). *Phonics they use: Words for reading and writing.* New York: HarperCollins.

Cunningham, P. M., & Allington, R. L. (1994). *Classrooms that work: They can all read and write.* Boston: HarperCollins.

Cunningham, P. M., & Cunningham, J. W. (1992). Making words: Enhancing the invented spelling-decoding connection. *Reading Teacher, 46,* 106–115.

Curtis, M. (2010). The role of word meanings in comprehension. In M. G. McKeown & L. Kucan (Eds.). *Bringing reading research to life.* New York: Guilford Press.

Curtis, M. E., & Longo, A. M. (1999). *When adolescents can't read: Methods and materials that work.* Boston: Brookline Books.

Curtis, M. E., & Longo, A. M. (2001, November). Teaching vocabulary to adolescents to improve comprehension. *Reading Online, 5*(4). Available online at http://www.readingonline.org/articles/art_index?.asp?HREF=curtis/index.html

Cutting, L. E., Materek, A., Cole, C. A. S., Levine, T. M., & Mahone, T. M. (2009). Effects of fluency, oral language, and executive function on reading comprehension performance. *Annals of Dyslexia, 59*(1), 34–54.

Dahl, K., & Farnham, N. (1998). *Children's writing, Perspectives from research.* Newark, DE: International Reading Association & National Reading Conference.

Dale, E., & O'Rourke, J. (1971). *Techniques of teaching vocabulary.* Chicago, IL: Field.

Dale, E., & O'Rourke, J. (1981). *Living word vocabulary.* Chicago: Field.

Daneman, M., & Carpenter, P. A. (1980). Individual differences in working memory and in reading. *Journal of Verbal Learning and Verbal Behavior, 19,* 450–466.

Davis, G., Jackson, J., & Johnson, S. (2000, May). *Guided writing-Leveling the balance.* Paper presented at the annual meeting of the International Reading Association, Indianapolis, IN.

Davis, N., Barquero, L., Compton, D. L., Fuchs, L. S., Fuchs, D., Gore, J. C., Powell-Smith, K. A., Kaminski, R., & Good, R. H. (2011). *DIBELS deep: In-depth diagnostic assessment of literacy skills.* Longmont, CO: Sopris Learning.

DeFord, D. E. (1997). Early writing: Teachers and children in Reading Recovery. In S. L. Swartz & A. F. Klein (Eds.), *Research in Reading Recovery* (pp. 148–172). Portsmouth, NH: Heinemann.

DePaulo, B., & Jordan, A. (1982). Age changes in deceiving and deceit. In R. Feldman (Ed.), *Development of nonverbal behavior in children* (pp. 140–180). New York: Springer-Verlag.

Dewitz, P. (2012, April). *New insights about students with comprehension problems: Let's focus on connecting ideas within a text.* Paper presented at the International Reading Association Convention, Chicago, IL.

Dewitz, P., & Dewitz, P. K. (2003). They can read the words, but they can't understand: Refining comprehension assessment. *Reading Teacher, 56,* 422–435.

Dickinson, D. K., & Smith, M. W. (1994). Long-term effects of preschool teachers' book reading on low-income children's vocabulary and story comprehension. *Reading Research Quarterly, 29,* 104–122.

Dickson, S. V. (2004, July). *Adaptations for struggling readers in the content areas:. Teacher-to-teacher initiative summer workshop.* Available online at http://www.ed.gov/teachers/how/read/list. html

Dixon, R. C., Carnine, D., & Kame'enui, E. (1993). Tools for teaching diverse learners: Using scaffolding to teach writing. *Educational Leadership, 5*(3), 100–101.

Dole, J. A., Brown, K. J., & Trathen, W. (1996). The effect of strategy instruction on the comprehension performance of at-risk students. *Reading Research Quarterly, 31,* 62–88.

Donovan, C. A., & Smolkin, L. B. (2011). Supporting informational writing in the elementary grades. *The Reading Teacher, 64,* 406–416.

Donovan, C., & Smolkin, L. (2012). *Explanatory writing development: Elementary school children explain the science of tornadoes and bicycles.* International Reading Association Convention, Chicago, IL.

Dorn, L. (2010, April). *Response to intervention: A comprehensive and systemic design.* Paper presented at the International Reading Association Convention, Chicago, IL.

Dorn, L. J., French, C., & Jones, T. (1998). *Apprenticeship in literacy: Transitions across reading and writing.* York, ME: Stenhouse.

Doyle, B. G., & Bramwell, W. (2006). Promoting emergent literacy and social–emotional learning through dialogic reading. *The Reading Teacher, 59,* 554–564.

Duffelmeyer, F. A., Baum, D. D., & Merkley, D. J. (1987). Maximizing reader-text confrontation with an Extended Anticipation Guide. *Journal of Reading, 35,* 654–656.

Duffy, G. G., & Roehler, L. R. (1987). Improving reading instruction through the use of responsive elaboration. *Reading Teacher, 40,* 514–520.

Duke, N. D., Pearson, P. D., Strachan, S. L., & Billman, A. K. (2011). Essential elements of fostering and teaching reading comprehension. In S. J. Samuels & A. E. Farstrup, *What research has to say about reading instruction* (4th ed., pp. 51–93). Newark, DE: International Reading Association.

Dunn, L., & Dunn, M. (1997). *Peabody Picture Vocabulary Test-Ill.* Circle Pines, MN: American Guidance Services.

Durrell, D., & Catterson, J. (1980). *Durrell analysis of reading difficulty.* San Antonio, TX: Psychological Corporation.

Durrell, D. D. (1980). Letter-name value in reading and spelling. *Reading Research Quarterly, 16,* 159–163.

Dutro, S., & Moran, C. (2003). Rethinking English language instruction: An architectural approach. In G. G. Garcia (Ed.), *English Learners* (pp. 227–258). Newark, DE: International Reading Association.

Dyson, A. H., & Freedman, S. W. (1991). Writing. In J. Flood, J. M. Jensen, D. Lapp, & J. R. Squire (Eds.), *Handbook of research on teaching the English language arts* (pp. 754–774). New York: Macmillan.

Early, M., & Sawyer, D. J. (1984). *Reading to learn in grades 5 to 12.* New York: Harcourt Brace Jovanovich.

Early Childhood-Head Start Task Force. (2002). *Teaching our youngest: Guide for preschool teachers and child care and family providers.* Washington, DC: U.S. Department of Education, U.S. Department of Health and Human Services. Available online at http://www.ed.gov/teachershow/early/teachingour youngest/index.html

Ehri, L. C. (1983). A critique of five studies related to letter-name knowledge and learning to read. In L. M. Gentile, M. L. Kamil, & J. S. Blanchard (Eds.), *Reading research revisited* (pp. 143–153). Columbus, OH: Merrill.

Ehri, L. C. (1992). Reconceptualizing the development of sight word reading and its relationship to reading. In P. B. Gough, L. C. Ehri, & R. Treiman (Eds.), *Reading acquisition* (pp. 107–143). Hillsdale, NJ: Erlbaum.

Ehri, L. C. (1994). Development of the ability to read words: Update. In R. B. Ruddell, M. R. Ruddell, & H. Singer (Eds.), *Theoretical models and processes of reading* (4th ed., pp. 323–358). Newark, DE: International Reading Association.

Ehri, L. C., Dreyer, L. G., Flugman, B., & Gross, A. (2007). Reading Rescue: An effective tutoring intervention model for language minority students who are struggling readers in first grade. *American Educational Research Journal, 44*(2), 414–448.

Ehri, L. C., & Robbins, C. (1992). Beginners need some decoding skill to read words by analogy. *Reading Research Quarterly, 27,* 12–26.

Ehri, L. C., & Saltmarsh, J. (1995). Beginning readers outperform older disabled readers in learning to read words by sight. *Reading and Writing: An Interdisciplinary Journal, 7,* 295–326.

Ehri, L. C., & Snowling, M. J. (2004). Developmental variation in word recognition. In C. A. Stone, E. R. Silliman, B. J. Ehren, & K. Apel (Eds.), *Handbook of language and literacy development and disorders* (pp. 433–460). New York: Guilford Press.

Elbro, C., & Arnbak, E. (1996). The role of morpheme recognition and morphological awareness in dyslexia. *Annals of Dyslexia, 46,* 209–240.

Elkonin, D. B. (1973). Reading in the USSR. In J. Downing (Ed.), *Comparative reading* (pp. 551–579). New York: Macmillan.

Elley, W. B. (1989). Vocabulary acquisition from listening to stories. *Reading Research Quarterly, 24,* 174–187.

Englert, C. S., & Hiebert, E. H. (1985). Children's developing awareness of text structures in expository materials. *Journal of Educational Psychology, 76,* 65–75.

Englert, C. S., Raphael, T. E., & Anderson, L. M. (1989). *Cognitive Strategy Instruction in Writing Project.* East Lansing, MI: Institute for Research on Teaching.

Englert, C. S., Raphael, T. E., Anderson, L. M., Anthony, H. M., Fear, K. L., & Gregg, S. L. (1988). A case for writing intervention: Strategies for writing informational text. *Learning Disabilities Focus, 8,* 98–113.

Englert, C. S., Mariage, T. V., Okolo, C. M., Shankland, R. K., Moxley, K. D., Courtad, C. A., Jocks-Meier, B. S., O'Brien, J. C., Martin, N. M., & Chen, H. (2009). The Learning-to-learn strategies of adolescent students with disabilities: Highlighting, note taking, planning, and writing expository texts. *Assessment for Effective Intervention, 34*(3), 147–161.

Enz, B. (1989, May). *The 90 percent success solution.* Paper presented at the annual convention of the International Reading Association, New Orleans, LA.

Fautsch-Patridge, T., McMaster, K. L., & Hupp, S. C. (2011). Are current reading research findings applicable to students with intellectual disabilities? In S. J. Samuels & A. E. Farstrup (Eds.), *What research has to say about reading instruction* (4th ed.). Newark, DE: International Reading Association.

Farr, R., & Carey, R. F. (1986). *Reading: What can be measured?* Newark, DE: International Reading Association.

Farr, R., & Farr, B. (1990). *Integrated assessment system.* San Antonio, TX: Psychological Corporation.

Fernald, G. M. (1943). *Remedial techniques in basic school subjects.* New York: McGraw-Hill.

Ferreiro, E. (1986). The interplay between information and assimilation in beginning literacy. In W. H. Teale & E. Sulzby (Eds.), *Emergent literacy* (pp. 15–49). Norwood, NJ: Ablex.

Feurstein, R., Rand, Y., & Hoffman, M. B. (1979). *The dynamic assessment of retarded performers: The Learning Potential Assessment Device—Theory, instruments, and techniques.* Baltimore, MD: University Park Press.

Fielding, L. G., Wilson, P. T, & Anderson, R. C. (1986). A new focus on free reading: The role of trade books in reading instruction. In T. E. Raphael (Ed.), *The contexts of school-based literacy* (pp. 149–160). New York: Random House.

Fielding-Barnsley, R. (1997). Explicit instruction in decoding benefits children high in phonemic awareness and alphabet knowledge. *Scientific Studies of Reading, 1*, 85–98.

Fisher, D. (2008). *Modeling thinking for older readers.* Paper presented at the National Reading Conference, Orlando, FL.

Fisher, D., & Frey, N. (2007). Implementing a schoolwide literacy framework: Improving achievement in an urban elementary school. *Reading Teacher, 61*, 32–43.

Fisher, D., Frey, N., & Lapp, D. (2011). What research says about intentional instruction. In S. J. Samuels & A. E. Farstrup (Eds.). *What research says about reading instruction* (4th ed., 359–378). Newark, DE: International Reading Association.

Fisher, D., Frey, N., & Lapp, D. (2012). *Text complexity, Raising rigor in reading.* Newark, DE: International Reading Association.

Fisher, J. B., Schumaker, J. B., & Deshler, D. D. (2002). Improving the reading comprehension of at-risk adolescents. In C. C. Block & M. Pressley (Eds.), *Comprehension instruction: Research-based best practices.* New York: Guilford Press.

Fitzgerald, J. (1951). *A basic life spelling vocabulary.* Milwaukee, WI: Bruce.

Fitzgerald, J., & Spiegel, D. (1983). Enhancing children's reading comprehension through instruction in narrative structure. *Journal of Reading Behavior, 15*, 1–17.

Five, C. L. (1992). *Special voices.* Portsmouth, NH: Heinemann.

Flanigan, K., Hayes, L., Templeton, S., Bear, D. R., Invernizzi, M., & Johnston, F. (2011). *Words their way with struggling readers: Word study for reading, vocabulary, and spelling instruction, grades 4–12.* Boston: Pearson/Allyn & Bacon.

Flanigan, K., Templeton, S., Hayes, L. (2012). What's in a word? Using content vocabulary to generate growth in general academic vocabulary knowledge. *Journal of Adolescent & Adult Literacy 56*, 132–140.

Fletcher, J. M., Lyon, G. R., Fuchs, L. S., & Barnes, A. (2007). *Learning disabilities: From identification to intervention.* New York: Guilford Press.

Fletcher, R., & Portalupi, J. (2001). *Writer's workshop.* Portsmouth, NH: Heinemann.

Flynt, E. S., & Cooter, R. B., Jr. (Eds.). (1995). *Flynt-Cooter inventory for the classroom.* Scottsdale, AZ: Gorsuch Scarisbrick.

Fong, P., Huebner, T., Fong, T., & Calisi , G. (2012). *CAPP expository literacy grant evaluation—Final report.* San Francisco, CA: WestEd.

Foorman, B. R., Fletcher, J. M., Francis, D. J., Schatschneider, C., & Mehta, P. (1998). The role of instruction in learning to read: Preventing reading failure in at-risk children. *Journal of Educational Psychology, 90*, 37–55.

Foorman, B. R., & Torgesen, J. (2001). Critical elements of classroom and small group instruction promote reading success in all children. *Learning Disabilities Research and Practice, 16*, 203–212.

Fountas, I., & Pinnell, G. S. (1996). *Guided reading: Good first teaching for all children.* Portsmouth, NH: Heinemann.

Fountas, I., & Pinnell, G. S. (1999). *Matching books to readers: Using leveled books in guided reading K–3.* Portsmouth, NH: Heinemann.

Fountas, I., & Pinnell, G. S. (2009). *The Fountas and Pinnell leveled book list K–8+ 2010–2012 edition.* Portsmouth, NH: Heinemann.

Fountas, I., & Pinnell, G. S. (2010). *The Fountas and Pinnell Benchmark Assessment System 1* (2nd ed.). Portsmouth, NH: Heinemann.

Fountas, I., & Pinnell, G. S. (2010). *The Fountas and Pinnell Benchmark Assessment System 2* (2nd ed.). Portsmouth, NH: Heinemann.

Fowler, M. C., Lindemann, L. M., Thacker-Gwaltney, S., & Invernizzi, M. (2002). *A second year of one-on-one tutoring: An intervention for second graders with reading difficulties* (CIERA Report No. 3-019). Ann Arbor: University of Michigan School of Education.

Francis, D., Rivera, M., Lesaux, N., Kieffer, M., & Rivera, H. (2006). *Practical guidelines for the education of English language learners: Research-based recommendations for instruction and academic interventions.* Portsmouth, NH: RMC Research, Center on Instruction. Available online at http://www.centeroninstruction.org/fdes/ELLl-Interventions.pdf

Fry, E. (1977a). *Elementary reading instruction.* New York: McGraw-Hill.

Fry, E. (1977b). Fry's readability graph: Clarifications, validity, and extension to level 17. *Journal of Reading, 21*, 242–252.

Fry, E., & Kress, J. E., (2006). *The reading teacher's book of lists* (5th ed.). Englewood Cliffs, NJ: Prentice Hall.

Fuchs, D., & Fuchs, L. S. (n.d.). *Letter sound fluency test.* Nashville, TN: Vanderbilt University.

Fuchs, D., & Fuchs, L. S. (2006). Introduction to response to intervention: What, why, and how valid is it? *Reading Research Quarterly, 41*, 93–99.

Fuchs, L. S., Fuchs, D., & Compton, D. L. (2004). Monitoring early reading development in first grade: Word identification fluency versus nonsense word fluency. *Exceptional Children, 7*(1), 7–21.

Fuchs, D., Fuchs, L. S., & Compton, D. L. (2012). Smart RTI: A next-generation approach to multilevel prevention. *Exceptional Children, 78*, 263–279.

Fuchs, L. S., Fuchs, D., & Deno, S. E. (1982). Reliability and validity of curriculum-based informal reading inventories. *Reading Research Quarterly, 18*, 6–26.

Fukkink, R. G., & de Glopper, K. (1998). Effects of instruction in deriving word meaning from context: A meta-analysis. *Review of Educational Research, 68*, 450–469.

Furth, H. G. (1970). *Piaget for teachers.* Englewood Cliffs, NJ: Prentice Hall.

Fusaro, J. (1988). Applying statistical rigor to a validation study of the Fry Readability Graph. *Reading Research and Instruction, 28*, 44–48.

Galvin, G. A. (1981). Uses and abuses of the WISC-R with the learning disabled. *Journal of Learning Disabilities, 14*, 326–329.

Gambrell, L. B., & Bales, R. J. (1986). Mental imagery and the comprehension monitoring performance of fourth- and fifth-grade poor readers. *Reading Research Quarterly, 21*, 454–464.

Gambrell, L. B., Wilson, R. M., & Gantt, W. N. (1981). Classroom observations of good and poor readers. *Journal of Educational Research, 24*, 400–404.

Ganske, K. (1993). *Developmental spelling analysis: A qualitative measure for assessment and instructional planning.* Barboursville, VA: Author.

Ganske, K. (2000). *Word journeys: Assessment-guided phonics, spelling and vocabulary instruction.* New York: Guilford Press.

García, G. E. (1991). Factors influencing the English reading test performance of Spanish-speaking Hispanic children. *Reading Research Quarterly, 26,* 371–392.

García, G. E., Pearson, P. D., & Jiménez, R. T. (1994). *The at-risk situation: A synthesis of reading research.* Champaign: University of Illinois, Center for the Study of Reading.

Gardner, H. (1983). *Frames of mind: The theory of multiple intelligences.* New York: Basic Books.

Gardner, H. (1999). *Intelligence reframed.* New York: Basic Books.

Garner, R. (1994). Metacognition and executive control. In R. B. Ruddell, M. R. Ruddell, & H. Singer (Eds.), *Theoretical models and processes of reading* (4th ed., pp. 715–732). Newark, DE: International Reading Association.

Garner, R., & Reis, R. (1981). Monitoring and resolving comprehension obstacles: An investigation of spontaneous text lookbacks among upper-grade's good and poor comprehenders. *Reading Research Quarterly, 16,* 569–582.

Garnett, K. (1986). Telling tales: Narratives and learning disabled children. *Topics in Language Disorders, 6*(2), 44–52.

Gaskins, I. W. (1998, May). *What research suggests are ingredients of a grades 1–6 literacy program for struggling readers.* Paper presented at International Reading Association convention, Orlando, FL.

Gaskins, I. W. (2003). Taking charge of reader, text, activity, and context variables. In A. Sweet & C. Snow (Eds.), *Rethinking reading comprehension* (pp. 141–165). New York: Guilford Press.

Gaskins, I. W. (2005). *Success with struggling readers: The Benchmark School approach.* New York: Guilford Press.

Gaskins, I. W. (2011). Interventions to develop decoding proficiencies. In A. McGill-Franzen & R. Allington (Eds.), *Handbook of reading disabilities* (pp. 289–306). New York: Routledge.

Gaskins, I. W., Ehri, L. C., Cress, C., O'Hara, C., & Donnelly, K. (1996–1997). Procedures for word learning: Making discoveries about words. *Reading Teacher, 50,* 312–327.

Gaskins, I. W., & Galloway, E. (2010). Beyond strategy instruction Looking at person, situation, task, and text variables. In J. L. Collins & T. G. Gunning (Eds.), *Building struggling students' higher level literacy: Practical ideas, powerful solutions* (pp. 199–229). Newark, DE: International Reading Association.

Gaskins, I. W., Gaskins, J. C., & Gaskins, I. W. (1991). A decoding program for poor readers and the rest of the class, too! *Language Arts, 63,* 213–225.

Gaskins, I. W., Satlow, E., & Pressley, M. (2007). Executive control of reading comprehension in the elementary school. In L. Meltzer (Ed.), *Executive function in education: From theory to practice* (pp. 194–215). New York: Guilford Press.

Gates, A. I. (1927). *The improvement of reading: A program of diagnostic and remedial methods.* New York: Macmillan.

Gates, A. I. (1931). *Interest and ability in reading.* New York: Macmillan.

Gathercole, S. E., & Baddeley, A. D. (1990). Phonological memory deficits in language disordered children: Is there a causal connection? *Journal of Memory and Language, 29,* 336–360.

Gelzheiser, L. M. (2010, April). *Interactive strategies approach: Part 2, older struggling readers.* Paper presented at the International Reading Association Convention, Chicago, IL.

Gelzheiser, L. M., Scanlon, D. M., & Hallgren-Flynn, L. (2010). Spotlight on RTI for adolescents: An example of intensive middle school intervention using the interactive strategies approach-extended. In M. Y. Lipson & K. K. Wixson (Eds.), *Approaches to response to intervention (RTI): Evidence-based frameworks for preventing reading difficulties* (pp. 211–230). Newark, DE: International Reading Association.

Gentile, L. M., & McMillan, M. M. (1987). *Stress and reading difficulties: Research, assessment, intervention.* Newark, DE: International Reading Association.

Gentry, J. R. (1997). *My kid can't spell.* Portsmouth, NH: Heinemann.

Gentry, J. R. (2004). *The science of spelling.* Portsmouth, NH: Heinemann.

Gentry, J. R., & Gillet, J. W. (1993). *Teaching kids to spell.* Portsmouth, NH: Heinemann.

Georgia Department of Education. (2000). *Developmental stages/scoring guidelines for writing.* Atlanta: Author.

German, D. J., & Newman, R. S. (2007). Oral reading skills of children with oral language (word finding) difficulties. *Journal of Reading Psychology, 28,* 397–442.

Gersten, R., & Jiménez, R. T. (1994). A delicate balance: Enhancing literature instruction for students of English as a second language. *Reading Teacher, 47,* 438–449.

Gersten, R., Baker, S. K., Shanahan, T., Linan-Thompson, S., Collins, P., & Scarcella, R. (2007). *Effective literacy and English language instruction for English learners in the elementary grades: A practice guide* (NCEE No. 2007-4011). Washington, DC: National Center for Education Evaluation and Regional Assistance, Institute of Education Sciences, U.S. Department of Education. Available online at http://ies.ed .gov/ncee

Geschwind, N. (1972). Disconnection syndromes in animals and man. In N. Geschwind (Ed.), *Selected papers on language and the brain* (pp. 106–236). Boston: Reidel.

Gibson, E. J., Gibson, J. J., Pick, A. D., & Osser, H. (1962). A developmental study of the discrimination of letter-like forms. *Journal of Comparative and Physiological Psychology, 55,* 897–906.

Gibson, E. J., & Levin, H. (1974). *The psychology of reading.* Cambridge, MA: MIT Press.

Gilger, J. W., & Wise, S. E. (2004). Genetic correlates of language and literacy impairment. In C. A. Stone, E. R. Silliman, B. J, Ehren, & K. Apel (Eds.), *Handbook of language and literacy development and disorders* (pp. 25–48). New York: Guilford Press.

Gillet, J. W., & Temple, C. (1994). *Understanding reading problems: Assessment and instruction* (4th ed.). New York: HarperCollins.

Gillingham, A., & Stillman, B. (1983). *Remedial training for children with specific disability in reading, writing, and penmanship* (7th ed.). Cambridge, MA: Educators Publishing Service.

Glass, G. G. (1976). *Glass analysis for decoding only: Teacher's guide.* Garden City, NY: Easier to Learn.

Glass, G. G., & Burton, E. H. (1973). How do they decode? Verbalizations and observed behaviors of successful decoders. *Education, 94,* 58–65.

Glazer, S. M. (1991). Behaviors reflecting emotional involvements during reading and writing activities. *Reading, Writing, and Learning Disabilities, 7,* 219–231.

Glenberg, A. M. (2011). How reading comprehension is embodied and why that matters. *International Electronic Journal of Elementary Education, 4*, 5–18.

Glenberg, A. M., Brown, E. M., & Levin, J. R. (2007). Enhancing comprehension in small reading groups using a manipulation strategy. *Contemporary Educational Psychology, 32*, 389–399.

Glenberg, A. M., Gutierrez, T., Levin, J. R., Japuntich, S., & Kaschak, M. P. (2004). Activity and imagined activity can enhance young children's reading comprehension. *Journal of Educational Psychology, 96*, 424–436.

Glenberg, A. M., Jaworski, B., Rischal, M., & Levin, J. R. (2007). What brains are for: Action, meaning, and reading comprehension. In D. McNamara (Ed.), *Reading comprehension strategies: Theories, interventions, and technologies* (pp. 221–240). Mahwah, NJ: Erlbaum.

Goerss, B. L., Beck, I. L., & McKeown, M. G. (1999). Increasing remedial students' ability to derive word meaning from context. *Reading Psychology, 20*, 151–175.

Gold, J., & Fleisher, L. S. (1986). Comprehension breakdown with inductively organized text: Differences between average and disabled readers. *Remedial and Special Education, 7*, 26–32.

Goldenberg, C. (1994). Promoting early literacy development among Spanish-speaking children: Lessons from two studies. In E. H. Hiebert & B. M. Taylor (Eds.), *Getting reading right from the start* (pp. 171–200). Boston: Allyn & Bacon.

Good, R. H., & Kaminski, R. A. (Eds.). (2003). *Dynamic indictors of basic early literacy skills* (6th ed.). Longmont, CO: Sopris West.

Good R., III, Kaminski, R. A., Dewey, E. N., Wallin, J., Powell-Smith, K. A., & Latimer, R. J. (2011). *DIBELS Next technical manual draft.* Dynamic Measurement Group, Inc. Available online at https://dibels.org/next/downloads/DIBELSNext_TechnicalManual.pdf

Goodman, K. S. (1969). Analysis of oral reading miscues: Applied psycholinguistics. *Reading Research Quarterly, 5*, 9–30.

Goodman, K. S. (1974). Miscue analysis: Theory and reality in reading. In J. E. Merritt (Ed.), *New horizons in reading* (pp. 15–26). Newark, DE: International Reading Association.

Goodman, K. S. (1982). Revaluing readers and reading. *Topics in Learning and Learning Disabilities, 7*(4), 87–93.

Goodman, K. S., & Goodman, Y. M. (1978). *Reading of American children whose language is a stable rural dialect of English or a language other than English.* Detroit, MI: Wayne State University Press (ERIC Document Reproduction Service No. ED 182-465).

Goodman, Y. S. (1992). Through the miscue window. In K. S. Goodman, L. B. Bird, & Y. M. Goodman (Eds.), *The whole language catalog: Supplement on authentic assessment* (pp. 20–21). Santa Rosa, CA: American School Publications.

Goodson, B., Wolf, A., Bell, S., Turner, H., & Finney, P. B. (2010). *The effectiveness of a program to accelerate vocabulary development in kindergarten (VOCAB)* (NCEE 2010-4014). Washington, DC: National Center for Education Evaluation and Regional Assistance, Institute of Education Sciences, U.S. Department of Education.

Gordon, W. C. (1989). *Learning and memory.* Belmont, CA: Brooks/Cole.

Goswami, U. (1988). Orthographic analogies and reading development. *Quarterly Journal of Experimental Psychology, 40*, 239–268.

Goswami, U. (2000). Phonological and lexical processes. In M. L. Kamil, P. B. Mosenthal, P. D. Pearson, & R. Barr (Eds.), *Handbook of reading research, Vol. III* (pp. 251–267). Mahwah, NJ: Erlbaum.

Gottlieb, J. (2004, March 9). North End's school success studied. *Hartford Courant,* pp. B1, B7.

Gough, P. B., & Hillinger, M. L. (1980). Learning to read: An unnatural act. *Bulletin of the Orton Society, 30,* 179–196.

Gough, P. B., Juel, C., & Griffith, P. L. (1992). Reading, spelling, and the orthographic cipher. In P. B. Gough, L. C. Ehri, & R. Treiman (Eds.), *Reading acquisition* (pp. 35–48). Hillsdale, NJ: Erlbaum.

Gough, P. B., Larson, K. C., & Yopp, H. (2001). *The structure of phonemic awareness.* Unpublished paper, Austin: University of Texas.

Graesser, A. C. (2007). An introduction to strategic reading comprehension. In D. S. McNamara (Ed.), *Reading comprehension strategies, theories, interventions, and technologies* (pp. 3–26). New York: Erlbaum.

Graesser, A. C., & Bertus, E. L. (1998). The construction of causal inferences while reading expository texts on science and technology. *Scientific Studies of Reading, 2,* 247–269.

Graham, S. (1999). Handwriting and spelling instruction for students with learning disabilities: A review. *Learning Disability Quarterly, 22,* 78–98.

Graham, S., Bollinger, A., Booth Olson, C., D'Aoust, C., MacArthur, C., McCutchen, D., & Olinghouse, N. (2012). *Teaching elementary school students to be effective writers: A practice guide* (NCEE 2012- 4058). Washington, DC: National Center for Education Evaluation and Regional Assistance, Institute of Education Sciences, U.S. Department of Education. Retrieved from http://ies.ed.gov/ncee/ wwc/publications_reviews.aspx#pubsearch

Graham, S., & Harris, K. R. (1993). Teaching writing strategies to students with learning disabilities: Issues and recommendations. In L. J. Meltzer (Ed.), *Strategy assessment and instruction for students with learning disabilities: From theory to practice* (pp. 271–292). Austin, TX: Pro-Ed.

Graham, S., Harris, K., & Olinghouse, N.G. (2007). Teaching effective writing strategies to students with executive function difficulties. In In L. Meltzer (Ed.), *Executive function in education: From theory to practice* (pp. 216–236). New York: Guilford Press.

Graham, S., & Hebert, M. A. (2010). *Writing to read: Evidence for how writing can improve reading.* A Carnegie Corporation Time to Act Report. Washington, DC: Alliance for Excellent Education. Available online at http://carnegie.org/fileadmin/Media/Publications/WritingToRead_01.pdf

Graves, D. H. (1983). *Writing: Teachers and children at work.* Exeter, NH: Heinemann.

Graves, D. H. (1991). All children can write. In S. Stives (Ed.), *With promise: Redefining reading and uniting to "special" students* (pp. 115–125). Portsmouth, NH: Heinemann.

Graves, D. H. (2004). What I've learned from teachers of writing. *Language Arts, 82,* 88–94.

Graves, M. F. (1987). Roles of instruction in fostering vocabulary development. In M. G. McKeown &

M. E. Curtis (Eds.), *The nature of vocabulary acquisition* (pp. 165–184). Hillsdale, NJ: Erlbaum.

Graves, M., & Silverman, R. (2011). Interventions to enhance vocabulary development. In A. McGill-Franzen & R. L. Allington (Eds.), *Handbook of reading disability research* (pp. 315–328). New York: Routledge.

Greaney, K., Tunmer, W. E., & Chapman, J. W. (1997). Effects of rime-based orthographic analogy training on the word recognition skills of children with reading disability. *Journal of Educational Psychology, 89,* 645–661.

Great Books Foundation. (1999). *An introduction to shared inquiry: A handbook for Junior Great Books leaders* (4th ed.). Chicago, IL: Author.

Great Books Foundation. (2006). *Junior Great Books.* Chicago, IL: Author.

Great Books Foundation. (2012). *Case studies: Measuring results of JGB program* [slideshow]. Chicago, IL: Author.

Greenwald, E. A., Persky, H. R., Campbell, J. R., & Mazzeo, J. (1999). *NAEP 1998 writing report card for the nation and the states.* Washington, DC: U.S. Department of Education.

Greenwood, C. R., Abbott, M., & Tapia, Y. (2001). *CWPT-LMS blueprint.* Juniper Gardens Children's Project, University of Kansas. Available online at http://www.lsi.ku.edu/jgprojects/ cwpdms/html2002/ProjectInfo/blueprint.htm

Grigg, W. S., Daane, M. C., Jin, Y., & Campbell, J. R. (2003). *The nation's report card: Reading 2002.* Washington, DC: U.S. Department of Education, Institute of Education Sciences, National Center for Education Statistics. Available online at http://nces.ed.gov/nationsreportcard

Gunning, T. (1975). *A comparison of word attack skills derived from a phonological analysis of frequently used words drawn from a juvenile corpus and an adult corpus.* Unpublished doctoral dissertation, Temple University, Philadelphia, PA.

Gunning, T. (1982). Wrong level test: Wrong information. *Reading Teacher, 35,* 902–905.

Gunning, T. (1988, May). *Decoding behavior of good and poor second grade students.* Paper presented at the annual meeting of the International Reading Association, Toronto.

Gunning, T. (1994a). *Word building: Beginnings.* Honesdale, PA: Phoenix Learning Resources.

Gunning, T. (1994b). *Word building, Book D.* Honesdale, PA: Phoenix Learning Resources.

Gunning, T. (1996). *Creating reading instruction for all children* (2nd ed.). Boston: Allyn & Bacon.

Gunning, T. (1998a). *Best books for beginning readers.* Boston: Allyn & Bacon.

Gunning, T. (1998b, December). *An analysis of the characteristics of the best-selling children's books.* Paper presented at the annual meeting of the National Reading Conference, Austin, TX.

Gunning, T. (1999, December). *Decoding behavior of good and poor second-grade students.* Paper presented at the annual meeting of the National Reading Conference, Orlando, FL.

Gunning, T. (2000a). *Best books for building literacy for elementary school children.* Boston: Allyn & Bacon.

Gunning, T. (2000b). *Phonological awareness and primary phonics.* Boston: Allyn & Bacon.

Gunning, T. (2000c, May). *The Primary Readability Index revised: Using subjective and objective factors to level books for primary grade students.* Paper presented at the annual meeting of the International Reading Association, Indianapolis, IN.

Gunning, T. (2001). *Building words: A resource manual for teaching word analysis and spelling strategies.* Boston: Allyn & Bacon.

Gunning, T. (2003). *Building literacy in the content areas.* Boston: Allyn & Bacon.

Gunning, T. (2005). *Assessing the comprehension processes of good decoding but poor comprehending students.* Paper presented at the National Reading Conference, Miami, FL.

Gunning, T. (2007). *Response to intervention in the primary grades: The role of the reading specialist in the successful implementation of RTI in an urban public school.* Paper presented at the International Reading Association Convention, Toronto.

Gunning, T. (2008a, May). *The construction of a text leveling system based on the scope and sequence of skills presented in today's beginning reading programs.* Poster session presented at the International Reading Association Convention, Atlanta, GA.

Gunning, T. (2008b). *Developing higher-level literacy in all students.* Boston: Allyn & Bacon.

Gunning, T. (2008c). *Teacher's guide for word building, book B* (2nd ed.). Honesdale, PA: Phoenix Learning Resources.

Gunning T., (2008d). *Read, reason, respond: Boosting literacy.* Unionville, CT: Galvin Publications.

Gunning, T. (2010). *Reading comprehension boosters: 100 lessons for building higher-level literacy.* San Francisco: Jossey-Bass.

Gunning, T. (2011). *Teacher's guide for word building book D* (2nd ed.). Unionville, CT: Galvin; Honesdale, PA: Phoenix Learning Resources.

Gunning, T. (2012). *Reading success for all students: Using formative assessment to guide instruction and intervention.* San Francisco: Jossey-Bass.

Gunning, T. (2013). *Creating literacy instruction for all students* (8th ed.). Boston: Allyn & Bacon.

Guthrie, J. (2003). *Classroom contexts in engaged reading: An overview.* Available online at http://www.cori.umd.edu/Research/Papers/ Classroom.htm

Guthrie, J. T. (2004, May). *Classroom practices promoting engagement and achievement in comprehension.* Keynote presentation at Reading Research 2004, Reno, NV.

Guthrie, J. T, Seifert, M., & Kline, L. W. (1978). Clues from research on programs for poor readers. In S. J. Samuels (Ed.), *What research has to say about reading instruction* (pp. 1–12). Newark, DE: International Reading Association.

Hall, L. A. (2008/2009). Research Connections: Understanding youth who struggle with middle school reading. *Journal of Adolescent and Adult Literacy, 52,* 353–355.

Hall, L. A. (2012). The role of reading identities and reading abilities in students' discussions about texts and comprehension strategies. *Journal of Literacy Research, 44,* 239–272.

Halsey, S., & Morris, E. (1977). *Macmillan beginning dictionary.* New York: Macmillan.

Halladay, J. L. (2012). Revisiting key assumptions of the reading level framework. *The Reading Teacher.* Advance online publication. doi: 10.1002/TRTR.01093

Hamilton, L., Halverson, R., Jackson, S., Mandinach, E., Supovitz, J., & Wayman, J. (2009). *Using student achievement data to support instructional decision making* (NCEE 2009-4067). Washington, DC: National Center for Education Evaluation and Regional Assistance, Institute of Education Sciences, U.S. Department of Education. Retrieved from http://ies.ed.gov/ncee/wwc/publications/practiceguides/

Hammill, D. D., Bryant, B. R. (1991). *Detroit Tests of Learning Aptitude-4.* Boston: Pearson.

Hampton, S., Murphy, S., & Lowry, M. (2009). *Using rubrics to improve student writing, grade 1* (rev.). Pittsburgh, PA: New Standards and National Center on Education and the Economy.

Hampton, S., & Resnick, L. B. (2009). *Reading and writing with understanding.* Newark, DE: International Reading Association.

Hansen, J. (1987). *When writers read.* Portsmouth, NH: Heinemann.

Hansen, J., & Pearson, P. D. (1980). *The effects of inference training and practice on young children's comprehension* (Technical Report No. 166). Urbana: University of Illinois, Center for the Study of Reading.

Hansen, J., & Pearson, P. D. (1982). *Improving the inferential comprehension of good and poor fourth-grade readers* (Report No. CSR-TR-235). Urbana: University of Illinois, Center for the Study of Reading (ERIC Document Reproduction No. ED 215-312).

Harcourt Educational Measurement. (2000). *Some things parents should know about testing: A series of questions and answers.* Available online at http://www.hbem.com/library/parents.htm

Hardy, M., Stennett, R. G. F., & Smythe, P. C. (1973). Word attack: How do they figure them out? *Elementary English, 50,* 99–102.

Harm, M., McCandliss, B. D., & Seidenberg, M. S. (2003). Modeling the successes and failures of interventions for disabled readers. *Scientific Studies of Reading, 7,* 155–182.

Harmon, J. W. (1998). Vocabulary teaching and learning in a seventh-grade literature-based classroom. *Journal of Adolescent and Adult Literacy, 41,* 518–529.

Harris, A. J., & Sipay, E. R. (1990). *How to increase reading ability* (9th ed.). New York: Longman.

Harris, K. R. (n.d.). *Self-regulated strategy development for writing: Initial research on classroom teacher implementation.* Available online at http://smu.edu/education/evidencebasededucation/research/KarenHarrisPresentationtoSMUMay2010.pdf

Harris, K. R., & Graham, S. (1992). *Helping young writers master the art: Strategy instruction and self-regulation in the writing process.* Cambridge, MA: Brookline Books.

Hart, B., & Risley, T. R. (1995). *Meaningful differences in the everyday experience of young American children.* Baltimore, MD: Brookes.

Hart, E. R., & Speece, D. L. (1998). Reciprocal teaching goes to college: Effects for postsecondary students at risk for academic failure. *Journal of Educational Psychology, 90,* 670–681.

Hasbrouck, J. (2012, October 2). *Reading fluency: We've come a long way, baby! Part two {Blog}.* Available online at http://soprislearning.wordpress.com/2012/10/02/reading-fluency-weve-come-a-long-way-baby-part-two

Hayes, J. R. (2000). A new framework for understanding cognition and affect in writing. In R. Indrisano & J. R. Squire (Eds.), *Perspectives on writing: Research, theory,*

*and practice* (pp. 6–44). Newark, DE: International Reading Association.

Haywood, H. C. (1993, November). *Interactive assessment: Assessment of learning potential, school learning, and adaptive behavior.* Paper presented at the Ninth Annual Learning Disorders Conference, Cambridge, MA.

Haywood, H. C., Brown. A. L., & Wingenfeld, S. (1990). Dynamic approaches to psychoeducational assessment. *School Psychology Review, 19,* 411–422.

Head, M. H., & Readence, J. E. (1986). Anticipation guides: Meaning through prediction. In E. K. Deshner, T. W. Bean, J. E. Readence, & D. W. Moore (Eds.), *Reading in the content areas* (2nd ed., pp. 229–234). Dubuque, IA: Kendall/Hunt.

Heiman, M., & Slomianko, J. (1986). *Methods of inquiry.* Cambridge, MA: Learning Associates.

Helen Keller International. (2002). *Vision Correction/ChildSight® The problem.* Available online at http://www.hki.org/preventing-blindness/vision-correction-childsight/

Helen Keller International. (2004). *ChildSight faces.* Available online at http://childsight.org/faces/index.htm

Henderson, E. H. (1990). *Teaching spelling.* Boston: Houghton Mifflin.

Henderson, E. H., & Templeton, S. (1986). A developmental perspective of formal spelling instruction through alphabet, pattern, and meaning. *Elementary School Journal, 86,* 305–316.

Henry, M. K. (1990). Reading instruction based on word structure and origin. In P. G. Aaron & R. M. Joshi (Eds.), *Reading and writing disorders in different orthographic systems* (pp. 25–49). Dordrecht, The Netherlands: Kluwer Academic.

Herber, H. L., & Herber, J. N. (1993). *Teaching in content areas with reading, writing and reasoning.* Boston: Allyn & Bacon.

Hess, K., McDivitt. P., & Fincher, M. (2008). *Who are the 2% students and how do we design test items and assessments that provide greater access for them? Results from a pilot study with Georgia students.* Available online at http://www.nciea.org/publications/CCSSO_KHPMMF08.pdf

Hidi, S., & Anderson, V. (1986). Producing written summaries: Task demands, cognitive operations, and implications for instruction. *Review of Educational Research, 56,* 473–493.

Hiebert, E. H. (1994). A small-group literacy intervention with Chapter 1 students. In E. H. Hiebert & B. M. Taylor (Eds.), *Getting reading right from the start* (pp. 85–106). Boston: Allyn & Bacon.

Hiebert, E. H. (1999). Text matters in learning to read. *Reading Teacher, 52,* 552–566.

Hiebert, E. H. (2010). Understanding the word-level features of texts for students who depend on schools to become literate. In M. G. McKeown, & L. Kucan (Eds.), *Bringing reading research to life.* New York: Guilford Press.

Hiebert, E. H., & Taylor, B. M. (2000). Beginning reading instruction: Research on early interventions. In M. L. Kamil, P. B. Mosenthal, P. D. Pearson, & R. Barr (Eds.), *Handbook of reading research, Vol. III* (pp. 455–482). Mahwah, NJ: Erlbaum.

Hochman, J. C. (2009). *Teaching basic writing skills: Strategies for effective expository writing instruction.* Boston, MA: Cambium Learning.

Hoffman, L. (1993, October). *Using readers' theatre in the general English classroom: Motivating reluctant readers and writers.* Paper presented at the annual meeting of the Connecticut Reading Association, Waterbury.

Honig, B., Diamond, L., & Gutlohn, L. (2008). *Assessing reading: Multiple measures for kindergarten through twelfth grade* (2nd ed.). Novato, CA: Consortium on Reading Excellence.

Horowitz, R. (1985). Text patterns. *Journal of Reading 28,* 534–542.

Hosp, M. L., Hosp, J. L., & Howell, K. W. (2007). *The ABCs of CBM: A practical guide to curriculum-based measurement.* New York: Guilford Press.

Hugdahl, K. (1993). Functional brain asymmetry, dyslexia, and immune disorders. In A. M. Galbruda (Ed.), *Dyslexia and development: Neurological aspects of extra-ordinary brains* (pp. 133–154). Cambridge, MA: Harvard University Press.

Hughes, M., & Searle, D. (1997). *The violent "e" and other tricky sounds: Learning to spell from kindergarten through grade 6.* York, ME: Stenhouse.

Hulme, C. (1981). *Reading retardation and multi-sensory teaching.* London: Routledge & Kegan Paul.

Hulme, C., & MacKenzie, S. (1992). *Working memory and severe learning difficulties.* Hillsdale, NJ: Erlbaum.

Hultquist, A. M. (1997). Orthographic processing abilities of adolescents with dyslexia. *Annals of Dyslexia, 47,* 89–104.

Hyerle, D. (2001). Visual tools for mapping minds. In A. L. Costa (Ed.), *Developing minds: A resource book for teaching thinking* (3rd ed., pp. 401–407). Alexandria, VA: Association for Supervision and Curriculum Development.

Hyman, R. T. (1978). *Strategic questioning.* Englewood Cliffs, NJ: Prentice Hall.

Idol, L. (Ed.). (1988). *Remedial techniques in basic school subjects.* Austin, TX: Pro-Ed. (Reprint of original publication by G. M. Fernald [1943]).

Ilg, F., & Ames, L. B. (1964). *School readiness.* New York: Harper & Row.

International Reading Association. (1999). *High stakes assessments in reading: A position statement of the International Reading Association.* Newark, DE: International Reading Association.

International Reading Association. (2000). Teaching all children to read: The roles of the reading specialist: A position statement of the International Reading Association. *Reading Teacher, 54,* 115–119.

International Reading Association. (2002). *What is evidence-based reading? A position statement of the International Reading Association.* Newark, DE: Author. Available online at http://www.reading.org/resources/issues/positions _evidence_based.html

Invernizzi, M., & Hayes, L. (2011). Developmental patterns of reading proficiency and reading difficulties. In R. Allington & A. McGill-Franzen (Eds.), *Handbook of reading disabilities* (pp. 196–207). New York: Routledge.

Irwin, J. W. (1986). *Understanding and teaching cohesion comprehension.* Newark, DE: International Reading Association.

Irwin, P. A., & Mitchell, J. N. (1983). A procedure for assessing the richness of retellings. *Journal of Reading, 26,* 391–396.

Iverson, S., & Tunmer, W. W. (1993). Phonological processing skills and the Reading Recovery program. *Journal of Educational Psychology, 85*(1), 112–126.

Ivey, G. (2000, May). *Dispelling myths associated with struggling middle school readers.* Paper presented at the Annual Meeting of the International Reading Association, Indianapolis, IN.

Jackson, M. D. (1980). Further evidence for a relationship between memory access and reading ability. *Journal of Verbal Learning and Verbal Behavior, 19,* 683–694.

Jenkins, J. R., Matlock, B., & Slocum, T. A. (1989). Approaches to vocabulary instruction. *Reading Research Quarterly, 24,* 215–235.

Jenkins, J. R., Stein, M. L., & Wysocki, K. (1984). Learning vocabulary through reading. *American Educational Research Journal, 2*(4), 767–787.

Jiménez, R. T. (1997). The strategic reading abilities and potential of five low-literacy Latina/o in middle school. *Reading Research Quarterly, 32,* 224–243.

Jiménez, R. T. (2004). More equitable literacy assessment for Latino students. *The Reading Teacher, 57,* 576–578.

Jiménez, R. T., García, G. E., & Pearson, P. D. (1995). Three children, two languages, and strategic reading: Case studies in bilingual/monolingual reading. *American Educational Research Journal, 52*(1), 31–61.

Jobe, F. W. (1976). *Screening vision in schools.* Newark, DE: International Reading Association.

Johns, J. L., & Elish-Piper, L. (2012). *Basic reading inventory* (11th ed.). Dubuque, IA: Kendall Hunt.

Johnson, D. (1993). *Diagnostic teaching: Implications for intervention.* Paper presented at the Ninth Annual Learning Disabilities Conference, Cambridge, MA.

Johnson, D. J., & Myklebust, H. R. (1967). *Learning disabilities: Educational principles and practices.* New York: Grune & Stratton.

Johnson, M. S. (1966). Tracing and kinesthetic techniques. In J. Money (Ed.), *The disabled reader: Education of the dyslexic child* (pp. 147–160). Baltimore, MD: Johns Hopkins University Press.

Johnson, M. S., & Kress, R. A. (1966). *Eliminating learning problems in reading disability cases.* Unpublished paper, Temple University, Philadelphia, PA.

Johnson, M. S., Kress, R. A., & Pikulski, J. J. (1987). *Informal reading inventories* (2nd ed.). Newark, DE: International Reading Association.

Johnston, P. H. (1992). *Constructive evaluation of literate activity.* New York: Longman.

Johnston, P. H. (2000). *Running records: A self-tutoring guide.* Portland, ME: Stenhouse.

Joint Task Force on Assessment. (1994). *Standards for the assessment of reading and writing.* Newark, DE: International Reading Association & Urbana, IL: National Council of Teachers of English.

Jongsma, E. (1980). *Cloze instruction research: A second look.* Newark, DE: International Reading Association.

Juel, C. (1991). Cross-age tutoring between student athletes and at-risk children. *Reading Teacher, 45,* 178–186.

Juel, C. (1994a). *Building a community of readers: University, community, and school partnerships.* Paper presented at the annual meeting of the International Reading Association, Toronto.

Juel, C. (1994b). *Learning to read and write in one elementary school.* New York: Springer-Verlag.

Juel, C. (2010). Taking a long view of reading development. In M. G. McKeown & L. Kucan (Eds.), *Bringing reading research to life*. New York: Guilford Press.

Juel, C., & Minden-Cupp, C. (2000). Learning to read words: Linguistic units and instructional strategies. *Reading Research Quarterly, 35*, 458–492.

Juel, C., & Roper-Schneider, D. (1985). The influence of basal readers on first-grade reading. *Reading Research Quarterly, 20*, 134–152.

Kaderavek, J. C., & Sulzby, E. (1999). *Issues in emergent literacy for children with language impairments* (CIERA Report No. 2-002). Ann Arbor: Center for the Improvement of Early Reading Instruction, University of Michigan School of Education.

Kamhi, A. G., & Catts, H. W. (2012). Language and reading: Convergences and divergences. In A. G. Kamhi & H. W. Catts (Eds.), *Language and Reading Disabilities* (3rd ed., pp. 1–23). Boston: Pearson.

Karasinski, C., & Weismer, S. (2010). Comprehension of inferences in discourse processing by adolescents with and without language impairment. *Journal of Speech, Language, and Hearing Research, 53*, 1268–1279.

Kearns, G., & Biemiller, A. (2010/2011). Two-questions vocabulary assessment: Developing a new method for group testing in kindergarten through second grade. *Journal of Education, 190*, 31–42.

Keene, E. O., & Zimmermann, S. (2007). *Mosaic of thought: The power of comprehension strategy instruction* (2nd ed.). Portsmouth, NH: Heinemann.

Keller, T. A., & Just, M. A. (2009). Altering cortical connectivity: Remediation-induced changes in the white matter of poor readers. *Neuron, 64*, 624–631.

Kelley, J. G., Lesaux, N. K., Kieffer, M. J., & Faller, S. E. (2010). Effective academic vocabulary instruction in the urban middle school. *Reading Teacher, 64*, 5–14.

Kephart, N. C. (1966). *The slow learner in the classroom* (2nd ed.). Columbus, OH: Merrill.

Kibby, M. (1995). *Practical steps for informing literacy instruction: A diagnostic decision-making model*. Newark, DE: International Reading Association.

Kibby, M. W., & Wieland, K. (2004). *How readers think during vocabulary acquisition: Findings from the verbal protocols of good readers when encountering unknown words in context with applications to instruction*. Paper presented at the International Reading Association Convention, Reno, NV.

Kids Count. (2011). *National fact sheet*. Available online at http://datacenter.kidscount.org/databook/2011/Online Books/2011NationalFactSheet.pdf

Kieffer, M. J., & Lesaux, N. K. (2007). Breaking down words to build meaning: Morphology, vocabulary, and reading comprehension in the urban classroom. *Reading Teacher, 61*, 134–144.

Kimmel, S., & MacGinkie, W. H. (1984). Identifying children who use a perseverative text processing strategy. *Reading Research Quarterly, 19*, 162–172.

Kincaid, J. P., Fishburne, R., Rogers, R. L., & Chissom, B. S. (1975). *Derivation of new readability formulas (Automated Readability Index, Fog Count, and Flesch Reading Ease formula) for Navy enlisted personnel* (Branch Report No. 8-75). Millington, TN: Chief of Naval Training.

Kinder, D., Bursuck, B., & Epstein, M. (1992). An evaluation of history textbooks. *Journal of Special Education, 25*, 472–491.

Kinnucan-Welsch, K., Magill, D., & Dean, M. (1999). Strategic teaching and strategic learning in first-grade classrooms. *Reading Horizons, 40*(1), 3–21.

Kintsch, W. (1994). Text comprehension, memory, and learning. *American Psychologist, 49*, 294–303.

Kissner, E. (n.d.). *Teaching text structure, A quick guide for teachers*. Slideshow presentation. Available online at http://www.slideshare.net/elkissn/teaching-text-structure

Klein, P. D., & Rose, M. A. (2010). Teaching argument and explanation to prepare junior students for writing to learn. *Reading Research Quarterly, 45*, 433–461.

Klenk, L., & Kibby, M. W. (2000). Re-mediating reading difficulties: Appraising the past, reconciling the present, constructing the future. In M. L. Kamil, P. B. Mosenthal, P. D. Pearson, & R. Barr (Eds.), *Handbook of reading research, Vol. III* (pp. 667–690). Mahwah, NJ: Erlbaum.

Kletzien, S. B. (1991). Strategy use by good and poor comprehenders reading expository text of differing levels. *Reading Research Quarterly, 26*, 67–86.

Kletzien, S. B., & Bednar, M. R. (1998). A framework for reader autonomy: An integrated perspective. *Journal of Reading, 32*, 30–33.

Knapp, N. F. (1998, December). *The reading apprenticeship intervention and its effect on reading skills and attitudes of delayed primary readers*. Paper presented at the 48th Annual Meeting of the National Reading Conference, Austin, TX.

Koskinen, P. S., Blum, I. H., Bisson, S. A., Phillips, S. M., Creamer, T. S., & Baker, T. K. (1999). Shared reading, books, and audiotapes: Supporting diverse students in school and at home. *Reading Teacher, 52*, 430–444.

Krashen, S. (1996). *Effective second language acquisition*. Torrance, CA: Education Centre.

Kuhn, M. R. (2011). Interventions to enhance fluency and rate of reading. In R. Allington & A. McGill-Franzen (Eds.), *Handbook of reading disabilities* (pp. 307–314). New York: Routledge.

Kuhn, M., & Stahl, S. (2000). Teaching children to learn word meanings from context: A synthesis and some questions. *Journal of Literacy Research, 30*, 119–138.

Labbo, L. D., & Teale, W. H. (1990). Cross-age reading: A strategy for helping poor readers. *Reading Teacher, 43*, 362–369.

Lake, J. H. (1973). The influence of wait time on the verbal dimensions of student inquiry behavior. *Dissertations Abstracts International, 34*, 6476A (University Microfilms No. 74-08866).

Langer, J. A. (2004). Beating the odds: Teaching middle and high school students to read and write well. In R. B. Ruddell & N. J. Unrau (Eds.), *Theoretical models and processes of reading* (5th ed., pp. 1040–1082). Newark, DE: International Reading Association.

Learning Media. (1991). *Reading in junior classes*. Wellington, New Zealand: Ministry of Education.

Lesaux, N. K., Kieffer, M. J., Faller, E., & Kelley, J. (2010). The effectiveness and ease of implementation of an academic vocabulary intervention for linguistically diverse students in urban middle schools. *Reading Research Quarterly, 45*, 198–230.

Leslie, L., & Allen, L. (1999). Factors that predict success in an early literacy intervention project. *Reading Research Quarterly, 34,* 404–424.

Leslie, L., & Caldwell J. (2011). *Qualitative reading inventory-5.* Boston: Pearson.

Levin, J. R. (1993). Mnemonic strategies and classroom learning: A twenty-year report card. *Elementary School Journal, 94,* 235–244.

Levin, J. R., & Pressley, M. (1978). A test of the developmental imagery hypothesis in children's associative learning. *Journal of Educational Psychology, 70,* 691–694.

Liberman, A. M., & Mattingly, I. G. (1989). A specialization for speech perception. *Science, 243,* 489–494.

Liberman, I. Y., Shankweiler, D., Fischer, F. W., & Carter, B. (1974). Explicit syllable and phoneme segmentation in the young child. *Journal of Experimental Child Psychology, 18,* 201–212.

Lindamood, C. H., & Lindamood, P. C. (1975). *The A.D.D. program: Auditory discrimination in depth.* Allen, TX: DLM Teaching Resources.

Lindamood, P., & Lindamood, P. (1998). *The Lindamood phoneme sequencing program for reading, spelling, and speech: LIPS.* Austin, TX: Pro-Ed.

Linden, M., & Wittrock, M. C. (1981). The teaching of reading comprehension according to the model of generative learning. *Reading Research Quarterly, 17,* 44–57.

Lipson, M. Y. (1984). Some unexpected issues in prior knowledge and comprehension. *Reading Teacher, 37,* 760–764.

Lipson, M. Y., & Wixson, K. K. (1991). *Assessment and instruction of reading disability: An interactive approach.* New York: HarperCollins.

Lipson, M. Y., & Wixson, K. K. (1997). *Assessment and instruction of reading disability: An interactive approach* (2nd ed.). New York: HarperCollins.

Lipson, M. Y., & Wixson, K. K. (2009). *Assessment and instruction of reading disability: An interactive approach* (4th ed.). Boston: Pearson.

Lonigan, C. J., Schatschneider, C., & Westberg, L. (2007). Identification of children's skills and abilities linked to later outcomes in reading, writing, and spelling. In *Report of the National Early Literacy Panel.* Washington, DC: National Institute for Literacy.

Lovett, M. W., Borden, S. L., DeLuca, T., Lacerenza, L., Benson, N. J., & Brackstone, D. (1994). Treating the core deficits of developmental dyslexia: Evidence of transfer-of-learning following phonologically and strategy-based reading training programs. *Developmental Psychology, 30,* 805–822.

Lovett, M. W., Warren-Chaplin, P. M., Ransby, M. J., & Borden, S. L. (1990). Training the word recognition skills of reading disabled children: Treatment and transfer effects. *Journal of Educational Psychology, 82,* 769–80.

Lovitt, T. C., Rudsit, J., Jenkins, J., Pious, C., & Benedetti, D. (1986). Adapting science materials for general and learning-disabled seventh graders. *Remedial and Special Education, 7*(1), 31–39.

Luria, A. R. (1970). The functional organization of the brain. *Science, 153,* 66–78.

Lyman, F. (1981). The responsive classroom discussion. In A. S. Anderson (Ed.), *Mainstreaming digest* (pp. 109–113). College Park: University of Maryland.

Lyons, C. (1995, December). *An analysis of the literacy behaviors of hard to accelerate Reading Recovery students.* Paper presented at the annual meeting of the National Reading Conference, New Orleans, LA.

Macartney, S. (2011). *Child Poverty in the United States 2009 and 2010: Selected race groups and Hispanic origin American community survey briefs.* Washington, DC: U.S. Census Bureau. Available online at http://www.census.gov/prod/2011pubs/acsbr10-05.pdf

MacGinitie, W., & MacGinitie, R. (1989). *Manual for scoring and interpretation of the Gates-MacGinitie reading tests* (3rd ed.). Chicago, IL: Riverside.

Manzo, A. V. (1969). The ReQuest procedure. *Journal of Reading, 13,* 123–126.

Manzo, A. V., & Manzo, U. C. (1993). *Literacy disorders: Holistic diagnosis and remediation.* Fort Worth, TX: Harcourt Brace Jovanovich.

Maria, K. (1990). *Reading comprehension instruction: Issues and strategies.* Parkton, MD: York Press.

Maria, K., & MacGinitie, W. (1987). Learning from texts that refute the reader's prior knowledge. *Reading Research and Instruction, 26,* 222–238.

Marley, S. C., Levin, J. R., & Glenberg, A. M. (2007). Improving Native American children's listening comprehension through concrete representations. *Contemporary Educational Psychology, 32,* 537–550.

Marley, S. C., Szabo, Z., Levin, J. R., & Glenberg, A. M. (2011). Investigation of an activity-based text-processing strategy in mixed-age child dyads. *The Journal of Experimental Education, 79,* 340–360.

Martin, M. (1995). *Spelling in the kindergarten.* Paper presented at the annual meeting of the International Reading Association, Anaheim, CA.

Mastropieri, M. A., & Scruggs, T. E. (1991). *Teaching students ways to remember: Strategies for learning mnemonically.* Cambridge, MA: Brookline.

Marzano, R. J. (2004). The developing vision of vocabulary instruction. In J. Baumann & E. Kame'enui (Eds.), *Reading vocabulary: Research to practice* (pp. 118–138). New York: Guilford Press.

Masterson, J. J., Apel, K., & Wasowicz, J. (2006). *Spelling performance evaluation for language and literacy* (2nd ed.). (SPELL-2). Evanston, IL: Learning By Design.

McArthur, T. (Ed.). (1992). *The Oxford companion to the English language.* New York: Oxford University.

McBride-Chang, C., Wagner, R. K., & Chang, L. (1997). Growth modeling of phonological awareness. *Journal of Educational Psychology, 89,* 621–630.

McCandliss, B., Beck, I. L., Sandak, R., & Perfetti, C. (2003). Focusing attention on decoding for children with poor reading skills: Design and preliminary tests of the word building intervention. *Scientific Studies of Reading 7,* 75–104.

McCormick, S. (1987). *Remedial and clinical reading instruction.* Columbus, OH: Merrill.

McCormick, S. (1992). Disabled readers' erroneous responses to inferential comprehension questions. *Reading Research Quarterly, 27,* 54–93.

McCormick, S. (1994). A nonreader becomes a reader. *Reading Research Quarterly, 29,* 157–176.

McCormick, S. (1995). *Instructing students who have literacy problems* (2nd ed.). Englewood Cliffs, NJ: Prentice Hall.

McCormick, S. (1999). *Instructing students who have literacy problems* (3rd ed.). Upper Saddle River, NJ: Prentice Hall.

McDaniels, M. (2008, March). Key concepts in spacing learning over time [transcript]. In U.S. Department of Education, What Works Clearinghouse, *Doing what works: How to organize your teaching.* Available online at http://dww.ed.gov/launcher.cfm?media/CL/OIS/SL/Learn/528_sl_video

McDonald, T., & Thornley, C. (2005). Literacy teaching and learning during the secondary years: Establishing a pathway for success to NCEA and beyond. *set: Research Information for Teachers, 2,* 9–14.

McGill-Franzen, A. (1994). Compensatory and special education: Is there accountability for learning and belief in children's potential? In E. H. Hiebert & B. M. Taylor (Eds.), *Getting reading right from the start* (pp. 13–35). Boston: Allyn & Bacon.

McGinley, W. J., & Denner, P. R. (1987). Story impressions: A prereading/writing activity. *Journal of Reading 31,* 248–253.

McGregor, K. K. (2004). Developmental dependencies between lexical semantics and reading. In C. A. Stone, E. R. Silliman, B. J. Ehren, & K. Apel (Eds.), *Handbook of language and literacy development and disorders* (pp. 302–317). New York: Guilford Press.

McGuinness, D. (1997). Decoding strategies as predictors of reading skill: A follow-up study. *Annals of Dyslexia, 47,* 117–150.

McIntyree, E. (2011). Sociocultural perspectives on children with reading difficulties. In A. McGill-Franzen & R. L. Allington (Eds.). *Handbook of reading disability research* (pp. 45–56). New York: Routledge.

McKeown, M. G., & Beck, I. L. (2004). Direct and rich vocabulary instruction. In J. Baumann & E. Kame'enui (Eds.), *Reading vocabulary: Research to practice* (pp. 13–27). New York: Guilford Press.

McKeown, M. G., Beck, I. L., & Blake, R. K. (2009). Rethinking reading comprehension instruction: A comparison of instruction for strategies and content approaches. *Reading Research Quarterly, 44,* 218–253.

McKeown, M. G., Beck, I. L., & Sandora, C. A. (1996). Questioning the author: An approach to developing meaningful classroom discourse. In M. F. Graves, P. van den Broek, & B. M. Taylor (Eds.), *The first R: Every child's right to read* (pp. 97–119). New York: Teachers College Press and International Reading Association.

McMackin, M. C., & Witherell, N. L. (2005). Different routes to the same destination: Drawing conclusions with tiered graphic organizers. *Reading Teacher, 59,* 242–252.

McNamara, T. P., Miller, D. L., & Bransford, J. D. (1991). Mental models and reading comprehension. In R. Barr, M. L. Kamil, P. Mosenthal, & P. D. Pearson (Eds.), *Handbook of reading research, Vol. II* (pp. 490–511). New York: Longman.

Medley, D. M. (1977). *Teacher competence and teacher effectiveness: A review of process-product research.* Washington, DC: American Association of Colleges for Teacher Education.

Meisel, S. J. (1998). *Assessing readiness* (Ciera Report 3-002). Ann Arbor: Center for the Improvement of Early Reading Instruction, University of Michigan School of Education.

Mellor, B., & Simons, M. (1991). As we see it: An interview with Kenneth S. & Yetta M. Goodman. In K. S. Goodman, L. B. Bird, & Y. M. Goodman (Eds.), *The whole language catalog* (pp. 100–101). Santa Rosa, CA: American School.

Meltzer, L. (1993). *Assessment of learning disabilities: The challenge of evaluating the cognitive strategies and processes underlying learning.* Paper presented at the Ninth Annual Learning Disorders Conference, Cambridge, MA.

Meltzer, L. (2007). Preface. In L. Meltzer (Ed.), *Executive function in education: From theory to practice* (pp. xi–xiii). New York: Guilford Press.

Meltzer, L., & Krishnan, K. (2007). Executive function difficulties and learning disabilities: Understandings and misunderstandings. In L. Meltzer (Ed.), *Executive function in education: From theory to practice* (pp. 77–105). New York: Guilford Press.

Meltzer, L., Pollica, L. S., & Barzillai, M. (2007). Executive function in the classroom: Embedding strategy instruction into daily teaching practice. In L. Meltzer (Ed.), *Executive function in education: From theory to practice* (pp. 165–193). New York: Guilford Press.

Memory, D. M., & Moore, D. W. (1992). Three time-honored approaches to study: An update. In E. K. Dishner, T. W. Bean, J. E. Readence, & D. W. Moore (Eds.), *Reading in the content areas: Improving classroom instruction* (3rd ed., pp. 326–340). Dubuque, IA: Kendall/Hunt.

Menon, S., & Hiebert, E. H. (2005). A comparison of first-graders' reading acquisition with little books or literature-based basal anthologies. *Reading Research Quarterly, 40,* 12–38.

Menyuk, P. (1991). Linguistics and teaching the language arts. In J. Flood, J. M. Jensen, D. Lapp, & J. R. Squire (Eds.), *Handbook of research on teaching the English language arts* (pp. 24–29). New York: Macmillan.

Merkley, D. M., & Jefferies, D. (2001). Guidelines for implementing a graphic organizer. *Reading Teacher, 54,* 350–357.

Mesmer, H. A. (1999). Scaffolding a crucial transition using text with some decodability. *Reading Teacher, 53,* 130–142.

Metsala, J. L. (1999). The development of phonemic awareness in reading-disabled children. *Applied Psycholinguistics, 20,* 49–58.

Meyer, B., Brandt, D., &: Bluth, G. (1980). Use of top-level structure in text: Key for reading comprehension of ninth-grade students. *Reading Research Quarterly, 16,* 72–103.

Meyer, B. J. F., & Ray, M. N. (2011). Structure strategy interventions: Increasing reading comprehension of expository text. *International Electronic Journal of Elementary Education, 4*(1), 127–152. Available online at http://www.iejee.com/4_1_2011/8_IEJEE_4_1_Meyer_Ray.pdf

Meyer, B. J. F., & Rice, G. E. (1984). The structure of text. In P. D. Pearson, R. Barr, M. L. Kamil, & P. Mosenthal (Eds.), *Handbook of reading research* (pp. 319–351). New York: Longman.

Miller, G. A. (1956). The magical number seven plus or minus two: Some limits on our capacity for processing information. *Psychological Review, 63,* 81–97.

Miranda, T., Johnson, K. A., & Rossi-Williams, D. (2012). E-readers: Powering up for engagement, *EL Online Educational Leadership, 69.* Available online at http://www.ascd.org/publications/educational_leadership/jun12/vol69/num09/E-Readers@_Powering_Up_for_Engagement.aspx

Mish, F. C. (1993). *Webster's tenth new collegiate dictionary.* Springfield, MA: Merriam-Webster.

Moats, L. C. (1995). *Spelling: Development, disabilities, and instruction.* Baltimore, MD: York Press.

Moats, L. C., & Farrell, M. L. (1999). In J. R. Birsh (Ed.), *Multisensory teaching and basic language skills* (pp. 1—18). Baltimore, MD: Brookes.

Monti, D., & Cicchetti, G. (1996). *TARA: Think-aloud reading assessment.* Austin, TX: Steck-Vaughn Berrent.

Moore, B. H., & Caldwell, H. (1991). Drama and drawing for narrative writing in primary grades., *Journal of Educational Research, 87,* 100–110.

Moore, D. W., & Moore, S. A. (1986). Possible sentences. In E. K. Dishner, T. W. Bean, J. E. Readence, & D. W. Moore (Eds.), *Reading in the content areas: Improving classroom instruction* (2nd ed., pp. 174–179). Dubuque, IA: Kendall/Hunt.

Moore, D. W., Readence, J. E., & Rickelman, R. J. (1989). *Prereading activities for content area reading and learning* (2nd ed.). Newark, DE: International Reading Association.

Moore, R. A., & Aspegren, C. (2001). Reflective conversations between two learners: Retrospective miscue analysis. *Journal of Adolescent and Adult Literacy, 44,* 492–503.

Moran, S., & Gardener, H. (2007). "Hill, skill, and will": Executive function from a multiple intelligences perspective. In L. Meltzer (Ed.), *Executive function in education: From theory to practice* (pp. 39–54). New York: Guilford Press.

Morgan, W. P. (1896). A case study of congenital word blindness. *British Medical Journal, 2,* 1378.

Morris, D. (1992). Concept of word: A pivotal understanding in the learning-to-read process. In S. Templeton & D. R. Bear (Eds.), *Development of orthographic knowledge and the foundations of literacy: A memorial festschrift for Edmund H. Henderson* (pp. 53–77). Hillsdale, NJ: Erlbaum.

Morris, D. (1999). *The Howard Street tutoring manual: Teaching at-risk readers in the primary grades.*

Morris, D. (2008). *Diagnosis and correction of reading problems.* New York: Guilford Press.

Morris, D., Blanton, L., Blanton, W. E., Nowacek, J., & Perney, J. (1995). Teaching low-achieving spellers at their "instructional level." *Elementary School Journal, 96,* 163–178.

Morris, D., Bloodgood, J. R., Lomax, R. G., & Perney, J. (2003). Developmental steps in learning to read: A longitudinal study in kindergarten and first grade. *Reading Research Quarterly, 38,* 302–328.

Morris, D., Trathen, W., Lomax, R. G., Perney, J., Kucan, L., Frye, E. M., Bloodgood, J. W., Ward, D., & Schlagal, R. (2012). Modeling aspects of print-processing skill: Implications for reading assessment. *Reading and Writing: An Interdisciplinary Journal, 25,* 189–215.

Moustafa, M. (1995). Children's productive phonological recoding. *Reading Research Quarterly, 30,* 464–476.

Murphy, L. L., Spies, R. A., & Plake, B. S. (Eds.). (2006). *Tests in print VII.* Lincoln: University of Nebraska Press.

Murray, B. A., Stahl, S. A., & Inez, M. G. (1993). *Developing phonological awareness through alphabet books.* Paper presented at the annual meeting of the National Reading Conference, Charleston, SC.

Muschla, G. R. (1993). *Writing workshop survival kit.* West Nyack, NY: The Center for Applied Research in Education.

Myers, C. A. (1980). Reviewing the literature on Fernald's technique of remedial reading. *Reading Teacher, 34,* 614–619.

Myers, J., & Lytle, S. (1986). Assessment of the learning process. *Exceptional Children, 53,* 138–144.

Nagy, W. E. (2010). The word games. In M. G. McKeown & L. Kucan (Eds.), *Bringing reading research to life.* New York: Guilford Press.

Nagy, W. E., & Scott, J. A. (2000). Vocabulary processes. In M. L. Kamil, P. B. Mosenthal, P. D. Pearson, & R. Barr (Eds.), *Handbook of reading research, Vol. III* (pp. 269–284). Mahwah, NJ: Erlbaum.

Nathenson-Mejia, S. (1989). Writing in a second language: Negotiating meaning through invented spelling. *Language Arts, 66,* 516–526.

Nation, P. (2001). *Learning vocabulary in another language.* Cambridge, England: Oxford University Press.

National Assessment Governing Board. (1985).*The reading report card: Progress toward excellence in our schools—Trends in reading over four national assessments, 1971–1984.* Princeton, NJ: Educational Testing Service.

National Assessment Governing Board. (2010). *Writing framework for the 2011 National Assessment of Educational Progress.* Washington, DC: Author.

National Association of School Psychologists. (2003). *Position statement on student grade retention and social promotion.* Available online at http://www.nasponline.org/ information/ pospapergraderetent.html

National Center for Education Statistics. (2011). *The nation's report card: Reading 2011* (NCES 2012–457). Washington, DC: Institute of Education Sciences, U.S. Department of Education.

National Dissemination Center for Children with Disabilities (2010). *Deafness and hearing loss.* Available online at http://nichcy.org/disabivlity/specific/hearingloss

National Governors Association Center for Best Practices and Council of Chief State School Officers. (2010a). *The standards: English language arts standards.* Available online at http://www.corestandards.org/the-standards/ englishlanguage-arts-standards

National Governors Association Center for Best Practices and Council of Chief State School Officers. (2010b). *Common Core State Standards for English language arts and literacy in history/social studies & science. Appendix A: Research supporting key elements of the standards.* Available online at http://www .corestandards.org/Files/K12ELAAppendixA.pdf

National Governors Association Center for Best Practices and Council of Chief State School Officers. (2010c). *Common Core State Standards for English language arts & literacy in history/social studies, science, and technical subjects. Appendix B: Text exemplars and sample performance, tasks.* Available online at http://www.corestandards.org/assets/Appendix_B.pdf

National High School Center, National Center on Response to Intervention, and Center on Instruction. (2010). *Tiered interventions in high schools: Using preliminary "lessons learned" to guide ongoing discussion.* Washington, DC: American Institutes for Research.

National Institute of Mental Health. (2008). *Attention deficit hyper-activity disorder.* Available online at http://www .nimh.nih.gov/ health/publications/adhd/cornplete-publication.shtml

National Reading Panel. (2000). *Report of the National Reading Panel.* Washington, DC: Author.

Neubach, A., & Cohen, A. (1988). Processing strategies and problems encountered in the use of dictionaries. *Dictionaries, 10,* 1–19.

Neubert, G. A., & Wilkins, E. A. (2004). *Putting it all together: The directed reading lesson in the secondary content classroom.* Boston: Allyn & Bacon.

Neuman, S. B. (1999). Books make a difference: A study of an access to literacy. *Reading Research Quarterly, 54,* 286–311.

Newcomer, P. L., & Barenbaum, E. M. (1991). The written composing ability of children with learning disabilities: A review of the literature from 1980 to 1990. *Journal of Learning Disabilities, 24,* 578–593.

Nichols, C. N. (2007). *The effect of three methods of introducing vocabulary words to elementary students: Traditional, friendly definitions, and parsing.* Unpublished doctoral dissertation, University of Pittsburgh, Pittsburgh, PA.

Nilsson, N. L. (2008). A critical analysis of eight informal reading inventories. *Reading Teacher, 61,* 526–536.

Nist, S. L., & Simpson, M. L. (2000). College studying. In M. L. Kamil, P. B. Mosenthal, P. D. Pearson, & R. Barr (Eds.), *Handbook of reading research, Vol. III* (pp. 645–666). Mahwah, NJ: Erlbaum.

Oakhill, J., & Yuill, N. (1996). Higher-order factors in comprehension disability: Processes and remediation. In C. Cornoldi & J. Oakhill (Eds.), *Reading comprehension difficulties: Process and Intervention* (pp. 69–92). Mahwah, NJ: Erlbaum.

O'Brien, C. A. (1973). *Teaching the language different child to read.* Columbus, OH: Merrill.

O'Connor, R. (2000). Increasing the intensity of intervention in kindergarten and first grade. *Learning Disabilities Research and Practice, 15,* 43–54.

O'Connor, R. E. (2011). Phoneme awareness and the alphabetic principle. In R. E. O'Connor & P. F. Vadasy (Eds.), *Handbook of reading interventions* (pp. 9–26). New York: Guilford Press.

O'Connor, R. E., & Bell, K. M. (2004). Teaching students with reading disability to read words. In C. A. Stone, E. R. Silliman, B. J. Ehren, & K. Apel (Eds.), *Handbook of language and literacy development and disorders* (pp. 481–498). New York: Guilford Press.

O'Connor, R. E., Bell, K. M., Harty, K. R., Larkin, L., Sackor, S., & Zigmond, N. (2002). Teaching reading to poor readers in the intermediate grades: A comparison of text difficulty. *Journal of Educational Psychology, 94,* 474–485.

Office of Elementary and Secondary Education. (2000). *The reauthorization of the Elementary and Secondary Education Act (ESEA).* Available online at http://www.ed.gov/legislation/ESEA

Office of Elementary and Secondary Education. (2008). *Early Reading First awards.* Available online at http://www.ed.gov/ programs/earlyreading/awards.html

Ogle, D., & Blachowicz, C. L. Z. (2002). Beyond literature circles: Helping students comprehend informational texts. In C. C. Block & M. Pressley (Eds.), *Comprehension instruction: Research-based best practices* (pp. 259–274). New York: Guilford Press.

Ogle, D. M. (1989). The know, want to know, learn strategy. In K. D. Muth (Ed.), *Children's comprehension of text* (pp. 205–223). Newark, DE: International Reading Association.

Olivares, R. (1993). *Using the newspaper to teach ESL learners.* Newark, DE: International Reading Association.

Olson, J. L. (1987). Drawing to write. *School Arts, 87,* 25–27.

Orellana, M. F., & Reynolds, J. (2008). Cultural modeling: Leveraging bilingual skills for school paraphrasing tasks. *Reading Research Quarterly, 43,* 48–65.

Orellana, M. F., Reynolds, J., & Martínez, D. (2011). Cultural modeling: Building on cultural strengths as an alternative to remedial reading approaches. In A. McGill-Franzen & R. L. Allington (Eds.), *Handbook of reading disability research* (pp. 273–276). New York: Routledge.

Orosco, M. J., & O'Connor, R. E. (2011). Cultural aspects of teaching reading with Latino English language learners. In R. E. O'Connor & P. F. Vadasy (Eds.), *Handbook of reading interventions* (pp. 356–379). New York: Guilford Press.

Orton, J. (1966). The Orton-Gillingham approach. In J. Money (Ed.), *The disabled reader: Education of the dyslexic child* (pp. 119–145). Baltimore, MD: Johns Hopkins University Press.

Orton, S. T. (1937). *Reading, writing, and speech problems in children.* New York: Norton.

Palincsar, A. S. (2003). Collaborative approaches to comprehension instruction. In A. Sweet & C. Snow (Eds.), *Rethinking reading comprehension* (pp. 99–114). New York: Guilford Press.

Palincsar, A. S., & Brown, A. L. (1986). Interactive teaching to promote independent learning from text. *Reading Teacher, 39,* 771–777.

Palincsar, A. S., & Klenk, L. (1992). Fostering literacy learning in supportive contexts. *Journal of Learning Disabilities, 25*(4), 211–225, 229.

Palincsar, A. S., Winn, J., David, Y., Snyder, B., & Stevens, D. (1993). Approaches to strategic reading instruction reflecting different assumptions regarding teaching and learning. In L. J. Meltzer (Ed.), *Strategy assessment and instruction for students with learning disabilities: From theory to practice* (pp. 247–292). Austin, TX: Pro-Ed.

PALS (Peer-Assisted Learning Strategies). (2004). *About PALS.* Available online at http://kc.vanderbilt.edu/pals/

Paratore, J. R. (1995). Implementing an intergenerational literacy project: Lessons learned. In L. M. Morrow (Ed.), *Family literacy, connections in schools and communities* (pp. 37–53). Newark, DE: International Reading Association.

Paratore, J. R. (2011). Parents and reading: What teachers should know about ways to support productive home-school environments. In S. J. Samuels & A. E. Farstrup (Eds.). *What research has to say about reading instruction* (4th ed.). Newark, DE: International Reading Association.

Paris, S. G. (1991). Assessment and remediation of metacognitive aspects of children's reading comprehension. *Topics in Language Disorders, 72*(1), 32–50.

Paris, S. G. (1993). *Classroom assessment for reading strategies, metacognition, and motivation.* Paper presented at the Ninth Annual Learning Disorders Conference, Cambridge, MA.

Paris, S. G., Cross, D. R., & Lipson, M. Y. (1984). Informed strategies for learning: A program to improve children's reading awareness and comprehension. *Journal of Educational Psychology, 76,* 1239–1252.

Paris, S. G., & Myers, M. (1981). Comprehension monitoring, memory, and study strategies of good and poor readers. *Journal of Reading Behavior, 13,* 5–22.

Paris, S. G., & Okra, E. (1986). Children's reading strategies, metacognition, and motivation. *Developmental Review, 6,* 25–56.

Pashler, H., Bain, P., Bottge, B., Graesser, A., Koedinger, K., McDaniel, M., & Metcalfe, J. (2007). *Organizing instruction and study to improve student learning* (NCER 2007–2004). Washington, DC: National Center for Education Research, Institute of Education Sciences, U.S. Department of Education. Available online at http://ies.ed.gov/ncee/wwc/pdf/practiceguides/20072004.pdf

Pauk, W. (1984). The new SQ3R. *Reading World, 23,* 386–387.

Paul, R., & Elder, L. (2001). *Critical thinking: Tools for taking charge of your learning and your life.* Upper Saddle River, NJ: Prentice Hall.

Pearson. (2009). *DRA2 K–8 technical manual* (2nd ed.). Upper Saddle River, NJ: Author.

Pearson Education. (2008). *The Longman dictionary of American English.* Essex, ENG: Pearson Education.

Pearson, P. D., & Gallagher, M. C. (1983). The instruction of reading comprehension. *Contemporary Educational Psychology, 5,* 317–345.

Pearson, P. D., & Johnson, D. D. (1978). *Teaching reading comprehension.* New York: Holt, Rinehart & Winston.

Perfetti, C. A. (1992). The representation problem in reading acquisition. In P. B. Gough, L. C. Ehri, & R. Treiman (Eds.), *Reading acquisition* (pp. 145–174). Hillsdale, NJ: Erlbaum.

Perfetti, C. (2010). Decoding, vocabulary, and comprehension: The golden triangle of reading skill. In M. G. McKeown, & L. Kucan (Eds.), *Bringing reading research to life.* New York: Guilford Press.

Perfetti, C. A., Beck, I., Bell, L., & Hughes, C. (1988). Phonemic knowledge and learning to read are reciprocal: A longitudinal study of first grade children. In K. E. Slanovich (Ed.), *Children's reading and the development of phonological awareness* (pp. 39–75). Detroit, MI: Wayne State University.

Persky, H. R., Daane, M. C., & Jin, Y. (2003). *The nation's report card: Writing 2002* (NCES No. 2003-529). Washington, DC: U.S. Department of Education, Institute of Education Services, National Center for Education Statistics.

Peters, C. (1979). The effect of systematic restructuring of material upon the comprehension process. *Reading Research Quarterly, 11,* 87–110.

Phillips, L. M. (1988). Young readers' inference strategies in reading comprehension. *Cognition and Instruction, 5*(3), 193–222.

Piasta, S., & Wagner, R. (2010). Developing early literacy skills: A meta-analysis of alphabet learning and instruction. *Reading Research Quarterly, 45,* 8–38.

Pike, M. M., Barnes, M. A., & Barron, R. W. (2010). The role of illustrations in children's inferential comprehension. *Journal of Experimental Child Psychology, 105,* 243–255.

Pinnell, G. S., & Fountas, I. C. (1998). *Word matters.* Portsmouth, NH: Heinemann.

Pinnell, G. S., & McCarrier, A. (1994). Interactive writing: A transition tool for assisting children in learning to read and write. In E. H. Hiebert & B. M. Taylor (Eds.), *Getting reading right from the start* (pp. 149–170). Boston: Allyn & Bacon.

Piolat, A., Roussey, J., & Gombert, A. (1999). The development of argumentative schema in writing. In J. Andriessen &

P. Coirier (Eds.), *Foundations of argumentative text processing* (pp. 117–136). Amsterdam: Amsterdam University Press.

Pittelman, S. D., Heimlich, J. E., Berglund, R. L., & French, M. P. (1991). *Semantic feature analysis: Classroom applications.* Newark, DE: International Reading Association.

Popham, W. J. (2000). *Modern educational measurement: Practical guidelines for educational leaders.* Boston: Allyn & Bacon.

Powell, W. R. (1971). The validity of the instructional reading level. In R. E. Liebert (Ed.), *Diagnostic viewpoints in reading* (pp. 121–133). Newark, DE: International Reading Association.

Powell-Smith, K. A. (2012, April 12). *DIBELS® Deep: In-depth diagnostic assessment of literacy skills* [Webinar]. Available online at http://www.soprislearning.com

Powell-Smith, K. A., Kaminski, R., Good, R. (2012). *DIBELS® Deep: In-depth diagnostic assessment of literacy skills.* Longmont, CO: Sopris Learning

Pressley, M. (1977). Imagery and children's learning: Putting the picture in developmental perspective. *Review of Educational Research, 47,* 585–622.

Pressley, M. (2000). Comprehension instruction in elementary school: A quarter-century of research progress. In B. Taylor, M. F. Graves, & P. van den Broek (Eds.), *Reading for meaning: Fostering comprehension in the middle grades* (pp. 32–51). New York: Teachers College Press.

Pressley, M., Johnson, C. J., Symons, S., McGoldrick, J. A., & Kurita, J. A. (1989). Strategies that improve children's memory and comprehension of what is read. *Elementary School Journal, 89,* 3–32.

Project CRISS. (2012, Spring). Strategy tips. *Comments from CRISS, 25*(2). Available online at http://www.projectcriss.com/central/wp-content/uploads/Comments-Newsletter-Spring-2012.pdf

Radencich, M. C. (1995). *Administration and supervision of the reading/writing program.* Boston: Allyn & Bacon.

Radencich, M. C., Beers, P. G., & Schumm, J. S. (1993). *A handbook for the K–12 resource specialist.* Boston: Allyn & Bacon.

RAND Reading Study Group. (2004). A research agenda for improving reading comprehension. In R. B. Ruddell & N. J. Unrau 2004. *Theoretical models and processes of reading* (5th ed., pp. 720–754). Newark, DE: International Reading Association.

Rapaport, W. J. (2004, May). *What is "context" in contextual vocabulary acquisition? Lessons learned from artificial intelligence and verbal protocol of good readers when they encounter unknown words in context.* Paper presented at the International Reading Association Convention, Reno, NV.

Raphael, T. E. (1984). Teaching learners about sources of information for answering questions. *Reading Teacher, 28,* 303–311.

Raphael, T. E. (1986). Teaching question-answer relationships, revisited. *Reading Teacher, 39,* 516–522.

Raphael, T. E., & Englert, C. S. (1990). Writing and reading: Partners in constructive meaning. *Reading Teacher, 43,* 388–400.

Raphael, T. E., Englert, C. S., & Kirschner, B. W. (1989). Acquisition of expository writing skills. In J. M. Mason (Ed.), *Reading and writing connections* (pp. 261–290). Boston: Allyn & Bacon.

Rashotte, C. A., &Torgesen, J. K. (1985). Repeated reading and reading fluency in learning disabled children. *Reading Research Quarterly, 20,* 180–188.

Rasinski, T. (2003). *The fluent reader: Oral reading strategies for building word recognition, fluency, and comprehension.* New York: Scholastic.

Rasinski, T., & Hamman P. (2010). Fluency: Why it is not hot. *Reading Today, 28*(1), 26.

Rasinski, T., & Padak, N. (1996). *Holistic reading strategies: Teaching children who find reading difficult.* Englewood Cliffs, NJ: Merrill.

Ratner, N. B. (1993). Atypical language development. In J. B. Berko (Ed.), *The development of language* (pp. 325–368). New York: Macmillan.

Read, C. (1971). Pre-school children's knowledge of English phonology. *Harvard Educational Review, 41,* 1–34.

Reading Recovery Council of North America. (2012). *Reading Recovery: Basic Facts.* Available online at http://readingrecovery.org/reading_recovery/facts/index.asp

Reitsma, P. (1989). Orthographic memory and learning to read. In P. G. Aaron & M. Joshi (Eds.), *Reading and writing disorders in different orthographic systems* (pp. 51–73). Dordrecht, The Netherlands: Kluwer.

Reschly, D. J., & Wood-Garnett, S. (2009). *Teacher preparation for response to intervention in middle and high schools.* Washington, DC: Learning Point Associates, National Comprehensive Center on Teacher Quality.

Resnick, L. B. (1999, June 16). Making America smarter. *Education Week on the Web, 18.* Available online at http://www.edweek.org/ew/vol-18/40resnick.hl8

Resnick, L. B., & Hall, M. W. (2001). *The principles of learning: Study tools for educators* [CD-ROM, version 2.0]. Pittsburgh, PA: University of Pittsburgh, Learning Research and Development Center, Institute for Learning. Available online at http://www.instituteforlearning.org

Resnick, L. B., & Hall, M. W. (2003). *The principles of learning: Study tools for educators* [CD-ROM version 3.1]. Pittsburgh, PA: University of Pittsburgh, Learning Research and Development Center. Institute for Learning.

Reutzel, D. R. (2008). *Effective letter recognition in kindergarten and first grade: Lessons learned from research and from working with early readers in high poverty settings.* Paper presented at the International Reading Association Convention, Atlanta.

Rhodes, L. K., & Dudley-Marling, C. (1988). *Readers and writers with a difference: A holistic approach to teaching learning disabled and remedial students.* Portsmouth, NH: Heinemann.

Rhodes, L. K., & Nathenson-Mejia, S. (1992). Anecdotal records: A powerful tool for ongoing literacy assessment. *Reading Teacher, 45,* 502–509.

Riccio, C. A., & Hynd, G. W. (1996). Neuroanatomical and neurophysiological aspects of dyslexia. *Topics in Language Disorders, 16,* 1–13.

Richek, M. A., Caldwell, J. S., Jennings, J. H., & Lerner, J. W. (1996). *Reading problems: Assessment and teaching strategies* (3rd ed.). Boston: Allyn & Bacon.

Richgels, D. J., & Hansen, R. (1984). Gloss: Helping students apply both skills and strategies in reading content texts. *Journal of Reading, 27,* 312–317.

Riedel, B. W. (2007). The relation between DIBELS, reading comprehension, and vocabulary in urban first-grade students. *Reading Research Quarterly, 42,* 546–567.

Rief, L. (2003). *100 quick writes.* New York: Scholastic.

Risley, T. (2003, May). *Meaningful differences in the everyday experiences of young American children.* Paper presented at the annual convention of the International Reading Association, Orlando, FL.

Ritchey, K. D., & Goeke, J. (2006). Orton-Gillingham and Orton-Gillingham based reading instruction: A review of the literature. *Journal of Special Education, 40,* 171–183.

Roach, E. G. (1966). *The Purdue perceptual-motor survey.* Columbus, OH: Merrill.

Robeck, M. C., & Wallace, R. R. (1990). *The psychology of reading: An interdisciplinary approach* (2nd ed.). Hillsdale, NJ: Erlbaum.

Roberts, R., & Mather, N. (1997). Orthographic dyslexia: The neglected subtype. *Learning Disabilities Research and Practice, 12,* 236–250.

Robinson, F. P. (1970). *Effective study* (4th ed.). New York: Harper & Row.

Roediger, H. L., McDaniel, K. B, & McDermott, M. A. (n.d.). *Using testing to improve learning and memory.* St. Louis, MO: St. Louis University.

Romance, N. R., & Vitale, M. R. (2001). Implementing an in-depth expanded science model in elementary schools: Multi-year findings, research issues, and policy implications. *International Journal of Science Education, 23*(4), 272–304.

Rosenberger, P. B. (1992). Dyslexia—Is it a disease? *New England Journal of Medicine, 326*(3), 192–193.

Rosenblatt, L. M. (1978). *The reader, the text, and the poem: The transactional theory of the literary work.* Carbondale: Southern Illinois University Press.

Rosenblatt, L. M. (1994). The transactional theory of reading and writing. In R. B. Ruddell, M. R. Ruddell, & H. Singer (Eds.), *Theoretical models and processes of reading* (4th ed., pp. 1057–1092). Newark, DE: International Reading Association.

Rosenshine, B., & Meister, C. (1994). Reciprocal teaching: A review of the research. *Review of Educational Research, 64,* 479–530.

Rosenthal, J., & Ehri, L. C. (2008). The mnemonic value of orthography for vocabulary learning. *Journal of Educational Psychology, 100,* 175–191.

Roser, N. (2011, May). *Teaching early learners: Remixing literacy, technology, and motivation.* Paper presented at the International Reading Association Convention, Orlando, FL.

Rosner, S., Abrams, J., Daniels, P., & Schiffman, G. (1991). Dealing with the reading needs of the learning disabled child. *Journal of Learning Disabilities, 14,* 436–448.

Roswell, F. G., & Chall, J. S. (1992). *Diagnostic assessments of reading.* Itasca, IL: Riverside.

Roswell, F. G., & Chall, J. S. (1994). *Creating successful readers: A practical guide to testing and teaching at all levels.* Itasca, IL: Riverside.

Roswell, F. G, & Natchez, G. (1989). *Reading disability: A human approach to evaluation and treatment of reading and writing difficulties* (4th ed.). New York: Basic Books.

Ross, R. J. (2004, April). *Effects on early literacy achievement of running records assessment: Results of a controlled experiment.* Paper presented at the annual meeting of the American Educational Research Association, San Diego, CA.

Rowe, M. B. (1969). Science, silence, and sanctions. *Science for Children, 6*(6), 11–13.

Rowell, C. G. (1992). *Assessment and correction in elementary language arts.* Boston: Allyn & Bacon.

Ruddell, M. R. (1992). Integrated content and long-term vocabulary learning with the vocabulary self-collection strategy. In E. K. Dishner, T. W. Bean, J. E. Readence, & D. W. Moore (Eds.), *Reading in the content areas: Improving classroom instruction* (3rd ed., pp. 190–196). Dubuque, IA: Kendall/Hunt.

Rumelhart, D. (1980). Schemata: The building blocks of cognition. In R. J. Spiro, B. C. Bruce, & W. F. Bruner (Eds.), *Theoretical issues in reading comprehension* (pp. 33–58). Hillsdale, NJ: Erlbaum.

Rumelhart, D. (1985). Toward an interactive model of reading. In H. Singer & R. B. Ruddell (Eds.), *Theoretical models and processes of reading* (3rd ed., pp. 722–750). Newark, DE: International Reading Association.

Rusnak, G. (1994). *Instructional conversations in the writing process.* Paper presented at the annual reading conference of the International Reading Association, Toronto.

Rye, J. (1982). *Cloze procedure and the teaching of reading.* London: Heinemann.

Sadowski, M., Goetz, E. T. X, & Fritz, J. B. (1993). Impact of concreteness on comprehensibility, interest, and memory for text: Implications for dual coding theory and text design. *Journal of Educational Psychology, 85,* 291–304.

Salahu-Din, D., Persky, H., & Miller, J. (2008). *The nation's report card: Writing 2007* (NCES No. 2008-468). Washington, DC: National Center for Education Statistics, Institute of Education Sciences, U.S. Department of Education.

Salvia, J., & Ysseldyke, J. E. (1998). *Assessment in special and remedial education* (7th ed.). Boston: Houghton Mifflin.

Salvia, J., Ysseldyke, J. E., & Bolt, S. (2007). *Assessment in special and inclusive education* (10th ed.). Boston: Houghton Mifflin.

Samuels, S. J. (1979). The method of repeated reading. *Reading Teacher, 32,* 403–408.

Samuels, S. J. (1994). Toward a theory of automatic information processing in reading revisited. In R. B. Ruddell, M. R. Ruddell, & H. Singer (Eds.), *Theoretical models and processes of reading* (4th ed., pp. 816–837). Newark, DE: International Reading Association.

Samuels, S. J. (2006). Fluency: Toward a model of reading fluency. In S. J. Samuels & A. E. Farstrup (Eds.), *What research has to say about fluency instruction* (pp. 24–46). Newark, DE: International Reading Association.

Samuelstuen, M. S., & Bråten, I. (2005). Decoding, knowledge, and strategies in comprehension of expository text. *Scandinavian Journal of Psychology, 46,* 107–117.

Sandora, C., Beck, I., & McKeown, M. (1999). A comparison of two discussion strategies on students' comprehension and interpretation of complex literature. *Journal of Reading Psychology, 20,* 177–212.

Santa, C. M., Havens, L. X., & Maycumber, E. M. (1996). *Creating independence through student-owned strategies* (2nd ed.). Dubuque, IA: Kendall/Hunt.

Santa, C. M., & Høien, T. (1999). An assessment of Early Steps: A program for early intervention. *Reading Research Quarterly, 34,* 54–79.

Santangelo, T., Harris, K. R., & Graham, H. (2008). Using self-regulated strategy development to support students who have "trubol giting thangs into werds." *Remedial and Special Education, 29,* 78–89.

Sawyer, D. J. (1985). *Language problems observed in poor readers.* Boston: College Hill Press.

Scanlon, D. M., Anderson, K. I., & Sweeney, J. M. (2010). *Early intervention for reading difficulties: The interactive strategies approach.* New York: Guilford.

Schiffini, A. (1999). *Successful strategies for your older struggling readers.* Torrance, CA: Staff Development Resources.

Schlagal, R. (1992). Patterns of orthographic development into the intermediate grades. In S. Templeton & D. Bear (Eds.), *Development of orthographic knowledge and the foundations of literacy: A memorial Festschrift for Edmund H. Henderson* (pp. 31–52). Hillsdale, NJ: Erlbaum.

Schnorr, J. A., & Atkinson, R. C. (1969). Repetition versus imagery instructions in the short- and long-term retention of paired associates. *Psychonomic Science, 15,* 183–184.

Schoenbach, R., Greenleaf, C., Cziko, C., & Hurwitz, L. (1999). *Reading for understanding.* San Francisco: Jossey-Bass.

Schoenbach, R., Greenleaf, L., & Murphy, L. (2012). Reading for understanding, *How reading apprenticeship improves disciplinary learning in secondary and college classrooms* (2nd ed.). San Francisco: Jossey-Bass.

Schunk, D. H., & Rice, J. H. (1987). Enhancing comprehension skill and self-efficacy with strategy value information. *Journal of Reading Behavior, 19,* 285–302.

Scott, J. A., & Nagy, W. E. (1997). Understanding the definitions of unfamiliar words. *Reading Research Quarterly, 32,* 184–200.

Scruggs, T., Mastropieri, M., Berkeley, S., &. Graetz, J. E. (2010). Do special education interventions improve learning of secondary content? A meta-analysis. *Remedial and Special Education, 31,* 437–449.

Seligman, M. E. P. (1975). *Helplessness.* San Francisco: Freeman.

Semel, E., Wiig, E., & Secord, W. A. (1995). *Clinical evaluation of language fundamentals.* Orlando, FL: Psychological Corporation.

Senechal, M., & Cornell, E. J. (1993). Vocabulary acquisition through shared reading experiences. *Reading Research Quarterly, 28,* 360–374.

Shanahan, T. (2008). Implications of RTI for the reading teacher. In D. Fuchs, L. S. Fuchs, & S. Vaughn (Eds.), *Response to intervention: A framework for reading educators* (pp. 105–122). Newark, DE: International Reading Association.

Shapiro, E. S. (1996). *Academic skills problems: Direct assessment and intervention.* New York: Guilford Press.

Shaywitz, B. A., Pugh, K. R., Jenner, A. R., Fulbright, R. K., Fletcher, J. M., Gore, J. C., & Shaywitz, S. E. (2000). The neurobiology of reading and reading disability (dyslexia). In M. L. Kamil, P. B. Mosenthal, P. D. Pearson, & R. Barr (Eds.), *Handbook of reading research, Vol. III* (pp. 229–249). Mahwah, NJ: Erlbaum.

Shearer, B. (1999). *The vocabulary self-collection strategy (VSS) in a middle school.* Paper presented at the 49th Annual Meeting of the National Reading Conference, Orlando, FL.

Shefelbine, J. (1990). A syllable-unit approach to teaching decoding of polysyllabic words to fourth- and sixth-grade disabled readers. In J. Zutell & S. McCormick (Eds.), *Literacy theory and research: Analysis from multiple paradigms* (pp. 223–230). Chicago, IL: National Reading Conference.

Shefelbine, J., & Newman, K. K. (2000a). *SIPPS (Systematic Instruction in Phoneme awareness, Phonics, and Sight words) manuals.* Oakland, CA: Developmental Studies Center.

Shefelbine, J., & Newman, K. K. (2000b). *SIPPS challenge level* (2nd ed.). Oakland, CA: Developmental Studies Center.

Sheffield, B. B. (1991). The structured flexibility of Orton-Gillingham. *Annals of Dyslexia, 41,* 41–54.

Siegel, L. (1998). The discrepancy formula: Its use and abuse. In B. K. Shapiro, P. J. Accardo, & A. J. Capute (Eds.), *Specific reading disability: A view of the spectrum* (pp. 123–135). Timonium, MD: York Press.

Simmons, J. (1990). Portfolios as large-scale assessment. *Language Arts, 67,* 262–268.

Simon, H. A. (1986). The role of attention in cognition. In S. L. Friedman, K. A. Klivington, & R. W. Peterson (Eds.), *The brain, cognition, and education* (pp. 105–115). Orlando, FL: Academic Press.

Sinatra, R. C., Berg, D., & Dunn, R. A. (1985). Semantic mapping improves reading comprehension of learning disabled students. *Teaching Exceptional Children, 17,* 310–314.

Singer, H. (1977). IQ is and is not related to reading. In S. Wanat (Ed.), *Issues in evaluating reading* (pp. 43–55). Arlington, VA: Center for Applied Linguistics.

Skjelfjord, V. (1976). Teaching children to segment spoken words as an aid in learning to read. *Journal of Learning Disabilities, 9,* 297–306.

Slater, W. H., Graves, M. F., & Piche, G. L. (1985). Effects of structural organizers on ninth grade students' comprehension and recall of four patterns of expository text. *Reading Research Quarterly, 20,* 189–202.

Slavin, R. E., Cheung, A., Groff, C., & Lake, C. (2008). Effective reading programs for middle and high schools: A best-evidence synthesis. *Reading Research Quarterly, 43,* 290–322.

Slingerland, B. H. (1971). *A multi-sensory approach to language arts for specific language disability children: A guide for primary teachers.* Cambridge, MA: Educators Publishing Service.

Smarter Balanced Assessment Consortium. (2011). *Content specifications for the summative assessment of the common core state standards for English language arts and literacy in history/social studies, science, and technical subjects.* Available online at http://www.smarterbalanced.org/wordpress/wp-content/uploads/2011/12/ELA-Literacy-Content-Specifications_010612.pdf

Smith, D. R. (2003). *Unveiling the WISC-IV.* Available online at harcourtassessment.com/handouts/WISC-IV-BasicHandout.pdf

Smith, L. (2006). Think-aloud mysteries: Using structured, sentence-by-sentence text passages to teach comprehension strategies. *Reading Teacher, 59,* 764–773.

Smith, S. D., Brower, A. M., Cardon, L. R., & DeFries, J. C. (1998). Genetics of reading disability: Further evidence for a gene on chromosome 6. In D. D. Drake (Ed.), *Reading and attention disorders: Neurological correlates* (pp. 63–74). Baltimore, MD: York Press.

Smolkin, L. B. (2011, May). *Introduction to a developmental framework to support children's informational writing.* Paper presented at the International Reading Association Convention, Orlando, FL.

Smolkin, L. B., & Donovan, C. A. (2011, May). *A developmental framework to support children's informational writing.* Paper presented at the International Reading Association Convention, Orlando, FL.

Snow, C. E., Burns, S. M., & Griffin, P. (1998). *Preventing reading difficulties in young children.* Washington, DC: National Academy Press.

Snowball, D., & Bolton, F. (1999). *Spelling K–8: Planning and teaching.* York, ME: Stenhouse.

Snyder, L. S., & Godley, D. (1992). Assessment of word-finding disorders in children and adolescents. *Topics in Language Disorders, 13,* 15–32.

Solan, H. A., Shelley-Tremblay, J. F., Hansen, P. C., & Larson, S. (2007). Is there a common linkage among reading comprehension, visual attention, and magnocellular processing? *Journal of Learning Disabilities, 40,* 270–278.

Spandel, V. (2005). *Creating writers through 6-trait writing assessment and instruction* (4th ed.). Boston: Allyn & Bacon.

Spear-Swerling, L. (2004). A road map for understanding reading disability and other reading problems: Origins, prevention, and intervention. In R. B. Ruddell & N. J. Unrau (Eds.), *Theoretical models and processes of reading* (5th ed., pp. 517–573). Newark, DE: International Reading Association.

Spear-Swerling, L. (2011). Patterns of reading disability across development. In A. McGill-Franzen & R. L. Allington (Eds.), *Handbook of reading disability research* (pp. 149–161). New York: Routledge.

Spear-Swerling, L., & Sternberg, R. J. (1996). *Off track: When poor readers become "learning disabled."* Boulder, CO: Westview Press.

Spies, R. A., Carlson, J. F., & Geisinger, K. F. (Eds.). (2010). *The eighteenth mental measurements yearbook.* Lincoln: University of Nebraska Press.

Spring, C., & French, L. (1990). Identifying children with specific reading disabilities from listening and reading discrepancy scores. *Journal of Learning Disabilities, 23,* 53–58.

Stainthorp, R., Powell, D., Stuart, M., Quinlan, P., & Garwood, H. (2010). Visual processing deficits in children with slow RAN performance. *Scientific Studies of Reading, 14,* 266–292.

Stahl, K. A. D. (2004). Proof, practice, and promise: Comprehension instruction in the primary grades. *Reading Teacher, 57,* 598–609.

Stahl, S. A. (1986). Three principles of effective vocabulary instruction. *Journal of Reading, 29,* 662–68.

Stahl, S. A., & Fairbanks, M. M. (1986). The effects of vocabulary instruction: A model-based meta-analysis. *Review of Educational Research, 56,* 72–110.

Stahl, S. A., Heubach, K. M., & Crammond, J. G. (1997). *Fluency-oriented reading instruction.* Athens: National Reading Research Center, University of Georgia (Reading Research Report No. 79, ED 405554).

Stahl, S. A., & Kapinus, B. A. (1991). Possible sentences: Predicting word meanings to teach content area vocabulary. *The Reading Teacher, 45,* 36–43.

Stahl, S. A., Stahl, K. A., & McKenna, M. C. (1998, December). *How do phonological awareness, spelling, and word recognition relate to each other?* Paper presented at the Annual Meeting of the National Reading Conference, Austin, TX.

Stanovich, K. E. (1986). Matthew effects in reading: Some consequences of individual differences in the acquisition of literacy. *Reading Research Quarterly, 21,* 360–407.

Stanovich, K. E. (1991). Discrepancy definitions of reading disability: Has intelligence led us astray? *Reading Research Quarterly, 26,* 7–29.

Stanovich, K. E., & Cunningham, A. E. (1992). Studying the consequences of literacy within a literate society: The cognitive correlates of print exposure. *Memory and Cognition, 20,* 51–68.

Stauffer, R. G. (1969). *Directing reading maturity as a cognitive process.* New York: Harper & Row.

Stein, J. (1996). Visual system and reading. In C. H. Chase, G. D. Rosen, & G. F. Sherman (Eds.), *Developmental dyslexia: Neural, cognitive, and genetic mechanisms* (pp. 107–125). Baltimore, MD: York Press.

Stein, J. (2001).The sensory basis of reading problems. *Developmental Neuropsychology, 20,* 509–534.

Stein, M., Johnson, M., & Gutlohn, L. (1999). Analyzing beginning reading programs: The relationship between decoding instruction and text. *Remedial and Special Education, 20,* 275–287.

Stein, N., & Glenn, C. G. (1979). An analysis of story comprehension in elementary school children. In R. Freedle (Ed.), *New directions in discourse processing Vol. II* (pp. 53–120). Norwood, NJ: Ablex.

Sternberg, R. J. (1987). Most vocabulary is learned from context. In M. G. McKeown & M. E. Curtis (Eds.), *The nature of vocabulary acquisition* (pp. 89–105). Hillsdale, NJ: Erlbaum.

Sternberg, R. J. (1996). *Successful intelligence: How practical and creative intelligence determine success in life.* New York: Penguin.

Stewart, R. A., & Cross, T. L. (1991). The effect of marginal glosses on reading comprehension and retention. *Journal of Reading, 35,* 4–12.

Stewart, R. A., & Cross, T. L. (1993). A field test of five forms of marginal gloss study guides: An ecological study. *Reading Psychology, 74,* 113–139.

Stewig, J. W., & Nordberg, B. (1995). *Exploring language arts in the elementary classroom.* Belmont, CA: Wadsworth.

Sticht, T. G., & James, J. H. (1984). Listening and reading. In P. D. Pearson, R. Barr, M. L. Kamil, & P. Mosenthal (Eds.), *Handbook of reading research* (pp. 293–317). New York: Longman.

Stieglitz, E. L. (2002). *The Stieglitz Informal Reading Inventory* (3rd ed.). Boston: Allyn & Bacon.

Stiggins, R. J. (2006). Assessment for learning: A key to motivation and achievement. *Edge, 2*(2), 3–19.

Stiggins, R. J. (2007). Assessment through the student's eyes. *Educational Leadership, 67*(8), 22–26.

Stiggins, R. J., & Chappuis, J. (2005). Using student-involved classroom assessment to close achievement gaps. *Theory Into Practice, 44*(1), 11–18.

Stone, C. A. (2004). Contemporary approaches to the study of language and literacy development: A call for the integration of perspectives. In C. A. Stone, E. R. Silliman, B. J. Ehren, & K. Apel (Eds.), *Handbook of language and literacy development and disorders* (pp. 3–24). New York: Guilford Press.

Stuart, M., & Colthheart, M. (1990). Does reading develop in a sequence of stages? *Cognition, 30,* 139–181.

Strategic Education Research Partnership. (2009). *An introduction to word generation.* Boston: Author. Available online at http://www.serpinstitute.org/tools-an-resources/wordgeneration.php

Sulzby, E., & Barnhart, J. (1992). The development of academic competence: All our children emerge as writers and readers. In J. W. Irwin & M. A. Doyle (Eds.), *Reading/writing connections: Learning from research* (pp. 120–144). Newark, DE: International Reading Association.

Sulzby, E., & Teale, W. (1991). Emergent literacy. In R. Barr, M. L. Kamil, P. Mosenthal, & P. D. Pearson (Eds.), *Handbook of reading research, Vol. II* (pp. 727–757). New York: Longman.

Swanborn, M. S. L., & de Glopper, K. (1999). Incidental word learning while reading: A meta-analysis. *Review of Educational Research, 69,* 261–285.

Swanson, H. L. (2011). Meta-analysis of research on children with reading disabilities. In R. Allington & A. McGill-Franzen (Eds.), *Handbook of reading disabilities research* (pp. 477–487). New York: Routledge.

Swanson, H. L., & Alexander, J. E. (2001). Cognitive processes as predictors of word recognition and reading comprehension in learning-disabled and skilled readers. *Journal of Educational Psychology, 89,* 128–158.

Taba, H. (1965). The teaching of thinking. *Elementary English, 42,* 534–542.

Taba, H. (1967). *Teacher's handbook for elementary social studies.* Reading, MA: Addison-Wesley.

Taylor, B. M., Strait, J., & Medo, M. A. (1994). Early intervention in reading: Supplemental instruction for groups of low-achieving students provided by first-grade teachers. In E. H. Hiebert & B. M. Taylor (Eds.), *Getting reading right from the start* (pp. 85–106). Boston: Allyn & Bacon.

Taylor, D., & Dorsey-Gaines, C. (1988). *Growing up literate, learning from inner-city families.* Portsmouth, NH: Heinemann.

Taylor, K. K. (1986). Summary writing by young children. *Reading Research Quarterly, 21,* 193–208.

Taylor, S. E., Klein, L. C., Lewis, B. P., Gruenewald, T. L., Gurung, R. A. R., & Updegraff, J. A. (2000). Biobehavioral responses to stress in females: Tend-and-befriend, not fight-or-flight. *Psychological Review, 107,* 411–429.

Temple, C., Nathan, R., Temple, F., & Burris, N. A. (1993). *The beginnings of writing* (3rd ed.). Boston: Allyn & Bacon.

Templeton, S., & Bear, D. (1992). A summary and synthesis: "Teaching the lexicon to read and spell." In S. Templeton & D. Bear (Eds.), *Development of orthographic knowledge and the foundations of literacy: A memorial festschrift for Edmund H. Henderson* (pp. 333–352). Hillsdale, NJ: Erlbaum.

Templeton, S., & Morris, D. (1999). Theory and research into practice: Questions teachers ask about spelling. *Reading Research Quarterly, 34,* 102–112.

Thames, D. G., & Reeves, C. K. (1994, May). *Preventing the progression of negative attitudes among poor readers.* Paper presented at the Annual Meeting of the International Reading Association, Toronto.

Thorndike, R. L., & Hagen, E. P. (1977). *Measurement and evaluation in psychology and education* (4th ed.). New York: Wiley.

Tierney, R. J., & Readence, J. E. (2000). Intervention programs for "at-risk" learners. In R. J. Tierney & J. E. Readence (Eds.), *Reading strategies and practices: A compendium* (5th ed., pp. 126–159). Boston: Allyn & Bacon.

Tierney, R. J., & Readence, J. E. (2005). Intervention programs for "at-risk" learners. In R. J. Tierney & J. E. Readence (Eds.), *Reading strategies and practices: A compendium* (6th ed., p. 244). Boston: Allyn & Bacon.

Tindal, G., Hasbrouck, J., & Jones, C. (2005). *Oral reading fluency: 90 years of measurement* (Technical Report No. 33). Eugene: University of Oregon, Behavioral Research and Teaching, College of Education.

Tompkins, G. E., & Hoskisson, K. (1991). *Language arts: Content and teaching strategies.* New York: Merrill.

Tonjes, M. J. (1991). *Secondary reading, writing, and learning.* Boston: Allyn & Bacon.

Topping, K. (1987). Paired reading: A powerful technique for parent use. *Reading Teacher, 40,* 608–609.

Topping, K. (1989). Peer tutoring and paired reading: Combining two powerful techniques. *Reading Teacher, 42,* 488–494.

Topping, K. (1998). Effective tutoring in America Reads: A reply to Wasik. *Reading Teacher, 52,* 42–50.

Torgensen, J. K. (1994). *Research based approach to prevention of reading disabilities.* Paper presented at the New York Branch of the Orton Dyslexia Society, 21st Annual Conference, Language and Medical Symposia on Dyslexia, New York.

Torgesen, J. K. (2000). Individual differences in response to early interventions in reading: The lingering problem of treatment resisters. *Learning Disabilities Practice, 15,* 55–64.

Torgesen, J. K. (2004a, May). *Adolescent literacy, reading comprehension,* and *the FCAT.* Paper presented at the CLAS Conference, Naples, FL.

Torgesen, J. K. (2004b, April). *Immediate intensive interventions: Their critical role within a whole school program to prevent reading difficulties.* Paper presented at the Regional Leadership Meeting, sponsored by the Eastern Regional Reading First Technical Assistance Center. Available online at http://www.fcrr.org/science/pptpresentations.htm

Torgesen, J. K. (2004c). *Struggling readers: What works for intermediate level students.* Paper presented at the Pennsylvania Summer Reading Conference, State College. Available online at http://www.fcrr.org/science/pptpresentations.htm

Torgesen, J. K., & Hecht, S. A. (1996). Preventing and remediating reading disabilities: Instructional variables that make a difference for special students. In M. F. Graves, P. van den Broek, & B. M. Taylor (Eds.), *The first R—Every child's right to read* (pp. 160–188). Newark, DE: International Reading Association.

Touchstone Applied Science Associates. (2006). The DRP model of reading. *TASA talk.* Available online at http://www.tasaliteracy.com/tasatalk/tasatalk-main.html

Tovani, C. (2000). *I read it but I don't get it* Portland, ME: Stenhouse.

Tracey, D. H., & Young, J. W. (2005). *An Internet-delivered, individually differentiated reading program: Effects on students' literacy achievement and technology skills.* Paper presented at the Annual Meeting of the National Reading Conference, Miami, FL.

Trachtenburg, P. (1990). Using children's literature to enhance phonics instruction. *Reading Teacher, 43,* 648–654.

Treiman, R. (1992). The role of intrasyllabic units in learning to read and spell. In P. B. Gough, L. C. Ehri, & R. Tremain (Eds.), *Reading acquisition* (pp. 65–106). Hillsdale, NJ: Erlbaum.

Troia, G. A. (2004). Phonological processing and its influence on literacy learning. In C. A. Stone, E. R. Silliman, B. J. Ehren, & K. Apel (Eds.), *Handbook of language and literacy development and disorders* (pp. 271–301). New York: Guilford Press.

Tunmer, W. E., & Chapman, J. W. (1999). Teaching strategies for word identification. In G. B. Thompson & T. Nicholson (Eds.), *Learning to read: Beyond phonics and whole language* (pp. 74–102). Newark, DE: International Reading Association.

Turbill, J. (1982). *No better way to teach writing!* Rozelle, AU: Primary English Teaching Association.

Tyre, P. (2012, October). The writing revolution. *Atlantic Magazine.* Available online at http://www.theatlantic.com/magazine/archive/2012/10/the-writing-revolution/309090/3/

Uhry, J. K., & Ehri, L. (1999). Ease of segmenting two-and three-phoneme words in kindergarten: Rime cohesion or vowel salience? *Journal of Educational Psychology, 91,* 594–603.

U. S. Census Bureau. (2012). *Income, poverty and health insurance in the United States: 2011—highlights.* Available online at http://www.census.gov/hhes/www/poverty/data/incpovhlth/2011/highlights.html

U.S. Department of Education. (2010). *A blueprint for reform: The reauthorization of the Elementary and Secondary Education Act.* Available online at http://www2.ed.gov/policy/elsec/leg/blueprint/index.html

U.S. Department of Education, National Center for Educational Statistics. (2005). *Components of oral reading: Accuracy, rate, and fluency.* Available online at http://nces.ed.gov/nationsreportcard/studies/ors/components.asp

U.S. Department of Health and Human Services, Health Resources and Services Administration, Maternal and Child Health Bureau. (2010). *The mental and emotional well-being of children: A portrait of states and the nation 2007.* Rockville, MD: U.S. Department of Health and Human Services.

Vadasay, P. F. (2011). Supplemental reading instruction by paraeducators and tutors: Recent research and applications. In R. E. O'Connor & P. F. Vadasy (Eds.), *Handbook of reading interventions* (pp. 300–325). New York: Guilford Press.

Valencia, S. (2001). *Integrated theme tests, Level 2.1.* Boston: Houghton Mifflin.

Valencia, S. (2011a). Reader profiles and reading disabilities. In A. McGill-Franzen & R. L. Allington (Eds.), *Handbook of reading disability research* (pp. 25–35). New York: Routledge.

Valencia, S. W. (2011b). Using assessment to improve teaching and learning. In S. J. Samuels & A. E. Farstrup (Eds.), *What research has to say about reading instruction* (4th ed.). Newark, DE: International Reading Association.

Valencia, S., & Buly, M. R. (2004). Behind test scores: What struggling readers really need. *Reading Teacher, 57,* 520–531.

Valencia, S. W., Smith, A. T., Reece, A. M., Li, M., Wixson, K. K., & Newman, H. (2010). Oral reading fluency assessment: Issues of construct, criterion, and consequential validity. *Reading Research Quarterly, 45,* 270–291.

Vandervelden, M. C., & Siegel, L. S. (1995). Phonological recoding and phoneme awareness in early literacy: A developmental approach. *Reading Research Quarterly, 30,* 854–876.

Vandervelden, M. C., & Siegel, L. S. (1997). Teaching phonological processing skills in early literacy: A developmental approach. *Learning Disabilities Quarterly, 20,* 63–81.

Vaughn, S., Denton, C. A., & Fletcher, J. M. (2010). Why intensive interventions are necessary for students with severe reading difficulties. *Psychology in the Schools, 47,* 432–444.

Vaughn, S., & Fletcher, J. M. (2012). Response to intervention with secondary school students with reading difficulties. *Journal of Learning Disabilities, 45,* 244–256.

Vaughn, S., & Linan-Thompson, S. (2003). Group size and time allotted to intervention: Effects for students with reading difficulties. In B. R. Foorman (Ed.), *Preventing and remediating reading difficulties: Bringing science to scale* (pp. 299–324). Baltimore, MD: York Press.

Vaughn, S., Wanzek, J., Murray, C. S., & Roberts, G. (2012). *Intensive interventions for students struggling in reading and mathematics: A practice guide.* Portsmouth, NH: RMC Research Corporation, Center on Instruction.

Vellutino, F. R. (1987). Dyslexia. *Scientific American, 256*(3), 34–41.

Vellutino, F. R. (2003, December 2). *Response to intervention as a vehicle for distinguishing between reading disabled and non-reading disabled children: Evidence for the role of kindergarten and first-grade intervention.* Paper presented at the National Research Center on Learning Disabilities Responsiveness-to-Intervention Symposium, Kansas City, MO. Available online at http://www.nrcld.org/html/symposium2003/ vellutino/ vellutino9.html

Vellutino, F. R., Fletcher, J. M., Snowing, M. J., & Scanlon, D. M. (2004). Specific reading disability (dyslexia): What have we learned in the past four decades? *Journal of Child Psychology and Psychiatry, 45,* 2–40.

Vellutino, F. R., & Scanlon, D. M. (1985). Verbal memory in poor and normal readers. In D. B. Gray & J. F. Kavanaugh (Eds.), *Biobehavioral measures of dyslexia* (pp. 177–214). Baltimore, MD: York Press.

Vellutino, F. R., & Scanlon, D. M. (1988). Phonological coding: Phonological awareness and reading ability: Evidence from a longitudinal and experimental study (pp. 77–119). In K. Stanovich (Ed.), *Children's reading and the development of phonological awareness.* Detroit, MI: Wayne State University Press.

Vellutino, F. R., Scanlon, D. M., Sipay, E. R., Small, S. G., Pratt, R., Chen, R., & Denckla, M. B. (1996). Cognitive profiles of difficult-to-remediate and readily remediated poor readers: Early intervention as a vehicle for distinguishing between cognitive and experiential deficits as basic causes of specific reading disability. *Journal of Educational Psychology, 88,* 601–638.

Vellutino, F. R., Scanlon, D. M., Small, S., & Fanuele, D. P. (2006). Response to intervention as a vehicle for distinguishing between children with and without reading disabilities: Evidence for the role of kindergarten and first-grade interventions. *Journal of Learning Disabilities, 39,* 157–169.

Vellutino, F. R., Scanlon, D. M., & Tanzman, M. S. (1998). The case for early intervention in diagnosing specific reading disability. *Journal of School Psychology, 36,* 367–397.

Venezky, R. L. (1965). *A study of English spelling-to-sound correspondences on historical principles.* Unpublished doctoral dissertation, Stanford University, Stanford, CA.

Vreeland, E. (1998). *Handwriting: Not just in hands: A comprehensive resource.* Hanover, NH: Maxanna Learning.

Vygotsky, L. S. (1978). *Mind and society: The development of higher psychological processes.* Cambridge, MA: MIT Press.

Wade, S. E. (1990). Using think-alouds to assess comprehension. *Reading Teacher, 43,* 442–451.

Walczyk, J. J., & Griffith-Ross, D. A. (2007). How important is reading skill fluency for comprehension? *Reading Teacher, 60,* 560–569.

Walker, B. G. (1992). *Diagnostic teaching of reading: Techniques for instruction and assessment* (2nd ed.). New York: Macmillan.

Walker, S. C., & Poteet, J. A. (1989). Influencing memory performance in learning disabled students through semantic processing. *Learning Disabilities Research, 5,* 25–32.

Walmsley, S. A. (1978–1979). The criterion referenced measurement of an early reading behavior. *Reading Research Quarterly, 14,* 574–604.

Walton, P. D. (1995). Rhyming ability, phoneme identity, letter–sound knowledge, and the use of orthographic analogy by prereaders. *Journal of Educational Psychology, 87,* 587–597.

Waters, K. C. (2010). Literacy initiatives in the urban setting that promote higher level thinking. In J. L. Collins & T. G. Gunning, (Eds.), *Building struggling students' higher level literacy: Practical ideas, powerful solutions.* Newark, DE: International Reading Association.

Watson, A. J. (1984). Cognitive development and units of print in early reading. In J. Downing & R. Valten (Eds.), *Language awareness and learning to read* (pp. 93–118). New York: Springer-Verlag.

Wechsler, D. (1974). *Manual for the Wechsler Intelligence Scale for Children–Revised.* Cleveland, OH: The Psychological Corporation.

Weaver, C. (1994). Understanding and educating students with attention deficit hyperactivity disorders: Toward a system-theory and whole language perspective. In C. Weaver (Ed.), *Success at last: Helping students with AD(H)D achieve their potential.* Portsmouth, NH: Heinemann.

Weaver, P. A. (1979). Improving reading comprehension: Effects of sentence organization instruction. *Reading Research Quarterly, 15,* 129–146.

Weinstein, C., & Mayer, R. (1986). The teaching of learning strategies. In M. C. Wittrock (Ed.), *Handbook of research on teaching* (pp. 315–327). New York: Macmillan.

West, J., Denton, K., & Germino-Hausken, E. (2000). *Early childhood longitudinal study: Kindergarten class of 1998–99.* Washington, DC: National Center for Educational Statistics. Available online at http://nces.ed.gov/ pubsearch/ pubsinfo.asp?pubid=200070

West, R. E., Stanovich, K. E., & Mitchell, H. R. (1993). Reading in the real world and its correlates. *Reading Research Quarterly, 28,* 34–50.

Westby, C. (1999). Assessing and facilitating text comprehension problems. In H. W. Catts & A. G. Kamhi (Eds.), *Language and reading disabilities* (pp. 154–223). Boston: Allyn & Bacon.

WestEd. (2012, October 16). *Meeting common core state standards and college-readiness expectations through academic literacy instruction* [Webinar]. Available online at http://www.schoolsmovingup.net/webinars/commoncore9

What Works Clearinghouse. (2007). *Dialogic reading.* Institute of Education Sciences. Available online at http://ies. ed.gov/ncee/wwc/InterventionReport.aspx?sid=135

What Works Clearinghouse. (2010a). *Literacy express.* Institute of Education Sciences. Available online at http://ies. ed.gov/ncee/wwc/interventionreport.aspx?sid=288

What Works Clearinghouse. (2010b). *Orton-Gillingham–based strategies (unbranded)*. Available online at http://ies.ed.gov/ncee/wwc/pdf/intervention_reports/wwc_ortongill_070110.pdf

Wheelock, A. (1999). Junior Great Books: Reading for meaning in urban schools. *Educational Leadership, 57*(2), 47–50.

Wheelock, W., & Campbell, C. (2012). *Classroom reading inventory* (12th ed). New York: McGraw-Hill.

White, T. G., & Kim, J. S. (2008). Teacher and parent scaffolding of voluntary summer reading. *The Reading Teacher, 62*, 116–125.

White, T. G., Sowell, J., & Yanagihara, A. (1989). Teaching elementary students to use word-part clues. *Reading Teacher, 42*, 302–308.

Whitehurst, G. J. (2012). Dialogic reading: An effective way to read to preschoolers. *Reading Rockets*. Retrieved June 23, 2012, http://www.readingrockets.org/article/400/

Wigfield, A., & Asher, S. R. (1984). Social and motivational influences on reading. In P. D. Pearson, R. Barr, M. L. Kamil, & P. Mosenthal (Eds.), *Handbook of reading research* (pp. 423–452). New York: Longman.

Wiig, E. H. (1994). The role of language in learning disabilities. In A. J. Capute, P. J. Accardo, & B. K. Shapiro (Eds.), *Learning disabilities spectrum: AD, ADHD, & LD* (pp. 139–154). Baltimore, MD: York Press.

Wilkinson, I. A. G. (2009, February). *Quality Talk about text to promote high-level reading comprehension*. Invited paper presented at the Research Conference of the International Reading Association, Phoenix, AZ.

Williams, J. P., & Pao, L. S. (2011). Teaching narrative and expository text structure to improve comprehension. In R. E. O'Connor, & P. F. Vadasy (Eds.), *Handbook of reading interventions* (198–219). New York: Guilford Press.

Willingham, D. T. (2009). *Why don't students like school?* San Francisco: Jossey-Bass.

Wilmer, J. B., Richardson, A. J., Chen, Y., & Stein, J. F. (2004). Two visual motion processing deficits in developmental dyslexia associated with different reading skills deficits. *Journal of Cognitive Neuroscience, 16*, 528–540.

Wilson, B. (1999). *Wilson reading system overview presentation* (3rd ed.) [Video recording]. Millbury, MA: Wilson Language Training.

Wilson, J. L. (2005). Interrupting the failure cycle: Revaluing two seventh-grade struggling readers. *Voices from the Middle, 12*(4), 25–30.

Wilson, M. M. (1979). The processing strategies of average and below average readers answering factual and inferential questions of three equivalent passages. *Journal of Reading Behavior, 11*, 235–245.

Winograd, P. N. (1984). Strategic difficulties in summarizing text. *Reading Research Quarterly, 19*, 404–425.

Wolf, M. A. (1991). Naming speed and reading: The contribution of the cognitive neurosciences. *Reading Research Quarterly, 26*, 123–141.

Wolf, M., & Goodglass, H. (1986). Dyslexia, dysnomia, and lexical retrieval. *Brain and Language, 28,*154–168.

Wolf, S., & Gearhart, M. (1994). Writing what you read: Narrative assessment as a learning event. *Language Arts, 71*, 425–444.

Wood, E., Pressley, M., & Winne, P. H. (1990). Elaborative interrogation effects on children's learning of factual content. *Journal of Educational Psychology, 82, 41*–48.

Wood, F. P. (1994). *Cortical activation patterns in normal reading and dyslexia: PET and ERR*. Paper presented at the New York Branch of the Orton Dyslexic Society Annual Conference, Language and Medical Symposia on Dyslexia, New York.

Wood, K. (1984). Probable passages: A writing strategy. *Reading Teacher, 37*, 496–499.

Wood, K. D., Lapp, D., Flood, J., & Taylor, D. B. (2008). *Guiding readers through text: Strategy guides for new times* (2nd ed.). Newark, DE: International Reading Association.

Word Generation. (2010). *Teacher's extended word form chart: Week 5 focus words*. Boston, MA: SERP.

Wright, J. (2007). *RTI toolkit: A practical guide for schools*. Port Chester, NY: National Professional Resources.

Yaden, D. B., Tarn, A., Madrigal, P., Brassell, D., Massa, J., Altamirano, S., & Armendariz, J. (2001). *Early literacy for inner-city children: The effects of reading and writing interventions in English and Spanish during the preschool years* (CIERA Article No. 00-04). Available online at http://www.ciera.org/ciera/publications/report-series

Yopp, H. K. (1995). A test for assessing phonemic awareness in young children. *Reading Teacher, 49*, 20–29.

Yopp, H. K., & Stapleton, L. (2008). Conciencia fonemica en Espanol (Phonemic awareness in Spanish). *Reading Teacher, 61*, 374–382.

Yoshimasu, K., Barbaresi, W. J., Colligan, R. C., Killian, J. M., Voigt, R. G., Weaver, A. L., & Katusic, S. K. (2010). Gender, attention-deficit/hyperactivity disorder, and reading disability in a population-based birth cohort. *Pediatrics, 126*, 788–795. Available online at http://www.ncbi.nlm.nih.gov/pmc/articles/PMC2995945/

Ysseldyke, J. E., & Christenson, S. L. (2002). *FAAB: Functional assessment of academic behavior*. Longmont, CO: Sopris West.

Yuill, N. (1996). A funny thing happened on the way to the classroom: Jokes, riddles, and metalinguistic awareness in understanding and improving poor comprehension in children. In C. Cornoldi & J. Oakhill (Eds.), *Reading comprehension difficulties: Processes and intervention* (pp. 193–220). Mahwah, NJ: Erlbaum.

Yuill, N., & Oakhill, J. (1991). *Children's problems in text comprehension: An experimental investigation* (Cambridge Monographs and Texts in Applied Psycholinguistics). New York: Cambridge University Press.

Zecker, S. G. (1991). The orthographic code: Developmental trends in reading-disabled and normally achieving children. *Annals of Dyslexia, 41*, 178–192.

Zeno, S. M., Ivens, S. H., Millard, R. T., & Duwuri, R. (1995). *The educator's word frequency guide*. Brewster, NY: Touchstone Applied Science.

Zentall, S. S. (1993). Research on the educational implications of attention deficit hyperactivity disorder. *Exceptional Children, 60*, 143–153.

Zwaan, R. A., Radvansky, G. A., Hilliard, A. E., & Curiel, J. M. (1998). Constructing multidimensional situation models during reading. *Scientific Studies of Reading, 20*(3), 199–220.

Zwiers, J. (2008). *Building academic language, Essential practices for content classrooms*. San Francisco: Jossey-Bass.

## CHILDREN'S BOOKS AND SCHOOL TEXTBOOKS

Abbye, S., & Donahue, B. C. (1991). *Our country's geography*. Austin, TX: Steck-Vaughn.

Bains, R. (1993). *Thurgood Marshall: Fight for justice.* Mahwah, NJ: Troll.

Blaine, M. (1986). Giants of the city. In J. Stanchfield and T. Gunning (Eds.), *Wings (New Directions in Reading)* (pp. 162–169). Boston: Houghton Mifflin.

AGS Secondary. (2004). *AGS general science-revised.* Englewood Cliffs, NJ: Pearson Education.

Bledsoe, L. J. (1988). *Biology, The kingdom of life.* Castro Valley, CA: Ojuercus.

Bledsoe, L. J. (1990). *Fearon's biology.* Paramus, NJ: Globe Fearon.

Bledsoe, L. J. (1994). *Fearon's general science* (2nd ed.). Paramus, NJ: Globe Fearon.

Block, D. (2013). *Exploring the solar system.* New York: PowerKids Press

Brown, C. (1989). *Big red barn.* New York: Greenwillow.

Brown, C. (1995). *Tractor.* New York: Greenwillow.

Bulla, R. C. (1987). *The chalk box kid.* New York: Random House.

Byars, B. (1970). *Summer of the swans.* New York: Viking.

Cameron, P. (1990). *Donna: A helping hand.* Hayward, CA: Alemany Press.

Carle, E. (1987). *Have you seen my cat?* New York: Scholastic.

Carroll, L. (1871/1969). *Alice in wonderland and through the looking glass.* Chicago, IL: Children's Press.

Cole, J. (1986). *Hungry, hungry sharks.* New York: Random House.

Cowley, J. (1990). *The hungry giant.* Bothell, WA: Wright Group.

Degen, B. (1983). *Jamberry.* New York: Harper.

Dodson, P. (2011). *Stegosaurus up close.* Cobble Hill, British Columbia: Bailey Books.

Domanska, J. (1969). *The turnip.* New York: Macmillan.

Duncan, L. (1976). *Summer of fear.* New York: Dell.

Eastman, P. D. (1961). *Go, dog, go.* New York: Random House.

Ehlert, L. (1987). *Growing vegetable soup.* Orlando, FL: Harcourt Brace.

Fajardo, A. (2012). *The dish on food and farming in colonial America.* Mankato, MN: Capstone Press.

Fleischman, P. (1988). *Joyful noise: Poems for two voices.* New York: HarperCollins.

Freeman, D. (1978). *A pocket for Corduroy.* New York: Puffin.

Freeman, M. S. (1999). *Polar bears.* Mankato, MN: Capstone.

Gág, W. (1928). *Millions of cats.* New York: Coward.

Geisel, T. S. (Dr. Seuss). (1974). *The cat in the hat.* New York: Beginner.

Geisel, T. S. (Dr. Seuss). (1974). *There's a wocket in my pocket.* New York: Beginner.

Gelman, R. G. (1977). *More spaghetti I say.* New York: Scholastic.

Goodall, J. (1992). *Writers' voices: Selected from In the Shadow of Man.* New York: Literacy Volunteers of New York City.

Greenfield, E. (1978). *Honey, I love and other poems.* New York: Harper.

Gutelle, A. (1990). *Baseball's best.* New York: Random House.

Hopkins, L. B. (1984). *Surprises.* New York: Harper.

Hopkins, L. B. (1987). *More surprises.* New York: Harper.

Kimmel, E. A. (1992). *Anansi goes fishing.* New York: Holiday House.

King, W., & Napp, J. (1998). *Our nation's history.* Circle Pines, MN: American Guidance Service.

King, W., & Napp, J. (1998). *United States history.* Circle Pines, MN: American Guidance Service.

Kuskin, K. (1992). *Soap soup and other verses.* New York: HarperCollins.

Leedy, L. (1992). *Blastoff to earth: A look at geography.* New York: Holiday House.

Lefkowitz, W. (1990). *Fearon's United States geography.* Belmont, CA: Globe Fearon.

Lionni, L. (1959). *Little blue and little yellow.* New York: Astor-Honor.

Lowery, L., & Lorbiecki, M. (1993). *Earthwise at home.* Minneapolis, MN: Carolrhoda Books.

Marshall, J. (1990). *Fox be nimble.* New York: Penguin.

Martin, B., Jr. (1983). *Brown bear, brown bear, what do you see?* New York: Holt.

McMullen, K. (1989). *Dinosaur hunters.* New York: Random House.

Minarik, E. H. (1958). *Little Bear.* New York: Harper.

Minarik, E. H. (1959). *A kiss for Little Bear.* New York: Harper.

Modesitt, J. (1990). *The story of Z.* New York: Simon & Schuster.

Morris, A. (1992a). *Tools.* New York: Lothrop, Lee & Shepard.

Morris, A. (1992b). *Vegetable soup.* New York: Lothrop, Lee & Shepard.

Morris, R. A. (1975). *Dolphins.* New York: Harper.

Murray, J. ( 2012). *Juneteenth.* Edina, MN: ABDO.

Nentl, J. A. (1983). *Big rigs.* New York: Crestwood House.

Nodset, J. L. (1963). *Who took the farmer's hat?* New York: Harper.

Parish, P. (1974). *Dinosaur time.* New York: Harper.

Person, S. (2011). *Polar bear: Shrinking ice.* New York: Bearpoint Publishing.

Rau, D. M. (2009). *Guess who swims.* New York: Marshall Cavendish Benchmark

Piper, W. (1961). *The little engine that could.* New York: Piatt.

Reef, C. (1991). *Ellis Island.* New York: Dillon Press.

Robart, R. (1986). *The cake that Mack ate.* Boston: Little, Brown.

Robinson, F. (1992). *We love fruit.* Chicago, IL: Children's Press.

Rockwell, A. (2001). *Bugs are insects.* New York: HarperCollins.

Roe, E. (1990). *All I am.* New York: Bradbury.

Sattler, H. R. (1993). *The earliest Americans.* New York: Clarion Books.

Schade, S. (1992). *Toad on the road.* New York: Random House.

Schade, S. (1994). *Railroad toad.* New York: Random House.

Scott, M. (1993). *A picture book of reptiles and amphibians.* Mahwah, NJ: Troll.

Shaw, N. (1986). *Sheep in a jeep.* Boston: Houghton Mifflin.

Shea, G. (1992). Amazing rescue underground. In G. Shea, *Amazing rescues* (pp. 28–48). New York: Random House.

Steele, P. (1991a). *Pocket facts: Birds.* New York: Crestwood House.

Steele, P. (1991b). *Pocket facts: Insects.* New York: Crestwood House.

Steele, P. (1991c). *Pocket facts: Wild animals.* New York: Crestwood House.

Stott, C. (1991). *Observing the sky.* Mahwah, NJ: Troll.

Strasser, T. (1993). *Help I'm trapped in my teacher's body.* New York: Scholastic.

Walker, A. (1992). *Writers' voices: Selected from The Temple of My Familiar.* New York: Literacy Volunteers of New York City.

Wang, M. L. (1989). *The ant and the dove.* Chicago, IL: Children's Press.

Wildsmith, B. (1982). *Cat on the mat.* New York: Oxford University Press.

Wiseman, B. (1959). *Morris and Boris.* New York: Harper.

Ziefert, H. (1988). *Dark night, sleepy night.* New York: Penguin.

Ziefert, H. (2008). *The boy who cried wolf.* New York: Sterling.

# Index